QuickBooks® 2013 IN DEPTH

Laura Madeira

800 East 96th Street,
Indianapolis, Indiana 46240
USA

QUICKBOOKS® 2013 IN DEPTH

ISBN-13: 978-0-7897-5039-6

ISBN-10: 0-7897-5039-2

Printed in the United States of America

Second Printing: July 2013

Library of Congress Cataloging-in-Publication Data is on file.

Trademarks

Warning and Disclaimer

Bulk Sales

Que Publishing offers excellent discounts on this book when ordered in quantity for bulk purchases or special sales. For more information, please contact

U.S. Corporate and Government Sales
1-800-382-3419
corpsales@pearsontechgroup.com

For sales outside of the U.S., please contact

International Sales
international@pearsoned.com

Editor-in-Chief
Greg Wiegand

Acquisitions Editor
Michelle Newcomb

Development Editor
Ginny Bess Munroe

Managing Editor
Sandra Schroeder

Project Editor
Mandie Frank

Copy Editor
Barbara Hacha

Indexer
Rebecca Salerno

Proofreader
Paula Lowell

Technical Editor
David Ringstrom

Editorial Assistant
Cindy Teeters

Designer
Anne Jones

Compositor
TnT Design, Inc.

CONTENTS AT A GLANCE

CONTENTS

ABOUT THE AUTHOR

Laura Madeira is the owner of ACS, Inc., a software sales and consulting firm located in the greater Dallas, Texas, area. She is one of the original members of the elite Intuit Trainer/Writer Network and a guest speaker for Intuit, sharing "What's New for QuickBooks" each fall. She was also a founding member of the Intuit Customer Advisory Council and a recent member of the Intuit Solution Provider Council. She is Advanced QuickBooks Certified ProAdvisor, Enterprise and Point of Sale Certified, and is also a Sage Certified Consultant representing Sage 100 Contractor (formerly Master Builder).

Laura is the author of *QuickBooks 2012 In Depth*, a 700+ page reference and training guide. She is also the author of *QuickBooks Solutions Guide*, *QuickBooks Essentials: For All QuickBooks Users*, a 6+ hours of self-paced video instruction, and co-author of *QuickBooks on Demand*—all offered by Que Publishing.

For more than 25 years, Laura has worked with companies of all sizes and from many varied industries. Her focus has been to help growing businesses become more successful by automating their internal accounting processes and improving their overall business financial reporting.

Additionally, Laura is a guest speaker for Intuit, providing training to thousands of consultants and accountants nationwide at numerous events. She is also a respected author for Intuit, writing technical training materials and presentations in addition to documenting and reviewing competing software.

Laura earned her accounting degree from Florida Atlantic University. She enjoys photography, art, and camping with her family. When Laura is not writing, she enjoys reading a good book or two!

More information can be found by visiting her website: www.quick-training.com or by email info@quick-training.com

ABOUT THE TECHNICAL EDITOR

David Ringstrom has worked behind the scenes as the technical editor for 27 books. David is a CPA and owner of Accounting Advisors, Inc., an Atlanta-based software consulting firm he started in 1991. He's slowly edging his way toward authoring a book himself and has written freelance articles on spreadsheets and other topics for more than 15 years. David also regularly presents continuing professional education webinars to CPAs on Microsoft Office and QuickBooks. More information about David can be found at www.acctadv.com

DEDICATION

My high school English teacher: Her assignment to write often in a journal provided the backdrop to my love of writing and reading.

My husband, Victor, who willingly made dinner, sat in front of the TV enjoying the dinner with me, and then cleaned up the kitchen as I went back to writing.

To my Mom, Joycelyn Demaree, who called me regularly to see how I was doing.

And to my Dad, Ronald Demaree, who proudly showed my book to everyone at his accounting office.

ACKNOWLEDGMENTS

I could not have completed this project without the expertise and tireless effort of my talented technical editor. (Try saying that fast three times in a row!)

Being a technical editor is not a "glamorous" job at all. The technical editor responsibilities include being completely familiar with the subject of the book, testing each documented step for technical accuracy, and verifying that the proper terminology is used for the specific audience.

These are just a few of the requirements. The technical editor must then communicate the change needed to the author in a clear and concise manner, while allowing the author the final word. Often weeks can go by between these reviews. Additionally, we write the original content during the beta release of the software, and then retest when the final software is released.

These details make for hours and hours of work. David did an excellent job, reading and rereading the content for clarity and accuracy.

A big thank you to William Murphy, a certified QuickBooks consultant, whose continued review and edits helped to define the content for Chapter 17, "Managing Your QuickBooks Database."

I appreciate Charlie Russell and our many late-night emails about the new features and how they work. Charlie was instrumental in his help to learn about and document QuickBooks Enterprise and Advanced Inventory Management features included in this edition.

Thanks to the entire Intuit Product Development Team who continues to keep me advised of new product features and helps me collect information during the beta testing of each new year's release of QuickBooks.

To all my QuickBooks peers in the many forums I belong to, thank you! You all play a part in this book, however unknowingly. In these forums I read your questions and answers and find it helps to guide what content I should include in the book.

For my family and friends who encouraged me to not lose sight of the goal—to share my knowledge of QuickBooks in this one-of-a-kind reference book, I could not have done this without your support.

Last, but very important, a big thanks to my acquisitions editor at Que, Michelle Newcomb, who has after all these years become a friend and who patiently works to keep me on schedule. Well, she tries anyway. And to the team at Que, including Ginny Munroe, development editor, who worked very closely with me to simplify the editing process, and Barbara Hacha, copy editor, who made sure my content was grammatically accurate.

—Laura

WE WANT TO HEAR FROM YOU!

As the reader of this book, *you* are our most important critic and commentator. We value your opinion and want to know what we're doing right, what we could do better, what areas you'd like to see us publish in, and any other words of wisdom you're willing to pass our way.

We welcome your comments. You can email or write to let us know what you did or didn't like about this book—as well as what we can do to make our books better.

Please note that we cannot help you with technical problems related to the topic of this book.

When you write, please be sure to include this book's title and author as well as your name and email address. We will carefully review your comments and share them with the author and editors who worked on the book.

Email: feedback@quepublishing.com

Mail: Que Publishing
ATTN: Reader Feedback
800 East 96th Street
Indianapolis, IN 46240 USA

Reader Services

Visit our website and register this book at quepublishing.com/register for convenient access to any updates, downloads, or errata that might be available for this book.

INTRODUCTION

Whether you are new to QuickBooks, an expert user, or somewhere in between, you will find this book to be a comprehensive reference guide to successfully complete your day-to-day QuickBooks tasks.

Having worked with many types of businesses the past 25 years, I know the importance of providing readers the "how and why" of common QuickBooks tasks. For both the inexperienced and expert user, this book includes easy-to-follow, step-by-step instructions accompanied by hundreds of illustrations. Additionally, using the provided instructions, you can practice what you learn with sample data installed with your QuickBooks software. In no time at all, you will be using QuickBooks like a pro!

What truly sets this book apart from the competition are the detailed instructions for managing and troubleshooting your QuickBooks data. For the business owner, this book provides step-by-step guides, checklists, and detailed advanced discussions of what information your QuickBooks data should provide.

For the accounting professional, learn how to work efficiently with your clients' QuickBooks files using Accountant's Copy, Client Data Review, QuickBooks Statement Writer, Send General Journal Entries and other useful features included with the QuickBooks Accountant 2013 software.

For the QuickBooks Enterprise 13.0 user, special focus has been provided in Appendix C, "QuickBooks Enterprise Solutions Inventory Features." Learn about using the robust inventory features, including those available with an Advanced Inventory subscription.

How This Book Is Organized

QuickBooks 2013 In Depth offers a wealth of information gathered from the author's years of working with business and accounting professionals who use QuickBooks software. So you can find just the right information, this book is organized into specific chapters, each focused on a particular task for working with your own or a client's QuickBooks data.

- **What's New**—Learn quickly about what's new in QuickBooks 2013.
- **Chapter 1, "Getting Started with QuickBooks"**—Learn how to create a new file, convert from other software, and set up users and permissions. *New!* Learn how to set up user security in QuickBooks Enterprise.
- **Chapter 2, "Getting Around QuickBooks"**—Navigation, setting preferences, using Help, and selecting a file to open are all discussed in this chapter.
- **Chapter 3, "Accounting 101"**—For the business owner, learn the basics of financial reporting. The included checklist helps you keep a close eye on the financial details.
- **Chapter 4, "Understanding QuickBooks Lists"**—Chart of accounts, items list, class list, managing lists, and fixing list errors are all detailed in this chapter.
- **Chapter 5, "Setting Up Inventory"**—Learn about the different features in each version of QuickBooks, defining inventory preferences, and using the proper inventory process.
- **Chapter 6, "Managing Inventory"**—How to adjust inventory, review inventory reports, and handle inventory backorders.
- **Chapter 7, "Setting Up Vendors"**—In this chapter, you learn how to use the Home page, set vendor preferences, and use the recommended accounts payable process.
- **Chapter 8, "Managing Vendors"**—Learn about vendor reporting, correcting vendor transactions, and handling unique accounts payable transactions, such as prepaying a vendor.
- **Chapter 9, "Setting Up Customers"**—From tracking customer leads, customizing the Home page, setting preferences, and properly invoicing and collecting payment from your customers—this is a very important chapter!
- **Chapter 10, "Managing Customers"**—This chapter provides a wealth of information about properly reporting your customer balances, paying sales tax, correcting transactions errors, and handling unique customer transactions.
- **Chapter 11, "Setting Up Payroll"**—Learn about the many payroll options, setting up payroll items and employees, and the proper payroll processing steps.
- **Chapter 12, "Managing Payroll"**—Prepare your quarterly and annual payroll tax forms, troubleshoot payroll errors, and record unique payroll transactions, such as a loan made to an employee.
- **Chapter 13, "Working with Bank and Credit Card Accounts"**—Learn about entering checks, credit card transactions, and bank transfers, as well as reconciling tasks. Save time using the Online Banking Center to download transactions directly into QuickBooks.
- **Chapter 14, "Reporting in QuickBooks"**—Setting preferences, using the Report Center, and modifying and memorizing reports are all discussed in this chapter.
- **Chapter 15, "Reviewing Your Data"**—Step-by-step guidance on reviewing the accuracy of your data. Don't miss this chapter!

- **Chapter 16, "Sharing QuickBooks Data with Your Accountant"**—Instructions for the business owner and accountant, plus a discussion of the different types of QuickBooks files.
- **Chapter 17, "Managing Your QuickBooks Database"**—Backing up your data and upgrading your data topics are explored. For the more advanced user, learn about troubleshooting database errors and monitoring your QuickBooks database.
- **Chapter 18, "Using Other Planning and Management Tools"**—Take advantage of all the tools available with your QuickBooks software, including loan management, planning, year-end guide, Microsoft Outlook contacts sync, and using the QuickBooks timer.
- **Appendix A, "Client Data Review"**—For the accounting professional, learn how to reclassify transactions in batch, track changes to lists, write off small customer balances in batch, fix beginning balance errors, and send journal entries by email, to name just a few tasks.
- **Appendix B, "QuickBooks Statement Writer"**—For the QuickBooks Enterprise user or accounting professional, learn how to prepare customized financials using Microsoft Excel and Word integration.
- **Appendix C, "QuickBooks Enterprise Solutions Inventory Features"**—*New Content!* Learn about managing inventory with the unique tools available only in QuickBooks Enterprise. Value-added content details features included with an Advanced Inventory Subscription.
- **Appendix D, "QuickBooks Shortcuts"**—Save time and work more efficiently.

Conventions Used in This Book

The book is straightforward enough so you can easily go to a specific chapter and find the needed information. It is worthwhile, however, to let you know how information is presented in this book.

Menu Commands

QuickBooks 2013 offers a variety of methods to accomplish a task. To simplify the instructions given, many steps use the top menu bar in QuickBooks.

Menu Bar

For example, the instructions for preparing a report might look like the following:

1. From the menu bar, select **Reports**, **Vendors & Payables**.

This directive refers to clicking Reports on the menu bar and then selecting Vendors & Payables as a submenu of Reports.

Another instruction method utilizes the new transaction ribbon toolbar, new for QuickBooks 2013.

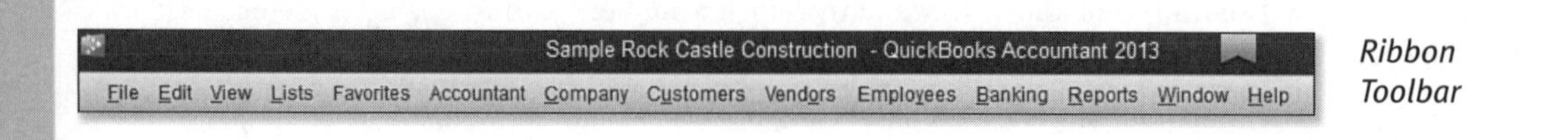

Ribbon Toolbar

For example, the instructions for modifying an invoice template might look like the following:

1. To continue with customizing your forms, select the **Customize Design** icon on the Formatting tab of the ribbon toolbar.

Instructions to select or type are **bolded** for easy identification in the text, and might look like the following:

1. In the Item column on the next available row, select the non-inventory part, **Flooring**.
2. In the Qty field, type **1**. Leave the U/M (Unit of Measure) field blank.

Additionally, for added clarity in the topic discussion, there are many screen illustrations that accompany the written steps.

Web Pages and Manufacturer Information

A few web pages are listed in this book, mostly directing you to the www.intuit.com website. These web addresses were current as this book was written; however, websites can change.

Special Elements

As you read through this book, you will note several special elements, presented in what we call "margin notes." Different types of margin notes are used for different types of information, as you see here.

tip
This is a tip that might prove useful for whatever you are in the process of doing.

note
Additional related information or alternative techniques that you might want to consider.

caution
This is a caution that something you might accidentally do could have undesirable results—so take care!

Sidebars

Learn quickly how to complete a task by following along with supplied step-by-step instructions using sample data installed with your QuickBooks software.

WHAT'S NEW IN QUICKBOOKS 2013

QuickBooks is both easy to learn and use. With improvements made in QuickBooks 2013, small businesses can complete their financial and accounting responsibilities with a minimum amount of effort so they can focus on growing their business.

All features detailed in this section are available in QuickBooks Pro, Premier, Professional Bookkeeper, Accountant, and Enterprise versions unless otherwise stated.

Easy to Learn and Use

The newest version of QuickBooks is designed to be easier to learn, thereby helping users complete accounting transactions efficiently. A more modern design boosts efficiency while retaining familiarity with common QuickBooks tasks.

To learn more, see "Getting Around QuickBooks," p. 61.

What's New Tips Overlay Help

New features in QuickBooks 2013 are easy to locate, with tips detailing the value the new feature provides. There is no need to search through menus to find What's New in QuickBooks for 2013.

Overlay tips display in orange when a user first opens QuickBooks 2013. Additionally, when a user clicks a window, a What's New tip overlay displays and then disappears automatically without disrupting the user's work. The tips can be minimized or dismissed (see Figure 1) on request with a single click. To reinstate the tips, from the menu bar select **Help**, **What's New**.

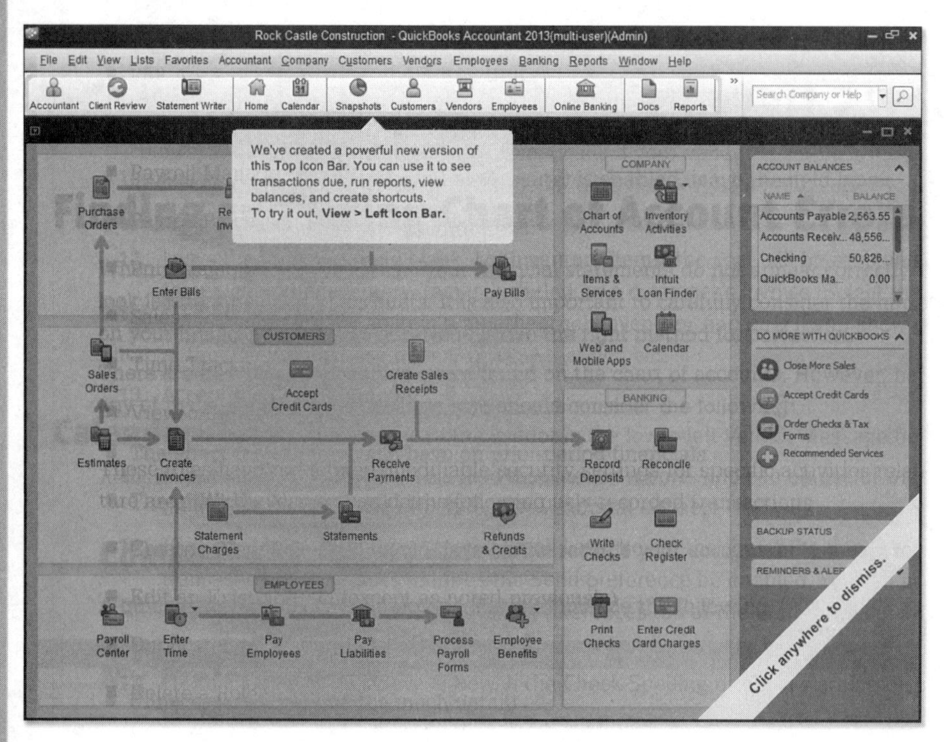

Figure 1 Never miss a new feature thanks to the What's New overlay tips!

New Modern Design

New, updated icons on the Home page (see Figure 2) and simplified navigation helps QuickBooks users get to the information they need, quickly and easily. Larger fonts improve readability. Click the top-right corner of a transaction to maximize the viewing area of the currently displayed transaction, helping to stay focused on the task at hand; see Figure 3.

Figure 2 New Home page icons and larger font makes it easier to work with QuickBooks.

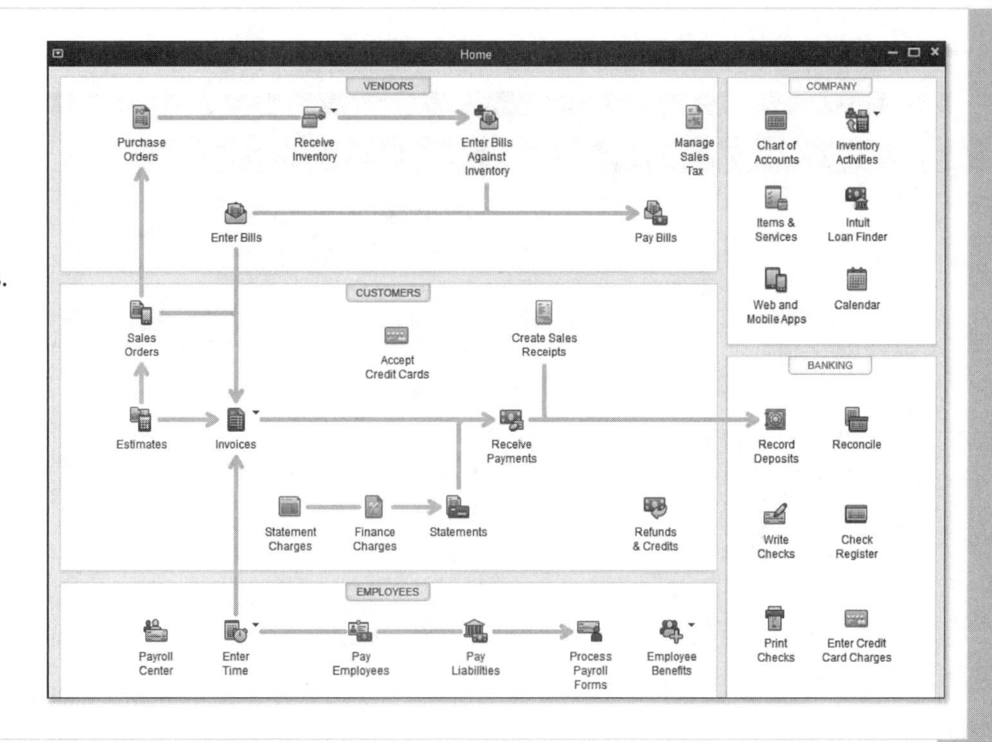

New Transaction Ribbon Toolbar

Invoices, Estimates, Sales Orders, and other forms now have a simplified layout, providing better access to actions that were previously hidden or required several clicks to execute. The new Ribbon Toolbar format shown in Figure 4 provides consistent placement of actions, helping to make it faster and easier to accomplish key tasks.

Icon Bar Selection

QuickBooks 2013 provides each user a personal choice when selecting which icon bar placement to use. Choose to keep the original icon bar at the top of the Home page or select the new icon bar placed to the left of the Home page.

 **note**

The light-colored icon bar is available after you have updated your QuickBooks file to maintenance release 4 or later. For more information see, "Installing a QuickBooks Maintenance Release," p. 618.

Top Icon Bar

For users who have grown accustomed to working with the customizable top icon bar, you can choose to display the top icon bar in a light color (as shown in Figure 5) or in the default darker color (shown in Figure 6). Manage this from the menu bar by selecting **Edit**, **Preferences**, **Desktop View**, **My Preferences** tab

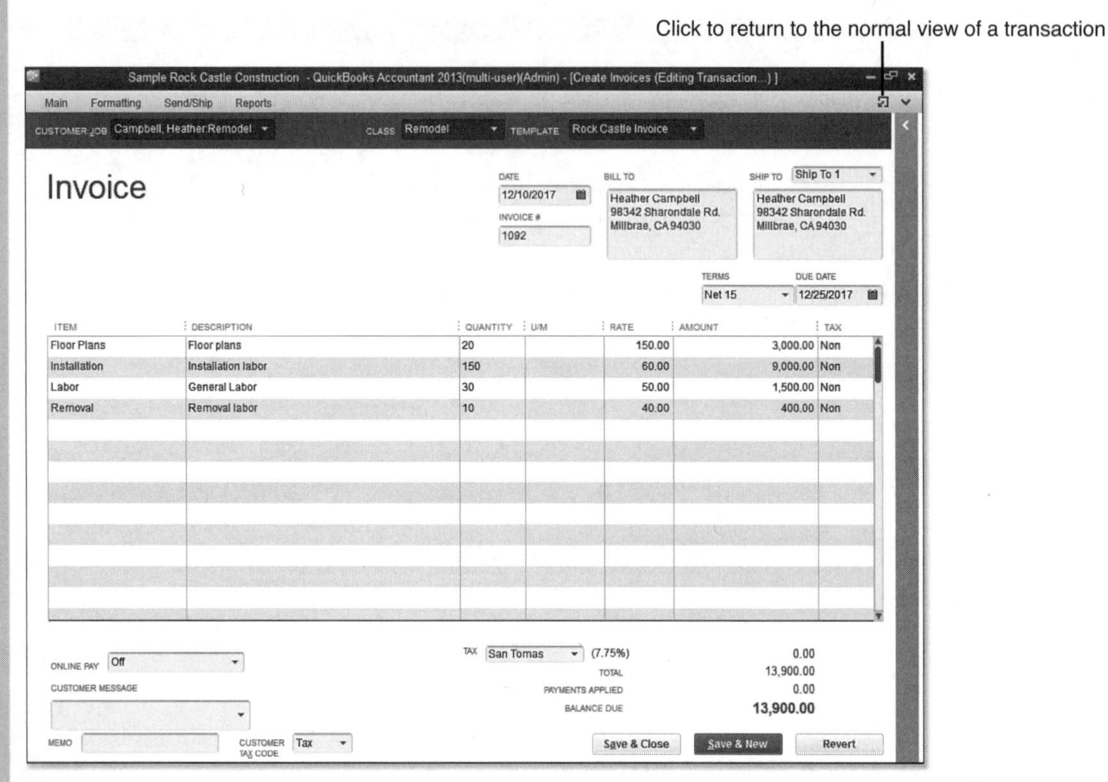

Figure 3
Stay focused on tasks by maximizing transaction windows.

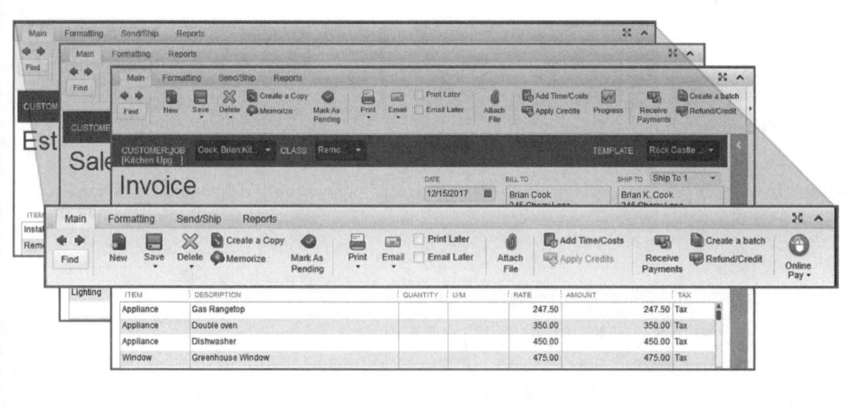

Figure 4
Save time and get instant access to related transaction functions on the new ribbon toolbar.

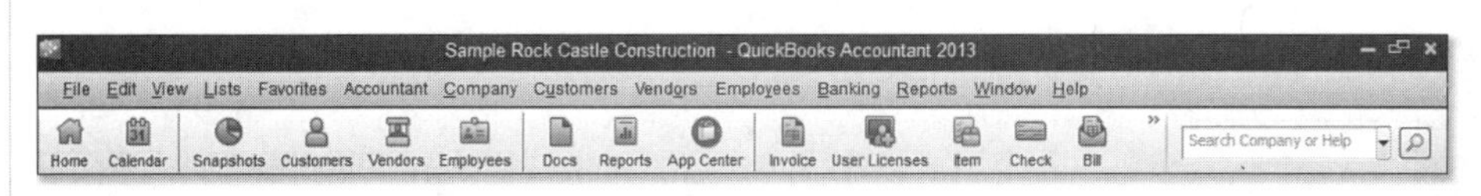

Figure 5
New, alternate-colored top placed icon bar.

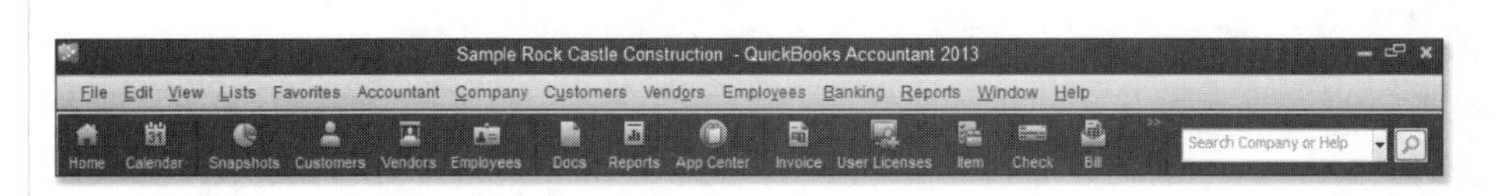

Figure 6
Default, darker-colored top placed icon bar.

Left Icon Bar

QuickBooks users can choose a new left-placed icon bar that takes advantage of newer, wider screen monitors; see Figure 7. Access integrated applications, favorite reports, important to do's, and much more! See Figure 8.

Figure 7
Improved features included with the new left icon bar.

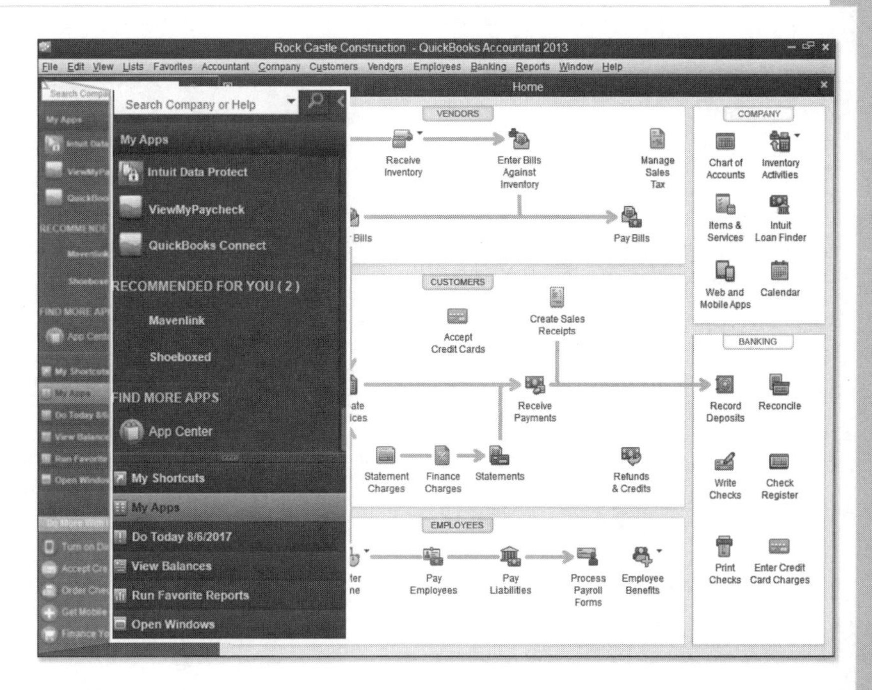

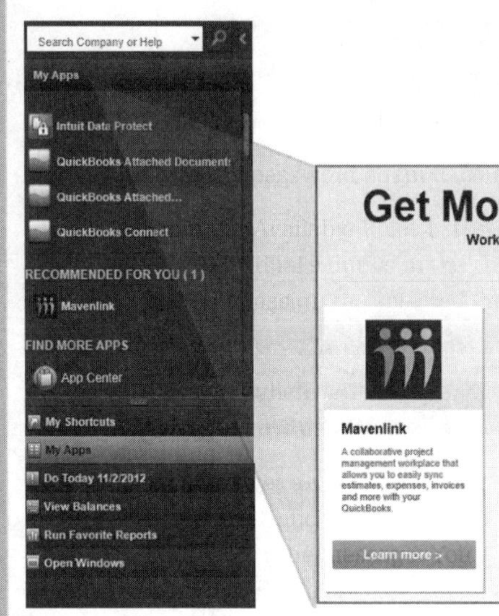

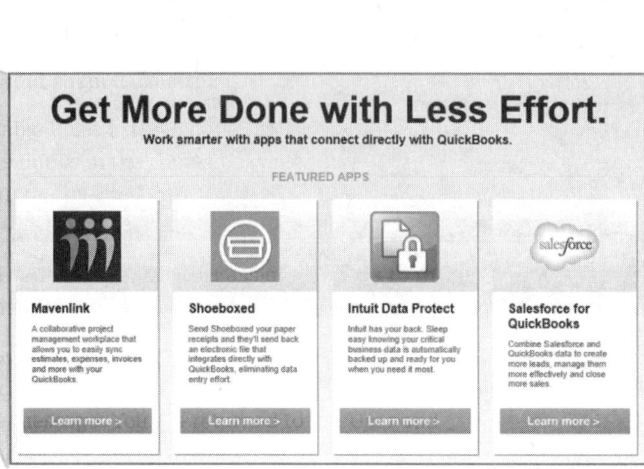

Figure 8
New, powerful left icon bar provides easy access to **My Apps**.

Assign a Company Flag Color

If your company has multiple QuickBooks data files, you may want to differentiate them from each other. Included with maintenance release 4 or newer, you can assign a Company Flag Color as shown in Figure 9. To add this to your file, from the menu bar select **Edit**, **Preferences**, **Desktop View**, My Preferences tab. From the Company Flag Color drop-down menu select a color of your choice.

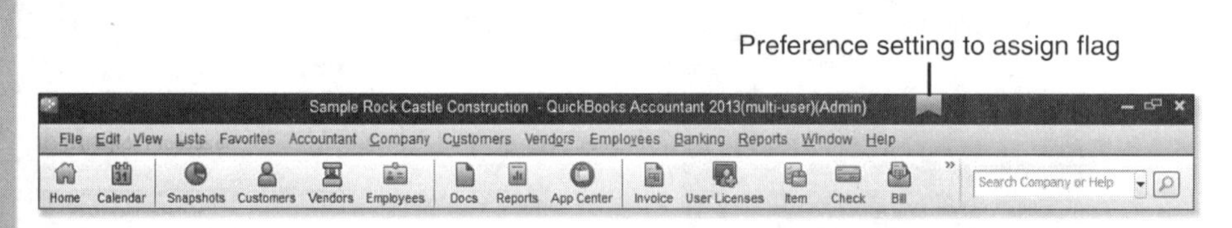

Figure 9
New Company Flag Color helps to visually differentiate one data file from another

New and Improved Features

QuickBooks adds to QuickBooks 2013 new and improved features designed to help businesses.

Time and Expenses Preference

Certain businesses invoice their customers using a method commonly referred to as "Time & Expense" or "Cost Plus" invoicing. Using Time & Expense billing, customer-related costs accumulate and are detailed on the invoice provided to the customer. With these new preference settings displayed in Figure 10, users will have the option to assign all costs or all time as billable to the customer. This setting can be overridden on a single transaction line as needed.

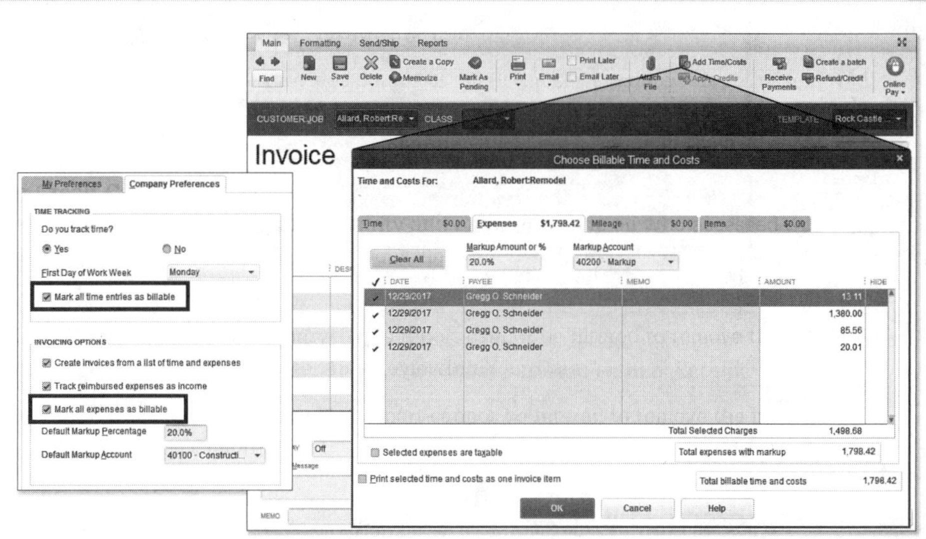

Figure 10
New Time & Expenses global preference defaults mark time and expenses as billable or not billable.

To learn more, see "Time and Expense Invoicing," p. 346.

Improved Customer, Vendor, and Employee Centers

Consolidate and organize more important information in the Customer, Vendor, and Employee Centers. Working in the Centers saves time searching for data as shown in Figure 11. Small businesses can now assign multiple contacts to customers and vendors, and assign To Dos to customers. In addition, users can track twice as many types of contact information for customers and vendors, such as Facebook pages or Twitter handles; see Figure 12.

To learn more, see "Working with the Customer Center," p. 305. Other chapters have information on the other Centers.

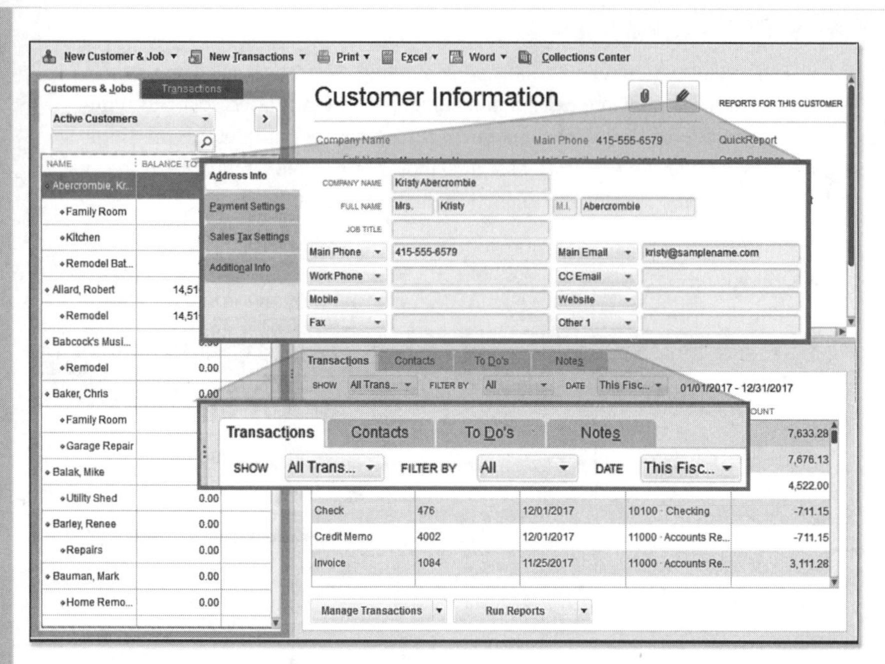

Figure 11
Updated Centers offer one-click access to managing details and running reports.

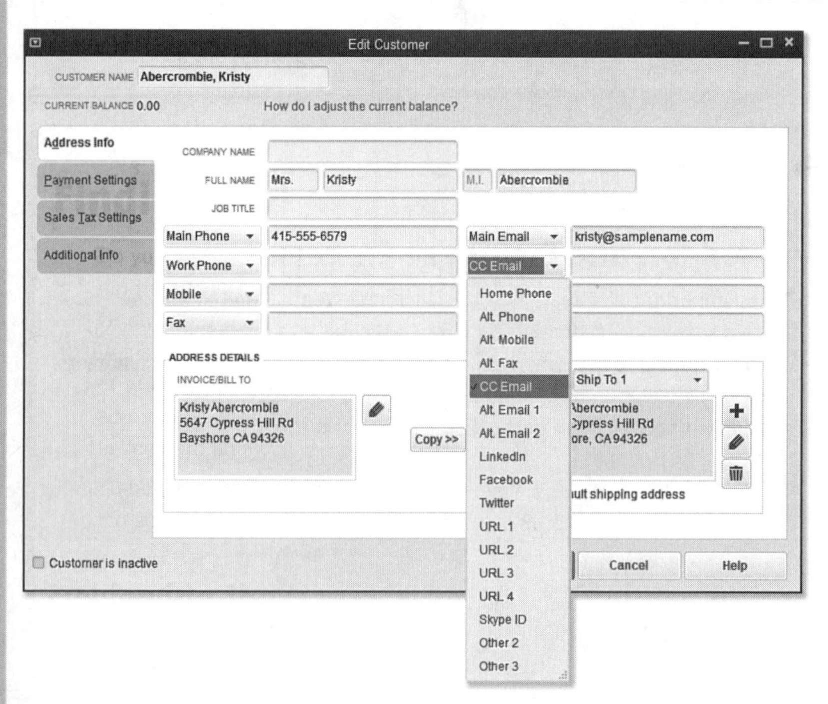

Figure 12
Track and report on customizable contact fields.

Assign Default Method of Payment for Customers

QuickBooks users can choose what type of payment methods they will accept online from customers. Choices include online check only or check and credit card. Users can also choose not to provide an online method of payment link on invoices for all or selected customers. These choices are displayed in Figure 13.

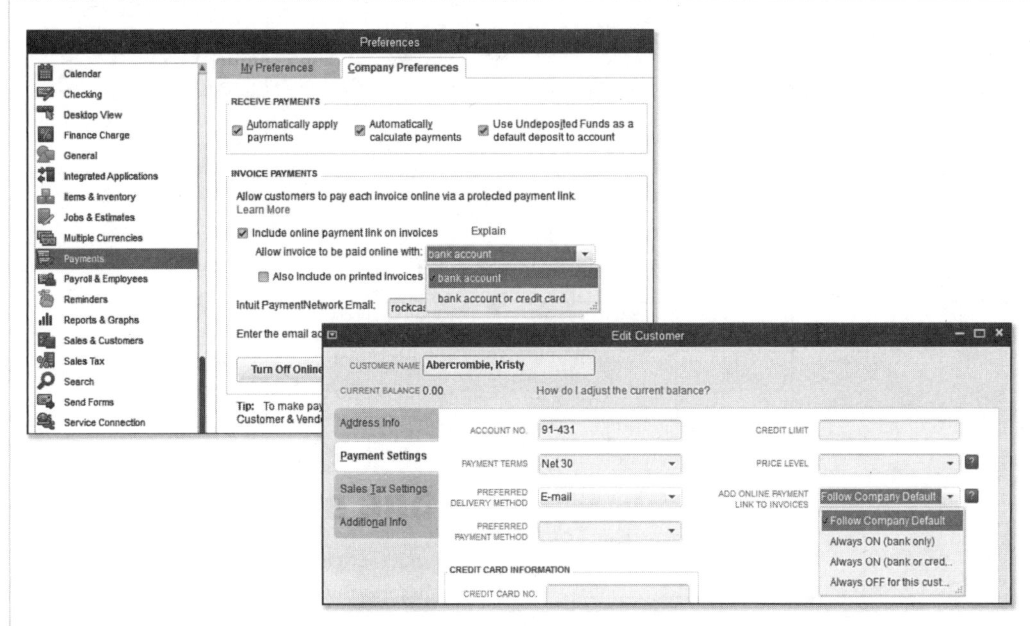

Figure 13
Global and by-customer preference for type of online payment accepted.

To learn more, see "Preferences that Affect Accounts Receivable," p. 292.

Print Vendor Bill

Certain businesses have an accounts payable process that includes approval by a manager of all bills entered. Companies that have intercompany transactions will find it useful to provide a copy of the bill paid (see Figure 14) by Company A to Company B for their record keeping.

To learn more, see "Recording Vendor Bills," p. 240.

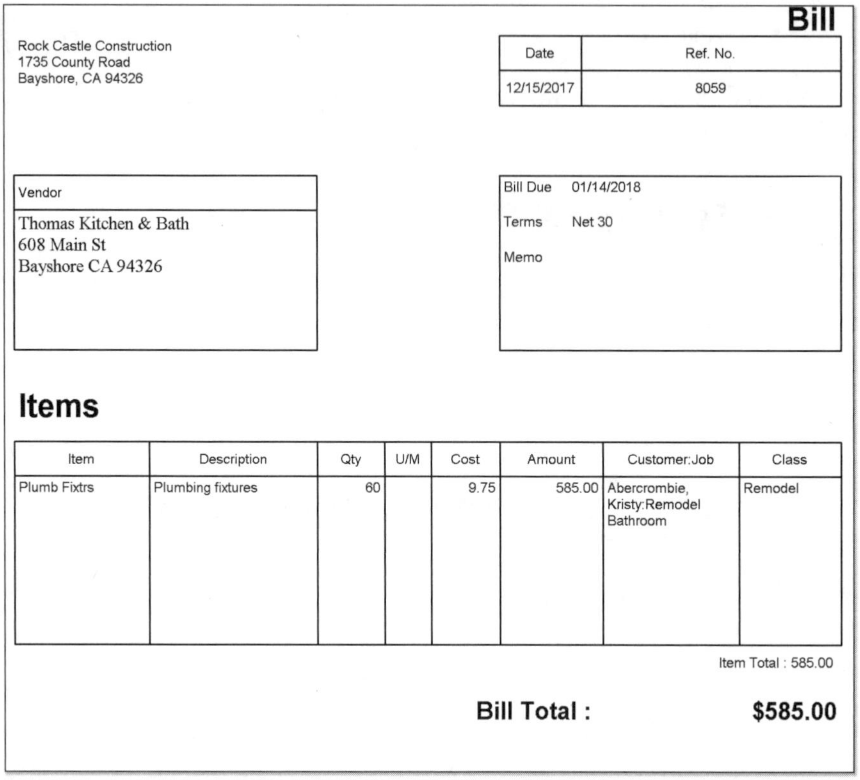

Bill

Rock Castle Construction
1735 County Road
Bayshore, CA 94326

Date	Ref. No.
12/15/2017	8059

Vendor

Thomas Kitchen & Bath
608 Main St
Bayshore CA 94326

Bill Due 01/14/2018
Terms Net 30
Memo

Items

Item	Description	Qty	U/M	Cost	Amount	Customer:Job	Class
Plumb Fixtrs	Plumbing fixtures	60		9.75	585.00	Abercrombie, Kristy:Remodel Bathroom	Remodel

Item Total : 585.00

Bill Total : $585.00

Figure 14
Print vendor bills for companies that do intercompany payables and for other purposes.

Reporting Preference for Item-Based Reports

QuickBooks users who use the Item Name field for the product number will find that including the description with or without the item name field (as shown in Figure 15) provides more meaningful reports without disrupting the workflow of the individual doing data entry.

To learn more, see "Inventory Reporting," p. 201.

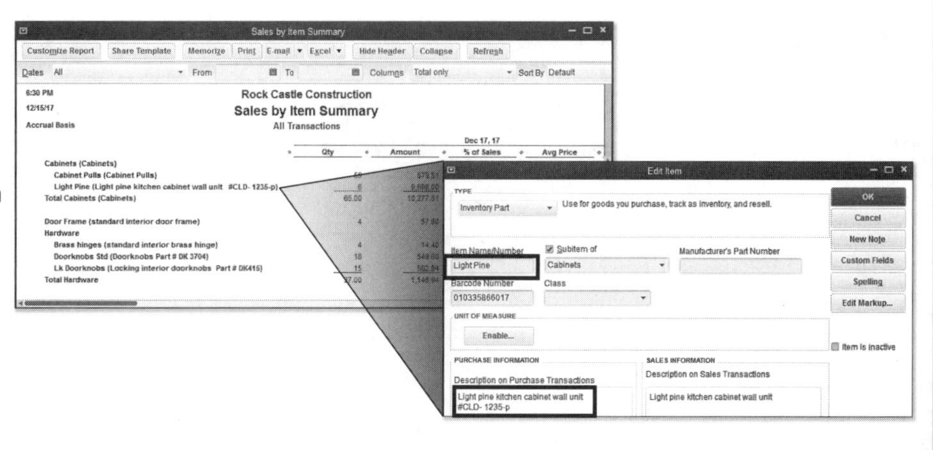

Figure 15 Select a new reporting preference to display name and description on item-based reports.

Hide Zero Quantity Items on Inventory Reports

Businesses with many inventory items can now choose to exclude zero-quantity items from inventory reporting. This feature is available with maintenance release 3 or later. To learn more about maintenance releases, see Chapter 17, "Managing Your QuickBooks Database." Figure 16 shows a report that includes both the Item Name/Number and Description.

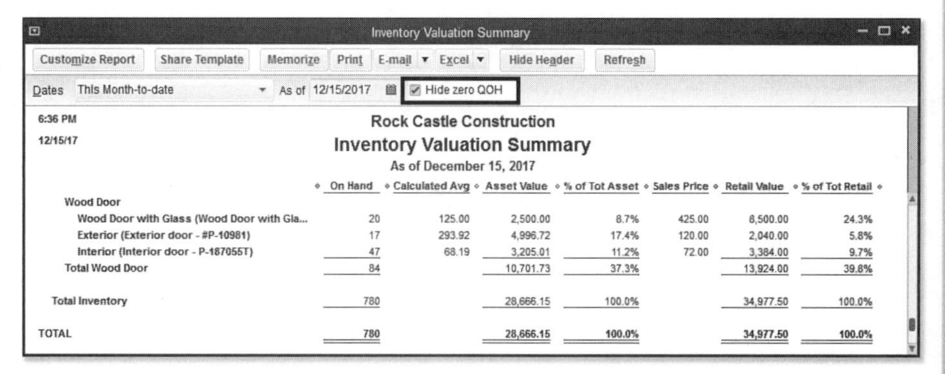

	On Hand	Calculated Avg	Asset Value	% of Tot Asset	Sales Price	Retail Value	% of Tot Retail
Wood Door							
Wood Door with Glass (Wood Door with Gla...	20	125.00	2,500.00	8.7%	425.00	8,500.00	24.3%
Exterior (Exterior door - #P-10981)	17	293.92	4,996.72	17.4%	120.00	2,040.00	5.8%
Interior (Interior door - P-187055T)	47	68.19	3,205.01	11.2%	72.00	3,384.00	9.7%
Total Wood Door	84		10,701.73	37.3%		13,924.00	39.8%
Total Inventory	780		28,666.15	100.0%		34,977.50	100.0%
TOTAL	780		28,666.15	100.0%		34,977.50	100.0%

Figure 16 Filter selected inventory reports to exclude items with no quantity on hand.

Use Available Quantity on Inventory Reorder Reports

Improved inventory reorder reports include the option to include or exclude available quantity (see Figure 17) from being considered in the items to be reordered.

This report improvement makes it easier to replenish inventory after factoring in committed inventory that may still be on the shelf. This feature is not available in QuickBooks Pro.

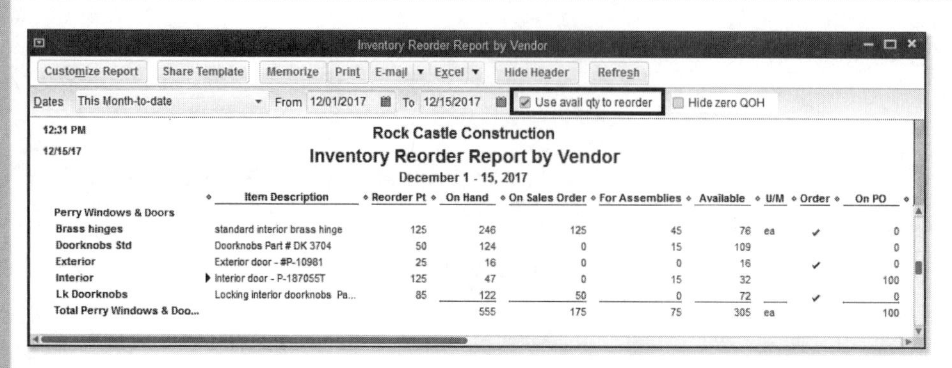

Figure 17 Capability to factor in available quantity when reviewing reorder points.

Collapse Summary Report Line Details

Summary reports can be prepared in QuickBooks that provide just the right amount of detail for management analysis without having to export the report to Excel for customization. If you are using QuickBooks Enterprise 13.0, you need to update your file to maintenance release 4 or later to access this feature. See Figure 18.

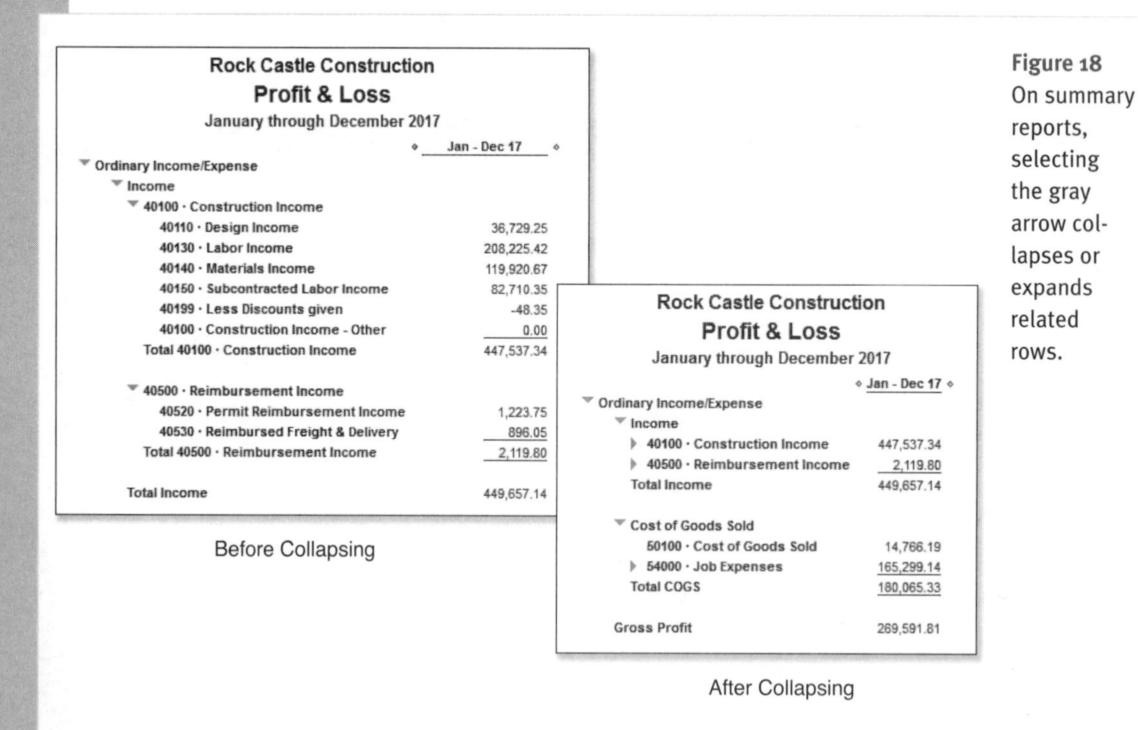

Figure 18 On summary reports, selecting the gray arrow collapses or expands related rows.

To learn more, see "Modifying Reports," p. 536.

Item Group Limit Increased

Businesses can enter more individual items into a single item group, improving data entry efficiency while retaining the ability to track item-level detail. See Figure 19 for more details.

Figure 19
Item groups automate streamlined entry on transactions. Now groups can include up to 50 items!

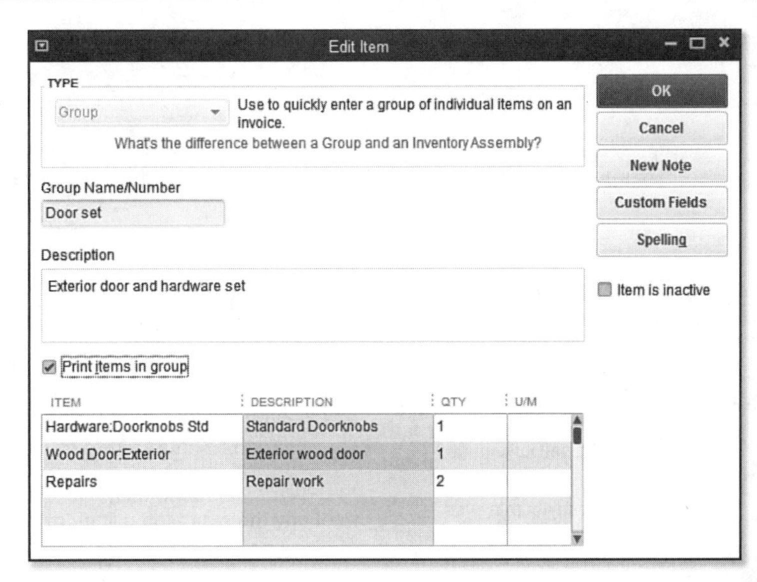

To learn more, see "Working with Group Items," p. 184.

Improved Upgrade Experience for Plus Subscribers

Improve the customer experience on upgrade by removing the need to enter the license key (see Figure 20) and register new versions of the software. Upgrade is a "side-by-side" install, meaning that the newest version of QuickBooks Pro or Premier will automatically be installed. This feature is only available for single user installs of Pro Plus or Premier Plus.

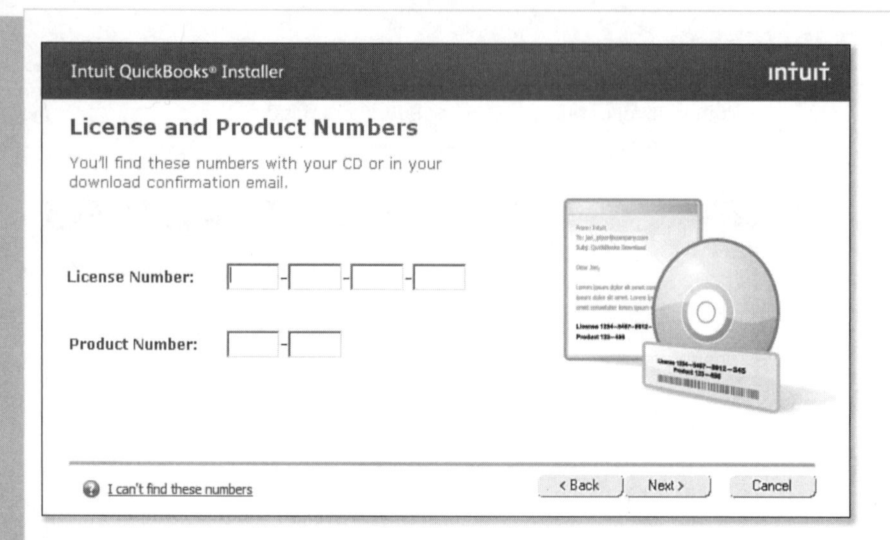

Figure 20
Plus subscribers will no longer need to enter License and Product Numbers or register when upgrading.

For the Accounting Professional

note

This feature is available with QuickBooks Accountant or QuickBooks Enterprise Accountant. For clients to import the journal entry, they must be using one of the QuickBooks for Windows 2013 solutions.

If you are an accounting professional, you will want to use the QuickBooks Accountant 2013 or QuickBooks Enterprise Solutions Accountant 13.0 software to take advantage of these new features.

Send General Journal Entries

Accounting professionals can now email changes to a client's data, which clients can import with a click on an email attachment. This means accountants can use a backup of a client's data, thereby avoiding the challenges and restrictions posed by an Accountant's Copy.

It is as easy as creating a journal entry, as shown in Figure 21. Next choose which entries to send to the client (see Figure 22). Last, your client receives an email with the entries attached as shown in Figure 23.

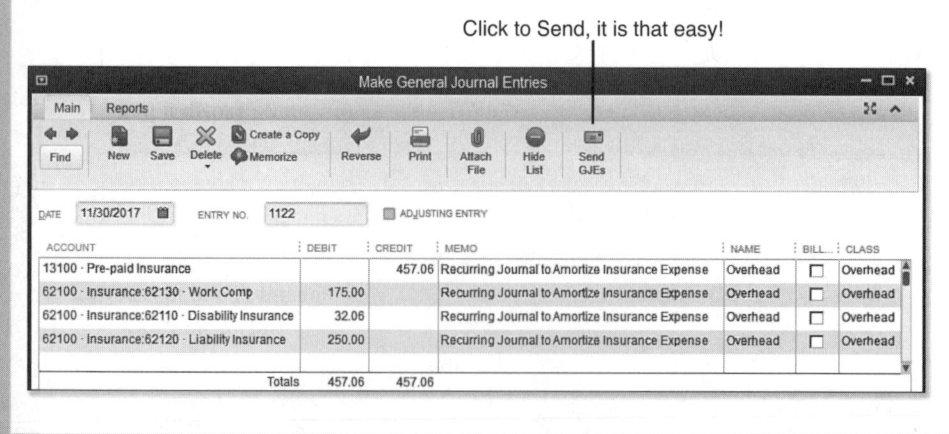

Figure 21
No fancy tools to learn; simply create the journal entry.

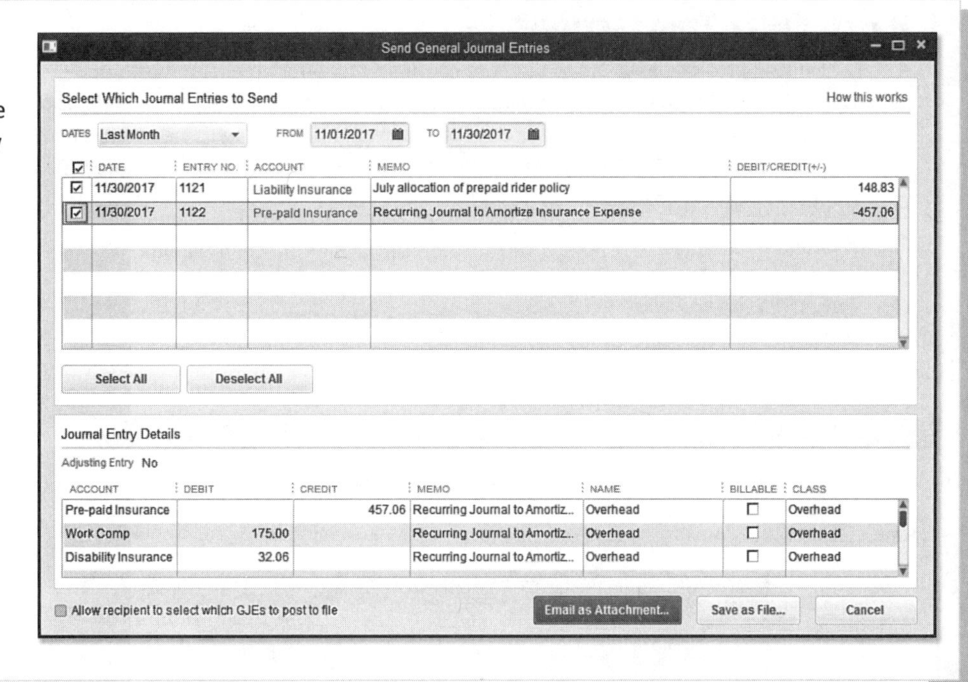

Figure 22 Choose to send a single journal entry or multiple entries in a single email attachment.

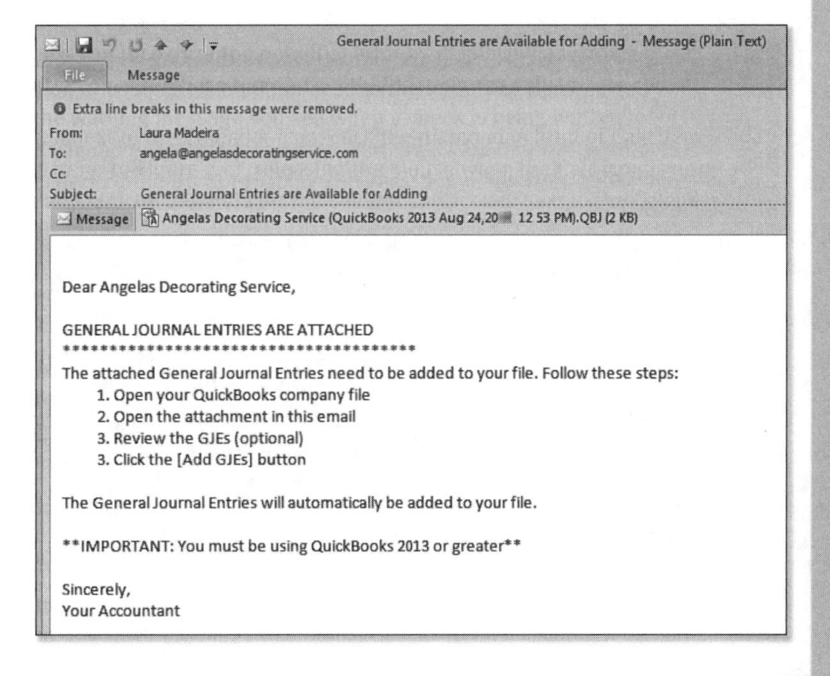

Figure 23 Double-click the email attachment to import the journal entry into QuickBooks. It's that easy!

To learn more, see "Send General Journal Entries," p. 576.

Batch Enter Transactions

Accounting professionals can work more efficiently by offering clients write-up services. Use this tool to copy and paste 1,000+ transactions from Excel, instead of entering them at one time. Easily customize the displayed columns of data to show only the fields you need, which saves you tabs and keystrokes; see Figure 24. Use the Batch Enter Transactions feature to add the following transactions to a QuickBooks file:

- Checks
- Deposits
- Credit Card Charges and Credits

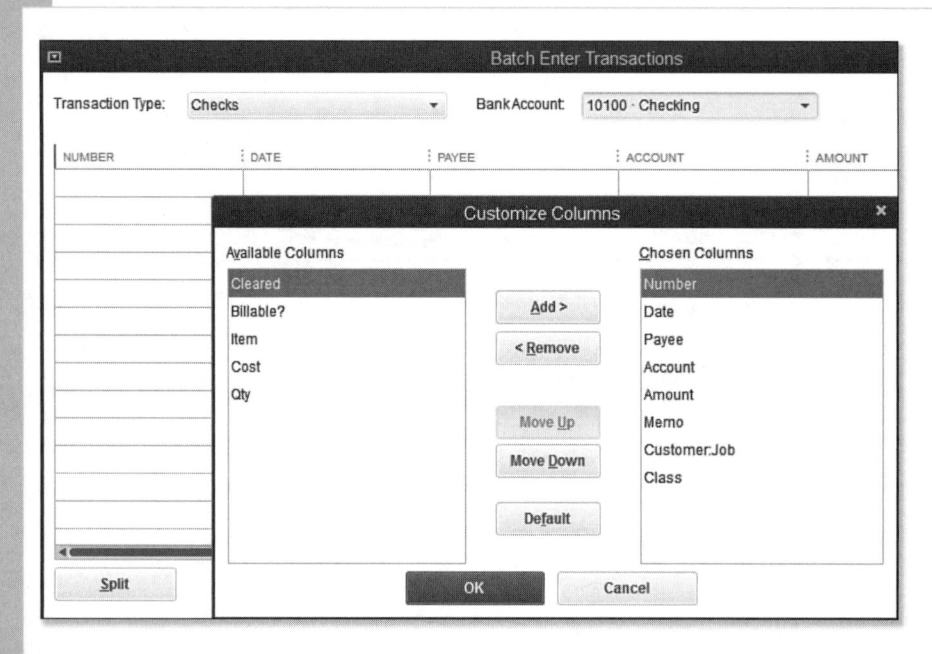

Figure 24 Customize the columns to display for easy data entry or to match your Excel spreadsheet.

Enter transactions quickly from data in an Excel spreadsheet as shown in Figure 25.

You stay in control, by reviewing and modifying the transactions before they are imported, as shown in Figure 26.

To learn more, see "Batch Enter Transactions," p. 606.

This feature is available with QuickBooks Accountant and QuickBooks Enterprise Accountant.

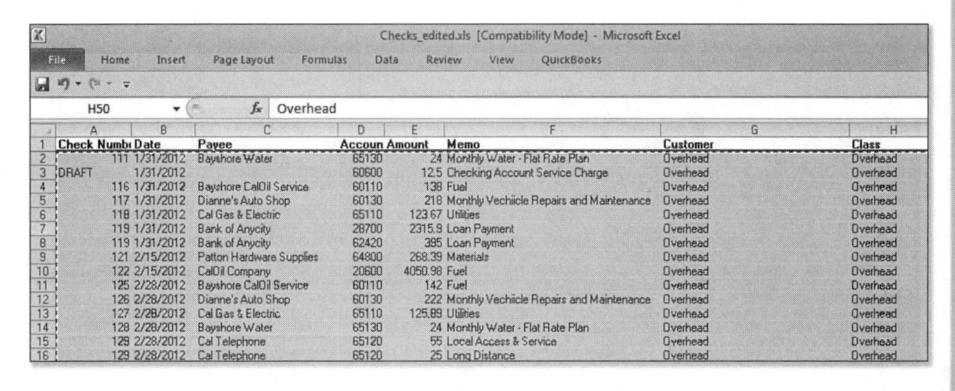

Figure 25 Copy and paste 1,000+ transactions from an Excel worksheet.

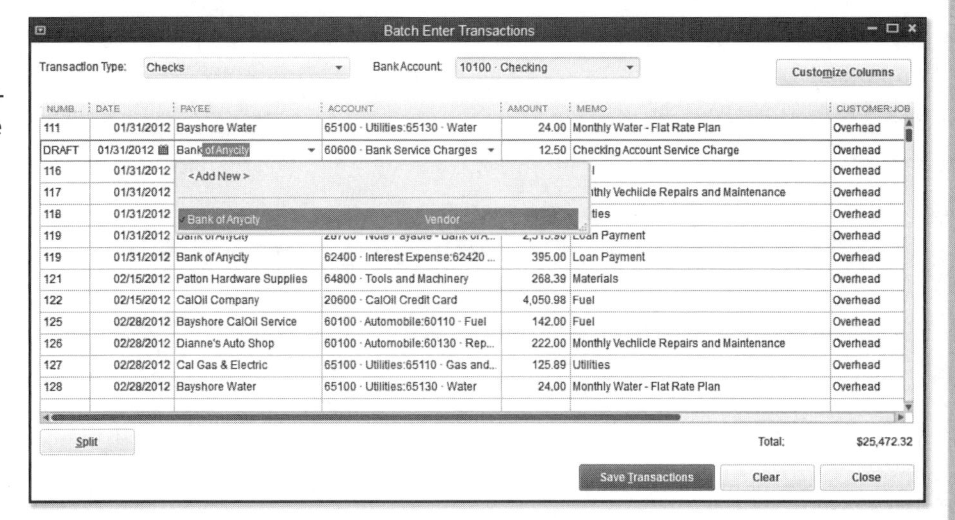

Figure 26 Manually enter transactions or make corrections before importing transactions.

Improved: Find and Fix Client Errors Faster

A few years ago, accounting professionals were provided with the Client Data Review feature. This feature is a collection of tools used by accounting professionals when working with their clients' data.

Included with Client Data Review is the Write Off Invoices feature. With this feature, accounting professionals can create a batch of credit memos, removing open, uncollectable balances efficiently in a batch for the client. New for QuickBooks 2013, confidently write off open invoices using an item (see Figure 27), knowing that all aspects of the accounting are handled correctly, including credits for accrual-based sales tax reporting.

To learn more, see "Write Off Invoices," p. 688.

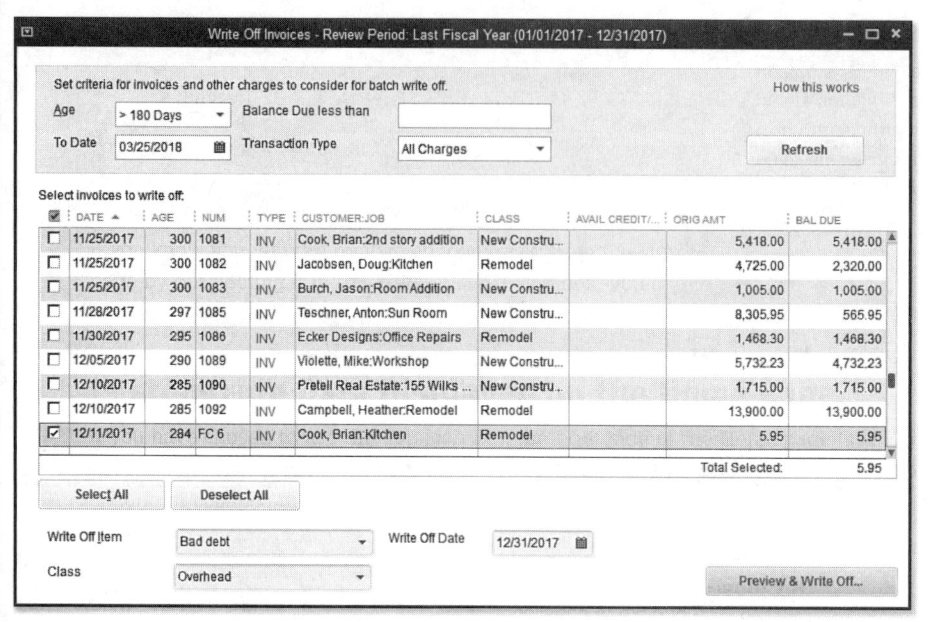

Figure 27
Utilizing an item when writing off invoices provides proper accounting for sales tax credits.

Easier Access to Creating New Data File from Template

Accounting professionals develop best practices when working with clients, helping them make the most of their QuickBooks data file. Share that effort by creating new company files patterned after other successfully created files as shown in Figures 28 and 29.

note

This feature is available with QuickBooks Accountant or QuickBooks Enterprise Accountant.

To learn more, see "Other Methods of Sharing Data," p. 603.

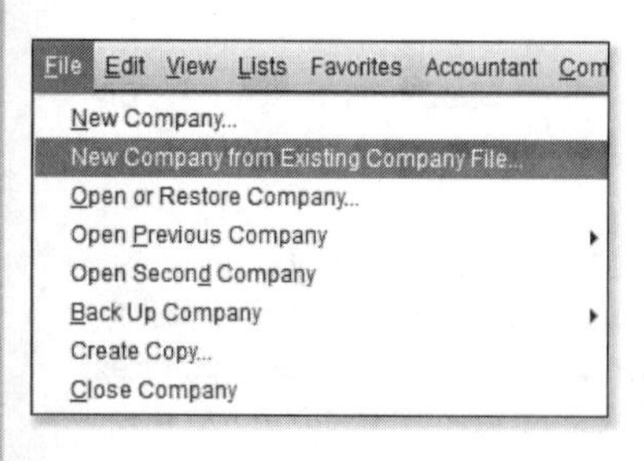

Figure 28
Easy access to creating a new file patterned after another file.

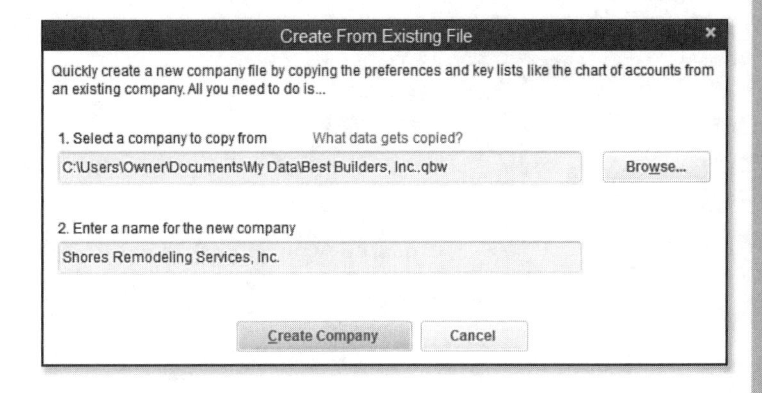

Figure 29
Select the preferred file to use as the template and provide a name for the new file.

For QuickBooks Enterprise Users

QuickBooks Enterprise users often push the limits of software because of their transaction volume, number of users, or other complexities. In that regard, QuickBooks Enterprise 13.0 builds on its slate of advanced features with these new additions for 2013.

note

The remaining features discussed in this section are available only when using the QuickBooks Enterprise Software.

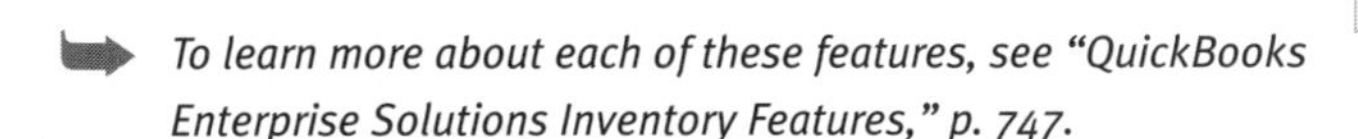

To learn more about each of these features, see "QuickBooks Enterprise Solutions Inventory Features," p. 747.

Default Class Assignment

Businesses that track data based on profit centers will save time with data entry by assigning a default class to *one* of the chosen lists, including Items, Accounts, or Names. Users can select one list to assign classes to, not all three, but can change that default at any time. See this preference setting in Figure 30 and assigning a class to an item in Figure 31.

To learn more about working with classes, see "Understanding QuickBooks Lists," p. 101.

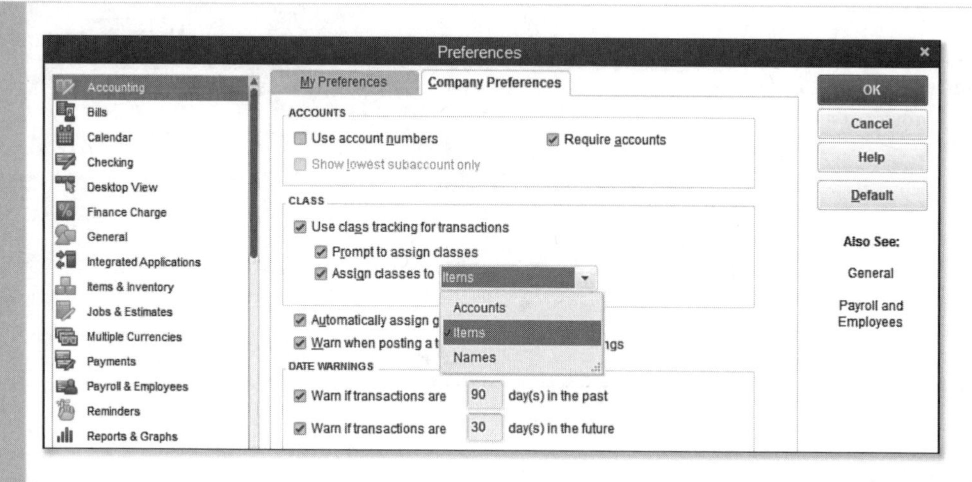

Figure 30 Assign default classes to either Account, Items, or Names.

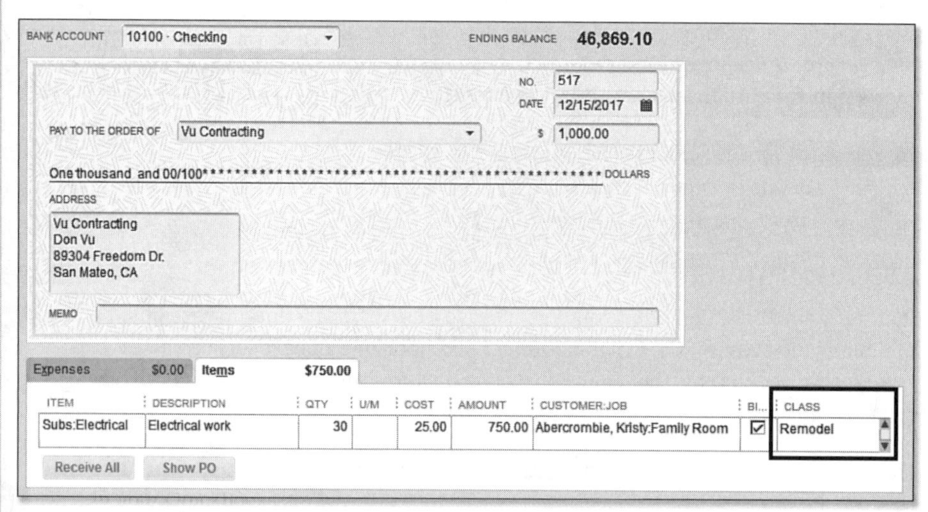

Figure 31 Classes are assigned to transaction lines for department profitability reporting.

Create Auto Purchase Orders

Simplify your inventory replenishing process by creating purchase orders in batch. Click Create Auto PO's from any inventory stock status report as shown in Figure 32.

To learn more about working with purchase orders in general, see "Entering a Purchase Order," p. 240.

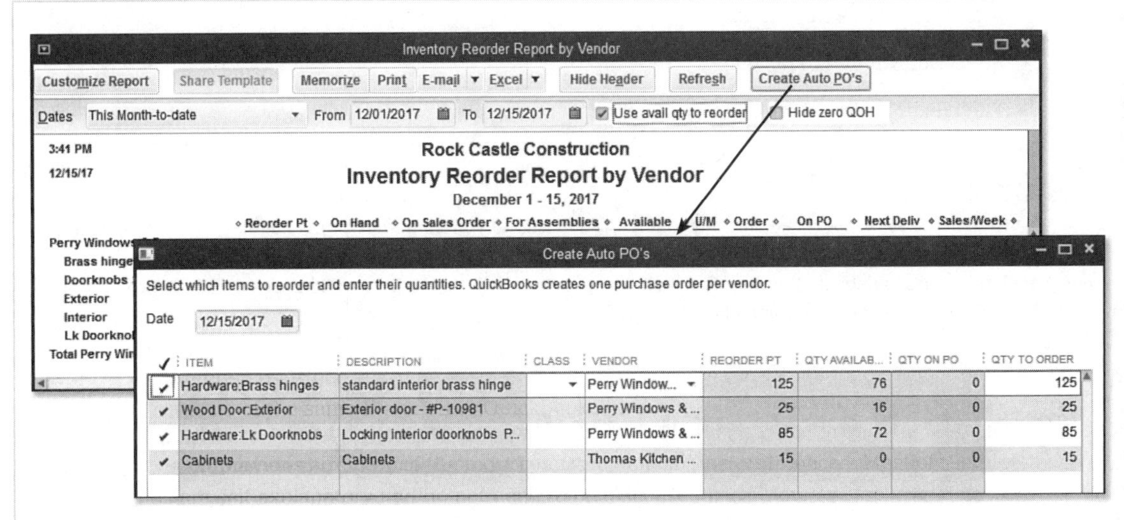

Figure 32
From the inventory stock status reports, conveniently auto-create PO's.

Increased List Limits

New list limits expand the capabilities of QuickBooks Enterprise Solutions as shown in the following table.

List Name	Previous Limits	New Limits
Chart of Accounts	10,000	100,000
Classes	10,000	100,000
Customer Types	10,000	100,000
Vendor Types	10,000	100,000
Memorized Transactions	29,000	50,000
To Dos	10,000	100,000
Customer Messages	10,000	100,000
Items in a Group or Sales Tax Item (also for Pro and Premier)	20	50

QuickBooks Enterprise with Advanced Inventory Subscription

Businesses with complex inventory needs may purchase an annual Advanced Inventory subscription for their QuickBooks Enterprise software to have access to the following features:

- Multiple Inventory Locations
- Serial/Lot Numbers Tracking
- FIFO (First in First Out) Inventory Costing

note

The Advanced Inventory module is an annually renewable subscription offering from Intuit and requires a current Full Service Plan. A current Full Service Plan provides you with the new software version each year, unlimited technical support from Intuit, and a variety of other benefits. Visit http://enterprisesuite.intuit.com and click the Full Service Plan link in the lower left of the web page for more details.

Row, Shelf or Bin Location Tracking

Use this new feature of Row, Shelf, or Bin Location Tracking for more sophisticated inventory tracking and reporting. Features include the ability to transfer product from one row, shelf, or bin to another; see Figure 33. Efficiently set a default row, shelf, or bin location per item by selecting **Lists**, **Add/Edit Multiple List Entries** from the menu bar. Inventory reports group products by location as shown in Figure 34.

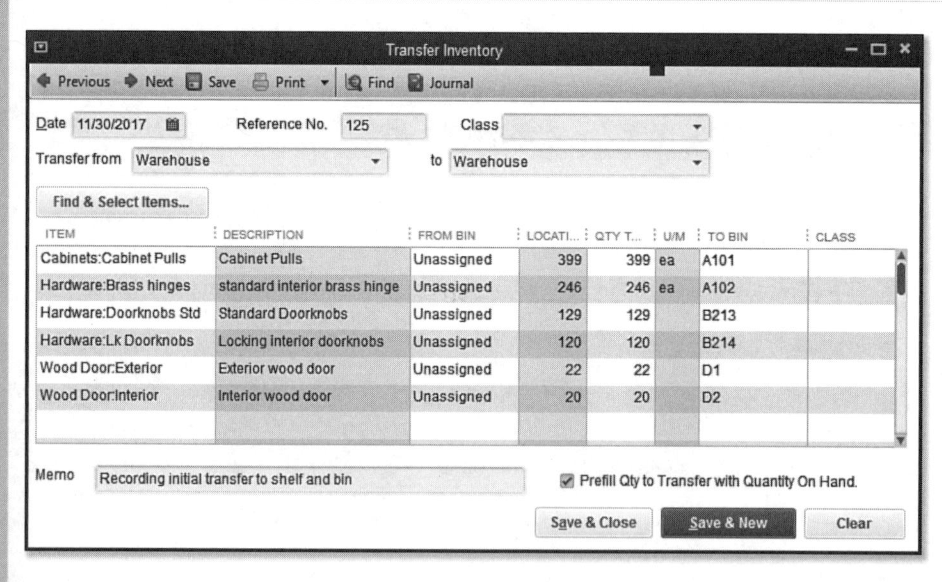

Figure 33 Transfer inventory from one row/shelf/bin to another.

To learn more, see "Add/Edit Multiple List Entries," p. 115.

Figure 34
Report and track inventory items by location and row, shelf, or bin.

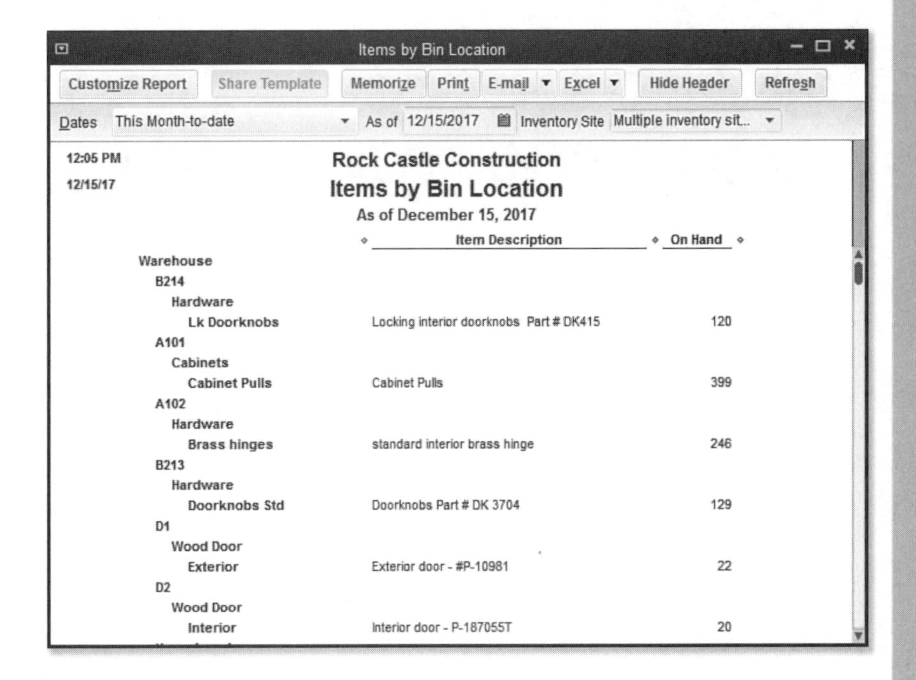

	Item Description	On Hand
Warehouse		
B214		
Hardware		
Lk Doorknobs	Locking interior doorknobs Part # DK415	120
A101		
Cabinets		
Cabinet Pulls	Cabinet Pulls	399
A102		
Hardware		
Brass hinges	standard interior brass hinge	246
B213		
Hardware		
Doorknobs Std	Doorknobs Part # DK 3704	129
D1		
Wood Door		
Exterior	Exterior door - #P-10981	22
D2		
Wood Door		
Interior	Interior door - P-187055T	20

Barcode Scanning

Small business owners can speed up the time required to input and track inventory transactions. You can even create a new item and automatically populate the barcode number as shown in Figure 35. Fewer keystrokes are needed from a keyboard, making it a perfect choice for a busy warehouse recording items received and shipped out. Use barcoding to complete transactions with the serial number and print a list of barcodes or barcode labels; see Figures 36, 37, and 38.

Figure 35
New Barcode Number field in the item record.

Edit Item
TYPE
Inventory Part
Use for goods you purchase, track as inventory, and resell.
OK
Cancel
New Note
Custom Fields
Spelling
Edit Markup...
Item Name/Number: Cabinet Pulls
Subitem of: Cabinets
Manufacturer's Part Number
Barcode Number: 010335866016
Class: Remodel
UNIT OF MEASURE
Enable...
Item is inactive
PURCHASE INFORMATION
Description on Purchase Transactions: Cabinet Pulls
SALES INFORMATION
Description on Sales Transactions: Cabinet Pulls

Main
Formatting
Reports
Find
New
Save
Delete
Create a Copy
Memorize
Mark As Closed
Print
Email
Print Later
Email Later
Attach File
Create Item Receipts
VENDOR
Perry Windows ...
CLASS
DROP SHIP TO
TEMPLATE
Custom ...
Purchase Or...
Date
12/15/2017
P.O. No.
6241
Vendor
Perry Windows & Doors
P.O. Box 5033
Bayshore CA 94326
Ship To
Rock Castle Constructi
1735 County Road
Bayshore, CA 94326
ITEM
DESCRIPTION
LOCATION
QTY
RATE
CUSTO...
U/M
AMOUNT
Cabinets:Cabinet Pulls
Cabinet Pulls
20
72.00
cs
1,440.00
Hardware:Brass hinges
standard interior brass hinge
15
72.00
cs
1,080.00
)103725147140
Total
2,520.00

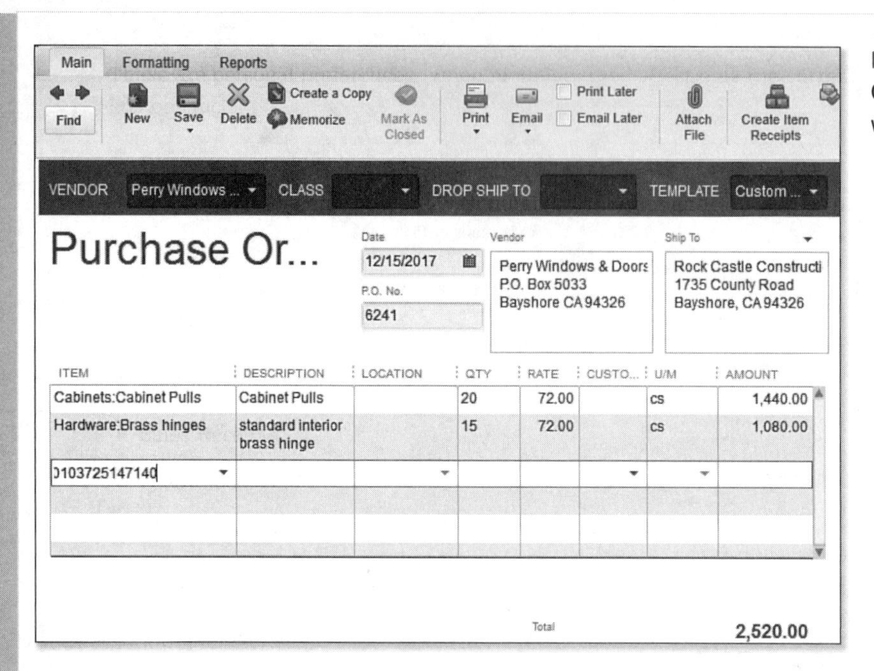

Figure 36
Complete transactions with ease by scanning.

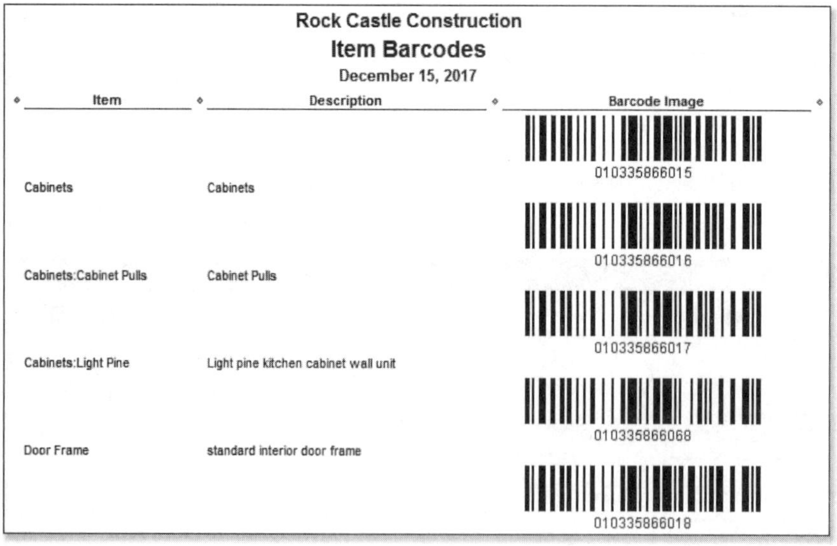

Rock Castle Construction
Item Barcodes
December 15, 2017
Item
Description
Barcode Image
010335866015
Cabinets
Cabinets
010335866016
Cabinets:Cabinet Pulls
Cabinet Pulls
010335866017
Cabinets:Light Pine
Light pine kitchen cabinet wall unit
010335866068
Door Frame
standard interior door frame
010335866018

Figure 37
Print a report of barcodes for scanning convenience.

To learn more about inventory items in general, see "Adding or Editing Inventory Items," p. 154.

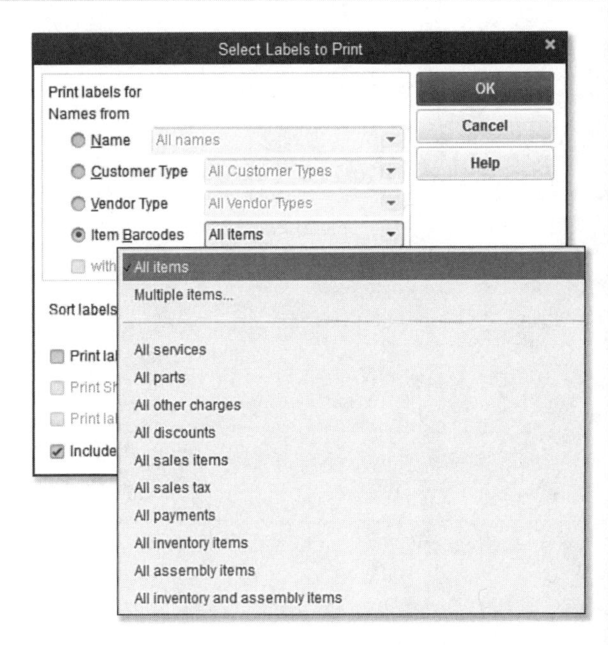

Figure 38
After updating to maintenance release 4 or newer, you can print the item barcodes on basic label stock.

FIFO Cost Lot History Report

Users can efficiently track the inventory acquisition (purchase, customer return, inventory adjustment, and so on) along with its cost as shown in Figure 39. This provides users with information so they can see that the oldest cost lot is being disbursed first.

FIFO Cost Lot History by Item

Customize Report | Share Template | Memorize | Print | E-mail | Excel | Hide Header | Refresh

Dates: This Month-to-date From 12/01/2017 To 12/15/2017

8:19 AM
12/15/17

Rock Castle Construction
FIFO Cost Lot History by Item
December 1 - 15, 2017

Item Description	Acq Date	Acq Trans Type	Acq From	Acq Amt	Qty	Disb Date	Disb Trans Type	Disb To	Disb Amt
Lk Doorknobs (Locking interior doorknobs Part # DK415)									
Locking interior doorknobs Pa...	01/01/2017			34.95	1	12/05/2017	Invoice	Violette, Mike:Work...	0.00
Locking interior doorknobs Pa...	01/01/2017			104.85	3	12/15/2017	Invoice	Robson, Darci:Rob...	114.00
Locking interior doorknobs Pa...	12/05/2017	Item Receipt	Patton Hardware Su...	209.70	6				0.00
Wood Do...									
Exterior (Exterior door - #P-10981)									
Exterior door - #P-10981	06/07/2017	Bill	Zeng Building Supplies	1,180.78	2	12/05/2017	Inventory Adjust	Pretell Real Estate:...	402.11
Exterior door - #P-10981	06/07/2017	Bill	Zeng Building Supplies	590.39	1	12/05/2017	Invoice	Violette, Mike:Work...	120.00
Exterior door - #P-10981	09/15/2017	Credit Card Char...	Patton Hardware Su...	590.39	1	12/14/2017	Invoice	Natiello, Ernesto:K...	599.50
Exterior door - #P-10981	10/25/2017	Bill	Perry Windows & Do...	840.00	8	12/05/2017	Inventory Adjust	Pretell Real Estate:...	1,608.44
Exterior door - #P-10981	12/05/2017	Inventory Adjust	Pretell Real Estate:15...	346.95	2	12/15/2017	Invoice	Robson, Darci:Rob...	240.00
Exterior door - #P-10981	12/05/2017	Inventory Adjust	Pretell Real Estate:15...	2,081.72	12				0.00
Exterior door - #P-10981	11/15/2017	Bill	Perry Windows & Do...	810.00	6	12/05/2017	Inventory Adjust	Pretell Real Estate:...	1,206.33

Figure 39
New report provides visibility into history of how FIFO cost lots was calculated.

1

GETTING STARTED WITH QUICKBOOKS

This comprehensive reference book offers the reader clear and concise step-by-step written instructions accompanied by detailed illustrations for using QuickBooks Pro, Premier 2013, Premier Accountant 2013, and QuickBooks Enterprise Solutions 13.0. Written for the business owner, accountant, or bookkeeper, *QuickBooks 2013 In Depth* offers readers a complete guide to the software they use every day.

Understanding QuickBooks

The QuickBooks software comes in a version that is just right for your business needs. For a complete comparison visit the following website: http://quickbooks.intuit.com/product/accounting-software/quickbooks-comparison-chart.jsp or from your Internet browser, Google **QuickBooks comparison**. A few of the differences are detailed in Table 1.1.

Table 1.1 QuickBooks Software Summary

Software Version	Number of Users	Invoice Customers, Pay Vendor Bills, Prepare Payroll	Industry-Specific Versions	Accountant-Specific Tools and Features
QuickBooks Online Plus	Up to 5			
QuickBooks for Mac	Up to 5	✓		
QuickBooks Pro	Up to 3	✓		
QuickBooks Premier	Up to 5	✓	✓	
QuickBooks Accountant	Up to 5	✓	Can toggle to all industry editions	✓
QuickBooks Enterprise	Up to 30	✓	✓	
QuickBooks Enterprise Accountant	Up to 30	✓	Can toggle to all industry editions	✓

This book does not cover the setup or use of QuickBooks Online or QuickBooks for Mac. The content in this comprehensive guide is from working with QuickBooks Pro, Premier, Accountant, and QuickBooks Enterprise. Most illustrations are from QuickBooks Accountant unless otherwise noted. In some sections, I note when the content or illustrations are from a specific version or industry edition of QuickBooks.

Additionally, this book is a perfect companion to the *QuickBooks Essentials LiveLessons* video training, combining the best of audio learning and book reference functionality. For more information, see the author's website:
www.quick-training.com

The primary purpose of this book is to teach business owners and accounting professionals how to use QuickBooks software quickly and accurately. Most chapters also include troubleshooting content that sets this book apart from other how-to books. This chapter helps you get started quickly and provides you with quick steps to begin using your QuickBooks software. If you would like to practice what you are learning, open one of the sample files installed with your QuickBooks software. I teach you how to do that first!

Over the years, I have helped hundreds of businesses troubleshoot problems with getting the proper financial and management information out of their QuickBooks data. I have found that improper setup of the data file is most often the primary cause of problems, second only to judgment errors in posting transactions to the incorrect account.

A word of caution: It is not my intention to offer you tax advice; I make comments throughout the text encouraging you to consult your accounting or tax professional before making any data corrections that might have a significant impact on a company's financials.

Using QuickBooks Sample Data

You can open one of the sample data files installed automatically with your QuickBooks software and begin trying what you are shown in this book. With this data you can test creating transactions, review how lists are set up, and process reports with ready-made data.

The number and type of sample data files installed differs, depending on the version of QuickBooks you purchased.

To open a sample file with sample data, follow these steps:

1. Launch QuickBooks from the icon on your desktop.
2. From the menu bar, select **File**, **Close Company**. The No Company Open dialog box displays.
3. Click the Open a Sample File button and choose a sample file from the drop-down list as shown in Figure 1.1.

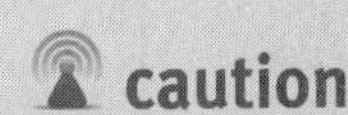

caution

Do not enter your own business data into the supplied sample files; they should be used for testing how to create transactions and reviewing reports populated with the sample data only. Additionally, any customizing that you do with the sample data is not saved to other files, including your own business files.

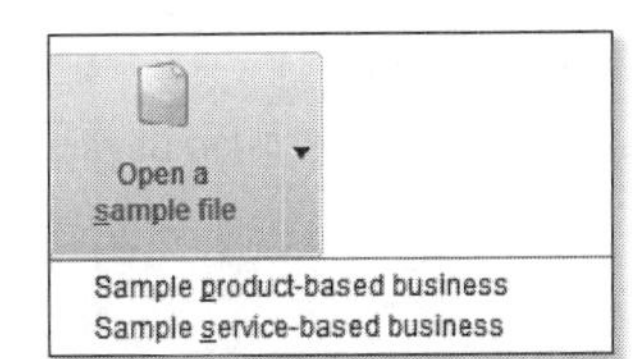

Figure 1.1
Practicing with sample data can help you feel more confident about using QuickBooks.

After creating your own data file, the next time you launch QuickBooks your file (not the sample file) will default as the file that QuickBooks opens.

If you want to quickly access previously opened QuickBooks files, including the sample file, select **File**, **Open Previous Company** from the menu bar. QuickBooks displays a list of previous files to choose from.

If you do not see other files listed, you might need to change the number of files displayed on this list. To do so, first open any data file. Then select **File**, **Open Previous Company**, **Set Number of Previous Companies** from the menu bar, and enter a number between 1 and 20. The No Company Open dialog box displays the most recent files you have opened with the software.

For more information, see "Selecting a Company File to Open," p. 77.

note

This book uses the Sample product-based business file included automatically when you install QuickBooks on the computer. The company name associated with this fictitious data file is Sample Rock Castle Construction. The images and exercises used in the book are from this sample file, but you can read along and practice with any of the installed sample files.

tip

Improved for QuickBooks 2013! Does the No Company Open dialog box include old, unused QuickBooks files? Would you like to see only the QuickBooks files you currently are using?

Click the Edit List link (see Figure 1.2) and place a checkmark next to each company file you want to hide. Click OK to save the changes. Note that the file remains on your computer or server and can later be opened by selecting **File, Open** or **Restore Company** from the menu bar.

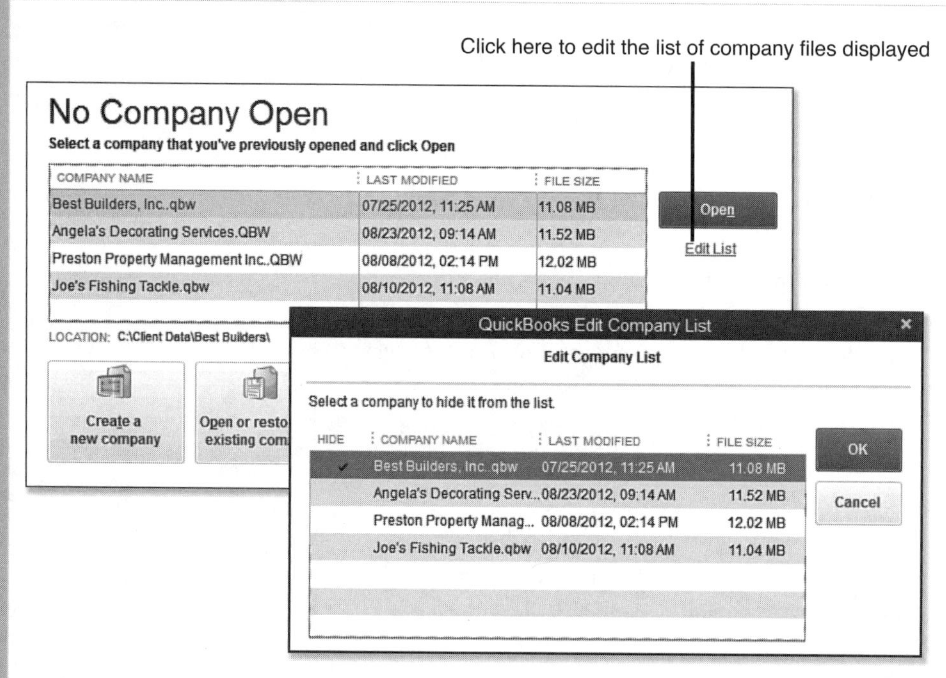

Figure 1.2 Edit the No Company Open dialog box to remove old, unused data files from the list.

Creating a New QuickBooks File

If you are new to QuickBooks, the first task is to create a data file. In the No Company Open dialog box, click the Create a New Company button. The QuickBooks Setup dialog box displays the following three options if you are using QuickBooks Pro, Premier (nonaccountant), or Enterprise (nonaccountant):

- **Express Start**—Create a file quickly with the least amount of initial setup time.
- **Advanced Setup**—Formerly called EasyStep Interview. Answer a series of questions to help you set up your new file. If you are using QuickBooks Accountant 2013, you will have additional methods as detailed in this section.

- **Other Options**—Open an Existing File, Convert Quicken Data, Convert from Other Accounting Software Data, or Set Upon Behalf of Someone Else.

To learn more about other options your accounting professional might have with QuickBooks Accountant 2013, see "Creating a New File from an Existing Company File," p. 45.

Choose from one of the three options that best suits your needs; each one is detailed in the following sections.

note

Are you working with QuickBooks Accountant 2013 or QuickBooks Enterprise Accountant 13.0? You have the previous options for creating a new file, plus the added method of creating a new company from an existing company file.

What information is copied from the existing company file to the new file? Sales tax items, chart of accounts (with the exception of bank or credit card accounts), and most preferences.

What information from the existing file is not copied to the new file? Memorized reports that contain data file-specific filters, memorized transactions, leads, customers, vendors, other names, and employees.

If instead of creating a new QuickBooks file you are upgrading your existing file, you can learn more about this process in "Upgrading Your QuickBooks Version," p. 617.

note

These steps detailed here are when using QuickBooks with maintenance release 4 or later. For more information see, "Installing a QuickBooks Maintenance Release," p. 618.

Express Start

With Express Start, you can use your new file in just three easy steps (outlined in the following sections). Express Start guides you through the basics of entering your company information, contact information, and—optionally—contacts, products, services, and bank accounts. From the menu bar select **File**, **Create a New Company**, and then click the Express Start button in the QuickBooks Setup dialog box. Alternatively, select the **Create a New Company** button in the No Company Open dialog box and then click the Express Start button.

Step 1—Tell Us

Enter the following information about your business as shown in Figure 1.3:

1. **Company Name**—This is the name that will be assigned to the file on your computer. This does not have to be your legal name.
2. **Industry**—QuickBooks uses this to provide you with a sample chart of accounts and for some industries, a sampling of ready-made items that are used throughout QuickBooks when invoicing customers and buying services or products from vendors. Click Help Me Choose to see the choices available for Industry selections.

3. **Company Type**—QuickBooks uses this to create specific equity accounts used primarily in tax preparation. Click Help Me Choose to see the choices available for Company Type.
4. **Tax ID#**—QuickBooks uses this information when processing payroll using one of Intuit's payroll subscription offerings.
5. **Do You Have Employees?**—Select Yes or No or No, but I might in the future.

When finished, click Continue to advance to the next step in the setup.

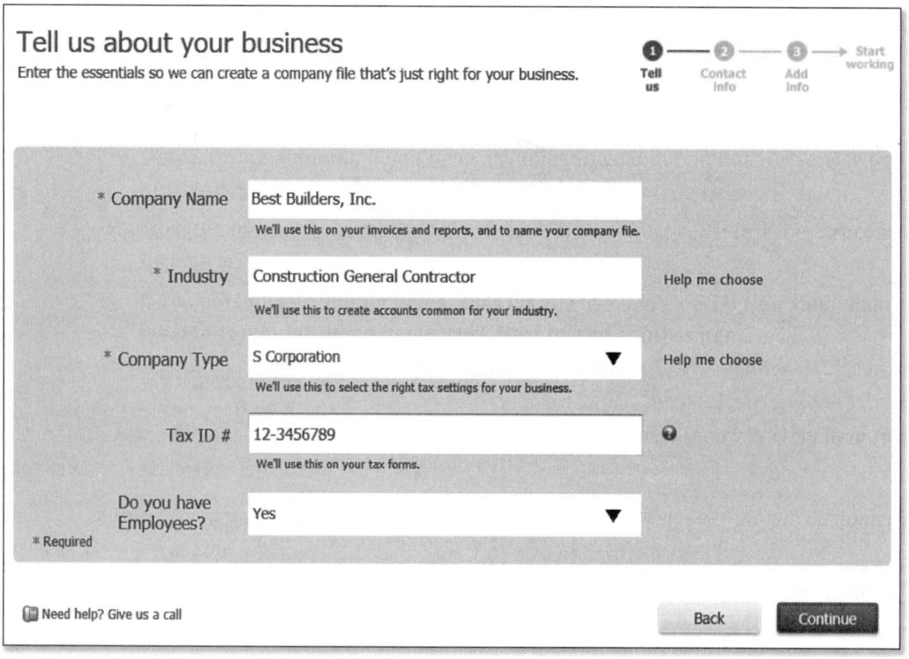

Tell us about your business

Enter the essentials so we can create a company file that's just right for your business.

Tell us — Contact Info — Add Info — Start working

* Company Name: Best Builders, Inc.

We'll use this on your invoices and reports, and to name your company file.

* Industry: Construction General Contractor — Help me choose

We'll use this to create accounts common for your industry.

* Company Type: S Corporation — Help me choose

We'll use this to select the right tax settings for your business.

Tax ID #: 12-3456789

We'll use this on your tax forms.

Do you have Employees?: Yes

* Required

Need help? Give us a call

Back | Continue

Figure 1.3 With Express Start, you can use your file in no time!

Step 2—Contact Info

Complete the following fields of information on the Contact Info dialog box shown in Figure 1.4:

1. Enter the legal name of the business. This will be used in payroll filings.
2. Enter other contact information. The zip code field and phone number field are required when setting up the file. This information will be used to set up a QuickBooks Payments account enabling you to receive payments online from your customers. More information will be sent to the email address you provide in this dialog box.

note

Intuit provides this information about their privacy practices: We value your privacy and security. This information is store safely on Intuit's servers.

3. You may choose to select the **Preview Your Settings** button. Click each of the displayed tabs to see the Features Selected, Chart of Accounts, and Company File Location QuickBooks suggests for you based on your answers in step 1. If you need to change the location where your QuickBooks data file will be stored, click the Change Location button on the Company File Location tab.

   Don't worry too much about the other settings just yet, because they are easy to modify later in your file and will be addressed in later chapters of the book.

4. Click OK to close the Preview Your Settings dialog box.

5. After completing the required fields, click the Create Company File button to continue to the next step. QuickBooks now creates your file and saves it on your hard drive or to a default location or to the specific location you selected in step 3. Optionally, click the Back button to review or change previous settings.

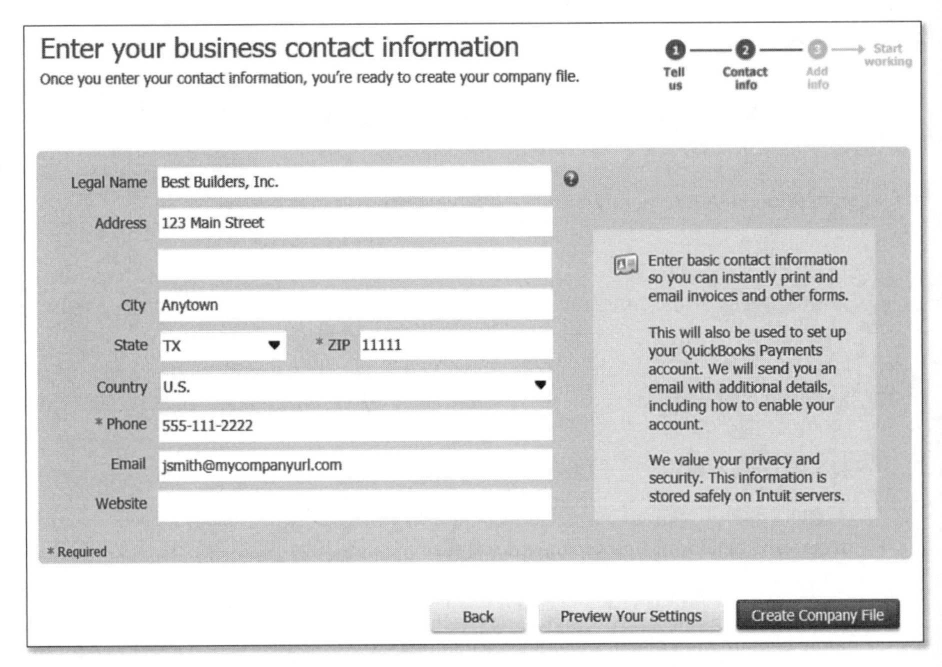

Figure 1.4 Complete the setup by entering your business contact information.

Step 3—Add Info

Continue with the QuickBooks Setup by adding the people you do business with, your products, services, and bank accounts to your new data file.

If you want to skip these steps, click the Start Working button on the bottom of the displayed dialog box (see Figure 1.5) to launch the QuickBooks Home page.

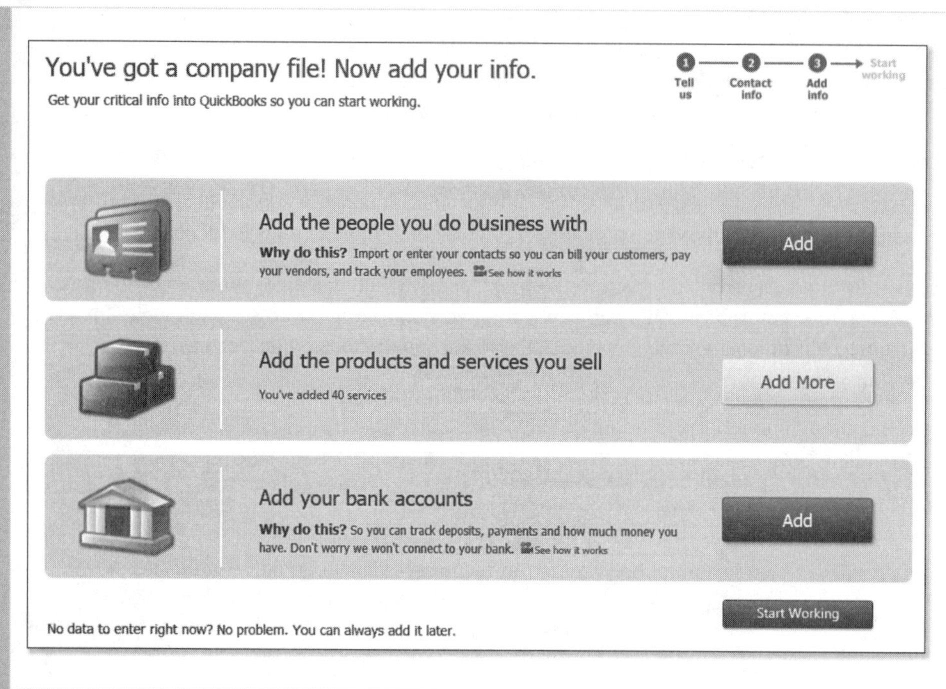

Figure 1.5 Adding your lists is easy with the QuickBooks Setup Wizard.

Adding People You Do Business With Now is the perfect time to add the people you do business with to your newly created file. This list includes customers, vendors, and employees. Adding contacts is a three-step process: choose how to add contacts, select who to add, and review and finish. Later, to learn more about these lists, see Chapter 7, "Setting Up Vendors" and Chapter 9, "Setting Up Customers."

To add contacts using the QuickBooks Setup Wizard, follow these steps:

1. Click the Add button in the Add the People You Do Business With box (or click Add More if you've already entered some names) to import or enter the names of people you do business with.
2. If you selected the Add option, you can choose how to add from these choices:
   - **Import from Outlook, Yahoo!, or Gmail Email**—Follow the instructions for importing from one of the listed email providers. You will be able to specify which contacts you want imported into QuickBooks. For Outlook, if you have more than one address book, you can choose which one to use for the import. For other email providers, you might receive an email message that you have shared your address book with QuickBooks.
   - **Paste from Excel or Enter Manually**—Your imported contacts display in the spreadsheet-like form shown in Figure 1.6. Be sure to scroll to the right to see additional data fields. You can also copy and paste from Excel or manually enter contacts directly in the form before importing.

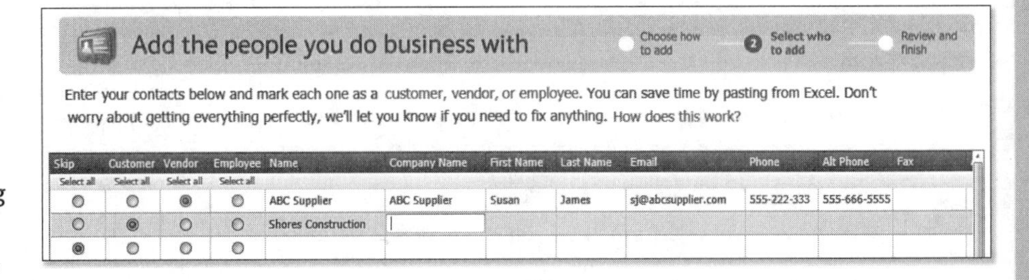

Figure 1.6 Adding the people you do business with is easy when getting started with QuickBooks.

3. If you selected **Add More**, you are returned to the Add the People You Do Business With dialog box with the same choices as listed in step 2.
4. After importing or entering manually, click Continue to review and finish. QuickBooks Setup checks your list for duplicate names or emails. If any duplicates are detected, you will need to change the Name field (not the Company Name field) so that no duplicates are imported.
5. Click the Fix button to have QuickBooks display any contacts that have duplicate names. Change the Name field to make each unique.
6. Click Continue after fixing. QuickBooks will show how many contacts are ready to be added and how many need to be fixed. Follow step 5 again if needed.
7. Click Continue. QuickBooks returns you to the dialog box for you to add more contacts or to add products, services, or bank accounts.

caution

If you choose, you can skip this step and then enter your contact information later. QuickBooks also makes it easy to later edit the information imported into your company data.

tip

QuickBooks does not allow you to have duplicated entries in the Name field across the various lists. For example, an employee name cannot be the same as a vendor name. An easy fix for this is to add a "V" to the end of the Name field for the vendor listing who is also included on the employee list.

Adding the Products and Services You Sell You can add the products and services you sell in just a few steps. If your business tracks inventory, you will not be able to enter your inventory items here.

note

Resist the temptation to click the Enter Opening Balances link on the dialog box displayed in step 6. Balances entered in this fashion are listed as a single amount due and not as individual customer invoices or vendor bill transactions. See Chapter 3, "Accounting 101," for more detailed information on properly setting up these beginning balances.

To add non-inventory products and services, follow these steps:

1. In the Add the Products and Services You Sell section, click Add (or click Add More if you've already entered some items).
2. Choose an item type and click the Continue button. Non-inventory types can be changed to inventory later. Item type options include the following:
   - **Service**—Work performed by you, such as an hour of labor
   - **Non-inventory part**—Products you sell but *do not* want to track as inventory
3. Copy and paste from a list you already have in Excel, or manually enter the item details including the name, description, price, and manufacturer's part number. Click Continue.
4. QuickBooks checks for any item duplicates, or if any items to be imported are already in your QuickBooks file. If necessary, click Fix. To add the items to your file, click Continue.

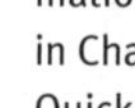

note

If you selected one of the selected industry types (as shown in Figure 1.3) your file may already contain industry-related items. You can find more information about working with items in Chapter 4, "Understanding QuickBooks Lists."

To learn more about setting up inventory, see Chapter 5 "Setting Up Inventory."

Adding Bank Accounts In the Add Bank Accounts panel, click Add to create accounts to track deposits, payments, and how much money you have. Type the Account Name (required) such as **Checking** or **Savings** and optional Account number. You can choose to enter your opening balance here or wait until you have reviewed the information in Chapter 3. If you choose to enter your opening balance, QuickBooks offsets the entry to the Opening Balance Equity account. Ask your accountant to help with this entry when it is time for your tax preparation.

tip

The bank account information you enter is necessary for you to properly reconcile your QuickBooks bank account. For example, if you are going to use 10/1/17 as your new start date, you would enter your Opening balance, which would be the 9/30/17 statement ending balance *not including* any uncleared checks or deposits. You will enter these individually later. For the Opening balance date you would use 9/30/17 in this example.

To add your bank accounts into your new QuickBooks file, follow these steps:

1. In the Add Your Bank Accounts dialog box (or the Add More dialog box if you've already entered an account), click the Add button.
2. Type your Account Name, Account Number (optional), Opening Balance (optional), and Opening Balance Date (optional).
3. Click Continue. QuickBooks displays information about ordering checks from Intuit. Select your reminder preference and click OK and Continue. QuickBooks adds the bank account to your data file.

You are now ready to begin working with your QuickBooks file. Click the Start Working button. The Quick Start Center dialog box displays with useful links to learn how to track money in and out using QuickBooks. Click the X in the top-right corner to close this dialog box.

Remember, everything you have entered so far is completely modifiable in your newly created QuickBooks file.

You can now skip to the section titled "Setting Up Users and Permissions" in this chapter.

Advanced Setup or Detailed Start—Formerly the EasyStep Interview

For help in creating a new file, earlier editions of QuickBooks did not have the Express Start option but instead offered the QuickBooks EasyStep Interview, which is now accessed from Advanced Setup in QuickBooks 2013 or Detailed Start when using QuickBooks Accountant 2013.

If you select the **Advanced Setup** or **Detailed Start** option, QuickBooks provides a series of question-and-answer type choices to help you properly set up your data file and certain default features.

Information to Collect

Having the following information on hand before starting the Advanced Setup or Detailed Start can help when entering the details:

- **Company name**—This should be the company name or a name that best describes the business. By default, this is the filename given to the data file (.QBW extension) on your computer.
- **Legal name**—The legal name displays on certain reports and federal tax forms.
- **Tax ID**—Although this ID is not required to begin using QuickBooks, it is required if you want to sign up for one of the QuickBooks payroll services or use QuickBooks to print 1099s.
- **Remaining information**—This includes a phone number, email address, website, and so on (see Figure 1.7). This information can optionally be added in QuickBooks, such as on a customer invoice.

If you need to leave the EasyStep Interview at any time after saving the file, QuickBooks returns to the point where you left off when you open the data file again.

The EasyStep Interview now prompts you for certain information based on what industry you selected. Your answers to the remaining questions will make certain features in QuickBooks the default. The purpose of this chapter is not to define each of these choices; most are self-explanatory or are included in various chapters in this book. However, discussing the effect of several important choices is useful at this time.

Using Advanced Setup or Detailed Start

You may prefer to have a bit more control of the setup process up front. This is exactly what the Advanced Setup (also known as the EasyStep Interview) offers.

To create a new file using Advanced Setup, from the menu bar, click File, Create a New Company, and then in the QuickBooks Setup dialog box, click the Advanced Setup button. Alternatively, in the No Company Open dialog box, click the Create a New Company button, and then click the Advanced Setup button.

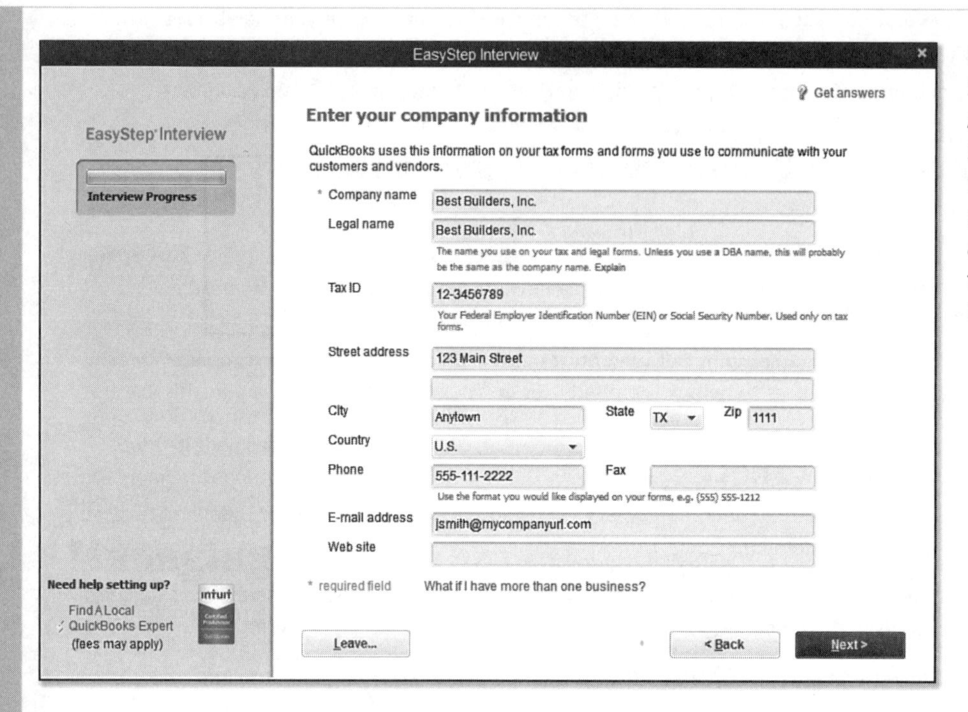

Figure 1.7 Selecting Advanced Setup or Detailed Start provides access to the EasyStep Interview.

You will then enter the following information when creating the new data file:

- **Enter Your Company Information**—Enter your Company Name, Legal Name, Tax ID, and other information that can be included on customer invoices and other forms within QuickBooks. Click Next.
- **Select Your Industry**—QuickBooks can help you get started quickly by providing basic information for particular industries (see Figure 1.8). Pick an industry that closely matches your own. Click Next.

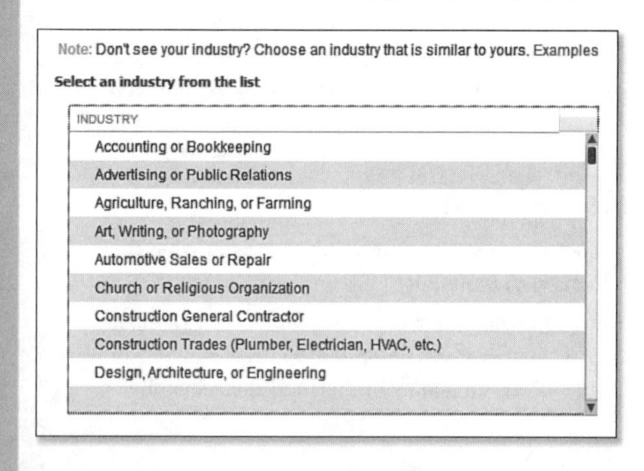

Figure 1.8 QuickBooks includes customized settings for your specific industry.

- **How Is Your Company Organized?**—Select the legal organization your company selected when obtaining your Federal Identification Number. This choice creates unique Equity accounts to match your legal selection. Click Next.

note

Do not worry if you cannot complete the entire set of questions at one time. After QuickBooks creates the file, you can click the Leave button. QuickBooks saves your choices and when you reopen QuickBooks, you return to where you left off.

- **Select the First Month of Your Fiscal Year**—Select the month your fiscal year starts in. Some reports will display the correct fiscal year dates by default when you select this option. Click Next.
- **Set Up Your Administrator Password**—It is recommended that you set up an administrator password. If you do not set one during the EasyStep Interview, you can open a QuickBooks file with the default username of Admin and leave the password blank. Using a blank password is fine during the initial setup, but you should put more security in place after you enter sensitive information. You can also set up or change this password later. Click Next and QuickBooks creates your company file.

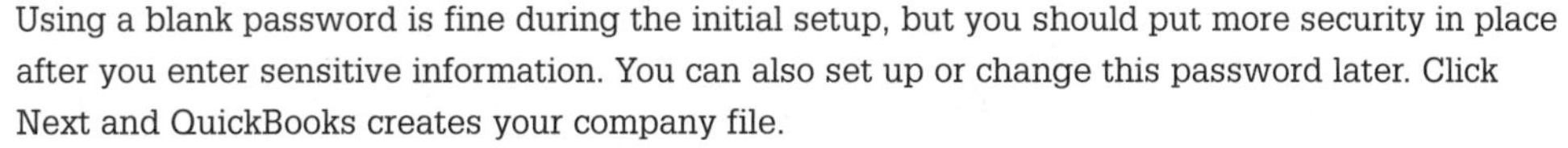

- **Create Your Company File**—QuickBooks requires that you decide where to store the company data file and provide a name for the file. Click Next. Browse to select a location to store your file or accept the default location and name suggested by QuickBooks. Click Save. QuickBooks displays a progressive message that your file is being created.
- **Customizing QuickBooks for Your Business**—After reading the information, click Next.
- **What Do You Sell?**—Choose from Services, Products, or Both Services and Products. This preference affects the type of default invoice form that is selected when you begin using QuickBooks. Click Next.
- **Do You Charge Sales Tax?**—Specify whether you want to charge sales tax, choosing from the Yes or No option button. (You can change this later if necessary). Click Next.
- **Do You Want to Create Estimates in QuickBooks?**—Select either the **Yes** or **No** option button. If you provide a proposal to your clients or multiple proposals, you will want to enable this feature. Click Next.
- **Tracking Customer Orders in QuickBooks**—Choose either the Yes or No options. (This feature is available only in QuickBooks Premier, Accountant, or QuickBooks Enterprise Solutions.) Click Next.

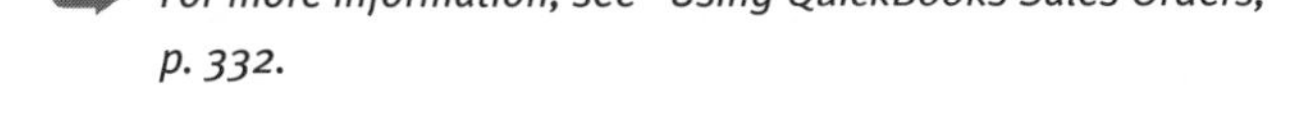

For more information, see "Using QuickBooks Sales Orders," p. 332.

note

Not certain which choice to make when completing the Advanced Setup (EasyStep Interview)? No worries; QuickBooks selects the recommended option based on the industry you selected in step 2.

- **Using Statements in QuickBooks**—Choose between Yes or No. This option enables you to print past-due statements for your customers. Click Next.
- **Using Invoices in QuickBooks and Using Progress Invoicing in QuickBooks**—Select **Yes or No**. Selecting Yes enables the use of customer invoices. In selected industries, you might also be prompted to enable progress invoicing. Progress invoicing is "milestone billing" (when you invoice a customer progressively during a job).

- **Managing Bills You Owe**—Choosing Yes enables the capability for you to enter vendor bills and pay those bills at a later date. Click Next.

Working with vendors is discussed in Chapter 7, "Setting Up Vendors."

- **Tracking Inventory in QuickBooks**—Select either **Yes** or **No** to enable this feature. Remember, these features can later be enabled in Preferences. Click Next.

To learn more about inventory, see Chapter 5, "Setting Up Inventory" and Chapter 6, "Managing Inventory."

- **Tracking Time in QuickBooks**—Tracking time enables you to bill customers for time, analyze time on projects, and pay hourly employees. Select either **Yes** or **No**. Click Next.
- **Do You Have Employees?**—Choose either W-2 employees or 1099 contractors. If you selected Yes to W-2 employees, QuickBooks will create the needed Chart of Accounts items. This setting can be modified later. Click Next.
- **Using Accounts in QuickBooks**—Click the link "Why Is the Chart of Accounts Important" to learn more about this list in QuickBooks. Click Next.

This list is also discussed in Chapter 4, "Understanding QuickBooks Lists."

- **Select a Date to Start Tracking Your Finances**—Choose from Beginning of This Fiscal Year: 01/01/2016 (for example) or Use Today's Date or The First Day of the Quarter or Month. These are examples of potential start dates.
  - You start using QuickBooks immediately upon starting your business with no prior expenses or income. This date is the easiest one to work with because you have no historical balances or transactions to consider. You begin by paying vendors and invoicing customers. Everything else falls into place.
  - At the beginning of a calendar year, such as January 1, 20xx. This choice is common when the decision to begin using QuickBooks is at the end of a year or not very far into the new year. Again, if the company has previously had business transactions, there will be beginning balances to enter.

To learn more, see "Setting Up a QuickBooks Data File for Accrual or Cash Basis Reporting," p. 88.

  - At the beginning of your fiscal year, (for companies whose tax year does not coincide with the calendar year).
  - The first day of a month during the current calendar or fiscal year. Click Next when you're finished with this selection.
- **Review Income and Expense Accounts**—You are provided the opportunity to include or exclude certain default charts of account from your new data file. Click Next.

tip

If you selected the incorrect first month of your fiscal year during the EasyStep Interview, you can easily change it by selecting **Company, Company Information** from the menu bar. Changing this month does not affect individual transactions but does ensure that the reports that are based on a fiscal year are correct.

- **Congratulations**—You are finished with the Advanced (or Detailed) Setup. Click Go to Setup.
- **You've Got a Company File!**—You can now add contacts, products, services, and bank accounts as discussed in the "Express Start" section earlier in this chapter.

Creating a New File from an Existing Company File

Available with QuickBooks Accountant 2013 and QuickBooks Enterprise Solutions Accountant 13.0 is the option to use an existing QuickBooks data file to create a new data file from, as shown in Figure 1.9. Your original file is left unchanged in the process.

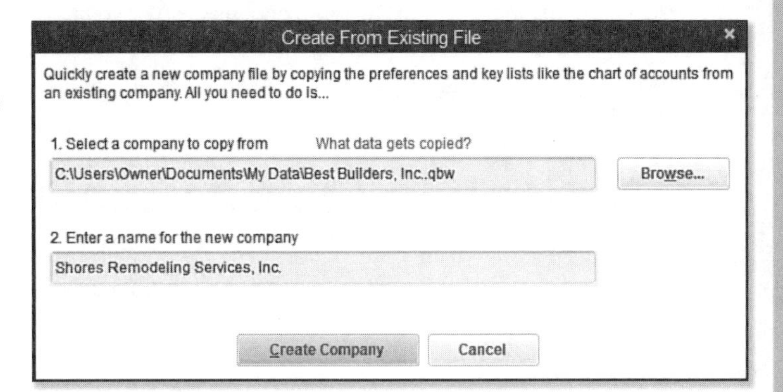

Figure 1.9
Convenient tool for accounting professionals who have a template file they want to copy for their clients to use.

To create a new file from an existing file, follow these steps:

1. From the QuickBooks Setup dialog box, click the Create button. The Create from Existing File dialog displays.
2. By default, the currently opened company is selected as the file to be copied from. To select a different QuickBooks file, click the Browse button.
3. Type a **Name** for the new company file.
4. Click Create Company.
5. Accept the default filename and location for saving your new file, or modify as needed.
6. Click Save.

note

The capability to create a new file from an existing file referenced in step 1 is available only if you are creating a new file from the Accountant 2013 or Enterprise Solutions Accountant 13.0 software.

Using the Create from Existing Company File process, QuickBooks copies the following information, from one file to another:

- **Preferences**—Not including those for bank or credit card accounts.
- **Items List**—Only sales tax items, no products or services.

- **Memorized Reports**—Only those that do not filter for specific accounts, customers or jobs, vendors, items, or employees.
- **Type of Tax Form**—Useful if you are going to integrate with tax preparation software.
- **Chart of Accounts**—No bank accounts are copied.

If you find that you wanted more details copied from the original file, or wanted to remove a specific year's transactions, ask your accounting professional to use QuickBooks Accountant 2013 software and provide you with a newly created "Condensed Data" file.

Hopefully, you found one of the three options best for your needs in starting your new QuickBooks file. The next section in this chapter covers converting other accounting software to a QuickBooks file.

tip

Not using the Accountant version of QuickBooks software? Or, would you like to be able to copy the products and services from one file to another? Consider using the IIF (Intuit Interchange Format) export. From the menu bar, select **File, Utilities, Export, Lists to IIF Files.**

With this option, you are able to select a specific list (not transactions) that you want to import into another QuickBooks file.

Converting from Other Accounting Software

QuickBooks has automated the process of converting files from other financial software into QuickBooks files. Other programs you can convert from include the following:

- Quicken
- Peachtree by Sage (recently renamed Sage 50)
- Microsoft Small Business Accounting
- Microsoft Office Accounting

This section provides specific details about how QuickBooks handles the conversions and what you need to consider when making the choice to convert existing data from one of the listed financial software programs to a QuickBooks data file.

Before converting your company data to QuickBooks, make sure you have QuickBooks installed and registered/licensed and updated to the latest release. For more information, see "Managing Your QuickBooks Database," p. 609.

Even with the automation of the process, you should consider finding a QuickBooks Certified ProAdvisor in your area to assist with the conversion. From the Help menu in QuickBooks, select **Find a Local QuickBooks Expert**.

Converting from Quicken to QuickBooks

To begin the conversion from Quicken, open QuickBooks, select **File**, **New Company** from the menu bar, and then from the Other Options drop-down list in the QuickBooks Setup dialog box, select **Convert Quicken Data**. The Conversion tool copies your Quicken data to a new QuickBooks file, leaving your original Quicken data file unchanged.

Table 1.2 shows you how the Quicken accounts are converted into QuickBooks accounts.

Table 1.2 Quicken Account Conversion

This type of account in Quicken:	Becomes this type of account in QuickBooks:
Checking	Bank
Credit Card	Credit Card
Asset	Other Current Asset
Liability	Other Current Liability
Investment	Other Current Asset

Because QuickBooks does not offer the Investment tracking feature that is in Quicken, you can choose whether to include or exclude the value of your investments in the resulting QuickBooks balance sheet. If you choose to include them, QuickBooks converts the investment accounts into the Other Current Asset chart of account type.

If you choose to exclude the investments, you are given the opportunity to delete the accounts before converting to QuickBooks. Any transfers that were recorded to or from the deleted accounts are recorded to your Opening Balance Equity account. This is in keeping with the "debits equal credits" accounting that is going on behind the scenes in QuickBooks.

During the conversion process QuickBooks asks you whether a Quicken Accounts Receivable account with customer payments exists. If you click Yes, the QuickBooks Conversion tool asks you to identify your Quicken Accounts Receivable account. QuickBooks then begins converting the Quicken transactions to QuickBooks Accounts Receivable transactions. This process can take several minutes.

During the conversion:

- QuickBooks creates an Opening Balance Equity account to compensate for deleted Quicken accounts.
- Memorized Invoices in Quicken might need to be reviewed, making sure the items memorized in Quicken remain on the invoice in QuickBooks.
- Duplicate check, invoice, or credit memo numbers are stored in a QBwin.log for review. You learn more about this log in Chapter 17.
- Every payee name in Quicken must be on a QuickBooks list.

Because QuickBooks cannot determine which list an item belongs to, it places all items on the Other Name list (see Figure 1.10).

From the menu bar, select **Lists**, **Other Names List** to open the Other Name List dialog box. Right-click this dialog box and then select **Change Other Name Types** for a one-time option to change the payee from an Other Name list item to a vendor, employee, or customer. If you do not need to use a name on vendor transaction or customer form, you can leave the name on the Other Names list.

caution

After you click OK to change the name type, you cannot undo the change. If you are not sure what list the payee belongs to, leave it as an Other Name.

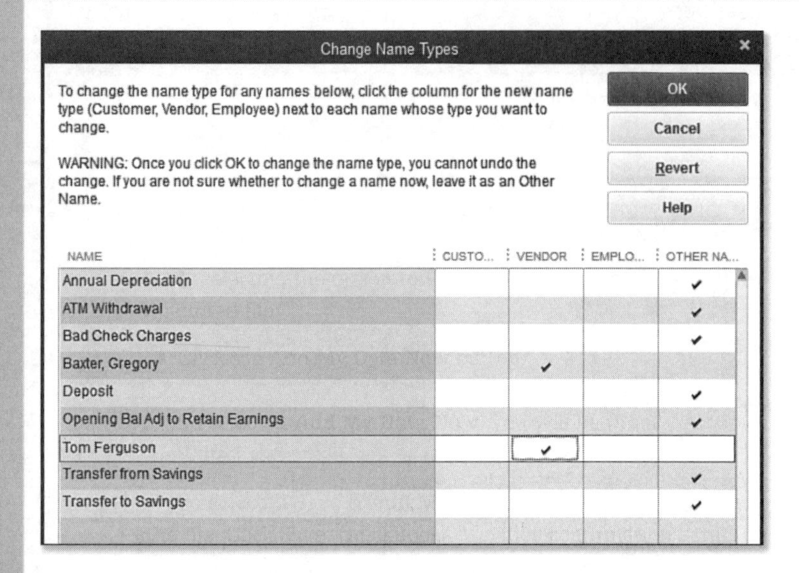

Figure 1.10
After converting from Quicken, you will need to reassign most of the names on the Other Names list to the Customer, Vendor, or Employee Lists.

Converting from Peachtree, Small Business Accounting, or Office Accounting to QuickBooks

Just as in the Quicken conversion, QuickBooks can convert your Peachtree/Sage 50, Small Business Accounting, or Office Accounting data to QuickBooks data directly from the Options drop-down menu on the QuickBooks Setup dialog box. The conversion process leaves your original Peachtree/Sage 50, Small Business Accounting, or Office Accounting data untouched.

To download the free conversion tool, follow these steps:

1. From the menu bar, select **File**, **New Company** or, alternatively, in the No Company Open dialog box, click the Create a New Company button. The QuickBooks Setup dialog box displays.
2. From the Other Options drop-down list, select **Convert Other Accounting Software Data**; you will need an Internet connection to complete this step.
3. Follow the helpful links to download the free conversion tool or to read the Conversion Tool FAQs document.

The free downloadable tool converts Peachtree/Sage 50 (2001 or later versions), Microsoft Small Business Accounting, or Office Accounting (2007–2009 versions). You can convert to QuickBooks Pro, Premier 2008 or later, or Enterprise Solutions 8.0 or later. The tool can be used to convert multiple company files from any of the named software.

The technical whitepaper available when downloading the free conversion tool is outdated as of the writing of this book, but still provides useful information about the conversion details.

In the conversion process, you can select the specific Peachtree/Sage 50, Microsoft Small Business Accounting, Microsoft Office Accounting, or Office Accounting Express file and the QuickBooks product version to which you will be converting it. Additionally, you can specify the conversion of lists and transactions (including historical transactions) or lists only.

You also choose a conversion date; any transactions dated after this date will not be converted.

Because of the differences between the two products, you are also given a choice to identify customers and vendors in QuickBooks with the name of the Peachtree/Sage 50, Microsoft Small Business Accounting, Microsoft Office Accounting, or Microsoft Office Express ID value. You must choose to use the name or the ID value in QuickBooks, so it's best to make this decision before performing the conversion.

Key lists that are converted include the following:

- Chart of accounts
- Customer/prospects
- Jobs
- Employees/sales reps
- Vendors
- Inventory item
- Custom fields
- Balance information

Open transactions include the following:

- Open invoices
- Open vendor bills

Customer transactions include the following:

- Estimates
- Sales orders
- Invoices
- Payment receipts
- Deposits
- Credit memos

Vendor transactions include the following:

- Purchase orders
- Bills
- Bill payments
- Checks
- Bill credits

Setting Up Users and Permissions

QuickBooks always creates a default user with the username Admin. The Admin user has full rights to all settings and preferences in QuickBooks. If your company is going to have multiple users accessing the QuickBooks data file, it is recommended that you create a unique user login for each person and assign specific permissions if needed. With unique usernames for each person, QuickBooks will be able to tell you who entered, modified, or deleted a transaction on the Audit Trail report.

External Accountant

Business owners who plan to share data with their accountant at tax time or for other purposes should create a unique user for your accountant. The External Accountant user type has all the controls of the Admin, except that the accountant cannot do the following:

- Add, delete, modify, or view sensitive customer credit card details
- Add, delete, or modify other QuickBooks user settings

note
Table 1.1 listed the number of users who can work in a company file at the same time, based on the version of the software that you have. If you need to buy additional licenses from the menu bar choose Help, Manage My License, Buy Additional User License.

To create a user login for your accountant, follow these steps:

1. From the menu bar, select **Company**, **Set Up Users and Passwords**, **Set Up Users**.
2. In the User List dialog box, click the Add User button.
3. Enter a User Name and Password (optional but recommended) and then enter the password again to confirm.
4. If you need to add additional licenses to your QuickBooks file, click the Explain link for more information about Intuit's licensing policy.
5. Click the Next button. If you didn't enter a password in step 3, QuickBooks opens the No Password Entered dialog box. Click Yes to create a password or No to skip this step.
6. Select the **External Accountant** option button, as shown in Figure 1.11, and click Next to continue.
7. In the Warning dialog box, click Yes to confirm you want to give the user access to all areas of QuickBooks, except credit card information.
8. Click Finish. If a Warning dialog box opens, click OK to confirm that you understand that the Admin user is being assigned to integrated applications.
9. Click Close to close the User List dialog box.

tip
If you are an accounting professional using QuickBooks Accountant 2013, you can use the QuickBooks File Manager 2013 to store your client's assigned username and password for you. When you open the client's file from within File Manager, QuickBooks automatically logs you in, bypassing the username and password dialog. This works with QuickBooks Pro, Premier, or Enterprise 2011 or newer files.

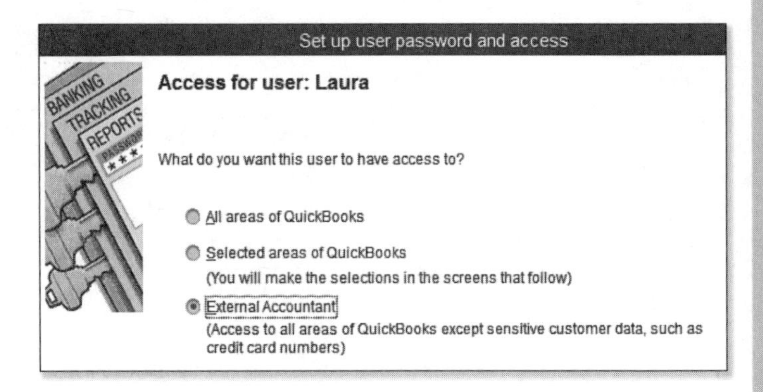

Figure 1.11
Creating an External Accountant user for your accounting professional limits access to sensitive customer information.

To log in to the file as the new External Accountant user, select **File**, **Close Company/Logoff** from the menu bar. From the No Company Open dialog box, select the file from the list. Click Open and enter the username and password.

Other QuickBooks Users

Setting up users with permissions is recommended when you have multiple users working in the same QuickBooks file. Transactions are assigned to users and many changes to the file are also tracked to the user who logged in to the file.

To create a user login and set permissions for additional users, follow these steps:

1. From the menu bar, select **Company**, **Set Up Users and Passwords**, **Set Up Users**.
2. From the User List dialog box, select **Add User**.
3. Enter a User Name and Password (optional but recommended) and enter the password again to confirm.
4. If you need to add additional licenses to your QuickBooks file, click the Explain link.
5. If you didn't enter a password, click Yes to create a password or No to skip this step.
6. Select the access option:
   - **All areas**—Provides access to all areas of QuickBooks except those which require Admin access.
   - **Selected areas**—Allows you to choose the options for access to each sensitive area of your QuickBooks data.
7. You now work through nine permission screens and on the tenth screen (see Figure 1.12) you can review the permission settings. Each dialog box offers details about the access levels and most include some or all of the following permission levels:

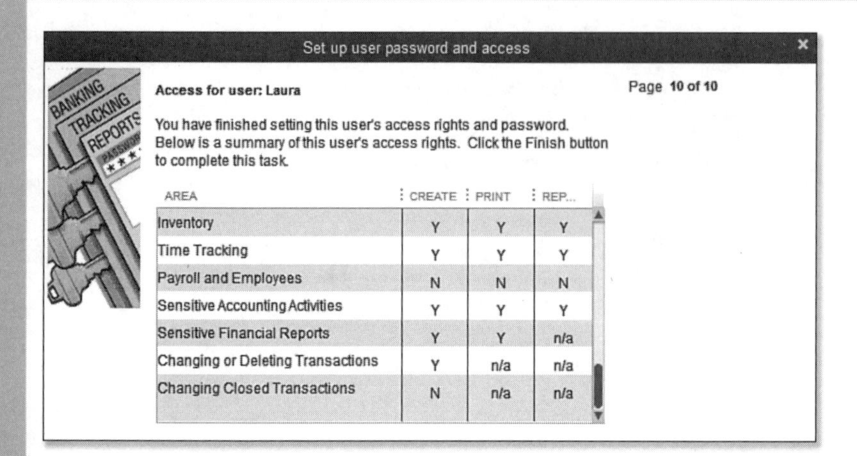

Figure 1.12
You can review a summary of the access rights assigned to a QuickBooks user.

- No Access
- Full Access
- Selective Access—Includes all or some of these options:
  - Create transactions only
  - Create and print transactions
  - Create transactions and create reports

If you are uncertain about the limitations of a permission setting in QuickBooks Pro or Premier, I recommend you set it for the Create Only option—the highest level of security. Then log in as that new user and attempt to access an area the employee will work in or an area she shouldn't be in to determine if the permissions assigned provide the controls you need. QuickBooks will tell you what level of permission is needed for any task you attempt.

note

Are you a QuickBooks Pro and Premier user intrigued by the extensive user security available in QuickBooks Enterprise? No worries; upgrade your data file to QuickBooks Enterprise with just a click. All your previous data will be available in QuickBooks Enterprise software. The user interface and menus in Enterprise are similar to QuickBooks Pro and Premier so you do not have to learn to use new software! For more information, see "Upgrading Your QuickBooks Version," p. 617.

User Security in QuickBooks Enterprise

If you have users other than yourself accessing QuickBooks enterprise data, you'll surely want to implement security controls. QuickBooks Enterprise allows granular control over user access to tasks, reports, and features.

QuickBooks Enterprise offers far more robust access control than QuickBooks Pro or Premier.

Overview

QuickBooks Enterprise Solutions 13.0 provides the capability to safeguard sensitive business data by giving employees access only to the specific information they need. These controls are robust with the capability to set individual user permissions for more than 115 different tasks in QuickBooks.

To use the QuickBooks Enterprise user security settings, you need to complete these steps:

1. Add to or modify the supplied user roles.
2. Set up named users.
3. Assign a role or multiple roles to the named user.

When defining access rights, you are modifying specific activity rights within an Area in QuickBooks. Areas are defined as a group of related tasks. Areas include the following:

- Accounting
- Banking
- Centers
- Company
- Customers & Receivables
- Employees & Payroll
- File Menu
- Lists
- Reports
- Time Tracking
- Vendors & Payables

Enable multiuser access if you want to have two or more users access your QuickBooks file simultaneously.

For more information, see "Changing to Multiuser Access," p. 613.

The next section discusses how to set up or modify user roles in QuickBooks Enterprise.

Set Up and Modify User Roles

In QuickBooks, a user role permits, limits, or blocks a user's access to reports, transactions, lists, centers, and so on. Roles can represent positions within a company and can be assigned to multiple QuickBooks users.

QuickBooks Enterprise comes with these predefined roles (similar to a position title) that can be modified (unless otherwise noted):

- Accountant
- Accounts Payable
- Accounts Receivable
- Admin (cannot be modified)
- Banking
- External Accountant (cannot be modified)
- Finance
- Full Access
- Inventory
- Payroll Manager
- Payroll Processor
- Purchasing
- Sales
- Time Tracking
- View-only

These roles have predefined, modifiable security settings for specific activities related to that feature area. With roles you can do the following:

- Create a New Role
- Edit an Existing Role (except as noted previously)
- Duplicate an Existing Role
- Delete a Role

The first step is to review the permissions assigned for a specific role or, optionally, create a new role. It is often easier to select an existing role and modify it. To modify an existing role, follow these instructions:

1. Log in to the QuickBooks file as the default Admin user, as discussed earlier in this chapter.
2. From the menu bar, select **Company**, **Users**, **Set Up Users**. The Users and Roles dialog box displays with the Users Tab selected.
3. To modify or create a Role, select the **Role List** tab. For this example, the Role Name of Accounts Payable was selected.
4. Click the Edit button on the right. The Edit Role dialog displays with the following information, as shown in Figure 1.13:

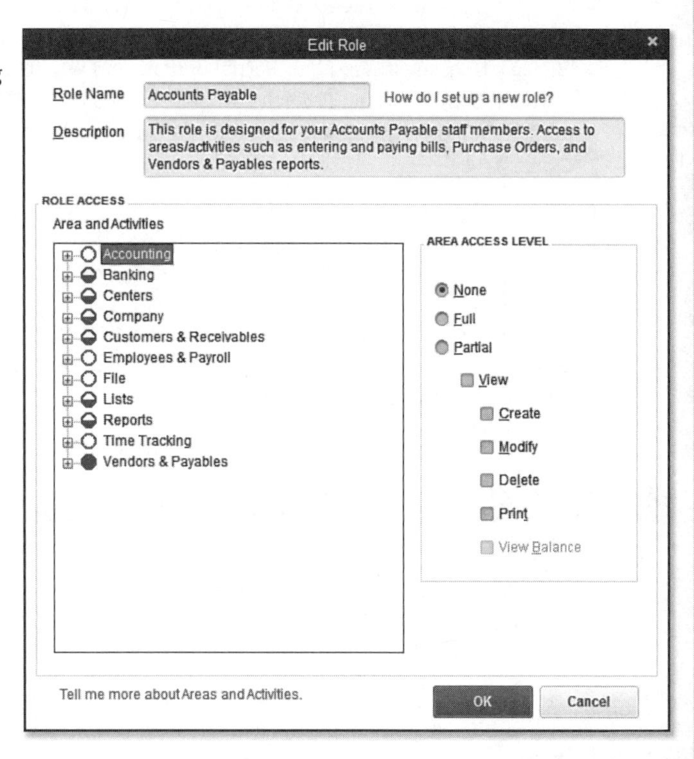

Figure 1.13
Edit the security settings for an existing Role.

- **Role Name**—This is the name you'll see when you choose from a list of roles to assign to a user.
- **Description**—Provide an overview of the role's rights and restrictions.
  - **Area and Activities**—Functional groupings of QuickBooks activities. Each area's general access level is noted by the coloring of the icon in front of the area, per the following:
    - **Shaded Circle**—Indicates that all activities in this area are allowed Full Access rights for the selected role.
    - **Partially Shaded Circle**—Indicates that some activity restrictions exist in that group for the selected role.
    - **Nonshaded Circle**—Indicates no access to any of the activities in this area.
  - **Area Access Level**—Assign more granular access controls.
  - **None**—No access to the selected Role Access Activity.
  - **Full**—Complete, unlimited access to the selected Role Access Activity.
  - **Partial**—View option, as well as access to Create, Modify, Delete, Print, View Balance, and other options unique to the selected Role Access Activity.

5. For this example, in the Area and Activities panel select the minus sign (–) in front of Custom Transaction to expand the choices. Choose either Full or Partial options and whether the user can both View and Print the report. You choices will differ depending on the specific activity you have selected. See Figure 1.14.

6. Make any other modifications to this Area and other Areas and Activities as needed. When finished with the changes, click OK.

After a role is created or modified, it can be assigned to one or more users of the company file. Conversely, a user can be assigned multiple roles.

tip

Do you want to provide users with the opportunity to create reports, but not have the report display information they do not have access to? When defining role access, in the Area and Activities section, select **Custom Transaction** and choose the **Custom Transaction Detail Limited** option, as shown in Figure 1.14.

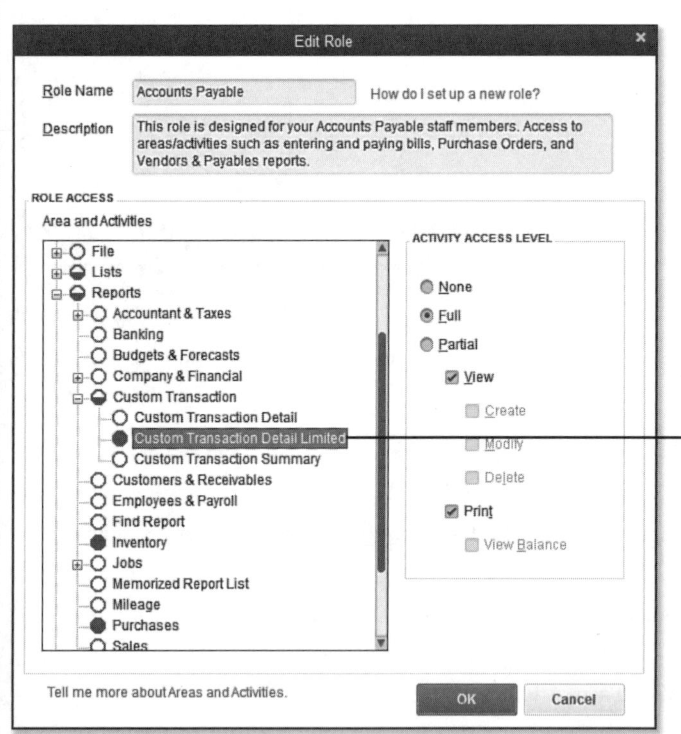

Figure 1.14
Define granular user security settings with QuickBooks Enterprise.

note

Are you uncertain how many User Licenses you have with your QuickBooks Enterprise software? With the file open, on your keyboard press F2 to display the Product Information dialog. Near the top and to the left the number of User Licenses will be listed. QuickBooks Enterprise offers simultaneous use by 5–30 users.

For example, to prevent a user from accessing sensitive payroll information, you must set user access levels as shown in Table 1.3 for the role assigned to the user:

Table 1.3 Limiting Access to Payroll

Area	Access Level
Employees & Payroll	None
Centers > Employee Center	None
Banking > Checks	None
Banking > Bank Accounts > Paycheck Bank Account	None
Reports > Company & Financial > Company & Financial Report Detail	None
Reports > Company & Financial > Company & Financial Report Summary	View only (If user needs it; otherwise, set to None)
Reports > Employees & Payroll	None
Reports > Custom Transaction	None

Now that you have set up roles that have the desired security settings for Activities, you can create users and assign these roles to the users.

Set Up Users

After creating or modifying user roles, you are ready to add named users to the file and assign the user roles to them.

1. Log in to the QuickBooks file as the default Admin user, as discussed earlier in this chapter.
2. From the menu bar, select **Company**, **Users**, **Set Up Users**. The Users and Roles dialog box displays with the Users Tab selected.
3. Select **User List** tab. From this tab you can do the following:
   - Add a new user
   - Edit an existing user's settings
   - Duplicate an existing user's settings for ease in adding a new, similar user
   - Delete a user (not recommended), instead if a user no longer is with the company: simply remove the user's roles.
4. Select **New**. The New User dialog displays.

caution

When someone no longer works for your company, resist the urge to delete the person's name. If you remove the name, transactions entered or modified by this user will be listed as "unknown user" on the audit trail reports. Instead, change the user's password and access level. Only active users in your file count toward your licensed user limit.

5. Type a User Name. This is the name the user will need to type to log in to the data file. The name typed is not case sensitive, but it must be spelled exactly as it is listed here, including any spaces.

6. Type a password (optional but recommended). This password is case sensitive.

7. Type the password again to confirm.

8. From the Available Roles list, select the applicable roles for this individual's duties in the QuickBooks file. Click the Add button to assign the selected Role to the Assigned Roles list to the right.

9. Click OK when you are finished with assigning Roles to the selected new user name.

10. You may get a warning message if you have previously instructed QuickBooks to log in to the file automatically. Click OK to close the message. You are returned to the User and Roles list displaying the newly created user and the roles assigned, as shown in Figure 1.15.

You can print a report detailing the permissions by employee or role. From the Users and Roles dialog box, click the View Permissions. You can choose to show permissions for the User or Role. Click Display to view the details.

Figure 1.15
From the Users and Roles dialog, you can see who is logged into the file and the roles assigned to each of the users.

Reporting on User Activity

Setting up users with the proper security access is important for any company that wants to have controls in place with its accounting data.

You can use these reports to track transactions that have been added, modified, or deleted using these reports accessible from the menu bar, by choosing **Reports**, **Accountant & Taxes**:

- **Audit Trail**—Listing of all transactions added or modified, grouped by username. You can learn more about this report in Chapter 15, "Reviewing Your Data."
- **Closing Date Exception Report**—Provides details of when the closing date was set or removed and transactions that were altered on or before the set closing date. More about working with the closing date can be found in Chapter 16, "Sharing QuickBooks Data with Your Accountant."
- **Customer Credit Card Audit Trail**—If you track credit card numbers for your customers in QuickBooks, you can enable credit card security and prepare reports on who accessed this sensitive information. To enable this security for your file, from the menu bar, choose Customer Credit Card Protection.
- **Voided/Deleted Transactions Summary**—This report cannot be filtered to remove the information. For more information, see Chapter 15, "Reviewing Your Data."
- **Voided/Deleted Transactions Detail**—This report cannot be filtered to remove the information. For more information, see Chapter 15.

Additionally, if you are using QuickBooks Accountant 2013 or QuickBooks Enterprise Solutions Accountant 13.0, you have access to Client Data Review, which includes a tool to track changes to lists. The previously listed reports do not report on changes to lists. See Appendix A, "Client Data Review," for more details.

With QuickBooks 2013, you have gotten off to a quick start in setting up your new file (or converting from other accounting software) and setting up users with specific permissions. You will also find it helpful to use the QuickBooks sample data when you want to practice or follow along with much of the content in this book.

2

GETTING AROUND QUICKBOOKS

You can make the most of your QuickBooks software when you learn how to navigate and customize the options available to meet your business's specific needs. This chapter shows you just how easy that task can be. For example, if your business does not need to track inventory, you can turn off that feature. However, as your business grows and the products and services you offer change, you can later enable these features once again.

Home Page and Navigation

QuickBooks 2013 makes it even easier to customize and navigate this easy-to-use and very popular accounting software. Let's start by making this *your* software!

Title Bar

At the top of your open QuickBooks file is the title bar, as shown on the Home page in Figure 2.1.

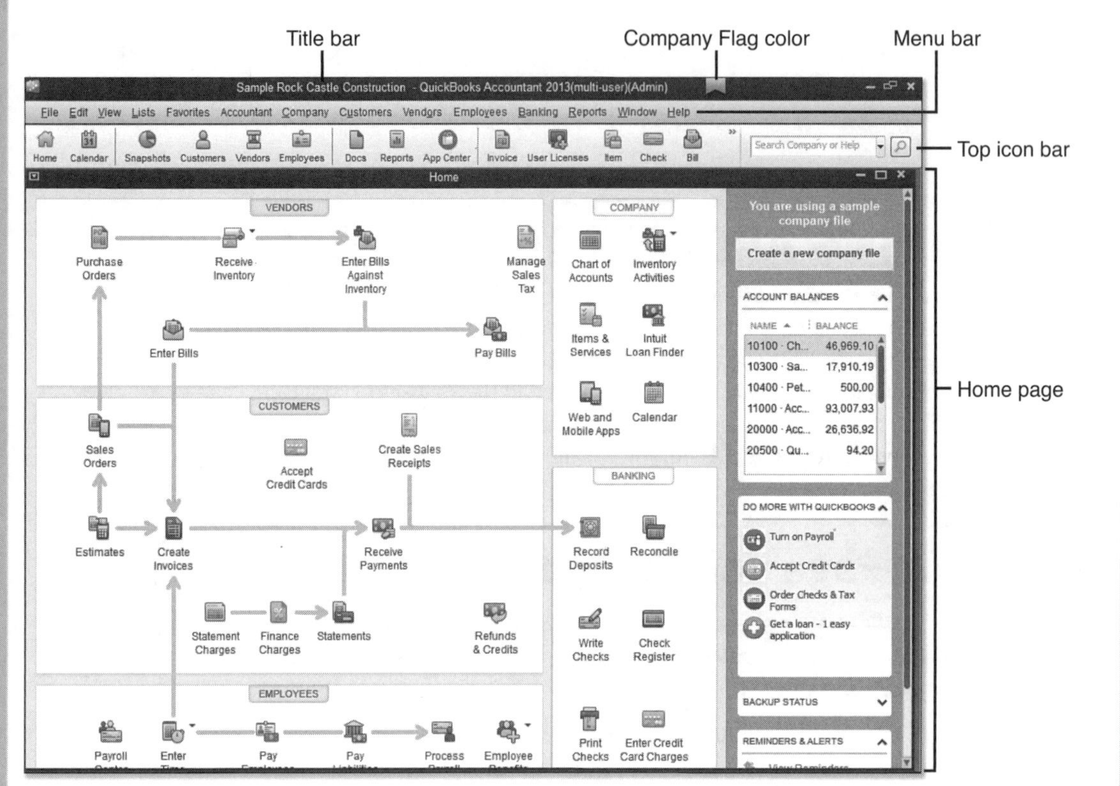

Figure 2.1
QuickBooks's many navigation points make it easy to work with.

The title bar indicates the following information about your file:

- The name of your file as it is assigned in the Company Name field, which is in the Company Information dialog box (from the menu bar, select **Company**, **Company Information** to open this dialog box).
- Your QuickBooks software year, and edition including Pro, Premier, or Enterprise. Also indicated (if applicable) is the industry specification, such as accountant, retail, professional services, and so on.
- Multiuser and the currently logged in username, if more than one user has access to the company file at a time.

caution

If you are following along with this text using one of the sample data files installed with your QuickBooks file, take note of any customization you do. This customization in the sample file will not affect your own QuickBooks file.

Menu Bar

The menu bar includes almost all the tasks, reports, forms, and functionality available in QuickBooks. If you are a new QuickBooks user, I encourage you to review all the menus and submenus. Look at what is included in the Company menu shown in Figure 2.2. Discovering these features can be valuable for your business because many of these additional QuickBooks tools are beyond the scope of this book.

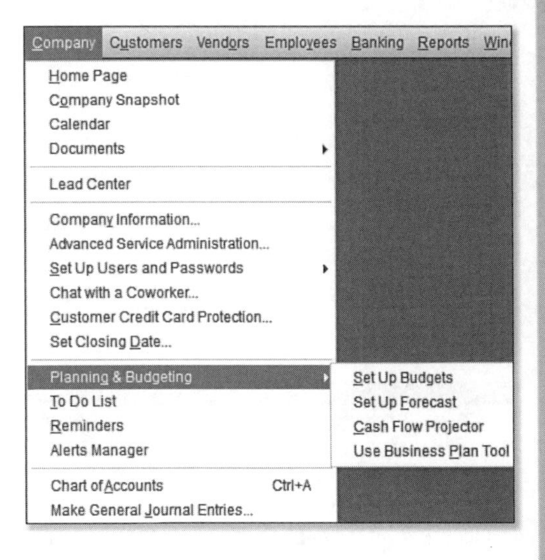

Figure 2.2
Review the menus for useful tools and features not shown on the Home page or icon bar.

Top Icon Bar

The Top Icon Bar (see Figures 2.1, 2.3, and 2.4) provides quick access to the tasks and reports you frequently use. You can customize the icon bar by selecting the color version, adding or removing shortcuts, and it is uniquely customizable for each user.

New for QuickBooks 2013, users can choose to have the icon bar placed to the top (as shown in Figure 2.1) or the left of the Home page (as shown in Figure 2.6). The choice is personal and can help maximize either vertical or horizontal working space for today's widescreen monitors.

The Top Icon Bar has two color choices to choose from:

- Default black with white icons and text
- Colored icons with light-colored background and black text

For companies that have multiple users accessing the same data file, the choice is an individual preference setting and will not affect all users. To select the Top Icon Bar with colored icons, follow these steps:

1. On the menu bar, select **View**, **Top Icon Bar**. The Top Icon Bar displays above the Home page. By default the icon bar is black with white icon as shown in Figure 2.3.

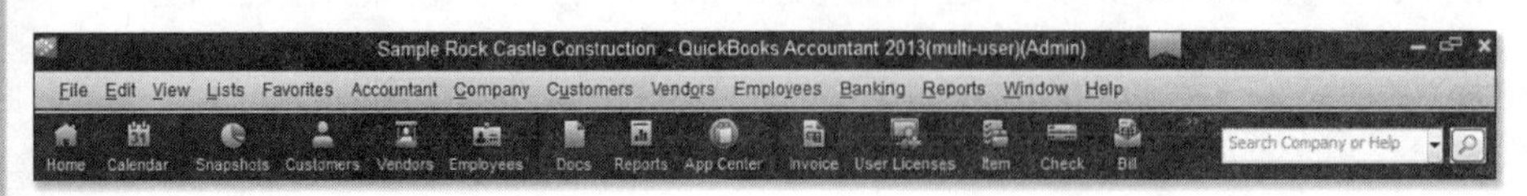

Figure 2.3
Top Icon Bar with dark background

2. To change to the top icon bar with colored icons, on menu bar select, **Edit**, **Preferences**, **Desktop View** and choose the My Preferences tab.
3. Place a checkmark next to the Switch To Colored Icons/Light Background on the Top Icon Bar in the Desktop settings.
4. Click OK to close the preferences dialog box. The icon bar now has color icons, see Figure 2.4.

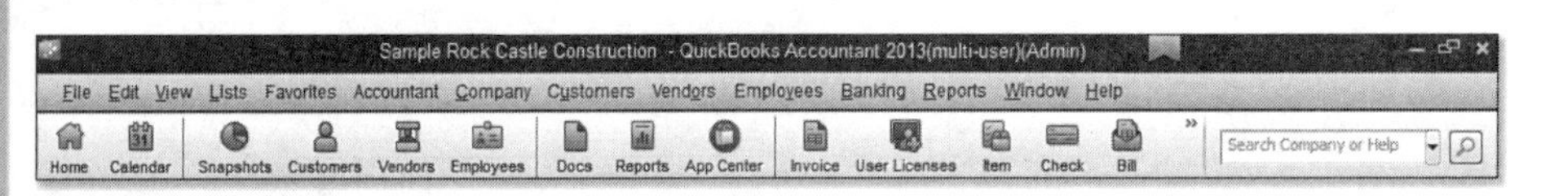

Figure 2.4
Top Icon Bar after enabling the color feature in preferences

To customize the icon bar for a particular user, make sure you are logged in to the file with that username before making any changes.

For more information about setting up users and permissions, see "Getting Started with QuickBooks," p. 31.

You can customize the icon bar by doing the following:

- Adding icons (shortcuts)
- Editing existing icons
- Rearranging the order of the icons
- Grouping icons
- Removing icons

The icon bar provides quick access to the most common tasks. You can customize the icon bar to be at the top or to the left in your QuickBooks data. Pick a style that works best for you and your specific monitor size.

tip

When you first begin working with QuickBooks 2013, a new tips banner may display. If you click the message to turn off the banners, you can bring them back by selecting **Help, What's New** from the menu bar.

note

QuickBooks 2013 menus and screens now use a larger size font for improved readability.

Customizing the Top Icon Bar

For QuickBooks 2013, the icon bar can either be on the top of your QuickBooks Home page or placed to the left. Follow these instructions for customizing the icon bar.

Use these steps to add the Calculator icon to the Top placed icon bar and reposition the new icon next to the Calendar icon:

1. From the menu bar, select **View, Top Icon Bar**. (If you selected the Left Icon Bar, view the instructions in the next section.)
2. On the top icon bar, click the small double arrows on the far right near the search box and select **Customize Icon Bar**. The Customize Icon Bar dialog box, shown in Figure 2.5, displays your currently selected icons.

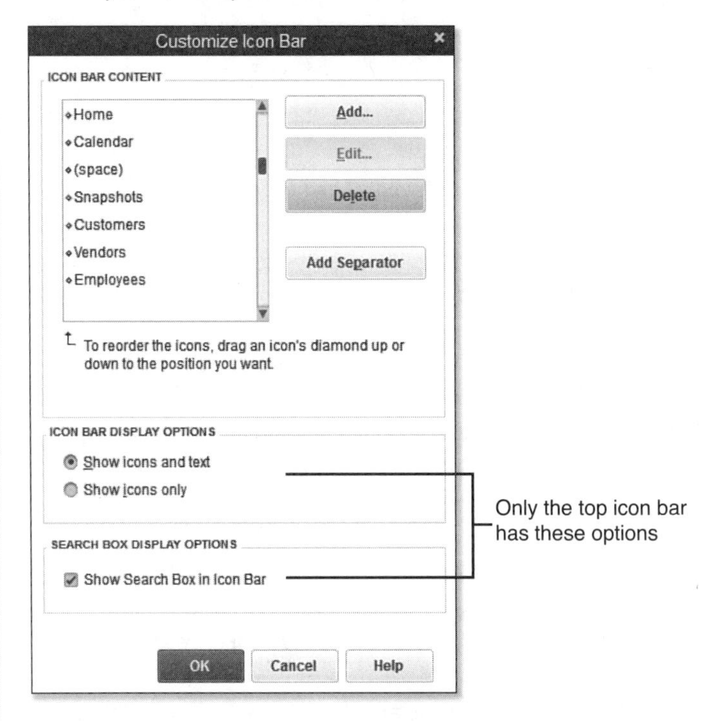

Figure 2.5
Add, remove, and reposition icons on your personal icon bar.

3. Click Add, and in the Add Icon Bar Item dialog box, select **Calculator**. The Calculator icon image is selected for you, but you can choose another icon image from the available choices.
4. Accept or edit the default Label. Keep the text as short as possible here; long labels can crowd the available space on the icon bar.
5. Accept or edit the default Description. The description displays when you hover over the icon with your cursor.
6. Click OK to close the Add Icon Bar Item dialog box.

7. To reposition the Calc icon next to the Calendar icon, click the diamond in front of Calc item. Drag the item up the list (refer to Figure 2.5), releasing the mouse when the Calc icon is next to the Calendar icon. Look at your icon bar and you will see the Calc icon is next to the Calendar icon. How easy was that!
8. (Optional) If you are modifying the settings for the top display of the icon bar, keep the default Show Icons and Text option or select Show Icons Only.
9. (Optional) If you are modifying the settings for the top display of the icon bar, select the Search Box Display Options checkbox to display the search bar on the far right of the icon bar.
10. Click OK to close the Customize Icon Bar dialog box.

Left Icon Bar

This new icon placement takes advantage of our wider computer monitor screens by allowing more space top to bottom for your QuickBooks transactions and reports. If you selected to use the new Left Icon Bar, from the View menu on the menu bar follow the nearby instructions.

The icon bar provides quick access to the most common tasks. You can customize the left icon bar similar to how you customized the top icon bar.

Now that you know how to "drag and drop" a list item by clicking on the diamond in front of an item, you will be able to rearrange many other QuickBooks lists this way!

Customizing the Left Icon Bar

Using the Left Icon Bar (see Figure 2.6) provides easy access to common tasks, reminders, reports, services. Another important benefit for using the Left Icon Bar is the added direct connection to Intuit applications. For example, you might be using Intuit Data Protect, an online backup service. From the new Left Icon Bar you can seamlessly access this and other connected services.

Use these steps to add the Calculator icon to the Left placed icon bar and reposition the new icon next to the Calendar icon:

1. From the menu bar, select **View**, **Left Icon Bar**. (If you selected the Top Icon Bar, view the instructions in the previous section.)
2. On the left icon bar, in the middle, click the My Shortcuts bar and scroll to the bottom link titled Customize Shortcuts. The Customize Icon Bar dialog box displays as previously shown in Figure 2.5; it displays your currently selected icons.
3. Click Add, and in the Add Icon Bar Item dialog box, select **Calculator**. The Calculator icon image is selected for you, but you can choose another icon image from the available choices.
4. Accept or edit the default Label. Labels can be longer than those on the Top Icon bar, but only the first 28 or so characters display.
5. Accept or edit the default Description. The description displays when you hover over the icon with your cursor.
6. Click OK to close the Add Icon Bar Item dialog box.

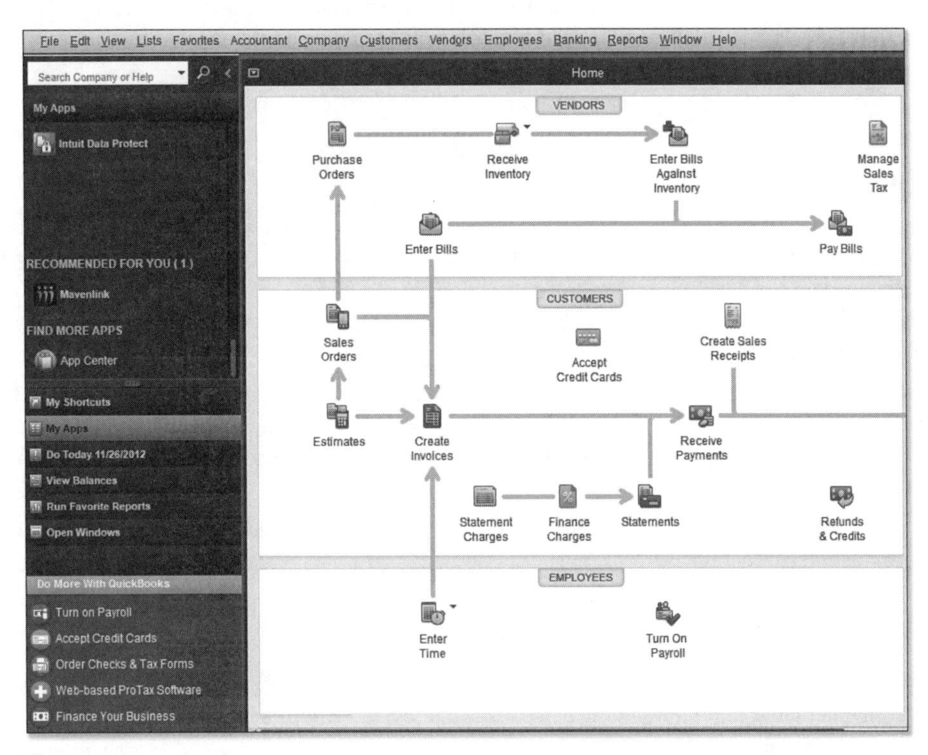

Figure 2.6
QuickBooks provides the option of using the Icon Bar placed to the left of the Home page.

7. To reposition the Calc icon next to the Calendar icon, click the diamond in front of Calc item. Drag the item up the list (refer to Figure 2.5), releasing the mouse when the Calc icon is next to the Calendar icon. Look at your icon bar and you will see the Calc icon is next to the Calendar icon. How easy was that!
8. Click OK to close the Customize Icon Bar dialog box.

An added benefit to using the Left Icon Bar is the ease in accessing your connected applications. My Apps provides access to integrated solutions that help you do more with your QuickBooks software. Follow these instructions in your own data file to access your connected apps or view trial versions of available applications.

1. From the Left Icon Bar, click My Apps.
2. Click the Sign In link and enter the email address you used when creating your Intuit Account.
3. Click Validate. If your email is recognized, you will be prompted for your password. If the email entered is not recognized, follow the prompts to create a password and assign a First and Last Name to your Intuit Account.

4. Select or deselect the box to connect your QuickBooks company file to Intuit's secure servers. Click the Learn More About Syncing link for more details.

5. Click Finish.

Home Page

The best place to start customizing QuickBooks specifically for your business needs is on the Home page. The Home page displays by default when you create a new QuickBooks file and include tasks and workflows you can customize (refer to Figure 2.1). You can add or remove icons from the Home page. You cannot rearrange the order or placement of icons on the Home page. (Some Home page icons cannot be removed if related preferences are enabled.)

When you customize the Home page to include or remove specific icons, you are often redirected to the related preference. For more detailed instructions on working with individual preferences, see the "Preferences" section in this chapter or the related preference section included with most chapters in this book.

To edit the Home page icons, you are required to be logged in to the file as the Admin or External Accountant user (see Chapter 1).

Customizing Icons (Tasks)

The QuickBooks Home page displays common tasks and workflow for vendors, customers, employees, and other activities and information. Some tasks can be added or removed depending on the needs of your business.

If your Home page did not automatically display, you can always open it by clicking the Home page icon on the icon bar, as displayed in Figure 2.1. In this section, you learn to manage the preference to display the Home page each time you launch QuickBooks.

The Admin User in QuickBooks

What if you're not sure whether you are logged in to the file as the Admin user? If you are working with a multiuser file (see Chapter 17, "Managing Your QuickBooks Database," for more details), the title bar shows the user currently logged in to the opened file (see Figure 2.1). However, if you are in the file in single-user mode, or if you renamed the Admin user, the username may or may not display "Admin."

To determine whether you are currently logged in to the file as the originally created default Admin user, on the menu bar, select **Company, Set Up Users and Passwords, Set Up Users** to open the User List dialog box. Figure 2.7 shows how the original Admin user was renamed to "Laura." A renamed Admin user still has all the same privileges as the original Admin user.

Many preferences and features require you to be logged in to the file as the Admin user. If you are not currently logged in as the Admin user, you can log off by selecting **File, Close Company/Logoff** from the menu bar.

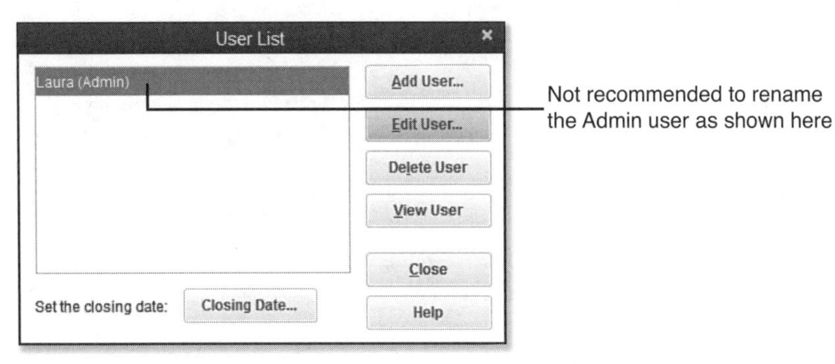

Figure 2.7
Viewing the User List shows whether the Admin user was renamed (not recommended).

To make changes to the Home page icons, follow these steps:

1. First, log in to your file as the default Admin or External Accountant user. Enter the appropriate password if one was set.
2. From the menu bar, select **Edit**, **Preferences** to open the Preferences dialog box, which displays the preferences available in your file.
3. Select the **Desktop View** preference in the left column.
4. At the top of the Preferences dialog box, select the **Company Preferences** tab. The following options are provided:
   - **Customers**—Choose to add or remove the following Home page icons:
     - **Invoices**—Can be removed only if Estimates, Sales Orders, and Sales Tax tracking is disabled. Either Sales Receipts or Statement and Statement Charges must be enabled to remove Invoices from the Home page.
     - **Sales Receipts**—Remove the checkmark if you do not want Sales Receipts included on the Home page.
     - **Statements and Statement Charges**—Remove the checkmark if you do not want these included on the Home page.
   - **Vendors**—Option to remove *both* the Enter Bills and Pay Bills icons. If this option is grayed out, it is because another preference is enabled that depends on using vendor bills. For example, if Inventory is enabled, you cannot remove the vendor icons of Enter and Pay Bills.
   - **Related Preferences**—Click the corresponding links to enable or disable features globally for all users. These preference settings are discussed in more detail in their related chapters.
     - **Estimates**—See Chapter 9, "Setting Up Customers."
     - **Sales Tax**—See Chapter 9.

- **Sales Orders**—See Chapter 9.
- **Inventory**—See Chapter 5, "Setting Up Inventory."
- **Payroll**—See Chapter 11, "Setting Up Payroll."
- **Time Tracking**—See Chapter 11.

5. Click OK to close the Preferences dialog box.

caution

Read the referenced chapter before adding a new Home page icon. Often, other unique settings will need to be defined when adding a new icon to your Home page.

If you know you want to remove an icon (task) from the Home page by deselecting it in the Preferences dialog box, you can safely do that. These icons can later be reinstated to your Home page.

Customizing Data Displayed on the Home Page

If you have chosen to use the Top Icon Bar, the right side of the Home page (see Figure 2.1) displays several additional panels of information as shown in Figure 2.8. Click the upward-facing arrow to expand or collapse the detail displayed.

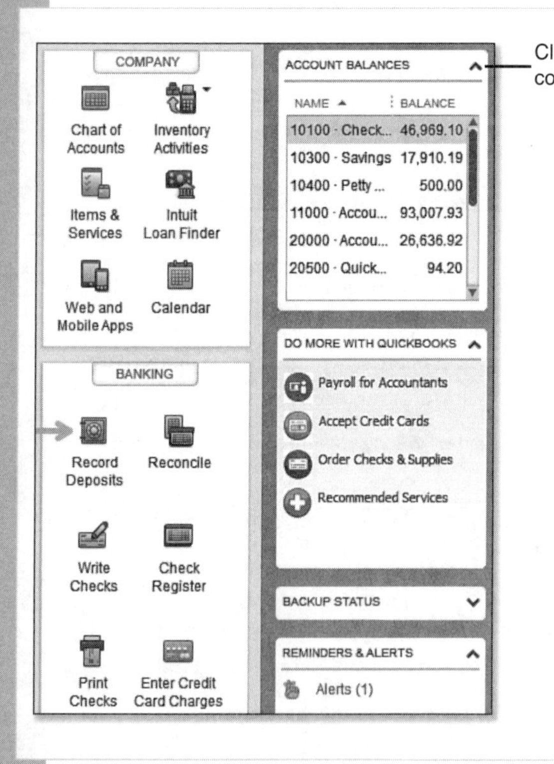

Figure 2.8
When using the Top Icon Bar, each panel of information can be expanded or collapsed.

These panels include the following:

- **Account Balances**—Click the column headers to sort the accounts by the Name or Balance column.
- **Do More with QuickBooks**—Links to other products or services offered for QuickBooks users.
- **Backup Status**—Notification of when the last backup was completed and links to information on storing your data online.
- **Reminders and Alerts**—Links to view the reminders and alerts you have enabled in your QuickBooks file.

Open Windows List

Are you ready for another personal preference for navigating in QuickBooks? Try the Open Windows list. With computer monitors getting larger and larger, you will most likely have plenty of room to use it with your QuickBooks file. This feature works with both the Top and Left positioned icon bar; how you access the feature depends on which icon bar you are using.

When Using the Top Icon Bar

From the menu bar, select **View**, **Open Window List**. The Open Windows list displays on the left side of your Home page (see Figure 2.9), which enables you to move between many open reports or transactions easily by clicking on their name in this list.

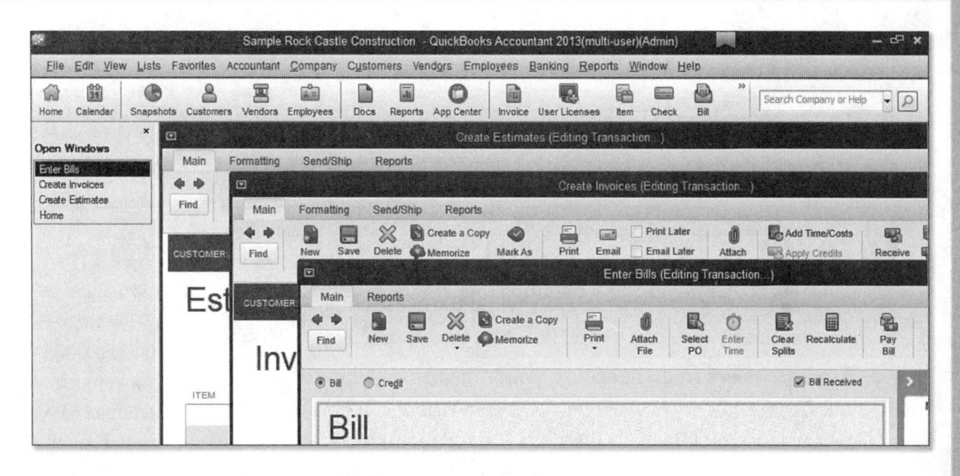

Figure 2.9 The Open Windows List view when using the Top Icon Bar.

Your open windows might cascade over the top of another open window. If you find this distracting, select **View**, **One Window** from the menu bar to make all the windows use the full QuickBooks desktop area. You can also resize an Open dialog box by dragging its top, bottom, sides, or corners.

When Using the Left Icon Bar

Some users with wide monitors might prefer to use the Left Icon Bar. As instructed previously, from View on the menu bar you can choose which icon bar to use. If you selected the Left Icon Bar, use these instructions to enable the same Open Windows list shown in Figure 2.10.

1. With the Left Icon Bar displayed, click Open Windows, in the My Shortcuts section of the Left Icon Bar.

2. You may also want to choose to view One Window or Multiple Windows from View, on the menu bar. Choosing Multiple Windows will float multiple open windows on top of each other.

Having the icon bar display the open windows makes it easy to work with multiple transactions or tasks at the same time. Your open windows might cascade over the top of another open window. If you find this distracting, select **View**, **One Window** from the menu bar to make all the windows use the full QuickBooks desktop area. You can also resize an Open dialog box by dragging its top, bottom, sides, or corners.

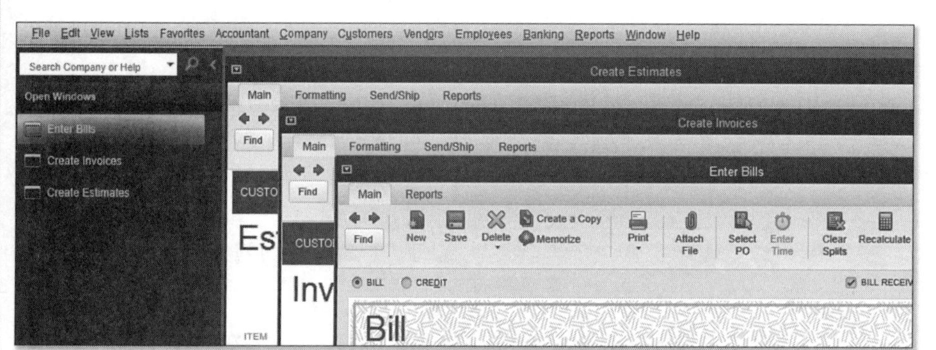

Figure 2.10 The Open Windows List view when using the Left Icon Bar

Tutorials

In your QuickBooks software are several tutorials to help you get started quickly. You can watch these as a supplement to this book.

To do so, select **Help**, **Learning Center Tutorials** from the menu bar. Click a category on the left or select **Quick Links** to jumpstart your use of QuickBooks. When you are finished viewing the tutorials, click Go to QuickBooks to close the Learning Center.

>  **tip**
>
> Click any icon on the Home page (other than the home icon) and see the Open Windows list on the left grow with each transaction or task that is opened. Would you like to close all open windows quickly? From the menu bar, select **Window, Close All.**
>
> After closing all open windows, if you want to return to the Home page, on the icon bar, click the Home icon.

Preferences

You can customize QuickBooks to suit your specific business needs while maintaining individual preferences.

You are required to save your changes as you work with each preference. Some preferences might have you close all open windows to effect the change. Simply return to the Preferences dialog box until you are finished specifying all your preferences by selecting **Edit**, **Preferences** from the menu bar.

To return to the original preference setting, select a preference on the left side of the Preferences dialog box and click the Default button. Be aware that the Default button is not available for all preferences. Click OK to close the Preferences dialog box.

Preferences come in two important types:

- **Company Preferences**—Affect all users of the currently opened QuickBooks file. Only the QuickBooks Admin and External Accountant user have full rights to set these preferences. Learn more about different types of users and user permissions in Chapter 1.
- **My Preferences**—Specific to the currently logged-in user; these do not affect the settings for other users of the same file or other QuickBooks files.

This section provides a review of the most common, general use preferences. Most of the preference settings are self-explanatory and do not need to be discussed here. However, specific details on important preferences are provided in each chapter.

Accounting—Company Preferences

These are global preferences and when modified, they affect all users of the opened QuickBooks file:

- **Date Warnings**—A new file defaults to Warn if Transactions Are 90 day(s) in the Past and Warn if Transactions Are 30 day(s) in the Future (see Figure 2.11). At times, you might want to edit these date ranges, such as when you are just starting to use QuickBooks and need to enter data for a period in the past.

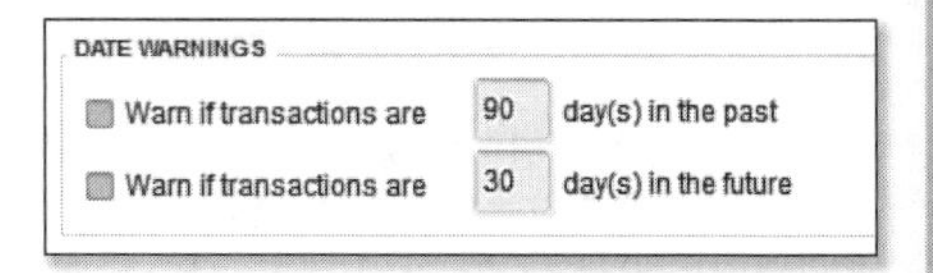

Figure 2.11
QuickBooks can warn when transaction dates do not fall within a specific date range.

Desktop View—My Preferences

These are personal preferences; when modified, they affect only the currently logged-in user (see Figure 2.12):

note

Several of these preferences will only be offered if your QuickBooks 2013 data is updated to maintenance release R4 or newer. To view the release you are using, from an open QuickBooks file press F2 on your keyboard. The release will display at the top of the Production Information Window. For more information see, "Installing a QuickBooks Maintenance Release," p. 618.

- **View**—One Window or Multiple Windows per user preference. This preference also can be selected from the View menu on the menu bar.
- **Desktop**—Includes the following options:
  - **Save When Closing Company**—Default setting that saves every open window when a QuickBooks session is closed. When QuickBooks is reopened, each report and transaction left open in the last session is restored. This preference is not recommended for a file that has multiple users logging into the file simultaneously. Restoring multiple windows, transactions, or reports at startup can slow down the time it takes for the QuickBooks file to open.
  - **Don't Save the Desktop**—Closes each open window automatically when the QuickBooks program is closed. This is the most efficient choice; if a transaction has not been completed, QuickBooks notifies you before closing the transaction and gives you the option to save any changes to custom report settings.
  - **Save Current Desktop**—When you reopen QuickBooks, any previously opened non transaction window is displayed.
  - **Keep Previously Saved Desktop**—Selected for you automatically when you choose the Save Current Desktop option.
  - **Show Home Page When Opening A Company File**—When you launch QuickBooks, the Home page will display automatically.
  - **Switch to Colored Icons/Light Background on the Top Icon Bar**—Preference available after updating to Release 4 or newer. Many prefer this new colored icon bar to the default black with white text icon bar.
- **Windows Settings**—Managing windows computer display and sound settings.
- **Company Flag Color**—Assign a colored flag (as shown previously in Figure 2.1) to help visually identify a data file. Useful if you have multiple QuickBooks data files.

> **tip**
> To simplify your daily QuickBooks use, select the **One Window** option and then on the menu bar, select **View, Open Window List**.

Certain preferences override these defaults, particularly if you have selected the Show Home Page When Opening a Company File. When this option is selected, the Home page always opens when you launch QuickBooks.

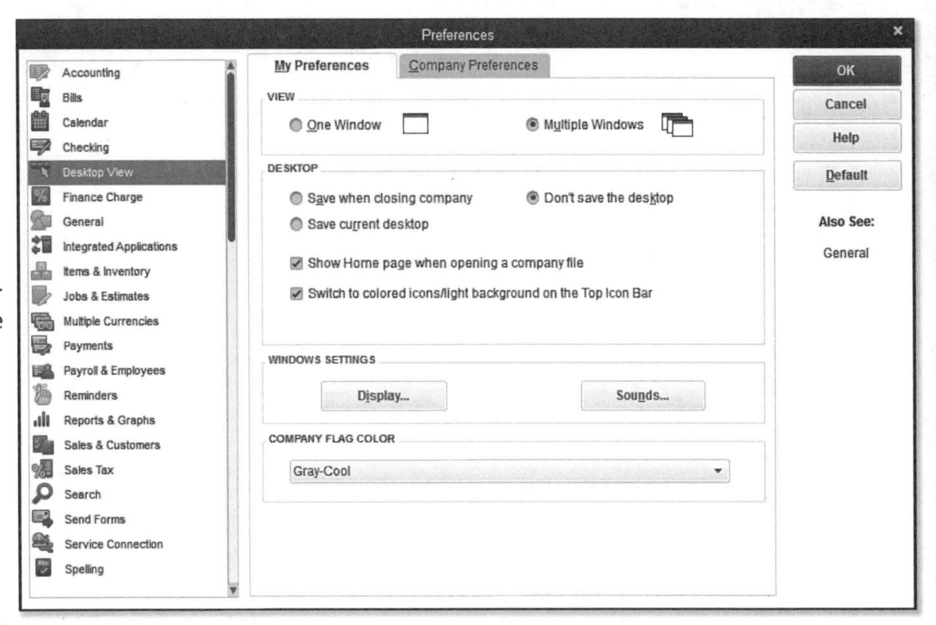

Figure 2.12 Make sure your data is updated to maintenance release 4 or newer, so that you have each of these preferences available

General—My Preferences

These are personal preferences; when modified, they affect only the currently logged-in user:

- **Pressing Enter Moves Between Fields**—When this is *not* selected, you use the Tab key to move between fields and the Enter key to save a transaction or activate a highlighted command.

  If you want to use the Enter key to move between fields (perhaps you have grown accustomed to using the Enter key in this way with other software) place a checkmark in this preference.

If you selected the preference **Pressing Enter Moves Between Fields** and you want to save a transaction or activate a highlighted command, use the combination of Ctrl + Enter from your keyboard.

- **Automatically Place Decimal Point**—When selected, .01 rather than 1.00 displays when you type the number "1" in QuickBooks.
- **Bring Back All One Time Messages**—If data entry mistakes have been ignored in the past, turning on this warning can call attention to possible mistakes in the future.
- **Keep QuickBooks Running for Quick Startups**—When selected, the QuickBooks software might open faster. This is the only preference that also affects other data files.

Spelling—My Preferences

These are personal preferences; when modified, they affect only the currently logged-in user. Options include:

- Always check spelling
- Ignore specific words or word with numbers, Internet address, and so on.

When enabled, the Description, Memo, Notes, and Message fields of the following transactions are spell checked:

- Invoices
- Estimates
- Sales Receipts
- Credit memos
- Purchase orders

If you do not select the option to always check spelling, on certain transactions you will be able to manually spell check.

Help Options

As a business owner or accounting professional new to QuickBooks, you will find many resources for getting the help you need. To access Help in QuickBooks, you can press the F1 key on your keyboard, or by selecting **Help**, **QuickBooks Help** from the menu bar.

Also, QuickBooks 2013 has a search tool on the right side of the icon bar (or located at the top of the left-placed icon bar). From the drop-down list on the icon bar search field, select **Search Company File** if you want to search through your lists or transactions, or select **Help** if you want to search technical resources. Select **Set Search Preferences** to default what type of search you normally perform.

QuickBooks provides help in several distinct ways and allows you to search each with a single dialog box, as shown in Figure 2.13.

Search results include how-to instructions from the in-product help content as well as related content shared in the Ask Community forums.

If the displayed search results do not answer your question, click the Ask Community and pose the question to other QuickBooks users.

Would you prefer to have a local QuickBooks experienced professional come to your place of business to help you get started quickly? If so, from the menu bar, choose Help, Find a Local QuickBooks Expert. You are asked for your zip code to help locate a list of QuickBooks Certified ProAdvisors in your area, and fees may apply.

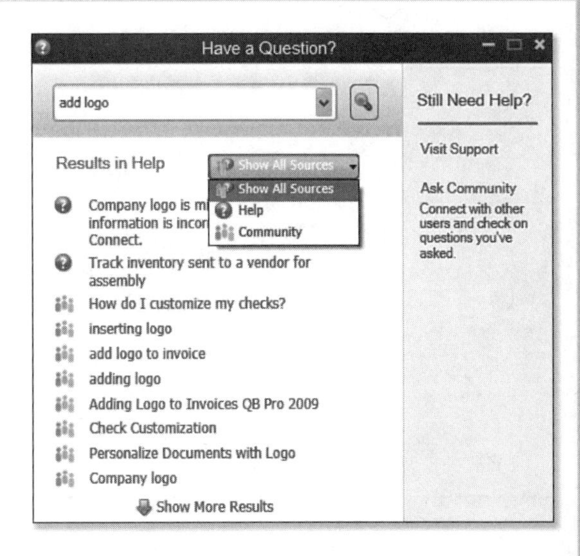

Figure 2.13
Search multiple help resources all at once.

Selecting a Company File to Open

In general, you should not have any trouble opening your QuickBooks file because the software automatically opens your file each time you launch QuickBooks. There are, however, several ways to open your QuickBooks data. Listed here are the most common.

Opening Your Data for the First Time

After creating your new file, QuickBooks will open your data file each time you launch the software. However, if you are opening your data for the first time on a new computer, you need to follow these steps:

1. Launch your QuickBooks software by clicking the QuickBooks icon on your desktop.
2. From the menu bar, select **File**, **Open or Restore Company**.
3. In the Open or Restore Company dialog box, select the **Open a Company File** option button, as shown in Figure 2.14.

   For more information about the other file actions shown in Figure 2.14, see p. 572.

4. Click Next.
5. QuickBooks defaults to the last known folder that a QuickBooks file was opened from, or you can browse to locate where you stored the file. Select the file and click Open. If required, enter your username and password to open the file.

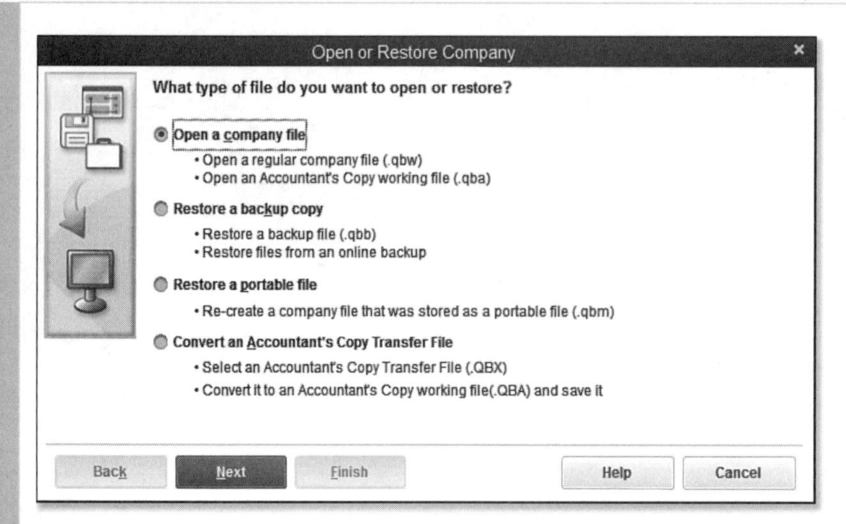

Figure 2.14
If you have moved your file to a new computer, select the Open a Company file option and browse to the location of the stored file.

Choosing from a List of Multiple Data Files

Chapter 1 introduced you to working with the QuickBooks sample data that installs automatically with your QuickBooks software. Using sample data can give you the freedom to practice what you learn and gain confidence in working with your software.

You also learned in Chapter 1 how to create your company's QuickBooks file using a variety of methods.

In this section, you learn how to open a QuickBooks file from a list, which is especially useful if you have multiple data files or want to open the sample data again after working in your own file.

tip

Chapter 16, "Sharing QuickBooks Data with Your Accountant," discusses in more detail different file types and their purposes. The QuickBooks instruction of selecting **File, Open** only opens a file with the extension of .QBW.

To choose from a list of multiple data files, follow these steps:

1. From the menu bar, select **File**, **Open Previous Company**. A list of previously opened files (up to a maximum of 20) displays, as shown in Figure 2.15.

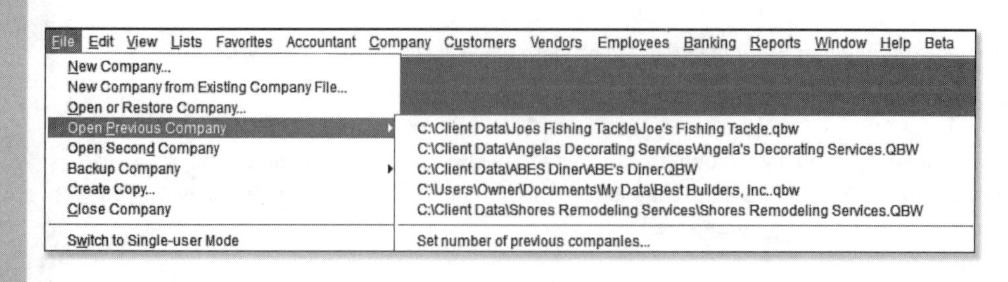

Figure 2.15
Access previously opened QuickBooks files easily.

2. Select a file in the list to open it.
3. Enter your username and password, if required.

If you need to increase the number of files shown, from an *opened* QuickBooks file, select **File**, **Open Previous Company**, **Set Number of Previous Companies** from the menu bar. QuickBooks can display up to 20 data files in this list. Enter the number you want to include in your list and click OK when finished.

In Chapter 1, you learned how to open and test with sample data and create your own file. In this chapter, you learned how to navigate the many features and tools found in QuickBooks. Let's take a quick break from QuickBooks and discuss some basic accounting in the next chapter, Chapter 3, "Accounting 101." I promise it will be worth your time and help you make better use of your QuickBooks file.

ACCOUNTING 101

In this chapter you will find a brief discussion of fundamental accounting principles for the non-accountant business owner. And, if you used another method or software for tracking your financials prior to QuickBooks, step-by-step instructions are provided for entering these beginning balances.

Basic Principles of Accounting

This chapter provides a quick review of some of the more important accounting concepts, written especially for the non-accountant business owner. Although there is much more to learn about accounting principles than this chapter covers, you learn enough to help you manage the financials of your business.

You made an important choice when you selected the QuickBooks software to help you track the day-to-day financial transactions of your business. QuickBooks completes most of the accounting behind-the-scenes, so you can focus on what you do best.

The Matching Principle

The *matching principle of accounting* refers to recognizing revenue and associated expenses in the same period. Matching income and costs in this manner gives you a much more accurate representation of your financial situation and performance.

Most businesses offer products or services that have related costs, such as the following:

- **Asset Purchases**—Inventory for sale, or fixed assets (equipment) used in the production of your product or services are examples.

- **Cost of Goods Sold Expenses**—Direct expenses incurred when making your product or providing a service. Cost of material or labor expenses are examples.
- **Expenses**—Overhead that has fixed costs and variable expenses; such as rent, office supplies, advertising, and so on.
- **Other Expenses**—Expenses of the business not related to the product or service you provide. For example, interest expense or depreciation expense.

note
This book does not offer tax or accounting advice. Be sure to consult your accounting professional when necessary.

note
Inventory you purchase is an asset purchase and later becomes a cost of goods sold expense when you sell it.

It is important to understand the different account types when recording costs, so that you categorize your bills or expenses correctly when entering them into QuickBooks.

For more information, see "Account Types," p. 102.

Any discussion of the matching principle isn't complete without defining revenue. *Revenue* (income) are the funds received from customers. Income is typically one of the following:

- **Operating Income**—Income derived from selling your business's product or service.
- **Other Income**—Income derived from sources other than selling your product or service. An example of other income might be interest earned on balances in your checking account.

You probably already understand the general concept of revenue versus expense. So what does the matching principle have to do with accounting? A retail bike store might keep parts, such as wheels, pedals, and chains on hand in its inventory so it can assemble bicycles for its customers. The matching principle requires this store to record the costs of the bike at the time of sale. The initial purchase of inventory is not an expense; it is simply trading one asset, cash, for another asset, inventory. When the asset is sold, the initial purchase cost becomes an expense, which reduces the resulting revenue.

Inventory management, as discussed in this example, is pretty straightforward. QuickBooks tracks your initial purchase as an asset, and then records the average cost of each part as an expense when you create an invoice to record the sale to a customer. If you are using QuickBooks Enterprise Solutions, you can opt to use First In First Out inventory costing. More information can be found in Appendix C, "QuickBooks Enterprise Solutions Inventory Features."

For more information, see "Setting Up Inventory," p. 145 and "Managing Inventory," p. 195.

However, let's tackle something a bit more difficult. In this same business, you are required to prepay six months of general liability insurance. Recording this entire balance as an expense in a single month would make that month's net income appear artificially lower, along with making net income for the next five months artificially higher. To match the expense, you would assign the initial payment to a prepaid expenses account on your balance sheet. You would then use a journal entry each month to record an increase in insurance expense and a decrease in the prepaid expenses account. Each month would then have the cost for insurance that belonged in a single month.

For more information, see "Recording Vendor Prepayments," p. 283.

QuickBooks accrual basis reporting can help view your financials in a format that matches revenue with expense. Accrual basis reporting is discussed in the next section.

Accrual Versus Cash Basis Reporting

Although the purpose of this book is not to give specific accounting or tax advice on any of the topics covered, it is worth discussing the nature of accrual versus cash basis reporting as it pertains to creating a new data file.

Cash basis accounting follows these rules:

- **Revenue**—Recognized when the customer payment is received, not necessarily the same day or month the service or product was provided.
- **Expenses**—Recognized when the payment is made to the vendor or employee, not necessarily the same day or month the expense relates to.

Accrual basis accounting follows these rules:

- **Revenue**—Recognized as income on the date of the customer invoice transaction regardless of when the customer pays the invoice.
- **Expenses**—Recognized as a cost on the date of the vendor bill, check, or credit card charge, regardless of when you make the payment.

Understanding the basics of these two types of reporting is important. When filing a tax return, businesses must specify cash or accrual as their accounting method. However, for management purposes, business owners can view one or both types of reports when making internal decisions. The capability to view reports in either accrual or cash basis is one of the features that sets the QuickBooks software apart from other accounting solutions.

Cash basis reporting can give you a sense of how cash flows through your business, whereas accrual basis reporting uses the matching principle to give you a much more accurate representation of how revenue and expenses are related.

The difference between the two methods is in the timing of when income and expenses are recognized in your financials. Table 3.1 shows how QuickBooks treats the different types of transactions in both reporting methods on the Profit & Loss statement.

Table 3.1 Accrual Versus Cash Accounting

Transaction Type	Profit & Loss Accrual Basis	Profit & Loss Cash Basis
Customer Invoice	Revenue is recognized as of the date of the invoice.	Revenue is recognized as of the date entered on the customer's payment transaction.
Customer Credit Memo	Revenue is decreased as of the date of the credit memo.	No impact.
Vendor Bill	Cost is recognized on the date entered on the vendor's bill.	Cost is recognized on the date of the bill payment check.
Vendor Credit Memo	Cost is decreased as of the date of the vendor credit memo.	No impact.
Check	Cost is recognized as of the date entered on the check transaction.	Cost is recognized as of the date entered on the check transaction.
Credit Card	Cost is recognized as of the date entered on the credit card transaction.	Cost is recognized as of the date entered on the credit card transaction.
General Journal	Cost or revenue is recognized using the date entered on the general journal transaction.	Cost or revenue is recorded using the date entered on the general journal transaction.
Inventory Adjustment	Date of inventory adjustment is the date the financials are affected.	Date of inventory adjustment is the date the financials are affected.

In QuickBooks preferences, you can set a global default basis for all reports. To do this, follow these steps:

1. Log in to the file as the Admin or External Accountant user type.
2. From the menu bar, select **Edit**, **Preferences**, **Reports & Graphs**.
3. Click the Company Preferences tab and choose Accrual or Cash from the Summary Reports Basis section.

You can also modify the basis of many reports individually. From a displayed report, select **Customize Report** and choose Accrual or Cash in the Report Basis section.

For management analysis, I encourage all business owners to view their financials often using accrual basis reporting. When you review accrual basis reports, you can see trends from one period to the next. Management decisions based on accrual basis reports might be different from decisions made when based on cash basis reports.

Basic Financial Reports

This section describes financial reports that are important to managing the financials of your business.

For more details on working with reports, see "Reviewing Your Data," p. 549.

Balance Sheet

The balance sheet represents the overall financial health of the business. Of the financial statements detailed here, the balance sheet is the only statement that applies to a single date in the business's calendar year.

A standard company balance sheet has three sections and is represented by this equation: Assets = Liabilities + Equity. The categories include the following:

- **Assets**—Cash, along with economic resources that can be converted to cash. Assets include:
  - **Current Assets**—Cash, accounts receivable, inventory, and prepaid expenses, to name a few.
  - **Fixed Assets and Depreciation**—Buildings and equipment and their depreciation.
  - **Other Assets**—Goodwill (typically the value of an asset that is intangible but has a quantifiable value), trademarks, and copyrights.
- **Liabilities**—A debt the business is obligated to pay. Liabilities include
  - **Current Liabilities**—Debt that typically is paid back within one year.
  - **Long-term Liabilities**—Debt that is expected to take longer than one year to pay back.
- **Equity**—Owner's investments, draws, and residual net income or loss in the business over time.

Business owners should review the balance sheet as often as they review the income statement. Most business owners who review the balance sheet will have a pretty good idea if the information is accurate just by looking at the balances.

Income Statement

The income statement also is referred to as a profit and loss statement in QuickBooks. My experience over the years is that business owners review this report often. In QuickBooks, a simple income statement includes these basic sections or totals:

- **Income**—Monies received from the sale of products and services.
- **Cost of Goods Sold**—Direct costs of producing your product or service.
- **Gross Profit**—Income less cost of goods sold.
- **Expense**—Costs associated with your business that are not directly related to producing goods or services, often referred to as overhead.
- **Net Ordinary Income (Loss)**—Income or loss from operations.
- **Other Income/Expense**—Income or expense not related to operations, such as interest income or interest expense.
- **Net Income (Loss)**—Income or loss from operations less other income/loss.

QuickBooks offers you the flexibility to review your Profit & Loss Standard report in either accrual or cash basis. Creating an income statement that shows 12-month periods on the accrual basis makes it easy to spot changes and trends from period to period.

Statement of Cash Flows

The primary purpose of this report is to show the sources and uses of cash in the business. The statement of cash flows includes the following groups:

- **Operating activities**—These include the production of the product, sales, and the delivery of it. It also includes those activities related to payment from the customer.
- **Investing activities**—These activities include the purchase or sale assets or loans. Assets and loans involve both suppliers and customers.
- **Financing activities**—These activities are related to the inflow and outflow of cash. Investors and shareholders are participants in these activities.

Additionally, the following information is included in the statement of cash flows report:

- Net cash increase for the period
- Cash at the beginning of the period
- Cash at the end of the period

QuickBooks automatically assigns a specific chart of accounts to cash flow report categories based on the account type assigned.

You also can manually assign a chart of accounts to a specific section of the statement. To do this, follow these steps:

1. Log in to the file as the Admin or External Accountant user to set this preference.
2. From the menu bar, select **Edit**, **Preferences**, **Reports & Graphs**, and select the Company Preferences tab.
3. Click the Classify Cash button and follow the instructions on the screen.

Other Accounting Reports

The reports referenced in this section are the basic reports used to analyze the financial health of a business. Many chapters in this book include sections that detail specific reports relevant to the topic of that chapter.

Accounting Checklist to Help You Manage Your Financials

This checklist is provided to help the business owner or accounting professional take an organized approach to periodically reviewing a QuickBooks file. This book includes several chapters that will help you learn how to accurately and efficiently manage your data, using this checklist.

Client Name: ______________________________

Date Due: ______________

Data for Year Ended: ___________ 201___

QuickBooks Version: __________ QuickBooks Release: ______

Method of Accessing Client Data (circle one):

On-site | .QBB Backup Data
.QBM Portable Co. File | .QBX Accountant's Copy
Remote Access | Send Journal Entry (*New* for 2013!)

External Accountant Username and Password: ____________________

Or Client Admin Password: _____________

___ Backup of Data Made Before Correcting Transactions

___ Review of Working Trial Balance Ending Balances from Prior Year

___ Prior-Year Balances Changed? Print Audit Trail, Voided/Deleted, Retained Earnings QuickReport

___ Review Chart of Accounts for Any Newly Created Accounts

- ___ Proper account type selected?
- ___ Duplicated accounts?
- ___ Assign as subaccount?

___ Item List Review—Print Reports—For the Item List Including Account and COGS Account

- ___ Proper accounts assigned?
- ___ Duplicated items?
- ___ Assign as subitem?

___ Review Accounts Receivable

- ___ Small open balances
- ___ Unapplied credits
- ___ Undeposited Funds

___ Review Accounts Payable

- ___ Paid open vendor bills
- ___ 1099-MISC. Income form setup
- ___ Unapplied vendor credits

___ Review Payroll

____ Non-payroll transactions ____ Employee defaults

____ Payroll item mapping

____ Completed Run Payroll Checkup

___ Review Completed Bank Reconciliations

____ Account(s) reconciled ____ Agrees with balance sheet?

____ Review uncleared bank transactions

___ Review Inventory Setup

____ Inv valuation summary asset total agrees with balance sheet

____ Old outdated item receipts ____ Journal entries posted to inventory asset account

Setting Up a QuickBooks Data File for Accrual or Cash Basis Reporting

This section is provided for the owner that has been tracking their business finances in other software or on paper prior to using QuickBooks. In this section you will learn about properly entering the startup balances from your previous records.

However, if you have recently started a new business and QuickBooks is the first financial tracking software you have used, rest easy. You can skip this section because QuickBooks does not require any complex entries to start using the software. Instead, you simply begin the daily tasks of paying vendors or employees and invoicing customers.

If instead you are converting to QuickBooks from a software application other than those currently supported with the QuickBooks conversion tool, you may have to manually enter open customer, vendor, bank account balances, and additional startup numbers. That is where this section will come in handy.

For more information, see "Converting from Other Accounting Software," p. 46.

When you begin using QuickBooks, you need to define a start date—the date you first want QuickBooks to track your financial accounting. If the business had expenses or sold products and services before this start date, you most likely have open transactions. For example, if your start date is January 1, 2017, your beginning balances would be dated as of December 31, 2016.

The following is a brief list of recommended information to collect when creating a new QuickBooks data file. These lists should represent their respective value as of the day before your QuickBooks start date:

- **Accounts Receivable**—List by customer of amounts owed you on the day before your start date, including any invoices where the payment was received but not deposited by the start date.

- **Accounts Payable**—List by vendor of those bills you had not paid as of your start date.
- **Bank Ending Balance**—Ending balance from your bank statement on the day before your start date.
- **Uncleared Checks and Deposits**—List of all checks and deposits that have not yet cleared your bank account as of your start date.
- **Other Balances**—List of all other assets, liabilities, and equity you have in the business.
- **Payroll**—Year-to-date totals for each employee (if using payroll in QuickBooks and you issued payroll checks prior to using QuickBooks).

To get your QuickBooks data ready for entering current transactions, you need to record these open balances. However, before doing so, you need to have a few things already set up in QuickBooks.

Before You Begin Entering Opening Balances

If you are converting your financials from information tracked in other software or on paper you will need to enter beginning balances. Before you begin entering these startup balances, make sure you have the following lists created in your QuickBooks data file. Each item in this list has its own chapter in this book to help you with this task:

- Chart of Accounts (see Chapter 4)
- Items List (see Chapter 4 and 5)
- Customer and Job Names (see Chapter 9)
- Vendor Names (see Chapter 7)
- Employee Names (see Chapter 11)
- Payroll Items (see Chapter 11)

The following sections detail these important startup balances that need to be entered when you convert to QuickBooks from some other accounting software or paper records.

Cash or Accrual Basis Startup Transactions: Accounts Receivable

After you have completed creating your new data file, you need to take some additional steps that are important to the successful setup of your new QuickBooks file. One of these steps is to create a list of customers or jobs that currently owe you money. You might want to review Chapter 9, "Setting Up Customers," before completing the activities in this section.

Creating a customer or job is easy in QuickBooks; follow these instructions:

1. From the menu bar, select **Customers**, **Customer Center**.

2. Select **New Customer & Jobs** (top left of the Customer Center) or select the menu to **Add Multiple Customer:Jobs**.

3. Type a Customer Name. By default, QuickBooks will sort the list numerically and alphabetically by this name.

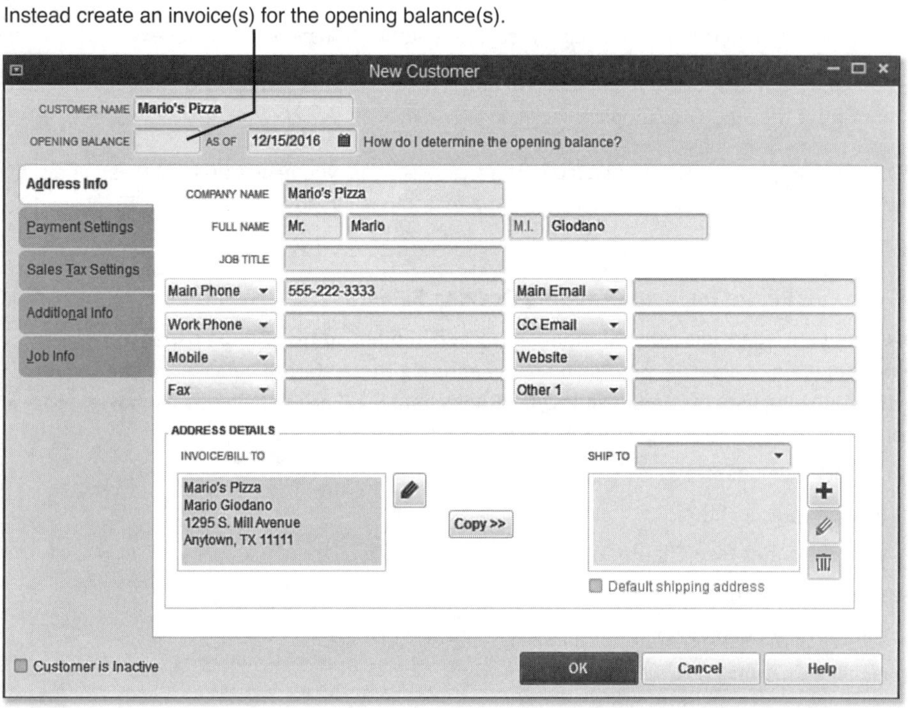

Instead create an invoice(s) for the opening balance(s).

Figure 3.1
Best practice is to not use the Opening Balance field in a New Customer dialog box.

4. Enter an amount in the Opening Balance field on a new Customer or Job record. QuickBooks creates a *single* invoice for the entire amount owed. This method can present a problem when your customer owes you for multiple invoices. The following also should be noted about using this field for recording the opening balances:

   - **Accrual Basis Reporting**—For this type of reporting, the Opening Balance field increases Accounts Receivable (debit) and increases Uncategorized Income (credit) assigned the date in the As Of field on the New Customer or New Job dialog box.

You might imagine that recording open customer invoices in the New Customer or New Job dialog box is generally not recommended. Instead, create individual invoices matching the open balance records from your previous accounting software for each customer.

- **Cash Basis Reporting**—For this type of reporting, the field has no effect until the date of customer payment. When the customer payment is received, it increases (debit) the account you assign to customer payments (either the QuickBooks Undeposited Funds or the bank account) and increases Uncategorized Income (credit).

Ctrl+I on your keyboard will open a customer invoice form or access it directly from the opening screen in QuickBooks, known as the Home page.

5. To create an individual customer invoice, from the menu bar, select **Customers**, **Create Invoices** (see Figure 3.2).

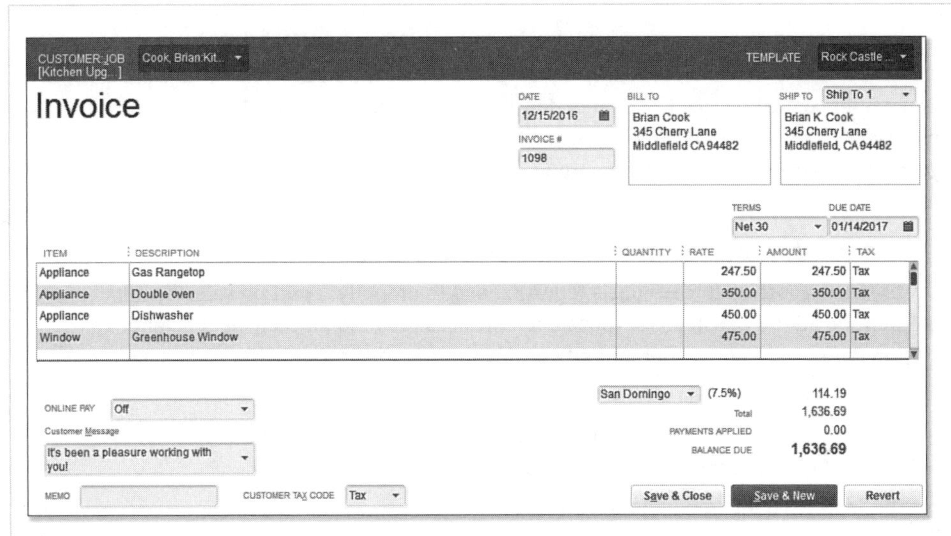

Figure 3.2
Record individual invoices for your customers' starting balances.

6. In the Customer:Job drop-down list, select the customer or job.
7. In the Date field (it should be before your start date), enter the original invoice date.
8. Enter the originally assigned invoice number.
9. In the Item column, enter the item(s)—the products or services that were sold—if you want to accurately track your revenue from this item. It should be the same item(s) that appeared on the original invoice to the customer.
10. If applicable, enter a value in the Quantity column.
11. If the rate did not prefill (because it was not included with list item record), enter a value in the Rate column.
12. The correct tax status on the line should prefill if the list item was set to the proper sales tax status. If some customers pay sales tax and others do not, you must first indicate the taxable status

of an item by selecting from the menu bar **Lists**, **Item List**. Highlight the item in question, click the Item button, and select Edit Item. The Edit Item dialog box opens, and you can mark the item with the appropriate sales tax code.

QuickBooks first determines whether an item is taxable, and then it checks whether the customer is a sales-tax-paying customer before assessing sales tax on a customer balance.

13. Check your Balance Due to make sure it agrees with the list item total from which you are working.
14. Click Save & Close if you are finished, or click Save & New if you have more invoice transactions to record.

QuickBooks offers useful Sales by Item reports that provide more granular detail about the items being sold. If you record a partially paid customer invoice only for the balance due your item sales reports will not offer complete sales information for the item. Instead, you can choose to follow the instructions provided in the next section. However, there are more steps to this process, so proceed only if you find the Sales by Item reports important for these partially paid customer invoices.

Partially Paid Open Customer Invoices on Cash Basis Reporting

To properly prepare reports with cash basis reporting and to properly report on sales by item, you should perform additional steps for those open invoices that had partially paid balances as of your startup date. These steps are required only if you want to accurately track sales by item:

1. From the menu bar, select **Lists, Chart of Accounts.**
2. In the Chart of Accounts dialog box, select **New** from the Account drop-down list. The Add New Account: Choose Account Type dialog box opens.
3. Select the **Bank** account type and click Continue.
4. In the Account Name field, type the name **Prior Year Payments Account.** If account numbering is enabled, enter an account number. Select **No** to the Set Up Online Services message. This is a temporary account that will later have the balances moved to the Opening Balance Equity account in step 15. Click Save & Close.
5. From the menu bar, select **Lists, Item List.**
6. In the Item drop-down list, select **New.** The New Item dialog box opens.
7. In the Type drop-down list, select **Payment,** and then in the Item Name/Number field, type the name **Prior Year Payments.**
8. Assign the Prior Year Payments account created in step 1 as the account to Deposit To (see Figure 3.3). Click OK.
9. To create a partially paid invoice with an open balance, from the menu bar, select **Customers, Create Invoices.**
10. In the drop-down list, choose the appropriate Customer:Job.
11. Enter the original invoice date (it should be before your QuickBooks start date), and enter the invoice number originally presented to the customer for payment.

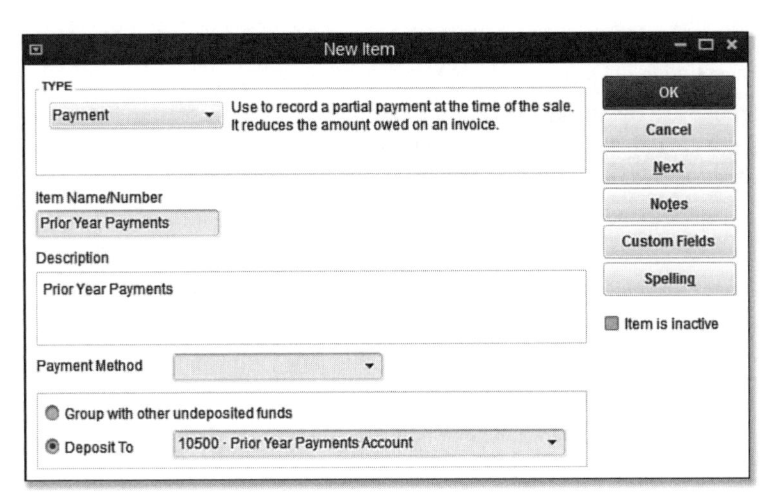

Figure 3.3
Create a payment item type to use on partially paid startup customer invoices.

12. On line 1 (or more if needed) of the customer invoice, enter your normal service or product item you sold to the customer. On the next available line, use the new Prior Year Payments item you created, and enter the total of the customer's prior payments as a negative amount (see Figure 3.4). Click Save & Close if you are finished, or click Save & New to create additional open customer invoices.

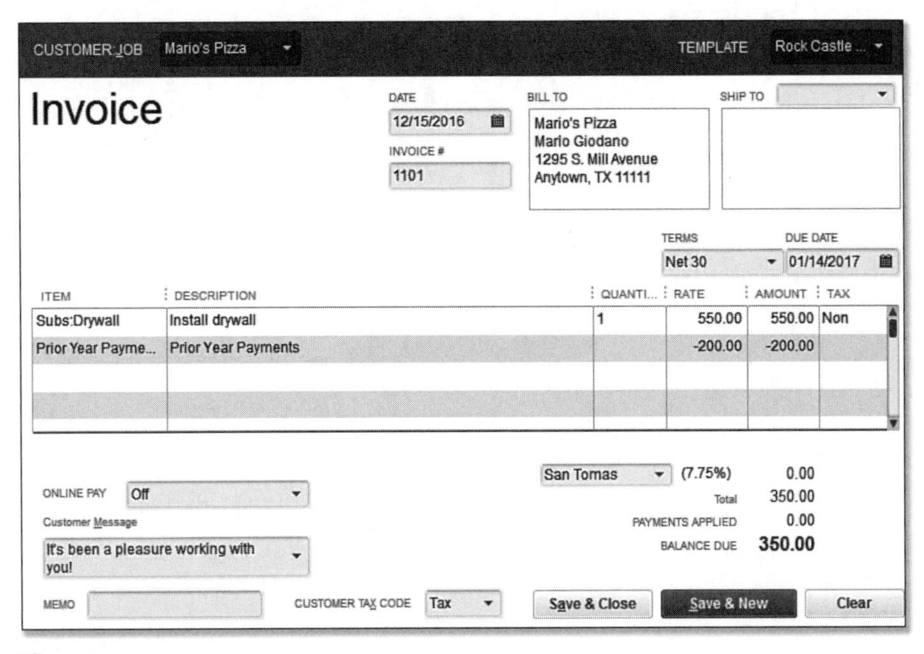

Figure 3.4
Creating an invoice that was partially paid before the date you started using QuickBooks.

13. Verify that the Balance Due amount on the invoice accurately matches the open invoice total from your prior accounting list or report.
14. Compare your QuickBooks A/R Aging Summary report to your open invoices startup list total. If the balances agree, go to step 15. If they do not agree, review either the Summary or Detail A/R Aging report and identify which customer(s) balances are incorrect.
15. When your totals agree, click Banking, Use Register, and select the Prior Year Payments Account.
16. To close the fictitious bank account balance to the Open Balance Equity account, enter the following on the next available line of the register.
    - For the date, enter the day before your startup date. Optionally for the number, use the term Closing.
    - In the payment column, enter the same dollar amount as the register total displayed prior to this transaction.
    - In the Account field, select the QuickBooks-created equity account named Opening Balance Equity.
17. Click Record to save the transaction.

Your Prior Year Payments bank register should now have a zero balance.

For more information, see "Closing Opening Balance Equity into Retained Earnings," p. 568.

Cash or Accrual Basis Startup Transactions: Accounts Payable

note

Entering invoices with partial payment detail provides you with sales reports by item. If this level of detail is not needed on past transactions, you could simply enter a net amount due on the invoice.

Accounts Payable startup refers to those vendor bills that were not paid as of your start date. These are the vendor bills you will be paying out in your first month of using QuickBooks. Correctly setting up the starting Accounts Payable balance is just as important to your financials as setting up Accounts Receivable.

1. From the menu bar, select **Vendors**, **Enter Bills**. In the Vendor drop-down list, choose the appropriate vendor (see Figure 3.5).
2. Enter the bill date. This date should be on or before your QuickBooks start date, and it is often the date on the vendor's bill you received.
3. In the Ref. No. field, enter the vendor's bill number. This serves two important purposes: One is to optionally print the reference number on the bill payment stub that is sent to the vendor, and the other is to allow QuickBooks to warn you if a duplicate bill is later entered with the same Ref. No.
4. Enter a number in the Amount Due field. If you previously paid part of the bill, the amount should equal the balance remaining to be paid. (See the sidebar "Partially Paid Open Vendor Bills on Cash Basis Reporting.")

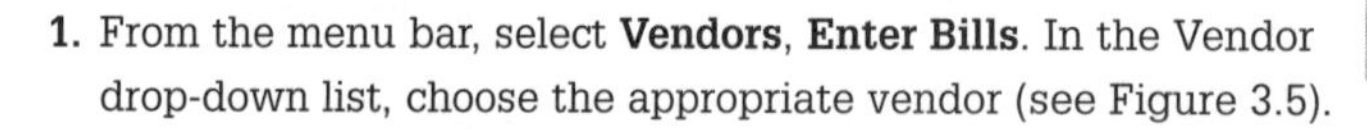

Figure 3.5
Enter a vendor bill that was unpaid at your startup date.

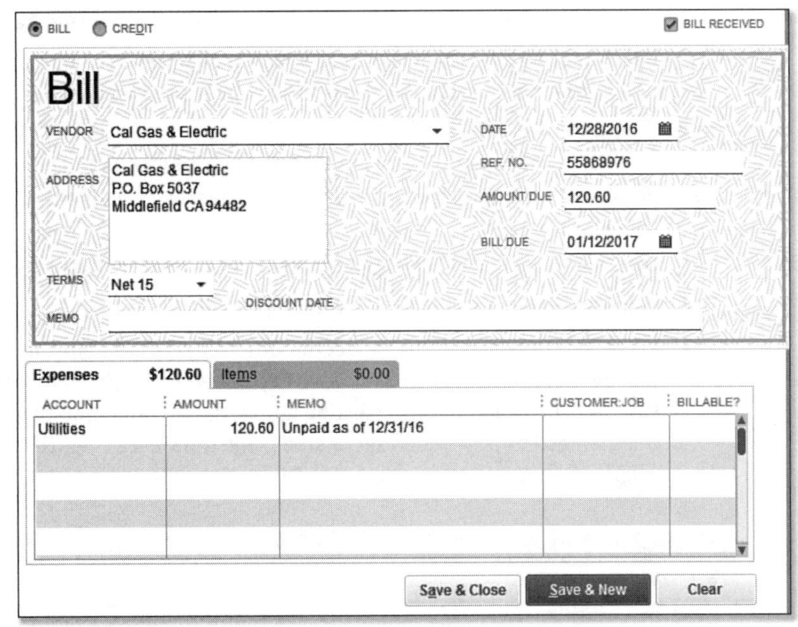

5. QuickBooks defaults the Bill Due date to the terms specified on the Payment Settings tab in the New Vendor or Edit Vendor dialog box; however, you also can override the Bill Due date on this screen, if necessary.

6. Click the Expenses tab and assign the appropriate expense account. If you are tracking costs by items, use the appropriate item on the Items tab. In accrual basis, the account or item selected is not as important because the expense was recorded on the vendor's bill date in your previous software or accounting method. For cash basis, it is most important because the cost is recorded to the expense account or item not when the bill is dated, but on the date of the bill payment check transaction, which should occur after the start date.

7. Click Save & Close or click Save & New to add additional transactions.

8. From the menu bar, select **Reports**, **Vendors & Payables**, **A/P Aging Summary** (or **A/P Aging Detail**), and compare the totals with your previous accounting software or manual records.

9. If the open bills you are entering are for inventory, make sure you read the details in Chapter 5, "Setting Up Inventory."

QuickBooks offers useful Purchase by Item reports that provide more granular detail about the items being purchased. If you record a partially paid vendor bill only for the balance due your item purchase reports will not offer complete purchase information for the item. Instead, you can choose to follow the instructions provided in the next section. However, there are more steps to this process, so proceed only if you find the Purchases by Item reports important for these partially vendor bills.

Partially Paid Open Vendor Bills on Cash Basis Reporting

To properly prepare reports on cash basis, you should perform additional steps for those open vendor bills that have partial payments as of your startup date. These steps are required if you want to accurately track your costs by item including in reports such as the Purchases by Item.

Use the Prior Year Payments bank account that you created in the previous set of steps. This is a temporary account that will later have the balances moved to the Opening Balance Equity account in step 9.

1. From the menu bar, select **Lists, Item List**. The Item List dialog box opens.
2. In the Item drop-down list, select **New**.
3. In the New Item dialog box, select the **Other Charge** item type. In the Item Name/Number field, type **Prior Year Vendor Payments** (see Figure 3.6). Assign it to the Prior Year Payments bank account by selecting it from the Account drop-down list. (This account was created in the previous set of steps. See the sidebar "Partially Paid Open Customer Invoices on Cash Basis Reporting.") Click OK to save.

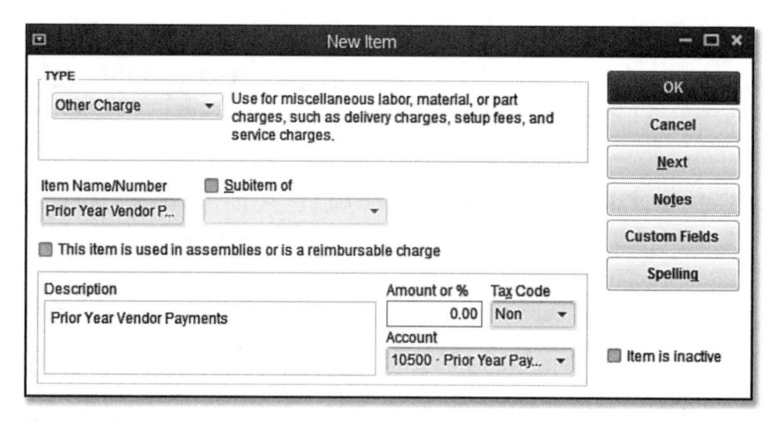

Figure 3.6
Create an Other Charge type item to record prior year vendor payments on startup vendor bills.

4. Follow steps 1–6 in the preceding section titled "Cash or Accrual Basis Startup Transactions: Accounts Payable," with the exception that you need to record the full amount of the original bill. You can use the Expenses tab and assign the appropriate expense account, or if you are tracking costs by item, use the Items tab and assign the correct item.
5. On the Items tab of the Enter Bills dialog box, add the Other Charge type item called Prior Year Vendor Payments. Enter a negative amount equal to the total of all previous bill payments (see Figure 3.7).

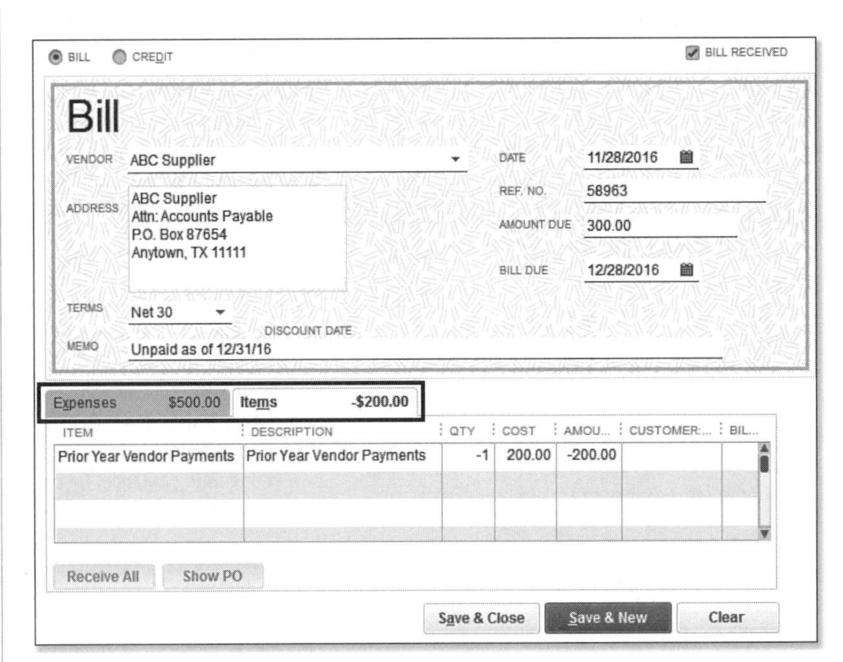
Bill

VENDOR	ABC Supplier
ADDRESS	ABC Supplier, Attn: Accounts Payable, P.O. Box 87654, Anytown, TX 11111
TERMS	Net 30
MEMO	Unpaid as of 12/31/16
DATE	11/28/2016
REF. NO.	58963
AMOUNT DUE	300.00
BILL DUE	12/28/2016

Expenses $500.00 | Items -$200.00

ITEM	DESCRIPTION	QTY	COST	AMOU...	CUSTOMER:...	BIL...
Prior Year Vendor Payments	Prior Year Vendor Payments	-1	200.00	-200.00		

Figure 3.7
Create an open vendor bill including any prior year vendor payment line detail.

6. Verify that the Amount Due amount on the Enter Bills dialog box accurately matches the open vendor invoice total from your previous software (or accounting method) report.
7. Compare your QuickBooks A/P Aging Summary report to the open vendor bill startup list total from your previous software. If the balances agree with each other, go to the next step. If they do not agree, review either the Summary or Detail A/P Aging report and identify which vendor(s) balances are incorrect; then make the needed changes.
8. When the totals of your prior accounting Payables agree with the new QuickBooks A/P Summary report, from the menu bar, click Banking, Use Register. In the Use Register dialog box, select the Prior Year Payments fictitious bank account. Click OK.
9. On the next available register line, enter the day before your startup date and the word **Closing** for the number. In the Deposit column, enter the total amount you see in the balance column of this register. In the Account field, select the QuickBooks-created equity account named **Opening Balance Equity**.
10. Click Record to save your transaction.

When completed, your Prior Year Payments account will have a zero balance.

For more information, see "Closing Opening Balance Equity into Retained Earnings," p. 568.

Cash or Accrual Basis Startup Transactions: Bank Account Statement Balance

In addition to setting up the Accounts Receivable and Payable startup transactions, you also must record the balance the bank had on record as of the start date. Having accurate information is necessary when you are ready to reconcile the bank account in QuickBooks to the bank's monthly statement.

To create your beginning bank balance, follow these steps:

1. From the menu bar, select **Banking**, **Make Deposits** to record your bank statement beginning balance (if a positive balance). However, if you have been using QuickBooks for recording payments before you entered your beginning bank balance, you may need to close the displayed Payments to Deposit dialog.
2. In the Deposit To field, enter your bank account from your chart of accounts list. The date should be the same as your bank statement ending date, usually the day before your QuickBooks start date.
3. In the From Account drop-down list (see Figure 3.8), select **Opening Balance Equity**. The balance belongs in Retained Earnings, but posting it here first gives you a chance to make sure the opening entries for your cash account are correct. (See Chapter 13, "Working with Bank and Credit Card Accounts," for a complete discussion on moving the Opening Balance Equity balance to Retained Earnings.)
4. Enter an optional Memo.

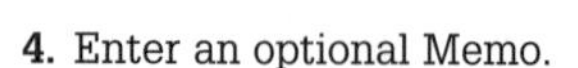

5. Enter the Amount. The amount recorded here is the ending balance from the bank statement the day before your QuickBooks start date. This amount *should not* include any uncleared checks or deposits; these will be added later individually.
6. Click Save & Close to record the transaction.

If you have outstanding deposits that did not clear your bank funds, the way you enter them depends on the basis of accounting used:

- Accrual basis users create the deposit(s) using the same steps as outlined for entering the beginning bank balance and date the transactions before the start date.
- Cash basis users select Customers, Receive Payment from the menu bar, and apply the deposit to an open invoice, which you created earlier in this chapter. Date this transaction *on* or *after* your start date.

tip

To check if your QuickBooks recorded bank balance is correct, from the menu bar, select **Banking, Use Register,** and then select your bank account to open the register.

If the amount is correct and agrees with your bank's statement ending balance, no further action is required. Otherwise, double-click the transaction and edit the amount. If the QuickBooks register does not yet have a beginning balance, follow the steps listed in this section.

tip

If your bank account had a negative balance as of your start date, you can use a check to record that amount.

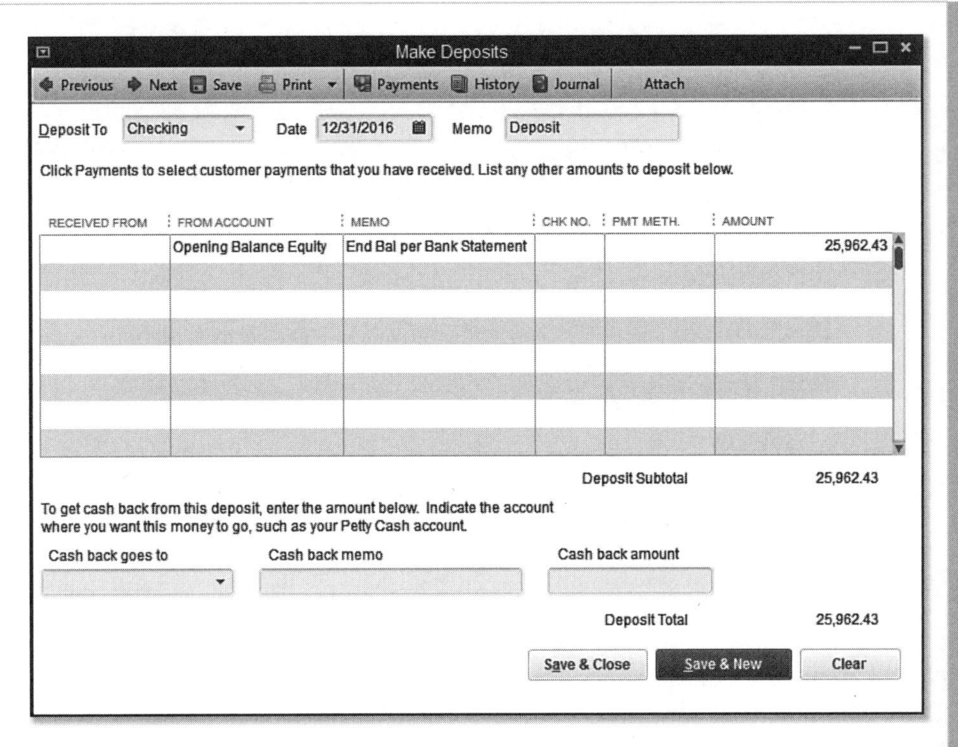

Figure 3.8 Enter the ending balance from the bank's statement.

Cash or Accrual Basis Startup Transactions: Recording Uncleared Bank Checks

You are almost finished with the startup entries. The last thing to do is to record the checking account's uncleared checks and debits, as shown in Figure 3.9. To complete the startup process for your banking transactions, follow these instructions to create your uncleared checks:

1. From the menu bar, select **Banking**, **Write Checks**.
2. In the Write Checks dialog box, enter the actual check number that was issued in the No. field.
3. In the Date field, enter the date of the original check, which should be before the start date.
4. In the Pay to the Order Of drop-down list, select the payee.
5. Enter the amount of the check.
6. On the Expenses tab (see Figure 3.9), select the **Opening Balance Equity** account. (This account is used because in both accrual and cash basis reporting, the check expense amount was included in our prior software or accounting method Profit & Loss totals.)
7. Click Save & Close (or Save & New) until you have completed this task.

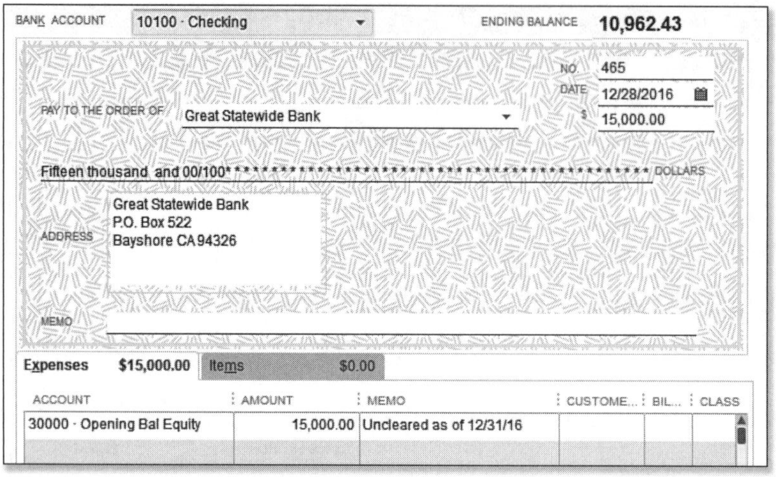

BANK ACCOUNT 10100 · Checking ENDING BALANCE 10,962.43

NO. 465
DATE 12/28/2016
PAY TO THE ORDER OF Great Statewide Bank $ 15,000.00

Fifteen thousand and 00/100*** DOLLARS

ADDRESS Great Statewide Bank
P.O. Box 522
Bayshore CA 94326

MEMO

Expenses $15,000.00 Items $0.00

ACCOUNT	AMOUNT	MEMO	CUSTOME...	BIL...	CLASS
30000 · Opening Bal Equity	15,000.00	Uncleared as of 12/31/16			

Figure 3.9
Details for entering a check that was not cashed by the bank as of the start date.

To verify the accuracy of the information, from the menu bar select **Reports**, **Company & Financial**, **Balance Sheet Standard**, and set the date to be one day before your start date. Your bank account balance(s) should be equal to Bank Statement Ending Balance plus Outstanding (uncleared) Deposits less Outstanding (uncleared) Checks.

UNDERSTANDING QUICKBOOKS LISTS

QuickBooks offers several methods for tracking and reporting on your accounting data so you can review how your business is doing financially.

With QuickBooks, you can use the following lists to analyze your business:

- **Chart of Accounts**—For organizing your daily transactions.
- **Items List**—For tracking the profitability of individual services and products sold.
- **Class List**—For tracking different corporate profit centers (divisions).
- **Customer Type List**—Capability to view your gross profit by user-defined customer types.

The QuickBooks chart of accounts is easy to set up. It might already exist if you created your file with the Express Start discussed in Chapter 1, "Getting Started with QuickBooks." What becomes problematic for some is how to efficiently use each of the available list types when you want to segment the business reporting activity in QuickBooks. We will start first with the chart of accounts.

Chart of Accounts

 tip

A well-defined QuickBooks data file most likely includes the use of items, classes, and customer types, in addition to the chart of accounts.

The chart of accounts is a list of asset, liability, equity, income, and expense accounts to which you assign your daily transactions.

This list is one of the most important lists you will use in QuickBooks; it helps you keep your financial information organized. When this list is created with summary accounts and you use the other list types for detail, you can capture information in a timely manner, which will help you make good financial and management decisions for the business.

Account Types

Understanding the chart of accounts isn't complicated. There are six standard account categories used for tracking the financial activity of your business: assets, liabilities, equity, income, cost of goods sold, and expense.

Assets

Assets include something you have purchased in the past that will be used in the future to generate economic benefit. QuickBooks offers these categories in the order of how liquid the asset is—or in simple terms, how quickly you can turn the asset into cash:

- **Bank**—Used to track your cash in and out of the business. This account type and the credit card account type are the only account types you can select as the payment account in the Pay Bills or Write Checks dialog box.
- **Accounts Receivable**—This account type requires a Customer or Customer and Job name with each entry. You use this account type when generating an invoice or credit memo transaction or when receiving a customer payment. You can create more than one Accounts Receivable account if needed. However, I do not recommend it because it adds the extra work of recording customer payments to the correct Accounts Receivable account.
- **Other Current Asset**—This account type is general in nature and includes the QuickBooks Inventory Asset and the Undeposited Funds account. The Undeposited Funds account is used like a "desk drawer" in that it holds customer payments to be totaled on a single deposit ticket.
- **Fixed Asset**—Used to track purchases of tangible property that will have a useful life of longer than one year. Accumulated Depreciation totals are also held in this account type as a negative fixed asset.
- **Other Assets**—Intangible assets that have a life of more than one year; also any asset that is not a Fixed Asset or Current Asset.

Liabilities

Liabilities are the debts the company has yet to pay. QuickBooks includes these subgroups:

- **Accounts Payable**—This account type is reserved for the QuickBooks Accounts Payable account where vendor bills and bill payments reside. You can create multiple Accounts Payable accounts. However, I do not recommend it as it adds complexity in the enter bill and pay bill processes.
- **Credit Cards**—Optionally, use this grouping to track the charges and payments made against a company credit card. One benefit is that you can reconcile this account as you do your bank account and also download your credit card transactions directly into QuickBooks.
- **Other Current Liability**—This is debt that is expected to be paid within one year. This grouping includes the QuickBooks-created Payroll Liabilities account and Sales Tax Payable account, in addition to other user-defined liability accounts.
- **Long-Term Liability**—This is debt that will not be paid within one year.

Equity

The Equity account category holds the owners (or owners') residual interest in the business after the liabilities are paid. Accounts in this category include common stock; owner's investments and draws; retained earnings; and opening balance equity (an account created by QuickBooks that is discussed in more detail in "Closing Opening Balance Equity into Retained Earnings" in Chapter 15, "Reviewing Your Data").

Income

Money earned from the sale of your products or services is recorded as income. Your company might have one income account or several, depending on the detail needed for your financial analysis. Another category of income is Other Income, or income generated from the sale of a product or service not normal to your operations. Interest Income is an example of an Other Income account type.

Cost of Goods Sold

The Cost of Goods Sold account is for costs directly related to producing a service or good for sale. There is a direct relationship between these costs and your revenue. If your company sells a product, your cost of goods sold (COGS) expenses would be the material, labor, and other costs incurred to make and sell the product. By contrast, your office expenses for rent or advertising are considered indirect and should not be posted to the Cost of Goods Sold account type.

tip

When you are creating your Cost of Goods Sold accounts, consider using summary accounts, such as material, labor, and subcontract, and letting your Item List track more detail. For example, if you are a construction company and you have expenses for site work, concrete, framing, painting, and so on, rather than having a Cost of Goods Sold account for each trade, use the Item List for these. See the section "Adding an Item" in this chapter for more details. Reports by item are available to break down the total of Cost of Goods Sold account into more detail.

Expense

An expense is recorded when an asset is used or there is an outflow of cash. The expense accounts were created during the Express Start or Advanced Setup and provide you with the basic classifications needed for properly tracking your expenses.

Although QuickBooks does not automatically create other groupings within the expenses category, a recommendation would be to group your expenses by fixed (or uncontrollable) and variable (or controllable) costs. When you review your costs, these additional groupings make easy work of determining which costs you have more control over.

You can also categorize an expense as an Other Expense, which is an expense that is not normal to your operations. You should contact your accountant for advice on what expenses are appropriate to record to an Other Expense category type.

Adding a New Account

If you created your own new data file using one of the methods taught in Chapter 1, you might already have the basics of your chart of accounts created for you. Let's think positively and use the example that your business is doing so well you have opened a new money market account with your bank. You know you need to create a new bank account in QuickBooks so that you can reconcile your banking activity with your financial institution's records.

Creating a New Account

To practice adding a new account record, open the sample data file as instructed in Chapter 1. If you are working in your own file, use these instructions to create a new bank (or other type of account) in your chart of accounts:

1. From the menu bar, select **Lists, Chart of Accounts,** or use the keyboard shortcut of Ctrl+A.
2. In the Chart of Accounts dialog box, select **New** from the Account drop-down list. Optionally, use the keyboard shortcut Ctrl+N.
3. In the Add New Account dialog box (see Figure 4.1), click the Bank option button and then click Continue.
4. In the Account Name field, type **Money Market** and in the Number field (if account numbering is enabled), type **10600** (see Figure 4.2).
5. Optionally, select the **Subaccount Of** checkbox and select the account you want to associate this account with. (Typically you would not make a bank account a subaccount of another account.)
6. Enter an optional description; this description will display in certain reports.
7. Accept the default Tax-Line Mapping, which comes from your sample data file or the choices you made when creating your own new file using the Express or Advanced Setup option discussed in Chapter 1. You can also select the drop-down list and choose a different tax line assignment, or click the "How do I choose the right tax line?" link for more information. If opened, close the help dialog box to continue.

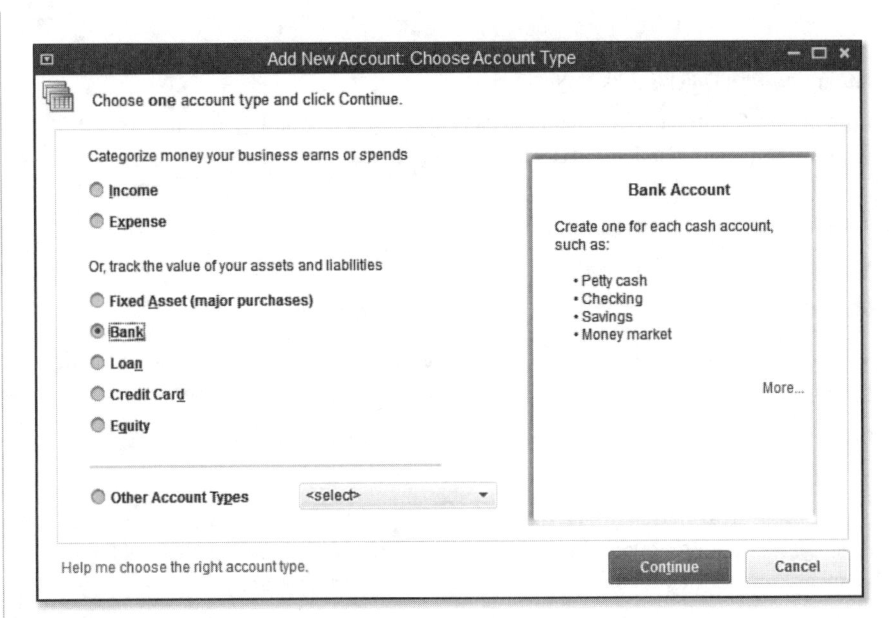

Figure 4.1
When creating a new account, useful information about the account type is displayed on the right.

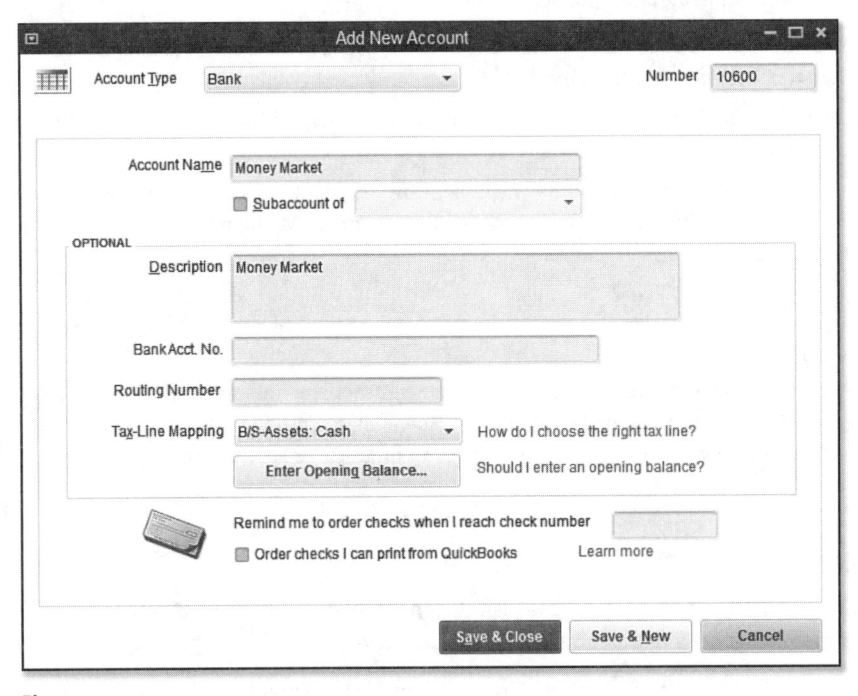

Figure 4.2
Adding a new account when account numbering is enabled.

The tax line is necessary only if you or your accountant prepares the business's tax return using software that integrates with QuickBooks.

8. Click No if the Set Up Online Services dialog displays. Or if you're working in your own data file, you might want to click Yes. More details are available in Chapter 13, "Working with Bank and Credit Card Accounts."
9. Click Save & Close.

The Add New Account dialog box also includes several other important fields:

- **Bank Acct No.**—This information is used if you set up your QuickBooks bank account for online banking downloads. For more information, see Chapter 13.
- **Routing Number**—This information is used if you set up your QuickBooks bank account for online banking downloads (see Chapter 13).
- **Enter Opening Balance**—This button opens the Enter Opening Balance dialog box where you can enter your Statement Ending Balance and Statement Ending Date. Click the "Should I enter an opening balance?" link for help in entering these important starting numbers.

For more information about beginning balances, see "Setting Up a QuickBooks Data File for Accrual or Cash Basis Reporting," pg. 88.

This dialog box also enables you to request a reminder to order checks when you reach a specific check number or order checks directly from Intuit.

The specific details required when creating a new account will vary depending on the type of account you are adding to the chart of accounts.

Creating a new account in the chart of accounts is simple. However, if after reviewing the content in this chapter you find the need to make corrections, read the section "Modifying an Account in the Chart of Accounts" in this chapter.

Items

Items are what you sell or buy and are used on all customer transactions and optionally on purchase transactions. Items provide a quick means for data entry. However, a more important role for items is to handle the behind-the-scenes accounting while tracking product- or service-specific costs and revenue detail.

Adding an Item

Adding items to your QuickBooks file takes some planning, but the effort will pay off with improved reporting on the different services or products your company provides.

Later in this chapter you will learn how to add multiple items at a time using the Add/Edit Multiple List Entries. In this example, you will be adding a single new Service item type to the sample data file.

Adding a New Service Item

To practice adding a new service item, open the sample data file as instructed in Chapter 1. If you are working in your own file, use these instructions to begin creating your own service items.

1. From the menu bar, select **Lists, Item List** to open the Item List dialog box.
2. Select **New** from the Item drop-down list. Optionally, use the keyboard shortcut Ctrl+N.
3. From the Type drop-down list select **Service**.
4. In the Item Name/Number field, type **Inspection**.
5. Select the **This Service Is Used in Assemblies or Is Performed by a Subcontractor or Partner** checkbox, as shown in Figure 4.3. This makes the item "two-sided," assigning both an expense account when used with a purchase transaction and an income account when used with a sales transaction.

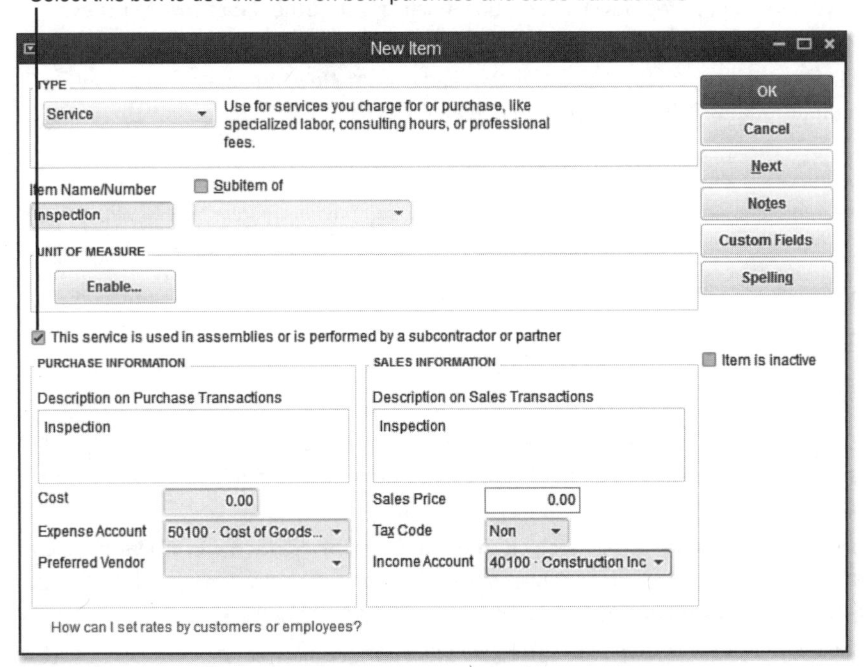

Figure 4.3
Items are used on customer sales transactions and purchase transactions.

6. In the Purchase Information text box, type **Inspection**.
7. Enter a default Cost. This amount will default on a purchase transaction, but can also be changed at the time of entry. If you do not want a default cost for the item, leave the box blank.

8. In the Expense Account field, select the appropriate account. For this example, we will use the Cost of Goods Sold account because the item is directly related to our Customers or Jobs.
9. In the Preferred Vendor field assign a vendor or leave blank. When a preferred vendor is assigned QuickBooks will pre-fill that vendor name on a purchase order transaction when the item is selected.
10. Accept the default description in the Sales Information text box or type a unique description. This description will default on your sales transactions for this item. Optionally, enter a default Sales Price. This amount will default on sales transactions, but can be changed at the time of entry.
11. From the Tax Code drop-down list, select **Non**. In your own file, select the tax code, choosing Tax if the item is subject to sales tax or Non for nontaxable services. Check with your state's taxing authority if you have any questions about an item or service you sell being taxable or not.
12. From the Income Account drop-down list, for this practice, select the **Subcontracted Labor Income** account.
13. If you are finished adding items, click OK to save and exit the New Item dialog box. If you want to continue adding items, click Next to add another item.

For more information about tracking product inventory, see "Inventory Item Type Descriptions," p. 152.

For more information about other uses of the items list, see "Unique Customer Transactions," p. 409.

Understanding Items

Using a construction business as an example, you can create an item for Site Work, Electrical, and Plumbing Subcontractor and assign each item to your single Cost of Goods Sold—Subcontractors account in the chart of accounts.

Using items enables you to capture cost detail by trade rather than by creating an account for each type of expense. When you view your Profit & Loss statement, you can easily see what your total Cost of Goods Sold—Subcontractors is for all trade labor expenses. See Figure 4.4.

From the menu bar, select **Reports, Jobs, Time & Mileage** for reports that provide detailed information about transactions assigned to items, including

- Job Profitability Summary or Detail
- Job Estimates vs. Actuals Summary or Detail
- Item Profitability
- Time by Item

tip

Use the Items tab on expense transactions such as Write Checks or Enter Bills to ensure that you have the detailed reporting you need to review customer or job profitability.

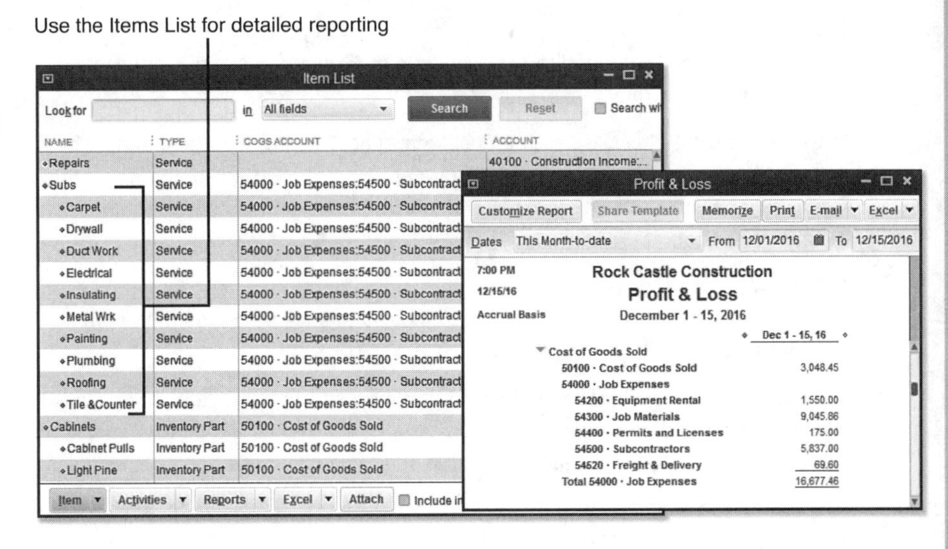

Figure 4.4 Item reports provide detail while keeping the Profit & Loss easy to read.

These reports are useful for a business owner who would like to know the profitability of individual customers or jobs.

Item Types

QuickBooks has 11 item types to choose from (not including the Fixed Asset Item), although some of the items might not be listed in your data file if the related feature is not enabled. You can choose the type to assign to a list item; however, each type has certain unique characteristics. Here are some general guidelines about the proper use for item types:

- **Service**—Create this type for services offered by you or your subcontractors.
- **Inventory Part**—This type displays only if you select the **Inventory and Purchase Orders Are Active** checkbox on the Items & Inventory—Company Preferences tab of the Preferences dialog box. (Access the dialog box from the menu bar by selecting **Edit**, **Preferences**.) Inventory is used to track products you make or buy, place in a warehouse location, and later sell to a customer. Inventory is increased with a received purchase order or bill and is decreased on a customer invoice.

  For more information, see Chapter 5, "Setting Up Inventory," and Chapter 6, "Managing Inventory."

- **Inventory Assembly**—This item type is an assembling of multiple inventory components, as in a Bill of Materials. When an inventory assembly is built, the individual items (components of the assembly) are deducted from inventory and the quantity of the finished assembly product is increased. The assembly functionality is available only in QuickBooks Premier, Professional Bookkeeper, Accountant, or Enterprise.

- **Non-inventory Part**—This type is used for products you purchase but do not track as inventory. Correct use of this type would include products you purchase that are ordered for a specific customer and directly shipped to the customer, or for materials and supplies you purchase but do not sell to the customer.
- **Other Charge**—This is a multipurpose item type. Freight, handling, and other miscellaneous types of charges are examples of the proper use of the Other Charge item type. Using this type makes it possible to segregate sales of your service or product from other types of revenue and expenses in reports.
- **Subtotal**—This type is used to add subtotal line items on sales and purchase transactions. This item is especially useful if you want to calculate a specific discount on a group of items on a customer invoice.
- **Group**—This type is used to quickly assign a grouping of individual items on sales and purchase transactions. Unlike assemblies, groups are not tracked as a separate finished unit. Groups can save you data entry time and enable you to display or hide details on a customer's printed invoice.
- **Discount**—This type facilitates dollar or percent deductions off what your customers owes. This item type cannot be used on purchase transactions.
- **Payment**—This item type is not always necessary to set up. You create this item type if you record the payment directly on an invoice as a line item, such as with a Daily Sales Summary (see the QuickBooks Help for more details). On typical customer invoices, you should not record payments in this manner because there is no tracking of the customer's check or credit card number.
- **Sales Tax Item**—This type is available only if you enabled sales tax on the Sales Tax—Company Preferences tab of the Preferences dialog box. (Access the dialog box from the menu bar by selecting **Edit**, **Preferences**.) In most cases, QuickBooks automatically assigns this item to an invoice. In some states or industries where there are multiple sales tax rates for a given sale, you can also add this item to an invoice as a separate line item.
- **Sales Tax Group**—This type is used to group multiple tax district flat-rate sales tax items that are combined and charged as one sales tax rate.

caution

Carefully determine the correct item type to use when creating items. After they are created, the following item types cannot be changed to any other item type: service, inventory assembly, subtotal, discount, payment, sales tax item, and sales tax group.

If you find you have set up the wrong item type, correcting it might require making an accounting adjustment. To avoid using the incorrect item on future transactions, mark the item as inactive by selecting **Lists**, **Item List** from the menu bar to open the Item List dialog box. Select **Edit Item** from the Item drop-down list and then select the **Item Is Inactive** checkbox. When this box is selected, as Figure 4.5 shows, the item is not included in any drop-down lists on transactions, but is included in reports if used during the period being reported.

However, do not make an inventory type inactive if QuickBooks still shows available inventory quantity.

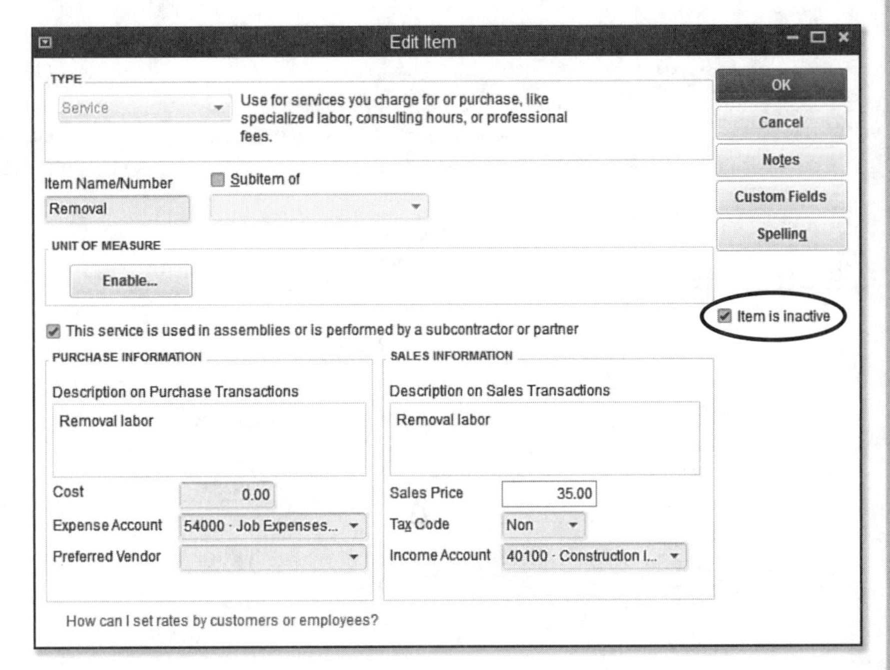

Figure 4.5 Marking a list item inactive only removes it from drop-down lists, not reports.

Class

Another method for segmenting your QuickBooks financial information is by using classes. The use of classes is a preference setting and must first be enabled by logging in to the data file as the Admin or External Accountant user.

To enable classes, follow these steps:

1. From the menu bar, select **Edit, Preferences**.
2. In the Preferences dialog box, select the **Accounting** preference on the left.
3. Select the **Company Preferences** tab.
4. Select the **Use Class Tracking for Transactions** checkbox, as shown in Figure 4.6.
5. Click OK to save your changes and close the dialog box.

Classes are typically used when a company has multiple revenue-generating business types or multiple profit centers. These class list items are then assigned to each transaction, as in Figure 4.7. Examples of classes might be a construction company that offers either new construction or remodeling services, or a restaurant with multiple locations. In both examples, using classes that are assigned to each transaction line for both revenue and costs enables you to report profit and loss by class.

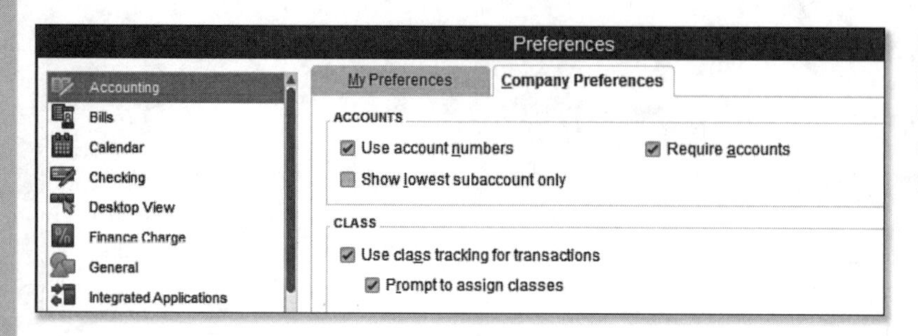

Figure 4.6
Class tracking provides another method for financial reporting for management purposes.

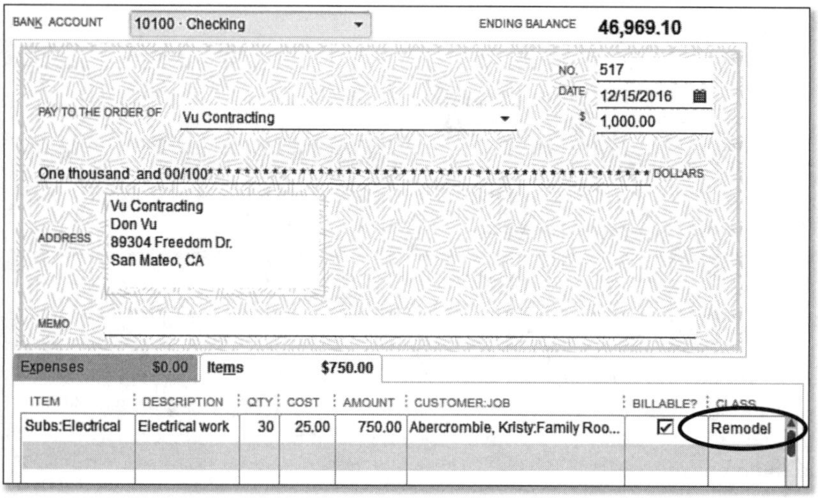

Figure 4.7
Assigning a class list item to a check transaction line provides additional management-reporting capabilities.

When deciding to use classes, it is important you have only one primary purpose for the class structure. If you try to track more than one "type" of class, the value in the reporting is diminished. For example, suppose your company has both an east coast and west coast division. These represent a single use of the QuickBooks class feature. However, using classes to also track the source of the business—for example, *Yellow Pages*, email marketing, and so on—would diminish the success of class reporting because you would be tracking two unrelated groupings. Instead, you can use classes for one purpose and customer types for another.

tip

When using class tracking, be sure to enable the preference to be prompted to assign a class. This preference can be found by selecting from the menu bar **Edit, Preferences, Accounting,** and the **Company Preferences** tab.

New for QuickBooks Enterprise Solutions 13.0 is the preference allowing users to assign default classes for one of the following:

- Accounts
- Items
- Names

For example if you selected to assign classes to items, when setting up an item you can identify the default class to be used on the transaction, as shown in Figure 4.8. This would save users time in data entry and improve the accuracy of assigning the desired default class.

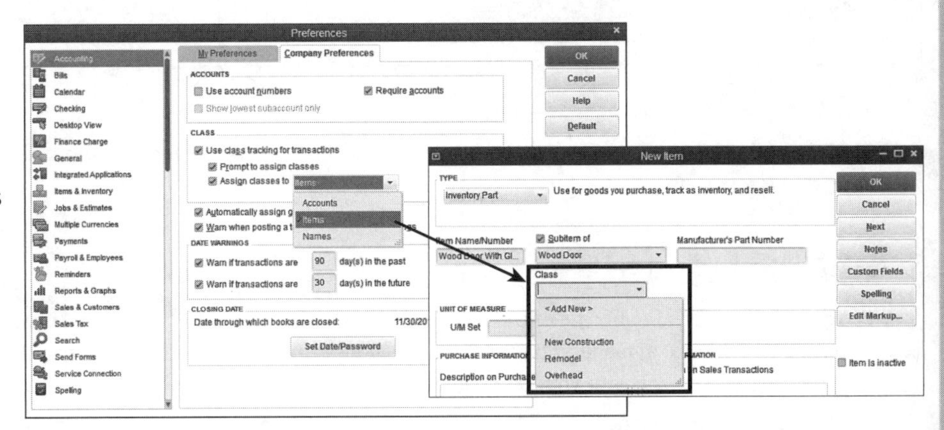

Figure 4.8 With QuickBooks Enterprise you can choose to default classes to accounts, items, or names.

Customer Type

You can use customer types to categorize your customers in ways that are meaningful to your business. A retailer might use customer types to track retail versus wholesale; a medical office might track types of services; a service company might track what marketing event brought in the customer. You can filter certain reports by these customer types, giving you critical information for making business management decisions. These customer types can also be useful for marketing purposes when you want to direct a letter to a specific customer type.

To create or edit a customer record and assign a customer type, follow these steps:

1. On the Home page, click the Customers button. Optionally, use the shortcut Ctrl+J.
2. Double-click to select a customer name in the list that displays.
3. In the Edit Customer dialog box, click the Additional Info tab and select a type from the Type drop-down list. Optionally, select **<Add New>** from the drop-down list to add a new type, as shown in Figure 4.9.
4. Click OK to save your changes.

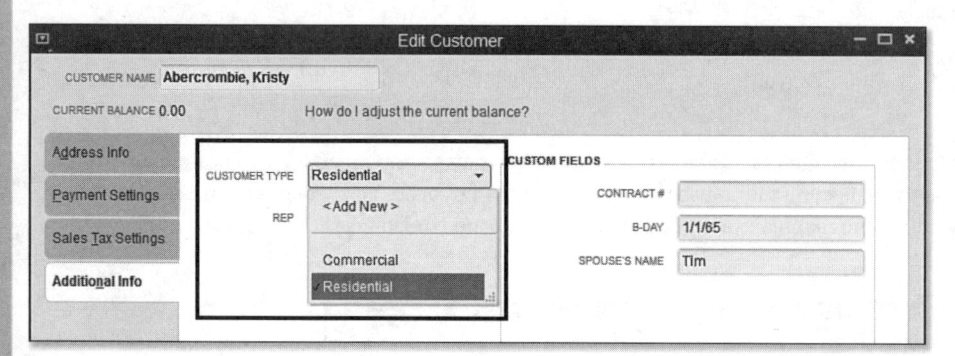

Figure 4.9 Assign a customer type for additional segmented reporting.

Many of the customer reports can be filtered by customer type, making it another useful list for management reporting.

Managing Lists

You have learned about some of the more important lists to set up in your QuickBooks file. This section shares details on managing these lists, including preference settings that can help you be more efficient and accurate with your daily data entry.

This section also provides you with multiple options for importing your lists (but not transactions) into your new QuickBooks file and managing these lists after they are in QuickBooks. When importing your lists, you can select from multiple methods, including the following:

- Adding or modifying the list directly in QuickBooks, one item at a time.
- Adding or modifying your lists using Add/Edit Multiple List Entries, or adding or modifying multiple records at a time in a single list.
- Using the Advanced Import tool in QuickBooks.
- Importing a list from another QuickBooks file using the IIF (Intuit Interchange File) format.

If you are starting with a new QuickBooks file, you might first want to review the preference settings that affect the chart of accounts.

Chart of Account Preferences

Setting preferences in QuickBooks can help you be more accurate and efficient with your data entry. In Chapter 2, "Getting Around QuickBooks," you learned about Company Preferences that are global for all users and My Preferences that affect only the settings for the currently logged-in user.

Using specific preferences, you can modify how many of the QuickBooks features work. To do so, from the menu bar, select **Edit, Preferences** and select the **Accounting—Company Preferences** tab as previously displayed in Figure 4.6.

Here is a list of the preferences found in the Accounting—Company Preferences tab that affect the chart of accounts:

- **Use Account Numbers**—Selecting this option turns on the data field that holds a numeric assignment for each chart of accounts. By default, this feature is not selected in a newly created QuickBooks file.

For accounts that have an account number assigned, deselecting the Use Account Numbers option does not remove the account number—it simply hides the field. For accountants, turn on the feature and assign your desired account numbers, and then turn the feature off when the file is returned to your client. When you review the file again, any accounts created since your last review will not have an account number, which makes locating them easy.

Alternatively, accountants who use the QuickBooks Accountant 2013 software can track changes made to the chart of accounts, including additions, renames, deletions, or merges made using the Client Data Review tools. More information is available in Appendix A, "Client Data Review."

- **Show Lowest Subaccount Only**—You can select this preference only if you selected the **Use Account Numbers** checkbox and if each account has been assigned an account number. If you have created a subaccount listing under a main (parent) listing, when you type the subaccount name, only the subaccount name and account number will display in transactions. Without the feature selected, when you type a subaccount name on an expense transaction, you will see both the main account name and subaccount name.
- **Require Accounts**—By default, this feature is selected in a newly created QuickBooks file. If this feature is not selected, any transactions saved without selecting an account will be posted to an automatically created uncategorized income or uncategorized expense account. This process follows the rule that there must always be a debit and credit side to each transaction. Fortunately, you do not have to know how to post a debit or credit because QuickBooks does this thinking for you with each transaction.

On a report, if you see an amount reporting to an "Other" subaccount row title under a main account, it is the result of posting to the main (or parent) account rather than to the appropriate subaccount.

Add/Edit Multiple List Entries

Adding or modifying several entries in a single QuickBooks list can be a daunting task when you have to work with one list entry at a time. In Chapter 1, you might have created your lists using the QuickBooks Setup to add the people you do business with, the products or services you sell, and your bank accounts.

When working in your own data, make sure your columns of data in Excel match the Add/Edit Multiple List Entries columns when cutting and pasting from Excel.

With the Add/Edit Multiple List Entries feature (see Figure 4.10), you can add to or modify customer or vendor records. You can also add or modify your service, inventory, and non-inventory items. Using this feature can save you precious time, particularly when you want to add or make changes to multiple entries on a list all at once.

If a sample file is not listed, select **File, Close Company or File, Close Company/Logoff.** In the No Company Open dialog box, select a file to practice with from the Open a Sample File drop-down list.

Practice Using the Add/Edit Multiple List Entries Feature

Learn how to use the Add/Edit Multiple List Entries feature by adding a customer record and customizing the columns of data displayed. To complete this task, open the sample data as instructed in Chapter 1.

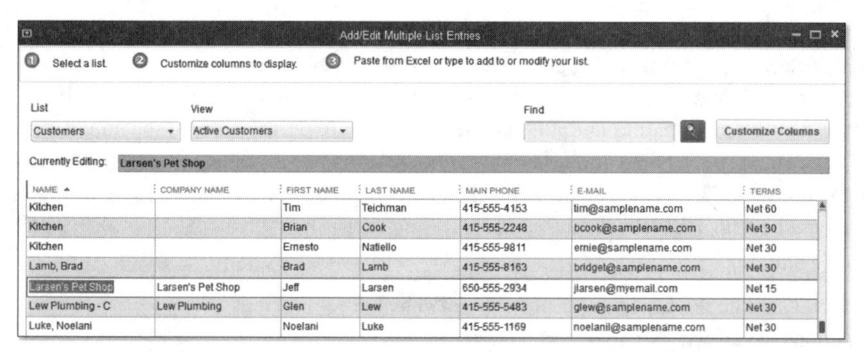

Figure 4.10
Use the Add/Edit Multiple Lists Entries to add or modify your lists efficiently.

1. From the menu bar, select **File, Open Previous Company** and select the sample data file you previewed in Chapter 1.
2. From the menu bar, select **Lists, Add/Edit Multiple List Entries**. In the Add/Edit Multiple List Entries dialog box that displays, the Customers list should default in the List drop-down. (If you are adding or modifying one of the other supported lists, your data fields will vary from the figures shown here.)
3. Click the Customize Columns button on the right side. The Customize Columns dialog box displays.
4. From the Available Columns panel on the left, select the **Terms** field and click Add. The Terms data field is now added to the Chosen Columns panel.

5. Click the Move Up or Move Down button with Terms selected to reposition the location of that data column. Adding, removing, or repositioning columns can be very useful if you are copying data from an existing Excel worksheet.
6. With your cursor, in the Chosen Columns panel, select the **M.I.** (middle initial) field. Click the Remove button.
7. Click OK to close the Customize Columns dialog box.
8. Optionally, select the **View** drop-down list to filter the list results or type in the Find box a specific search term to add as an additional filter to the resulting list.
9. For practice in this sample data, right-click and select **Insert Line**. Complete the data entry fields as displayed for this practice adding a customer record. Or, if your own business's customer list is already in an Excel spreadsheet, you may also use Excel's cut and paste functionality to add the customer details from an existing Excel spreadsheet. From the grid, you can right-click with your cursor for other functionality. From this menu, you can use Copy Down, Duplicate Row, Clear Column, and other useful features.
10. Click Save Changes. QuickBooks indicates the number of customer record(s) that have been saved. Click OK. If you are modifying several records, you might want to save your work often.
11. Click Close to close the Add/Edit Multiple List Entries dialog box when you have completed your additions or modifications.

Using the Add/Edit Multiple List Entries dialog box for importing via Excel's cut and paste can be an efficient way to get started and to update existing lists.

caution

On the Customers list, the Name field is the "look-up" or internal name you give a customer. It can be the same as the Company Name field or different. The customer invoice will display the name you type in the Company Name field, so be sure not leave it blank.

If you type a name in the Name column that already exists, QuickBooks highlights the duplicate name and requires you to amend the name. You cannot have the same Name field duplicated on a single list or other lists. For example, a customer named ABC Services cannot exist more than once on the customer list and cannot also be a vendor with the same spelling. If you have a customer that is also a vendor, modify the vendor listing to ABC Services-V and put the actual name of the vendor in the Company Name field and Print on Check As field in the vendor record.

Add Your Excel Data to QuickBooks Utility

Lists can also be added to QuickBooks for Vendors, Customers, and Products You Sell (Items) directly from a ready-made Excel spreadsheet using the Add Your Excel Data to QuickBooks utility. If you choose to use the Advanced (Excel) Import feature of this utility, you can also import a chart of accounts list, something you cannot do using the Add/Edit Multiple Lists Entries feature.

Enter Data into Preformatted Spreadsheets

Follow these steps to import lists using the preformatted Excel spreadsheets included with this utility:

1. From the menu bar select **File**, **Utilities**, **Import**, **Excel Files**.
2. An information message may display regarding the Add/Edit Multiple List Entries feature discussed in the prior section. Optionally, place a checkmark in the Do Not Display This Message in the Future box.
3. Click No to continue with using the Add Your Excel Data utility. The Add Your Excel Data to QuickBooks Wizard displays, shown in Figure 4.11.

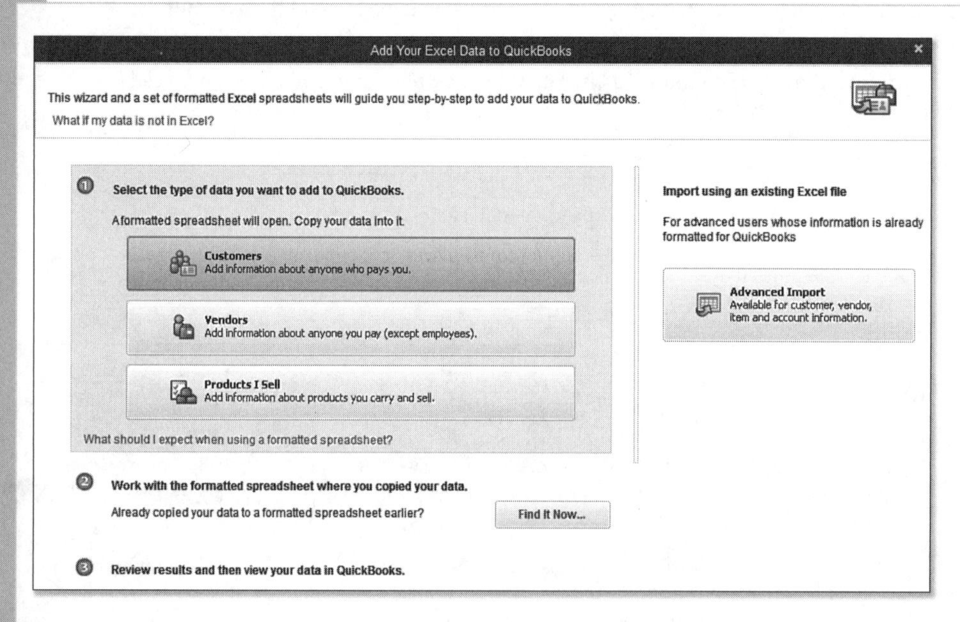

Figure 4.11 Choose which type of list you want to add information to using this utility.

4. Click to select the type of data you want to add to QuickBooks. You can choose from

   - Customers
   - Vendors
   - Products I Sell

5. In this example, click Customers. QuickBooks might display an information message about not being able to undo this import. It is prudent to make a backup of your data file before proceeding. Click Yes.

For more information, see "Creating a QuickBooks Backup," p. 619.

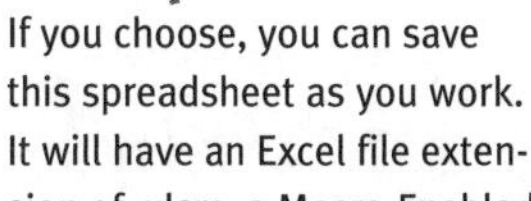

tip

If you choose, you can save this spreadsheet as you work. It will have an Excel file extension of .xlsm, a Macro-Enabled Workbook. When you are ready to return to finish adding to the data, return to step 1 of this section, click the Find It Now button, and then browse to the stored workbook.

6. Optionally, click the Show or Hide Coach Tips and Show or Hide Detailed Instructions. Both provide onscreen details about working with this preformatted spreadsheet. See Figure 4.12.

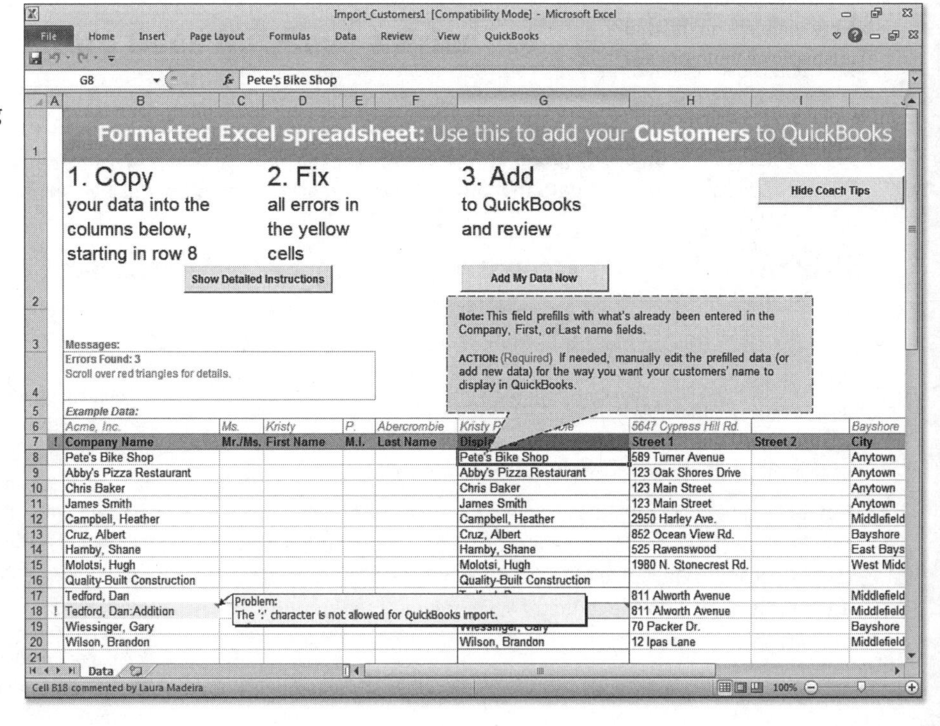

Figure 4.12 Preformatted spreadsheets make entering data with this utility easy.

7. Begin adding data to the spreadsheet using one of these two methods:
   - Copying and pasting from an existing Excel worksheet.
   - Manually type your data into the spreadsheet.
8. When your work is complete, you have the following options:
   - Save the workbook and later open it by returning to step 1, selecting the option to Find It Now, and browsing to the stored file.
   - Click the Add My Data Now button.

Although manually adding or copying data from Excel are both options using this utility, you may find that working with the Add/Edit Multiple List Entries (from the prior section) is a more efficient method for this type of entry.

9. If you selected **Add My Data Now**, you will be prompted to Save & Add My Data Now or I'll Add My Data Later.
10. If you selected **Save & Add My Data Now** you will be prompted to select a location to store the file. Click Save. QuickBooks provides confirmation listing the number of records that were imported successfully.
11. Select the **View Customer List** button to view the data that was imported.
12. Click Close to leave the Add Your Excel Data to QuickBooks.

This utility has been available for many years and will help you get your lists quickly into a new QuickBooks file. I personally prefer working with the Add/Edit Multiple List Entries dialog because I can arrange the columns of data to match my existing spreadsheet I might be copying from.

Advanced Import from an Existing Excel Worksheet

The advantage to using the Advanced Import is the capability to import a chart of accounts list into a new QuickBooks file from an existing Excel worksheet. This is a common practice among accounting professionals. The other methods of importing discussed in this chapter so far do not offer the capability to import one of the most important lists, the chart of accounts.

However, most users will not necessarily need to import this list. When you use the Express Start feature for creating a new QuickBooks file, QuickBooks automatically creates a chart of account list based on the industry type you selected during that process.

For more information, see "Express Start," p. 35.

Follow these instructions to import the chart of accounts from an Excel spreadsheet.

tip

Accounting professionals have another method for creating a new file using a previously set-up chart of accounts. Create a template QuickBooks file with the chart of accounts and other settings as desired. If you're using QuickBooks Accountant, from the menu bar select **File, New Company, From Existing Company File,** and then follow the onscreen prompts.

1. From the menu bar select, **File**, **Utilities**, **Import**, **Excel Files**. The Import a File dialog displays with the Set Up Import tab selected.

2. In the Select a File pane, browse to the location of your saved Excel spreadsheet that contains the chart of accounts.

3. If there are multiple sheets in the workbook, select the appropriate sheet to use from Choose a Sheet in This Excel Workbook, as shown in Figure 4.13.

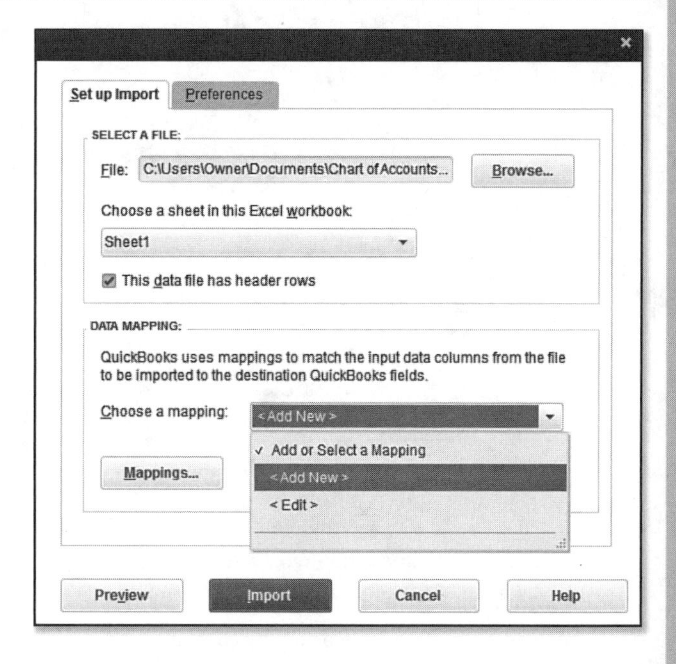

Figure 4.13
The Advanced Import is a useful utility if you already have your lists in an Excel worksheet. This utility does not require that you copy and paste the details.

4. If this is your first time using this utility, in the Data Mapping pane, select **Add New** in the Choose a Mapping drop-down. The Mappings dialog box displays.

5. Type a name into the Mapping Name field. This enables you to select this mapping for use again.

6. For the Import Type, in this example select **Account**.

7. The fields available in QuickBooks will be listed in the left column (see Figure 4.14). The fields in your selected spreadsheet will be displayed in the Import Data pane on the right. From the drop-down, select the matching field.

8. Click Save to store this mapping for future use. You are returned to the Import a File dialog box.

tip

It helps when creating the Excel worksheet to type data labels that will be easy to match to the QuickBooks fields.

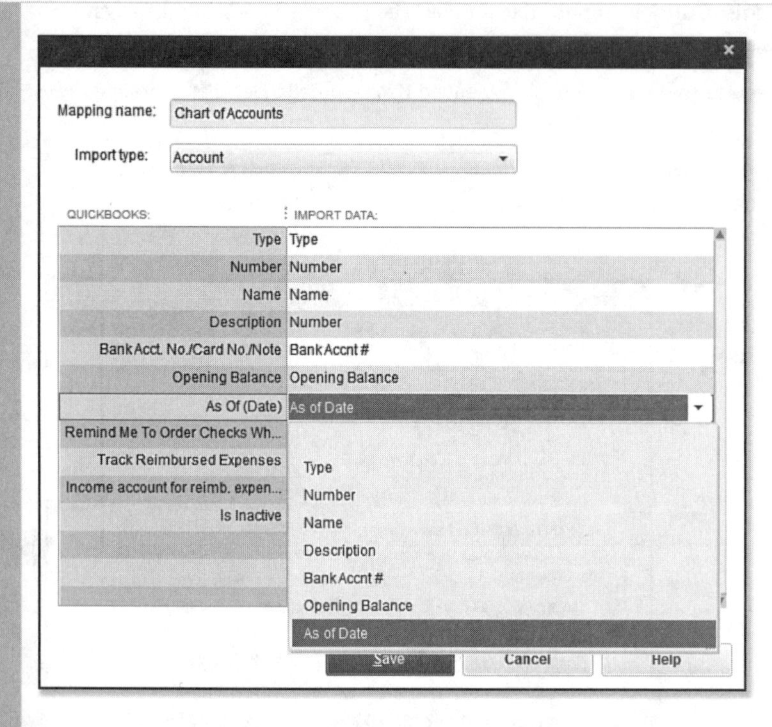

Figure 4.14
When using the Advanced Import, map the columns of an existing spreadsheet to the fields in QuickBooks.

9. Click Preview to see the results of what the import will be prior to completing this step. Any errors in the import file will have the word Error displayed in red text. Click any row with an error, and QuickBooks details the reason so you can fix it before importing.

10. Select how to handle errors by choosing from the following:

    - Import Rows with Errors and Leave Error Fields Blank
    - Do Not Import Rows with Errors

11. Click Import to complete the process. Or click OK to close the Preview dialog box, and Cancel to not make any changes. See Figure 4.15.

12. If you selected Import, QuickBooks displays an information dialog recommending that you back up your data prior to the import. The import process cannot be undone. Click Yes to continue the import, or No to make a data backup first.

13. If you selected Yes to the Import message, QuickBooks confirms the records that were imported. Select **Save** to save the Error Log (browse to a location to store the file) or **Don't Save**.

14. To view the chart of accounts that was imported, from the menu bar select **Lists**, **Chart of Accounts**.

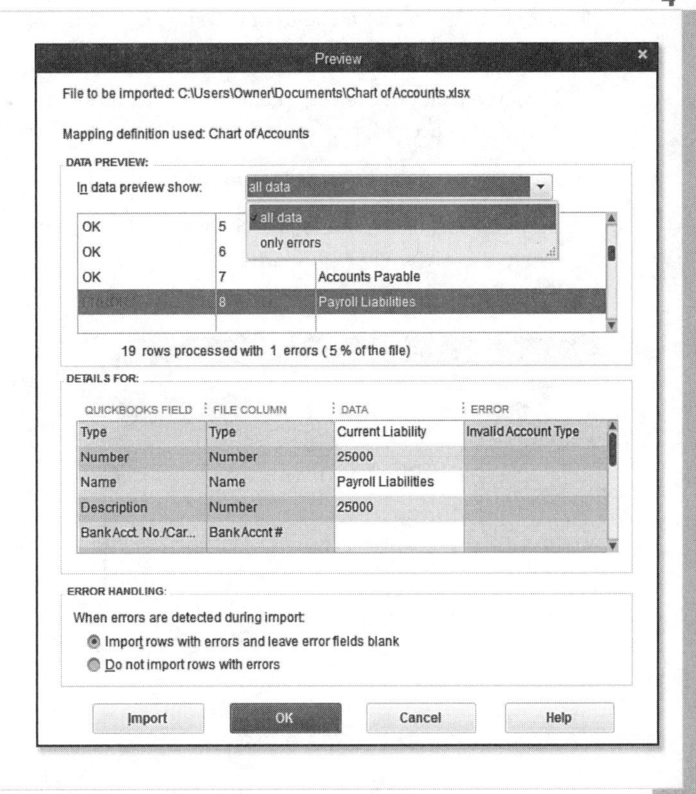

Figure 4.15
Preview the import, and view any rows with errors.

With QuickBooks 2013 you have several options for importing your lists. Getting started using QuickBooks is fast and easy. The next section details another method you may choose to use, especially if you are choosing to copy lists from one QuickBooks file to another.

Importing an Intuit Interchange Format File (IIF)

The term *Intuit Interchange Format (IIF)* refers to data exchange functionality that has been around for some time. It is a method for exporting lists from one QuickBooks file and importing these lists into a new QuickBooks file. The process creates a tab-delimited value format file with the extension of .iif. You can view and edit this file using Excel.

The most common use for this tool is to export lists from one QuickBooks data file to a new QuickBooks data file. The process is easy and relatively error free. Other uses for the tool include transaction imports. This book does not cover the topic of transaction imports using IIF formatted files; however, you can find more information about this utility by typing **IIF** into the search field at www.quickbooks.com/support.

The IIF format is a preferred and easy method to use if you already have a QuickBooks file with a chart of accounts (or other lists) that you want to replicate in another file.

The only disadvantage to working with an IIF format file is all the extra information that is in the text file, making it awkward to edit or add to the existing information.

To export an IIF-formatted chart of accounts file from an existing QuickBooks file, follow these steps:

1. From the menu bar select, **File**, **Open** or **Restore Company** to open the QuickBooks file that has the chart of accounts (or other lists) you want to export and duplicate in another file.
2. From the open QuickBooks file, on the menu bar select, **File**, **Utilities**, **Export**, **Lists to IIF Files**.
3. In the Export dialog box, select the **Chart of Accounts** checkbox (or other type of list you want to export), as shown in Figure 4.16.

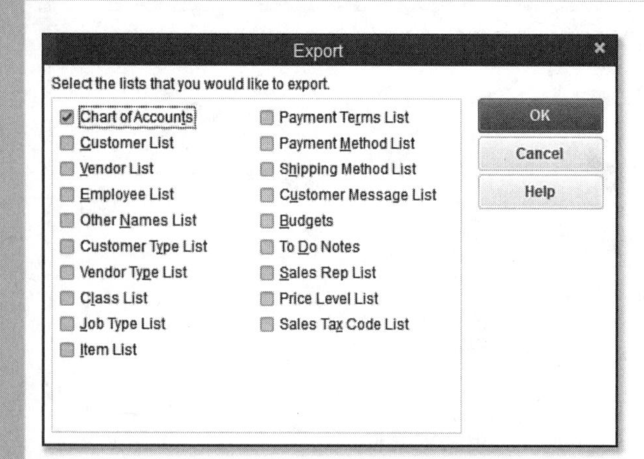

Figure 4.16
The Export dialog box shows choices of lists available for export.

4. Click OK. You will be prompted to provide a filename and to save the file. Remember the location you stored the file in; you will need to browse to the file to import into another QuickBooks file.

tip

Creating individual IIF files for each of the master lists you want to export is preferable to creating one combined file. In other words, create one file for your chart of accounts separate from a file for vendors or customers. This way, if one list has trouble importing, it won't prevent the other lists from importing.

Figure 4.17 shows the exported QuickBooks chart of accounts in the IIF format in an Excel workbook. You can see it is not as user friendly as the Add/Edit Multiple List Entries dialog box discussed previously.

note

The Add/Edit Multiple List Entries feature does not include modifying the chart of accounts list. To import the chart of accounts, see the section "Advanced Import from an Existing Excel Worksheet" in this chapter.

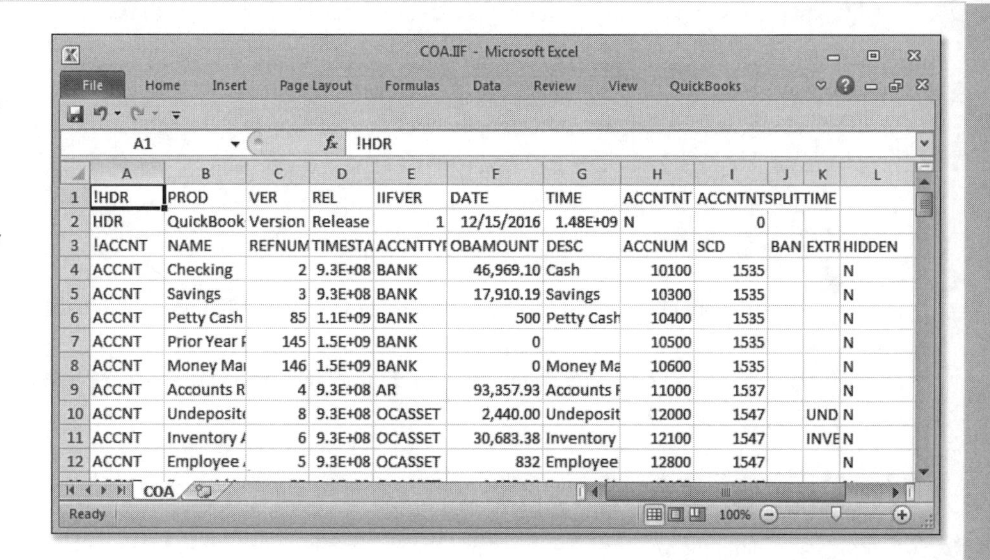

	A	B	C	D	E	F	G	H	I	J	K	L
1	!HDR	PROD	VER	REL	IIFVER	DATE	TIME	ACCNTNT	ACCNTNTSPLITTIME			
2	HDR	QuickBook	Version	Release	1	12/15/2016	1.48E+09	N	0			
3	!ACCNT	NAME	REFNUM	TIMESTA	ACCNTTYI	OBAMOUNT	DESC	ACCNUM	SCD	BAN	EXTR	HIDDEN
4	ACCNT	Checking	2	9.3E+08	BANK	46,969.10	Cash	10100	1535			N
5	ACCNT	Savings	3	9.3E+08	BANK	17,910.19	Savings	10300	1535			N
6	ACCNT	Petty Cash	85	1.1E+09	BANK	500	Petty Cash	10400	1535			N
7	ACCNT	Prior Year F	145	1.5E+09	BANK	0		10500	1535			N
8	ACCNT	Money Mai	146	1.5E+09	BANK	0	Money Ma	10600	1535			N
9	ACCNT	Accounts R	4	9.3E+08	AR	93,357.93	Accounts F	11000	1537			N
10	ACCNT	Undeposit	8	9.3E+08	OCASSET	2,440.00	Undeposit	12000	1547		UND	N
11	ACCNT	Inventory A	6	9.3E+08	OCASSET	30,683.38	Inventory	12100	1547		INVE	N
12	ACCNT	Employee A	5	9.3E+08	OCASSET	832	Employee	12800	1547			N

Figure 4.17 A chart of accounts IIF format file that can be imported into another QuickBooks file.

To import the saved IIF file into a new QuickBooks file, follow these steps:

caution

The IIF file format is a tab-delimited text file with an extension of .iif. Be sure to keep this format when saving your changes; do not save as an .xls or .xlsx Excel file type.

1. From the menu bar, select **File**, **Open or Restore Company**, and select the QuickBooks file you want to import the previously exported list into.

   If you have not already created your new file select, **File**, **New**, and follow the prompts. (See Chapter 1 for more information.)

2. From the menu bar select, **File**, **Utilities**, **Import**, **IIF Files**.

3. In the Import dialog box, browse to the location of the stored IIF formatted file.

4. With your cursor, select the file and click Open.

5. QuickBooks then imports the IIF formatted file into the QuickBooks data file. Click OK to close the Your Data Has Been Imported message box.

Now that you have your new data file with new lists from another file, you are ready to begin entering transactions. Think of all the time you saved by not having to manually create each list item in the new file.

Reporting on Lists

With a QuickBooks file created and lists entered, you can now review the efforts of your work. Let's start with a simple listing of your vendors.

1. From the menu bar select **Reports**, **List**. Take a moment of your time to review the many lists available for reporting on in this menu. Some lists will display only if the associated preference in QuickBooks is enabled.
2. Select the **Vendor Contact List**. Optionally, click the Customize Report button.
3. The Modify Report dialog opens with the Display tab selected. From the Columns listing, add or remove checkmarks to include or exclude information from the list report.
4. Click OK when finished.

You will learn more about modifying these and other reports in Chapter 14, "Reporting in QuickBooks."

Reviewing your lists before you begin entering transactions can ensure that the information provided in reports is correct.

Finding and Fixing Chart of Account Errors

When searching for reasons why your financial statements do not appear correctly, the first place to look is often the chart of accounts. It is also important to carefully consider the impact of the change on your financials and make sure you choose the right method for correction.

There are many ways to resolve errors found on the chart of accounts. However, before attempting any of the suggested methods here, you should consider the following:

- The effect the change could have on prior-period financials
- The effect the change could have on previously recorded transactions
- The impact the changes would have on the records your accountant has kept for the company

A quick review of the chart of accounts should include the following:

- Duplicated accounts
- Unnecessary accounts (too much detail)
- Accounts placed in the wrong account type category
- Misplaced subaccounts

QuickBooks Required Accounts

The chart of accounts listed here is required for specific functionality of a transaction. If you have previously removed the account, QuickBooks re-creates it when you use a transaction that depends on that specific account. Additionally, these accounts are automatically created when a related transaction is opened for the first time:

- Accounts Receivable
- Inventory Asset
- Undeposited Funds
- Accounts Payable
- Payroll Liabilities
- Sales Tax Payable
- Opening Balance Equity
- Retained Earnings
- Cost of Goods Sold
- Payroll Expenses
- Estimates (nonposting)
- Purchase Orders (nonposting)

note

In earlier versions of QuickBooks, you might have accounts that have an asterisk (*) in front of the name to indicate a duplicate account name. This situation usually happens only when you did not select to use one of the sample charts of accounts. QuickBooks has certain accounts that it creates automatically.

For example, if you did not select a sample default chart of accounts, and you created your own Accounts Receivable account, QuickBooks automatically adds another Accounts Receivable account when an invoice transaction is opened. Because QuickBooks recognizes that you already have an Accounts Receivable account (the one you created), QuickBooks appends the name with an asterisk. You should merge your created account (the one without the *) into the QuickBooks-created account. See the later section titled "Merging Duplicated Accounts" for instructions on how to merge two like accounts.

Making an Account Inactive

Marking an account inactive is usually the best choice when you have duplicate or extra list entries on your chart of accounts. Making an account inactive removes it from any drop-down list where the item can be selected. However, for reporting periods where the account has a value, any reports generated will include the inactive account balance.

Do you need to mark several accounts as inactive? Select the **Include Inactive** checkbox at the bottom of the chart of accounts list, as shown in Figure 4.13. You can mark any list items you want to become inactive by clicking in front of the list item name. If Include Inactive is grayed out, right-click an account and choose Make Account Inactive. You will now have the option to place a checkmark in the Include Inactive box.

In the future, if you try to use an inactive account, QuickBooks prompts you to choose between Use It Once or Make It Active.

Merging Duplicated Accounts

Another method to remove duplicated accounts is to merge the similar accounts. To perform a chart of accounts merge, both accounts must be in the same chart of accounts category; in other words, you cannot merge an Asset with a Liability-type account.

Before merging accounts, perform a backup of your data, just in case the result is not what you expected. When the accounts are merged, all transactions previously assigned to the removed account now appear as if they were always assigned to the remaining account.

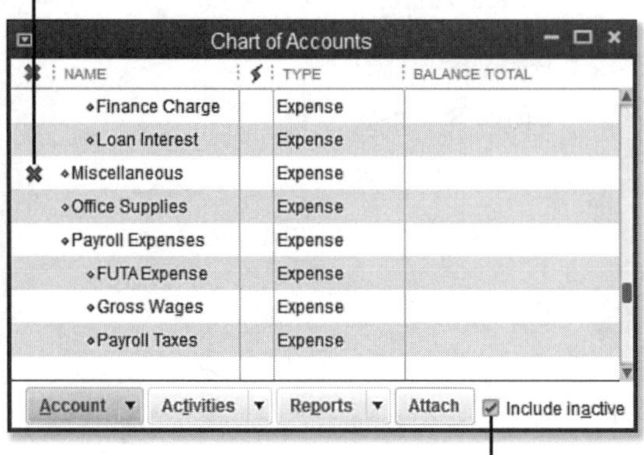

Figure 4.18
Easily mark accounts inactive from the Chart of Accounts dialog box.

To merge two accounts, follow these steps:

1. From the menu bar select **Lists**, **Chart of Accounts**, and highlight the account you want to remove with the merge. With the account highlighted, press Ctrl+E on your keyboard to open the Edit Account dialog box.
2. If you are using account numbering, replace the account number with the account number for the account you want to retain. Optionally, you can type the exact spelling of the name of the other account you are merging with this one into the Account Name field.

   QuickBooks cautions you that the name is already being used and asks whether you want to continue (see Figure 4.19). If you do not get this message, you didn't accurately type the name or account number. You need to try again.
3. Click Yes to merge the accounts.

caution
This method potentially changes your financials and should be cautiously performed only after you have discussed the effect with the company's accountant and have made a backup of the data file.

caution
Chart of accounts, customers, jobs, vendors, and other names lists can all be merged within their own type or category. Be careful—there is no undo function, making the action irreversible.

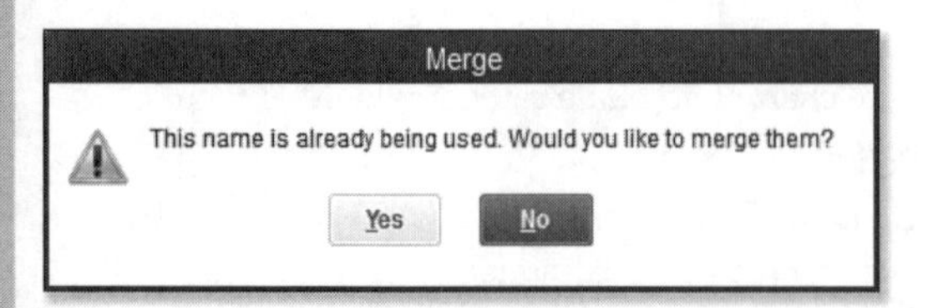

Figure 4.19
QuickBooks offers a word of caution when you are merging two charts of accounts lists.

Modifying an Account in the Chart of Accounts

The mistake most often made when creating your own chart of accounts is assigning the wrong account type. QuickBooks provides additional subcategories under the six standard accounting categories, as identified in the "Account Types" section at the beginning of this chapter.

The Add New Account dialog box, previously shown in Figure 4.1, can help you reduce errors that occur when creating a new account. When you select an account type, QuickBooks provides a general description of the proper use of the selected account.

Changing an account type can also be advantageous when you want to fix future transactions and prior-period transactions. For example, suppose you created a Current Asset account type instead of the correct Expense account type. Simply changing the account type via the Edit Account dialog box (see the following steps) corrects all prior-period and future transactions to be assigned to the new account type.

However, you will not be able to change an account type or merge a chart of an account if subaccounts are associated with that chart of account list item. For more information, refer to the note on page 131.

caution

Exercise caution before changing an account type. The change affects any prior-period financials. If this consequence is a limitation for your company, a simple solution is to create a general journal entry to remove the amount from one account and assign it to another, dating the transaction in the current period. This method preserves the integrity of prior-period financials.

The Audit Trail report in QuickBooks does not track that a change was made to an account type. However, if your accountant views your data with QuickBooks Accountant 2013 software, the accountant can view the changes you or your employees made to an account type.

To change an account type, follow these steps:

1. From the menu bar select **Lists**, **Chart of Accounts** (or press Ctrl+A). The Chart of Accounts dialog box displays.
2. Select the account for which you want to change the type.
3. From the Account drop-down list, select **Edit Account** (or press Ctrl+E to open the account for editing). The Edit Account dialog box displays.
4. Click the drop-down arrow next to Account Type (see Figure 4.20) and choose a new account type from the list.
5. Click Save & Close.

note

Not all account types can be changed. Accounts Receivable, Accounts Payable, Credit Cards (with online access configured), and any of the default accounts created by QuickBooks cannot be changed to a different type. In addition, for any Balance Sheet account that the account type is changed to a non-Balance Sheet account type, QuickBooks warns that you can no longer use a register for this account or enter transactions directly into this account.

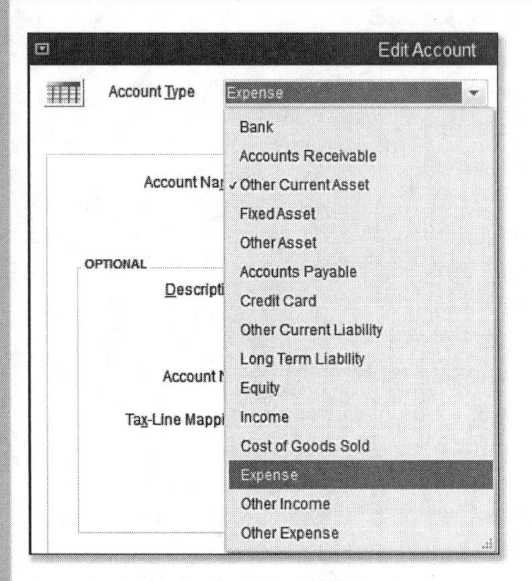

Figure 4.20
You can usually, but not always, change an account type.

Assigning or Removing a Subaccount Relationship

Often in accounting reports, you have specific accounts for which you want to see a more detailed breakdown of the costs. You can get this breakdown easily by creating the main account and associating subaccounts with the main account.

Figure 4.21 shows Utilities as a main account with an indented subaccount for each type of utility expense.

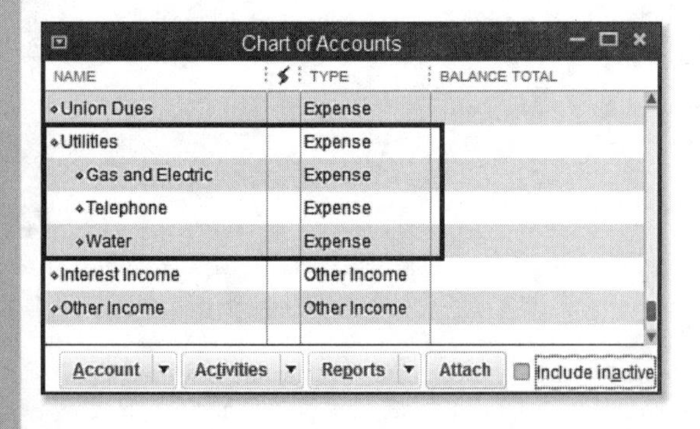

Figure 4.21
Chart of Accounts showing a subaccount relationship to parent account.

To edit an existing account to be a subaccount of another main account, follow these steps:

1. From the menu bar select **Lists**, **Chart of Accounts** (or press Ctrl+A). The Chart of Accounts dialog box displays.
2. Select the account that you want to be a subaccount of another account.

3. From the Account drop-down list, select **Edit Account** (or press Ctrl+E to open the account for editing). The Edit Account dialog box displays.

4. Select the **Subaccount Of** checkbox and choose the account you want it to be associated with from the drop-down box. (It must be of the same account type.)

5. Click Save & Close.

Users can assign a subaccount that is only in the same general account type. For example, an Expense type cannot be a subaccount of a Current Asset type account (see Figure 4.22).

Figure 4.22
Assigning a subaccount to a parent account.

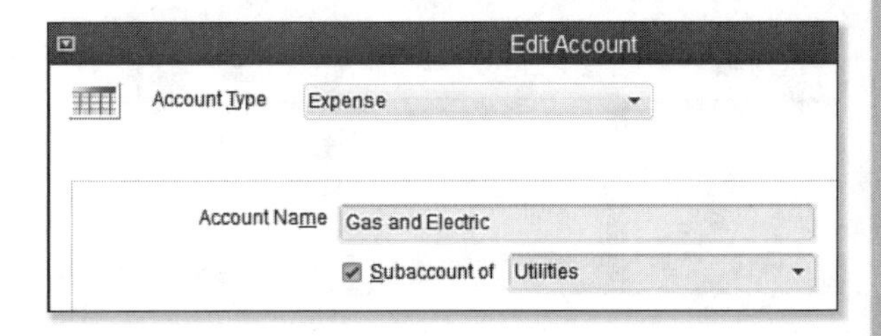

note

If you need to change the subaccount to another General Ledger account type, first deselect the Subaccount Of checkbox. Click Save & Close to save the change. Then edit the account and change the type. You cannot change subaccount types when they are associated with a main account. You also cannot change the account type when that account has subaccounts associated with it.

Another method for changing the assignment of a subaccount to a main account is easily done directly from the list view.

To remove or add a subaccount directly from the list, follow these steps:

1. In the Chart of Accounts dialog box, click with your cursor over the diamond in front of the list item (see Figure 4.23).

2. Drag the diamond so the selected account is immediately below the main account grouping.

3. Drag the diamond to the right to create a subaccount-account relationship to the main account. Or optionally, drag the diamond to the left to remove the subaccount relationship.

   The chart of accounts list shows the corrected relationship (see Figure 4.24).

Financial reporting is more accurate when you take the time to review and correct your chart of accounts setup. Often, you can manage the information better when you group similar income or expense accounts using the subaccount feature.

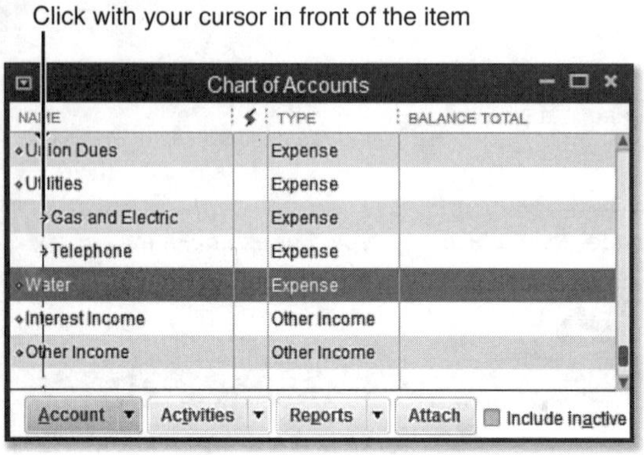

Click with your cursor in front of the item

Figure 4.23
Dragging the diamond in front of an account is an easy way to change the subaccount relationship within the same category type.

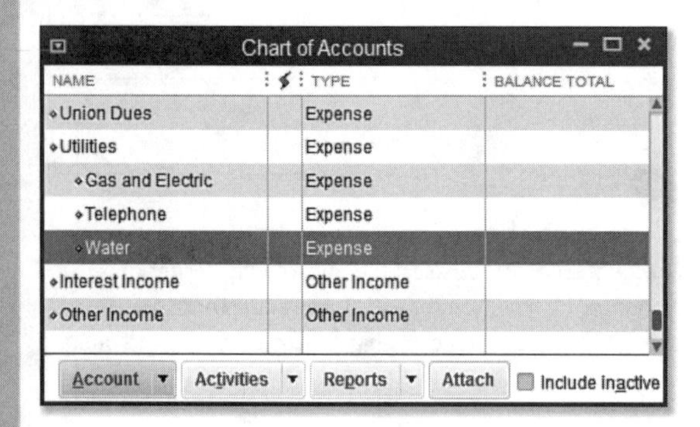

Figure 4.24
The chart of accounts viewed after changing the subaccount relationship.

Finding and Fixing Item List Errors

Do you want to quickly fix some of the most common errors in QuickBooks? Reviewing and correcting items in QuickBooks can be an efficient way to repair a company's data file accounting errors. Often the reason or misstatement on a company's financials can be traced to incorrect setup of items. Some indicators of this might be understated revenue, negative costs, or just an overall lack of confidence in the financials. This is because QuickBooks items are "mapped" to the chart of accounts, if an item is improperly assigned to the wrong type of an account, this could create errors in accurate financial reporting.

To help you in those instances where incorrectly set-up items might not be so apparent, the following sections offer a few methods for reviewing the item list.

Reviewing the Item List on the Computer Screen

Adding and removing columns you view in the Item List can help you notice any setup errors that exist.

Customizing the View of the Item List

To modify the columns that display on the items list, follow these instructions:

1. In the Item List dialog box (select **Lists**, **Item List** from the menu bar), right-click and select **Customize Columns**.
2. In the Customize Columns dialog box, as shown in Figure 4.25, add the COGS Account by highlighting it in the Available Columns pane and clicking Add to include the account in the Chosen Columns pane on the right. Add (or remove) from the Chosen Columns pane those fields that you want (or don't want) to see when viewing the Item List dialog box.

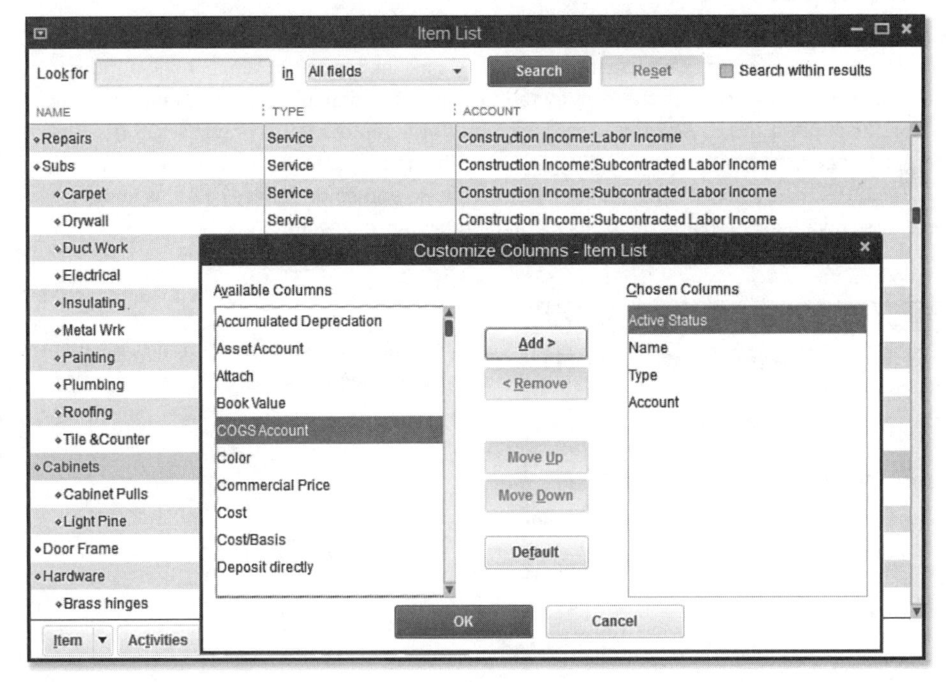

Figure 4.25
Right-click the items list to customize the columns to display.

3. Click the Move Up or Move Down buttons in the center of the dialog box to customize the order in which you want to view the columns, and then click OK.
4. Optionally, to widen columns of displayed data on your computer screen, place your mouse on the right edge of a column header and drag to make the column wider or smaller.
5. Optionally, click a header column to sort the displayed data by the selected column.
6. Click the X in the top-right corner to close the Item List.

Now you can conveniently review the list on the computer screen for those items that do not have a cost of goods sold or expense account assigned, or that might have the wrong account assigned. Not having an expense account assigned becomes problematic when the item is both purchased and sold; both types of transactions will report only to the single account selected as the Income Account.

See the "Correcting One-Sided Items" section of this chapter for a more detailed discussion of how to properly fix this issue. Refer back to Figure 4.3 for details on creating a two-sided item in QuickBooks.

Item Listing Report

Another method to review the item list setup is the Item Listing report (by choosing Reports, List, Item Listing from the menu bar). Click Customize Report from the top left of the displayed report. In the dialog box that displays, click the Display tab to select the columns to view. Useful columns include Item, Description, Type, Account, Asset Account (for inventory items only), COGS Account, and Sales Tax Code, as shown in Figure 4.26. Whenever the item is used on a purchase or sales transaction (such as an invoice, a sales receipt, a bill, a check, and so on), these columns show to which accounts QuickBooks records the transaction on the chart of accounts.

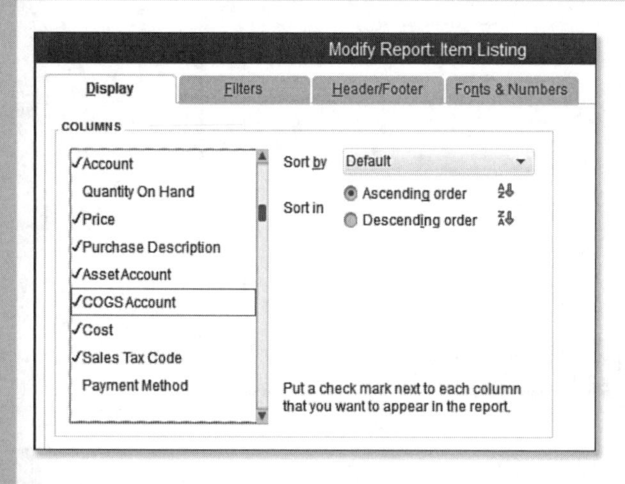

Figure 4.26
Modify the item listing report to provide just the details you need.

What exactly are you looking for on the list item report? First, look for items that you use on both purchase and sales transactions, but that are missing the COGS Account, as shown in Figure 4.27. Alternatively, you might also look for items with the incorrect account assigned. If you collect sales tax, be sure the correct sales tax code is selected.

For a more detailed discussion of sales tax in QuickBooks, see "Setting Up Sales Tax," p. 314.

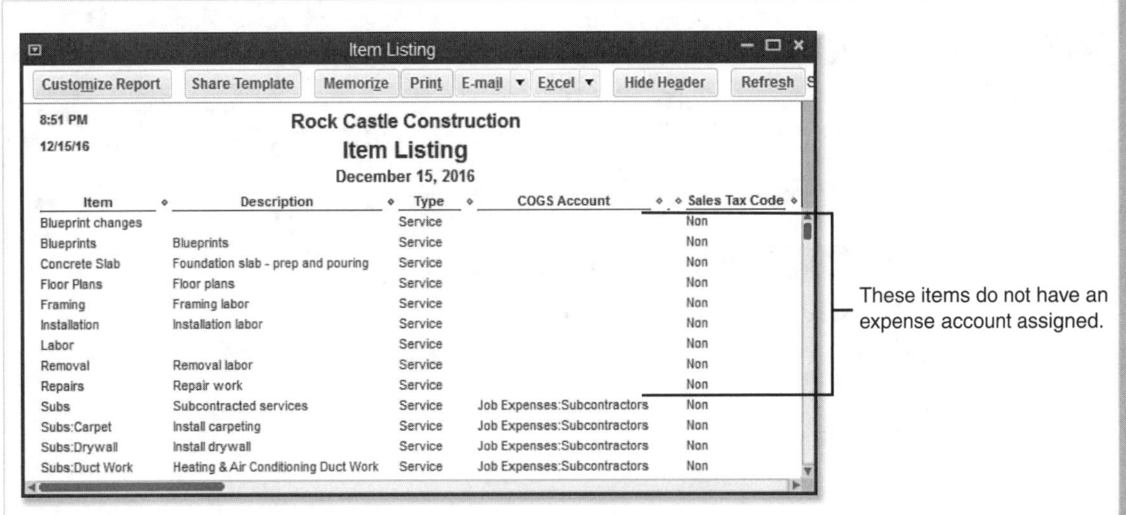

8:51 PM
12/15/16

Rock Castle Construction
Item Listing
December 15, 2016

Item	Description	Type	COGS Account	Sales Tax Code
Blueprint changes		Service		Non
Blueprints	Blueprints	Service		Non
Concrete Slab	Foundation slab - prep and pouring	Service		Non
Floor Plans	Floor plans	Service		Non
Framing	Framing labor	Service		Non
Installation	Installation labor	Service		Non
Labor		Service		Non
Removal	Removal labor	Service		Non
Repairs	Repair work	Service		Non
Subs	Subcontracted services	Service	Job Expenses:Subcontractors	Non
Subs:Carpet	Install carpeting	Service	Job Expenses:Subcontractors	Non
Subs:Drywall	Install drywall	Service	Job Expenses:Subcontractors	Non
Subs:Duct Work	Heating & Air Conditioning Duct Work	Service	Job Expenses:Subcontractors	Non

Figure 4.27
Review the Item Listing report for item setup errors or missing information.

Profit & Loss Standard Report

If you suspect errors with your financials, drilling down (double-clicking with your cursor) on the Total Income, Cost of Goods Sold, or Expense totals from a Profit & Loss Standard report might provide clues to the mistakes. To generate this report for your data, follow these steps:

1. From the menu bar select, **Reports**, **Company & Financial**, **Profit & Loss Standard**.
2. On the Profit & Loss Standard report, double-click the Total Income subtotal, as shown in Figure 4.28. A Transaction Detail by Account report displays, showing each line of detail that makes up the amount you viewed on the original Profit & Loss Standard report.
3. On the Transaction Detail by Account report, click Customize Report. In the dialog box that displays, click the Filters tab. In the Choose Filter pane, scroll down to select **Transaction Type**.
4. In the Transaction Type drop-down list, select **Multiple Transaction Types**, as shown in Figure 4.29. The Select Transaction Type dialog box displays. Click to place a check next to each transaction type that normally would *not* be reported to an income account, such as a check, bill, credit card, and so on, and then click OK.

The resulting report now shows all purchase type transactions (or whatever transaction types you selected) that were recorded to income accounts. In the example shown in Figure 4.30, a vendor bill transaction type displays in the totals for income. This is because on the vendor bill an item was used that had only an income account assigned. After you determine you have these types of errors in posting, you should review your item list for any one-sided items. This topic is discussed in the next section.

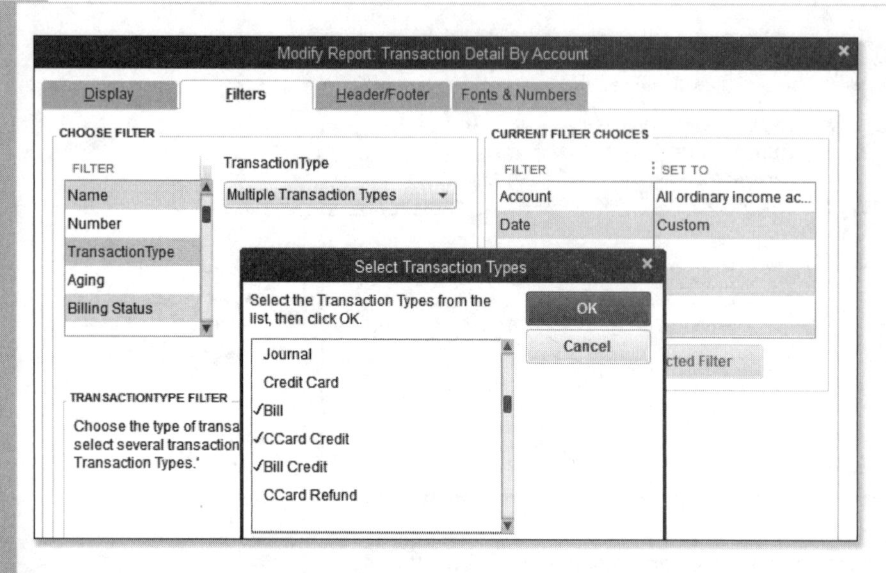

Figure 4.28 Drill down to review the details of your business's Total Income dollars.

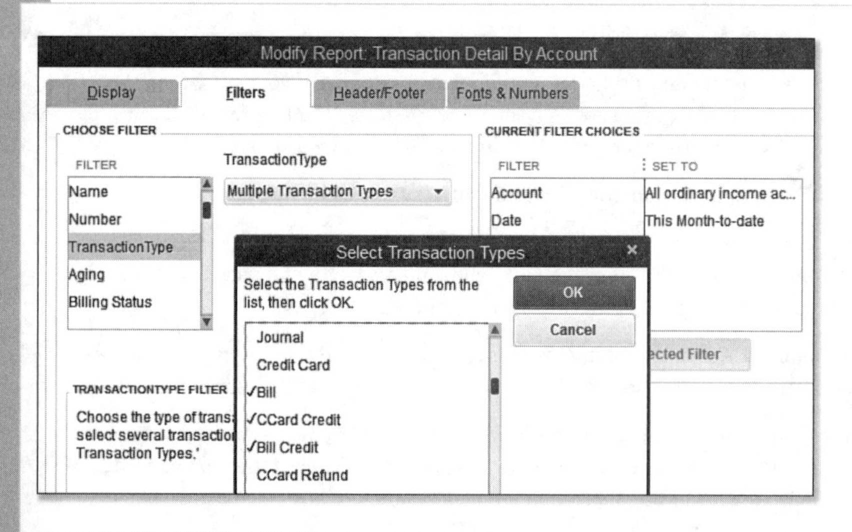

Figure 4.29 Filter the report to include transaction types that should not be reporting to income accounts.

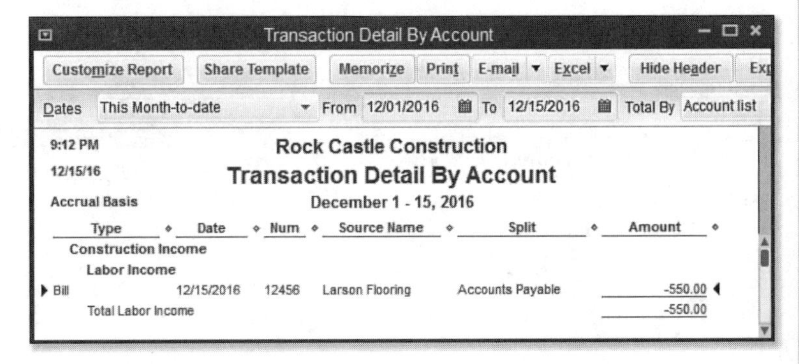

Figure 4.30
The Transaction Detail by Account report shows a purchase type (vendor bill) transaction reporting to an income account in error.

As with any data correction in QuickBooks, you should make a backup of the data before attempting these methods. The preferred backup method is a QuickBooks backup (a file with the extension of .QBB). You can create a data backup by selecting **File**, **Create Backup** from the menu bar. If the result after fixing items is not what you expected, you can easily restore the backup file.

> **tip**
>
> These methods might affect your financials for prior accounting periods. You should take care when selecting a method that will impact financial periods that have already been used to prepare your tax documents. Discuss these choices with your accountant before making the changes.
>
> If you would like to be warned when making changes to prior periods, consider entering a Closing Date into your file. For more information, see Chapter 16, "Sharing QuickBooks Data with Your Accountant."

This section showed some effective ways to determine whether your items were incorrectly set up. In the next section, you learn the methods of fixing these item setup errors in QuickBooks.

If you are an accounting professional, you will want to review your client's item setup and possible errors using the Client Data Review features and tools available only with QuickBooks Accountant 2013. More information can be found in Appendix A, "Client Data Review."

Correcting One-Sided Items

A one-sided item is an item that has only one account assigned. See Figure 4.31, which shows the Framing item setup. Notice the only account assigned to this item is Income:Labor. When this item is used on a customer invoice, it increases the Income:Labor amount. However, if the same item is used on a check or bill, the amount of the expense records directly to the Income:Labor income account as a negative number. This would cause both income and cost of goods sold to be understated.

You should not have one-sided items if you plan to use the same item on both purchase transactions and sales transactions.

You might have several items on your list that can qualify to be one sided because they are used only on sales transactions and never on purchase transactions, or always on purchase transactions and never on sales transactions. What can become problematic is that at some time, a user may mistakenly use the item on the other transaction type.

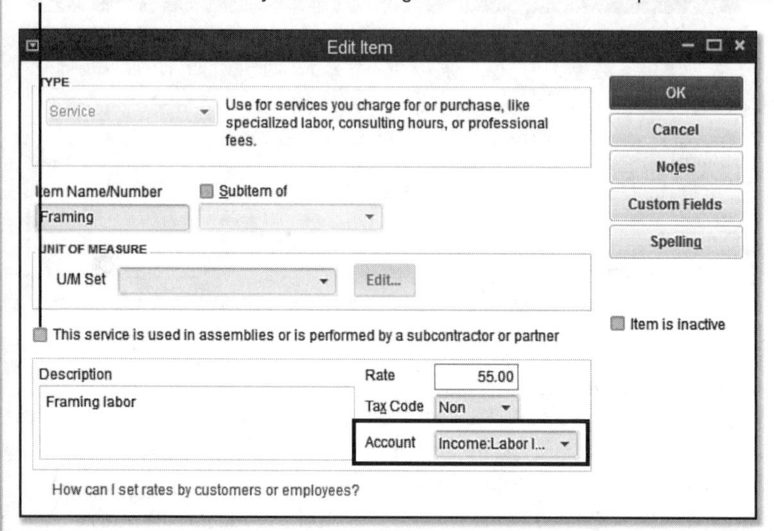

Figure 4.31
Items with only one account assigned can misstate financials if used on both purchase and sales transactions.

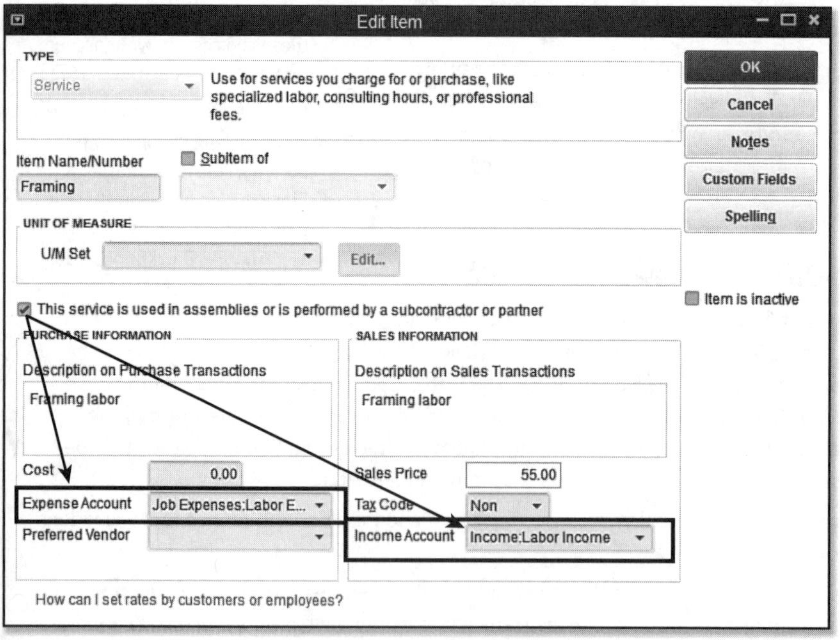

Figure 4.32
The corrected one-sided item now has both an expense and income account assigned.

Inventory items will default as two sided. For the other item types, I recommend you create them all as two-sided items (see Figure 4.32). You do so by selecting the checkbox labeled **This Service Is Used in Assemblies or...** (the rest of the label depends on what item type is selected) in the New or Edit Item dialog box.

The results are new Purchase Information and Sales Information panes. Now, the "Account" has become an "Income Account" and you have a new Expense Account field to assign your proper expense account. This way, if you use the item on both a vendor bill or check and a customer sales transaction, your financials show the transaction in the proper account.

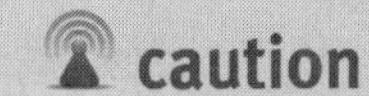

caution

Before making these suggested changes, have you made a backup of your data? Remember, some of the recommended changes are not reversible.

You might even consider printing reports before and after to compare and verify that you achieved the desired end result with your change.

The decision made at this time to change the account assignment is critical to your financials. Clicking Yes to updating existing transactions causes all previous transactions to now report to the new account assigned. If you are attempting to fix historical transactions, this can be a timesaving feature because you do not have to change each individual transaction manually.

Click No if you do not want to update prior period transactions. This option might be recommended if you have already prepared your tax data with QuickBooks financial information. The change then takes effect only for future transactions.

Additional Warnings for One-Sided Items

You aren't completely on your own when it comes to locating one-sided item errors in item assignments. QuickBooks helps you recognize the potential error by displaying a warning message when you are using an item on a purchase transaction that is assigned only to an income account. Figure 4.33 shows the warning message you see when a check is being written to a vendor but the item used is assigned only to an income account. Be aware that this warning displays only if you have not checked the Do Not Display This Message in the Future checkbox.

Figure 4.33
The warning message displayed when you use an item on a purchase transaction that is mapped only to an Income Account.

If you ignore the message, in this example QuickBooks posts the expense to the revenue account selected in the New or Edit Item dialog box. The effect of this is to understate revenue (an expense is a negative amount in the revenue account) and to understate your costs (because no cost was recorded to an expense account). Both of these messages distort your financial details, so be sure you don't disregard this important message.

note

Users often ignore these one-time messages and select the **Do Not Display This Message in the Future** check box (refer to Figure 4.33). To enable these messages again, select **Edit, Preferences** from the menu bar. In the Preferences dialog box, select the **Bring Back All One Time Messages** checkbox on the General—My Preferences tab, as shown in Figure 4.34. This preference setting is only for the currently logged in user; so don't forget to have other users enable this same preference, if desired.

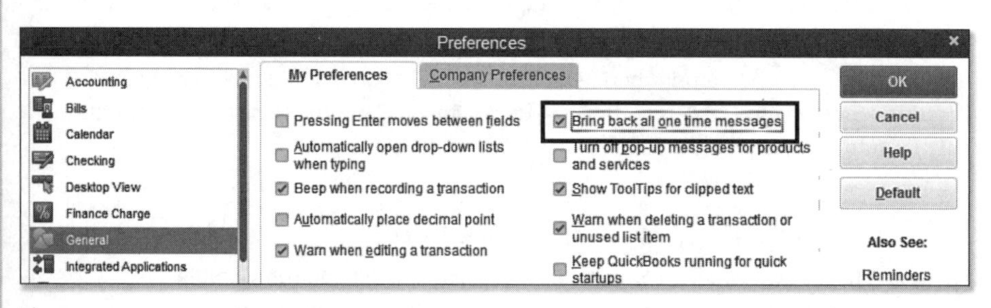

Figure 4.34
To be notified of transaction errors previously disregarded, select the **Bring Back All One Time Messages** checkbox.

Making an Item Inactive

If you have found errors in your item list, a safe method for avoiding future mistakes by using the incorrect items is to make them inactive. An inactive item still displays in reports, but is not included in any drop-down lists on sales or purchase transactions.

To mark an item as inactive:

1. From the menu bar, select **Lists**, **Item List**.
2. Select the item you want to make inactive by clicking it once.
3. Right-click the selected item.
4. Select **Make Item Inactive**.
5. If a warning message displays (such as the item being part of a group), click Yes to make the item inactive or click No to cancel your change.

Making an item inactive does not have any impact on the company's financials. If you want to correct your financials, you need to choose one of two options:

- Edit the account assignment on each item. This gives you the option to fix all previous transactions that used this item retroactively. (Use this cautiously because it changes prior-period financials.) The effect of changing an account assignment on an item is the same as the one discussed in the section "Correcting One-Sided Items" in this chapter.
- Create a General Journal Entry transaction to reassign the amounts from one account to another. This method is typically completed by your accountant.

Before making changes, make a backup of your data and always discuss the method you choose with your accountant.

tip

Open the Item List by selecting **Lists, Item List** from the menu bar. Select the **Include Inactive** checkbox (in the lower center of the dialog box). Click once to the left of any list item to make the item inactive, as shown in Figure 4.35.

If the checkbox is grayed out, you have not yet made any item inactive. After making the first item inactive, you can select the checkbox.

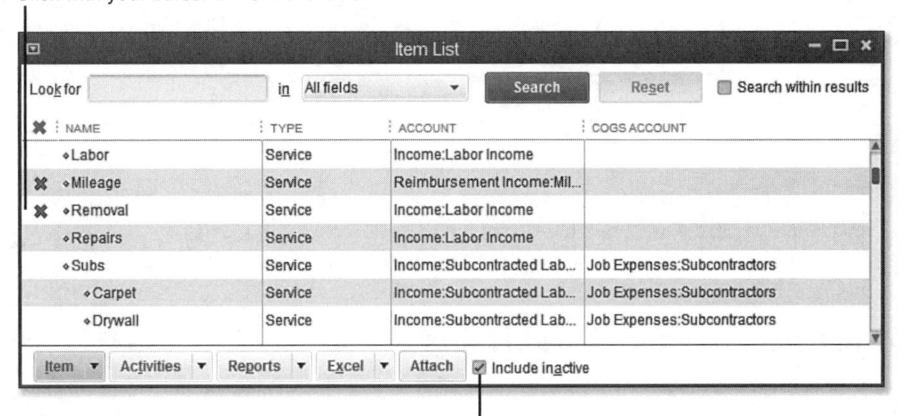

Figure 4.35 Marking Item List elements as inactive causes the item not to show on drop-down lists.

Except for inventory items, there are generally no ramifications for marking a list item inactive. Only inventory items with a zero quantity on hand should be made inactive. See Chapter 6, "Managing Inventory," for more details on handling inventory errors.

Merging Items

If you have duplicated items, one easy method for fixing the problem is to merge items of the same type. When merging two items, you first need to decide which item is going to be merged into the other item. The item merged will no longer exist on your item list.

To merge two items, follow these steps:

1. From the menu bar, select **Lists**, **Item List**.
2. Review the list for duplicate items; note the name of the item you want to remain.
3. Double-click the item you want to merge into another item. The Edit Item dialog box displays.
4. Type in the Item Name/Number field the name exactly as you noted it in step 2. You can also use the copy and paste command to avoid typing lengthy names or long numbers.
5. Click OK to save your change. QuickBooks provides a warning message that you are merging items (see Figure 4.36).

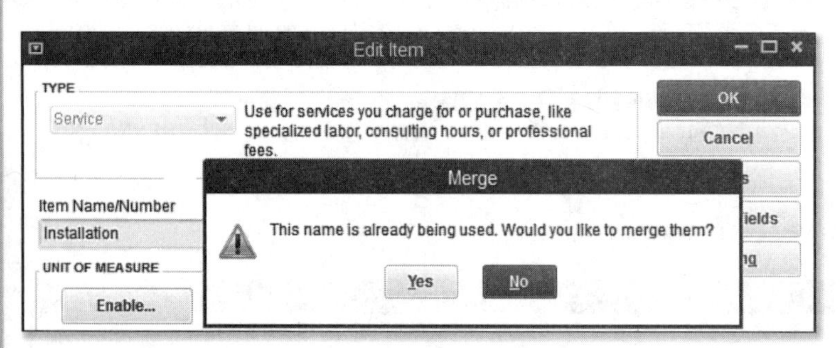

Figure 4.36
A warning displays when you merge two items.

Carefully consider the consequences of merging before you do it (and be sure you have a backup of your QuickBooks file). All the historical transactions merge into the remaining list item.

caution

You can merge only items of the same type. Duplicate service item types can be merged together, but a service item type cannot be merged with a non-inventory item type. It is not recommended to merge inventory items; see Chapter 6 for more detail.

Creating Items as Subitems

Creating an item as a subitem of another item is one way to easily organize reports for a group of similar items. Your accounting data is not affected by having or not having items as subitems.

To make an item a subitem of another item, follow these steps:

1. From the menu bar, select **Lists**, **Item List**.
2. Double-click the item you want to assign as a subitem. The Edit Item dialog box opens.
3. Select **Subitem Of** checkbox, as shown in Figure 4.37.
4. From the drop-down list, select the item you want to relate this subitem to.

You can create a subitem only within the same item type. For example, service items cannot be subitems of inventory items.

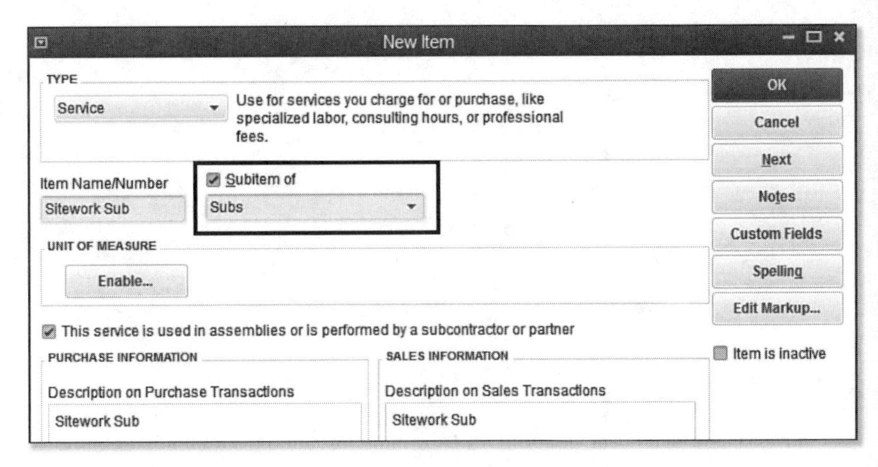

Figure 4.37
The Sitework Sub service item is being made a subitem of Subs (short for Subcontracted).

You can also rearrange the list by assigning a subitem to another item by using your mouse pointer on the Item List to move the item up or down and to the right or left. This functionality is the same as the example discussed in the section "Assigning or Removing a Subaccount Relationship" in this chapter.

You have now completed the important steps in getting your file ready to work with. In the next few chapters, you will learn about inventory, vendor, customer activities, and much more!

5

SETTING UP INVENTORY

Inventory can be described as a company's merchandise, raw materials, and finished and unfinished products that have not yet been sold.

QuickBooks can track the products you purchase, stock, and then later sell to customers. QuickBooks can also track the products you assemble (a component) and use to create a product for sale (finished good). QuickBooks has a perpetual inventory system, meaning each time you record a purchase transaction, inventory is increased, and when you record a sales transaction, inventory is decreased. (See the "Proper Inventory Processes" section later in this chapter.)

QuickBooks Pro, Premier, and Enterprise Solutions record the cost of inventory using the Average Cost method in contrast to LIFO (Last In First Out) or FIFO (First In First Out). This means that the cost recorded at the time a product is sold is equal to the number of inventory units purchased divided by the total cost of the units. QuickBooks automates this process for you. As long as you record your documents correctly and date them appropriately, QuickBooks assigns the correct average cost.

If you are using QuickBooks Enterprise Solutions 13.0, you also have the *option* to use FIFO costing, or First In First Out method. The feature differences between the editions of QuickBooks can be found in the upcoming section titled "Inventory Features by QuickBooks Edition."

If you are using QuickBooks Enterprise for inventory management, refer to Appendix C, "QuickBooks Enterprise Solutions Inventory Features," pg. 747.

Ask yourself these important questions to differentiate between using inventory or non-inventory items in QuickBooks:

- **Will you be selling what you buy, and do you not know the customer at the time of purchase?**—An example is a furniture store that purchases furniture for resale to customers, or a retail store that purchases medical supplies that are sold to customers. These qualify as the proper use of inventory items.

- **Are you manufacturing what you sell?**—In other words, you buy components (raw materials) and later assemble the components into a finished product that is sold to a customer. An example is a bike store that purchases wheels, steering columns, chains, and so on and then assembles the components into a completed bike for sale to the customer. This qualifies as the proper use of inventory items.
- **Are you purchasing materials that you use, but do not sell?**—For example, a car detailing business purchases buffing pads and paint supplies. These items are stored in inventory but are not sold directly to a customer. This example is a more appropriate use of non-inventory items.
- **Is the dollar value of your inventory not significant?**—Often, companies carry a small amount of inventory, but the majority of their vendor product purchases are drop-shipped directly to the customer's address. For example, a construction company can order appliances for a new home but generally does not stock them. Instead, it has the appliances shipped directly from the vendor to the new home. This example is a more appropriate use of a non-inventory item.

Making the decision to track inventory takes commitment on your part. QuickBooks can help you efficiently and accurately track your inventory with features unique to each edition of QuickBooks.

Inventory Features by QuickBooks Edition

The release of QuickBooks 2013 has again dramatically changed the features available when your business tracks inventory. Now, more than ever, you need to review those features you need the most and make sure you are working in the right QuickBooks edition for your business inventory tracking needs.

Many other feature differences exist among the versions that are not discussed in this chapter or book. You can view the differences by visiting http://quickbooks.intuit.com/product/accounting-software/small-business-software.jsp

If you are using the QuickBooks Pro or Premier editions and later decide your business would benefit from the features available only with QuickBooks Enterprise Solutions, you can expect the transition to be seamless. When you are ready to upgrade, you open your company file in Enterprise Solutions, and your lists, data, report templates, and user permissions automatically transfer.

QuickBooks Pro 2013

QuickBooks Pro 2013 is easy to set up and learn to use. With QuickBooks Pro you can have up to three simultaneous users working in the same data file. QuickBooks Pro *does not* come in industry-specific editions.

QuickBooks Pro has the most basic of inventory features, including the following:

- **Inventory Items**—Including Inventory Part and Non-inventory Part.
- **Purchase Orders**—Commitment to purchase from a vendor.
- **Change Item Prices in Batch**—Feature to change more than one item price at a time by a fixed amount or percentage.

- **Warn If Not Enough Inventory to Sell**—Found in the Inventory Preference Settings.
- **Integrate Your FedEx, UPS, and USPS Software**—From the menu bar select **File**, **Shipping**.

Inventory features such as Multiple Unit of Measure can be viewed in a Pro file (after the feature has been enabled in a Premier edition of QuickBooks), but you cannot add, edit, or modify the Unit of Measure settings in a QuickBooks Pro file.

You can easily convert a QuickBooks Pro file to QuickBooks Premier or Enterprise.

More information about upgrading your file can be found in Chapter 17, "Managing Your QuickBooks Database."

QuickBooks Premier 2013

QuickBooks Premier 2013 offers several industry-specific editions. The inventory features include everything offered with QuickBooks Pro 2013 and in addition the following:

- **Inventory Center**—Central location for inventory activities and reporting.
- **Inventory Assembly**—Creating a finished good from a bill or materials.
- **Sales Orders**—Handling customer preorders.
- **Quantity Available**—Preference settings for handling how quantity available is calculated.
- **Multiple Unit of Measure**—When you purchase one unit and sell in another. (Available only in selected Premier or Enterprise editions.)

If you have purchased the QuickBooks Premier Manufacturing & Wholesale 2013 edition, you will have all the preceding features plus the following:

- **Sales Order Fulfillment Worksheet**—Ease in filling orders.
- **Create Customer Return Materials Authorization Form**—Creates a Word template for you to enter information into.
- **Report on Nonconforming Material Report**—Creates a Word template for you to enter information into.
- **Damaged Goods Log**—Creates a Word template for you to enter information into.
- **Several Industry-Specific Reports**—Includes Inventory Reorder Report by Vendor.

QuickBooks Enterprise Solutions 13.0

The release of QuickBooks Enterprise Solutions 13.0 has created the most excitement in years, specifically for companies that track inventory. This chapter lists the features for the following versions of QuickBooks. More specific details can be found in Appendix C:

- QuickBooks Enterprise Solutions 13.0
- QuickBooks Enterprise Solutions Manufacturing & Wholesale 13.0
- Either of the preceding two versions with an Advanced Inventory subscription

QuickBooks Enterprise Solutions 13.0

QuickBooks Enterprise Solutions 13.0 includes all the features mentioned previously, as well as the following:

- **NEW! Auto Create POs**—From the inventory stock status reports (and others), option to create multiple purchase orders at one time.
- **NEW! Default Class Assignment**—Preference to default class (departments) assignment to Accounts, Items, or Names.
- **Enhanced Inventory Receiving**—Optional workflow that improves how you receive and pay for inventory. Item receipts increase inventory and inventory offset (current liability) account until the vendor bill is received and entered.
- **Automatic Cost and Price Updates**—When an item's cost changes, set a preference for automatically handling changes to the default cost, sales price, and markup as recorded with the item record.
- **Edit Markup**—Define how markup is calculated from cost.
- **Inventory Center Add Image**—Ability to attach an image to an item record. (Currently, you cannot attach an image to a transaction.)
- **Custom Fields**—Used to track additional specific detail for your inventory items. Custom fields can be required upon entry and can be defined by type of data, numbers, date, phone, and so on.

QuickBooks Enterprise Solutions Manufacturing & Wholesale 13.0

If you purchased the QuickBooks Enterprise Solutions Manufacturing & Wholesale 13.0 edition, you will have the same industry-specific tools available with QuickBooks Premier Manufacturing & Wholesale 2013, including the following:

- **Sales Order Fulfillment Worksheet**—Ease in filling orders.
- **Create Customer Return Materials Authorization Form**—Creates a Word template for you to enter return information into.
- **Report on Nonconforming Material Report**—Creates a Word template for you to enter non-confirming information into.
- **Damaged Goods Log**—Creates a Word template for you to enter inventory damage information into.
- **Inventory Reorder Report by Vendor**—One of a few industry-specific reports.

Advanced Inventory Subscription

QuickBooks Enterprise Solutions 13.0 or QuickBooks Enterprise Solutions Manufacturing & Wholesale 13.0 with an Advanced Inventory subscription includes these additional features:

- **NEW! Bin/Shelf/Row Location Tracking**—Tracks specific items to bin/shelf/row location within one or more inventory locations. Sort pick lists and item receipts by location.
- **NEW! Barcode Scanning**—Increases efficiency and reliability of data entry by scanning items and serial numbers without a keyboard. Create your own barcodes. (Requires any simple USB barcode scanner).
- **Multiple Inventory Sites**—Reports and tracks inventory in multiple locations.
- **Lot or Serial Number Tracking**—Tracks one or the other and a variety of related preference settings.
- **FIFO**—First In First Out Inventory Costing. This means that the oldest inventory items are recorded as sold first but do not necessarily mean that the exact oldest physical object has been tracked and sold.

The optional Advanced Inventory functionality is built into QuickBooks Enterprise Solutions, has an annual fee, and requires a current Full Support Plan (annual fee).

For more details see, "QuickBooks Enterprise Solutions Inventory Features," p. 747.

QuickBooks has a version right for your business inventory tracking needs. You can also visit http://quickbooks.intuit.com/product/accounting-software/small-business-software.jsp to compare the different editions feature by feature.

Enabling Inventory Preferences

To begin using QuickBooks to track inventory, you must first turn on the feature found in the Items & Inventory preference in QuickBooks. By default, when you create a new company data file, inventory management is not enabled.

To turn on the inventory feature, follow these steps:

1. Log in to the data file as the Admin or External Accountant user.
2. From the menu bar, select **Edit**, **Preferences** to open the Preferences dialog box.
3. On the Items & Inventory—Company Preferences tab, select the **Inventory and Purchase Orders Are Active** checkbox.
4. Click OK to save the preference.

The preferences displayed in Figure 5.1 do not affect the accounting for inventory; rather, they enable specific features and preferences within inventory management. The preferences available in your QuickBooks data might differ depending on the year and edition of QuickBooks you are using.

Your QuickBooks Home page now shows the inventory workflow (see Figure 5.2). To have the Home page display automatically when you open your QuickBooks file, from the menu bar select **Edit**, **Preferences**. Click the My Preferences tab. On the Desktop View select the **Show Home Page When Opening a Company File** checkbox.

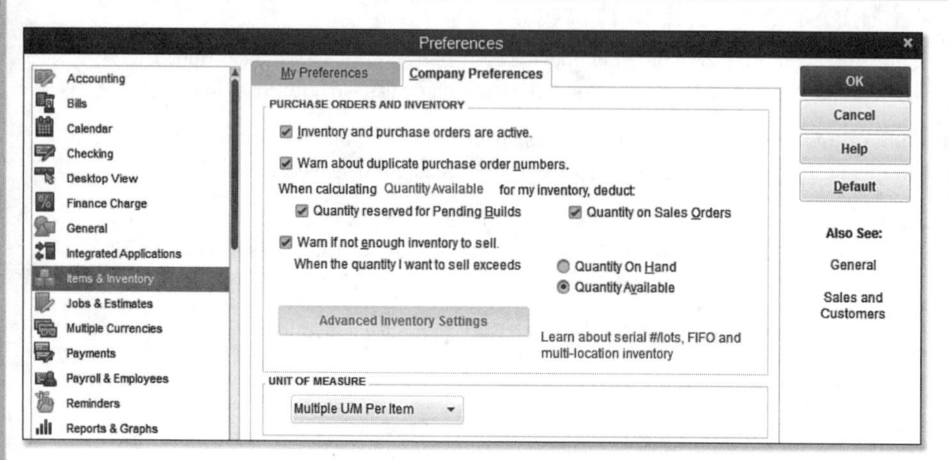

Figure 5.1 Preferences that enable QuickBooks inventory vary by version of QuickBooks being used.

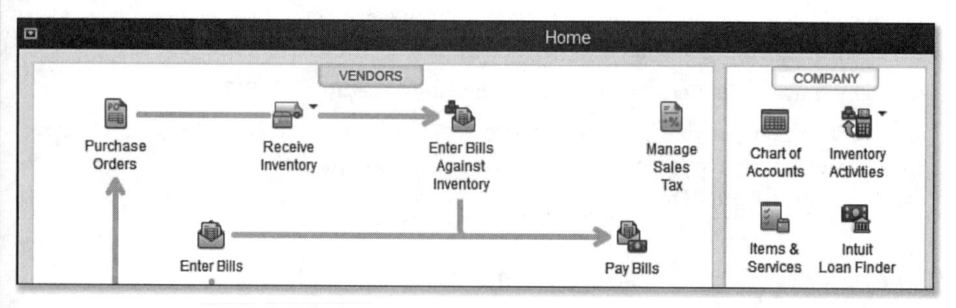

Figure 5.2 Home page workflow with inventory and purchase orders enabled.

One additional preference that can affect your setup of inventory is found in the Time & Expenses—Company Preferences tab (accessed as you did previously for the Items & Inventory preference). When you enter a percentage in the Default Markup Percentage field, QuickBooks automatically makes the default Sales Price to be the cost multiplied by the markup on a new item when the cost is first recorded (see Figure 5.3). As part of the setup, you will be required to select an account for the Markup amount; usually this is an income account type.

For example, when you create a new inventory list item and enter a cost of $3.00, QuickBooks will default the sales price of $3.90, or $3.00 + 30% markup, as shown in Figure 5.4.

Another feature for inventory management is the Unit of Measure (on the Items & Inventory—Company Preferences tab). When selecting this preference (see Figure 5.5), you can define the following for inventory items or non-inventory items in QuickBooks:

note

QuickBooks Enterprise 13.0 includes more robust preferences for automatically handling markups when item costs change on purchase documents.

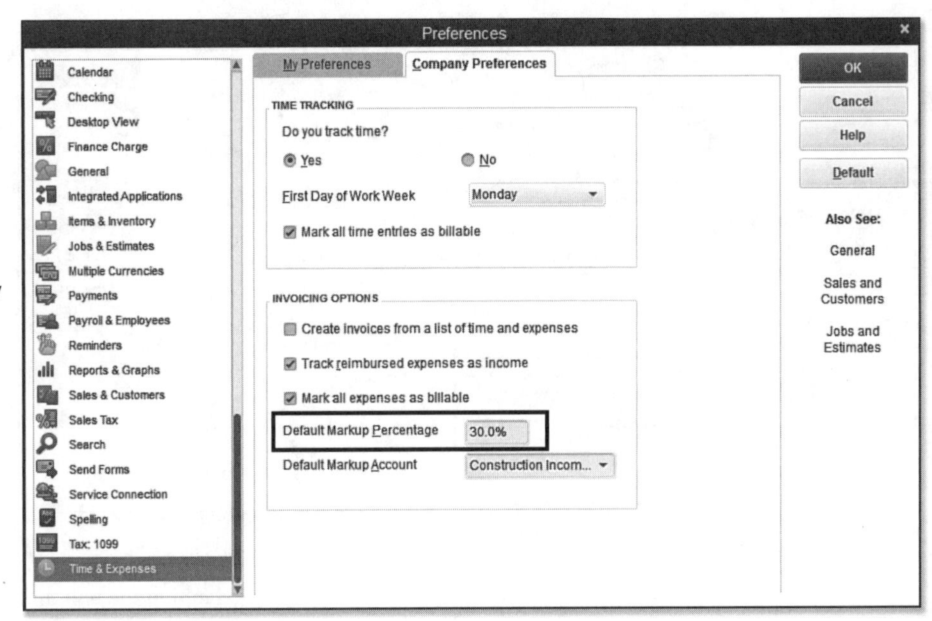

Figure 5.3 Including a Default Markup Percentage will make the sales price of a newly created inventory item to be cost multiplied by the markup.

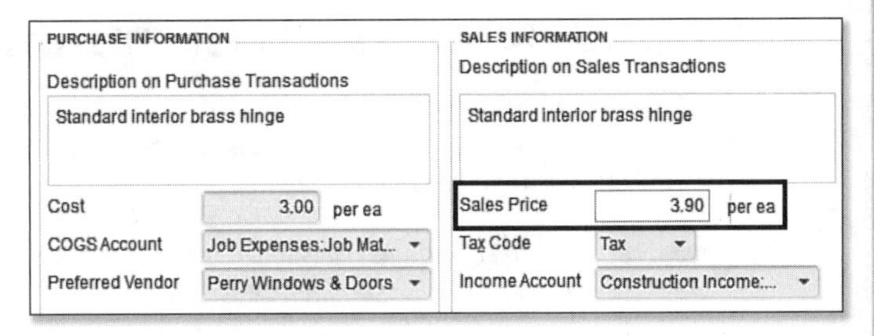

Figure 5.4 QuickBooks automatically calculates the sales price when you set the preference for default markup in the Time & Expenses preference.

- **Single Unit of Measure**—Choose this if you buy, stock, and sell each item by the same unit of measure. For example, if you buy by the pound, sell by the pound, and track your inventory by the pound, this option is the best choice.
- **Multiple Unit of Measure**—If you buy in one measurement, for example, you purchase by the skid (multiple cases of soda) and sell to the customer in single units (a can of soda), but ship by the case (multiple cans of soda), the Multiple Unit of Measure option is the best choice.

When you select Multiple Unit of Measure and assign it to an inventory or non-inventory item, you can also define your default units of measure for purchase, sales, and shipping transactions.

For more information, see "Setting Up Multiple Unit of Measure," p. 168.

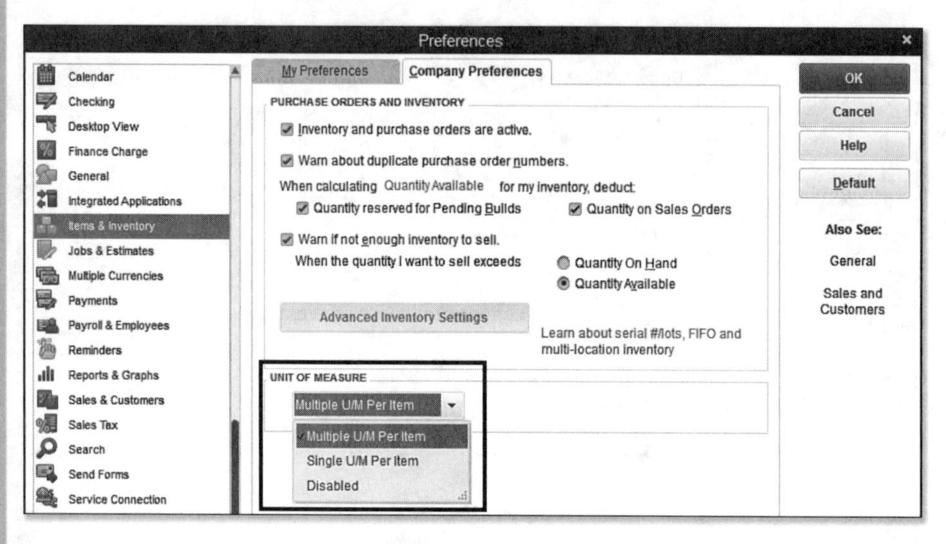

Figure 5.5 QuickBooks Premier or Enterprise includes Multiple Unit of Measure (U/M) preference.

Unit of Measure settings indirectly affect your accounting by defaulting the unit and the associated cost and sales price. Using this feature can improve your buying and selling accuracy on your documents and can help ensure that proper inventory quantities are recorded.

Inventory Item Type Descriptions

QuickBooks provides several item types for use in the management of inventory and non-inventory. These items can be used on purchase and sales transactions. This section details the purpose of these QuickBooks item types used primarily with inventory management.

➡ *For details on additional types of QuickBooks items, see Chapter 4, "Understanding QuickBooks Lists" and Chapter 9, "Setting Up Customers."*

Inventory Part

Create an inventory part if any of the following applies to your business:

- Items are purchased and sold.
- Items are stored in stock and later sold.
- Items are purchased and used as components of a finished product (assembled).

The capability to create an assembled good and track the quantity on hand of the finished product is available only in QuickBooks Premier (all editions) and QuickBooks Enterprise (all editions).

Non-inventory Part

Create a non-inventory part if any of the following applies to the specific part:

- Purchased but not sold
- Sold but not purchased
- Purchased and resold, but not tracked as stock (drop-shipped directly to the customer)

For more information, see "Adding or Editing Inventory Items," p. 154.

Group Items and Inventory Assemblies

The group item types and inventory assembly types are similar in that they both let you record multiple items with a single entry on purchase or sales transactions. The group item type is included with QuickBooks Pro, Premier (all editions) or Enterprise (all editions). Inventory assemblies are included only with QuickBooks Premier (all editions), Accountant, or QuickBooks Enterprise (all editions).

Here are a few reasons you might want to use assemblies in QuickBooks:

- Track finished goods separately from individual inventory items.
- Customize the price of assembled items. You can specify a price for an assembly, which is different from the sum of the default prices of its component items.
- Get detailed information about your finished goods, including date they were assembled, quantity and cost, and list of component items.
- Set reminders for future builds.

If you are using QuickBooks Premier (all editions) or QuickBooks Enterprise Solutions (all editions), you may benefit from creating group items.

What are some reasons you would work with a group item? They might include the following:

- Get detailed sales, cost, and budget reporting for multiple items.
- Use the option to show a single line of detail when invoicing the customer.

Inventory assemblies can be added to both purchase and sales transactions. Group Items can be added only to sales transactions. Both help to automate the process of entering multiple items on transactions.

Table 5.1 compares the details of using the Group Item or Inventory Assembly Item. This should help you determine the proper type to use for your business:

Table 5.1 Comparing Group and Assembly Items

Group Item	Inventory Assembly Item
Can include any item type except other groups.	Can include any of the following item types: service, inventory part, inventory assembly (subassemblies), non-inventory part, and other charge.
Ability to print on sales transactions the individual items in the group item or a single line summary.	Prints only the assembly name, not the component part names on sales transactions.
No reports specific for group items.	On standard inventory reports, including pending builds report.
Quantity on hand of each individual item is adjusted at the time of sale.	Quantity on hand of each individual item is adjusted at the time of build.
Sales tax is calculated by individual items.	One sales tax code (rate) applies to the entire assembled (finished) good.
Cannot be included in another group item.	Can be included (nested) in other assemblies and in group items.
Does not track the finished item; only the individual parts are tracked.	Tracks the quantity of the finished product and depletes the quantity of components.
Price of the group item is the sum of the parts (you can include another item to adjust the sales price).	Sales price of an assembly item defaults to the sales price of the sum of the parts, but can be manually adjusted.
Can include both taxable and nontaxable items.	Must be entirely designated as either taxable or nontaxable.

Included in the next section are details on creating both the group item and inventory assembly. Both are used to save data entry time and improve accuracy when recording purchase and sales transactions with the same multiple items.

Adding or Editing Inventory Items

With inventory and purchase order tracking enabled in your QuickBooks file, you can add your inventory or non-inventory products to the Item list. You will have several options for adding or modifying your list of products. Choose the method that best meets your needs.

Before you begin tracking inventory, you should know the commitment you are making to additional accounting responsibilities. When choosing to track inventory in the normal course of your business, you need to use purchase transactions to increase inventory, and use sales transactions to decrease inventory. You also need to commit to periodic inventory counts because your inventory can often get out of sync with your accounting information.

Adding or Editing Individual Items

Efficiently add or modify individual inventory or non-inventory items in your QuickBooks data, or use one of several tools detailed in this chapter for working with multiple items at a time.

Inventory Part

When you purchase or build your product, and then stock it in your warehouse for future sale to your customer, you should create an inventory part (see Figure 5.6).

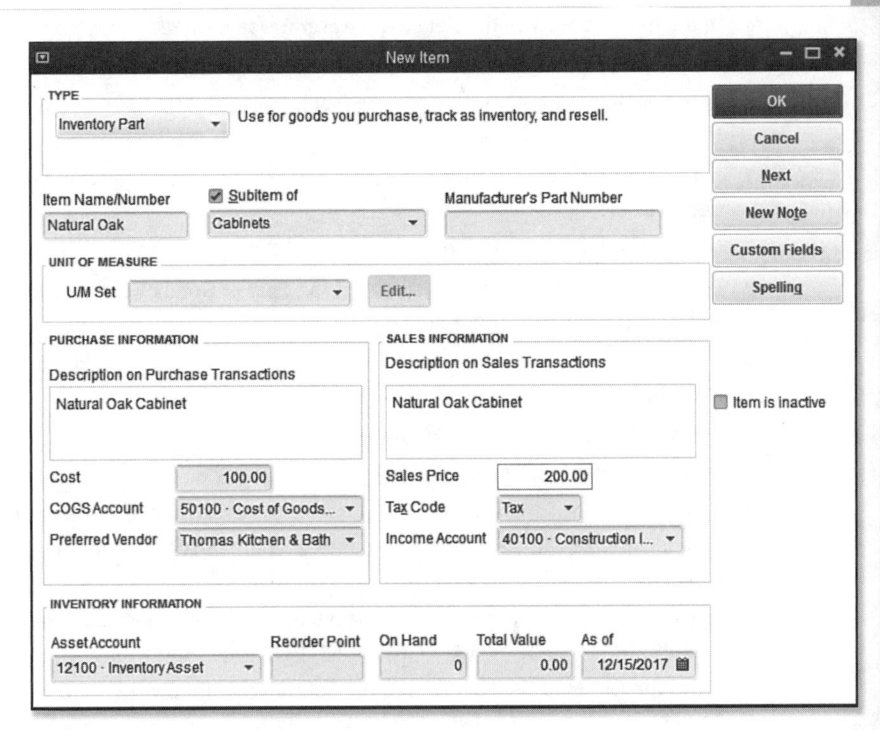

Figure 5.6
Adding a new inventory part item.

When inventory is used, an Inventory Asset account is increased when you purchase and stock the product. The income and related cost is not recorded until you include the inventory item on your customer's invoice.

Adding an Inventory Part

To practice adding a new inventory part item, open the sample data file as instructed in Chapter 1, "Getting Started with QuickBooks":

1. On the Home page, click the Items & Services icon. The Item List displays.
2. Click the Item button in the lower-left corner, and select New or use the keyboard shortcut of Ctrl+N. The New Item dialog box displays.
3. In the Type drop-down list, select **Inventory Part**.
4. In the Item Name/Number field, type **Natural Oak Cabinet**.
5. Check the Subitem Of checkbox and then select **Cabinets** from the drop-down list.
6. Leave the boxes for Manufacturer's Part Number and U/M Set (for Unit of Measurement) blank.
7. In the Description on Purchase Transactions box, select the newly created **Natural Oak Cabinet**.
8. In the Cost field, type **100.00**.
9. From the Account drop-down list, select the **Cost of Goods Sold** account if it isn't automatically selected by QuickBooks.
10. In the Preferred Vendor field, select or begin typing **Thomas Kitchen & Bath**, and the existing vendor name populates the field.
11. In the Sales Price field, type **200.00**.
12. Leave the default of Tax assigned in the Tax Code field.
13. In the Income Account drop-down list, select the **Construction Income:Materials Income** account. You can also select the account by typing **40100** (the account number) in this example.
14. In the Asset Account drop-down list, leave the Inventory Asset account that displays by default. (Optional) Enter a quantity for Reorder Point reporting.
15. Leave the On Hand field blank. See the Caution that follows about entering your quantity on hand in this manner. If you choose to enter an On Hand quantity, QuickBooks enters a financial transaction that increases the inventory asset account and increases the Opening Balance Equity account.
16. If you entered an On Hand quantity (not recommended), QuickBooks automatically calculates the Total Value field by taking the On Hand quantity times the amount recorded in the Cost field. You can override this calculated Total Amount field, but you should do so only if the resulting value is the proper amount to record for this asset. (See the Caution following this sidebar.)
17. If you entered an On Hand quantity, select the As Of date you want to record the increase in your inventory asset value.
18. Click OK to save your changes and close the New Item dialog box.

Following are optional fields or actions in an item record (depending on the version of QuickBooks you are using) that are useful:

- **U/M Set**—Used to assign default units of measure for purchases, sales, and shipping of the selected item.
- **Notes**—Internal notes for the currently selected item.
- **Custom Fields**—Flexibility to add information that is not already tracked by QuickBooks. Review the section in this chapter titled "Inventory Features by QuickBooks Edition" to see if the custom field you need is already tracked in a different edition of QuickBooks than the edition you are currently using.
- **Spelling**—Click Spelling, and QuickBooks will spell check the description fields of the individual item being added or edited.
- **Item Is Inactive**—Should be used only when the item inventory count for the selected item is zero and when you no longer want the item to be included in drop-down lists. More information on efficiently managing your items is included in Chapter 4, in the section titled "Making an Item Inactive."

tip

The Cost field in a new (or edit) inventory part record is optional. Entering a default cost can be useful for automating entry on purchase transactions, and in some instances can help with properly reporting a change in value when an inventory adjustment record is recorded.

caution

Converting to QuickBooks after having used other software to track inventory? It is recommended you use an Inventory Adjustment transaction to enter your opening quantity on hand instead of entering a quantity in the On Hand field of a new inventory item record. For more information, see "Adjusting Inventory," p. 195.

Offering a new product for sale to your customers? You should not enter an amount in the On Hand field; instead use a Create Purchase Orders, Enter Bills, or Write Checks transaction to record the purchase of this new inventory item.

After you save a new item record, many fields cannot be edited, including the On Hand and Total Value fields.

Non-inventory Part

Your company might want to create non-inventory items. For example, a construction company that orders appliances for the new homeowner but does not stock the appliance would create non-inventory items.

When non-inventory is used, the expense account on the non-inventory item record is used to record the cost at the time of purchase. These items never increase your inventory asset balances.

Adding a Non-inventory Part

To practice adding a new non-inventory item, open the sample data file as instructed in Chapter 1:

1. On the Home page, click the Items & Services icon. The Item List displays.
2. Click the Item button in the lower-left corner, and select **New** or use the keyboard shortcut of Ctrl+N. The New Item dialog box displays.
3. From the Type drop-down list that displays, select **Non-inventory Part.**
4. In the Item Name/Number field, type **Stain.**
5. Select the **Subitem Of** checkbox and then select **Lumber** from the drop-down list.
6. Leave the boxes for Manufacturer's Part Number and U/M Set (for Unit of Measurement) blank.
7. Check the This Item Is Used in Assemblies or Is Purchased for a Specific Customer checkbox. See more details about the importance of this in the caution that follows these instructions.

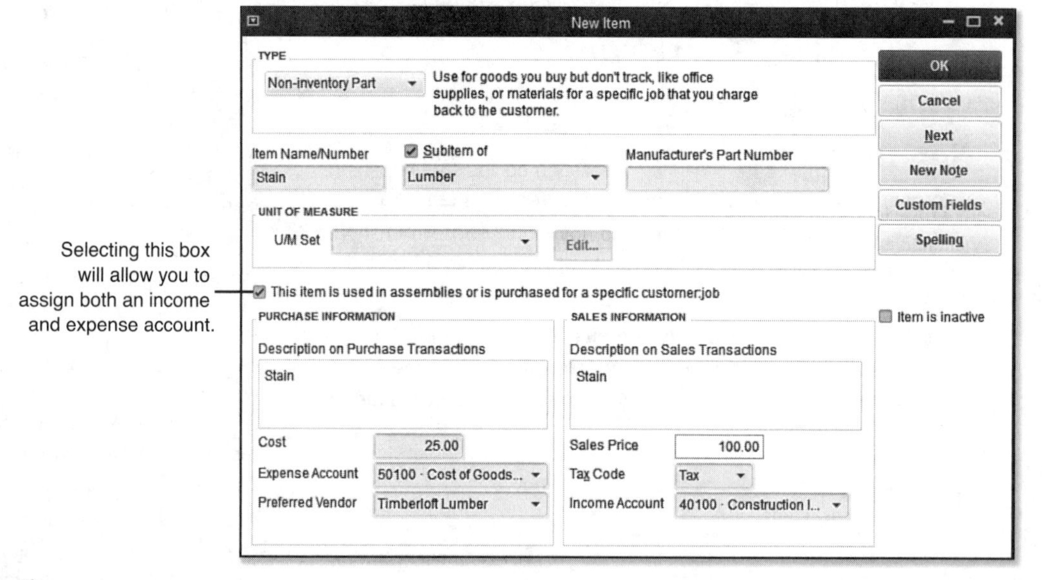

Figure 5.7
Use Non-inventory Part type for items you stock but do not sell.

8. In the Description on Purchase Transactions box, type **Stain.**
9. In the Cost field, type **25.**
10. In the Expense Account drop-down list, select the **Cost of Goods Sold** or, if you prefer, the expense account of your choice.

11. In the Preferred Vendor field, select or type **Timberloft Lumber.**
12. In the Sales Price field, type **100.00.**
13. Leave the default of Tax assigned in the Tax Code field.
14. From the Income Account drop-down list, select the **Construction Income:Materials Income** account. You can also select the account by typing the account number **40100** (the account number) in this example.
15. Click OK to close the New Item dialog box.

If you are tracking inventory in your business, non-inventory parts are also a great way to track items you consume as part of your business operations.

Entering or editing each inventory item can be time-consuming and take you away from more important tasks. The next few sections provide alternatives for adding or editing multiple inventory items at one time.

caution
Non-inventory parts require only one account by default. This is okay if you do not purchase and sell the item. To ensure proper accounting, I recommend that when you create a non-inventory item type, you place a checkmark in the This Item Is Used in Assemblies or Is Purchased for a Specific Customer:Job box, as shown in Figure 5.7. This enables you to assign both an expense and income account in the event you purchase and sell the item.

Using Add/Edit Multiple List Entries

Adding or modifying several list items in a single QuickBooks list can be a daunting task when you have to work with one list item at a time. In Chapter 1, you might have created your lists using the QuickBooks Setup to add the people you do business with, the products or services you sell, and your bank accounts.

With the Add/Edit Multiple List Entries feature (see Figure 5.8), you can add to or modify service items or inventory and non-inventory parts. Using this feature can save you precious time, particularly when you want to add or make changes to multiple items on a list all at once.

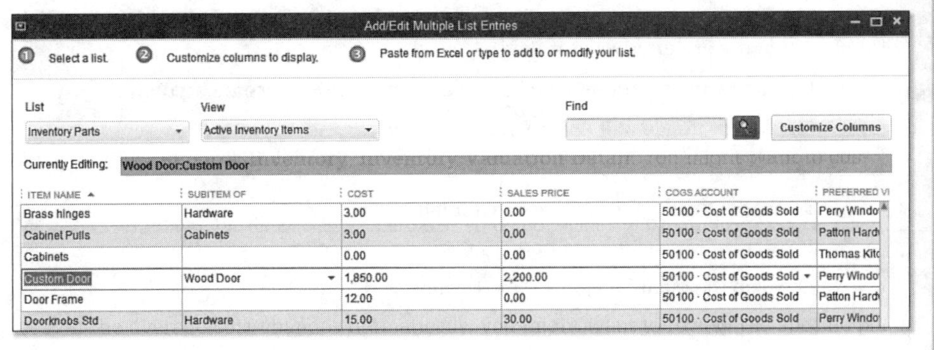

Figure 5.8
Use the Add/Edit Multiple Lists Entries to add or modify multiple inventory parts efficiently.

Add/Edit Multiple Items at Once

Practice using the Add/Edit Multiple List Entries feature by adding a Custom Door inventory item and customizing the columns of data displayed for editing.

Open the sample data as instructed in Chapter 1:

1. From the menu bar, select **Lists, Add/Edit Multiple List Entries.**
2. In the List drop-down list, select **Inventory Parts.**
3. In the View drop-down list, select **Active Inventory Items.**
4. Click the Customize Columns button on the right to open the Customize Columns dialog box.
5. View the fields in the Chosen Columns pane. These fields are currently displayed in the Add/Edit Multiple List Entries grid.
6. To add a column to the grid, select **Purchase Description** and click the Add> button in the center.
7. To rearrange the order of the columns, select the newly added Purchase Description in the Chosen Columns pane and click the Move Up button several times until the Purchase Description field is immediately below the Subitem Of field.
8. Click OK to close the Customize Columns dialog box.
9. Use the scrollbar at the bottom of the Add/Edit Multiple List Entries dialog box to view the fields available.
10. Click in the next available blank row in the Item Name field. Or optionally, with your cursor right-click to insert a line and access other features for using this tool.
11. In the Item Name field, type **Custom Door.**
12. In the Subitem Of drop-down list, select **Wood Door.**
13. In the Purchase Description field, type **Custom Wood Door.**
14. In the Cost field, type **1,850.00.**
15. In the Sales Price field, type **2,200.00.**
16. Accept the default account: Cost of Goods Sold. (Optional) Select Perry Windows & Doors in the Preferred Vendor field.
17. In the Income drop-down list, select **Construction Income** account.
18. Accept the default Asset Account: Inventory Asset.
19. Type **10** in the Reorder Point field.
20. Leave the default Total Value column blank.
21. Accept the default Tax in the Sales Tax Code column.
22. Skip the Manufacturer's Part Number field.
23. Skip the Qty on Hand field.
24. Click Save Changes.
25. QuickBooks displays the number of record(s) saved. Click OK, and then click Close.

To view your newly added inventory item, select **Lists**, **Item List**, type **Wood Door** in the Look For field at the top of the Item List, and press the Enter key on your keyboard. Do you see the newly created Custom Door listed? Click the Reset button to return to the original list.

You can also enter your inventory data into an Excel spreadsheet and then copy and paste it into the Add/Edit Multiple List Entries dialog box.

tip

When using the Add/Edit Multiple List Entries tool, use the Tab key on your keyboard to move efficiently from one field to the next.

From the grid, you can right-click for other functionality. From the right-click menu, you can choose from Copy Down, Duplicate Row, Clear Column, and other useful features.

Importing an Intuit Interchange Format File (IIF)

The term *Intuit Interchange Format (IIF)* refers to data exchange functionality that has been around for some time. It is a method for exporting lists from one QuickBooks file and importing these lists into a new QuickBooks file. The process creates a tab-delimited text file with the extension of .iif. You can view and edit this file using Excel.

The IIF format is a preferred and easy method to use if you already have a QuickBooks file with an items list you want to replicate in another QuickBooks file.

caution

When cutting and pasting from Excel, make sure your columns of data in Excel match the order of the Add/Edit Multiple List Entries columns in QuickBooks.

To export an IIF-formatted items file from an existing QuickBooks file, follow these steps:

1. Open the QuickBooks file that has the items list you want to export and duplicate for another file.
2. From the menu bar, select **File**, **Utilities**, **Export**, **Lists to IIF Files**.
3. Select the **Item List** checkbox.
4. Click OK. You are prompted to provide a filename and to save the exported file. Remember the location you stored the file in; you will need to browse to the .iif file to import it into another QuickBooks file.
5. Click OK to the message that your data was exported successfully.

Figure 5.9 shows the exported items list in the IIF format in an Excel workbook. You can see that it is not as user friendly as the Add/Edit Multiple List Entries previously discussed.

Exported Items List.IIF - Microsoft Excel

File Home Insert Page Layout Formulas Data Review View QuickBooks

B30 Removal

	A	B	C	D	E	F	G	H	I	J	K	L	M	N	O	P
28	INVITEM	Labor	63	1.07E+09	SERV			Construction Income:Labor Income					0	0	N	Non
29	INVITEM	Mileage	70	1.2E+09	SERV			Reimbursement Income:Mileage Income					0.365	0	N	Non
30	INVITEM	Removal	3	9.33E+08	SERV	Removal I	Removal I	Construction Income:Labor Income					35	0	N	Non
31	INVITEM	Repairs	4	9.33E+08	SERV	Repair wo	Repair wo	Construction Income:Labor Income					35	0	N	Non
32	INVITEM	Subs	5	9.33E+08	SERV	Subcontra	Subcontra	Construction Income		Job Expenses:Subcontractors			0	0	N	Non
33	INVITEM	Subs:Carp	6	9.33E+08	SERV	Install car	Install car	Construction Income		Job Expenses:Subcontractors			0	25	N	Non
34	INVITEM	Subs:Dryw	7	9.33E+08	SERV	Install dry	Install dry	Construction Income		Job Expenses:Subcontractors			0	25	N	Non

Figure 5.9
An exported items list in IIF format can be imported into another QuickBooks file.

To import the saved IIF file into a new QuickBooks file, follow these steps:

1. Open the QuickBooks file you want to import the previously exported list into. If you have not already created your new file, select **File**, **New** from the menu bar and follow the prompts. (For more information, see Chapter 1.)
2. From the menu bar, select **File**, **Utilities**, **Import**, **IIF Files**.
3. When the Import dialog box opens, browse to the location of the stored IIF formatted file.
4. Select the file and click Open.
5. QuickBooks then imports the IIF formatted file into the QuickBooks data file. Click OK to the Your Data Has Been Imported message.

> **caution**
> The IIF file format is a tab-delimited text file format with an extension of .iif. If you edit the details of the file, be sure to keep this format when saving your changes; do not save as an .xls or .xlsx Excel file type.

Now that you have your new data file with new lists from another file, you are ready to begin entering transactions. Just think of all the time you saved by not having to manually create each list item in the new file.

Changing Item Prices

Your business might have a variety of items, including Service, Inventory, Non-inventory Parts, and even Other Charge items. During the course of doing business, your costs of supplying these products or services will change, and you might want to update your item sales prices.

Included with QuickBooks Pro, Premier, or Enterprise is the Change Item Prices tool (see Figure 5.10).

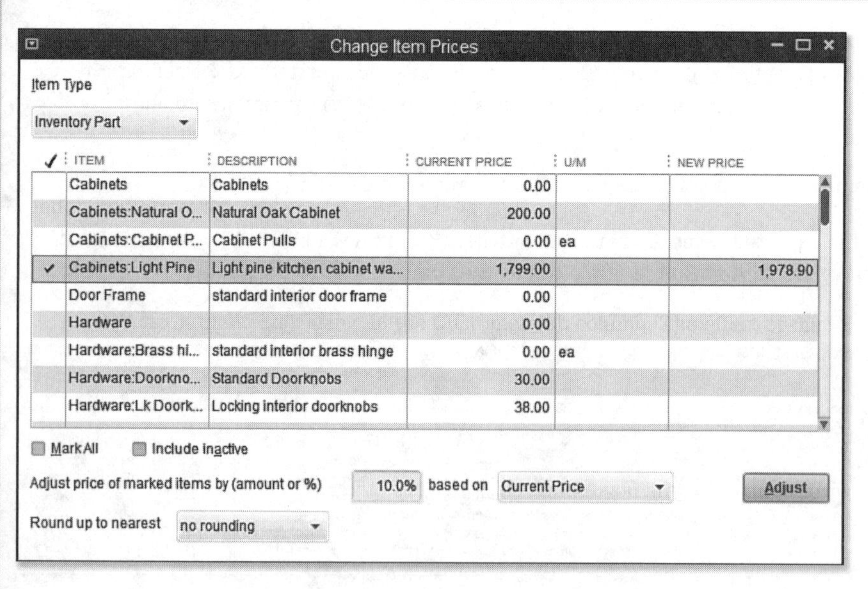

Figure 5.10
You can efficiently manage multiple inventory part sales price changes with Change Item Prices.

With this feature you can change the price of the following:

- One item at a time
- More than one item at a time
- Several items by a fixed amount based on Current Price or Unit Cost
- Several items by a percentage based on Current Price or Unit Cost

Practice Using the Change Item Prices

To practice using the Change Item Prices feature, open the sample data as previously instructed in Chapter 1:

1. From the menu bar, select **Customers, Change Item Prices.**
2. In this example, in the Item Type drop-down list, select **Inventory Part**.
3. Place a checkmark next to the Cabinets:Light Pine item.
4. In the Adjust Price of Marked Items by (Amount or %) field, type **10%**. See the Caution that follows for including the % symbol.
5. Leave the default of Based On Current Price selected. The other option available is to base the change on the Unit Cost.
6. Click Adjust. Notice the New Price is calculated based on your specifications in step 4.
7. In the Round Up to Nearest drop-down list, leave the No Rounding option selected. Other options include the ability to round up or down by a specific increment.
8. Click OK to close the Change Item Prices dialog box.

caution

When using the Change Item Prices, if you want to increase the Current Price by a percentage, be sure to type the amount with the percentage symbol. For example, if you want to increase the New Price by 15 percent, you would type 15% because without the % symbol, QuickBooks assumes you want to raise the price by a fixed amount of $15.

Using the Change Item Prices dialog box can be an efficient way of updating your pricing for multiple items at one time. QuickBooks Enterprise Solutions 13.0 provides more control over changes to the default part cost, sales price, and markup when an item's cost changes. When entering a cost on a purchase transaction that differs from the cost in the item record, QuickBooks prompts the user to set a preference for updating the item record and sales price. See Figures 5.11 and 5.12.

 **caution**

In Chapter 9, "Setting Up Customers," you learn about working with memorized transactions. It is important to note that changes made to item prices *do not* automatically change the prices you have previously recorded on a memorized customer invoice.

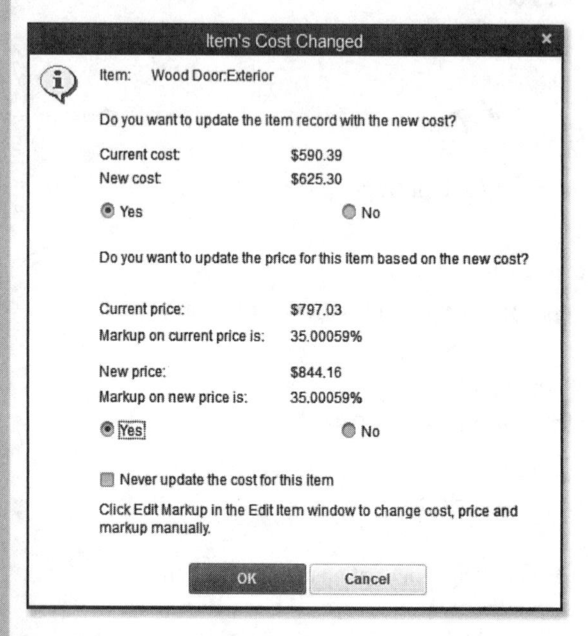

Figure 5.11
Available only in QuickBooks Enterprise is the option to update the default cost and sales price when recording a purchase transaction.

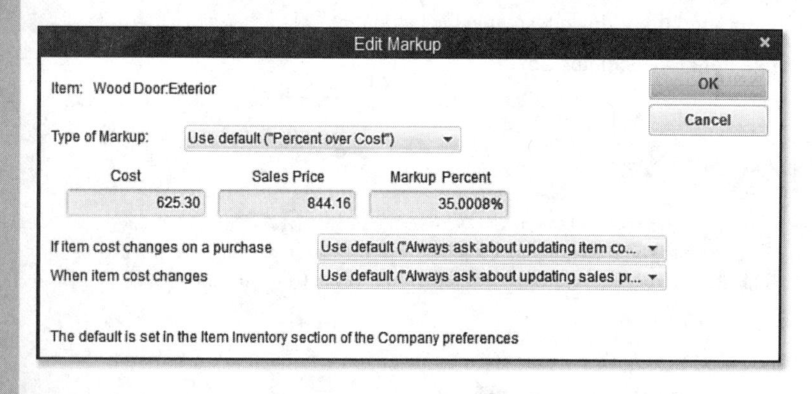

Figure 5.12
Define specific settings for handling markup % or amount, available with QuickBooks Enterprise.

Creating Inventory Assemblies

The inventory assembly (see Figure 5.13) can include the following item types:

- Other Assemblies (Subassemblies)
- Inventory Parts
- Non-inventory Parts
- Service Items
- Other Charge Items

Figure 5.13
Inventory Assembly items are available in QuickBooks Premier, Accountant, or Enterprise.

Practice Using Inventory Assemblies

To practice adding a new inventory assembly (only if you have QuickBooks Premier or Enterprise), open the sample data file as instructed in Chapter 1:

1. On the Home page, click the Items & Services icon. The Item List displays.
2. In the lower-left corner, click the Item button, and then select **New** or use the keyboard shortcut of Ctrl+N.

For more information, see "Using Add/Edit Multiple List Entries," p. 159.

3. In the Type drop-down list, select **Inventory Assembly**.
4. In the Item Name/Number field, type **Deck**.
5. Leave the I Purchase This Assembly Item from a Vendor checkbox and Unit of Measure (U/M) Set field blank.
6. Leave the Cost field blank.
7. Accept the default COGS Account of Cost of Goods Sold.
8. In the Description field, type **Decking**.
9. Leave the Sales Price blank.

10. Leave the default Tax Code of Tax.
11. In the Income Account drop-down list, select account number **40140** or **Construction Income:Materials Income**.
12. In the Item drop-down list, enter the Bill of Materials by selecting the following items:
    - Select **Trim** from the Lumber item group. Type **5** in the Qty column.
    - On the next row, select the new item you created in an earlier exercise in this chapter, **Stain**. Type a Qty of **8**.

    Notice how QuickBooks calculates the Total Bill of Materials Cost, which is the sum total of the individual default costs recorded with each item record. Knowing the cost of the items can help you assign a proper Sales Price.
13. Type **1,125.00** in the Sales Price field.
14. Leave the default Asset Account.
15. Type **3** in the Build Point.
16. Leave the On Hand and Total Value fields blank. Leave the default date value in the As Of field.
17. Click OK to close the New Item dialog box.

caution

Working with assemblies requires some care and attention on your part. Here are a couple of items worth noting:

- Future changes to the Item default cost will update the costs of all assemblies that use that item.
- An assembly with items included that have 0 (zero) for quantity will not be able to be built until the QTY has a number greater than zero.

Carefully review the details of your assemblies by selecting the Full View on the Add or Edit Assembly dialog box.

Creating the assembly is only part of the process. You also need to "build" the assembly.

Using inventory assemblies can help your business track whether you have enough components in inventory to build the finished product for your customers. You can edit inventory assemblies, but QuickBooks does not track the revision history for an item. If you are no longer selling a particular assembled item, you can make the item inactive so it cannot be used on future purchase or sales transactions.

Creating Group Items

Previously, Table 5.1 listed the differences between working with Group Items (see Figure 5.14) versus an Inventory Assembly. In this section, you will learn how to work with Group Items.

note

New for QuickBooks 2013, you can now include up to 50 different items in a Group Item. In previous versions of QuickBooks you could only have up to 20 individual items in a Group Item.

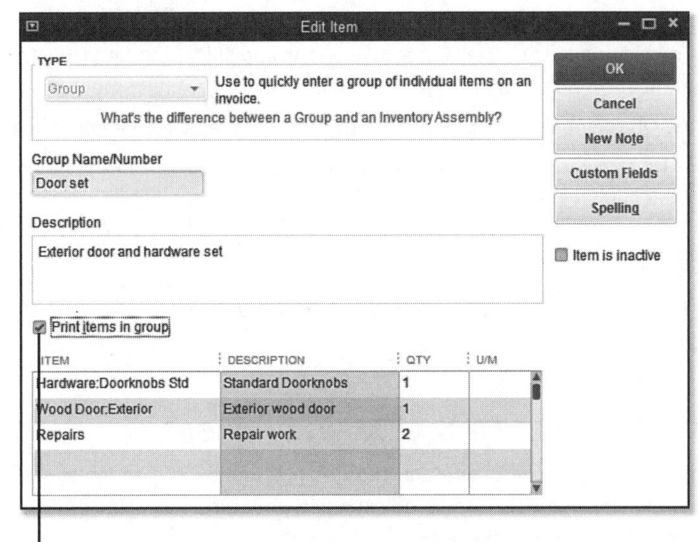

Figure 5.14
Creating Group items can save you time when you need to enter multiple items.

Unlike working with assemblies, when creating or editing Group Item, you do not assign a cost for each item or a sales price for the Group Item. The cost and sales price is calculated for you from the respective totals for each of the included items. The sales priced recorded on the invoice can be modified at the time you create the invoice, if necessary.

Practice Using Group Items

In this exercise, you will edit an existing Group item. Open the sample data as previously instructed in Chapter 1:

1. On the Home page, click the Items & Services icon. The Item List displays.
2. Scroll down the list and select the **Door Set** group (near the bottom of the list in the Group section). (Optional) You can also begin selecting Door Set in the Look For box at the top of the Item List and click the Search button.
3. Double-click to select the Door Set group. The Edit Item dialog box displays.
4. When working with your own data, enter a Group Name/Number of your choosing that will serve as reminder of what items are included in this Group.
5. In the Description box is the desired detail that will display on a customer's invoice. You can modify the description on the invoice if needed.
6. Don't select the Print Items in Group checkbox. This is one unique feature of working with the Group item type. When the Print Items in Group checkbox is *not selected,* the customer's invoice will show only the Description from step 5.

7. Currently, two items are included in the Group: Doorknobs Std and Exterior Wood Door. In the Item column, click the next available row and select the Service item named **Repairs** from the drop-down list.
8. In the Qty. column, type **2**, assigning two hours of repair labor when installing this door.
9. Click OK to close the Edit Item dialog box. You are returned to the Item List and your new group is highlighted (selected).

To practice using this Group item on an invoice, see the section titled "Working with Group Items," p. 184.

Setting Up Multiple Unit of Measurement

If you are using QuickBooks Premier or Enterprise, you have the option to set up Multiple Unit of Measure. A benefit of this feature is the capability to assign a specific unit default for purchases, shipping, and sales transactions.

To begin using Multiple Unit of Measure in your Premier or Enterprise file, you need to enable the preference setting. To do so, follow these steps:

1. Log in to the file as the Admin or External Accountant user.
2. From the menu bar, select **Edit**, **Preferences**.
3. Select the **Items & Inventory—Company Preferences** tab.
4. In the Unit of Measure box, click the Enable button. This button will not be present if the feature is already enabled.
5. Select either **Single U/M Per Item** or **Multiple U/M Per Item** (as shown in Figure 5.15). For more information, see "Enabling Inventory Preferences," p. 149.
6. Click Finish. Click OK to close the Preferences dialog box.

Now that the preference is enabled, create the different unit measurements you will be tracking.

Figure 5.15
To begin using Multiple Unit of Measure, first enable the preference.

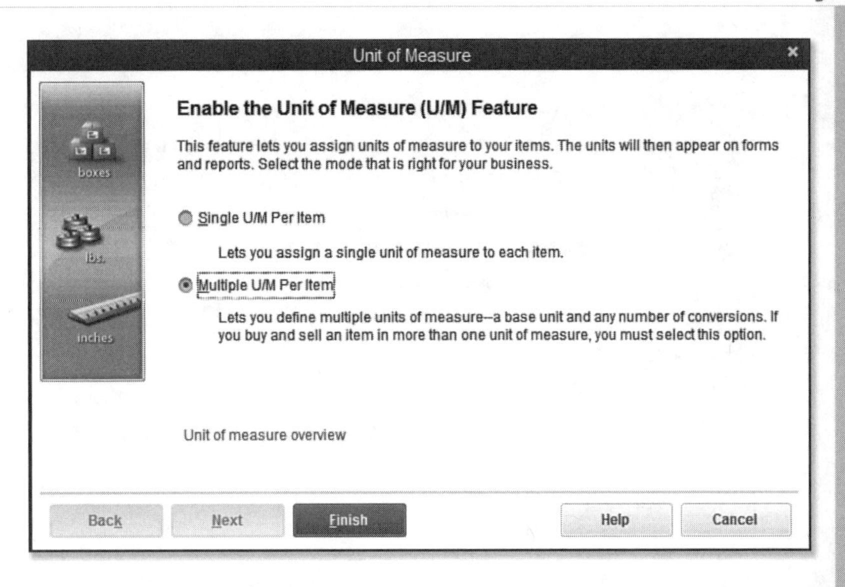

Using Multiple Unit of Measure

After enabling the Unit of Measure preference, let's create Multiple Unit of Measure for the Stain non-inventory part. This part was created in the section of this chapter titled "Non-inventory Part":

1. From the menu bar, select **Lists, Item List**.
2. Select the **Stain** non-inventory part created earlier. Double-click the stain item to open the Edit Item dialog box.
3. From the Unit of Measure drop-down list on an existing item, select **Add New** to open the Unit of Measure dialog box.
4. The Unit of Measure dialog box displays. Select **Count** (each, box, case, dozen, and so on). When working in your own file, if you do not see the desired unit displayed, select the **Other** option, as shown in Figure 5.16, and follow the instructions after you click Next to create a new base unit.

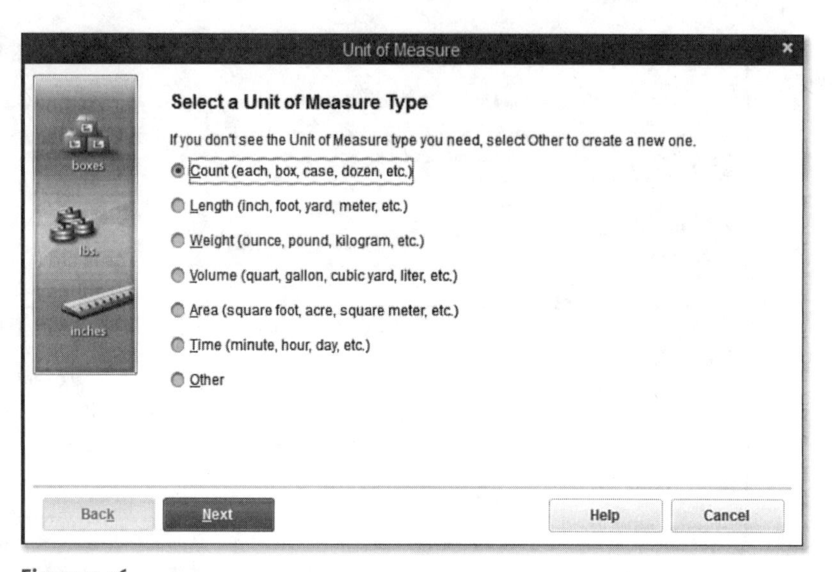

Figure 5.16
QuickBooks provides multiple units of measure types, or you can select Other to create your own.

5. Click Next and select **Each** (ea) as the Base Unit of Measure for this practice.
6. Click Next to display the Add Related Units screen (see Figure 5.17).

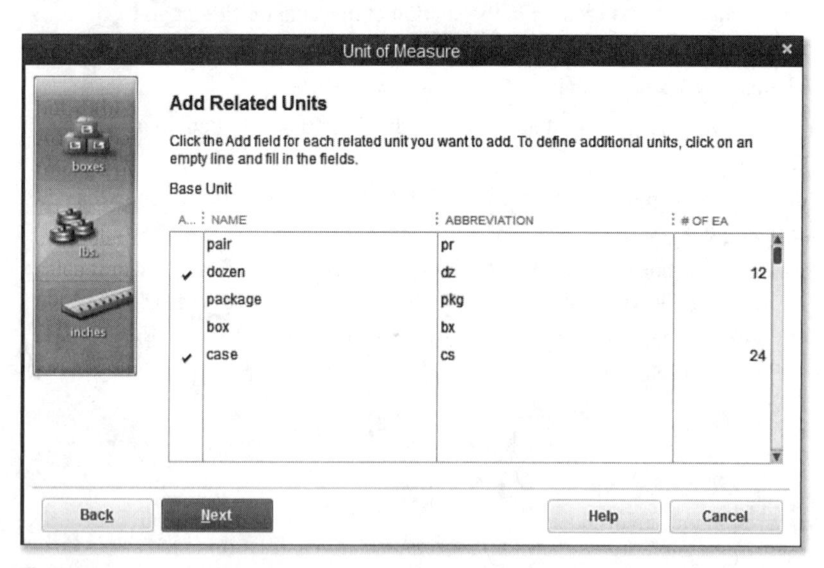

Figure 5.17
For the unit of measure created, you define the number of base units (in this example # of ea).

7. Place a checkmark next to the individual units of measurement you want to add to the selected item (see Figure 5.17 for the quantities used in this practice). Click Next when it's complete.

8. The Select Default Units of Measure screen displays. In the drop-down list, select the default units for Purchase, Sales, and Shipping transactions, as shown in Figure 5.18.

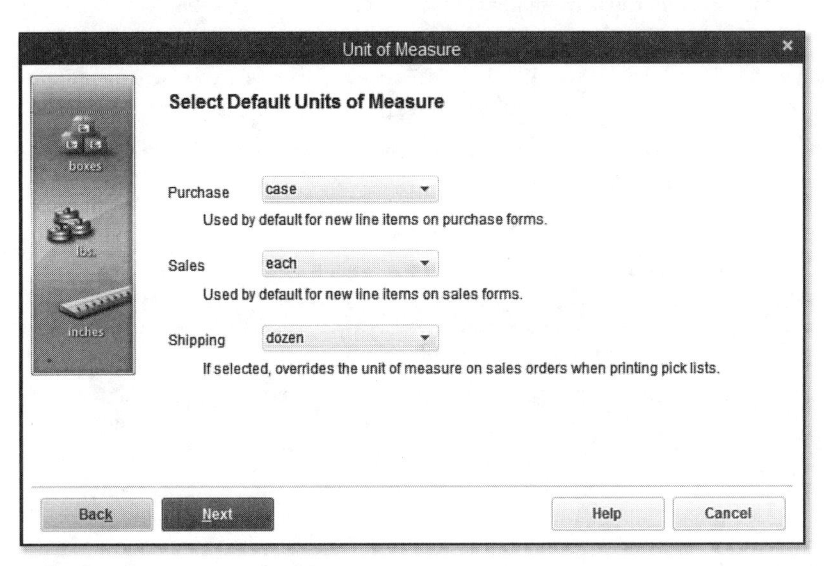

Figure 5.18
The benefit of working with Multiple Unit of Measurement is the capability to define the default units for specific transaction types.

9. Click Next.
10. The Name the Unit of Measure Set screen displays. Type a name for the unit of measure set or accept the default that is displayed.
11. Click Finish, and the U/M Set now shows the configured Multiple Unit of Measurement assigned to the selected item.
12. Click OK to close the New Item dialog box or Edit Item dialog box.

With Multiple Unit of Measure defined for this item, entering inventory on transactions will be easier and more accurate.

caution
When working with Multiple Unit of Measures, if you edit an existing unit of measure assigned to an item, you will be warned "Any changes you make to this unit of measure set will affect all items that use this set."

Proper Inventory Processes

Understanding the recommended inventory process and the associated transactions can help you properly use the inventory feature. If you are new to inventory management, QuickBooks makes getting started with it easy, via the workflow outlined on the Home page, as shown previously in Figure 5.2.

Use a purchase order if you want to compare the bill the vendor sends with the original agreed quantity and cost. With purchase orders, you can also keep track of what items have been ordered and have not yet been received.

You can receive inventory in one of two ways. With one method, you receive inventory with the vendor's final bill. If you record full receipt of the quantity, QuickBooks then marks the purchase order as closed. You can also choose to receive inventory without a bill. QuickBooks will create an Item Receipt document that is included in the accounts payable reports but cannot yet be paid in the Pay Bills dialog box.

Rest assured that as you create the vendor's final bill, QuickBooks recognizes if you have outstanding purchase orders or item receipts you want to associate with the vendor's bill.

Table 5.2 shows a listing of all transaction types you should use when working with Inventory and their related effects on the company's accounting.

Table 5.2 Inventory Transaction Types

Transaction Type	Purpose of Transaction	Effect with Accounting
Purchase Order	Record order placed with vendor	No effect
Item Receipt without Bill	Record receipt of inventory items	Increases inventory, increases accounts payable (bill cannot be selected in the Pay Bills dialog box)
Item Receipt with Bill	Record receipt of inventory items	Increases inventory, increases accounts payable (bill can be selected in the Pay Bills dialog box)
Bill	Record bill (optionally, assign purchase order or item receipt)	Increases inventory, increases accounts payable
Check	Items tab used (optionally, assign purchase order or item receipt)	Increases inventory, decreases cash
Estimates	Record quote for sales of items to a customer	No effect
Sales Order	Manage sales of inventory by committing it for sale (used to manage back orders of inventory)	No effect, except to show the items in inventory as committed
Invoice	Record sale of inventory to customer	Decreases inventory, increase accounts receivable, increases cost of goods sold, and increases income
Sales Receipt	Record sale of inventory to customer	Decreases inventory, increases cash, increases cost of goods sold, and increases income
Inventory Adjustment—Quantity	Record a change to the quantity of stock on hand	Decreases or increases inventory quantity and decreases or increases Inventory Adjustment account (Cost of Goods Sold type or Expense account type)
Inventory Adjustment—Value	Record a change to the value of the stock on hand	Decreases or increases inventory value and decreases or increases Inventory Adjustment account (Cost of Goods Sold type or Expense account type)

QuickBooks Enterprise Solutions 13.0 (all industry versions) includes the option to use Enhanced Inventory Receiving. When enabled, this feature records an item receipt as an increase to Inventory and an increase to an Inventory Offset account (other current liability account created automatically by QuickBooks). Later when the vendor bill is entered, Accounts Payable is increased and the Inventory Offset account is decreased.

As a business owner, you do not need to worry about the details; QuickBooks Enterprise does all the behind-the-scenes accounting for you.

Purchasing, Receiving, and Entering the Vendor Bill

One other transaction type can be used to pay for your inventory purchase: Write Checks. If you use the Write Checks transaction type to enter your inventory purchases, you must use the Items tab to enter the items being purchased. However, the Write Checks transaction does not track the vendor's bill reference number.

An important reason to purchase accounting software is having the capability to track the expenses incurred in providing products or services to your customers. In fact, the business's profitability can be improved by effectively managing your purchasing costs. In this section, you learn a recommended purchasing process specifically for inventory items and non-inventory items. This process is similar to the steps outlined in Chapter 7, "Setting Up Vendors."

Review Table 5.2 in the previous section for how QuickBooks handles the accounting for inventory. To manage your inventory purchasing with the greatest level of control, follow these three steps:

1. Create a purchase order recording a commitment to purchase.
2. Receive inventory without a vendor bill to create an item receipt.
3. Enter a vendor bill upon receipt and associate it with the open item receipt.

Creating the Purchase Order

If you are practicing in your own data file, make sure you have read the section in this chapter titled "Enabling Inventory Preferences."

Practice Creating a Purchase Order

Using the sample company referred to in Chapter 1, let's practice creating a purchase order and receiving the inventory:

1. On the Home page, shown in Figure 5.2, click the Purchase Orders icon to open the Create Purchase Order transaction.
2. In the Vendor drop-down list, begin typing the letters **Th.** QuickBooks automatically prefills with the vendor Thomas Kitchen & Bath. Alternatively, you can scroll through the drop-down list and click to select a vendor for the purchase order.

3. Use the Tab key to move to the Class field and select **New Construction**. If you have not enabled class tracking in your file, you will not have this field.
4. In this example, leave the Drop Ship To field blank. Accept the default Template, Date, P.O. No., Vendor, and Ship To details.
5. From the Item drop-down list, select the **Light Pine** item, a subitem of Cabinets.
6. Accept the default description.
7. In the Qty field, click the icon (see Figures 5.19 and 5.20) to view the Current Availability of the item. This useful feature is available only with QuickBooks Premier or Enterprise. Click Show Details. From the Show Details for drop-down list, select **Sales Orders**.
8. Click Close to close the Current Availability dialog box.
9. In the Qty field, type **2**.
10. For this exercise, if U/M (Unit of Measure) is enabled, leave the field blank.
11. Accept the default Rate.
12. Leave the Customer field blank. For inventory items, the cost will be assigned to the customer when the inventory item is included on a customer's invoice. Select the customer only if you are using an item type *other than* inventory, and *only* if you know the customer at the time of purchase.
13. Accept the default Amount.
14. (Optional) Type a message to the vendor in the lower-left Vendor Message field.
15. (Optional) Enter a Memo. This field displays on reports and can be useful when you have multiple open purchase orders for one vendor at a time.
16. (Optional) Select the Print Later or Email Later box at the top of the transaction. Emailing transactions and reports requires the Send preference be enabled. You can access this preference from the Send Forms—My Preferences tab of the Preferences dialog box (from the menu bar select Edit, Preferences).
17. For this practice, click Save & New. If the Check Spelling on Form warning displays, select the **Ignore All** option.
18. Let's preview the purchase order just created. From the Create Purchase Orders transaction, click the Previous arrow (top left) pointing to the left. The purchase order you just created is displayed.
19. Click the Print button (at the top) and select **Preview**.
20. Your newly created purchase order displays using the default purchase order template.

For more information, see "Customizing QuickBooks Forms," p. 322.

21. Click Close to close the preview, and click Save & Close to close the Create Purchase Orders transaction.

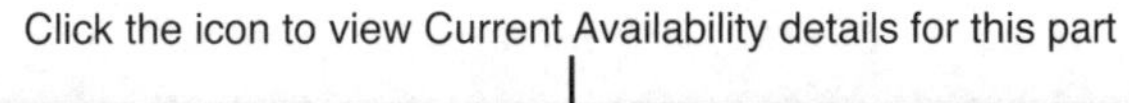

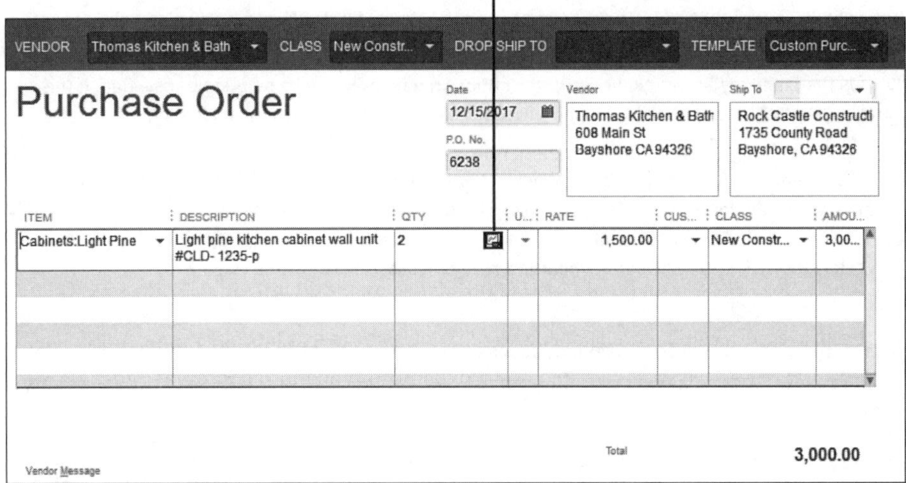

Figure 5.19
Creating a purchase order helps you manage your expected costs.

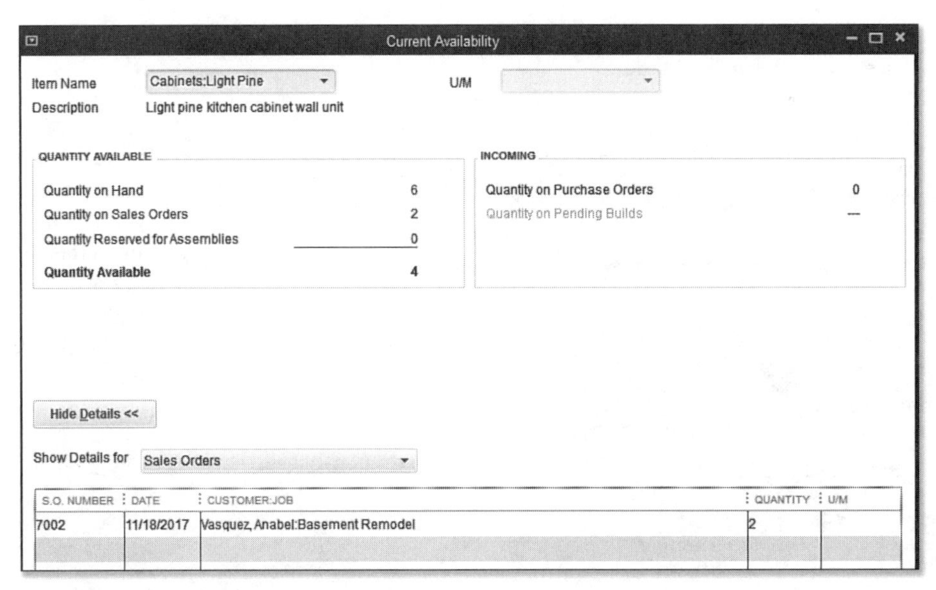

Figure 5.20
Current Availability information for inventory items is conveniently included on purchasing and sales transactions in Premier or Enterprise editions only.

 **tip**

Did you know that by default, QuickBooks would have you use the Tab key on your keyboard to advance from one field to another with certain transactions?

If you inadvertently used the Enter key on your keyboard, QuickBooks might store the incomplete transaction. If this happens to you, use the arrows at the top left of the open transaction to find the transaction you had not fully completed.

If you prefer to use the Enter key on your keyboard to advance between fields, you can set that preference on the General—My Preferences tab of the Preferences dialog box (select **Edit, Preferences** from the menu bar). Select the **Pressing Enter Moves Between Fields** check box and click OK to save your preference setting. Later, when recording transactions, you can select the Ctrl+Enter on your keyboard to save a transaction.

To simplify creating purchase orders, you can access useful tasks from the ribbon toolbar on the top of the Create Purchase Orders transaction. The ribbon toolbar includes the following tabs, as shown in Figure 5.21:

- **Main**—Central location for common tasks related to working with purchase orders. From this tab you can Find, Save, Print, Email, and access other purchase order functions.
- **Formatting**—Preview, manage, download, and customize the purchase order form. More information can be found in Chapter 9.
- **Reports**—Quick access to common reports for the displayed purchase order and useful purchase order reporting on all purchase orders.

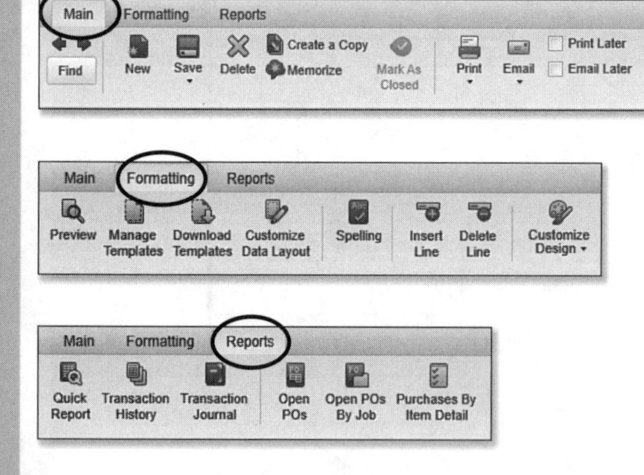

Figure 5.21 Use the new transaction ribbon toolbar to access commonly used tasks and reports.

To the right of a displayed purchase order, you may see the following tabs as shown in Figure 5.24. If you do not see these tabs, click the small arrow pointing to the right next to the Template to view them:

- **Vendor**—Provides summary and recent transaction information for the vendor selected on the Purchase Order. Also includes links to edit the vendor record, create a QuickReport, and enter notes for the current transaction.
- **Transaction**—View summary information, related transactions, and notes for the currently displayed purchase order.

tip

If you want to minimize the ribbon toolbar at the top of a displayed transaction, click the arrow on the top right that is pointing up. Clicking expands or collapses the ribbon toolbar, depending on its present state.

New for 2013, if you are using QuickBooks Enterprise software, you have the added feature of automatically creating purchase orders from your inventory stock status reports.

To use QuickBooks Enterprise to automatically create multiple purchase orders, follow these steps:

1. From the menu bar, select **Reports**, **Inventory**, **Inventory Stock Status by Item or Vendor**.
2. On the top of the displayed stock status report, click the Create Auto PO's button as shown in Figure 5.22.

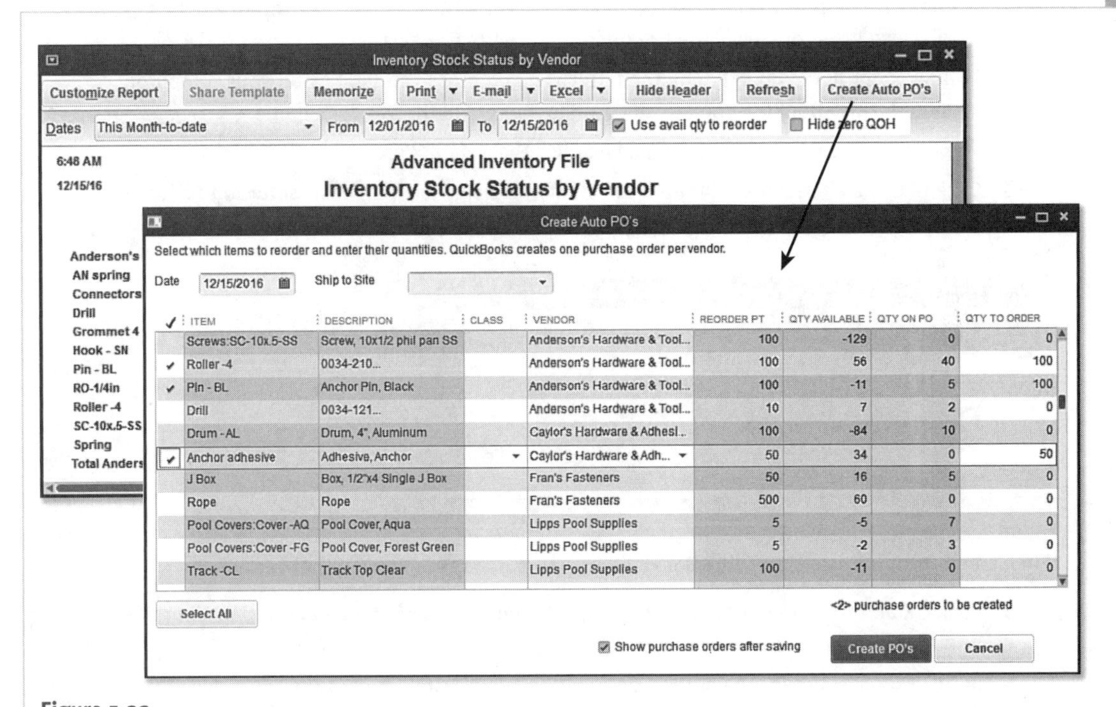

Figure 5.22
With QuickBooks Enterprise, review your stock status reports and prepare replenishing purchase orders easily.

3. The Create Auto PO's dialog box displays as shown in Figure 5.22.
4. Items with Preferred Vendors stored on the part record will display with that vendor's name. In the vendor column, change the vendor as needed.

5. Place a checkmark next to the parts you want to include on the purchase orders. QuickBooks creates one purchase order per vendor.

For more information on how easy it is to upgrade your Pro or Premier file to QuickBooks Enterprise, see "Upgrading Your QuickBooks Version," p. 617.

Congratulations on taking the first step to successfully managing your inventory!

Receiving Item(s) into Inventory

Next, you will work with receiving your items into inventory, and you will find many of the same ribbons on top and tabs to the right that were available on the purchase order transaction.

Practice Receiving Items

Continuing with our practice using QuickBooks sample data and building on the previous exercise, let's record the receipt of the inventory:

1. From the Home page, select **Receive Inventory Without Bill** from the drop-down list next to the Receive Inventory icon. The Create Item Receipts transaction opens.
2. In the Vendor field, begin typing the letters **Th** and press the Tab key on your computer keyboard. QuickBooks automatically prefills the rest of the vendor's name.
3. The Open POs Exist dialog box displays. Click the default Yes.
4. Click to place a checkmark in the first column to assign the purchase order to this Item Receipt, as shown in Figure 5.23.

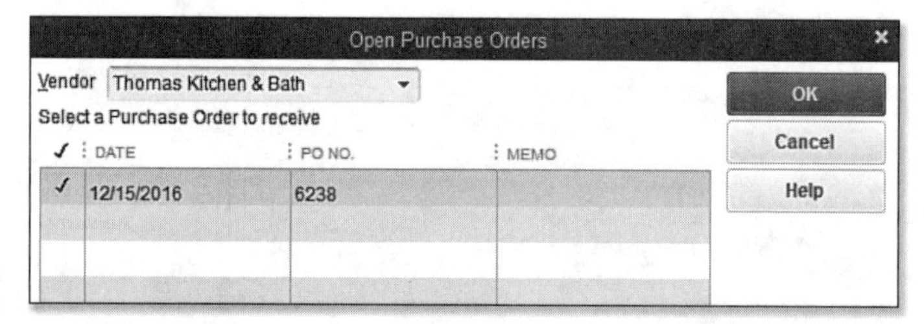

Figure 5.23
When creating an item receipt, QuickBooks lists open purchase orders for that vendor.

5. Click OK and the Create Item Receipts transaction prefills with the information from the original purchase order.
6. In this exercise, accept the default date. In the Ref. No. field, type **1234**.
7. To continue with the practice example here, record only a partial receipt of the inventory items, and replace the 2 in the Qty field by typing **1** as displayed in Figure 5.24.
8. Leave the Customer:Job and Billable? fields blank. Accept the default Class and PO No. assigned.

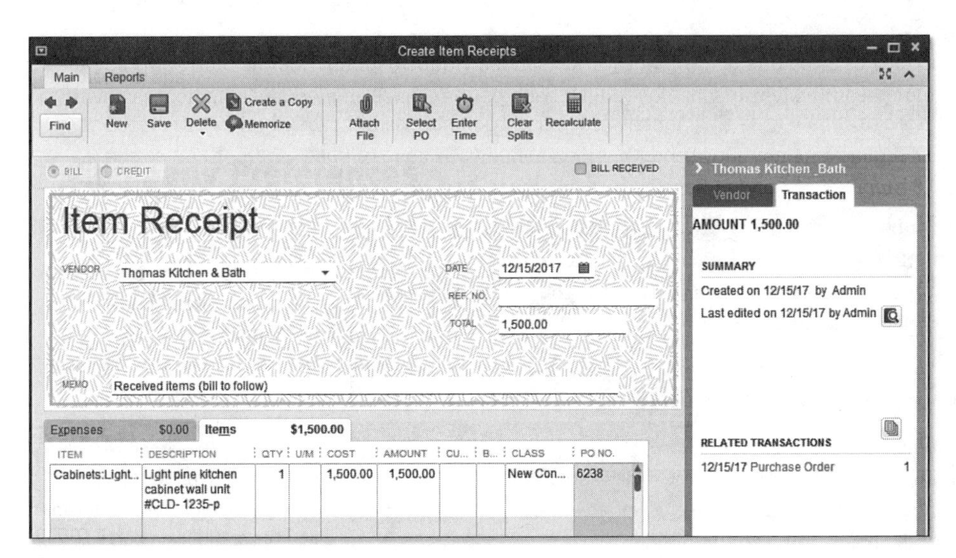

Figure 5.24
When receiving inventory without the final vendor bill, QuickBooks creates an Item Receipt.

9. Notice other useful buttons on the Create Item Receipts transaction:
   - **Clear Qtys**—Click this if you want to clear all quantity fields and enter them manually.
   - **Show PO**—Click this to open the selected purchase order. Useful if you need to make changes to the purchase order details.
10. To continue with the practice, click Save on the Main tab of the ribbon toolbar on the Create Item Receipts transaction. This saves the details, but leaves the current transaction displayed for this exercise. (Normally, you will be selecting Save & New or Save & Close at the bottom of the transaction.)
11. Click the Transaction tab to the right to view Related Transactions, including a link to the Purchase Order used to create this item receipt. Another option is to select Transaction History on the Report tab of the ribbon toolbar.
12. Click the Purchase Order link in the Related Transactions section of the Transaction tab to view the Purchase Order that the Item Receipt is linked to.
13. The Create Purchase Orders transaction now includes a column with the Backordered quantity.
14. Click Save & Close to close the Create Purchase Orders transaction.
15. Click Save & Close to close the Create Item Receipts transaction.

Notice other useful features or reports found on the Create Item Receipts ribbon toolbar:

- **Main**—Central location for common tasks related to working with item receipts. From this tab you can find, save, create new item receipts, enter time (from time sheets), and clear splits (remove the line detail), to name just a few of the additional functions available.
- **Reports**—Quick access to common reports for the displayed item receipt.

Did your vendor not supply you with a vendor bill number (same as Ref. No.)? You might want to use the same date as the vendor bill in the Ref. No. field. The primary purpose of the Ref. No. field is to warn you if you enter a bill with the same reference number more than once.

Now might be a good time to advance to the section titled "Inventory Reporting," p. 201. Specifically look for reports in the Report Center, Vendors and Payable section. You can review several excellent purchasing reports.

Do you have freight, shipping, or handling charges to add the vendor's item receipt? To track them as an added expense but not as part of the average cost of this inventory item, click the Expenses tab on the vendor bill, or write a check transaction and add the additional charges.

Entering the Vendor Bill

When it comes to inventory, the more controls you have in place surrounding your purchasing process the more accurate your accounting data will be. In the next step, you learn how to enter a vendor bill and assign it to the previously recorded item receipt.

Practice Entering a Vendor Bill and Assigning the Item Receipt

Continuing with our practice using QuickBooks sample data (as discussed in Chapter 1), let's record the vendor bill and assign it to the open item receipt from the previous exercise:

1. On the Home page, click the Enter Bills Against Inventory icon. The Select Item Receipt transaction opens.
2. In the Vendor field, select **Thomas Kitchen & Bath** as the vendor from the drop-down list.
3. (Optional) Select the Use Item Receipt Date for the Bill Date check box. Because QuickBooks removes the item receipt and replaces it with a bill, you want to be sure to use the date you want your financials affected. You can also set a Default Date to Use for New Transactions by selecting Edit, Preferences, General—My Preferences tab from the menu bar.
4. Select the appropriate Item Receipt to associate with this bill, as shown in Figure 5.25.

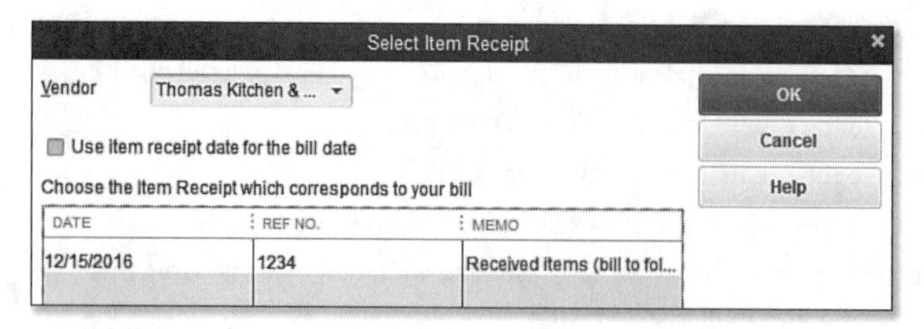

Figure 5.25
Be certain your item receipt is highlighted before clicking OK.

5. Click OK to close the Select Item Receipt transaction. The Enter Bills transaction displays, and the item receipt no longer exists as an item receipt transaction.
6. In this exercise, accept the vendor's Ref. No., Qty, and Cost. When you are creating your own vendor bill transactions, you should carefully inspect that the vendor's bill details for Ref. No., Qty, and Cost agree with your records generated by the original purchase order.
7. Click Save & Close. If the message stating you have changed the transaction displays, click Yes.

Your business will benefit from the added cost controls put in place when you use a purchase order and receive item transactions. This process is particularly useful when the vendor sends the final bill separately from the original shipment. When you do get the vendor bill in the mail, you can review the details to make sure they agree with your records.

Paying for Inventory

You have now learned how to efficiently manage your inventory beginning with the purchase order that tracks the quantity ordered and the agreed-to cost. Next, when the product is delivered to your warehouse, you enter an item receipt with or without the vendor bill.

After creating a vendor bill in the previous section, you are now ready to process a payment by check, credit card, or electronic funds transfer (ACH) to your vendor.

Practice Paying for Inventory

Using the sample company referred to in Chapter 1, you will now create a payment to the vendor for the bill created in the earlier exercise:

1. On the Home page, click the Pay Bills icon. The Pay Bills dialog box displays.
2. Leave selected the Show All Bills option.
3. In the Filter By drop-down list, select **Thomas Kitchen & Bath**. When you are ready to pay your bills in your own QuickBooks file, you will probably not need to filter for a specific vendor because you will process multiple checks for many vendors at once.
4. In the Sort By drop-down list, view the other options for sorting the bills in the Pay Bills dialog box.
5. Place a checkmark next to both of the bills in the first column on the left. Notice that after you place a checkmark, the Amt. to Pay column for each bill is now equal to the Amt. Due column (see Figure 5.26).
6. With a bill selected, click the Go to Bill button. Notice how easy it is to get to the original transaction. Press the Esc key on your keyboard to close the Enter Bills transaction and return to the Pay Bills dialog box.

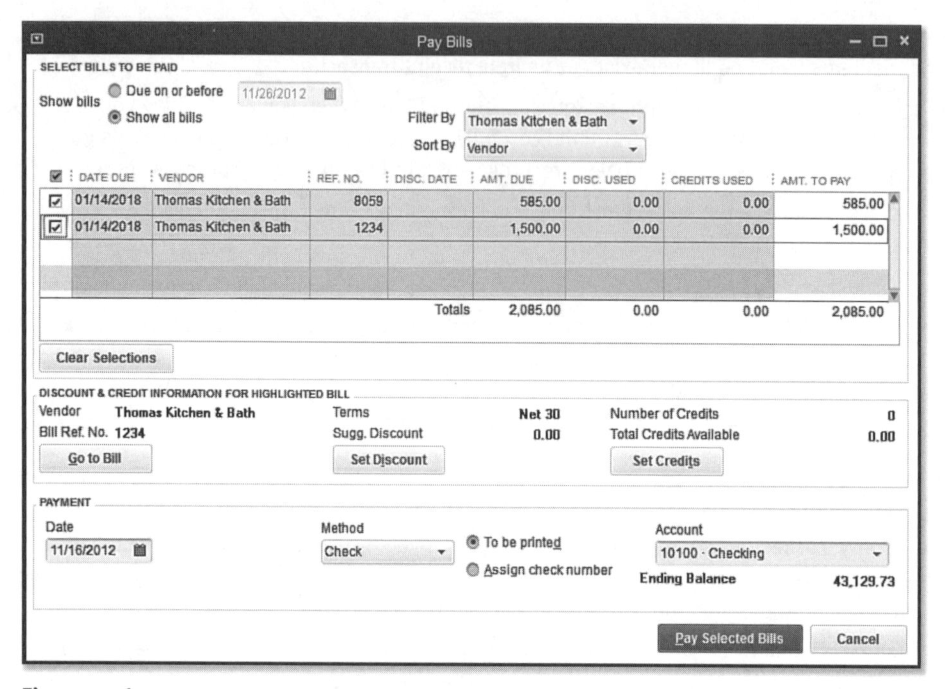

Figure 5.26
You can filter the Pay Bills dialog box for a single vendor.

7. The Set Discount and Set Credits options are discussed in Chapter 7, in the section titled "Applying Vendor Credits."
8. For this exercise, leave the default Payment Date. When working in your own data, enter the date you want to print on the vendor checks.
9. Accept the default of Check for Payment Method.
10. In the Account field, accept the default of Checking account. (When working with your own data, you will select the account you are recording the payment from.) Notice that QuickBooks displays your projected Ending Balance for your bank account.
11. Click Pay Selected Bills. QuickBooks opens the Payment Summary dialog box.
12. Review the details displayed, including payment date, account, and method.
13. Click the Print Checks button or click Done if you do not want to practice printing (using plain paper).
14. If you selected the option to Print Checks, the Select Checks to Print dialog box displays. Accept the defaults for Bank Account and First Check Number.
15. Review the list of checks to be printed. Each will have a checkmark in the column to the left. Remove the checkmarks from any checks you do not want to print at this time.

16. Click OK to open the Print Checks dialog box. Select your printer from the Printer Name drop-down list, and then choose the proper Check Style from Voucher, Standard, or Wallet. More detailed instructions on setting check printing preferences are included in Chapter 13.
17. Click Print. For this exercise, make sure you have plain paper in your printer. A check printed to plain paper is not a negotiable document.
18. The Print Checks—Confirmation dialog box displays. In this exercise, click OK to close the confirmation.

See how easy it is to print checks paying your vendors? You can order checks from most reputable check suppliers or order directly from Intuit. To order checks from Intuit, select the Print Checks icon on the lower right of the Home page if using the Top placed icon bar. Or at the bottom of the Left placed icon bar. Click the Order Checks button. Internet connection is required.

In the next section, you learn how to handle selling inventory on a customer invoice.

 **tip**

When selecting vendor bills to pay, you can override the Amt. to Pay and type an amount of your choosing. QuickBooks will keep track of the remaining balance due to the vendor.

Selling Inventory

For your business to survive, you need to sell your products (or services) to customers. The next important task discussed in this chapter shows just how easy it is to prepare invoices for your customers in QuickBooks.

First, it might be helpful for a little review on the proper accounting for inventory at the time of sale. You will recall that Table 5.2 detailed the impact an invoice or sales receipt has on accounting—namely, to decrease inventory, increase accounts receivable (or cash) depending on the transaction type used, increase cost of goods sold, and increase income.

Your inventory item setup does all this complicated work for you behind the scenes. First, each inventory item in QuickBooks is assigned an inventory asset account, COGS (cost of goods sold account), and income account. Second, QuickBooks uses the average cost method for calculating the cost of your product at the time of the invoice.

Did you know that you can pay your vendors by any one of a number of methods? The methods include printing a check, recording a manually written check, by credit card, and even as an online bank payment. To learn more about preferences for printing checks or making online payments directly from your QuickBooks file, see Chapter 13, "Working with Bank and Credit Card Accounts."

For more information, see "Reviewing the Recorded Average Cost Valuation," p. 206.

Practice Selling Inventory

Follow these steps to practice creating an invoice for a customer using the sample data installed with QuickBooks and discussed in Chapter 1:

1. On the Home page, click the Create Invoices or Invoices icon. The icon name will differ, depending on whether you have enabled specific Time and Expenses preferences. If another menu drop-down list displays, select Create Invoices.
2. In the Customer:Job drop-down list, select **Garage Repair** for the customer Baker, Chris.
3. In the Class drop-down list, select **New Construction.**
4. Accept the default Template, Date, Invoice #, Bill To, Ship To, Terms, and Due Date fields.
5. In the Item column drop-down list, select the **Doorknobs Std** inventory part from the Hardware parent inventory part.
6. In the Quantity field, type **1**. If you are using the QuickBooks-supplied sample data for this practice, you will have an invoice for 1 doorknob inventory part with tax.
7. For this practice, click Save on the top of the form. This saves the invoice and assigns the invoice number, but keeps the invoice open for viewing. See the tip that follows this exercise.
8. From the top of the open invoice, select **Preview** from the Print drop-down list. Click Close when you're done with the Print Preview dialog box.
9. Click Save & Close (or Save & New) to practice creating another invoice.

QuickBooks truly makes it easy to create invoices for your customers. Now, getting your customers to pay them is another task! Join me later in Chapter 10, in the section titled "Using the Collections Center," p. 370.

tip

When recording customer invoices in your own data, you have the option to select the Save button at the top. Typically, you do not need to do this each time. Instead, you can choose between the Save & Close button and the Save & New button on the lower right.

Working with Group Items

Using Group items can save time when you need to enter several items on a purchase or sales transaction.

Practice Using Group Items

Using the sample company referred to in Chapter 1, let's practice creating an invoice with the Group item modified in an earlier exercise:

1. On the Home page, click the Create Invoices or Invoices icon. The icon name will differ, depending on whether you have enabled specific Time and Expenses preferences. If another menu drop-down list displays, select Create Invoices.
2. In the Customer:Job drop-down list, select the **Barley, Renee:Repairs** job. Select **Remodel** for the Class field. Accept the default Template, Date, Invoice #, Bill To, Ship To, Terms, and Due Date fields.
3. In the Item column, select **Door Set**.
4. QuickBooks adds multiple rows to the invoice. For this exercise, click the Save button at the top of the invoice so that it can easily be previewed. When working with your own data, you can ignore this step and choose one of the save options in the lower right of the transaction.
5. In the Print drop-down list at the top of the invoice, select **Preview**.
6. Click Zoom In at the top to enlarge the detail displayed. Notice that the QuickBooks customer invoice includes one line of detail for the customer, but your internal reports and transaction screens show multiple lines of detail.
7. Click Close to close the preview. Click Save & Close to close the Create Invoices transaction.

Using Group items makes data entry more efficient when you need to enter multiple items at one time. An added benefit is that using Group items also provides the option to hide individual line details on the invoice provided to the customer.

Next, continue your practice by working with assembly items.

Working with Assemblies

Assemblies are used when you want to enter multiple items at one time and track the on-hand quantity for the finished good. Inventory Assemblies are available only with QuickBooks Premier (all editions), Accountant, and Enterprise (all editions).

Working with assemblies is a two-step process:

1. Create the assembly.
2. Build the assembly.

Practice Using Assemblies

Using the sample company referred to in Chapter 1, let's practice building an assembly and creating an invoice with an assembly item in your sample data:

1. From your Home page, select **Build Assemblies** from the drop-down list next to the Inventory Activities icon. The Build Assemblies dialog box opens (see Figure 5.27).

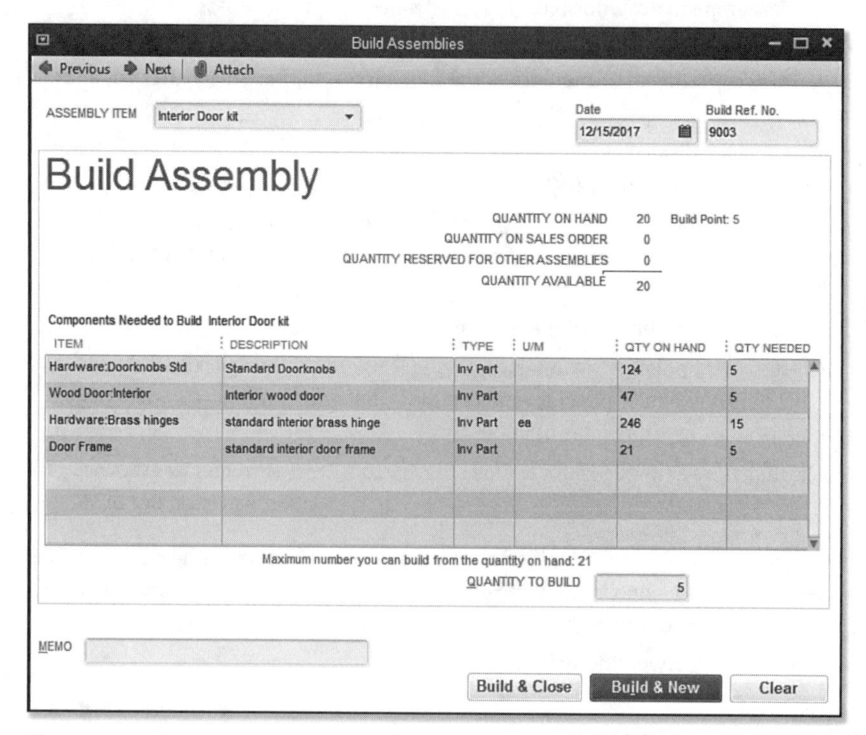

Figure 5.27
You must first build the assembly to track the quantity of finished product.

2. In the Assembly Item drop-down list, select **Interior Door Kit.**
3. Accept the default Date and Build Ref. No.
4. Review the individual items and note the reported maximum number of items that can be built with the stock on hand (lower right).
5. In the Quantity to Build box, type **5**. Enter an optional memo for your own reporting.
6. Click Build & Close.

With the assembly now built, you are ready to add the assembly to a customer's invoice. To do so, follow these steps:

1. On the Home page, click the Create Invoices or Invoices icon. The icon name will differ depending on whether you have enabled specific Time and Expenses preferences. If another menu drop-down list displays, select Create Invoices.
2. In the Customer:Job drop-down list, select the **Baker, Chris:Family Room** job. Select **Remodel** for the Class field. Accept the default Template, Date, Invoice #, Bill To, Ship To, Terms, and Due Date fields.
3. In the Item column, select **Interior Door Kit.**
4. In the Quantity field, type **1.**
5. In the Rate field, type **125.00.** This rate would have prefilled if a sales price was associated with the inventory assembly.
6. Click Save & Close to close the Create Invoices transaction.

How do you handle your accounting when you do not have enough inventory on hand to ship to a customer? Join me in the next section for details on working with sales orders to track these backorders.

Handling Inventory Backorders

Do you want to "commit" inventory to a customer ahead of purchasing the inventory? Handling backorders for your customers is best tracked using the QuickBooks sales order transaction available with QuickBooks Premier (all editions), QuickBooks Accountant, or QuickBooks Enterprise Solutions (all editions).

With a sales order transaction, you can record that you have committed inventory (backordered) for sale to the customer, provide the customer details of the sale for prepayment, and then later create the customer invoice directly from the sales order details. If you do take a prepayment from a customer, you will want to review the instructions included in Chapter 9, in the section "Recording the Customer Payment," p. 352.

Sales orders are considered a nonposting document, meaning that when they are created they do not affect inventory, revenue, or costs until the sales order is converted to an invoice, whereas, if you use a sales receipt, you affect your inventory, revenue, and costs when the sales receipt is recorded.

Using this sales order transaction type is the best solution if you must provide a sales document to a customer before the customer receives the merchandise.

tip

The sales order transaction type is available only in QuickBooks Premier (all editions), QuickBooks Accountant, or QuickBooks Enterprise Solutions (all editions). If you need this functionality, consider upgrading your file to Premier or Enterprise. For more information, see "Upgrading Your QuickBooks Version," p. 617.

Additionally, working with sales orders is a preference that is enabled by logging in to the file as the Admin or External Accountant. From the menu bar select **Edit, Preferences, Sales & Customers—Company Preferences,** and click the Enable Sales Orders checkbox.

Practice Working with Sales Orders

Using the same sample data discussed in Chapter 1, let's create a sales order after enabling this in preferences:

1. On the Home page, click the Sales Orders icon. If you do not have this icon, make sure sales orders are enabled in the Sales & Customers—Company Preferences.
2. In the Customer:Job drop-down list, select the **Home Remodel** job for the customer Bauman, Mark, as displayed in Figure 5.28.

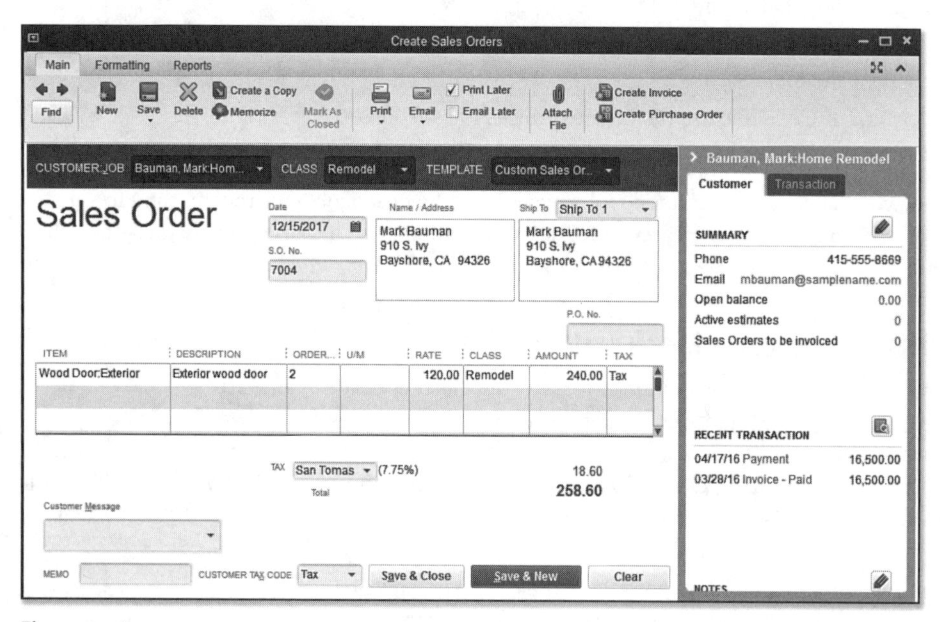

Figure 5.28
Use a Sales Order to commit inventory for a future sale.

3. For the Class field, select **Remodel**.
4. Leave the default template, date, S.O. No., Ship To, and P.O. details.
5. In the Item column drop-down list, select the **Exterior** inventory part subitem of Wood Door. Accept the default description.
6. In the Ordered column, type **2**. Leave the other fields on the row as the default. If you are using the QuickBooks-supplied sample data for this practice, you will have a Sales Order for 2 Exterior Wood Doors with tax.
7. For this exercise, click Save on the top of the transaction. This saves the sales order and assigns the sales order number, but keeps the sales order open for viewing.
8. In the Print drop-down list, at the top of the open sales order, select **Preview**. Click Close when done with the Print Preview dialog box.
9. Click Save & Close (or Save & New) to practice creating another sales order.

10. Next, create an invoice for the open sales order. On the Home page, click the Create Invoices or Invoices icon. (Optional) From an open sales order, you can click the Create Invoice icon at the top of the transaction to create the invoice.
11. In the Customer:Job drop-down list on the Create Invoices transaction, select the **Home Remodel** job for the customer Bauman, Mark. The Available Sales Orders dialog box shown in Figure 5.29 displays.

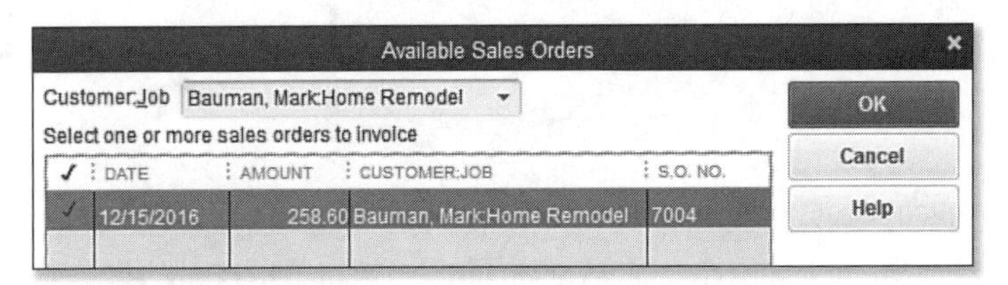

Figure 5.29
Don't forget to place a checkmark next to each available sales order you want to invoice.

12. Click in the first column to place a checkmark next to the listed open sales order(s) you want to include on the invoice to the customer.
13. Click OK. The Create Invoice Based on Sales Order(s) dialog box displays. For this exercise, select the **Create Invoice for Selected Items** option button, as shown in Figure 5.30.

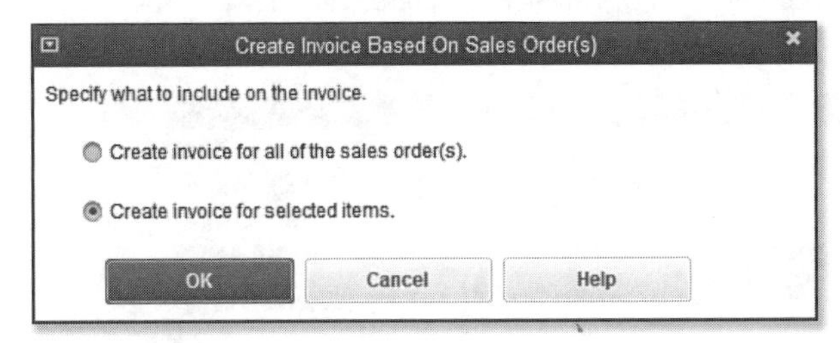

Figure 5.30
Invoicing a partial sales order.

14. Click OK. QuickBooks displays the Specify Invoice Quantities for Items on Sales Order(s) dialog box, as displayed in Figure 5.31.

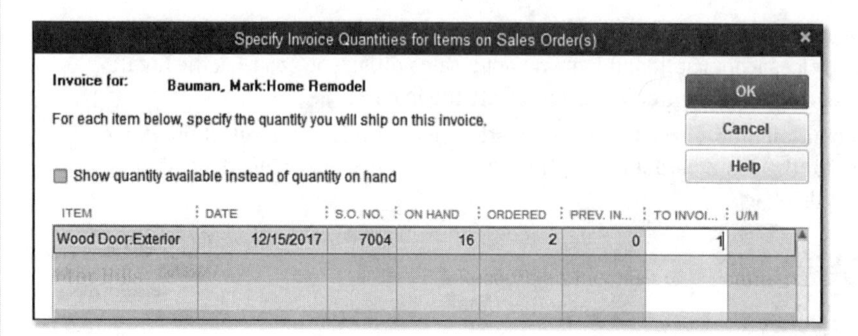

Figure 5.31
Use this dialog box to specify the quantity of the sales order items you want to invoice.

15. (Optional) Select the Show Quantity Available Instead of Quantity on Hand checkbox. How quantity available and quantity on hand differ is determined by your settings in Inventory preferences (see Figure 5.1).
16. In the To Invoice column, type **1** (to record a partial invoice).
17. Click OK to return to the Create Invoices transaction.
18. Review the details on the invoice (see Figure 5.32) for the Wood Door:Exterior with details for Ordered, Prev. Invoiced, and Invoiced. If you selected multiple sales orders to invoice, you will also have a column for Backordered on the invoice template. Click Save on the top of the transaction.

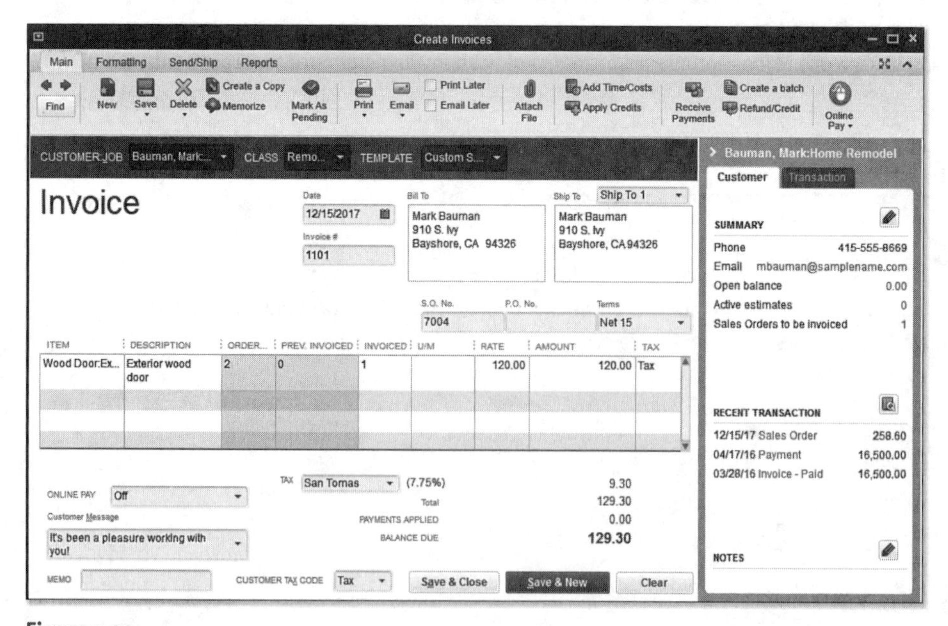

Figure 5.32
The invoice now shows separate columns for Ordered, Prev. Invoiced, and Invoiced.

19. In the Recent Transactions section on the Customer tab (on the right side of the dialog box), click the link to the Sales Order you created in this exercise. (Optional) From a displayed transaction, select Transaction History from the Report tab on the ribbon toolbar.
20. The Create Sales Order transaction displays with the details of the original sales order. Notice the new columns of detail for Backordered and Invoiced on the sales order.

If your customer orders inventory before you have made or ordered the part, using the sales order transaction can keep track of these committed sales. Reviewing your open sales orders is important for effective inventory management.

Handling Customer Inventory Returns

When your company offers an inventory product for sale, you will probably also have the occasion when a customer returns the product. In QuickBooks you use a credit memo transaction to record the return.

Processing your customer returns correctly can be very important to your company's financials. A returned inventory product from your customer affects the following:

- Inventory physical count and inventory valuation on the balance sheet
- Accounts receivable balance on the balance sheet
- Income and cost of goods sold
- Sales tax payable (if applicable to your business and product)

To help you be more efficient with this process, you can create a credit memo directly from the original customer invoice. This functionality can help QuickBooks users be more accurate when recording customer returns.

Practice Recording Customer Returns

Using the same sample data discussed in Chapter 1, you can continue with the practice exercise you completed earlier when creating an invoice:

1. On the Home page, click the Customers icon to open the Customer Center (see Figure 5.33).

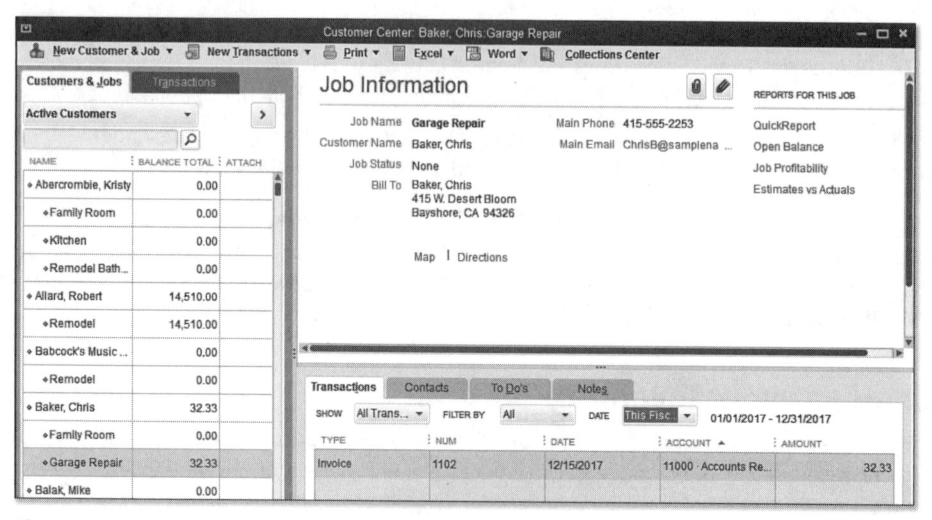

Figure 5.33

The Customer Center can be the easiest place to find specific transactions.

2. On the Customers & Jobs tab, select the **Garage Repair** job for the customer Baker, Chris.
3. On the right side of the Customer Center, you should see the invoice you created in the earlier practice. Double-click it to open the selected invoice.
4. With the customer invoice open, from the Main tab of the ribbon toolbar (at the top of the Create Invoices transaction) select **Refund/Credit.**
5. The Create Credit Memos/Refunds transaction displays with the same item(s) that was included on the original invoice. Review and leave the default information. In your own data you might need to add or remove items from the Create Credit Memos/Refunds transaction.
6. Click Save & Close. The Available Credit dialog box displays, as shown in Figure 5.34, with these options:
   - Retain as an available credit
   - Give a refund
   - Apply to an invoice

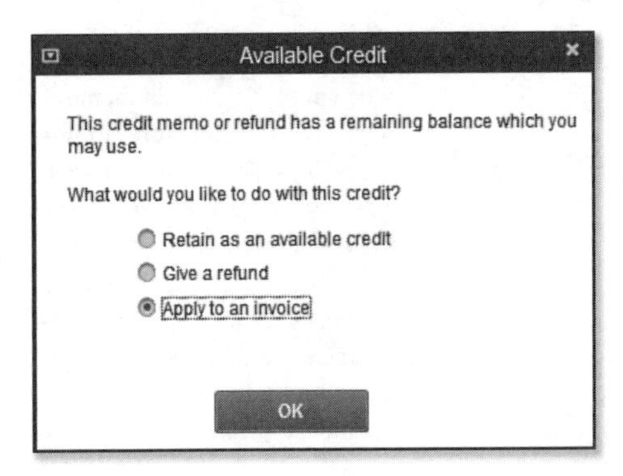

Figure 5.34
Multiple options are available for handling customer credits.

7. For this practice, select the **Apply to an Invoice** option button. Click OK. The Apply Credit to Invoices dialog box displays (see Figure 5.35). In this practice example, QuickBooks has automatically selected the invoice you created in the previous practice.

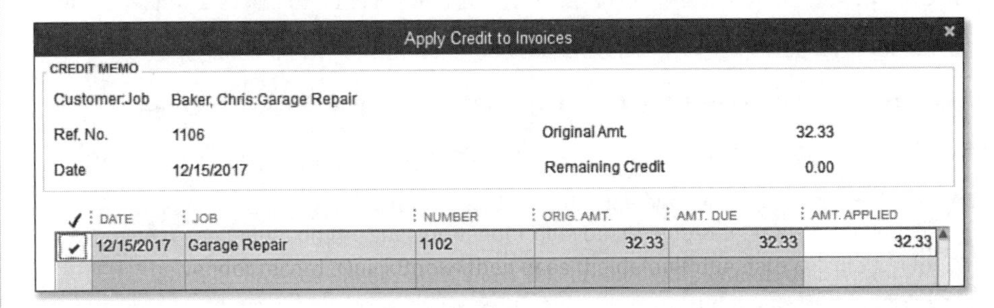

Figure 5.35
You can manually override the amount or invoice selection in how a customer credit is applied.

8. Click Done. You are returned to the Create Invoices transaction that, for this exercise, shows a Balance Due of 0.00 in the lower-right corner with a Paid stamp on the invoice.
9. Click Save & Close.

Creating credit memos for product returns is much easier when you're working in QuickBooks 2013.

tip

When applying a credit memo to an invoice in the Apply Credit to Invoices dialog box, shown in Figure 5.35, QuickBooks matches the credit to an invoice of the same amount if there are multiple invoices with open balances by default. If no match is found, QuickBooks applies the credit to the oldest invoice(s) first.

Handling Vendor Inventory Returns

Perhaps after receiving the returned inventory from your customer, you find the product was not manufactured to your specifications and needs to be returned to the vendor.

Handling these types of returns properly is important and can affect these financial balances:

- Inventory physical count and inventory valuation on the balance sheet
- Accounts payable balance on the balance sheet

To create a vendor return in your QuickBooks data file, follow these steps:

1. On the Home page, click the Enter Bills icon.
2. Select the **Credit** radial button at the top of the Enter Bills transaction to create a vendor credit.
3. From the Vendor drop-down list, select the vendor you are returning the product(s) to.
4. For the Date field, enter the date you want to record for the return of the inventory.
5. In the Ref. No. field, enter your vendor's credit authorization number if supplied.
6. Click the Items tab and select the inventory item(s) being returned.
7. In the Qty field, type the number of units being returned.
8. Review the default Cost and adjust as needed to agree with your vendor's credit authorization.
9. Click Save & Close (or Save & New) to enter another vendor credit.

Entering a credit memo is the first step in the process. When you know to which bill your vendor applied the credit, you can assign the credit to the same bill. For more detail, see "Applying Vendor Credits," p. 248.

MANAGING INVENTORY

Inventory management requires adherence to a strict process to monitor the items being purchased into stock and later being sold. Failure to have these processes in place can wreak havoc on the company's financials by misstating the value of the inventory or the associated costs for that inventory. This chapter provides details on how to use QuickBooks to properly manage your inventory activities.

Adjusting Inventory

For companies that track inventory, I find inventory balances receive less attention compared to the watchful eye over the company's receivables and payables. You review your accounts receivable because you have customers that need to pay you. You keep up with your accounts payable because you have vendors that won't supply you without first getting paid. Why exactly is it, that inventory "reconciling" is often at the bottom of the list, yet it can have the greatest impact on your company's financials?

Experience has taught me that most companies are unaware that QuickBooks can be used to properly review and audit their inventory balances. This section outlines specific reports and methods you can use in QuickBooks to make sure inventory balances are correct.

If you are using inventory in your QuickBooks data, it is recommended that you view your financial reports in accrual basis. Most companies that have inventory also report their tax financials on an accrual basis. However, a more important reason is that on accrual basis reporting, QuickBooks matches the cost with the related sale. The exception is when using non-inventory items. These items, when purchased, do not increase an Inventory Asset account. Instead, they are recorded directly to the Cost of Goods Sold account or the Expense account that was assigned when the item was created.

Any company that manages inventory needs to minimize inventory errors. Business owners list any of the following reasons for having to correct their accounting inventory errors:

- Errors in the physical counted results
- Damaged goods
- Theft of inventory
- Open vendor item receipts or bills that are not due to the vendor
- Incorrect valuation given to the inventory at the startup of a data file

This section discusses the methods for correcting inventory errors you might find in your QuickBooks data.

Performing a Physical Inventory Count

If you have a good inventory count commitment from your team and manage the resulting information from the QuickBooks Inventory Valuation Summary report, you should see little to no data entry errors; instead, you probably will be adjusting inventory only for damage or theft.

All too often, here is where I find a complacent attitude about inventory management. I agree that performing a physical inventory count is a time-consuming task. However, if effort is put to this task, your overall financials will be more accurate.

To make recording the count easier, on the menu bar, click Reports, Inventory, Physical Inventory Worksheet. The report cannot be modified or filtered for specific dates (see Figure 6.1), so you should run the report at the moment you start to do your physical count and be certain that all your inventory-related transactions have been entered. If you want to keep a record of the original worksheet, you can export it to Excel or email it as a PDF attachment.

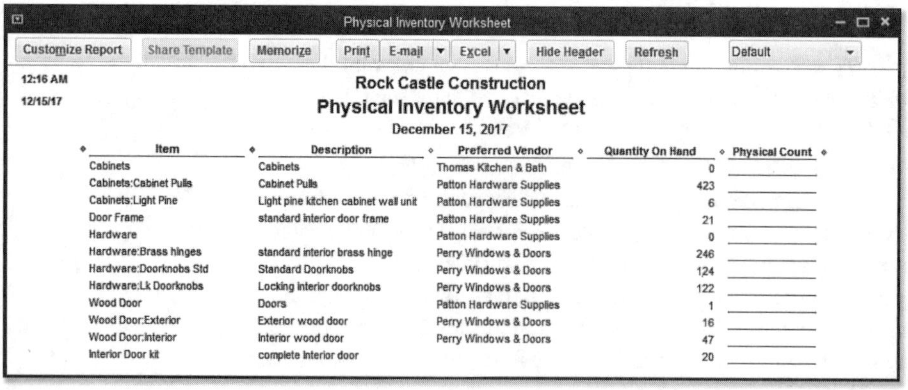

Physical Inventory Worksheet

Customize Report | Share Template | Memorize | Print | E-mail | Excel | Hide Header | Refresh | Default

12:16 AM
12/15/17

Rock Castle Construction
Physical Inventory Worksheet
December 15, 2017

Item	Description	Preferred Vendor	Quantity On Hand	Physical Count
Cabinets	Cabinets	Thomas Kitchen & Bath	0	
Cabinets:Cabinet Pulls	Cabinet Pulls	Patton Hardware Supplies	423	
Cabinets:Light Pine	Light pine kitchen cabinet wall unit	Patton Hardware Supplies	6	
Door Frame	standard interior door frame	Patton Hardware Supplies	21	
Hardware		Patton Hardware Supplies	0	
Hardware:Brass hinges	standard interior brass hinge	Perry Windows & Doors	246	
Hardware:Doorknobs Std	Standard Doorknobs	Perry Windows & Doors	124	
Hardware:Lk Doorknobs	Locking interior doorknobs	Perry Windows & Doors	122	
Wood Door	Doors	Patton Hardware Supplies	1	
Wood Door:Exterior	Exterior wood door	Perry Windows & Doors	16	
Wood Door:Interior	Interior wood door	Perry Windows & Doors	47	
Interior Door kit	complete Interior door		20	

Figure 6.1
Create a physical inventory worksheet to record the actual inventory counts.

After completing a physical inventory count, you can confidently create an inventory adjustment so the accounting records match your actual physical inventory.

Quantity Adjustments

If you discovered quantity differences between your accounting records and your physical inventory account, you should record an inventory quantity adjustment to correct your accounting records.

To create an inventory quantity adjustment in your data, follow these steps:

1. On the Home page, in the Company section, click the Inventory Activities icon and then from the menu select **Adjust Quantity/ Value on Hand**. The Adjust Quantity/Value on Hand dialog box opens, as shown in Figure 6.2.

caution

Before creating the accounting adjustment, make sure you have created an account in the chart of accounts to hold the value of the inventory adjustment. The account type can be either a Cost of Goods Sold type or an Expense type. Business owners should consult their accountant when making this decision.

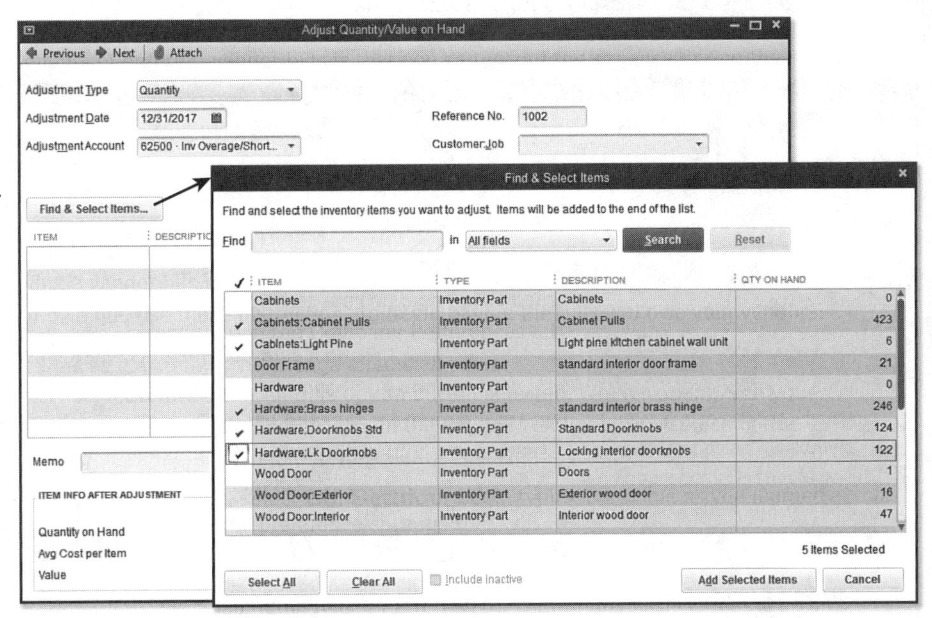

Figure 6.2
Use the Find & Select Items button to efficiently select multiple inventory items to adjust quantity.

2. From the Adjustment Type drop-down list, select **Quantity**.
3. Select an **Adjustment Date** and type an optional **Ref. No**.
4. Select the appropriate **Adjustment Account**. This account is usually a Cost of Goods Sold account or an Expense account named Inventory Overage/Shortage.
5. (Optional) Assign a Customer:Job and/or specify a Class if it's being tracked. However, Job Profitability reports will not include inventory adjustment transactions; only the Profit & Loss by Job reports include the value of these adjustments.

caution

Inventory (and Value) adjustments assigned to a customer or job will be included in the Profit & Loss by Job reports, but will not be included in any of the other reports offered when you select **Reports, Jobs, Time & Mileage** from the menu bar.

6. To efficiently select multiple items at once, click the Find & Select Items button. Click with your cursor to place a checkmark (see Figure 6.2) next to those items you want to create a quantity adjustment for.

7. Click Add Selected Items to return to the Adjust Quantity/Value on Hand dialog box.

8. In the New Quantity column, enter your count from the completed physical inventory or, optionally, enter the change in the Qty Difference column.

9. Click Save & Close when finished.

QuickBooks provides details on the Item Info After Adjustment and summarizes the Total Value of the Adjustment and the Number of Item Adjustments.

The accounting effect of the transaction in Figure 6.3 is to adjust the quantity on hand for each of the items shown, the net effect of this adjustment is to increase the Inventory value on the books with the offset to the assigned Adjustment Account.

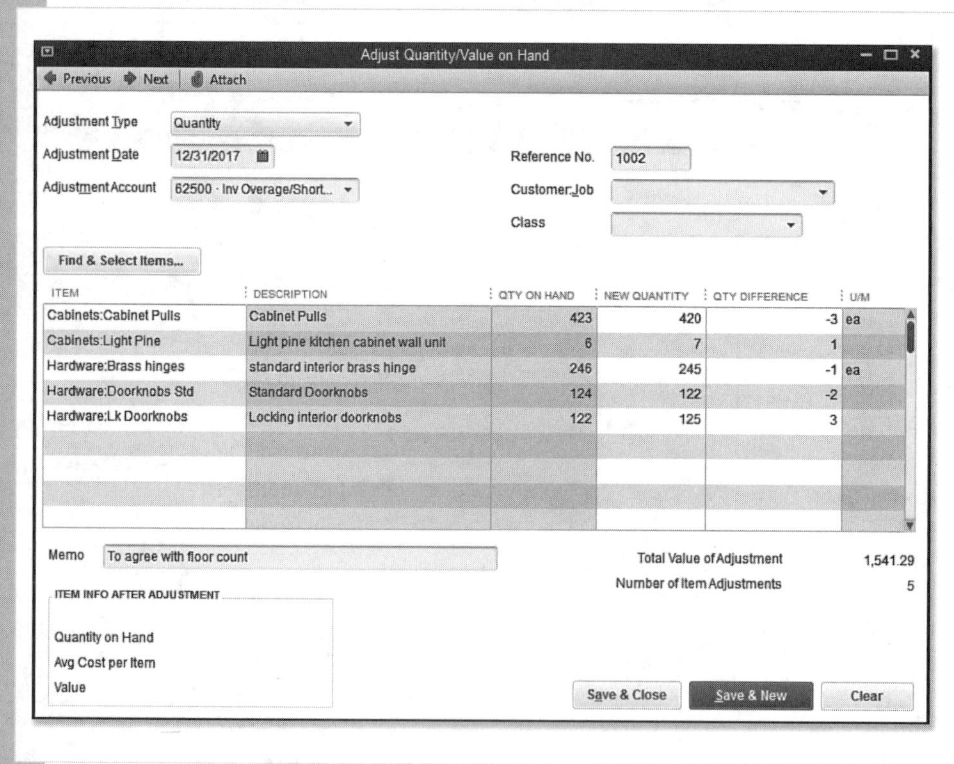

Figure 6.3 Use Inventory Adjustments to properly adjust your inventory in your accounting to match your physical counts.

Value Adjustments

Timing is important when doing a valuation adjustment. Value adjustments, if appropriate, should be carefully considered for their impact on the company's resulting financials.

Value adjustments differ from quantity adjustments because they do not adjust the quantity but instead adjust the recorded value of the specific items in inventory.

> **caution**
>
> Generally, value adjustments are not done as often as quantity adjustments. The purpose of this book is not to explore or offer tax advice, but certain guidelines determine when an inventory valuation adjustment is appropriate. Ask your tax accountant to provide them for you.

To create a value-only inventory adjustment in your data, follow these steps:

1. From the menu bar, select **Vendors**, **Inventory Activities**, **Adjust Quantity/Value on Hand**. A dialog box with the same name opens, as shown in Figure 6.4.

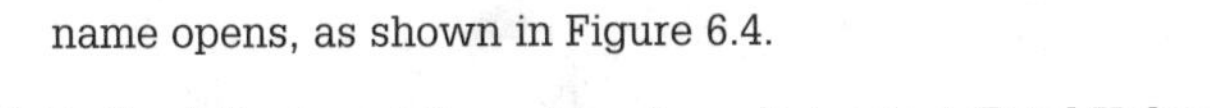

2. In the Adjustment Type drop-down list, select **Total Value**.
3. Select an **Adjustment Date** and type an optional **Ref. No**.
4. Select the appropriate **Adjustment Account**. This account is usually an Expense account named Inventory Overage/Shortage.

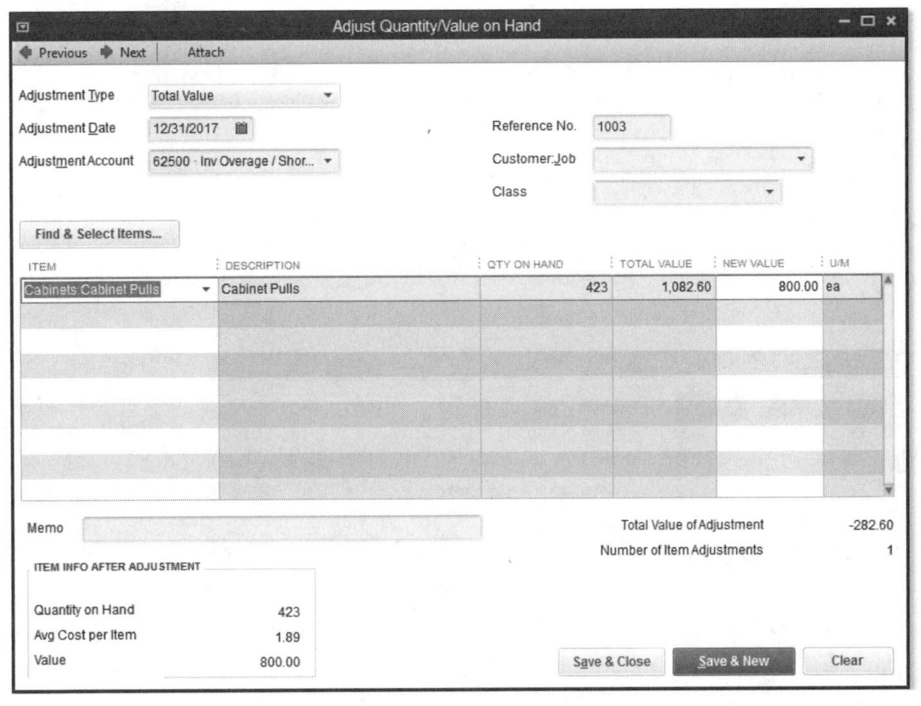

Figure 6.4
Value adjustments are not used often; be sure to ask your accountant first if it is appropriate for your needs.

5. (Optional) Assign a Customer:Job and/or specify a Class if it's being tracked. However, Job Profitability reports will not include inventory adjustment transactions; only the Profit & Loss by Job reports include the value of these adjustments.
6. To efficiently select multiple items at once, click the Find & Select Items button. Click with your cursor to place a checkmark next to those items you want to create a quantity adjustment for.

7. Click Add Selected Items. You are returned to the Adjust Quantity/Value on Hand dialog box.
8. In the New Value column, enter the new calculated total value you want assigned to the item.
9. Click Save & Close when finished.

The accounting result of this inventory value adjustment, as shown in Figure 6.4, is no net change to inventory quantities, a decrease (credit) to your Inventory Asset account, and an increase (debit) to your Inventory Adjustments account (either a Cost of Goods Sold type or Expense type). A new average cost will be computed based on the (Original Asset Value + or - the Value Difference)/Quantity on Hand as recorded on the inventory value adjustment. You can view the newly assigned average cost in the lower left of the inventory adjustment.

caution

Did you know how important the date is when assigning the inventory adjustment? If you backdate your inventory adjustment, QuickBooks will recalculate your Cost of Goods Sold from that date forward, using the new average cost as of the date of the sales transaction. Care should be taken not to date an inventory adjustment in a prior year where tax returns have already been filed.

tip

There are two preferences to control dating transactions. To access them, log in as the Admin or External Accountant user in single-user mode. From the menu bar, select **Company, Set Closing Date** to open the Preferences dialog box with Accounting—Company Preferences tab selected (see Figure 6.5).

Setting Date Warnings enables a user to be warned when a transaction is either dated so many days in the past or in the future. Set Date/Password is another option to "close" QuickBooks to prevent adding, modifying, voiding, or deleting transactions prior to a selected closing date. Setting a closing date and related features is discussed more fully in Chapter 16, "Sharing QuickBooks Data with Your Accountant."

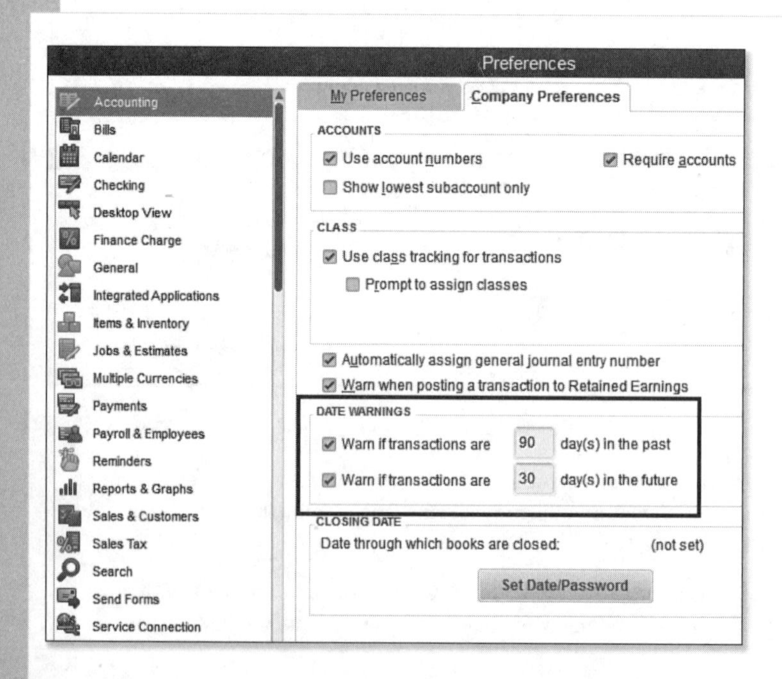

Figure 6.5
Choices for controlling past- or future-dated transactions.

The new average cost will be recorded when a sales transaction uses this item *on or after* the date of the inventory adjustment.

Inventory Reporting

You have learned just how easy it is to buy, sell, and adjust your inventory. Good inventory management also includes frequent reviews of inventory-specific reports available in QuickBooks.

In this section, you are introduced to some of the more common reports. However, take the time to review all available reports, because you may have a specific reporting need in addition to those mentioned here.

Inventory Center

To access the Inventory Center, from the Home page, in the Company section, click the Inventory Activities icon, and from the menu bar, select the Inventory Center (see Figure 6.6). Similar to the other "centers" in QuickBooks, the Inventory Center offers one convenient location to manage your inventory reporting and activities, including the following:

- **New Inventory Item**—Quick access to creating an individual new inventory item or to the Add/ Edit Multiple List Entries functionality.
- **New Transactions**—Quick access to all inventory-related transactions.
- **Print**—Quick access to printing the item list, information, or transaction list.
- **Excel**—Exporting to Excel the item or transaction list. Importing item list from Excel. In addition, you can add new items from Excel via import or by pasting.

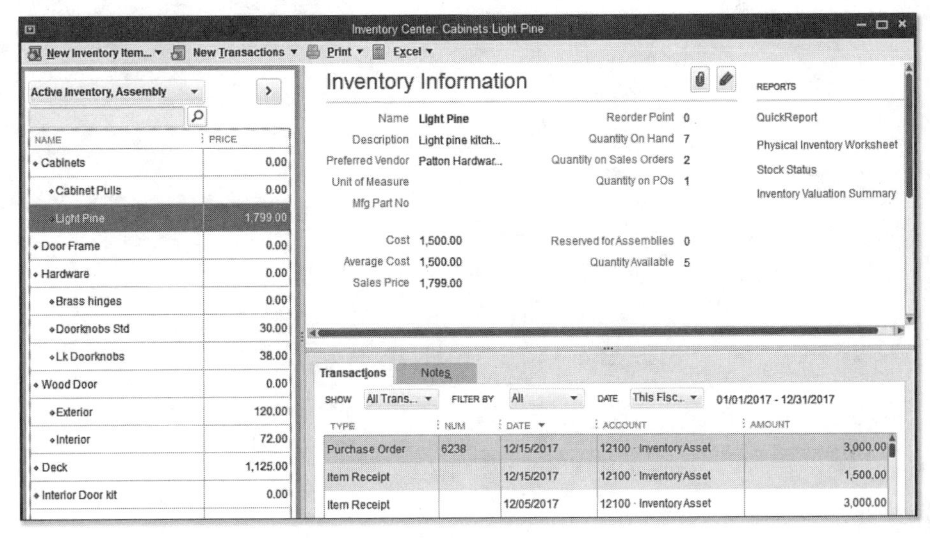

Figure 6.6 Access the most common transactions and reports for your inventory from the Inventory Center.

Click with your cursor on a specific inventory item, and to the right you will see displayed detailed information, transactions, and links to some of the more common reports for managing your inventory.

You can also attach a document to the inventory item using the free QuickBooks attachments feature. Click the Docs icon on your icon bar to open the Doc Center.

Click the Edit button after you select an item in the Inventory Center to make changes, as discussed previously in Chapter 5 in the section titled "Adding or Editing Inventory Items," p. 154.

tip

The Inventory Center allows you to filter your inventory list by ready-made filters or custom filters of your choosing. One important selection is the capability to filter for inventory with a negative inventory quantity on hand (QOH <= zero). You will learn later in this chapter how important it is to accurate financials not to let your inventory get negative (where you have the appearance of having sold more than you have on hand).

Report Center

Use the Report Center to find the right report for your inventory management needs. See Figure 6.7.

To open the Report Center, follow these steps:

1. From the menu bar, select **Reports**, **Report Center**.
2. On the Report Center's Standard tab, select **Sales**.
3. Scroll down to the bottom of the page to find the Open Sales Orders—by Customer or by Item report, which is useful when managing inventory. This report is available only if you are using QuickBooks Premier, Accountant, or Enterprise Solutions.

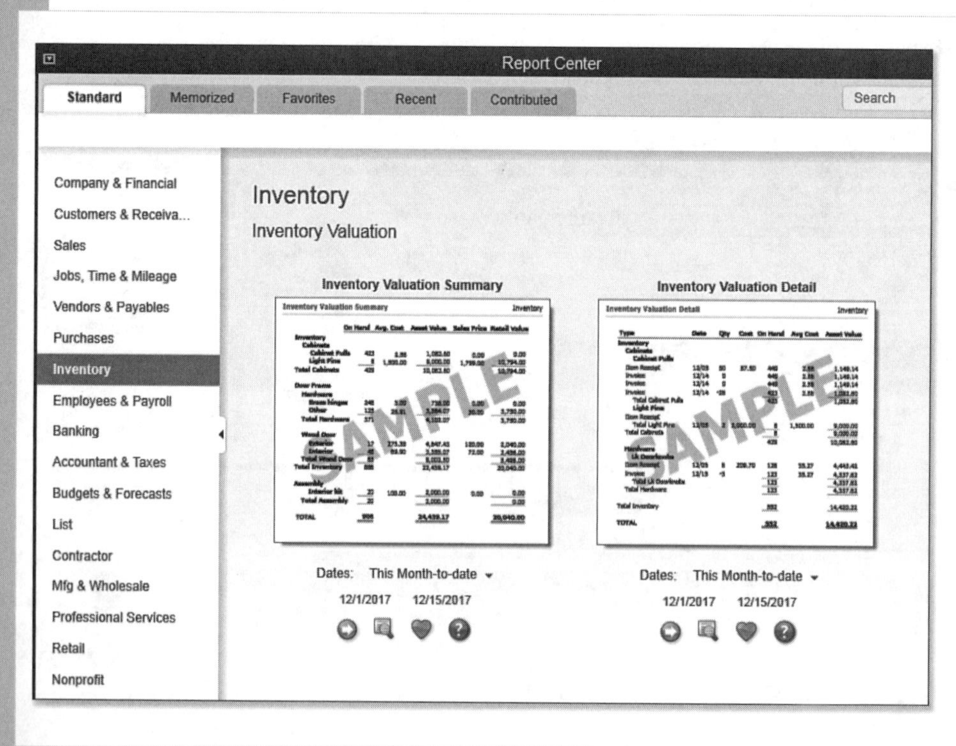

Figure 6.7 The Report Center makes finding the right inventory management report simple.

4. On the Standard tab of the Report Center, select **Purchases** to view these inventory management reports:

   - **Purchases by Vendor**—Summary or Detail
   - **Purchases by Item**—Summary or Detail
   - **Open Purchase Orders**—Summary or Detail

The Report Center provides a thumbnail image of how the data would look in the report.

5. Below each report you can change the dates, click Run to prepare the report with your data, click Info to preview a larger thumbnail image, click Fave to include the report in the Favorites section of the Reports Center, or click Help for more details.
6. On the Standard tab of the Report Center, select Inventory to view these inventory management reports:

   - **Inventory Valuation**—Summary or Detail. More details in the next section.
   - **Inventory Stock Status**—By Item or Vendor.
   - **Physical Inventory Worksheet**—Used for recording your physical inventory count totals.
   - **Pending Builds**—For QuickBooks Premier, Accountant, or Enterprise users who have assembly inventory items.

7. If you are using the Manufacturing & Wholesale edition of QuickBooks Premier or Enterprise Solutions, click Mfg & Wholesale on the Standard tab of the Report Center for additional useful inventory management reports.

Inventory Valuation and Your Financials

Another equally important task in inventory management is to compare your Inventory Valuation Summary report to your Inventory Asset balance on your accrual basis Balance Sheet.

tip

Because you might want to compare the following reference reports side-by-side; from the menu bar, select **Window, Tile Vertically.** Both reports are displayed side-by-side (shown later in this book in Figure 10.40) if these reports are the only currently open windows.

Comparing Inventory Reports to Financials

Using the sample company referred to in Chapter 1, "Getting Started with QuickBooks," use this exercise to practice how to compare the Inventory Valuation Summary report to the Balance Sheet Inventory Asset balance.

1. From the menu bar, select **Reports, Report Center**. From the Standard tab, select **Inventory**. Find the Inventory Valuation Summary report and click the Run icon to display the report. Accept the default report date; as shown in Figure 6.8, "As of December 15, 2017" data is displayed.
2. Take note of the Asset Value column Total. In Figure 6.8, the total Asset Value is $30,683.38. Your sample data total might differ.
3. From the Report Center, on the Standard tab, select **Company & Financial**, and then, under the Balance Sheet Standard report (scroll down to find this report), click Run. Accept the default report date.
4. Compare the balance in the Inventory Asset account (in the Other Current Assets group) to the total from step 2.

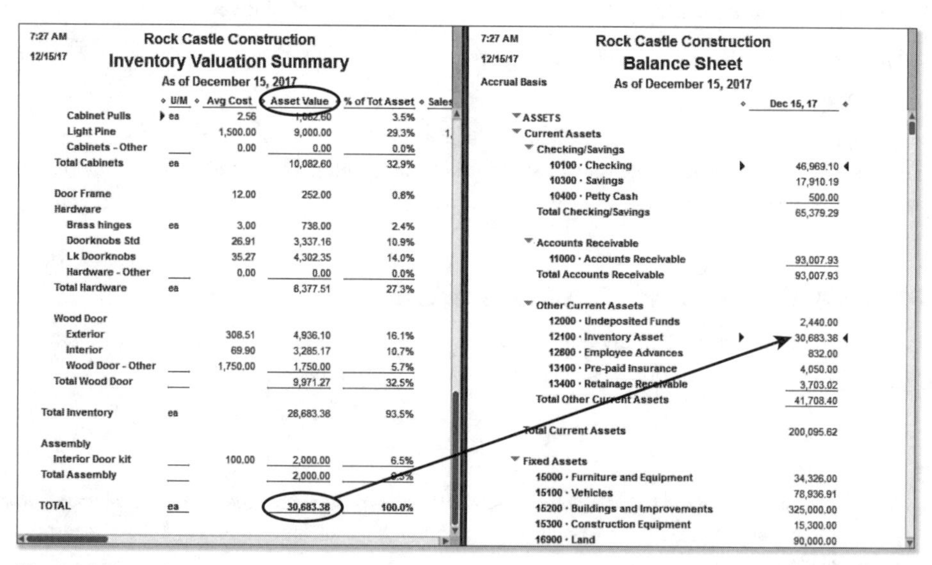
7:27 AM 12/15/17 Rock Castle Construction
Inventory Valuation Summary
As of December 15, 2017

	U/M	Avg Cost	Asset Value	% of Tot Asset	Sales
Cabinet Pulls	ea	2.56	1,082.60	3.5%	
Light Pine		1,500.00	9,000.00	29.3%	1,
Cabinets - Other		0.00	0.00	0.0%	
Total Cabinets	ea		10,082.60	32.9%	
Door Frame		12.00	252.00	0.8%	
Hardware					
Brass hinges	ea	3.00	738.00	2.4%	
Doorknobs Std		26.91	3,337.16	10.9%	
Lk Doorknobs		35.27	4,302.35	14.0%	
Hardware - Other		0.00	0.00	0.0%	
Total Hardware	ea		8,377.51	27.3%	
Wood Door					
Exterior		308.51	4,936.10	16.1%	
Interior		69.90	3,285.17	10.7%	
Wood Door - Other		1,750.00	1,750.00	5.7%	
Total Wood Door			9,971.27	32.5%	
Total Inventory	ea		28,683.38	93.5%	
Assembly					
Interior Door kit		100.00	2,000.00	6.5%	
Total Assembly			2,000.00	6.5%	
TOTAL	ea		30,683.38	100.0%	

7:27 AM 12/15/17 Rock Castle Construction
Balance Sheet
Accrual Basis As of December 15, 2017

	Dec 15, 17
ASSETS	
Current Assets	
Checking/Savings	
10100 · Checking	46,969.10
10300 · Savings	17,910.19
10400 · Petty Cash	500.00
Total Checking/Savings	65,379.29
Accounts Receivable	
11000 · Accounts Receivable	93,007.93
Total Accounts Receivable	93,007.93
Other Current Assets	
12000 · Undeposited Funds	2,440.00
12100 · Inventory Asset	30,683.38
12800 · Employee Advances	832.00
13100 · Pre-paid Insurance	4,050.00
13400 · Retainage Receivable	3,703.02
Total Other Current Assets	41,708.40
Total Current Assets	200,095.62
Fixed Assets	
15000 · Furniture and Equipment	34,326.00
15100 · Vehicles	78,936.91
15200 · Buildings and Improvements	325,000.00
15300 · Construction Equipment	15,300.00
16900 · Land	90,000.00

Figure 6.8
Compare your total Asset Value with your Balance Sheet Inventory Asset balance.

caution

When working with inventory adjustments, never use a General Journal transaction. The specific reason is because a General Journal transaction does not use Items, and any adjustments using this transaction affect only the Balance Sheet balance, not the Inventory Valuation Summary report.

It is also not appropriate to use the Inventory Asset account on the Expense tab of a Vendor Bill, Credit, or Write Checks transaction. To properly use these transactions, use the Items tab with the appropriate inventory item.

If you need to adjust inventory, from the menu bar, select **Vendors, Inventory Activities, Adjust Quantity/Value on Hand,** as discussed earlier in this chapter.

What if the two balances do not match? The most common cause for the two reports not to match is entering a transaction that affects the Inventory Asset account but does not affect inventory items. The Inventory Summary report shows only the results of transactions that use inventory items. For example, if a General Journal has been used to adjust the Balance Sheet balance, those transactions will not affect the Inventory Valuation Summary report.

To find General Journal entries in your own data that might be causing the out-of-balance amount, follow these steps:

1. On your Balance Sheet report, double-click the Inventory Asset balance. QuickBooks creates the Transactions by Account report.

2. From the Dates drop-down list, scroll to the top and select **All**.

3. To locate the General Journal entries, from the Sort By drop-down list (in the upper-right corner of the report), select **Type**, as shown in Figure 6.9. QuickBooks now organizes the data by transaction type. Look for General Journal type transactions.

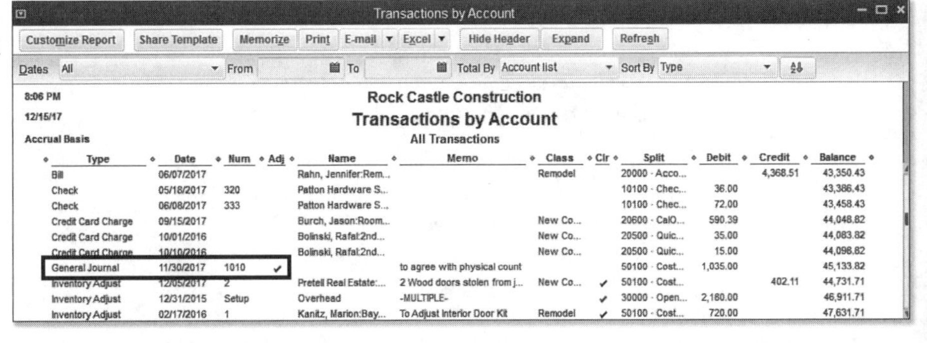

8:06 PM
12/15/17
Accrual Basis

Rock Castle Construction
Transactions by Account
All Transactions

Type	Date	Num	Adj	Name	Memo	Class	Clr	Split	Debit	Credit	Balance
Bill	06/07/2017			Rahn, Jennifer:Rem...		Remodel		20000 · Acco...		4,368.51	43,350.43
Check	05/18/2017	320		Patton Hardware S...				10100 · Chec...	36.00		43,386.43
Check	06/08/2017	333		Patton Hardware S...				10100 · Chec...	72.00		43,458.43
Credit Card Charge	09/15/2017			Burch, Jason:Room...		New Co...		20600 · CalO...	590.39		44,048.82
Credit Card Charge	10/01/2016			Bolinski, Rafal:2nd...		New Co...		20500 · Quic...	35.00		44,083.82
Credit Card Charge	10/10/2016			Bolinski, Rafal:2nd...		New Co...		20500 · Quic...	15.00		44,098.82
General Journal	11/30/2017	1010	✓		to agree with physical count			50100 · Cost...	1,035.00		45,133.82
Inventory Adjust	12/05/2017	2		Pretell Real Estate:...	2 Wood doors stolen from j...	New Co...	✓	50100 · Cost...		402.11	44,731.71
Inventory Adjust	12/31/2015	Setup		Overhead	-MULTIPLE-		✓	30000 · Open...	2,180.00		46,911.71
Inventory Adjust	02/17/2016	1		Kanitz, Marion:Bay...	To Adjust Interior Door Kit	Remodel	✓	50100 · Cost...	720.00		47,631.71

Figure 6.9
General Journal transactions should not be used to adjust inventory balances.

You should not modify, delete, or void these transactions, especially if they were used in accounting periods that have already had tax returns prepared using the current financial information. Continue with the remaining methods in the sections that follow, before making any corrections.

Reviewing the Recorded Average Cost Valuation

As mentioned earlier in this chapter, QuickBooks uses the Average Cost method for valuing inventory. From the menu bar, select **Reports**, **Inventory**, **Inventory Valuation Summary**. Figure 6.10 shows the value assigned to your costs when you sell an inventory item.

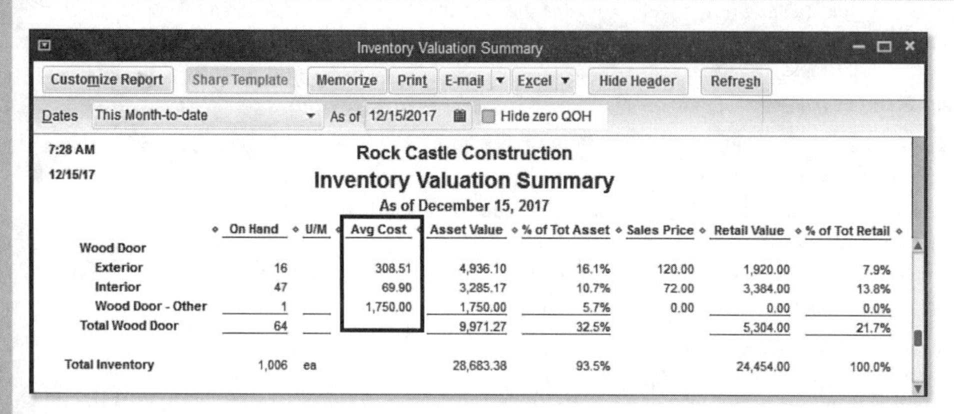

	On Hand	U/M	Avg Cost	Asset Value	% of Tot Asset	Sales Price	Retail Value	% of Tot Retail
Wood Door								
Exterior	16		308.51	4,936.10	16.1%	120.00	1,920.00	7.9%
Interior	47		69.90	3,285.17	10.7%	72.00	3,384.00	13.8%
Wood Door - Other	1		1,750.00	1,750.00	5.7%	0.00	0.00	0.0%
Total Wood Door	64			9,971.27	32.5%		5,304.00	21.7%
Total Inventory	1,006	ea		28,683.38	93.5%		24,454.00	100.0%

Figure 6.10 Use the Inventory Valuation Summary report to verify the cost being recorded when an inventory item is sold.

If you are using QuickBooks Enterprise Solutions 13.0 with FIFO (First In First Out) costing enabled, it might not be necessary to review this section because FIFO costing replaces Average Costing. Beginning with QuickBooks Enterprise 13.0, you can review your inventory valuation reports using either the Average Cost method discussed here or First In First Out (FIFO) method. FIFO costing in QuickBooks Enterprise is a preference setting that can be enabled or disabled.

To learn more about this and other inventory features, see Appendix C, "QuickBooks Enterprise Solutions Inventory Features," p. 747.

For example, assume you are selling an inventory product with the following transactions, as shown in Table 6.1.

note

New for QuickBooks 2013, the Inventory Valuation Summary report and others now include the option to hide (exclude from the report) inventory items when the quantity on hand is zero.

This was a feature added in the R3 maintenance release of all Windows versions of QuickBooks 2013. You can learn more about maintenance releases in Chapter 17, "Managing Your QuickBooks Database."

Table 6.1 Calculating Average Cost

Date	Quantity Purchased	Actual Cost per Unit	Total Cost	QuickBooks Calculated Average Cost per Unit
12/15/17	100	$10.00	$1,000.00	$10.00
12/25/17	50	$8.50	$425.00	$9.50
TOTAL	150		$1,425.00	(1425/150)

Sales transactions that are dated on or between 12/15/17 and 12/24/17 for this item will record cost of goods sold at $10.00 per unit (assuming no other replenishing purchases are made during that time).

The average cost of the 150 units will be $9.50 each if none are sold prior to 12/26. However, any quantity sold from the first order will change the weighting of the unit cost, so a different average cost will result when the second order is received.

To further explain how important it is to enter your inventory transactions daily (and not retroactively), Table 6.2 shows the resulting Average Cost calculations used when selling more inventory than is available.

In Table 6.2, the cost recorded on 12/20/17 is $10.00 per unit. However, after the replenishing transaction the actual average cost is $7.00 per unit. The costs in 2017 will be overstated by $3.00 per unit, with the correcting entry to Cost of Goods Sold reported in the 2018 financials.

These details assume that no other transactions were recorded for this item except as noted in the following transactions.

Table 6.2 Calculating Average Cost When Selling Negative Inventory

Date	Quantity Purchased	Quantity Sold	Actual Cost per Unit	Inventory Value	Calculated Average Cost
12/15/17	100		$10.00	$1,000.00	$10.00
12/20/17		–125	$10.00	($1,250.00)	$10.00
01/05/18	50		$8.50	$425.00	$9.50
Remaining Quantity	25		Remaining Value	$175.00	$7.00

Average costing is a perfect fit for a business that sells a product that does not fluctuate significantly in cost from one period to the next. However, this is not always the case, so it becomes important that you verify the relative accuracy of the average cost QuickBooks has recorded on the Inventory Valuation Summary report.

In Figure 6.10, shown previously, the average cost for the Interior Wood Door is listed as $69.90. Compare this amount to a recent vendor bill. If the amount is significantly different, you should review the purchase details for the item.

From the menu bar, select **Reports, Inventory, Inventory Valuation Detail**. You might want to customize and filter the report for specific dates or items. More about working with reports is available in Chapter 14, "Reporting in QuickBooks."

In Figure 6.11, the Inventory Valuation Detail is shown for the Interior Wood Door. Reviewing the individual lines in the Average Cost column can help you determine whether an issue exists with the average cost. If the average cost changes dramatically, you might want to review the specific bill or check details recorded when the product was purchased.

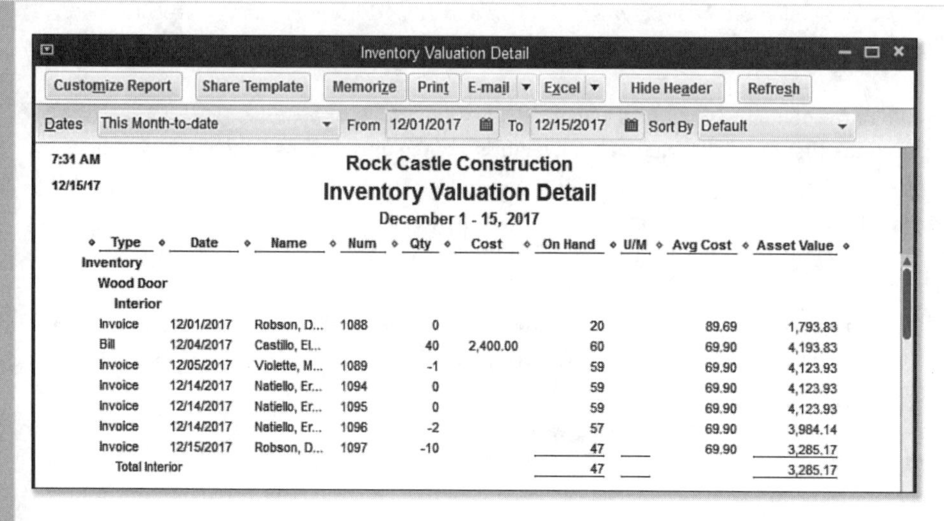

Inventory Valuation Detail

Rock Castle Construction
Inventory Valuation Detail
December 1 - 15, 2017

7:31 AM
12/15/17

Type	Date	Name	Num	Qty	Cost	On Hand	U/M	Avg Cost	Asset Value
Inventory									
Wood Door									
Interior									
Invoice	12/01/2017	Robson, D...	1088	0		20		89.69	1,793.83
Bill	12/04/2017	Castillo, El...		40	2,400.00	60		69.90	4,193.83
Invoice	12/05/2017	Violette, M...	1089	-1		59		69.90	4,123.93
Invoice	12/14/2017	Natiello, Er...	1094	0		59		69.90	4,123.93
Invoice	12/14/2017	Natiello, Er...	1095	0		59		69.90	4,123.93
Invoice	12/14/2017	Natiello, Er...	1096	-2		57		69.90	3,984.14
Invoice	12/15/2017	Robson, D...	1097	-10		47		69.90	3,285.17
Total Interior						47			3,285.17

Figure 6.11 Create an Inventory Valuation Detail report to research changes in average cost.

Reviewing and correcting the average cost of items is as equally important as adjusting the quantity on hand.

Reviewing Aged Item Receipts

The "Purchasing, Receiving, and Entering the Vendor Bill" section of Chapter 5, "Setting Up Inventory," provided details about the inventory process; one of the methods of receiving inventory is without the vendor's bill.

The effect of receiving inventory without a bill is to increase your inventory asset (debit) and increase your accounts payable (credit). The unique feature of this method is that QuickBooks creates an item receipt transaction that *will not* show in the Pay Bills window. QuickBooks recognizes that because you did not receive the bill, it is not likely you should be paying it without the final bill details.

Often, goods will arrive at your business without a bill. A couple of reasons exist for a vendor to ship the goods to your place of business without a final bill:

- Shipping charges need to be added to the bill. Often, the vendor will not know the shipping charges when the goods are initially shipped.
- Vendors do not want to disclose the value of the inventory so that those who handle the inventory during shipping will not know the value of the goods being shipped.

What you might not know is that item receipts age just like an outstanding accounts payable bill. To see whether you have open, outdated item receipts, go to the Vendor Center and click the Transactions tab (see Figure 6.12). Select the Item Receipts transaction type. Filter by All Dates and click the Date column to sort the transactions by date.

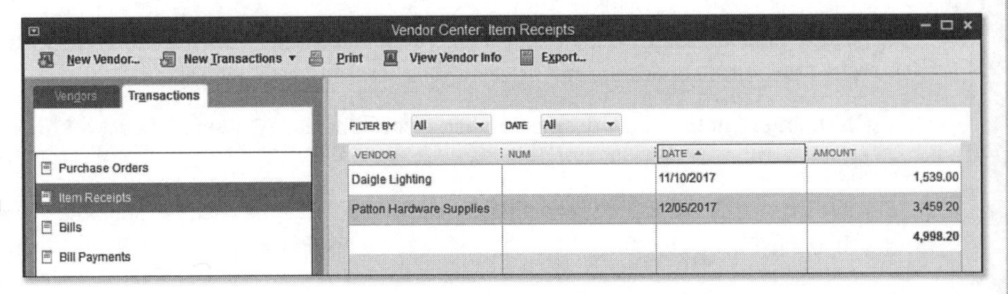

Figure 6.12 Use the Transactions tab of the Vendor Center to see all open item receipts.

If you find you have aged item receipts and you know you have paid the vendor, use the following steps to assign the check to the open item receipt. If you have paid your vendors with a credit card, you might also want to use these same instructions, substituting the credit card transaction for the check transaction:

1. From the Vendor Center, select the **Item Receipts** transaction type on the Transactions tab.
2. Unapplied item receipts display on the right. Click the header for the Date column to sort by date. You are looking for any old, outdated item receipts.
3. If you find an aged item receipt that you know was paid to the vendor, double-click the item receipt to open the Create Item Receipts transaction.
4. Select the Bill Received checkbox (top right), as shown in Figure 6.13. The Item Receipt now becomes a vendor bill transaction type.

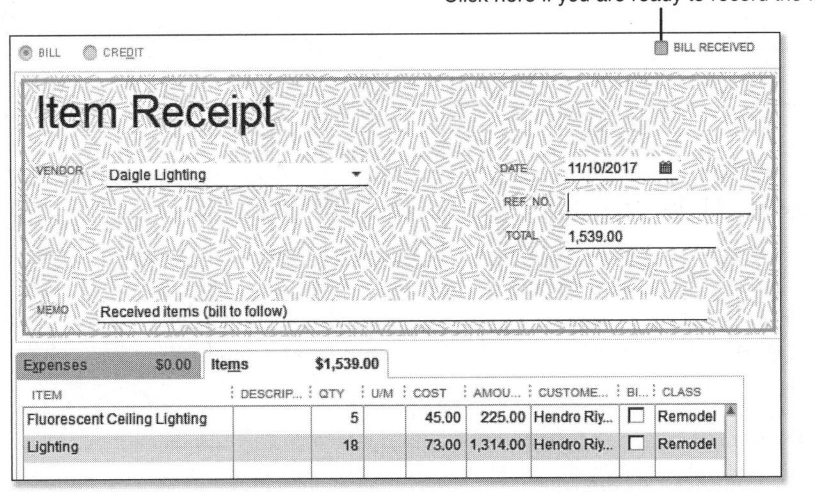

Figure 6.13 Item receipts do not show up in bills to be paid.

5. Click Save & Close.

6. Locate the check that was written to the vendor. From the Vendors tab on the Vendor Center, select the same vendor the item receipt was created for.

7. On the right, in the Show drop-down list, select **Checks**. (Optional) Select a **Filter By** and **Date range**.

8. After locating the check in the Vendor Center, double-click the check to open the Write Checks transaction. Modify the Account on the Expenses tab to be Accounts Payable, as shown in Figure 6.14.

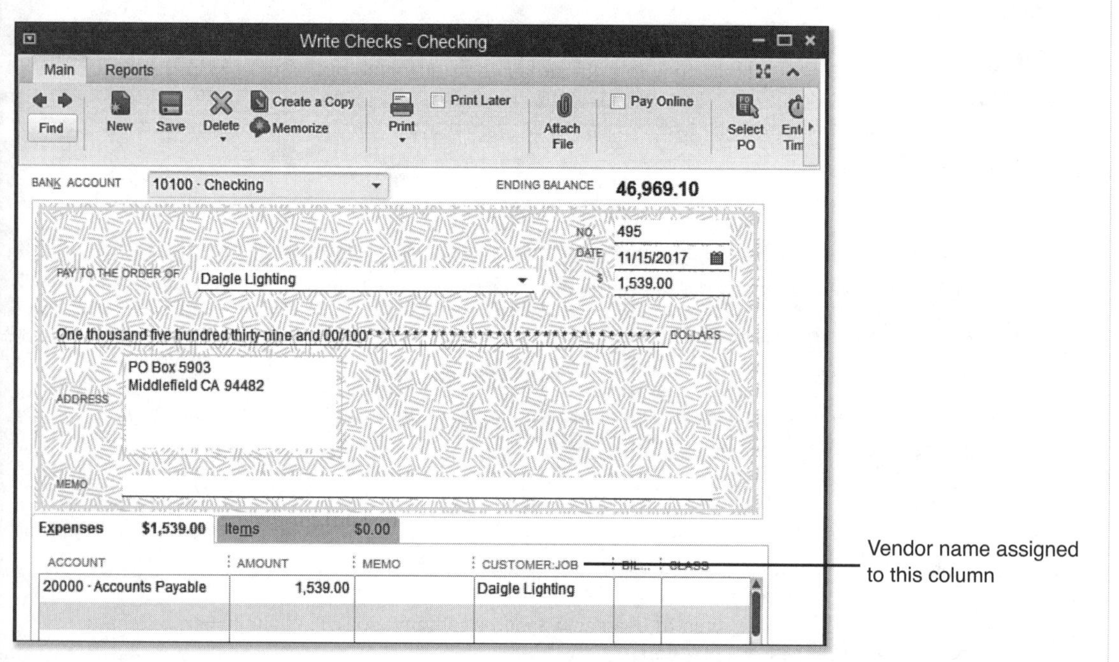

Figure 6.14
Changing the Expenses account to Accounts Payable and adding the vendor name on the same line creates a vendor credit from the check.

9. Assign the Vendor name in the Customer:Job column. The effect of this updated transaction is to decrease (debit) Accounts Payable and decrease (credit) Cash.

10. Click Save & Close.

11. From the Home page, click the Pay Bills icon. The Pay Bills dialog box opens.

12. In the Filter By drop-down list, select the vendor you are correcting the records for.

13. Place a checkmark next to the bill (see Figure 6.15).

14. Click the Set Credits button to assign the modified check transaction from step 7 to the open vendor bill (see Figure 6.16).

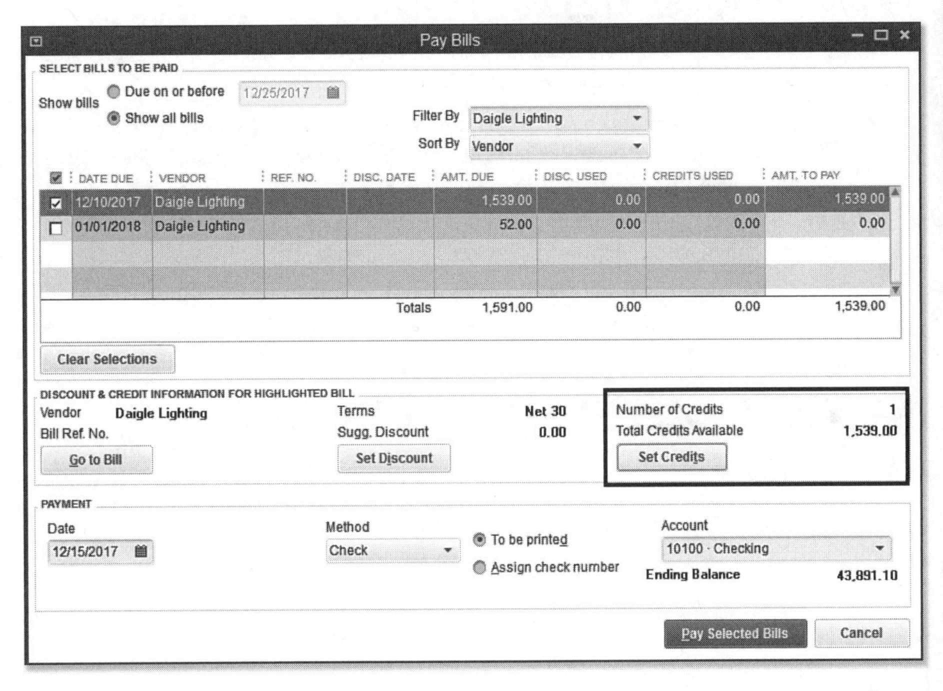

Figure 6.15
After the bill is selected, the Set Credits option is available.

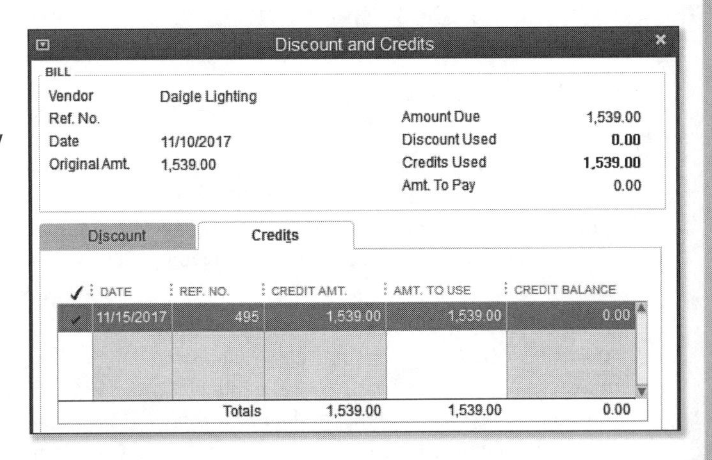

Figure 6.16
QuickBooks automatically matches a credit with a bill of the same amount, or you can select the credit and modify the amount assigned.

15. Click Done to return to the Pay Bills dialog box. If your credit is the same amount as the open vendor bill, the Amt. To Pay column will be zero.

16. Click Pay Selected Bills. Click Done to close the Payment Summary dialog box.

Reviewing Aged Accounts Payable

At the same time you review your open item receipts, you should also review your accounts payable open invoices that have aged more than 60 days.

To review your accounts payable, from the menu bar, select **Reports**, **Vendors & Payables**, **Unpaid Bills Detail**. If you see open vendor bills you are sure you have paid, it might be because you used the Write Checks transaction to pay your vendor bills instead of using the Pay Bills dialog box (accessed from the Vendors, Pay Bills menu). Having both an open vendor bill and check paying for the same purchase overstates your costs or inventory.

QuickBooks tries to prevent you from doing this by providing a warning message when you try to write a check to a vendor for whom you have an unpaid bill, as shown in Figure 6.17.

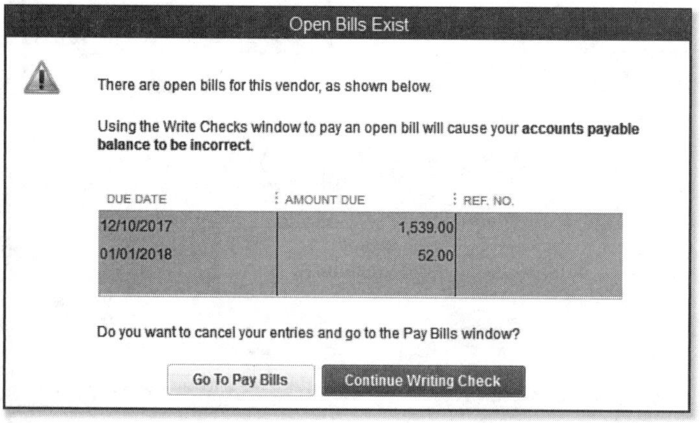

Open Bills Exist

There are open bills for this vendor, as shown below.

Using the Write Checks window to pay an open bill will cause your **accounts payable balance to be incorrect.**

DUE DATE	AMOUNT DUE	REF. NO.
12/10/2017	1,539.00	
01/01/2018	52.00	

Do you want to cancel your entries and go to the Pay Bills window?

Go To Pay Bills | Continue Writing Check

Figure 6.17
A warning displays if you try to use the Write Checks transaction to pay a vendor instead of creating a bill payment from the Pay Bills dialog box.

If you did use the Write Checks transaction to issue a vendor payment for a currently open vendor bill, you can resolve this problem by reassigning it. To do so, follow the steps outlined in the "Reviewing Aged Item Receipts," section p. 208, starting with step 7.

After completing the steps, you will have successfully assigned the check you wrote using the Write Checks transaction to the open vendor bill that should have been paid by a check in the Pay Bills dialog box. This correction has now removed the expected overstatement in your costs and removed the bill from being included in your open accounts payable balances.

tip

If you are an accounting professional using the QuickBooks Accountant 2013 software, you will find a tool in Client Data Review that will simplify the steps outlined in this section. For more information, refer to Appendix A, "Client Data Review."

How QuickBooks Handles Negative Inventory

QuickBooks allows you to oversell your inventory, which results in negative inventory. What it means is that you can include an inventory item on a customer invoice or sales receipt before you have recorded the item receipt or bill for the purchase of the item into your inventory.

When a transaction will cause you to have a negative inventory balance, you will see the warning message shown in Figure 6.18. The warning does not prevent the user from completing the intended transaction, but should be viewed as a need to research why QuickBooks does not have enough stock of that item in inventory to record the sale.

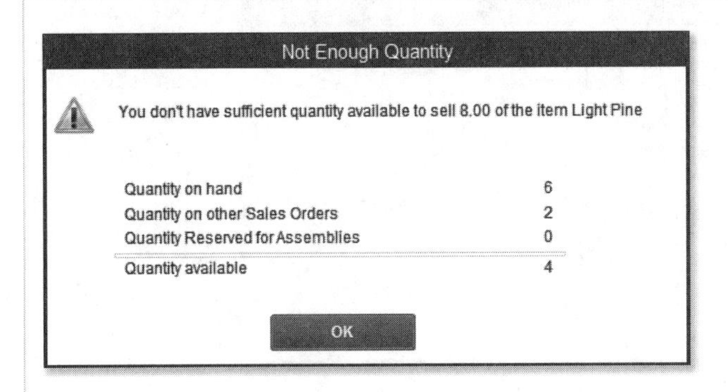

Figure 6.18
Not enough quantity warning indicates an issue with not following the recommended processes for proper inventory management.

Although ignoring the warning message can be useful for getting the invoice to the customer, it can create issues with your company's financials. The following sections detail how QuickBooks handles the costing of the inventory behind the scenes when you sell negative inventory and provides information on how to avoid or minimize the negative effect it can have on your company's financials.

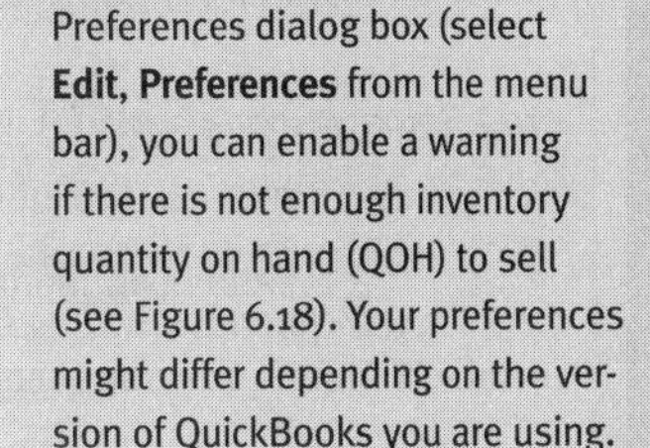

caution
On the Items & Inventory—Company Preferences tab of the Preferences dialog box (select **Edit, Preferences** from the menu bar), you can enable a warning if there is not enough inventory quantity on hand (QOH) to sell (see Figure 6.18). Your preferences might differ depending on the version of QuickBooks you are using.

When Inventory Has an Average Cost from Prior Purchase Transactions

If you review the Inventory Valuation Detail report (select **Reports**, **Inventory**, **Inventory Valuation Detail** from the menu bar) for the item(s) that have negative values, and there are previously recorded average cost amounts, QuickBooks assigns the most recent average cost dated on or before the invoice date that created negative inventory. When the purchase transaction is later recorded, QuickBooks adjusts the Cost of Goods Sold or Expense type for any difference.

tip

With the QuickBooks Accountant 2013 Client Data Review feature, you can troubleshoot inventory discrepancies between the Inventory Valuation Summary report and the inventory balance on the Balance Sheet. This troubleshooting tool automatically compares the balances from the two reports and details which transactions are potentially causing the discrepancy.

Additionally, this new tool identifies which items are negative (you have sold more than you have purchased) for the specific accounting period being reviewed, as well as for a current date. You learn in this chapter just how important it is to not let your inventory go negative.

For more information, see Appendix A, "Client Data Review," p. 659.

Figure 6.19 shows the average cost on the date of the invoice was $150.00 per unit. QuickBooks records a decrease (credit) to inventory for the two units of $300.00 total and an increase (debit) to Cost of Goods Sold of $300.00 for the two units sold.

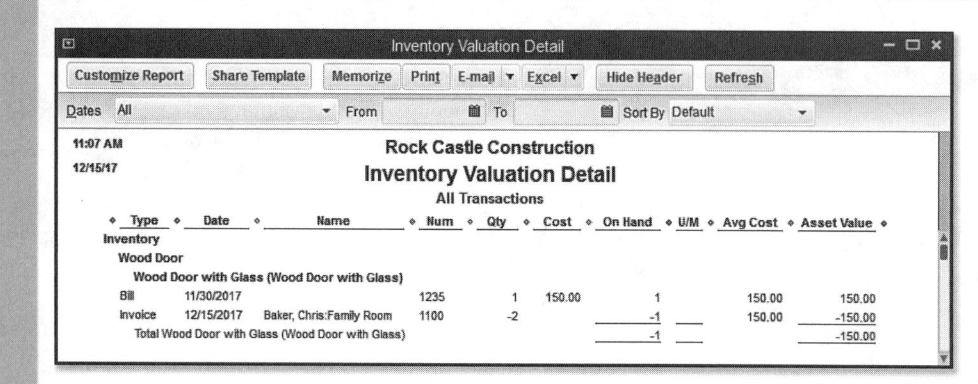

Inventory Valuation Detail

Customize Report | Share Template | Memorize | Print | E-mail | Excel | Hide Header | Refresh

Dates: All | From | To | Sort By: Default

11:07 AM
12/15/17

Rock Castle Construction
Inventory Valuation Detail
All Transactions

Type	Date	Name	Num	Qty	Cost	On Hand	U/M	Avg Cost	Asset Value
Inventory									
Wood Door									
Wood Door with Glass (Wood Door with Glass)									
Bill	11/30/2017		1235	1	150.00	1		150.00	150.00
Invoice	12/15/2017	Baker, Chris:Family Room	1100	-2		-1		150.00	-150.00
Total Wood Door with Glass (Wood Door with Glass)						-1			-150.00

Figure 6.19
QuickBooks records the Cost of Goods Sold for negative inventory items at the last known average cost.

To show how important the date of the replenishing purchase transaction is, review the details provided next. This example assumes that no additional transactions were recorded except as noted:

The new inventory asset value is calculated as

($150.00) Inventory asset value as of 12/15/17 due to selling "negative inventory"

$600.00 12/25/17 replenishing purchase of 3 units @ $200.00/unit

$450.00 Asset value before the QuickBooks automatic adjustment to COGS

Actual inventory value is 2 remaining units at $200 each, or $400.00 total.

$(50.00) On the date of the replenishing vendor bill, QuickBooks automatically creates a transaction that decreases (credits) Inventory asset and increases (debits) COGS. See Figure 6.20. This increase in cost adjustment is not associated with the recorded per unit cost to the customer.

$400.00 Resulting Inventory Asset value on 12/25/17 as shown in Figure 6.21.

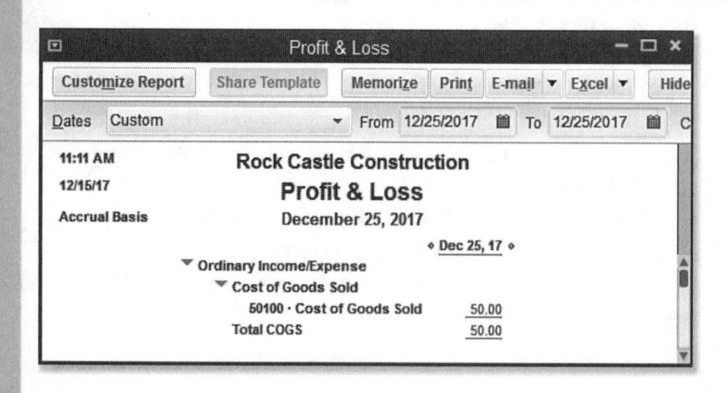

Profit & Loss

Customize Report | Share Template | Memorize | Print | E-mail | Excel | Hide

Dates: Custom | From 12/25/2017 | To 12/25/2017

11:11 AM
12/15/17
Accrual Basis

Rock Castle Construction
Profit & Loss
December 25, 2017

	Dec 25, 17
Ordinary Income/Expense	
Cost of Goods Sold	
50100 · Cost of Goods Sold	50.00
Total COGS	50.00

Figure 6.20
When you replenish inventory shortages, QuickBooks automatically makes an adjustment to agree with what the average cost would have been.

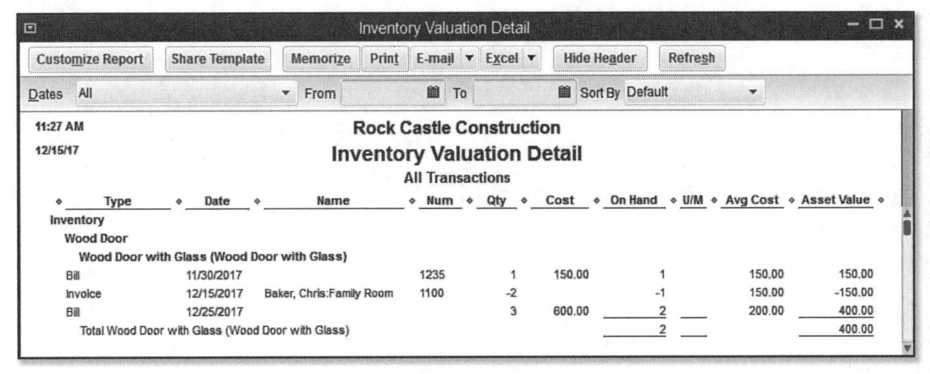

Figure 6.21 The Inventory Valuation Detail report shows the actual inventory value after recording the replenishment transaction.

When QuickBooks creates an adjustment to reflect what the average cost should have been, the adjustment is *not* assigned to customers or jobs—making it even more important to not sell negative inventory.

tip

It is important to note that QuickBooks does not retroactively record the additional cost back to the customer's negative inventory invoice date. In fact, QuickBooks records the adjustment as of the date of the purchase transaction and will not associate the adjustment with the original customer at all, thereby overstating gross profit on a Profit & Loss by Job report.

The date of the replenishing purchase transaction becomes increasingly important to manage when you let inventory go negative in your data at the end of a fiscal or tax year.

When Inventory Does Not Have a Prior Average Cost

There might be times when you stock a new item and you add it to a customer invoice before recording any purchase activity for the item. If this happens, you should at least record a default cost on the New or Edit Item dialog box.

When an Inventory Item Has a Default Cost

If you have assigned an inventory item that you have not yet purchased (that is, the quantity on hand is zero) to a customer invoice, and if you *did* define a default cost when you first created the inventory item, QuickBooks uses this default cost as the suggested per-unit cost when the invoice is recorded.

Suppose you stock a new inventory item for a Wood Door with Glass. When creating the item, you record a default cost of $150.00, as shown in Figure 6.22.

Before any purchase is recorded for this item, it is sold on a customer invoice. When you create an invoice where there is not enough quantity on hand, QuickBooks provides a warning, as previously shown in Figure 6.18.

QuickBooks has to estimate the cost of the item and, in this example, uses the cost assigned to the item in the New or Edit Item dialog box, as shown in Figure 6.23. When you save this invoice, QuickBooks creates the following entry as shown in Table 6.3.

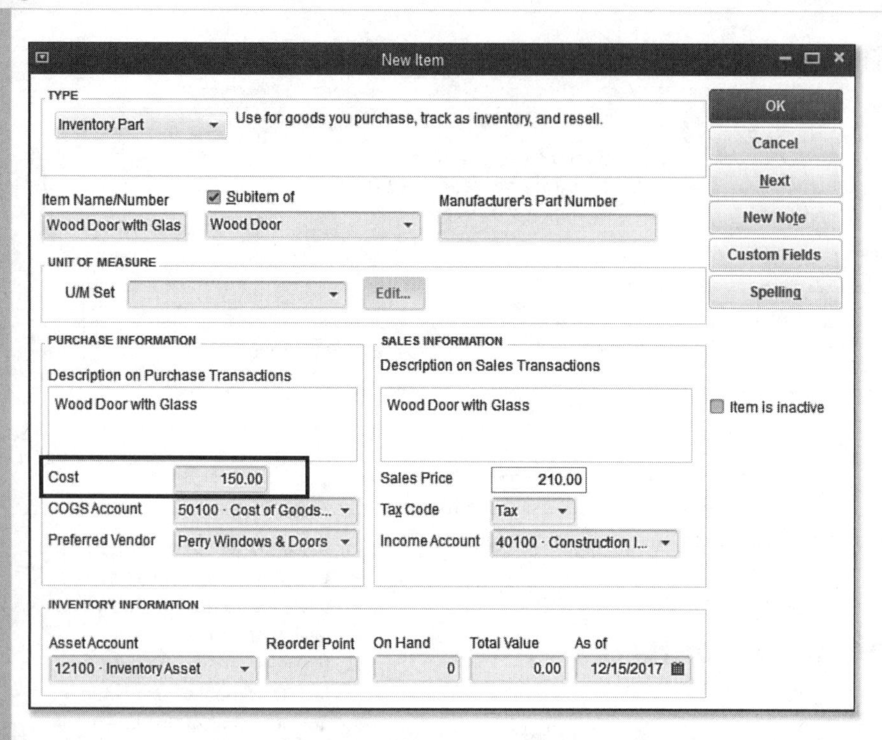

Figure 6.22
New stock item created in QuickBooks with a default cost of $150.00.

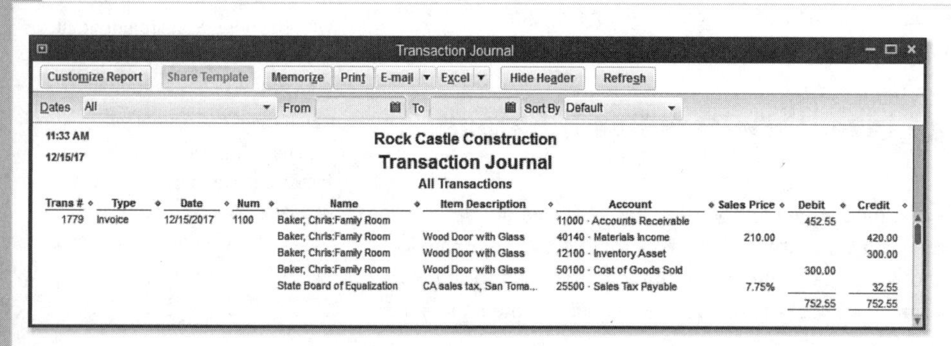

Rock Castle Construction
Transaction Journal
All Transactions

Trans #	Type	Date	Num	Name	Item Description	Account	Sales Price	Debit	Credit
1779	Invoice	12/15/2017	1100	Baker, Chris:Family Room		11000 · Accounts Receivable		452.55	
				Baker, Chris:Family Room	Wood Door with Glass	40140 · Materials Income	210.00		420.00
				Baker, Chris:Family Room	Wood Door with Glass	12100 · Inventory Asset			300.00
				Baker, Chris:Family Room	Wood Door with Glass	50100 · Cost of Goods Sold		300.00	
				State Board of Equalization	CA sales tax, San Toma...	25500 · Sales Tax Payable	7.75%		32.55
								752.55	752.55

Figure 6.23
QuickBooks uses the cost assigned in the New or Edit Item dialog box when you sell inventory that you have not recorded any purchase transactions for.

Table 6.3 Accounting When Inventory Is Sold

Debit	Credit
Accounts Receivable (increase)	Income (increase)
Cost of Goods Sold (increase)	Inventory Asset (decrease)
	Sales Tax Payable (if applicable) (increase)

To view this report, on the Reports tab of any transaction window, choose Transaction Journal.

This impact to your financials (positive or negative) can be significant if the actual purchase price is different from the recorded default cost on the New or Edit Item dialog box.

When an Inventory Item Does Not Have a Default Cost

If you have assigned an inventory item you have not yet purchased (that is, the quantity on hand is zero) to a customer invoice, and if you *did not* define a default cost when you first created the inventory item, QuickBooks will use -0- as the default cost per unit when the invoice is recorded, showing a 100% profit margin for your financials and for that customer!

Now, using the same previous example, only *not* recording a default cost when setting up the item, as shown in Figure 6.24, QuickBooks will not calculate any cost or inventory reduction with the sale of the inventory (see Figure 6.25).

Figure 6.24
Setting up an item without including a default cost is not recommended.

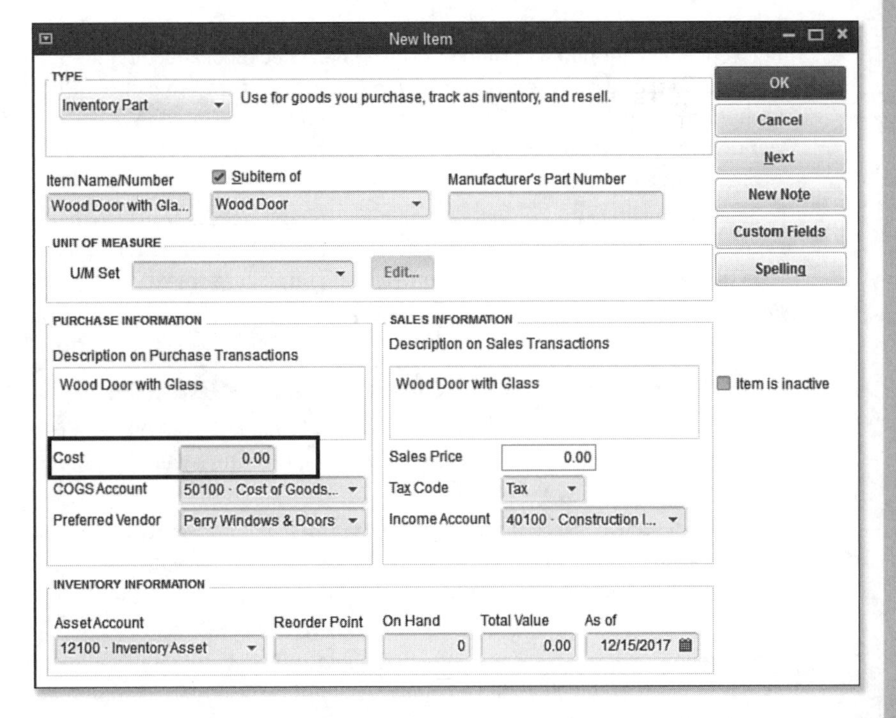

Imagine the impact this can have on your financials and the profitability reports you might review for your business or clients. Simply heeding the warnings QuickBooks provides about the errors of selling negative inventory can prevent this from happening in your data file.

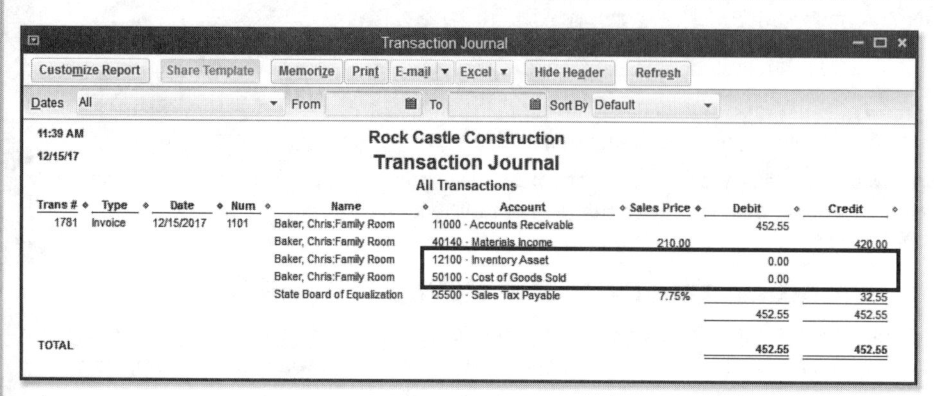

11:39 AM
12/15/17

Rock Castle Construction
Transaction Journal
All Transactions

Trans #	Type	Date	Num	Name	Account	Sales Price	Debit	Credit
1781	Invoice	12/15/2017	1101	Baker, Chris:Family Room	11000 · Accounts Receivable		452.55	
				Baker, Chris:Family Room	40140 · Materials Income	210.00		420.00
				Baker, Chris:Family Room	12100 · Inventory Asset		0.00	
				Baker, Chris:Family Room	50100 · Cost of Goods Sold		0.00	
				State Board of Equalization	25500 · Sales Tax Payable	7.75%		32.55
							452.55	452.55
TOTAL							452.55	452.56

Figure 6.25 No inventory decrease or cost is recorded when selling an item you do not have in inventory, have not purchased, and did not record a default cost for.

When a Replenishing Purchase Transaction Is Created

Exactly what happens when you do record purchase transactions? The date recorded on the purchase transaction has significant impact on how QuickBooks will handle this transaction.

For example, if a sale resulting in negative inventory was dated in October and the replenishing transaction (vendor bill) was dated in November, QuickBooks records the revenue in the month of October and the cost in the month of November. From month to month, it might not be noticeable, but if the transactions cross years, revenue would be overstated in one year and costs in another. Additionally, the revenue is tracked by the customer assigned to the invoice, but the cost *is not* tracked by the customer because the cost is recorded on the date of the purchase transactions.

To limit the negative impact, date your replenishing purchase transactions *before* the date of the customer invoice that caused the negative inventory. QuickBooks recalculates the average cost of all sales transactions dated after this "replenishing" purchase transaction. Of course, it is simply best not to sell negative inventory at all.

How to Avoid Incorrect Inventory Valuation

Troubleshooting negative inventory can be an eye opener to show how important proper inventory management is. To help with this task, rely on the Inventory Valuation Detail report, shown previously in Figure 6.21.

You can avoid these issues if the purchase transactions or inventory adjustments are dated on or prior to the date of the sales transactions creating the negative inventory. Backdating inventory adjustment transactions can be a powerful solution for correcting months of misstated financials, so use it where appropriate after discussing it with your accountant.

Solid inventory management processes and being current with your data entry will avoid recording negative inventory. If you do have negative inventory, be sure to correct it at the end of your tax year, or your tax return information will potentially be incorrect.

7

SETTING UP VENDORS

Your business is off to a great start using the QuickBooks software. Tracking the expenses your company makes is important to the overall financial health of the business. This chapter will help you work more effeciently with the vendors whom are the suppliers of your product or services.

Customizing Your Home Page for Vendor Activities

QuickBooks makes performing vendor activities easy with a customizable list of tasks on the Home page, as shown in Figure 7.1.

When working with accounts payable, you can customize the Home page to include or exclude the following:

- The option to enter bills and pay bills
- Inventory-related activities
- Time tracking, which is useful if you pay vendors for time worked on jobs

For more information on customizing the Home page, refer to Chapter 2, "Getting Around QuickBooks."

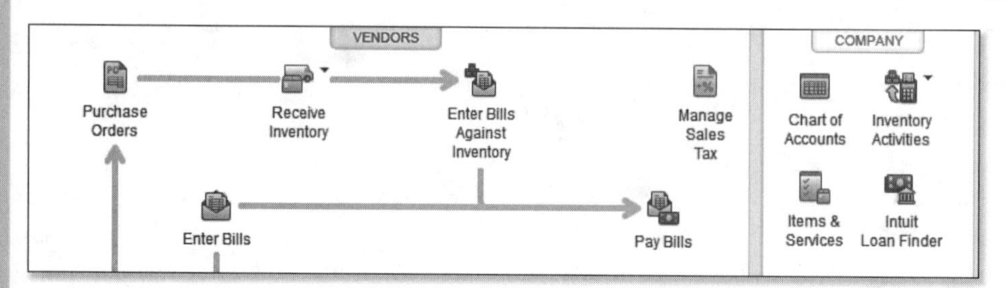

Figure 7.1 Access common vendor activities from the Home page.

Preferences That Affect Accounts Payable

note

To set company preferences, you need to open the file as the Admin or External Accountant user and switch to single-user mode (if you are using the data file in a multi-user environment). The Admin user is the default user created when you begin using QuickBooks for the first time.

Proper data entry security includes limiting which employees have access to logging in as the Admin and setting company preferences that are global for all users.

Did you know that you can streamline accounts payable processes by setting certain QuickBooks preferences? Setting preferences saves keystrokes, which in turn can save data entry time.

Not every preference that affects accounts payable impacts your financials; some preferences enable specific features. To view and modify these QuickBooks settings, from the menu bar choose Edit, Preferences.

Preferences in QuickBooks come in two forms:

- **My Preferences**—Settings that are unique to the current user logged in to the data file and are not shared by other users. Click the My Preferences tab to modify the user-specific settings for the logged-in user.
- **Company Preferences**—Settings that are common for all users. Click the Company Preferences tab to modify settings globally for all users.

The following sections detail the preferences that can affect your use of the accounts payable functionality.

Accounting

The Accounting preferences are important to review when you first create your data file. These choices affect much of how your accounting information is recorded in accounts payable.

Company Preferences

Company preferences are shared globally by all users. The Accounting preferences include the following:

- **Accounts**—These settings are important for proper management of recording revenue and expenses. The following are the preference settings for Accounts:

    - **Use Account Numbers**—Requires the use of an account number in addition to the account name when creating a new chart of account list item. Users can type either the number or the name when referencing an account on a transaction line.
    - **Show Lowest Subaccount Only**—You can choose this option if account numbering is enabled and all the chart of account items have a number assigned. This setting changes how the account name is displayed. If you see an "other" named account on your financials, users recorded a transaction to the parent account and not to one of the available subaccounts.
    - **Require Accounts**—Use this option to determine whether QuickBooks displays a prompt when you forget to choose an account on a transaction line. If you leave the option turned off, QuickBooks assigns the transaction to Uncategorized Income or Uncategorized Expense. When you create a new data file, this default is automatically selected.
- **Use Class Tracking for Transactions**—Classes in QuickBooks provide a secondary means of grouping transactions, such as into profit centers. The optional Prompt to Assign Classes allows you to enforce class tracking in a similar fashion to the aforementioned Require Accounts option. See the QuickBooks Help menu for more information on how you can use class tracking to track multiple profit centers on your income statement and for some balance sheet accounts.
- **Automatically Assign General Journal Entry Number**—This preference sequentially numbers any general journal entries automatically. Each entry number can be modified at the time of input.
- **Warn When Posting a Transaction to Retained Earnings**—You can post to the Retained Earnings account, but you should not because QuickBooks uses this account at year's end to close out the year's Profit or Loss totals. Note: When creating a new data file, this option is enabled by default.
- **Date Warnings**—When you create a new data file, the default date range set is from 90 days in the past to 30 days in the future, calculated from your current computer system date. Users can modify these date ranges, and QuickBooks warns users when they enter or modify a transaction outside these dates.
- **Closing Date**—The Admin or External Accountant user login can set a date in the past for which transactions cannot be modified, added, or deleted prior to that date without entering the closing date password (if one was created).

My Preferences

My Preferences are unique to the username currently logged in to the data file. These settings are not shared globally.

Autofill Memo In General Journal Entry—When this is selected, QuickBooks will repeat the memo detail from the first line in the journal entry to all other lines in the same journal entry.

Bills

Review your Bills preferences to determine whether the defaults set by QuickBooks are appropriate for your company's needs.

Company Preferences

Company preferences are shared globally by all users. The following are the Bills preferences:

- **Entering Bills, Bills Are Due**—Specifies the default number of days vendor bills should be paid within. You can change this global default on each vendor's record information or on a specific transaction. By default, QuickBooks sets the default due date for bills (where a vendor record does not have payment terms set) to 10 days. Users can modify this for their company's specific bill-paying terms.
- **Warn About Duplicate Bill Numbers from Same Vendor**—Ensures you don't pay the same bill twice. This safeguard is an important reason for entering bills first, rather than skipping a step and instead using the Write Checks transaction type when you pay vendors.
- **Paying Bills, Automatically Use Discounts and Credits**—Enables QuickBooks to apply the discount to your vendor bill payments automatically if your vendor is set up with discount terms and the bill is being paid within the discount date defined. Be sure to select your preferred chart of account for recording these credits.

My Preferences

There are no My Preferences in the Tax:1099 that you can set.

Calendar

Review and set preferences for the calendar view for upcoming transactions.

Company Preferences

There are no Company Preferences in the Calendar preferences that you can set.

My Preferences

My Preferences are unique to the username currently logged in to the data file. These settings are not shared globally. For Upcoming and Past Due Settings, you have these options:

- **Display**—Choose from Hide, Show, Show Only if Data Exists, or Remember Last.
- **Upcoming Events & Past Due Settings**—Set the default to show upcoming and past due data.

Checking

The Checking preferences improve the accuracy of your day-to-day data entry. Be sure to review them when setting up a new data file.

Company Preferences

Company preferences are shared globally by all users. The following are the Checking preferences:

- **Print Account Names on Voucher**—The default is to print the General Ledger account when using the Write Checks transaction. General Ledger accounts do not appear on checks printed via the Pay Bills transaction.
- **Change Check Date When a Non-Cleared Check Is Printed**—If you use the Pay Bills feature to queue bill payment checks ahead of printing them, this setting will change the check date to the current system date when you print the checks.
- **Start with Payee Field on Check**—This time-saving option places your curser in the Payee field when you use the write checks transaction type.
- **Warn About Duplicate Check Numbers**—QuickBooks warns if the user is using a check number that the system has already recorded.
- **Autofill Payee Account Number in Check Memo**—You can assign the account number your vendor has assigned to you and have this number print on the memo field of the bill payment check. For more information, see the section "Assigning the Vendor Account Number to the Vendor Record" later in this chapter.
- **Select Default Accounts to Use**—You can assign the default bank accounts QuickBooks uses when creating paychecks or payroll liability checks.
- **Online Banking**—Users can select from two data viewing options when downloading transactions.

My Preferences

My Preferences are unique to the username logged in to the data file. These settings are not shared globally:

- **Select Default Accounts to Use**—Assign what account you want to use for the following:
  - Open the Write Checks transaction
  - Open the Pay Bills transaction
  - Open the Pay Sales Tax transaction
  - Open the Make Deposits transaction

General

Everyone using QuickBooks should review the settings in General Preferences. Although I have named a couple here, many are worth selecting and customizing for your company's specific needs.

Company Preferences

Company preferences are shared globally by all users. Following are the General Preferences that might affect your use of accounts payable functions:

- **Time Format**—If you track your vendors' time with QuickBooks time sheets, you can set a default for how portions of an hour display.
- **Never Update Name Information When Saving Transactions**—When not selected and you change the payee name or address, QuickBooks asks whether you want to update the payee's information. By default, this preference is not selected in a newly created QuickBooks file.
- **Save Transactions Before Printing**—By default, this preference is selected in a newly created QuickBooks file.

My Preferences

My Preferences are unique to the username currently logged in to the data file. These settings are not shared globally:

- **Pressing Enter Moves Between Fields**—When this setting is not selected, the Tab key advances through fields in a transaction; using the Enter key saves a completed transaction. If selected, both the Tab and Enter keys advance through fields on a transaction. The keyboard combination of Ctrl+Enter saves a completed transaction.
- **Automatically Open Drop-Down Lists When Typing**—This is a time-saving feature that is selected by default. This is useful if the chart of accounts has subaccounts.
- **Warn When Editing a Transaction**—By default, this is selected. It helps to avoid unintentional changes to a transaction being reviewed.
- **Warn When Deleting a Transaction or Unused List Item**—By default, this is selected. This setting helps avoid the unintentional deletion of a transaction being reviewed.
- **Automatically Recall Information**—Check this option to recall both the previously assigned account and the amount, or just the account, when creating a new vendor transaction.
- **Default Date to Use for New Transactions**—Exercise caution to ensure that the appropriate choice is selected. If you are entering transactions from the past, you might want to choose the last entered date. Otherwise, I recommend setting the default to use today's date.

Reminders

When setting the Company Preferences for reminders, do not forget to also set the My Preferences for this section.

The Company Snapshot is a digital dashboard that includes a view of your reminders. Defining these preferences specifically for your company affects the information users see on the Company Snapshot, reminding them of important tasks.

Company Preferences

On the Reminders preference page, you set the default for QuickBooks reminders to show a summary, a list, or not to be reminded of all checks to print, bills to pay, or purchase orders to print.

My Preferences

If you would like reminders to display when you open the QuickBooks data file, select the My Preferences tab of the Reminders preference and choose to Show Reminders List when opening a Company file.

Reports and Graphs

The person responsible for how QuickBooks reports your accounts payable aging should review these preferences choices.

Company Preferences

Company preferences are shared globally by all users. The Reports and Graphs preferences include the following:

- **Summary Reports Basis**—This feature is important because it tells QuickBooks what basis you want to view your Balance Sheet and Profit & Loss report in by default. You can always override the default when you prepare the report. More details about the differences between accrual and cash report basis are included in Chapter 3, "Accounting 101."
- **Aging Reports**—You can choose to age your reports from the due date or from the transaction date.

The remaining preferences affect the appearance of your reports.

My Preferences

My Preferences are unique to the username logged in to the data file. These settings are not shared globally:

- **Prompt Me to Modify Report Options Before Opening a Report**—By default, this preference is not selected. If it's selected, each time you open a report the Modify Report dialog will display.
- **Report and Graphs**—These settings determine how a report is refreshed when the data used in the report changes. The default in a newly created QuickBooks file is Prompt Me to Refresh. I recommend selecting the refresh automatically. You can make this decision for yourself depending on the size of your QuickBooks data file and the speed of your computer's processor.
- **Graphs Only**—Specify to draw graphs in 2D (faster) and whether to use patterns.

Tax:1099

Setting up your vendors for proper 1099 status is important. However, be assured that if after reviewing this information you determine the original setup was incorrect, any changes made to this preference will correct prior- and future-dated reports and transactions.

The Internal Revenue Service requires a business to provide a Form 1099-MISC at the end of the tax year to any person or unincorporated business paid $600 or more for services in a given calendar year. Most incorporated businesses are not required to get a Form 1099-MISC. You should contact your accountant for the most current IRS guidelines.

Company Preferences

You can select the Do You File 1099-MISC Forms? option to let QuickBooks know that you will be providing 1099 forms to your vendors at the end of the year.

The dialog box shown in Figure 7.2 is the first step in getting ready to track your Form 1099-MISC payments.

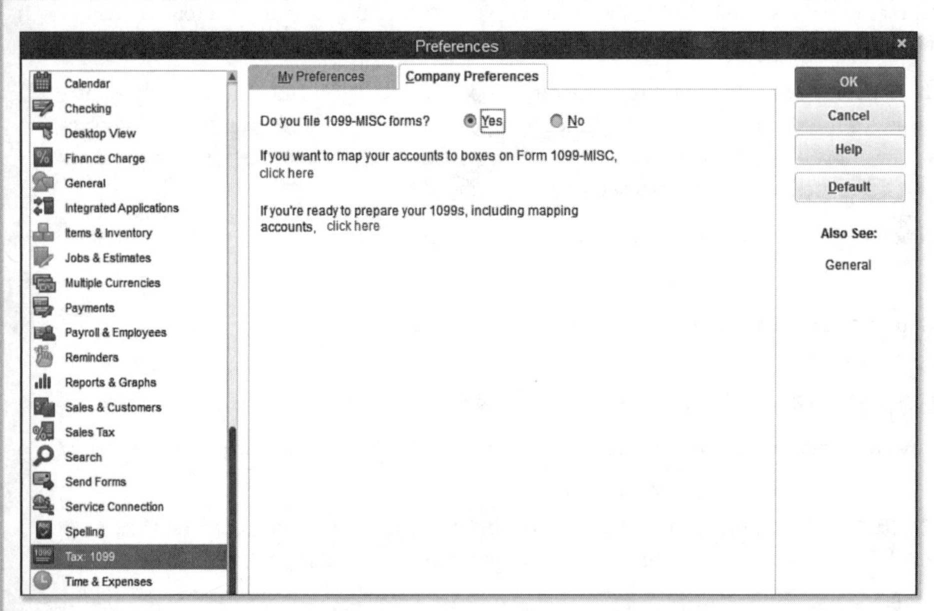

Figure 7.2 Choose Yes if you are required to submit 1099-MISC forms to the Internal Revenue Service.

For more information, see "Tracking and Reporting Vendor 1099-MISC Payments," p. 263.

My Preferences

There are no My Preferences in the Tax:1099 that you can set.

Time & Expenses

If you track time or your vendor's supply services or if you add time and costs to your customers' invoices, commonly known as Time and Expense billing, you should review these preferences.

Company Preferences

Company preferences are shared globally by all users. The Time & Expenses preferences as displayed in Figure 7.3 includes the following:

- **Time Tracking**—This preference enables the use of time sheets (for both vendor and employee time tracking) and the First Day of Work Week assignment. The Mark All Time Entries as Billable preference is new for QuickBooks 2013. With this preference selected, you can include employees' or vendors' time details on your customer's invoices.
- **Invoicing Options**—Include the improved functionality of creating invoices from a list of time and expenses. Additionally, when using the time and expense method of billing your customers, these options offer added functionality:
    - **Create Invoices from a List of Time and Expenses**—Enables the use of a single dialog box displaying all unbilled time and expenses for batch invoicing to customers.
    - **Track Reimbursed Expenses as Income**—When selected, the purchase transaction line that is marked billable to a customer is treated as income. This is the preferred method for billing in the legal profession as well as other industries.
    - **Mark All Expenses as Billable**—Do you provide your customers with details of your expenses? If you do, you should select this preference.
    - **Default Markup Percentage**—Enter a percentage, and each time you add a time or cost to a customer's invoice, QuickBooks adds this amount as a default markup embedded in the invoice line amount (not displayed separately).
    - **Default Markup Account**—Select a preferred default account (usually an Income category type).

note

When Track Reimbursed Expenses as Income is selected, you can define unique income accounts on the Expense chart of account, as shown in Figure 7.4. When setting Time & Expenses preferences for Invoicing Options, if no Default Markup Account is selected, when the cost is included on a customer's invoice, the original expense account is decreased (credited).

My Preferences

There are no personal preferences for Time & Expenses.

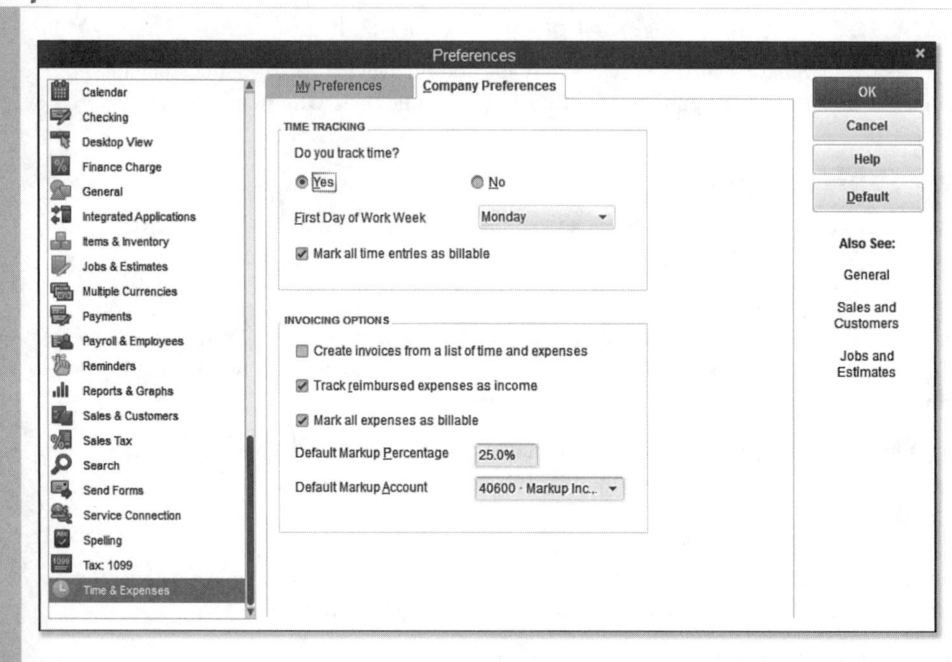

Figure 7.3 Review the Time & Expense preferences if your invoices to your customer include detailed line-item time and costs.

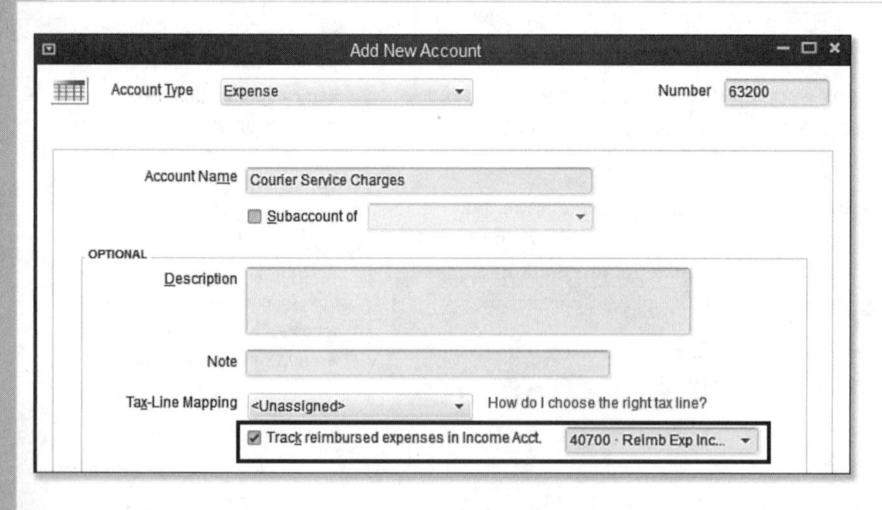

Figure 7.4 Optionally, choose to have invoiced reimbursed expenses post to an income account.

Working with the Vendor Center

QuickBooks makes adding, modifying, and researching vendor activity easy using the Vendor Center. Vendors are individuals or companies that you purchase services or products from, and they are managed in the Vendor Center as displayed in Figure 7.5.

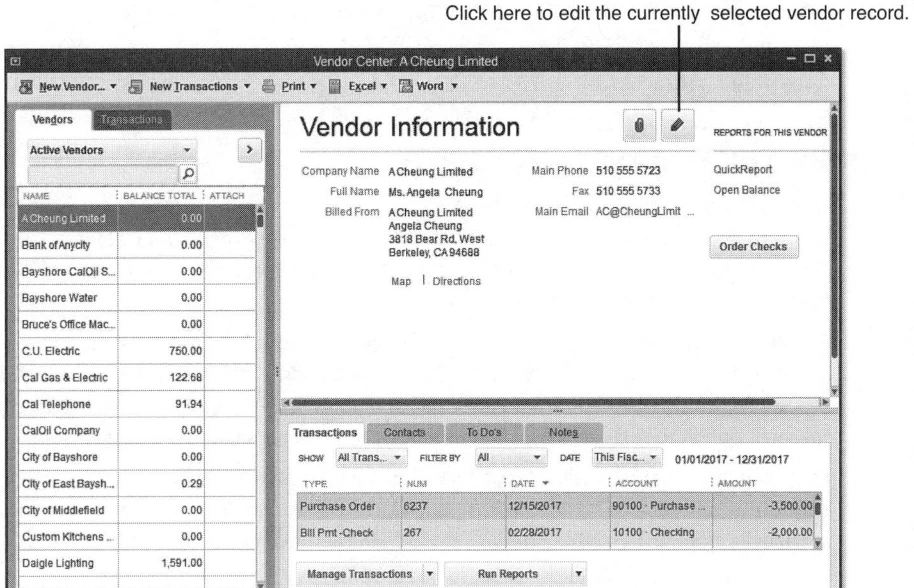

Figure 7.5
Complete common vendor tasks from the Vendor Center.

From the Vendor Center, you view contact details for your vendors and can access many tasks, including the following:

- Create a new vendor or edit an existing one.
- Add Multiple Vendors (using the Add/Edit Multiple List Entries feature discussed in Chapter 4, "Understanding QuickBooks Lists").
- Record commonly used vendor transactions.
- Print the vendor list, information, or transactions.
- Export the vendor list or transactions; import or paste vendors from Excel.
- Prepare vendor letters and customize the vendor letter templates.
- Filter your list of vendors to include All Vendors, Active Vendors, Vendors with Open Balances, or a custom filter of your choice.
- Attach documents to vendor records, such as attaching a copy of the signed subcontractor agreement.
- Access a map and driving directions to a vendor's location.
- Add and edit vendor contact names, to-do reminders, and notes.
- View and filter a list of transactions by vendor or by transaction type.
- Prepare a QuickReport or Open Balance Report for a given vendor.

Use the Vendor Center to access many of the common vendor transactions and reports you will learn about in this chapter and in Chapter 8, "Managing Vendors."

The following sections provide more detail about creating a vendor and using the Vendor Center for researching transactions.

Adding or Modifying Vendors

When you are ready to purchase materials or services for your business, you need to create a vendor. You might already have a head start on adding vendors to your file if you used the Adding Contacts feature available with the Express Start QuickBooks setup discussed in Chapter 1, "Getting Started with QuickBooks."

However, another less frequently used list in QuickBooks is worth mentioning here: the Other Names list. One occasion when you might choose to add a payee to the Other Names list is when you are recording a one-time purchase. Later, if you begin using the vendor regularly, you have a one-time option to remove the payee from the Other Names list and add it to your Vendor list.

This section offers instructions specific to setting up vendors. If your company will be using the Enter Bills process, you have to use a payee from the vendor list; the vendor bill transaction does not allow you to use an Other Names list item in the payee field.

 **tip**

Would you like to efficiently create new vendor records? Start with entering data in the Company Name field. When you move your cursor out of the Company Name field, QuickBooks also automatically populates the Vendor Name, Billed From, and Print on Check As field (found on the Payment Settings tab).

The Vendor Name field in QuickBooks is a "look-up" name; this field also controls how your vendors are automatically sorted in the Vendor Center.

If you prefer to use a different vendor look-up name, be sure to enter the proper vendor name in the Print On Check As field on the Payment Settings tab.

Adding a New Vendor

To practice adding a new vendor record, open the sample data file as instructed in Chapter 1. If you are working in your own file, use these instructions to begin entering the vendors you purchase goods and services from:

1. Click the Vendors button on the Home page. Alternatively, from the menu bar select **Vendors, Vendor Center.**
2. If the New Feature highlights display, read the information provided. To dismiss these message in the future, click the X in the What's New dialog box. You can re-enable help from the menu bar by selecting **Help, What's New.**
3. In the New Vendor drop-down list in the upper-left corner of the Vendor Center, select **New Vendor.**

4. The New Vendor dialog box displays (see Figure 7.6). In the Vendor Name field, type **ABC Subcontractor**. It is important to mention that no two names from any of the lists in QuickBooks can be the same.

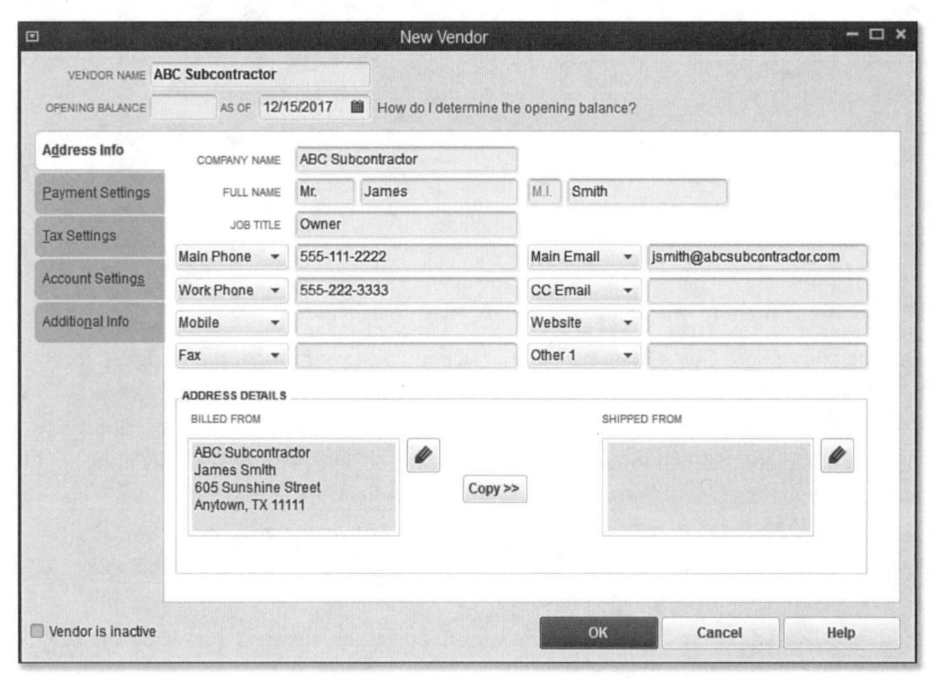

Figure 7.6
Completing the contact information for your vendor is good practice for your record keeping.

5. Leave the Opening Balance field blank. Chapter 3 discusses entering beginning balances in a new QuickBooks file (when there have already been previous accounting transactions recorded in some other accounting software or method). If you are a new business, you will later enter a vendor bill to increase the balance owed to the vendor instead of entering an Opening Balance amount in the New Vendor record.

   The As Of (date) field does not have any effect in your QuickBooks file if a dollar value was not entered in the Opening Balance field.

6. On the Address Info tab, consider completing the Salutation, First Name, and Last Name fields so you have the option to send letters to your vendors in the future.
7. Complete any remaining fields you deem applicable, such as contact information and address.
8. Click the Payment Settings tab as shown in Figure 7.7. In the Account No. field, enter the account number your vendor has assigned to you, if applicable. This account number can optionally be printed on the memo line of a vendor bill payment check.

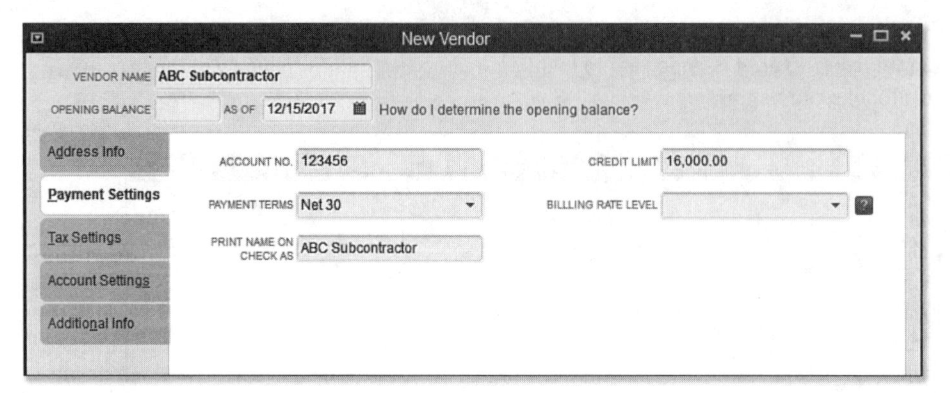

Figure 7.7
QuickBooks can add the Account No. field to the memo line of voucher style checks.

9. Select the appropriate payment terms, such as Net 30 days, your vendor has assigned to your account. If the specific term needed is not displayed, select **Add New** to add additional payment terms to the list.
10. (Optional) Complete the Print Name on Check As field. This field is necessary only if the printed name on the check differs from the Vendor Name field.
11. If you are using QuickBooks Premier, Accountant, or Enterprise, you have the option of selecting a Billing Rate Level for your vendor. Billing rates allow you to mark up billable time you will later add to a customer invoice.
12. Click the Tax Settings tab to enter the Vendor's Tax ID and assign the vendor as eligible for 1099 reporting. Note that if you do not have this information handy when you first create the vendor, you can add this information at a later date without any loss of tracking the details.
13. Click the Account Settings. Select the **Repairs:Building Repairs** expense account. You can assign up to three different accounts that will display automatically when you create a new transaction using this vendor as the payee. If you also download transactions from your bank or credit card, click the link to review the information provided about how Account Prefill works with Online Banking.
14. Click the Additional Info tab. From the drop-down Vendor Type menu, select from the provided types or select **Add New** to create a new vendor type. Use the Vendor Type field to categorize your vendors, which you can then use to filter your vendor and transaction reports.
15. If you have created a Custom Field, complete the value for that field. Custom fields allow you to track supplemental information about your vendors. Click the Define Fields button to add or remove custom fields.
16. At any time, you can select or deselect the Vendor Is Inactive checkbox. In such cases, the vendor still appears on reports, but will not appear in most drop-down lists you use for creating new transactions.
17. Click OK to save your changes and close the New Vendor dialog box, or click Cancel to discard your work.

Are you using QuickBooks Enterprise? With this edition, you can choose from more robust settings when you use Custom Fields. Custom fields are assigned to items. For example, you might use custom fields when your inventory items have multiple sizes or colors. With Enterprise, you can have up to 15 custom fields. These custom fields are then assigned to items; they can be selected on transactions and can be reported on.

QuickBooks Enterprise adds more robust custom field functionality by permitting you to assign the custom field to be used for specific transaction types. With each custom field you can specify the characteristics of the data, such as a text, date, number field with or without decimals, or offer a multichoice list for the user to select when entering an item. These are just a few of the available data field types that can be assigned. More information on working with custom fields can be found in Appendix C, "QuickBooks Enterprise Solutions Inventory Features."

Now that you have created a new vendor in the sample file, you are prepared to create a list of your own vendors. Return to the Vendor Center anytime you need to update a vendor's information.

QuickBooks does not keep a time stamp on revisions made to your vendors' contact information. After you make a change, all previous records reflect the change to the address or contact information.

However, changes to the Account Prefill selection affect only the newly created transactions.

Finding Vendor Transactions

The Vendor Center not only provides access for adding to or modifying your vendor records in QuickBooks, but also includes convenient access to finding vendor transactions.

With the Vendor Center open, select a vendor to display a list of that vendor's transactions on the right. In the previously displayed Figure 7.5, vendor A Cheung Limited is selected, and to the right are the individual transactions.

You can filter the resulting transactions by selecting options in the Show, Filter By, and Date drop-down lists. The options in the Filter By list change as you make a selection from the Show list.

Figure 7.8 shows representative vendor transaction types. Your transaction types might differ from the displayed types if you do not have the related feature enabled in Preferences. The only transaction type that can have a vendor record assigned that is not included in these options is Make Journal Entry.

The Transactions tab in the Vendor Center allows you to review transactions by type, rather than by vendor.

Figure 7.8
Filter the displayed vendor transactions based on multiple criteria.

Researching Vendor Transactions

To practice finding vendor transactions by type, open the sample data file as instructed in Chapter 1. If you are working in your own file, use these instructions to easily locate vendor transactions:

1. On the Home page, click the Vendors button to open the Vendor Center. Click the transactions tab on the left.
2. Select the **Purchase Orders** transaction type, as shown in Figure 7.9.

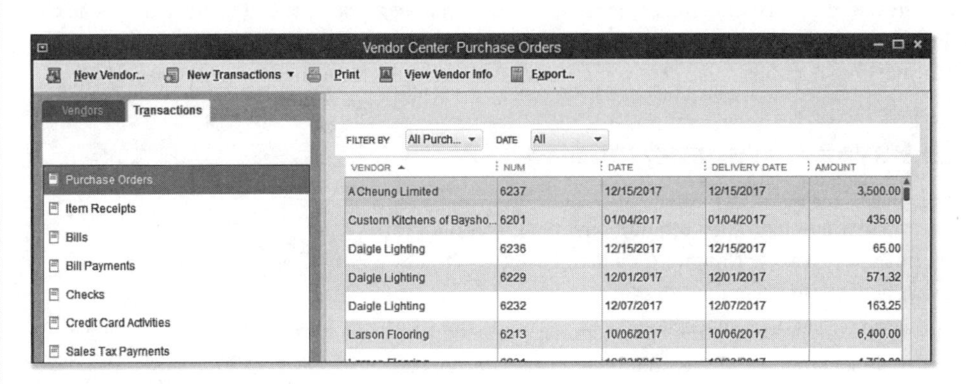

Figure 7.9
Use the Transactions tab of the Vendor Center to find like transaction types.

3. (Optional) From the Filter By drop-down list, select **Open Purchase Orders**.
4. (Optional) Filter for a specific date range. This might be useful if you are looking specifically for older dated open purchase orders.
5. (Optional) Click any column header to sort that column.
6. To view a transaction, double-click or right-click, and select **Edit Transaction**.
7. Click the Print icon to print the listed transactions.
8. (Optional) Click the View Vendor Info button and click OK if the New Feature message displays. QuickBooks opens the Edit Vendor dialog box for the currently selected vendor. Click OK to close and return to the Vendor Center:Purchase Orders listing.
9. Click the Export icon to export the list of transactions to an Excel worksheet or to a comma-separated value file.

The Vendor Center provides one location to create or modify your vendor records and even research vendor transactions.

Next, you learn about the proper accounts payable process so you can successfully track your vendor business expenses.

The Accounts Payable Process

QuickBooks includes a flexible payable process. Your company can choose to use the purchase order and receive item transactions for controlling and monitoring costs and delivery, or you can skip these steps and create a bill to be paid later.

An important reason for using a vendor bill to record your business expenses is the ability to track the vendor's bill reference number. In the event your vendor invoices you more than once for the same services or items, QuickBooks preferences for Bills includes the option to be warned about duplicate bill numbers from the same vendor.

If you created your data file using the Express Start option, you might need to enable the features as discussed in the earlier section "Preferences That Affect Accounts Payable" of this chapter. If you are ready to work in your own data file, make sure you have created your new file as discussed in Chapter 1.

Accounts Payable Transactions

Many of the accounts payable transactions use QuickBooks items. If you are considering using the accounts payable process for the first time, be sure to review Chapter 4, which discusses the use of items and how to set them up properly.

If you choose to use purchase order transactions, you need to create items. Items are a list of the products or services you sell to customers or purchase from vendors. The primary purpose of items is to perform the accounting behind the scenes and to automate the data entry process by prefilling descriptions, costs, and sales price on purchase and sales transactions.

Should you use items even if you do not plan to use purchase order or item receipt transactions? I recommend that you do, especially if you follow the instructions in the nearby tip. A powerful feature of items is that each time the item is purchased or sold, QuickBooks records the amount to the specific account(s) defined in the Add New or Edit Item dialog box, reducing or eliminating potential errors created from recording the transaction to the wrong account when using the Expense tab of a purchase transaction.

tip

Many users inadvertently post revenue and expenses to the same account for Services, Non-Inventory Parts, Other Charges, and Discounts when selecting a single chart of account. The New or Edit Item dialog box includes a checkbox (see Figure 7.10) that enables you to avoid this problem and provides separate revenue and expense account fields. Choosing to set up items correctly can be one of the most important decisions you make in using accounts payable.

How can items help you track your customer's profitability? Many of the QuickBooks reports that provide profitability information are based on transactions recorded using items on the Items tab and will not provide the same information if the transaction is recorded using the Expenses tab.

For example, a home builder creates a budget for the project (using an estimate transaction) and wants to track actual versus budgeted expense. To take advantage of the many customer and job profitability reports, you must enter your expenses using the Items tab on an accounts payable bill (and use the same process for the Write Checks transaction), as shown in Figure 7.11.

Table 7.1 lists the transaction types available in accounts payable and the purpose each type serves. You also should review Table 8.1 in Chapter 8, "Managing Vendors," which outlines the accounting that goes on behind the scenes with these same transactions.

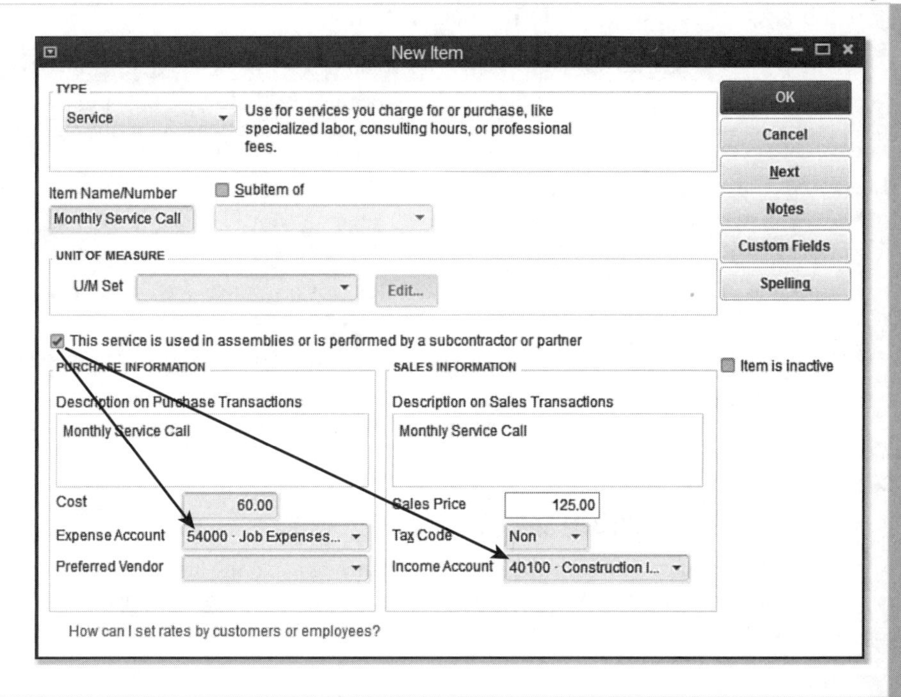

Figure 7.10
Set up items with both an income and expense account.

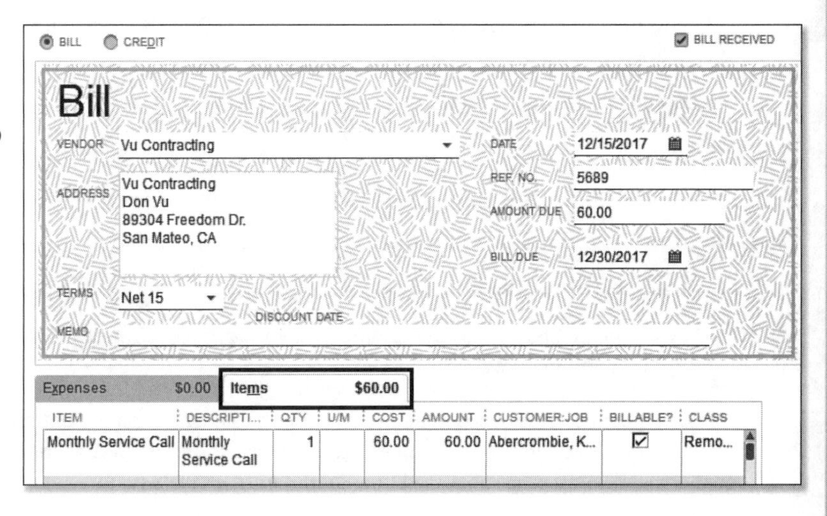

Figure 7.11
Use the Items tab to record expenses you want to track in customer or job profitability reports.

Table 7.1 Accounts Payable Transactions

Accounts Payable Transaction Name	Primary Purpose of Transaction
Purchase Order	Document issued by a buyer to a seller indicating the products or services, quantity, and amounts the buyer has agreed to pay.
Item Receipt (Receiving inventory, non-inventory, or other item recorded on a purchase order)	Records receipt of inventory, non-inventory items, or other item types when the goods arrive before the vendor's final bill.
Enter Bills	Records an increase to accounts payable and the associated expense.
Vendor Credit Memo	Records a decrease of what is owed to a vendor.
Bill Payment Check	Pays the vendor bill and decreases accounts payable and cash account balances.

Accounts Payable Workflow

In this section, you learn about the importance of using the accounts payable process in place of using the write check transaction type for recording business expenses. The QuickBooks Home page and Vendor Center, as shown in Figures 7.1 and 7.5, respectively, make managing all your purchasing activities easy.

Your Home page workflow might vary, depending on the version of QuickBooks you are using and the preferences you have enabled.

To perform typical vendor-related activities from the QuickBooks Home page, as shown in Figure 7.1, follow these steps:

1. Access the Vendor Center.
2. (Optional) Create a purchase order to the vendor.
3. (Optional) Receive inventory with or without the final vendor bill.
4. Enter bills against inventory (does not create an item receipt).
5. Enter a bill to the vendor.
6. Pay the bill (typically within the agreed-upon payment terms for that vendor; for example, 30 days from the bill date).

Some companies choose not to use accounts payable transactions, but instead pay their vendors via the check transaction (from the menu bar selecting **Banking**, **Write Checks**). Often, this choice is made because the process of paying a vendor with a check is quick and easy and takes fewer steps than creating and paying a vendor bill.

However, by choosing *not* to use accounts payable transactions, you ignore several important controls for managing the purchases your company makes. These purchasing controls include the following:

- **Associating the bill with the purchase order (or item receipt) to automatically calculate quantity and cost**—When you enter the vendor's name on a bill, QuickBooks prompts you with an open purchase order (or item receipt) dialog box, as shown in Figure 7.12, and prefills the bill for you.

- **Receiving a warning when entering a vendor invoice number twice**—It can happen: or more likely, the user inadvertently enters it twice. However, when you use a vendor bill (versus the write checks transaction) and you enter the vendor's invoice number in the Ref No. field, QuickBooks warns you if the vendor's reference number was used on a previous bill, as shown in Figure 7.13.

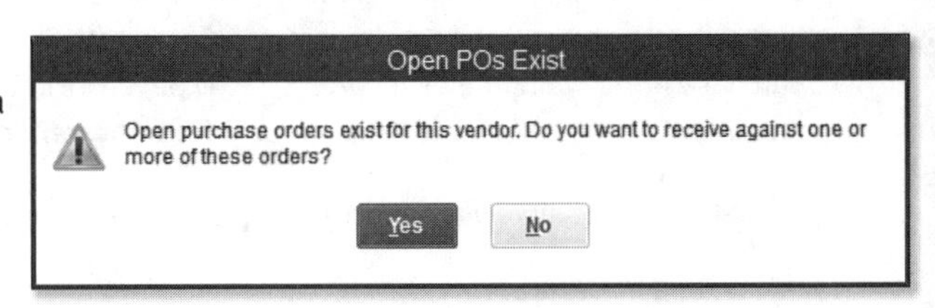

Figure 7.12
Warning provided when you enter a bill for a vendor that has an open purchase order.

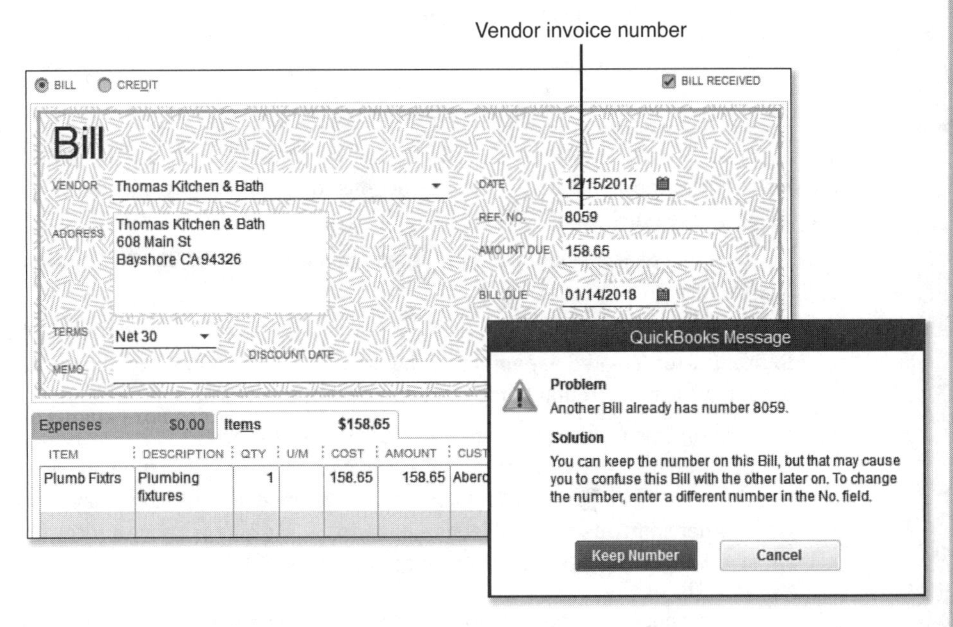

Figure 7.13
QuickBooks provides a warning message when you enter a bill with the same reference (vendor invoice) number.

- **Not recognizing costs in the month they were incurred**—When you opt to use the write checks transaction instead of a vendor bill, QuickBooks uses the date of the check as the date the expense is recorded (recognized). How often do you pay the vendor's bill the same day or month you receive it? You might be overstating or understating the expenses incurred in a specific month if you use the check instead of the bill transaction type.
- **Taking advantage of discounts offered by your vendor**—Only if you use vendor bills can you set a preference to have QuickBooks automatically calculate and record the discount if paying the bill within the vendor's discount terms.

The purchasing controls and warnings provided in QuickBooks make using the accounts payable process a smart choice for your company. Additionally, your company benefits from having financial statements that can be viewed in cash and accrual basis.

Entering a Purchase Order

Your business might choose to record purchase orders to track the expected product or service cost. Purchase orders are nonposting, which, in accounting vernacular, means that when you record a purchase order, you are not recording an expense or liability. Instead, a purchase order serves as a reminder that you expect to receive a bill from the vendor at a later date.

➡ *To learn more about working with purchase orders, see "Creating the Purchase Order," p. 173.*

Recording Vendor Bills

You are on your way to properly using accounts payable transactions to help track and report on your business expenses. Learn how to enter your vendor bills in this section.

Practice Entering a Vendor Bill

To practice adding a new vendor bill, open the sample data file as instructed in Chapter 1. If you are working in your own file, use these instructions to begin entering bills for the products and services you have purchased:

1. On the Home page, click the Enter Bills icon to open the Enter Bills transaction, as shown in Figure 7.14.
2. From the Vendor drop-down list, type the first few letters of the vendor name **ABC Subcontractor** (created earlier in this chapter). You might also select the vendor from the drop-down list by scrolling through the list and selecting a specific vendor.
3. Use the Tab key on your keyboard to advance to the Date field. If you are practicing, accept the default date; otherwise, enter the actual date for your transaction. In your file, you can use the (+) or (-) key on your keyboard to change the date by a single day forward or backward. Other shortcuts are detailed in Appendix C. This date is used to record the expense when viewing your financial reports in accrual basis.

   ➡ *See more information on the accounting for transactions in Table 8.1 in Chapter 8.*

4. Type **1234** in the Ref. No. field. This represents the invoice number supplied by your vendor on his bill. If your vendor did not provide an invoice number, I often recommend using the digits of the bill date. For example, I might use 121517 as the Ref. No. if I am also dating the bill 12/15/2017.
5. Using the Tab key again, advance to the Amount Due field and type **100**. QuickBooks automatically formats the amount as 100.00. In your own file, you can manage this preference from the menu bar by selecting, **Edit, Preferences, General, My Preferences** tab. If you enabled the Automatically Place Decimal Point option, QuickBooks would have formatted your input of 100 as 1.00 instead.

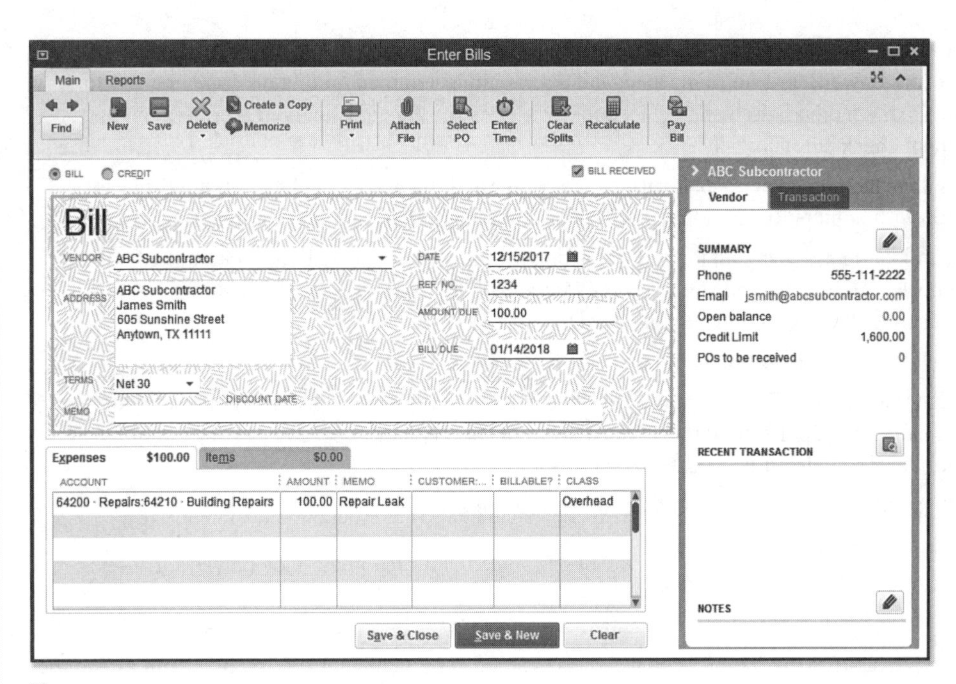

Figure 7.14
Using the Bill allows you to record the expense when incurred, but pay the vendor at a later date.

6. The Bill Due, Terms, and Discount Date will prefill from the vendor's record. You can override these inputs on the specific vendor bill you are entering. If no defaults are included in the vendor record, QuickBooks then uses the default due date calculation found on the Bills—Company Preferences tab of the Preferences dialog box (see Figure 7.15). You must be logged in to the file as the Admin user or External Accountant to change the Company Preferences settings for bills.

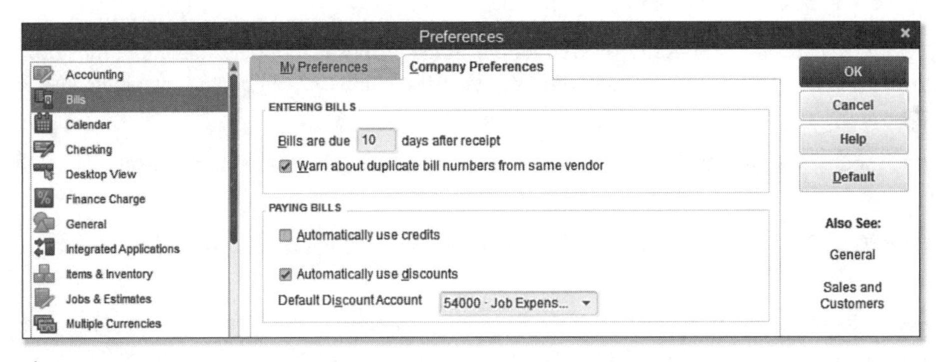

Figure 7.15
QuickBooks uses the Company Preferences term when a vendor record doesn't specify terms.

7. (Optional) Enter a memo. This memo prints on the bill payment check. If your vendor record has a stored Account No. as detailed in the section on Adding or Modifying Vendors, leave the memo field blank; QuickBooks includes the Account No. on the printed bill payment check automatically.
8. In this exercise, QuickBooks automatically prefilled the Account column on the Expenses tab with Repairs:Building Repairs. This account was set as a default for this vendor.
9. (Optional) Enter a memo for your reporting needs. This memo will not print on the final check. Although named similar to the Memo field on the check, this field allows you to describe the transaction line for your reporting.
10. Select a customer or job name from the list when applicable.
11. Use the Billable? field when you specify a customer or job and you want to include this expense on a future customer invoice. New for QuickBooks 2013, you can set a preference for always having this checkmark selected.
12. If you are using Class tracking, enter the appropriate class.
13. Click Save & Close.

The ribbon toolbar at the top of a displayed transaction is new for QuickBooks 2013. The ribbon toolbar includes access to commonly used transaction features that in previous editions of QuickBooks were hidden or hard to find. The ribbon toolbar on an enter bill transaction includes the following tabs:

- **Main**—Use this tab to access the following:
  - Browse or search saved vendor bills or credits using the arrows.
  - Access to create, save, delete, copy, or memorize vendor bills. The Save option on the ribbon toolbar keeps the transaction open. You'll still use Save & Close or Save & New at the bottom of the dialog box after you complete your transaction.
  - *New for QuickBooks 2013*—print the vendor bill. Some purposes for doing this might include: providing details to a sister company that is paying the bill, or when needing management's approval before paying.
  - Attach source documents. This is a free service and offers local document storage on your computer.
  - Select PO or Enter Time to autofill the vendor bill with stored information from these transaction types.
  - Clear Splits removes the line detail on the Expenses or Items tab but retains the vendor name, date, and other information on the header portion of the vendor bill.
  - Recalculate updates the Amount Due field, which is helpful when you have added additional line items.

- Pay Bills opens the Pay Bills dialog box with Filter By selected for the same vendor displayed in the transaction and the bill marked ready to be paid.

- **Reports**—From this tab on the ribbon toolbar, create a QuickReport, Transaction History, or Journal Report.

tip

Did you know that by default, QuickBooks requires you to use the Tab key on your keyboard to advance from one field to another on certain transactions?

If you inadvertently used the Enter key on your keyboard, QuickBooks might save and close the transaction. If this happens to you, from an open transaction dialog box, click the arrows found on the Main tab of the ribbon toolbar in the top-left corner.

If you prefer to use the Enter key on your keyboard to advance between fields, you can set that preference from the menu by selecting **Edit**, **Preferences**, **General Preferences**. On the My Preferences tab, select the **Pressing Enter Moves Between Fields** checkbox. You can save a transaction using the Ctrl+Enter keyboard shortcut. Click OK to save and close your preference setting.

Recording Vendor Credits

Now that you are recording your business expenses with vendor bills, what about returning a product to the vendor or receiving a credit for a service not performed to your specifications? The next section shows you how easy it is to create a vendor credit.

Practice Entering a Vendor Credit

To practice entering a vendor credit, open the sample data file as instructed in Chapter 1. If you are working in your own file, use these instructions to begin entering credits you receive from your vendors:

1. On the Home page, click the Enter Bills icon.
2. Select the Credit option at the top of the Enter Bills dialog box (see Figure 7.16). The dialog box now displays a credit, decreasing accounts payable and decreasing the account(s) assigned on the Expenses tab, or if you are using the Items tab, the account assigned to the item(s) being used.

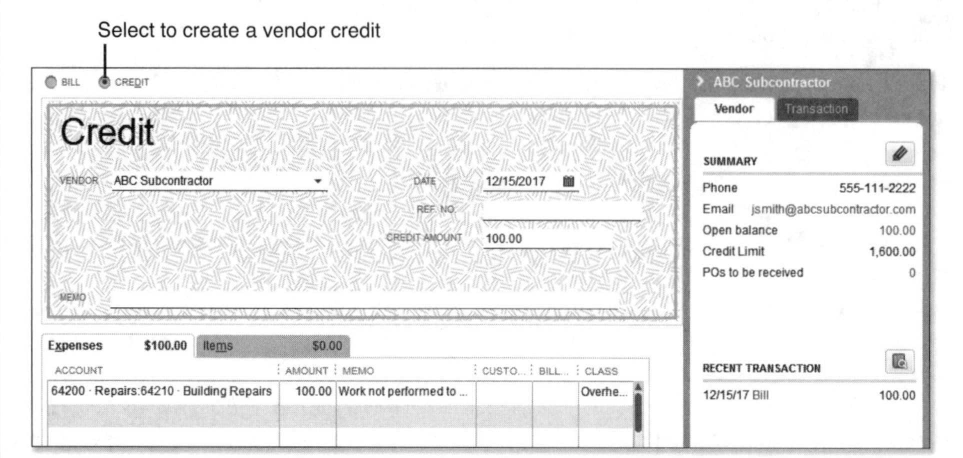

Figure 7.16
Credits reduce both what you owe your vendor and the account assigned on the credit or associated with the item.

3. To continue with the practice example we used earlier, begin typing the vendor name **ABC Subcontractor**. Press the Tab key on your keyboard to advance to the Date field.
4. If you are practicing, accept the prefilled date. In your own file, you can select the date from the calendar.
5. In the Ref. No. field, type **1223**. This is the credit memo number your vendor has assigned this record.
6. In the Credit Amount field, type **100.00**.
7. Enter an optional memo. If you want the memo to display in reports based on your expense lines, be sure to use the memo field in the Expenses tab or the Description field on the Items tab.
8. In this exercise, QuickBooks used the Repairs:Building Repairs expense account assigned to the vendor record and the amount entered in the Credit Amount field. If needed, you can change the account or add additional lines.
9. Click Save & Close.

This vendor credit is currently unapplied and available to be applied when you record a bill payment. If you know that a vendor has an unpaid bill pending, you can apply the credit against that bill now, or wait until the next time you need to pay the vendor.

If you would like to view this unpaid bill on a report, select **Reports**, **Vendors & Payables**, **Unpaid Bills Detail** report from the menu bar. An unapplied credit will be listed in this report, as shown in Figure 7.17.

note

For ease in typing, QuickBooks formats the date for you. For example, if your current computer system year is 2017, you would need to type only **1220** in a date field and QuickBooks will format the date as 12/20/17.

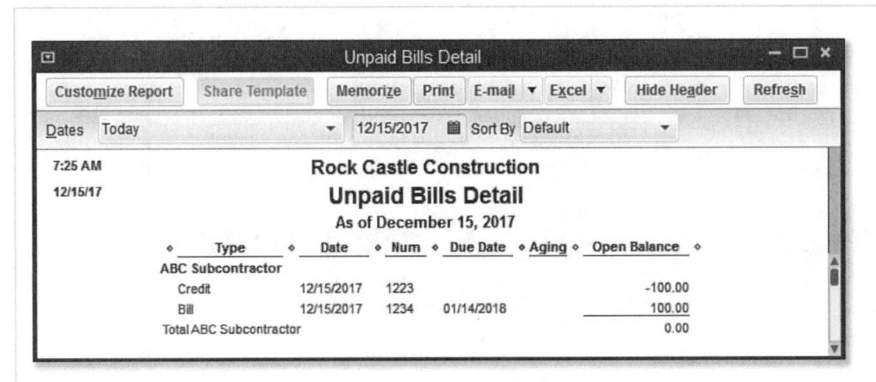

Figure 7.17
The Unpaid Bills Detail report makes it easy to see open vendor credits.

Paying Vendor Bills

One of the benefits of entering vendor bills is that you can record the expense during the month you incur it, but pay the balance owed at a later date.

If you are ready to pay your bills, make sure you have a vendor bill or some record of the expense being incurred. Develop a process at your business for accurately reviewing your unpaid bills.

Practice Paying Vendor Bills

To practice paying a vendor bill, open the sample data file as instructed in Chapter 1. If you are working in your own file, use these instructions to begin paying the bills you owe your vendors:

1. On the Home page, click the Pay Bills icon.
2. For this exercise, leave the Show All Bills option button selected. When working with your own data, you can filter the bills that display in the Pay Bills dialog box by selecting the Due On or Before option button and entering a date (see Figure 7.18).
3. In the Filter By drop-down list, select **C.U. Electric** or begin typing the name as you learned in an earlier exercise.
4. Review the choices available in the Sort By drop-down list, but leave Vendor selected.
5. Place a checkmark next to each of the bills for C.U. Electric, or optionally click the Select All Bills button. If you are printing checks, QuickBooks creates one check for the two selected bills displayed in Figure 7.18.
6. When working with your own data, if you did not want to pay the full balance, you can manually type an amount in the Amt. To Pay column on a specific bill's row. Later when you are prepared to pay the balance, QuickBooks will include the remaining balance due in the Amt. To Pay column.
7. With a bill selected, click the Go to Bill button. QuickBooks opens the Enter Bills dialog box where, if necessary, you can make changes. Click Save & Close to return to the Pay Bills dialog box.
8. (Optional) View the discount terms or credits available. More details are provided about working with discounts and credits in the next section.

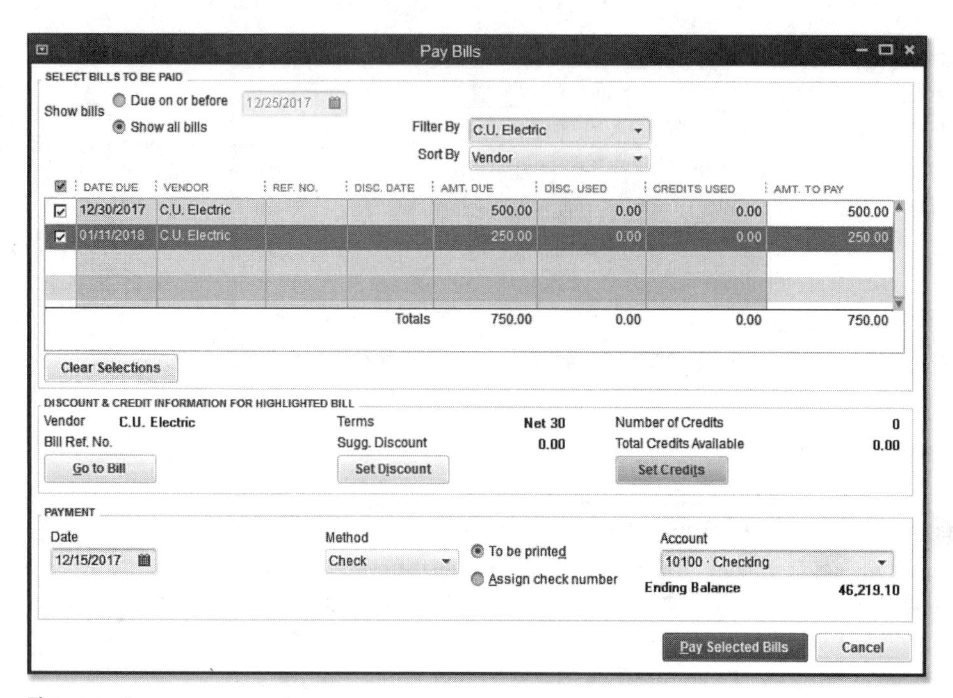

Figure 7.18
Use the Pay Bills dialog box to record payment by check, credit card, or online payment to your vendor.

9. When working with your own data, you can specify payment options in the Payment section of the Pay Bills dialog box, including the following fields (for this exercise, leave the choices as displayed in Figure 7.18):

   - **Date**—This is the date that will print on your checks or will be assigned to the transactions in your accounting.
   - **Method**—Select Check if you will be printing a check or recording a manually written check. Select Credit Card if you are paying the bill with the company's corporate credit card. Select Online Bank Pmt if you are using online banking.
   - **To Be Printed** or **Assign Check Number**—If you selected Check as your method of payment, you can select the To Be Printed option button. If you manually wrote the check, you can select Assign Check Number.
   - **Account**—Depending on your Method selection, you can assign either the bank account or credit card account used to make the payment.
   - **Ending Balance**—QuickBooks displays the ending balance for the bank or credit card account selected.

10. Click Pay Selected Bills. QuickBooks opens the Payment Summary dialog box.
11. Review the details displayed in the Payment Summary dialog box, including payment date, account, and method.

12. Click the Print Checks button on the Payment Summary dialog box. (Optional) You can click the Pay More Bills button to return to the Pay Bills dialog box, or click Done if you do not want to practice printing (using plain paper).
13. If you selected the Print Checks button, the Select Checks to Print dialog box displays (see Figure 7.19). Leave selected the default Bank Account and the prefilled First Check Number.

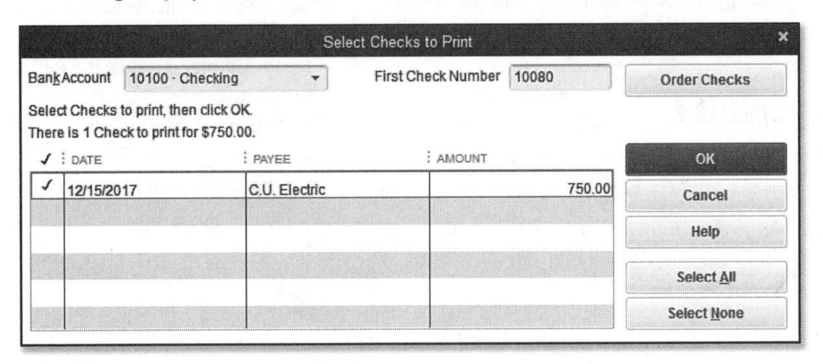

Figure 7.19
When printing checks, specify the first check number to print.

14. Review the list of checks to be printed. Each will have a checkmark in the column to the left. Remove the checkmarks from any checks you do not want to print at this time.
15. Click OK to open the Print Checks dialog box. Select your printer from the Printer Name drop-down list as shown in Figure 7.20, and then choose the proper Check Style from Voucher, Standard, or Wallet.

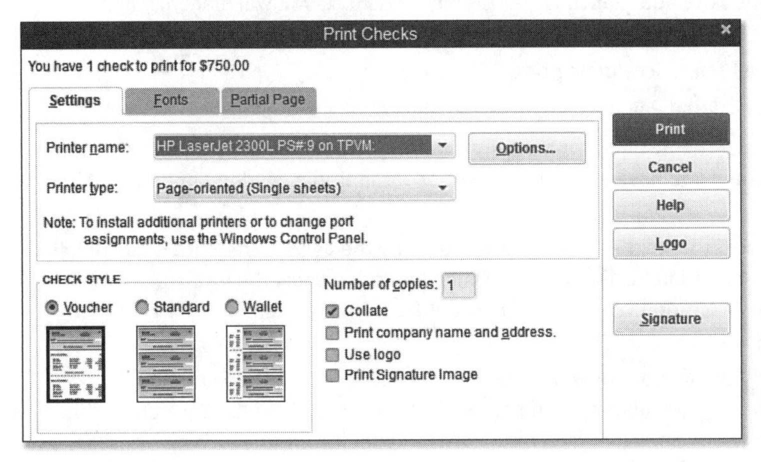

Figure 7.20
Select the printer name, check style, and other printer settings for preparing checks from QuickBooks.

16. Click Print. For this exercise, make sure you have plain paper in your printer. A check printed to plain paper is not a negotiable document.
17. The Print Checks—Confirmation dialog box displays. In this exercise, click OK to close the confirmation.

To learn more about printer settings for checks, see "Printing Checks," p. 496.

You have now learned how to complete basic accounts payable tasks, including using bills to record your expenses and preparing the payment for the vendor. In the next sections, you learn how to work with vendor discounts and credits.

tip

Efficiently prepare a bill payment check for a single vendor.

To do so, open a previously saved vendor bill; on the Main tab on the transaction ribbon toolbar at the top, click the Pay Bill icon. The Pay Bills dialog box opens with the Filter By field already selected for the same vendor as the open vendor bill.

Applying Vendor Credits

Your vendor might offer discounts for timely payment or issue a credit for products or services that did not meet your expectations.

Continue your QuickBooks practice by applying the vendor credit created in an earlier practice section of this chapter.

Practice Applying Vendor Credits

To practice applying a credit, open the sample data file as instructed in Chapter 1. If you are working in your own file, use these instructions to apply vendor discounts or credits to your vendor's open balances:

1. Review your preference for applying credits. From the menu bar, select **Edit, Preferences,** and go to the Bills—Company Preferences tab on the Preferences dialog box. (You must log in to the file as the Admin or External Accountant user type.) See the previous Figure 7.15. These settings determine whether QuickBooks automatically applies any open credits for you. If you don't select the Automatically Use Credits checkbox, you will manually apply the credits. Pick the selection that best meets your business needs.
2. Click OK to close the Preferences dialog box.
3. On the Home page, click the Pay Bills icon. The Pay Bills dialog box opens.
4. For this practice, select the **ABC Subcontractor** vendor in the Filter By drop-down list. Filtering can be useful if you have many open invoices for multiple vendors, but it is not required.
5. Place a checkmark next to the open bill you want to apply the vendor credit to. If you didn't select to apply credits automatically in step 1, QuickBooks will show the total number of available credits and their total value in the Discount & Credit Information for Highlighted Bill section (see Figure 7.21).
6. If you want to modify the amount or which credits are selected, click the Set Credits button. The Discount and Credits dialog box displays as shown in Figure 7.22. You can modify which credit is selected by changing the checkmark from one credit to another or by manually overriding the Amt. To Use.
7. Click Done to close the Discount and Credits dialog box. Click Pay Selected Bills to exit the Pay Bills dialog box. If the AMT. TO PAY column is 0.00, you have associated a credit memo with a vendor bill, and no additional check transaction will be created.
8. Click Done in the Payment Summary dialog box or click Pay More Bills if you want to return to the Pay Bills dialog box.

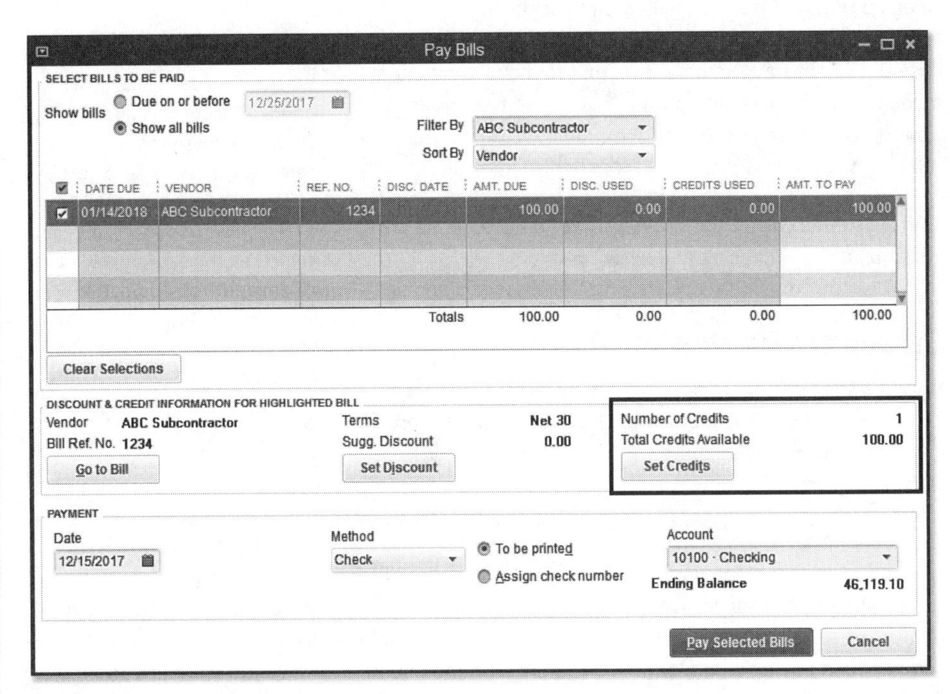

Figure 7.21
With paying vendor bills, QuickBooks will show the number of available credits for the selected vendor.

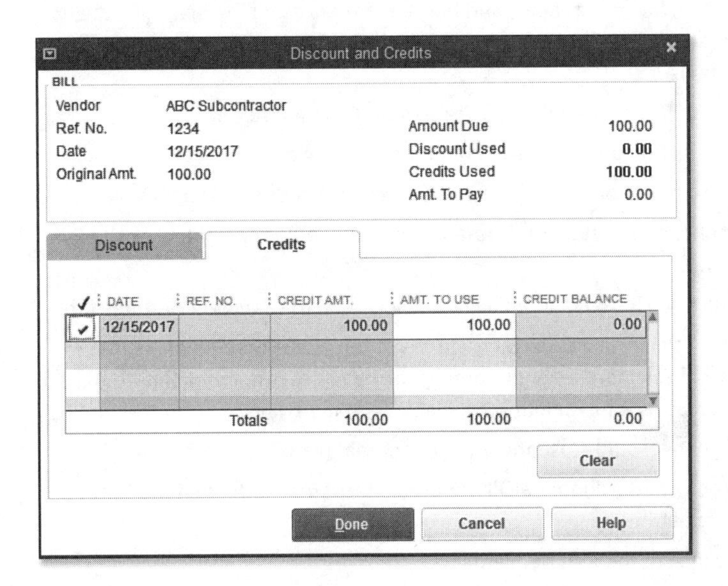

Figure 7.22
The Discount and Credits dialog box allows you to manage how the credits are applied to open vendor bills.

If you are an accounting professional using QuickBooks Accountant or QuickBooks Enterprise Accountant, you might want to use the Client Data Review feature. From one convenient window, you can assign the vendor unapplied credit memo to the open accounts payable bill, replacing the previous steps numbered 3–8.

To learn more about time-saving features for accounting professionals, see "Client Data Review," p. 659.

note

When you need to change a prior year's open balance for a vendor, credit memos can be the safest way to not inadvertently affect prior year financials. With a credit memo you can date the correcting transaction in the current year, which is important if you have already used the prior year's data to prepare and file a tax return.

Taking Discounts on Vendor Bills

Your company might be able to save money by paying your vendors within their allowed discount terms. Discounts are offered by some vendors to encourage quick payment of their invoices.

Practice Taking Discounts on Vendor Bills

To practice applying a vendor discount, open the sample data file as instructed in Chapter 1. For this practice we will complete all the steps necessary for QuickBooks to automatically calculate the discount when paying a vendor bill. If you are working in your own file, you will need to log in as the Admin or External Accountant user type to set the preference mentioned. You can then use these instructions to apply discounts to your vendors' open balances:

1. From the menu bar, click **Edit, Preferences,** and in the Preferences dialog box, click the Bills—Company Preferences tab. Check the Automatically Use Discounts checkbox, as displayed previously in Figure 7.15.
2. Select **Job Expenses:Less Discounts Taken** as the Default Discount Account.
3. Click OK to save your selection and close the Preferences dialog box.
4. Assign discount terms to a vendor. From the menu bar, select **Vendors, Vendor Center.**
5. In the QuickBooks sample data, select **Bayshore CalOil Service.** To the right, click the Edit icon (looks like a pencil).
6. In the Edit Vendor dialog box for Bayshore CalOil Service, click the Payment Settings tab.
7. If not already assigned, select the **2% 10 Net 30** terms in the Terms drop-down list. When selected, QuickBooks will calculate a 2% discount if the payment is dated within 10 days of the invoice date. Otherwise, the full amount is payable within 30 days.
8. Click OK to save your changes and close the Edit Vendor dialog box.
9. From the Vendor Center, with Bayshore CalOil Service, select **Enter Bills** from the New Transactions drop-down list.
10. Using the Tab key, advance to the Ref. No. field. Type **567**.
11. In the Amount Due field, type **1,000.00**. QuickBooks assigns the Terms and Discount Date and adds the amount to the Expenses tab.

12. Assign Overhead to the Class column on the Expenses tab.
13. On the Main tab of the transaction ribbon toolbar, select **Save**. This will keep the transaction displayed for this exercise. Normally, you would select the Save & Close or Save & New buttons at the bottom of the transaction.
14. On the same Main tab of the transaction ribbon toolbar, select **Pay Bill**.
15. The Pay Bills dialog box displays with the vendor bill you just created already selected. Notice that as a result of selecting Automatically Use Discounts in step 1, QuickBooks displays the terms and the Sugg. Discount (see Figure 7.23).

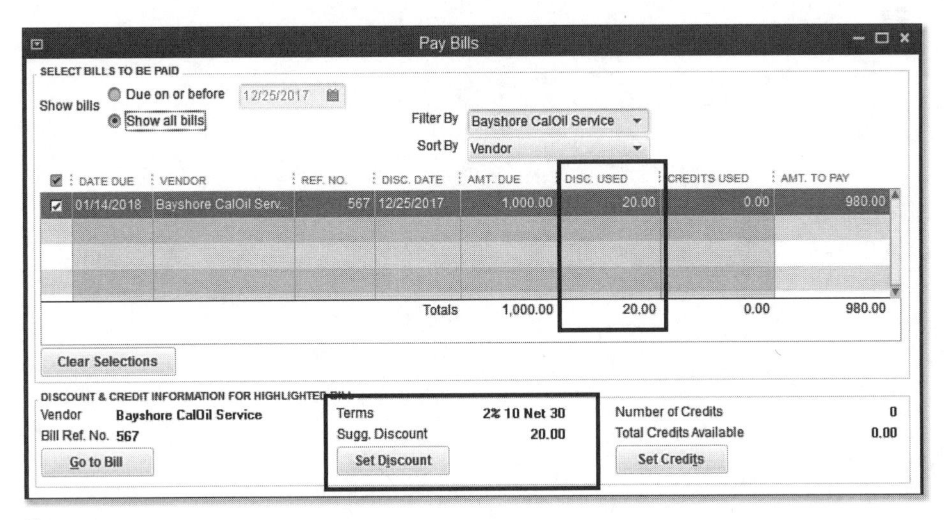

Figure 7.23
Set QuickBooks preferences to automatically calculate early payment discounts.

16. (Optional) You can click the Set Discount button to change the amount of the discount, assign a different discount account, and assign a discount class. Click Done to close the Discounts and Credits dialog box.
17. For this practice, click Cancel to close the Pay Bills dialog box. If you are assigning discounts to your own vendor bills, continue with the check printing process.

If you are going to assign discounts to your vendor bills, record your bills at the "gross" amount or total amount before any discount. Then, over time you can watch the amount you have saved grow!

caution

If you decide to add discount terms to your vendor's record after creating vendor bills, you will need to edit any unpaid vendor bills and manually change the terms or discount date.

8

MANAGING VENDORS

In Chapter 7, "Setting Up Vendors" you learned the particulars for adding, editing, and creating transactions for vendors. In this chapter you will learn how to best manage the vendor details in your QuickBooks file. Additionally, I share with you how to handle unique vendor transactions.

Accounts Payable Reporting

Accounts payable mistakes often can be one of the primary reasons for misstated company financials. Knowing which reports are best to review will make you much more efficient at keeping your accounts payable "clean," meaning the data is correct and up to date. Often, the thing that makes troubleshooting data errors most difficult is not knowing exactly what you should be looking for. This problem is addressed in the next section, which explains some of the more common reports used to identify whether your accounts payable information is correct.

Reconciling Balance Sheet Accounts Payable Balance to A/P Aging Summary Report Total

With QuickBooks, you don't have to worry that the Balance Sheet accounts payable balance will not match the A/P Aging Summary report total because any transaction posting to the accounts payable account must have a vendor assigned. When providing year-end documentation to your accountant, be sure to include the A/P Aging Summary or Detail report and compare the total amount from these reports to the Balance Sheet balance for accounts payable.

To compare the Balance Sheet Standard report balance for accounts payable with the A/P Aging Summary report total, follow these steps:

1. From the menu bar, select **Reports**, **Company & Financial**, **Balance Sheet Standard**. On the Balance Sheet report that opens, select the **As of Date** you want to compare to. To accurately compare the Balance Sheet report Accounts Payable balance and the A/P Aging Summary report total, you *must* create your Balance Sheet in accrual basis. If your reporting preference default was for cash basis, you can change the reporting basis temporarily by clicking the Customize Report button on the active report window and selecting Accrual as the report basis. Click OK to return to the report.

2. Note the balance of your Accounts Payable account(s) on the Balance Sheet (see Figure 8.1).

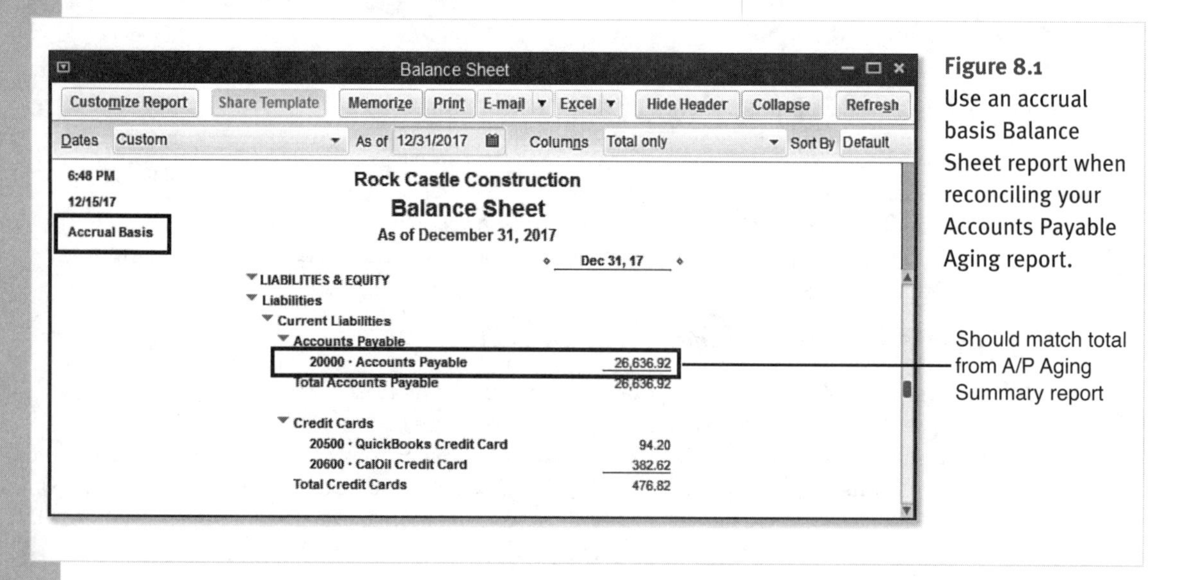

Figure 8.1
Use an accrual basis Balance Sheet report when reconciling your Accounts Payable Aging report.

3. From the menu bar, select **Reports**, **Vendors & Payables**, **A/P Aging Summary**. See Figure 8.2. Make sure the date is the same as the date you selected in step 1.

Your Accounts Payable balance on the Balance Sheet Standard report should match the total on the A/P Aging Summary report. If it does not, the reason might be a data integrity issue. If you find the two balances do not match, first make sure your Balance Sheet Standard report is created in the accrual basis. Then verify your data by selecting **File**, **Utilities**, **Verify Data** from the menu bar. This is discussed in more detail in Chapter 17, "Managing Your QuickBooks Database."

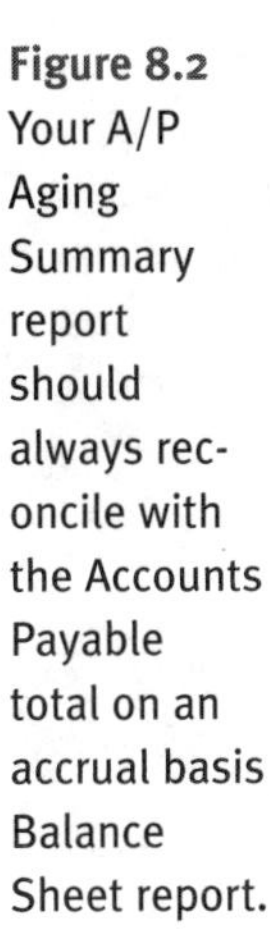

Figure 8.2 Your A/P Aging Summary report should always reconcile with the Accounts Payable total on an accrual basis Balance Sheet report.

A/P Aging Summary

Customize Report | Share Template | Memorize | Print | E-mail | Excel | Hide Header | Collapse | Refresh

Dates Custom | 12/31/2017 | Interval (days) 30 | Through (days past due) 90 | Sort By Default

6:49 PM
12/15/17

Rock Castle Construction
A/P Aging Summary
As of December 31, 2017

	Current	1 - 30	31 - 60	61 - 90	> 90	TOTAL
C.U. Electric	250.00	500.00	0.00	0.00	0.00	750.00
Cal Gas & Electric	0.00	122.68	0.00	0.00	0.00	122.68
Cal Telephone	0.00	91.94	0.00	0.00	0.00	91.94
Daigle Lighting	52.00	1,539.00	0.00	0.00	0.00	1,591.00
Hamlin Metal	670.00	0.00	0.00	0.00	0.00	670.00
Hopkins Construction Rentals	0.00	700.00	0.00	0.00	0.00	700.00
Lew Plumbing	0.00	1,330.00	0.00	0.00	0.00	1,330.00
Middlefield Drywall	0.00	1,200.00	0.00	0.00	0.00	1,200.00
Patton Hardware Supplies	1,020.00	3,459.20	0.00	0.00	0.00	4,479.20
Perry Windows & Doors	2,580.00	2,325.00	1,800.00	0.00	0.00	6,705.00
Sergeant Insurance	4,050.00	0.00	0.00	0.00	0.00	4,050.00
Sloan Roofing	1,047.00	0.00	0.00	0.00	0.00	1,047.00
Thomas Kitchen & Bath	585.00	0.00	0.00	0.00	0.00	585.00
Timberloft Lumber	195.50	19.60	0.00	0.00	0.00	215.10
Vu Contracting	0.00	1,250.00	0.00	0.00	0.00	1,250.00
Washuta & Son Painting	600.00	0.00	0.00	0.00	0.00	600.00
Wheeler's Tile Etc.	0.00	1,250.00	0.00	0.00	0.00	1,250.00
TOTAL	11,049.50	13,787.42	1,800.00	0.00	0.00	26,636.92

Should agree with your Balance Sheet report

Reviewing the Unpaid Bills Detail Report

If you need more detail than the A/P Aging Summary report offers, consider the Unpaid Bills Details report instead. This report is helpful because it displays individual vendor bill and credit memo lines for each open vendor transaction instead of summarizing amounts by aging interval.

By default this report is perpetual, which means that even if you create it using a date in the past, QuickBooks will show those open vendor bills, or unapplied credit memos, as of *today's* computer system date, including all payments recorded before and after the report date. You can override this default, and then properly reconcile the Unpaid Bills Detail report to your Balance Sheet and your A/P Aging Summary report for a date prior to today's date. To do so, follow these steps:

1. From the menu bar, select **Reports**, **Vendors & Payables**, **Unpaid Bills Detail**. As mentioned previously, this report includes all payments made before and after the report date you have chosen.
2. If you are creating this report for a date other than today, you will likely want to have the report match your Balance Sheet totals as of that same date. To do so, click the Customize Report. The Modify Report dialog box opens, with the Display tab selected.
3. Click the Advanced button to open the Advanced Options dialog box.
4. Under Open Balance/Aging, select the **Report Date** option, as shown in Figure 8.3, and click OK to close the Advanced Options dialog box.
5. Click OK to return to the report.

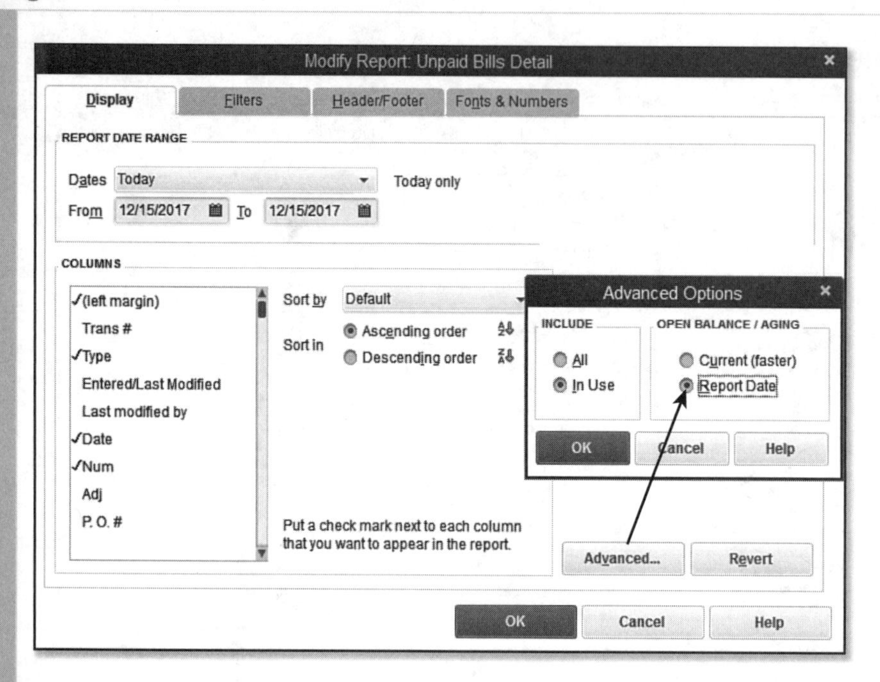

Figure 8.3
Modify the Unpaid Bills Detail report so it will agree with the Balance Sheet for a date in the past.

Modifying this report enables you to see each open vendor bill or unapplied credit detail as of some date in the past. This report becomes useful for reconciling your accounts payable unpaid bills or open credit detail to your Balance Sheet accounts payable total. You might want to send a copy of this modified report to your accountant after verifying that it agrees with the Balance Sheet for the same date.

If an amount is listed on this report, it is presumed you owe the money, or in the event of a credit, your vendor owes you.

Reviewing Aged Open Item Receipts

Often, when goods are purchased for inventory, non-inventory, or other item types, your vendor will ship the product with a packing slip and then send the final vendor bill later. One reason for doing this is that receiving departments in a warehouse should not necessarily know the value of the goods being delivered. Another reason is that the vendor might need to add freight and handling to the final bill before sending it to your company.

The QuickBooks Create Item Receipts transaction is used to record the receipt of the stock into your place of business, increase the quantity on hand for this item (if an inventory item), and increase your accounts payable due to that vendor.

However, because you have not yet received the final bill from the vendor, QuickBooks does not include these item receipts in the Pay Bills dialog box. This is because QuickBooks recognizes an item receipt transaction as not yet having received the final bill to be paid.

An error in your accounting can result if you entered a bill, ignored the warning message that outstanding item receipts existed for that vendor, and created another bill. Or perhaps you used the Write Checks transaction to pay for the same charge as recorded on the original item receipt. Both of these types of mistakes will overstate your expenses or inventory value.

note

QuickBooks Enterprise Solutions 13.0 offers an Enhanced Inventory Receiving feature that allows you to specify a different method of accounting for item receipts.

With Enhanced Inventory Receiving enabled, when an item receipt is recorded without the final bill, QuickBooks increases (debits) the Inventory Asset and increases (credits) the Inventory Offset account, a current liability account created automatically by QuickBooks when the feature is enabled.

Later when you enter the final vendor's bill, QuickBooks decreases (debits) the Inventory Offset account and increases (credits) Accounts Payable. For more information see, "Enhanced Inventory Receiving," p. 757.

First, to see if this issue is a problem for your data file, from the menu bar select **Reports**, **Vendors & Payables**, **Unpaid Bills Detail**. On the report, do you have line items with a transaction type of Item Receipt (see Figure 8.4)? If you do, these are from receiving inventory, non-inventory, or other types of items *without* receiving (or recording) the final vendor bill.

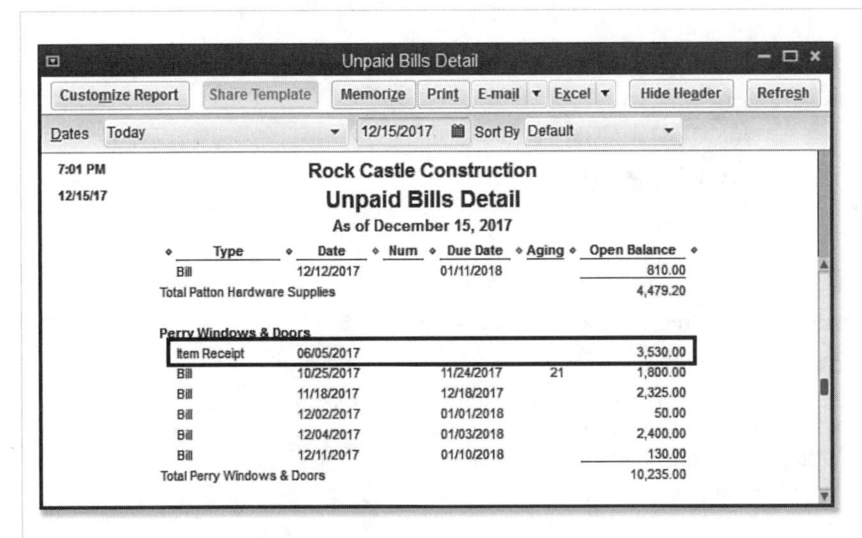

Type	Date	Num	Due Date	Aging	Open Balance
Bill	12/12/2017		01/11/2018		810.00
Total Patton Hardware Supplies					4,479.20
Perry Windows & Doors					
Item Receipt	06/05/2017				3,530.00
Bill	10/25/2017		11/24/2017	21	1,800.00
Bill	11/18/2017		12/18/2017		2,325.00
Bill	12/02/2017		01/01/2018		50.00
Bill	12/04/2017		01/03/2018		2,400.00
Bill	12/11/2017		01/10/2018		130.00
Total Perry Windows & Doors					10,235.00

Figure 8.4
Aged item receipts are acceptable only when you have not yet received the vendor's final bill.

After reviewing your Unpaid Bills Detail report, if you find outdated item receipts that you do not owe the vendor, determine whether they have been paid by requesting an open payables statement from your vendor. To see if the bill was paid with a Write Checks transaction instead of the proper Pay Bills transaction, follow these steps:

1. On the Home page, click the Vendors button.
2. Click the Vendor name on the left. If you don't initially see the vendor you want, click any vendor on the list, and then type the first letter of the name to advance to the first list entry with that letter.
3. On the Transaction tab, on the right, click the Show drop-down list to select the **Checks** transaction type, as shown in Figure 8.5.

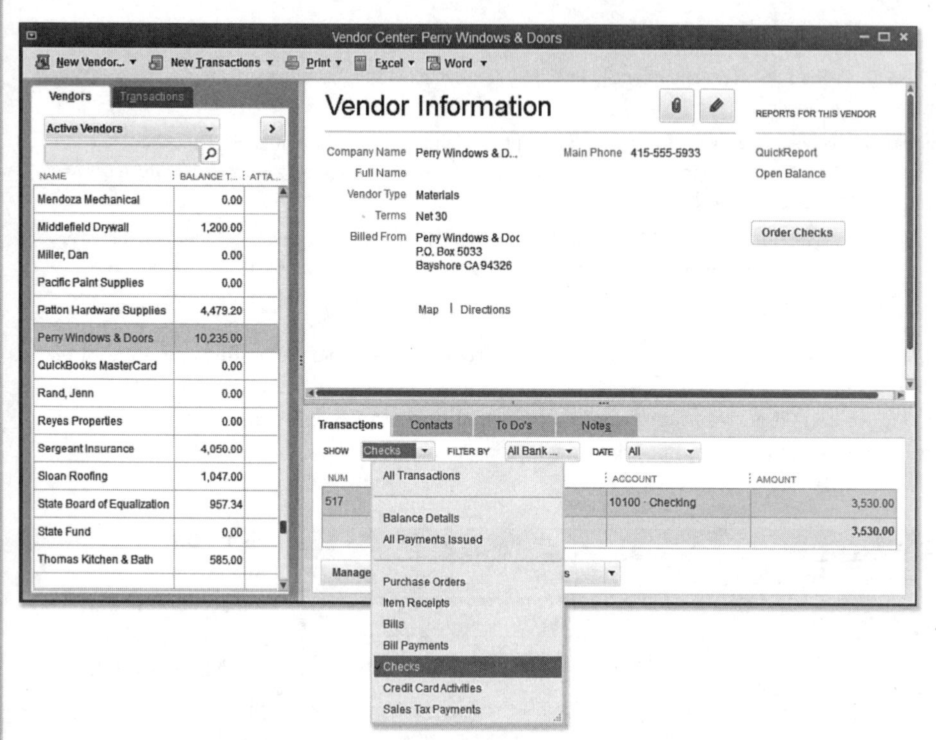

Figure 8.5
Use the Vendor Center to easily review checks written to a vendor as opposed to bill payment checks.

You can optionally print the vendor transaction list via the Print drop-down list at the top of the Vendor Center dialog box.

In Figure 8.4, shown previously, Perry Windows has an open item receipt dated 06/05/17. To see whether a check was used to pay this vendor, follow the steps listed previously to see any Write Checks transaction (not Pay Bills) transaction type that was written to the vendor.

For more information, see "Correcting Accounts Payable Errors," p. 273.

caution

How exactly does QuickBooks manage the use of Item Receipt transactions?

- Item receipts age like other open payables on the A/P Aging Summary report.
- The Unpaid Bills Detail report does not show any days in the aged column, yet item receipts are aging.
- QuickBooks does not let you pay an item receipt in the Pay Bills dialog box.

Reviewing Item Setup

Items play an important part in the accounts payable process if you use purchase orders, item receipts, or the Items tab on a vendor bill or check.

Figure 7.10 (as shown in the previous chapter) pictured a service type item with a checkmark placed in the box titled This Service Is Used.... It is important to select this option if you buy and sell the same item. If this option is not selected and you use the same item on a purchase and a sales transaction, QuickBooks records both the revenue and the expense to the single account selected on the New Item dialog box or Edit item dialog box. In this case, total revenues and total expenses will both be understated because QuickBooks nets the two amounts together into a single general ledger account.

It is acceptable to create an item with only one account if you know you will never buy and sell the same item. However, I usually recommend that each item be set up as two-sided, where the item record requires both an expense and an income account.

Properly setting up items is discussed in more detail in Chapter 4, "Understanding QuickBooks Lists." This section focuses on how you can determine whether your items are the cause of errors on your financials for a company data file with transactions. If your data file does not have transactions in it yet, you should use this report to check your item setup.

Presume that an item was created with only an income account assigned. The item was used on a vendor bill, and the user has to decide whether to ignore the warning shown in Figure 8.6.

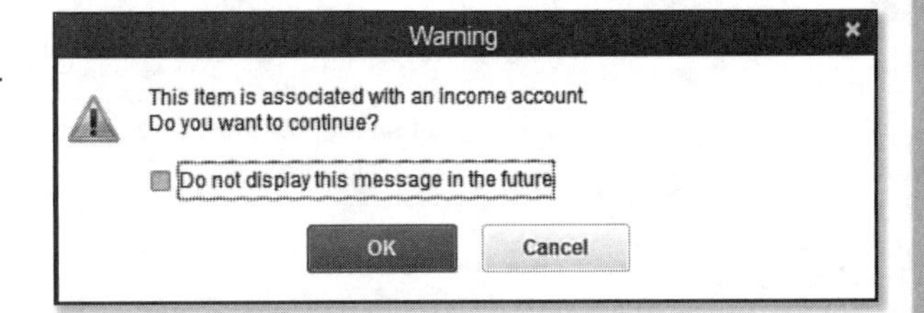

Figure 8.6
The warning you receive on an expense transaction when using an item that only has an income account assigned.

To see whether this type of error affects your data, create the following report:

1. From the menu bar, select **Reports**, **Company & Financial**, **Profit & Loss Standard**.
2. Double-click the Total Income account (see Figure 8.7). QuickBooks creates a Transaction Detail by Account report, as displayed in Figure 8.8.
3. On the top right of the resulting Transaction Detail by Account report, select **Type** from the Sort By drop-down list. QuickBooks groups all transactions by type within each income account or subaccount. Notice in Figure 8.8 that the Labor Income account has a vendor bill transaction posting to an income account.

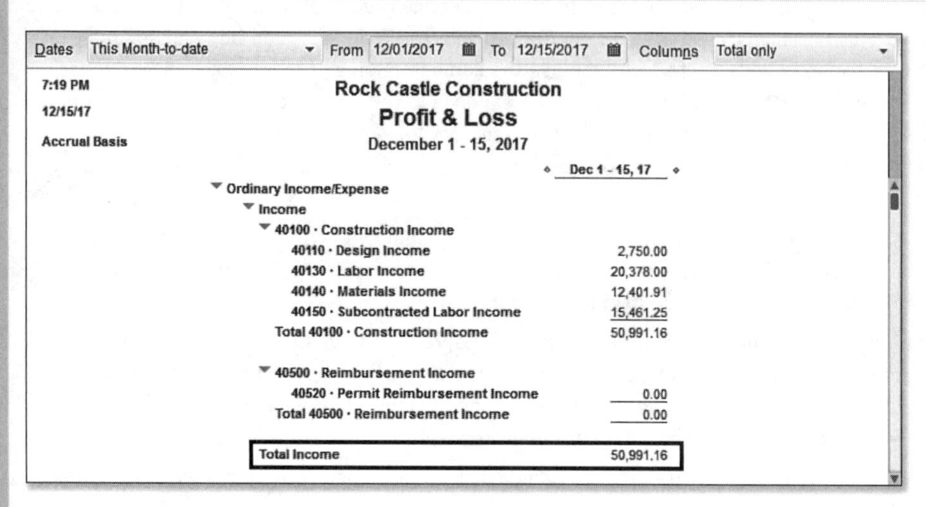

Dates: This Month-to-date | From 12/01/2017 | To 12/15/2017 | Columns: Total only

7:19 PM
12/15/17
Accrual Basis

Rock Castle Construction
Profit & Loss
December 1 - 15, 2017

	Dec 1 - 15, 17
Ordinary Income/Expense	
Income	
40100 · Construction Income	
40110 · Design Income	2,750.00
40130 · Labor Income	20,378.00
40140 · Materials Income	12,401.91
40150 · Subcontracted Labor Income	15,461.25
Total 40100 · Construction Income	50,991.16
40500 · Reimbursement Income	
40520 · Permit Reimbursement Income	0.00
Total 40500 · Reimbursement Income	0.00
Total Income	50,991.16

Figure 8.7
Double-click the Total Income amount to create a Transaction Detail by Account report.

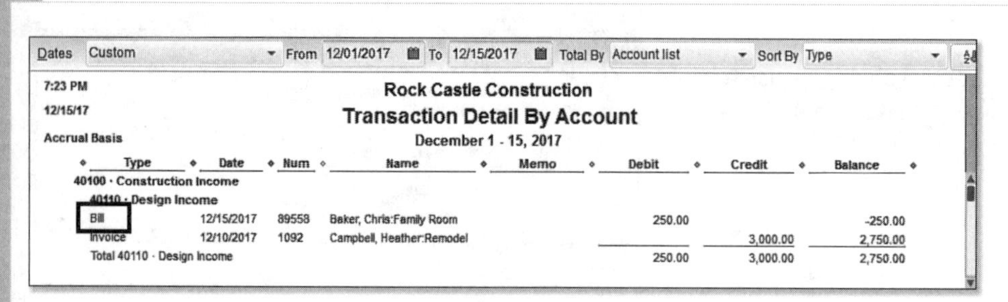

Dates: Custom | From 12/01/2017 | To 12/15/2017 | Total By: Account list | Sort By: Type

7:23 PM
12/15/17
Accrual Basis

Rock Castle Construction
Transaction Detail By Account
December 1 - 15, 2017

Type	Date	Num	Name	Memo	Debit	Credit	Balance
40100 · Construction Income							
40110 · Design Income							
Bill	12/15/2017	89558	Baker, Chris:Family Room		250.00		-250.00
Invoice	12/10/2017	1092	Campbell, Heather:Remodel			3,000.00	2,750.00
Total 40110 · Design Income					250.00	3,000.00	2,750.00

Figure 8.8
A Bill transaction type should not post to an income account, unless the item does not have an expense account assigned.

Accounts Payable Balance on Cash Basis Balance Sheet

The nature of accounts payable suggests that when you review your financials in cash basis, you would not see an accounts payable balance. See Table 8.1 for a listing of the transactions you can use in accounts payable and the effect the transaction has on both accrual and cash basis reporting.

Table 8.1 Accounts Payable on Accrual or Cash Basis Balance Sheet

Transaction Name	Accrual Basis	Cash Basis
Create Purchase Orders	No effect	No effect
Create Item Receipt (Receiving inventory ***without*** the vendor's bill)	Date of Item Receipt—increase (debit) account assigned to the item usually cost of goods sold (or expense account); increase (credit) accounts payable. Note: Item Receipts *will not* display in the Pay Bills dialog box.	No effect
Create Item Receipt (Receiving inventory ***with*** the vendor's bill)	Date of Item Receipt—increase (debit) account cost of goods sold (or expense account); increase (credit) accounts payable. Note: Item Receipt has now become a Bill and *will* display in the Pay Bills dialog box.	No effect
Enter Vendor Bill for Non-inventory, Other Item Types or General Expenses	Date of Bill—increase (debit) account assigned to item, or account used on the Expense tab; increase (credit) accounts payable.	No effect until date of bill payment check
Enter Bills (Credit)	Date of Credit—decrease (debit) accounts payable; decrease (credit) inventory, account assigned to item, or account used on the Expenses tab of the credit	No effect until date credit is applied against a bill payment

What can cause an accounts payable balance to appear on a cash basis Balance Sheet report? Any of the following:

- A/P transactions have expenses or items posting to other balance sheet accounts.
- Inventory items on an invoice or credit memo (typically, inventory management should be done in accrual basis reporting).
- Transfers between balance sheet accounts.
- Unapplied accounts payable vendor payments.
- Payments applied to future-dated vendor bills.
- Preferences that contradict each other. (This can happen if you select cash basis on your summary reports and accrual basis as your sales tax preference.)
- Data corruption. To confirm, (and hopefully resolve) this problem, from the menu bar select **File**, **Utilities**, **Verify Data**. More details are included in Chapter 17.

What can you do if you do have an accounts payable balance on your cash basis Balance Sheet? The following steps will help you locate the transactions making up this balance:

1. From the menu bar, select **Reports**, **Company & Financial**, **Balance Sheet Standard**.
2. Click the Customize Report button to open the Modify Report dialog box with the Display tab selected.
3. Select **Cash** for the report basis.
4. Click OK.
5. Double-click the Accounts Payable amount in question. See Figure 8.9. The Transactions by Account report is created.
6. Click the Customize Report button to open the Modify Report dialog box with the Display tab selected.
7. For the Report Date Range, remove the From date and leave the To date.
8. Click the Advanced button and from the Open Balance/Aging box, select **Report Date**, as shown in Figure 8.10. Click OK to close the Advanced Options dialog box.
9. Click the Filters tab.
10. In the Choose Filter box, scroll down to select **Paid Status**.
11. Select **Open** for Paid Status.
12. Click OK to return to the report and look for transactions that fall into any of the categories described earlier. The Transaction Detail report in Figure 8.11 shows several inventory transactions and a pre-paid insurance transaction. All of these transactions post to other balance sheet accounts, one of the common causes of having an Accounts Payable balance on a cash basis Balance Sheet report.

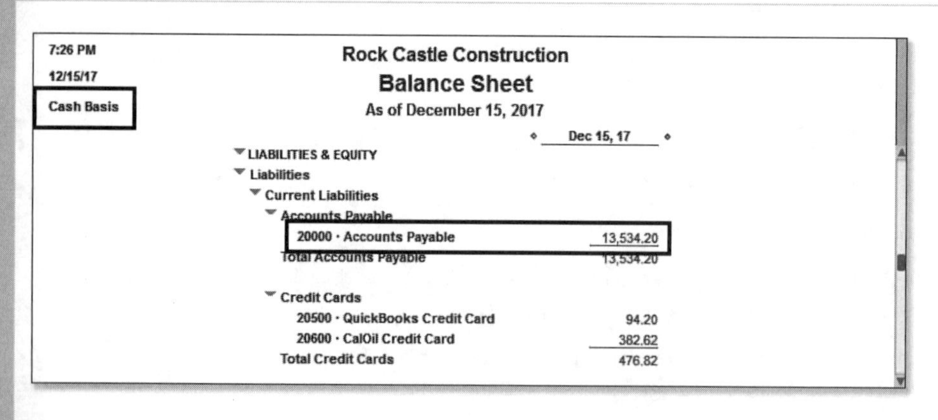

Figure 8.9 Cash basis Balance Sheet report with an Accounts Payable balance.

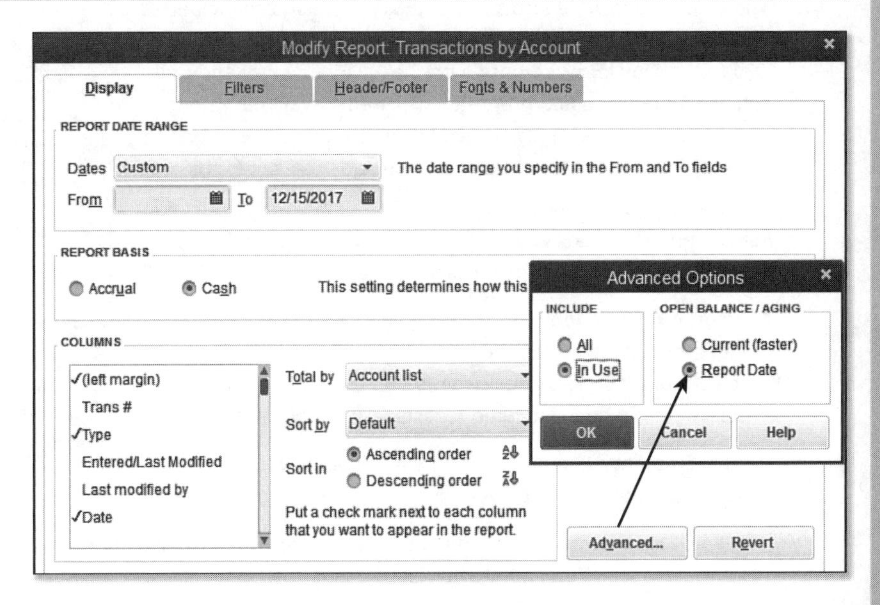

Figure 8.10 Use the Advanced button on the Modify Report dialog box to filter a report for transaction status as of a specific date in the past.

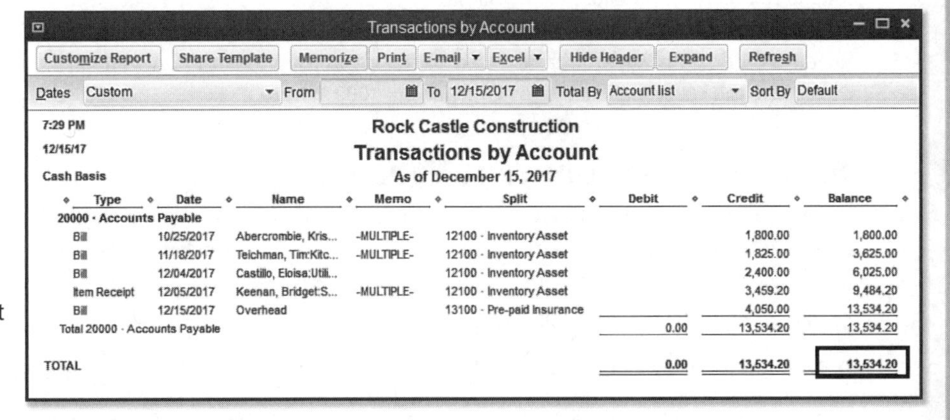

Type	Date	Name	Memo	Split	Debit	Credit	Balance
20000 · Accounts Payable							
Bill	10/25/2017	Abercrombie, Kris...	-MULTIPLE-	12100 · Inventory Asset		1,800.00	1,800.00
Bill	11/18/2017	Teichman, Tim:Kitc...	-MULTIPLE-	12100 · Inventory Asset		1,825.00	3,625.00
Bill	12/04/2017	Castillo, Eloisa:Utili...		12100 · Inventory Asset		2,400.00	6,025.00
Item Receipt	12/05/2017	Keenan, Bridget:S...	-MULTIPLE-	12100 · Inventory Asset		3,459.20	9,484.20
Bill	12/15/2017	Overhead		13100 · Pre-paid Insurance		4,050.00	13,534.20
Total 20000 · Accounts Payable					0.00	13,534.20	13,534.20
TOTAL					0.00	13,534.20	13,534.20

Figure 8.11 Filter for transactions that make up the Accounts Payable amount on a cash basis prepared Balance Sheet report.

Tracking and Reporting Vendor 1099-MISC Payments

If your company pays individuals and certain types of businesses, you might need to file a Form 1099-MISC at the end of each calendar year. Currently, only vendors paid $600 or more in a given year are required to be reported to the IRS.

note

Did you just start using QuickBooks during the calendar year? Did you previously pay your 1099-MISC eligible vendors using some other software? If yes, review the section titled "Entering Midyear 1099 Balances," later in this chapter for help in reporting the proper amount of calendar year payments.

When submitting 1099 forms to the IRS, you must also include Form 1096. This transmittal document summarizes the individual 1099 forms. QuickBooks prints both the 1096 summary and individual 1099 forms, using preprinted tax forms available through Intuit or most office supply stores. Intuit also offers the option to use its E-File Service for filing your 1099 and 1096 tax forms.

caution

The QuickBooks 1099 Wizard helps you comply with ever-changing IRS regulations. Be sure to check for QuickBooks software updates before you issue 1099s or other tax documents. Instructions on updating your data file are included in Chapter 17.

Press Ctrl+1 on your keyboard to view the Product Information dialog box. The Product field lists the QuickBooks version, year, and release you are currently using.

Before you begin using the QuickBooks 1099 Wizard, review your vendor settings using the following reports. To access these, select **Vendors**, **Print/E-file 1099s** from the menu bar.

- **Review 1099 Vendors**—Lists each vendor's Tax ID, Address, and other useful information. Sort by Eligible for 1099 at the top of the report to help verify you have all the vendors selected for whom you need to issue a Form 1099-MISC.
- **1099 Summary Report**—Lists Box 7:Nonemployee Compensation details by vendor.
- **1099 Detail Report**—Lists individual transactions that are used to calculate the amount reported for the vendor's Form 1099-MISC earnings.

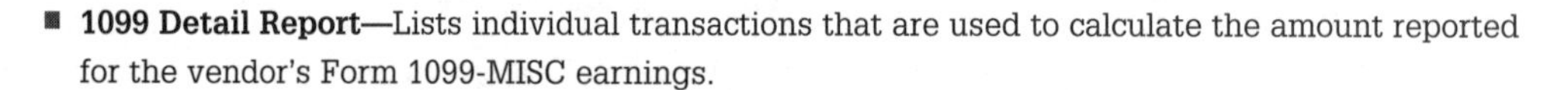

Properly setting up your 1099 tax form preferences in QuickBooks will ensure compliance with federal tax reporting guidelines. If you have specific questions about what type of vendor should receive this document, refer to the www.irs.gov website or contact your company's accountant or tax advisor. Next, let's get your file ready to track and report your Form 1099-MISC payments to vendors using the six steps in the new QuickBooks 1099 Wizard.

Step 1—Select Your 1099 Vendors

Not all vendors are required to receive a Form 1099-MISC at the end of the year. Make sure you have reviewed the reporting requirements on the IRS website or have asked for advice from your company's accountant or tax advisor.

To select your 1099 vendors, follow these steps:

1. Log in to your file as the Admin or External Accountant user.
2. From the menu bar, select **Edit**, **Preferences** to open the Preferences dialog box, as previously shown in Figure 7.2 in Chapter 7.
3. Select the **Tax:1099—Company Preferences** tab. Select the **Yes** option for Do You File 1099-MISC Forms?
4. Select the **Click Here** link for If You're Ready To Prepare Your 1099s, Including Mapping Accounts.
5. Click Yes to the Save Changes message if displayed. QuickBooks opens the 1099 Wizard, displayed in Figure 8.12.
6. Review the steps and click Get Started.
7. Place a checkmark in front of those vendors you want to track Form 1099-MISC earnings for. (Optional) Click the Select All button. See Figure 8.13.

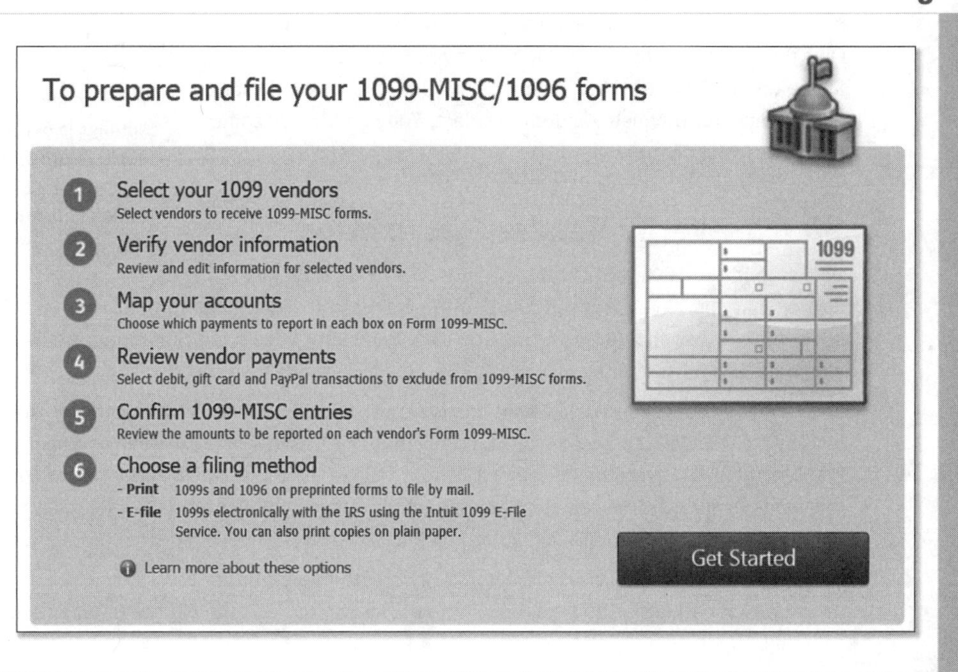

Figure 8.12 In a few simple steps, you can use the 1099 Wizard to review eligible payments and generate 1099 forms.

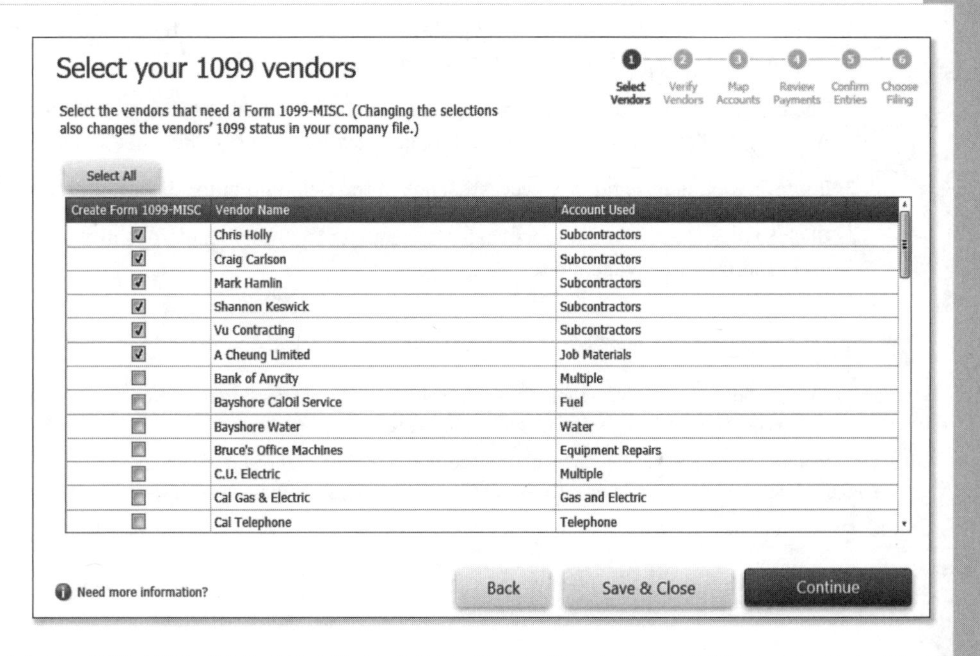

Figure 8.13 Select the vendors that will receive a Form 1099-MISC.

8. Click Save & Close if you are not ready to complete the remaining steps in the 1099 Wizard, or click Continue to advance to the next step.

Select all the vendors that should get the required tax form. QuickBooks automatically excludes any vendors whose payments fall below the IRS threshold (currently $600). Do not worry here if you are uncertain which vendors to select. You can always come back and make changes.

tip

If you do not complete the 1099 settings in one sitting, you can easily return to the 1099 Wizard. On the menu bar, select **Vendors, Print/E-Files 1099s, 1099 Wizard.**

Step 2—Verify Vendor Information

This step in the 1099-MISC Income setup wizard displays each vendor that you have assigned needing the 1099-MISC Income tax form at year end. If you do not see a vendor that should be on this list, click Back and place a checkmark next to those vendors whom qualify for the form.

You can also update the Tax Settings tab within the vendor record for any vendors that should receive a 1099. This includes recording the vendor's Tax ID number, as well as clicking the "Vendor Eligible for 1099" checkbox on the Tax Settings tab of a New or Edit Vendor record. You can request the vendor's address and tax identification number using the IRS form W-9, Request for Taxpayer Identification Number and Certification. This form can be downloaded from the www.irs.gov website.

If you omitted these steps when you initially created your vendor record, you can add this information at any time during the year, and QuickBooks will include the vendor payments in your 1099 reporting.

To verify vendor information, follow these steps:

1. If you selected Continue after step 7 (select your 1099 vendors) in the previous section, you should now verify your 1099 vendors' information.
2. The list shows only those vendors you selected. Confirm that the Tax ID, Company Name, Address, and other fields are all completed correctly for each vendor. See Figure 8.14.
3. If information is missing or inaccurate, click in the field and enter the appropriate information.
4. Click Save & Close if you are not ready to complete the remaining steps in the 1099 Wizard, or click Continue to advance to the next step.

tip

The end of any calendar year is a busy time. Consider reviewing your vendors' 1099 information throughout the year so you have time to collect the missing information before the tax forms are due.

Businesses must provide eligible vendors with their Form 1099-MISC by the end of January following a calendar year. Some vendors will want their forms as early as possible in January, so prepare in advance.

Figure 8.14 Changes made in the 1099 Wizard will automatically update the corresponding vendor record in QuickBooks.

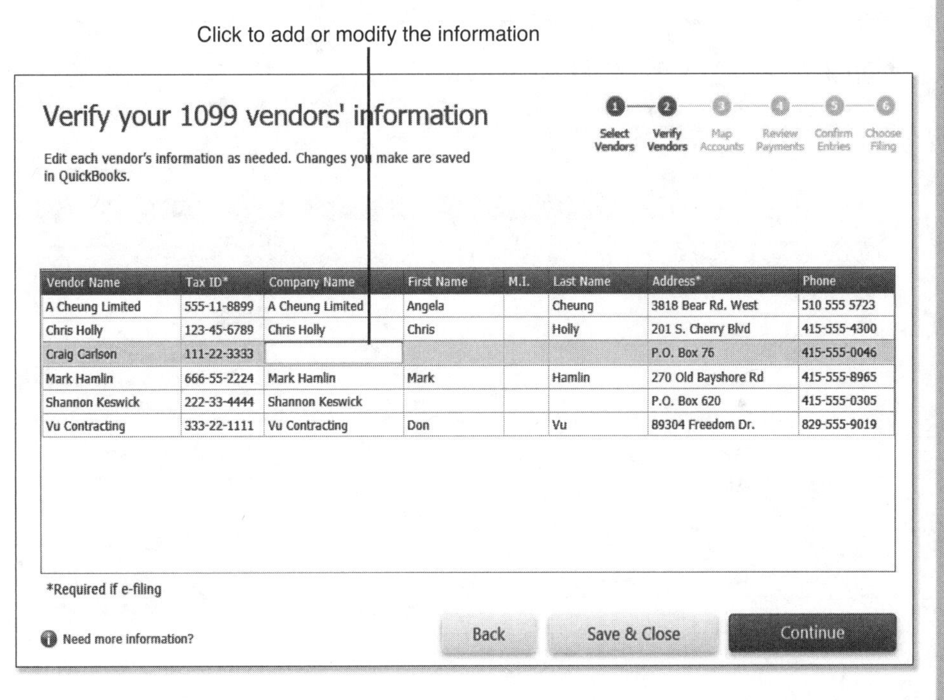

Step 3—Map Accounts

QuickBooks provides the option of including or excluding specific general ledger accounts from being used when reporting your vendor's payments. For example, you might pay your vendor for services and record it to a specific Subcontractors expense account. You might also reimburse that same vendor for materials purchases and record that portion of the expense to a different expense account.

caution

It is not the intent of this book to provide tax filing advice, so check with the IRS website for more details or ask your company's accountant or tax advisor.

To map your accounts, follow these steps:

1. After verifying your 1099 vendors' information, click Continue.
2. For the vendors you have selected, the 1099 Wizard displays the accounts that were assigned on the vendor payments. For each account displayed, you can choose to Omit these payments from Form 1099-MISC income reporting or select from several 1099 box reporting options. See Figure 8.15.
3. (Optional) Click the Show 1099 Accounts drop-down list and select **Show All Accounts** if you want to omit or map your 1099 reporting for all your accounts on your chart of accounts.
4. (Optional) Select the **Report All Payments** in Box 7 checkbox. When you do so, all the displayed accounts will be assigned to Box 7:Nonemployee Compensation.

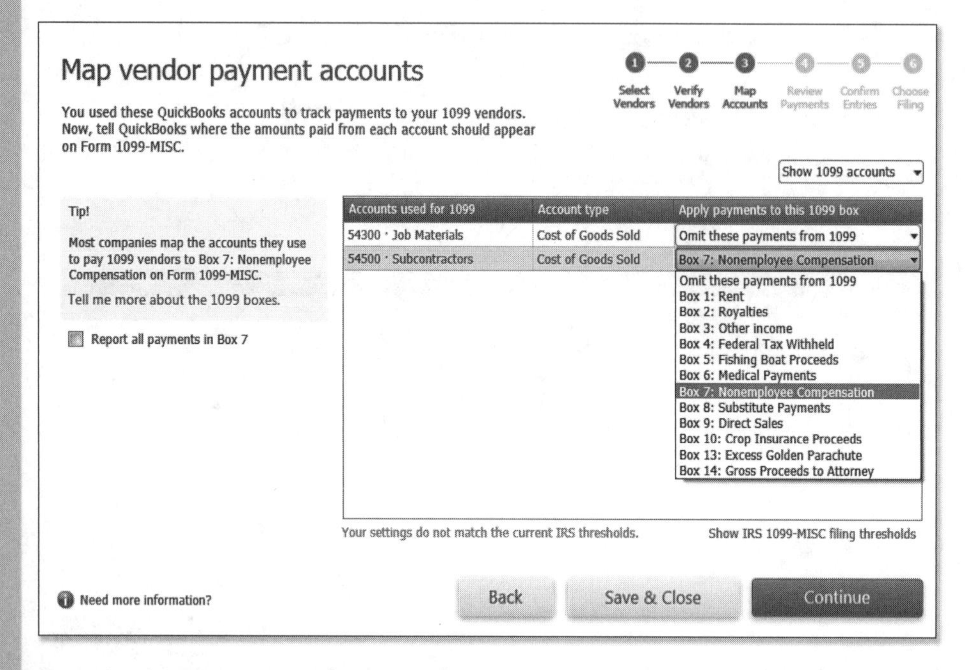

Figure 8.15 Selectively choose which accounts are reported or omitted from your 1099 reporting.

caution

The only 1099 form that QuickBooks will print or that can be processed by Intuit 1099 E-File Service is the Form 1099-MISC. However, general ledger in QuickBooks can be assigned to any of the 14 boxes on the Form 1099-MISC.

Multiple cost of sales, ordinary expense, and other expense accounts can be assigned (mapped) to a single box on the Form 1099-MISC. However, a single account cannot be assigned to more than one reporting box on the form.

If a Balance Sheet account (such as a vendor prepayment) is used when recording a payment to a 1099 eligible vendor; that account will not display by default in the Map Vendor Payment Accounts dialog box. However, if you select **Show All Accounts,** you are provided the option to omit the payments recorded to Balance Sheet accounts from 1099 or assign to the appropriate Form 1099-MISC box.

5. If you see the warning message Your Settings Do Not Match the Current IRS Thresholds, click the Show IRS 1099-MISC Filing Thresholds link.

6. Read the information displayed in the 1099-MISC IRS Thresholds dialog box. Click the Reset to IRS Thresholds button. QuickBooks updates the thresholds with current tax information.

7. Click Save & Close to return to the 1099 Wizard.

8. Click Save & Close if you are not going to complete the remaining steps in the 1099 Wizard, or click Continue to advance to the next step.

Step 4—Review Vendor Payments

Do you pay your vendor bills by credit card? Beginning with the 2011 reporting tax year, the IRS established new rules to exclude from Form 1099-MISC any payments you made by credit card, debit card, gift card, or third-party payment network such as PayPal. (The IRS now requires that card issuers and third-party payment networks report these transactions on Form 1099-K.) You should review both included and excluded payments on the Review Payments for Exclusions screen in the 1099 Wizard, displayed in Figure 8.16.

Payments to vendors should always be recorded in QuickBooks via the Enter Credit Card Charges form. If instead you use the Pay Bills or Write Checks transaction forms, you'll need to take special guidelines into account. To record a vendor payment made with a credit card, debit card, or gift card, or using a third-party payment network such as PayPal, you should note the payment method in the No. field of a Write Checks dialog box. QuickBooks recognizes, and automatically excludes from Form 1099-MISC, these payments if the following notations in the check number field (limited to eight characters) are used:

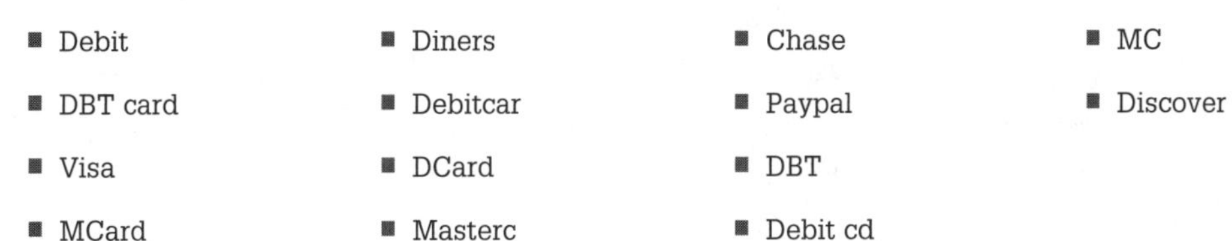

- Debit
- DBT card
- Visa
- MCard
- Diners
- Debitcar
- DCard
- Masterc
- Chase
- Paypal
- DBT
- Debit cd
- MC
- Discover

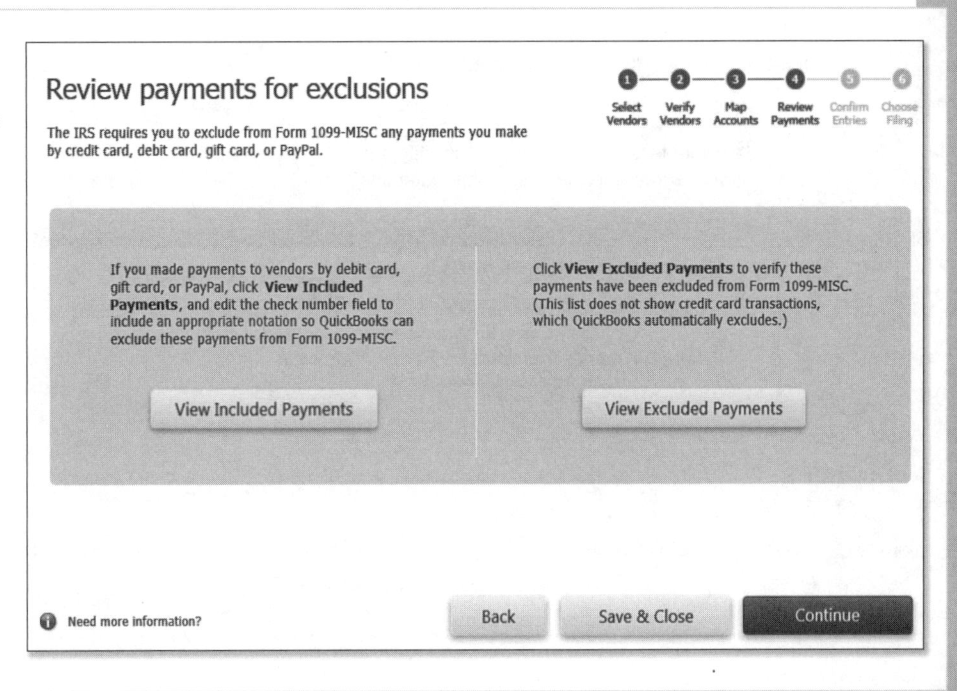

Figure 8.16 The 1099 Wizard allows you to verify whether payments should be included or excluded in the year's 1099 reporting.

To view the transactions included in your 1099 reporting, follow these steps:

1. Click View Included Payments. QuickBooks creates a report titled "Check Payments Included on Forms 1099-MISC" (see Figure 8.17).
2. If any of these payments were made by credit card, debit card, gift card, or third-party payment network such as PayPal, you need to edit the check number, which is displayed in the Num column on this report.
3. Double-click to open a single transaction that was paid by credit card. The associated check displays. Modify the information in the No. field using one of the accepted notations listed previously.
4. Click Save & Close to save your changes. QuickBooks no longer includes this payment in your 1099-MISC Income reporting.
5. Click the View Excluded Payments button. QuickBooks creates a report titled Check Payments Excluded from Forms 1099-MISC. Verify that the transactions listed on this report qualify to be excluded from 1099-MISC Income reporting.
6. Click the X in the top-right corner to close the report(s).
7. Click Save & Close if you are not going to complete the remaining steps in the 1099 Wizard, or click Continue to advance to the next step.

tip

Save yourself time from having to modify the check number assigned to bill payment checks or other checks when recording vendor 1099 payments made by credit card using these transaction types. Instead, when paying a vendor bill, assign the payment to a credit card account or use the Enter Credit Card Charges dialog box to record the expense (from the menu bar select **Banking, Enter Credit Card Charges**).

QuickBooks automatically excludes from Form 1099-MISC reporting any bill payment made using the credit card payment method.

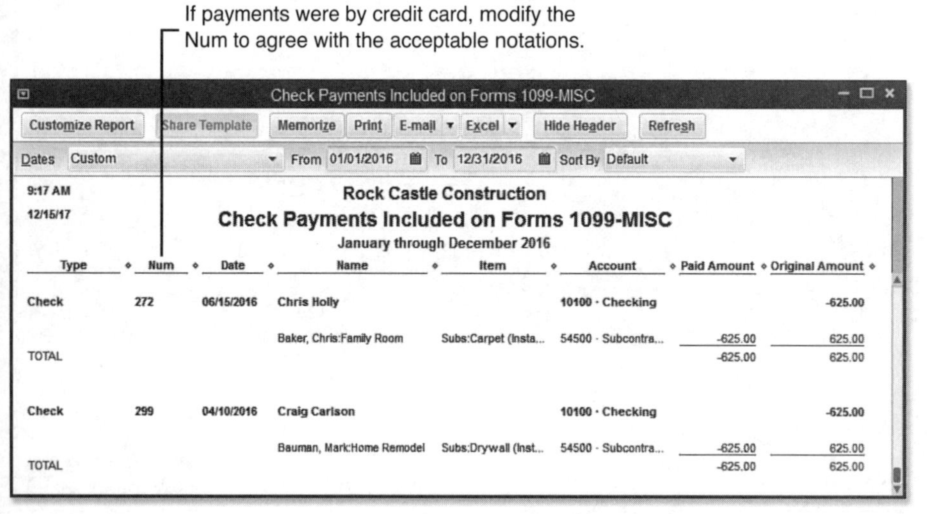

Figure 8.17
Review checks recorded as payments to vendors that might have been paid by credit card.

Step 5—Confirm 1099-MISC Entries

The 1099 Wizard displays a list of the Vendors that will receive a Form 1099-MISC (see Figure 8.18).

To confirm 1099-MISC entries, follow these steps:

1. Click the Summary Report link to see a summary for all vendors included in your Form 1099-MISC income reporting. Modify the dates and filters as needed.
2. Click the X in the top right to close the 1099 Summary Report.
3. Click the Detail Report to see a list of all transactions grouped by vendor. Modify the dates and filters as needed.
4. Click the X in the top right to close the 1099 Detail Report.
5. Click Save & Close if you are not going to complete the remaining steps in the 1099 Wizard, or click Continue to advance to the next step.

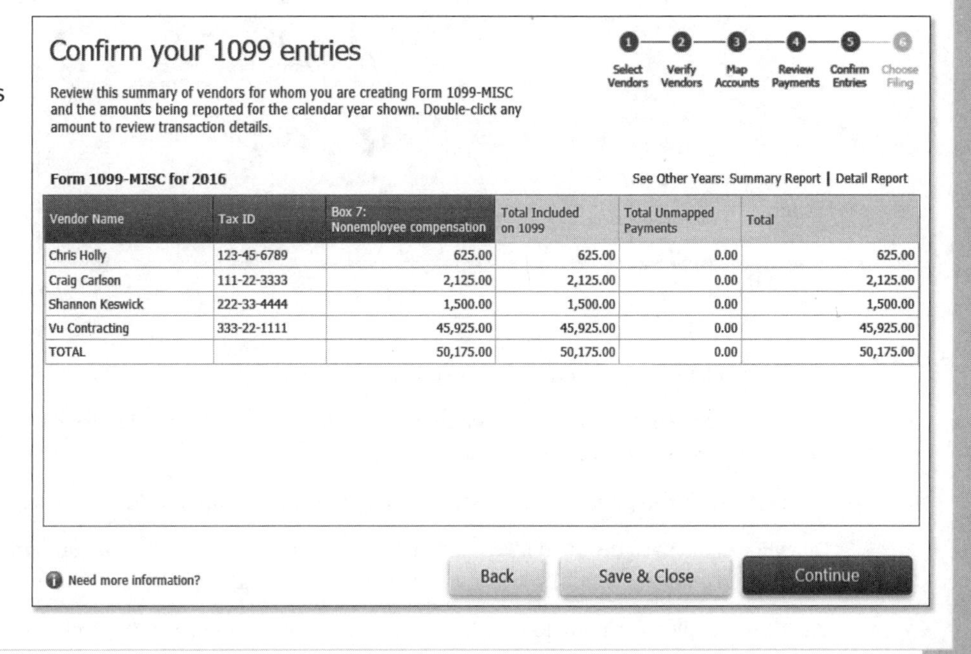

Vendor Name	Tax ID	Box 7: Nonemployee compensation	Total Included on 1099	Total Unmapped Payments	Total
Chris Holly	123-45-6789	625.00	625.00	0.00	625.00
Craig Carlson	111-22-3333	2,125.00	2,125.00	0.00	2,125.00
Shannon Keswick	222-33-4444	1,500.00	1,500.00	0.00	1,500.00
Vu Contracting	333-22-1111	45,925.00	45,925.00	0.00	45,925.00
TOTAL		50,175.00	50,175.00	0.00	50,175.00

Figure 8.18 Preview vendor payments that will be included or not included in your Form 1099-MISC income reporting.

Step 6—Choose a Filing Method

The QuickBooks 1099 Wizard provides information to help you choose a filing method, either printing or electronically filing the forms (see Figure 8.19).

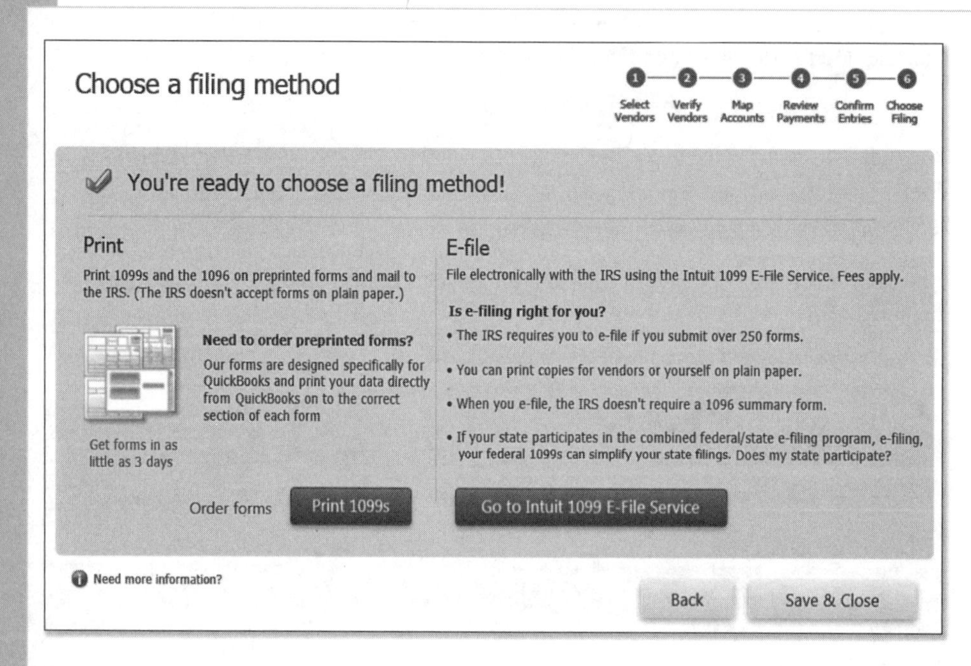

Figure 8.19
The 1099 Wizard makes it easy to print 1099 forms or file electronically.

To print your 1099-MISC Income forms, follow these steps:

1. Click the Order Forms link to order your tax forms from Intuit. You might also purchase tax forms from your local office supply store.
2. Click Print 1099s to print the documents on the preprinted forms you have purchased.
3. QuickBooks displays the 1099-MISC and 1096 Forms dialog box. Select the appropriate year you are printing your forms for. Typically, you will select **Last Calendar Year**.
4. The Select 1099s to Print dialog box displays with each vendor selected. (Optional) Click Select All or Select None if needed.
5. QuickBooks displays the number of vendors selected and the total dollar amount for the selected vendors.
6. If you will be e-Filing your 1099s, skip to the instructions that follow step 11. If you are printing, continue with step 7.
7. Click Print 1099. The Print 1099s settings display. Place the tax forms in your printer and select **Print**. You will need to print on preprinted forms; unlike W-2s, the IRS does not accept 1099 forms on plain paper.

8. View the documents that printed. When you have completed printing 1099s, click Print 1096 and insert the preprinted form into your printer.
9. Enter the Contact Name in the 1096 Information dialog box. If circumstances warrant, select **This is My Final Return**.
10. Choose your printer and click Print. QuickBooks returns to the Select 1099s to Print.
11. When the printing is complete, click the X in the top-right corner to close the Select 1099s to Print dialog box.

If you will be E-Filing, click the Go to Intuit 1099 E-File Service. Follow the instructions for filing. You will complete three steps:

1. **Sign up for the Service**—Use your Intuit Account username and password.
2. **Set up Intuit Sync Manager**—Enable QuickBooks to send your information to the Intuit E-File 1099 Service.
3. **Purchase, Print and E-File**—Print and E-File your returns with a click of a button.

The information window provides a toll-free number to call if you have any questions. 1099 forms for a given tax year cannot be filed until January of the following year.

You have successfully completed the steps to properly track and report your vendors' Form 1099-MISC income payments.

Correcting Accounts Payable Errors

Chapter 7, "Setting Up Vendors," provided a recommended workflow and preference settings that will help you avoid making mistakes with your accounts payable transactions. This chapter provides specific details about methods you can use to correct existing accounts payable errors.

The purpose of this book is not to give you business-specific accounting or tax advice, but rather to introduce you to ways you might use to fix specific mistakes you have found.

Open Vendor Bills Paid with a Write Checks Transaction

Earlier in this chapter, in the "Reviewing the Unpaid Bills Detail Report" section, you learned a way to reconcile your A/P Aging Summary report total to your Balance Sheet accounts payable total (refer to Figures 8.1 and 8.2). As important as this task is, it is also necessary for you to review those items listed as unpaid to your vendor. If you notice an open vendor bill that you know is no longer due, it might be because you paid the vendor with a Write Checks transaction instead of the proper Pay Bills transaction type.

 **caution**

Before making any of the suggested changes, be sure you have made a backup of your data in case the change does not give you the desired result. Additionally, obtaining your accountant's advice regarding the changes you are contemplating is always prudent.

You should experience fewer of these types of mistakes in recent years because QuickBooks directs you to the Pay Bills dialog box, as shown in Figure 8.20, when you attempt to write a check to a vendor with open bills.

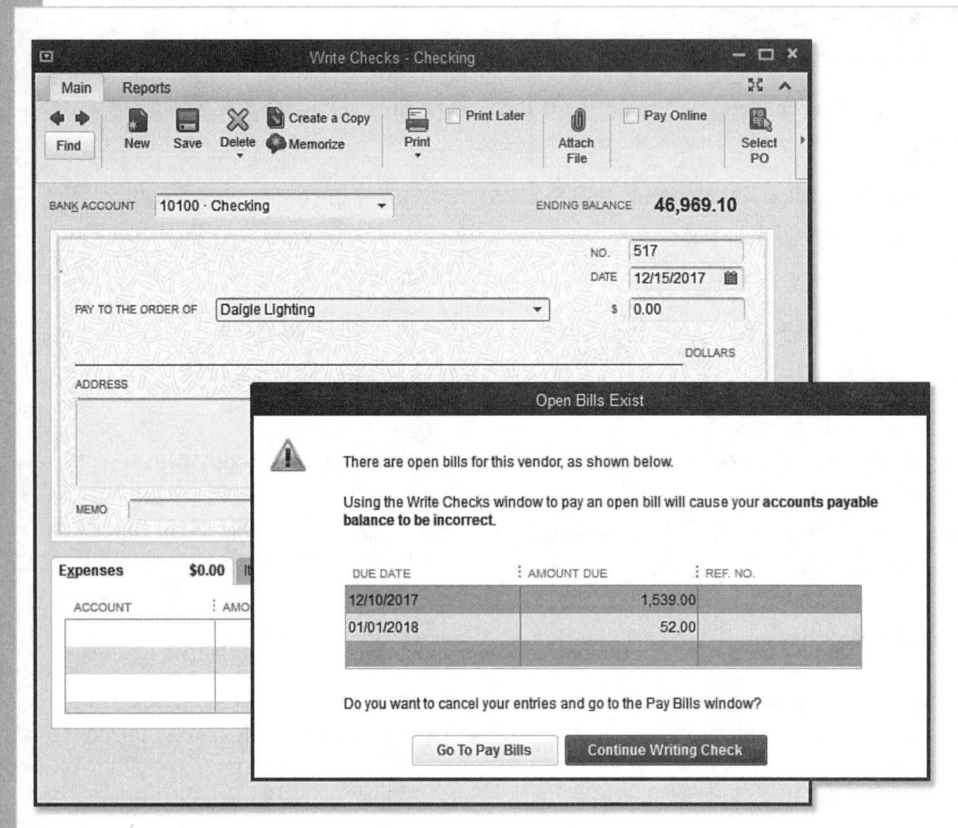

Figure 8.20
The warning provided if you attempt to create a write check transaction when paying a vendor with open bills.

If you choose to modify the original vendor check, carefully consider the accounting effect this type of correction will have on your financials:

- Is the change a significant dollar amount? Both cash and accrual basis reports will be affected.
- Consider the date of the check and the date of the bill—are they in different tax years?
- Is the correction going to affect a year where the data has already been used to prepare a tax return?

If you answered yes to any of these questions, be sure to discuss with your accountant the impact this change could have on your financials.

You can modify this check, making it become a vendor credit. In other words, it will decrease (debit) accounts payable and maintain the original decrease (credit) to your cash account. To do so, follow these steps:

1. Locate the Write Checks transaction used to pay the vendor. One easy way is to click the Vendors button on the Home page to open the Vendor Center. Choose your vendor from the list on the left, and select **Checks** from the Show drop-down list, as displayed previously in Figure 8.5.
2. Double-click the check to open the Write Checks transaction.
3. On the Expenses tab, in the account column, replace the currently listed account with the accounts payable account as shown in Figure 8.21. This creates a decrease (debit) to the accounts payable account.

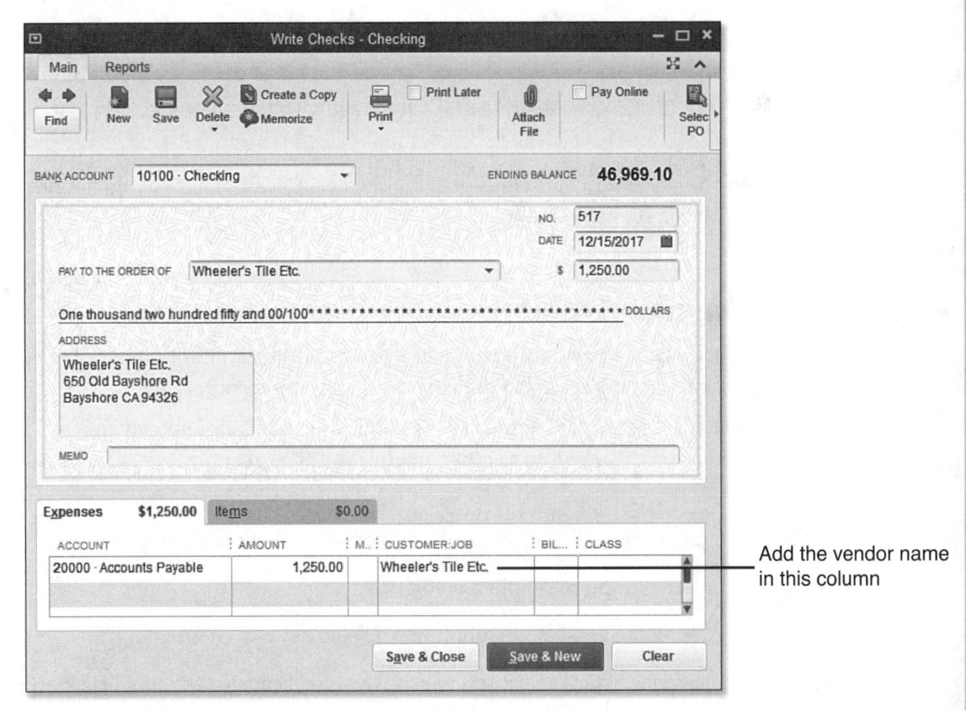

Figure 8.21 Using a check to record a vendor prepayment (debit to Accounts Payable).

4. In the drop-down list in the Customer:Job column, select the vendor name. If you had previously listed a Customer:Job in this field, you will be warned to choose a Vendor name instead. This assigns the accounts payable decrease to a specific vendor. You cannot save the transaction without assigning a vendor name.
5. Click Save & Close, and then click Yes to record your changes.

6. From the menu bar, select **Vendors**, **Pay Bills**, and use the arrow key on your keyboard to move up and down through the list of vendors in the Pay Bills dialog box. Or, optionally, select the vendor name from the Filter By drop-down list. Before placing a checkmark in the box next to the vendor's specific invoice, QuickBooks shows the total number of credits and their total value in the Discount & Credit Information for Highlighted Bill section. (See Figure 7.21 in Chapter 7.)

7. When you have located the correct bill, place a checkmark in the box to the left of the Date Due column. When an invoice is selected, QuickBooks automatically applies the available credits to the selected vendor invoice (if the preference was set). If not, and you want to modify the amount or which credits are selected, click the Set Credits button. The Discount and Credits dialog box displays (previously shown in Figure 7.22 in Chapter 7). Users can modify which credit is selected by changing the checkmark from one credit to another or by manually overriding the amount of the credit.

8. Click the Done button when the credit is assigned.

9. QuickBooks shows in the Pay Bills dialog box that the bill is paid by a credit (if the entire bill is being paid by the credit, QuickBooks will not create a check). Click Pay Selected Bills when you are finished.

10. QuickBooks offers you Pay More Bills or Done choices. Click Done if you do not have any other transactions to correct using this method.

Misapplied Vendor Credit

Have you ever been given a credit from a vendor, only to find out later that your vendor applied the credit to a different open bill than you did in your accounting records?

QuickBooks makes it easy to reassign a vendor credit from one accounts payable bill to another bill. You temporarily assign the credit to another vendor, and then reapply it to the correct vendor. To do so, follow these steps:

1. On the Home page, click the Vendors button to open the Vendor Center.

2. Select the vendor with the misapplied credit.

3. In the Show drop-down list, select **Bills** (this will also list vendor credits).

4. From the transactions listed, select the misapplied credit memo by double-clicking it. The Enter Bills dialog box, with the word *Credit* displayed, opens for the selected transaction.

5. On the vendor line of the credit, select a different vendor. (Remember to whom you assign it.)

6. Click Save & Close. QuickBooks removes the credit transaction from the vendor bill it was previously associated with.

7. QuickBooks also warns that the transaction you edit will no longer be connected. Click Yes to continue (see Figure 8.22).

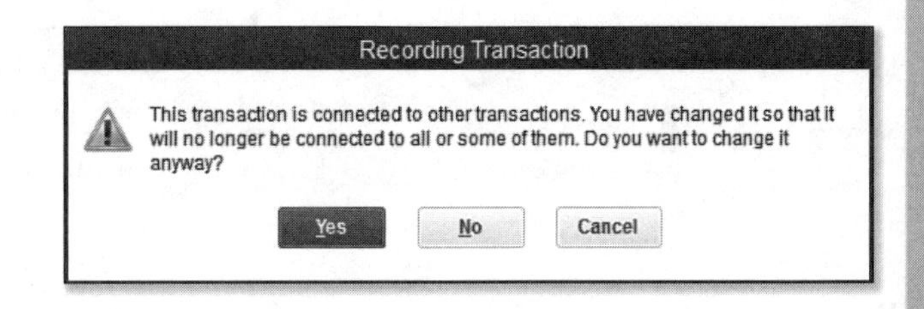

Figure 8.22
Warning when you unapply a previously applied vendor credit.

8. From the same Vendor Center, select the other vendor to which you assigned the credit. From the Show drop-down list, select **Bills** and double-click the credit you just assigned in step 5. The Enter Bills dialog box, with the word *Credit* displayed, opens for the selected transaction.
9. On the vendor line, select the original vendor.
10. Click Save & Close, and click Yes to making the change.

QuickBooks now shows the credit as unapplied to your original vendor, and you can follow the steps outlined previously for applying the credit to the correct open vendor bill.

Removing Aged Open Item Receipts or Vendor Bills

One of the more important tasks you can do to maintain a correct accounting records is to remove old, aged item receipts or payables you do not owe or will not collect.

You have three options when you want to remove these aged (old) transactions:

- Create a credit memo and apply it
- Void the item receipt or bill
- Delete the item receipt or bill

To create and apply a credit memo to a vendor bill, follow the same steps as listed in the earlier section titled "Applying Vendor Discounts or Credits."

You must give special consideration to applying a credit memo to an open item receipt. First, convert the item receipt to a bill. To do so, follow these steps:

1. Locate the open item receipt using any of the methods suggested in Chapter 7.
2. When you select the open item receipt, QuickBooks opens the Create Item Receipts dialog box. Place a checkmark in the Bill Received box at the top right, as shown in Figure 8.23.

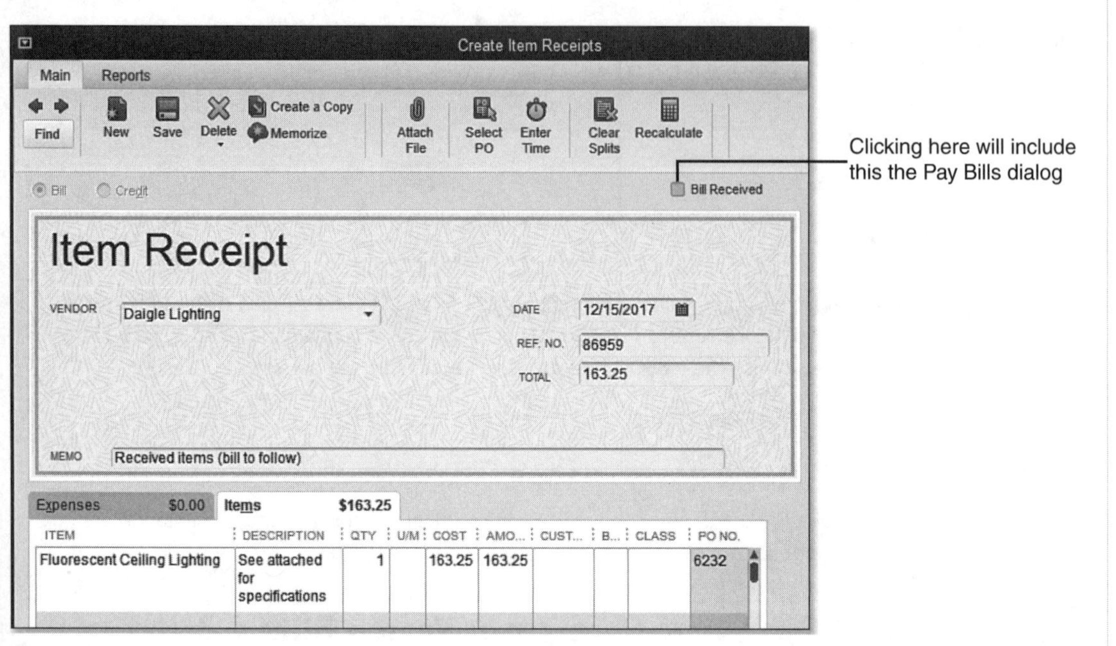

Figure 8.23
Converting an open Item Receipt to a bill is necessary before applying a vendor credit memo.

You can now apply your credit memo to the item receipt, which has been converted to a bill.

When considering whether to void it or delete it, I always prefer the void option because it leaves a record of the original transaction. Before voiding or deleting, you need to verify that the aged open item receipts or bills do not have any other transactions associated with them. To verify this, follow these steps:

1. Open the item receipt or bill using any one of the many methods discussed in Chapter 7.
2. Open a previously recorded bill or create item receipt transaction, the transaction tab to the right will include information about linked transactions. QuickBooks displays in the Summary box information about when the transaction was created and edited (if applicable). In the Related Transactions box, links are provided to the original transactions (if any).

If you had voided or deleted the vendor bill shown in Figure 8.24, you would have created an unapplied vendor payment (the Bill Pmt-Check listed in the Related Transactions section). In effect, you would have traded one correction for another problem. So be careful when making corrections to your accounts payable transactions.

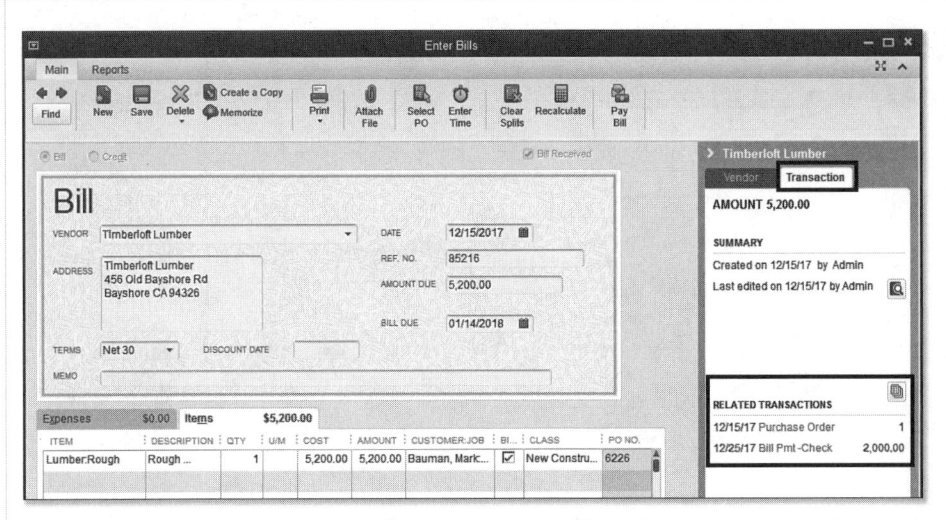

Figure 8.24 Before voiding, deleting, or modifying a bill, click the Transaction tab to the right to see whether any transactions are associated with this bill.

Making General Journal Adjustments to Accounts Payable

All too often, I find that accounting professionals are quick to make adjustments to accounts payable using the Make General Journal Entries transaction, also referred to as a journal entry. The following are some of the issues surrounding the use of the journal entry for accounts payable adjustments:

- Only a single vendor or a customer name can be in the Make General Journal Entries transaction, not both a vendor and customer in the same transaction, minimizing the usefulness of the transaction for large volume corrections.
- General journal entries do not include the option to assign an item, including service, non-inventory, inventory, and so on. The adjustment would affect the Profit & Loss reports, but not specific QuickBooks reports that use item information, such as the Job Profitability reports or Inventory Valuation reports.
- You will still need to go to the Pay Bills dialog box to assign the balance generated by the general journal to the other related vendor transactions.

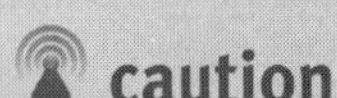

Often, the use of the general journal entries does not provide the desired results in your reporting. Did you know that the first line of any general journal entry is considered a "source" line? Specifically, this means that if the first line of a multiple-line general journal entry includes a vendor, customer, or any list item name in the Name column, as shown in Figure 8.25, that name element will display in reports on the lines below the first line, even if there is no relationship (see Figure 8.26).

This type of error is more apparent when a Customer:Job Name is included on the first line of a multiple-line general journal entry form. When preparing a Profit & Loss by Job report, QuickBooks would include all lines of the general journal entry as belonging to that job!

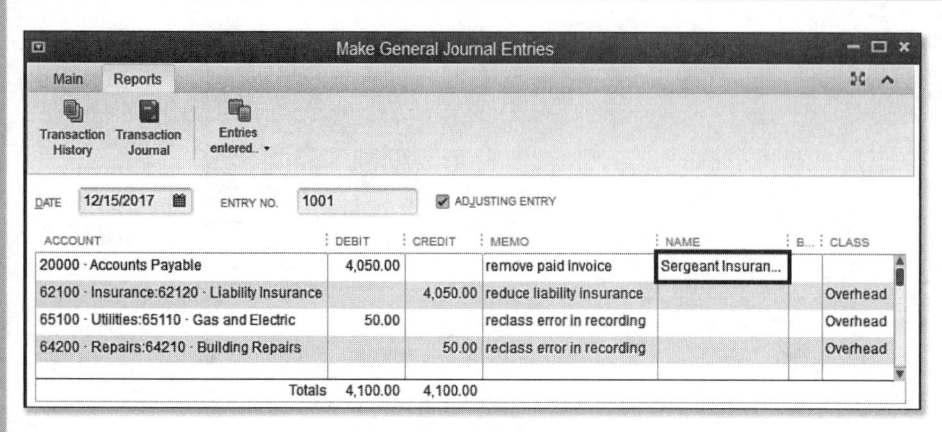

Figure 8.25 When the first line of a multiple-line general journal includes a list name in the Name column, QuickBooks associates the name entry with all lines of the transaction.

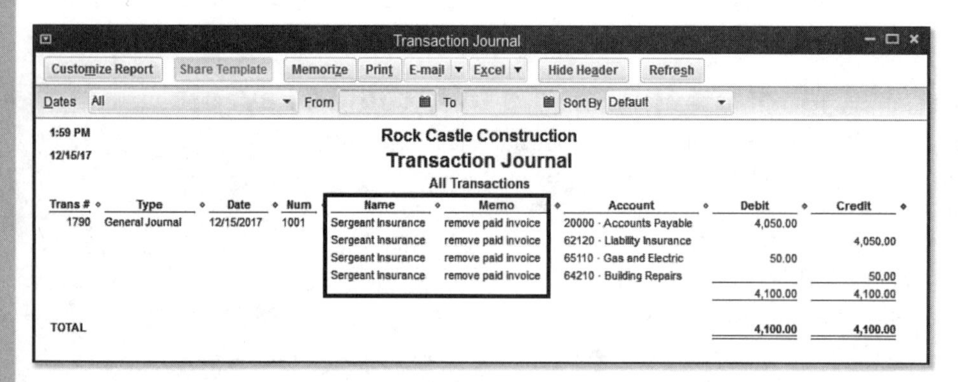

Figure 8.26 QuickBooks associated the vendor's name with all lines of the journal entry because the vendor list name was on the first line of the general journal.

A quick fix is to add a blank line at the beginning of each general journal entry. Another recommendation is to create a fictitious bank account and call it Adjusting Entries, but then leave the debit and credit fields blank. If you assign the first line of the entry to this account, QuickBooks provides a "register" for you to locate these types of transactions and at the same time avoid the issue addressed in this section. See Figures 8.27 and 8.28 to see how adding the line at the beginning of the transaction solves the problem in reporting.

Often, these simple tips can help make your QuickBooks reporting much more accurate!

If you have journal entries recorded to your accounts payable, your unpaid bills report might look something like Figure 8.29.

If your Unpaid Bills Detail report includes journal entries, see "Applying Vendor Credits," p. 248.

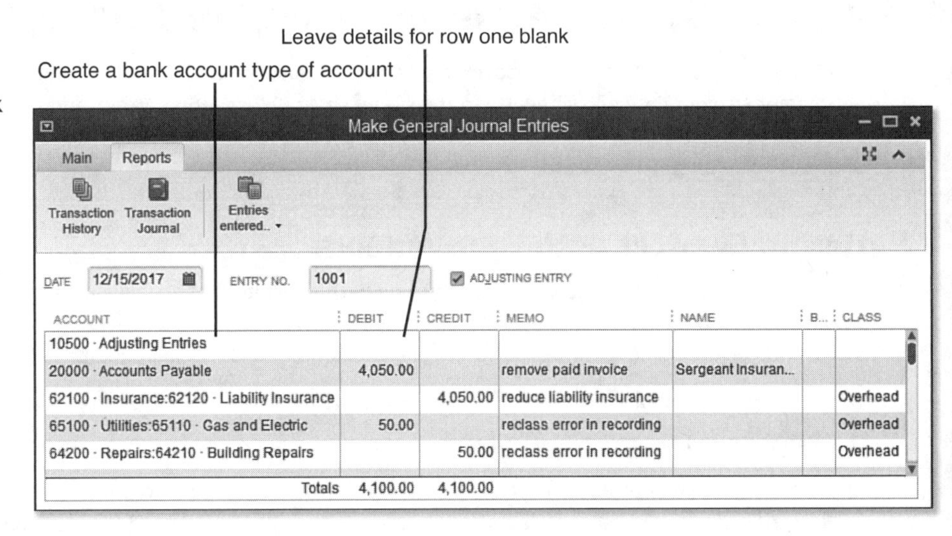

Figure 8.27 Including the fictitious bank account on the first line of a general journal entry prevents the source line (line 1) from being associated with each additional unrelated line.

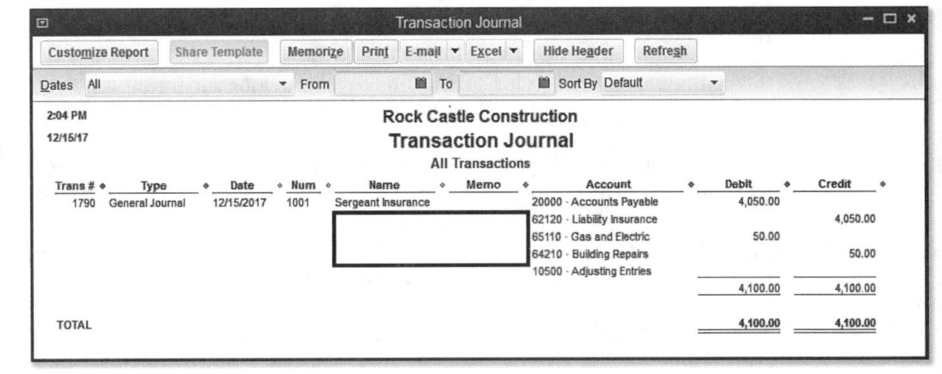

Figure 8.28 QuickBooks no longer associates the vendor's name with the unrelated general journal lines.

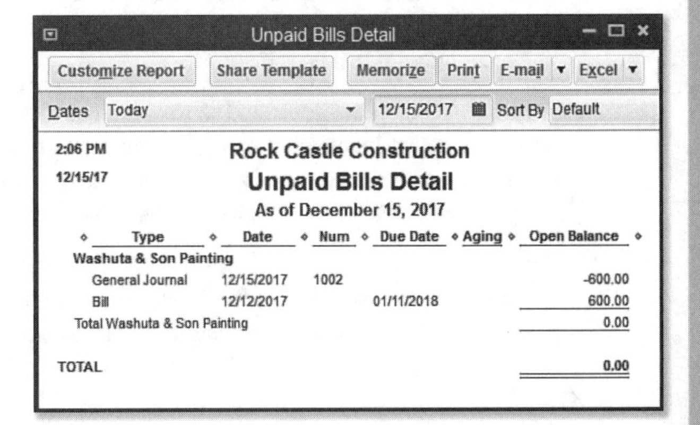

Figure 8.29 Your Unpaid Bills Detail report might show the general journal entry as unapplied.

Handling Unique Accounts Payable Transactions

So far you have learned about the accounts payable transactions and workflow, preferences you can set to improve your data entry, reports to review when troubleshooting errors, and methods of correcting accounts payable errors. This section offers specific solutions to some of those unique transactions you might need to record.

Bartering Services with Your Vendors

Exchanging goods or services on a noncash basis with a vendor that is also a customer is commonly referred to as bartering. A common scenario is that your vendor also purchases your goods or services, and you are going to "swap" and not pay each other for the items purchased from each other.

To track the exchange of goods, follow these steps:

1. From the menu bar, select **Lists**, **Chart of Accounts**.
2. From the Account drop-down list, select **New** to create a new bank account and type the name **Bartering**. If you have account numbering turned on, you will also need to assign an account number. This bank account will always have a net zero balance if the transactions are recorded properly.
3. Click Save & Close.
4. From the menu bar, select **Vendor**, **Enter Bills** to record your vendor bill as if you were going to make the purchase from the vendor.
5. From the menu bar, select **Vendor**, **Pay Bills**. The Pay Bills dialog box opens. Select the bill for the vendor you will barter with.
6. In the Pay Bills dialog box, select the **Bartering Account** as the payment account (as displayed in Figure 8.30). You can then choose to assign a fictitious check number.
7. On the Home page, click the Customers button to open the Customers Center.
8. From the New Customer & Job drop-down list, select **New Customer** and complete the contact information for the new customer; otherwise, double-click the customer or job you will be bartering with to select it.
9. From the Customers Center, in the New Transactions drop-down list, select **Invoices**. Prepare the invoice to the new customer (also your vendor) using the same items on the invoice as if you were selling them to a customer. Click Save & Close.
10. From the Customers Center, in the New Transactions drop-down list, select **Receive Payments**. Record the fictitious payment from the customer (your vendor). Click Save & Close.

note

QuickBooks will not allow the same name to reside on multiple lists. To get around this limitation, when creating the customer name for your vendor, follow this convention: Johns Plumbing–C. I have added a –C after the "vendor name" on my customer list. This is helpful when picking the name from a list and you need to be certain to select the customer list item.

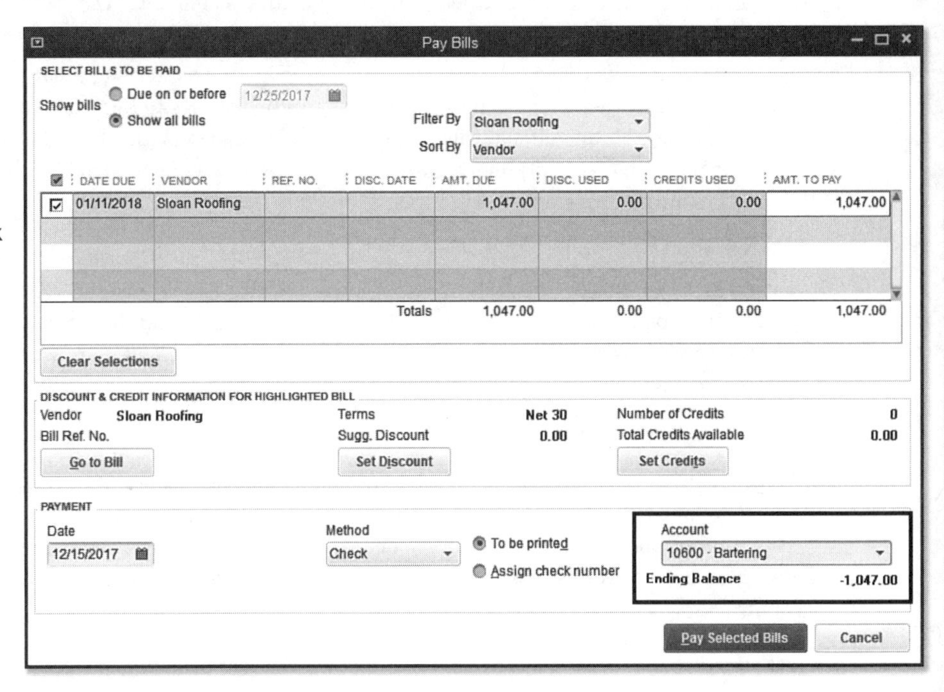

Figure 8.30 When you are bartering goods with your vendor, choose the fictitious bank account when recording the "payment" of the vendor bill.

11. Depending on how your preferences are set up for customer payments, deposit the fictitious customer payment into the same Bartering bank account created earlier.

12. If the value of what you purchased is equal to the value of what you sold, your Bartering bank account will have a net zero ending balance. If not, you will need to enter an adjusting entry to remove the balance or adjust your purchase or sales transaction total. If needed, you can create this entry by selecting **Banking**, **Use Register** from the menu bar and selecting the newly created **Bartering** bank account from the Use Register drop-down list. On the next available line in the account register, record a payment or deposit as needed to clear the account. You will want to ask your accountant what account is appropriate for the adjustment.

Recording Vendor Prepayments

If your business is required to prepay a vendor for purchases, you can choose from a couple of methods:

- Assign expenses to the other current asset type account typically named Prepaid Expenses.
- Record a decrease (debit) transaction to the accounts payable account.

Often you will have expenses that must be paid in advance of the benefit of the service or product being purchased. An example is a business's general liability insurance. Typically, you pay several months in advance for this type of insurance. To record this annual or semiannual expense all in one month would make that month unfairly take on the total expense.

A preferred method is to record the expense in equal monthly increments. The following steps show you how to record the original prepaid expense and record the expense to the individual months.

To accomplish this task, you pay the insurance vendor, assign the expense to other current asset type account, and then create a recurring entry that QuickBooks uses to remind you to enter the expense. Or QuickBooks can automatically enter the expense each month, depending on how you set up the reminder. This example shows how you would prepay a general liability insurance bill of $12,000 for 12 months of coverage.

To record vendor prepayments, follow these steps:

1. Complete an Enter Bills or Write Checks transaction payable to your insurance provider (or whatever type of prepaid expense you are recording). Instead of assigning the usual expense account on the transaction, assign the prepaid other current asset type account. In this example, the account is Prepaid Insurance.

2. Pay the bill to the vendor as normal.

3. Set up a recurring transaction to charge 1/12 of the total to each month. If the amount remains the same from month to month, set up the recurring entry to automatically post to QuickBooks. To do so, select **Company**, **Make General Journal Entries** from the menu bar. Create a journal entry with a debit to your expense account and a credit to the prepaid other current asset type account.

The next step is to memorize the transaction so that QuickBooks can automatically record it each month, or remind you to do so. To do so, follow these steps:

1. Create the transaction you want to memorize. You can also use this process to memorize icons for any of the QuickBooks transaction types, checks, bills, invoices, and so on.

2. From the ribbon toolbar, Main tab on most transactions, click Memorize and the Memorize Transaction dialog displays. (Optional) With the transaction displayed, press Ctrl+M on your keyboard, or from the menu bar, select **Edit**, **Memorize** to open the Memorize Transaction dialog box.

3. Choose to have QuickBooks remind you of a specific frequency or choose to have QuickBooks automatically enter the transaction (see Figure 8.31).

Figure 8.31
Memorized transactions can automate repetitive transactions or serve as a reminder to enter the transaction.

The other method discussed here is to record a debit balance to the vendor's accounts payable account. This is appropriate if you are going to be using the prepayment soon as payment toward the final vendor bill. To do so, follow these steps:

1. From the menu bar, select **Banking**, **Write Checks**.
2. In the Pay to the Order Of field, select the vendor's name.
3. Enter the amount of the prepayment.
4. On the Expenses tab, in the account detail area, select the **Accounts Payable** account (see Figure 8.32).
5. In the Customer:Job column, enter the vendor's name (must be a vendor type for this method to work).
6. Click Save & Close.

QuickBooks now records a vendor credit (debit to accounts payable) as shown in Figure 8.33.

tip

QuickBooks displays memorized transactions on the Memorized Transaction List, which is available by pressing Ctrl+T on your keyboard. You can also select **Lists, Memorized Transaction List** from the menu bar.

You might want to check your company reminders to be sure you enable a reminder for showing your memorized transactions. To do so, select **Edit, Preferences** from the menu bar, and then select the **Reminders** tab on the Preferences dialog box.

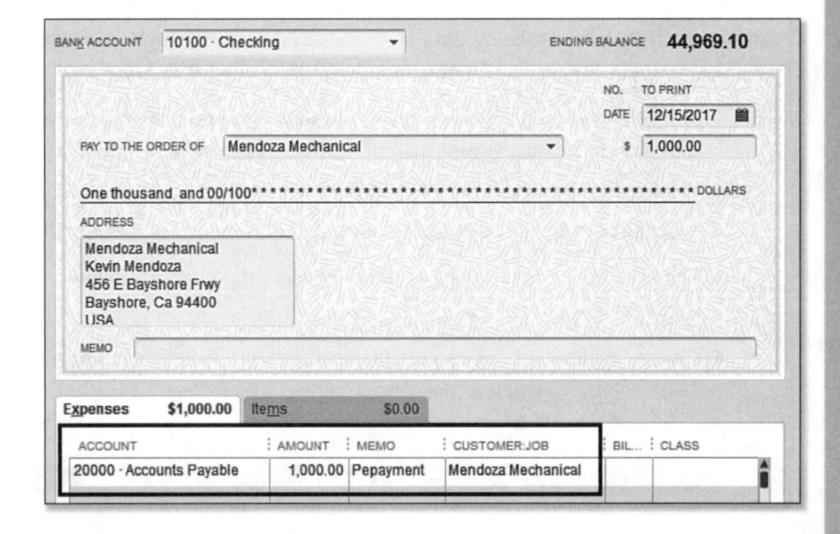

Figure 8.32
Assign the Accounts Payable account and the vendor name to a check when recording a vendor prepayment.

At a later date, you would record a bill for the full purchase price and apply this credit, detailed previously in Chapter 7.

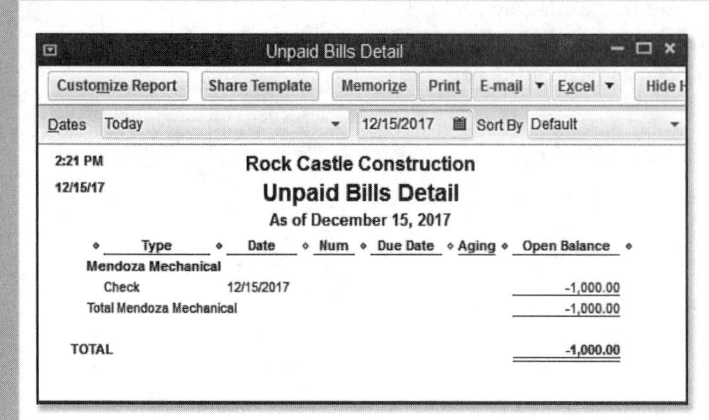

Figure 8.33
QuickBooks records the vendor prepayment as a negative entry to accounts payable (or a debit to accounts payable).

Entering Midyear 1099 Balances

If you start your QuickBooks data file midyear (or at some other time than the first of a new calendar year), you might have amounts paid previously to vendors who are eligible to receive the Form 1099-MISC.

To properly record the amounts paid to vendors in your prior accounting software, and to make sure that QuickBooks reports all amounts paid to the vendor on the Form 1099-MISC, follow these steps:

1. From the menu bar, select **Company**, **Make General Journal Entries**. If you use any of the job profitability reports, leave the first line (source line) of the journal entry blank.
2. On the following lines (one line per vendor), in the Account column, enter the cost of goods sold account or expense account assigned in the preferences for Tax:1099.
3. For each Debit line amount, be sure to select the vendor's list name (this must be a vendor type) in the Name column.
4. On the last line, enter one line total assigning the same account as the other lines so that the Debit column is equal to the Credit column (see Figure 8.34).

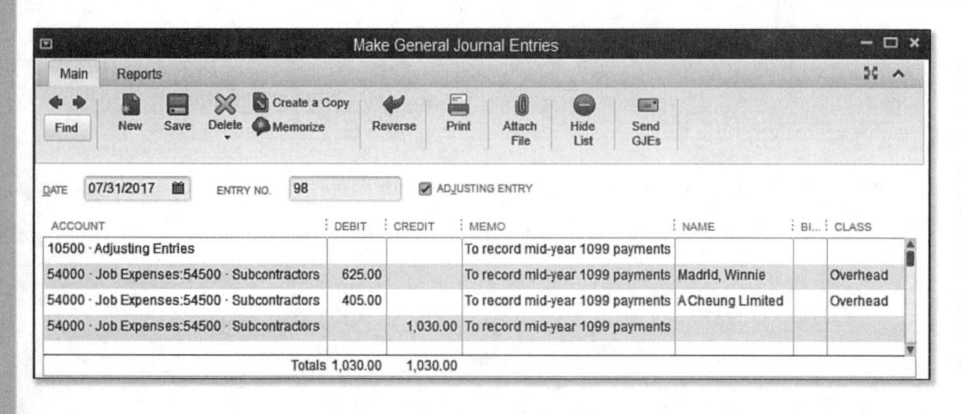

Figure 8.34
When starting a QuickBooks file midyear, create a general journal entry to record year-to-date vendor Form 1099-MISC Income tax payments.

Your overall financials will not change because the same account was used for both the debit and credit side of the transaction. Including the vendor name on the debit side of the transaction lines causes QuickBooks to include the amount in the reported Form 1099-MISC income amount.

Memorizing Recurring Transactions

QuickBooks can also help you not forget a recurring accounts payable bill. Memorized bills work best if the amount being paid is the same from month to month (or whatever frequency you set). An example is your rent payment.

To memorize a recurring accounts payable transaction, follow these steps:

1. Create a vendor bill as normal, assigning the amount and expense account that you want it to be associated with.
2. With the Enter Bills dialog box open, press Ctrl+M to open the Memorize Transaction dialog box (see previous Figure 8.31).
3. Enter a name that identifies this transaction in the memorized transaction list.
4. Choose one of the available options:
   - **Add to My Reminders List**—If you select this option, you need to choose how often and the next date you want to be reminded.
   - **Do Not Remind Me**—Use this option if you want to stop permanently, or even temporarily, your reminders for this transaction.
   - **Automate Transaction Entry**—Use this option if you want QuickBooks to create the entry automatically.
   - **Add to Group**—You can assign multiple transactions to a group and then process them with one keystroke. First, create a group by choosing Lists, Memorized Transaction List from the menu bar. From the Memorized Transaction drop-down list, select **New Group**. Give the group a name and choose options for the group from the following options: Remind Me, Do Not Remind Me, or Automatically Enter.
5. Click OK to close the Schedule Memorized Transaction dialog box.
6. Click Save & Close on your bill only if you want to create the vendor bill now and also add it to your memorized transaction list. If not, select **Clear** to remove the bill details, knowing that QuickBooks will prompt you to enter it on the frequency and date you selected.

 **note**

If you assign the Automate Transaction Entry option for memorizing a transaction, QuickBooks provides a reminder dialog box that displays when you log in to the QuickBooks file.

From the Enter Memorized Transactions dialog box, you can enter all the selected transactions, select those you want to enter, or enter them all later (see Figure 8.35).

To manually enter the transactions (if they're not set to Automate Transaction Entry), from the menu bar, select **Lists**, **Memorized Transaction List**, or press Ctrl+T on your keyboard to quickly call up the list. Select the group or individual transactions you want to post by double-clicking the group or individual item from the memorized transaction list.

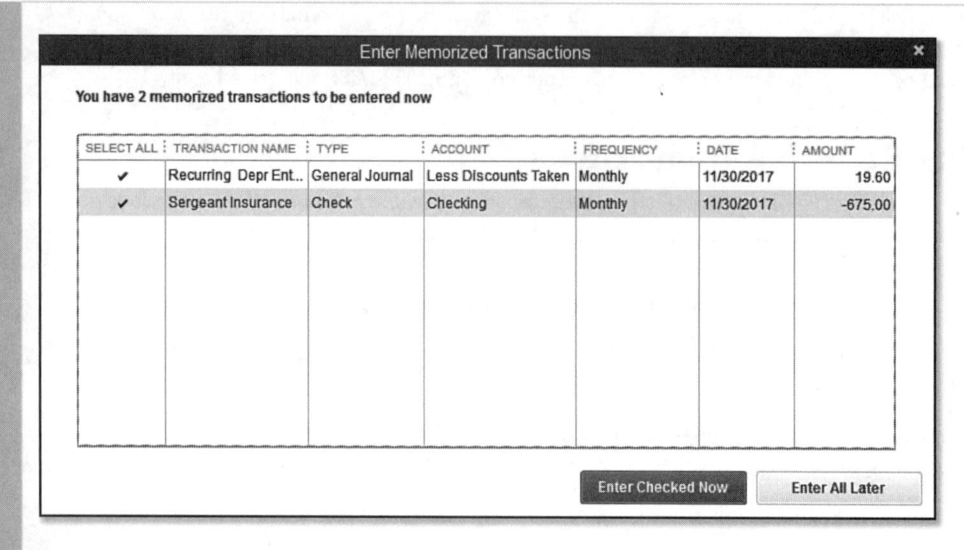

Figure 8.35 QuickBooks reminds you to process Memorized repeating transactions.

If you clicked a memorized group, QuickBooks creates each of the transactions in the group, asking you to assign a transaction date globally to all the transactions in the group. Use the memorized transaction tool to save time and to remind yourself to pay those important recurring bills.

Depositing a Vendor Refund

On occasion, you might receive a refund from your vendor whom you previously paid. To add a vendor refund check to your bank deposit, follow these steps:

1. Create your deposit (normally done with customer invoice payments) as usual.
2. On the next available deposit line, enter the vendor name in the Received From column, and then choose one of these two options:
   - If you do not have an open vendor credit in your Accounts Payable, select the expense account you want to reduce in the From Account column.
   - If you do have an open vendor credit that you want to associate this refund with, select the **Accounts Payable** account in the From Account column. Then apply the deposit to the open credit.
3. Enter an optional memo.
4. Enter the amount.
5. Click Save & Close when the total of the deposit agrees with the bank deposit total.

Although this method is quite easy to use, it does not allow you assign an item, so any refund recorded this way will not be included in certain job cost reports that are prepared from the use of items.

Instead, you would create a vendor credit memo to record the reduction in a job cost, and then follow the preceding instructions for applying the deposit to the open vendor credit.

Paying and Recording a Credit Card Bill

You have flexibility in how you choose to record and pay your credit card bills. The decision is based on your own circumstances because several ways can be appropriate.

Options for recording credit card expenses include the following:

- Enter a bill to the credit card vendor, summarizing the total charges on one bill and entering a separate line for each expense account amount.
- Enter individual credit card charges. From the menu bar, select **Banking**, **Enter Credit Card Charges**. You might be prompted to add a credit card account to QuickBooks.
- Use the QuickBooks Online Banking feature and automatically download your credit card charges and payments directly into your QuickBooks data file. Not all credit card providers offer this functionality. To see whether your card offers this option, select **Banking**, **Online Banking**, **Participating Financial Institutions** from the menu bar.

For more information, see "Online Banking Center," p. 502.

Options for paying your credit card bill include the following:

- If you selected to enter a bill to your credit card vendor, pay the bill as you do other bills, paying it partially or in full.
- If you selected one of the other two options, you need to create a vendor bill or check and in the Account column of the transaction assign the Credit Card type account you previously recorded the transactions to. The vendor bill simply decreases the balance owed on the credit card liability account.

The cash basis Balance Sheet might show this credit card payment amount if it is not paid by the date you prepare your financials.

For more information about how QuickBooks handles certain accounts on a cash basis, see "Accounts Payable Balance on Cash Basis Balance Sheet," p. 260.

Have you ever found that QuickBooks users assign a different expense account each time they create a check or bill to pay for costs of the business? This can make reviewing your specific expenses for the business less accurate.

QuickBooks offers two choices with the Automatically Recall Information preference (select **Edit**, **Preferences** from the menu bar and select the **General—My Preferences** tab):

- **Automatically recall last transaction for this name**—Recalls both the account and the previous amount.
- **Prefill accounts for vendor based on past entries**—Recalls only the account(s) used and will not recall the amount.

A more efficient process is to assign up to three default chart of accounts to each vendor record. To add these accounts, follow these steps:

1. From the Home page, click Vendors to open the Vendor Center.
2. Select the vendor to which you want to assign accounts, and click Edit Vendor to open the Edit Vendor dialog box.
3. Click OK to close the New Feature message if it displays.
4. Click the Account Settings tab. In the fields provided, select the desired account(s) from the drop-down list.

If you rarely use the additional accounts, you might want to consider adding them only when needed. All newly created transactions include up to the three lines assigned. If these lines are not removed, they result in blank lines of data in many reports.

The selected accounts will override any preference setting for Recall or Prefill and will instead insert these accounts automatically on a Write Checks or Enter Bills transaction. This is just another method you will find to help you keep your accounting accurate.

SETTING UP CUSTOMERS

It is not surprising to me—and perhaps not to you, either—that the accounts receivable process is the most organized and "cared for" task in QuickBooks. The process of producing a customer invoice is completed quickly because you have to provide a document to a customer to get paid.

In this chapter, you will find useful information to help you do the following:

- Customize and set important preferences
- Work with prospecting activities
- Set up customers, jobs, and supporting lists

In Chapter 10, "Managing Customers," you will find information useful for managing your customers by

- Creating accounts receivable reports
- Troubleshooting accounts receivable issues
- Handling unique customer transactions

Whether you are a first-time QuickBooks user or you have been using the software for years, the details in this chapter will help you set up your customers correctly.

Customizing Home Page Customer Activities

QuickBooks makes performing customer activities easy with a customizable list of tasks on the Home page (see Figure 9.1).

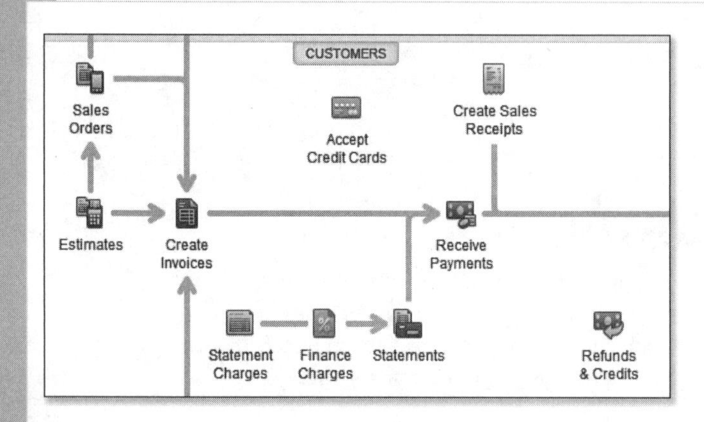

Figure 9.1
The Home page provides easy access to common customer activities.

Depending on your version of QuickBooks, you can add or remove the following transaction types or tasks from your Home page:

- **Sales Orders**—Use this transaction to commit a sale to a customer (QuickBooks Premier, Accountant, or Enterprise).
- **Estimates**—Use this transaction type to provide customers with quotes for your product or service, and most importantly, provide the basis for Customer or Job budgets.
- **Sales Tax Tracking**—Use this task to collect sales tax from your customers and remit to the taxing authority.

For more information on customizing the Home page, refer to Chapter 2, "Getting Around QuickBooks."

Details about the selected features that can be enabled or disabled on the Home page are discussed in the next section.

Preferences That Affect Accounts Receivable

You can simplify your Accounts Receivable tasks by setting certain QuickBooks preferences. Some of these preferences save you keystrokes, which can save data entry time.

Not every preference that affects Accounts Receivable impacts your financials. Some preferences enable specific features such as those shown in Figure 9.2. To set preferences in QuickBooks, from the menu bar select **Edit**, **Preferences**, and then choose the type of preference on the left side of the Preferences dialog box.

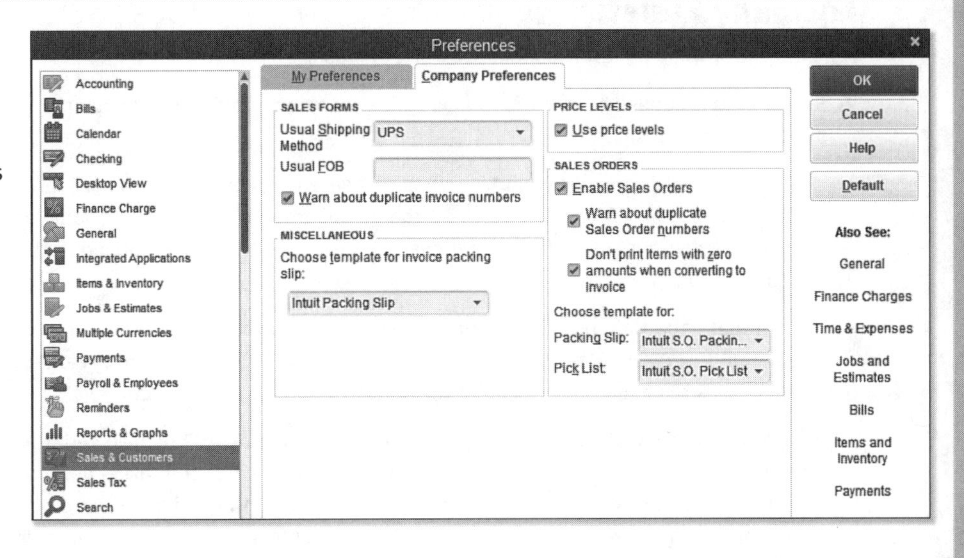

Figure 9.2 Preferences enable features and specific types of customer transactions.

Preferences in QuickBooks come in two forms:

- My Preferences are settings that are unique to the user logging in to the data file and are not shared by other users.
- Company Preferences are settings that are common for all users. When a preference is modified on the Company Preferences tab of the Preferences dialog box, the change affects all users.

To set company preferences, open the file as the Admin or External Accountant user and switch to single-user mode (if you are using the data file in a multiuser environment).

The sections that follow outline the preference settings that will improve your QuickBooks Accounts Receivable workflow. Many preferences can help you work more efficiently in QuickBooks. Be sure to have each user log in to QuickBooks with his or her username and review all the available preferences.

caution

The Admin user is the default user that is created when you first start using QuickBooks. Proper controls should be in place to allow only certain individuals to log in to the data file as the Admin user. For more information, see "Setting Up Users and Permissions," p. 50.

Payments

Payments preferences help you with customer payment processing and improve your overall process for receiving money from customers. From the menu bar, select **Edit**, **Preferences**, and then select **Payments** on the left side of the Preferences dialog box.

Company Preferences

Here are the specific preferences that are set for all users:

- **Receive Payments**—These settings make it easier for you to assign customer payments to the customers' invoices:
  - **Automatically Apply Payments**—When you select this option and record the receive payment transaction, QuickBooks applies the payment to an invoice of the same amount, or if no invoice amount matches the exact dollar amount, the payment is applied to the oldest invoice first. See Figure 9.3.
  - **Automatically Calculate Payments**—When selected, you do not need to put a total in the Amount box on the Receive Payments dialog box. QuickBooks calculates and prefills the amount as the sum total of each of the invoices marked as received.
  - **Use Undeposited Funds as a Default Deposit to Account**—When selected, this preference causes QuickBooks to place all customer payments into a current asset account that is created by QuickBooks. Undeposited Funds are like a safe that holds your customer payments before they are taken to the bank for deposit. When you record a Make Deposit transaction, QuickBooks removes the funds from the Undeposited Funds account and places them in your bank account.
- **Invoice Payments**—After signing up for Intuit PaymentNetwork, your customers can pay your invoices online by ACH (Automated Clearing House), or a debit to their bank account (similar to paying with a company check). Following are the invoice payments options:
  - **Sign Up for Intuit PaymentNetwork**—Click the Learn More to sign up for the Intuit PaymentNetwork service.
  - **Include Online Payment Link on Invoices**—Adds a payment web address to all invoices you email from QuickBooks. New for QuickBooks 2013, you can select to allow payments to be made by bank account only or bank account and credit card. Select the **Explain** link to learn more. You can modify this file preference for selected customers.
  - **Include on Printed Invoices**—Adds a payment web address on invoices printed or emailed.
  - **Intuit PaymentNetwork Email**—Enter the email address you use (or plan to use) to sign into Intuit PaymentNetwork.
  - **Turn Off Online Payments**—This action turns links off for all invoices and all customers. If you resend a past invoice that includes the link, the newly sent invoice will not include the online payment link.

My Preferences

There are no My Preferences for Payments settings.

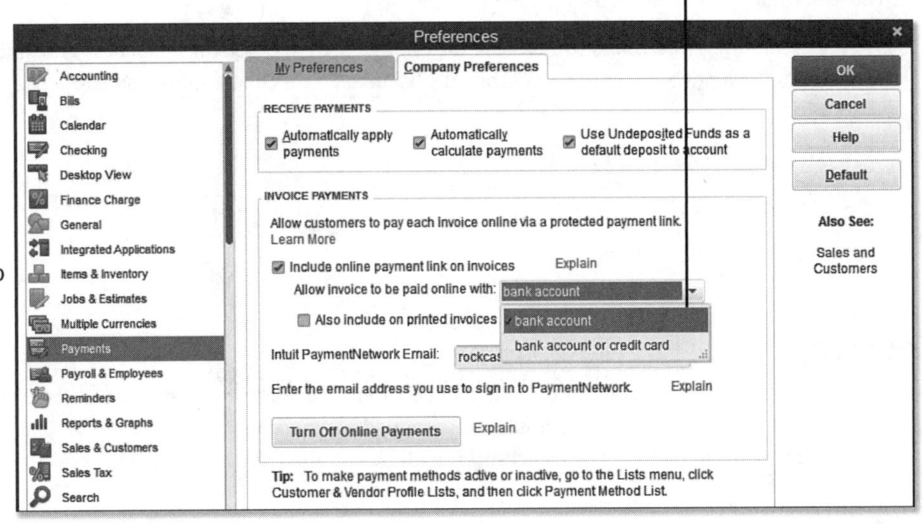

Figure 9.3 Payment preferences are important to review and set before sending invoices to your customers.

Sales & Customers

The Sales & Customers preference settings enable you to customize QuickBooks around the tasks you use to manage customer activities. You can also make it easier for your employees to do their daily tasks by customizing the Home page so the needed transactions types are available. From the menu bar select **Edit**, **Preferences,** and then select the **Sales & Customers** preference on the left side of the Preferences dialog box.

Company Preferences

Here are the specific preferences that are available for all users:

- **Sales Forms**—These settings enable you to set a default shipping method that displays on customer forms. You can also choose to be warned when duplicate invoice numbers are detected.
- **Miscellaneous**—A drop-down list allows you to select the default packing slip form.
- **Price Levels**—Click the Use Price Levels checkbox to enable the use of price levels. Price levels are assigned to your customers and automate unique customer pricing. An example is using price levels to offer wholesale pricing to certain customers and charging retail to others.
- **Sales Orders**—Available with QuickBooks Premier, Accountant, or QuickBooks Enterprise Solutions, use the Sales Order transaction type to commit sales to customers and track backorders. Preferences include warning about duplicate sales order numbers, printing options for items with zero amounts, and choosing templates for Packing Slips and Pick Lists.

My Preferences

These settings affect the current logged-in user:

- **Add Available Time/Costs to Invoices for the Selected Job**—Determines how QuickBooks prompts the logged-in user when unbilled costs exist for a Customer or Job. Options include the following:
  - Prompt for time/costs to add
  - Don't add any
  - Ask what to do

Checking

The Checking Preferences are for defining specific bank accounts for sales-related activities, such as depositing a customer's payment into a predefined bank account. From the menu bar, select **Edit**, **Preferences**, and then select the **Checking** preference on the left side of the Preferences dialog box.

Company Preferences

There are no Checking Company Preferences that affect your workflow for Accounts Receivable.

My Preferences

The Open the Make Deposits default account preference is optional. Use this preference to specify the default bank account selected for making deposits. If you have multiple bank accounts you make deposits to, you might not want to set a default on this tab. When no preference is set, the first bank account on the list will default.

Finance Charge

Does your company charge late-paying customers finance charges on open balances? If so, you will want to set these preferences. From the menu bar, select **Edit**, **Preferences**, and then select the **Finance Charge** preference on the left side of the Preferences dialog box.

Company Preferences

These preferences set your company's annual interest rate, minimum finance charge, grace period, and income account you want to credit.

These settings will affect your financial reports and how QuickBooks will calculate and report on finance charges as shown in Figure 9.4:

- **Annual Interest Rate (%)**—Enter the interest rate you want to use when calculating finance charges on late payments.
- **Minimum Finance Charge**—Enter a dollar amount that will be used as the minimum finance charge.

- **Grace Period (days)**—Use this setting to calculate a grace period before finance charges apply.
- **Finance Charge Account**—Enter the account you will use to track the finance charges you collect from your customers. Typically you would select an income account type.
- **Assess Finance Charges on Overdue Finance Charges**—When selected, this option includes unpaid finance charge amounts previously invoiced in the new amount used to calculate additional late fees. In my experience, when you do this, you become the "squeaky wheel" that gets paid.
- **Calculate Charges From**—The choices are Due Date or Invoice/Billed Date. For example, if you create an invoice for a customer for $1,000 that is due in 30 days, and you select the **Calculate Charges from Due Date** option, the amount is not considered overdue until 30 days from the invoice due date.
- **Mark Finance Charge Invoices "To Be Printed"**—If this option is not selected, you can send a statement to the customer at the end of your billing cycle to communicate the amounts that are owed instead of sending an invoice for the finance charges assessed.

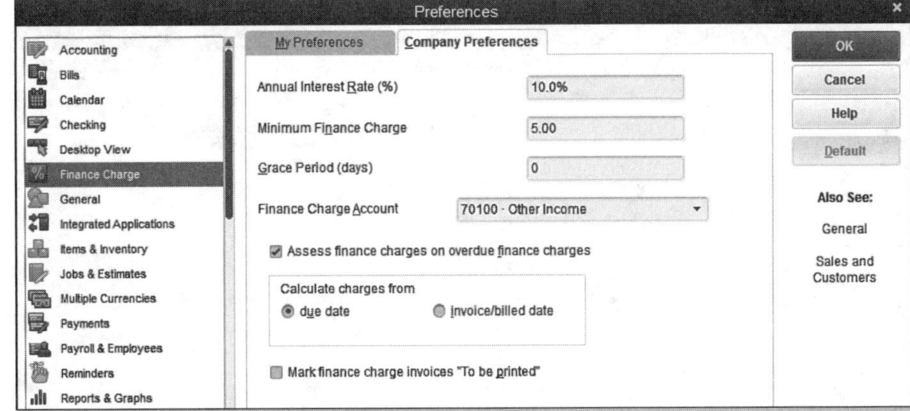

Figure 9.4 Assess finance charges, and remember that the "squeaky wheel" is the one that gets paid!

My Preferences

There are no My Preferences for Finance Charge settings.

Jobs & Estimates

The preference settings found in this section enable certain accounts receivable transaction types in QuickBooks. From the menu bar, select **Edit**, **Preferences**, and then select the **Jobs & Estimates** preference on the left side of the Preferences dialog box.

Company Preferences

These choices have to do with enabling specific estimating and invoicing features in QuickBooks as well as defining custom job status descriptions (see Figure 9.5):

- **Job Status Descriptions**—You can choose to modify the job status descriptions, such as changing Not Awarded to Lost.
- **Do You Create Estimates?**—Selecting Yes adds an icon to the Home page for Estimates.
- **Do You Do Progress Invoicing?**—Selecting Yes enables a dialog box when creating an invoice from an estimate. The dialog box includes the options to create an invoice for all, a percentage, or selected items from a multiline estimate.
- **Warn About Duplicate Estimate Numbers**—Selecting this option provides good internal controls over your documents.
- **Don't Print Items That Have Zero Amount**—This option is useful when creating a progress invoice with many lines. This selection is available if you selected Yes to the Progress Invoicing option.

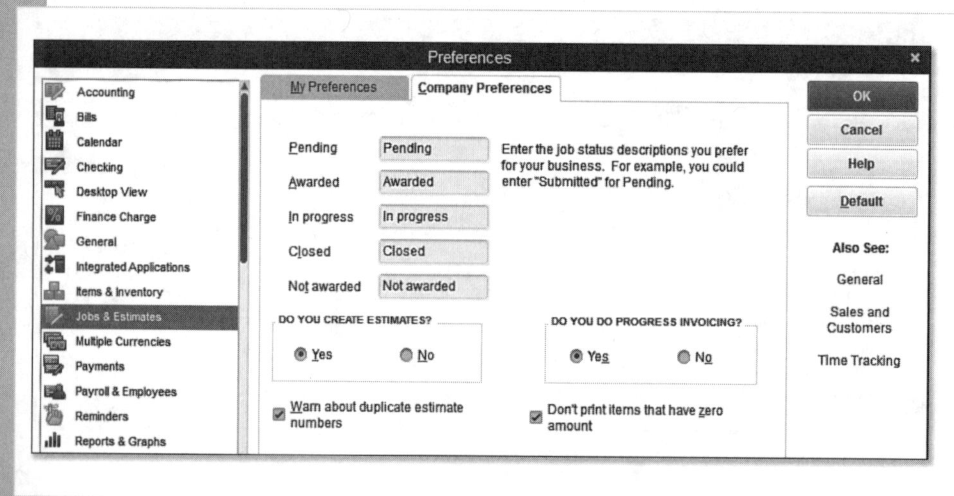

Figure 9.5 Jobs & Estimates preferences enable specific transaction types for you to use.

My Preferences

There are no My Preferences for Jobs & Estimates.

Reminders

The Reminders Preferences can be useful if you want QuickBooks to prompt you when certain accounts receivable tasks are due. Select **Edit**, **Preferences** from the menu bar, and then select the **Reminders** preference on the left side of the Preferences dialog box.

Company Preferences

The Company Preferences for Reminders, as shown in Figure 9.6, determines how QuickBooks shows reminders. Options include Summary, List, or Don't Remind Me. Accounts Receivable reminders include Invoices/Credit Memos to Print, Overdue Invoices, Almost Due Invoices, and other customer activity–related reminders.

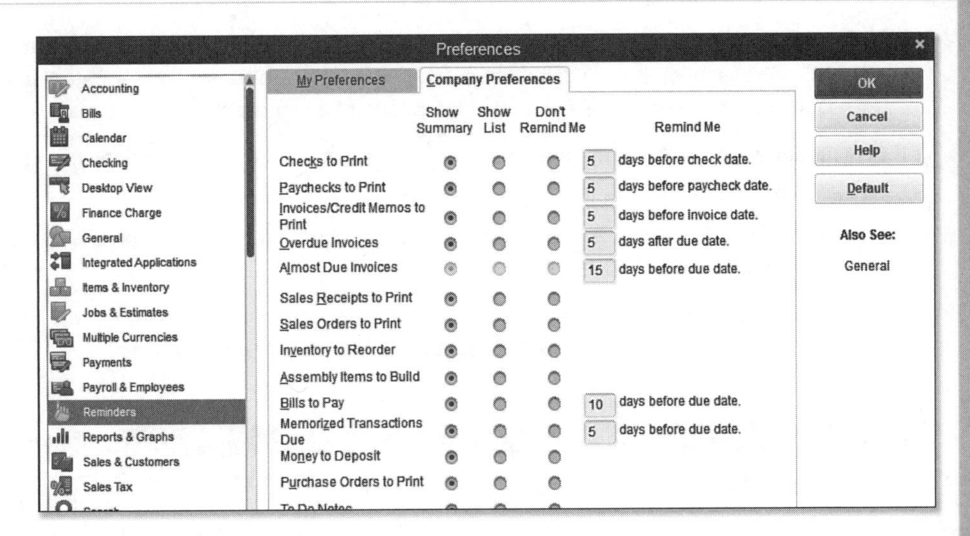

Figure 9.6 The selections on the Company Preferences tab determine how QuickBooks reminds all users.

My Preferences

Users can specify whether they want to see the reminders when they open the QuickBooks data file. Regardless of this setting, users can select **Company**, **Reminders** from the menu bar at any time to review the reminder list contents.

Reports & Graphs

Review the personal preferences and company preferences for working with reports and graphs. The defaults set here can be overridden at the time a particular report is prepared. From the menu bar, select **Edit**, **Preferences,** and then select the **Reports & Graphs** preference on the left side of the Preferences dialog box.

Company Preferences

Review each of the listed preferences; they will often affect how certain accounts receivable reports will calculate:

- **Summary Report Basis**—Choose to have the default basis for reports selected for you. Although this setting affects many reports in QuickBooks, selected reports can be prepared only on the accrual basis; for example, accounts receivable or accounts payable reports.
- **Aging Reports**—This option sets the default for calculating overdue invoices. You can choose to age from due date or from transaction date. Typically, aging from transaction date causes invoices to show as overdue earlier than if you aged from due date.
- **Format**—This option enables you to override the default header, footer, and font for all QuickBooks reports. You should not override the Report Title, Subtitle, or Date Prepared because QuickBooks will accurately fill in this information for you each time you prepare a report.
- **Reports—Show Accounts By**—This setting offers you the following options for displaying reports:
  - **Name Only**—Reports display the name and account number (if the preference to enable account numbers is selected).
  - **Description Only**—Reports display the description typed in the New or Edit Account dialog box (see Figure 9.7). No account numbers are displayed on the reports.

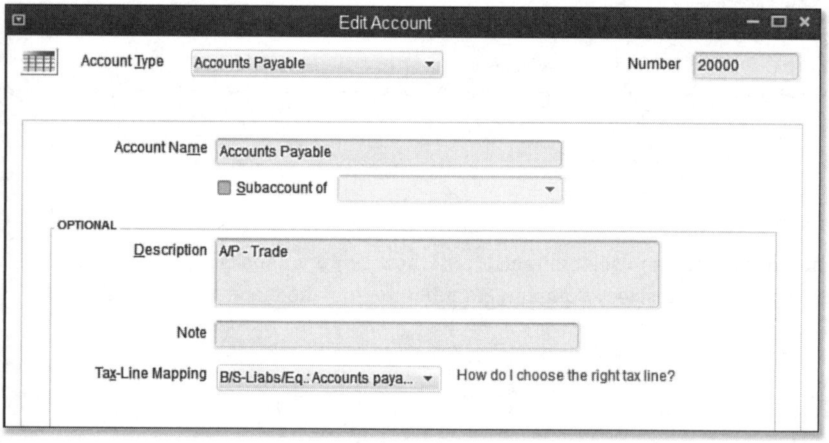

Figure 9.7
Enter an optional description on the New or Edit Account dialog box; reports can display this description.

  - **Name and Description**—Reports display the account number (if enabled in preferences), the name, and the description as typed in the New Account or Edit Account dialog box in parentheses (see Figure 9.8).
- **Classify Cash**—If you need to prepare a cash flow statement, QuickBooks uses these settings to determine which accounts are considered Operating, Investing, or Financing. This preference does not specifically relate to accounts receivable.

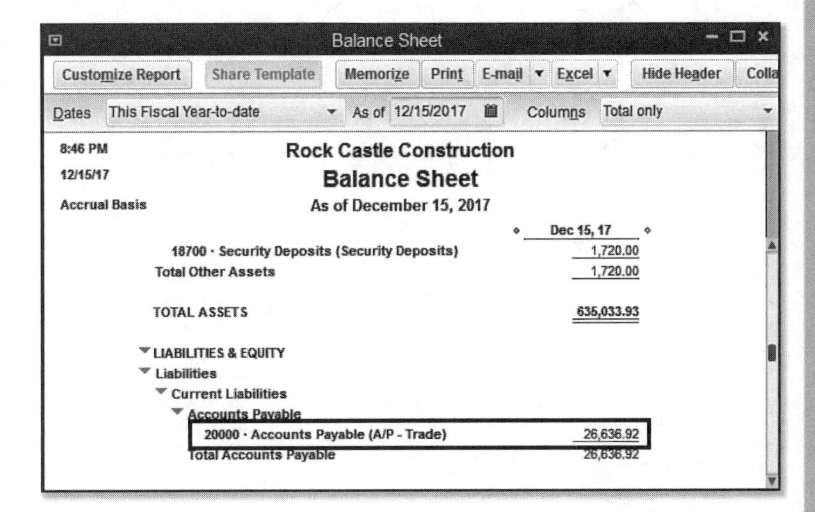

Figure 9.8
Reports show the additional description when you select the Name and Description reporting preference.

My Preferences

The My Preferences selections include the following:

- **Prompt Me to Modify Report**—Selecting this opens the Modify Report dialog box with each created report. (This action is the same as selecting Customize Report from a displayed report.)
- **Reports & Graphs**—Refresh options for reports and graphs when data changes. These prompt the user to refresh or to not refresh.
- **Graphs Only**—Specific display settings when preparing graphs.

Sales Tax

The Sales Tax preference shown in Figure 9.9 is important if your business is required to collect sales tax on sales made to your customers. Be sure to research each state's sales tax regulations so you can comply with the laws and avoid penalties. From the menu bar select **Edit**, **Preferences**, and then select the **Sales Tax** preference on the left side of the Preferences dialog box.

Company Preferences

To enable sales tax tracking, select Yes next to the Do You Charge Sales Tax? field. Additionally, complete the following selections:

- **Set Up Sales Tax Item**—When you click the Add Sales Tax Item button, QuickBooks opens the New Item dialog box with the Sales Tax item type selected. Here you define a name for the sales tax item, type a description, a rate, and assign the tax agency you will be remitting the collected tax to. A separate drop-down list allows you to select your most common sales tax item.

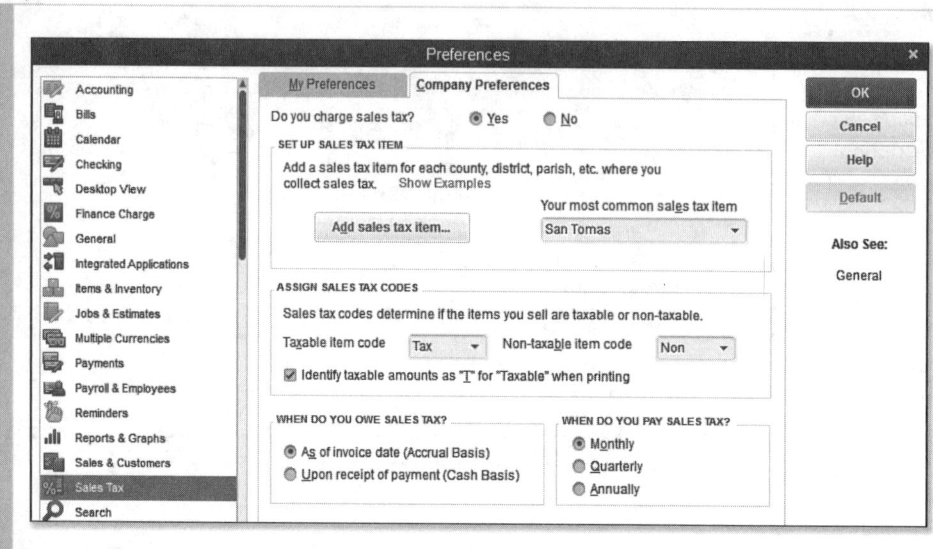

Figure 9.9 Use these Company Preferences to configure Sales Tax defaults in QuickBooks.

- **Assign Sales Tax Codes**—This is the name of the code that will be assigned to your product or service items. Usually the default of Tax and Non are considered appropriate. You can select to have a "T" print on your customer invoices for items that are taxable. This option is useful if on one invoice you sell both taxable and nontaxable items.
- **When Do You Owe Sales Tax?**—If you are not sure what each state department of revenue requires, review their websites or call to get the correct information.
- **When Do You Pay Sales Tax?**—This setting tells QuickBooks what date range to select automatically when paying your sales tax. For example, if you select **Monthly**, QuickBooks computes the amount owed for the previous month in the Pay Sales Tax Liability dialog box.

My Preferences

There are no My Preferences for Sales Tax.

Send Forms

For sending forms, users have the option to use Web Mail, Outlook, or QuickBooks E-mail. From the menu bar, select **Edit**, **Preferences**, and then select the **Send Forms** preference on the left side of the Preferences dialog box.

Company Preferences

This preference, as shown in Figure 9.10, enables you to set email defaults, including a default message when sending supported forms or reports. Select the different forms from the Change Default For drop-down list. Click the Spelling button to check your template content for spelling errors.

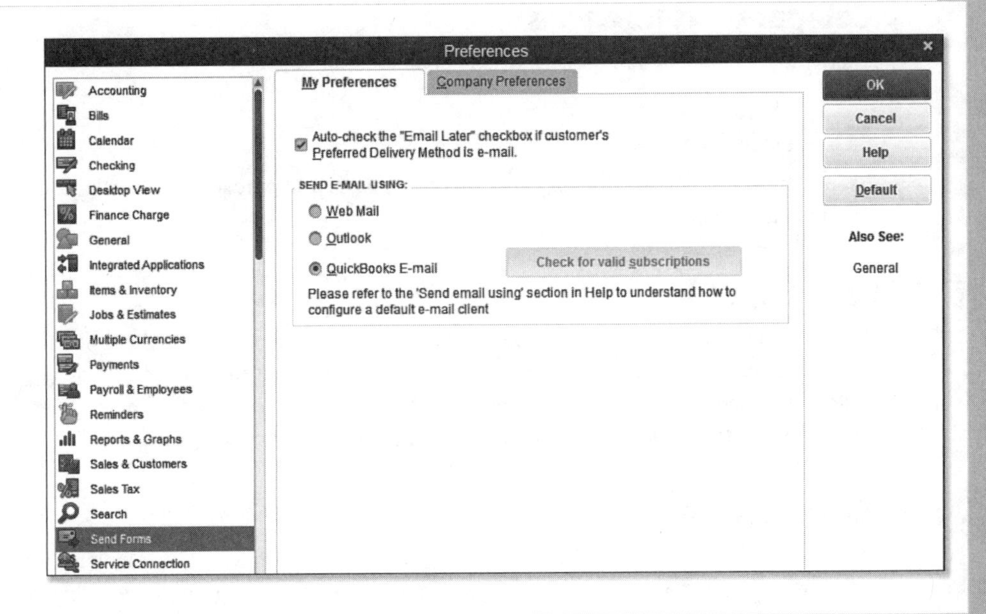

Figure 9.10 QuickBooks provides multiple choices for using email to send reports or forms.

My Preferences

These settings affect the current logged-in user:

- **Auto-Check the "To Be E-Mailed"...**—If enabled, QuickBooks automatically selects the To Be E-Mailed checkbox on newly created invoices.
- **Send E-mail Using—**You can select your preferred method for sending transactions and reports:
  - Web Mail
  - Outlook
  - QuickBooks Email (Using Billing Solutions)

QuickBooks users can use Outlook, Outlook Express, other web-based email (such as Gmail or Hotmail), or the QuickBooks email server as the preferred method for sending reports and transactions from within QuickBooks. If you select **Outlook**, however, your preference can affect certain Billing Solutions features. From the menu bar, select **Help** and type **billing solutions** into the search box.

Spelling

This preference determines how QuickBooks assists you with spelling on accounts receivable transactions. From the menu bar, select **Edit**, **Preferences**, and then select the **Spelling** preference on the left side of the Preferences dialog box.

Company Preferences

There are no Company Preferences for the Spelling Preference.

My Preferences

Users can set QuickBooks spelling preferences for sales and purchase transactions and include custom-added spelling words.

Time & Expenses

Time & Expenses is a specific method of invoicing common to the professional services industry, where customers' sales are invoiced based on hours or costs of the project plus an agreed-to markup and/or overhead fee. Select **Edit**, **Preferences** from the menu bar, and then select the **Time & Expenses** preference on the left side of the Preferences dialog box.

Company Preferences

If your company needs to provide customers with an invoice showing your individual costs plus an added markup,.enable this preference (see Figure 9.11) by selecting from the following:

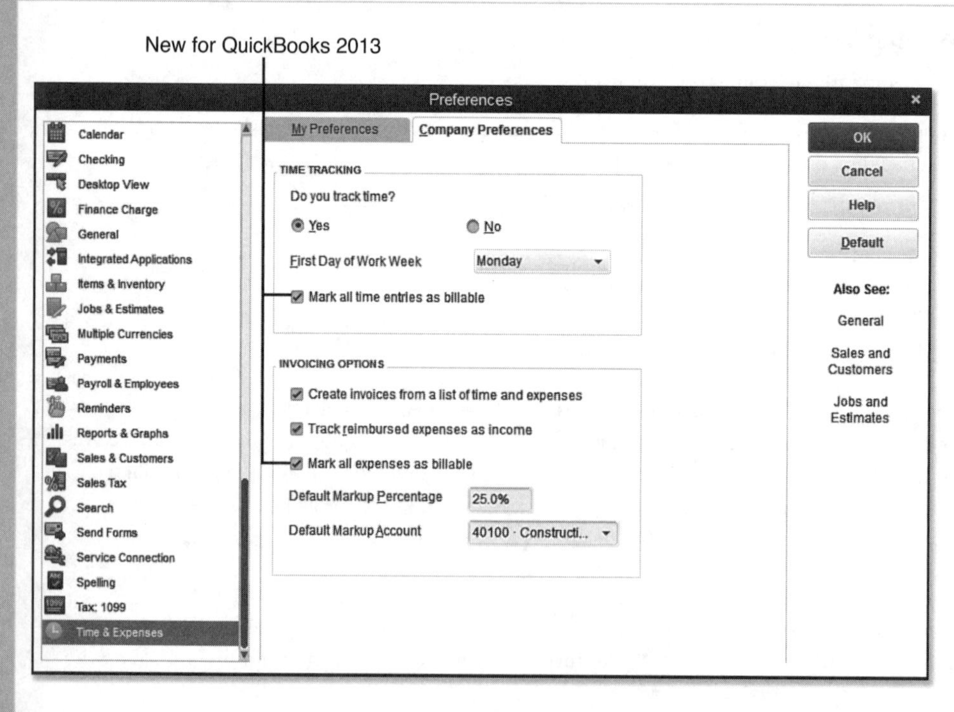

Figure 9.11 Enable these preferences if your company tracks time or bills customers for reimbursement of costs.

- **Time Tracking**—The Time Tracking options include the following:
  - **Yes**—Selecting Yes enables time recording on timesheets, which can be transferred to vendor and employee payment transactions and customer invoices.
  - **First Day of Work Week**—Define the first day of the work week.
  - **Mark All Time Entries as Billable**—*New for QuickBooks 2013:* This feature is useful if you list detailed vendor or employee time on the invoices to your customers.
- **Invoicing Options**—The Invoicing Options include the following:
  - **Create Invoices from a List of Time and Expenses**—Select Yes for Do You Track Time to enable time recording on timesheets, which can be transferred from payment transactions to customer invoices. This is useful when your company will be detailing on a customer's invoice specific amounts paid to vendors, employees, or payees on the other names list.
  - **Track Reimbursed Expenses as Income**—Select this checkbox if you want to track costs invoiced to customers as income. An example might be a law firm that charges the customer for costs incurred for shipping charges and wants to show the amount as income. The income would be offset by the expense, usually in an overhead expense account.
  - **Mark All Expenses as Billable**—*New for QuickBooks 2013:* You can use this option to mark all expense line transactions as billable. This feature is useful if you list detailed costs on the invoices to your customers.
  - **Default Markup Percentage**—Use this option to define a percentage to add to the customer's invoice when billing for time and costs. An example is including a 10% markup, adding $10.00 to a $100.00 cost reimbursement invoice.
  - **Default Markup Account**—Option to select a default account (typically an Income category) for tracking all amounts charged to the customer as markup.

My Preferences

There is no My Preferences for the Time & Expenses settings.

Working with the Customer Center

The Customer Center provides quick access to common customer tasks and reporting.

Are you new to using QuickBooks? I expect one of the first lists you have already added to in QuickBooks is the customer list. You might have imported your customers while creating your new file using the Express Start.

The Customer Center (see Figure 9.12) provides one location for viewing contact details and accessing many customer tasks and reports, including the following:

- Create a new or edit an existing Customer or Job.

- Access the Add Multiple Customers:Jobs feature.
- Record commonly used customer transactions.
- Print the Customer & Job list, information, or transactions.
- Export the Customer list or transactions as an Excel or CSV file; import or paste customers from Excel.
- Prepare customer letters and customize the built-in letter templates.
- Access the Collections Center.
- Filter your list of customers to include All Customers, Active Customers, Customers with Open, Overdue or Almost Due Balances, or a custom filter of your choice.
- Attach documents to the customer record, such as a copy of a signed agreement.
- Access a map and driving directions to the Customer or Job location.
- Add or edit customer notes and to-do reminders.
- View and filter transactions by customer or by transaction type.
- Prepare a QuickReport, Open Balance Report for the currently selected customer.
- Show Estimates and Customer Snapshot for the currently selected customer.

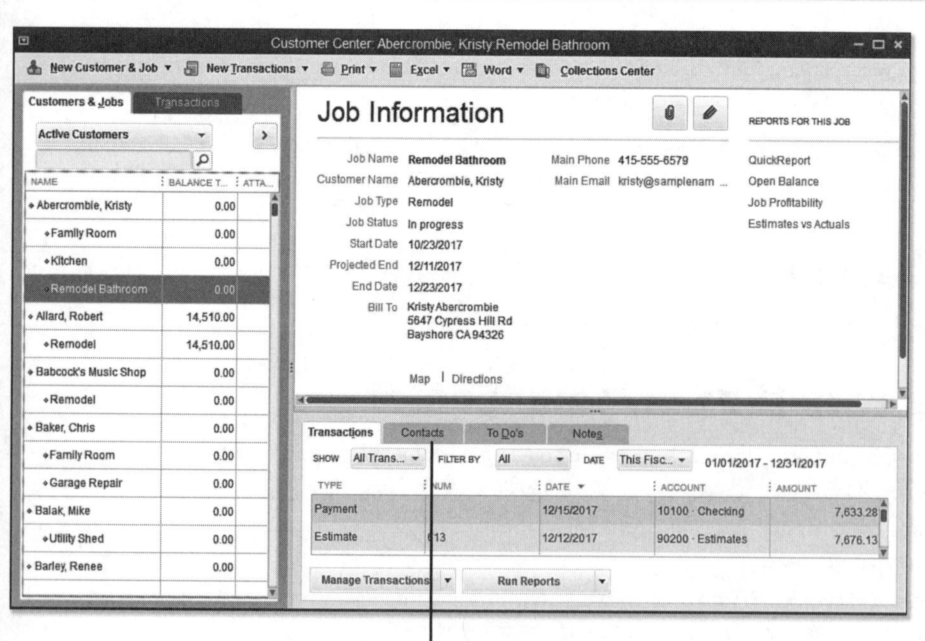

Figure 9.12 From the Customer Center, you can access most customer activities and useful reports.

tip

You can customize the information displayed on the Customers & Jobs tab (left side of the Customer Center).

1. On the displayed list of customers, right-click with your cursor and select **Customize Columns.**
2. The Customize Columns dialog box displays. Click a data field listed in the Available Columns box and then in the center of the dialog box click the Add button. Your selected field is now added to the Chosen Columns.
3. To reposition the placement of the columns of data, highlight a field in the Chosen Columns box and use the Remove, Move Up or Move Down buttons.

The following sections provide more details about creating a customer or job and using the Customer Center for researching transactions.

Adding or Modifying Customers and Jobs

Customers are the individuals or businesses you sell your product or service to. QuickBooks can also track a job for a customer, in the event you want to track the profitability for different projects for the same customer. For example, if you're renovating a house, you might create a job for each room. Or, an attorney might track the revenue and costs for individual legal matters for the same customer.

tip

Efficiently enter multiple customers or jobs at one time using an Excel-like data entry grid. Do you have a ready-made list of customers in an Excel file? To learn more about adding multiple customer records, see "Add/Edit Multiple List Entries," p. 115.

Or, if you are just setting up your QuickBooks file, review the information provided in Chapter 1, "Getting Started with QuickBooks," in the section titled "Adding People You Do Business With." In this referenced section you will learn how to import your contacts from Outlook, Gmail or other email providers.

Creating jobs is not required in QuickBooks, but is helpful when you have multiple projects for a single customer. This section offers instruction specifically for setting up customers and jobs of customers.

tip

If you begin typing the name of your customer or job in the Company Name field, QuickBooks populates the Customer Name and Bill To name field.

New for QuickBooks 2013, with a customer listing on the left selected in Customer Center, you can access the following:

- **Transactions**—From this tab you can view and filter the transactions assigned to the currently selected customer or job record.
- **Contacts**—*New for QuickBooks 2013*, you can store multiple contact names for each customer or job record.
- **To Dos**—Keep track of important To Dos by assigning the event an action, such as a call, meeting, task, and so on. Associate the To Do with a lead, customer, vendor, or employee. Assign the task a due date and time with details that will display on your QuickBooks calendar (from the menu bar, select **Company**, **Calendar**).

Creating a Customer and Job Record

To practice adding a new customer record and assigning a job to that customer, open the sample data file as described in Chapter 1. If you are working in your own file, use these instructions to begin entering the customers you sell your product or service to:

1. Click the Customers button on the Home page, or, from the menu bar, select **Customers, Customer Center**.
2. In the New Customer & Job drop-down list, select **New Customer**.
3. The New Customer dialog box displays with the Address Info tab selected (see Figure 9.13). In the Customer Name field, type **Angela's Decorating**. It is important to mention that no two names from any of the lists in QuickBooks can be the same. For more information, see "When Your Vendor Is Also Your Customer," p. 282.

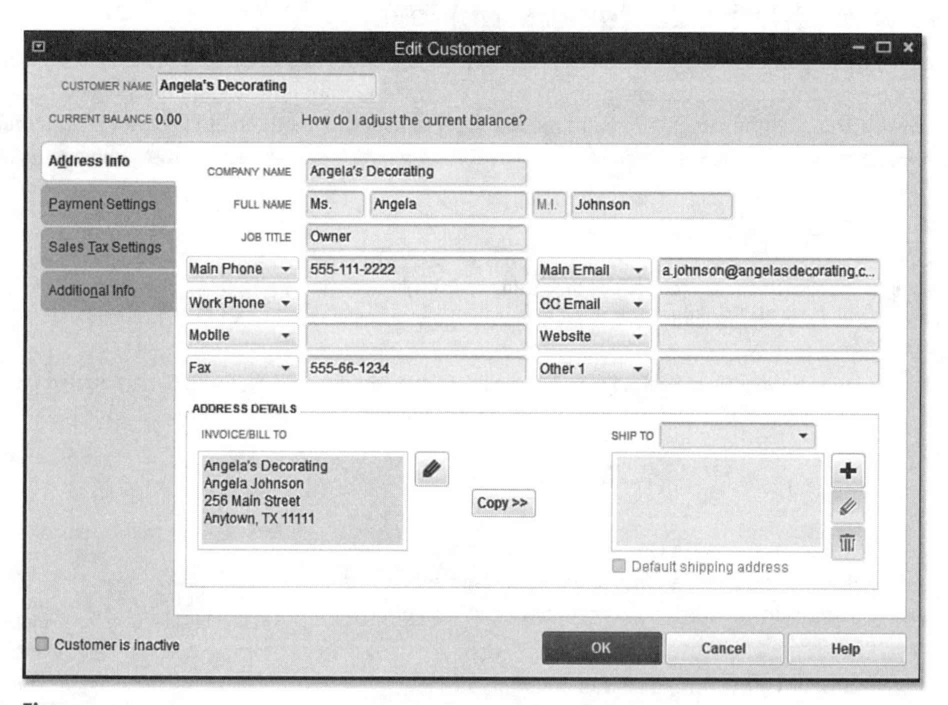

Figure 9.13
Completing the contact information for your customer is good practice for your record keeping.

4. Leave the Opening Balance field blank. To learn more about entering opening balances in QuickBooks, see Chapter 3, "Accounting 101." If you are a new business, the amounts your customer owe you will be recorded using the accounts receivable transactions detailed in this chapter.
5. The As Of (date) field supports the Opening Balance field and has no effect when no dollar value is entered in the Opening Balance field.

6. Complete the remaining fields for this practice by adding the contact information and address. Consider completing the salutation, first name, and last name fields. Doing so enables you to send professional-looking letters to your customers in the future. *New for QuickBooks 2013*: Customer and job records now have multiple contact data fields.
7. For this exercise, on the Payment Settings tab, for Payment Terms, select **Net 30** from the drop-down list. This instructs QuickBooks to calculate due dates that are 30 days from your invoice dates. In your own data, use the Add New choice to create terms that suit your specific needs. Leave the remaining Payment Settings as defaulted for this exercise.

   When you are working with your file, you can define these additional fields:

   - **Account No**—This is the account number you assign to your customer; it can optionally be printed on a customer transactions.
   - **Preferred Delivery Method**—It is important to select this if you will be using the Create Batch Invoices feature available with QuickBooks Premier, Accountant, and Enterprise.
   - **Preferred Payment Method**—Prefill the customer payment transaction with this default.
   - **Credit Card Information**—Safely and securely store your customer's credit card numbers for ease in processing payments. However, be sure to review the instructions for setting up user rights in the file to limit who can modify or view this information. See more information in Chapter 1.
   - **Credit Limit**—Setting this limit enables QuickBooks to warn you when a transaction will exceed the allowed credit.
   - **Price Level**—Available with QuickBooks Premier, Accountant, or Enterprise. Offers the capability to default a specified rate for the items or services you sell. For example, you might offer a 10% discount on all purchases made by this customer. You can have only one price level assigned per customer, and it cannot be based on volume pricing. Refer to Figure 9.25 for the information used to create a Price Level.
   - **Add Online Payment Link to Invoices**—Choices include using the company default set in preferences, bank only, bank or credit card payment links, or turning off the links on invoices for this customer.
8. Click the Sales Tax Settings tab. The information on this dialog defaults from the Sales Tax preferences discussed earlier in this chapter.
9. Click the Additional Info tab. If you're working in the practice file, select **Commercial** from the Customer Type field, or select **Add New** to create your own customer type. Many sales reports can be filtered by customer type.
10. Leave the Rep field blank for this exercise. In your own data, you can select the Rep field if you will be tracking sales by Rep.
11. For this exercise, leave the custom fields blank. When working with your data you can select the Define Fields button and add custom fields that you assign to your Customer, Vendor, or Employee records. These custom fields can also be added to your sales transactions and be included in many reports.

12. Select the **Job Info** tab. For this exercise, leave the Job Status information blank. In your own file, if you are tracking project activity at the customer level, complete the fields as needed. Some of the job profitability reports can be filtered by these fields.
13. Click OK to close the New Customer dialog box. You are returned to the Customer Center, and Angela's Decorating will be selected.
14. From the New Customer & Job drop-down list, select **Add Job**.
15. Type **Office Remodel** for the Job Name. Complete any other fields as desired on each of the New Job tabs.
16. Click OK to add this job record to the Angela's Decorating customer record. You will be returned to the Customer Center and Office Remodel will appear beneath Angela's Decorating, as shown in Figure 9.14.

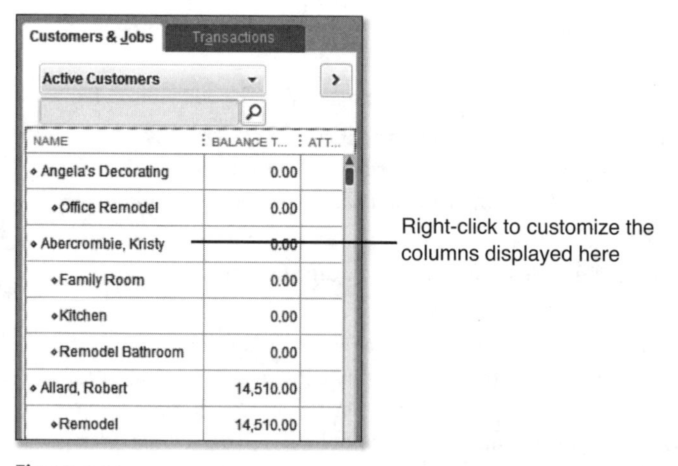

Figure 9.14
Create jobs to track costs and revenue for multiple projects for the same customer.

caution

Specifying terms is part of the process for managing your accounts receivable balances. You should also review the Reporting—Company Preferences tab on the Preferences dialog box for settings that affect A/R Aging reports. You can select to have the A/R Aging or Detail reports age from the invoice due date or age from invoice transaction date.

- **Notes**—Keep track of any additional information in these dated notes. The notes list can be filtered for specific dates, and notes can be edited or deleted as needed.

Now that you have created a new customer in the sample file, you are prepared to create a list of your own customers. When your customer's address or contact information changes, you can return to the Customer Center to edit the same information.

Finding Customer Transactions

The Customer Center provides access for adding to or modifying your customer or job records in QuickBooks, but also includes convenient access to finding customer transactions.

With the Customer Center open, select a customer or job with your cursor. Then click the Transactions tab on the right, and the individual transactions assigned to that customer or job display. In the previously displayed Figure 9.12, the job Remodel Bathroom for customer Abercrombie, Kristy is selected, and to the right are individual transactions for that job.

You can filter the resulting transactions by selecting options in the Show, Filter By, and Date drop-down lists. The options available differ depending on the type of transaction being filtered for.

In Figure 9.15, the options available for filtering include customer transactions. Your transaction types might differ from the displayed types if you do not have the related feature enabled in preferences. The only transaction type that can have a customer or job record assigned that is not included in these options is the Make Journal Entry.

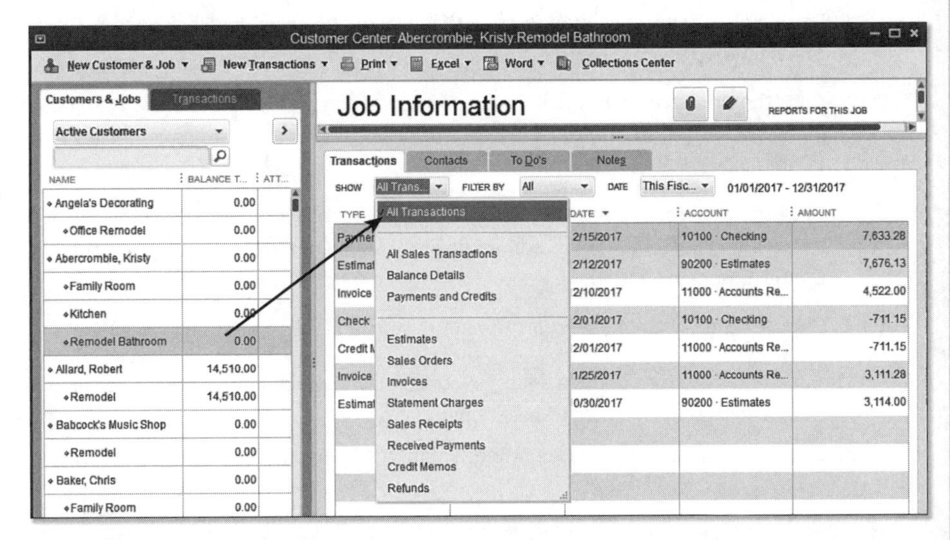

Figure 9.15 Conveniently filter for specific transactions types and dates for the selected customer.

Another useful feature of working with the Customer Center is available on the Transactions tab. On the Transactions tab, you can locate similar transaction types for all customers.

To do so, follow these steps:

1. From the Customer Center, click the Transactions tab.
2. Select the **Estimates** type, as shown in Figure 9.16.
3. From the Filter By drop-down list, select **Open Estimates**.
4. (Optional) Filter for a specific date range.

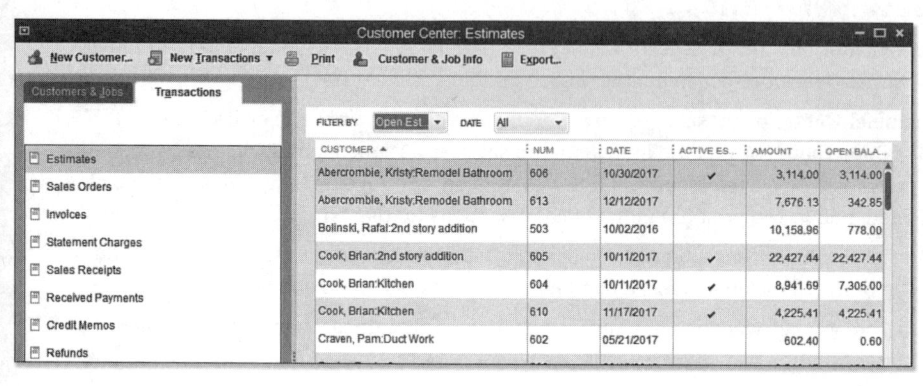

Figure 9.16 Use the Transactions tab of the Customer Center to find like transaction types.

5. Click any column header to sort the data by that column.
6. Double-click any transaction to open the selected transaction. Click Save & Close to return to the Transactions tab details.
7. Click the Print button to print the listed transactions. Click OK to close the Transaction Report message. Click Print to print the list of transactions, or click Cancel to return to the Customer Center's Transactions tab.
8. Click the Customer & Job Info tab. QuickBooks displays the Edit Customer or Job dialog box for the selected customer or job edit as needed. Click OK to close and be returned to the Customer Center:Estimates listing.
9. Click the Excel button to export the list of transactions to an Excel worksheet or CSV file format.

The Customer Center provides a single location from which you can create or modify your customer records or research customer transactions.

In the next section, you learn about managing your prospects using the Lead Center.

Working with Prospects in the Lead Center

The Lead Center helps you keep track of your business prospecting activities. From the menu bar select **Customers**, **Lead Center** to open the Lead Center (see Figure 9.17).

From the Lead Center, you can click the following options, which perform various functions:

- **New Lead**—Enter a single new lead.
- **Import Multiple Leads**—Using a preformatted grid you can enter multiple leads row by row, or copy and paste from an existing Excel worksheet.
- **Excel**—Export a Lead Contact List, Lead Status List, or a list of Converted Leads (those leads that become customers).

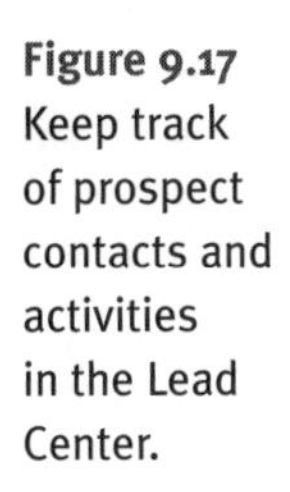

Figure 9.17 Keep track of prospect contacts and activities in the Lead Center.

Use the new Lead Center to track important business prospecting activities and save time when creating customer records from your lead base.

Creating a New Lead

To practice creating a new lead record, open the sample data file as instructed in Chapter 1. You might also use these instructions if you are getting started with lead management in your own data file:

1. In the Lead Center, click New Lead.
2. In the Name field, type your own name.
3. Complete the remaining fields on the Company and Contacts tab.
4. (Optional) Add additional locations or contacts for this new lead.
5. Click OK to complete adding the lead.
6. With the lead selected on the left, click the To Do button on the To Do List to add a new reminder activity. See Figure 9.18. These To Do activities are included in your calendar reminders. See Chapter 18, "Using Other Planning and Management Tools."

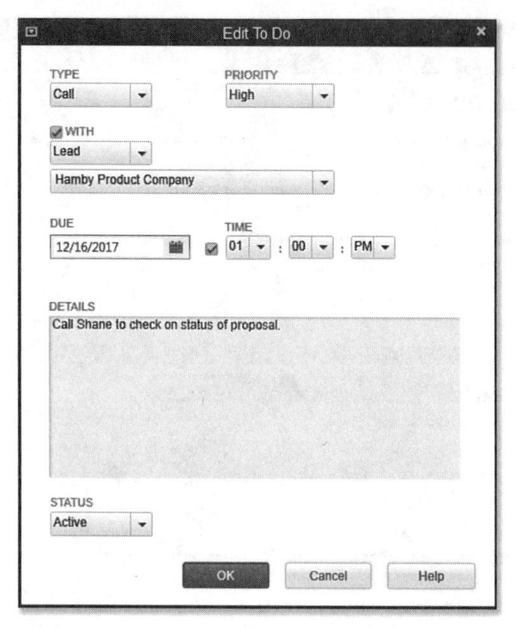

Figure 9.18
Stay organized with your prospecting activities by adding To Dos to the lead record.

7. Click any header column to sort the data by that column.
8. Click the Contacts, Locations, or Notes tab to view additional information about your lead.
9. Continue adding a few more leads using any of the mentioned methods.
10. In this exercise, select a lead from the list and click the icon in the top right to Convert to Customer. QuickBooks creates a new customer record from the details in the Lead Center. Select Yes to the Convert Lead message, confirming that that action cannot be undone.
11. The lead is no longer listed in the Lead Center. Open the Customer Center to view the new customer record, contacts, and notes that transferred with the lead.

Setting Up Sales Tax

In QuickBooks you can collect and remit sales tax on behalf of governmental authorities. To do so, you need to establish sales tax items and codes. You might also need to create sales tax groups.

Do not forget to register with the department of taxation for the state(s) you will be selling in. Each state has specific rules and guidelines, as well as providing you with a unique filing identification number for your business. Not all states require sales tax to be charged to your customers on specific items sold. To see if the taxing authority has special guidelines to follow, call their sales tax department; my experience is they are quite helpful and can direct you to the needed documentation.

tip

Each state has different requirements and rates for reporting sales tax. It is critical you research the applicable regulations and set up QuickBooks correctly. Otherwise, your business can be subjected to expensive—and avoidable—penalties.

Creating Sales Tax Items

Sales tax items are used to identify specific rates charged to your customers and the tax authority vendor to which you remit the sales tax. You might have one sales tax item, or several, on your item list.

After enabling Sales Tax in preferences, to create a sales tax item in your data file, follow these steps:

1. From the menu bar select **Lists**, **Item List**.
2. In the Item drop-down list, select **New** to open the New Item dialog box.
3. In the Type drop-down list, select **Sales Tax Item** as shown in Figure 9.19.
4. Enter a sales tax name for the sales tax item; the name should identify the applicable jurisdiction (see Figure 9.20).
5. Enter a Description you want printed on the customer's invoice.

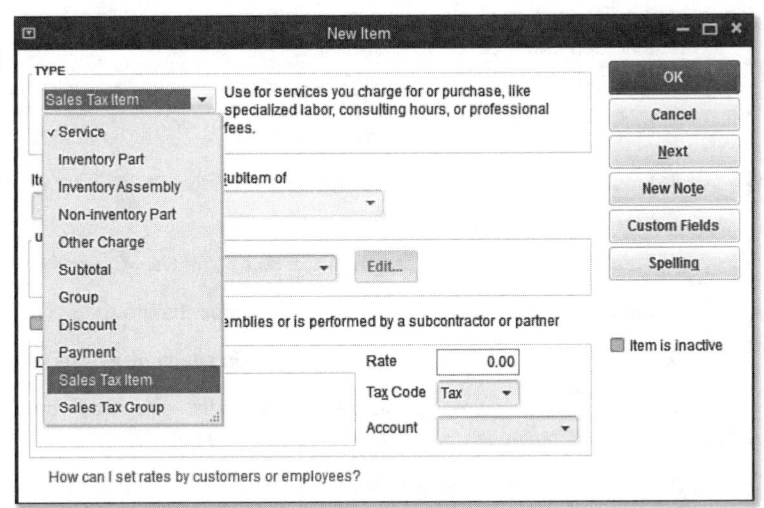

Figure 9.19
Sales tax is properly calculated and tracked in QuickBooks when you use the Sales Tax Item type.

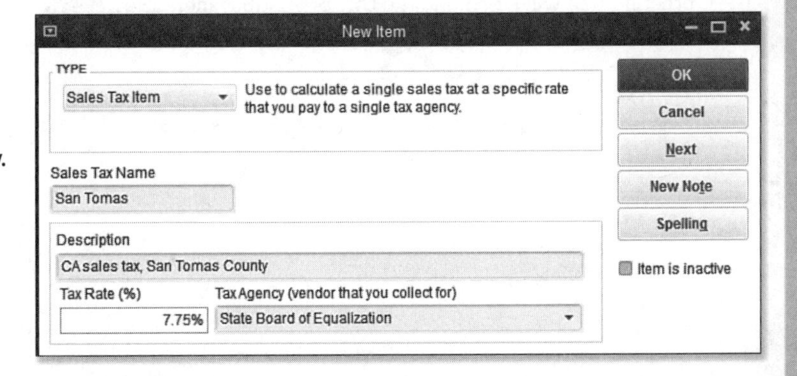

Figure 9.20
Setting up your sales tax item with the proper rate and vendor ensures that you collect and remit sales taxes correctly.

6. In the Tax Rate (%) box, enter the rate the taxing authority charges.
7. In the Tax Agency (vendor you collect for) drop-down list, select the vendor to which you remit your sales tax payments. If your vendor is not set up in QuickBooks, select **Add New** at the top of the list to create a sales tax vendor record.
8. Click OK to save the sales tax item.

With sales tax items created, you can group them into sales tax groups if the state requires collection and reporting on multiple tax entities.

Creating Sales Tax Group Items

Sales tax groups are optional in QuickBooks. In many states, you are required to report the collection of sales tax for a combination of city, county, and state, but you want to show the customer a single tax rate. In QuickBooks, you can accomplish this by first creating your individual city, county, and state sales tax items, and then assigning them to a Sales Tax Group item type. The Sales Tax Group item is then assigned to the customer.

To create a Sales Tax Group item in your data file, follow these steps:

1. From the menu bar, select **Lists**, **Item List**.
2. From the Item drop-down list, select **New** to open the New Item dialog box. If necessary, click OK to close the New Feature message.
3. In the Type drop-down list, select the **Sales Tax Group** item.
4. Enter a Group Name or Number that identifies the group.
5. In the Description box, enter the description you want printed on the customer's invoice.
6. In the Tax Item column, from the drop-down list, select the appropriate city, county, or state sales tax items previously created (refer to Figure 9.20).
7. Click OK to save the new Sales Tax Group item.

In the example shown in Figure 9.21, you are going to collect and remit the sales tax at a rate of 8.05%. In this example, part of the payment will be made to the State Board of Equalization and the other portion will be paid to the City of East Bayshore. However, when this tax group is assigned to a customer, the invoice will show a single rate of 8.05%.

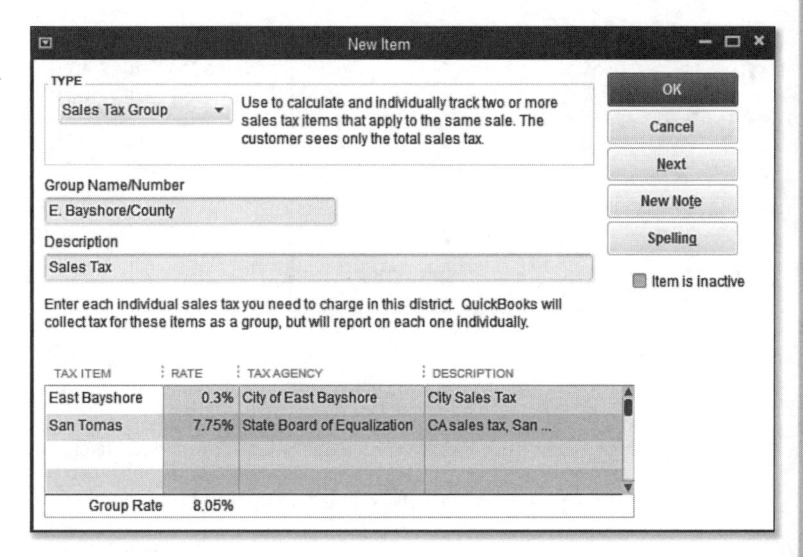

Figure 9.21
Use sales tax groups to track multiple taxes, but show one tax rate on a customer's invoice.

Creating Sales Tax Codes

The primary purpose of sales tax codes in QuickBooks is to identify a product or service as taxable or nontaxable and identify a customer as taxable or nontaxable. If you track sales tax, you must have at least one taxable code but might have multiple nontaxable tax codes.

Another use of sales tax codes is for when the state has reporting requirements on the types of non-taxable sales you make. Creating a unique nontaxable sales code for each of these nontaxable sales types enables you to report the total sales by nontaxable sales tax type.

Examples of nontaxable tax codes might include some or all of the following:

- Nontaxable reseller
- Out-of-state sales
- Sale to a nonprofit organization
- Government entity

To see a list of suggested nontaxable tax codes, select **Help** from the drop-down list to the right of the search box on the icon bar. Type **Sales Tax Code** and select the **Nontaxable Sales Tax Codes Examples** topic. QuickBooks provides a list of commonly used sales tax codes. See Figure 9.22 for a sample Sales Tax Code List.

When creating a customer invoice and before charging sales tax to the customer, QuickBooks determines whether the item being sold is taxable and whether the customer is assigned a taxable or nontaxable sales tax code before computing any sales tax charge on an invoice.

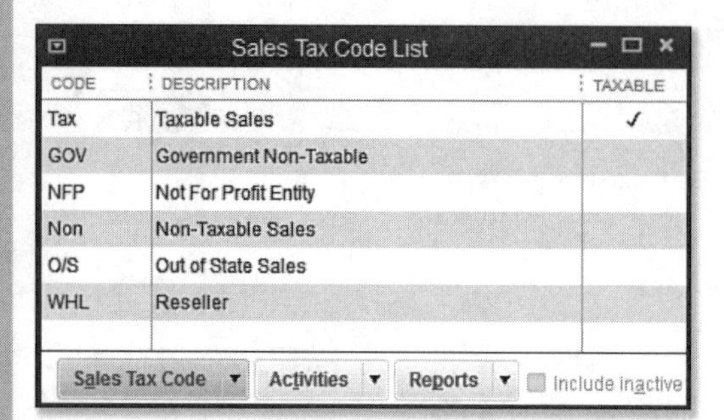

Figure 9.22
Sales Tax Codes are assigned to your customers and help with reporting requirements by your taxing authority.

To create a sales tax code list or edit the existing sales tax codes in your data file, follow these steps:

1. Make sure you have enabled the sales tax preference as discussed earlier in this chapter.
2. From the menu bar select **Lists**, **Sales Tax Code List**.
3. In the Sales Tax Code drop-down list, select **New** to create a new code. Alternatively, select a sales tax code from the list and then in the Sales Tax Code drop-down list, select **Edit Sales Tax Code**. (Note that a new QuickBooks data file defaults with one taxable tax code and one nontaxable tax code.)
4. In the New Sales Tax dialog box (or Edit Sales Tax dialog box), in the Sales Tax Code field, enter a three-character code. Make the three-character code something meaningful. You will see this code on the following dialog boxes: New Item, Edit Item, New Customer, or Edit Customer; and optionally, on the lines of the customer's invoice.

In the next section, you will complete the process and assign the appropriate code to your customer record.

Assigning Sales Tax Codes to Products or Services

Items are created in QuickBooks for use on sales and purchase transactions. The primary purpose of creating items is to handle the behind-the-scenes accounting and to assign the taxable status for an item on a customer invoice.

The following items in QuickBooks enable you to assign a taxable code, as shown in Figure 9.23:

- Service Item
- Inventory Part
- Inventory Assembly
- Non-inventory Part
- Other Charge
- Discount

If you expect to charge sales tax on an item, it should be marked as taxable even if it is sold to a nontaxable customer. QuickBooks validates whether an item is taxable and then verifies that the customer is taxable before it charges sales tax.

note

Items are typically assigned a generic taxable or nontaxable sales tax code. You might create other sales tax codes for resellers or out-of-state sales, which you will assign to customers, but not items.

If the item is always nontaxable, even if it is sold to a taxable customer (for example, labor), it should be assigned a nontaxable sales tax code so it will never have sales tax calculated on the sale of that item.

Some states require the sale of labor services to be taxed if they are invoiced with products and not taxed if they are invoiced separately. Although this might not be the requirement for the state jurisdictions you sell in, to handle this situation, create two Labor Service type items—one named Taxable Labor and assigned a taxable tax code, and another named Nontaxable Labor and assigned a nontaxable tax code. You can then select the appropriate item when you invoice your customers.

Figure 9.23
When an item is set up with a Non-Tax Code, no tax will be calculated even if the customer is taxable.

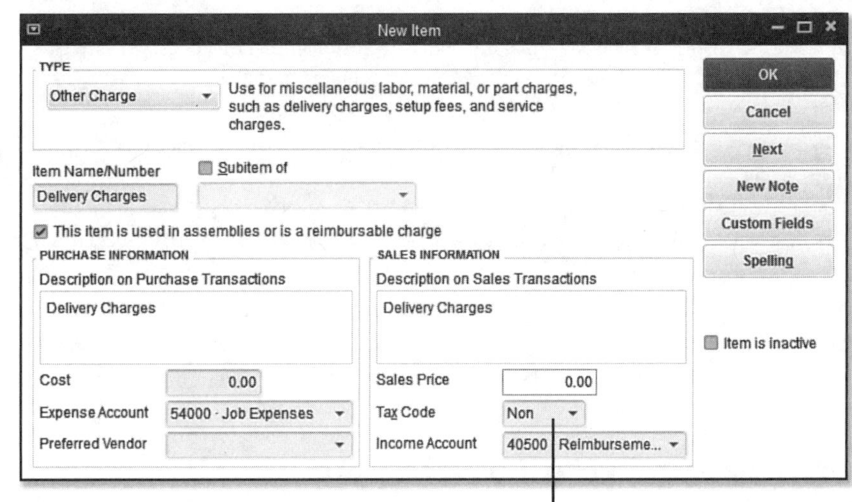

Select the proper tax status for this item

Assigning Sales Tax Codes and Sales Tax Items to Customers

Enabling the sales tax preference and creating sales tax items, groups, and codes are part of the sales tax setup. You also need to assign a tax code and a tax item to each customer.

To assign or edit an existing customer's tax code (as well as tax item), as shown in Figure 9.24, follow these steps:

Figure 9.24
Assign the proper sales tax code and sales tax item to each of your customers.

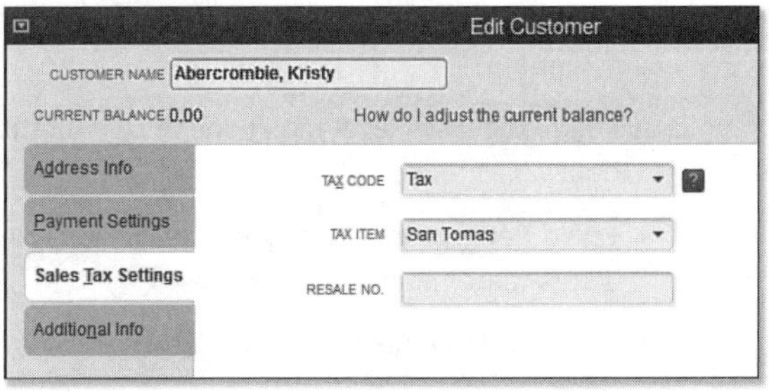

1. On the Home page, click the Customers button to open the Customer Center.
2. Select the customer for whom you want to assign or edit a tax code.
3. Click the Edit Customer button.
4. In the New or Edit Customer dialog box, click the Sales Tax Settings tab.
5. In the drop-down lists in the Sales Tax Information box, select the appropriate Tax Code and Tax Item. If the customer is a reseller of your product, for best record-keeping practices record the Resale No. you might be required to provide in the event of a sales tax audit.

caution

You can assign one tax code and one tax item to each customer. You cannot assign a tax code or tax item to a job. If you have a customer with multiple locations, and you are required to charge different sales tax rates for each location, you need to create a unique customer for each location.

The sales tax code defines the customer as taxable or not. The sales tax item defines the sales tax rate to be charged to the customer.

Because QuickBooks enables you to save a customer record without one or both of these settings, be sure to review your customer sales tax list often to ensure your sales tax is assigned to each of your customers.

Creating Price Level Lists

Each time you sell a product or service to a customer with an assigned price level, QuickBooks defaults the sales price to match the price level. (This feature is available in the QuickBooks Premier, Accountant, or Enterprise Solutions editions.) The price level assigned to a customer affects all sales to the customer for the selected item(s). Price levels cannot be based on discounts earned from buying a product in bulk.

To create a price level, follow these steps:

1. Enable the use of Price Levels. From the menu bar, select **Edit**, **Preferences**, **Sales & Customers**. On the Company Preferences tab place a checkmark in the Use Price Levels setting. Click OK to save your selection.
2. From the menu bar select **Lists**, **Price Level List**. After creating the price level, assign the price level to the appropriate customers.
3. Calculate the price level using one of two methods as shown in Figure 9.25:
   - **Fixed Percentage Price Levels**—An example is creating a Price Level that awards a customer a 10% discount on all purchases.
   - **Per Item Price Levels**—You might have preferred customers who get a specific rate for a particular item.

note

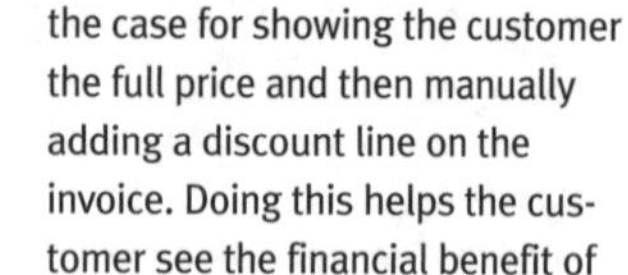
Using Price Levels is truly a time saver! However, I would also make the case for showing the customer the full price and then manually adding a discount line on the invoice. Doing this helps the customer see the financial benefit of doing business with your company.

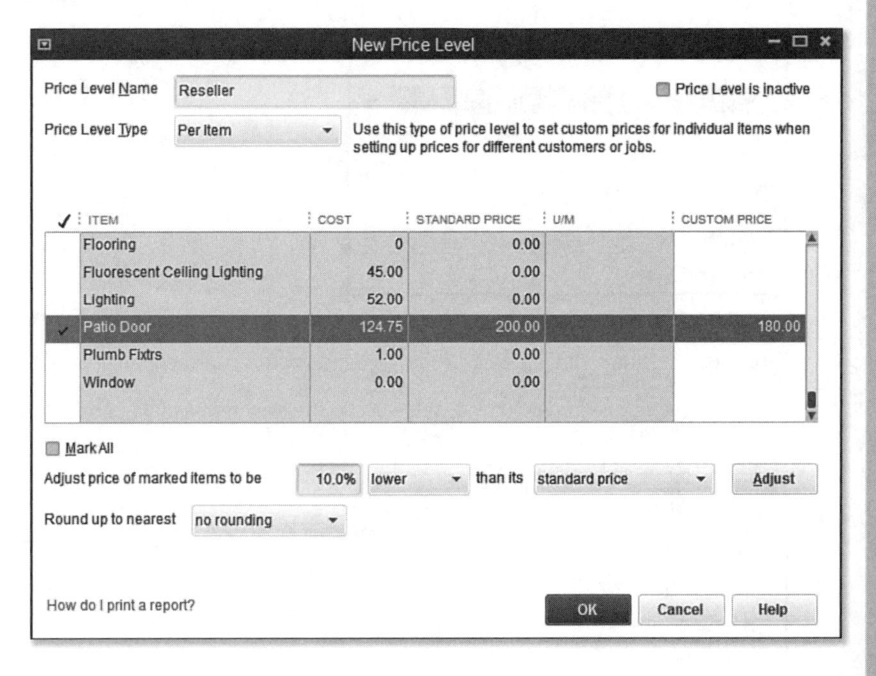

Figure 9.25
Price levels automate custom sales prices and can be assigned to specific customers.

4. To assign a price level to a customer, from the Customer Center select a customer list item on the left.
5. Click the Edit Customer button and choose the Additional Info tab.
6. From the Price Level drop-down list, select the proper price level to assign to this customer. You can assign one price level per customer.

It is important to note that Price Levels do not work with the batch invoicing method, discussed later in this chapter.

Creating Payment Terms

QuickBooks terms offer a shortened description and calculate on an invoice when you expect to receive payment from a customer or when a vendor expects to receive payment from you. For example, 1% 10 Net 30 is an expression for payment due in 30 days, 1% discount if paid within 10 days.

Creating a Payment Term

To practice creating a payment term, open the sample data file as instructed in Chapter 1. You might also use these instructions if you are creating a new payment term in your own data file:

1. From the menu bar select **Lists, Customer & Vendor Profile Lists, Terms List**. A list of terms displays, as shown in Figure 9.26.

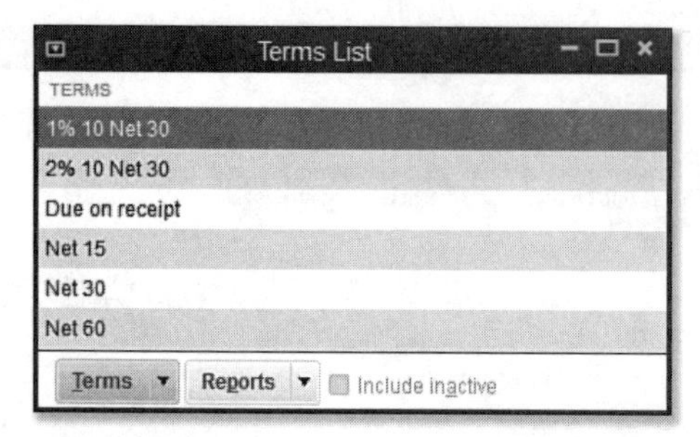

Figure 9.26
Terms lists calculate due dates on customer and vendor transactions.

2. In the Terms drop-down list, select **New**. The New Terms dialog box displays (see Figure 9.27).

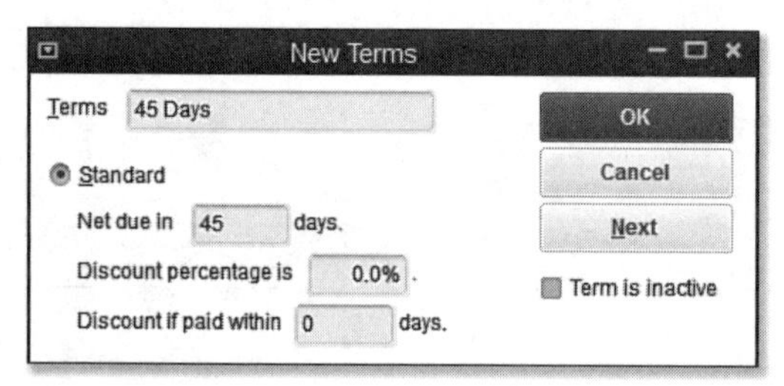

Figure 9.27
Complete all the fields when creating a new payment term.

3. In the Terms field, type **45 Days**.
4. Select the **Standard** option and type **45** in the Net Due In field.
5. Click OK. You are returned to the Terms List.
6. (Optional) Click the Reports button and then select **QuickReport** to prepare a report of transactions using the selected term.
7. You can now assign this term to customer and vendor transactions.

If you want the due date to be a specific date, use the Date Driven terms and complete the necessary fields.

Customizing QuickBooks Forms

You can customize most forms in QuickBooks, such as sales orders and customer invoices. *New for QuickBooks 2013,* you can access these powerful, yet previously hidden, features from the Ribbon Toolbar tabs displayed at the top of most transactions.

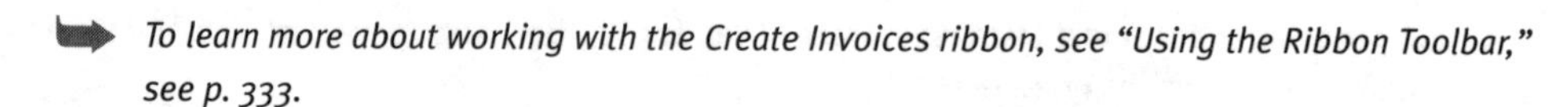
To learn more about working with the Create Invoices ribbon, see "Using the Ribbon Toolbar," see p. 333.

When customizing the QuickBooks invoice form, you can use these options:

- **Overall Design**—Includes how the form looks, if the form has a design imprint, or if field titles are shaded, as well as other format options.
- **Data Fields**—Customizing the data layout on a form.

Let's first tackle customizing the overall design of the invoice using the Customize My Forms Wizard.

Using the Customize My Forms Wizard

To create a consistent look and feel for your printed forms, consider using the Intuit—Customize My Forms Wizard. This feature is free for the first 30 days for each QuickBooks data file. After 30 days, if you need to make changes to a design, the fee is $4.99 per design. Any changes you pay for come with a 60-day satisfaction guarantee.

In just a few simple steps, you can add a professional look to all the QuickBooks forms.

To customize QuickBooks forms, follow these steps:

If you would like to "practice" using this tool before committing the changes to your own forms, use the Rock Castle Construction file as instructed in Chapter 1.

When using the sample data for this exercise, you will not be able to save the design or apply it to your own data's QuickBooks forms.

1. From the menu bar select, **Customers**, **Create Invoices**.
2. *New for QuickBooks 2013* is the Ribbon Toolbar at the top of a displayed transaction. To continue with customizing your forms, select the **Customize Design** icon on the Formatting tab.
3. The QuickBooks Forms Customization dialog box opens (see Figure 9.28). An Internet connection required. Choose a background that is specific to your business from the Industry drop-down list. As you select a background, the resulting design is displayed on the right.

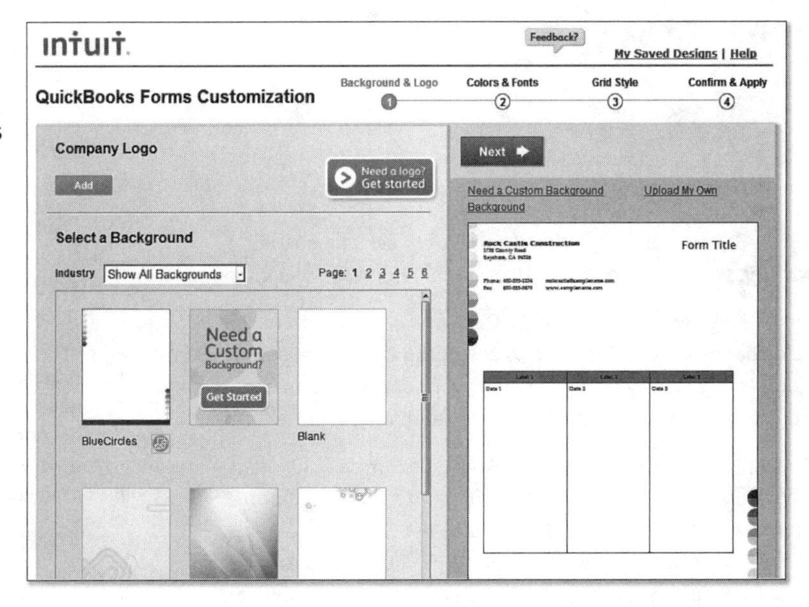

Figure 9.28 Add a professional look to your business forms.

4. Click the Add button under Company Logo to browse for your logo file. If you do not have a company logo, click the Need a Logo? Get Started button. Intuit has partnered with 99designs to offer very affordable custom design services.

note

Our firm uses this same Intuit design service partnered with 99designs to create the logo displayed on our website, www.quick-training.com.

5. Click Next to display Step 2—Colors and Fonts, as shown in Figure 9.29. Select your font and grid colors overall or for specific fields by clicking the appropriate drop-down list. A grayed-out field indicates the data for that field does not exist in your QuickBooks data file. (Optional) Place a checkmark in the box to indicate that you mail your invoices in window envelopes. Click Next.

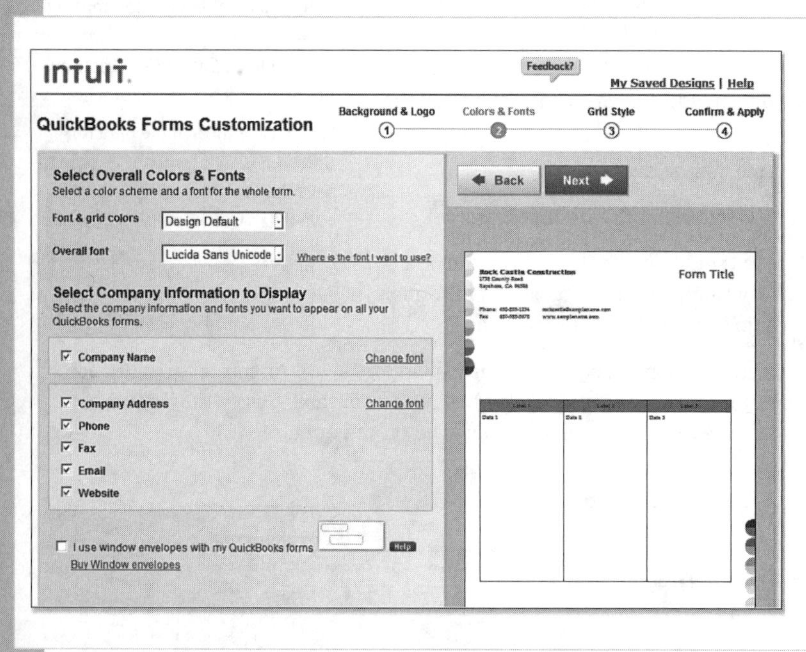

Figure 9.29
Select font and grid colors and other design options for your customized forms.

6. Step 3—Select a Grid Style displays. Click to select a shaded style grid of your choice. Click Next on the top of the dialog box.

7. Step 4—Review Design displays. Click the Back button to make changes. Click Continue to select the forms to assign the design to. Click No Thanks to cancel your changes. You are redirected to a website that displays matching business forms.

8. The Apply Design dialog box displays (see Figure 9.30). Place a checkmark next to each of the forms to which you want to apply the customized design. You can select from the many QuickBooks forms (Invoice, Sales Receipt, Purchase Order, and so on), making it easy to customize several forms all at once!

note

If you are prompted for payment to apply the designs to your forms, this indicates that you have previously used the initial free service. After a period of time, the service is available but requires a minimal fee.

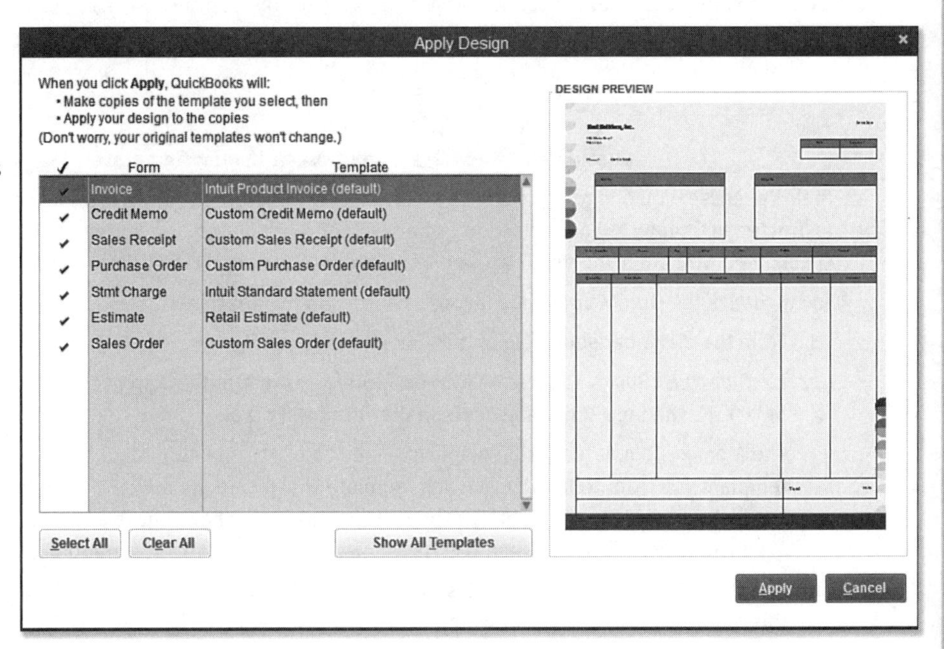

Figure 9.30 Apply the design customization to multiple forms all at once.

9. Click Apply, and the Design Applied dialog box displays with instructions for identifying your customized templates on the Templates list. After reading the details, click OK to close the message.
10. The Save Design Online (Recommended) dialog box displays with these options:
    - **Save**—The design is available for future editing; you will be prompted to define a name for the design and to create a secure login for future editing. A message displays showing the date the form was customized and the last day to make changes without an additional fee. Click OK to close.
    - **No Thanks**—Select this if you do not want to save the design. A warning message displays; click OK to close, and you are redirected to a website showing other business items that match your customized style. Close the open web pages when completed reviewing the information.
11. The Intuit Business Forms web page displays. Click the X in the top-right corner to close the web page when you're finished with your review of the information.

Now that you have customized the overall design of your invoice form, let's look at managing the data that is both displayed on the screen during input and printed on the customer's invoice.

Using the Customize Data Layout Tool

Use the Customize Data Layout tool to create a new template or edit the layout and design of an existing invoice, purchase order, or other template. One distinct difference from the method taught previously is that the changes you make now are only for the currently selected form. If you want to make changes to the format for multiple forms at one time, use the method discussed in the previous section.

Customizing the Data Layout on an Invoice Template

In this exercise, you are going to create a new invoice template using the sample data as instructed in Chapter 1. Your selection options might differ depending on the version of QuickBooks you are using and if you are using a different sample data file:

To customize the QuickBooks data layout on forms, follow these steps:

1. From the menu bar select **Customers, Create Invoices.**
2. *New for QuickBooks 2013* is the Ribbon Toolbar at the top of a displayed transaction. Select the **Manage Templates** icon on the Formatting tab.
3. The Manage Templates dialog displays. Scroll through the list of templates to select the template you want to modify. As each template is selected, a preview of the finished template displays to the right. For the instructions that follow, I have selected the Intuit Product Invoice. Click OK when you have selected the template you want to modify.
4. The Basic Customization dialog displays. Review the information that can be modified from this dialog, including the following:
   - **Use Logo**—Browse for your logo image file to attach to the form. QuickBooks copies the logo to a folder that resides in the same location as your QuickBooks data file.
   - **Select Color Scheme and Apply Color Scheme**—Alter the color of borders and header fonts.
   - **Change Font For and Change Font**—Select a data field and choose the Change Font to change the font for that specific field.
   - **Company & Transaction Information and Update Information**—Click to select the fields you want to display on your form, and then select the Update Information button.
5. Click the Additional Customization button at the bottom of the screen.
6. If prompted with the Locked Template message, click the Make a Copy button. Intuit protects the original templates and does not allow you to edit them without making a copy first. The Additional Customization dialog box displays with the Selected Template name in the top left.
7. Click the following tabs to modify the respective information:
   - **Header**—Each field selection offers the option to view onscreen, print on the invoice, and add a title. See Figure 9.31.
   - **Columns**—Each field offers the option to select which columns appear onscreen and in print, and in what order. Accept the default title or assign a new title to each field. See Figure 9.32.

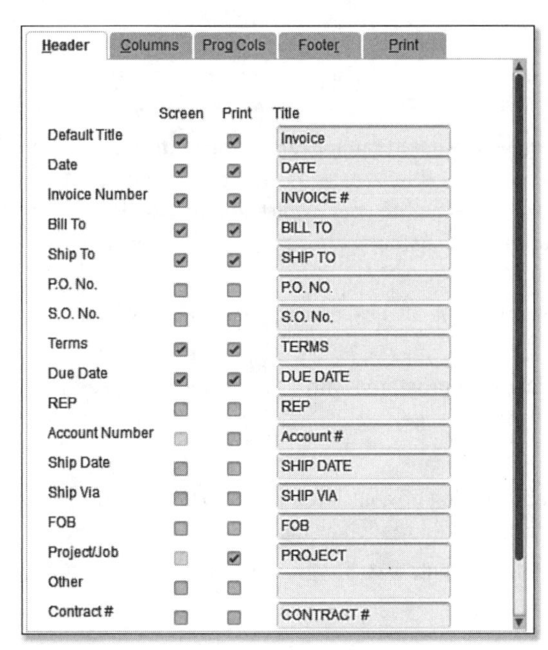

Figure 9.31
Customize your forms for which fields to display onscreen and print on the invoice.

Header | Columns | Prog Cols | Footer | Print

	Screen	Print	Order	Title
Service Date			0	SERVICED
Item	✓		1	ITEM
Description	✓	✓	2	DESCRIPTION
Quantity	✓	✓	3	QUANTITY
Unit of Measure	✓	✓	4	U/M
Rate	✓	✓	5	RATE
Amount	✓	✓	6	AMOUNT
Class			0	CLASS
Other 1			0	
Other 2			0	
Color			0	COLOR
Material			0	MATERIAL

Figure 9.32
For your customized forms, define the label and order of the displayed and printed fields.

- **Prog Cols**—If you have enabled Estimates or Sales Orders, these fields allow you to select which columns appear onscreen or in print, and in what order. Accept the default title or type a new title in the field.
- **Footer**—These fields allow you to manage the data that appears at the bottom of forms onscreen and in print. Accept the default title or assign a new title to the field. Optionally, select to include a long text disclaimer on your invoice and to include the Intuit PaymentNetwork link (allowing your customers to pay online by check) on printed invoices.
- **Print**—Settings for managing the printing of the invoice, adding page numbers, and the option to print trailing zeros.

8. If you added any fields to your form, you might be prompted with a Layout Designer message. For this exercise, click OK to dismiss the message.
9. Click Print Preview to take a closer look at the changes.
10. At the bottom of the Additional Customization dialog box, click the Layout Designer button. Use the layout designer as shown in Figure 9.33 to do the following:
    - Modify the properties for the selected field's font, text, border, and background.
    - Add a text box, data field, or image.
    - Copy or remove a field.
    - Use the Copy Format button to apply formatting from one field to others. Click End Format to turn off this feature.
    - Make multiple fields the same height, width, or size by holding down the Ctrl key on your keyboard while selecting the desired fields.
    - Click Center to place a selected field in the center of the form.
11. Click Undo or Redo as needed.
12. Use the Zoom In or Out buttons to see the detail more closely.
13. Click the Margins button to set the margins for the form. Click OK to close.
14. Click the Grid button to various options related to the grid. Click OK to close.
15. If you use window envelopes, click Show Envelope Window to determine whether the business address is positioned correctly.
16. Click OK to save your changes, or select **Cancel** or **Help**. Select **Yes** to the Layout Designer message and to be returned to the Additional Customization dialog box.
17. Click OK to close the Additional Customization window. Click OK to close the Basic Customization dialog box. You are returned to the Create Invoices dialog box (in this example).

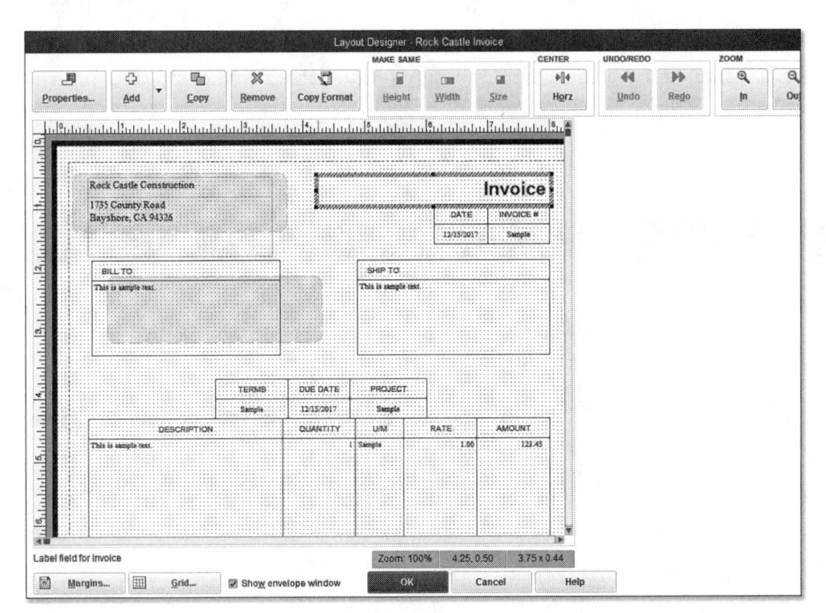

Figure 9.33
Use the layout designer to rearrange the fields or modify the attributes of the field.

The newly created or modified invoice format can be used when preparing an invoice for your customers.

QuickBooks can help you put on a professional look for your communications with suppliers and customers. To download ready-made customized forms, from the Ribbon Toolbar at the top of a displayed Create Invoices transaction, click the Formatting tab and choose Download Templates. An Internet connection is required.

The Forms Intuit Community site displays. Scroll through the list of forms that you can download and use with your QuickBooks data.

Forms include Credit Memos, Estimates, Invoices, Purchase Orders, Sales Orders, Sales Receipts, Statements, and specifically for nonprofit entities, Donation forms.

Accounts Receivable Processes

Within QuickBooks, you have some flexibility in how you handle your company's receivables workflow. Your company might use some or all of the transaction types listed in this chapter, depending on the product or service that you sell.

In the section "Preferences That Affect Accounts Receivable" in this chapter, I discussed the preferences you can define after you determine what sales transaction type or feature you need.

Table 9.1 details the transactions that are used in the Accounts Receivable module and their primary purpose.

Table 9.1 Accounts Receivable Transactions

Transaction Types	Primary Purpose
Estimates	Create a job budget and proposal.
Sales Orders	Record a committed sale.
Invoices	Record the sale of services or products on account.
Sales Receipt	Record the sale of services or products COD (cash at the time of delivery).
Receive Payment	Record customer payment of invoices.
Online Payments	Download online customer payments (requires a monthly subscription).
Record Deposits	Record the bank account deposit.
Statement Charges	Assess customers' recurring charges.
Finance Charges	Assessed to customers with a past-due balance.
Statements	Periodic statement provided to the customer of account activity.
Refunds & Credits	Returns or credits given to customers.

So whether you start with an estimate, a sales order, or prepare an invoice for a customer, the proper workflow for recording a sale has some or all of these steps:

1. (Optional) Create a quote using an estimate. Estimates are useful if you will be providing a quote or multiple quotes for a prospect. Estimates not won can be marked as inactive.
2. (Optional) Create a sales order. Sales orders are best when you have a commitment for sale to a customer, but you cannot fulfill it at the time the order comes in. Sales orders can be created directly from an estimate.
3. Prepare an invoice, sales receipt, or statement charge. The invoice transaction can be created directly from the estimate or sales order.
4. Receive the customer payment into an Undeposited Funds account.
5. Record the deposit into your bank account.

Performing these related tasks in QuickBooks is easy from the Home page, as shown in Figure 9.1. Whether you are new to QuickBooks or are an experienced user, you will find the Home page useful in getting around QuickBooks and in determining what the next transaction process should be.

What I have noticed over the years of consulting with clients is that many do not know the proper Accounts Receivable process. By following a recommended workflow, some of the more common errors can be avoided, rather than having to be fixed at a later date.

Using QuickBooks Estimates

Use a QuickBooks estimate to provide prospects a quote for your product or services. The estimate helps you keep track of the sales price you have quoted. In accounting terms, the estimate is considered "nonposting," which means when you record an estimate you are not yet recording revenue.

Estimates also provide the means for QuickBooks to prepare a budget (expected costs and revenue) for a customer or job. There are many job costing reports that use the estimate details. You can view these reports using the sample data referred to in Chapter 1. From the Reports menu, select **Jobs**, **Time & Mileage**, and view the Job Estimates vs. Actuals Summary or Detail (to name just a couple).

Do you need to track Active vs. Inactive Estimates? From the Ribbon Toolbar on the Create Estimates dialog box, select the **Main** tab and toggle the checkmark on or off for Mark as Active or Mark as Inactive.

When an Estimate is inactive, it will not display on drop-down lists.

Creating an Estimate

To practice creating a new estimate, open the sample data file as instructed in Chapter 1. If you are using your own data file, make sure you have enabled estimates as discussed in the preferences section of this chapter:

1. On the Home page, click the Estimates icon. The Create Estimates transaction displays (see Figure 9.34).

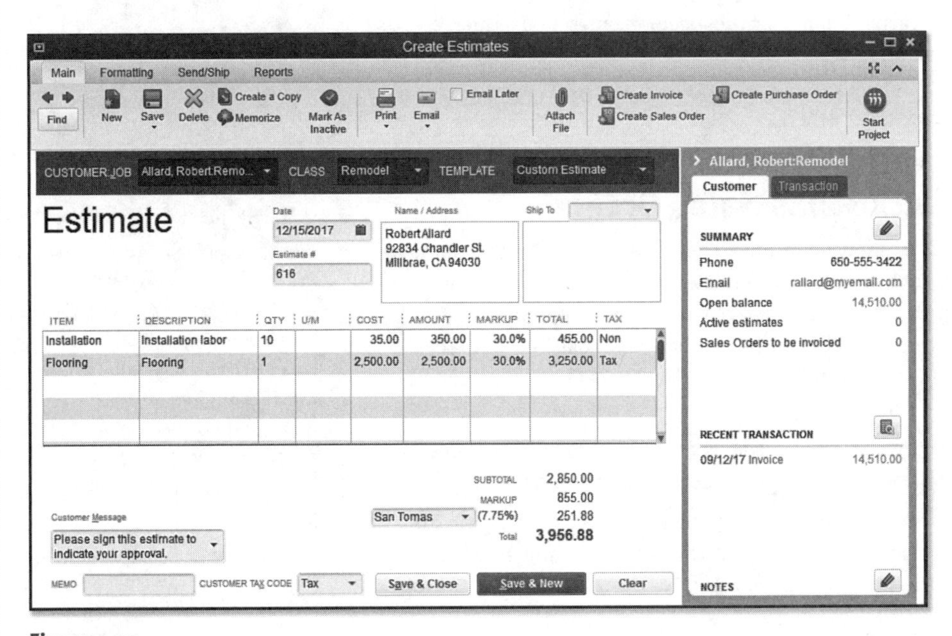

Figure 9.34
Use estimates to track your projected job costs and to save time creating invoices when the quote becomes a sale.

2. In the Customer:Job drop-down list, select the customer **Allard, Robert:Remodel job**.
3. For this exercise, leave the prefilled values in the Template, Date, Estimate #, and Name/ Address fields.
4. Click the first field in the Item column and use Installation. Accept the prefilled description of Installation Labor.
5. In the Qty field, type **10**.
6. Leave the U/M (Unit of Measure) field blank.
7. Accept the Cost field default of $35.00.
8. In the Markup field, type **30%**. (See the caution that follows this sidebar.) Accept the default Tax line assignment.
9. In the Item column on the next available row, select the non-inventory part, **Flooring**.
10. In the Qty field, type **1**. Leave the U/M (Unit of Measure) field blank.
11. In the Cost field, type **2,500.00**.
12. In the Markup field, type **30%**. Accept the default Tax line assignment.
13. Click Save & Close to complete the estimate, or click Save & New to practice creating another estimate.

You now have an estimate and can track quotes you provide to your prospects. When your prospect becomes a customer, create the invoice from the estimate.

Estimates can also be used to create Sales Orders referred to in the next section.

caution

When working with Estimates, if you want the markup to be % over cost, you must also type the percentage (%) character. To charge a fixed dollar amount over cost, type the dollar amount.

If you do not include anything in the Markup column, QuickBooks job budget vs. cost reports will consider the amount in the Cost column the same as the Total, which is, in effect, the Sales Price. Best practice is to include a markup % or dollar amount.

Using QuickBooks Sales Orders

Sales orders are used to record the sale of products you do not have in stock or services you have scheduled to provide at some future date. Sales orders are perfect for tracking "back orders." Sales orders are not available with QuickBooks Pro, but are included with all other editions of the QuickBooks for Windows desktop products.

You can start with a blank sales order, of if you created an estimate, you can create the sales order from the estimate.

The Sales & Customers—Company Preferences tab on the Edit Preferences dialog box offers settings you can adjust, which will make working with Sales Orders more efficient for your business.

For instructions on creating sales orders, see "Handling Inventory Backorders," p. 187.

Creating Customer Invoices

If my guess is correct, this is one of the first sections of the book you have turned to. My clients typically are quick to get an invoice to a customer for payment for the product or service being sold.

This section provides some basic instruction in using multiple methods of invoicing in QuickBooks. You might even learn some new techniques.

Using the Ribbon Toolbar

New for QuickBooks 2013 is a ribbon toolbar that is accessible from the Create Invoices dialog box and on other transaction types. The features displayed will differ depending on the particular transaction type that is displayed.

The ribbon centralizes previously lost or underutilized features relating to the displayed transaction (form).

When working with the Create Invoices transaction, on the ribbon toolbar at the top of the transaction you have the following available:

- **Main**—On this tab, access these commonly used transaction tools and features:
  - **Find**—Search for a specific invoice, or use the arrows to move backward or forward one record at a time.
  - **New**, **Save or Delete**—Create new, save, or delete the currently displayed transaction.
  - **Create a Copy**—Duplicate the currently displayed invoice.
  - **Memorize**—Assign the displayed transaction to a list of memorized transactions. More information follows in this section.
  - **Mark as Pending or Mark as Final**—When an invoice is marked pending, it is considered non-posting and does not affect accounts receivable or the accounts assigned to the items used. I would recommend not using this method and instead using Sales Orders when needing to record a committed sale that you cannot fulfill at the time of the commitment.
  - **Print or Email (with option for Later)**—Options for providing the invoice to your customers. When you select the box for Print Later or Email Later, you can then efficiently process these multiple transactions at one time.
  - **Attach File**—Free document storage (local on your server or computer hard drive) of scanned documents, emails, and so on.
  - **Add Time/Costs**—Useful if you do Time and Expense Invoicing, discussed later in this section.
  - **Apply Credits**—Click to apply open credits for the selected Customer or Job.
  - **Receive Payments**—Record money in from your customer for this specific invoice.
  - **Create a Batch**—Create a batch of invoices, where the customers being invoiced all share the same invoice template, date, items and rates. More about this in the section "Batch Invoicing" in this chapter.

- **Refund/Credit**—Selecting this icon opens the Create Credit Memos/Refunds dialog box. If you click the icon with a saved create invoices transaction displayed, QuickBooks creates a new Credit Memo with the same lines as on your original invoice.
- **Online Pay**—Learn about how you can sign up (no monthly fee) for taking online payments from your customers. Our company wouldn't be without this service! If you are not presently accepting credit cards from your customers, let the author's company provide you with a quote and any current giveaways for signing up for a merchant services account. Email the author at info@quick-training.com.

- **Formatting**—On this tab you can access the following:
  - **Preview**—View the format as your customer would see it.
  - **Manage Templates**—See a list of all the templates available with the currently opened QuickBooks file.
  - **Download Templates**—Intuit offers many customized forms already; do not miss checking this out! An Internet connection is required.
  - **Customize Data Layout**—Settings to control what data displays, what date prints, and many other settings you will find useful.
  - **Spelling**—Spell checks the currently displayed transaction. Customize your spell checker list by selecting **Edit**, **Preferences**, **Spelling**, and choosing the My Preferences tab.
  - **Insert Line**—Inserts a line directly above where your cursor is placed on the displayed transaction. A shortcut to this same task is available by pressing the Ctrl+Insert keys on your keyboard.
  - **Delete Line**—Deletes the currently selected line. A shortcut to this same task is available by pressing the Ctrl+Delete keys on your keyboard.
  - **Customize Design**—Self-service and paid-for service for customizing multiple forms in just a few steps. Use this to create a new customized design or apply a saved design.

- **Send/Ship**—QuickBooks offers several options for managing distribution of your invoice to your customers, including the following:
  - **Email**—Email a single invoice or a batch of invoices at one time.
  - **FedEx**, **UPS**, **USPS**—Include options when working with these shipping vendors to send, find, schedule, track, and print postage on shipping labels or directly on envelopes (fees may apply).
  - **Mail Invoice**—Use your own web mail account to send invoices by email. Sign up for Intuit QuickBooks Billing Solution and send your customer an invoice with a tear-off remittance slip, as shown in Figure 9.35.
  - **Prepare Letter**—Efficiently communicate in letter form with your customers by preparing letters directly from your QuickBooks file. Customize the letter templates to meet your business's specific needs.

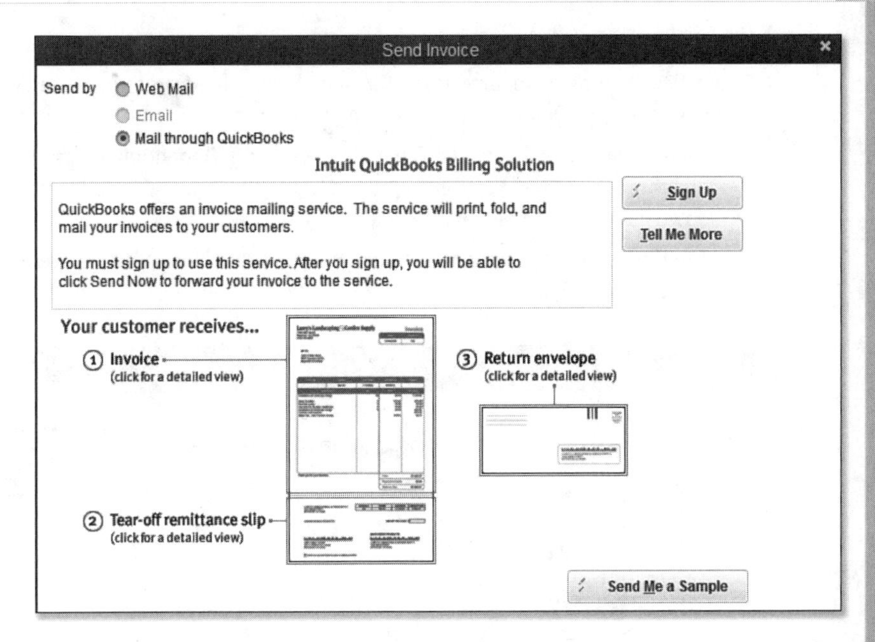

Figure 9.35
Using Intuit's QuickBooks Billing solutions, provide your customers with an invoice with a tear-off remittance slip.

- **Reports**—Access these reports detailing the currently displayed transaction:
  - **Quick Report**—Displays only if a Create Invoices transaction is open.
  - **Transaction History**—Displays related transactions (if any). This information is also available on the Transaction tab to the right of the invoice details.
  - **Transaction Journal**—Detailed report showing the behind-the-scenes transaction accounting.

You are now ready to create a basic invoice to provide to your customers.

Creating a Basic Invoice

QuickBooks makes it easy to prepare and send invoices to your customers. A basic invoice might contain a single line or many lines, depending on the nature of the products and services you provide.

 **tip**

When entering data, you can use common keyboard shortcuts to complete transactions. For this exercise, start typing **Rice** into the Customer:Job field, and the customer Rice, Linda displays.

Without leaving the field, press the Ctrl key while you tap the down-arrow key to navigate through the list from that point forward.

When you have the proper job selected, use the Tab key to advance to the next field.

Creating an Invoice

To practice creating an invoice, open the sample data file as instructed in Chapter 1. You might also use these instructions if you are creating an invoice for your own customers:

1. On the Home page, click the Create Invoices icon. Depending on the sales and customer preferences you have enabled, you might have to select Create Invoices from the drop-down list next to the Invoices icon.
2. The Create Invoices transaction displays as shown in Figure 9.36. Select the **Rice, Linda:Repairs job**.

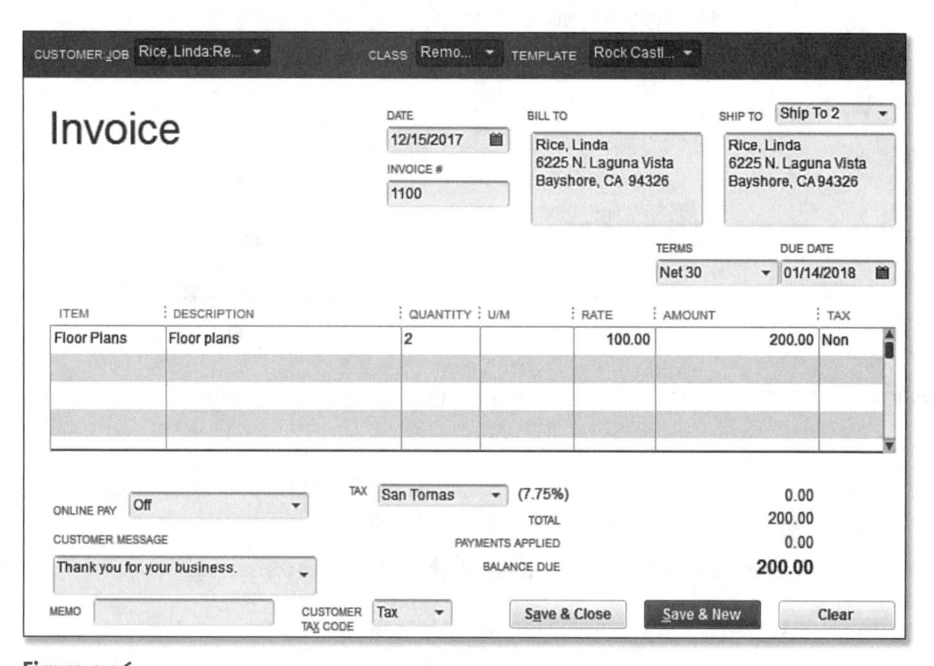

Figure 9.36
Creating a basic invoice is simple using QuickBooks.

3. In the Class field, select **Remodel**.
4. Leave the prefilled Template, Date, Invoice #, Bill To, and Ship To details. If you are working in your own data, optionally choose a different template.
5. Select the **Floor Plans** item in the Item column.
6. Accept the prefilled description.
7. In the Quantity field, type **2** and leave the U/M (Unit of Measure) field blank.
8. In the Rate field, type **100.00**. QuickBooks did not include a rate because the item record did not have a value recorded in the Sales Price field of the stored item record. QuickBooks automatically calculates the row total. The item used, Floor Plans, is a nontaxable item (per the original setup of this item), even though the customer is taxable.

9. (Optional) Select to include a link on the invoice for your customer to pay online. Links include options for your customer to pay with a business check only or allowing your customer to choose between paying by check or credit card.
10. (Optional) Select or create a new Customer Message that will display on the invoice for your customer.
11. (Optional) Type a Memo. This detail will be included in your reports and will not be included on the customer's invoice.
12. Leave the Sales Tax item selected. This location is assigned to the original setup of your customer on the Sales Tax Settings tab of the customer (not job) record.
13. Leave the assigned Customer Tax Code; this is also set up with the customer's record.
14. To preview this invoice, on the Main tab of the ribbon at the top of the Create Invoices dialog box, for this exercise click Save. Choosing Save at this time will make it easier to preview the invoice in the next step. Normally you will be selecting the Save & Close or Save & New options at the bottom of the transaction when working in your own data.
15. In the Print drop-down list, select **Preview**. (Optional) Click the Zoom In button to see more details.
16. Click Close to return to the Create Invoices dialog box.
17. Click Save & Close if you have completed this task, or click Save & New to practice creating another invoice.

Do you routinely add multiple items to your invoices? QuickBooks Enterprise Solutions 12.0 (all editions) includes the capability to select multiple items (see Figure 9.37) in one easy, searchable window.

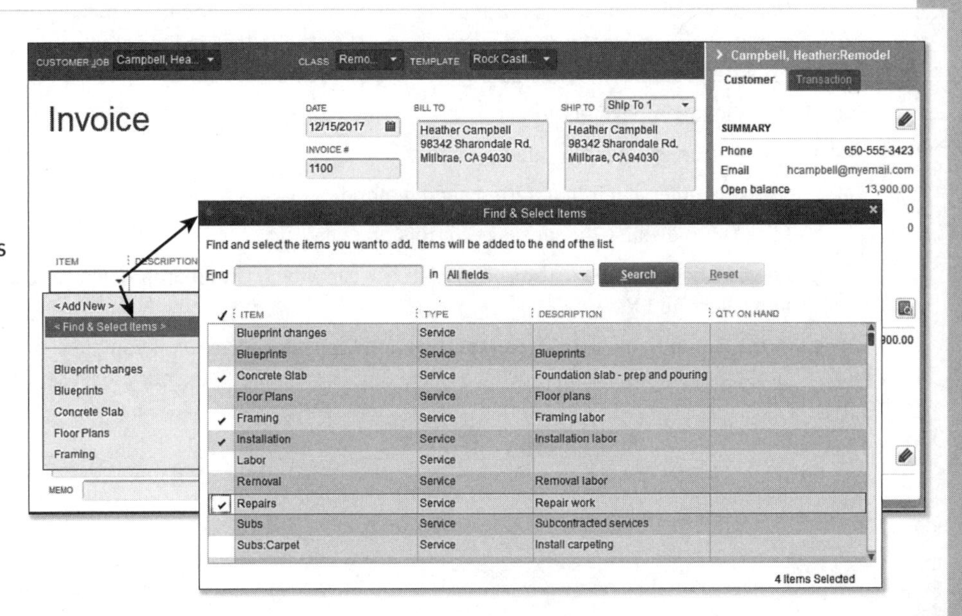

Figure 9.37 QuickBooks Enterprise includes the capability to quickly add multiple items to an invoice.

Batch Invoicing

Do you issue recurring invoices to a group of customers for the following?

- Same service or product item
- Same price
- Same billing frequency
- Same invoice template

 **note**

To successfully use Batch Invoicing, make sure that each customer or job has important information in their records, including Terms, Send Method, and Tax Status. These items are more difficult to change after processing a batch of invoices.

If you answered yes to each of these questions, you will save time invoicing using the QuickBooks Batch Invoicing feature.

There are three basic steps when working with Batch Invoicing:

1. Creating your billing group involves naming the group and then assigning customers and/or jobs.
2. Selecting the line items and rates for the batch invoices.
3. Reviewing the list of invoices to be prepared.

Using Batch Invoicing

To practice using Batch Invoicing, open the sample data file as instructed in Chapter 1. You might also use these instructions if you are creating Batch Invoicing with your own data:

1. From the menu bar select, **Customers, Create Batch Invoices.**
2. If the warning message Is Your Customer Info Set Up Correctly? displays, read the information provided. Your success with using Batch Invoicing is dependent on how well your customer records are set up. The message refers to the following fields that should be defined for each customer before creating invoices using the Batch Invoicing feature:
   - Customer payment terms
   - Customer sales tax rates
   - Customer and Job preferred send method
3. Click OK to dismiss the message for this practice.
4. The Batch Invoice dialog box displays. Click the Billing Group drop-down list (top right), and select **Add New.**
5. In the Group Name field, type **Monthly**, and then click Save. Or, if you are creating a Billing Group in your own data, provide a name that is meaningful to your business. Click Save.

6. In the Search Results box, which displays all active jobs, select a few jobs of your choice. In this example, three jobs were selected as displayed in Figure 9.38. Notice you can search for a specific list of customers or choose **Select All** or **Clear All** for ease in setting up your Billing Group.

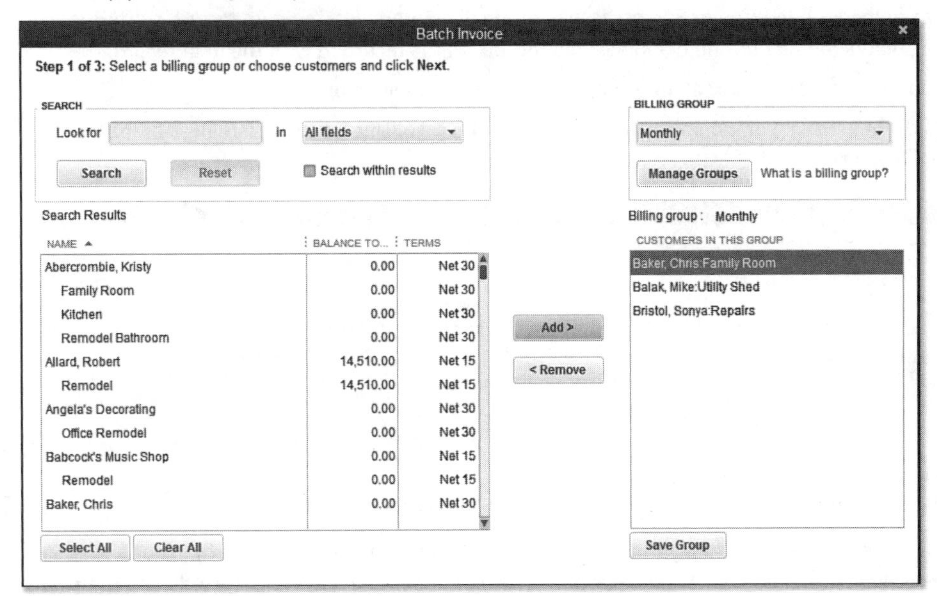

Figure 9.38
When creating a Billing Group, select the Customers or Customer:Jobs you want to issue a recurring invoice for.

7. Click Save Group. You can return to this dialog box at any time to modify the list of customers or jobs included.
8. Click Next. Step 2 of 3 displays as shown in Figure 9.39. Leave the Rock Castle invoice template selected. If you are working in your own data, select the invoice template you want to use.

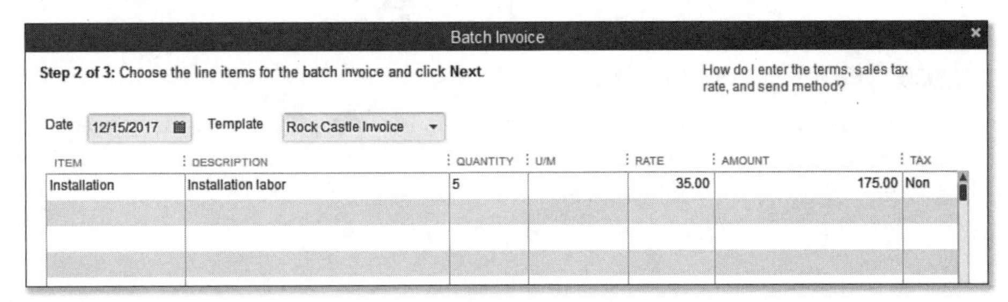

Figure 9.39
Batch invoices share the same item, description, quantity, rate, and tax status.

9. In the Item column, select **Installation**.
10. In the Quantity column, type **5**.
11. Leave the U/M (Unit of Measure) blank.
12. Leave the prefilled rate of $35.00 as was originally stored with the item record. QuickBooks calculates the Amount field and assigns the Tax status recorded with the item record.
13. (Optional) Select or add a new Customer Message (not shown).
14. Click Next. Step 3 of 3 displays as shown in Figure 9.40. Unclick any customers or jobs you don't want to invoice at this time.

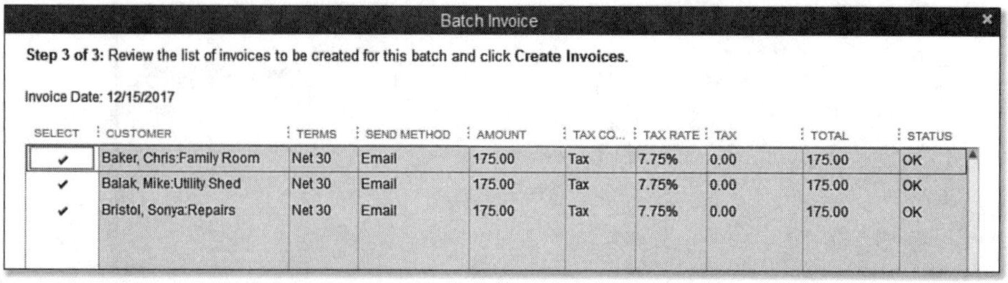

Batch Invoice

Step 3 of 3: Review the list of invoices to be created for this batch and click **Create Invoices**.

Invoice Date: 12/15/2017

SELECT	CUSTOMER	TERMS	SEND METHOD	AMOUNT	TAX CO...	TAX RATE	TAX	TOTAL	STATUS
✔	Baker, Chris:Family Room	Net 30	Email	175.00	Tax	7.75%	0.00	175.00	OK
✔	Balak, Mike:Utility Shed	Net 30	Email	175.00	Tax	7.75%	0.00	175.00	OK
✔	Bristol, Sonya:Repairs	Net 30	Email	175.00	Tax	7.75%	0.00	175.00	OK

Figure 9.40
Review the listed terms, send method, and tax settings before creating the invoices.

15. Click Create Invoices when you are ready. If any of the fields displayed are blank or show incorrect information, click Cancel. Update the corresponding customer records and then return to the Batch Invoicing menu to complete the steps listed here.
16. After you click Create Invoices, the Batch Summary dialog box displays. Here you can print or email the newly created invoices. If a Preferred Send method was not indicated in the Customer or Job record, the invoice will be included in the unmarked total.

You might be asking, what if my customers have different items or rates, but on a recurring basis? The next section details how to use Memorized Invoice transactions when Batch Invoicing won't meet your specific needs.

Memorized Transaction Group

Memorized transactions offer a recurring invoice alternative to Batch Invoicing. With memorized transactions you can assign different items or prices to each customer, yet still create a group of invoices all at once.

When working with a memorized group, you need to do the following:

1. Create a memorized group.
2. Define the frequency of the recurring transactions.
3. Assign memorized transactions to the group.

Creating Memorized Transactions

To practice using a Memorized Transaction Group of customer invoices, open the sample data file as instructed in Chapter 1. This practice will build on the exercise completed in the section titled "Basic Invoicing":

1. From the menu bar, select **Lists, Memorized Transaction List.**
2. In the Memorized Transaction drop-down list, select **New Group.**
3. Type a group name. In this practice, type **Monthly**. See Figure 9.41.

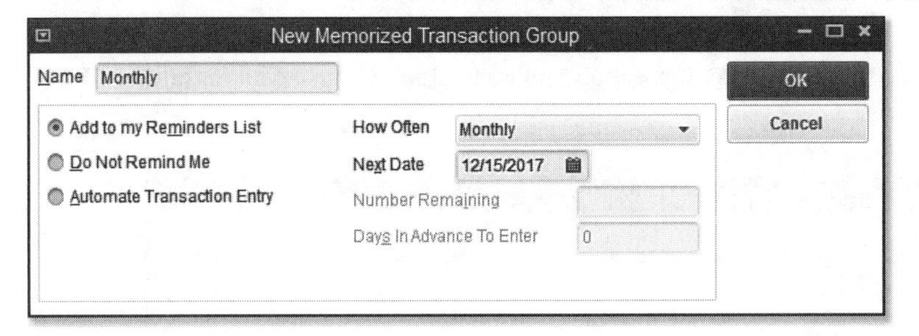

Figure 9.41
Create the Memorized Transaction Group first.

4. In the How Often drop-down list, choose Monthly.
5. For this exercise, you can accept the date that QuickBooks prefills in the Next Date field, or assign a different date if you are using your own data.
6. Click OK to close the New Memorized Transaction Group message. You are returned to the Memorized Transaction List and your newly created Group name is in bold text. Next you will add a previously recorded invoice to your memorized group.
7. On the Home page, click the Create Invoices icon. Depending on the sales and customer preferences you have enabled, you might have to select Create Invoices from the drop-down list next to the Invoices icon.
8. On the top left, on the Main tab of the ribbon toolbar, click the arrow pointing to the left. A previously recorded invoice is displayed. Alternatively, create a new invoice from scratch.
9. From the Main tab of the ribbon toolbar, select **Memorize Transaction.**
10. In the Name field, type a descriptive name, such as the customer or job name on the invoice. When creating a memorized transaction (see Figure 9.42) in your own data file, type a name that will be helpful for you to identify the transaction in a group.
11. Click to select **Add to Group** and then select your newly created group from the Group Name drop-down list.
12. Click OK.
13. Return to the Memorized Transaction List (see Figure 9.43) to see your memorized transaction now part of the memorized transaction group.

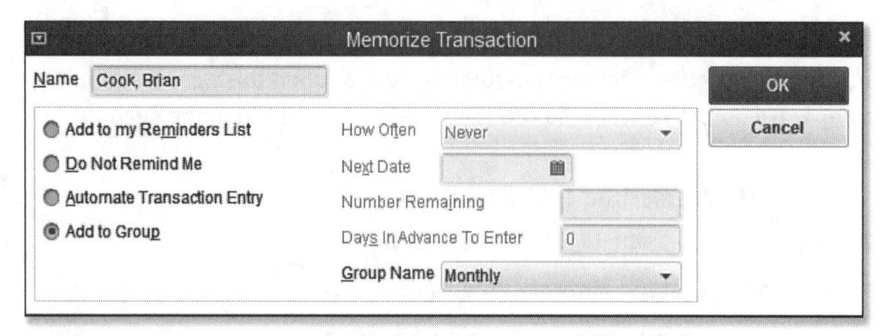

Figure 9.42
Click the Memorize icon on the Main tab of the ribbon toolbar to store a transaction for future recurring use.

Memorized Transaction List

TRANSACTION NAME	TYPE	SOURCE ACCOUNT	AMOUNT	FREQUEN...	AUTO	NEXT DATE
◆ Overhead	General Journal	13100 · Pre-paid Insurance	675.00	Monthly		01/01/2018
◆ **Monthly**	**Group**			**Monthly**		**12/15/2017**
◆Cook, Brian	Invoice	11000 · Accounts Receivable	1,636.69			
◆ Sergeant Insurance	Check	10100 · Checking	1,265.00	Monthly		01/15/2018

Memorized Transaction ▾ | Enter Transaction

Figure 9.43
The Memorized Transaction Group name will be in bold text, with the transactions assigned to that group indented to the right.

14. To process this recurring Memorized Transaction Group, double-click the group name, Monthly.
15. The Using Group dialog displays, and QuickBooks prefills the Date that will be assigned to each of the transactions in the group. Alternatively, choose another date.
16. Click OK and QuickBooks creates the transactions in the group. Click OK to close the message indicating that the transactions in the group were entered. Review the tip on emailing these forms that follows these steps.

tip

Do you need to print or email your newly created forms? Select **File, Print Forms**, or **Send Forms** and follow the instructions.

note

Use your mouse cursor on the sides or corners of the Memorized Transaction list to expand the information, or click the top-right box (next to the X) to expand the list contents.

You have learned several easy techniques for invoicing your customers: how to create and send a basic invoice, use the batch invoicing feature, and memorize recurring invoices. Let's get a little more complex with the next invoice method named Progress Invoicing. This type of invoice is often used in the construction industry or any industry that invoices customers based on % (or $) completion of the work contracted.

Progress Invoicing

The Progress Invoicing feature allows you to generate multiple invoices from a single estimate. To use progress invoicing, you must first enable the preference on the Jobs & Estimates—Company Preferences tab of the Preferences dialog box. (You must log in to the file as the Admin or External Accountant User type.)

Certain industries you do business with might require the work performed or products being made to be invoiced in stages of completion. This method of invoicing is often referred to as *percentage of completion*. Conversely, you would not need to use Progress Invoicing in cases where you present a single invoice at point of delivery or project completion.

Creating a Progress Invoice

To practice creating a progress invoice for a customer, open the sample data file as instructed in Chapter 1. If you are working in your own data, the company preferences for progress invoicing must be enabled on the Jobs & Estimates—Company Preferences tab of the Preferences dialog box.

This practice exercise will continue with the estimate created earlier:

1. On the Home page, click the Create Invoices icon. Depending on the sales and customer preferences you have enabled, you might have to select Create Invoices from the drop-down list next to the Invoices icon.
2. In the Customer:Job drop-down list, select the **Allard, Robert:Remodel customer**.
3. In the Available Estimates dialog box, select the estimate. The selected row will be shaded as shown in Figure 9.44.

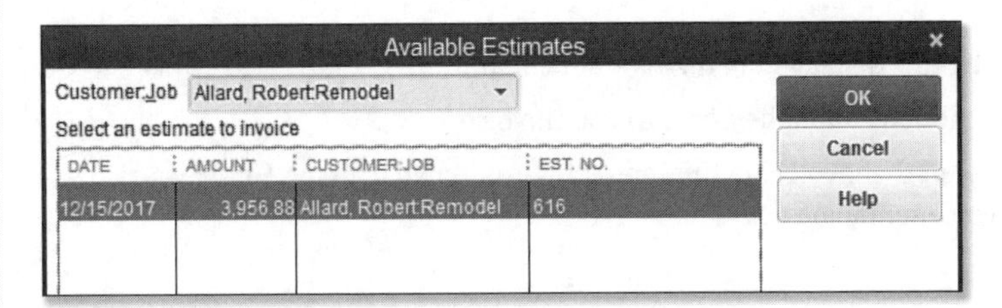

Figure 9.44
Select the Estimate you want to use for creating the progress invoice.

4. Click OK, and QuickBooks displays a Create Progress Invoice Based on Estimate message.
5. For this exercise, select **Create Invoice for Selected Items or for Different Percentages of Each Item** and then click OK. You might also want to familiarize yourself with the other options. See Figure 9.45. Click OK.

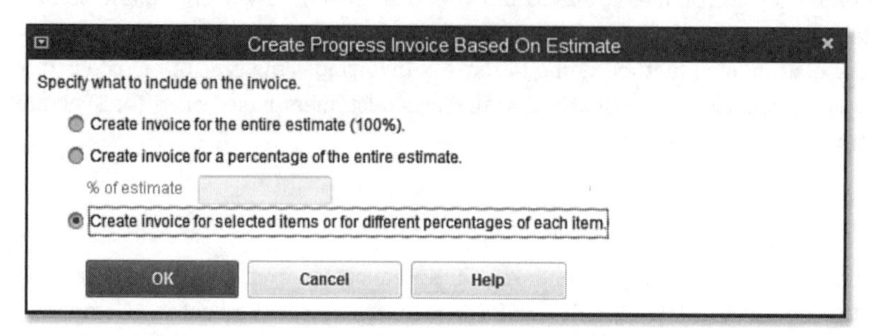

Figure 9.45
When progress invoicing is enabled, you can choose from these options when creating an invoice.

6. QuickBooks opens the Specify Invoice Amounts for Items on Estimate dialog box.
7. Toggle the Show Quantity and Rate and Show Percentage options to see how the displayed view changes.
8. In the Qty column for Installation, type **7**. In the same column for Flooring, type **.50** (invoicing for 50% of the materials). Figure 9.46 displays the result of entering these values.

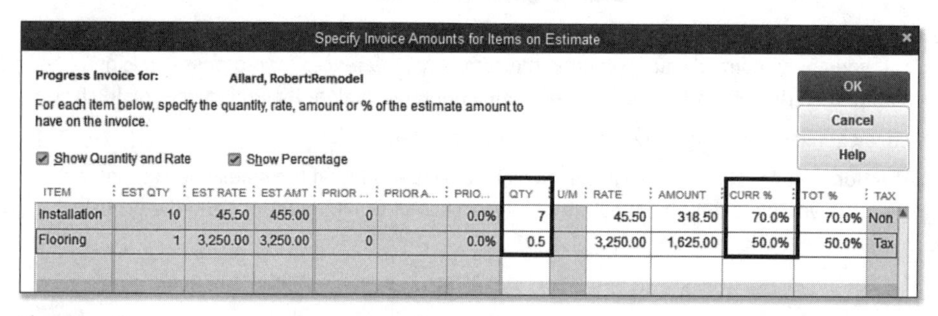

Figure 9.46
Enter either a Qty or a percentage in the Curr % column to add line items to the customer's progress invoice.

9. Review the dollar total by row displayed in the Amount column.
10. When you click OK, QuickBooks adds the items to your invoice.
11. From the top-right corner of the invoice, in the Template drop-down list (see Figure 9.47), select the **Progress Invoice** template.

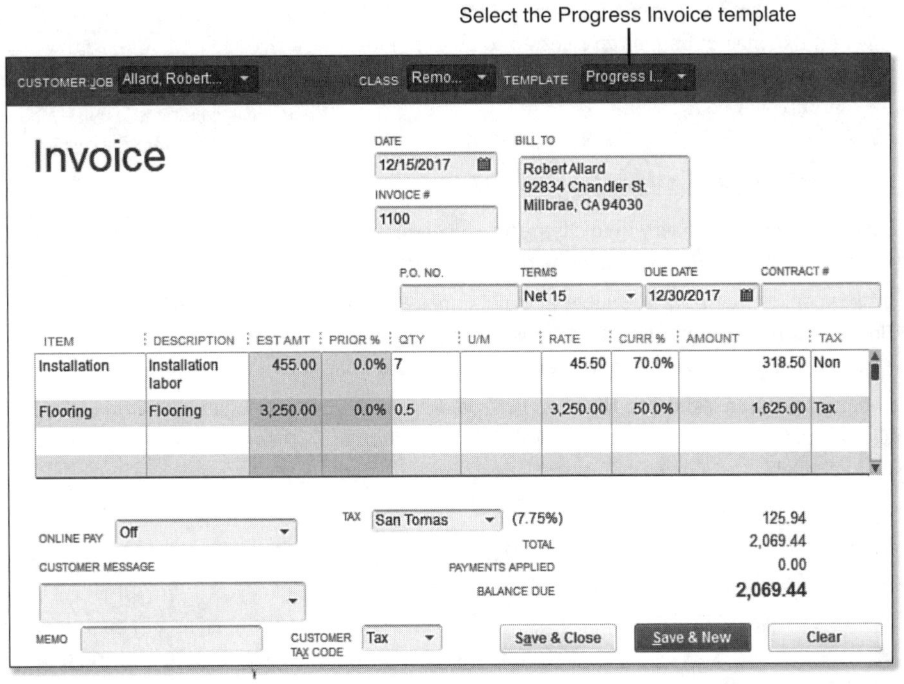

Figure 9.47
The Progress Invoice template includes columns for Estimate Amount and Prior Percentage invoiced.

12. For this exercise, click Save & New to practice creating a second invoice. A blank Create Invoice dialog box displays.
13. Repeat the preceding steps 2–4.
14. On the Create Progress Invoice Based on Estimate dialog box, select **Create an Invoice for the Remaining Amounts of the Estimate** (see Figure 9.45). Click OK.
15. QuickBooks prepares the transaction. Click Save on the Main tab of the ribbon. The transaction remains displayed.
16. In the Main tab on the ribbon toolbar, click the Print, Preview option to see the completed invoice.
17. Click Close to return to the Create Invoices dialog box. Click Save & Close.

caution

Are you tracking inventory in your QuickBooks data file? Be careful to progressively bill only whole increments of inventory part items, such as 3 wheels, rather than 2.5 wheels.

If instead, you are trying to create a printable document to record a customer's deposit or prepayment, use the instructions later in this chapter in the section "Unique Customer Transactions."

With progress invoicing, your customers can see the percentage of the quoted contract that they are being invoiced for. The next method, Time and Expense billing, often referred to as Cost Plus Invoicing, will meet the needs of those customers for whom you quote a fixed markup over your costs.

> **caution**
> If the Est Amt and Prior % columns do not appear on your invoice, confirm that you have selected the Progress Invoice template.

Time and Expense Invoicing

Time and Expense invoicing allows you to charge your customers the costs you incur on their behalf plus an agreed-upon markup (to cover for overhead costs and profit).

The Time and Expenses feature is available in QuickBooks Pro, Premier (all editions), Accountant, and QuickBooks Enterprise Solutions (all editions). You can enable this feature on the Time & Expenses—Company Preferences tab of the Preferences dialog box.

Before you begin creating a Time and Expense invoice, you must first have billable charges for your customer. The Write Checks, Enter Bills, and Make General Journal Entries transactions can all have costs selected as billable, as shown in Figure 9.48.

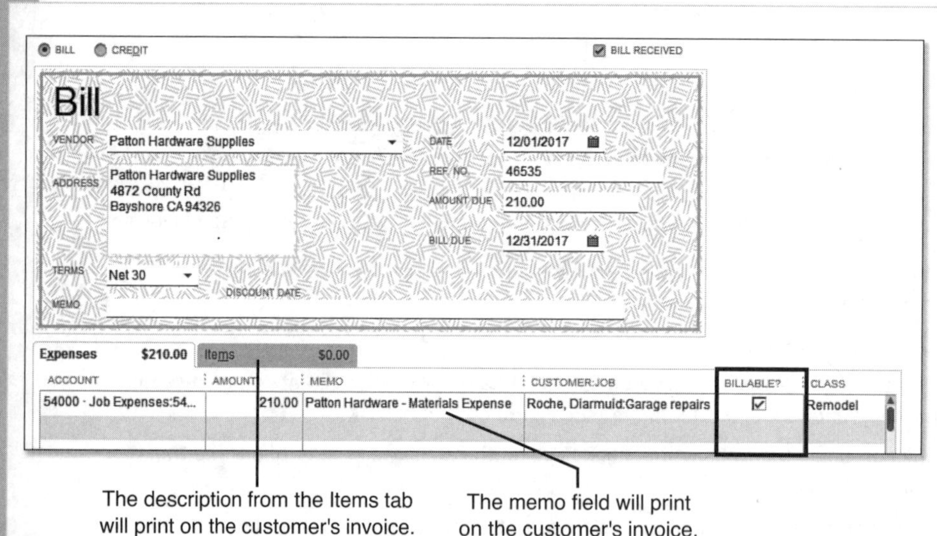

Figure 9.48 When creating a customer- or job-related expense, place a checkmark in the Billable column if you need to add the charge to a future customer invoice.

New for QuickBooks 2013, you can set a preference that defaults all time or all expense entries as billable to your customers when a customer or job is assigned to the transaction line. On the menu bar, select **Edit**, **Preferences**, **Time & Expenses** and select the **Company Preferences** tab.

You can review the costs marked as billable by selecting **Reports**, **Jobs**, **Time & Mileage**, **Unbilled Costs by Job** from the menu bar.

> **note**
> It is not necessary to remove (or add) the checkmark in the billable column if you are not providing your customers a Time and Expense type of invoice.

Creating a Time and Expense Invoice

To practice creating a Time and Expense invoice, open the sample data file as instructed in Chapter 1. You might also use these instructions if you are creating a Time and Expense invoice for your own customers:

1. Review the preference setting for working with Time and Expense invoicing. On the menu bar select **Edit, Preferences, Time & Expenses** (at the end of the list) and select the **Company Preferences** tab. You must be logged in to the file as the Admin or External Accountant user type.

   For more information on selecting the proper preference setting, see "Time & Expenses," see p. 304.

2. Click OK to close the Time & Expenses Preferences dialog box.
3. On the Home page, in the drop-down list next to the Invoices icon, select **Invoice for Time & Expenses.** A message about this improved feature may display. Read and optionally select the **Do Not Display This Message in the Future** checkbox. Click OK to close the message.
4. The Invoice for Time & Expenses dialog box displays. Select a **Date Range.** For this practice exercise, accept the prefilled To Date of 12/15/2017 as shown in Figure 9.49.

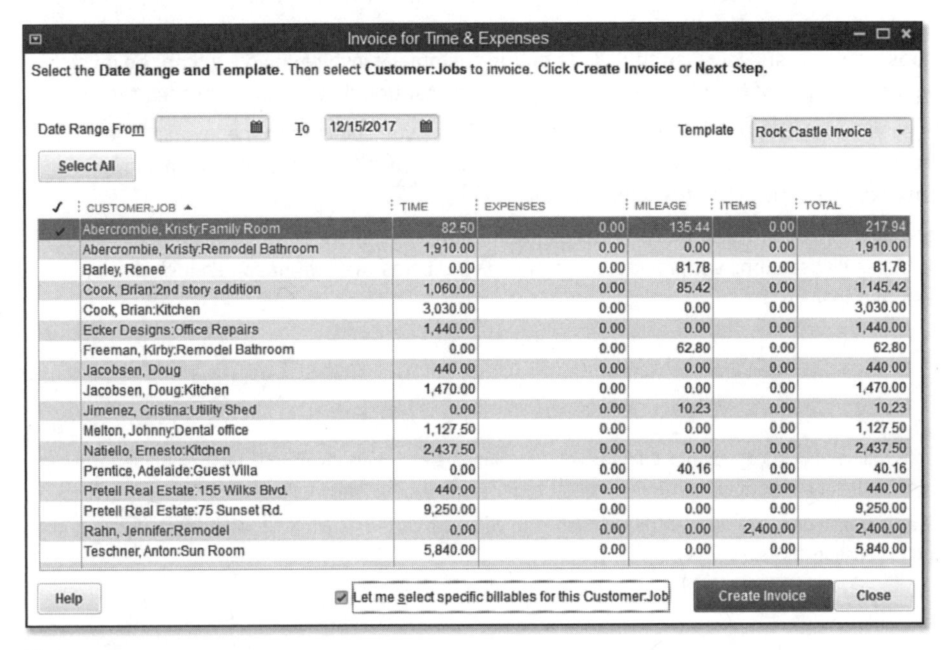

Figure 9.49
Invoice multiple customers more efficiently after enabling the preference to create invoices from a list of time and expenses.

5. In the sample company, select the **Rock Castle Invoice** template, or select a template from your data that suits your needs.
6. (Optional) Click any header column to sort the list by the selected column. For example by clicking on the Total column, the list will sort in ascending or descending order of the amount to be invoiced.
7. For this exercise, place a checkmark next to the Abercrombie, Kristy:Family Room. In your own file you could select multiple customers at once, if desired.
8. Select the **Let Me Select Specific Billables for This Customer:Job** checkbox at the bottom of the dialog box.
9. Click Create Invoice. QuickBooks displays the Choose Billable Time and Costs dialog box. From here, you can view expenses marked billable from the following tabs:
   - **Time**—Employees' time from paychecks; click the Options button to see choices for transferring employee time to the customer's invoice. Click OK to return to the Choose Billable Time and Costs dialog box.
   - **Expenses**—Costs from the Expense tab of a write check, vendor bill, or journal entry.
   - **Mileage**—Costs recorded using the menu Company, Enter Vehicle Mileage.
   - **Items**—Costs from the Items tab of a write check or vendor bill.
10. From the Time tab, place a checkmark in the first column next to the time entry for Gregg O. Schneider. Or, optionally, click Select All for this practice. In your own data, you can choose which costs you want to include on the customer's invoice. If you will not be invoicing the client any of the displayed costs, review the caution that follows these instructions.
11. When you click OK, QuickBooks transfers the charges you selected to the invoice. The Description on the invoice will default from the item record or the memo field included in most expense transactions (see previous Figure 9.48).
12. Click Save & Close. QuickBooks replaces the Billable checkmark on the originating expenses transactions with an invoice icon. This indicates the cost has been included on a customer invoice.

The Choose Billable Time and Costs dialog box enables you to review the expenses invoiced to your customer. You can then click the Hide column at the right to indicate you won't be invoicing the customer for certain charges.

Choosing to Hide an expense does not remove the expense from your own records; instead it will be excluded from this or future Time and Expense invoices.

Do you invoice your customers for the services of vendors or employees? If necessary, you can create billing rate levels (see Figure 9.50) that you associate with your vendors and/or employees. In turn, QuickBooks applies the proper billing rate when you add expenses marked as billable (refer to Figure 9.48) to an invoice.

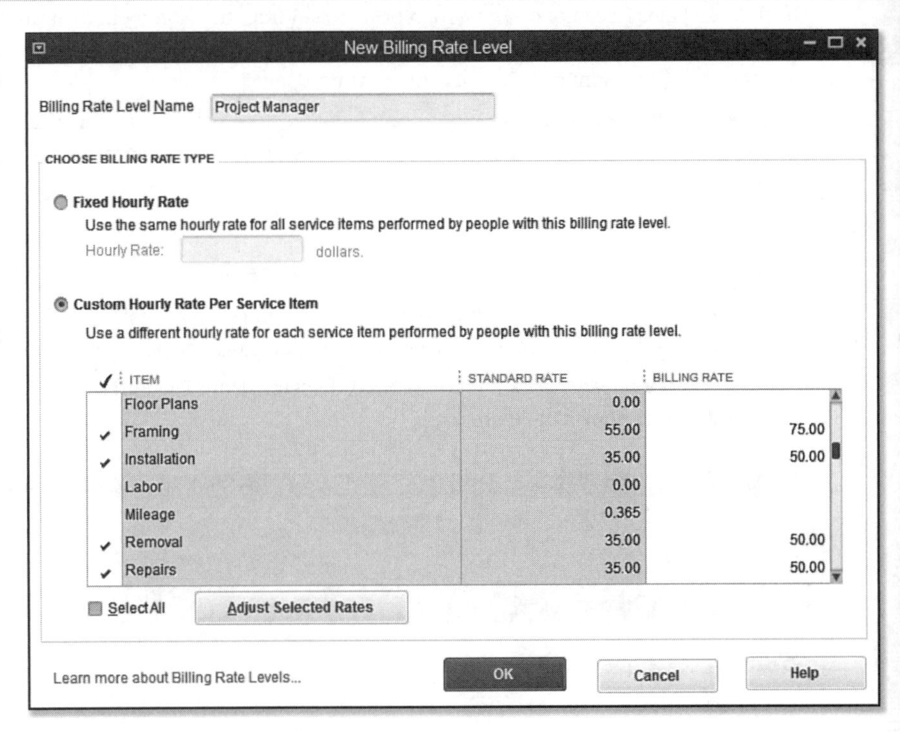

Figure 9.50 Billing Rate Levels are assigned to vendors, customers, and other names lists and default the sales price for a person when time is tracked to specific service items.

To use billing rates, follow these steps:

1. Create your service items.
2. Create your billing rate levels.
3. Assign each billing rate level to vendors, employees, or other names as needed.
4. Invoice your customers using Add Time/Costs. QuickBooks will use the corresponding billing rate you have assigned.

Use Time and Expense invoicing when you are permitted to add a markup to job expenses.

Recording a Sales Receipt

Use a QuickBooks Sales Receipt when you are recording a sale and taking payment at the time of sale, commonly referred to as Cash on Delivery, or COD. Recording a sales receipt does not increase Accounts Receivable because you are receiving payment at the time of sale.

QuickBooks Sales Receipts can be added or removed from the Home page on the Desktop view—Company Preferences tab of the Preferences dialog box. To change this preference, you need to log in to the file as the Admin or External Accountant User.

Sales receipts are a perfect choice for a company that does not offer terms to its customers. Some retail establishments might summarize the day's cash register tally into a Sales Receipt for a generic customer named "Daily Sales."

Creating a Sales Receipt

To practice creating a sales receipt, open the sample data file as instructed in Chapter 1. You might also use these instructions if you are creating a sales receipt in your own data:

1. On the Home page, click the Create Sales Receipts icon. The Enter Sales Receipts dialog displays, as shown in Figure 9.51.

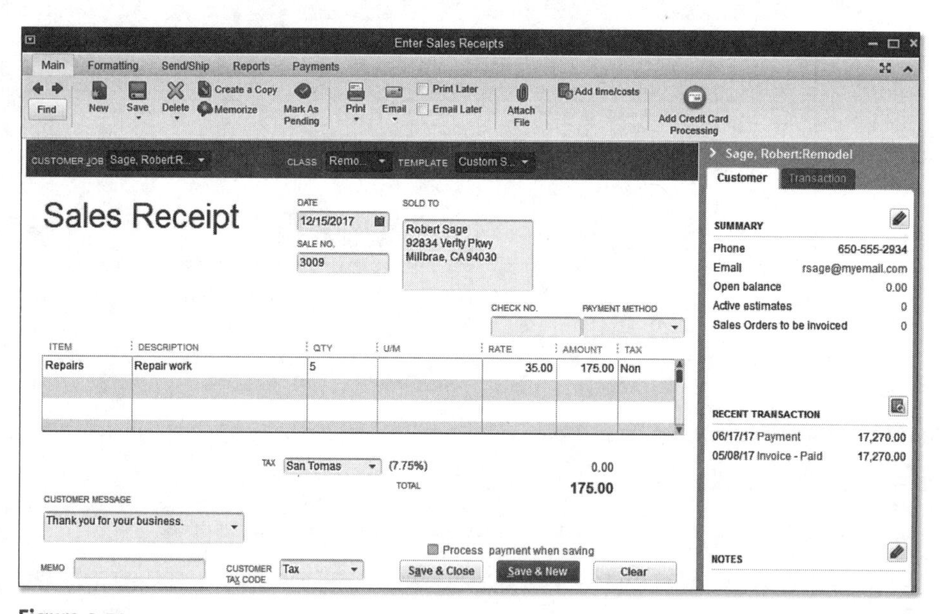

Figure 9.51
Enter sales receipts when payment is collected at the time of sale.

2. In the Customer:Job drop-down list, select **Sage, Robert:Remodel job.**
3. In the Class field, select **Remodel.**
4. For this exercise, leave the Template, Date, and Sale No. as prefilled by QuickBooks.

5. In the Check No. field, type **1234**. In the Payment Method drop-down list, select **Check**.
6. In the Item column, select **Repairs**.
7. Using the Tab key on your keyboard, advance to the Qty field and type **5**. QuickBooks prefills the Amount column. Accept the defaulted Tax column data. This tax assignment is assigned to the Repairs item setup.
8. (Optional) Select a **Customer Message**.
9. For this exercise, click Save. In the Print drop-down list on the Main tab of the ribbon, you can preview, print, or choose from other useful commands.
10. Click Save & Close to complete the Sales Receipt, or click Save & New to practice creating another sales receipt transaction.

You might be asking, where did the money go that I just recorded go in my accounting records? First, you will want to review your Payments preference as discussed earlier in this chapter and then learn how to add these payments to a bank deposit in the section "Making the Bank Deposit."

Recording a Statement Charge

Statement charges are useful if you want to accumulate charges before requesting payment, or if you assess a regular monthly charge to your customer. Use statement charges when you are not going to be providing the customer with an invoice, but instead will provide the customer with a periodic statement.

Recording statement charges one customer at a time can be very time consuming. If this charge is recurring, consider adding them to a Memorized Transaction Group discussed previously.

Recording a Statement Charge

To practice recording a statement charge, open the sample data file as instructed in Chapter 1:

1. On the Home page, click the Statement Charges icon.
2. In the Customer:Job drop-down list, select the **Babcock's Music Shop:Remodel job**. See Figure 9.52.
3. For this exercise, place your cursor in the next available row and accept the prefilled date. The selected customer's Accounts Receivable register displays.
4. Leave the Number field blank. In the Item field, type **Repairs**.
5. In the Qty field, type **5**.
6. In the Class field, type **Remodel**.

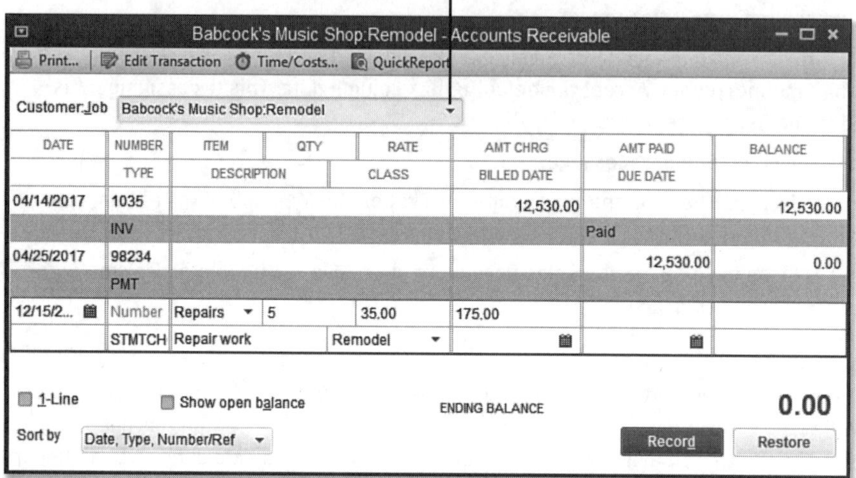

Figure 9.52
Use statement charges for a customer or job when you are not providing an invoice for the charges.

7. Click Record to save the charge on the customer's register. Repeat steps 2–7 as needed to add additional statement charges.

Recording the Customer Payment

Sales Receipts record your customer's payment at the time of the sale. However, businesses issue invoices or statement charges and expect the customer to remit payment within an agreed-upon number of days.

When your customer pays in full or in part an amount that is due, you will record a receive payment transaction.

When a customer payment is posted to your bank account will depend on your payment preference settings.

You can watch a demonstration of the many online customer payment methods that work with your QuickBooks file at http://payments.intuit.com/products/quickbooks-payment-solutions/quickbooks-online-billing.jsp

To review your current payment settings, choose **Edit**, **Preferences** from the menu bar and select the **Payments** preference, **Company Preferences** tab. You will need to be logged in to the file as the Admin or External Accountant User type. See Figure 9.53.

note

Does your company accept credit card payments from your customers? Although a discount fee is charged, the benefit can be getting paid more quickly when providing your customers this choice.

Intuit offers a Merchant Service that permits your customers to pay online by check or credit card. You can learn more by clicking the Add Credit Card Processing on the Main tab of the ribbon toolbar. If you would like to receive our discounted rates and receive our current credit card processing promotions, contact the author at info@quick-training.com

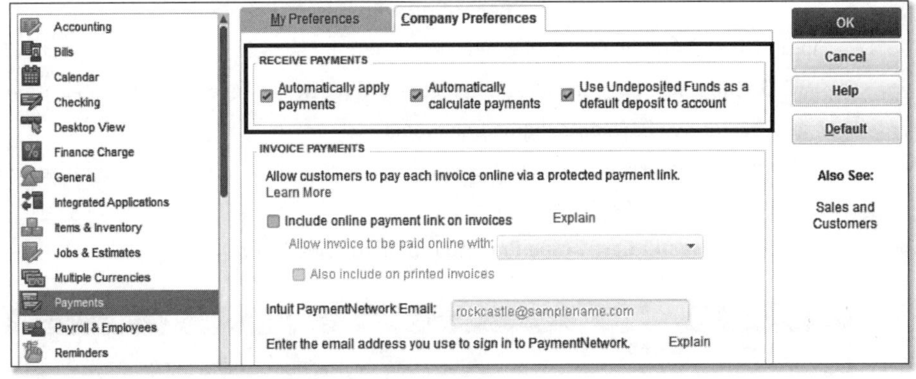

Figure 9.53 The Company Preferences for Receive Payments determines how QuickBooks records money received from customers.

New for QuickBooks 2013 is the ribbon toolbar that displays at the top of most QuickBooks transactions. Access these additional features from the following tabs on the Receive Payments transaction:

- **Main**—Access common payment actions from the following tabs:
  - **Find**—Click Find to open the Simple and Advanced find dialog. Or click the arrows to move forward and backward through previously recorded transactions.
  - **New**, **Delete**—Complete the selected task for the currently displayed transaction.
  - **Print**—Print a payment receipt.
  - **Attach File**—Free document storage (local on your server or computer hard drive) of scanned documents, emails, and so on.
  - **Look Up Customer/Invoice**—Use to find a customer or specific invoice.
  - **Un-Apply Payment**—Clears the payment details in the grid below.
  - **Discounts and Credits**—Opens the Discount and Credit dialog box. More details are provided in the next section.
  - **Add Credit Card Processing**—Select this to learn about Intuit Merchant Service for QuickBooks.
- **Reports**—Access commonly used reports, including a Processed Payment Receipt and an Open Invoices report.
- **Payments**—Links to adding credit card processing or accepting eCheck processing. Get paid faster!

This Receive Payments transaction reduces the balance your customer owes you and increases the balance in your Undeposited Funds account. In the next section, you learn how to add this and other monies received to complete the deposit transaction in QuickBooks.

tip

Often your customer will send in a payment but will not indicate on the payment what invoice he is paying for.

Click the Look Up Customer/Invoice icon on the Main tab of the ribbon toolbar for searching selected fields.

From the displayed results, select any of the matches and click the Use Selected Customer or Transaction.

Recording a Customer Payment

To practice recording a customer payment, open the sample data file as instructed in Chapter 1:

1. On the Home page (as shown in Figure 9.1), click the Receive Payments icon.
2. The Receive Payments dialog box displays.
3. From the Received From drop-down list, select **Melton Johnny:Dental office.**
4. In the Amount field, type **5,000.00.**
5. Select **Master Card** in the Pmt. Method field. See Figure 9.54.

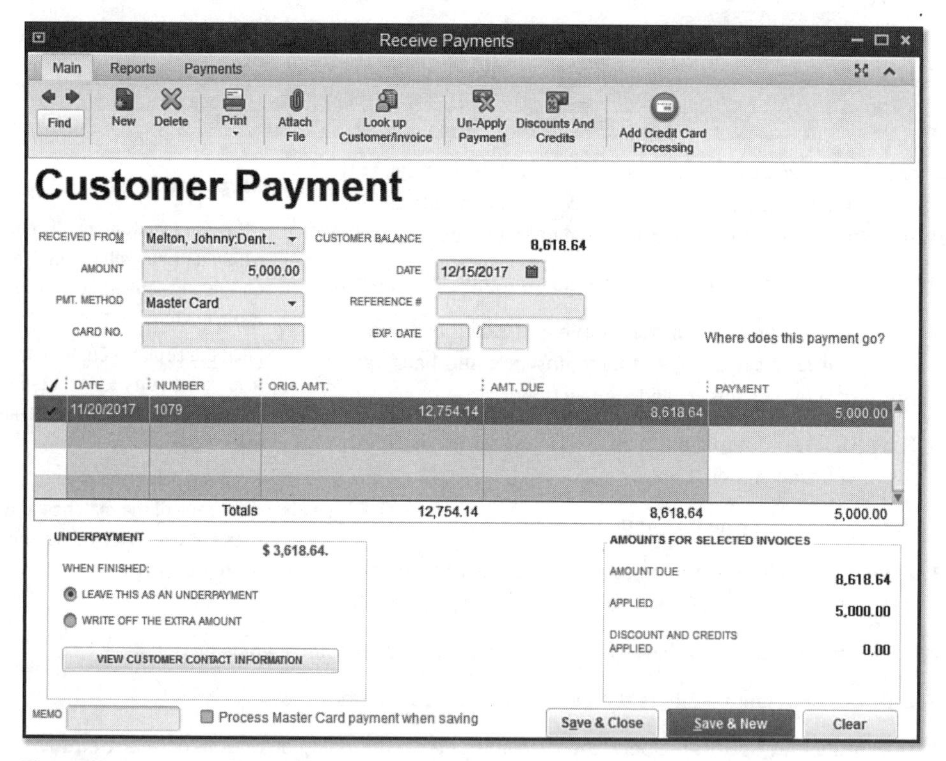

Figure 9.54
Record a Receive Payments transaction when a customer remits funds to you.

6. If you selected the preference to Automatically Apply Payments, QuickBooks first tries to match the payment with an invoice for the same amount. If a match is not found, it applies the payment to the oldest invoice.
7. For this practice, QuickBooks displays an underpayment message as well as a link to View Customer Contact Information. Accept the default choice of Leave This as an Underpayment.
8. Click Save & Close to complete this exercise or lick Save & New to practice adding more customer payments.

Making the Bank Deposit

When receiving payments from your customers, you will record the payments and then physically store the checks or cash received in a safe place until you can go to the bank.

Depending on the preferences you set, QuickBooks uses an account titled Undeposited Funds to hold payments received, but not yet included on a bank deposit ticket.

The Undeposited Funds account also plays an important role in making the bank reconciliation process easier and more accurate. If you list multiple customer payments on one deposit ticket taken to the bank, you need to match this deposit ticket total to the make deposit transaction recorded in QuickBooks. By setting the preference to have QuickBooks forward all your customer payments into a temporary Undeposited Funds account (see Figure 9.53), you can then "group" these individual payments in QuickBooks using the Make Deposits transaction. The deposits in your bank account register will now match the deposit amounts on your bank statement.

Check and Cash Payment Deposits

Creating a bank deposit for your cash and check payments correctly is one of the important tasks necessary to properly track the balance of funds you have in your bank account.

Recording a Bank Deposit

To practice making a deposit, open the sample data file as instructed in Chapter 1:

1. On the Home page, click the Record Deposits icon.
2. Using the sample data for practice, the Payments to Deposit dialog box displays a listing of payments received that have not yet been recorded as a deposit into the bank account. When you are working in your data, if this message does not display, you do not have any payments that were recorded to the Undeposited Funds account.
3. From the View Payment Method Type drop-down list, select **Cash and Check**. This step is optional, but it helps to group the payments by the type of deposit.
4. Click the Select All button to place a checkmark next to each of the amounts listed. See Figure 9.55. Your total might differ if you did not complete the exercise in the previous section.
5. Compare your deposit ticket total to the payments subtotal on the Payments to Deposit dialog box. See Figure 9.56.
6. When you click OK, QuickBooks adds the selected payments to the Make Deposits dialog box.
7. Confirm that the Deposit To account is correct, and select the Date your bank will credit your account with the funds. Entering details in the Memo field will display in reports.
8. From the Print drop-down list, select to print a deposit slip (preprinted forms are necessary) or print a deposit summary for your file. See Figure 9.57.
9. Click Save & Close to complete the task or click Save & New to record another bank deposit.

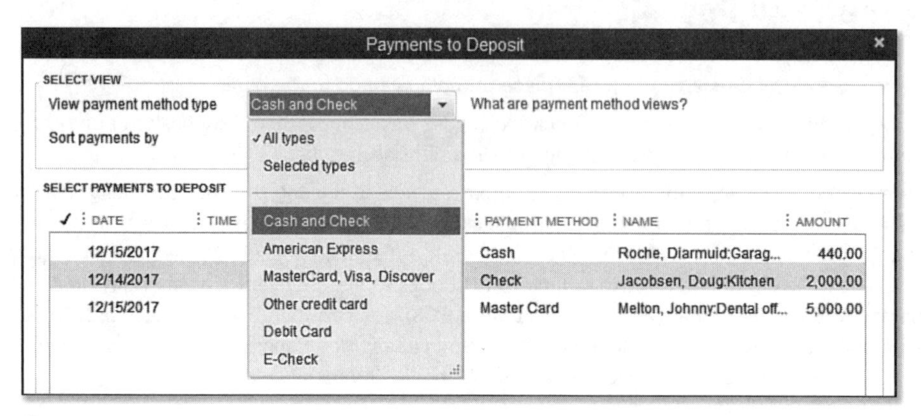

Figure 9.55
The Payments to Deposit can be filtered for specific payment types, helping you group the payments to agree with your bank's deposit records.

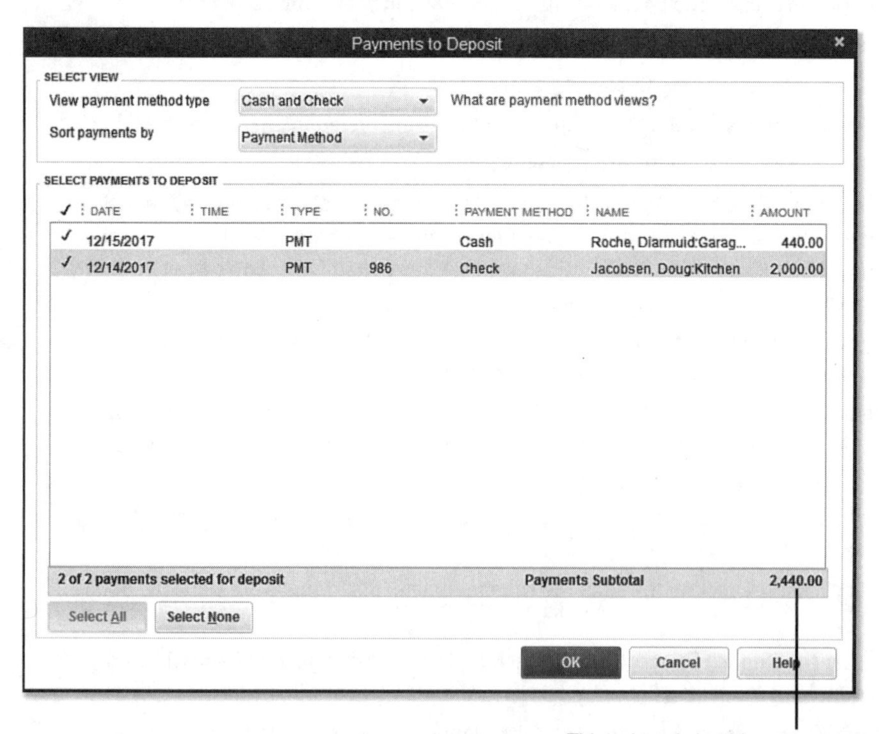

Figure 9.56
Place a checkmark next to each payment item that is included on your deposit ticket.

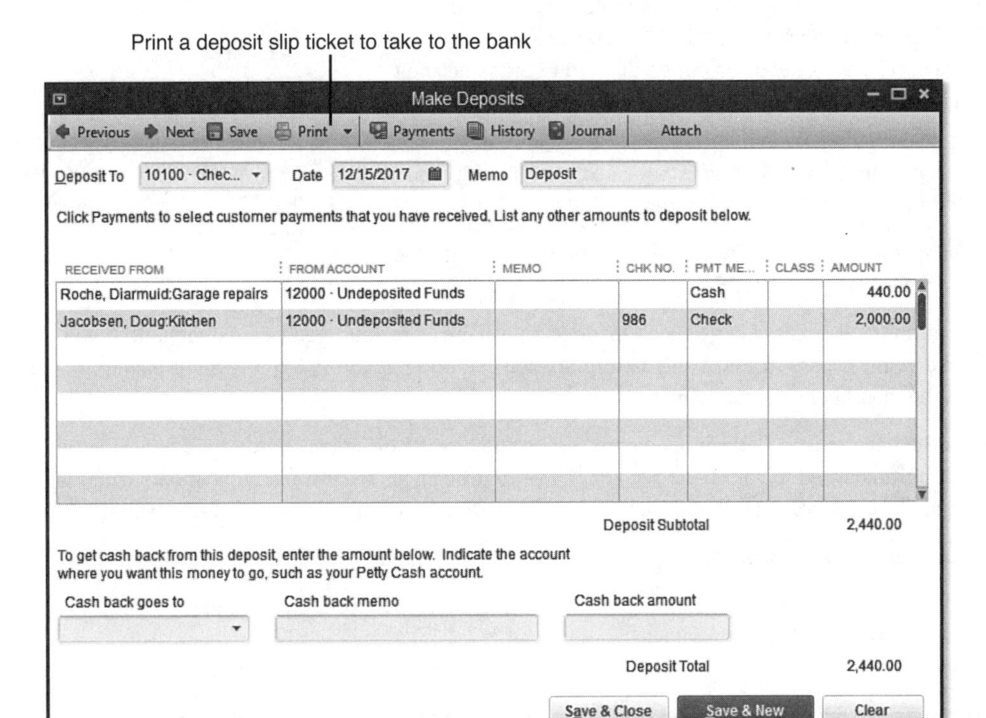

Figure 9.57
Using the Make Deposits dialog box is the final step in recording customer payments.

It's really that simple! Create an invoice, receive the customer's payment, and make the deposit into your bank account records. Next we look at another kind of deposit: when your customer pays you by credit card.

Recording Credit Card Deposits Less a Discount Fee

If you collect credit card payments from your customers, having a defined Receive Payments and Make Deposits process you can consistently follow is important. Because you don't physically hold the payment from your customer as you do with cash or check payments, tracking these credit card payments accurately and reconciling with the bank's monthly statement helps you avoid some common mistakes.

When your business accepts credit card payments from your customers, your merchant account vendor charges you, the seller, a discount fee. Your credit card processor might charge the fee at the time of the deposit, at the end of the billing cycle, or a combination of both.

If you are charged a fee at the end of the month, you can enter the fee into your checkbook register in QuickBooks or create a journal entry with a debit to your credit card expense account and a credit to your bank account.

What if your merchant vendor reduces the amount of your customer's payment credited to your bank account? To help you keep accurate records, follow these steps:

tip

I teach my clients to leave credit card deposits in the QuickBooks Undeposited Funds account until they know the exact amount and date that money was deposited to their bank.

1. Follow the instructions in the section titled "Recording the Customer Payment," p. 352.
2. Confirm the amount of the deposit made to your bank from your credit card merchant. If you have online access to your bank institution, you can find this information without having to wait for the monthly bank statement.
3. On the Payments to Deposit dialog box, select the credit card payments that were included in the batch transmitted to your bank account. Does your business receive many payments by credit card? It can be helpful to have a printout of the batch details from your merchant vendor.
4. Click OK and QuickBooks includes these credit card payments on a make deposits transaction.
5. On the next available line, in the From Account column, enter your credit card discount fees expense account. See Figure 9.58.

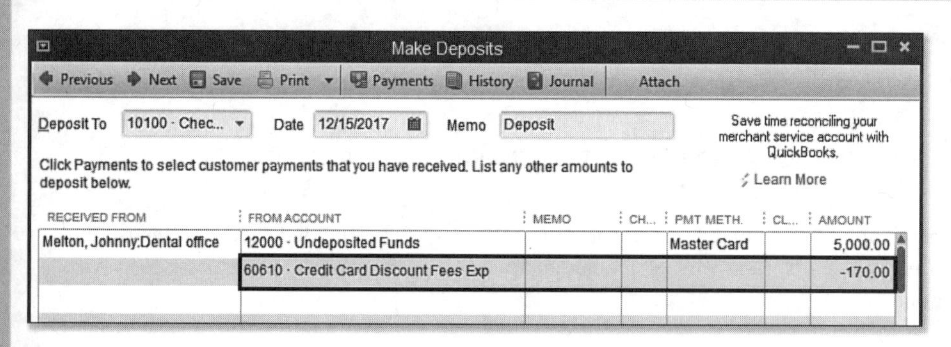

Figure 9.58 Record discount fees as part of your credit card deposit.

6. In the Amount column, enter a negative amount equal to the fee charged.
7. Confirm that the deposit total on the make deposits transaction agrees with the exact amount credited to your bank account by the merchant. Click Save & Close if you are done. Click Save & New to record another deposit.

Timely recording of credit card deposits and in agreement with your bank's deposit records will help your business better manage the monies received in your bank account.

Recording and Applying a Customer Credit Memo

Use the Create Credit Memos/Refund transaction when a customer returns a product or you want to record a credit toward a future purchase.

Creating a Customer Refund Check

To practice refunding an overpayment with a check, open the sample data file as instructed in Chapter 1:

1. On the Home page, click the Customers button to open the Customer Center.
2. For this exercise, scroll through the Customers & Jobs list and select the **Hendro Riyadi:Remodel Kitchen job**.
3. Double-click the invoice listed on the right.
4. From Main tab on the ribbon toolbar, select **Refund/Credit** (see Figure 9.59). QuickBooks duplicates the details from the original invoice to a new Create Credit Memos/Refunds transaction.

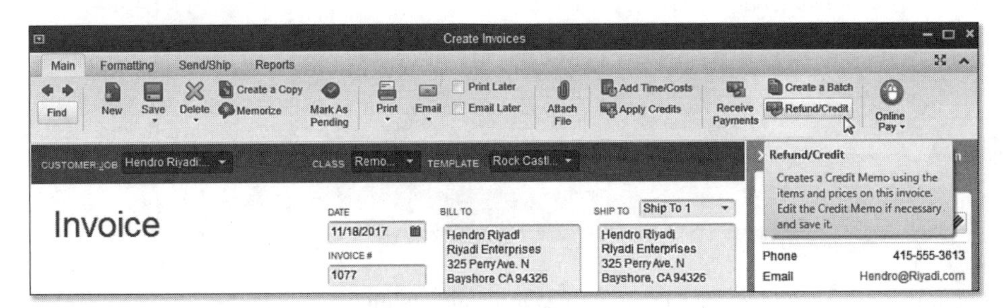

Figure 9.59
QuickBooks duplicates the invoice lines and creates a credit memo.

5. Review the lines included on the newly created credit memo. When working in your own data, remove individual lines as needed to agree with the products returned or services to be credited.
6. Click Save & Close. QuickBooks displays the Available Credit message.
7. Select the option to **Apply to an Invoice** as shown in Figure 9.60.
8. QuickBooks displays the Apply Credit to Invoices dialog box. From here, you can change which invoice or how much of the credit is applied. For this exercise, leave the transaction as shown in Figure 9.61.
9. Click Done.
10. QuickBooks returns to the Create Invoices dialog box. In this practice exercise, a paid stamp is displayed on the invoice. Click Save & Close to complete the activity or click Save & New to create another credit memo.

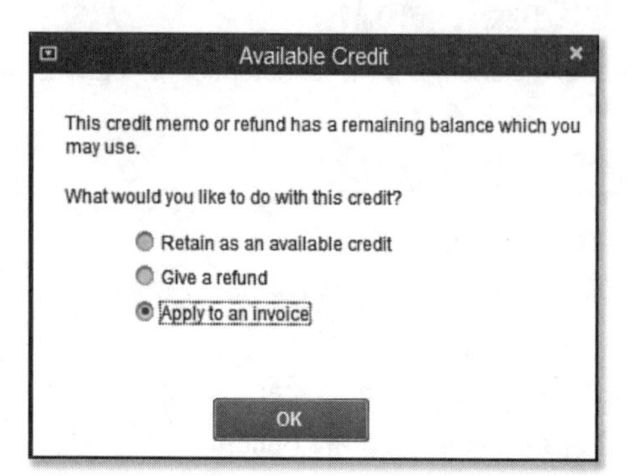

Figure 9.60
Choose how you will record the available credit in QuickBooks.

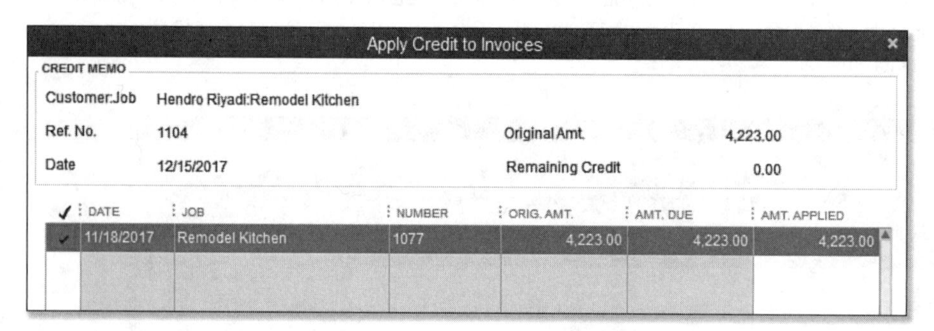

Figure 9.61
Make sure your records for applying the credit agree with your customer's.

tip

To efficiently remove lines on a newly created transaction, with your cursor select a row and press the Ctrl+Delete keys on your keyboard to remove an entire line one at a time.

Refunding a Customer's Overpayment

Has your company received an overpayment from a customer? Although it is rare during difficult economic times, knowing how to handle the transaction can help keep your financial records correct and your customer happy.

When you receive an overpayment, you can leave the overpayment in your books and apply it to future invoices, similar to the process for applying credit memos to open invoices.

However, your customer might request that you refund the overpayment.

Refunding a Customer's Overpayment

To practice refunding an overpayment with a check, open the sample data file as instructed in Chapter 1:

1. Record an overpayment in this sample file you are using. On the Home page, click the Receive Payments icon.
2. In the Received From drop-down list, select the **Robson, Darci:Robson Clinic job**.
3. The customer balance displays on the Receive Payments dialog box. In the Amount field, type **12,500.00**. Leave the other fields as they default.
4. QuickBooks displays a message in the lower left about the overpayment. Select **Refund the Amount to the Customer**.
5. (Optional) Click the View Customer Contact Information to edit the customer's address that will print on the check. Click OK to return to the Customer Payment transaction.
6. Click Save & Close.
7. QuickBooks opens the Issue a Refund dialog box as shown in Figure 9.62. In the Issue This Refund Via drop-down list, select **Check**.

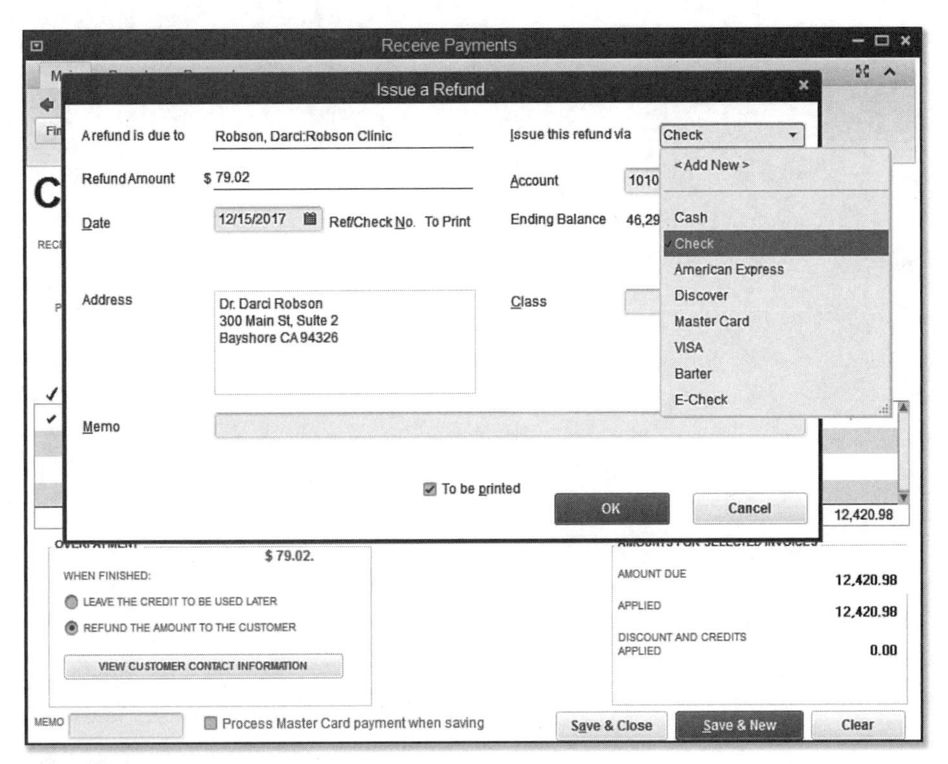

Figure 9.62
Be sure to specify a method when you issue a customer refund.

8. Leave selected the prefilled bank account as is.
9. (Optional) Enter a Class and Memo.
10. Check or remove the checkmark from the To Be Printed checkbox.
11. Click OK.
12. To print the check, from the menu bar select **File, Print Forms, Print Checks,** and enter the check number you are placing in your printer.
13. You can also modify the To Be Printed status of a transaction in the Number/Type field in the bank register by selecting **Banking, Use Register** from the menu bar.

If you did not apply the credit when you first created it, you can later process the credit as a refund or apply it to an open invoice by selecting the **Credit To** drop-down list from the Create Credit Memos/Refunds dialog box.

10

MANAGING CUSTOMERS

As a business owner, you are going to do your best to take care of those that keep you in business, your customers. Customers are one of the most valuable assets you have and necessary to stay in business.

This chapter is going to focus on managing the accounting that goes on behind-the-scenes in the back office for customer-related transactions. You will learn what reports to be reviewing, how to handle sales tax, and how to work with unique customer transactions to name just a few of the details covered in this chapter.

Accounts Receivable Reporting

You have learned how to use some of the most common customer-related transactions and carry out important customer-related activities in your QuickBooks data file.

QuickBooks provides a wide variety of reports for documenting sales, customer balances, and other useful management reporting. Details on working with QuickBooks reports are included in Chapter 14, "Reporting in QuickBooks," including accessing a variety of customer-related reports from the following menus:

- From the menu bar select **Reports**, **Report Center**; select the **Customers & Receivables** or **Sales** reports from the Standard tab.
- From the menu bar select **Company**, **Company Snapshot**; select the **Payments** or **Customer** tab.

The next several sections in this chapter will help you review and troubleshoot your own data for accuracy. Following are some of the more common reports used to identify whether your Accounts Receivable information is correct.

Reviewing A/R Aging Summary and Detail Reports

Preparing your customer invoices and recording payments from customers is important to the accuracy of your financials. Several reports summarize the status of unpaid or unapplied customer transactions included in your Accounts Receivable balance on the Balance Sheet report. You can prepare these reports with your own data, or review the report details using the sample data discussed in Chapter 1, "Getting Started with QuickBooks."

From the menu bar, select **Reports**, **Customers & Receivables**, and then select one of the following from the submenu:

- **A/R Aging Summary**—Report groups open customer transactions by job into a series of aged date ranges (see Figure 10.1). Use this report for a quick view of those customers who have older unpaid balances.

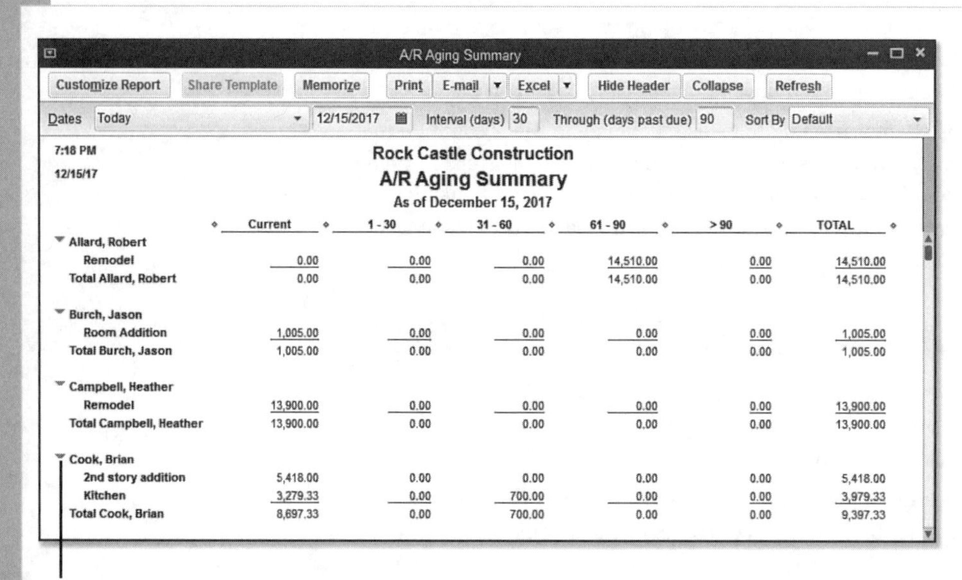

Rock Castle Construction
A/R Aging Summary
As of December 15, 2017

	Current	1 - 30	31 - 60	61 - 90	> 90	TOTAL
Allard, Robert						
Remodel	0.00	0.00	0.00	14,510.00	0.00	14,510.00
Total Allard, Robert	0.00	0.00	0.00	14,510.00	0.00	14,510.00
Burch, Jason						
Room Addition	1,005.00	0.00	0.00	0.00	0.00	1,005.00
Total Burch, Jason	1,005.00	0.00	0.00	0.00	0.00	1,005.00
Campbell, Heather						
Remodel	13,900.00	0.00	0.00	0.00	0.00	13,900.00
Total Campbell, Heather	13,900.00	0.00	0.00	0.00	0.00	13,900.00
Cook, Brian						
2nd story addition	5,418.00	0.00	0.00	0.00	0.00	5,418.00
Kitchen	3,279.33	0.00	700.00	0.00	0.00	3,979.33
Total Cook, Brian	8,697.33	0.00	700.00	0.00	0.00	9,397.33

Figure 10.1 Use the A/R Aging Summary report to identify which customers have overdue balances.

- **A/R Aging Detail**—The report shown in Figure 10.2 provides detail for all open customer transactions, grouped by aging status.

Use these reports to identify those customers who are in need of collection efforts, and use the tools discussed in the section "Using the Collections Center" in this chapter.

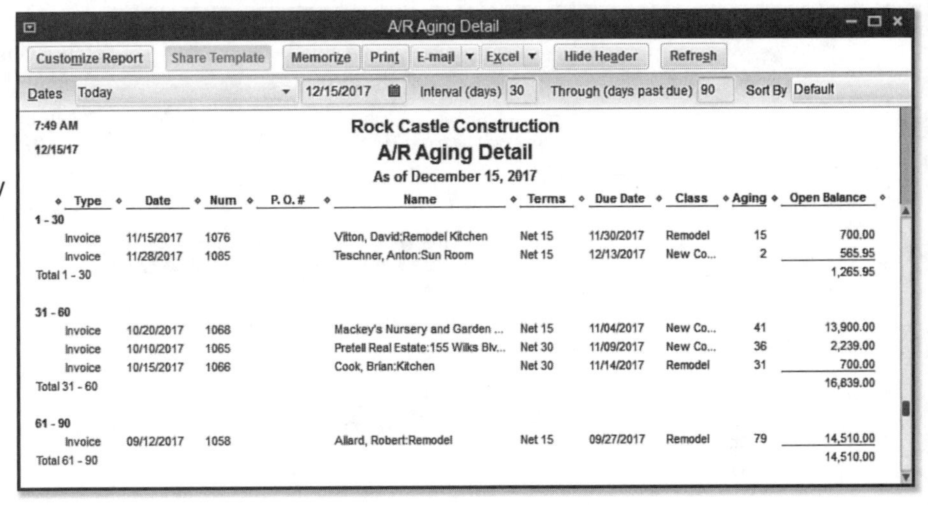

A/R Aging Detail

Customize Report | Share Template | Memorize | Print | E-mail | Excel | Hide Header | Refresh

Dates Today 12/15/2017 Interval (days) 30 Through (days past due) 90 Sort By Default

7:49 AM
12/15/17

Rock Castle Construction
A/R Aging Detail
As of December 15, 2017

Type	Date	Num	P. O. #	Name	Terms	Due Date	Class	Aging	Open Balance
1 - 30									
Invoice	11/15/2017	1076		Vitton, David:Remodel Kitchen	Net 15	11/30/2017	Remodel	15	700.00
Invoice	11/28/2017	1085		Teschner, Anton:Sun Room	Net 15	12/13/2017	New Co...	2	565.95
Total 1 - 30									1,265.95
31 - 60									
Invoice	10/20/2017	1068		Mackey's Nursery and Garden ...	Net 15	11/04/2017	New Co...	41	13,900.00
Invoice	10/10/2017	1065		Pretell Real Estate:155 Wilks Blv...	Net 30	11/09/2017	New Co...	36	2,239.00
Invoice	10/15/2017	1066		Cook, Brian:Kitchen	Net 30	11/14/2017	Remodel	31	700.00
Total 31 - 60									16,839.00
61 - 90									
Invoice	09/12/2017	1058		Allard, Robert:Remodel	Net 15	09/27/2017	Remodel	79	14,510.00
Total 61 - 90									14,510.00

Figure 10.2
The A/R Aging Detail report groups aged customer transactions by aging status.

Reviewing the Open Invoices Report

Different from the A/R Aging Summary report, the Open Invoices report is particularly useful because it shows individual lines for each open (unapplied) transaction grouped by customer and job. This report is a perpetual report, meaning it will show open invoices as of today's date and not some fixed time in the past unless you modify the reports as detailed here.

To modify an Open Invoices report so you can compare it to your Balance Sheet report for some specific date in the past, follow these steps:

1. From the menu bar select, **Reports**, **Customers & Receivables**, **Open Invoices**. By default, this report includes all payments made by your customer as of today's computer system date.
2. If you are creating this report for some date in the past, click the Customize Report button and then click the Advanced button on the Display tab of the Modify Report dialog box.
3. In the Open Balance/Aging box of the Advanced Options dialog box, select the **Report Date** option (see Figure 10.3). This modification to the report enables you to see each invoice balance detail as of the prior report date. If you do not modify this report, QuickBooks displays the prior date on the report, but also reduces the balances owed for payments made after the report date.
4. On the Open Invoices report (see Figure 10.4), view details of all open balances and any unapplied credits grouped by customer and job.

note

Changing the date on the Open Invoices report does not change the detail displayed. This Open Invoices report is perpetual. If you need to document your balances for a date in the past, use the Accounts Receivable Aging reports.

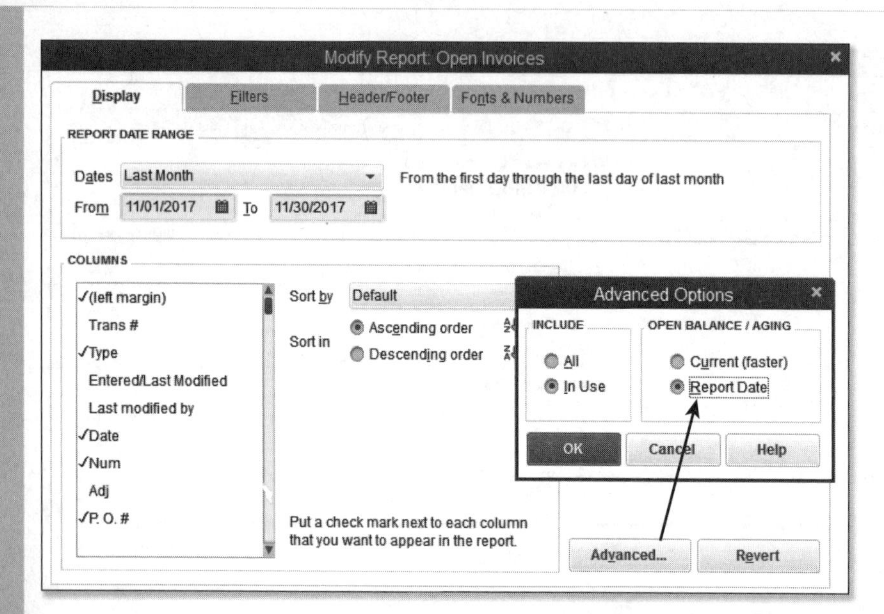

Figure 10.3
The Open Invoices report, when modified, can be compared to the totals on your Balance Sheet report for a previous date.

Open Invoices

Customize Report | Share Template | Memorize | Print | E-mail | Excel | Hide Header | Refresh

Dates Today 12/15/2017 Sort By Default

7:54 AM
12/15/17

Rock Castle Construction
Open Invoices
As of December 15, 2017

Type	Date	Num	P. O. #	Terms	Due Date	Class	Aging	Open Balance
Allard, Robert								
Remodel								
Invoice	09/12/2017	1058		Net 15	09/27/2017	Remodel	79	14,510.00
Credit Memo	12/15/2017	1100			12/15/2017	Remodel		-500.00
Total Remodel								14,010.00
Total Allard, Robert								14,010.00
Burch, Jason								
Room Addition								
Invoice	11/25/2017	1083		Net 30	12/25/2017	New Construct...		1,005.00
Total Room Addition								1,005.00
Total Burch, Jason								1,005.00
Campbell, Heather								
Remodel								
Invoice	12/10/2017	1092		Net 15	12/25/2017	Remodel		13,900.00
Total Remodel								13,900.00

Figure 10.4
Unlike the Aging Summary report, the Open Invoices report subtotals open or unapplied transactions by customer or job rather than by aging date.

Reconciling Balance Sheet Accounts Receivable Amount to A/R Aging Summary Total

With QuickBooks, you don't have to worry that the Balance Sheet report and Accounts Receivable Aging Summary report match, because any transaction posting to the Accounts Receivable account must have a customer assigned. You want to make sure you always create your Balance Sheet with the accrual basis because the A/R Aging Summary report can be prepared only on accrual basis:

tip

To compare your Balance Sheet report with the A/R Aging Summary report, you must create your Balance Sheet in accrual basis. If your reporting preference default is for cash basis, you can still run any report using accrual basis. Just click the Customize Report button at the top of the report and select **Accrual** as the reporting basis.

To prepare the reports needed for this comparison, follow these steps:

1. From the menu bar, select **Reports**, **Company & Financial**, **Balance Sheet Standard**. The selected report is displayed. For the date, select the As of Date you want to compare to.
2. In the Balance Sheet report that displays, note the balance in the Accounts Receivable account (see Figure 10.5).

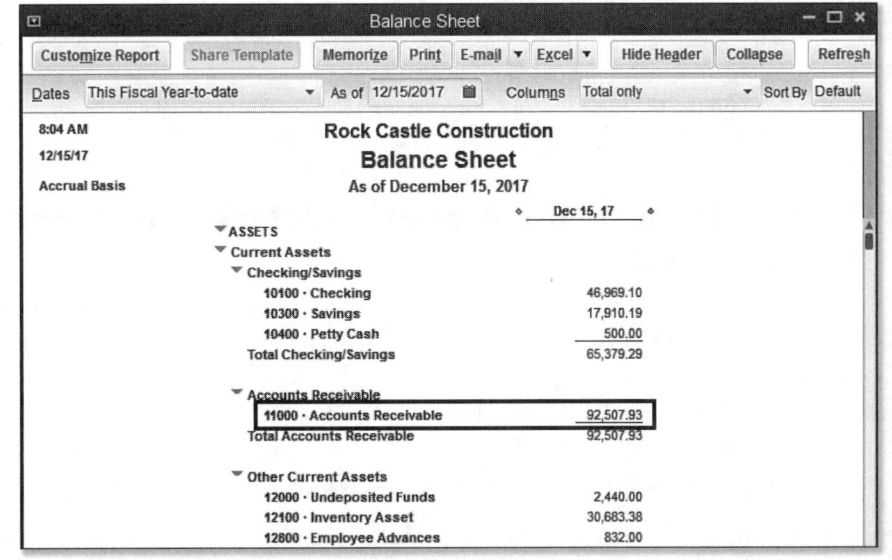

Figure 10.5 Use your Balance Sheet report (accrual basis) to reconcile your Accounts Receivable report.

3. From the menu bar select, **Reports**, **Customers & Receivables**, **A/R Aging Summary**, making sure the field shows the same date as the date selected in step 1. The image shown in Figure 10.6 has been "collapsed" to make viewing the information easier. To expand to see more detail, click the Expand button at the top of the report.

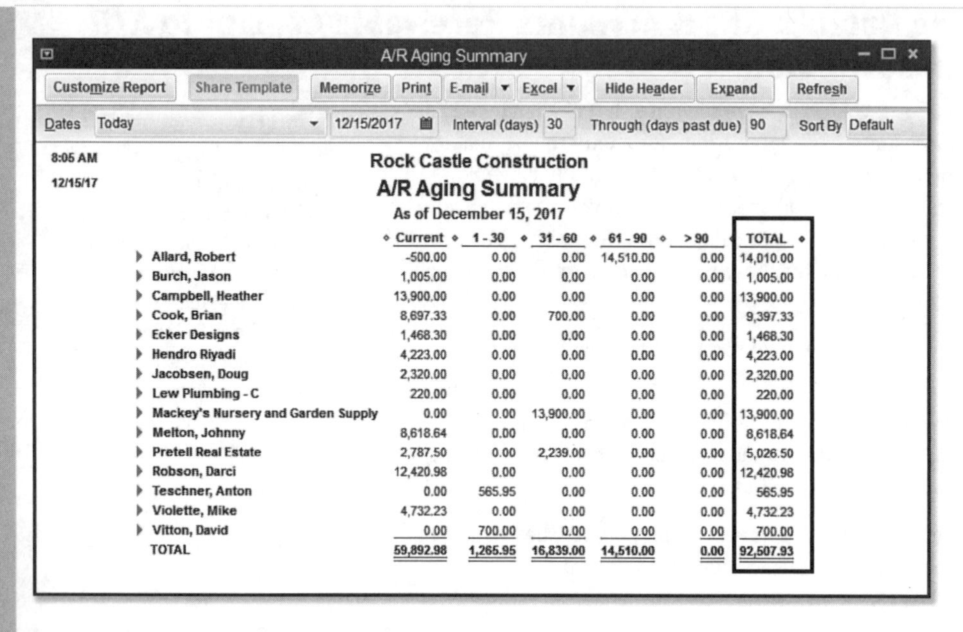

A/R Aging Summary

Customize Report | Share Template | Memorize | Print | E-mail | Excel | Hide Header | Expand | Refresh

Dates: Today | 12/15/2017 | Interval (days): 30 | Through (days past due): 90 | Sort By: Default

8:05 AM

12/15/17

Rock Castle Construction

A/R Aging Summary

As of December 15, 2017

	Current	1 - 30	31 - 60	61 - 90	> 90	TOTAL
Allard, Robert	-500.00	0.00	0.00	14,510.00	0.00	14,010.00
Burch, Jason	1,005.00	0.00	0.00	0.00	0.00	1,005.00
Campbell, Heather	13,900.00	0.00	0.00	0.00	0.00	13,900.00
Cook, Brian	8,697.33	0.00	700.00	0.00	0.00	9,397.33
Ecker Designs	1,468.30	0.00	0.00	0.00	0.00	1,468.30
Hendro Riyadi	4,223.00	0.00	0.00	0.00	0.00	4,223.00
Jacobsen, Doug	2,320.00	0.00	0.00	0.00	0.00	2,320.00
Lew Plumbing - C	220.00	0.00	0.00	0.00	0.00	220.00
Mackey's Nursery and Garden Supply	0.00	0.00	13,900.00	0.00	0.00	13,900.00
Melton, Johnny	8,618.64	0.00	0.00	0.00	0.00	8,618.64
Pretell Real Estate	2,787.50	0.00	2,239.00	0.00	0.00	5,026.50
Robson, Darci	12,420.98	0.00	0.00	0.00	0.00	12,420.98
Teschner, Anton	0.00	565.95	0.00	0.00	0.00	565.95
Violette, Mike	4,732.23	0.00	0.00	0.00	0.00	4,732.23
Vitton, David	0.00	700.00	0.00	0.00	0.00	700.00
TOTAL	59,892.98	1,265.95	16,839.00	14,510.00	0.00	92,507.93

Figure 10.6 A/R Aging Summary report collapsed for reviewing report totals.

The balance from the Balance Sheet report should match the total on the A/R Aging Summary. If it does not, the cause might be a "broken" transaction link. You can detect these types of issues by selecting **File**, **Utilities**, **Verify Data** from the menu bar; additional details are provided in Chapter 17, "Managing Your QuickBooks Database."

Viewing the Accounts Receivable Balance on a Cash Basis Balance Sheet

The nature of cash basis reporting implies you would not see an Accounts Receivable balance on your Balance Sheet. In short, cash basis accounting doesn't recognize revenue until you deposit the funds.

What should you do if you see an Accounts Receivable balance on a cash basis Balance Sheet? Any of the following can be the cause:

- A/R transactions have items posting to other Balance Sheet accounts.
- Inventory items on an invoice or credit memo (inventory management should be reported in accrual basis reporting).
- Transfers between Balance Sheet accounts.
- Unapplied Accounts Receivable customer payments.
- Customer payments applied to future-dated Accounts Receivable invoices.

- Preferences that contradict each other. (This situation can happen if you select Cash Basis on your Summary Reports, but Accrual Basis as your Sales Tax preference.)
- Data corruption (select **File**, **Utilities**, **Verify Data** from the menu bar to check for data corruption).

Preparing reports on Accounts Receivable balances is easy with the QuickBooks software. However, if you review a cash basis Balance Sheet, you might have an Accounts Receivable balance. Use the next section to learn more about discovering what makes this happen.

Accounts Receivable Balances on Cash Basis Balance Sheet

To determine why an Accounts Receivable balance displays on a cash basis Balance Sheet, follow these steps:

1. From the menu bar select **Reports, Company & Financial, Balance Sheet Standard,** as displayed in Figure 10.7.

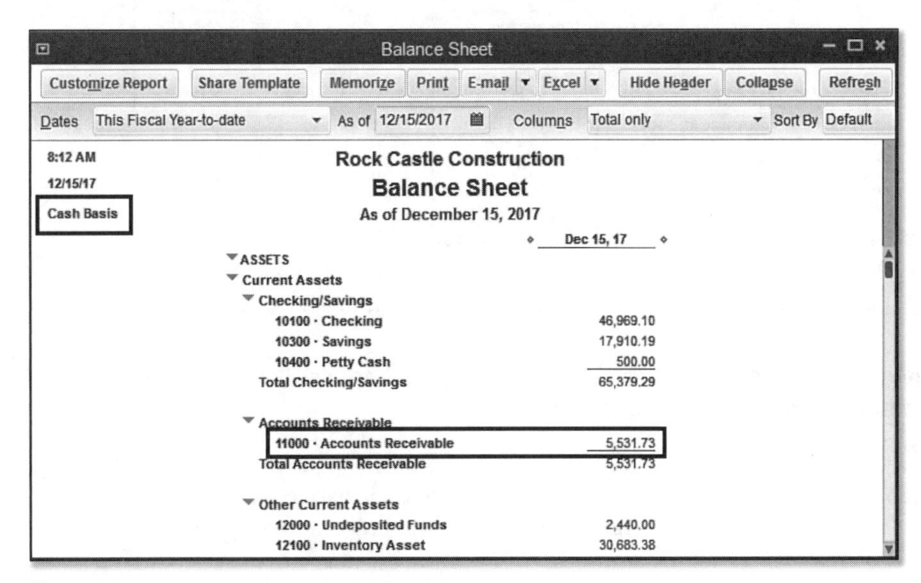

Figure 10.7
The cash basis Balance Sheet shows an Accounts Receivable balance.

2. Click the Customize Report button.
3. The Modify Report dialog box opens with the Display tab selected. Select **Cash** for the report basis.
4. Click OK.
5. Double-click the Accounts Receivable amount in question. The Transaction by Account report is created.
6. Click the Customize Report button. The Modify Report dialog box opens with the Display tab selected.

7. For the Report Date Range, remove the From date and leave the To date.
8. Click the Advanced button, and from the Open Balance/Aging box, select **Report Date.**
9. Click the Filters tab.
10. In the Choose Filters box, scroll down to select **Paid Status** and select the **Open** option.
11. Click OK.

Look for transactions that fall into any of the categories described previously. Figure 10.8 shows transactions that affected other Balance Sheet accounts. Any item used on a customer invoice that is mapped to another Balance Sheet account (including inventory) will display on a cash basis Balance Sheet report.

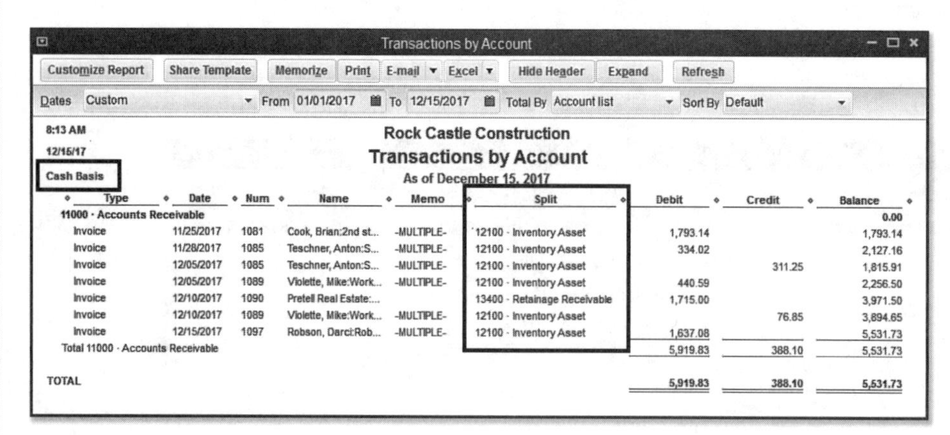

Rock Castle Construction
Transactions by Account
As of December 15, 2017

Type	Date	Num	Name	Memo	Split	Debit	Credit	Balance
11000 · Accounts Receivable								0.00
Invoice	11/25/2017	1081	Cook, Brian:2nd st...	-MULTIPLE-	12100 · Inventory Asset	1,793.14		1,793.14
Invoice	11/28/2017	1085	Teschner, Anton:S...	-MULTIPLE-	12100 · Inventory Asset	334.02		2,127.16
Invoice	12/05/2017	1085	Teschner, Anton:S...	-MULTIPLE-	12100 · Inventory Asset		311.25	1,815.91
Invoice	12/05/2017	1089	Violette, Mike:Work...	-MULTIPLE-	12100 · Inventory Asset	440.59		2,256.50
Invoice	12/10/2017	1090	Pretell Real Estate:...		13400 · Retainage Receivable	1,715.00		3,971.50
Invoice	12/10/2017	1089	Violette, Mike:Work...	-MULTIPLE-	12100 · Inventory Asset		76.85	3,894.65
Invoice	12/15/2017	1097	Robson, Darci:Rob...	-MULTIPLE-	12100 · Inventory Asset	1,637.08		5,531.73
Total 11000 · Accounts Receivable						5,919.83	388.10	5,531.73
TOTAL						5,919.83	388.10	5,531.73

Figure 10.8
This modified report identifies the individual transactions that are included in the Accounts Receivable amount showing on a cash basis Balance Sheet.

Now that you have been reviewing your customers' open and aged balances, you will appreciate the tools available in your QuickBooks software to help you with critical collection tasks.

Using the Collections Center

If your business sends invoices to customers for payment, you have offered the customer terms of payment. Those terms might be Net 30 or Net 60 and might include discounts if early payment is received.

Using the A/R Aging Summary, Detail or Open Invoices reports will help you to identify customers who are late in paying. Other useful reports included in the Reports, Customers & Receivables menu that assist with collections analysis are the following:

- Customer Balance Summary
- Customer Balance Detail

- Collections Report
- Average Days to Pay Summary
- Average Days to Pay

The QuickBooks Collections Center as shown in Figure 10.9 provides a place for you to record notes about your collection efforts and prepare reminder notices for clients with overdue and almost due balances.

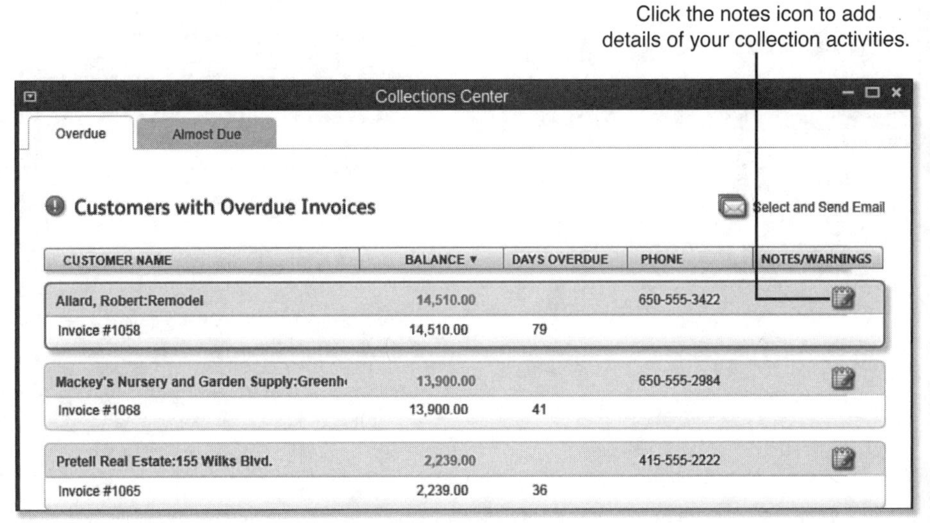

Figure 10.9 Managing collection activities is more efficient with the Collections Center.

1. On the Home page, click the Customers button.
2. The Customer Center opens with the Customers & Jobs tab selected. From the top of the Customer Center, click the Collections Center icon.
3. The Collections Center opens with the Overdue tab selected. Click any column header to sort by that column.
4. Click the Notes/Warnings icon next to any open item; QuickBooks populates the date and time, and you can add your collection notes. Click Save. These notes become part of the customer or job notes record and can be viewed from the Customer Center. After the note is saved, hover your mouse over the Notes/Warnings icon, and QuickBooks displays the contents without opening the note.
5. Click the Select and Send Email link as displayed in Figure 10.9.
6. Place a checkmark next to each overdue invoice you want to send a collection notice for. Select all or deselect all using the checkmark in front of the Customer Name column header.

7. To the right, modify the boilerplate text that will be included in the email communication. Add the From, Cc:, and Bcc: email addresses. You can set your default text for these communications on the Send Forms—Company Preferences tab of the Preferences dialog box, as shown in Figure 10.10.

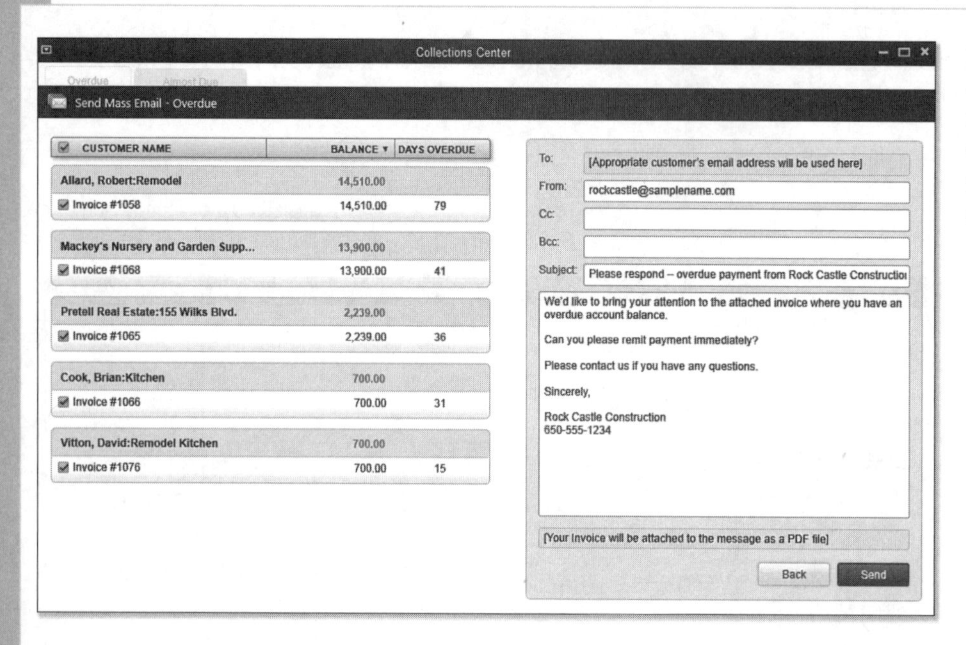

Figure 10.10 Manage email communications in batch for past-due customers.

8. QuickBooks uses the email provider you designated on the Send Forms—My Preferences tab of the Preferences dialog box.

9. Repeat steps 4–7 for customers with open invoices listed on the Almost Due tab.

10. Click the X in the top right to close the Collections Center.

The notes assigned to the overdue invoice can also track the day and time an email was sent.

Even with your best efforts, sometimes you are not able to collect the money that is owed to you. For these instances, you will want to accurately write off the balance to your Bad Debt expense account. Review the "Removing an Open Balance from a Customer Invoice" section for details.

Generating the Missing Customer Invoices Report

Most companies establish some control over the process of creating customer invoices. One control, if invoices are created manually in the field and later entered into QuickBooks, is to maintain a numeric invoicing pattern. Usually each invoice is one number larger than the prior invoice. This method of invoice record keeping can be an important process to have if your company is ever audited and you are required to provide a list of all invoices.

To see whether your data has any missing numbers in the invoicing sequence, follow these steps:

1. From the menu bar select, **Reports**, **Banking**, **Missing Checks**.
2. In the Missing Checks dialog box, in the Specify Account drop-down list, select **Accounts Receivable** and click OK to generate the report (see Figure 10.11).
3. Rename the report by choosing Customize Report, clicking the Header/Footer tab, and typing a new title for the Report Title field, such as Invoice List.
4. Click OK to display the newly renamed report.

This customized report makes the process of identifying missing or duplicated invoice numbers easy (see Figure 10.12). Use this information to determine whether you need better company practices to avoid this situation.

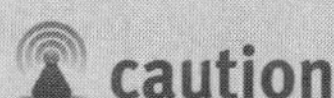

caution

The customized Missing Invoices report filter omits credit memos. With the customized report displayed, you can add credit memos to the transactions reported. Click the Customize Report button and select the **Filters** tab. In the Choose Filter box, select **Transaction Type.** From the Transaction Type drop-down list, select **Multiple Transaction Types** including invoice, credit memo, and others you want included.

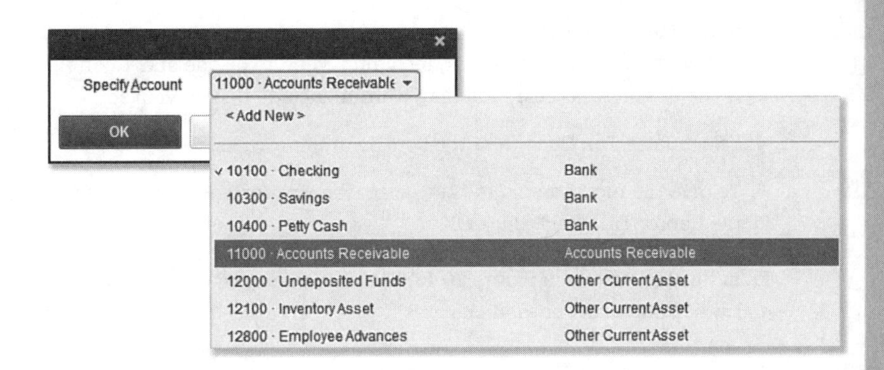

Figure 10.11
Create a report that lists all your customer invoices by invoice number.

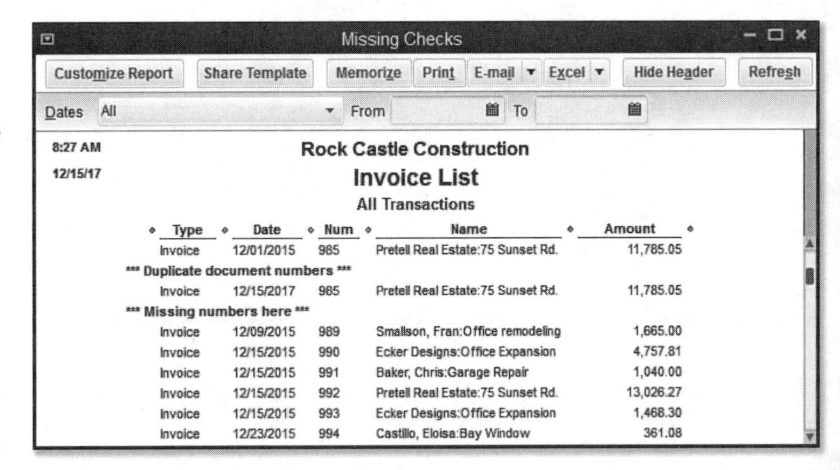

Figure 10.12
This modified report shows a list of all missing or duplicated invoice numbers.

Sales Tax Payable Reports

When your company is required to collect sales tax from your customers you become and agent for the state. As an agent you have an obligation to maintain proper records of your sales and taxes collected. This section provides you with easy-to-follow instructions on properly reporting on sales tax and correcting common sales tax data entry errors.

I recommend that you review these reports each time you prepare to pay your sales and use tax to the taxing authority. Properly "reconciling" these reports to each other helps minimize any chance that your QuickBooks data will not support what you filed on your sales tax return.

Reviewing Customer Lists for Tax Code and Tax Item Assigned

Check your customers' taxable status often. This task is quite easy to do and helps prevent the costly mistakes caused by not charging sales tax or charging the incorrect rate.

1. From the menu bar select **Reports**, **List**, **Customer Phone List**.
2. Click the Customize Report button on the top left of the report.
3. In the Modify Report dialog box that opens, place a checkmark in the Columns box next to items you want to review for the list, including Sales Tax Code and Tax Item. Not shown in the image is the Resale Num field; you may want to include this on your report.
4. Select **Sales Tax Code** from the Sort By drop-down list.
5. To give the report a unique title, select the **Header/Footer** tab and type a name for the report in the Report Title field. Click OK.

From this list, shown in Figure 10.13, double-click any line item detail to open the Edit Customer dialog box and make needed changes.

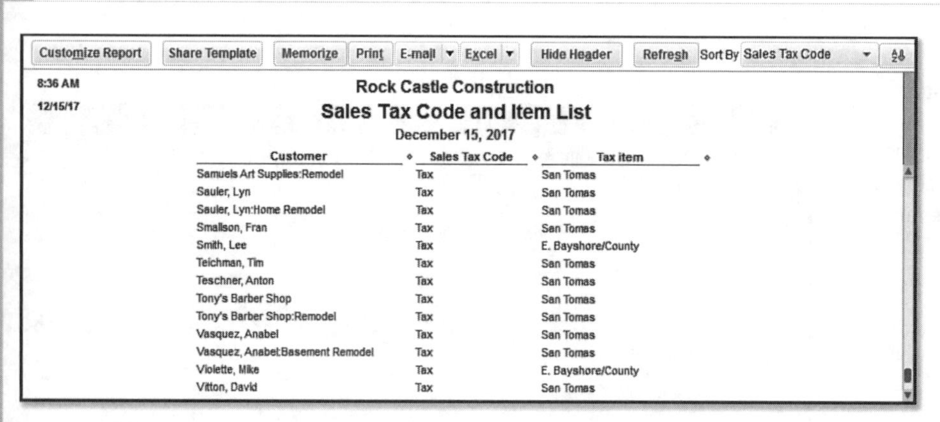

8:36 AM
12/15/17

Rock Castle Construction
Sales Tax Code and Item List
December 15, 2017

Customer	Sales Tax Code	Tax item
Samuels Art Supplies:Remodel	Tax	San Tomas
Sauler, Lyn	Tax	San Tomas
Sauler, Lyn:Home Remodel	Tax	San Tomas
Smallson, Fran	Tax	San Tomas
Smith, Lee	Tax	E. Bayshore/County
Teichman, Tim	Tax	San Tomas
Teschner, Anton	Tax	San Tomas
Tony's Barber Shop	Tax	San Tomas
Tony's Barber Shop:Remodel	Tax	San Tomas
Vasquez, Anabel	Tax	San Tomas
Vasquez, Anabel:Basement Remodel	Tax	San Tomas
Violette, Mike	Tax	E. Bayshore/County
Vitton, David	Tax	San Tomas

Figure 10.13 Prepare this report often to review the accuracy of the sales tax codes and items assigned to your customers.

Reviewing the Item List for Tax Code Assigned

Another review that I recommend you do periodically is to look at the list of services and products you sell and determine whether the proper tax code has been assigned (see Figure 10.14).

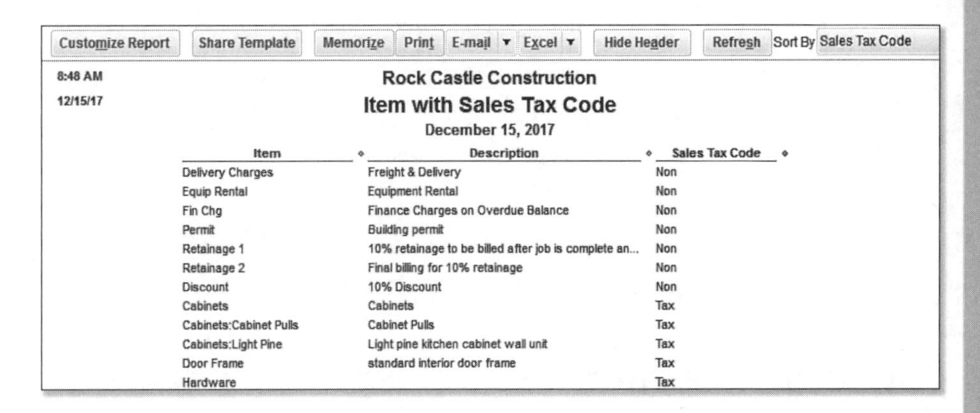

Customize Report | Share Template | Memorize | Print | E-mail | Excel | Hide Header | Refresh | Sort By Sales Tax Code

8:48 AM
12/15/17

Rock Castle Construction
Item with Sales Tax Code
December 15, 2017

Item	Description	Sales Tax Code
Delivery Charges	Freight & Delivery	Non
Equip Rental	Equipment Rental	Non
Fin Chg	Finance Charges on Overdue Balance	Non
Permit	Building permit	Non
Retainage 1	10% retainage to be billed after job is complete an...	Non
Retainage 2	Final billing for 10% retainage	Non
Discount	10% Discount	Non
Cabinets	Cabinets	Tax
Cabinets:Cabinet Pulls	Cabinet Pulls	Tax
Cabinets:Light Pine	Light pine kitchen cabinet wall unit	Tax
Door Frame	standard interior door frame	Tax
Hardware		Tax

Figure 10.14 Prepare a report of the sales tax codes assigned to your items.

Follow these steps to customize the Item Price List report:

1. From the menu bar select **Reports**, **List**, **Item Price List**.
2. Click the Customize Report button at the top left of the report.
3. In the Columns box of the Modify Report dialog box, remove checkmarks from those data fields you do not want displayed on this report. Place a checkmark next to date fields you want to review for the list, including Sales Tax Code.
4. In the Sort By drop-down list, select **Sales Tax Code**.
5. If desired, click the Header/Footer tab to change the report title. Click OK.

caution

When you make a change to a customer's assigned tax code or tax item or to the tax code assigned to a product or service you sell on your item list, QuickBooks will *not* correct or modify prior saved transactions. Only new transactions will show the change in the sales tax status or rate.

Reconciling Total Sales to Total Income

The term *reconciling* (also known as proofing) refers to the act of comparing two related numbers from two different reports. The importance of this task cannot be overstated. If your company is selected to have a sales tax audit, one of the first numbers the auditor will want to determine is the total sales you reported on your tax returns for the time period being audited.

For more information, see "Setting Up Sales Tax," p. 314.

When comparing these two reports, it is imperative that you know the reporting basis you have selected for your sales tax. To compare your total sales on the Sales Tax Liability report to your total income on the Profit & Loss report using the same basis as your sales tax preference, follow these steps:

1. From the menu bar select **Reports, Vendors & Payables, Sales Tax Liability**. This report will not be listed if you have not yet enabled your Sales Tax preference as discussed in the "Sales Tax Setup" section of Chapter 9, "Setting Up Customers."
2. Make a note of the date range and total sales on this report.
3. From the menu bar select **Reports, Company & Financial, Profit & Loss Standard**.
4. Select the same date range used for your Sales Tax Liability report in step 1.
5. Verify that the same reporting basis is used on this report as was used on the Sales Tax Liability report. If necessary, click Customize Report and then choose Cash or Accrual from the Report Basis section of the Display tab.
6. Compare total income (see Figure 10.15) to the total sales from the Sales Tax Liability report. Note: You might have to deduct any nonsales income on your Profit & Loss Total Income amounts. Also, make sure you prepare the reports using the same reporting basis.

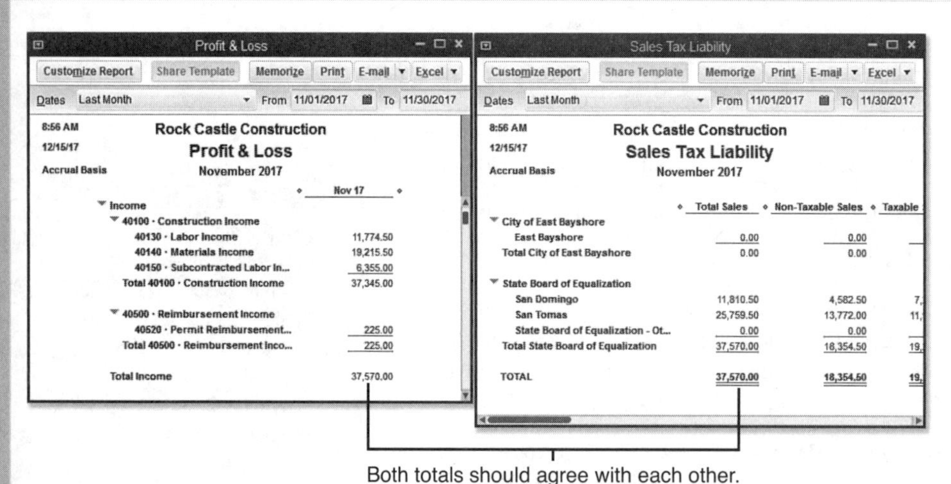

Figure 10.15 Compare the total income on the Profit & Loss report to the total sales on the Sales Tax Liability report.

If your totals on these two reports do not match, review the instructions included in the "Correcting Sales Tax Errors" section of this chapter.

Reconciling Sales Tax Liability to Balance Sheet Sales Tax Payable

Another important comparison to make is between the amount reported for Sales Tax Payable on the Balance Sheet report and the Sales Tax Payable total on the Sales Tax Liability report. Carefully check that you are using the same cash or accrual basis for each report when completing this review.

If you created your own Sales Tax Payable account, you might not be able to accurately compare the two reports. QuickBooks creates a Sales Tax Payable account automatically.

To compare the Balance Sheet Sales Tax Payable account balance with the Sales Tax Payable total on the Sales Tax Liability report, follow these steps:

1. From the menu bar select **Reports**, **Company & Financial**, **Balance Sheet Standard** (see Figure 10.16).

Figure 10.16 Balance Sheet Sales Tax Payable amount should agree with your Sales Tax Liability report.

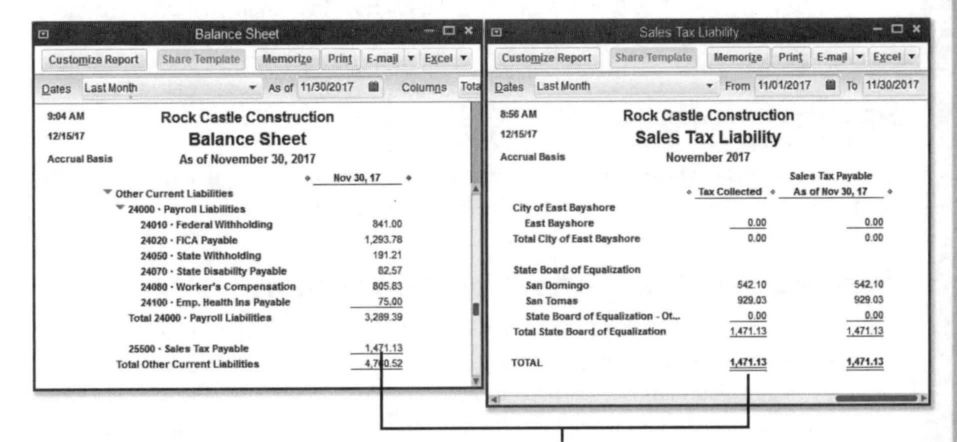

2. On the report, select the **As of Date** you are comparing to (this date must be the same ending date you will use when you prepare your Sales Tax Liability report in the next step).

3. From the menu bar select **Reports**, **Vendors & Payables**, **Sales Tax Liability**. See Figure 10.16. QuickBooks defaults the date range depending on your sales tax preference setting.

Each month before preparing your sales tax return, compare the total of these two reports. Later in this chapter, you learn about methods you can use to troubleshoot these totals when they do not match.

When a Check or Bill Was Used to Pay Sales Tax

A common mistake when recording payment of the sales tax payable is to use a Write Checks or Enter Bills transaction. If these types of transactions are used and the Sales Tax Payable account is assigned on the form, QuickBooks reduces the Sales Tax Payable amount on the Balance Sheet, but does not make the same adjustment in the Pay Sales Tax dialog box. Instead, this type of transaction will be included in the Pay Sales Tax dialog box as a negative Amt. Due.

To find the transaction(s) that might be the cause of differences between the Balance Sheet Sales Tax Payable amount to your Sales Tax Liability report amount to be paid, follow these steps:

1. On the Home page, click the Vendors button to open the Vendor Center.
2. Select your sales tax vendor from the Vendors list.
3. From the Show drop-down list, select **Checks** (or Bills), making sure you are looking in the appropriate date range.

Any checks or bills that appear here could be the reasons your two reports do not agree with each other. The correct sales tax payment transaction is named TAXPMT when viewing transactions in your bank register. The following section details how to properly record the payment of the collected sales tax in your QuickBooks data.

Paying Sales Tax

Now that you have your sales tax correctly set up and you have reviewed your sales tax payable reports, you need to know how to properly pay your sales tax.

Paying Sales Tax Without an Adjustment

As mentioned earlier, when you collect sales tax, you are acting as an agent for the state. Most often, you will pay the state or city taxing authority the same amount that you collected from your customers. Sometimes the state might allow you to discount the sales tax due for prompt payment or charge a penalty for paying late. Each of these situations is discussed in detail in this section.

Paying Sales Tax Without an Adjustment

To practice paying sales tax without an adjustment, open the sample data file as instructed in Chapter 1. Use these instructions when creating your own sales tax payments—selecting accounts and dates that are correct for your needs:

1. From the menu bar select, **Vendors, Sales Tax, Pay Sales Tax.** The Pay Sales Tax dialog box displays (see Figure 10.17).

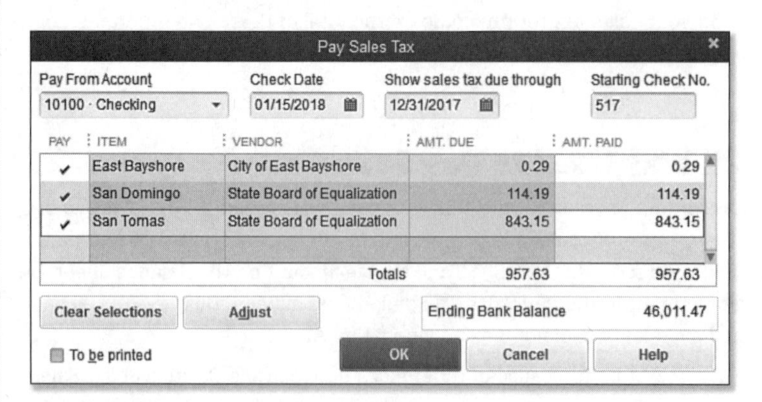

Figure 10.17
Use this transaction type to properly remit your sales tax payable amount.

2. For this exercise, in the Pay from Account field, leave Checking account selected.
3. In the Check Date field, select **January 15, 2018** or whatever date you are assigning on the check.
4. In the Show Sales Tax Due field, select **December 31, 2017**. This date should default to your preference setting. You can change this date if necessary.
5. Leave the Starting Check No. unchanged. We will assume that a manual check was written and this was the check number. If instead you are printing your check, place a checkmark in the To Be Printed box in the lower left.
6. Place a checkmark in the Pay column on the left for the individual items you want to pay. QuickBooks creates or prints a separate check transaction for each line item with a different vendor.
7. Verify that the Amt. Paid column is in agreement with your Sales Tax Liability report for the same period.
8. Click OK; QuickBooks creates a transaction with the TAXPMT type viewable from your checkbook register, as shown in Figure 10.18.

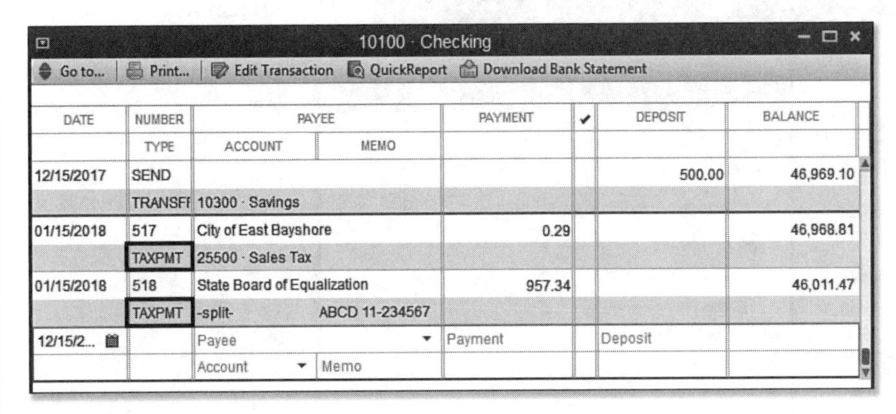

Figure 10.18
Sales Tax Payment transactions displayed in a checkbook register.

 **tip**

You can set a user-specific default account for paying the sales tax liability. From the menu bar select **Edit, Preferences, Checking** and choose the My Preferences tab.

Paying Sales Tax with an Adjustment

There are many reasons why your Sales Tax Payable doesn't agree with the actual amount you need to pay (the agency can't know in advance what it expects you to pay), including the following:

- Discount offered for early payment
- Penalty or fee assessed for late payment
- Credit received for overpayment on a prior period's sales tax return
- State sales tax holiday or rate reduction
- Rounding errors

note

If you select the items to be paid *first*, and then click the Adjust button recording the discount or increase, QuickBooks provides a warning that your previously selected checkmarks will be removed, and you will need to select the line items again, including the new adjustment to be included with the payment.

If any of these apply to your business, follow these steps:

1. Perform steps 1–5 listed in the preceding section ("Paying Sales Tax Without an Adjustment") making sure to select the proper accounts and dates for your specific needs.
2. In the Pay Sales Tax dialog box, click Adjust to open the Sales Tax Adjustment dialog box, as shown in Figure 10.19.

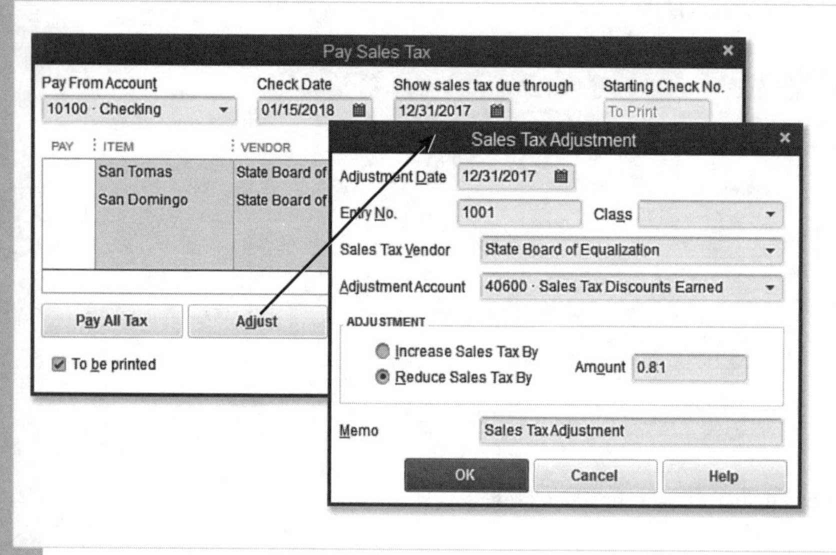

Figure 10.19
Use the Sales Tax Adjustment dialog box to increase or decrease your sales tax payment.

3. Select the appropriate Adjustment Date. This date should be on or before the Show Sales Tax Through date.
4. Enter an Entry No. or QuickBooks will default a number if that preference is set.
5. Select the Sales Tax Vendor for which you are decreasing or increasing your payment.
6. Select from your chart of accounts the Adjustment Account. Ask your accountant what is preferred; the account might be either of the following:

- Other Income, if you are recording a discount for early payment.
- Expense, if you are recording a penalty or fine.

7. Select the option to **Increase Sales Tax By** or **Reduce Sales Tax By** and enter the appropriate dollar amount.
8. In the Memo section, enter a description for your reports or accept the default description.
9. Click OK to record the sales tax adjustment.
10. Click OK to close the warning message when recording a sales tax adjustment.
11. QuickBooks now shows the Pay Sales Tax dialog box with an additional line showing the adjustment. This example shows a reduction in sales tax due (see Figure 10.20).

Figure 10.20
When preparing your sales tax payment, select the sales tax lines and the adjustment line.

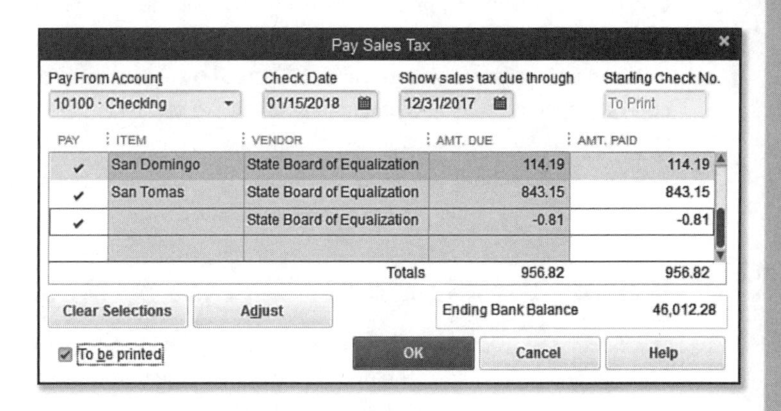

QuickBooks creates a general journal entry when the sales tax adjustment is recorded.

Correcting Accounts Receivable Errors

After reviewing your accounts receivable reports, you might have identified some data entry errors. Before you can fix these, you need to determine the best method to correct the errors. When deciding which method is best, you should ask yourself the following:

- **Are the errors in an accounting year that I have already filed a tax return for?**—If yes, then adjusting these transactions by dating the modifying entry in the current tax year and not modifying the original transaction is best. Some methods listed in this section do not enable you to select a date different from the original transaction date.
- **Are the errors significant in the dollar amount, collectively or individually?**—If yes, you should obtain the advice of your accountant before making any adjustments so changes that will affect your tax status are carefully considered.

- **Am I going to fix detail or summary information?**—In other words, are you going to fix individual invoices or correct a group of customer invoices with one adjusting transaction?
- **Am I modifying an invoice with sales tax recorded on the invoice?**—If yes, refer to the "Correcting Sales Tax Errors" section in this chapter for a detailed discussion on adjusting invoices with sales tax. These corrections should be made only with transactions dated in the current accounting month.

Removing an Open Balance from a Customer Invoice

There are several reasons you might have open balances on your Accounts Receivable invoices. There are also several methods to correct overstated or understated balances, each with its own effect on your company's financials.

If you are an accounting professional and you are using QuickBooks Accountant 2013 or QuickBooks Enterprise Solutions Accountant 13.0 software, you should review Appendix A, "Client Data Review."

Included in the Client Data Review (CDR) used by accountants are useful tools that streamline applying open customer payments and credits to open customer invoices and simplify writing off small open balances in batch.

The following sections are methods you can use to remove open customer balances with your QuickBooks Pro, Premier, or Enterprise software.

Writing Off a Customer Balance by Modifying the Original Customer Receive Payments Transaction

This method of modifying the original customer payment to write off a customer balance records the change as of the date of the Receive Payments transaction and permits a write-off amount equal to the underpayment amount. You can write off the amount at the time you first record the payment or at a later date.

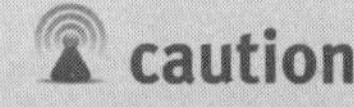

Writing off amounts on the Receive Payment transaction affects your financials as of the date recorded on the Receive Payment transaction. Ask your accountant first about making these types of changes for prior years that you have already filed your company's income tax returns.

Follow these steps to write off a balance due from a customer directly from the Receive Payment transaction:

1. On the Home page, click the Customers button to open the Customer Center.
2. From the list on the left, select the appropriate customer.
3. In the Show drop-down list, select **Payments and Credits** or just **Received Payments** and any other date criteria you want to use, as shown in Chapter 9, Figure 9.15.
4. Double-click the selected customer payment to open it. In the example shown in Figure 10.21, the customer paid $10.00 less than the amount due. Write off this amount by selecting **Write Off The Extra Amount** option on the lower left of the Receive Payments dialog box.
5. Select **Save & Close**. QuickBooks prompts you for an account to assign for the write-off amount.

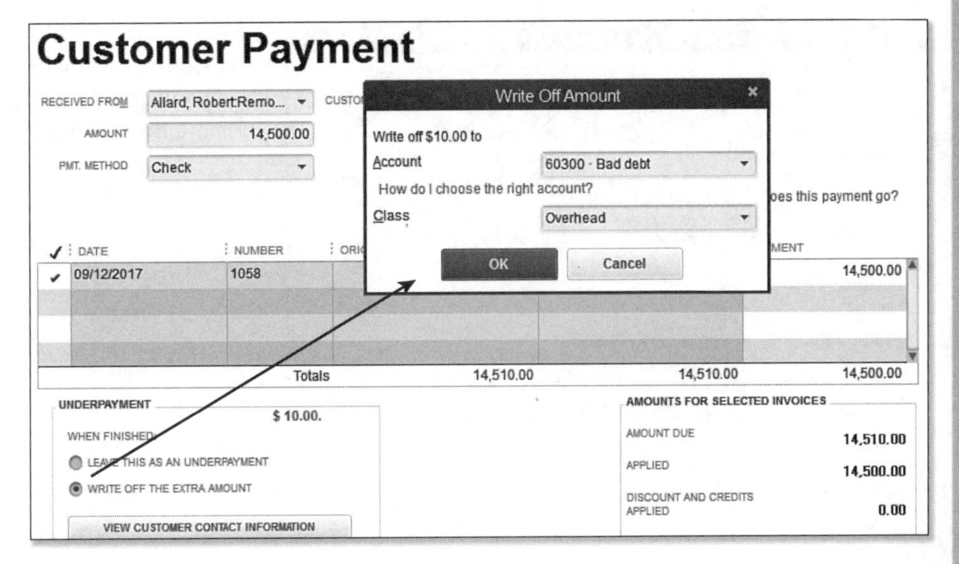

Figure 10.21 When you select to write off an amount due, QuickBooks requires you to assign the amount to an account and optionally to a class.

Recording a Discount to Remove a Customer Balance

Another way to remove an open customer balance is to record a discount. This method records the change as of the date of the Receive Payments transaction. A discount can be recorded initially when the customer's short payment is recorded, or on a later date by creating a new payment without placing any dollars in the Amount field and choosing the Discounts & Credits option. However, the discount amount cannot be in excess of the amount due.

If the amount due is an insignificant amount, you might not want to take the time to collect it. The easiest method of dealing with it would be to write off the remaining amount on the date the payment is recorded. If you do not write off the remaining amount, QuickBooks will warn you of the underpayment.

The difference between a write-off and discount is the placement on the Profit & Loss statement. A write-off is used when the debt has gone bad and cannot be collected and is often an expense type. In contrast, the discount is used when you decide to reduce the sale price, and this account is typically an income type.

To record a discount, click the Discount & Credits button on the Receive Payments dialog box. Similar to the Write Off Amount dialog box, you will be asked to identify an account to post the amount to (see Figure 10.22).

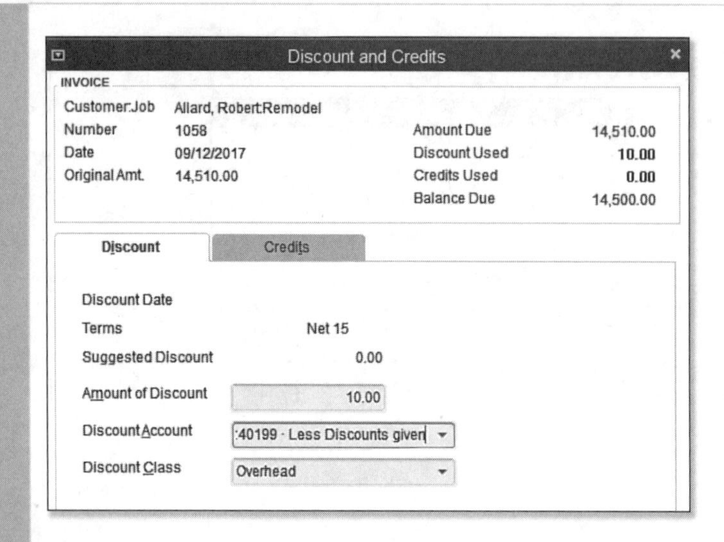
INVOICE
Customer:Job Allard, Robert:Remodel
Number 1058
Date 09/12/2017
Original Amt. 14,510.00
Amount Due 14,510.00
Discount Used 10.00
Credits Used 0.00
Balance Due 14,500.00
Discount
Credits
Discount Date
Terms Net 15
Suggested Discount 0.00
Amount of Discount 10.00
Discount Account :40199 · Less Discounts given
Discount Class Overhead

Figure 10.22
For small unpaid balances, recording a discount can be an easy method to remove the balance.

Recording a Credit Memo to Remove a Balance Due

The most accurate method for removing a balance due is to record a credit memo, because it creates a good audit trail. You can date the credit in a period you want to reduce the appropriate income account and, if applicable, sales tax due.

For more detailed instructions on working with customer credit memos, "Recording and Applying a Customer Credit Memo," p. 359.

Recording a Journal Entry to Remove (or Increase) a Customer Balance

Another way to remove or increase a customer balance is to record a journal entry. This type of transaction is often created by the company's accountant when adjusting Accounts Receivable.

If you are going to record a journal entry adjustment, you need to keep in mind the following:

- Only one customer is allowed per journal entry.
- If the general journal entry has other noncustomer-related adjustments, the first line of the journal entry should remain blank. For more information read the caution in this section.
- The date of the general journal entry is the date the transaction will impact your financials for accrual or cash basis.
- If you print cash basis reports, make sure the income account is *not* recorded on the first line of the journal entry.
- You can enter and apply one lump sum to multiple open customer invoices.

caution

Did you know that if you use a customer on the first line of a journal entry, every other adjustment made—even noncustomer adjustments—will display on the Profit & Loss by Job report for that customer? This situation is due to the first line of any journal entry being a source line and causing a relationship with transactions below the first line.

To avoid this problem, always leave the first account line of a journal entry blank, as shown in Figure 10.23. Including a memo on the first line is acceptable.

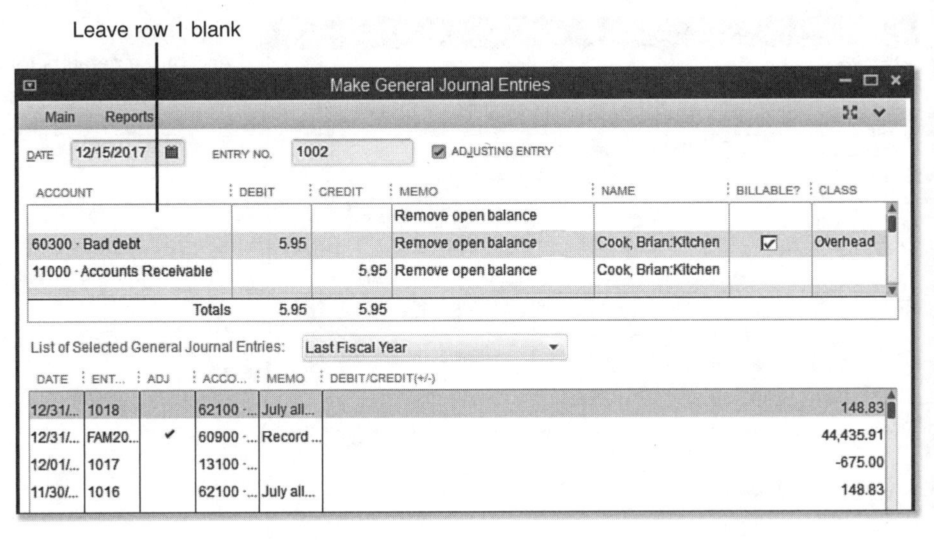

Figure 10.23 Journal entries that adjust accounts receivable balances should then be applied against a customer's open invoice(s).

To record a journal entry adjustment to a customer balance, follow these steps:

1. From the menu bar select **Company**, **Make General Journal Entries**.
2. In the Make General Journal Entries dialog box, record a debit to increase Accounts Receivable or credit to reduce Accounts Receivable (refer to Figure 10.23). Be sure to assign the customer name to each line (except the first line, see the previous caution) so a Profit & Loss by Job report will show the adjustment.
3. Assign the General Journal Entry to the appropriate customer invoice. From the menu bar, select **Customers**, **Customer Center**.
4. Select the correct customer from the list on the left, and in the Show drop-down list, select **Invoices**. Double-click the appropriate invoice with the open balance.
5. The Create Invoices dialog box opens. From the Main tab on the ribbon toolbar at the top, select **Apply Credits**. QuickBooks then provides a list of available credits to choose from (see Figure 10.24).
6. On the Apply Credits dialog box that opens, select the appropriate credits by placing a checkmark next to the credit. Click Done to assign the credit(s) to the customer invoice.
7. Click Save & Close.

Correcting Customer Payments

Applying the customer's payments exactly as the customer intended is important. If you apply the customer's payment to an invoice of your own choosing, communicating any discrepancies with open invoice balances can be more confusing than necessary.

However, many times your customer does not provide you with the correct invoice number, and you might apply his payment to an incorrect invoice. QuickBooks makes changing how you applied the payment to an invoice easy.

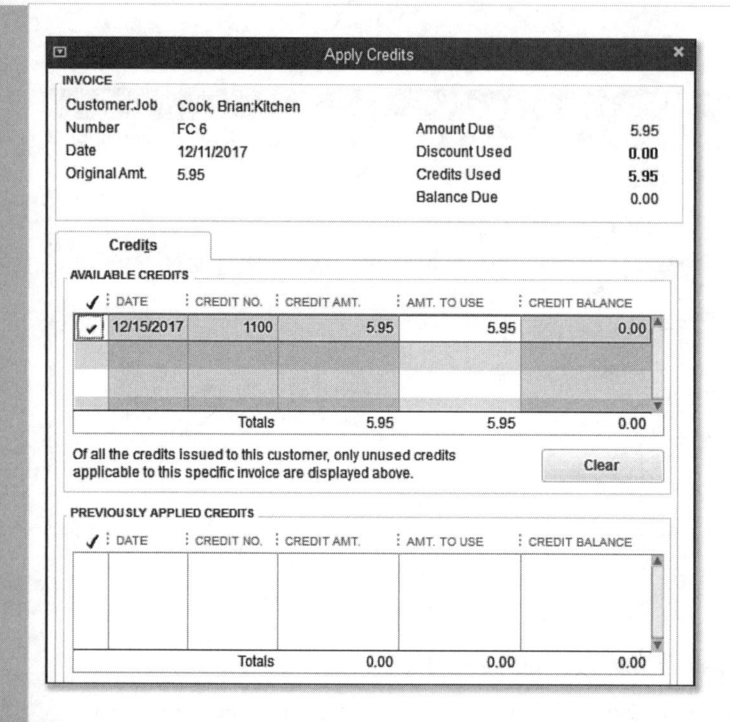

Figure 10.24
Accept the defaults for applying open credits, or manually assign them.

Fixing Unapplied Customer Payments and Credits

You might notice that your Open Invoice report includes unapplied payments (see Figure 10.25). This happens when the payment is recorded by a QuickBooks user who does not assign the payment to an open invoice.

To correct this, double-click the Payment transaction listed on the report, and add the checkmarks to the invoice(s) being paid. This transaction change affects prior year financials in cash basis reporting, so be sure to notify your accounting professional of the change.

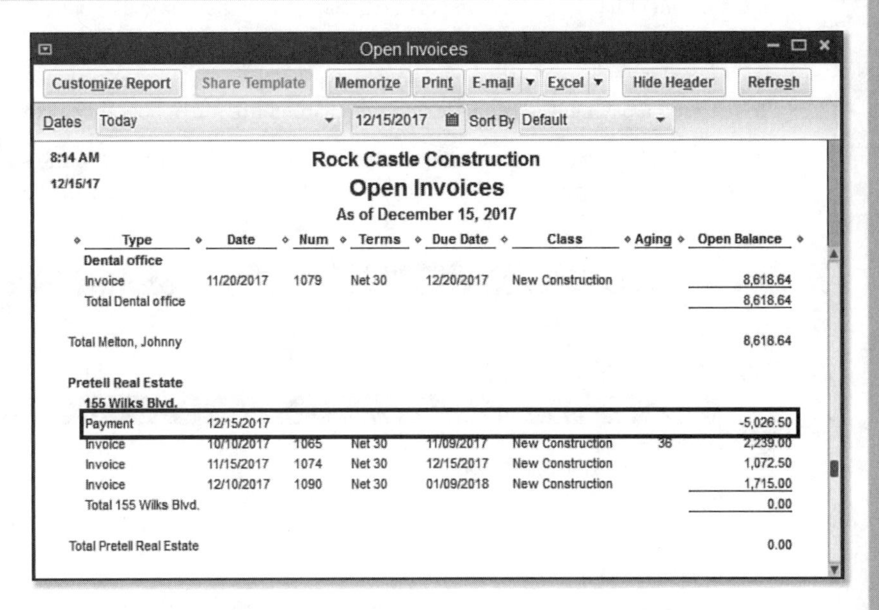

Figure 10.25
Unapplied Receive Payments transactions will show on the Open Invoices report as a credit for that customer.

Fixing a Payment Applied to the Wrong Invoice Number

If, after you compare your customer's records with yours, you find you have applied the payment to the wrong invoice, follow these steps to unapply the payment and then reapply it to the correct invoice:

1. From the menu bar select **Customers**, **Customer Center**.
2. On the list on the left, select the appropriate customer.
3. In the pane to the right of the customer list, in the Show drop-down list, select **Payments and Credits**.
4. Optionally, select specific payment methods or select a specific date range from the appropriate drop-down list. QuickBooks lists all received payment transactions for this customer.
5. Double-click the payment that was misapplied.
6. The Receive Payments dialog box opens. Remove the checkmark from one invoice and place it next to the correct invoice. Ensure that the amount of the payment total does not change. Click Save & Close.

Fixing a Payment Applied to the Wrong Customer or Job

From the Customer Center, find the appropriate customer, filter for Received Payments, and locate the payment in question as instructed in previous sections.

Determine whether the payment has already been included on a deposit by clicking Transaction History on the Reports tab of the transaction ribbon. If you attempt to change the customer name on the payment screen, QuickBooks warns you that the payment first needs to be deleted from the deposit.

If the payment has been included on a deposit, follow these steps to correct the customer or job assigned. You will temporarily remove the amount from a deposit and then add back in the corrected payment.

To reassign a payment received to another customer or job, follow these steps:

1. From the Receive Payments dialog box for the payment assigned to the incorrect customer or job, on the Reports tab of the ribbon toolbar, click Transaction History, as shown in Figure 10.26.

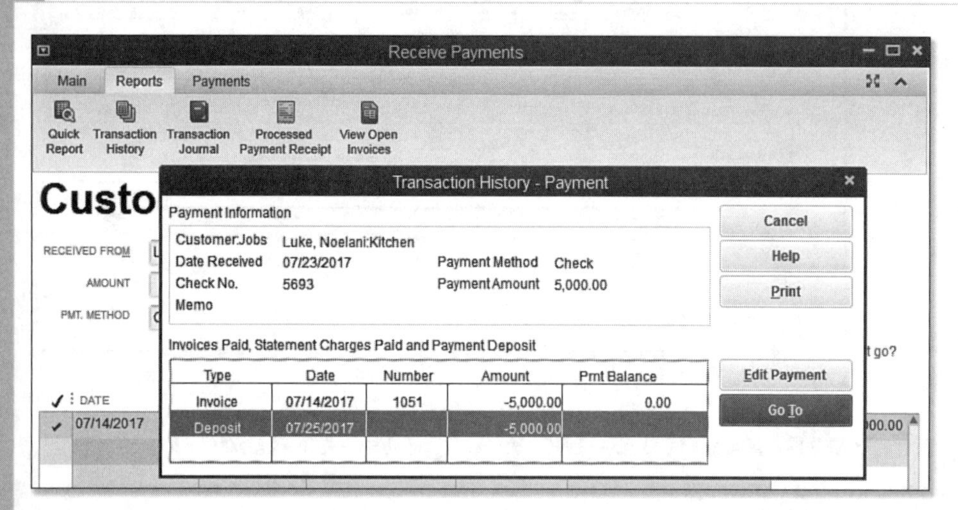

Figure 10.26
To reassign a recorded payment to a different customer or job, you first have to remove the payment from the deposit.

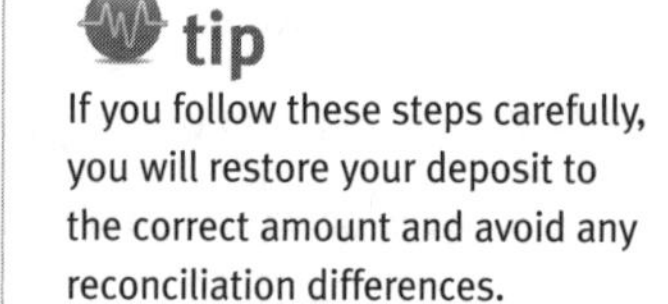

tip

If you follow these steps carefully, you will restore your deposit to the correct amount and avoid any reconciliation differences.

2. From the Transaction History—Payment dialog box, select the deposit and click Go To. The deposit dialog opens.
3. Record on paper the total deposit amount and date. You will need this information later in step 8.
4. If multiple payments are on the deposit, go to step 5. If the payment amount being corrected is the only deposit line item, go to step 9.
5. Highlight the line item to be removed, as in Figure 10.27, and press Ctrl+Delete on your keyboard. Click OK to the Delete warning message. Then click Save & Close. This step removes the line item from the deposit. QuickBooks will also warn you if the item has previously been cleared.
6. Locate the customer payment that was in error and change the Customer or Job assigned.
7. Return to the bank register and locate the deposit. Double-click the deposit. With the deposit open, select **Payments** at the top and place a checkmark next to the payment with the corrected Customer or Job (see Figure 10.28). Click OK to add the payment to the deposit.
8. Verify that the total of the deposit agrees with the original amount you recorded on paper. When this transaction is saved with the same original amount, your bank reconciliation will not show a discrepancy. The process is now complete (see Figure 10.29).

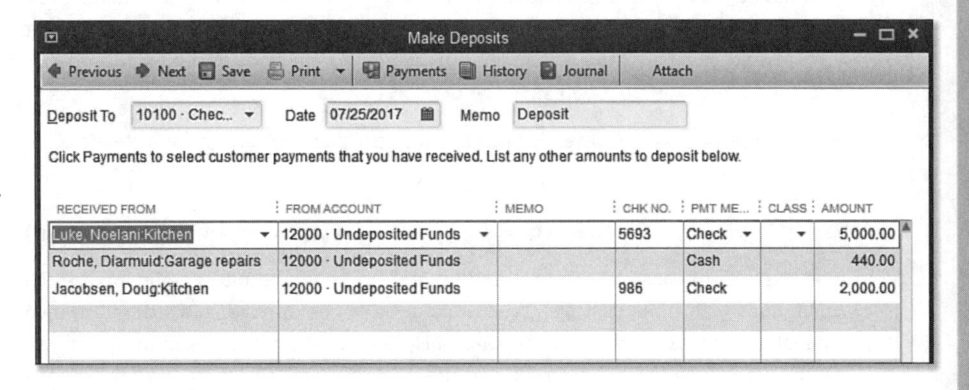

Figure 10.27 Use Ctrl+Delete on your keyboard to remove an entire transaction line.

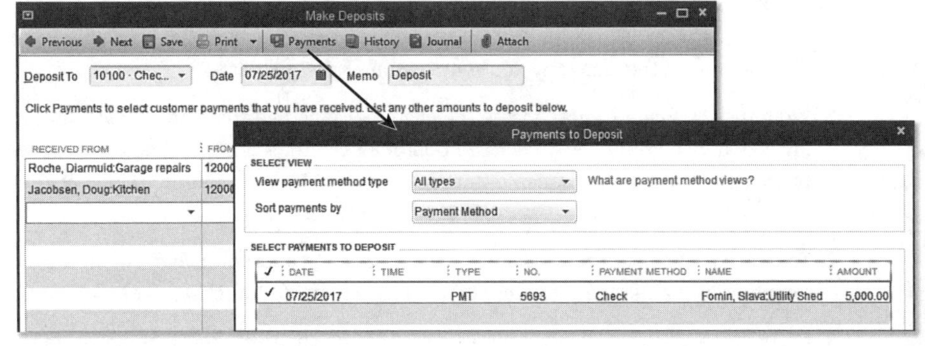

Figure 10.28 With the original deposit open, click the Payments icon to add back the corrected payment.

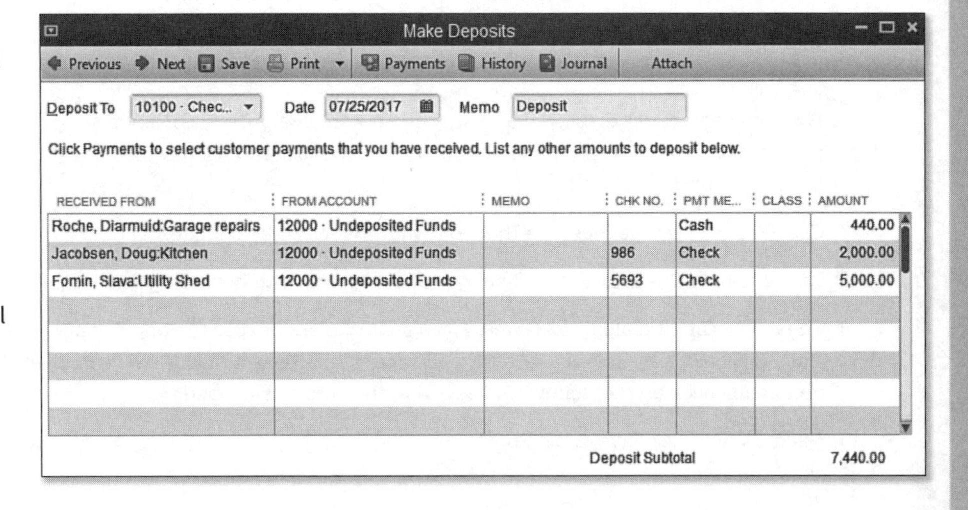

Figure 10.29 The corrected payment has been added to the original deposit, preserving the cleared bank status of the original deposit.

9. If the payment you are correcting is the only deposit line item, from the menu bar, select **Customers**, **Receive Payments** and record the information for the correct customer or job. Then follow steps 7 and 8 to assign your newly created payment to the existing deposit. Next, delete the incorrect line item and save the deposit.
10. From the Customer Center, locate the incorrect payment and void or delete it.

When a Credit Memo Is Applied to the Wrong Customer Invoice

It often happens that you create a credit memo and apply it to a specific invoice. Then, when you communicate with the customer, you find out he or she applied it to a different invoice. When you are making those credit and collections calls, the discrepancy can end up costing you critical time in outstanding invoices paid. If in the end the total due from the customer remains the same, I find it easier to defer to the customer's records when applying credit memos.

Without agreeing with the customer, your collections process would be delayed as both parties sort out what remains unpaid. This process will temporarily have you reassign the credit memo to another customer. The steps that follow will help you reassign the credit memo to the correct invoice, or at least the same invoice your customer assigned it to:

1. From the Customer Center, locate the customer who had the credit memo applied to the wrong invoice. If you are not sure, click the Customer Center's Transactions tab and select **Credit Memos** from the list of available transaction types. You can filter for Open or All Credit Memos as well as transaction dates to narrow your search.
2. To reassign the incorrectly assigned credit memo to another invoice, open the credit memo and temporarily change the Customer or Job name to any other customer or job name.
3. Make a note of the new customer assigned to the changed credit memo. From the Main tab of the ribbon toolbar at that top, select **Save**.
4. Click Yes to close the message that you want to record the change.
5. Click OK to the Available Credit message, leaving the Retain as an Available Credit option selected.
6. With the open credit displayed and showing a Remaining Credit balance assigned to the temporary customer, click the Customer:Job drop-down list and choose the correct Customer or Customer:Job.
7. Click Yes to close the message that you want to record the change.
8. The Available Credit message displays. Click the Apply to Invoice option.
9. The Apply Credit dialog box opens. Place a checkmark next to the appropriate credit amounts. QuickBooks will, by default, select the invoice with an exact match. You can override this selection by unchecking the default and applying the credit as needed.
10. Select **Done**. Click Save & Close.

When Deposits Were Made Incorrectly

Many users follow these four steps to properly managing most Accounts Receivable tasks:

1. Create a quote using an estimate or sales order (optional).
2. Prepare an invoice, sales receipt, or statement charge.
3. Receive the customer payment into an Undeposited Funds account.
4. Record the deposit into your bank account.

This section details how to correct your QuickBooks data when the receive payments step was skipped in recording deposits to the bank account.

How can you know when this situation happens? You need to do a little troubleshooting first to identify the problem:

- Do you have open invoices for customers who you know have paid you?
- Is your bank account balance reconciled and correct?
- Does Income on your Profit & Loss Report appear to be too high?

If you answered yes to these questions, you need to determine just how the deposits in the bank account register were recorded.

Viewing Deposits in the Bank Register

To determine how deposits were made to the bank account, view the deposits in your bank register. To open a bank register, select **Banking**, **Use Register** from the menu bar and select the appropriate bank account.

The two deposits dated 12/15/17 (see Figure 10.30) were each individually recorded to the account by assigning the checking account directly on the receive payment transaction. This would be acceptable if the individual checks were on different deposit tickets taken to your bank and if the date of the receive payment was also the same date as the deposit. Often these are not the normal conditions, and having the payment recorded to the Undeposited Funds would be the best process.

In the checkbook register view, the account shown represents the account from which the transaction originated. You might see Accounts Receivable, an income account, or you will see "-Split-," which indicates that there are several lines of detail for this single transaction. To view the "-Split-" detail, double-click the transaction itself to open the originating QuickBooks transaction.

By contrast, look at the deposit dated 12/16/2017 for $2,000.00 in Figure 10.30. The account shown is Undeposited Funds, which is the account where the transaction originated.

To summarize, look for a "pattern" of how deposits were made to your QuickBooks data. The examples here show two types of deposits: those that were recorded to the checking account and others that first went through the Undeposited Funds account. You might have others in your data where the account shown is your income account. This type of transaction is discussed in the next section, "Viewing the Deposit Detail Report."

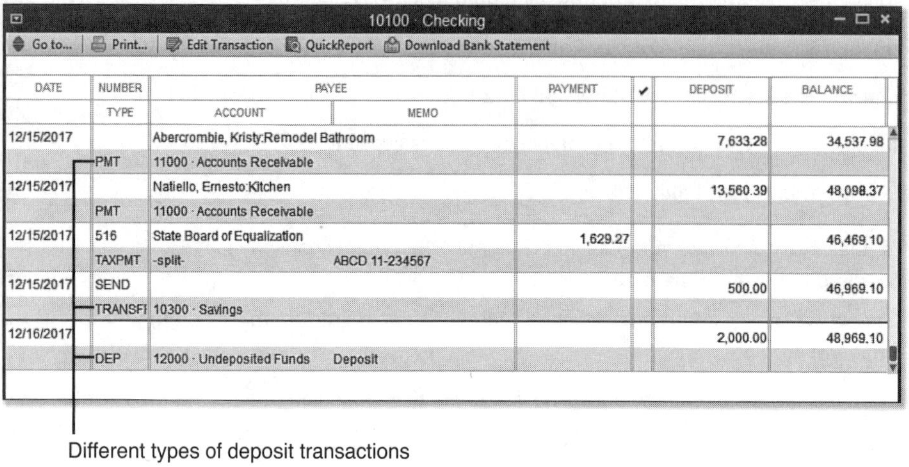

10100 · Checking

Go to... | Print... | Edit Transaction | QuickReport | Download Bank Statement

DATE	NUMBER / TYPE	PAYEE / ACCOUNT	MEMO	PAYMENT	✔	DEPOSIT	BALANCE
12/15/2017		Abercrombie, Kristy:Remodel Bathroom				7,633.28	34,537.98
	PMT	11000 · Accounts Receivable					
12/15/2017		Natiello, Ernesto:Kitchen				13,560.39	48,098.37
	PMT	11000 · Accounts Receivable					
12/15/2017	516	State Board of Equalization		1,629.27			46,469.10
	TAXPMT	-split-	ABCD 11-234567				
12/15/2017	SEND					500.00	46,969.10
	TRANSFI	10300 · Savings					
12/16/2017						2,000.00	48,969.10
	DEP	12000 · Undeposited Funds	Deposit				

Different types of deposit transactions

Figure 10.30 The checkbook register indicates the record type for each deposit.

You will also be looking to see which transactions have been cleared in the bank reconciliation and which deposits remain uncleared. Chapter 13 discusses the bank reconciliation topic. In fact, it would be best if the reconciliation task were completed before you begin fixing your deposit details. Why? If you see an uncleared deposit, it would help you identify your potential errors in the Undeposited Funds account.

Viewing the Deposit Detail Report

Use this report to review how deposits were recorded to the bank account in QuickBooks and identify deposits that did follow the recommended process of being recorded first to the Undeposited Funds account.

To open the Deposit Detail report, follow these steps:

1. From the menu bar select **Reports**, **Banking**, **Deposit Detail**.
2. Click the Customize Report button at the top of the report.
3. Click the Filters tab. In the Choose Filter box, the Account filter is already selected. In the drop-down list, select your bank account or use the default all bank accounts. Click OK to prepare the report.

In Figure 10.31, the deposit for $2,000.00 on 12/16/17 was recorded using the recommended process of automatically assigning the payment to the Undeposited Funds account. The other payments did not follow this same process, and details for correcting these are provided in the next sections.

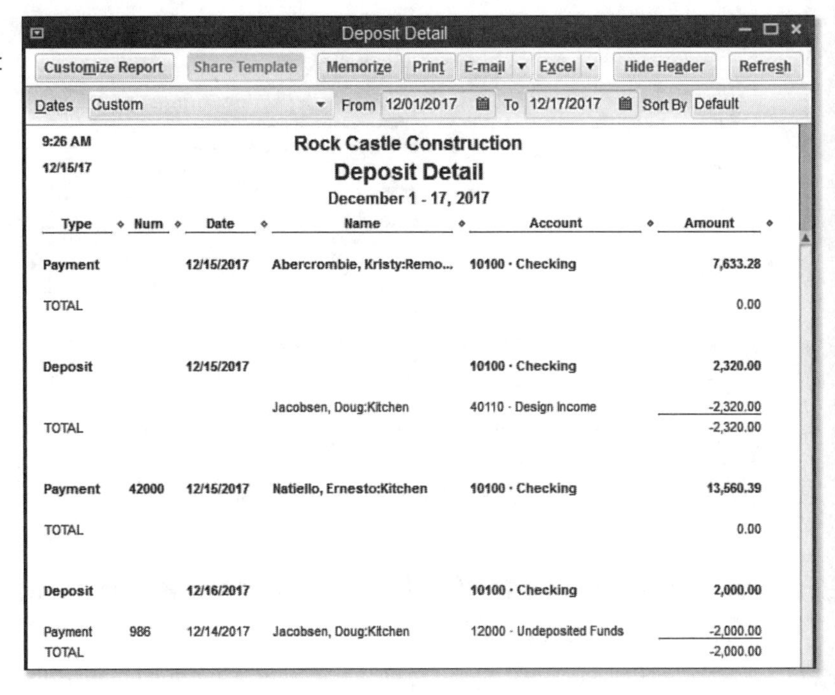

Figure 10.31
The Deposit Detail report also indicates the record type of each deposit.

Creating a Payment Transaction List Detail Report

Do you find the Deposit Detail report too lengthy and difficult to read? You can create a report that shows the detail in a list form and provides a total of the column detail using these steps:

1. From the menu bar, select **Reports, Custom Reports, Transaction Detail**. The Modify Report dialog opens with the Display tab selected.
2. Select the **Report Date Range** you want to view, as well as the columns you want to see on the report.
3. From the Filters tab, in the Choose Filter box, select **Account** and choose a specific bank account.
4. Set an additional filter for Multiple Transaction Types, including the deposit, payment, and journal (although it's less likely a journal was used).
5. Click OK to close the Transaction Type filter and optionally select the **Header/Footer** tab to modify the Report Title.
6. Click OK to display the report with the selected filters.

Now you can view in a list format all payments that were recorded to the Checking account (see Figure 10.32).

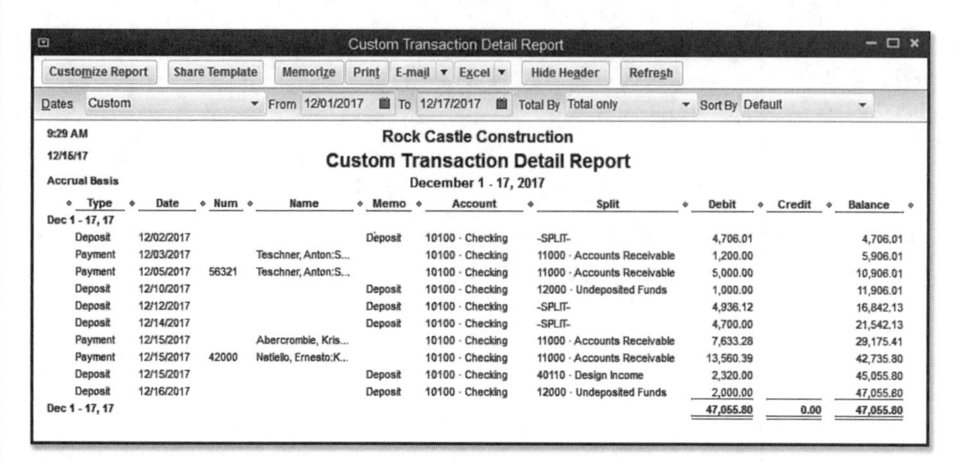

9:29 AM
12/15/17
Accrual Basis

Rock Castle Construction
Custom Transaction Detail Report
December 1 - 17, 2017

Type	Date	Num	Name	Memo	Account	Split	Debit	Credit	Balance
Dec 1 - 17, 17									
Deposit	12/02/2017			Deposit	10100 · Checking	-SPLIT-	4,706.01		4,706.01
Payment	12/03/2017		Teschner, Anton:S...		10100 · Checking	11000 · Accounts Receivable	1,200.00		5,906.01
Payment	12/05/2017	56321	Teschner, Anton:S...		10100 · Checking	11000 · Accounts Receivable	5,000.00		10,906.01
Deposit	12/10/2017			Deposit	10100 · Checking	12000 · Undeposited Funds	1,000.00		11,906.01
Deposit	12/12/2017			Deposit	10100 · Checking	-SPLIT-	4,936.12		16,842.13
Deposit	12/14/2017			Deposit	10100 · Checking	-SPLIT-	4,700.00		21,542.13
Payment	12/15/2017		Abercrombie, Kris...		10100 · Checking	11000 · Accounts Receivable	7,633.28		29,175.41
Payment	12/15/2017	42000	Natiello, Ernesto:K...		10100 · Checking	11000 · Accounts Receivable	13,560.39		42,735.80
Deposit	12/15/2017			Deposit	10100 · Checking	40110 · Design Income	2,320.00		45,055.80
Deposit	12/16/2017			Deposit	10100 · Checking	12000 · Undeposited Funds	2,000.00		47,055.80
Dec 1 - 17, 17							47,055.80	0.00	47,055.80

Figure 10.32
Use a filtered custom transaction detail report for a simple view of all deposits into the bank account.

Assigning the Make Deposits Transaction to the Open Customer Invoice

Did your research reveal Make Deposits transactions recorded directly to an income account instead of using the Receive Payments transaction? For the business owner, assigning the deposits to the customer invoice is a two-step process. If you have the time to correct individual transactions, this method retains your bank reconciliation status and identifies the payment with the customer's open invoice. Be prepared for a bit of tedious work. You need to have a good record of which deposit was paying for which customer invoice. Remember, these steps are to correct transactions that have been recorded incorrectly.

To manually correct recorded Make Deposits and apply them to the correct open invoice, follow these steps:

> **tip**
> I like using the Reports, Customers & Receivable, Open Invoices report because I can see both the unapplied credits and open invoices grouped by customer or job.

1. From the menu bar, select **Banking**, **Use Register**.
2. The Use Register dialog box opens. Select the bank account to which the deposit was made.
3. Locate the deposit in the checkbook register and double-click it to open the Make Deposits transaction. Change the account assigned in the From Account column from Income to Accounts Receivable. The effect of this step is to "credit" or decrease, Accounts Receivable (see Figure 10.33). Click Save & Close.
4. From the menu bar select **Reports**, **Customers & Receivables**, **Open Invoices**, and double-click the unpaid invoice.
5. From the Main tab of the ribbon toolbar, click the Apply Credits icon and select the credit that pertains to this invoice.
6. Click Done to close the Apply Credits dialog box. Click Save & Close.

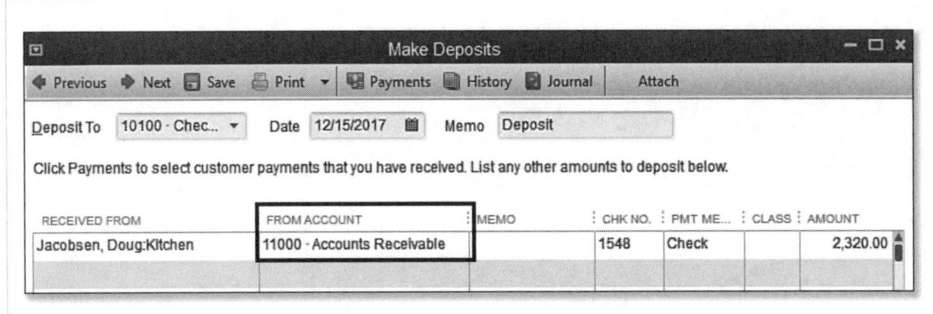

Figure 10.33
Changing the From Account on a deposit to Accounts Receivable will create a credit for the customer listed in the Received From column.

You have now corrected the deposit and assigned the amount to the open customer invoice, all without changing your bank reconciliation status of the item. This process works well, but can be tedious if you have many transactions with this type of error.

Grouping Deposited Items to Agree with Bank Deposit

Unless you take each and every check or cash payment from your customers to the bank on a separate bank deposit ticket, your customer payments should be grouped together with the total matching your bank deposit slip.

If you group your customer payments on the same deposit transaction and match the total deposited to your bank deposit ticket, your bank reconciliation will be much easier to complete each month.

You should not attempt this correcting method if you have reconciled your bank account in QuickBooks. Also, if you are correcting years of unreconciled transactions, this method might just be too tedious.

The easiest place to see the problem is in your bank account register. From the menu bar, select **Banking**, **Use Register**, and select the appropriate bank account.

As shown in Figure 10.30, assume the deposit total per the bank records on 12/15/17 was $21,193.67, but in the QuickBooks checkbook register, you recorded two individual deposits.

This situation was caused by choosing Checking as the Deposit To account when receiving the customer's payment (see Figure 10.34). The preferred method would have been to select Undeposited Funds and group them on one deposit transaction.

To correct these errors (be aware, it is a time-intensive process if you have many months or years of transactions), follow these steps:

1. From the displayed Receive Payments transaction that was originally deposited directly to the bank account, select the **Deposit To** drop-down list and choose Undeposited Funds.

2. From the menu bar select **Banking**, **Make Deposits**. QuickBooks displays a list of all the payments received, but not yet included in a deposit (included in the Undeposited Funds balance sheet account balance).

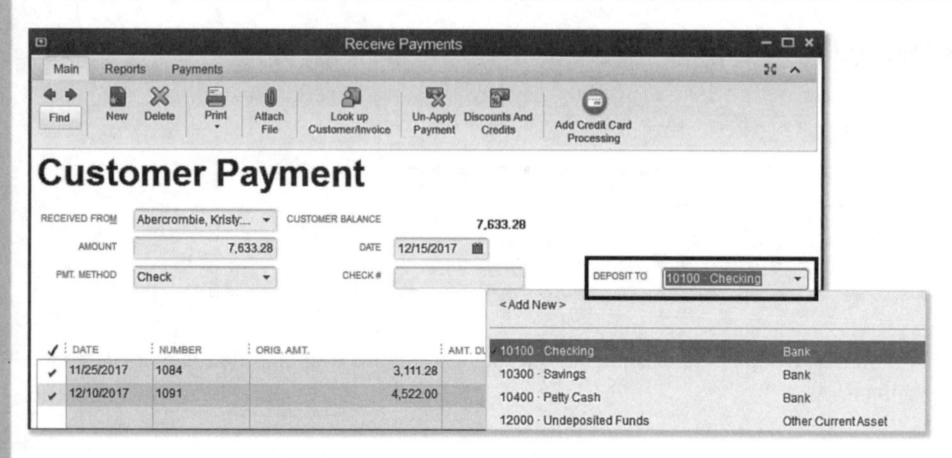

Figure 10.34
This customer payment won't be grouped with other customer funds on the same bank deposit ticket.

3. Click to place a checkmark next to the grouped payments, and verify that the total deposit agrees with each individual bank deposit.

4. Click OK. The make deposit transaction now agrees with the actual bank deposit recorded by the bank.

Eliminating the Print Queue for Customer Invoices Marked to Print

On the Main tab of the ribbon toolbar on each customer invoice is the option to select **Print Later**. QuickBooks remembers the setting from the last stored invoice, which can sometimes hinder your own company process.

If you find that you have many invoices selected to print and you don't intend to print them, try this easy solution:

1. Place one or two sheets of paper in your printer. From the menu bar, select **File**, **Print Forms**, **Invoices**. The Select Invoices to Print dialog box displays the invoices that are marked to be printed (see Figure 10.35).

Select Invoices to Print

A/R Account 11000 · Accounts Receiva...

Select Invoices to print, then click OK.
There are 5 Invoices to print for $24,894.03.

✓	DATE	TYPE	NO.	CUSTOMER	TEMPLATE	AMOUNT
✓	12/14/2017	INV	1094	Natiello, Ernesto:K...	Rock Castle Invoice	2,080.11
✓	12/14/2017	INV	1095	Natiello, Ernesto:K...	Rock Castle Invoice	8,656.25
✓	12/15/2017	INV	1097	Robson, Darci:Ro...	Progress Invoice	12,420.98
✓	12/15/2017	INV	1098	Cook, Brian:Kitchen	Rock Castle Invoice	1,636.69
✓	12/15/2017	INV	1100	Abercrombie, Krist...	Rock Castle Invoice	100.00

OK
Cancel
Help
Select All
Select None
Print Labels

Figure 10.35
View the invoices selected to print.

2. The checkmark next to the invoice tells QuickBooks you want to print the invoice on paper. Click OK to send the forms to the printer.

3. After a couple of invoices print, a message displays showing a list of the forms that did not print. Because you don't want to print them, click OK and each transaction will be marked in QuickBooks as if it were printed. You might also need to cancel the print job at your printer. Another option is to print the invoices to a PDF printer (file).

Correcting Sales Tax Errors

Sales tax errors can be a bit tricky to fix, so make sure you can answer the following questions:

- Have you made a backup of your data?
- Have taxes or financials been prepared using the current data? If yes, then you need to be concerned about the dates and types of the corrections you make.
- If the QuickBooks sales tax due is incorrect, have you determined outside QuickBooks how much was or is due?

Print your sales tax reports before you begin to make corrections to your data file. Then, when your corrections are complete, print the same reports to be sure you achieved the desired end result. Of course, keep good paper documentation of why you did what you did in case you are subject to a sales tax audit.

When a Check or Bill Was Used to Pay the Sales Tax

In newer versions of QuickBooks, the error of using a check or bill to pay sales tax should happen less often. QuickBooks provides messages to users attempting to pay their sales tax vendors incorrectly.

When you pay a vendor and assign the Sales Tax Payable account (created by QuickBooks) on a check or bill, QuickBooks provides the warning shown in Figure 10.36.

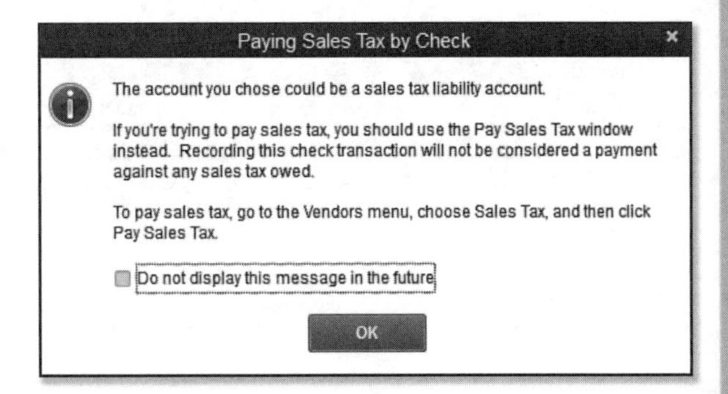

Figure 10.36
Warning when using a check to record a sales tax payment.

When you locate a sales tax payment made by check (or bill), first determine whether the check has been included in the bank reconciliation. If it has not, void the check and re-create the check per the instructions in the section titled "Paying Sales Tax."

If the check has already been included in the bank reconciliation, use the following method to assign the check or bill to the line items in the Pay Sales Tax dialog box:

1. From the menu bar select **Vendors**, **Vendor Center**. Select the vendor to whom sales tax payments were made using the incorrect transaction type.
2. From the Show drop-down list to the right, double-click the check or bill to open the Write Checks dialog box or Enter Bills dialog box.
3. Assign the Sales Tax Payable liability account in the Account column of the Expenses tab.
4. In the Customer:Job column, select the Sales Tax Vendor from the list of vendors (make sure it is a vendor and not an "other name" list item).
5. Click Save & Close to close the check (or bill).
6. From the menu bar select **Vendors**, **Sales Tax**, **Pay Sales Tax**. The corrected transaction will display in the Pay Sales Tax dialog box if it is dated on or prior to the Show Sales Tax Due Through date.
7. When you are ready to pay your next period's sales tax, place a checkmark next to each sales tax line item, including the line item with the correction to associate the check or bill payment with the sales tax due (see Figure 10.37). If the net total amount is zero, wait and select each of the items for the next period you pay your sales tax.

note

If you are an accounting professional working with QuickBooks Accountant 2013 software, review Appendix A, "Client Data Review." CDR includes a tool that will help you efficiently correct sales tax payments that were recording using the incorrect payment transaction type.

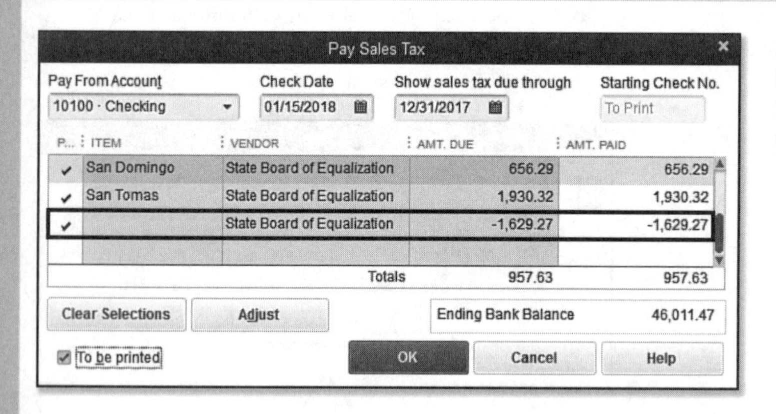

Figure 10.37
Include the corrected check (or bill) with your next period sales tax payment.

If the net Amt. Due is zero, place a checkmark next to each item and QuickBooks will associate your check or bill payment with the related sales tax due. When you return to the Pay Sales Tax dialog box, the amount previously showing as unpaid will no longer be there. If the Amt. Due does not agree with your records, you might need to create a sales tax adjustment before making your next sales tax payment.

When the Sales Tax Liability Report Shows Past Sales Tax Due

If your collected sales tax amount and the amount showing payable on the Sales Tax Liability report do not match, as shown in Figure 10.38, it is because there are sales taxes collected prior to the current report's Show Sales Tax Through date that remain unpaid. Perhaps the payments were incorrectly paid using a check or bill, in which case you should correct these errors following the instructions provided in the previous section.

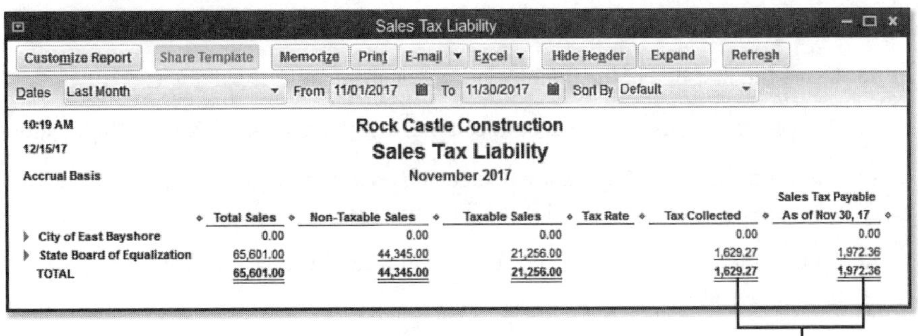

Figure 10.38 When the tax collected and the sales tax payable do not match, prior sales taxes have not been properly recorded or remitted.

To verify the totals and to make the needed corrections, follow these steps:

1. From the menu bar select **Vendors, Sales Tax, Sales Tax Liability**.
2. From the Dates drop-down list, select **This Month-to-Date**.
3. If the Tax Collected and Sales Tax Payable totals agree with each other for today's date, your sales tax payment made previously was given the wrong Show Sales Tax Through date. To fix this error, you can void and reissue the payment or know that the QuickBooks report prepared for a future date should reflect the payment accurately.
4. If the two totals do not match, verify that the tax collected for the current period is correct. You can verify this amount by reviewing the invoices you have issued for the month.
5. Verify that the tax collected for the prior period was correct.
6. Determine to what account(s) your sales tax payments were incorrectly recorded. The previously made payments would cause these accounts to be overstated.

   In the correcting entry example in Figure 10.39, your research found that a Sales Tax Expense type account was used when recording a sales tax payment in error.
7. From the menu bar select **Company, Make General Journal Entries** to create a correcting entry.

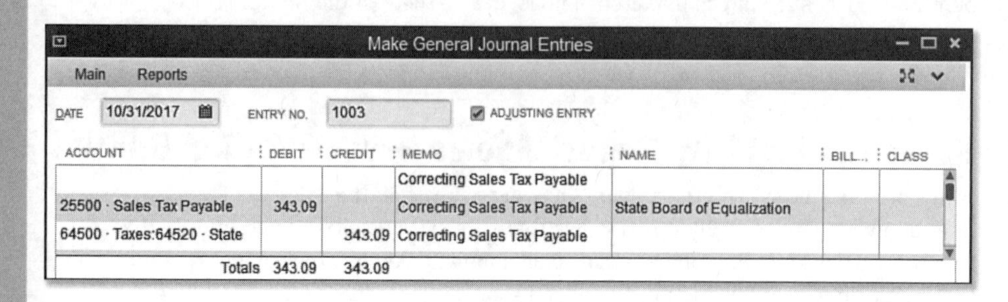

Figure 10.39 Journal entries can correct sales tax payable errors.

8. Date the entry in the period you are correcting.
9. Give the entry a number, or let QuickBooks automatically number it if you've set that preference.
10. Leave the first line of the general journal blank.
11. On the second line in the Account column, select the **Sales Tax Payable** liability account.
12. Enter a debit amount if you are decreasing your sales tax payable amount. Enter a credit amount if you are increasing your sales tax payable amount.
13. On the third line, select the account that was discovered to be overstated or understated in your review (see step 6).
14. Enter the same amount from line 2 in the opposite column (debit or credit) from the previous line. Verify that your debits are equal to your credits.
15. Click Save & Close to close the general journal.

You will now be able to select this line item with other sales tax lines for future tax payments, similar to what was shown in Figure 10.37.

You might opt for this method to fix many months' errors with one journal entry and then put in place better controls for future sales tax management.

When Total Sales Does Not Equal Total Income

One of the important comparisons to make is the Sales Tax Liability total sales with the Profit & Loss Standard total income. Both of these reports were discussed in the section "Reconciling Total Sales to Total Income." Before comparing the reports, be sure to create both using the same accounting basis: accrual or cash. The default basis for the sales tax report comes from the Sales Tax Preference discussed earlier in this chapter. With the report displayed, you can click the Customize Report button to change the basis being used for that report.

What can cause your total sales on your Sales Tax Liability report not to match your total income on your Profit & Loss report? Some of the reasons might be the following:

- **Different accounting basis between reports**—Your Sales Tax Liability report basis is in conflict with your Profit & Loss reporting basis. The basis of the report is by default printed on the top left of the report. Both reports must be either accrual basis or both must be cash basis before comparing.
- **Nonsales-type transactions recorded to income accounts**—A method to locate these transactions is to double-click the total income amount on your Profit & Loss report. Doing so opens the Transaction Detail by Account report. At the top right of the report, select **Sort By** and choose Type. Within each income account group, QuickBooks sorts the transactions by transaction type. Review the report for nonsales transaction types, such as General Journal or Bill (to name a couple). If you find an expense transaction in this report, often the cause is from using items on expense transactions, when the item record only has an assigned income account. More details on properly setting up items can be found in Chapter 4, "Understanding QuickBooks Lists."
- **Using items on sales forms that are assigned to a non-income account**—For example, a company that collects customer deposits might be using an item that is assigned to a current liability account. Total sales on the Sales Tax Liability report would include this amount, but the Profit & Loss would not.
- **Income recorded as a result of vendor discounts**—If you have set up an income account for your vendor discounts in your bills preferences setting, you will need to deduct this amount from your total revenue when you compare the two totals. If you are using an income account, create a separate income account for these discounts so that you can easily identify them.

The first two previous bullet points can be corrected by changing the reporting basis or correcting the original item record (from the menu bar, select **Lists**, **Item List**) to include both an income and an expense account.

Because you want to compare the totals, try this: From the menu bar, select **Window, Tile Vertically.** Both reports will be displayed side-by-side as shown in Figure 10.40 if these reports are the only currently open windows.

The last two bullet points are less likely to be changed in your process. You might instead need to prepare specific reports to proof your totals, making sure that when you file your sales tax return you are using the correct information.

In the following exercise, use the sample data to see how these reports can help you reconcile the differences.

Now that you have identified the difference, what exactly does it mean? If your state requires you report total sales as income earned on your sales tax reports, in this example, the proper amount to report would come from your Profit & Loss report. Your company's results might differ and might be more difficult to identify.

Instead, you might want to try customizing the Sales Tax Liability report. Click the Customize Report button, select the **Filters** tab in the Modify Report dialog box, and select **All Ordinary Income Accounts** from the Accounts drop-down list as shown in Figure 10.43. From here, review the amount displayed in the Total Sales Column. If this amount now agrees with your Profit & Loss report, you can be sure there are items on invoices that are mapped to account other than ordinary income accounts.

Reconciling Financials and Sales Tax Reports

To practice reconciling (proofing) the Profit & Loss total income to the sales tax payable on the Sales Tax Liability report, open the sample data file as instructed in Chapter 1. Your totals might differ from those shown in the figures here, but the process remains the same:

1. From Reports menu, open these two reports:
   - **Company & Financial, Profit & Loss Standard**—In the Dates drop-down list, select **Last Month.**
   - **Vendors & Payables, Sales Tax Liability**—By default, the Last Month is selected in the Dates field.
2. Notice in this exercise that the Total Sales from the Sales Tax Liability report and Total Income from the Profit & Loss report (on the right in Figure 10.40) do not match. The difference between the two amounts in this example is $2,174.50.

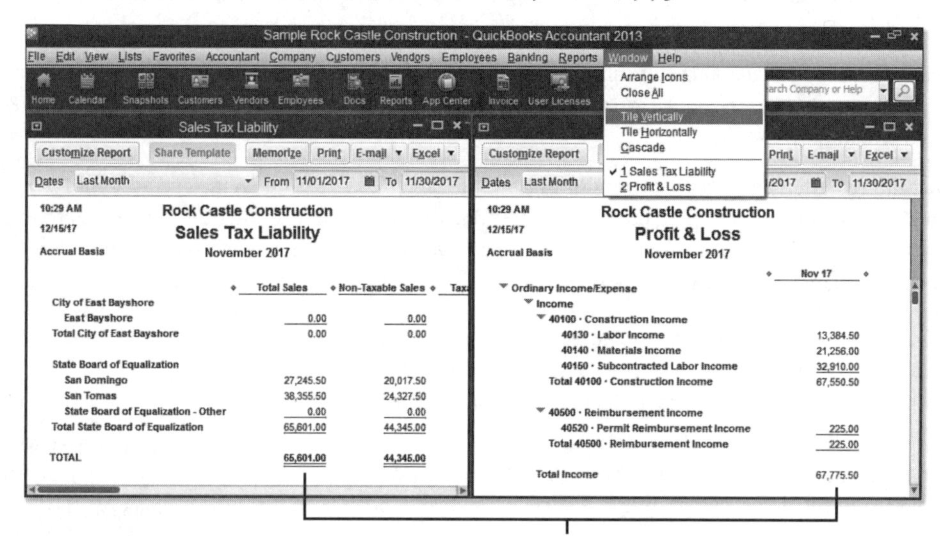

Figure 10.40
When comparing two reports; select **Window, Tile Vertically.**

3. Select **Reports, Sales, Sales by Item Summary** from the menu bar. In the Dates drop-down list, select **Last Month.** See Figure 10.41.
4. Click Customize Report and remove the checkmarks for COGS, Ave. COGS, Gross Margin, and Gross Margin % because we do not need this information for our analysis. Click OK.
5. To make this report easier to read, you might consider clicking the Collapse button at the top right of the open report.
6. What exactly are you looking for? Because this report shows all items sold on customer sales forms during the same month being "reconciled," you are looking for items that do not map to ordinary income accounts. In Figure 10.42, the difference is easy to spot: The Retainage 1 item was used on sales transactions during the month. A review of the item record shows the account assigned is a Balance Sheet account (see Figure 10.42).

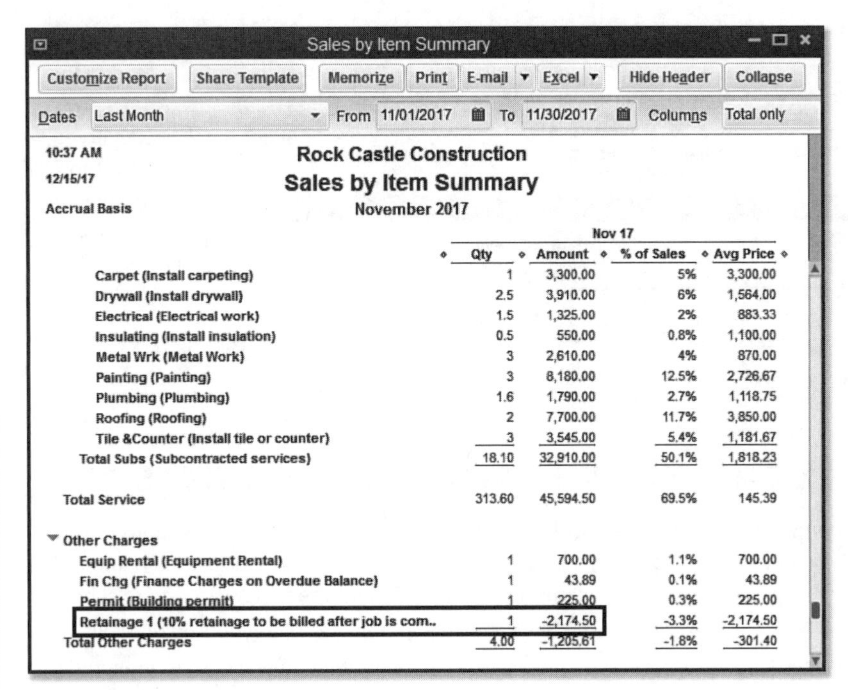

Sales by Item Summary

Customize Report | Share Template | Memorize | Print | E-mail | Excel | Hide Header | Collapse

Dates: Last Month | From 11/01/2017 | To 11/30/2017 | Columns: Total only

10:37 AM

12/15/17

Accrual Basis

Rock Castle Construction

Sales by Item Summary

November 2017

	Nov 17			
	Qty	Amount	% of Sales	Avg Price
Carpet (Install carpeting)	1	3,300.00	5%	3,300.00
Drywall (Install drywall)	2.5	3,910.00	6%	1,564.00
Electrical (Electrical work)	1.5	1,325.00	2%	883.33
Insulating (Install insulation)	0.5	550.00	0.8%	1,100.00
Metal Wrk (Metal Work)	3	2,610.00	4%	870.00
Painting (Painting)	3	8,180.00	12.5%	2,726.67
Plumbing (Plumbing)	1.6	1,790.00	2.7%	1,118.75
Roofing (Roofing)	2	7,700.00	11.7%	3,850.00
Tile &Counter (Install tile or counter)	3	3,545.00	5.4%	1,181.67
Total Subs (Subcontracted services)	18.10	32,910.00	50.1%	1,818.23
Total Service	313.60	45,594.50	69.5%	145.39
Other Charges				
Equip Rental (Equipment Rental)	1	700.00	1.1%	700.00
Fin Chg (Finance Charges on Overdue Balance)	1	43.89	0.1%	43.89
Permit (Building permit)	1	225.00	0.3%	225.00
Retainage 1 (10% retainage to be billed after job is com..	1	-2,174.50	-3.3%	-2,174.50
Total Other Charges	4.00	-1,205.61	-1.8%	-301.40

Figure 10.41
Report differences might arise when items with non-income accounts assigned are included on sales transactions.

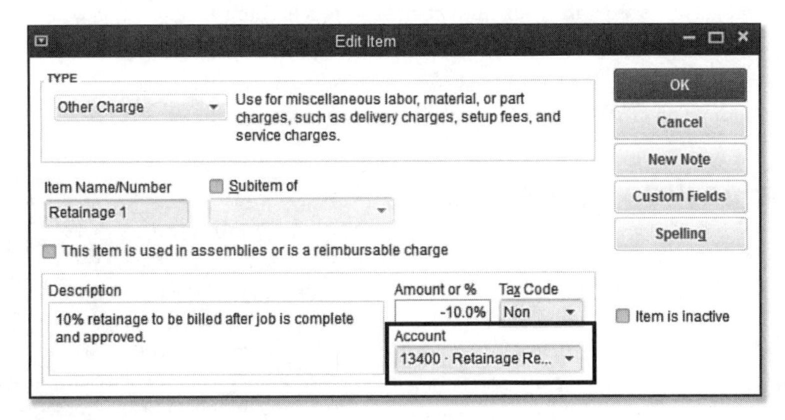

Figure 10.42
When reviewing differences, review the account assigned to items sold during the period.

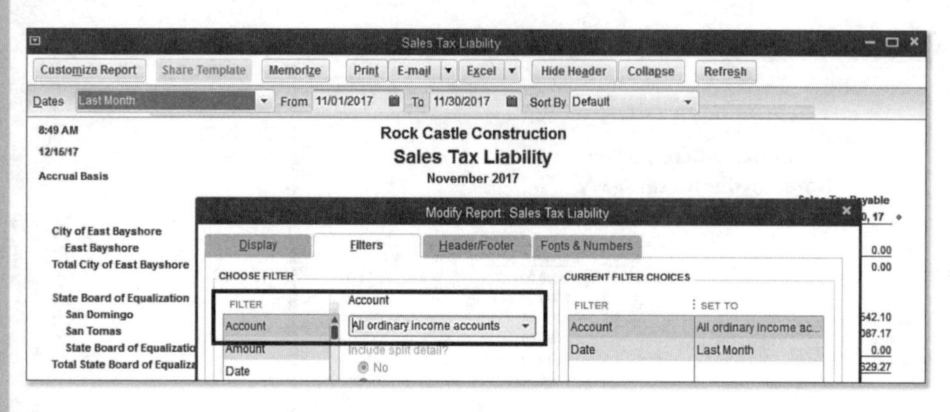

Figure 10.43 Modify the Sales Tax Liability report to troubleshoot discrepancies.

Correcting Undeposited Funds Account Errors

Did you make it through the review of each of the referenced reports in the earlier sections of this chapter? You don't want to jump into fixing transactions that affect accounts receivable without due diligence in researching what the correct balance should be. Without the review and troubleshooting time, you might hastily delete, void, or modify a transaction only to compound the problem.

This section details specific steps for correcting the errors you might find. It is important to first discover why the error was made and then fix it so you can avoid the same error on future transactions.

Reviewing the Balance in the Undeposited Funds Account

Before you can begin to agree or disagree with your Undeposited Funds account balance, it is best to review your QuickBooks data, concentrating on certain reports that will help you simplify the review process.

This section provides instructions on creating specific reports you can use for this task.

Creating an Undeposited Funds Detail Report

The first report I create for a client is a custom report titled "Undeposited Funds Detail." This is not a prebuilt report in QuickBooks, but it is easy to create, as you will see.

This report is fundamental because you cannot troubleshoot a total balance for the undeposited funds you see on a balance sheet report without knowing the detail behind the numbers. If you print the register for the account, too much data will display, making it difficult to identify what is not deposited.

How do transactions get to this account? When you select the Undeposited Funds account as the deposit-to account (or you set

 **caution**

Before you troubleshoot your Undeposited Funds Detail, reconcile your bank account. Identify what transactions have cleared your bank and which transactions have been recorded in QuickBooks but did not clear your bank in a timely manner.

For more information, see "Reconciling the Bank or Credit Card Account," p. 512.

the preference to have QuickBooks automatically do this), QuickBooks increases the balance in the Undeposited Funds account. Then, when you complete a make deposit, QuickBooks reduces the Undeposited Funds account balance, and behind the scenes, it marks the original increase and the new decrease as cleared. Table 10.1 shows the relationship of these transactions to your accounting.

Table 10.1 Transaction Effect on Undeposited Funds Account

Transaction Type	Accounts Receivable	Undeposited Funds	Bank Account
Customer Receive Payments with Undeposited Funds Account Selected as the "Deposit to" Account	Decreases (credit)	Increases (debit)	No effect
Make Deposits	No effect	Decreases (credit)	Increases (debit)

Before we dig too deeply, let's see if you agree with the detail of the Undeposited Funds balance in your QuickBooks data. You also might want to memorize this report for the convenience of reviewing the detail often, avoiding any data entry errors this section might help you uncover.

For the date range field, type the letter **a** to make the date range default to All.

To create this Undeposited Funds Detail report, follow these easy steps:

1. From the menu bar select **Reports**, **Custom Reports**, **Transaction Detail**. The Modify Report dialog box opens.
2. Display the date range as All.
3. For Total By, from the bottom of the list, select **Payment Method**.
4. For Columns, select those you want to view on the report.
5. Click the Filters tab. In the Choose Filter box, select **Account**, and choose the account named **Undeposited Funds** from the drop-down list.
6. Also from the Filters tab, select **Cleared** and click the No button.
7. Click the Header/Footer tab. Type **Undeposited Funds Detail** as the report title. Click OK.

caution

The modified custom report you named Undeposited Funds Detail will always show the present state of the transaction, which means when a payment is received and is included on a Make Deposits transaction, the report for a prior date will no longer show that item as undeposited. Behind the scenes, QuickBooks marks the transaction as "cleared" as of the transaction date; therefore, you cannot get a historical snapshot with this report.

This report provides the details of the amounts that are included in the Undeposited Funds account balance. You might want to include preparing this report at the end of each month for your records. Following are other reports you might also find useful when reviewing the balance in your Undeposited Funds account.

Creating a General Ledger Report of the Undeposited Funds Account

You can review a General Ledger report of the Undeposited Funds account balance that will agree with the ending balance on your Balance Sheet report, but without quite a bit of manual work, you cannot identify each individual transaction that makes up the Undeposited Funds account for a specific prior period. Why? Because each time you deposit a receive payment, QuickBooks marks the original dated line item as cleared. This is why we first create a custom report to see if the current (today's date) detail is correct.

If you review your balances monthly, you need to print out the Undeposited Funds Detail report you created earlier in this chapter, on the last day of your accounting month. Save this report in your paper file for future reference because you cannot go back to a historical date and get the same information.

If you take credit cards as payments from your customers, I recommend that you do not complete the "Make Deposits" task until you view a bank statement showing the funds deposited into your bank account. This does not mean waiting a month for the statement to arrive, because most financial institutions now offer online account access to your account statements.

For those clients, particularly retail businesses, where there is often a large volume of customer receipts in any day, I recommend reviewing the modified report as part of the month, quarter, or year-end process. Notice whether any old dated transactions are on the list. If you find none, you can assume the Balance Sheet balance in Undeposited Funds as of the prior period date is probably correct.

To generate a General Ledger report, follow these steps:

1. From the menu bar select **Reports**, **Accountant & Taxes**, **General Ledger**.
2. Select **Customize Report** from the report screen.
3. In the Modify dialog box that opens, enter an appropriate Report Date Range.
4. From the Columns box, select the columns you want to see. (You might want to include Clr for seeing the cleared status of transactions.)
5. Click the Advanced button and from the Include box select **In Use**. This will streamline the data that results on the report.
6. Click the Filters tab, choose to filter for Account, and select the **Undeposited Funds** account from the drop-down list.
7. Click OK.

You can use this General Ledger report to see details for the Undeposited Funds account and to verify if the running balance in this report agrees with your Balance Sheet report. However, you still cannot use this report to identify which Receive Payments transaction was not deposited as of the report date because QuickBooks does not capture the information with an "as of" date.

Removing Old Dated Payments in the Undeposited Funds Account

Did your review of the data uncover old dated payment transactions still in the Undeposited Funds account? If yes, use the following method to remove these payments without editing or modifying each transaction.

This method of correcting makes the following assumptions:

- Your bank account is reconciled before making these changes.
- You have reviewed your Accounts Receivable Aging reports, and if necessary have made corrections.
- You have identified which payment amounts are still showing in the Undeposited Funds account, and these are the same amounts that have already been deposited to your bank register by some other method.
- You have identified the specific chart of accounts (typically income accounts) to which the deposits were originally incorrectly recorded.

The date you assign the Make Deposits transaction is the date the impact will be recorded in your financials. You have several important considerations to take into account when selecting the appropriate date:

- Are the corrections for a prior year?
- Has the tax return been prepared using current financial information from QuickBooks for that prior period?
- Has another adjustment to the books been done to correct the issue?

If you answered yes to any of these, you should contact your accountant and ask advice about the date this transaction should have.

This method enables you to remove the unwanted balance in your Undeposited Funds account with just a few keystrokes. To remove old payments in the Undeposited Funds account, follow these steps:

1. If the funds that remain in your Undeposited Funds account are from more than one year ago, you first should identify the total amount that was incorrectly deposited for each year. See the sidebar "Creating a Payment Transaction List Detail Report" in this chapter. Filter the report for the specific date range.
2. Now start the process of removing these identified Undeposited Funds items by selecting **Banking**, **Make Deposits** from the menu bar. The Payments to Deposits dialog displays. From the Sort Payments By drop-down list, select **Date**. See Figure 10.44.
3. In the Payments to Deposit dialog box, select all the payments for deposit with dates in the date range you are correcting by placing a checkmark next to the payment items. Click OK.

   The Make Deposits dialog box opens with each of the previously selected payments included on a new make deposit.
4. On the next available line, enter the account to which the incorrect deposits were originally recorded. In this example, you discovered that the Construction Income account was overstated by the incorrectly recorded deposits. The effect of this new transaction is to decrease (debit) the Construction Income account and decrease (credit) the Undeposited Funds account without any effect on the checking account, as shown in Figure 10.45.
5. Make sure to mark as cleared this net -0- deposit in your next bank reconciliation.

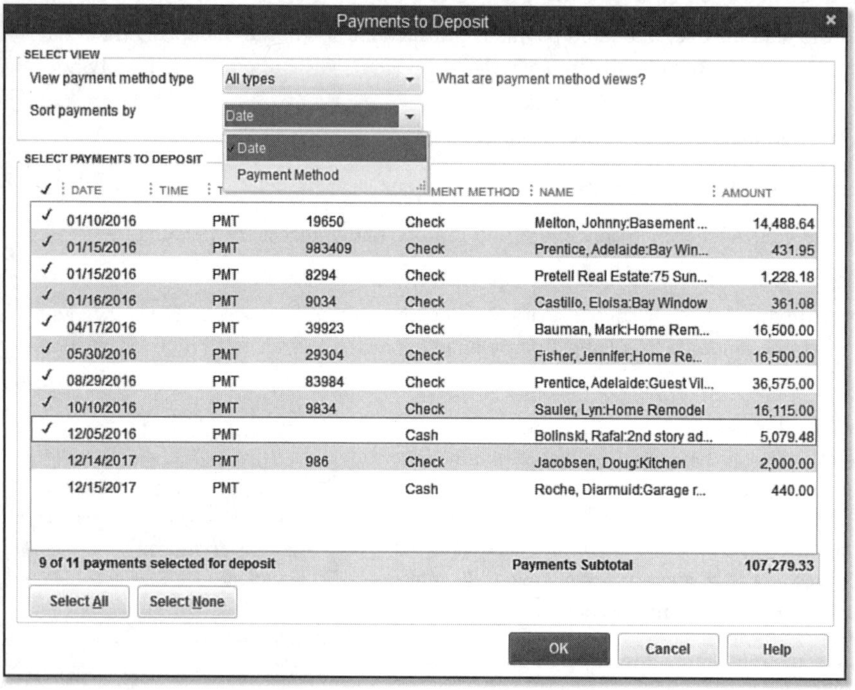

Payments to Deposit

SELECT VIEW

View payment method type: All types — What are payment method views?

Sort payments by: Date (Date / Payment Method)

SELECT PAYMENTS TO DEPOSIT

✓	DATE	TIME	TYPE	NO.	PAYMENT METHOD	NAME	AMOUNT
✓	01/10/2016		PMT	19650	Check	Melton, Johnny:Basement ...	14,488.64
✓	01/15/2016		PMT	983409	Check	Prentice, Adelaide:Bay Win...	431.95
✓	01/15/2016		PMT	8294	Check	Pretell Real Estate:75 Sun...	1,228.18
✓	01/16/2016		PMT	9034	Check	Castillo, Eloisa:Bay Window	361.08
✓	04/17/2016		PMT	39923	Check	Bauman, Mark:Home Rem...	16,500.00
✓	05/30/2016		PMT	29304	Check	Fisher, Jennifer:Home Re...	16,500.00
✓	08/29/2016		PMT	83984	Check	Prentice, Adelaide:Guest Vil...	36,575.00
✓	10/10/2016		PMT	9834	Check	Sauler, Lyn:Home Remodel	16,115.00
✓	12/05/2016		PMT		Cash	Bolinski, Rafal:2nd story ad...	5,079.48
	12/14/2017		PMT	986	Check	Jacobsen, Doug:Kitchen	2,000.00
	12/15/2017		PMT		Cash	Roche, Diarmuid:Garage r...	440.00

9 of 11 payments selected for deposit — Payments Subtotal 107,279.33

Select All | Select None | OK | Cancel | Help

Figure 10.44 The older payments in Undeposited Funds were posted to the cash account by some other method.

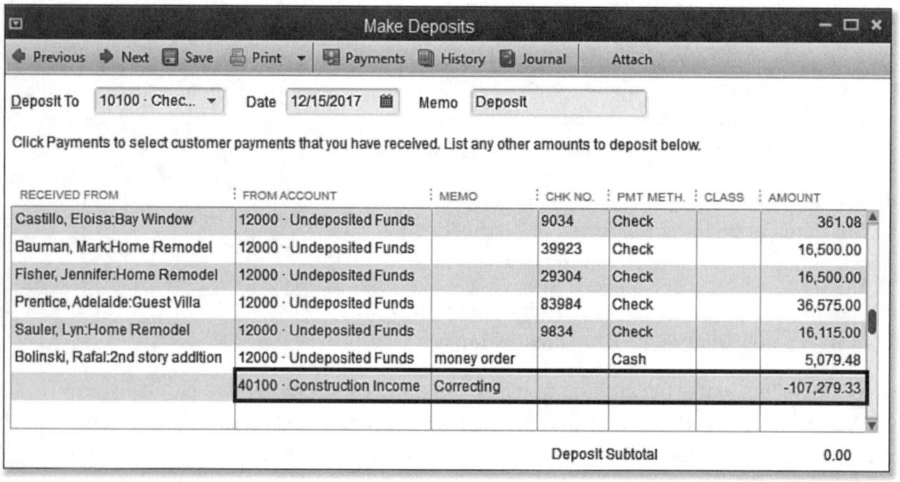

Make Deposits

Previous | Next | Save | Print | Payments | History | Journal | Attach

Deposit To: 10100 · Chec... Date: 12/15/2017 Memo: Deposit

Click Payments to select customer payments that you have received. List any other amounts to deposit below.

RECEIVED FROM	FROM ACCOUNT	MEMO	CHK NO.	PMT METH.	CLASS	AMOUNT
Castillo, Eloisa:Bay Window	12000 · Undeposited Funds		9034	Check		361.08
Bauman, Mark:Home Remodel	12000 · Undeposited Funds		39923	Check		16,500.00
Fisher, Jennifer:Home Remodel	12000 · Undeposited Funds		29304	Check		16,500.00
Prentice, Adelaide:Guest Villa	12000 · Undeposited Funds		83984	Check		36,575.00
Sauler, Lyn:Home Remodel	12000 · Undeposited Funds		9834	Check		16,115.00
Bolinski, Rafal:2nd story addition	12000 · Undeposited Funds	money order		Cash		5,079.48
	40100 · Construction Income	Correcting				-107,279.33

Deposit Subtotal 0.00

Figure 10.45 Enter a line with a negative amount recorded to the account that was previously overstated.

You should now be able to review the Undeposited Funds Detail report and agree that the items listed on this report as of today's date are those you have not yet physically taken to your bank to be deposited or the credit card vendors have not yet credited to your bank.

Unique Customer Transactions

This chapter provides ways you can review and troubleshoot your data, and instructions on how to fix many of the common Accounts Receivable errors. This section of the chapter shares some ways to handle unique transactions—the type of transaction you might come across but are not sure how to enter.

Recording Your Accountant's Year-End Adjusting Journal Entry to Accounts Receivable

Often, adjustments at tax time might include adjustments to your Accounts Receivable account. This transaction is typically created by your accountant using a general journal transaction. What can make the entry more difficult for you is when no customer(s) are identified with the adjustment.

You can request a breakdown by customer of the adjustments made to the Accounts Receivable account. If that is not available, and you need to enter the adjustment, you might want to consider using the following method:

1. From the Customer Center, enter a fictitious customer name—something such as **Accountant YE Adj**.
2. Use this customer to apply the line item to in the make journal entry. Remember that this is a temporary fix, and the balance for the fictitious customer will display on your Open Invoices report.

Later, when you are able to collect from the actual customer(s) who make up the adjustment, you can enter a reversing entry to the fictitious customer and new entries to the correct customers.

When a Customer Is Also a Vendor

Often, I am asked how to handle a transaction when you are selling your company's product or service, but instead of getting paid, you are trading it for the products or services of your customer.

To keep track of the both the revenue and costs in this bartering arrangement, follow these steps:

1. From the menu bar select **Lists**, **Chart of Accounts** to open the Chart of Accounts dialog box.
2. Click the Account button. Select **New** and create an account named Barter Account as a bank account type following the instructions on the screen. Click Save & Close.
3. Create a new customer record for your vendor. (Or a new vendor record for your customer) using instructions found in previous chapters and using the naming tip provided in the caution in this section. The following instructions assume that you are selling your product or services to your vendor in a bartering agreement.

caution

You can add new customers by selecting the Customer Center from the QuickBooks Home page.

However, QuickBooks does not let you use the same name on the customer list as the vendor list. A little trick can help with this; when naming the new "fictitious" customer, enter a "- C" after the name. This naming convention will not display on invoices, but when selecting this name from lists, it will bring to your attention that you are using the "customer" list item.

4. From the menu bar select **Customers**, **Create Invoices**. Select the new customer you created (your vendor that was added to the customer list). Enter the information as if you were selling your products or services to this customer. Click Save & Close.

5. From the menu bar select **Customers**, **Receive Payments**. Select the new customer you created and record the amount of the payment, placing a checkmark next to the appropriate "fictitious" invoice.

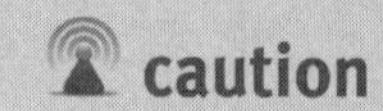

If your default preference is set to assign the specific bank account when you receive the payment, you should select the **Barter Account** for this type of transaction.

6. From the menu bar select **Banking**, **Make Deposits** to open the Payments to Deposit dialog box. Place a checkmark next to the fictitious transaction, and click OK to advance to the Make Deposits dialog box.

7. In the Make Deposits dialog box, select the **Barter Account** as the Deposit To account and select the date you want this transaction recorded. Click Save & Close when done. See Figure 10.46.

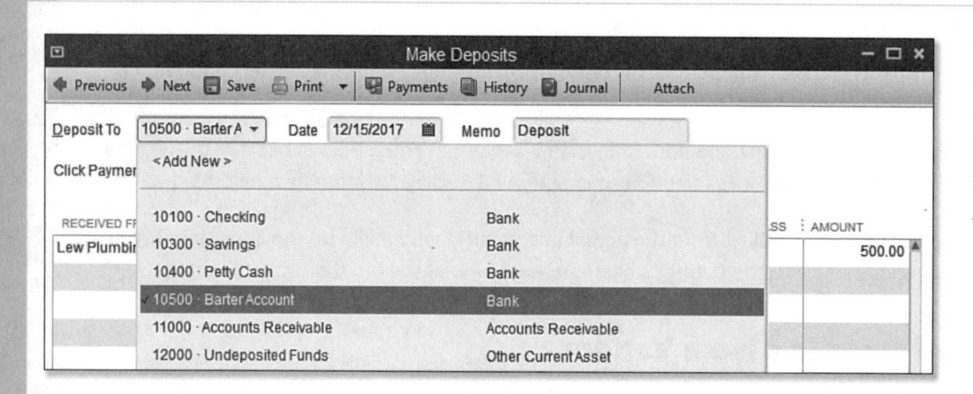

Figure 10.46 Deposit the "fictitious" payment into the Barter Account.

You have recorded the "potential" revenue side as well as the "fictitious" payment of the invoice of the barter agreement. Now you need to record the expense side of the transaction.

I recommend that the transactions going in and out of the barter account are equal in value; if not, you will need to make an adjustment in the register. Select **Banking**, **User Register** from the menu bar. Select the **Barter Account** and increase or decrease the amount to an income or expense account as determined by the amount left in the account.

To continue with the example presented previously, let's record the "fictitious" payment to our vendor whom we are bartering with. When working with your own data, you might instead be bartering with your customer:

1. Enter your expense transaction as you normally would, as if you were going to pay your vendor for the products or services being purchased.

2. If you are using a write check transaction, select the **Barter Account** as the checking account. If you are using the enter bill transaction, complete the bill entry as you normally would.

3. For the check or reference number, use any number or alphanumeric characters you want.
4. For the payee, select your vendor whom you are bartering with. This should be the same vendor that you entered the write check or enter bill transaction for in step 2.
5. Record to the normal expense account an amount as if you were purchasing the goods or services with a check.
6. Click Save & Close. If paying by check, the process is complete. If you recorded a vendor bill, continue with the following steps.
7. To pay the bill, select **Vendors**, **Pay Bills** from the menu bar. Optionally filter the Pay Bills dialog box with the vendor's name.
8. Place a checkmark next to the appropriate bill that has been paid by providing the vendor with your product or services.
9. In the Payment Method box, select the choice to assign check number because we don't expect to print a check to give to the vendor.
10. In the Payment Account box, select the newly created Barter Account as the payment account.
11. Click **Pay Selected Bills** to open the Assign Check Numbers dialog box. Assign a fictitious check number of your choosing. You can even put the term "Barter" in for the check number. Click OK and QuickBooks displays a payment summary. Click Done.

When this process is finished, your Barter Account should have a zero balance (see Figure 10.47) as indicated earlier in this section. You might even want to perform a bank reconciliation of the Barter Account to clear both equal sides of the transaction.

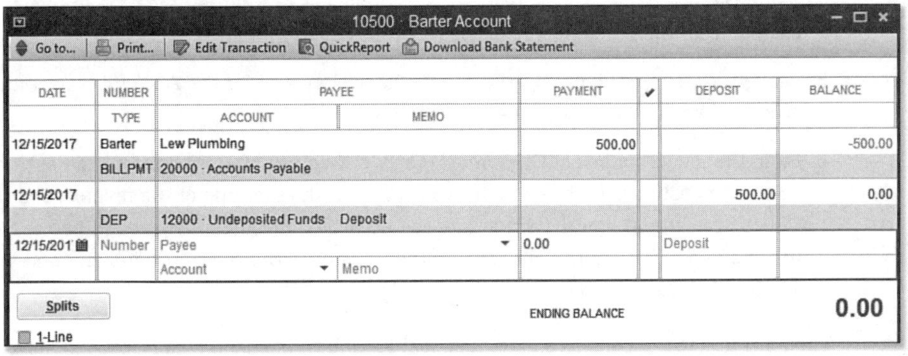

Figure 10.47 The Barter Account will have a net -o- balance when all transactions are recorded properly.

10500 · Barter Account

Go to... | Print... | Edit Transaction | QuickReport | Download Bank Statement

DATE	NUMBER / TYPE	PAYEE / ACCOUNT	MEMO	PAYMENT	✔	DEPOSIT	BALANCE
12/15/2017	Barter	Lew Plumbing		500.00			-500.00
	BILLPMT	20000 · Accounts Payable					
12/15/2017						500.00	0.00
	DEP	12000 · Undeposited Funds	Deposit				
12/15/2017	Number	Payee		0.00		Deposit	
		Account	Memo				

Splits — ENDING BALANCE 0.00

1-Line

Recording a Customer's Bounced Check

If you have ever had a customer's payment check bounce, you know how important correct accounting is. When a check is bounced, often your banking institution automatically debits your bank balance and might also charge an extra service fee.

So just how do you record these transactions and also increase the balance your customer now owes you? Follow these steps:

1. To create a bounced check item, select **Lists, Item List** from the menu bar. Click the Item button and select **New**. If necessary, click OK to dismiss the New Feature message.
2. The New Item dialog box displays. Select an **Other Charge** item type. In both the Number/Name field and Description field, type **Bounced Check**.
3. Leave the Amount field blank; assign Non as the Tax Code. For the Account, select the bank account that was deducted for the returned check (see Figure 10.48).

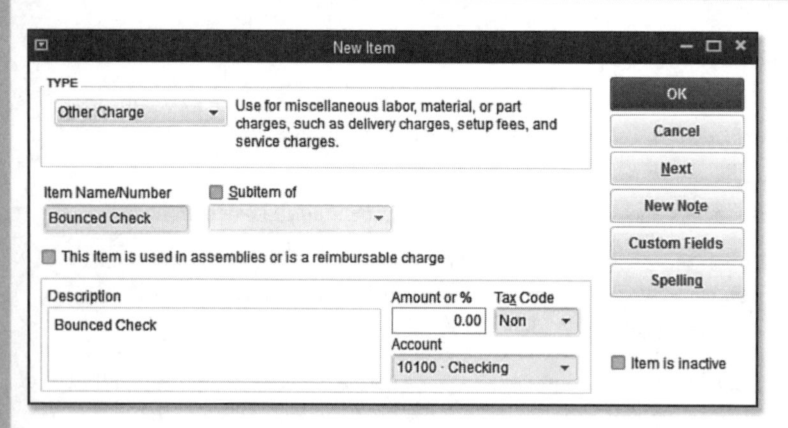

Figure 10.48
This item will be used to record the deduction to your bank account for the bounced check amount.

4. Using the preceding steps, create an additional Other Charge item type to be used to invoice the customer for the bank fee you incurred. Name the item Bad Chk Chg.
5. Leave the Amount blank, set the Tax Code as Non, and for the Account, select an income account, such as **Returned Check Charges**.
6. From the menu bar select **Customers, Create Invoices**, and in the transaction that displays, select the customer with the bounced check. On the first line of the invoice, use the Bounced Check item and assign the amount of the bounced check. On the second line of the invoice, use the Bad Chk Chg item and assign the amount of the fee your bank charged you (see Figure 10.49). Click Save & Close.

The impact is to increase Accounts Receivable (debit), increase Income for the bank fee (credit), and decrease your bank account (credit). The reduction in the bank account is to record the fact that the bank deducted the amount from your account.

When you reconcile your bank account, be sure to enter the service fee charged.

Although this method provides a process to charge your customer again for the returned check as well as the bank fee, it does have one side effect you might want to consider. When you create a Balance Sheet on a cash basis, you might see this amount in Accounts Receivable.

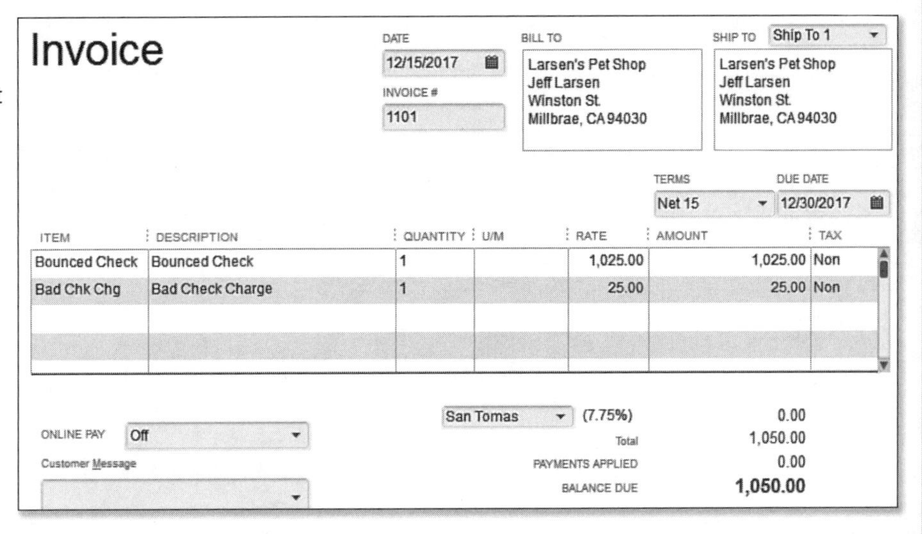

Figure 10.49 Create an invoice to collect the NSF funds and recover the bank fee from the customer.

Tracking Customer Deposits in QuickBooks

Do you require your customers to pay a deposit in advance of the product shipping or the service being provided? You might want to track these in one of two ways:

- As a credit to Accounts Receivable for the specific customer
- As a credit to an Other Current Liability account

You might want to ask your company accountant which method is preferred. Using the first method is often easier and takes fewer steps. The second method of using a current liability account reports the prepayment in the proper category on the business's balance sheet.

If you are choosing the first method listed previously, you would create a receive payment when your customer pays and not assign the payment to an invoice. In effect, this debits (increases) your Undeposited Funds account or bank account and credits (reduces) accounts receivable.

If you choose to use the second method, follow these steps:

1. If needed, start the process to create a Customer Deposits account by selecting **Lists**, **Chart of Accounts** from the menu bar.
2. Click the Account button at the bottom of the screen and select **New**.
3. In the Add New Account dialog box that opens, from the Other Account Types drop-down list, select the **Other Current Liability** type account and follow the remaining steps on the screen.
4. Create an item to be used on invoices for this prepayment. From the menu bar, select **Lists**, **Item Lists**.
5. Click the Item button on the bottom of the list and select **New**.
6. In the New Item type drop-down list, select **Other Charge**.

7. In the Item Name/Number field, type a name such as **Customer Deposits**. Enter an optional description and select the **Customer Deposits** other current liability account from the Account drop-down list.

8. Prepare your invoice to the customer for the amount of the prepayment you are requiring. When the customer pays, record the Receive Payments transaction.

9. When the project is completed and you are ready to recognize the revenue associated with the sale, create your invoice using the item(s) that were sold to the customer. On the next available line of your invoice, use the Customer Deposit item, only this time enter a negative amount. See Figure 10.50.

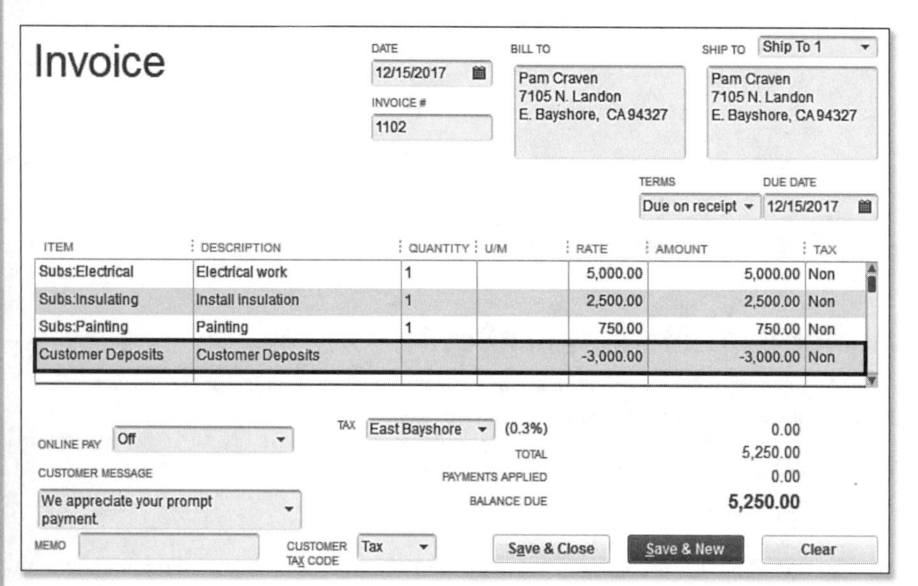

Figure 10.50 Proper accounting for customer deposits paid on the final invoice when you track the original payment as a liability.

QuickBooks records the revenue in the period the sale was complete, and the final invoice will be reduced by the amount of the deposit previously paid.

Using the method described here does have a trade-off. If you are a cash basis taxpayer, you would not expect to see a balance in your Accounts Receivable account when the Balance Sheet report is prepared on a cash basis. However, when you use this method, you will see an Accounts Receivable balance on a cash basis Balance Sheet report. One of the causes of this is that QuickBooks reports an Accounts Receivable balance on a cash basis Balance Sheet report when items are used that map to other Balance Sheet accounts.

Unique Sales Tax Transactions

Over the years, I have come across some unique sales tax transaction tracking needs. This section addresses several that you might find useful if your state has similar guidelines.

As always, because you are acting as the agent for the state in collecting sales tax from your customers, you should take the time to research the sales tax regulations for each state where you do business.

The state you sell in might require you to collect and track multiple sales tax rates depending on where the customer is located. If you have a customer with different tax rate locations, you need to create a customer for each tax location if you want QuickBooks to automatically calculate the correct tax amount, because QuickBooks tracks the sales tax rate by customer and not by job.

When Your State Imposes a Maximum Sales Tax

I have encountered having to track a state-imposed maximum sales tax a few times. If your state imposes a maximum sales tax for a certain type of sale, I recommend the following method:

1. From the menu bar select **Lists**, **Item List**. The New Item dialog box displays.
2. If you do not have a subtotal item on your list, select **Subtotal** from the Type drop-down list.
3. To create the invoice to your customer, select **Customers**, **Create Invoices** from the menu bar.
4. Enter the taxable items on the invoice, making sure the Tax column has "Tax" listed.
5. Enter a subtotal item—you might even want to type in the description that this amount is subject to sales tax.
6. Enter the next sale item that is normally taxed. If you have met a threshold defined by your state, select **Non** in the Tax column. See Figure 10.51

QuickBooks now records the total sales (in this example) of $6,000.00, but it shows only $5,000 in the Taxable Sales column of the Sales Tax Liability report, as shown in Figure 10.52.

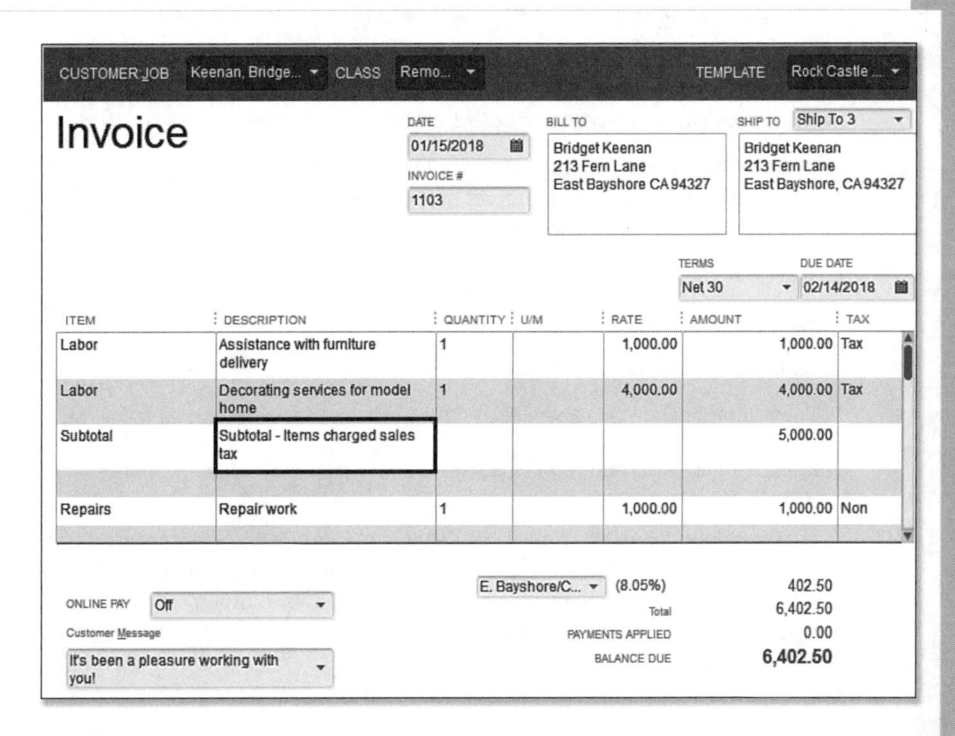

Figure 10.51 Adding a subtotal and adjusting the Tax column helps when your state has a threshold for sales tax charges on a single invoice.

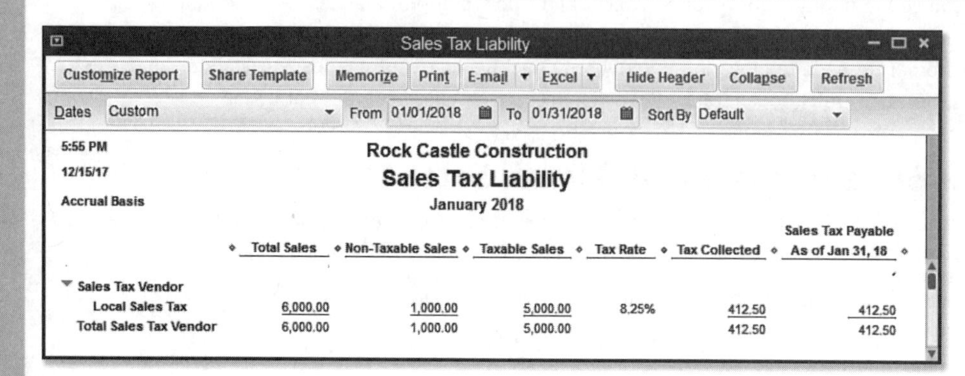

Figure 10.52 QuickBooks properly separates the taxable revenue amount from the nontaxable sale amount.

Multiple Sales Tax Rates on One Invoice

In particular, if your business sells retail items, liquor, and food all on one sales form, chances are each item type is subject to a unique sales tax rate. Follow these steps for creating the subtotal item and 0% sales tax item. Assign this newly created 0% sales tax item to your customer's record on the sales tax settings tab.

Next, create your customer's invoice as detailed in the previous section, following these additional steps:

1. Create these items:
   - **Subtotal Item**—Using the steps outlined in the previous section.
   - **Sales Tax Item**—Use the name See Above and the same, See Above, for the description. Tax Rate will be 0.0%. Tax Agency should be your most common Tax Agency vendor.
   - **Sales Tax Items**—Representing the tax jurisdictions you are required to collect and report on. Name them clearly so your customer can identify them.
2. Enter the line item(s) subject to one tax rate.
3. Enter a subtotal line.
4. Enter the appropriate sales tax item.
5. Enter additional invoice lines, each with a subtotal and appropriate sales tax items.

tip

If you would like more information on this, you can press the F1 key on your keyboard to open QuickBooks Help. Click the Search tab and on the top search bar, type **sales summaries**, and follow the link for more information on this topic.

QuickBooks calculates and reports on the correct amount of sales tax charged for the different item types being sold.

To further clarify this point, the example shown in Figure 10.53 does not track sales by customer, but just a retail summary for the day's sales. The example also shows how to charge multiple sales tax rates on a single invoice by placing a subtotal after each group of sales and then placing the correct sales tax rate after the subtotal.

Figure 10.53 Creating a Daily Sales Summary is a perfect choice for a retail establishment that does not track individual customer activity.

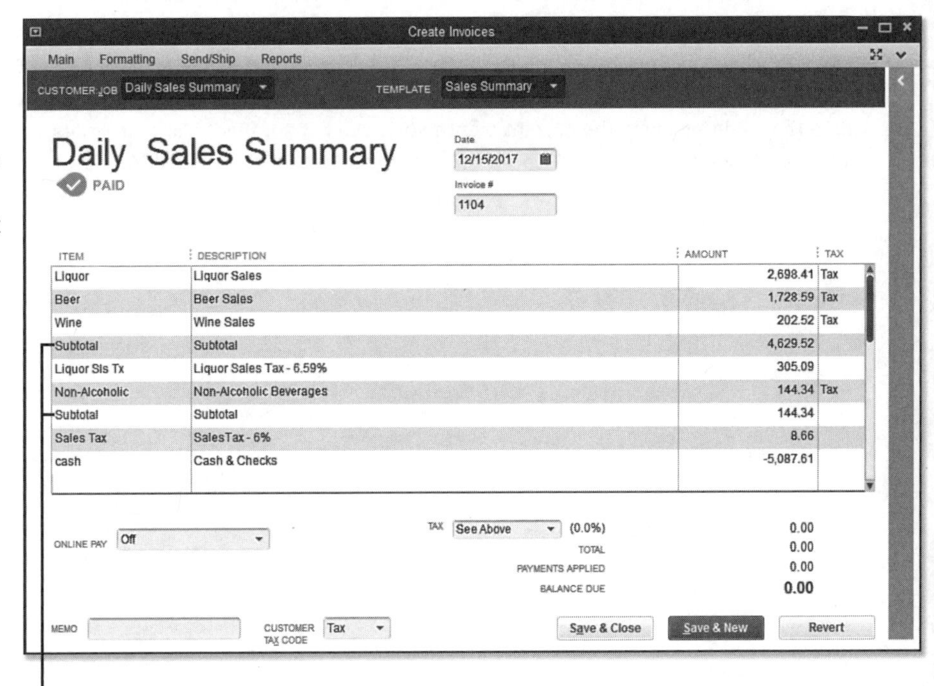

Add subtotals before using multiple sales tax rates on the same invoice

Issuing Credit Memos When Sales Tax Should Not Have Been Charged

Issuing customer credit memos is necessary for correct reporting when you file your sales tax on accrual basis (sales tax payment liability accrued as of the date of the customer invoice) and is not required when you report sales tax liability on cash basis (sales tax payment liability not accrued until the date of customer's payment). However, I still recommend having controls in place that limit the ability to modify an invoice from a prior month.

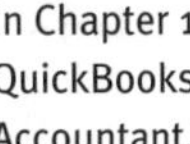

note

In Chapter 16, "Sharing QuickBooks Data with Your Accountant," I discuss setting a closing date for your data. I recommend this same control be placed in your file after preparing your monthly or quarterly sales tax returns for your state.

After you have filed your sales tax return with your state, you should not adjust any invoices or sales tax payments recorded on or before your file-through date. If you do, QuickBooks recalculates the taxable sales, nontaxable sales, and amount owed, and your return as filed with the state will no longer agree with your QuickBooks data.

Instead of adjusting a customer's invoice, consider using the QuickBooks customer credit memos/refund. For example, suppose you charged sales tax to a nontaxable customer by mistake. Let's also assume you have filed your accrual basis sales tax return for the month of that invoice, overstating taxable sales.

Creating a credit memo reduces taxable sales, increases nontaxable sales, and credits the customer's invoice for the sales tax amount, all within the current sales tax month.

Follow the same steps outlined in the section "Recording and Applying a Customer Credit Memo" in Chapter 9 for creating a credit memo from the original customer invoice. You want to be sure you date the credit memo in the current month you have not yet filed your state sales tax reports for. The credit memo will then reduce the sales tax you owe for the current period.

11

SETTING UP PAYROLL

When your business hires employees, one of the more important tasks you will have is making sure your QuickBooks data is set up correctly to handle this responsibility. This chapter details for you the proper way to set up your payroll. In Chapter 12, "Managing Payroll," you learn how to efficiently review your payroll data and handle some of those unique payroll transactions.

Getting Started

For the new business owner, here is a common definition of an employee: "a person in the service of another under any contract of hire, express or implied, oral or written. The employer also has the power or right to control and direct the employee in the material details of how the work is to be performed." If your company hires individuals who meet this criteria, your company is responsible for paying wages, collecting and paying certain federal and state payroll taxes, and filing quarterly and annual forms.

Your company becomes an agent of the federal and state governments because the company must collect certain payroll-related taxes and pay these on predetermined payment schedules.

Payroll Process Overview

QuickBooks is designed to help you set up and manage your company's payroll. Payroll tasks are easily completed using the Employee Center and Payroll Center. Scheduling your payrolls and related liability payments practically eliminates the chance of making errors.

The recommended payroll workflow detailed here, when combined with the frequent review of reports, can help you manage your company's payroll efficiently and accurately:

1. Sign up for an Intuit QuickBooks payroll subscription.
2. Set Payroll and Employee preferences for your company.
3. Complete (if your data is new) the Payroll Setup process or use the Run Payroll Checkup diagnostic tool included with your QuickBooks software.
4. Set up scheduled payrolls to pay your employees.
5. Pay your scheduled payroll liabilities.
6. Reconcile your bank account each month verifying that the paychecks distributed were cleared for the proper amounts.
7. Review and compare your business financials and payroll reports.
8. Prepare your quarterly and annual state and federal payroll forms directly in QuickBooks (depending on which payroll subscription you have purchased).

note

Are you already using QuickBooks for your payroll processing? Why not start with the QuickBooks Run Payroll Checkup on pg. 439.

When managing payroll in QuickBooks, you use these transactions:

- **Paycheck**—Record payment to an employee and automatically calculate all additions and deductions. You can identify these in your bank register as the transactions with a PAY CHK transaction type, as shown in Figure 11.1.

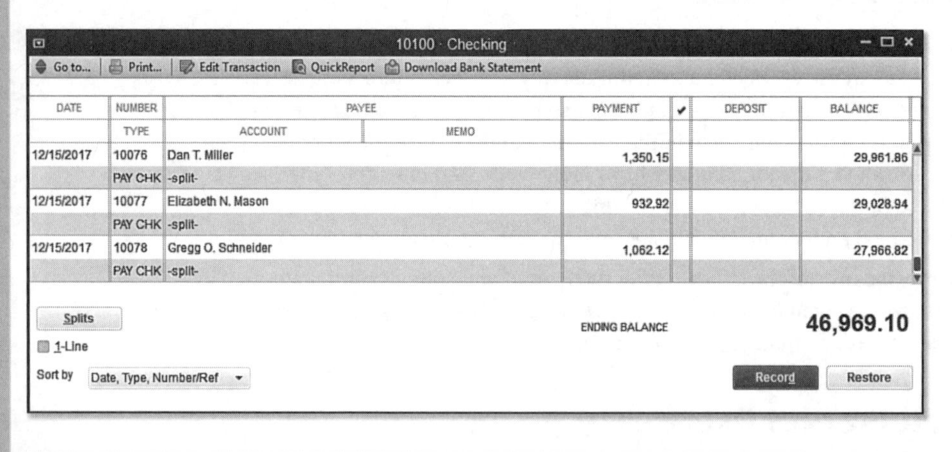

Figure 11.1 Properly created employee paychecks have PAY CHK as the transaction type.

- **Liability Adjustment**—Used to modify the payroll liability amounts computed from actual paychecks. You can identify these transactions in your bank register as transactions with a LIAB CHK transaction type.
- **Refund Deposit for Taxes and Liabilities**—Record any refund received from overpaying your payroll liabilities. You learn more about this transaction type in Chapter 12.

Each of these transactions is accessible from the Payroll Center or by selecting submenus from Employees on the menu bar.

When you use the proper payroll transactions, QuickBooks includes the amounts in preparing payments of payroll liabilities due or when preparing state and federal payroll reports in QuickBooks.

Selecting and Activating a Payroll Service Subscription

For QuickBooks to automatically calculate your payroll, you need to purchase a payroll service subscription from Intuit in addition to the purchase of your QuickBooks financial software.

QuickBooks financial software partnered with an Intuit-provided payroll service makes setting up payroll, collecting taxes, remitting timely payments of the collected taxes, and filing the required payroll reports trouble free.

tip

The payroll offerings are detailed here, or you can visit http://payroll.intuit.com/compare/compare-quickbooks-payroll.jsp for a graphical comparison.

Purchase your payroll service subscription at www.payroll.com, or click the Turn On Payroll icon on the Home page and select a plan that works for your company. You can choose from several payroll subscriptions that start at these levels:

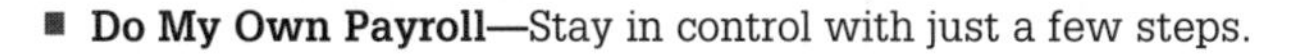

- **Do My Own Payroll**—Stay in control with just a few steps.
- **Intuit Provided Payroll Services**—Worry-free payroll; you enter the hours and Intuit does the rest.

note

You can enable manual payroll in QuickBooks without purchasing a subscription. With manual payroll, QuickBooks will not calculate the payroll taxes or prepare the payroll forms. I do not recommend this method unless you have only a few payroll checks that are always the same amounts each pay period.

From the menu bar, select **Help, QuickBooks Help.** In the search box, type **process payroll manually** and select the link with the same name. Read the information and follow the provided instructions.

As of the writing of this book, Intuit offers four payroll service options, one of which is sure to meet the needs of your company.

Preparing and Printing Paychecks Only

On the Home page, select **Turn On Payroll**. Choose the **I Want My Accountant...** option. This option is the Intuit Payroll Basic subscription and includes the following:

- The capability to enter employee hours and let QuickBooks automatically calculate payroll taxes, additions, and other deductions.
- The option to print checks; or, for a small per check fee, you can direct deposit the earnings into your employees' bank accounts.
- A variety of reports your accountant can use to complete payroll tax forms.

Preparing and Printing Paychecks and File Tax Forms

On the Home page, select **Turn On Payroll**. Choose the **I Want To Pay & File...** option. This service is the Intuit QuickBooks Payroll Enhanced subscription and includes the following:

- Capability to enter employee hours and let QuickBooks automatically calculate payroll taxes, additions, and other deductions.

- Option to print checks, or for a small per check fee, direct deposit the earnings into your employee's bank accounts.
- Automatic preparation of federal and most state tax forms for you to print or E-File.

If you are an accounting professional, you can select the **Intuit QuickBooks Payroll Enhanced for Accountant's** subscription. With this subscription you can do all the preceding tasks named plus the following:

- Create after-the-fact payroll
- Calculate net-to-gross paychecks
- Support up to 50 Federal Employer Identification Numbers (FEINs) with your paid payroll subscription
- Prepare Client Ready Payroll Reports (using Excel)

More details about the ProAdvisor program can be found by visiting the http://proadvisor.intuit.com website.

Allowing Intuit Payroll Experts to Prepare Your Payroll

On the Home page, select **Turn On Payroll**. Choose the **I Want Intuit Payroll Experts...** option. This is the Intuit Full Service Payroll Subscription and it includes:

- One-on-one guidance with Intuit payroll experts will set up or transfer all your employee data.
- Enter hours into QuickBooks to create paychecks. Intuit reviews the payroll for accuracy. All your taxes, additions, and deductions are calculated automatically.
- Get instant alerts when you enter hours significantly different from your usual hours.
- Print checks or offer direct deposit into your employees' bank accounts.

- Allow Intuit to process tax payments and forms for you, guaranteed to be accurate and on time.

note

If you currently use an outsourced payroll solution that does not integrate with QuickBooks, consider the Full Service payroll subscription. Entering payroll into QuickBooks can save time and improve accuracy.

Using Intuit Online Payroll

With an Intuit Online Payroll subscription you can prepare payroll anytime, anywhere with an Internet connection. With Intuit Online Payroll you can

- Enter employee hours online and make paycheck additions, and deductions automatically calculate.
- Receive email reminders when it's payday or for tax filing deadlines.
- Print paychecks or direct deposit employees' paychecks into their bank accounts.
- Process electronic payments and tax filings.
- Allow employees to view their pay stub information online.
- Process payroll using your mobile device.
- Prepare many detailed payroll reports.
- Process an unlimited number of payrolls each month.
- Import the transactions into QuickBooks (as a Write Checks transaction).

note

Are you an accounting professional? Would you like to share responsibility with your client for payroll processing?

With Intuit Online Payroll for Accounting Professionals subscription, your client can enter the payroll hours and leave the responsibility for tax filings to you. Visit www.accountant.intuit.com and select the Payroll & Payments tab to learn about each of the payroll offerings.

Updating Payroll Tax Tables

Your purchase of an Intuit payroll subscription includes periodic tax table updates. When the federal or state government makes changes to payroll taxes or forms, you will be notified that a new tax table is available.

To update your tax tables, make sure you are connected to the Internet and you have a current payroll subscription.

To update payroll tax tables, follow these steps:

1. From the menu bar select, **Employees**, **Payroll Center**. Your payroll subscription status is detailed to the left. See Figure 11.2.

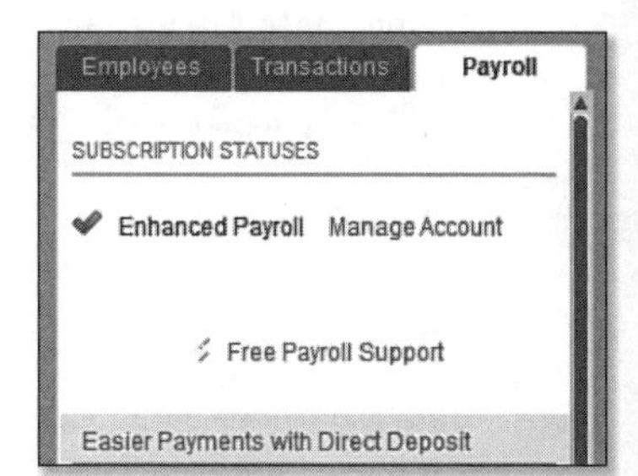

Figure 11.2
Check the status and manage your payroll subscription from the Payroll Center.

2. From the menu bar select **Employees**, **Get Payroll Updates**.
3. (Optional) Click the Payroll Update Info button for details about the currently installed tax table version.
4. (Optional) Click the Account Info button. You will need to sign into your account to view the QuickBooks Payroll Account Maintenance information about your subscription, including type of service, payroll company FEIN information, billing details, and direct deposit details. Click the X in the top-right corner to close the QuickBooks Payroll Account Maintenance dialog.
5. Select the option to download only changes and additions to the installed payroll files or download the entire payroll update. Click the Update button.
6. Click OK to close the Payroll Update message that tells you a new tax table or updates were installed. Click Troubleshooting Payroll Updates if the update does not install successfully.
7. QuickBooks opens the Payroll Update News dialog box. Click through the tabs of information to learn more about changes made with the installed update. Press the Esc key on your keyboard to close.
8. From the menu bar select **Employees**, **Payroll Center**.
9. On the left side of the Payroll Center, view information about your payroll subscription status.

tip

Because payroll requirements are changing all the time, make sure you have an accounting professional who can review your payroll setup or who can file the returns for you.

Employer Resources

Getting started with payroll can seem like a daunting task. This section discusses the many resources that can help you successfully get started with payroll.

Classifying Workers as Employees

Your business might hire employees and independent contractors (discussed in Chapter 7, "Setting Up Vendors"). Use these IRS guidelines when classifying a worker as an employee:

- **Behavioral**—Does the company control or have the right to control what the worker does and how the worker does his or her job?
- **Financial**—Are the business aspects of the worker's job controlled by the payer? (These include things like how the worker is paid, whether expenses are reimbursed, and whether the business owner provides tools and supplies.)
- **Type of Relationship**—Are there written contracts or employee-type benefits (pension plan, insurance, vacation pay, and so on)? Will the relationship continue, and is the work performed a key aspect of the business?

The IRS provides additional comments on this topic on its website, www.irs.gov. Type **contractor or employee** into the help search box and click the links provided for more details.

Federal and State Required Identification

Your business will likely have identification numbers assigned by federal, state, and local governments. The identification numbers detailed here represent the basic identification numbers you will need to properly report and pay payroll liabilities.

The reporting regulations for federal and state governments can be time consuming to learn about. Hiring legal and accounting professionals to guide you through the process can save you time and allow you to concentrate on building your business.

As mentioned earlier, your company becomes an agent of the state and federal government when it collects from employees certain taxes that are required to be reported and paid to the respective legal entity. Your company needs the following identification numbers for properly reporting and remitting your payroll taxes:

- **Federal Employer Identification Number**—Commonly referred to as FEIN. This number is obtained from the Internal Revenue Service. Visit www.irs.gov for instructions.
- **State Withholding Tax ID**—Issued by the states you do business in and used to file and pay state income tax withheld from your employees' paychecks. Some jurisdictions might also require IDs by city, county, or both. Call your state tax department or search your state's website for more details.
- **State Unemployment ID**—Issued by the states you do business in and used to pay and file state unemployment reports. Call your state tax department or search your state's website for more details.
- **Other identification numbers**—These may be required by the state, county, or city jurisdictions you do business in.

You might process your first payrolls before you have your assigned identification numbers. Check with your state taxing authority for instructions on paying these liabilities while you wait for your proper identification number to be assigned.

IRS and Other Forms

Your business is required to have on file for each employee a Form W-4: Employee's Withholding Allowance Certificate. You can access this form and other useful forms for your business in the Your Taxes section of the http://payroll.intuit.com/support/forms website. If the forms provided at this site are not the most current, you can also go to www.irs.gov.

State Reporting

Each state that you have employees working in will have specific filing requirements. You are even required to report new hires and in some states report independent contractors. Your state might also require city and county reporting. You can access information from each state's website, or Intuit provides useful information on the following websites:

- http://payroll.intuit.com/support/compliance
- http://payroll.intuit.com/support/PTS/statelocaltax.jsp

There are many other requirements of the business owner when paying employees, including displaying the most current federal and state labor law posters at your place of business. More information can be found at www.freeposteraudit.com.

Properly tracking and reporting to the state your payroll activity will help you avoid costly penalties for not filing timely.

Creating Payroll Accounts in the Chart of Accounts

Proper payroll tracking includes having the necessary payroll liability and expense accounts in the chart of accounts.

Review your data to make sure you have these accounts, or create them as needed. Adding subaccounts (see Figure 11.3) to the default accounts created by QuickBooks can help you track the financial details of payroll more efficiently.

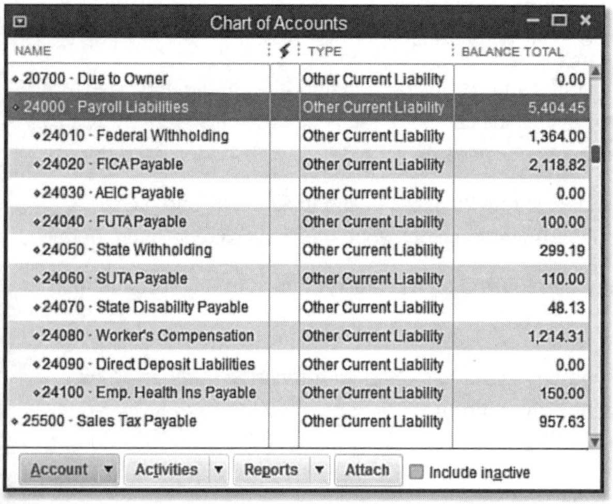

Chart of Accounts

NAME	⚡	TYPE	BALANCE TOTAL
◆ 20700 · Due to Owner		Other Current Liability	0.00
◆ 24000 · Payroll Liabilities		Other Current Liability	5,404.45
◆ 24010 · Federal Withholding		Other Current Liability	1,364.00
◆ 24020 · FICA Payable		Other Current Liability	2,118.82
◆ 24030 · AEIC Payable		Other Current Liability	0.00
◆ 24040 · FUTA Payable		Other Current Liability	100.00
◆ 24050 · State Withholding		Other Current Liability	299.19
◆ 24060 · SUTA Payable		Other Current Liability	110.00
◆ 24070 · State Disability Payable		Other Current Liability	48.13
◆ 24080 · Worker's Compensation		Other Current Liability	1,214.31
◆ 24090 · Direct Deposit Liabilities		Other Current Liability	0.00
◆ 24100 · Emp. Health Ins Payable		Other Current Liability	150.00
◆ 25500 · Sales Tax Payable		Other Current Liability	957.63

Account ▾ Activities ▾ Reports ▾ Attach ☐ Include inactive

Figure 11.3
Create subaccounts for payroll liability and expenses for more detailed reporting.

➡ See "Chart of Accounts," p. 102 for more information on creating these subaccounts.

Typical accounts to create for working recording payroll transactions include the following:

- **Bank Account**—QuickBooks does not require that you have a separate bank account for payroll transactions. Companies with large amounts of funds from operations might choose to have another bank account for payroll transactions. Having a separate bank account for payroll can limit the business's financial exposure from fraud.
- **Payroll Liabilities—Other Current Liability**. QuickBooks uses this account type to track the amount owed to federal or state governments, health insurance providers, and the like.

tip

Have you been recording QuickBooks payroll transactions without using these recommended subaccounts? Create the desired subaccounts, and then edit the payroll items, assigning the newly created subaccount.

QuickBooks will reassign all previous transactions to the newly created subaccounts. Always make a backup of your data before attempting a procedure such as this.

QuickBooks creates this account for you automatically. Include the following as subaccounts to this account and add additional subaccounts as needed:

- FICA/Medicare Payable (also referred to as 941 taxes). For simplicity, I recommend a single account combining the employee deductions and employer contributions.
- State Unemployment Payable (also referred to as SUTA).
- Federal Unemployment Payable (also referred to as FUTA).
- Health Insurance Payable.
- Wage Garnishments.

- **Job Costs—Cost of Goods Sold**. Many industries track the costs associated with providing a service or product to their customers or jobs. To track these properly on your Income Statement, use the Cost of Goods Sold account category. Do not overuse this category by adding too many to the chart of accounts; instead use QuickBooks items for greater detail.

For more information, see " Understanding Items," p. 108.

- **Overhead Costs**—Expense. When you create a company paid payroll item, you will assign an account for the expense. Payroll items are used on paycheck transactions and have account(s) assigned to them. QuickBooks automatically creates a Payroll Expenses account. Typically, you would add the following as subaccounts:
  - **Salaries & Wages**—Assign to payroll compensation items.
  - **Payroll Taxes**—Assign to the employer Social Security and Medicare payroll items.
  - **State Unemployment**—Assign to your state(s) unemployment payroll item.
  - **Federal Unemployment**—Assign to the Federal Unemployment payroll item.
  - **Employee Benefits**—Assign to company-paid benefits, including health, dental, life insurance, and other types of benefits.

A comprehensive chart of accounts that includes subaccounts for liabilities and expenses will make it easy for you to review your payroll and fix any errors.

caution

Do you have employees who work in the office doing administrative tasks and other employees who perform work related to customers and jobs? If you do, proper recording of payroll costs would assign the costs of administrative payroll to an overhead expense account and customer or job payroll expenses to cost of goods sold account.

However, QuickBooks has a limitation with this process. Company-paid payroll tax items allow only a single-expense account. The result is that each specific company paid payroll tax expense is reported to a single account. Keep this in mind when you are reviewing your financials.

Setting Up Payroll Tax Vendors

Tracking, paying, and reporting payroll liabilities balances can be improved if you identify the vendors by the tax or benefit being paid. This is important for states or other agencies that have the same payee name for multiple state tax liabilities.

Creating separate vendor records is recommended. When processing the payroll liability payments from the Payroll Center, QuickBooks will prepare a separate liability check for each:

- Unique liability payroll item assigned to a specific payee
- Liability payments with different due dates

When preparing the Federal 941/944 and Federal 940 payments, QuickBooks will create a separate check for each type of liability or for same payroll item types but with different due dates. See the Pay Scheduled Liabilities section in Figure 11.4. This is necessary so that the reporting and payment for these liabilities follow strict due date guidelines dictated by the state, federal government, or other entity being paid.

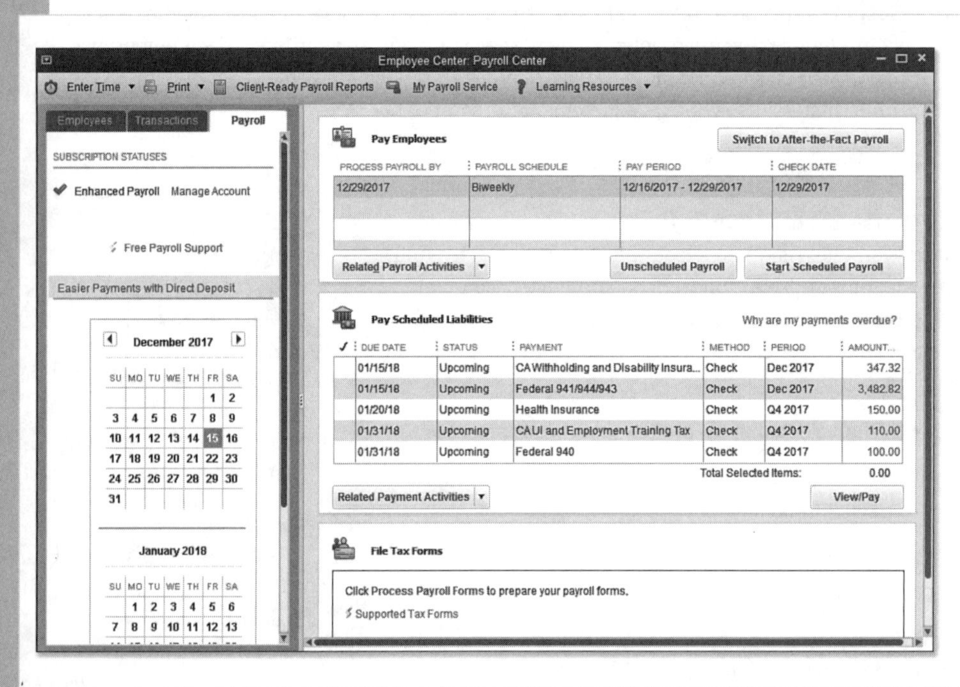

Figure 11.4 QuickBooks will prepare individual checks for the different payroll items and for the same payroll items but with different due dates.

To learn more about creating your vendor records, see "Adding or Modifying Vendors," p. 230.

The following is a list of some of the more common payroll vendors you should create when you are managing payroll:

- United States Treasury—941
- United States Treasury—940
- State income tax department
- State unemployment tax department
- Health insurance vendor

Payroll Preferences

After you sign up for one of the Intuit Payroll Service subscriptions, you need to enable payroll and set some payroll-specific and employee-specific preferences. There are two types of preferences in QuickBooks:

- **My Preferences**—Settings that are unique to the user logged in to the data file and are not shared by other users.
- **Company Preferences**—Settings that are common for all users. When a preference is modified on the Company Preferences tab, the change affects all users.

For this section, reference is made only to preferences on the Company Preferences tab. The My Preferences settings do not directly affect the payroll process. Log in to the file as the Admin or External Accountant user in single-user mode to set the following preferences.

Payroll and Employee Preferences—Company Preferences

These specific preferences are set for all users. To set up payroll and employee preferences, follow these steps:

1. From the menu bar select **Edit**, **Preferences** to open the Preferences dialog box. Select the **Payroll & Employees—Company Preferences** tab as shown in Figure 11.5.

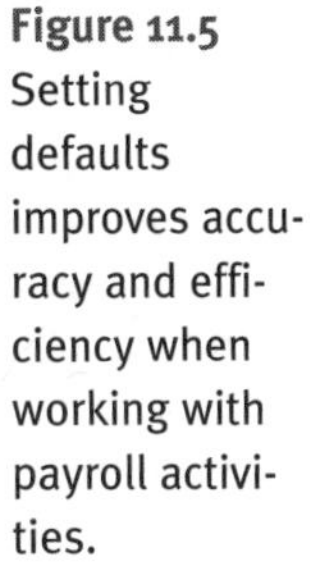
Figure 11.5 Setting defaults improves accuracy and efficiency when working with payroll activities.

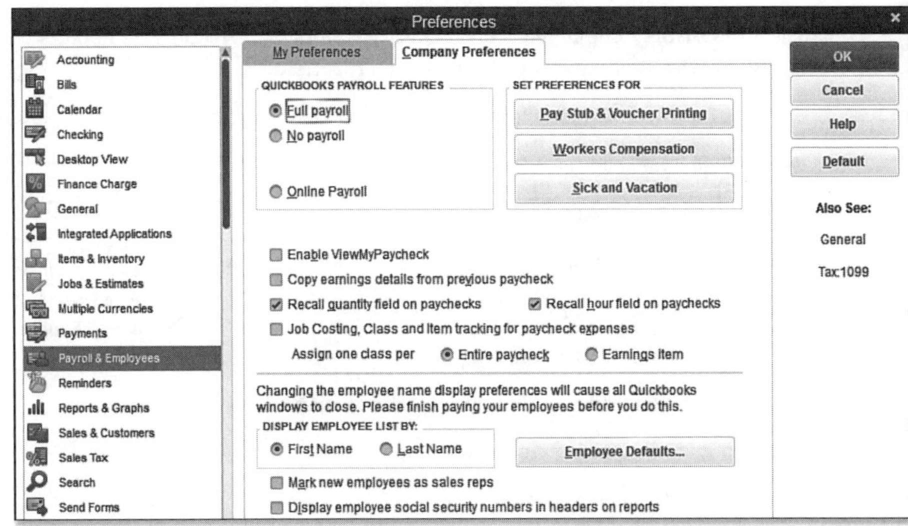

2. Select the **Full Payroll** option in the QuickBooks Payroll Features box. This enables the remaining features in the Preferences dialog box.

3. Select the checkbox next to the features that are appropriate to your business:

   - **Enable ViewMyPaycheck**—Give your employees online access to their pay stubs, W-2s, and other payroll info—free with your QuickBooks Payroll subscription! More information is provided later in this chapter.
   - **Copy Earnings Details from Previous Check**—Copies hours, rates, and Customer:Job from prior paycheck.
   - **Recall Quantity Field on Paychecks**—Recalls line 1 of a previous paycheck, payroll item, and rate only; no Customer:Job recalled.
   - **Recall Hour Field on Paychecks**—Recalls total hours only and places total number of hours on a single line even if prior paycheck had several lines.
   - **Job Costing, Class, and Item Tracking for Paycheck Expenses**—Enables QuickBooks to add the cost of company-paid taxes to the burdened costs for time that is assigned to a Customer:Job. QuickBooks also offers the Class Tracking by Paycheck or Earnings Item option if you have the class tracking preference enabled.

4. Choose the default for displaying employee names on reports. Choose to display by First Name or Last Name.

5. Select the **Mark New Employees as Sales Reps** checkbox if you want new employees automatically added to the sales rep list. An employee who is also a sales rep can be listed on a customer invoice transaction so you can report on sales by rep.

6. Select the **Display Employee Social Security Numbers in Headers on Reports** checkbox if you want to display this sensitive information on reports.

7. Click the Employee Defaults button to set the following defaults for new employees:

   - Earnings items and rate
   - Time data to create paychecks
   - Additions, deductions, or company contributions payroll items
   - Employee coverage by qualified pension plan
   - Payroll schedule or pay frequency
   - Class (if the QuickBooks Class preference is enabled)
   - Taxes for federal and state tax settings
   - Sick and vacation settings

tip

Setting these payroll defaults ensures consistency and saves time when setting up employees in QuickBooks.

8. Click OK to close the Employee Defaults dialog box.

9. Click the Set Preferences for Pay Stub and Voucher Printing button to open the Payroll Printing Preferences dialog box shown in Figure 11.6. In this dialog box, you can customize what detail will print on employees' paycheck stubs.

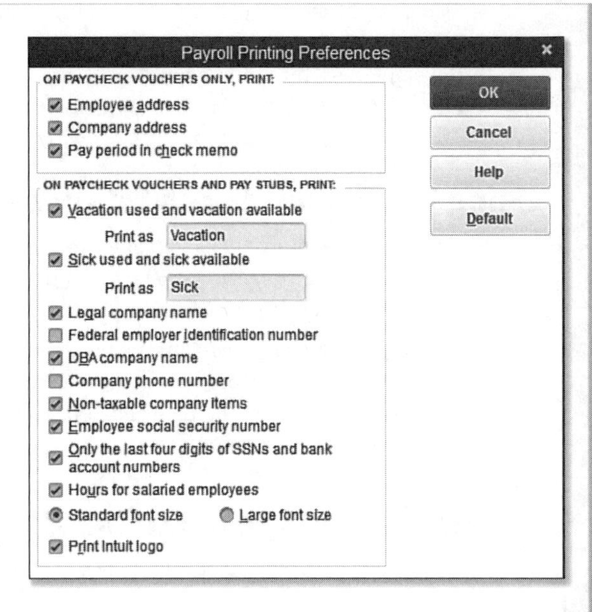

Figure 11.6
Customize the information that will print on the employee's paychecks or paystubs.

10. Click the Workers Compensation button to set the preference to track worker's comp, to be warned when worker's comp code is not assigned, and to exclude overtime hours from worker's compensation calculations.

11. Click the Sick and Vacation button to set default accrual period, hours accrued, maximum number of hours, and if the hours should be reset each new year.

Checking—Company Preferences

The Checking-specific preferences are set for all users. From the menu bar, select **Edit**, **Preferences** to open the Preferences dialog box. Select the **Checking** preference from the left side and click the Company Preferences tab.

In the Select Default Accounts to Use box, select the **Open the Create Paychecks** checkbox or the **Open Pay Payroll Liabilities** checkbox and specify a bank account from the drop-down list.

Time and Expense—Company Preferences

The Time and Expense preferences are set for all users. To set up time and expense preferences, follow these steps:

1. From the menu bar select **Edit**, **Preferences** to open the Preferences dialog box and select the **Time & Expenses—Company Preferences** tab.

2. Select **Yes** in the Time Tracking box if you plan to use timesheets to record employee work hours.

3. If necessary, change the First Day of Work Week from the drop-down list.

4. Placing a checkmark in the Mark All Time Entries as Billable is helpful if you create invoices for your customers that include the employees' time on the invoice. This type of billing is often referred to as Cost Plus or Time and Expense billing.

Do you invoice customers for time, expense, and a markup percentage? If yes, the Invoicing Options will help you with this task. For more information, see "Time and Expense Invoicing," p. 346.

Using the Payroll Setup Interview

The Payroll Setup Interview is helpful for new and existing QuickBooks payroll users. New users will appreciate how it walks you through setting up your first payroll.

For existing QuickBooks Payroll users, the Payroll Setup feature will help you by identifying missing information necessary for properly preparing, reporting, and paying payroll. If you do not have all the information needed at the time of setup, select **Finish Later** to exit the Payroll Setup. You can return later to update the information.

Information Needed to Set Up Payroll

The following information should be collected, where possible, before you begin to set up your payroll:

- **Compensation types**—Compile a list of the types of pay you offer, such as hourly, salary, overtime, vacation, and so on. You will be establishing a QuickBooks payroll item for each of these.
- **Other additions or deductions to payroll**—Some examples are dental insurance, uniforms, and union dues.
- **Employee names, addresses, and Social Security numbers**—Form W-4: Employees Withholding Allowance Certificate.
- **Payroll tax payment schedules and rates**—That is, what frequency your business is required to pay payroll taxes, including the rate you pay for your state unemployment tax and other taxes.
- **A year-to-date payroll register from your previous payroll system**—If you're transferring your payroll process to QuickBooks at any other time than the first of a calendar year, request a year-to-date payroll register from your previous payroll system.

  For more information, see "Midyear Payroll Setup," p. 436.

- **Any year-to-date payroll tax and other liability payments made prior to using QuickBooks**—These will help you to prepare your startup payroll records in QuickBooks.

note

If you have been using QuickBooks for preparing payroll, consider using the Run Payroll Checkup diagnostics. From the menu bar select **Employees, My Payroll Services, Run Payroll Checkup.** To learn more about working with this feature, see "Using the Run Payroll Checkup Diagnostic Tool," p. 439.

With this information collected, you are ready to begin using the Payroll Setup Interview. This handy tool uses a question-and-answer format to walk you through customizing your payroll settings. When it's completed, you can begin preparing payroll checks for your employees.

Introduction

The Payroll Setup Interview will guide you through adding the necessary payroll items needed to begin processing payroll.

After purchasing a payroll service subscription, launch Payroll Setup (see Figure 11.7) by selecting **Employees**, **Payroll Setup** from the menu bar. Optionally, click the link Payroll Item Checklist (not shown in Figure 11.7). Click Continue.

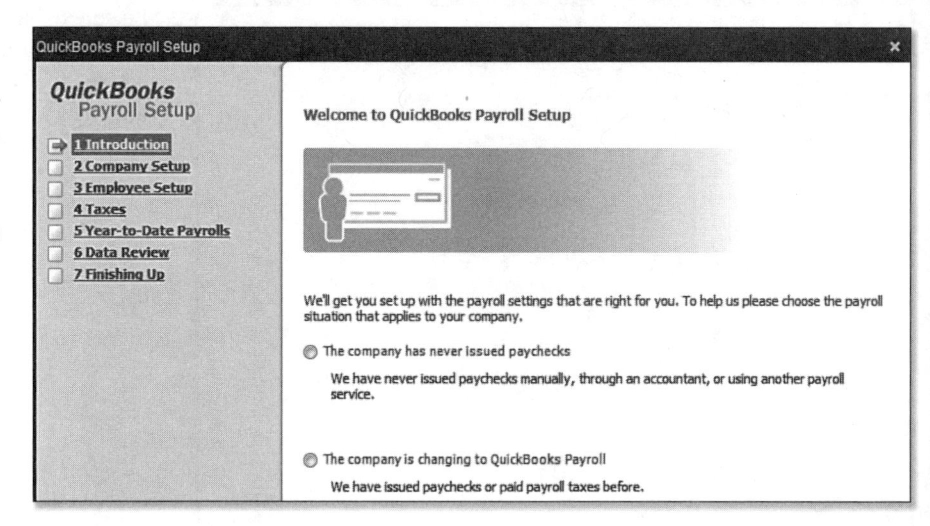

Figure 11.7 Selecting the right option for setting up payroll will affect the menus provided in the QuickBooks Payroll Setup dialog box.

Choose one of the following that best describes your business payroll setup needs:

- **The Company Has Never Issued Paychecks**—Not manually nor through an accountant or using another payroll service.
- **The Company Is Changing to QuickBooks Payroll**—Paychecks have been issued in same year you are starting to use QuickBooks payroll.

The instructions that follow assume that no prior paychecks have been issued. Your menu options will differ if you selected the Company Is Changing to QuickBooks Payroll.

Company Setup

The Company Setup introduction provides two methods for creating pay types and benefits:

- **Typical New Employer Setup**—QuickBooks automatically creates common payroll items, and then you can later add additional items. I recommend selecting this option.
- **Custom Setup**—Selecting this option allows you to custom create your payroll items. If you are familiar with setting up payroll, you could use this method. You can make changes to your setup later in your QuickBooks file if needed.

To learn more about adding custom payroll items, see "Adding or Editing Payroll Items," p. 448.

The instructions that follow assume that you selected **Typical New Employer Setup**. Click Continue to begin setting up your employees (see Figure 11.8).

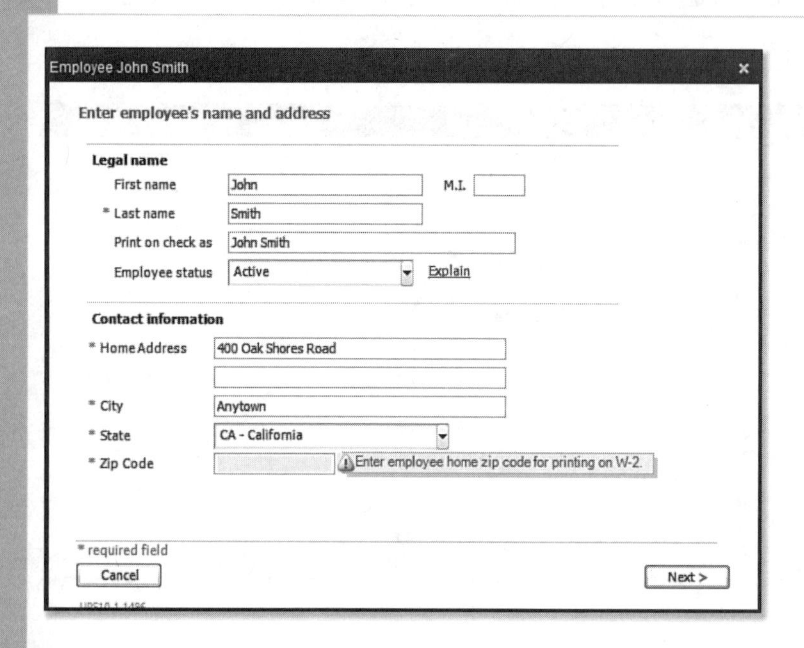

Figure 11.8
Be sure to have your employees' information ready when you run the Payroll Setup Interview so you can complete each of the required fields.

Employee Setup

You can work most efficiently with entering your employees if you have all the required information listed here. Complete the following information:

- Legal Name.
- Contact Information.
- Employee type: Regular, Officer, Statutory, or Owner and other hiring information.
- Payroll schedule, pay type, and rate (see Figure 11.9).
- Additions or deductions to employees' payroll.
- Determine what method of payment will be made for the payroll—check, direct deposit to an Intuit Pay Card, bank account, or splitting the amount into multiple direct deposit bank accounts.
- Assign the employee's state worked and state subject to withholding taxes.

tip

After completing some of the information, you will have the option to Finish Later (lower left). When you choose to Finish Later, QuickBooks retains the information you have entered, and you can return later to the Payroll Setup Interview to complete the missing information.

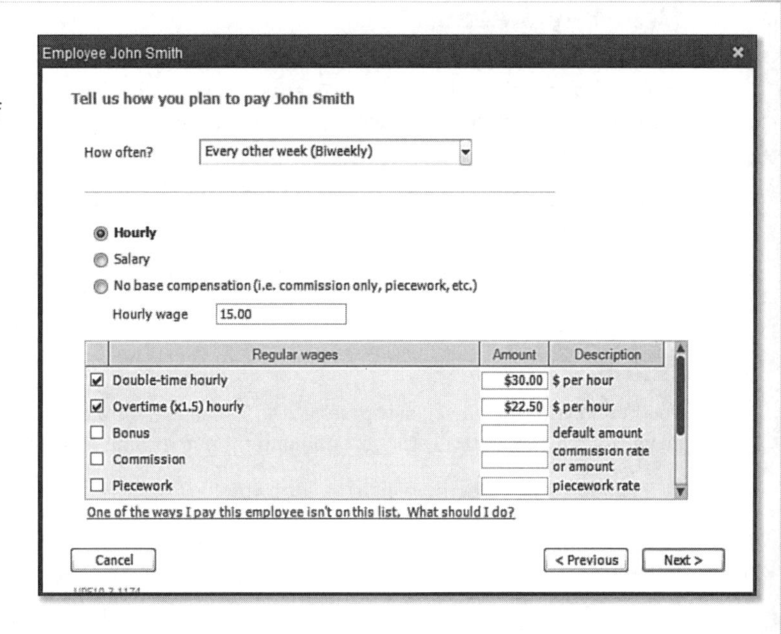

Figure 11.9
Assign the pay frequency and rate to improve the accuracy of the prepared paycheck.

- Federal tax information from the employee's Form W-4, and then select the proper withholdings and credits. Most employees' wages are subject to Medicare, Social Security, and Federal Unemployment.
- Whether the employee is subject to any special local taxes.

Information required will differ from state to state.

Click Finish (not shown in Figure 11.9) to complete the setup for employees. If you have not completed all the information, you might get a Missing Information error message, as shown in Figure 11.10. Read the information and click OK to close the message or Cancel to return to the setup. Choose Add New to continue with the next employee setup or select an employee from the list and click Edit, Delete, or Summary.

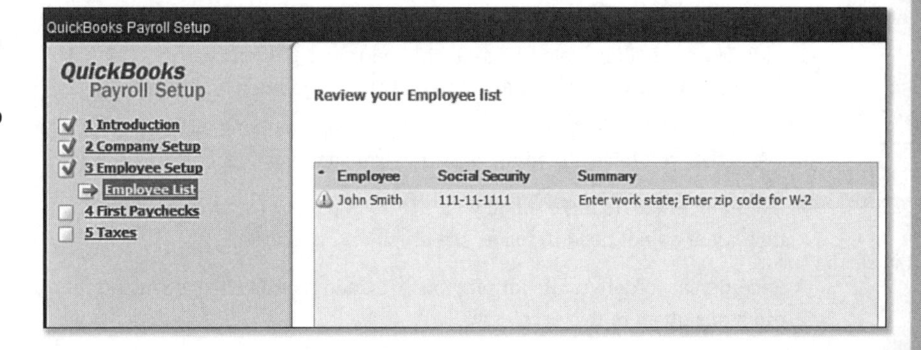

Figure 11.10
The QuickBooks Payroll Setup detects any setup errors or missing information.

First Paychecks

With the few steps you have completed, you can immediately create paychecks. If you are in a hurry to prepare paychecks, click First Paychecks, step 4 on the QuickBooks Payroll Setup dialog. You will have the following choices; however, I recommend completing the setup by selecting the second option listed next:

- Click the Create Paychecks button to be returned to the Payroll Center where you can immediately pay your employees.
- Click the Continue button to Continue to Tax Setup, providing agency information (recommended).

Taxes

Continuing with the payroll setup, select the **Taxes** menu item in the Payroll Setup, review the tax items created automatically for you, and enter the rates your business pays for federal and state taxes:

- **941/944 Form**—Identify which tax form you file.
- **Federal Taxes**—Review the federal payroll tax items created for you (you will add to or edit them later).
- **State Tax**—Click Add New to create a specific local/custom tax and define the state you are creating a payroll tax item for. Click Finish. Click Add New, Edit, or Delete. Click Continue when you have finished setting up state tax payroll items.
- **Schedule Payments**—Assign the tax item deposit method of check or E-pay, payee, and payment frequency. If you are uncertain what payment schedule your business should follow, contact your tax accountant or click How Often Should I Pay These Taxes? for additional resources.

caution

When a Fix This Error Now icon displays during Payroll Setup, heed the warning. If you don't, your payroll transactions or reporting might be incorrect. See Figure 11.10 previously displayed.

Midyear Payroll Setup

In the accounting community, the term "midyear" refers to setting up payroll at any time other than at the beginning of the current calendar year.

This method is needed only for companies converting to QuickBooks payroll in a calendar year that had prior payroll produced using software or through a payroll service provider.

When you make the decision to begin using QuickBooks payroll in a year that you have already had payroll transactions, you can

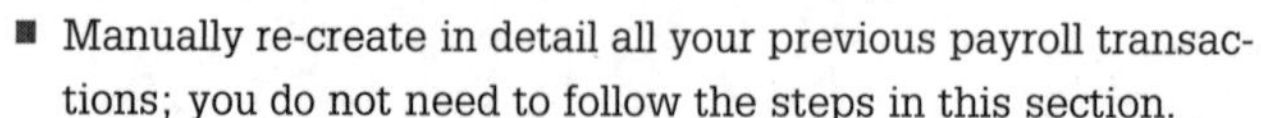

- Manually re-create in detail all your previous payroll transactions; you do not need to follow the steps in this section.

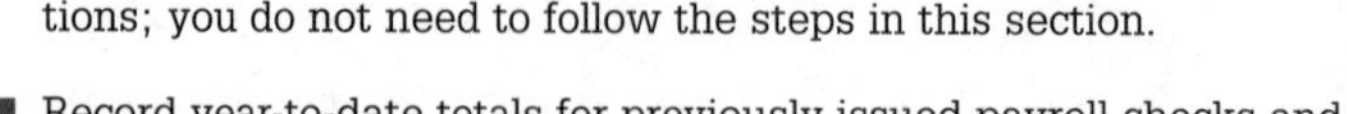

- Record year-to-date totals for previously issued payroll checks and liability payments, following the steps given in this section.

caution

If creating midyear payroll records, you will need to complete each of the following: paychecks, tax payments, and nontax payments. Failure to complete each of these may result in misleading information in the QuickBooks payroll module.

note

The Enter Paychecks by Employee option *will not* create any accounting entries (no effect on Balance Sheet or Profit & Loss). However, the entries *will* affect payroll reports and forms you file for your state and the federal government. The transactions entered here are used to enter year-to-date totals so that certain taxes on future paychecks calculate correctly and for completing quarterly and annual payroll forms using QuickBooks.

You will separately record the payroll liability balances for the Balance Sheet and payroll expenses for the Profit & Loss reports with a beginning trial balance entry provided by the company accountant.

Before beginning this process, make sure you have accurate records of the prior period payrolls, preferably subtotaled by calendar quarter. To set up midyear payroll totals using the Payroll Setup, follow these steps:

1. On step 1 of the Payroll Setup (select **Employees**, **Payroll Setup** from the menu bar), select **The Company Is Changing to QuickBooks Payroll**. QuickBooks will add additional menus to the Payroll Setup necessary for completing YTD entries.
2. Complete steps 2–4, entering the required information for Company, Employee, and Taxes setup as detailed previously.
3. On step 5 (Year-to-Date Payrolls), select **Determine if Needed**.
4. Click Yes to Has Your Company Issued Paychecks This Year?
5. Click Continue. QuickBooks opens the Enter Paychecks by Employee dialog box, as shown in Figure 11.11. This dialog box, with functionality similar to Microsoft Excel, streamlines the task of entering year-to-date payroll totals for your employees.

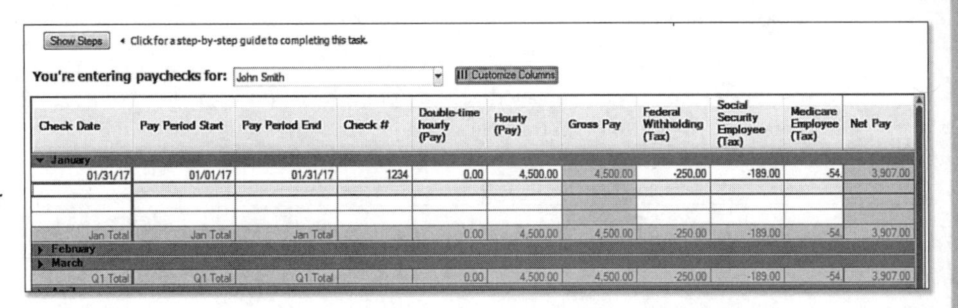

Figure 11.11 Use this worksheet in QuickBooks Payroll Setup to record prior year paychecks.

note

If you previously started using the Payroll Setup, step 5 will instead display the Payroll Summary. Click Edit next to the desired information you need to complete including paychecks, tax payments, or nontax payments.

6. Click the Show Steps button to have QuickBooks provide a pop-up dialog box of the steps for entering the information to be typed in each cell.

7. Click the Customize Columns button to arrange the columns of data to match the reports from your prior software or payroll provider, which simplifies the data entry process.

8. To begin entering data for your employees, click the drop-down list for You're Entering Paychecks For and select the employee name.

9. Right-click to conveniently copy, paste, delete, or insert rows. This functionality is especially useful when entering repeating information, such as for salaried employees.

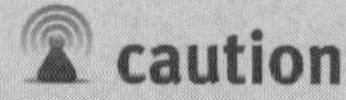

The Enter Paychecks by Employee dialog box will only allow you to enter payroll check dates in the current calendar year (determined by the year on your computer).

10. Conveniently check your monthly and annual totals as you type directly from the Enter Paychecks by Employee dialog box to make sure your data entered agrees with your prior payroll records.

11. Click View Reports, and QuickBooks includes the following two reports to help report on the accuracy of the setup details:

   - **Historical Paycheck Report—Basic**—The report details the gross pay and any deductions or company expenses. This report should be reviewed carefully to make sure the totals match your prior payroll records.

   - **Historical Paycheck Report—Advanced**—Click the Switch to Advanced Report. The Advanced report compares the combination of historical paycheck detail with any employee or company payroll liability adjustments. If your historical payroll and adjustments (if needed) were correctly entered, the QuickBooks-Calculated amount column should equal your totals for those payroll tax items as reported to your federal and state governments.

After clicking View Reports, if your computer has Internet security settings enabled, you might see a yellow bar near the top of your Internet browser. Click the yellow bar, select **Allow Blocked Content**, and click Yes if prompted.

After the reports are displayed you can print the report, export the report to Excel, or compress the report to fit on the printed page. See Figure 11.12.

Check Date		Gross Pay	Federal Withholding (Tax)	Social Security Company (Tax)	Social Security Employee (Tax)	Medicare Company (Tax)	Medicare Employee (Tax)	Federal Unemployment (Tax)	CA - Withholding (Tax)	Net Pay
2017 Paychecks		4,500.00	-250.00	279.00	-189.00	65.25	-54.00	27.00	-100.00	3,907.00
Q1 Jan-Mar		4,500.00	-250.00	279.00	-189.00	65.25	-54.00	27.00	-100.00	3,907.00
January		4,500.00	-250.00	279.00	-189.00	65.25	-54.00	27.00	-100.00	3,907.00
1/31/17										
	John Smith	4,500.00	-250.00	279.00	-189.00	65.25	-54.00	27.00	-100.00	3,907.00
	1/31 Total	4,500.00	-250.00	279.00	-189.00	65.25	-54.00	27.00	-100.00	3,907.00
February		0	0	0	0	0	0	0	0	0
March		0	0	0	0	0	0	0	0	0

Figure 11.12
The Historical Paycheck Report—Basic is useful to review and compare to the payroll records you have before using QuickBooks.

12. Click the X in the top-right corner to return to the Enter Paychecks by Employee dialog box.
13. Click the Done Entering Paychecks button to return to the QuickBooks Payroll Setup dialog box. As each paycheck, tax payment, and nontax payment are entered, the boxes will be shaded green progressively until each task is complete, making it easy to return where you left off.

Congratulations, you have completed the tasks necessary to set up your year-to-date payroll; you can now process new payroll transactions. This is a good time to complete the Run Payroll Checkup diagnostics discussed in the next section.

Using the Run Payroll Checkup Diagnostic Tool

After you complete the payroll setup and you have created payroll checks or year-to-date entries in QuickBooks, you are ready to review your data using the Run Payroll Checkup diagnostic tool. This feature is similar to the previously listed Payroll Setup feature. In fact, when you open the Run Payroll Checkup diagnostic tool, it also opens the Payroll Setup feature, but some of the menu choices are different.

What makes the Run Payroll Checkup tool different from the Payroll Setup tool? After you have set up your payroll, you will most likely use the Run Payroll Checkup tool to diagnose errors with setup and transactions.

The QuickBooks Run Payroll Checkup enables you to "Finish Later" and return where you left off. Before you begin the Run Payroll Checkup dialog box, make sure you have the following information available in case any of it is missing or incorrect:

- Employees' names, addresses, and Social Security numbers.
- Compensation, benefits, and other additions or deductions your company offers.
- Missing or incomplete information when you originally set up the employees; an example was shown previously in Figure 11.10.
- Compensation items, other additions, and deductions for missing or incomplete information.
- For existing data, review of actual wage and tax amounts provides an alert if any discrepancy is found, as shown in Figure 11.13.

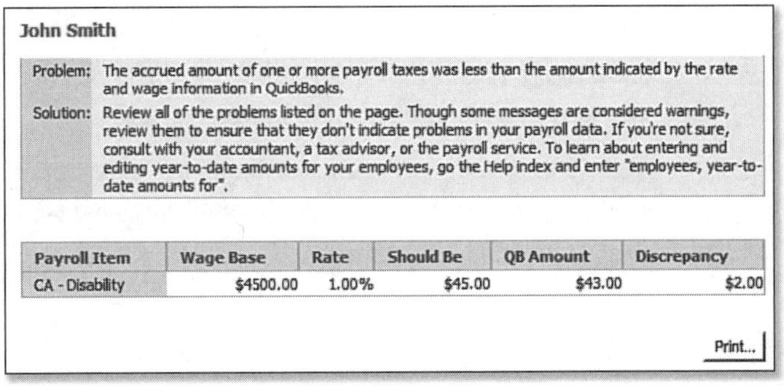

Figure 11.13
QuickBooks Payroll Setup detects certain payroll tax computation errors.

John Smith

Problem: The accrued amount of one or more payroll taxes was less than the amount indicated by the rate and wage information in QuickBooks.

Solution: Review all of the problems listed on the page. Though some messages are considered warnings, review them to ensure that they don't indicate problems in your payroll data. If you're not sure, consult with your accountant, a tax advisor, or the payroll service. To learn about entering and editing year-to-date amounts for your employees, go the Help index and enter "employees, year-to-date amounts for".

Payroll Item	Wage Base	Rate	Should Be	QB Amount	Discrepancy
CA - Disability	$4500.00	1.00%	$45.00	$43.00	$2.00

Print...

To have the payroll diagnostic tool in QuickBooks review your payroll setup for missing information and paycheck data discrepancies, do the following:

1. From the menu bar select **Employees**, **My Payroll Service**, **Run Payroll Checkup**. Follow each of the dialog boxes, clicking Continue through each step.
2. In the Data Review dialog box, click Yes. QuickBooks reviews the wages and taxes in the payroll records.
3. If errors are detected, click the View Errors button. QuickBooks opens the error detail, as shown in Figure 11.13.
4. Click the Print button in the Payroll Item Discrepancies dialog box.
5. If you click the Continue button, some errors will require you to fix them before you can proceed.
6. Click the Finish Later button to close the Run Payroll Checkup diagnostic tool so you can create correcting entries.

tip

The Run Payroll Checkup diagnostic tool is optional for Intuit's Basic or Enhanced Payroll subscribers. However, I recommend you process the Run Payroll Checkup regardless of what payroll subscription you select. Using the tool as often as once a quarter before preparing quarterly payroll tax returns can help ensure your data is correct.

Be prepared to take the time to fix the errors that are detected. The QuickBooks Run Payroll Checkup diagnostic tool allows you to ignore warnings, but doing so might result in additional payroll calculation errors.

Using the errors displayed earlier in Figure 11.13 as an example, the following are the typical steps for correcting them. (Your errors will be different and might require adjustments to other types of payroll items than the ones detailed here.)

1. From the menu bar select **Reports**, **Employees & Payroll**, **Payroll Summary**. Review this report for either prior or current payroll quarters (depending on where the error was detected). In Figure 11.14, compare the Payroll Summary report to the Payroll Item Discrepancies report in shown earlier in Figure 11.13. The Should Be amount should equal what your Payroll Summary report shows when prepared today.
2. From the menu bar select **Employees**, **Payroll Taxes and Liabilities**, **Adjust Payroll Liabilities** as shown in Figure 11.15.
3. Enter the Date and Effective Date. Both should be dated in the quarter you want to effect the change.
4. Select either **Company** or **Employee** for the adjustment. Company indicates it is a company-paid adjustment. Employee indicates an employee-paid adjustment and affects W-2 reported amounts.
5. (Optional) Assign a class if your business tracks different profit centers.

caution

Carefully consider the adjustments that need to be made if they affect a prior calendar quarter you have already filed with the state or federal government.

Be prepared to promptly file a correcting return with the appropriate agency when you adjust your QuickBooks payroll data from what was previously reported.

Correcting prior quarters can often be the best choice, especially if your data is ever audited.

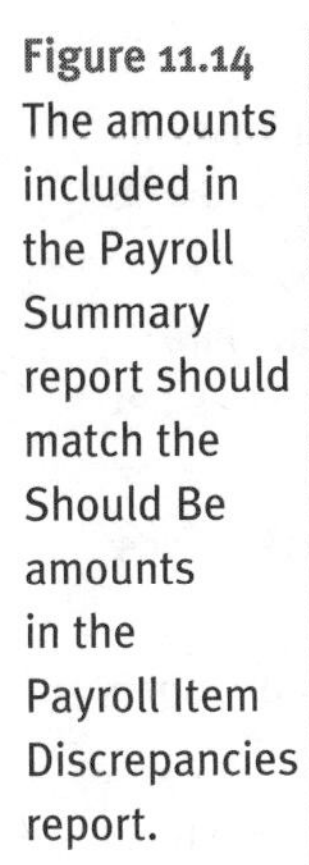

Figure 11.14 The amounts included in the Payroll Summary report should match the Should Be amounts in the Payroll Item Discrepancies report.

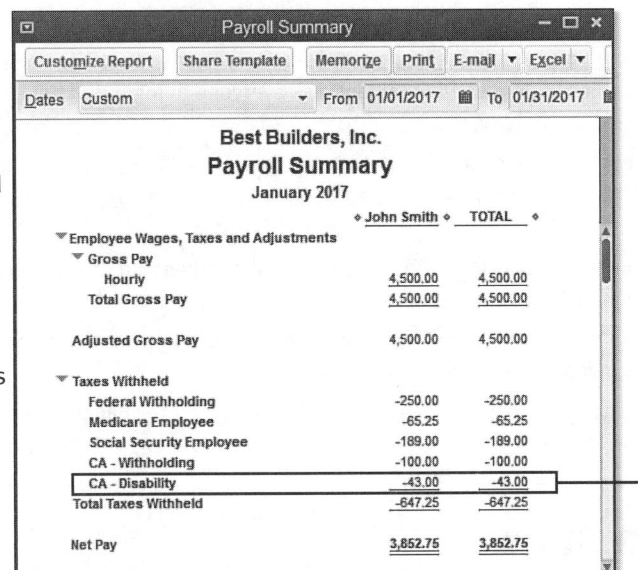

Best Builders, Inc.
Payroll Summary
January 2017

	John Smith	TOTAL
Employee Wages, Taxes and Adjustments		
Gross Pay		
Hourly	4,500.00	4,500.00
Total Gross Pay	4,500.00	4,500.00
Adjusted Gross Pay	4,500.00	4,500.00
Taxes Withheld		
Federal Withholding	-250.00	-250.00
Medicare Employee	-65.25	-65.25
Social Security Employee	-189.00	-189.00
CA - Withholding	-100.00	-100.00
CA - Disability	-43.00	-43.00
Total Taxes Withheld	-647.25	-647.25
Net Pay	3,852.75	3,852.75

The Payroll Checkup calculated this amount to be $45.00.

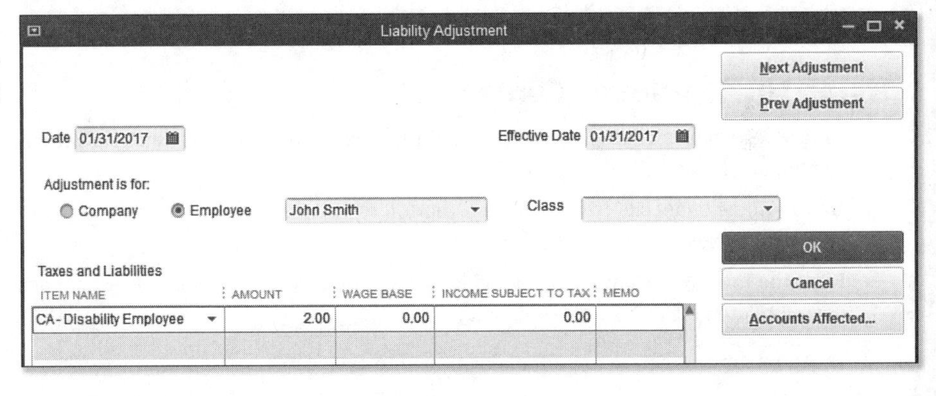

Figure 11.15 Create a liability adjustment to correct any errors found in the Payroll Item Discrepancies report.

6. Click Accounts Affected only if you do not want the adjustment to affect liability and expense account balances. This would be necessary if your Balance Sheet is correct, but the Pay Scheduled Liabilities balances in the Payroll Center are incorrect. Click OK to close the Accounts Affected dialog box if displayed.
7. Click OK to save the transaction.
8. Return to the Run Payroll Checkup menu to review your payroll data again after the correction. If your adjustments were successful, QuickBooks displays a Congratulations message showing all adjustments have corrected the discrepancies.

Do You Need to Run Payroll Checkup for a Prior Year?

If you need to complete a Run Payroll Checkup diagnostic for a prior year, follow these instructions. If you are working in a multiuser environment, ask everyone to log out of the QuickBooks file and close the data file.

Next, change your computer system date to a date in the prior year. When selecting the date, keep in mind how QuickBooks will review and report on "prior quarters" dependent on this new system date.

Run the Payroll Checkup diagnostic; QuickBooks now checks the payroll data that corresponds to the year of your computer's system date.

Don't forget to close the file and then reset your computer date to the current date before opening the file again and allowing other users into the system.

You might want to contact your computer hardware professional before changing the system date in a networked environment, because it might impact other running programs.

Setting Up Employees

If you are a new QuickBooks payroll user, I recommended using the Payroll Setup for adding payroll items and employees. You can return to the Payroll Setup to add additional employees or use the following instructions to add or edit employee information. Refer to the instructions in the "Employee Setup" section of "Using the Payroll Setup Interview" in this chapter.

Using the Employee Center

QuickBooks makes adding, modifying, and researching employee activity easy from the Employee Center, as displayed in Figure 11.16.

On the Home page, click the Employees button to open the Employee Center. Alternatively, you can click the Employees icon on the icon bar.

From the Employee Center, you can view contact details for your employees and access many payroll-related tasks to do the following:

- Add a new employee or edit an existing employee's information.
- Manage employee sales rep information and new employee defaults.
- Print paychecks, paystubs, and other useful list information.
- Enter time for employees.
- Export to Excel employee lists and transactions.
- Export to Excel Client-Ready Payroll Reports (requires a payroll service subscription for accounting professionals).
- Prepare employee letters and customize vendor letter templates using Word.

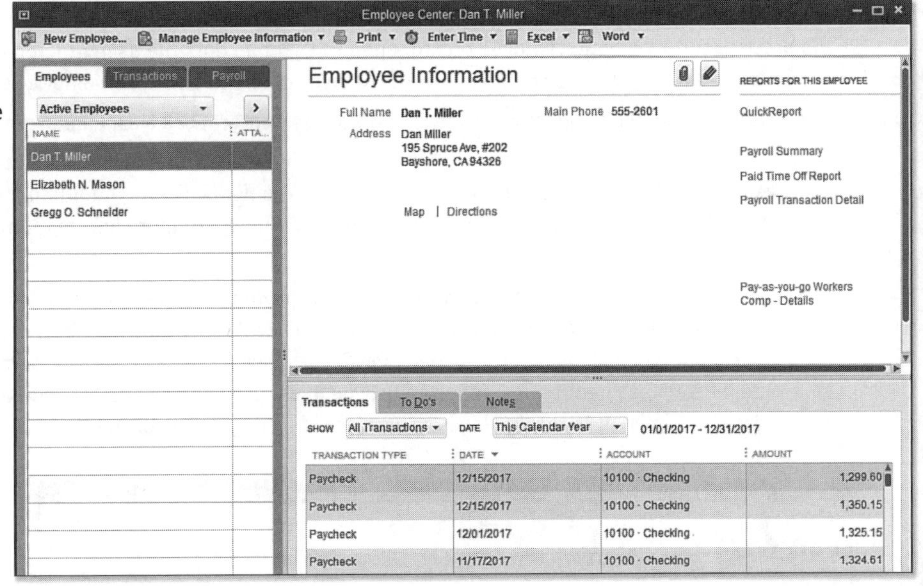

Figure 11.16 The Employee Center provides one place to access common employee tasks and reports.

- Filter the list of employees to include All Employees, Active Vendors, or Released Employees.
- Attach documents to the employee record.
- Access a map and driving directions to the employee's address.
- Add and edit employee notes and to-do reminders.
- View and filter the list of transactions by employee or by transaction type.
- Schedule To Do's reminding you of important employee-related tasks.
- Record miscellaneous Notes in the employee's record.
- Prepare a QuickReport, Payroll Summary, Paid Time Off Report, or Payroll Transaction Detail report for the selected employee.

Use the Employee Center to access many of the common employee transactions and reports you will learn about in this chapter.

Adding or Editing Employee Information

Have you completed the steps outlined in the Payroll Setup? You can now easily add a new employee or modify the information for an existing employee in the Employee Center.

 **caution**

Is this your first time setting up employees in QuickBooks? You might want to start by using the Payroll Setup. For more information, see "Using the Payroll Setup Interview," p. 432.

Adding an Employee

To practice adding a new employee record, open the sample data file as instructed in Chapter 1. If you are working in your own file, follow these instructions to add a new employee:

1. From the menu bar select **Employees, Employees Center**. Click New Employee.
2. Complete the fields in the Personal, Address and Contact, and Additional Info tabs. For this exercise, enter fictitious information into each of the fields. On the Additional Info tab, your QuickBooks version might offer a Billing Rate Level field. For more information, see "Billing Rate Levels," p. 349.
3. Select the **Payroll Info** tab. Select **Biweekly** for the payroll schedule, as shown in Figure 11.17. In your own file, click Add New to create a payroll schedule. Payroll schedules help you keep track of the next payroll processing date. Payroll schedules also facilitate grouping employees into different pay frequencies. For example, you might pay your field labor every week and your administrative staff biweekly. This is an example of setting up two different payroll schedules.

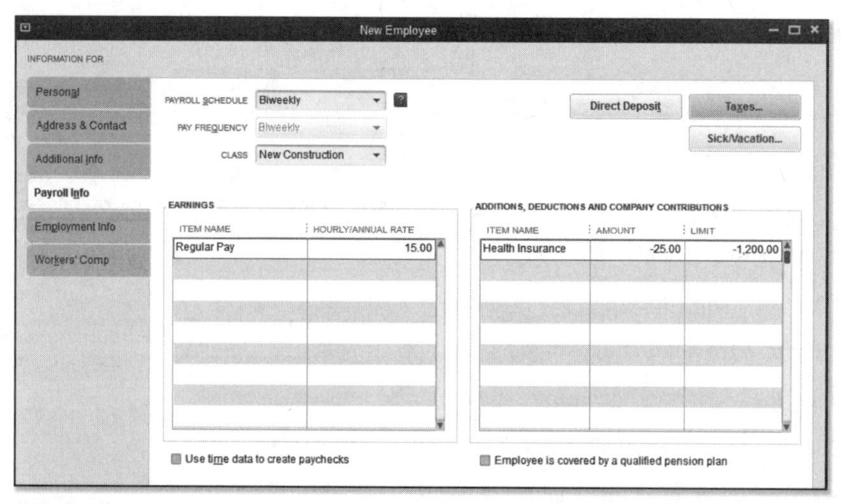

Figure 11.17
The Payroll Info tab should include each pay period's earnings and deduction items.

4. In the Class field, select **New Construction**. The option to assign a single class (department) to the entire paycheck or assign multiple classes to a single paycheck is defined in the Payroll & Employee preferences section. From the menu bar, select **Edit, Preferences, Payroll & Employees, Company Preferences.**
5. The Regular Pay wage item defaults in the Item Name column of the Earnings box. Type **15.00** into the Hourly/Annual column. To view other compensation items, click the down arrow next to Regular Pay.
6. For this exercise, do not select either of these options: Use Time and Expense Data to Create Paychecks, or Employee is Covered by a Qualified Pension Plan.
7. Record other Additions, Deductions, and Company Contributions for this employee. In the Item Name drop-down list for this exercise, select **Health Insurance**. Type **25.00** into the

amount column and accept the defaulted Limit—QuickBooks will deduct this amount from each paycheck. The Limit allows you to set an upper limit and if the limit is reset annually. The Limit amount can be defined globally for all employees when setting up the deduction, or the Limit can be a specific amount for each employee.

8. The Direct Deposit button is inactive in the sample data being used for this exercise. If this button is enabled in your own file, clicking it will display a QuickBooks dialog box to verify your company information, enter bank information, and select check security limits.
9. Click the Taxes button to see the information displayed in Figure 11.18. The information selected in the fields on the Federal, State, and Other tabs determines how the respective taxes are calculated. Use the information on the employee's completed Form W-4 when selecting Filing Status, Allowances, and Extra Withholding settings. Click OK to close. If you did not select a State Worked, you might be prompted to complete the setup.

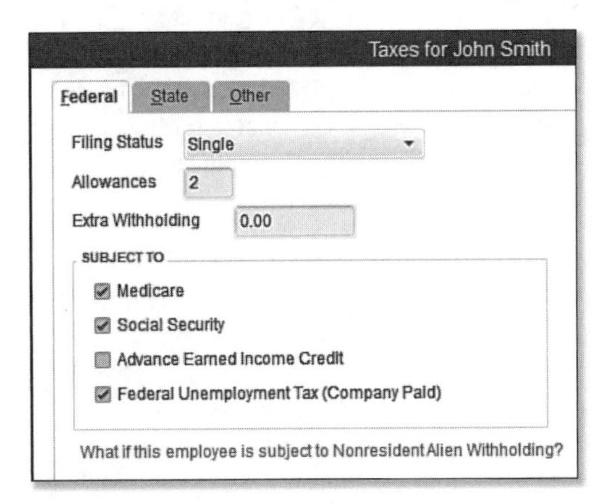

Figure 11.18
Assign the employee's federal, state, and other tax status.

10. Click the Sick/Vacation button. Use these settings to accrue and track employees sick and vacation time. Click OK to close.
11. (Optional) Click the Employment Info tab to record Employment Dates and Employment Details.
12. (Optional) Click the Worker's Comp tab to assign the Worker's Comp Code available with selected Intuit payroll subscriptions.
13. Click OK to close the New Employee dialog box.

tip

Working in your own file, if you select **Use Time and Expense Data to Create Paychecks**, QuickBooks uses that time data from time cards to prefill the hours on a paycheck. This can save you time making your payroll processing more efficient.

Learn more about using the QuickBooks Timer, p. 654.

Managing your employees' information from the Employee Center is easy. To edit an employee's information, select an employee on the left side of the dialog box and click the Edit Employee icon above and to the right of the employee's contact information.

Finding Payroll Transactions

The Employee Center provides a central location for maintaining employee records and reviewing payroll transactions in QuickBooks.

On the Home page, click the Employees button to open the Employee Center. Select an employee on the left side of the dialog box to display individual transactions assigned to that employee on the right. With the employee Dan T. Miller selected in the Employee Center, QuickBooks displays individual transactions for that employee. See Figure 11.19.

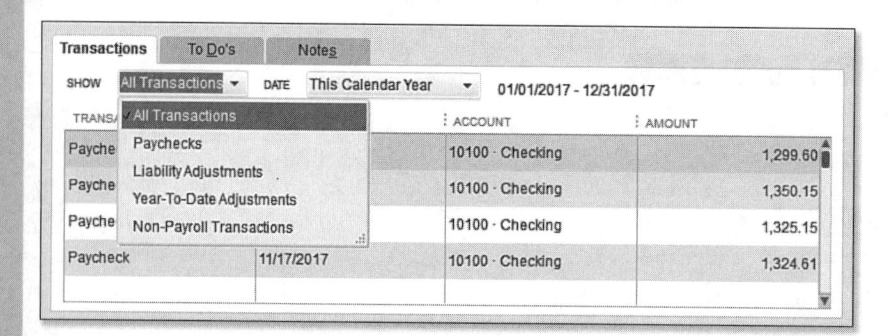

Figure 11.19
Filter for specific transactions types and dates for the selected employee.

Another useful feature of working with the Payroll Center is found on the Transactions tab. From the Transactions tab in the Employee Center, you can easily locate payroll and non-payroll transactions for all employees. When reviewing payroll, it can be helpful to see what payments, if any, were paid to the employees using payroll transactions or payments made with other transaction types. Payments made to an employee not through a payroll transaction type will not be included in state and federal payroll reporting.

You are now proficient in adding or editing an employee's information. In the next section you learn about managing your payroll items.

Researching Payroll and Non-payroll Transactions

To practice finding employee transactions by type, open the sample data file as instructed in Chapter 1. If you are working in your own file, use these instructions to locate your own employee's transactions.

1. From the Employee Center, click the Transactions tab.
2. Select the **Liability Checks** type as shown in Figure 11.20.

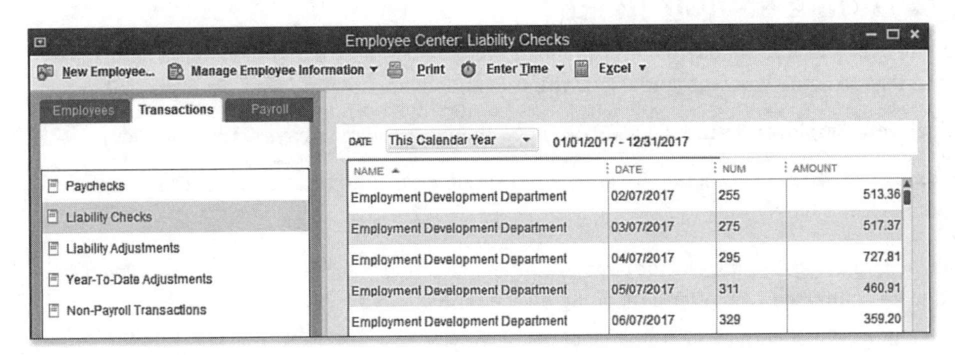

Figure 11.20
Use the Transactions tab of the Employee Center to research by transaction type.

3. From the Date drop-down list, select **This Calendar Quarter**. (If you are using the QuickBooks-supplied sample data, the date selected might be some time in the future.)
4. Click any column header to sort the data by that column.
5. Double-click any transaction to open it. Click Save & Close to return to the Transactions tab details.
6. Click the Print button to print the listed transactions.
7. Click the Enter Time drop-down list to enter a Weekly Timesheet or Time/Enter Single Activity.
8. Click the Excel drop-down list to choose from the following:
    - Export Transactions—Exports the displayed transactions to an Excel worksheet.
    - Client-Ready Payroll Reports—Available if you are using QuickBooks Accountant 2013 or QuickBooks Enterprise Accountant 13.0. A robust set of payroll reports created for you using Excel.
    - Summarize Payroll Data in Excel—A collection of useful payroll reports.

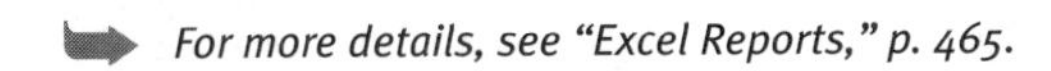
For more details, see "Excel Reports," p. 465.

tip

To customize the information displayed, right-click in the column area of the transaction display and select **Customize Columns**. You can then choose to add or remove available columns of data and change the order the information is displayed.

Setting Up Payroll Items

QuickBooks uses payroll items to calculate and track compensation, additions, deductions, and company expenses that result from paying employees. You need to set up your payroll items only once, which in turn makes processing payroll as easy as reporting the time an employee works.

Adding or Editing Payroll Items

If you are new to QuickBooks payroll, I recommend that you begin by using the Payroll Setup. During the Payroll Setup you were provided with two options for creating your list of payroll items:

- **Typical New Employer Setup**—QuickBooks adds the most common payroll items for you.
- **Custom Setup**—Select this option if you need to set up sick time, vacation time, or insurance benefits.

If you have been using QuickBooks for payroll, you will no longer see these two options. The fields required to be completed will differ depending on the type of payroll item.

To add or edit a deduction payroll item, follow these steps:

1. From the menu bar select **Lists**, **Payroll Item List**.
2. Select **New** from the Payroll Item menu (or use the Ctrl+N keyboard shortcut). You can also right-click a payroll item and choose Edit Payroll Item if you need to make changes.
3. Select one of the following methods:
   - **EZ Setup**—Opens the Payroll Setup using standard settings, recommended for most users. To learn more about using this option, see "Using the Payroll Setup Interview," p. 432.
   - **Custom Setup**—Offers a more traditional approach to setting up payroll items, recommended for expert users.
4. If you selected Custom Setup in step 3, the Add New Payroll Item dialog box displays.
5. Select a payroll item type, such as **Deduction** (shown in Figure 11.21), and then click Next.

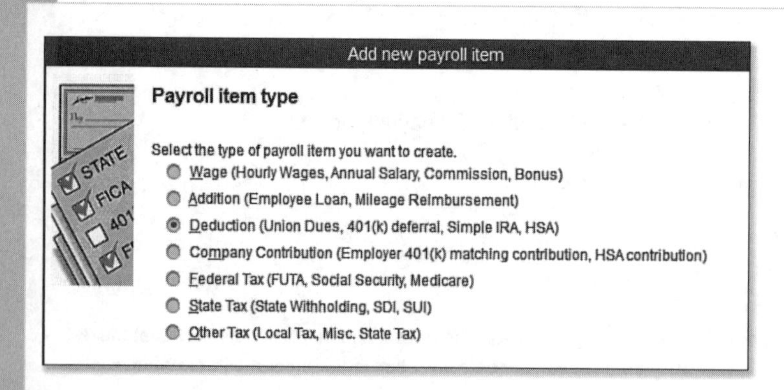

Figure 11.21
Select the appropriate payroll item type to be created.

6. Type a name for the payroll item. This name will display on paychecks and in reports. Selecting the Track Expenses by Job might be suitable for most company contribution and addition items and would include costs to this payroll item in Job Profitability reports. Click Next.

7. On the Agency for Employee-Paid Liability screen, enter the following:

   - From your vendor list, select the agency or vendor to which you pay the liability. If necessary, click Add New to create a new vendor record. Skip this field if the deduction is not being paid to anyone. For instance, Figure 11.22 shows how to establish a cell phone reimbursement item.

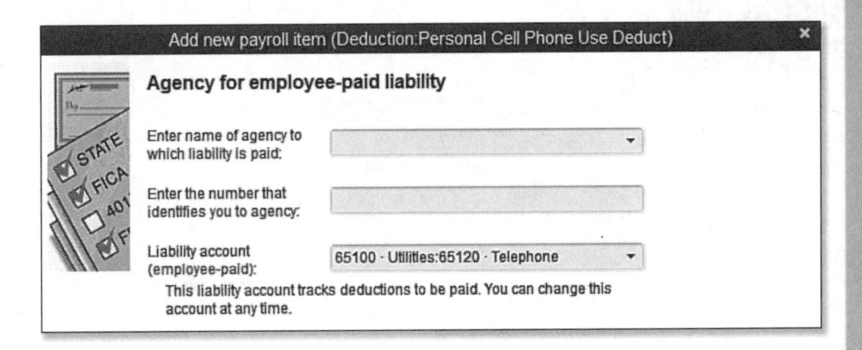

Figure 11.22
Payroll deductions can recover a portion of a business paid expense.

   - If your liability vendor assigns an account number to your business, enter it into the account number field.

   - Make a selection from your chart of accounts. In this example, the Telephone Expense account is selected. If the deduction payroll item is used to recover a business paid expense from employees, select the corresponding expense account. Normally you would accept the default account of Payroll Liabilities. If you followed the previously recommended process for creating detailed payroll accounts on your chart of accounts, select the appropriate subaccount. Click Next.

8. Select the appropriate Tax Tracking Type, or select **None** if none of the types applies, as shown in Figure 11.23. This choice is important to properly set up your payroll items. If you are unsure, ask your accountant for advice. Click Next.

9. The Taxes screen displays. In most cases, you will not need to modify the settings in this screen. Click Default to return to the original settings. Click Next.

note

You can always edit the settings for a specific payroll item. However, some changes will affect only future payroll checks and not those recorded prior to making the change.

10. The Calculate Based on Quantity screen offers the following choices:

    - Calculate This Item Based on Quantity
    - Calculate This Item Based on Hours
    - Neither

11. After making a selection, click Next.

12. Select to calculate the deduction from Gross Pay or Net Pay. If you are unsure, ask your accountant, because the correct selection will depend on the item being set up. Click Next.

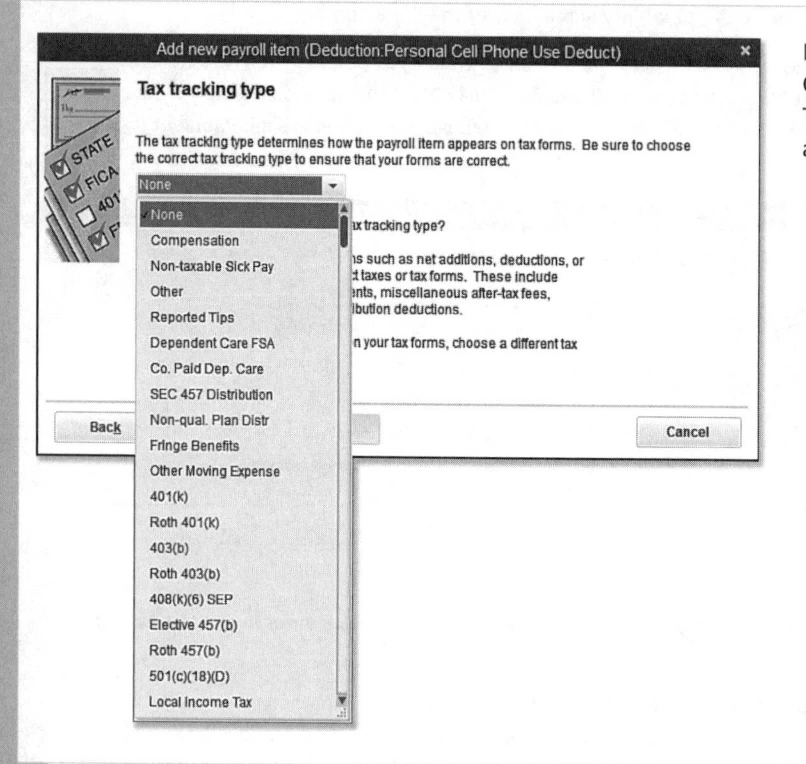

Figure 11.23
Carefully reviewing the Tax Tracking Types can help with accurately setting up payroll.

13. Enter a Default Rate, optional Default Upper Limit, and specify whether the limit is annually reset. If the rate or upper limit differs for each employee, do not enter amounts here. The rate and limit can be added individually to each employee's record. Click Finish.

14. Click OK after reading the Schedule Payments message. For more information, see "Creating or Editing a Payroll Schedule," p. 455.

Now that you have properly set up your payroll items, let's learn about reporting on them. In the early stages of your payroll use, you should carefully inspect your setup to avoid any mistakes with payroll payments.

Reporting About Payroll Items

Reviewing your payroll items list after adding to or modifying it would be prudent to make sure the changes are correct. Follow these steps for reviewing the Payroll Item List:

1. From the menu bar select **Lists**, **Payroll Item List** (see Figure 11.24). QuickBooks displays the Payroll Item List dialog box.

2. To expand the report for better viewing, double-click the words *Payroll Item List* in the title bar of the dialog box.

3. To add or remove columns, right-click and select **Customize Columns**.

Figure 11.24 View the Payroll Item List for information about the setup and accounts assigned to the payroll items.

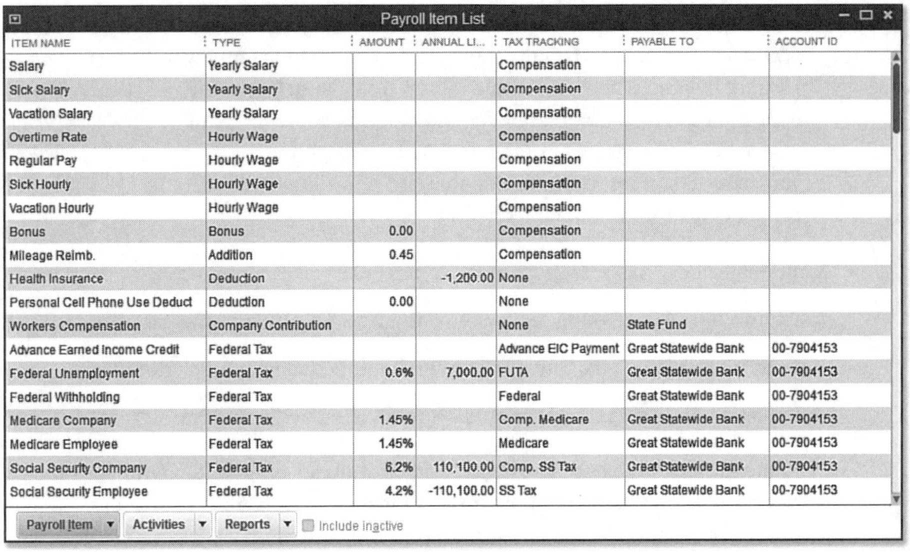

Payroll Item List

ITEM NAME	TYPE	AMOUNT	ANNUAL LI...	TAX TRACKING	PAYABLE TO	ACCOUNT ID
Salary	Yearly Salary			Compensation		
Sick Salary	Yearly Salary			Compensation		
Vacation Salary	Yearly Salary			Compensation		
Overtime Rate	Hourly Wage			Compensation		
Regular Pay	Hourly Wage			Compensation		
Sick Hourly	Hourly Wage			Compensation		
Vacation Hourly	Hourly Wage			Compensation		
Bonus	Bonus	0.00		Compensation		
Mileage Reimb.	Addition	0.45		Compensation		
Health Insurance	Deduction		-1,200.00	None		
Personal Cell Phone Use Deduct	Deduction	0.00		None		
Workers Compensation	Company Contribution			None	State Fund	
Advance Earned Income Credit	Federal Tax			Advance EIC Payment	Great Statewide Bank	00-7904153
Federal Unemployment	Federal Tax	0.6%	7,000.00	FUTA	Great Statewide Bank	00-7904153
Federal Withholding	Federal Tax			Federal	Great Statewide Bank	00-7904153
Medicare Company	Federal Tax	1.45%		Comp. Medicare	Great Statewide Bank	00-7904153
Medicare Employee	Federal Tax	1.45%		Medicare	Great Statewide Bank	00-7904153
Social Security Company	Federal Tax	6.2%	110,100.00	Comp. SS Tax	Great Statewide Bank	00-7904153
Social Security Employee	Federal Tax	4.2%	-110,100.00	SS Tax	Great Statewide Bank	00-7904153

Payroll Item ▾ | Activities ▾ | Reports ▾ | Include inactive

The following information is displayed by default when viewing the Payroll Item List:

- **Item Name**—Displayed on paychecks and reports.
- **Type**—This is from a predefined list in QuickBooks. The types are more wide ranging than that, because they describe pay types and tax types, as well as additions and deductions.
- **Amount**—This figure is often determined by the QuickBooks-provided payroll tax tables, with the exception of addition and deduction calculations, which include amounts that can be set by the user as well.
- **Annual Limit**—This figure is often determined by the QuickBooks-provided tax tables and is not modifiable by the user. Incorrect limits for standard tax calculations could be due to a payroll tax table that is not current.
- **Tax Tracking**—When you create a new payroll item and select a payroll item type, QuickBooks provides a predetermined list of tax tracking types associated with that item type. Tax tracking determines how QuickBooks treats the item on the W-2 year-end employee tax form.
- **Payable To**—Checks are payable to the named entity.
- **Account ID**—The identification number your tax payment agency has assigned to your company.
- **Expense Account**—If the payroll item type is considered an expense, users can define the default expense account from the chart of accounts list in the payroll setup. QuickBooks defaults this account to a generic Payroll Expense account, which is created automatically by QuickBooks when payroll is enabled.

tip

On the displayed Payroll Item List, to add or remove specific columns of data, right-click and select **Customize Columns.**

- **Liability Account**—This account is used for payroll items that are accrued with payroll and paid to the state or federal government. QuickBooks defaults these items to a generic liability account created when payroll is enabled. You can define what liability account is assigned. If you are creating a new account, it should be a subaccount of the one QuickBooks provides if you want to see certain warnings that are provided when you try to create a transaction incorrectly.

Additionally, from this screen view of the payroll items list you can access the following:

- **Payroll Item**—Add, edit, delete, make item inactive, find in transactions, and print list.
- **Activities**—Access the Payroll Setup and other common payroll item tasks.
- **Reports**—Access summary or detail reports of payroll item transactions.

Congratulations! You have the needed items set up for preparing payroll for your employees. In the next section you learn how to prepare and process your payroll. Take your time with the details; accuracy is everything when it comes to payroll processing.

Paying Employees

Having completed your Payroll Setup and Run Payroll Checkup, you are ready to begin paying your employees. If you previously paid your employees' payroll with other software or by a payroll agency, record the year-to-date payroll totals for each employee.

For more information, see "Midyear Payroll Setup," p. 436.

The next sections provide details on preparing payroll for your employees.

Payroll Home Page Workflow

With a paid payroll subscription you might have all or some of the following icons on your Home page, providing easy access to the typical payroll workflow. Your icons might differ from Figure 11.25 depending on the payroll subscription purchased and the preferences you have set in QuickBooks.

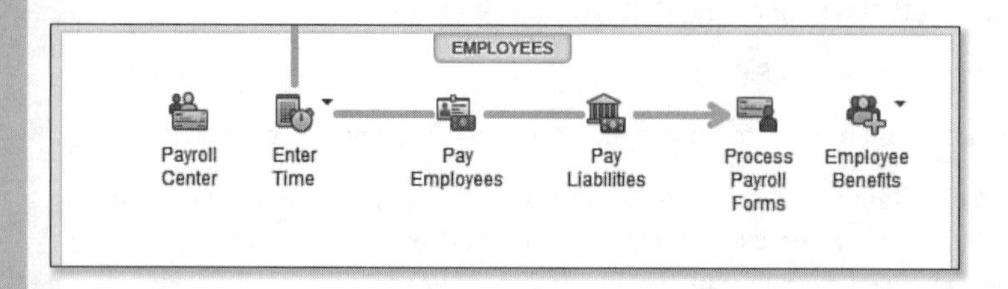

Figure 11.25
The Home page provides access to the proper payroll workflow.

Entering Employee Time

QuickBooks includes weekly or single activity timekeeping you can use to record employee work time and create paychecks. You can access timesheets by clicking the Enter Time icon on the Home page.

Using timesheets will simplify the process of creating payroll records if you track employees' time by customers, jobs, or service items. Timesheets are not necessary if your employees are paid a fixed amount (salary) or work the same hours each pay period. Features of using timesheets in QuickBooks include the following:

- Using a stopwatch to time an activity as it is performed.
- Entering the time manually using a weekly timesheet or individually by the activity, as shown in Figures 11.26 and 11.27.
- Adding the time to a customer's invoice. For more information, see "Time and Expense Invoicing," p. 346.

 **note**

Time tracking is enabled in the Preferences dialog box. From the menu bar, select **Edit, Preferences** to open this dialog box and select the **Time & Expenses—Company Preferences** tab.

Time sheet entries can help you efficiently create payroll records each pay period. On the Payroll Info tab for each employee (refer to Figure 11.17), select the **Use Time Data to Create Paychecks** check-box.

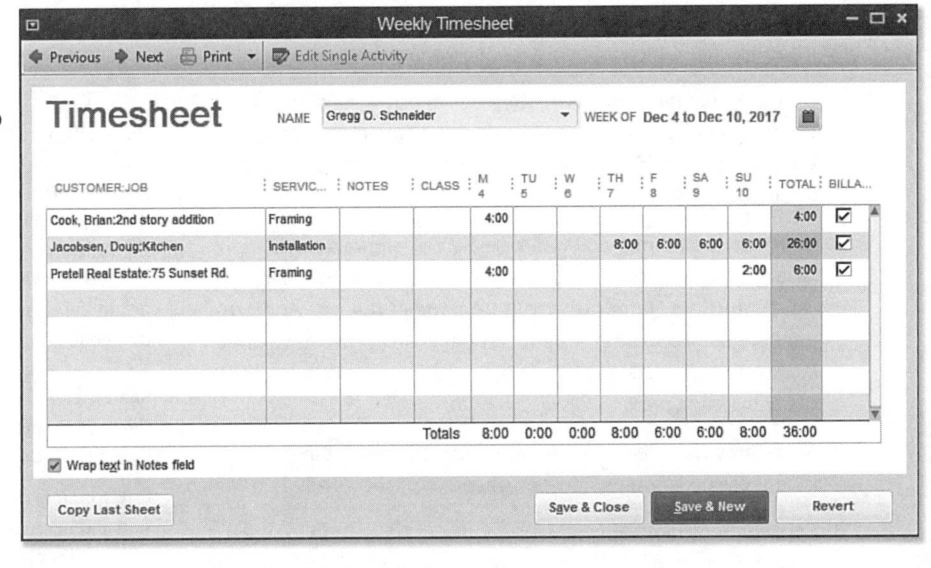

Figure 11.26 Weekly timesheets can be used to create payroll transactions.

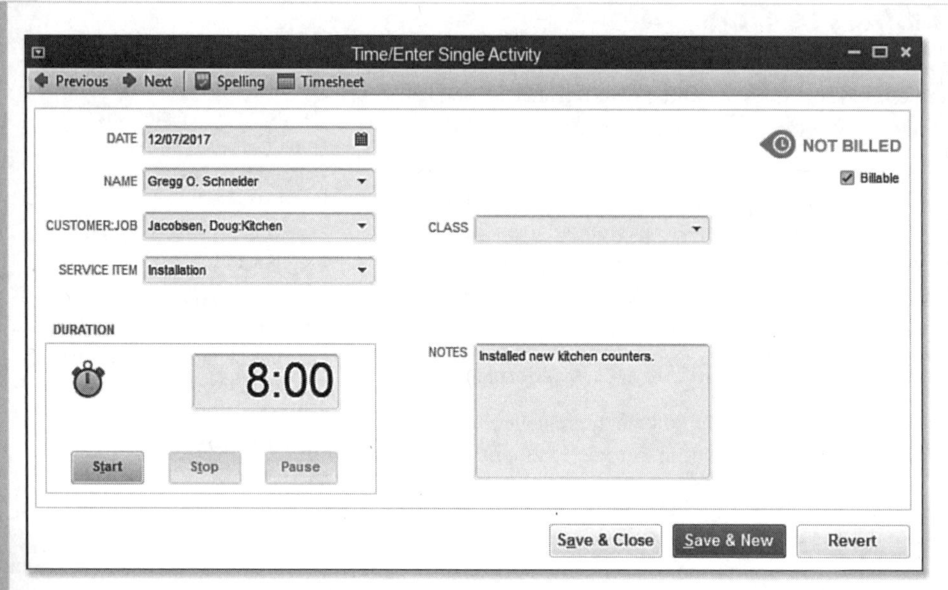

Figure 11.27 The Time/Enter Single Activity dialog box includes a stopwatch.

To record payroll timesheet activity, follow these steps:

1. On the Home page, click the drop-down arrow next to the Enter Time icon and select **Use Weekly Timesheet** or **Time/ Enter Single Activity**. The following instructions presume you selected the Weekly Timesheet.
2. From the Name drop-down list, select the employee whose time you want to enter. If you want to enter multiple names, select **Multiple Names (Payroll)** from top of the list. Adding multiple names to a timesheet can be useful if you have crew labor that works the same hours, on the same service items for the same customers or jobs.
3. Click Copy Last Sheet if you would like to repeat the detail from a previously recorded timesheet.
4. Enter data as needed (the user might not have time for each day, for instance) in each of the columns. Your columns might differ depending on your purchased payroll subscription and payroll preferences you enabled.

tip

Do you want to have employees track their own time on jobs at their computer, even if they do not have access to the QuickBooks file? Enter **QuickBooks Timer** in the search box in the upper-right corner of the menu bar, select **Help** from the drop-down list, and click the Search icon to the right. Follow the links for installing and working with the QuickBooks Timer.

For more detailed information and instructions, see "Using the QuickBooks Timer," p. 654.

5. (Optional) Click the Print button to print the current timesheet with a signature line. If you want to print a blank timesheet, click the down arrow to the right of the Print button and select **Print Blank Timesheet**.
6. Click Save & Close when completed with the timesheet entry.

Using timesheets can help you enter payroll more efficiently and can be printed for the employees to sign, approving of the hours that they will be paid.

Preparing Employee Paychecks

You are now ready to create paychecks for your employees. Following the instructions provided in this chapter can help to make this process efficient and accurate.

Creating or Editing a Payroll Schedule

A payroll schedule defines the payroll frequency, the pay period end date, and the date that should print on the employee's paycheck. If you create at least one payroll schedule, the Payroll Center will display the next scheduled payroll. Another use for payroll schedules is to separate your employees into different groups. If your business pays the administrative staff biweekly but your operations employees weekly, you would set up two payroll schedules.

To create or edit a payroll schedule, from the menu bar select **Employees**, **Add or Edit Payroll Schedules**. Complete the information required and click OK to save the schedule. Press the Esc key on your keyboard to close the Payroll Schedule List.

Next, assign your employees to the newly created scheduled payroll.

For more information see, "Adding an Employee" pg. 444.

Paying Employees

To prepare your QuickBooks payroll paychecks, follow these steps. To help you along, when you prepare your first payroll, QuickBooks displays a Welcome to Your First Payroll message. After you review the details, click OK, I'm Ready!

1. On the Home page, click the Pay Employees icon. The Payroll Center opens (refer to Figure 11.4).
2. Select a **Payroll Schedule** and click Start Scheduled Payroll.
3. From the Enter Payroll Information dialog box:
   - Accept the default Pay Period Ends and Check Date or change as necessary.
   - Place a checkmark next to each employee you want to pay. Optionally, click the Check All or Uncheck All button, as shown in Figure 11.28.
   - Optionally, use Sort By and Show/Hide Columns to customize how the information is displayed.
   - If time entered on a QuickBooks timesheet doesn't appear for a given employee, verify that the employee record has the Use Time Data to Create Paychecks option selected (refer to Figure 11.17).

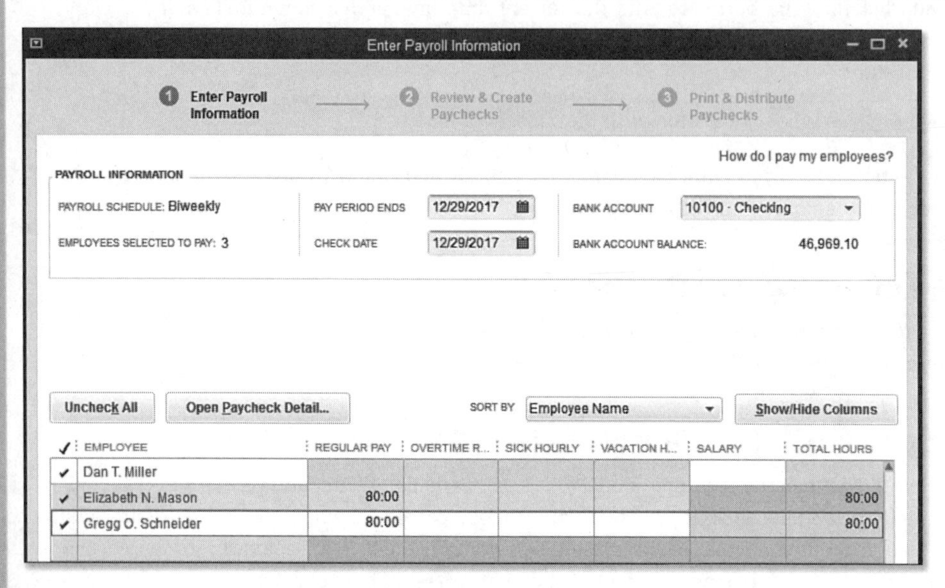

Figure 11.28 The payroll information defaults from the scheduled payroll setup and employee's salary or time sheet details.

- Optionally, enter your employee's hours in the Enter Payroll Information dialog box.
- Optionally, click the Open Paycheck Detail, to review and or edit information not displayed on the Enter Payroll Information dialog box. Click Save & Next or Save & Close to return to the Enter Payroll Information dialog box.

4. Click Continue. The Review and Create Paychecks dialog box displays as shown in Figure 11.29.

How do I pay my employees?

PAYROLL INFORMATION

PAYROLL SCHEDULE: Biweekly | PAY PERIOD ENDS 12/29/2017 | BANK ACCOUNT 10100 · Checking

NUMBER OF PAYCHECKS: 3 | CHECK DATE 12/29/2017 | BANK ACCOUNT BALANCE: 46,969.10

PAYCHECK OPTIONS

Print paychecks from QuickBooks | Assign check numbers to handwritten checks | Explain Printing Options

First Check Number 518 | Printing Preferences

Open Paycheck Detail...

Employee	Gross Pay	Taxes	Deductions	Net Pay	Employer Taxe	Contributions	Total Hours	Direct De
Dan T. Miller	1,596.15	-125.74	0.00	1,470.41	122.11	266.11		
Elizabeth N. Mason	1,180.00	-166.56	0.00	1,013.44	90.27	121.18	80:00	
Gregg O. Schneider	1,380.00	-212.27	-12.50	1,155.23	105.57	13.11	80:00	
	4,156.15	-504.57	-12.50	3,639.08	317.95	400.40	160:00	

Figure 11.29 Select paycheck printing options and review paycheck details.

5. Change the Bank Account if necessary.
6. Choose to Print Paychecks from QuickBooks or Assign Check Numbers to Handwritten Checks.
7. Click Create Paychecks.

The following section details printing of paychecks or paystubs.

Printing Paychecks or Paystubs

The last step in preparing payroll for your employees is printing the checks. There are two options:

- **Print Paychecks**—Prints on check stock for employees to deposit or cash.
- **Print Paystubs**—Creates a nonnegotiable document detailing the employee's earnings. Use this dialog box when an employee is paid by direct deposit.

When you click Create Paychecks, the Confirmation and Next Steps dialog box displays as shown in Figure 11.30.

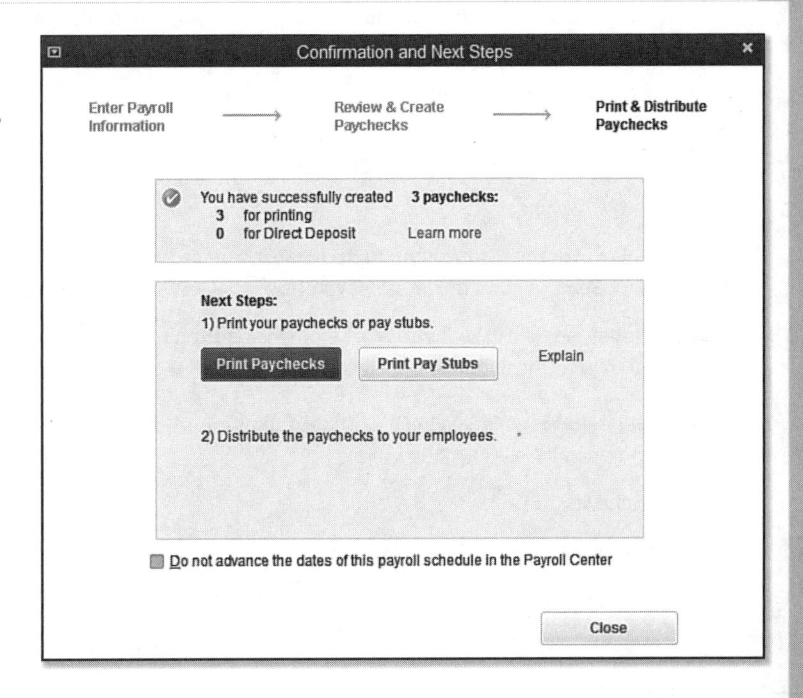

Figure 11.30
You can print paychecks now or print later by selecting **File, Print Forms, Print Paychecks, or Print Paystubs** from the menu bar.

After successfully printing your employees' paychecks, you should promptly pay the payroll liabilities to avoid costly penalties and late fees.

To learn more about printer settings in QuickBooks, see "Setting Form Defaults and Making Printing Adjustments," p. 496.

Do your employees ask for information about previously paid payroll? Check out the next section for details on using the free service ViewMyPaycheck.

ViewMyPaycheck

With ViewMyPaycheck, a free service included with your QuickBooks Payroll subscription, give your employees online access to their pay stubs, W-2s, and other payroll info. Access the information from any Internet connection or on your mobile device.

How does the ViewMyPaycheck service work? Following are the steps:

1. After subscribing to one of QuickBooks's integrated payroll subscriptions, from the menu bar, select **Employees**, **Send To ViewMyPaycheck.com**. This is a free service for companies that have a paid QuickBooks payroll subscription.
2. The ViewMyPaycheck dialog displays. Click Connect.
3. The Intuit App Center displays where you create an Intuit Account or sign in to an existing account. Complete the fields as required.
4. You might get an If You're Almost Ready... message, indicating you have more than one Intuit Account and need to associate this service with the correct account. Click Continue.
5. A message displays with details about how the application ViewMyPaycheck will access your Intuit company data. Click Authorize.
6. A message displays that you are securely connected to ViewMyPaycheck. Click Return to ViewMyPaycheck.
7. If this is your first time signing up for this service, you will see a ViewMyPaycheck message. Select **Send** to send the latest paystubs to the service so employees can view and print them.
8. If prompted, click the Invite My Employees button or the I'll Do This Later button. The ViewMyPaycheck dialog displays as shown with the administrator view in Figure 11.31.

Logging in to ViewMyPaycheck as the Administrator (the original user that signed up for the service), you can access the following:

- Paychecks Tab
  - Print Pay Stub or Download/Save PDF.
  - Filter paychecks listed for a specific date range.
  - View paystub information, including Used and Available Paid Time Off.
- Taxes Tab
  - Enabling W-2 Access. If you are an employee of the company as well as the ViewMyPaycheck administrator, you will need to set yourself up as an employee and sign into the service.
  - A link is provided for sending your QuickBooks W-2 data to ViewMyPaycheck.

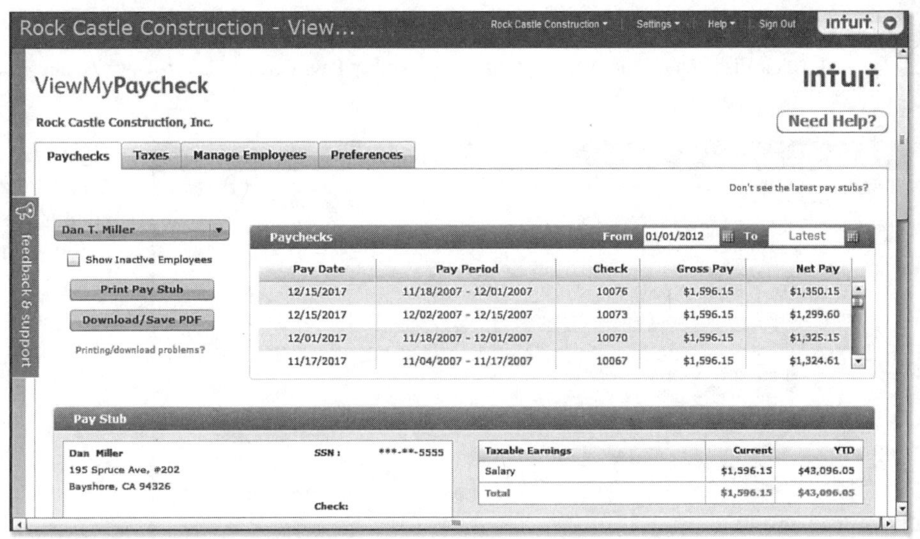

Figure 11.31 Invite employees to access their payroll information using the free ViewMyPaycheck service on the Internet or mobile device.

- Manage Employees Tab
  - Manage administrators by adding new administrators or removing access.
  - Enter employees' email addresses and send invitations to set up access to view their own payroll information.
- Preferences Tab
  - Option to send email notification to employees when pay stubs are uploaded.
  - Show all paychecks dated through today's date or the latest paycheck date.

If you would like more information about this service, go to this website: http://viewmypaycheck.intuit.com/

Preparing Payroll Liability Payments

When your business pays employees, you also become responsible for paying the liabilities associated with the payroll to governmental and other entities.

Paying Scheduled Liabilities

To pay scheduled payroll liabilities, follow these steps:

1. On the Home page, click the Pay Liabilities icon. QuickBooks opens the Payroll Center. The Pay Scheduled Liabilities lists each payroll liability (amount you owe), with the Due Date, Status, Payment Description, Method, Period, and Amount (refer to Figure 11.4).

2. To process a payment, place a checkmark next to the payroll item you want to pay. (Optional) Double-click the Amount to view a listing of the transactions that are included in the amount due.

3. Click View/Pay. QuickBooks prepares a Liability Payment for your review, as shown in Figure 11.32.

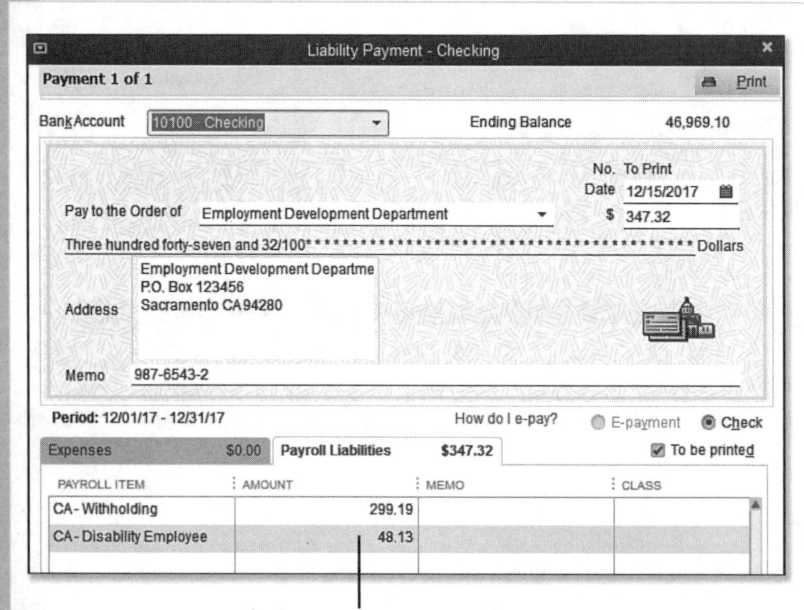

Figure 11.32
QuickBooks payroll calculates the tax payments automatically.

4. Change the Bank Account if needed. The payroll items and amount included on the liability payment are calculated from payroll transactions. Check E-Payment to process your payment electronically, or for more information click the How Do I E-Pay link.

5. Print the checks from the top-right Print icon, or later by selecting **File**, **Print Forms**, **Print Checks** from the menu bar.

6. Click Save & Close when finished to return to the Payroll Center, Pay Scheduled Liabilities dialog box.

caution

If you do not see all the payroll liabilities you accrue each pay period, you might not have the correct payroll liability due date assigned. From the Payroll Center, in the Pay Scheduled Liabilities dialog box, select the **Related Payment Activities** drop-down list.

When you select **Edit Payment Due Dates/Methods,** QuickBooks opens the Payroll Setup. Review and edit the Scheduled Tax Payments List.

Adjusting Payroll Liabilities

QuickBooks automatically calculates payroll liabilities as you process paychecks. If you determine that an amount is not calculating correctly, review the settings for that payroll item.

Your accounting professional might choose to create a journal entry to correct the business financials. However, this type of transaction will not affect the amounts included in the Pay Scheduled Liabilities in the Payroll Center or the payroll reporting forms. Instead, use the Liability Adjustment dialog box for changes to the amounts that are reported as liabilities and to affect federal and state reporting forms.

After reviewing your payroll reports detailed in Chapter 12, you can adjust payroll liabilities. To do so, follow these steps:

1. From the menu bar select **Employees**, **Payroll Taxes and Liabilities**, **Adjust Payroll Liabilities** (refer to Figure 11.15).
2. Select the **Date** and **Effective Date**. These dates might affect your payroll reporting forms, so specify the date carefully.
3. Select **Company** if the adjustment is for a company-only payroll item, such as a company-paid health insurance benefit.
4. Select **Employee** if the adjustment is for an employee-reported liability or if you need to affect a change to the employee's W2 amounts. Select **Class** if using this feature in QuickBooks.
5. From the Item Name drop-down list, select the payroll item or items to be adjusted.
6. Enter an Amount (positive or negative).
7. Enter the Wage Base (positive or negative) if the payroll item being adjusted is subject to a wage threshold similar to federal or state unemployment.
8. Enter the Income Subject to Tax (positive or negative) to adjust the amount reported on tax forms.
9. (Optional) Enter a Memo.
10. (Optional) Click Accounts Affected. The default is to affect liability and expense accounts. If your financials are correct, but the payroll reporting and liabilities are incorrect, select **Do Not Affect Accounts**. Click OK to close the message.
11. Click Next Adjustment to add an additional record, or click OK to close the Adjust Payroll Liabilities dialog box.

It's a good practice to review your payroll reports again after making the adjustments to be certain they display the expected results.

This chapter has prepared you well for working with payroll processes. Join me in the next chapter for details on managing your payroll, including what reports to review and how to verify that your payroll data is correct.

12

MANAGING PAYROLL

There are many areas in QuickBooks that deserve a thorough review and one in particular is payroll. Managing your payroll includes verifying you are paying your employees properly and that you remain in compliance with state and federal regulations regarding your company's payroll obligations.

If your company process payroll for employees, this chapter will help you better manage the many facets of providing payroll.

Report Center Payroll Reports

You will find that reporting on payroll activity is necessary to properly manage your business payroll activity. QuickBooks offers several payroll reports that can be customized to suit your needs. For more details on customizing reports, see Chapter 14, "Reporting in QuickBooks." Whether you are new to QuickBooks, or an expert, you will benefit from the payroll reports in the Report Center. To open the Report Center, from the menu bar, select **Reports**, **Report Center**. Select any of the icons on the top right to change the viewing method for the Report Center:

- Carousel View
- List View
- Grid View

By default, the Report Center opens with the Standard tab selected and displays several report categories. Click Employees & Payroll. To the right you'll see sample payroll reports, as shown in Figure 12.1, using the Grid View.

Underneath each sample report, you can click the corresponding icons to prepare the report using your data and a date you select, get more information about the report, mark the report as a favorite, or access help information for the report. Icon descriptions appear when you hover your cursor over a report.

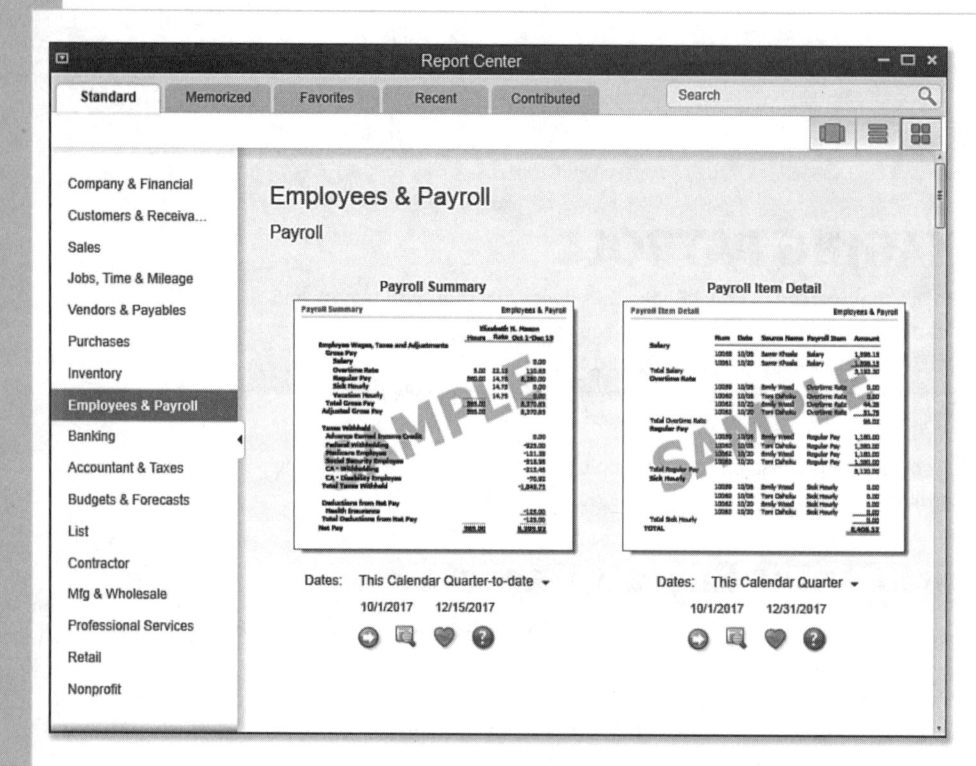

Figure 12.1 Preview and prepare payroll reports in the Report Center.

The Report Center also offers these additional tabs:

- **Memorized**—From any displayed report, click Memorize to add the report to this tab in the Report Center.
- **Favorites**—Mark a report as a Favorite (or Fave) to include the report in this tab group.
- **Recent**—QuickBooks lists reports you have recently prepared here.
- **Contributed**—Custom reports created by Intuit or other QuickBooks users can be downloaded and used with your data. You can also share reports you create with the community at large. When sharing a report, you are not sharing sensitive information, just the format of the report.

You can also type a descriptive search term into the search box in the Report Center to display a list of relevant reports. Additional payroll reports are available in QuickBooks using pivot tables in Microsoft Excel. The next section details these reports.

Excel Reports

If you did not find the report you needed in the Report Center, check out the many reports that use pivot tables in Microsoft Excel. These reports are included with your QuickBooks software.

To access these reports follow these steps:

1. From the menu bar, select **Reports**, **Employees & Payroll**, **Summarize Payroll Data In Excel**. QuickBooks launches Excel and provides a dialog box to:
   - Select Date ranges for collecting payroll data
   - Select Options/Settings that include updating worksheet headers, column widths, and enabling drilldown on data and other useful settings.
   - Select Optional Reports including 8846 Worksheet, Effective Rates by Item, YTD Recap, and Deferred Compensation report.
2. Click Get QuickBooks Data. Excel then collects data for the selected date range and creates a Workbook with several worksheets, see Figure 12.2, including the following:
   - Employee Journal
   - YTD Summary (two versions)
   - Hours
   - Rates & Hours by Job
   - State Wage Listing
   - Deferred Comp
   - Quarterly details
   - 8846 Worksheet
   - Calculated % By Payroll Item and Employee

You can save this report as an Excel worksheet for future reference. However, this report cannot be updated with more current data unlike many other exported Excel reports.

In addition to these reports, there are other reports that QuickBooks creates using Excel.

From the menu bar, select **Reports**, **Employees & Payroll**, **More Payroll Reports in Excel**. Choose which specific report you want from the following:

- Payroll Summary by Tax Tracking Type
- Employee Time & Costs
- Employee Sick & Vacation History
- Employee Direct Deposit Listing
- Tax Form Worksheets
- New! Certified Payroll Report

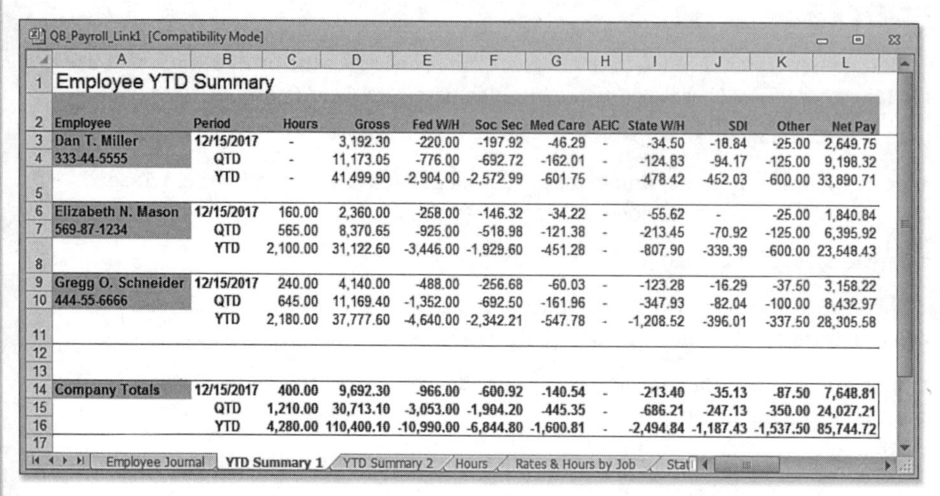

Employee YTD Summary

Employee	Period	Hours	Gross	Fed W/H	Soc Sec	Med Care	AEIC	State W/H	SDI	Other	Net Pay
Dan T. Miller	12/15/2017	-	3,192.30	-220.00	-197.92	-46.29	-	-34.50	-18.84	-25.00	2,649.75
333-44-5555	QTD	-	11,173.05	-776.00	-692.72	-162.01	-	-124.83	-94.17	-125.00	9,198.32
	YTD	-	41,499.90	-2,904.00	-2,572.99	-601.75	-	-478.42	-452.03	-600.00	33,890.71
Elizabeth N. Mason	12/15/2017	160.00	2,360.00	-258.00	-146.32	-34.22	-	-55.62	-	-25.00	1,840.84
569-87-1234	QTD	565.00	8,370.65	-925.00	-518.98	-121.38	-	-213.45	-70.92	-125.00	6,395.92
	YTD	2,100.00	31,122.60	-3,446.00	-1,929.60	-451.28	-	-807.90	-339.39	-600.00	23,548.43
Gregg O. Schneider	12/15/2017	240.00	4,140.00	-488.00	-256.68	-60.03	-	-123.28	-16.29	-37.50	3,158.22
444-55-6666	QTD	645.00	11,169.40	-1,352.00	-692.50	-161.96	-	-347.93	-82.04	-100.00	8,432.97
	YTD	2,180.00	37,777.60	-4,640.00	-2,342.21	-547.78	-	-1,208.52	-396.01	-337.50	28,305.58
Company Totals	12/15/2017	400.00	9,692.30	-966.00	-600.92	-140.54	-	-213.40	-35.13	-87.50	7,648.81
	QTD	1,210.00	30,713.10	-3,053.00	-1,904.20	-445.35	-	-686.21	-247.13	-350.00	24,027.21
	YTD	4,280.00	110,400.10	-10,990.00	-6,844.80	-1,600.81	-	-2,494.84	-1,187.43	-1,537.50	85,744.72

Figure 12.2 You can prepare this and many other payroll reports with your data using Excel spreadsheets.

As you can see, QuickBooks provides plenty of options for finding the right payroll report for your needs, either within QuickBooks or using the automatically generated Microsoft Excel reports.

Tax Forms and Filings

Up to this point, you have set up payroll, managed employees and payroll items, paid your employee and the liabilities, and prepared payroll reports. You will now see how QuickBooks helps you to comply with the required payroll reporting.

In Chapter 11, "Setting Up Payroll," you learned about the many payroll subscription offerings you can choose from. If you want your QuickBooks software to automatically calculate your payroll transactions and prepare federal and state forms, you need to have the Intuit QuickBooks Payroll Enhanced subscription. For accounting professionals who prepare payroll for multiple clients, Intuit QuickBooks Payroll Enhanced for Accountants is the subscription most suitable.

QuickBooks can print required federal and state payroll forms or E-File them for you; it couldn't be easier to complete your payroll reporting tasks.

Preparing and Printing Tax Forms

Before preparing your first payroll tax form, complete the Payroll Tax Information box on the Company Information dialog box. To do so, from the menu bar, select **Company**, **Company Information**. In the lower-right corner confirm the Contact Name, Title, and Phone # that will be included on the prepared payroll tax forms, as displayed in Figure 12.3.

To prepare your federal or state forms, follow these steps:

1. On the Home page, click the Process Payroll Forms icon.

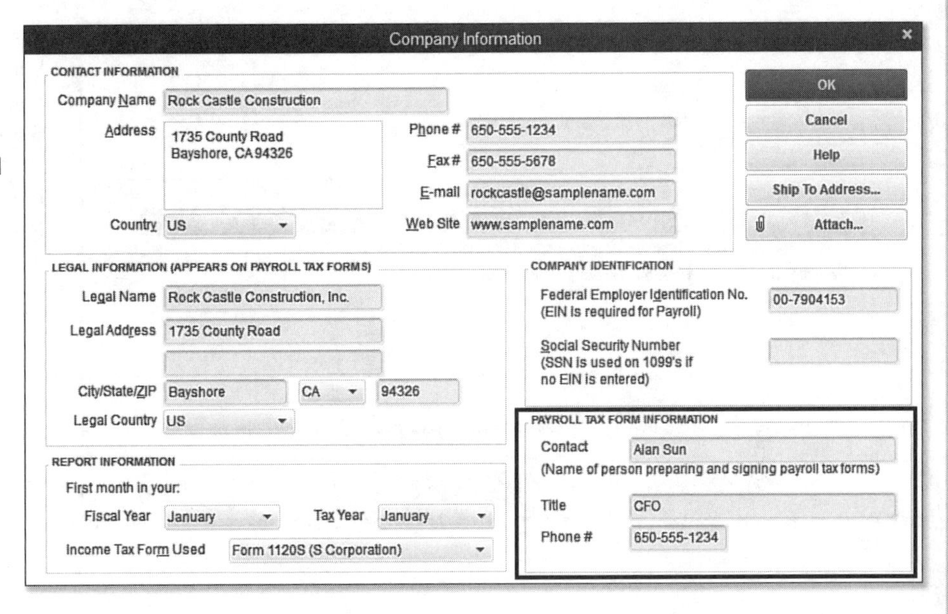

Figure 12.3 QuickBooks prefills payroll tax forms with specified contact information.

2. Select Federal Form or State Form. Click OK. If a Payroll Subscription Alert message displays, informing you to update your tax tables, go to step 3; otherwise, go to step 5.
3. Click Get Updates or Skip. I recommend that you select the Get Updates to ensure you have the latest tax tables and forms.
4. Click OK to close the Payroll Update message.
5. On the Home page, click the Process Payroll Forms icon.
6. Select a Federal Form or State Form. Click OK. See Figure 12.4.
7. Choose a form to prepare. Accounting professionals should choose the report forms labeled For Reporting Agents.
8. Select Filing Period, Quarter, and Quarter Ending date. Click OK.
9. Complete any required fields on the displayed form. If you have questions about the form details, click the provided links. When you have completed the form, click the Check for Errors button (see Figure 12.5). If any errors display, click the error, and QuickBooks will advance to that section of the form for you to complete or correct.
10. Click Next to advance to the next form page.
11. Click Save & Close if you need to return later to your saved work.
12. Click Save as PDF to save a PDF for your records; click Print for Your Records to prepare a paper copy; or click Submit Form if you have signed up for (discussed in the next section).

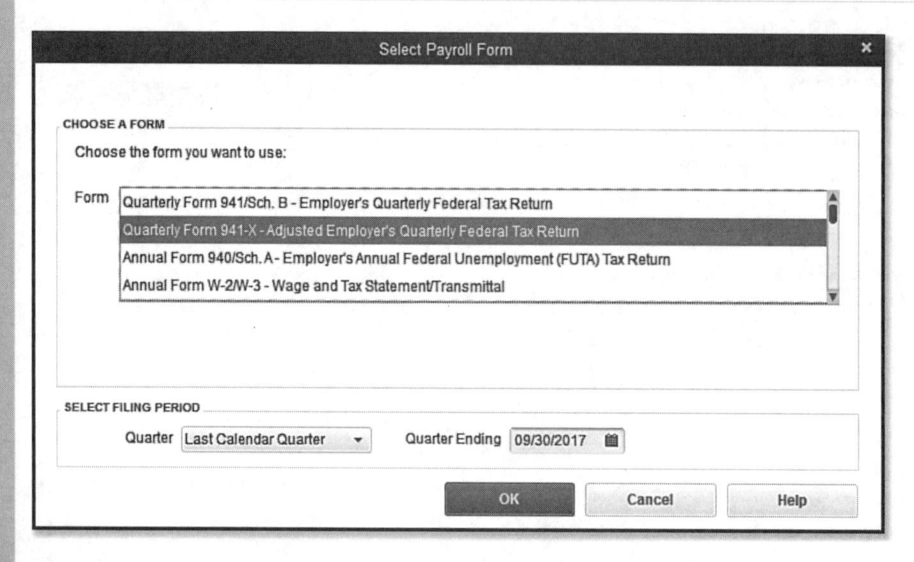

Figure 12.4 With the Enhanced Payroll Subscription, QuickBooks can prepare all your federal forms and many state forms.

Payroll Tax Form

Form **941** | **Employer's Quarterly Federal Tax Return** | **2017**

Name (not your trade name): Rock Castle Construction, Inc.
Employer Identification No. (EIN): 00-7904153
Trade Name (if any): Rock Castle Construction
Address: 1735 County Road
City: Bayshore **State**: CA **ZIP Code**: 94326

Report for this Quarter (Check one)

1 January, February, March ☐
2 April, May, June ☐
3 July, August, September ☒
4 October, November, December ☐

Part 1 – Answer These Questions For This Quarter

1	**Number of employees who received wages, tips, or other compensation for the pay period including March 12 (Quarter 1), June 12 (Quarter 2), September 12 (Quarter 3), December 12 (Quarter 4)**	1	0
2	**Wages, tips, and other compensation**	2	25,176.95
3	**Income tax withheld from wages, tips, and other compensation**	3	2,509.00
4	**If no wages, tips, and other compensation are subject to social security or Medicare tax, check here and go to line 6** ☐		

Column 1 *Column 2*

View details about this form · View filing and printing instructions · <<< Previous · Next >>>
Save and Close · Save as PDF... · Print for Your Records... · Check for Errors · Submit Form...

Click here before printing or filing

Figure 12.5 Save time and prepare accurate payroll tax forms using the Enhanced Payroll subscription.

E-Filing Tax Payments and Forms

If you selected the Intuit QuickBooks Payroll Enhanced subscription or the Intuit QuickBooks Payroll Enhanced for Accountant's subscription for your business, you can sign up for the E-File and E-Pay service.

With E-File and E-Pay, you prepare your payroll liability payments in QuickBooks and select E-Pay. Intuit debits your bank account for the funds and remits them directly to the IRS on your behalf.

With E-File of your payroll forms, you can select Submit Form and QuickBooks will process your payroll form and send it to the IRS. You will receive email notification that the form was accepted (or rejected) by the IRS. To take advantage of the E-File and E-Pay Service, you need the following:

- An active Enhanced Payroll subscription.
- A supported version of QuickBooks (typically not older than three years back from the current calendar year).
- An Internet connection.
- The most recent payroll tax update.
- Enrollment with the Electronic Federal Tax Payment System (EFTPS), used by the IRS for employer or individual payments. For more information, visit www.eftps.gov.

More detailed information is provided by clicking the Find Out About E-File & Pay link on the Payroll Center. As your business E-Pays and E-Files, you can click the link to Check E-Filing Status, which displays documentation that the payments and forms were successfully transmitted to the IRS.

Troubleshooting Payroll

Using the QuickBooks Run Payroll Checkup diagnostic tool is a recommended way to review and validate the accuracy of your payroll data. You can also review your data setup and accuracy manually by reviewing the reports detailed in this section.

Reviewing the Payroll Item Listing can also be helpful when needing to troubleshoot payroll issues.

 *For more information, see "Reporting About Payroll Items," p. 450.*

Comparing Payroll Liability Balances to the Balance Sheet

It's important to periodically compare your Balance Sheet payroll liabilities account balance to the amount on the Payroll Liabilities Balances report. To do so, follow these steps:

1. From the menu bar, select **Reports**, **Company & Financial**, **Balance Sheet Standard**.
2. Select the As Of date for the period you are reviewing.
3. From the menu bar, select **Reports**, **Employees & Payroll**, **Payroll Liability Balances**.
4. From the Dates drop-down list select **All** from the top of the list. Leave the From date box empty. In the To date box, enter the same date that was used on the Balance Sheet Standard report.

Doing so ensures you are picking up all transactions for this account, including any unpaid balances from prior years. Click Print if you want to have a copy of this report to compare to your Balance Sheet payroll liabilities balance.

These two reports should have matching totals. In the examples shown in Figure 12.6, the Balance Sheet and Payroll Liabilities reports do not match.

The totals might not match because of nonpayroll transactions being used to record adjustments or payments to payroll liabilities using nonpayroll transactions, including make journal entry, enter bill, or write check transaction types.

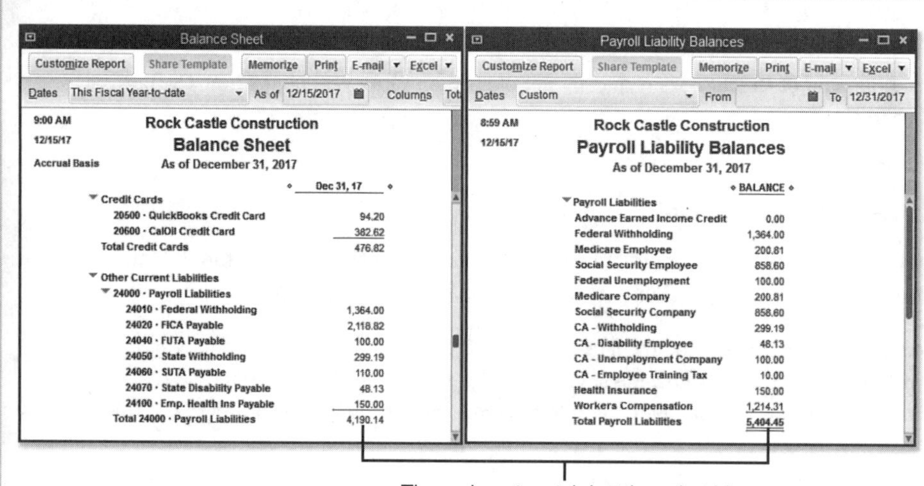

Figure 12.6 Compare the Balance Sheet payroll liabilities amount to the payroll liability balances report.

To troubleshoot payroll liabilities differences, you can use the Custom Transaction Detail report. To access the report, follow these steps:

1. From the menu bar, select **Reports**, **Custom Reports**, **Transaction Detail**. The Modify Report dialog box opens.
2. In the From date box leave the field blank; in the To date box, enter the date you used on the Balance Sheet Standard report.
3. Select the same Report Basis as the Balance Sheet report.
4. In the Columns box, remove or add a checkmark for the information you want to display on the report. Be sure to include Type.
5. In the Sort By drop-down list, select **Type**.

6. Click the Filters tab; in the Choose Filters box, the Accounts filter is already selected. From the Accounts drop-down list to the right, select the **Payroll Liabilities** account.

7. Click OK to create the report.

QuickBooks creates a useful and telling report, as shown in Figure 12.7. When this report is sorted by type of transaction, you can easily see what nonpayroll-related transactions are affecting your Balance Sheet Standard report Payroll Liability balance and are not affecting your Payroll Liability Balances report.

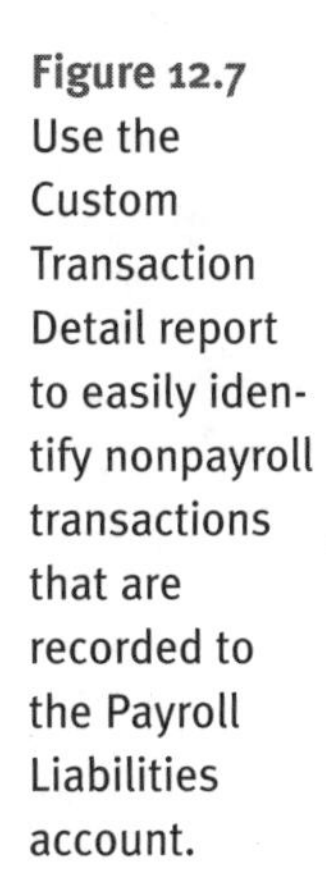

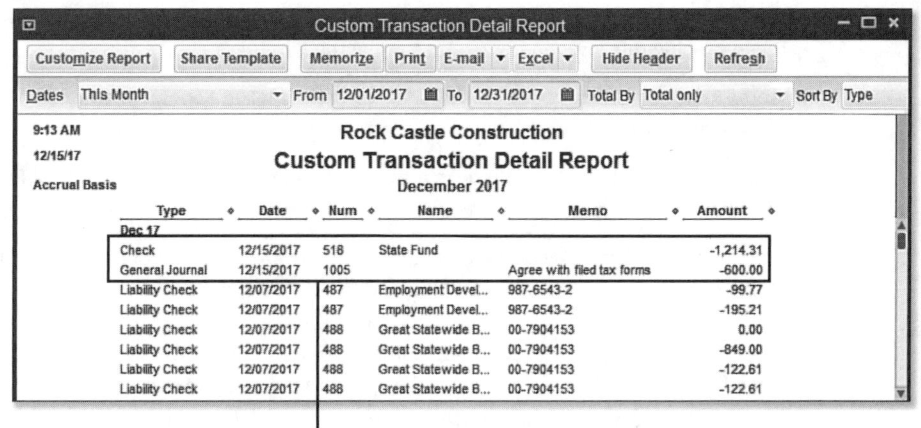

Type	Date	Num	Name	Memo	Amount
Dec 17					
Check	12/15/2017	518	State Fund		-1,214.31
General Journal	12/15/2017	1005		Agree with filed tax forms	-600.00
Liability Check	12/07/2017	487	Employment Devel...	987-6543-2	-99.77
Liability Check	12/07/2017	487	Employment Devel...	987-6543-2	-195.21
Liability Check	12/07/2017	488	Great Statewide B...	00-7904153	0.00
Liability Check	12/07/2017	488	Great Statewide B...	00-7904153	-849.00
Liability Check	12/07/2017	488	Great Statewide B...	00-7904153	-122.61
Liability Check	12/07/2017	488	Great Statewide B...	00-7904153	-122.61

Figure 12.7 Use the Custom Transaction Detail report to easily identify nonpayroll transactions that are recorded to the Payroll Liabilities account.

If you are an accounting professional working with the Client Data Review feature, you can also select the Find Incorrectly Paid Payroll Liabilities custom report from the menu bar by selecting **Accountant**, **Client Data Review**, **Find Incorrectly Paid Payroll Liabilities**.

For more information, see "Find Incorrectly Paid Payroll Liabilities," p. 703.

You can double-click any of the listed transactions to see more detail about the transaction that was used to create the adjustment to the Balance Sheet. If the Balance Sheet is correct and the Payroll Liability Balances report is not, you can choose between the following options:

- If there are only a few nonpayroll transactions, you might consider voiding them and re-creating them with the correct payroll liability payment transaction. However, if the transactions have been included in bank reconciliations, you would have other factors to consider and should consider the next option.
- Create an Adjust Payroll Liabilities transaction.

For more information see, "Preparing Payroll Liability Payments," p. 459.

Comparing Payroll Summary to Filed Payroll Returns

Has your company ever received a notice from the IRS indicating that your year-end payroll documents do not agree with your quarterly payroll return totals, or have you received a similar notice from your state payroll tax agency?

Listed in this section are some basic comparisons you should do both before filing a payroll return and after, in the event you allow users to make changes to transactions from previous payroll quarters.

For more information about preventing these changes, see "Set a Closing Date," pg. 587.

Compare the following items routinely while doing payroll in QuickBooks and ensure that

- Each calendar quarter QuickBooks payroll totals agree with your filed payroll return totals. Look at these specific totals when reviewing the Payroll Summary:
  - Total Adjusted Gross Pay in QuickBooks agrees with the Federal 941 Form, Wages, Tips, and Other Compensation.
  - Federal Withholding in QuickBooks agrees with the Federal 941 Form, Total Income Tax Withheld from Wages, and so on.
  - Employee and Company Social Security and Medicare in QuickBooks agree with the computed Total Taxable Social Security and Medicare on the Federal 941 Form.
- Total payroll tax deposits for the quarter in QuickBooks agrees with your paper trail. Whether you pay online or use a coupon that you take to the bank, make sure you recorded the correct calendar quarter with the IRS for your payments.
- Total Adjusted Gross Pay for the calendar year in QuickBooks agrees with the reported Gross Wage total on the annual Federal Form W-3, Transmittal of Wage, and Tax Statements.
- Total Adjusted Gross Pay for the calendar quarter in QuickBooks agrees with the Total Gross Wage reported to your state payroll agency.
- Total Payroll expense from the Profit & Loss report agrees with total Adjusted Gross Pay on the Payroll Summary report.

Comparing these critical reports with your federal and state tax filings will ensure your data agrees with the payroll tax agency records.

Reconciling Payroll Reports to Business Financials

When applying for a business loan from your bank, your company might be required to produce reviewed or audited financials. One of the many items that will be reviewed is the comparison of payroll costs included in the business financials to those in the payroll returns filed with federal or state governments.

If you are uncertain about which accounts within your chart of accounts to review, refer to the account you assigned to the payroll item. Here are a few selected comparisons you can do yourself as a business owner:

- Compare Federal Form 941 Wages, Tips, and Other Compensation (Box 2) to the expense accounts used to report salaries and wages. You might need to add multiple accounts to match the total in Box 2.
- Compare the company portion of the payroll taxes reported to federal or state governments. If you are uncertain about the amount, ask your accountant or view information about payroll taxes on the www.irs.gov website.

This section has provided you with several critical comparisons to make and reports to review. No matter how proficient you are with QuickBooks, review these reports often. The next section of this chapter provides instructions on handling unique payroll transactions.

Recording Unique Payroll Transactions

The following sections detail several common payroll transactions you might need in your business.

Employee Loan Payment and Repayment

Your business might offer a loan to an employee in advance of payroll earnings. This amount should not be taxed at the time of payment if you expect the loan to be paid back to the company.

Paying an Employee Paycheck Advance

When you offer to pay employees an advance on their earnings, you are creating a loan payment check. If this is a loan to be paid back to the company, follow these steps:

1. From the menu bar, select **Employees**, **Pay Employees**, **Unscheduled Payroll**. The Enter Payroll Information dialog box opens.
2. Place a checkmark next to the employee you are creating the loan check for.
3. QuickBooks might warn that a paycheck for that period already exists. Click Continue if you want to create the loan payment check. You are returned to the Enter Payroll Information dialog box.
4. To modify the check to be an employee loan check, click the Open Paycheck Detail button.
5. In the Preview Paycheck dialog box, remove any amounts from the Earnings box (if you expect to be repaid this amount, the amount is not considered taxable earnings).
6. In the Other Payroll Items drop-down list, select the Employee Advances (in this example it was an Addition type payroll item), as shown in Figure 12.8, and skip to step 15.

   If you do not have an employee advance payroll item, you can easily create one right from the Preview Paycheck dialog box. In the Other Payroll Items box drop-down list, click Add New.
7. In the Add New Payroll Item dialog box, select the button for the Addition type and click Next.
8. The Add New Payroll Item (Addition) dialog box opens. Name the item Employee Advance (if displayed, do not select the Track Expenses by Job box). Click Next.

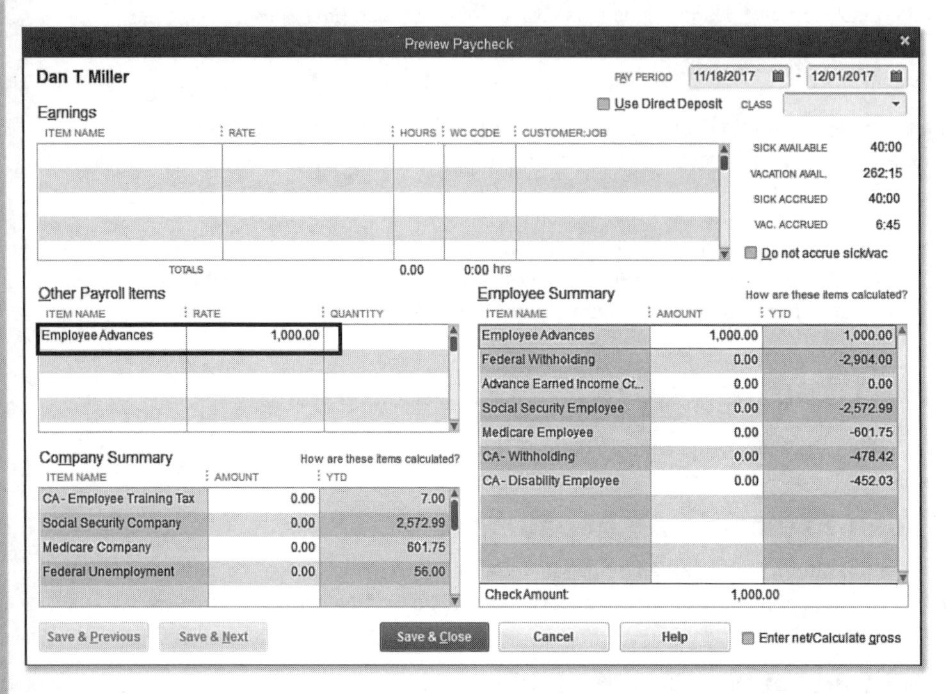

Figure 12.8 Use an Addition type payroll item when preparing a nontaxable loan (advance) to an employee.

9. In the Expense Account drop-down list, select Employee Advances, Other Current Asset account. You can also scroll to the top of this list and click Add New in this dialog box to create the Other Current Asset account if needed. Click Next.

10. On the Tax Tracking Type screen, select None (at the top of the list) and click Next.

11. Do not place a checkmark next to any of the Taxes options. Click Next.

12. The Calculate Based on Quantity screen opens. Leave the default of Neither selected and click Next.

13. On the Gross vs. Net screen, leave the default of Gross. This setting has no impact because you are setting it up with a tax tracking type of None. Click Next.

14. The Default Rate and Limit screen opens. Leave it blank because you define the limit amounts individually for each employee. Click Finish to close the Add New Payroll Item (Addition) dialog box.

15. You are returned to the Preview Paycheck dialog box. From the Other Payroll Items box, in the Item Name column, select the Employee Advance payroll addition item from the drop-down list.

caution

Carefully consider what option you choose when selecting the Tax Tracking type for a new payroll item or editing an existing payroll item. The selection you choose here affects how QuickBooks taxes or doesn't tax the payroll item on paychecks and how QuickBooks handles reporting the payroll item on forms, such as the W-2 form given to employees at the end of a calendar year.

When you select each Tax Tracking type, QuickBooks provides detailed information about how it will be treated for tax calculations and form preparation. Be sure to take the time to read these. If you are unsure of the proper tax tracking type, consult your accounting professional.

Enter the dollar amount of the loan you are providing the employee in the Rate column. QuickBooks creates a payroll advance check without deducting any payroll taxes (see Figure 12.8 shown previously). Note that you do not need to enter anything in the Quantity column.

QuickBooks now has on record a loan paid to the employee. If you have defined payment terms with the employee, you need to edit the employee's record so that on future payroll checks the agreed-to amount will be deducted. Learn more about this task in the following section.

Automatically Deducting the Employee Loan Repayments

When a company provides an advance to an employee that is to be paid back in installments, you can have QuickBooks automatically calculate this amount and even stop the deductions when the total of the loan has been completely paid back to the company. QuickBooks will automatically deduct the loan repayments from future payroll checks. Follow these steps to record a payroll deduction on the employee's setup:

1. From the menu bar, select **Employees**, **Employee Center**.
2. Select the employee who was given a payroll advance or loan. Click the Edit icon in the top right. The Edit Employee dialog box opens.
3. From the Change Tabs drop-down list, select Payroll and Compensation Info. The Payroll Info tab displays.
4. In the Item Name column of the Additions, Deductions, and Company Contributions box, select your Employee Loan Repay deduction item (and skip to step 14) or click Add New to open the Add New Payroll Item dialog box.
5. If creating a new item, select type Deduction and click Next.
6. The a name for the item such as **Employee Loan Repay** and click Next.
7. The Add New Payroll Item (Deduction) dialog box opens. Leave the agency name and number fields blank. For the Liability Account, select the drop-down list and select your Employee Loans, Other Current Asset account created when you made the employee advance check. (See Figure 12.9.) Click Next.

Figure 12.9
Assign the Other Current Asset Employee Loan Advances as the liability account for the paycheck deduction.

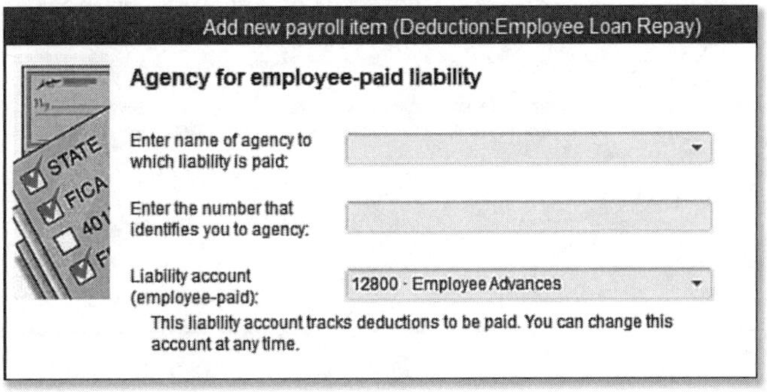

Add new payroll item (Deduction:Employee Loan Repay)

Agency for employee-paid liability

Enter name of agency to which liability is paid:

Enter the number that identifies you to agency:

Liability account (employee-paid): 12800 · Employee Advances

This liability account tracks deductions to be paid. You can change this account at any time.

8. The Tax Tracking type screen displays. Leave the default for Tax Tracking type of None and click Next.

9. The Taxes screen displays. Accept the default of no taxes selected and click Next.

10. The Calculate Based on Quantity screen displays. Leave the default of Neither selected and click Next.

11. The Gross vs. Net screen displays. Leave the default of Gross Pay. This setting has no impact because you are setting it up with a tax tracking type of None. Click Next.

12. The Default Rate and Limit screen displays. Leave it blank because you define the limit amounts individually for each employee. Click Finish to return to the New Employee dialog box or Edit Employee dialog box.

13. In the Item Name column of the Additions, Deductions, and Company Contributions box, select the Employee Loan Repay deduction item you just created.

14. In the Amount column, enter the per-pay-period amount you want to deduct.

15. In the Limit column, enter the amount of the total loan. QuickBooks stops deducting the loan when the limit is reached. Click OK to record your changes to the employee setup.

QuickBooks is now properly set up to deduct the stated amount on each paycheck until the employee loan has been fully paid back. If you provide additional employee loans, do not forget to go back to step 15 to add the new amount to the previous loan total.

Reporting Employee Loan Details

It is equally important to track the actual details of the employee loan. To open a modified version of my favorite report, the Transaction Detail report (as shown in Figure 12.10), follow these steps:

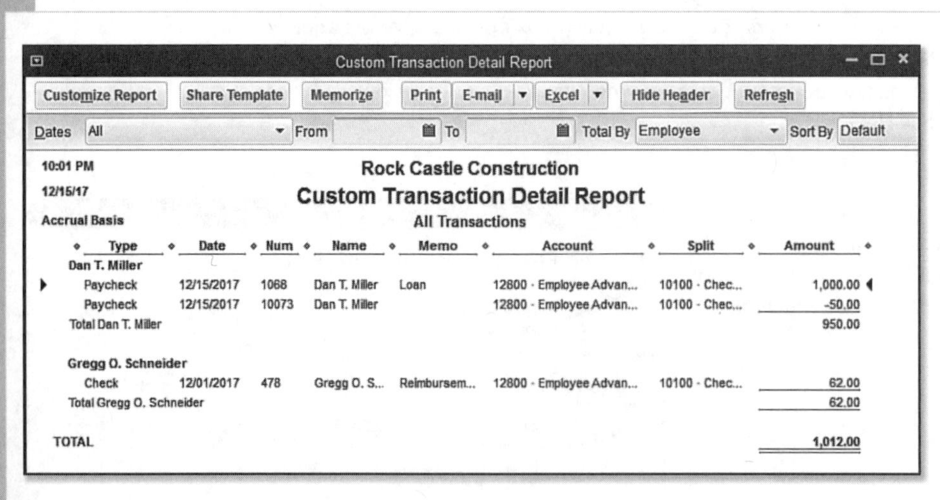

10:01 PM
12/15/17
Accrual Basis

Rock Castle Construction
Custom Transaction Detail Report
All Transactions

Type	Date	Num	Name	Memo	Account	Split	Amount
Dan T. Miller							
Paycheck	12/15/2017	1068	Dan T. Miller	Loan	12800 · Employee Advan...	10100 · Chec...	1,000.00
Paycheck	12/15/2017	10073	Dan T. Miller		12800 · Employee Advan...	10100 · Chec...	-50.00
Total Dan T. Miller							950.00
Gregg O. Schneider							
Check	12/01/2017	478	Gregg O. S...	Reimbursem...	12800 · Employee Advan...	10100 · Chec...	62.00
Total Gregg O. Schneider							62.00
TOTAL							1,012.00

Figure 12.10 Create a report to track your employee loan details.

1. From the menu bar, select **Reports**, **Custom Reports**, **Transaction Detail**. The Modify Report dialog box displays.

2. In the Report Date Range drop-down list, select the date range you are reviewing.

3. In the Columns box, select or deselect the detail you want to see displayed on the report.

4. In the Total By drop-down list, select **Employee**.

5. Click the Filters tab; Account is already selected in the Choose Filters box. In the Account drop-down list to the right, select the **Employee Loans**, Other Current Asset account.

6. In the Choose Filters box, select the Amount filter and optionally select an amount greater than or equal to .01. Doing so provides a report of only those employees with nonzero balances.

7. If you want to change the report title, click the Header/Footer tab and customize the report title.

8. Click OK to view the modified report.

9. If you want to use this report again, click Memorize to save the report for later use.

You are now prepared to advance money to an employee and track the employee's payments against the loan accurately. Don't forget to review the balances and to increase the limit when new loans are paid out.

Reprinting a Lost Paycheck

When any other check in QuickBooks is lost, you typically void the check in QuickBooks and issue a stop payment request to your bank so it cannot be cashed.

With payroll, you need to be a bit more cautious about voiding the transaction because when you void a payroll transaction and then reissue it, payroll taxes can be calculated differently on the replacement check compared to the original paycheck.

Certain payroll taxes are based on limits; for example, Social Security, Federal Unemployment, and State Unemployment taxes are examples of taxes that are charged to employees or to the company up to a certain wage limit. When you void a previously issued check, QuickBooks recalculates these taxes for the current replacement check, and these amounts might differ from the original check, potentially affecting the net amount of the check.

Proper control would be to issue a stop payment request for the missing check to your bank so it cannot be cashed. In QuickBooks, instead of voiding the payroll check and then re-creating it, print a new payroll check (from the same original payroll check details), record the new check number, and then separately create a voided check for the lost check.

To record these transactions, follow these steps:

1. Locate the lost check in your checking register from the menu bar by selecting **Banking**, **Use Register**.

2. In the Select Account drop-down list, select the bank account that has the missing check and click OK to open the bank register.

3. Find the check in the register that was reported missing. Double-click the specific check to open the Paycheck dialog box (see Figure 12.11). Make a note of the check number, date, and payee.

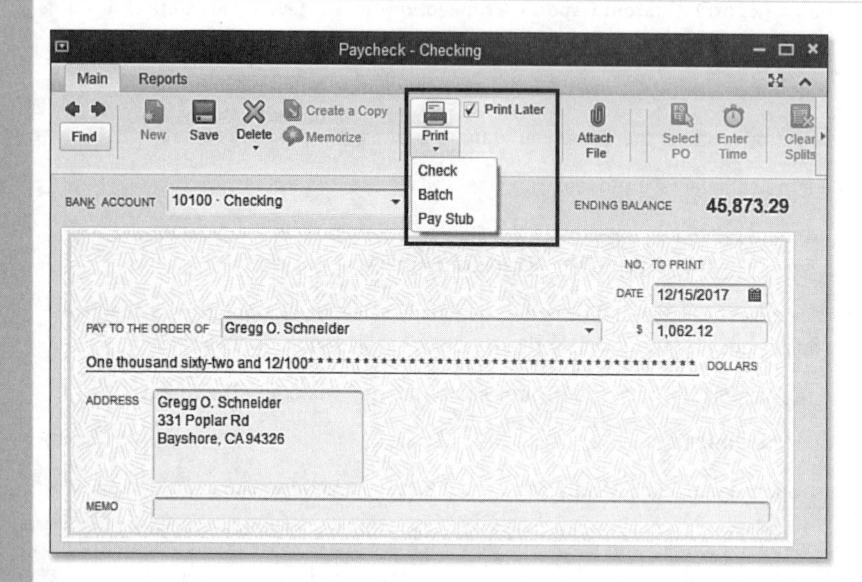

Figure 12.11
Do not re-create a lost paycheck; instead, select Print Later on the original paycheck.

4. In the open Paycheck dialog box, on the Main tab of the ribbon toolbar at the top of the transaction, select the **Print Later** checkbox.
5. Print the paycheck singly or with others by clicking the Print button at the top of the check on the Main tab of the ribbon toolbar.
6. Enter the Printed Check Number. After printing the check, QuickBooks assigns the new check number and uses the check date and totals assigned to the original check.
7. To keep track of the lost check in your accounting, select Banking, Write Checks from the menu bar. Using the original check number, date, and payee, record the check with a zero amount to an account of your choosing. You might get a message warning not to pay employees with a check, but because you are recording a zero transaction, you can ignore this warning.
8. With the lost check created in step 7 still open, from the menu bar select **Edit**, **Void Check**. QuickBooks prefills with a "0" amount and the Memo line of the check with "Void." This now shows this check as voided in your register, just in case the employee was able to cash the check. You would notice when reconciling that you have marked it as voided.

Using this method for printing a lost payroll check ensures you do not inadvertently change any prior period payroll amounts and reported payroll totals; at the same time, recording the lost check helps keep a record of each check issued from your bank account.

Paying a Taxable Bonus

Use an unscheduled payroll to issue bonuses to your employees. This payroll is included in their total taxable wages. To do so, follow these steps:

1. From the menu bar, select **Employees**, **Pay Employees**, **Unscheduled Payroll**. The Enter Payroll Information dialog box displays.

2. Place a checkmark next to the employee(s) receiving a bonus check.

3. If the employee is paid hourly, you can adjust the hours from the regular pay column.

4. Often, you want to edit or remove the default Gross Earnings or Federal Taxes Withheld on a bonus check. To adjust this detail, click the Open Paycheck Detail button to modify the default amounts.

note

When issuing a bonus paycheck, QuickBooks might display a warning that a paycheck already exists for the date you have selected. Click Continue to close the warning. You are returned to the Enter Payroll Information dialog box.

5. If you are using the Intuit QuickBooks Payroll Enhanced subscription, you can also select the checkbox to Enter Net/Calculate Gross on the paycheck detail. Selecting this option enables you to specify the net amount, and QuickBooks then calculates what the gross amount should be to cover taxes and withholdings.

6. QuickBooks might display a warning dialog box titled Special Calculation Situation to inform you that certain payroll items have reached their limits.

7. In the example shown in Figure 12.12, the Federal Withholding amount that was automatically calculated was removed. QuickBooks now shows that this paycheck was adjusted.

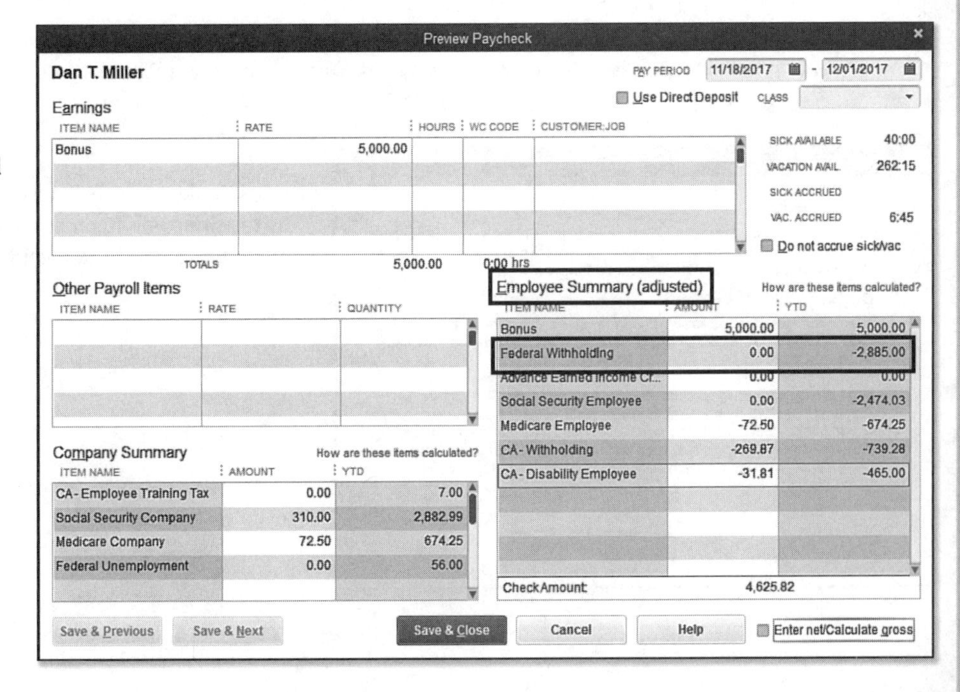

Figure 12.12 QuickBooks identifies when automatic payroll calculations have been manually adjusted.

Adjust paychecks cautiously, making sure you do not adjust those items that have a predefined tax table amount, such as Social Security and Medicare. If you do, and the adjustment causes the calculated totals to be incorrect for the year, QuickBooks "self-corrects" the taxes on the next payroll check you create for this employee. You should also obtain the advice of your tax accountant before adjusting taxes withheld on bonus payroll checks.

Adjusting an Employee Paycheck

You should rarely need to adjust a paycheck record in QuickBooks. One example is where you hand-prepare a check, and then later discover QuickBooks calculated a different net pay amount.

In this example, the check amount cashed by the employee differs from what QuickBooks computed, so adjusting the QuickBooks paycheck is acceptable.

To adjust a prepared employee check before it is printed, or to adjust a paycheck that had the wrong amount in QuickBooks from what was recorded on the actual check, follow these steps:

1. Locate the paycheck in your checking register by clicking the Check Register icon on the QuickBooks Home page.
2. If you have multiple checking accounts, select the account the paycheck was recorded to and click OK to open the bank register.
3. Find the check with the incorrect amount; open the paycheck transaction by double-clicking the check.
4. Click the Paycheck Detail button to display the detail of the check to be modified.
5. Click Unlock Net Pay and review the caution message QuickBooks provides about changing net pay on existing checks. Click OK to close the message, as shown in Figure 12.13.

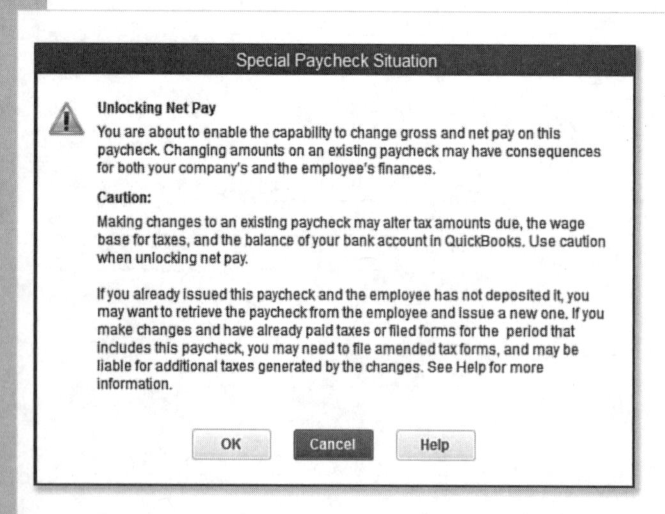

Figure 12.13
QuickBooks protects inadvertent changes by requiring you to unlock net pay before modifying a paycheck record.

6. Modify the check as needed, being careful not to modify the Social Security or Medicare taxes. Modify the check to reflect the actual check amount that cleared.

7. Click OK to close the dialog box.

8. Click Save & Close to save the changes to the paycheck.

Cautiously consider the effect of changes you make to existing paychecks will have on previously filed payroll tax returns.

Allocating Indirect Costs to Jobs Through Payroll

This section provides instructions for allocating "indirect" job costs, or those costs that your company incurs but that cannot be easily associated with a job. The term "allocating" used here is referring to distributing costs to jobs independent of the original cost record. Costs such as cell phone, automobile fuel, training fees, uniforms, and small tools are practically impossible to assign to jobs.

However, don't confuse these costs with the general and administrative costs of the business. These costs are essential to your overall operations and are relatively stable.

Why do I mention this at all? If you review your Profit & Loss report and total the collective value of these costs, it can be significant, and when these costs are not associated with jobs, your job's profitability is overstated.

To begin with, you need to make sure that you assign a customer or job to each line on expense transactions. Additionally, by using the Items tab as displayed in Figure 12.14, these costs will be included in a variety of Job Profitability reports that are item based. To access these reports, from the icon bar select **Reports**, **Jobs**, **Time & Mileage**.

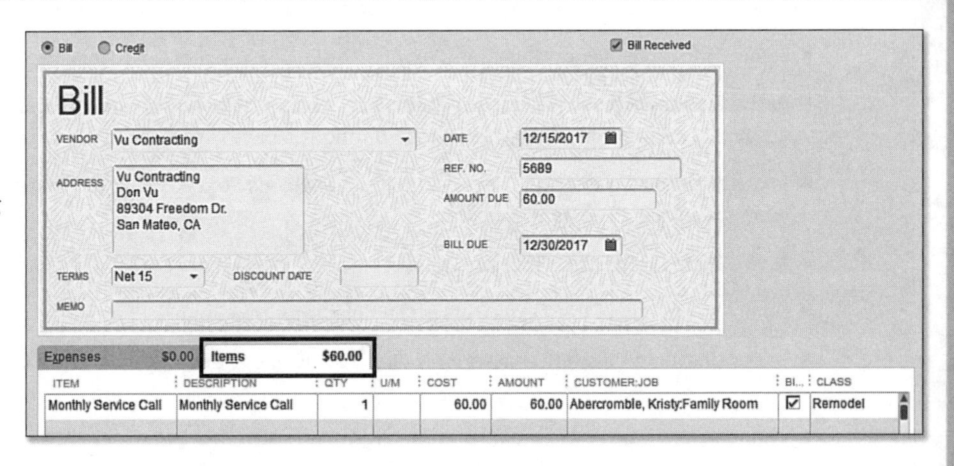

Figure 12.14 Properly recorded job costs using the Items tab and assigning a customer or job to the line.

If your company performs much of the labor associated with your service or product (instead of subcontracting the work to a vendor), you can use the payroll records to automatically allocate these costs. It is easy using just a few steps, as discussed in the following sections.

Identify Costs and Allocation Rate

The first step in this process is to review your Profit & Loss report and identify which expense accounts you post your indirect job expenses to without assigning a customer or job. These costs are easy to identify; they increase when you have more jobs and decrease when you have fewer jobs.

Because this method uses payroll as the tool to automatically allocate the costs, next you need to estimate the number of payroll hours in the period you will be allocating expenses.

Here is an example that you should be able to replicate with your own data. After reviewing my company's Profit & Loss report, I estimate the cost of paying for employee's cellular phones yearly is $15,000.00. I also estimate the yearly labor hours to be 16,000 hours. To arrive at the overhead allocation rate as a per hour cost, divide the estimated cost by the estimated hours. In this example, the per-hour cost is rounded to $.94 cents per hour.

Create Payroll Items for Allocating

After identifying the indirect expenses and the per hour allocation rate, you are ready to create list items. You need to create the following:

- **Chart of Accounts Allocation Account**—I recommend that you create a new chart of account specifically for the allocation amount, see Figure 12.15. Having a separate account helps you identify over time whether the allocation estimate is closely matched to the like expense being recorded. The normal balance for this type of account is a negative expense balance.
- **Company Contribution Payroll Item**—This item will not affect the employee's gross earnings or net pay. The newly created payroll item provides the means to automatically allocate the cost to a job through the payroll record. When creating this item, follow these guidelines:
    - Select Track Expense by Job checkbox.
    - In the Liability Account (Company-Paid) field, assign the newly created allocated expense account. This account will be "credited" during the payroll process.
    - In the Expense Account field, assign the Cost of Goods Sold account, or whatever account you want the allocated costs to record to.
    - Select None for the Tax Tracking Type.
    - Do not select any of the Taxes (this is the default for this item).
    - Select Calculate This Item Based on Hours. This is important, because your allocation is based on hours.
    - Enter Default Rate; this would be your allocation rate. In the example detailed here the rate would be .94.

To learn more about working with these lists, see "Chart of Accounts," p. 102 and "Setting Up Payroll Items," p. 447.

Figure 12.15
Creating a unique account for the allocated costs helps to identify them when viewing reports.

Chart of Accounts

NAME	TYPE
◆65110 · Gas and Electric	Expense
◆65120 · Telephone	Expense
◆65130 · Water	Expense
◆65200 · Small Tools	Expense
◆65300 · Allocated Small Tools	Expense
◆69000 · Miscellaneous	Expense
◆70100 · Other Income	Other Income
◆70200 · Interest Income	Other Income
◆80100 · Other Expenses	Other Expense

Allocating Through Payroll Records

The method discussed in this section presumes that your company performs the labor, versus hiring vendors to provide the labor for your product. For those laborers whom you included in your estimated hours, add the newly created company contribution calculation to their employee record, Payroll Info tab. See Figure 12.16 and the added Allocated Small Tools calculation.

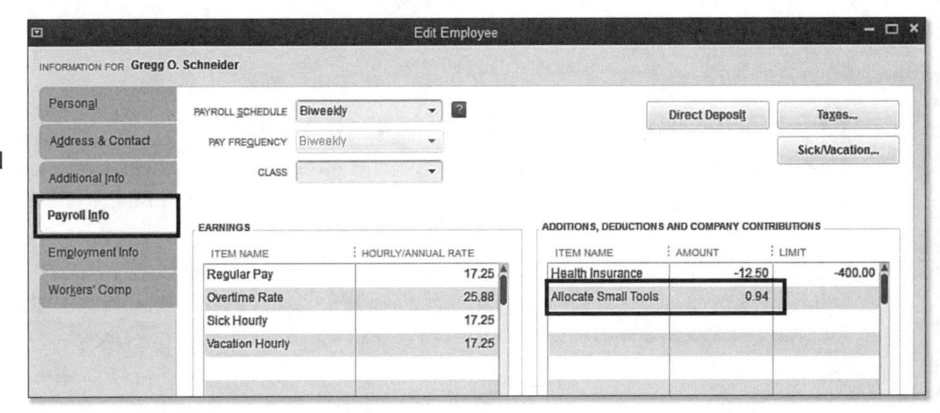

Figure 12.16
Using payroll calculations, you can allocate overhead expenses to jobs.

When you create a paycheck, QuickBooks uses this allocation payroll item in calculating the company's costs. This payroll item had a tax tracking type of None and does not affect the employee's gross or net wages.

Assigning the Calculate This Item Based on Hours option when you set up the payroll item distributes the estimated hourly cost of the small tools to the two jobs reported on the paycheck shown in Figure 12.17.

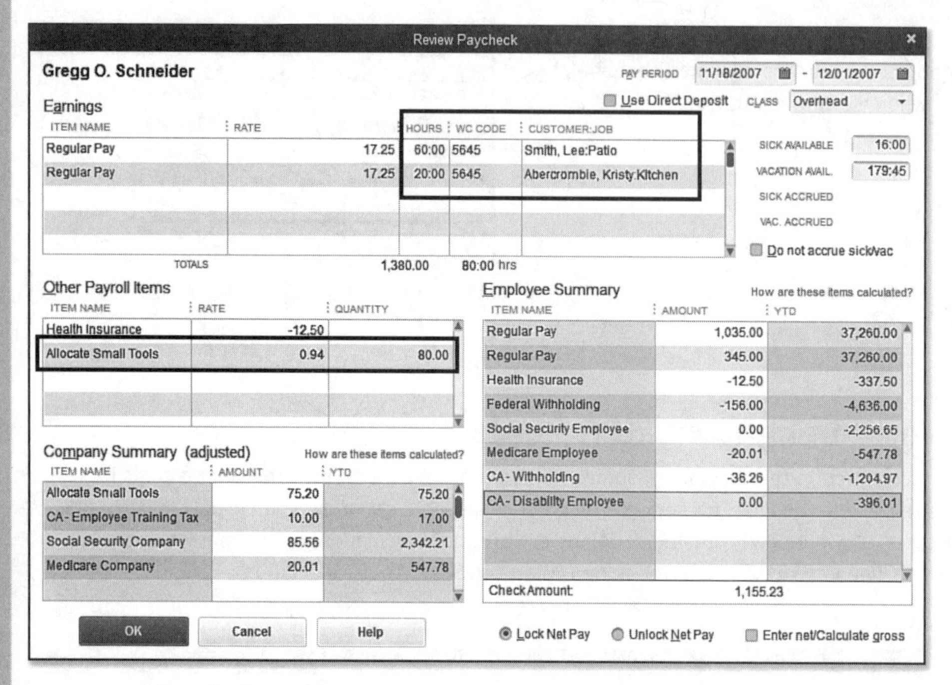

Figure 12.17 QuickBooks automatically uses the hours on the paycheck to allocate the estimated costs to the jobs.

Reporting on Actual and Allocated Costs

When you first begin using this method, you will want to verify the payroll item provided for the desired accounting. I find the transaction journal the easiest way to see the accounting that goes on "behind-the-scenes" with the payroll items.

From the checkbook register, select a paycheck record that used this newly created allocation item. From the ribbon toolbar at the top of the displayed check, select the **Reports** tab, **Transaction Journal**. The Transaction Journal for the paycheck shown previously in Figure 12.17 is shown in Figure 12.18.

In this example, QuickBooks calculates 80 hours at the .94/hour allocation rate. The total amount is then distributed to the two jobs using a weighted average. The job with the most hours receives the highest allocated cost.

Allocating indirect job expenses takes just a few steps and will provide more accurate job profitability reporting.

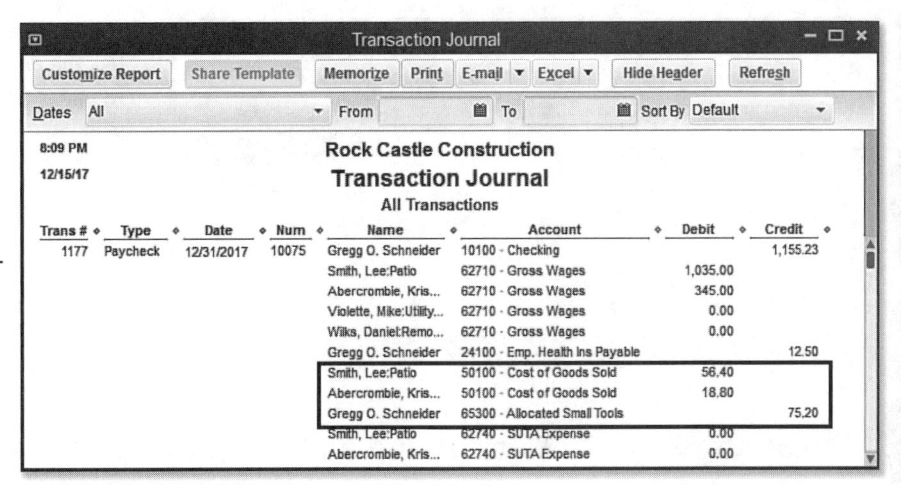

Rock Castle Construction
Transaction Journal
All Transactions

Trans #	Type	Date	Num	Name	Account	Debit	Credit
1177	Paycheck	12/31/2017	10075	Gregg O. Schneider	10100 · Checking		1,155.23
				Smith, Lee:Patio	62710 · Gross Wages	1,035.00	
				Abercrombie, Kris...	62710 · Gross Wages	345.00	
				Violette, Mike:Utility...	62710 · Gross Wages	0.00	
				Wilks, Daniel:Remo...	62710 · Gross Wages	0.00	
				Gregg O. Schneider	24100 · Emp. Health Ins Payable		12.50
				Smith, Lee:Patio	50100 · Cost of Goods Sold	56.40	
				Abercrombie, Kris...	50100 · Cost of Goods Sold	18.80	
				Gregg O. Schneider	65300 · Allocated Small Tools		75.20
				Smith, Lee:Patio	62740 · SUTA Expense	0.00	
				Abercrombie, Kris...	62740 · SUTA Expense	0.00	

Figure 12.18 Review the Transaction Journal report, verifying the accuracy of your payroll item setup for allocating overhead costs.

Depositing a Refund of Payroll Liabilities

If you received a refund from an overpayment of payroll taxes, you should not add it to a Make Deposits transaction (like other deposits you create). If you do, the refunded amount will not correct your overpayment amount showing in the payroll liability reports and in certain payroll forms.

This type of payroll error should rarely, if at all, occur in current versions of QuickBooks, thanks to improved messaging and ease of creating payroll transactions from the Payroll Center.

However, if you were paying your payroll liabilities outside the QuickBooks payroll menus, and you had an overpayment you requested and received a refund for, you can record the deposit to reflect receipt of the overpayment in your payroll reports. To do so, follow these steps:

1. From the menu bar, select **Employees**, **Payroll Taxes and Liabilities**, **Deposit Refund of Liabilities**. The Refund Deposit for Taxes and Liabilities dialog box displays.
2. Select the name of the payroll tax liability vendor.
3. Enter the Refund Date (the date of your deposit).
4. Enter the For Period Beginning date (this should be the payroll month or quarter the overpayment was in).
5. Enter the Deposit Total of the refund.
6. Select the Group with Other Undeposited Funds button if this item is included on a bank deposit ticket with other deposit amounts; or select the Deposit To button to create a single deposit entry and select the appropriate bank account from the drop-down list.
7. Select the Payroll Item that needs to be adjusted.
8. It would be wise to add a Memo so that you have a record of why this transaction occurred. Click OK.

See Figure 12.19 for a completed Refund Deposit for Taxes and Liabilities transaction.

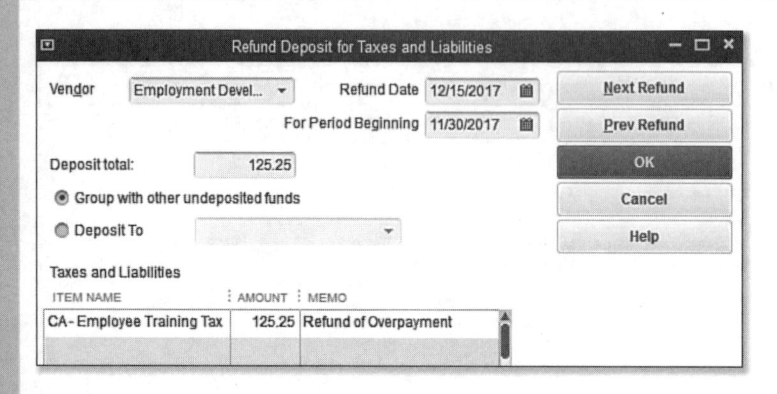

Figure 12.19
Use the proper transaction when recording a refund of overpaid payroll liabilities.

Recording Payroll When Using an Outside Payroll Service

In Chapter 11, you learned about several-Intuit provided payroll subscription offerings that integrate with your QuickBooks software. If, however, your company uses another payroll provider, you might find these instructions handy for recording the payroll activity in your QuickBooks file.

When using an outside payroll service, I encourage you to request comparative pricing for either Intuit's Assisted or Full Service Payroll offerings. One of the primary benefits of using an Intuit-provided payroll service is that you can track your employees' time to jobs in QuickBooks and let Intuit take care of the rest of the payroll responsibility.

The method I recommend for recording this payroll makes the following assumptions:

- You want to track your employees' time to customers or jobs.
- You value the customer or job profitability reports found by selecting **Reports**, **Jobs**, **Time & Mileage** from the menu bar.
- You subscribe to one of Intuit's payroll offerings.
- Your outside payroll vendor consolidates the charges to your bank account, usually two large debits. A typical payroll provider will debit your bank account one lump sum for the net amount of the checks and another for payment of taxes to the IRS on your behalf.

If your company does not need or want any of the previously listed items, you can continue recording the payroll using your current method. Be aware that if you use a journal entry to record these payroll expenses, many of the Job Profitability reports will not reflect the information properly. Instead, use the Items tab on a check or vendor bill (refer to Figure 12.14) so that your Job Profitability reports provide complete details, as shown in Figure 12.20.

The following steps can help you track payroll costs to customers or jobs, and record the company's payroll expense. Detailed instructions for each of these steps can be found in Chapter 11.

1. Create a bank account on the chart of accounts list and name it **Payroll Clearing**. The purpose of this account is to record individual net payroll checks. Many payroll vendors will debit your bank account for the lump-sum total of the payroll checks, not individually.

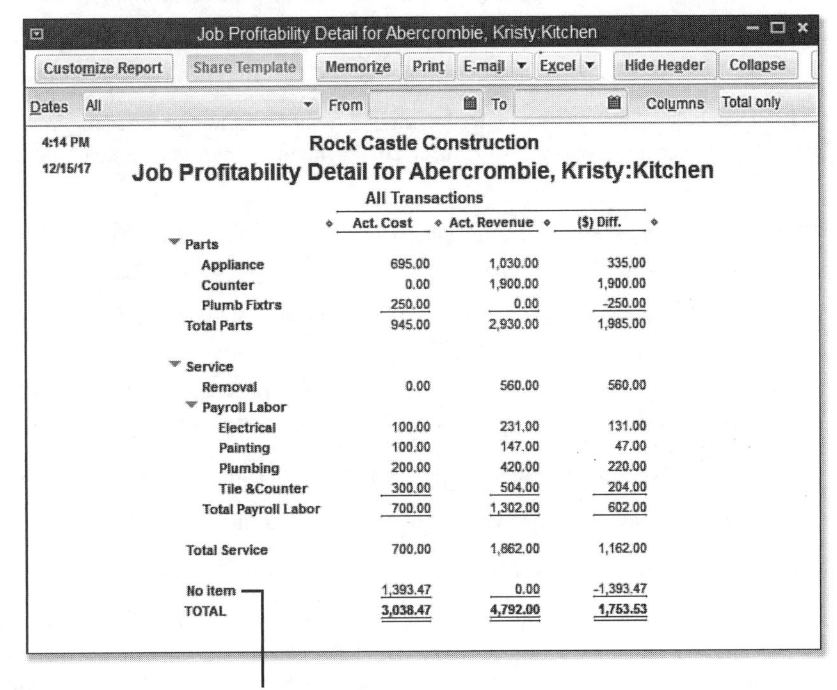

	Act. Cost	Act. Revenue	($) Diff.
Parts			
Appliance	695.00	1,030.00	335.00
Counter	0.00	1,900.00	1,900.00
Plumb Fixtrs	250.00	0.00	-250.00
Total Parts	945.00	2,930.00	1,985.00
Service			
Removal	0.00	560.00	560.00
Payroll Labor			
Electrical	100.00	231.00	131.00
Painting	100.00	147.00	47.00
Plumbing	200.00	420.00	220.00
Tile &Counter	300.00	504.00	204.00
Total Payroll Labor	700.00	1,302.00	602.00
Total Service	700.00	1,862.00	1,162.00
No item	1,393.47	0.00	-1,393.47
TOTAL	3,038.47	4,792.00	1,753.53

Figure 12.20 Using paycheck transactions provides job profitability reports by labor type.

2. Sign up for one of Intuit's payroll subscriptions. Without signing up for a subscription, you will have to manually type the payroll calculation amounts that your payroll provider details for you. Your time is worth the expense!

3. Complete the payroll setup as detailed in Chapter 11. One exception: Because a payroll service is controlling your payroll, use a single Payroll Liabilities account for all taxes due.

4. Prepare timesheets, or record time directly on a paycheck transaction. QuickBooks calculates the expected additions or deductions for you based on your setup.

5. Assign the fictitious bank account named Payroll Clearing to each paycheck.

6. Compare your current payroll totals in QuickBooks to your vendor's payroll reporting by selecting **Reports**, **Employees & Payroll**, **Payroll Summary**. It is expected that there might be minor differences due to rounding.

7. To record your vendor's lump-sum debit to your bank account, select **Banking**, **Transfer Funds** from the menu bar.

8. Enter the date the vendor debits (charges) your bank account.

9. In the Transferred Funds From drop-down, select the bank account that will be charged.

10. In the Transfer Funds To drop-down, select the **Payroll Clearing** bank account.
11. Review the remaining balance in the Payroll Clearing account. From the menu bar, select **Banking**, **Use Register**, and select the **Payroll Clearing** bank account. Click OK.
12. If the balance is not zero, enter an adjusting entry in the next available row. Enter **ADJ** in the Number column; enter an amount in the Payment column to decrease or in the Deposit column to increase.
13. Assign an expense account of your choosing for this small adjustment and click Record. Your payroll clearing account should now have a net zero balance.
14. Record the payment of the payroll taxes by your vendor by selecting **Banking**, **Write Checks** from the menu bar.
15. From the Bank Account drop-down list, select the bank account from which your payroll taxes are withdrawn.
16. Enter the word **Debit** in the No. field and select the date the charge is made to the bank account.
17. Select your payroll service vendor in the Pay to the Order Of drop-down list.
18. Enter the Amount in the field next to the payee name.
19. In the Account column on the Expenses tab, select your payroll liability account. I recommend simplicity here, using a single payroll liability account. You have a payroll service closely monitoring your payments; you might not need the same level of detail on your own balance sheet.
20. Click Save & Close to finish recording the payroll tax payment.

Check your work for accuracy. Your payroll clearing account should have a zero balance. The payroll liability account on your Balance Sheet should have a zero balance. Your job profitability reports accurately track payroll costs, and your bank register shows the debit transactions your payroll vendor made.

13

WORKING WITH BANK AND CREDIT CARD ACCOUNTS

Incorrect bank account balances are one of the most common problems I find when troubleshooting a client's QuickBooks data. One of the first questions I ask new clients is whether they have reconciled their bank or credit card accounts in QuickBooks. Most tell me they have. I then review any transactions that are not marked as cleared and I will usually find older, dated transactions that have not cleared. For more information, see "Reviewing Uncleared Transactions," in this chapter.

One of the most important reconciliations you should do in QuickBooks is match your bank or credit card transactions recorded in QuickBooks with the same transactions reported by the financial institution in their monthly statement. Just reconciling your account balances can correct many errors on the Profit & Loss statement.

Preferences That Affect Banking and Credit Card Management

Did you know that you can streamline your banking and credit card processes by setting certain QuickBooks preferences? Setting preferences saves keystrokes, which in turn can save data entry time.

Not every preference that affects banking or credit card management impacts your financials; some preferences enable specific features. To set preferences in QuickBooks from the menu bar select **Edit**, **Preferences**.

Preferences in QuickBooks come in two forms:

- **My Preferences**—Settings that are unique to the current user logged in the data file and are not shared by other users.
- **Company Preferences**—Settings that are common for all users.

➡ *For a detailed review of the preferences that affect working with banking and credit card activities, see "Preferences That Affect Accounts Payable," p. 220.*

Working with Write Check Transactions

An important task for any financial management software is the capability to record the expenses that a business has in providing the product or service to its customers.

QuickBooks offers multiple transaction types for recording your business expenses. The Write Checks transaction offers a quick method for entering costs. Another transaction for recording expenses is the Enter Bills transaction.

➡ *For more information, see "The Accounts Payable Process," p. 235.*

Both the Write Checks transaction and the Enter Bills transaction can be used to record expenses. However, some notable differences exist between the two:

- Using a vendor bill transaction allows you to track what is owed until you pay an invoice, whereas using a write check transaction simply records the cost as of the date of the check.
- If you use a vendor bill, QuickBooks warns you if you enter the same reference number (vendor's invoice number) that has already been recorded. This warning helps to control inadvertently paying a vendor more than once for the same invoice.

You might want to use a vendor bill for selected vendor costs rather than writing a check. This chapter is specific to working with the costs you will be recording using the Write Checks or Enter Credit Card Charges transactions.

note

To set company preferences, you must log in to the file as the Admin or External Accountant user and switch to single-user mode (if you are using the data file in a multiuser environment). The Admin user is the default user created when you begin using QuickBooks for the first time.

Proper data entry security includes limiting which employees have access to logging in as the Admin and setting company preferences that are global for all users. For more information see, "Setting Up Users and Permissions," p. 50.

caution

The Write Checks transaction is *not* the proper type of transaction for recording payment of a bill entered into QuickBooks, sales tax liability payments, paychecks for employees or payroll liability payments. More detailed information about using the proper transaction type for these specific transactions can be found in the following chapters:

- Chapter 7, "Setting Up Vendors"
- Chapter 9, "Setting Up Customers"
- Chapter 11, "Setting Up Payroll"

Using the Expenses Tab and Items Tab

The QuickBooks Write Checks transaction includes an Expenses and Items tab. The information entered on these tabs provides financial detail about the cost being recorded as well as other useful information. See Figure 13.1.

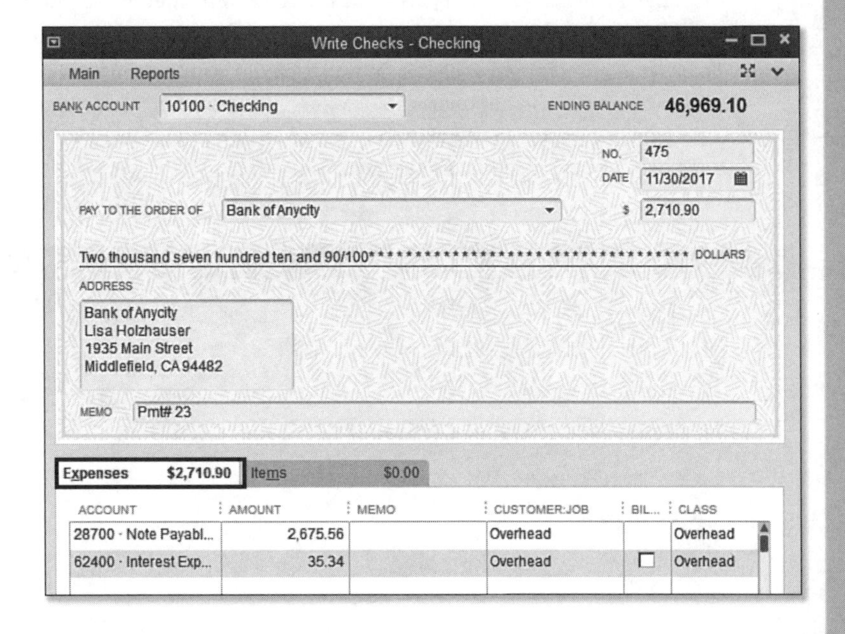

Figure 13.1
Use the Expenses tab to record administrative or overhead costs.

The Expenses and Items tabs on a write check or vendor bill affect QuickBooks reports in different ways. Costs recorded on either tab are included in all the Profit & Loss reports. However, if your business wants to use the many job profitability reports, you must consistently use the Items tab for recording job-related expenses as shown in Figure 13.2. If you use the Expenses tab, you will see these costs on a Profit & Loss by Job, but not itemized on the Job Profitability reports.

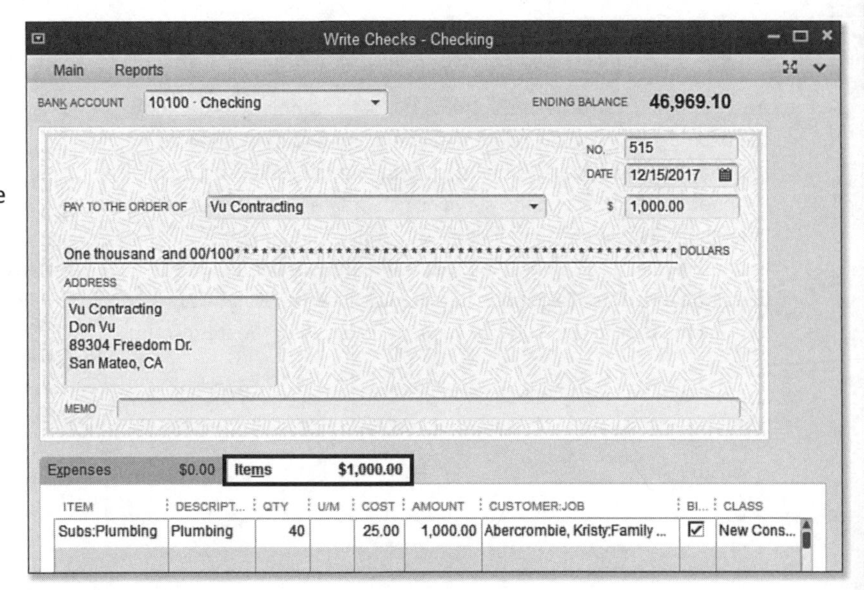

Figure 13.2
Use the Items tab to record customer- or job-related expenses to take advantage of the reporting available with job profitability reports.

From the menu bar, select **Reports**, **Jobs**, **Time & Mileage**. These job profitability reports depend on the information entered on the Items tab of the write checks transaction.

Tracking job profitability includes setting a budget and tracking costs for the same budgeted items. When you do not use the Items tab on expense transactions (see Figure 13.3), the costs display as a No Item line on Job Profitability reports, as shown in Figure 13.4. Doing so makes it impossible to track profitability by the budgeted item.

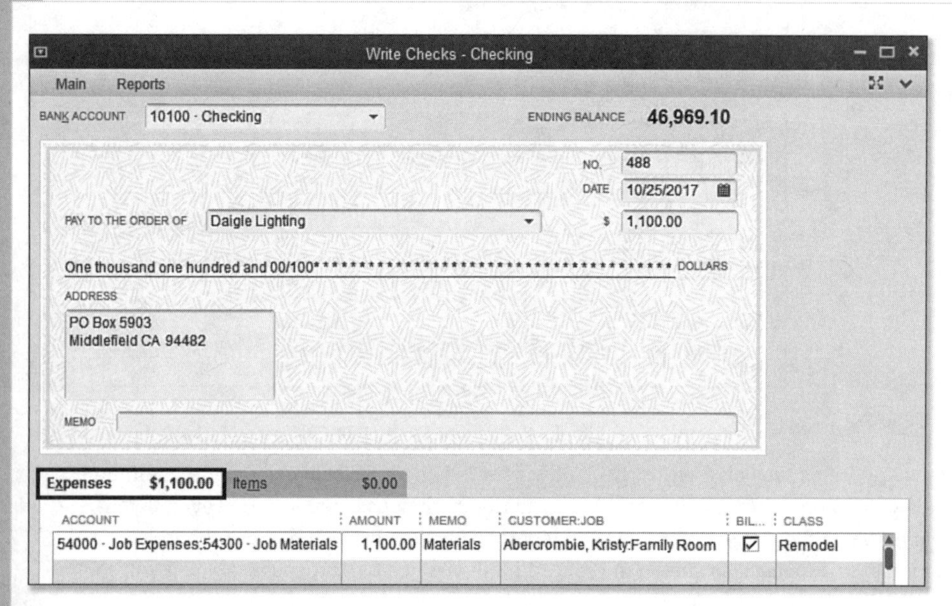

Figure 13.3 Using the Expense tab for job expenses will make Job Profitability reports less meaningful.

For more information, see "Items," p. 106.

Another useful purpose of the Items tab is to automate assigning the expense to a specific chart of account. An example is recording telephone expenses. A business that has multiple vendors for telephone, fax, or cell phone services can create an item named Telephone. This item is mapped to the appropriate chart of account. When a bill is received, the cost can be recorded on the Items tab using the Telephone item. QuickBooks automatically assigns the cost to the expense account included in the item setup.

tip

QuickBooks can automatically open drop-down lists when you're typing. From the menu bar, select **Edit, Preferences,** and select the **General—My Preferences** tab on the Preferences dialog box. Place a checkmark in the Select the Automatically Open Drop-Down Lists When Typing. Click OK to close the dialog box and save your changes.

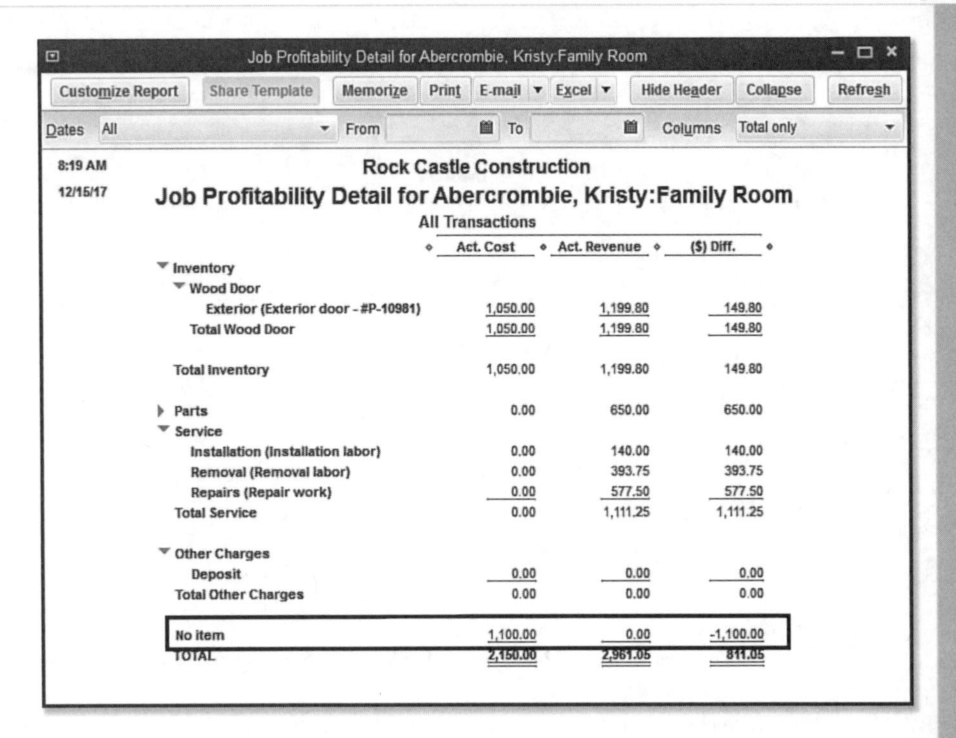

Figure 13.4 Job Profitability report when the Expense tab was used instead of the preferred Items tab when job costing expenses.

Writing a Check

Writing a check is an easy way to record expenses. I recommend using it for one-time purchases from a supplier or service provider, or for recording debit card or ACH payments from your bank account.

Writing a Check

To practice creating a write check transaction, open the sample data file as instructed in Chapter 1, "Getting Started with QuickBooks." If you are working in your own file, use these instructions:

1. From the menu bar, select **Banking, Write Checks**.
2. On the Write Checks transaction that displays, leave the prefilled Bank Account—Checking.
3. In the Pay to the Order Of field, begin typing **Davis Business Associates** until the appropriate vendor displays. QuickBooks will prefill if the name is recognized in any of the lists in QuickBooks (see Figure 13.5). To continue with the sample exercise, skip to step 9; if you're working in your own file, continue to step 4.

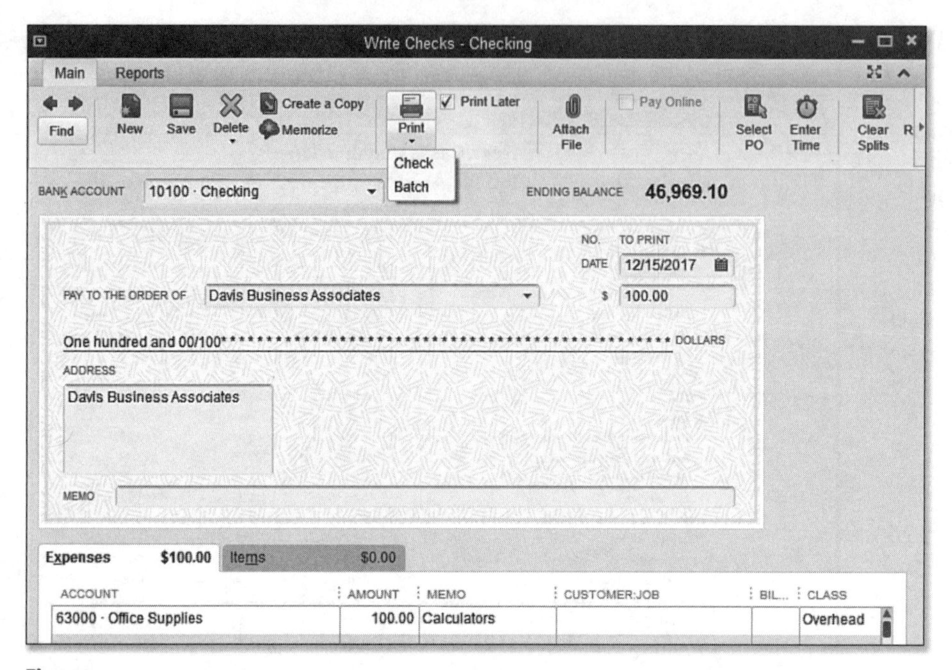

Figure 13.5
Create a write check transaction to record a business expense.

4. When you are entering checks in your own file and the payee is not included in a list, select **Add New** at the top of the Pay to the Order Of drop-down list.
5. When you're adding a new payee, the Select Name Type message displays where you will assign the new payee as a Vendor, Customer, Employee, or Other. After selecting the appropriate list, click OK.
6. Complete the details for the newly created list item.
7. (Optional) Instead of selecting Add New in step 4, if you begin typing the new vendor name in the payee field, QuickBooks offers these choices:
    - **Quick Add**—Creates a new list record with just the name field.
    - **Set Up**—Opens up the Select Name Type. Choose from Vendor, Customer, Employee, or Other names list.
    - **Cancel**—Select to not add the new payee.
8. Complete the remaining fields for adding the new name to the selected list. This process varies depending on whether you are adding a new vendor, employee, customer, or other name. Click OK to return to the Write Checks transaction.
9. Accept the prefilled Date. The cost is recorded in the business financials as of this date.
10. In the amount field, type **100.00**.

11. (Optional) Complete the address details. (When you save the record, QuickBooks prompts you if you want to save the changes for future transactions.)
12. Enter an optional Memo (the field below the address box). This memo prints on the check. If the Memo field is left blank, QuickBooks can insert the Account Number from the vendor record. For more information, see the section "Adding or Modifying Vendors," in Chapter 7.
13. On the first line of the Expenses tab, begin typing the account **Office Supplies**.
14. Use the Tab key on your keyboard to advance to the following fields:
    - **Memo**—Enter an optional memo that will be included in reports (not on the printed check).
    - **Customer:Job**—Leave blank for this exercise. It is recommended you use the Items tab when assigning costs to jobs with budgets.
    - **Billable**—Leave blank for this exercise. For more information, see "Time and Expense Invoicing," p. 346.
    - **Class**—Select Overhead.
15. Leave the following fields unselected on the Main tab of the ribbon toolbar at the top of the transaction:
    - **Print Later**—When selected, QuickBooks removes any prefilled check number. The check number will be assigned when the check is printed.
    - **Pay Online**—Select if you've established electronic bill payment through your QuickBooks file. For more information, see the section in this chapter titled "Online Banking Center."
16. (Optional) Click any of the following also found on the Main tab of the ribbon toolbar to help complete the transaction:
    - **Clear Splits**—Consolidates multiple amounts into a single line item.
    - **Recalculate**—Useful if, after entering an amount at the top of the record, you add additional lines of detail to the Expenses or Items tab, including the following:
        - **Clear**—Remove all data entered in fields and start over.
        - **Save & Close**—Save and close the dialog box.
        - **Save & New**—Save and continue with another record.

You will not have the Class field in your data if Class Tracking in the Preferences dialog box is not enabled. To enable class tracking, from the menu bar select, **Edit, Preferences, Accounting, Company Preferences** tab.

Printing Checks

Printing checks from QuickBooks can save you time over manually writing checks and later recording them in your software. Printing also helps to limit any confusion about the amount the transaction is approved for.

Ordering QuickBooks Checks

Many check printing suppliers offer QuickBooks-compatible checks. When ordering, confirm with your check supply source that they guarantee the format supplied will work with the QuickBooks software. In QuickBooks, only a few minor adjustments can be made to the placement of data on the printed check.

You can also purchase checks directly from Intuit. For more information, click the Order Checks icon on the Main tab of the Write Checks ribbon toolbar.

Setting Form Defaults and Making Printing Adjustments

Before printing checks from your QuickBooks file, review the printing defaults assigned to checks or paychecks.

To review the printing defaults in your file follow these steps:

1. From the menu bar, select **File**, **Printer Setup**.
2. From the Form Name drop-down list, select **Check/PayCheck**, as shown in Figure 13.6.

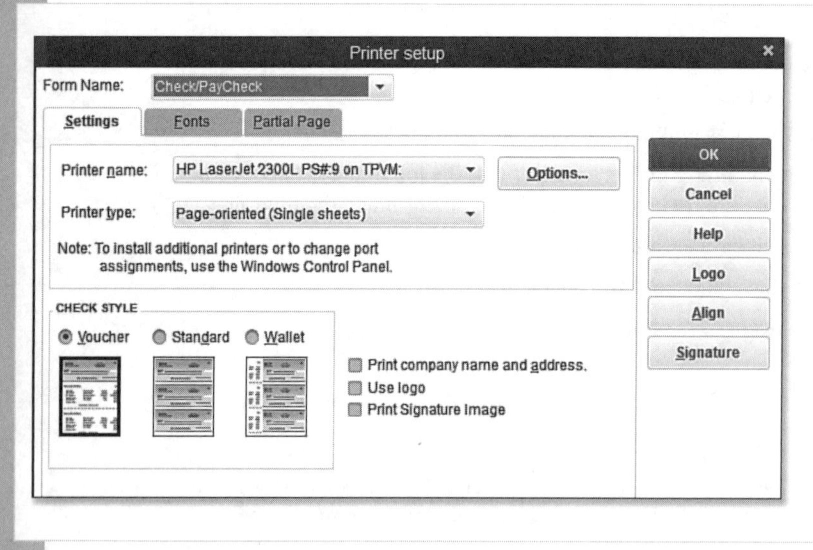

Figure 13.6
Select the check style you will be printing and other settings.

3. From the Settings tab, you can select the following:
   - **Printer Name and Printer Type**
   - **Check Style**—Select from Voucher, Standard, or Wallet.

- **Print Company Name and Address, Use Logo, or Print Signature Image**—Click the Signature button to the right to locate the electronically stored signature image.

4. Select the **Fonts** tab to modify the Font used on the check.
5. Select the **Partial Page** tab if you print standard or wallet format style checks. Use this setting to define how a single check is to be positioned in the printer.
6. After printing a check, you might find it necessary to make minor alignment modifications to the printed check. Click the Align button. Select amounts to move the text in 1/100-inch increments (as shown in Figure 13.7).
7. Click Print Sample to check your new settings. Click OK to close the Printer Setup when you're finished with this task.

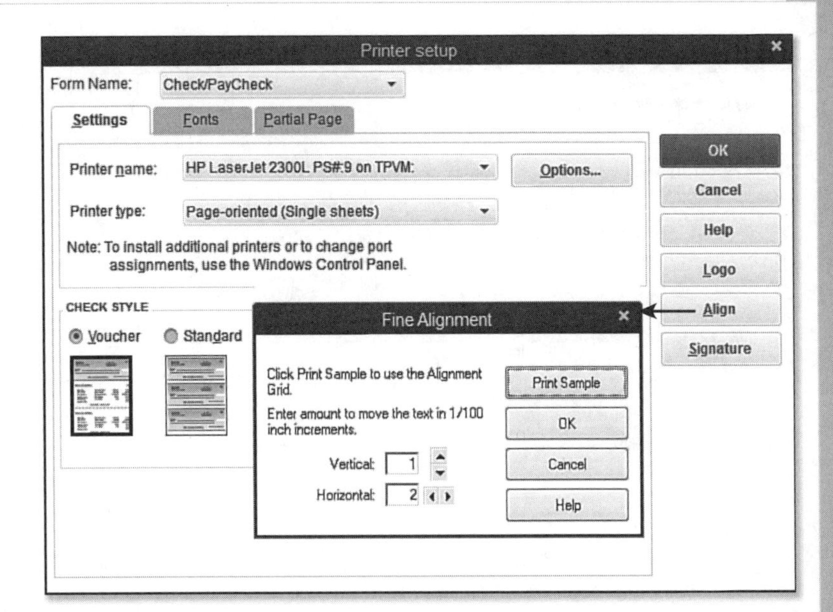

Figure 13.7
From the Printer Setup you can choose to make minor alignment adjustments.

Printing Checks

With QuickBooks, you can print checks individually or in a batch of checks all at one time as shown in Figure 13.5.

To print a check or a group of checks, follow these steps:

1. If the Write Checks transaction isn't already open, select **Banking**, **Write Checks** from the menu bar, and prepare your check for printing.

2. In the Print drop-down list, select from the following:
   - **Print**—Enter the check number you are printing to.
   - **Print Batch**—Select the Bank Account. Enter the First Check Number and remove the checkmark for any check you will not be printing in the batch.
3. The Print Checks dialog box displays. Change the defaults as necessary.
4. If you are printing a single check using the Standard or Wallet check style, click the Partial Page tab. Review the settings specific for how your printer needs the single check to be positioned before printing.
5. Click the Print button to print your checks. The Print Checks—Confirmation dialog box displays as shown in Figure 13.8.

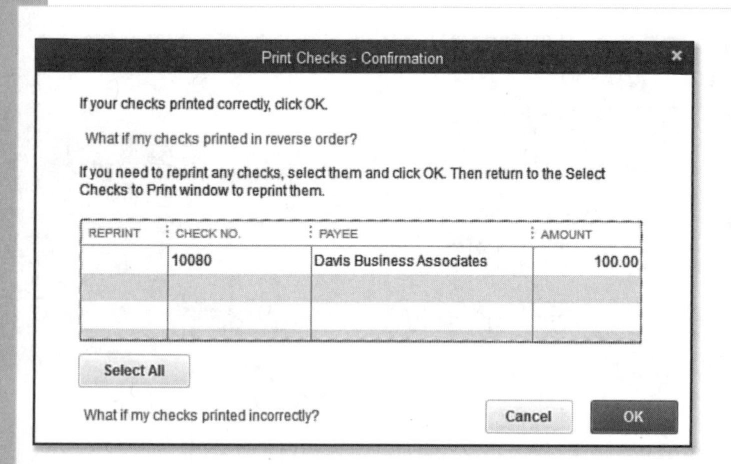

Figure 13.8
Make sure that each check printed correctly before selecting OK on the Print Checks—Confirmation dialog box.

6. Review the checks that just printed. If each check printed successfully, click OK on the Print Checks—Confirmation dialog box. If any check did not print successfully, place a checkmark in the Reprint column. You can return to step 2 and reprint the checks selected.

tip

You can review both printed and to be printed check transactions by clicking the Check Register icon on the Home page and selecting the appropriate bank account.

Entering a Bank Debit Charge

If your business uses a debit card for making purchases, you need to record these expenses like any other purchase transaction. A debit card transaction is debited from your bank's available cash balance, unlike a credit card where the payment for the purchase is made at some later date.

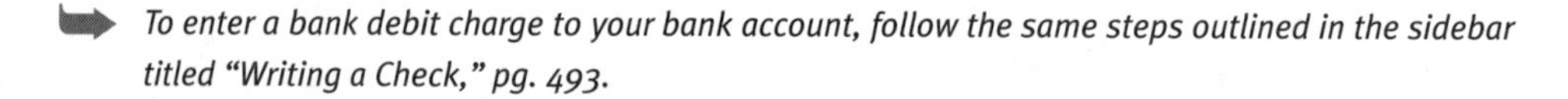
To enter a bank debit charge to your bank account, follow the same steps outlined in the sidebar titled "Writing a Check," pg. 493.

Instead of printing a check, remove the Print Later checkmark and in the No. field enter a notation as described in the Caution in this section. Or, you can enter some notation of your own that will help you identify the charge as a debit when reconciling the bank account.

caution

If you are recording a debit card payment made to a vendor for whom you issue a year-end Form 1099-MISC, specific notations should be used in the No. field. For more information, see "Tracking and Reporting Vendor 1099-MISC Payments," p. 263.

Entering Credit Card Charges

QuickBooks uses the Enter Credit Card Charges transaction to record business purchases made on credit. Has your business been using this transaction type? If not, you might have recorded credit card purchases using a vendor bill payable to the credit card merchant. Listed here are a few of the reasons to use a credit card receipt to record payments made by credit card:

- Track the vendors paid for the service or product.
- Track the date the purchase was made.
- Reconcile the credit card activity to the monthly statement from your credit card provider.

Recording a Credit Card Charge

To practice recording a credit card charge, open the sample data file as instructed in Chapter 1. If you are working in your own file, use these instructions to enter a credit card charge:

1. From the menu bar, select **Banking, Enter Credit Card Charges.**
2. Leave the prefilled QuickBooks Credit Card account (see Figure 13.9).

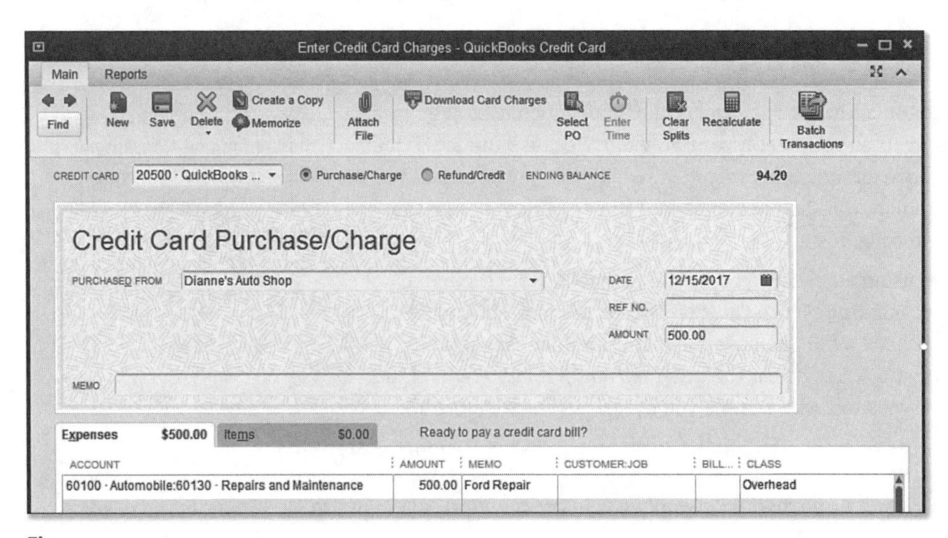

Figure 13.9
Recording expenses made with the company credit card.

3. For this exercise, leave Purchase/Charge selected. When working in your own data, you can select Refund/Credit when necessary.
4. In the Purchased From drop-down list, start typing **Dianne's Auto Shop**. To add a new payee when necessary, select **Add New** at the top of the list. Select an appropriate type from the Select Name Type dialog box that displays.
5. For this exercise, leave the prefilled date. When working with your own data, use the date the charge was incurred.
6. If you want to record a reference number enter it into the Ref. No. field.
7. Type the amount of **500.00.**
8. For details in your reporting enter a Memo.
9. On the Expenses tab, the account has prefilled from the default settings with that vendor or from past credit card purchases.
10. For this exercise, leave the Memo and Customer:Job blank.
11. For this exercise, leave the Billable column blank and select the Overhead class.
12. (Optional) Click any of the following to help complete the transaction:
    - **Clear Splits**—Consolidates multiple amounts into a single line item.
    - **Recalculate**—Recalculate the Amount field from the total of the rows.
    - **Clear**—Remove all data entered in fields and start over.
    - **Save & Close**—Save and close the dialog box.
    - **Save & New**—Save and continue with another record.

Paying the Credit Card Bill

As you enter credit card charges, QuickBooks increases the amount you owe your credit card provider. Because the individual charges have already been recorded, when you pay your bill, you need to reduce your bank balance and the amount you owe the credit card company.

tip

Often credit card purchases are made from one-time suppliers. I recommend that you select the Other name type when adding this type of payee. This will keep your vendor list limited to those you frequently do business with.

If you are using a check to record the payment, from the menu bar, select **Banking**, **Write Checks**. Follow the instructions for writing a check, with one exception. On the Expenses tab, in the Account column, select the other current liability credit card account associated with the bill you are paying (see Figure 13.10).

If you choose to enter a bill, from the menu bar, select **Vendors**, **Enter Bills**.

For more information on working with vendor records, see "Recording Vendor Bills," p. 240.

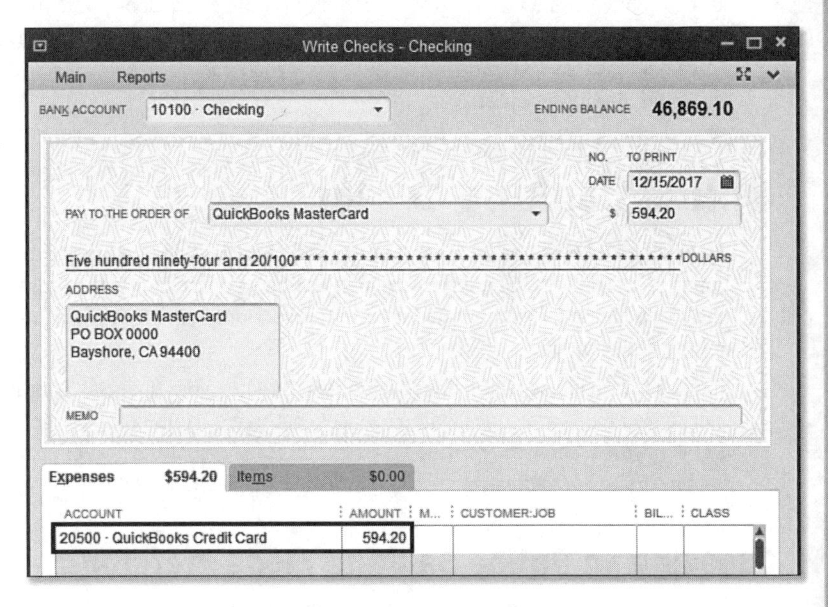

Figure 13.10
Properly record the payment of your credit card bill by assigning the credit card liability account on the Expenses tab.

On the Expenses tab, in the Account column, select the other current liability credit card account. Process the payment for the vendor bill as with other bills.

Include reconciling your credit card account in your list of monthly accounting tasks; doing so will help you manage your credit card activity as discussed in this chapter.

Transferring Funds Between Bank Accounts

If your business has more than one bank account, at some time you will probably need to transfer funds from one account to another account. If you need to physically take a printed check to the bank, use the instructions in the sidebar "Writing a Check" earlier in this chapter. Or create a bill and pay the bill as instructed in Chapter 7. The exception with these two types of transactions is on the Expenses tab. In the Account column, select the bank account you are depositing the funds into.

If you transfer the funds between accounts using your bank's online portal, you can record the transaction using the Transfer Funds Between Accounts transaction type using these steps:

1. From the menu bar, select **Banking**, **Transfer Funds**.
2. Enter the date the transfer is effective.
3. Select the Transfer Funds From account and the Transfer Funds To account.
4. Enter the Transfer Amount $.
5. (Optional) Enter a memo, which will display in reports.

6. If you have signed up for Online Banking within QuickBooks and you are transferring funds between two accounts at the same bank, select **Online Funds Transfer**. QuickBooks automatically processes the transfer the next time you synchronize your records with the bank via the Online Banking Center.

Online Banking Center

QuickBooks makes it easy to send or receive financial information among your bank or credit card financial institutions. The interface enables you to download your transactions for easy matching and reconciliation, examine recent bank transactions, transfer money between two online accounts, and pay bills online.

You don't have to use all the online services offered by your financial institution. Checking balances and transferring funds are typically free services, but many banks charge a monthly fee or per-transaction fee for bill payment services. You should weigh this fee against the cost of postage and paper supplies and the time you save to determine whether the service is worthwhile to you.

Choosing an Online Banking Mode Preference

QuickBooks users have the option to choose between two methods of viewing the information that is to be downloaded. Try both methods and see which one works best for you.

From the menu bar, select **Edit**, **Preferences**, **Checking**, **Company Preference** tab. The Online Banking box offers two choices:

- Side-by-Side Mode
- Register Mode

Click the What's the Difference? link for more information, or give them both a try. You can choose to work with one and then later switch back to the other method.

The remaining sections on the QuickBooks Online Banking feature will be shown using the side-by-side mode.

Activating Online Services with Your Financial Institution

The first step in using online banking services is getting access to a bank that provides the services you need. After you have opened a bank account and established online privileges, you are ready to put QuickBooks to work. With an Internet connection, you will be able to access your bank account directly from your QuickBooks program.

To initiate the QuickBooks online banking feature after creating a bank (or credit card) account, follow these steps:

1. From the menu bar, select **Banking**, **Online Banking**, **Set Up Account for Online Services**. If necessary, wait until the Updating Branding Files prompt disappears.
2. From the Select Your QuickBooks Account drop-down list, select the QuickBooks bank account (or credit card) for which you want to set up online services, or select **Add New** if you are creating a

new bank or credit card type account. (Remember, you must have online services enabled with your financial institution before you can set up the services within QuickBooks.) Click Next.

3. In the Enter the Name of Your Financial Institution drop-down list, select your banking or credit card institution. *Hint:* You can also begin typing the name and QuickBooks will prefill the list with possible matches. Click Next.

> **tip**
>
> QuickBooks uses your bank or credit card institution's legal or formal name; keep that in mind when you are looking at the list of financial institutions.

4. You might be prompted with a Select Option dialog box if your financial institution has multiple related financial entities. Choose where the account is held, if applicable, and click OK.

5. If your financial institution provides more than one method for connecting, you will be given the option to choose which connection to use. Select **Direct Connect** if you want to connect to your bank or credit card directly from within QuickBooks. (This is the most efficient method but may require a fee.) See Figure 13.11.

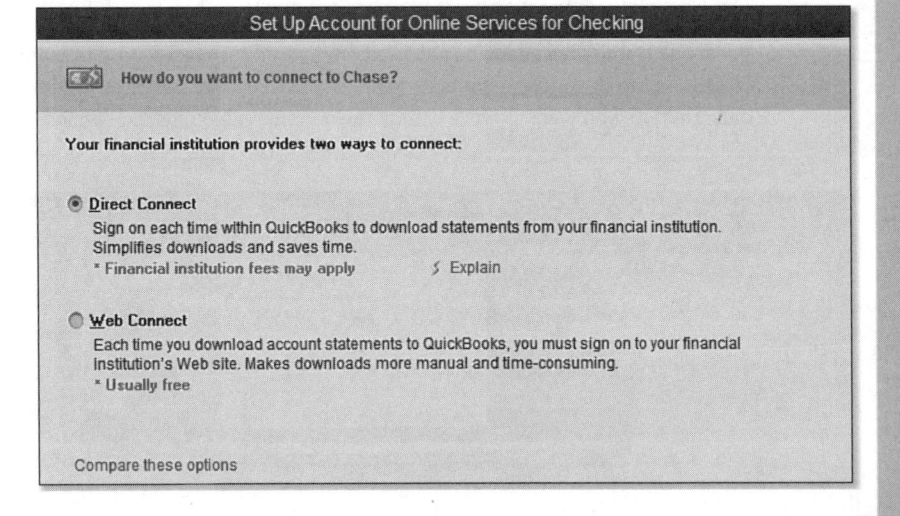

Figure 13.11 Choose between two methods for downloading transactions into QuickBooks.

6. Select **Web Connect** if you want to first sign into your financial institution's website before downloading transactions (this method is more manual and time consuming).

7. Click the Compare These Options link if you are unsure which to choose. Click Next.

8. If prompted, select **Yes** if you have already activated your online access with your financial institution. Select **No** if you need the contact information for your financial institution. If you selected No, a dialog box will open in which you can view your bank's contact information.

9. If you selected Yes, you are prompted to enter your Customer ID and Password. Click Sign In.

10. Click to select the account you want to log on to from the list.

11. Click Next and QuickBooks processes the request for your online financial services connection to QuickBooks.

12. Click Activate Online Bill Payments to set up the capability to pay your bills directly from QuickBooks (fees might apply).

13. Click Finish, and QuickBooks opens the Online Banking Center.

note

You can also download credit card transactions directly into your QuickBooks data file.

Retrieving Online Transactions

After you have activated online services with your bank, you can request to review and download your bank or credit card transactions that have recently cleared your financial institution.

1. From the menu bar, select **Banking**, **Online Banking**, **Online Banking Center**.

2. If the Choose Your Online Banking Mode dialog box displays, select **Continue** to use your existing mode, or switch the mode by selecting **Change Mode**. The selection is not permanent, so you can test each method and pick what works best for you.

3. If you have more than one online account, verify that the correct account name displays in the Financial Institution box. If you have multiple online services, use the Select drop-down list to select the proper online service you want to work with in the current online banking session. See Figure 13.12.

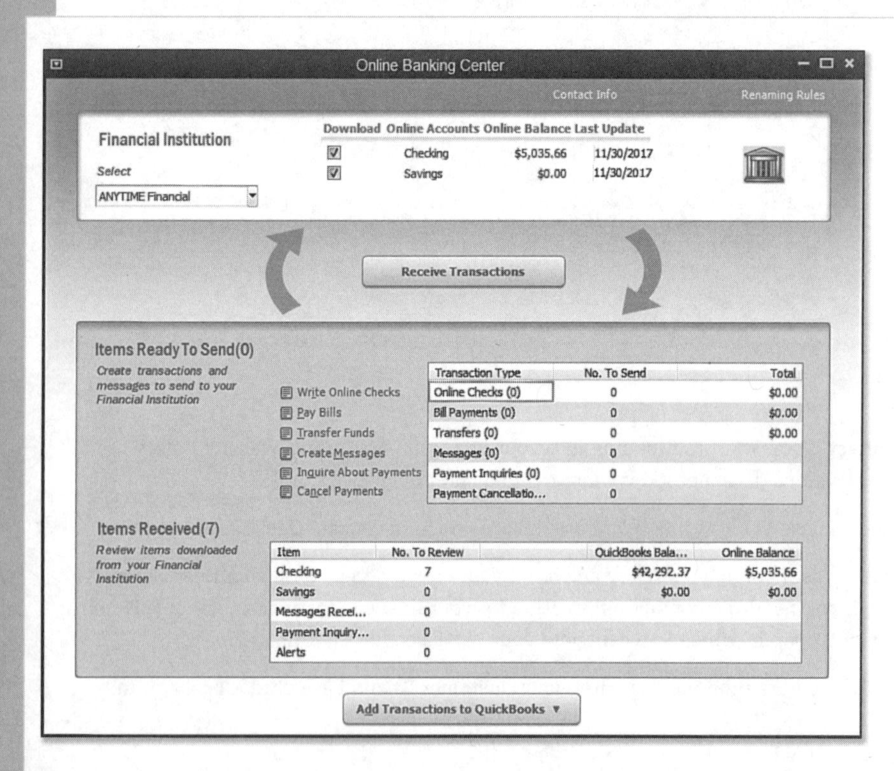

Figure 13.12
Receive, review, and add downloaded transactions to your QuickBooks file.

4. Click the Receive Transactions button to automatically connect through the Internet with your selected financial institution.
5. Enter your PIN into the Access dialog box for your financial institution that displays.
6. Click OK.
7. QuickBooks provides a status message as it downloads current transactions into the QuickBooks Online Banking Center. In the Online Banking Center, you can control which transactions you download into the corresponding QuickBooks banking register.

Now that you have successfully retrieved your financial institution's transactions, follow the steps in the next few sections to properly download the transactions into your QuickBooks file.

Adding Downloaded Transactions to QuickBooks

You can conveniently add transactions one at a time to your QuickBooks data file (see Figure 13.13). Activating Online Banking Services can save you time and improve your data entry accuracy.

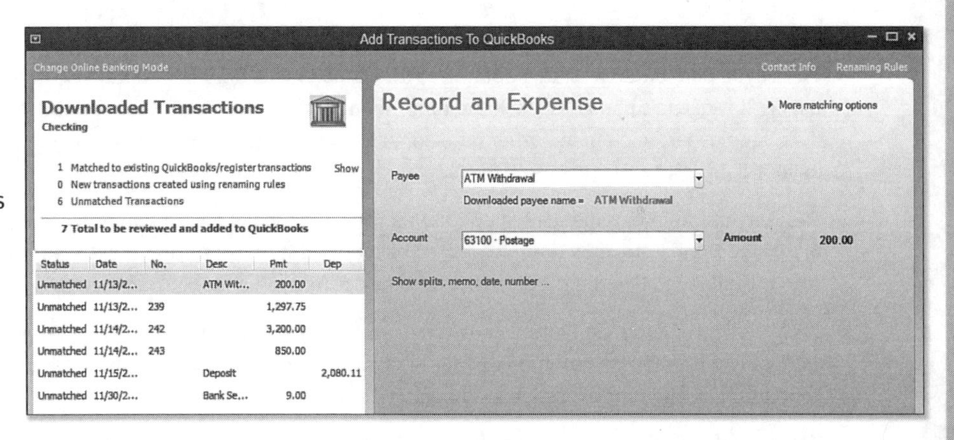

Figure 13.13 Choose to add the downloaded transactions to QuickBooks one at a time.

Follow these steps to download transactions into your QuickBooks file:

1. To open the Online Banking Center, from the menu bar, select **Banking**, **Online Banking**, **Online Banking Center**.
2. To review the items downloaded, in the Items Received section, click any of the listed Bank or Credit Card accounts, Messages Received, or Alerts. The Add Transactions to QuickBooks dialog box displays the transactions, messages, or alerts.
3. Click a single transaction on the left. (You might optionally click Add Multiple. A list of Renamed or Unmatched transactions displays, as shown in Figure 13.14.)

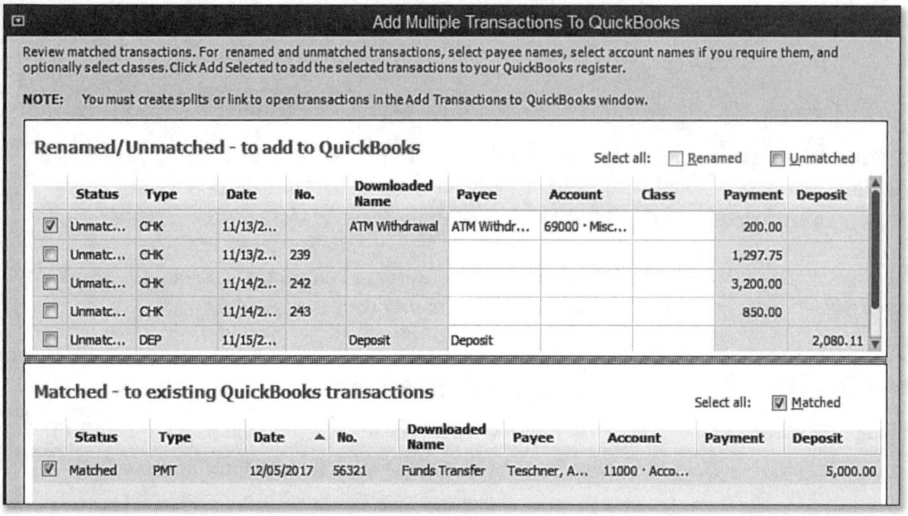

Add Multiple Transactions To QuickBooks

Review matched transactions. For renamed and unmatched transactions, select payee names, select account names if you require them, and optionally select classes. Click Add Selected to add the selected transactions to your QuickBooks register.

NOTE: You must create splits or link to open transactions in the Add Transactions to QuickBooks window.

Renamed/Unmatched - to add to QuickBooks

Select all: ☐ Renamed ☐ Unmatched

	Status	Type	Date	No.	Downloaded Name	Payee	Account	Class	Payment	Deposit
☑	Unmatc...	CHK	11/13/2...		ATM Withdrawal	ATM Withdr...	69000 · Misc...		200.00	
☐	Unmatc...	CHK	11/13/2...	239					1,297.75	
☐	Unmatc...	CHK	11/14/2...	242					3,200.00	
☐	Unmatc...	CHK	11/14/2...	243					850.00	
☐	Unmatc...	DEP	11/15/2...		Deposit	Deposit				2,080.11

Matched - to existing QuickBooks transactions

Select all: ☑ Matched

	Status	Type	Date	No.	Downloaded Name	Payee	Account	Payment	Deposit
☑	Matched	PMT	12/05/2017	56321	Funds Transfer	Teschner, A...	11000 · Acco...		5,000.00

Figure 13.14 Work efficiently by adding multiple downloaded transactions at once into QuickBooks.

4. The Payee field automatically populates if the QuickBooks online banking services recognizes the payee. If it doesn't populate, click the drop-down list to select from your QuickBooks lists (vendors, employees, customers, other names), or begin typing the name and have QuickBooks add it to your lists.

5. The Account field automatically populates if the QuickBooks online banking service recognizes the payee from a previous downloaded transaction. If it doesn't populate, begin typing the account name or click the drop-down list to select from a list of your accounts.

6. Click the More Matching Options link to select to record the expense, assign the payment to an open vendor bill, or match to an existing QuickBooks transaction. (Your options might differ depending on the type of transaction being added.)

7. If you need to add additional lines or details, click Show Splits, Memo, Date, and Number and modify as needed.

8. In the Account field, if the account did not automatically populate, type the account name or select one from the drop-down list.

9. Accept the default amount that displays, or click in the amount column to modify if needed.

10. (Optional) Assign the expense to a customer using the Customer:Job field. However, as discussed earlier in this chapter assigning expenses to jobs using the Items tab takes advantage of many job profitability reports.

11. Select the Billable checkbox if you use the QuickBooks Add Time and Costs feature to invoice the customer for the expense.

12. Assign a class with the Class field if you departmentalize your company's Income Statement (and use Classes for other reporting).

13. Click Remove Selected to clear the line detail above the currently selected line.

14. Click Hide Splits, Memo, Date, Number to return to the less-detailed entry dialog box.

15. Click Add to QuickBooks, and the transaction will now be included in the QuickBooks register for that financial institution.

16. Click Finish Later to return to QuickBooks and exit the Online Banking Center.

Renaming Rules in Online Banking

Would you like QuickBooks to "remember" the name and account you previously assigned to a downloaded transaction? QuickBooks does this with Renaming Rules that automate and standardize the names of downloaded banking transactions into QuickBooks. For example, your financial institution might include a transaction number in the downloaded Payee name field. In such cases, QuickBooks might then create a new vendor for each transaction; when you assign a name from one of your QuickBooks lists to this transaction, QuickBooks automatically creates the renaming rule to use for this same transaction in the future.

For example, suppose you purchase mobile phone services from Verizon Wireless. When the transaction is downloaded, the vendor name is "Verizon Wireless - <*transaction code or location*>." You can create a renaming rule that instructs QuickBooks to ignore the transaction code and assign it to the proper vendor. Renaming rules are based on several options: begins with, ends with, contains, or exactly matches.

To modify the renaming rules created automatically by QuickBooks Online Banking, follow these steps:

1. In the top-right corner of the Online Banking Center, click Renaming Rules.

2. In the Edit Renaming Rules dialog box (see Figure 13.15), click the name for which you are modifying the renaming rule from the list on the left. Or click the Create New button to manually create a renaming rule.

3. In the If a Downloaded Name drop-down list, choose from the Begins With, Ends With, Contains, or Exactly Matches options.

4. Type the criteria to be used. This can be useful for vendors that append their name with a unique transaction number for each charge.

5. Click Remove if you want to clear your selection. Click Save to assign the renaming rule.

note

Did you know that the QuickBooks Online Banking feature creates a renaming rule automatically when you assign the transaction to an existing QuickBooks name for the first time? You can then modify the renaming rule created.

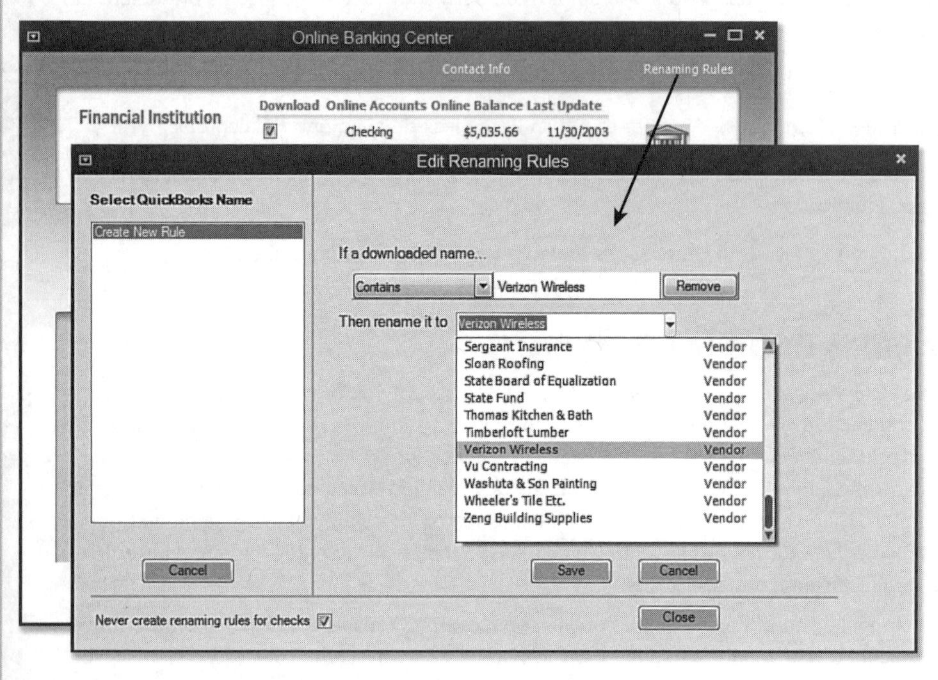

Figure 13.15 Renaming rules help QuickBooks recognize the payee name on your list and accounts assigned for future transactions.

Other Online Banking Features

There are many other features of working with QuickBooks Online Banking. These are discussed in the following sections.

Assigning Transactions to Open Vendor Bills

If you would like to associate a downloaded transaction to an open vendor bill in QuickBooks, effectively paying the open vendor bill with the downloaded transaction, you can use the Add Transactions dialog box.

To assign downloaded transactions to open vendor bills, follow these steps:

1. In the Online Banking Center, click the Add Transactions to QuickBooks button.
2. At the top right of the Add Transactions to QuickBooks dialog box, select the **More Matching Options** link.
3. Click Select Open Bills to Pay.
4. Select the payee from the drop-down list, or begin typing the payee name. QuickBooks finds list names that match. See Figure 13.16.
5. Accept the prefilled Accounts Payable account, or select the proper account if you have more than one Accounts Payable type account.

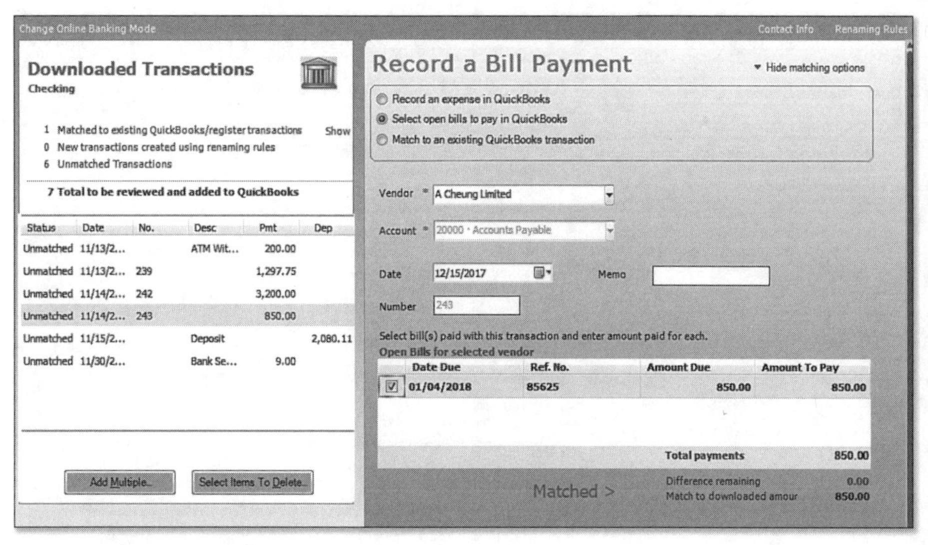

Figure 13.16 Assign downloaded payments to open vendor bills.

6. Accept the prefilled Date or change as needed.
7. Enter an optional Memo for your reporting needs.
8. Enter an optional transaction number or name in the Number field if no number displays.
9. Place a checkmark next to the open bill or bills that are being paid by this downloaded transaction.
10. Click the Add to QuickBooks button to record this transaction to your financial institution register in QuickBooks.
11. Click Finish Later to leave the dialog box.
12. Select **Yes** or **No** to saving the changes you made.

Assigning Deposits to Open Customer Invoices

QuickBooks Online enables you to match your downloaded banking deposits to open customer invoices or previously recorded deposits into your bank account using the Make Deposit forms.

To assign downloaded deposits to open customer invoices, follow these steps:

1. In the Online Banking Center, click the Add Transactions to QuickBooks button.
2. In the Add Transactions to QuickBooks dialog box, click a deposit transaction item from the list on the left, as displayed in Figure 13.17.
3. Accept the default Date or modify as needed.

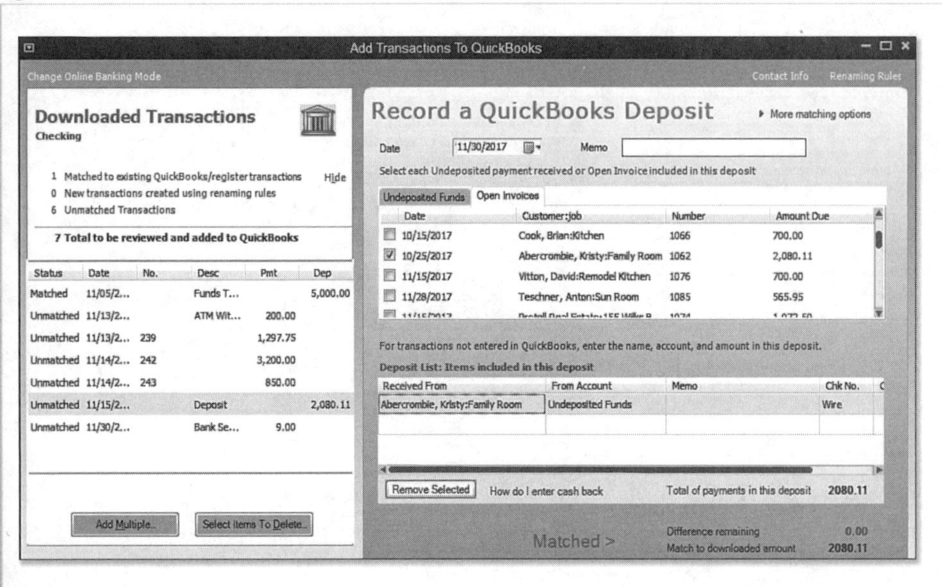

Figure 13.17 Assign downloaded bank deposits to open customer invoices.

4. Enter an optional Memo.
5. Click to place a checkmark next to each invoice that was included in the deposit downloaded. Modify the amount in the Deposit List pane if you are not receiving full payment.
6. Click Remove Selected to clear the contents of the Deposit List box.
7. Click Add to QuickBooks, and your transaction will be included in your financial institution's register in QuickBooks.
8. Click Finish Later to exit and return later to finish recording.
9. If you opt to finish recording information later, QuickBooks presents a prompt box. Click Yes to discard your changes.
10. Click No to save your changes and return to the dialog box.
11. When you finish assigning deposits, close the Online Banking Center dialog box by clicking the (x) in the upper-right corner.

Adding or Deleting Multiple Transactions

QuickBooks Online Banking Services can save you data entry time by enabling you to add multiple transactions at once. To add or delete multiple transactions, follow these steps:

1. In the Online Banking Center, click the Add Transactions to QuickBooks button.
2. In the Add Transactions to QuickBooks dialog box, click the Add Multiple button.
3. If you choose, in the No. field, you can add a transaction number.

4. Click the Payee field to select the payee from your QuickBooks lists.
5. Click the Account field to select the account from your QuickBooks chart of accounts.
6. If you plan to track classes in your data file, select the Class field and choose a class.
7. To select all the transactions, place a checkmark in the Renamed or Unmatched boxes. If not selected, you can manually add or remove individual checkmarks for individual items you want to add to your financial institution register.

 note

You can also delete selected transactions. After they are deleted, those transactions will no longer be included in future downloads. Click the Select Items to Delete button and place a checkmark next to those transactions you want to remove.

8. Leave the default checkmark in Select All Matched, and QuickBooks Online Banking removes these "matched" transactions from future downloads.
9. (Optional) Click the checkboxes to add or remove individual checkmarks.
10. Click Add Selected to add the selected transactions to your QuickBooks register for this financial institution.
11. If you click Cancel, you will be given the choice to keep or discard your changes to the transactions.

Making or Canceling Online Payments

Online Bill Payment from the QuickBooks Online Services lets you pay your vendors electronically though QuickBooks.

After the service is enabled (your bank might charge a fee for this), you can use QuickBooks to record the bills being paid and send instructions to your financial institution. Your financial institution's payment processor will make the payments electronically or print and mail the check for you.

To make or cancel online payments, follow these steps:

1. If you activated your online bill payment service, as discussed in the "Activating Online Services with Your Financial Institution" section, you will have a link to Write Online Checks or Pay Bills in the Online Banking Center.
2. Click Write Online Checks to create a check that will be sent to your financial institution for payment directly to the vendor. (Optional) Click Pay Bills to write a bill payment check in QuickBooks. Click Save and Close.
3. The Online Payment dialog box displays, instructing you to click the Send/Receive Transactions to complete the process. (Optional) Click Do Not Display the Message in the Future. Click OK.
4. Click Send/Receive Transactions in the Online Banking Center.

 note

What if your financial institution doesn't offer bill pay service? Consider signing up for the Intuit QuickBooks Bill Pay Service. From the menu bar select **Banking, Online Banking, Learn About Online Bill Payment.** Information and instructions are provided for signing up for the service.

5. Enter your PIN if requested.
6. The Online Transmission Summary dialog box displays. Click Print to optionally print the summary.
7. Click Close to exit the Online Transmission Summary details and return to the Online Banking Center.

Reconciling the Bank or Credit Card Account

Are you reconciling your bank or credit accounts in QuickBooks? If the answer is no, are you reconciling these accounts on the monthly paper statement provided by the financial institution? If you still answered no, you will certainly find value in learning how easy it is to reconcile these accounts in QuickBooks.

Why exactly is it so important? Most businesses record a significant amount of income and expenses through bank or credit card activity. When the reconciliation is not completed in the software, how certain are you that the financial reports are accurate?

There are a few exceptions to income and expenses flowing through a bank account. For example, a restaurant or bar might manage a significant amount of cash during the course of doing business. Do not limit yourself to thinking the task of reconciling is limited to bank or credit card accounts. If you have a cash safe, drawer, or box at the office, reconcile the ins and outs of the cash in your QuickBooks data.

note

If your work is interrupted while you are reconciling a bank or credit card statement, you can click Leave in the Reconcile–Account dialog box. Clicking Leave will keep the checkmarks you have assigned to transactions and let you return to finish your work later.

To begin reconciling your bank or credit card accounts, follow these steps:

1. From the menu bar, select **Banking**, **Reconcile** to open the Begin Reconciliation dialog box, as shown in Figure 13.18.

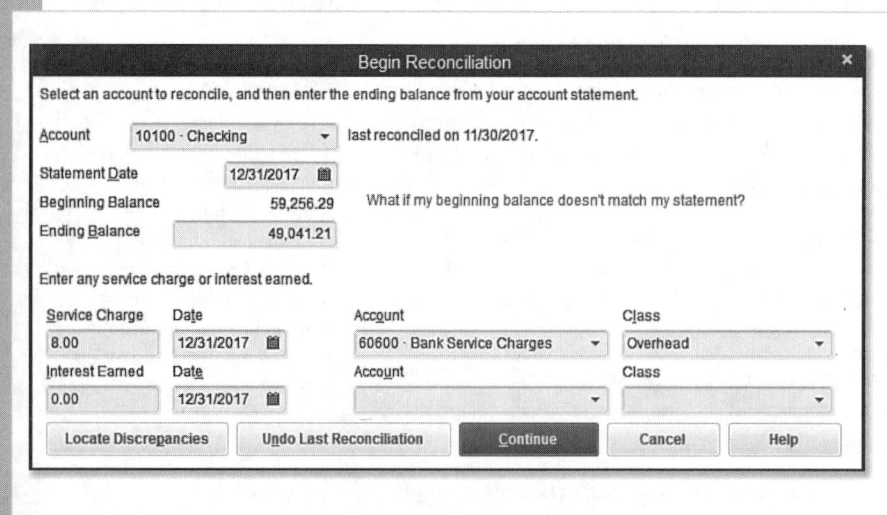

Figure 13.18 Reconcile your accounting records to your financial institution's monthly statement.

2. From the Account drop-down list, select the appropriate account. (Any Balance Sheet type account can be reconciled.)
3. Select the **Statement Date** that matches the ending statement date from your financial institution.
4. Review the Beginning Balance, which should equal the same number provided by your financial institution. Later sections in this chapter will detail methods of troubleshooting errors in the Beginning Balance.

note

Where does the beginning balance originate from on the Begin Reconciliation dialog box? It is the sum total of all previous transactions for the selected account that are marked as cleared.

5. Enter the ending balance from your financial institution's period statement.
6. (Optional) Enter any Service Charge or Interest Earned, selecting the appropriate date, account, and Class if tracking the use of Classes.
7. Click Continue. The Reconcile–*Account Name* dialog box opens.
8. Place a checkmark in the Hide Transactions After the Statement's End Date. This makes the task of reconciling much easier.
9. Place individual checkmarks next to each cleared Checks and Payments and Deposits and Other Credits that are included in the statement from your financial institution.
10. Click Reconcile Now only when the Difference is 0.00. See Figure 13.19. This indicates that your cleared transactions match those provided by the financial institution.

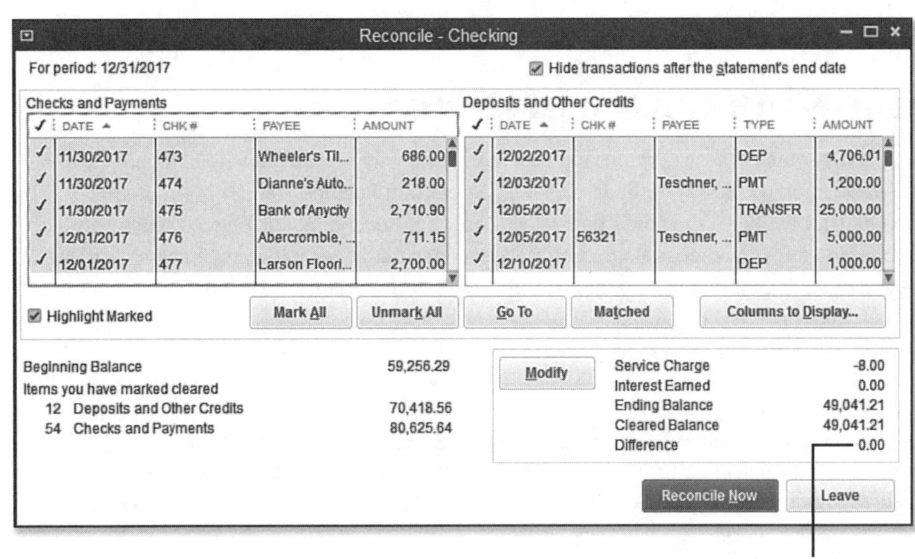

Figure 13.19
Reconcile your QuickBooks transactions to your financial institution's for a specific month.

For more information, see "Reconciling with an Adjustment," p. 525.

11. Follow the prompts to print the reconciliation report to attach to your financial institution's statement for safekeeping.

Other useful features of working with the Reconcile feature in QuickBooks include the following:

- **Highlight Marked**—Make it easier to differentiate the cleared from the noncleared transactions on the computer screen.
- **Mark All or Unmark All**—Use to automatically add or remove checkmarks from transactions during the bank reconciliation process.
- **Go To**—Open the currently selected transaction. Useful if you need to modify the transaction.
- **Matched**—Match downloaded transactions to the transactions in QuickBooks.
- **Columns to Display**—Add or remove the columns of data displayed.
- **Modify**—Click to change the reconcile For Period date or the Ending Balance amount.
- **Leave**—Click to save your work and close the Begin Reconcile window.

You can also click any column header to sort the data in that column.

Reconciliations are easiest when done each month. However, you might have been using QuickBooks for some time before learning how to complete the reconciliation task. The following section of this chapter helps you learn how to troubleshoot the first reconciliation or fix errors in previous reconciliations.

Troubleshooting Reconciliations

A simple way to determine whether your bank account is correctly reconciled is to compare your bank statement beginning balance to the QuickBooks Beginning Balance amount in the Begin Reconciliation dialog box. From the menu bar, select **Banking**, **Reconcile**, and select the appropriate Account. If you find your QuickBooks Beginning Balance does not agree with your bank statement, you can use one or a combination of several methods listed in this chapter to figure out why.

 **note**

What makes up the Beginning Balance, as shown in Figure 13.18? The beginning balance is the sum of all previously cleared checks, deposits, and other transactions. A checkmark next to a transaction item in the bank account register indicates it has previously been cleared in the bank reconciliation in QuickBooks. An asterisk indicates the item is currently being reconciled, as shown in Figure 13.20. A lightning bolt (not shown) next to a transaction indicates it has been downloaded and matched, but has not yet been marked as cleared.

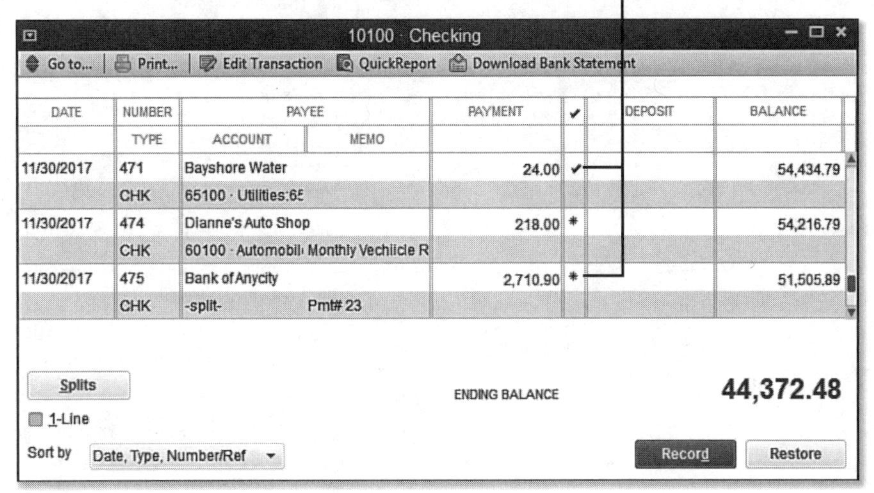

Figure 13.20 View the cleared status of transactions in your account register.

Determining Whether the Account Has Been Reconciled

If your business is just starting, it is a good time to make it part of your regular routine to reconcile your bank account in QuickBooks with the statement you receive each month. However, what if you have been using QuickBooks for years or months and have never reconciled the bank account in the software?

How can you tell whether your bank account has been reconciled? An easy method is to begin the bank reconciliation. From the menu bar, select **Banking**, **Reconcile**, and select the desired account. Review the Last Reconciled On (date) in the Begin Reconciliation window. A month/day/year indicates that the account has previously been reconciled (see Figure 13.18). If you have a Beginning Balance amount but no Last Reconciled On (date), no reconciliation has been completed. This beginning balance was most likely from entering your bank balance when you first created your QuickBooks file.

 **tip**

Are you an accounting professional? Included with QuickBooks Accountant 2013 and QuickBooks Enterprise Accountant 13.0 is the Accountant Center, as shown in Figure 13.21.

Open a client's file and the Accountant Center summarizes important information about your client's account reconciliations.

 *For more information, see "Express Start," p. 35.*

Have there been no reconciliations completed? First, determine how many months have gone by. Catching up with a few months of bank statement reconciliations takes much less effort than having to do several years or months of bank statement reconciliations. If you are going to go back to the beginning of the business and reconcile each month, you need to start with the first month of your bank activity and work your way month by month to the current month. Completing your bank reconciliation for each month is the most accurate and thorough process and provides a separate reconciliation report for each month.

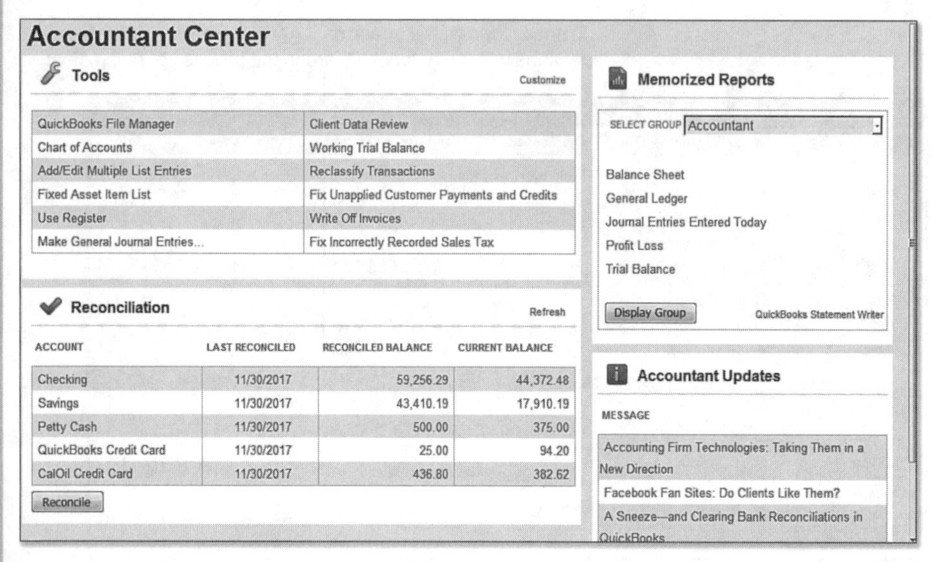

Figure 13.21 The Accountant Center is available with the Accountant editions of QuickBooks.

However, it is often not practical to go back to the start of your business when you simply want to get the bank account reconciled in the current month.

Complete the recommendations in the following sections before attempting to complete a multiyear or multimonth bank reconciliation.

caution

As with any major task or adjustment you plan to make in your QuickBooks data, I recommend you make a backup copy. You can easily create this backup by selecting **File, Create Backup** from the menu bar, and then follow the instructions on the screen.

Verifying That All Account Transactions Have Been Entered

Ensuring that all checks, bill payments, payroll checks, customer payments, and any other banking-related transactions have been entered in the QuickBooks data file is critical to the success in accurate reporting in your own or your client's QuickBooks file. You don't want to complete a multiyear or multimonth bank reconciliation if handwritten checks or other bank transactions have not been recorded in the data.

Creating a Missing Checks Report

To help you determine whether any check transactions are missing, create a Missing Checks report. To do so, follow these steps:

1. From the menu bar, select **Reports**, **Banking**, **Missing Checks** report.
2. In the Missing Checks dialog box, select the bank account from the drop-down list.

The resulting Missing Checks report shows all check or bill payment check type transactions sorted by number (see Figure 13.22). Look for any breaks in the detail with a ****Missing* or ****Duplicate* warning.

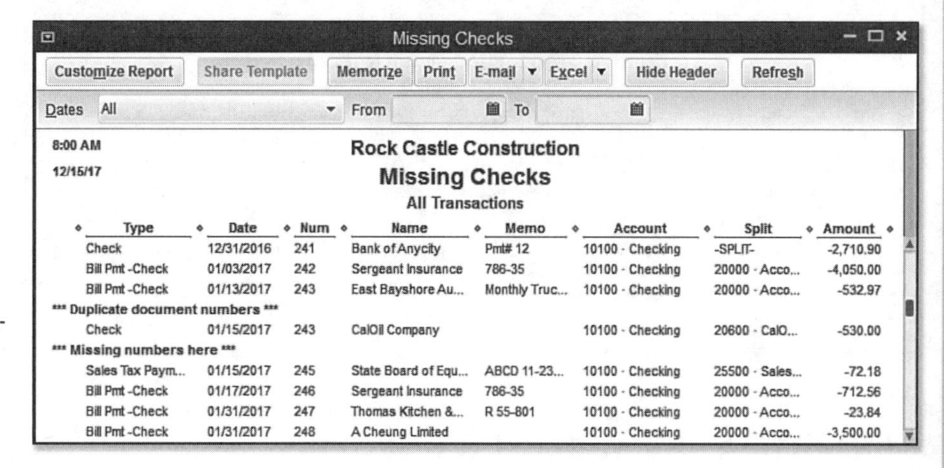

Type	Date	Num	Name	Memo	Account	Split	Amount
Check	12/31/2016	241	Bank of Anycity	Pmt# 12	10100 · Checking	-SPLIT-	-2,710.90
Bill Pmt -Check	01/03/2017	242	Sergeant Insurance	786-35	10100 · Checking	20000 · Acco...	-4,050.00
Bill Pmt -Check	01/13/2017	243	East Bayshore Au...	Monthly Truc...	10100 · Checking	20000 · Acco...	-532.97
*** Duplicate document numbers ***							
Check	01/15/2017	243	CalOil Company		10100 · Checking	20600 · CalO...	-530.00
*** Missing numbers here ***							
Sales Tax Paym...	01/15/2017	245	State Board of Equ...	ABCD 11-23...	10100 · Checking	25500 · Sales...	-72.18
Bill Pmt -Check	01/17/2017	246	Sergeant Insurance	786-35	10100 · Checking	20000 · Acco...	-712.56
Bill Pmt -Check	01/31/2017	247	Thomas Kitchen &...	R 55-801	10100 · Checking	20000 · Acco...	-23.84
Bill Pmt -Check	01/31/2017	248	A Cheung Limited		10100 · Checking	20000 · Acco...	-3,500.00

Figure 13.22 The Missing Checks report can help you determine whether you need to enter any missing transactions before you reconcile.

Creating a Custom Transaction Detail Report

Another method used to verify you have recorded all your transactions requires a bit more effort on your part. Manually add the total of all deductions and additions from the statements your bank provides you and compare to the Custom Transaction Detail report.

To do so, follow these steps:

1. From the menu bar, select **Reports**, **Custom Reports**, **Transaction Detail**. The Modify Report dialog box opens.
2. Select the From and To dates to match the period you are reconciling. If it's from the beginning of the file, you might want to leave the From date blank and enter only the To date.
3. Click the Filters tab.
4. In the Choose Filter box, with the Account filter highlighted, choose the bank account from the drop-down list.
5. Click OK.

This report (see Figure 13.23) totals all debits (money into your bank account) and credits (money out of your bank account). To these totals, you have to add in checks and deduct deposits that have not yet cleared the bank. If the resulting totals are exact or close to your manual totals, you can feel confident reconciling multiple years or months at one time.

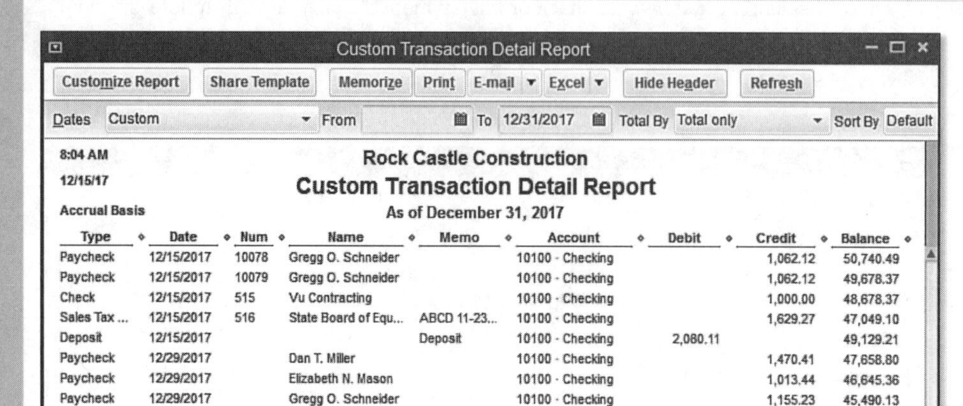

Custom Transaction Detail Report

Customize Report | Share Template | Memorize | Print | E-mail | Excel | Hide Header | Refresh

Dates Custom From To 12/31/2017 Total By Total only Sort By Default

8:04 AM
12/15/17
Accrual Basis

Rock Castle Construction
Custom Transaction Detail Report
As of December 31, 2017

Type	Date	Num	Name	Memo	Account	Debit	Credit	Balance
Paycheck	12/15/2017	10078	Gregg O. Schneider		10100 · Checking		1,062.12	50,740.49
Paycheck	12/15/2017	10079	Gregg O. Schneider		10100 · Checking		1,062.12	49,678.37
Check	12/15/2017	515	Vu Contracting		10100 · Checking		1,000.00	48,678.37
Sales Tax ...	12/15/2017	516	State Board of Equ...	ABCD 11-23...	10100 · Checking		1,629.27	47,049.10
Deposit	12/15/2017			Deposit	10100 · Checking	2,080.11		49,129.21
Paycheck	12/29/2017		Dan T. Miller		10100 · Checking		1,470.41	47,658.80
Paycheck	12/29/2017		Elizabeth N. Mason		10100 · Checking		1,013.44	46,645.36
Paycheck	12/29/2017		Gregg O. Schneider		10100 · Checking		1,155.23	45,490.13
Paycheck	12/31/2017		Elizabeth N. Mason		10100 · Checking		1,037.65	44,452.48
Total						654,177.56	609,725.08	44,452.48

Figure 13.23 The modified Custom Transaction Detail Report shows the total of all money in and out of a bank account for the time period selected.

Identifying All Uncleared Transactions

Make a list of all the uncleared bank transactions as of the month and year you are reconciling. If you have been manually reconciling your bank account, simply find the paper statement for the selected month and look for the list of uncleared transactions.

For example, suppose it is April 2017 and you want to reconcile multiple years or months through December 31, 2016. Collect your bank statements for January through March of 2017. Identify any cleared transactions from these 2017 bank statements where the transaction date was on or before December 31, 2016, but did not clear your bank until year 2017.

tip

If you are choosing to complete a multiyear or multimonth bank reconciliation, consider reconciling through the last month of your previous fiscal year, which for most companies would be your statement ending December 31, 20xx. Choosing a month to reconcile through that is two to three months in the past will make identifying the transactions that have not cleared the bank as of the month you are reconciling much easier.

Completing the Multiyear or Multimonth Bank Reconciliation

To complete the multiyear or multimonth bank reconciliation, follow these steps:

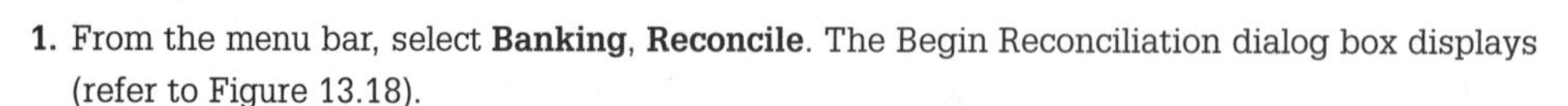

1. From the menu bar, select **Banking**, **Reconcile**. The Begin Reconciliation dialog box displays (refer to Figure 13.18).

2. Select the desired Account from the drop-down list, and type the Statement Date you want to reconcile through. Enter the Ending Balance from the bank statement and click Continue. The Reconcile–*Account* dialog box displays. Figure 13.19 shows the bank reconciliation in progress for the period ended December 31, 2017.

3. Place a checkmark in the Hide Transactions After the Statement's End Date at the top right. Checking this box makes working with the remaining transactions easier.

4. Click the Mark All button. Now each transaction is marked as if it has cleared. Remove the checkmark from any transaction you previously identified as uncleared. Your work is complete when the reconciliation shows a Difference of 0.00 at the lower right of the Reconcile–*Account* dialog box.

5. Click Reconcile Now. QuickBooks creates a bank reconciliation report you can print.

For added convenience when reconciling, you can sort the uncleared transactions by clicking once on any of the column headers in the Reconcile–*Account* dialog box.

Not all bank account reconciliations are this easy to troubleshoot and correct. Often, you need to dig deeper into the possible causes of reconciliation errors. QuickBooks makes this task much easier by providing many tools and reports to help with this important process.

caution

What if the reconciled difference is not 0.00? First determine whether the amount is significant. If the answer is yes, the best method for finding errors is to review each item marked cleared in QuickBooks with the transactions listed on your bank statements.

If you choose to record the adjustment, QuickBooks records this amount into an automatically created Expense account called Reconciliation Discrepancies. For more information, see "Reconciling with an Adjustment," p. 525.

Reviewing Uncleared Transactions

If your bank account has previously been reconciled, reviewing your uncleared bank transactions is the best place to start when troubleshooting an incorrectly reconciled bank account.

Creating an Uncleared Transactions Detail Report

This report is one of the most useful to you as you research your bank reconciliation errors. You might want to memorize this report so it can be reviewed again if needed.

To create an uncleared bank transactions report, follow these steps:

1. From the menu bar, select **Reports**, **Custom Reports**, **Transaction Detail**. The Display tab of the Modify Report dialog box displays. In the Report Date Range box, select **All Dates**. If you have more than one bank account, in the Total By drop-down list, select **Account List** to keep each bank account with separate totals. From the Columns box, select the data you want to appear in the report.

2. Click the Filters tab. In the Choose Filter box, with Account highlighted, select **All Bank Accounts**. Scroll down the Choose Filter list and select **Cleared**, and then click No next to the list, as shown in Figure 13.24.

3. This report will be useful to you in the future, so go ahead and give it a specific name by clicking the Header/Footer tab and changing the Report Title as desired.

4. Click OK to create the report (see Figure 13.25).

5. To store this report for future use, click Memorize. QuickBooks asks you to provide a name for the report. Click OK to close the Memorize Report dialog box.

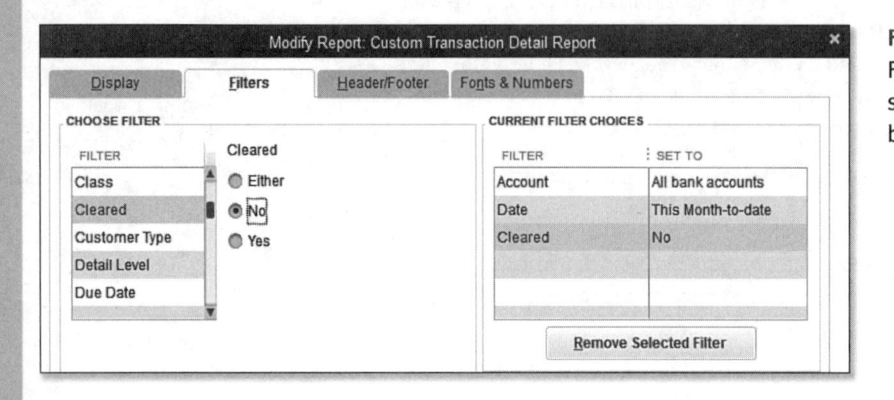

Figure 13.24
Filter the report to show only uncleared bank transactions.

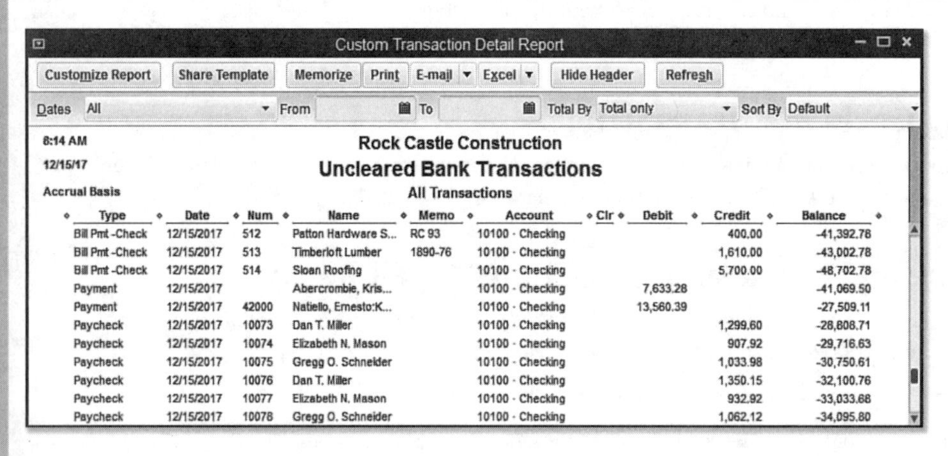

Type	Date	Num	Name	Memo	Account	Clr	Debit	Credit	Balance
Bill Pmt -Check	12/15/2017	512	Patton Hardware S...	RC 93	10100 · Checking			400.00	-41,392.78
Bill Pmt -Check	12/15/2017	513	Timberloft Lumber	1890-76	10100 · Checking			1,610.00	-43,002.78
Bill Pmt -Check	12/15/2017	514	Sloan Roofing		10100 · Checking			5,700.00	-48,702.78
Payment	12/15/2017		Abercrombie, Kris...		10100 · Checking		7,633.28		-41,069.50
Payment	12/15/2017	42000	Natiello, Ernesto:K...		10100 · Checking		13,560.39		-27,509.11
Paycheck	12/15/2017	10073	Dan T. Miller		10100 · Checking			1,299.60	-28,808.71
Paycheck	12/15/2017	10074	Elizabeth N. Mason		10100 · Checking			907.92	-29,716.63
Paycheck	12/15/2017	10075	Gregg O. Schneider		10100 · Checking			1,033.98	-30,750.61
Paycheck	12/15/2017	10076	Dan T. Miller		10100 · Checking			1,350.15	-32,100.76
Paycheck	12/15/2017	10077	Elizabeth N. Mason		10100 · Checking			932.92	-33,033.68
Paycheck	12/15/2017	10078	Gregg O. Schneider		10100 · Checking			1,062.12	-34,095.80

Figure 13.25
Create a customized report to easily view uncleared bank transactions.

Memorizing customized reports for later use is easy. First, make sure your Dates selection is appropriate. If your Dates selection is Custom, each time you create this report, it uses the custom dates. Selecting Dates, such as the generic This Month-to-Date or any of the other choices, makes the memorized report more valuable in future months.

With the report displayed, click Memorize. QuickBooks offers to save the report with the header name, or you can rename it.

For more information, see "Reporting in QuickBooks," p. 527.

tip

Another useful option is to add this report to your icon bar. With the report displayed, select **View, Add** *<name of report>* **to Icon Bar**. If you use the Top Icon bar, you may need to click the right-facing double arrows to see this icon and others that do not fit on the icon bar.

If you are using the Left Icon bar placement, scroll down to the bottom of the My Shortcuts list to see the report added.

Sorting Transactions

Another method for reviewing uncleared bank transactions is to open your bank register and follow these steps:

1. From the menu bar select **Banking**, **Use Register**.
2. Select the desired bank account in the Use Register dialog box.
3. On the lower left of the register is a Sort By drop-down list. Select the Cleared status from the drop-down list.
4. Scroll through the register and view those transactions that are either
   - **Cleared**—Denoted by a checkmark
   - **In process of being cleared**—Denoted by an asterisk (*)
   - **Not cleared**—No checkmark or *

Often, either a transaction that is cleared and should not have been cleared or a transaction that is uncleared and should have been cleared can be the cause of the opening balance not matching.

If you need to unclear a transaction or two, double-click the checkmark next to the item in the bank register. QuickBooks replaces the checkmark with an asterisk. You can also click once more to remove the asterisk if desired.

If you attempt to make a change to the cleared status of a transaction while in the bank register, QuickBooks provides a warning message.

Using additional reporting tools in QuickBooks can help you find changes made to previously reconciled transactions. You will find that using a combination of the following reports when troubleshooting reconciliation errors is useful.

Reviewing Previous Bank Reconciliation Reports

If you determine that the file has been previously reconciled but no paper copy was kept, no need to worry. This feature is available for QuickBooks Premier and Enterprise. From the menu bar, select **Reports**, **Banking**, **Previous Reconciliation**. In the Select Previous Reconciliation Report dialog box, choose a Statement Ending Date to view (see Figure 13.26). QuickBooks displays the last stored reconciliation report (available only in QuickBooks Premier, Accountant, and Enterprise). Choose from the following view options: Summary, Detail, or Both.

Additionally, you can view the reports in two ways:

- **Transactions Cleared at the Time of Reconciliation**—This stored report shows the bank reconciliation details in PDF form as they were completed at the time the account was reconciled.
- **Transactions Cleared Plus Any Changes**—View this report to see how the bank reconciliation would look today.

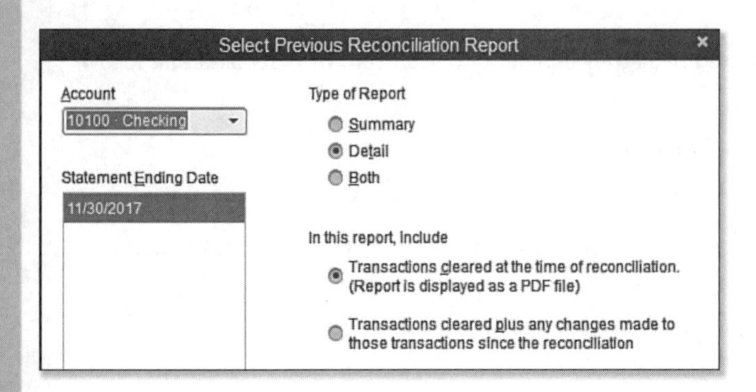

Figure 13.26
Select the previous bank reconciliation report when troubleshooting errors.

Compare the stored PDF with the Transactions Cleared Plus Changes report. Any differences between the two should indicate what your discrepancies are. You might be able to find these discrepancies easily with the Reconciliation Discrepancy report, as discussed next.

Locating Bank Account Reconciliation Discrepancies

Finding bank reconciliation discrepancies in QuickBooks is made easier with the Reconciliation Discrepancy report. To prepare this report:

1. From the menu bar select **Reports**, **Banking**, **Reconciliation Discrepancy**. The Reconciliation Discrepancy Report displays.
2. Choose the bank account from the drop-down list and select **OK** to create the report.

   This report identifies any transaction modified after being cleared in the bank reconciliation process. For each transaction on this report, you see the modified date, reconciled amount, type of change (amount added, deleted, or voided), and the financial effect of the change (see Figure 13.27).

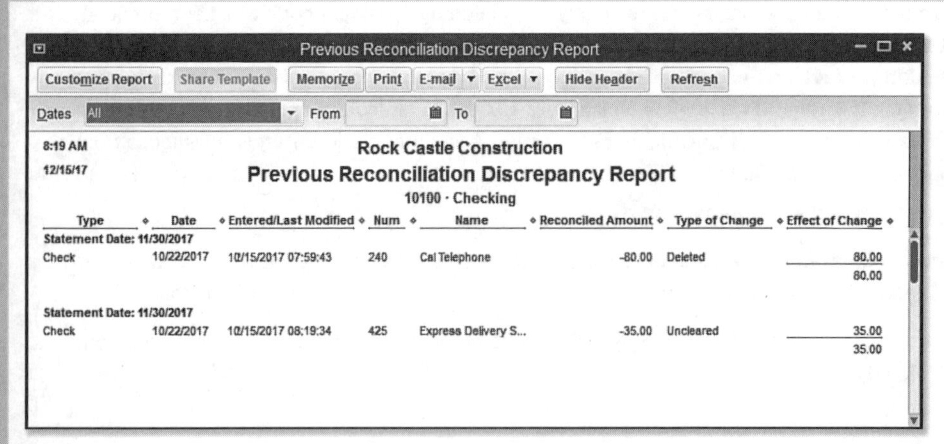

Figure 13.27
View details of previously cleared transactions that have been modified, deleted, or voided.

3. You can click Modify Report and add the username that modified the transaction to help in identifying who made the change to the transaction.

After you have found the reconciliation discrepancy, you can view the Voided/Deleted Report (discussed in the next section) to help re-create the transaction(s).

caution

Troubleshoot your bank reconciliation beginning balance differences with the previous Reconciliation Discrepancy report before completing the next month's reconciliation. Doing so is important because QuickBooks removes all detail from the discrepancy report when you complete a new reconciliation. This is due to QuickBooks determining that you have solved the issue, or you would not have completed the next month's bank reconciliation.

This report does *not* track discrepancies caused by changing the bank account associated with a transaction.

Reviewing the Voided/Deleted Transactions Reports

Other reporting tools that help locate problem transactions are the Voided/Deleted Transactions Summary report and the Voided/Deleted Transactions Detail reports.

To create the Voided/Deleted Transactions Summary report, shown in Figure 13.28, from the menu bar select **Reports**, **Accountant & Taxes**, **Voided/Deleted Transactions Summary**. Alternatively, you can select **Voided/Deleted Transactions Detail** from the submenu to view the detailed reported.

If you are having trouble finding the problem, particularly when the beginning balance has changed, this report can help you find the problem transaction(s).

Use this report for re-creating the voided or deleted transactions as part of the process of fixing your bank reconciliations.

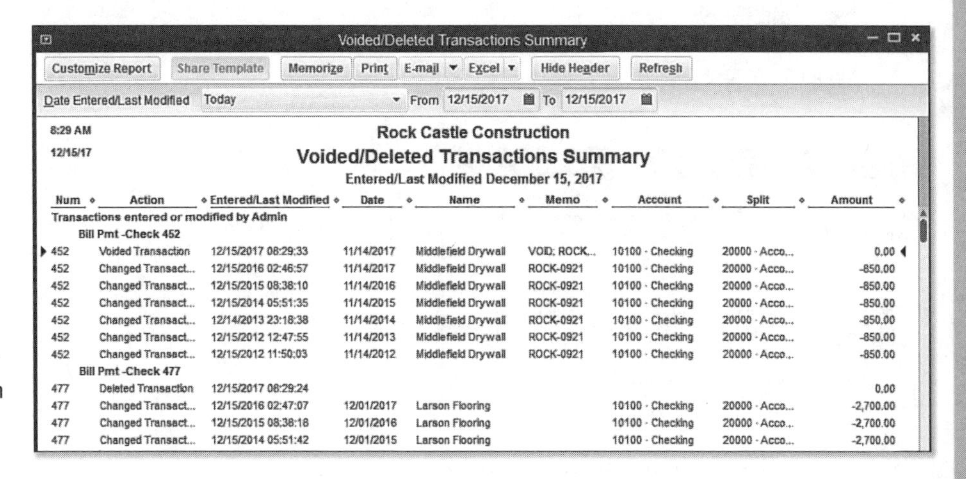

Voided/Deleted Transactions Summary

Customize Report | Share Template | Memorize | Print | E-mail | Excel | Hide Header | Refresh

Date Entered/Last Modified: Today | From 12/15/2017 | To 12/15/2017

8:29 AM
12/15/17

Rock Castle Construction

Voided/Deleted Transactions Summary

Entered/Last Modified December 15, 2017

Num	Action	Entered/Last Modified	Date	Name	Memo	Account	Split	Amount
Transactions entered or modified by Admin								
Bill Pmt -Check 452								
452	Voided Transaction	12/15/2017 08:29:33	11/14/2017	Middlefield Drywall	VOID: ROCK...	10100 · Checking	20000 · Acco...	0.00
452	Changed Transact...	12/15/2016 02:46:57	11/14/2017	Middlefield Drywall	ROCK-0921	10100 · Checking	20000 · Acco...	-850.00
452	Changed Transact...	12/15/2015 08:38:10	11/14/2016	Middlefield Drywall	ROCK-0921	10100 · Checking	20000 · Acco...	-850.00
452	Changed Transact...	12/15/2014 05:51:35	11/14/2015	Middlefield Drywall	ROCK-0921	10100 · Checking	20000 · Acco...	-850.00
452	Changed Transact...	12/14/2013 23:18:38	11/14/2014	Middlefield Drywall	ROCK-0921	10100 · Checking	20000 · Acco...	-850.00
452	Changed Transact...	12/15/2012 12:47:55	11/14/2013	Middlefield Drywall	ROCK-0921	10100 · Checking	20000 · Acco...	-850.00
452	Changed Transact...	12/15/2012 11:50:03	11/14/2012	Middlefield Drywall	ROCK-0921	10100 · Checking	20000 · Acco...	-850.00
Bill Pmt -Check 477								
477	Deleted Transaction	12/15/2017 08:29:24						0.00
477	Changed Transact...	12/15/2016 02:47:07	12/01/2017	Larson Flooring		10100 · Checking	20000 · Acco...	-2,700.00
477	Changed Transact...	12/15/2015 08:38:18	12/01/2016	Larson Flooring		10100 · Checking	20000 · Acco...	-2,700.00
477	Changed Transact...	12/15/2014 05:51:42	12/01/2015	Larson Flooring		10100 · Checking	20000 · Acco...	-2,700.00

Figure 13.28 Use the Voided/Deleted Transactions Summary report to locate transactions that are possibly causing your reconciliation errors.

If there are more than a few transactions in error, restarting or undoing the previous bank reconciliation might be easier than researching each transaction marked as cleared. However, if previously cleared transactions were voided or deleted, they will have to be recreated.

Restarting a Previously Completed Bank Reconciliation

If your review shows a few minor issues with bank reconciliation accuracy, restarting your reconciliation might be the best action to take. To do so, select **Banking**, **Reconcile**, **Locate Discrepancies** from the menu bar. The Locate Discrepancies dialog box displays. From this dialog box, click Restart Reconciliation.

Restarting your bank reconciliation retains your checkmarks on the cleared transactions, but enables you to put in a new statement date and ending balance. You can restart only the last month's banking reconciliation.

If you need to restart the reconciliation for more than one banking month, click Undo Last Reconciliation. You can repeat this undo for multiple months in a row—all the way back to the first reconciliation if desired.

Undoing a Previous Bank Reconciliation

If you have determined that the integrity of one or more completed bank reconciliations is in question, you can easily undo previous reconciliations, one month at a time. From the menu bar select **Banking**, **Reconcile**, and click Undo Last Reconciliation.

QuickBooks opens the Undo Previous Reconciliation dialog box, providing you with ample information about what to expect, and recommending that you back up your company data file first. As each month is undone, QuickBooks shows you the Previous Beginning Balance. You should undo bank reconciliations only until you reach a statement where this amount agrees with the same month's bank statement beginning balance, so watch it closely.

Click Continue after reviewing the message in Figure 13.29. You can undo the bank reconciliation one month at a time. You will know you are back to the first statement when the Undo Previous Reconciliation dialog box shows the Previous Beginning Balance as 0.00. When you return to the Begin Reconciliation dialog box, you no longer see a Last Reconciled On (date) or a Beginning Balance amount.

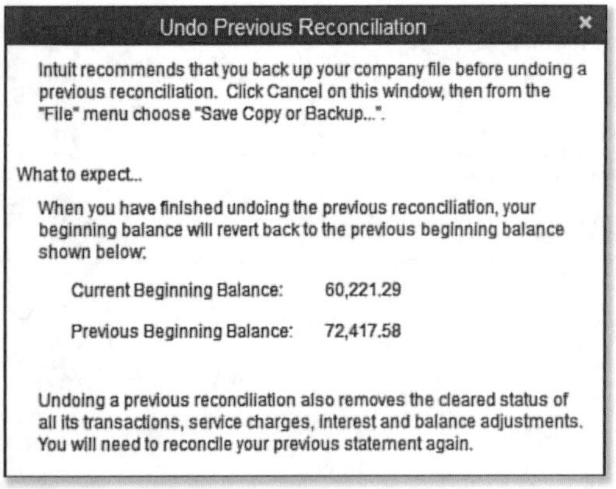

Undo Previous Reconciliation

Intuit recommends that you back up your company file before undoing a previous reconciliation. Click Cancel on this window, then from the "File" menu choose "Save Copy or Backup...".

What to expect...

When you have finished undoing the previous reconciliation, your beginning balance will revert back to the previous beginning balance shown below:

Current Beginning Balance: 60,221.29

Previous Beginning Balance: 72,417.58

Undoing a previous reconciliation also removes the cleared status of all its transactions, service charges, interest and balance adjustments. You will need to reconcile your previous statement again.

Figure 13.29
Details of what you can expect when you complete an Undo Previous Reconciliation transaction.

Reconciling with an Adjustment

QuickBooks creates an adjustment to your bank account and financials if you choose to reconcile a bank account that does not have 0.00 in the Difference row of the Reconcile dialog box.

When you decide to reconcile with an adjustment for the difference amount (see Figure 13.30), you need to first consider the following:

- Have you made every attempt to find the difference using those techniques and reports you have read in this chapter?
- Is the difference as reported on the QuickBooks Reconcile dialog box not a significant dollar amount?

tip

Use the Undo a Previous Bank Reconciliation transaction when an incorrect statement date was entered on the bank reconciliation. QuickBooks defaults the next bank statement date to 30 days from the last statement date. Before beginning the bank reconciliation in QuickBooks, verify that the statement date and beginning balance are correct.

If you can answer *yes* to these two items, let QuickBooks make an adjustment to your financials for the difference.

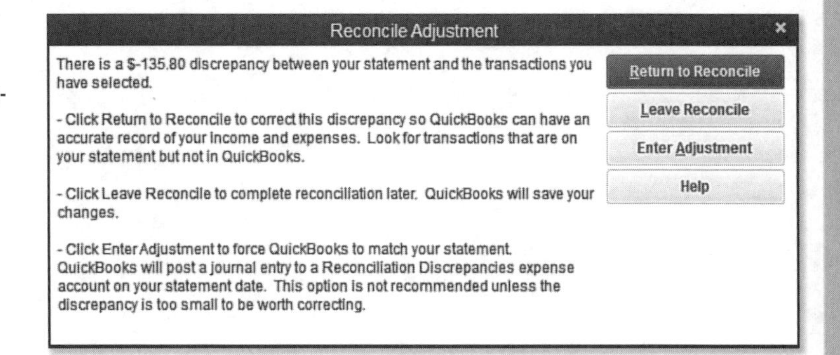

Figure 13.30
Letting QuickBooks enter an adjustment for the reconciliation difference.

To reconcile with an adjustment created by QuickBooks, click Reconcile Now in the Reconcile–Account dialog box or the Enter Adjustment in Reconcile Adjustment dialog box.

QuickBooks details the amount of the adjustment and limits your choices to do the following:

- **Return to Reconcile**—Click this option if you want to return to the reconciliation window to look for the difference.
- **Leave Reconcile**—QuickBooks saves your changes so you can return later and review your work.
- **Enter Adjustment**—This option forces QuickBooks' accounting to match your bank statement.
- **Help**—This option provides useful links to information about reconciling your accounts.

tip

One of my favorite tricks for tracking down an unreconciled balance is this: If the amount is evenly divisible by 9, there's a very strong probability the digits of a transaction amount were transposed when the transaction was entered.

When you choose Enter Adjustment, QuickBooks creates a journal entry and posts the difference to a Reconciliation Discrepancies expense account on the profit and loss report.

I don't recommend reconciling with an adjustment. Sooner or later, you will have to identify where the adjustment came from and where it should be posted. However, making an adjustment for a small balance can often save time that would be better spent on activities that grow the business. Always put in place better processes so these types of errors do not occur again.

note

Any Balance Sheet type account can be reconciled, not just bank account types. Reconciling credit card accounts provides the same control over the accuracy of your financials. Did you know that any account that transactions flow in and out of can be reconciled? Do you have a car loan? Have you reconciled your car loan account to the lending institution's statement? Do you loan money to employees and then have them pay the loan back? These are all examples of accounts that would benefit from the same reconciliation process used for bank accounts.

14

REPORTING IN QUICKBOOKS

One of the reasons QuickBooks is so popular is the ease in which you can get reports of your financial activity. On summary reports you can "drill down" on a specific number in a report to see the underlying transactions; taking out the guess work of where a number came from.

In this chapter you will learn about the many ways you can access, modify, and memorize often-used reports.

Using the Company Snapshot

The Company Snapshot (see Figure 14.1) is one convenient place to review company information and perform important tasks. The QuickBooks Company Snapshot offers a real-time view of your company's critical information. The Company Snapshot provides insight into your business using a variety of analytic and performance indicators ready-made for your use.

Customizing the Company Snapshot

QuickBooks offers the capability to customize the snapshot information on both a user and company-file specific basis, which can be helpful in multiuser environments. To customize your Company Snapshot, follow these steps:

1. From the menu bar, select **Company**, **Company Snapshot** to view the default graphs and reports.
2. Click Add Content to view and select from additional graphs and reports. See Figure 14.2.
3. Click the + Add button next to a graph or report to add it to your Company Snapshot.

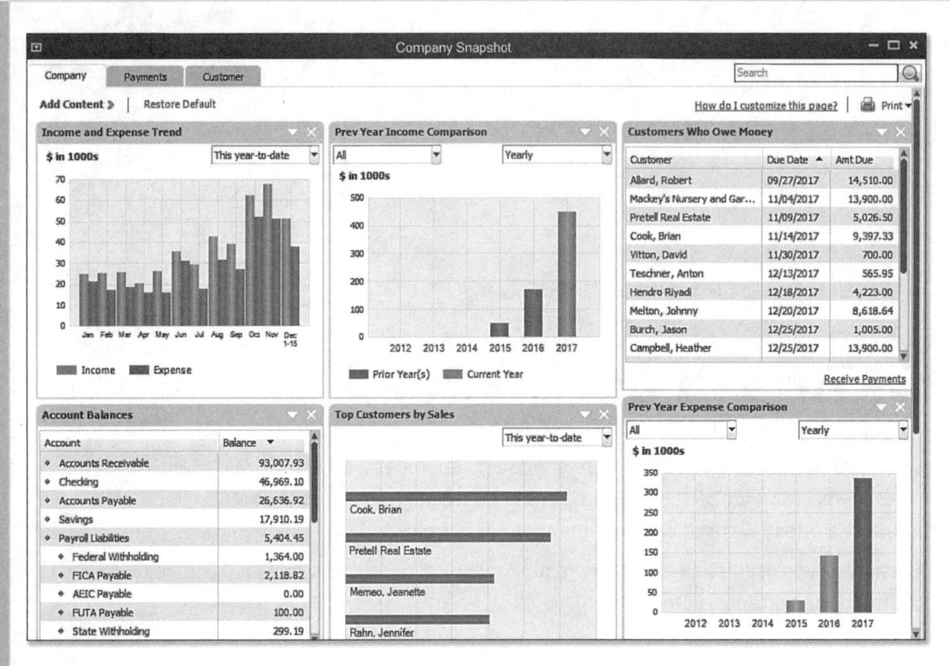

Figure 14.1 The Company Snapshot offers a wealth of useful information.

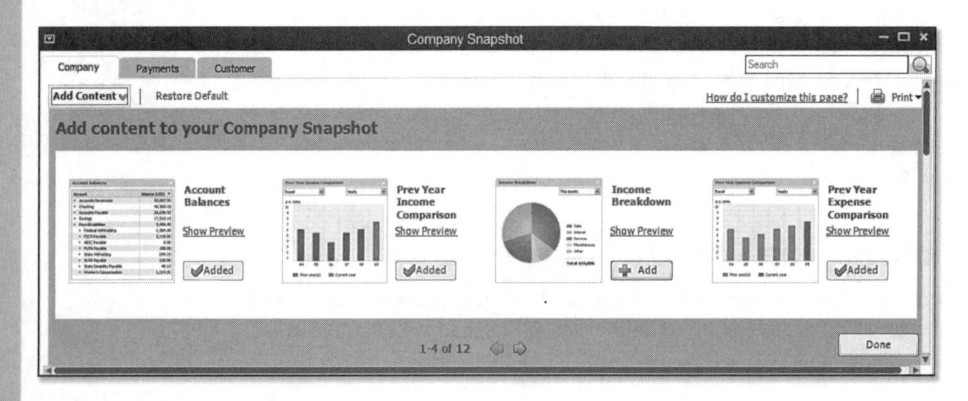

Figure 14.2 Customize the Company Snapshot by adding or removing content.

4. Click Restore Default to remove any graphs or reports you added.
5. Click Done to view your modified Company Snapshot.
6. To rearrange the order or placement of a graph and report, click and hold your left mouse button (a four-pointed arrow displays), drag the item to a new location, and release the button.
7. If you wish to print the details of the snapshot, select one of the following options from the Print menu in the upper-right corner to print your snapshot or prepare it for printing: Print, Print Preview, or Set Orientation.

Get an immediate view of the bottom line of your business with these reports available on the QuickBooks Company Snapshot:

- **Account Balances—**View Balance Sheet accounts by default is shown. You can add any other account type to this view by clicking the Select Accounts link.
- **Previous Year Income Comparison—**View how much money you are making this year compared to previous years for any or all accounts. You can view monthly, quarterly, weekly, or yearly comparisons.
- **Income Breakdown—**View your company's largest sources of income.
- **Previous Year Expense Comparison—**Compare how much money you are spending this year to previous years for any or all accounts. You can view monthly, quarterly, weekly, or yearly comparisons.
- **Expense Breakdown—**View your company's biggest expenses.
- **Income and Expense Trend Graph—**View where the money goes in and out of your business.
- **Top Customers by Sales—**Easily report on who your top five customers are based on sales for a given period of time.
- **Best Selling Items—**Know which items and services customers are buying the most during a given period of time. You can view the data by amount or by units.
- **Customers Who Owe Money—**Review those customers who owe your company money. Overdue items are shown in red. To sort any of the columns, click the column header in any of the panes. The Due Date shown is the earliest due date for all invoices or statement charges for that customer.
- **Top Vendors by Expense—**View your top five vendors based on expenses for a given period of time.
- **Vendors to Pay—**Skip running the aged payables report by adding this section to your Company Snapshot. Amounts shown in red are past due. To sort any of the columns, click the column header. The Due Date shown is the earliest due date that the vendor bills are due. The Amt Due column is the total ending balance for that vendor.
- **Reminders—**Never forget important tasks. Include these critical reminders on your Company Snapshot. Click the Set Preferences link in the Reminders box to customize what information you want displayed.

caution

If your company has created user restrictions in QuickBooks, users will have access only to activities of the Company Snapshot that they have permission to access. If you do not want users to see the Income and Expense of the company, you will have to set restrictions for both the Sensitive Accounting Activities and Sensitive Financial Reporting. To modify a user's security rights, you must be logged in to the data file as the Admin user.

After you have set up the security, log in as that user and verify whether the behavior is what you were expecting. For more comprehensive user security settings, consider using QuickBooks Enterprise Solutions 13.0.

Defaulting the Company Snapshot as Home Page

If you want to have the Company Snapshot display when you first open a company file, follow these steps:

1. Click the Company Snapshot icon on the icon bar to open the Company Snapshot. Alternatively, select **Company**, **Company Snapshot** from the menu bar.
2. With the Company Snapshot displayed, from the menu bar select **Edit**, **Preferences**, and then on the left side of the Preferences dialog box, select **Desktop View**.
3. On the My Preferences tab, select the **Save Current Desktop** option button. See Figure 14.3.

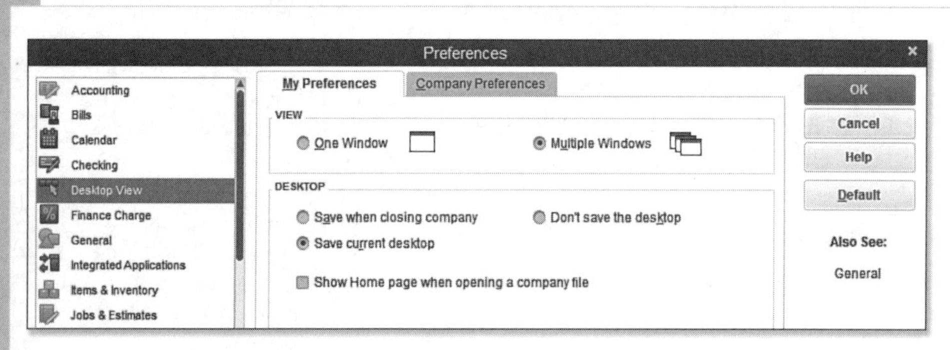

Figure 14.3 The desktop preference settings control what opens automatically when you launch QuickBooks.

4. Uncheck the option to Show Home Page When Opening Company File. When you open your data file, the Company Snapshot automatically displays.

Report Center

Up to this point in the book, you have learned how to get started with QuickBooks and create a variety of transactions. In this chapter, you learn from step-by-step instructions to create specific reports to assist you with your QuickBooks setup or review.

If you are new to QuickBooks or if you have never reviewed the QuickBooks Report Center, in this section you can find out about the many features available for simplifying your reporting needs in QuickBooks.

The Report Center is available in the following editions of QuickBooks: Pro, Premier, Accountant, and Enterprise.

To open the Report Center, on the icon bar click Reports, or from the menu bar, select **Reports**, **Report Center**. The Report Center displays. Features of the Report Center include the following:

- Option to view the reports or graphs in Carousel view (see Figure 14.4), List view (see Figure 14.5), or Grid view (see Figure 14.6) by selecting one of the icons on the top right of the Report Center.

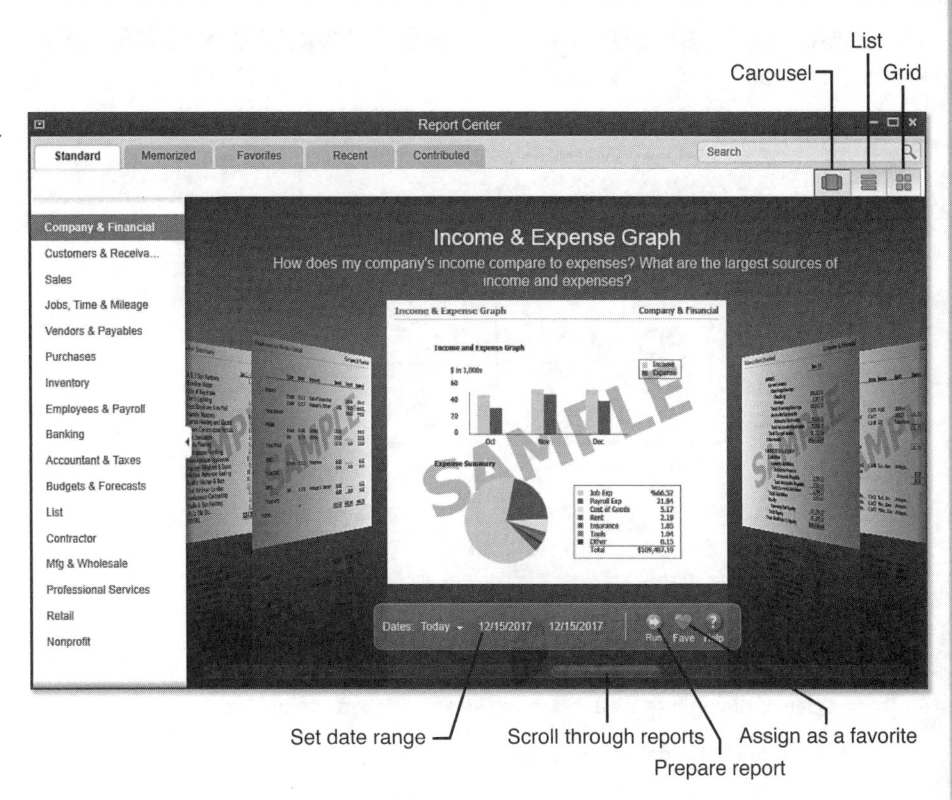

Figure 14.4 The QuickBooks Report Center in Carousel view.

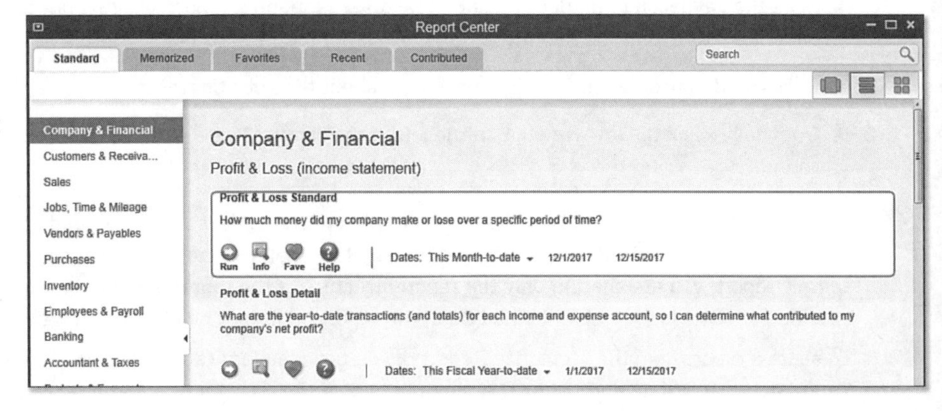

Figure 14.5 Optionally view your reports in List view.

- From the Standard tab, select a grouping of reports. Your displayed report groups might differ from those shown in Figure 14.4 depending on the version of QuickBooks you are using.

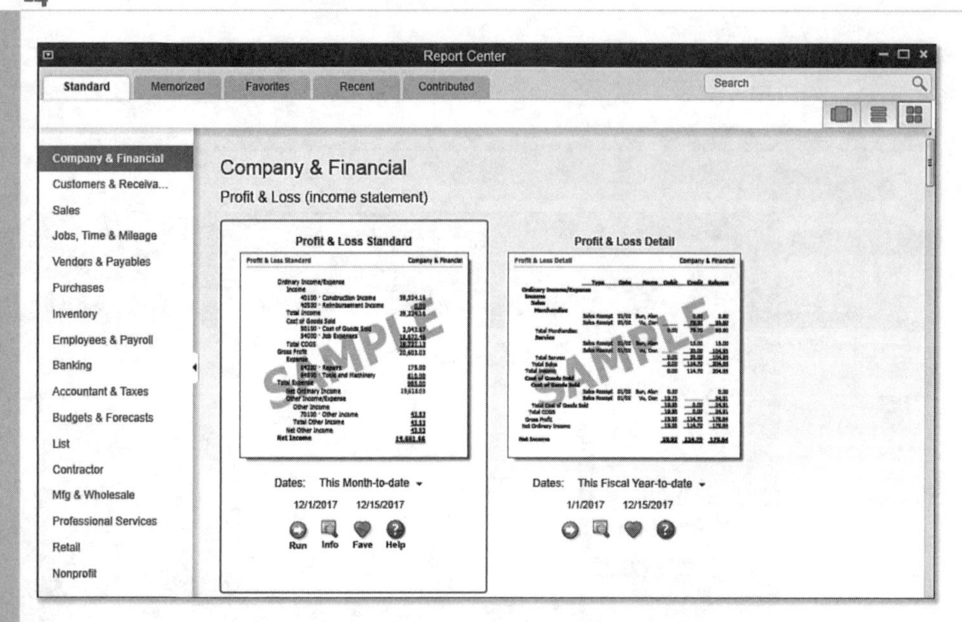

Figure 14.6 Use the Grid view to find reports for your business.

- In Carousel view, use the scrollbar at the bottom of the displayed report to move through samples of the reports available in the selected report group. Data displayed is sample data.
- Click the Dates drop-down list to select a specific date, or accept the default date. (You can also click the dates to modify.)
- Click the Run icon to display the report details with your company data.
- Click the Fave icon to mark or unmark a favorite. Marking a report as a favorite places it on the Favorites tab within the Report Center.
- Click the Help icon to open Help information about the specific report.
- Optionally, click the arrow notch on the left of the carousel view to close the menu report group listing.

The Report Center also includes a Contributed tab, which displays reports shared by other QuickBooks users. QuickBooks does not share any financial data from your company file. When you share a report, you are sharing only the report structure. If the report is filtered for specific chart of accounts or other unique user defined data, the report might not be able to be shared.

To share a report from the Memorize Report dialog box (see Figure 14.16), select **Share the Report Template with Others** and follow the prompts to give the report a title and brief description.

Reports & Graphs Preferences

QuickBooks makes it easy for you to customize reports globally through the use of the Reporting Preferences. Reporting Preferences come in two types: My Preferences, which are unique to a logged-in user, and Company Preferences, which can be set only by the Admin or External Accountant user and represent global settings for all users.

My Preferences

The My Preference setting for reports is user specific. To access user-specific preferences for reports, from the menu bar select **Edit**, **Preferences**. In the Preferences dialog box, select **Reports & Graphs** and click the My Preferences tab.

You can specify the following settings that will be unique for the currently logged-in user (if using QuickBooks in a multiuser mode):

- **Prompt Me to Modify Report Options Before Opening a Report**—When selected, this option causes QuickBooks to open the Modify Report dialog box each time a report is opened.
- **Reports and Graphs**—You have a choice, when report details have changed, to request QuickBooks to select one of the following options: **Prompt Me to Refresh** (this is the default option for a new data file), **Refresh Automatically**, or **Don't Refresh**. I usually choose the Refresh Automatically option. However, if the report is lengthy and you have multiple users entering data, you might want to review a report, make changes, and not have QuickBooks refresh at the time the change is made.
- **Graphs Only**—This option offers settings for drawing in 2D or using patterns.

Company Preferences

Different from the My Preference setting for Reports and Graphs, the Company Preferences can be set only by the Admin or External Accountant user and are global settings for all users.

To access Company Preferences for reports, log in as the Admin or External Accountant user in single-user mode and select **Edit**, **Preferences** from the menu bar. In the Preferences dialog box, select **Reports & Graphs**, click the Company Preferences tab, and set global defaults (for all users) for the following items:

- **Summary Report Basis**—You can choose Accrual (default) or Cash Basis. For business owners, I suggest that you discuss this option with your accountant.
- **Aging Reports**—You can choose to age from the due date (default) or age from the transaction date. This setting determines the aged status of your accounts receivable and accounts payable reports.

- **Format**—Click the Format button to set the following options globally for all reports:
  - **Show Header Information**—Leave the default information in place. QuickBooks will then populate the report with this current information automatically.
  - **Show Footer Information**—Enter an extra footer line, such as **Confidential Information** or the like.
  - **Page Layout**—Adjust the alignment from the default of Standard to left, right, or center justified.
  - **Fonts**—Set this on the Fonts & Numbers tab and use this to set fonts for all text or specific text lines. As you select the text line on the left, QuickBooks displays the current font choice and size for that text.
  - **Show Negative Numbers**—Use these settings for defining how numbers will be formatted on reports. Format choices include normal −300.00; in parentheses (300.00) or with a trailing minus 300.00−. Optionally, you can select to have these numbers print in red.
  - **Show All Numbers**—Use this setting to divide all numbers by 1,000, to not show zero amounts, or to show numbers without the cents. These options are most often used by accounting professionals when providing a statement to a bank and so on.

You can display accounts by Name Only (the default), Description Only, or Name and Description. These are fields you completed in the Add New Account or Edit Account dialog boxes, as shown in Figure 14.7.

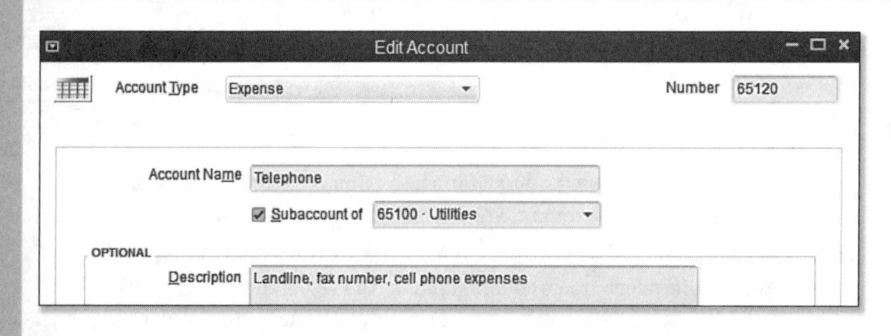

Figure 14.7
Optionally, include a description in addition to the account name.

- **Reports—Show Accounts By**—Choose from the following options for displaying the account name on reports:
  - **Name Only**—Shows account name and account number, as shown in Figure 14.8 (if the Use Account Numbers preference is enabled).
  - **Description Only**—Shows only the information typed in the Description field (see Figure 14.9).
  - **Name and Description**—Shows account number, account name, and description, as shown in Figure 14.10.

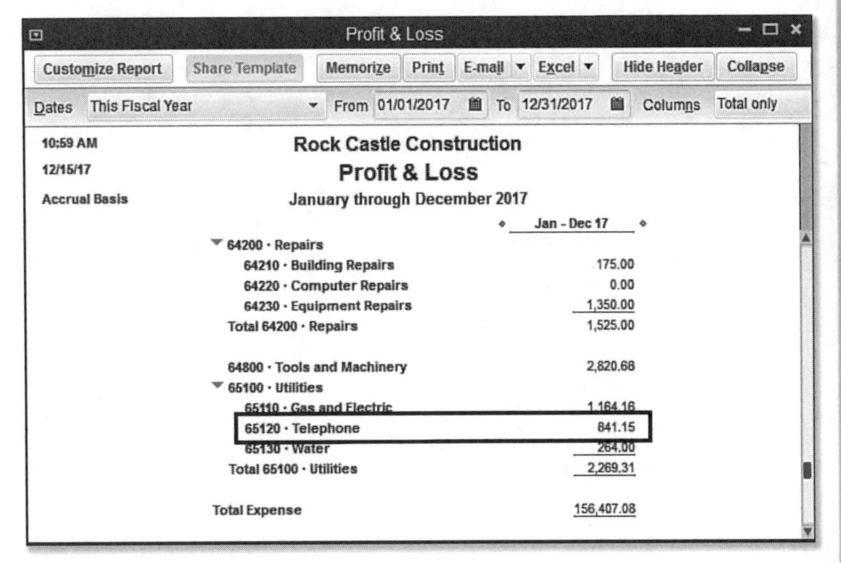

Figure 14.8
Resulting report when the Name Only report preference is selected in addition to having the account numbering preference enabled.

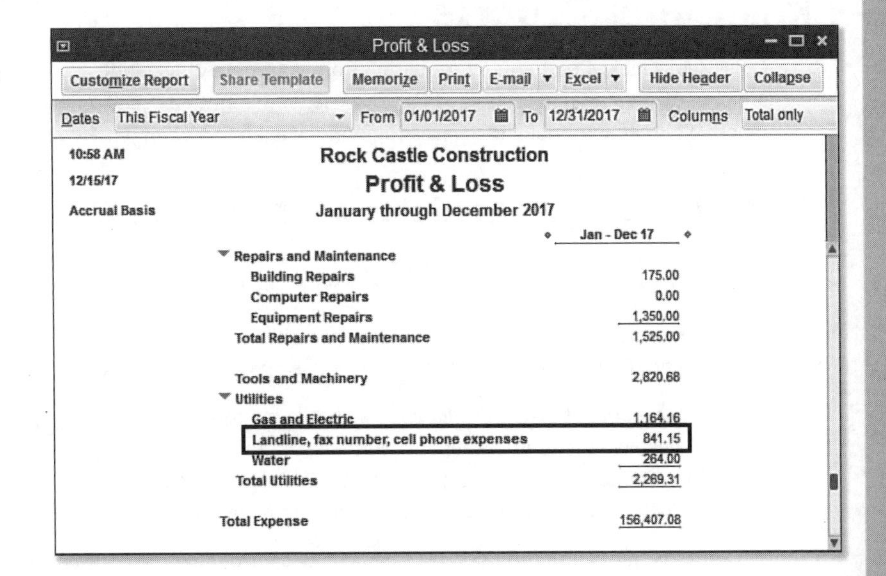

Figure 14.9
Resulting report when the Description Only report preference is selected.

- **Statement of Cash Flows**—View information about uses of Cash for Operating, Investing, and Financing activities. Click the Classify Cash button to open the Classify Cash dialog box and specify which accounts you want included in the Cash Flow analysis.

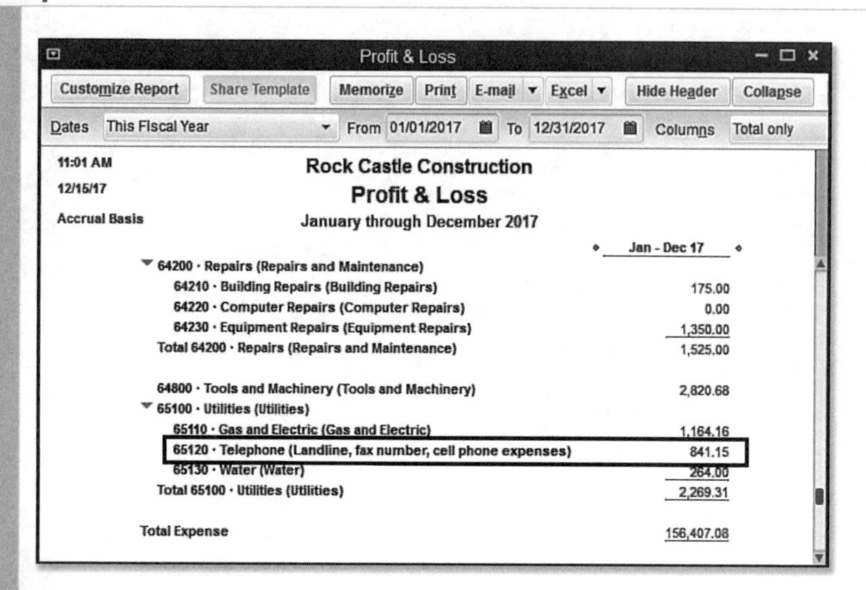

Profit & Loss

Customize Report | Share Template | Memorize | Print | E-mail | Excel | Hide Header | Collapse

Dates: This Fiscal Year | From 01/01/2017 | To 12/31/2017 | Columns: Total only

11:01 AM
12/15/17
Accrual Basis

Rock Castle Construction
Profit & Loss
January through December 2017

	Jan - Dec 17
64200 · Repairs (Repairs and Maintenance)	
64210 · Building Repairs (Building Repairs)	175.00
64220 · Computer Repairs (Computer Repairs)	0.00
64230 · Equipment Repairs (Equipment Repairs)	1,350.00
Total 64200 · Repairs (Repairs and Maintenance)	1,525.00
64800 · Tools and Machinery (Tools and Machinery)	2,820.68
65100 · Utilities (Utilities)	
65110 · Gas and Electric (Gas and Electric)	1,164.16
65120 · Telephone (Landline, fax number, cell phone expenses)	841.15
65130 · Water (Water)	264.00
Total 65100 · Utilities (Utilities)	2,269.31
Total Expense	156,407.08

Figure 14.10 Resulting report when the Name and Description report preference is selected in addition to having the account numbering preference enabled.

Modifying Reports

QuickBooks makes gathering information from your data quick and easy. Though many reports are already created and organized for your use, you might on occasion want to modify an existing report. This section briefly discusses the options available when you want to modify a report.

Modifying Options Available on the Report Window

A few of the options to modify a report are available directly on any active report dialog box. The options include the following:

- **Hide Header**—Removes the header, or report title section, from the report. Click Show Header when you want it to appear.
- **Collapse**—Collapse the information, as shown in Figure 14.11. This allows you to toggle a report between summary and detail views on-the-fly. When you click the Collapse button, QuickBooks removes the subaccount detail from view only.

tip

Did you know that each line on a report can be collapsed or expanded manually? To do this, click the gray arrow in front of any row report detail.

- **Columns**—For certain reports, you can easily control how the data is subtotaled or grouped and add additional columns or subcolumns.
- **Sort By**—Use this to group the detail in useful ways for your review. I use this frequently, especially when looking at reports with many lines of detail. Your sort by options will vary based on the type of report you have displayed.

Other options on the active report window are also discussed in this chapter including customizing, memorizing, and exporting reports to Excel.

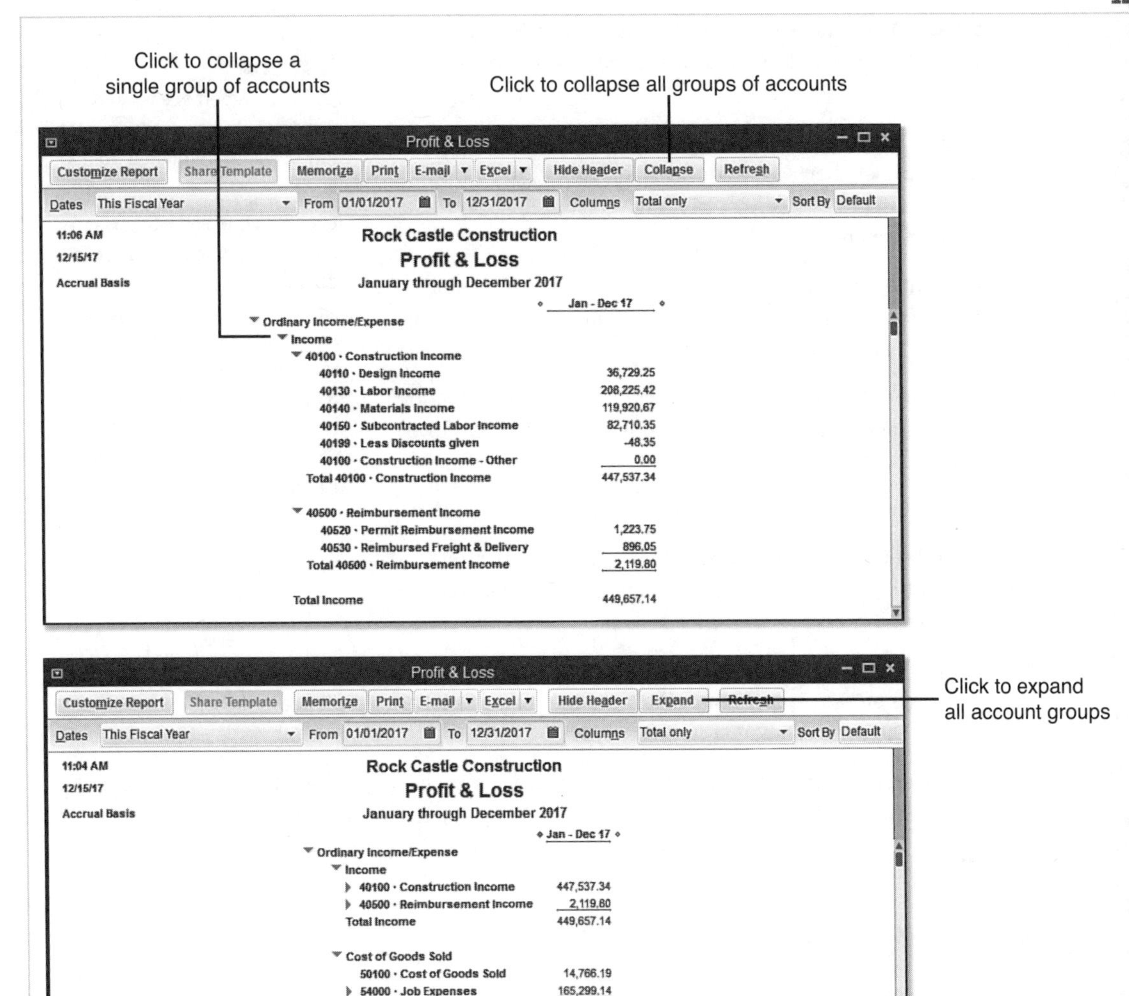

Figure 14.11
Click the Collapse button on a report to roll up the subaccounts into the main account.

Customizing Reports

Click the Customize Report button at the top left of the open report dialog box. The options for modifying reports vary by report type. Some reports offer the following choices (others might not offer the same report modification choices):

- **Display tab**—This tab opens automatically when you choose to customize an existing report. Depending on the report that you choose, some or all of the following options will be available:

- **Report Date Range**—Choose from the QuickBooks predefined date ranges or set a custom date range for your report.
- **Report Basis**—You can choose Accrual or Cash. This option is not available on all reports. This allows you to override the default preference you might have set in Reports & Graphs preferences.
- **Columns**—This setting is useful for selecting what information you want to see and whether you want it sorted or totaled by a specific field on the resulting report.
- **Advanced Button**—This button is often overlooked, but its settings enable users to display active, all, or nonzero rows and columns as well as the desired reporting calendar.
- **Revert Button**—Undo of any changes made to the settings.

tip

Filtering a report is easy and convenient to do when you want only specific information from a longer report.

If you do filter, you might want to modify your report title so it identifies what has been filtered. For example, if you are filtering a report to show employee advances detail, you might want to modify the report title on the Header/Footer tab to **Employee Advances Detail** so those who read the report will know it is pulling out specific information.

- **Filters tab**—Use these options to filter for specific accounts, names, or transaction types as well as many other fields that can be filtered on.
- **Header/Footer tab**—Use this tab to modify the report title and the appearance of the information that displays on the report. You can set this information globally for all users; see the section "Company Preferences" earlier in this chapter.
- **Fonts & Numbers tab**—Use this tab to specify fonts for specific line text as well as how numbers appear in your reports. You can set this information globally for all users; see the section "Company Preferences" earlier in this chapter.

Report Groups

Users often overlook report groups, which allow you to run two or more reports in QuickBooks at once. This feature can streamline your reporting process. This section highlights how to create, use, and manage report groups.

tip

From time to time I'll encounter a mistake-prone client. In such instances, I advise them on proper procedures and provide a grouping of reports for them to review prior to my appointment.

Creating Report Groups

For accountants, this feature can save you precious time each period you work with your client's data. You can create a group of reports that you review each time you work with the client's file.

To create a report group, follow these steps:

1. From the menu bar, select **Reports**, **Memorized Reports**, **Memorized Report List**. The Memorized Report List dialog box displays (showing predefined groups and associated reports).
2. Click the Memorized Report drop-down button at the bottom of the list and then select **New Group**.

3. In the New Memorized Report Group dialog box, provide a name for the group. Click OK to return to the Memorized Report List. QuickBooks places your new group alphabetically in the existing list of report groups.

4. Click the X in the upper right to close the Memorized Report List.

> **note**
>
> If you work in the file with Multiuser access enabled, select **File, Switch to Single User Access** before attempting to move a group of reports on the list.

If you are going to create several reports that are included as part of this report group, you should move this newly created report group to the top of the list. To move a report group, with your cursor, click on the diamond in front of the report group name. You will have to be logged into the file in single-user mode. As you memorize reports for this group, QuickBooks defaults the report group in the Memorize Report dialog box to the first Report Group on the list.

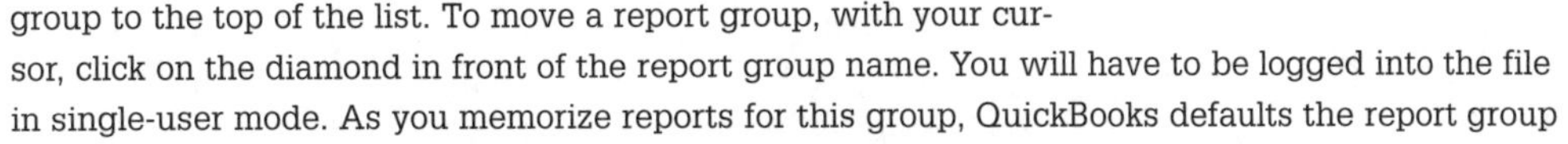

When you are done memorizing the reports to this report group (see the next section), you can move the group list item back alphabetically within the rest of the memorized reports or groups.

To move a report group up or down the list, place your cursor over the diamond shape in front of the report group name. Drag the item up or down. Figure 14.12 shows the new Monthly Reports group being moved to the top of the list.

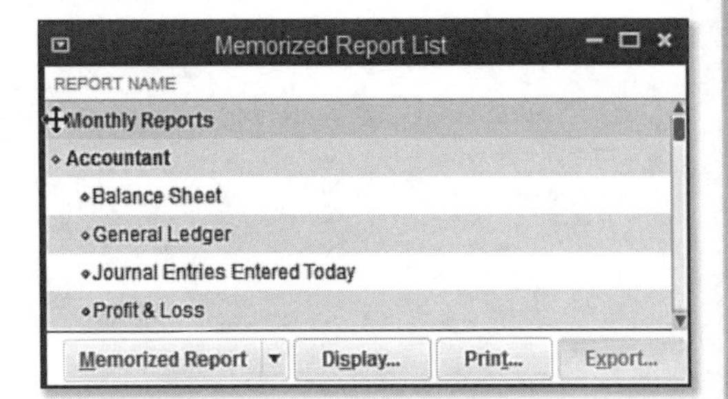

Figure 14.12
Create a report group so you can easily display or print multiple reports at one time.

Using Report Groups

The primary purpose of report groups is to simplify displaying or printing multiple reports at one time.

To display a group of reports, follow these steps:

1. From the menu bar, select **Reports**, **Process Multiple Reports**. The Process Multiple Reports dialog box displays.

2. In the Select Memorized Reports From drop-down list, select the specific report group you want to create, as shown in Figure 14.13.

3. Remove the checkmark for any report you do not want to process in the group. Figure 14.14 shows a sample of selected reports.

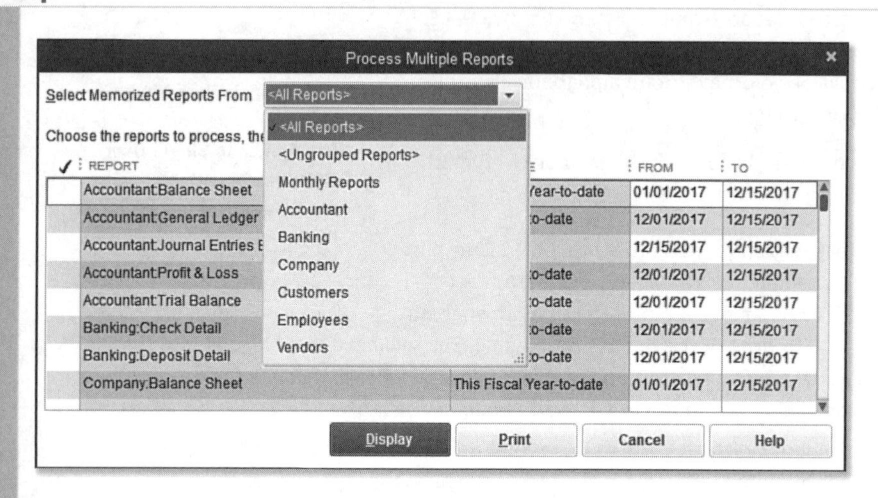

Figure 14.13
The Process Multiple Reports dialog box enables you to choose what group of reports to display or print.

Process Multiple Reports

Select Memorized Reports From Monthly

Choose the reports to process, then press Display or Print.

✓	REPORT	DATE RANGE	FROM	TO
✓	Balance Sheet	This Month-to-date	12/01/2017	12/15/2017
✓	Profit & Loss Month to Date	This Month-to-date	12/01/2017	12/15/2017
✓	Missing Invoices	All		
✓	Unpaid Bills Detail	Today	12/15/2017	12/15/2017
✓	Customer Balance Summary	All		
✓	Payroll Liabilities	Custom	01/01/2003	11/30/2003

Display Print Cancel Help

Figure 14.14
The Monthly report group has been selected, and those reports memorized with this group are shown.

4. In the From and To columns, change the date as needed. Be aware that these changes are not permanent. The next time you create the report group, the original date range stored with the report appears. If you want the new dates to appear next time, you need to memorize the report again and select the Replace button to replace the previously stored report with the new date range.

5. Click Display to view the reports on your computer screen, or click Print to send the selected reports to your printer.

 caution

When memorizing a report you will add to a report group, be aware of the date range selected. If you want to generate a report for the current month-to-date, select **This Month-to-Date** as the default date range. When the report is generated, QuickBooks uses data from the current month-to-date.

If you select a specific range of dates on a memorized report, QuickBooks considers those dates to be a default setting and will always generate the report with those specific dates.

Your report group generates the multiple reports for you to view or print. I often create a report group for my clients named either Monthly or Quarterly Reports. In this group, I put certain reports I want them to review before my appointment. This method helps them help me in keeping their QuickBooks data reporting organized.

Managing Report Groups

To manage a report group, follow these steps:

1. From the menu bar, select **Reports**, **Memorized Reports**, **Memorized Report List**. The Memorized Report List dialog box displays (showing predefined groups and associated reports).
2. At the bottom of the list, click the Memorized Report button to choose the following memorized report list options:
   - **Edit Memorized Report**—Edit the name of an existing report list item or which group it is associated with (you do not edit the date ranges or filters from this dialog box).
   - **New Group**—Create an association of multiple reports, discussed in the previous section.
   - **Delete a Memorized Report**—Manage the list and changes over time.
   - **Print the List**—Create a printed list of your memorized reports.
   - **Re-sort the List**—Return the list to its original order before any custom changes to the organization of the list items. This option isn't needed that often.
   - **Import or Export a Template**—Create and then use reports for multiple client data files.

   For more information, see "Exporting and Importing Report Templates," p. 543.
3. To rearrange your reports, place your cursor on the diamond in front of the report name, and click and drag down and to the right, as shown in Figure 14.15. Release the mouse button when the report is in the desired position.

From the memorized report list, you can also export your reports to Excel without first displaying them in QuickBooks. Use these report groups to streamline your data review. You can use the Memorize feature for many of the special reports discussed in this book and place them in a report group for easy and frequent access.

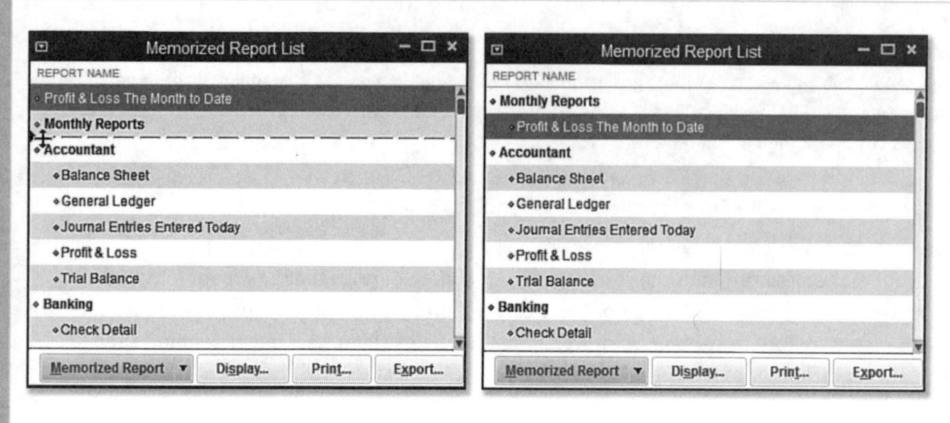

Figure 14.15 Click and drag the diamond in front of any report or group to rearrange the list manually.

Memorized Reports

After you have created a report group, you can use the memorize feature for the reports you want in that group. Placing your memorized reports in a group is optional, but using groups helps keep your memorized reports organized.

To memorize a report, click the Memorize button at the top of an open report, as shown in Figure 14.16. QuickBooks requires you to give the report a name and optionally lets you assign it to a report group or share it with others (optional). (You must first create the report group so it displays in the drop-down list in the Memorize Report dialog box.)

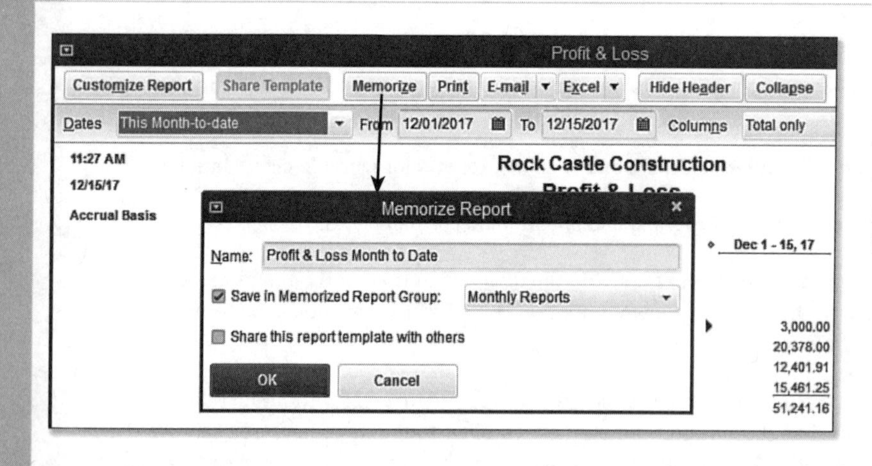

Figure 14.16 Click Memorize on any displayed report, give the report a name, and (optionally) assign it to a report group or share the template with others.

If you choose not to assign a report group, your memorized reports are listed individually on the Memorized Report List, as shown previously in Figure 14.15.

Exporting and Importing Report Templates

QuickBooks offers the option to export and import report templates. This feature is useful for accountants who want to save time by having several clients use the same report template.

Only the format and filter settings are stored with report templates. If you create a report template and then have several clients use it, when the client imports it, the desired report is generated with the current client's data, not the data it was created with.

You can export and import a single report or a group of reports only from the Memorized Report List. Thus you must first memorize any reports that you want to export.

Exporting a Report or Report Group Template

To export a report or report group template, follow these steps:

1. From the menu bar, select **Reports**, **Memorized Reports**, **Memorized Report List**.
2. In the Memorized Report drop-down list, select **Export Template**.
3. The Specify File Name dialog box displays, enabling you to select a location to store the template (.QBR extension).
4. Attach the stored report template or report group to an email, or copy it to a removable storage device such as a USB drive to share with other QuickBooks data files.

caution

Certain restrictions exist when creating a template for export. For example, if you filter for a specific chart of account or customer name that might not be present in every customer's file, QuickBooks provides the message shown in Figure 14.17, warning that this report cannot be exported.

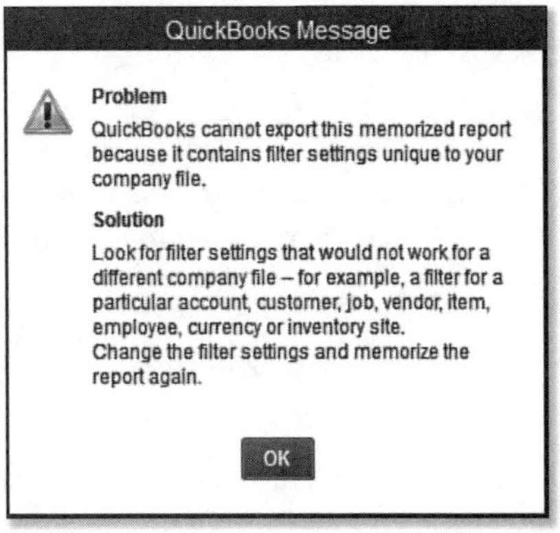

Figure 14.17
If your report has specific filters, you might not be able to export and share it with multiple data files.

QuickBooks Message

Problem

QuickBooks cannot export this memorized report because it contains filter settings unique to your company file.

Solution

Look for filter settings that would not work for a different company file – for example, a filter for a particular account, customer, job, vendor, item, employee, currency or inventory site.
Change the filter settings and memorize the report again.

OK

Importing a Report or Report Group Template

To import a report or report group template, follow these steps:

1. From the menu bar, select **Reports**, **Memorized Reports**. The Memorized Reports List dialog box displays.
2. In the Memorized Reports List drop-down list, select **Import Template**.
3. The Specify File Name dialog box displays, enabling you to select the stored location of the .QBR template.
4. Select the appropriate .QBR report or report group template.
5. Click Open. The Memorize Report dialog box displays for you to assign a name for the report and optionally assign it to a group.
6. Click OK to add the report to your memorized report list.

tip

Did you know that an abundance of reports are already created for you to import into your or your client's data file? Both business owners and accountants will find these reports useful and unique to what you already have in QuickBooks. Go to http://community.intuit.com/quickbooks

On the right, from the More Resources section select **Library**. Select the Reports for **QuickBooks 2012 and Above** link in the Reports section. From the Search drop-down menu, select **All Reports** or select a specific category.

Exporting Reports to a .CSV File or to Excel

You might have occasions where you want to export your reports to Excel to manipulate them in some more extensive manner than is available within QuickBooks.

To export a report to either .CSV or Excel format, follow these steps:

1. From any report window, click the Excel button at the top of the report.
2. Click Create New Worksheet. (If you are updating a previously exported report, select **Update Existing Worksheet** and follow the prompts to browse to the file location.)
3. The Send Report to Excel dialog box displays with these options:
   - Create New Worksheet, in a new workbook or in an existing workbook
   - Update an existing worksheet
   - Create a comma separated values (.csv) file
4. (Optional) Click the Advanced tab of the Export Report dialog box for options to preserve QuickBooks formatting, enabling certain Excel features, and printing options. Try different configurations of these settings to see what best suits your needs. See Figure 14.18. Changes made to the Advanced tab settings affect future exported reports. Click OK.

caution

I generally try to discourage exporting to Excel and do my best with a client to find the appropriate report in QuickBooks, simply because any changes you make to your report in Excel do not "flow" back into your QuickBooks data file. However, you can link exported reports, so changes made in your QuickBooks data will update your Excel spreadsheet.

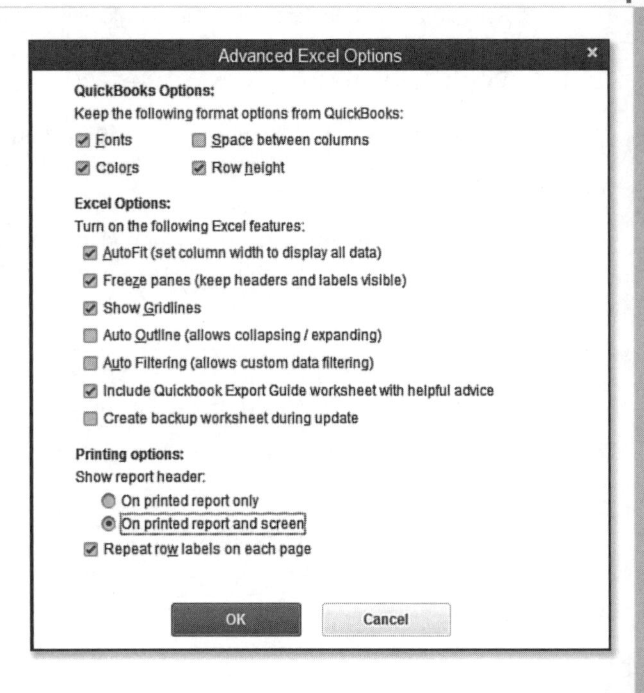

Figure 14.18
Advanced Excel Options includes automatically formatting the exported QuickBooks report.

5. Click Export to create the exported report, shown in Figure 14.19.

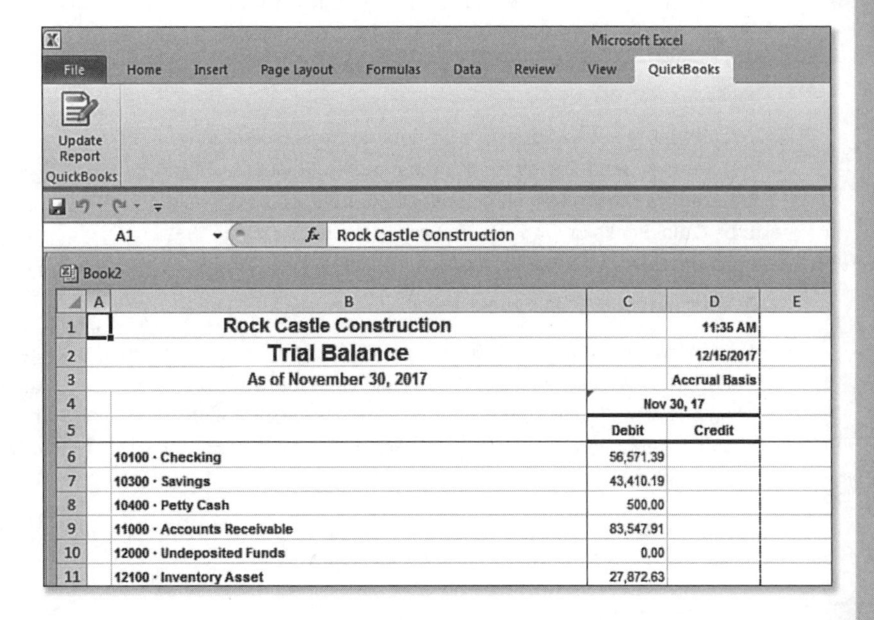

Figure 14.19
Easily convert any QuickBooks report or list to an Excel or .CSV format.

6. Select the **QuickBooks Export Tips** worksheet tab for additional useful hints in working with exported reports. The Advanced button includes an option to Turn Off creating the QuickBooks Export Tips worksheet.

Remember, however, that changes made in Excel to the exported report details are "static"—their information is fixed in time. Changes made to the Excel report do not transfer back into QuickBooks.

However, you can send changes in QuickBooks out to your Excel report by selecting Update an Existing Worksheet. Another method for updating a saved Excel exported report is to click the **QuickBooks tab** in Excel's ribbon interface and select **Update Report**. See Figure 14.20.

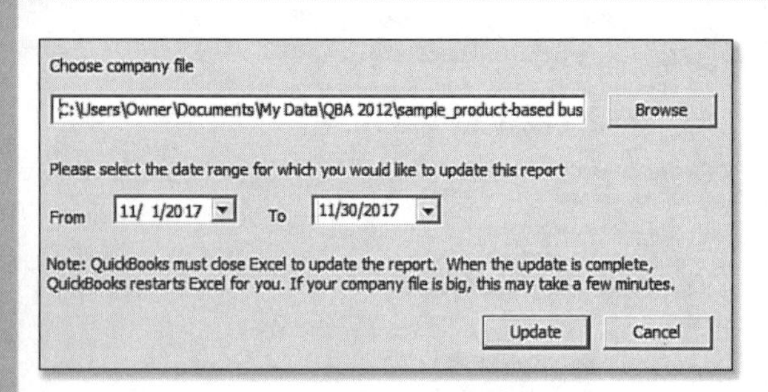

Figure 14.20
Update the saved file from the QuickBooks tab in Excel.

Emailing Reports

Did you know that you can email reports from within QuickBooks? This can be a convenient way to get information to your customers, vendors, management, owners, and even the company accountant. You can email reports as two types of attachments: individual Adobe PDF files or Excel workbooks.

If you want to set Outlook as your default email, select **Edit**, **Preferences**, **Send Forms** from the menu bar. Select the **My Preferences** tab where you can set the default email application to be QuickBooks or Outlook. You can also choose from other email providers.

note

If you do not use Outlook for your email, QuickBooks will send the email through QuickBooks Business Solutions, which has been available for years. Figure 14.22 shows how the email is created within QuickBooks when Outlook is not your default email program.

To email a report, follow these steps:

1. From the open report, click Email and choose whether to Send Report as Excel or to Send Report as PDF. Figure 14.21 shows how the email would appear if you are using Outlook 2010 as your default send method. In this example, Send Report as PDF is selected.

2. If a security message displays, indicating that sending information over Internet email is not secure, click OK to continue or click Cancel.

Figure 14.21 Reports can be sent as PDF or Excel attachments using your own email account.

Report from Rock Castle Construction - Message (Plain Text)
File
Message
Insert
Options
Format Text
Review
Cut
Copy
Paste
Format Painter
Clipboard
Basic Text
Address Book
Check Names
Names
Attach File
Attach Item
Signature
Include
Follow Up
High Importance
Low Importance
Tags
Zoom
Send
To...
johnsmith@smithcpa.com
Cc...
Subject:
Report from Rock Castle Construction
Attached:
Report from Rock Castle Construction.pdf (42 KB)
Please review the attached report. Feel free to contact us if you have any questions.
Thank you.

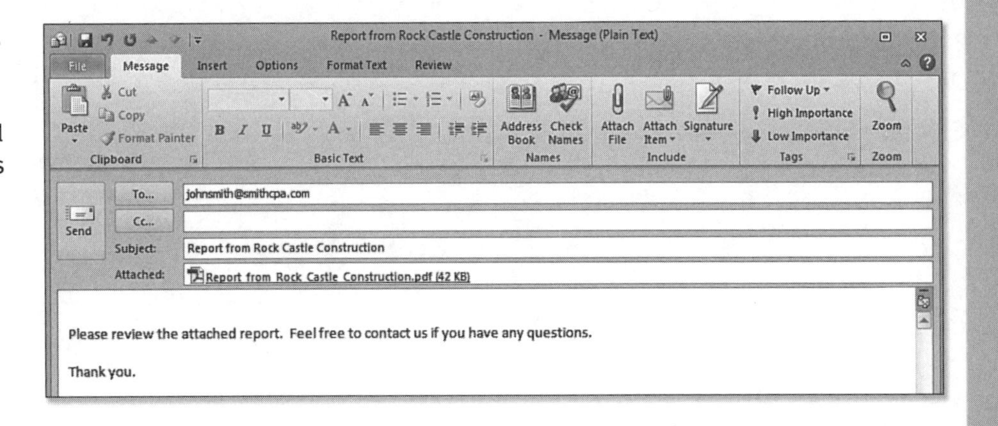

Figure 14.22 Send a report as an attachment through QuickBooks (when you don't use Outlook).

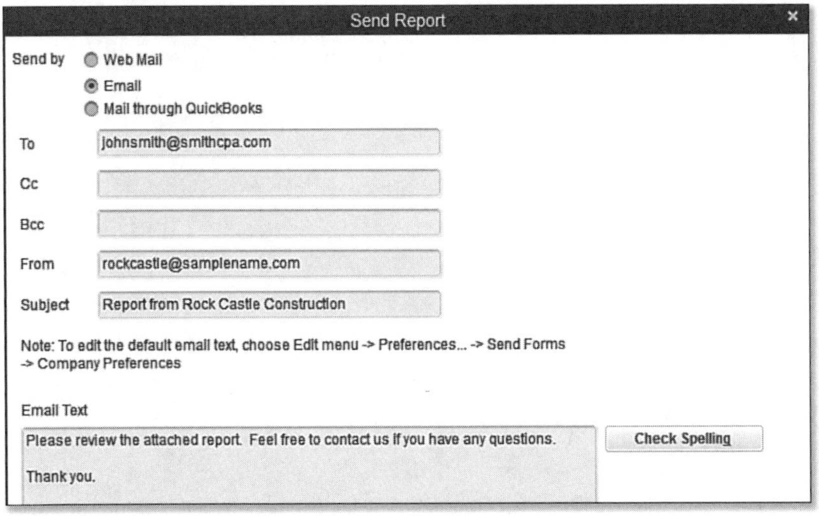

Send Report
Send by
Web Mail
Email
Mail through QuickBooks
To
johnsmith@smithcpa.com
Cc
Bcc
From
rockcastle@samplename.com
Subject
Report from Rock Castle Construction
Note: To edit the default email text, choose Edit menu -> Preferences... -> Send Forms
-> Company Preferences
Email Text
Please review the attached report. Feel free to contact us if you have any questions.
Thank you.
Check Spelling

3. If you are sending the report through Outlook, add your email address and any additional comments to the email. Click Send when you're done. You are returned to your QuickBooks data file, and the email is stored in your Outlook Sent folder.

   If you are not using Outlook for email, click Send Now (not shown) and QuickBooks transmits the email for you.

As a business owner, learning how to work with reports is valuable and helps you efficiently manage reporting in your QuickBooks file. Next, in Chapter 15, "Reviewing Your Data," you will learn about specific data reviews you should do in your file that can help with management decisions for your company.

15

REVIEWING YOUR DATA

This book would not be complete without a few pages of instructions about what reports you should review for your business. These reports are not the only reports you will find useful in QuickBooks, but they are important for you to review in your file periodically.

These reports are only a subset of the many reports in QuickBooks, but are typically used by accounting professionals to verify the accuracy of your data. This chapter is devoted to the business owner, helping you properly review your data for accuracy. Each section provides what the review is to accomplish and what reports in QuickBooks will help with these reviews.

Reviewing the Balance Sheet

Did you know that the report a business owner is least likely to look at is also one of the most important? To the business owner, the Balance Sheet report shows the balance of assets (what the business owns), liabilities (what the business owes others), and equity (what was put into the business or taken out of the business). Because these numbers are important, a business owner should first review this report.

This section details specific reports to use when reviewing your data. Each report is prepared in accrual basis unless otherwise mentioned. Begin by creating a Balance Sheet report of your data; this is the primary report we use for review.

From the menu bar, select **Reports**, **Company & Financial**, **Balance Sheet Standard**.

Leave the report with today's date on it. You are going to first review your data with today's date before using any other date. In the following instructions, if a different date is needed, it will be noted in the step-by-step details. Verify that the top left of the report shows Accrual Basis. If not, click the Customize Report button on the report, and select **Accrual Basis** from the Report Basis options.

Figure 15.1 shows a sample data Balance Sheet Standard report.

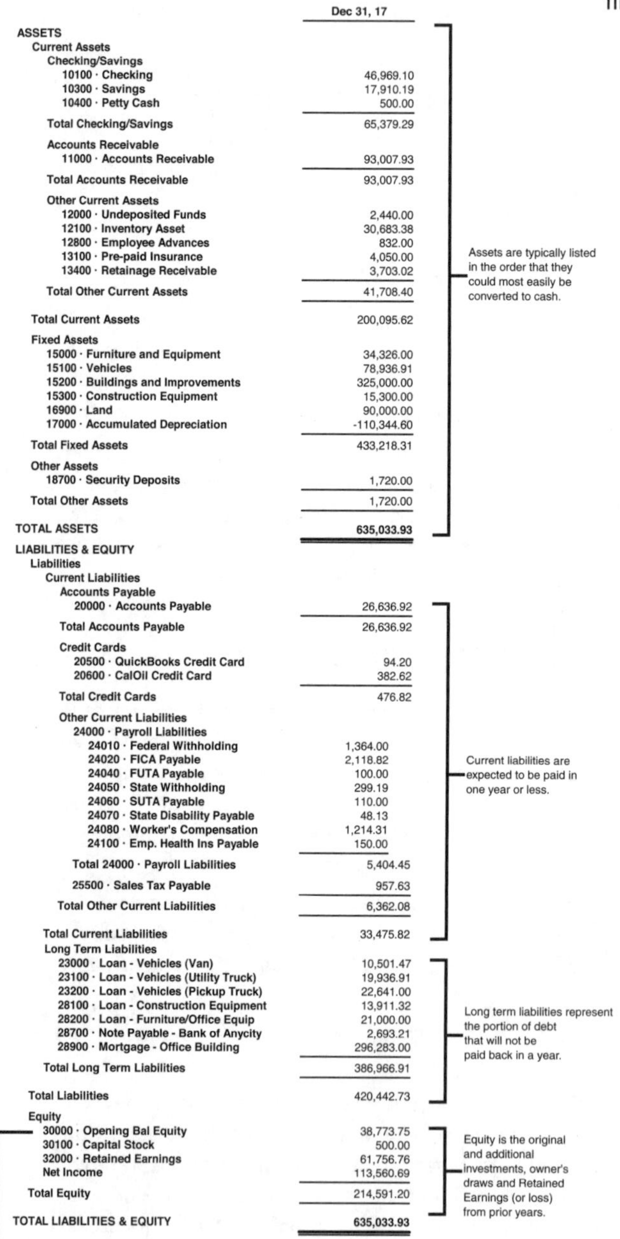

2:07 PM
12/15/17
Accrual Basis

Rock Castle Construction
Balance Sheet
As of December 31, 2017

	Dec 31, 17
ASSETS	
Current Assets	
Checking/Savings	
10100 · Checking	46,969.10
10300 · Savings	17,910.19
10400 · Petty Cash	500.00
Total Checking/Savings	65,379.29
Accounts Receivable	
11000 · Accounts Receivable	93,007.93
Total Accounts Receivable	93,007.93
Other Current Assets	
12000 · Undeposited Funds	2,440.00
12100 · Inventory Asset	30,683.38
12800 · Employee Advances	832.00
13100 · Pre-paid Insurance	4,050.00
13400 · Retainage Receivable	3,703.02
Total Other Current Assets	41,708.40
Total Current Assets	200,095.62
Fixed Assets	
15000 · Furniture and Equipment	34,326.00
15100 · Vehicles	78,936.91
15200 · Buildings and Improvements	325,000.00
15300 · Construction Equipment	15,300.00
16900 · Land	90,000.00
17000 · Accumulated Depreciation	-110,344.60
Total Fixed Assets	433,218.31
Other Assets	
18700 · Security Deposits	1,720.00
Total Other Assets	1,720.00
TOTAL ASSETS	**635,033.93**
LIABILITIES & EQUITY	
Liabilities	
Current Liabilities	
Accounts Payable	
20000 · Accounts Payable	26,636.92
Total Accounts Payable	26,636.92
Credit Cards	
20500 · QuickBooks Credit Card	94.20
20600 · CalOil Credit Card	382.62
Total Credit Cards	476.82
Other Current Liabilities	
24000 · Payroll Liabilities	
24010 · Federal Withholding	1,364.00
24020 · FICA Payable	2,118.82
24040 · FUTA Payable	100.00
24050 · State Withholding	299.19
24060 · SUTA Payable	110.00
24070 · State Disability Payable	48.13
24080 · Worker's Compensation	1,214.31
24100 · Emp. Health Ins Payable	150.00
Total 24000 · Payroll Liabilities	5,404.45
25500 · Sales Tax Payable	957.63
Total Other Current Liabilities	6,362.08
Total Current Liabilities	33,475.82
Long Term Liabilities	
23000 · Loan - Vehicles (Van)	10,501.47
23100 · Loan - Vehicles (Utility Truck)	19,936.91
23200 · Loan - Vehicles (Pickup Truck)	22,641.00
28100 · Loan - Construction Equipment	13,911.32
28200 · Loan - Furniture/Office Equip	21,000.00
28700 · Note Payable - Bank of Anycity	2,693.21
28900 · Mortgage - Office Building	296,283.00
Total Long Term Liabilities	386,966.91
Total Liabilities	420,442.73
Equity	
30000 · Opening Bal Equity	38,773.75
30100 · Capital Stock	500.00
32000 · Retained Earnings	61,756.76
Net Income	113,560.69
Total Equity	214,591.20
TOTAL LIABILITIES & EQUITY	**635,033.93**

Assets are typically listed in the order that they could most easily be converted to cash.

Current liabilities are expected to be paid in one year or less.

Long term liabilities represent the portion of debt that will not be paid back in a year.

Equity is the original and additional investments, owner's draws and Retained Earnings (or loss) from prior years.

Did you know that proper accounting would have the Open Bal Equity account with no balance? See "Troubleshooting Opening Balance Equity" section of this chapter.

Figure 15.1
Review your Balance Sheet first, as in this example.

Account Types

Reviewing the account types assigned requires some basic knowledge of accounting. If you're unsure of what to look for, ask your accountant to take a quick look at how your accounts are set up.

Review the names given to accounts. Do you see account names in the wrong place on the Balance Sheet? For example, does an Auto Loan account show up in the current asset section of the Balance Sheet?

To correct the category (account type) assigned follow these steps:

1. From the menu bar, select **Lists**, **Chart of Accounts**.
2. Select the account in question with one click. From the Account drop-down menu, select **Edit**. On the Edit Account dialog box (see Figure 15.2), you can select the drop-down menu for **Account Type** to change the currently assigned account type.

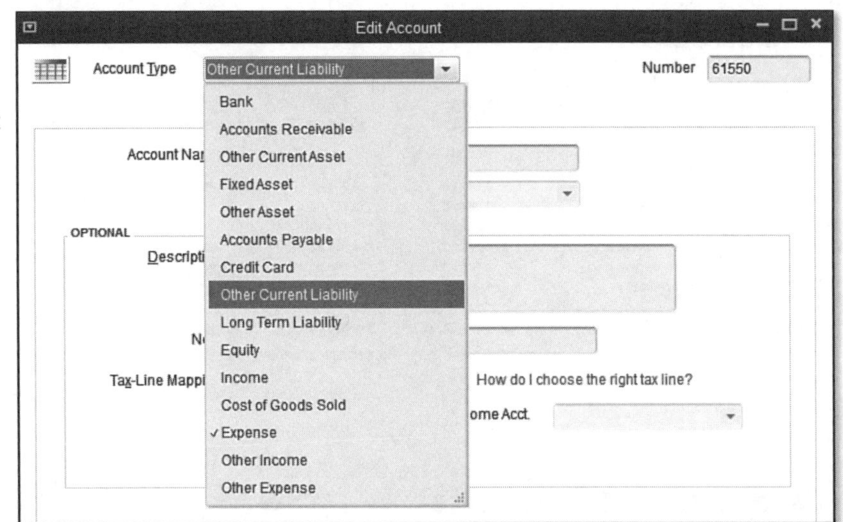

Figure 15.2 In the Edit or New Account dialog box, you assign the account type for proper placement of financial reports.

Prior Year Balances

You should provide a copy of your Balance Sheet dated as of the last day of your *prior* tax year (or fiscal year) to your accountant and request that she verify that the balances agree with her accounting records used to prepare your tax return. This is one of the most important steps to take in your review because Balance Sheet numbers are cumulative over the years you are in business.

For more information, see "Accrual Versus Cash Basis Reporting," p. 83.

You can also create a two-year balance sheet to provide to your accounting professional:

From the menu bar, select **Reports**, **Company & Financial**, **Balance Sheet Prev Year Comparison** (see the report displayed in Figure 15.3). If necessary, click the Customize Report button to change the Report Basis.

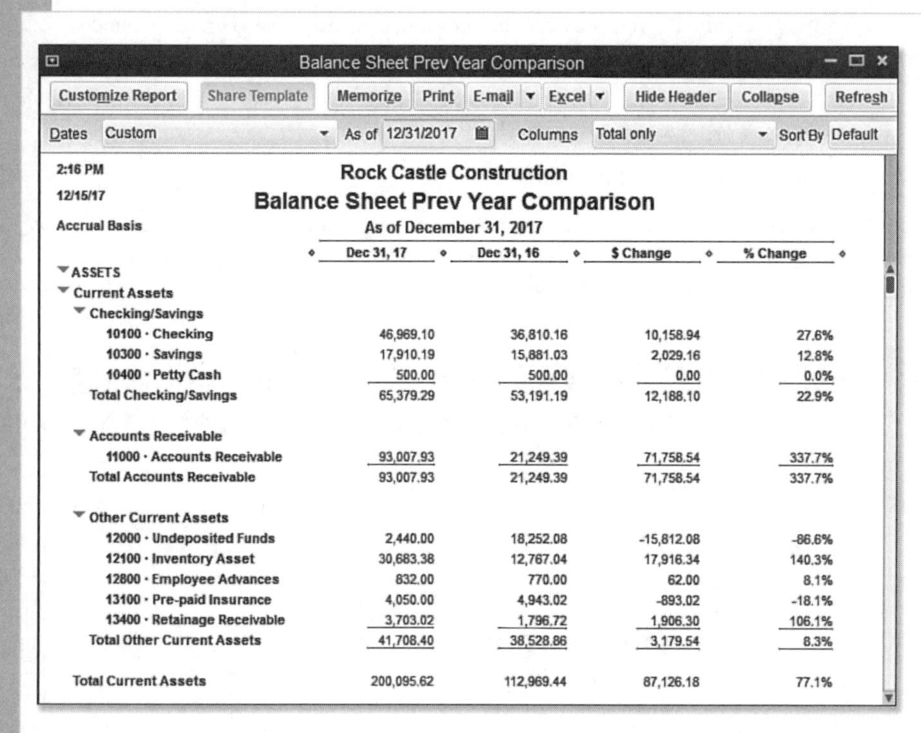

Balance Sheet Prev Year Comparison

Customize Report | Share Template | Memorize | Print | E-mail | Excel | Hide Header | Collapse | Refresh

Dates Custom | As of 12/31/2017 | Columns Total only | Sort By Default

2:16 PM
12/15/17
Accrual Basis

Rock Castle Construction
Balance Sheet Prev Year Comparison
As of December 31, 2017

	Dec 31, 17	Dec 31, 16	$ Change	% Change
ASSETS				
Current Assets				
Checking/Savings				
10100 · Checking	46,969.10	36,810.16	10,158.94	27.6%
10300 · Savings	17,910.19	15,881.03	2,029.16	12.8%
10400 · Petty Cash	500.00	500.00	0.00	0.0%
Total Checking/Savings	65,379.29	53,191.19	12,188.10	22.9%
Accounts Receivable				
11000 · Accounts Receivable	93,007.93	21,249.39	71,758.54	337.7%
Total Accounts Receivable	93,007.93	21,249.39	71,758.54	337.7%
Other Current Assets				
12000 · Undeposited Funds	2,440.00	18,252.08	-15,812.08	-86.6%
12100 · Inventory Asset	30,683.38	12,767.04	17,916.34	140.3%
12800 · Employee Advances	832.00	770.00	62.00	8.1%
13100 · Pre-paid Insurance	4,050.00	4,943.02	-893.02	-18.1%
13400 · Retainage Receivable	3,703.02	1,796.72	1,906.30	106.1%
Total Other Current Assets	41,708.40	38,528.86	3,179.54	8.3%
Total Current Assets	200,095.62	112,969.44	87,126.18	77.1%

Figure 15.3 The Balance Sheet Prev Year Comparison report is a useful report to give your accounting professional at tax time.

Bank Account Balance(s)

Compare your reconciled bank account balances on the Balance Sheet report to the statement your bank sends you. Modify the date of the Balance Sheet to be the same as the ending statement date on your bank statement. Your QuickBooks Balance Sheet balance for your bank account should be equal to the bank's ending statement balance plus or minus any uncleared deposits or checks/withdrawals dated on or before the statement ending date.

At tax time, provide your last month's bank statement and QuickBooks bank reconciliation report to your accounting professional.

You might want to provide the Balance Sheet Prev Year Comparison report to your accountant using both Accrual and Cash Basis reporting. To change the basis of the report, click the Customize Report button and select the desired Report Basis on the Display tab.

Accounts Receivable

The Accounts Receivable balance on your Balance Sheet report should agree with the A/R Aging Summary Report total, as shown in Figure 15.4.

To create the A/R Aging Summary report, from the menu bar, select **Reports**, **Customers & Receivables**, **A/R Aging Summary or A/R Aging Detail**. On the top of the report, click Collapse to minimize (remove from view) the line detail, making the report easier to view at a glance. The total should match the Accounts Receivable balance on the Balance Sheet report, as shown in Figure 15.1.

Figure 15.4
Use Expand or Collapse at the top of the report to change the level of detail displayed.

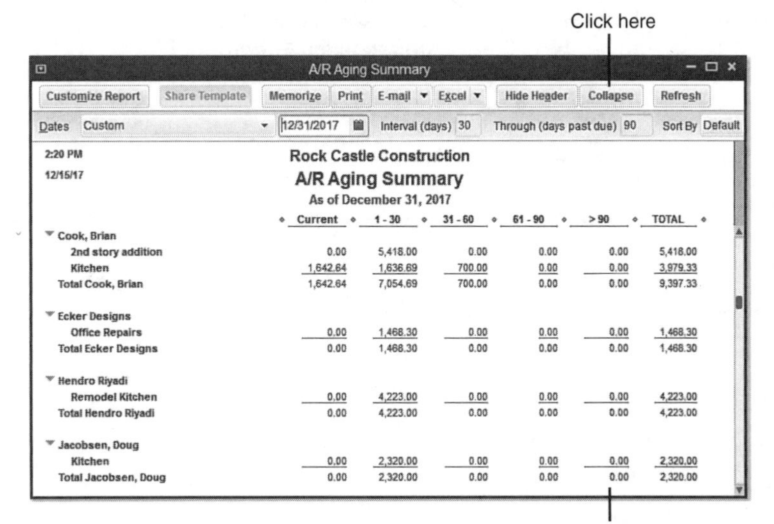

Rock Castle Construction
A/R Aging Summary
As of December 31, 2017

	Current	1 - 30	31 - 60	61 - 90	> 90	TOTAL
Cook, Brian						
2nd story addition	0.00	5,418.00	0.00	0.00	0.00	5,418.00
Kitchen	1,642.64	1,636.69	700.00	0.00	0.00	3,979.33
Total Cook, Brian	1,642.64	7,054.69	700.00	0.00	0.00	9,397.33
Ecker Designs						
Office Repairs	0.00	1,468.30	0.00	0.00	0.00	1,468.30
Total Ecker Designs	0.00	1,468.30	0.00	0.00	0.00	1,468.30
Hendro Riyadi						
Remodel Kitchen	0.00	4,223.00	0.00	0.00	0.00	4,223.00
Total Hendro Riyadi	0.00	4,223.00	0.00	0.00	0.00	4,223.00
Jacobsen, Doug						
Kitchen	0.00	2,320.00	0.00	0.00	0.00	2,320.00
Total Jacobsen, Doug	0.00	2,320.00	0.00	0.00	0.00	2,320.00

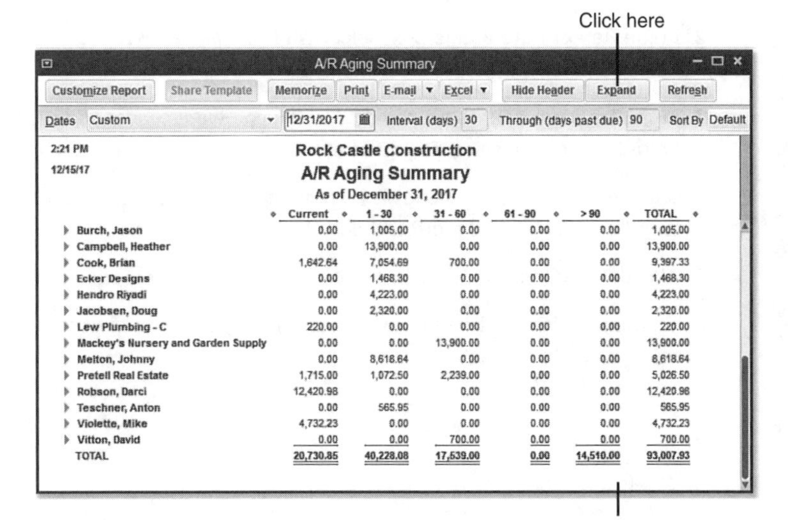

Rock Castle Construction
A/R Aging Summary
As of December 31, 2017

	Current	1 - 30	31 - 60	61 - 90	> 90	TOTAL
Burch, Jason	0.00	1,005.00	0.00	0.00	0.00	1,005.00
Campbell, Heather	0.00	13,900.00	0.00	0.00	0.00	13,900.00
Cook, Brian	1,642.64	7,054.69	700.00	0.00	0.00	9,397.33
Ecker Designs	0.00	1,468.30	0.00	0.00	0.00	1,468.30
Hendro Riyadi	0.00	4,223.00	0.00	0.00	0.00	4,223.00
Jacobsen, Doug	0.00	2,320.00	0.00	0.00	0.00	2,320.00
Lew Plumbing - C	220.00	0.00	0.00	0.00	0.00	220.00
Mackey's Nursery and Garden Supply	0.00	0.00	13,900.00	0.00	0.00	13,900.00
Melton, Johnny	0.00	8,618.64	0.00	0.00	0.00	8,618.64
Pretell Real Estate	1,715.00	1,072.50	2,239.00	0.00	0.00	5,026.50
Robson, Darci	12,420.98	0.00	0.00	0.00	0.00	12,420.98
Teschner, Anton	0.00	565.95	0.00	0.00	0.00	565.95
Violette, Mike	4,732.23	0.00	0.00	0.00	0.00	4,732.23
Vitton, David	0.00	0.00	700.00	0.00	0.00	700.00
TOTAL	20,730.85	40,228.08	17,539.00	0.00	14,510.00	93,007.93

Undeposited Funds

The Undeposited Funds amount should agree with funds not yet deposited into your bank account, as shown in the custom report displayed in Figure 15.5 (use today's date on your Balance Sheet report).

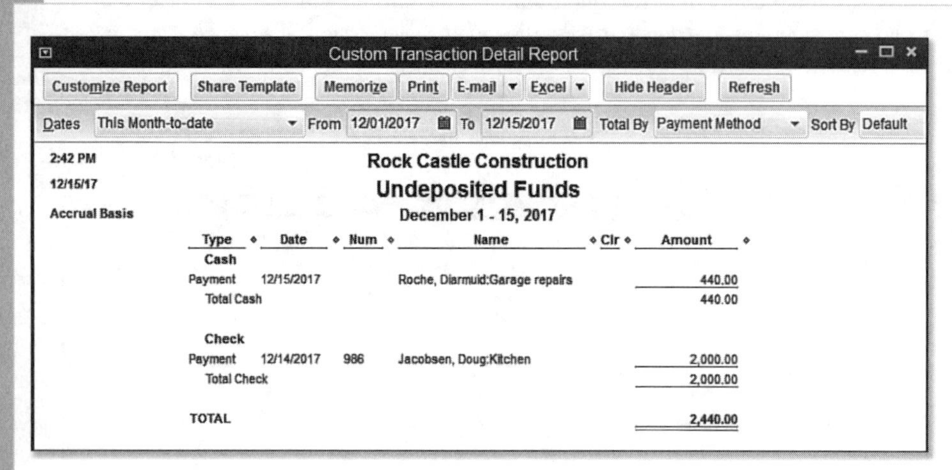

Figure 15.5 The amount of funds shown on this report should agree with the amount of funds you have not yet taken to the bank.

Create the following custom report to review the Undeposited Funds detail sorted by payment method:

1. From the menu bar, select **Reports**, **Custom Reports**, **Transaction Detail**. The Modify Report dialog box opens.
2. In the Report Date Range box, select **All** (type an "a" without the quote marks to change the date range to All).
3. In the Columns box, select the data fields you want to view on the report and in the Total By drop-down menu, select **Payment Method**.
4. Click the Filters tab; Account is already highlighted in the Choose Filter box. In the Account drop-down menu to the right, choose Undeposited Funds.
5. Also in the Choose Filter box, scroll down to select **Cleared**; on the right, choose Cleared No.
6. (Optional) Click the Header/Footer tab and change the report title to Undeposited Funds. Click OK to view the report.

Inventory

The Inventory balance on the Balance Sheet report (refer to Figure 15.1) should agree with the Inventory Valuation Summary Asset Value report total, as shown in Figure 15.6. The ending dates of both reports need to be the same.

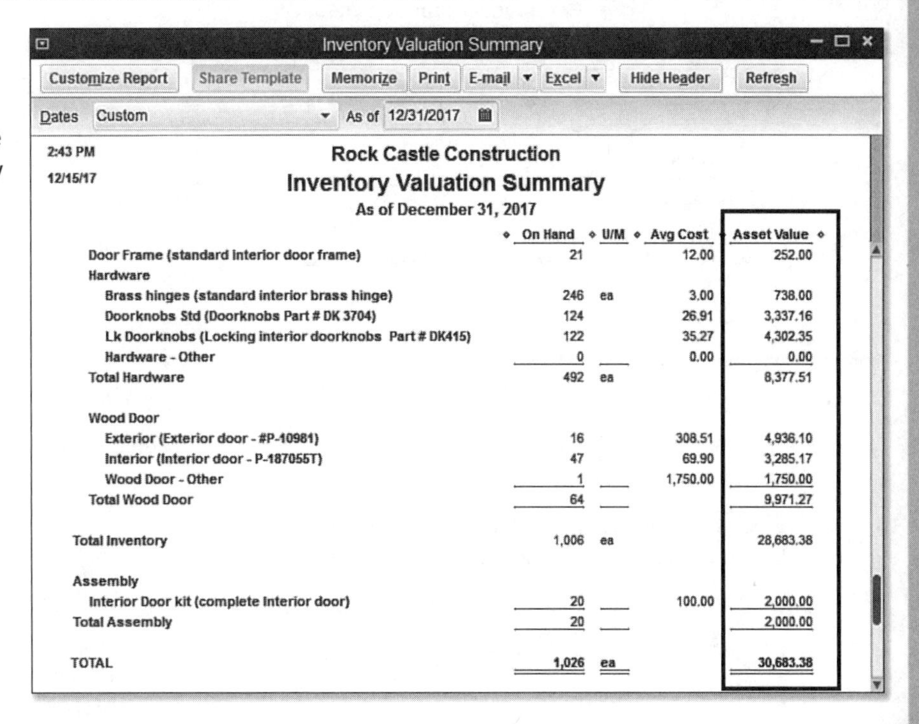

2:43 PM
12/15/17

Rock Castle Construction
Inventory Valuation Summary
As of December 31, 2017

	On Hand	U/M	Avg Cost	Asset Value
Door Frame (standard interior door frame)	21		12.00	252.00
Hardware				
Brass hinges (standard interior brass hinge)	246	ea	3.00	738.00
Doorknobs Std (Doorknobs Part # DK 3704)	124		26.91	3,337.16
Lk Doorknobs (Locking interior doorknobs Part # DK415)	122		35.27	4,302.35
Hardware - Other	0		0.00	0.00
Total Hardware	492	ea		8,377.51
Wood Door				
Exterior (Exterior door - #P-10981)	16		308.51	4,936.10
Interior (Interior door - P-187055T)	47		69.90	3,285.17
Wood Door - Other	1		1,750.00	1,750.00
Total Wood Door	64			9,971.27
Total Inventory	1,006	ea		28,683.38
Assembly				
Interior Door kit (complete Interior door)	20		100.00	2,000.00
Total Assembly	20			2,000.00
TOTAL	1,026	ea		30,683.38

Figure 15.6
The total of the Asset Value column should agree with the Inventory balance on the Balance Sheet report.

To create the Inventory Valuation Summary report, from the menu bar, select **Reports**, **Inventory**, **Inventory Valuation Summary**. More details about working with inventory reporting can be found in Chapter 6, “Managing Inventory.”

Other Current Assets

The Other Current Asset accounts can differ widely by company. If you have employee advances, make sure your employees concur with your records. For any other accounts in the Other Current Assets category, look to documentation within QuickBooks to verify the reported balances.

Do you need an easy report to sort the detail in these Other Current Asset accounts by a list name? In this example, I created a detail report of the Employee Advances account sorted and subtotaled by payee, as shown in Figure 15.7. You can create this same report for any of your accounts, sorting in a way that improves the detail for your review.

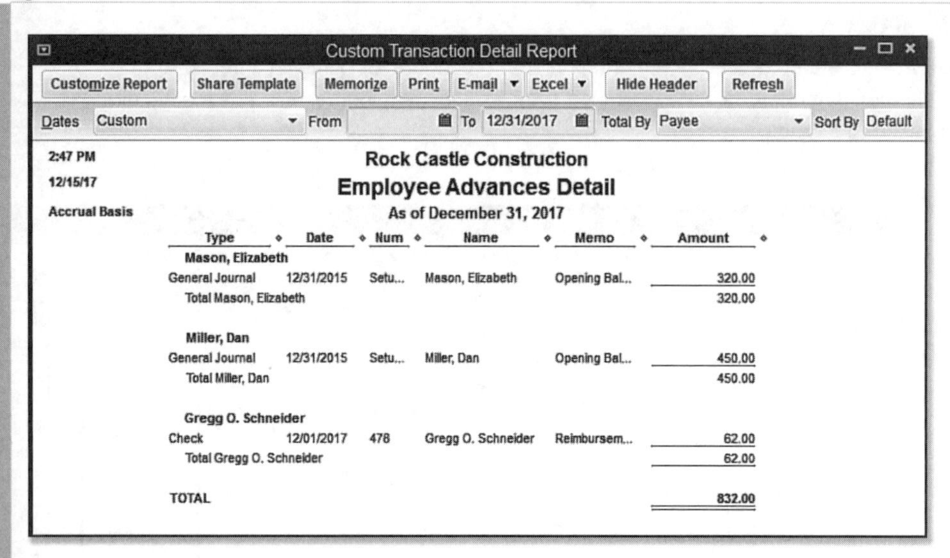

Figure 15.7 Create a custom report to review balances in an Employee Advances account or any other asset account.

To create a detail report of your Other Current Asset accounts (in addition to other types of accounts), follow these steps:

1. From the menu bar, select **Reports**, **Custom Reports**, **Transaction Detail**. The Modify Report dialog box displays.
2. On the Date Range drop-down menu, select **All**.
3. In the Columns box, select the specific data you would like to see in the report.
4. Also in the Columns box, in the Total By drop-down menu, select **Payee**.
5. Click the Filters tab.
6. The Choose Filter box already has selected the Account filter. On the right, in the Account drop-down menu, select the **Employee Advances** account (or select the specific account for which you want to see detail).
7. (Optional) Click the Header/Footer tab and provide a unique report title. Click OK to create the modified report.

tip

Reconciling accounts like these can be useful. An example is when an employee pays back in full the loan. Complete a reconciliation for this account, marking each transaction for this employee as “cleared.” You can then filter the report for “uncleared” only, limiting the amount of information that is displayed.

Verify the balances reported here with either the employees or outside source documents.

Fixed Assets

Fixed assets are those purchases that have a long-term life and for tax purposes cannot be expensed all at once but instead must be depreciated over the expected life of the asset.

Accountants can advise business owners on how to classify assets. If the account balances have changed from year to year, you might want to review what transactions were posted to make sure they are fixed asset purchases and not expenses that should be reported on the Profit & Loss report.

If you have properly recorded a fixed asset purchase to this account category, provide your accountant with the purchase receipt and any supporting purchase documents for their depreciation schedule records.

If you see a change in the totals from one year to the next, you can review the individual transactions in the account register by clicking Banking, Use Register, and selecting the account you want to review. Figure 15.8 shows the register for Fixed Assets—Furniture Equipment. If a transaction was incorrectly posted here, you can edit the transaction by double-clicking the line detail and correcting the assigned account category.

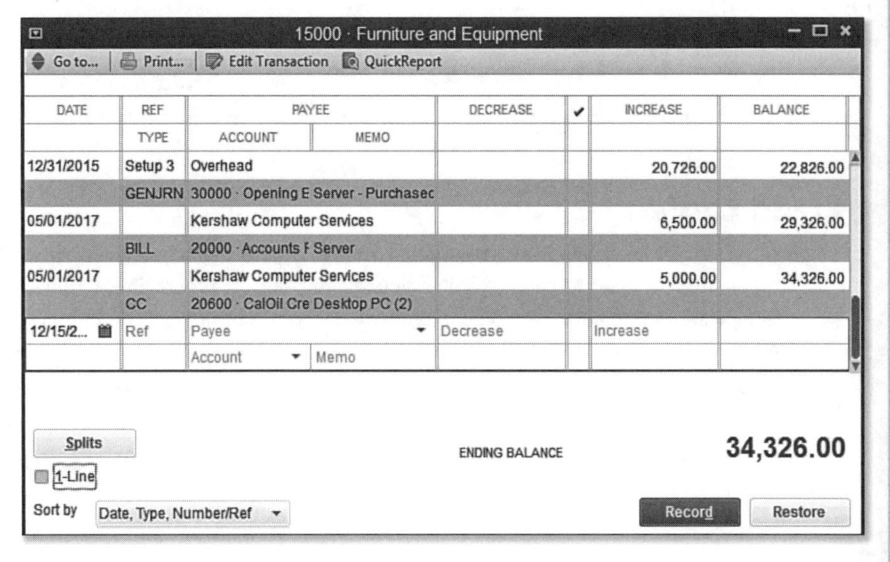

Figure 15.8
Use registers for certain accounts to see the transactions that affect the balances.

Accounts Payable

The Accounts Payable balance on the Balance Sheet report should agree with the A/P Aging Summary report total, as shown in Figure 15.9.

To create the A/P Aging Summary or Detail report, from the menu bar, select **Reports**, **Vendors & Payables**, **A/P Aging Summary** or **Detail**. For more information, see Chapter 8, "Managing Vendors."

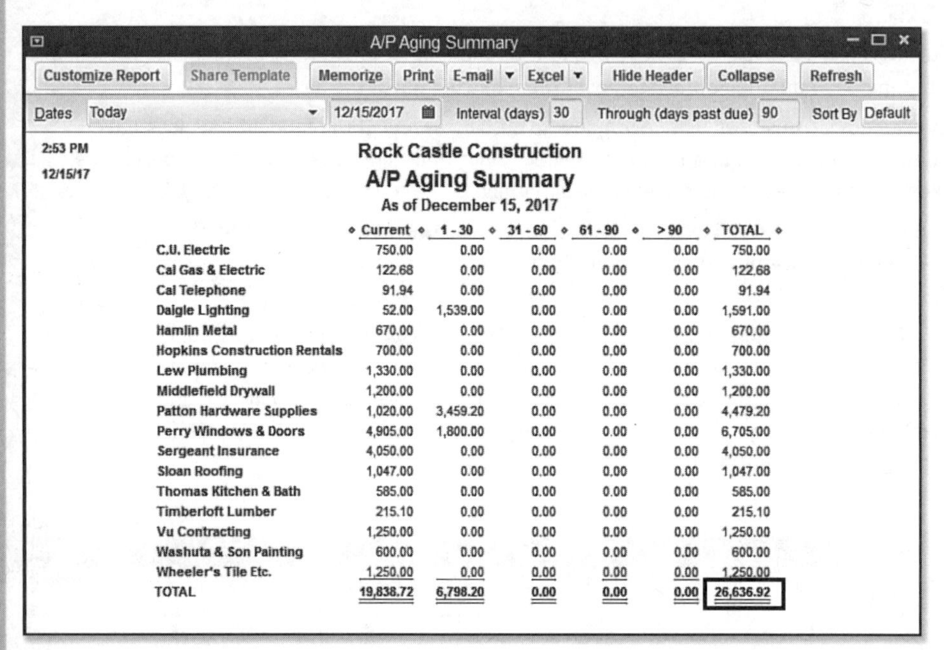

A/P Aging Summary

Customize Report | Share Template | Memorize | Print | E-mail | Excel | Hide Header | Collapse | Refresh

Dates: Today | 12/15/2017 | Interval (days) 30 | Through (days past due) 90 | Sort By Default

2:53 PM
12/15/17

Rock Castle Construction
A/P Aging Summary
As of December 15, 2017

	Current	1 - 30	31 - 60	61 - 90	> 90	TOTAL
C.U. Electric	750.00	0.00	0.00	0.00	0.00	750.00
Cal Gas & Electric	122.68	0.00	0.00	0.00	0.00	122.68
Cal Telephone	91.94	0.00	0.00	0.00	0.00	91.94
Daigle Lighting	52.00	1,539.00	0.00	0.00	0.00	1,591.00
Hamlin Metal	670.00	0.00	0.00	0.00	0.00	670.00
Hopkins Construction Rentals	700.00	0.00	0.00	0.00	0.00	700.00
Lew Plumbing	1,330.00	0.00	0.00	0.00	0.00	1,330.00
Middlefield Drywall	1,200.00	0.00	0.00	0.00	0.00	1,200.00
Patton Hardware Supplies	1,020.00	3,459.20	0.00	0.00	0.00	4,479.20
Perry Windows & Doors	4,905.00	1,800.00	0.00	0.00	0.00	6,705.00
Sergeant Insurance	4,050.00	0.00	0.00	0.00	0.00	4,050.00
Sloan Roofing	1,047.00	0.00	0.00	0.00	0.00	1,047.00
Thomas Kitchen & Bath	585.00	0.00	0.00	0.00	0.00	585.00
Timberloft Lumber	215.10	0.00	0.00	0.00	0.00	215.10
Vu Contracting	1,250.00	0.00	0.00	0.00	0.00	1,250.00
Washuta & Son Painting	600.00	0.00	0.00	0.00	0.00	600.00
Wheeler's Tile Etc.	1,250.00	0.00	0.00	0.00	0.00	1,250.00
TOTAL	19,838.72	6,798.20	0.00	0.00	0.00	26,636.92

Figure 15.9 The A/P Aging Summary report total should agree with your Balance Sheet, Accounts Payable balance.

Credit Cards

Your Credit Card account balances should reconcile with those balances from your credit card statement(s). You might have to adjust your Balance Sheet report date to match your credit card vendor's statement date. Or, you can request that your credit card company provide you with a statement cut-off at the end of a month.

You should provide your accountant with a copy of the most recent credit card statement, so that he can verify the accuracy of your credit card balance.

For more information on working with reconciliation tasks, see Chapter 13, "Working with Bank and Credit Card Accounts."

Payroll Liabilities

The Payroll Liabilities balance on the Balance Sheet report should agree with your Payroll Liability Balances report total. Be careful with the dates here. If you have unpaid back payroll taxes, you should select a date range of All for the Payroll Liability Balances report. See Figure 15.10.

To create the Payroll Liability Balances report, from the menu bar, select **Reports**, **Employees & Payroll**, **Payroll Liability Balances**. Totals on this report should match your Balance Sheet report for the Payroll Liabilities account.

Figure 15.10
The Payroll Liability Balances report total should agree with the same total on the Balance Sheet report.

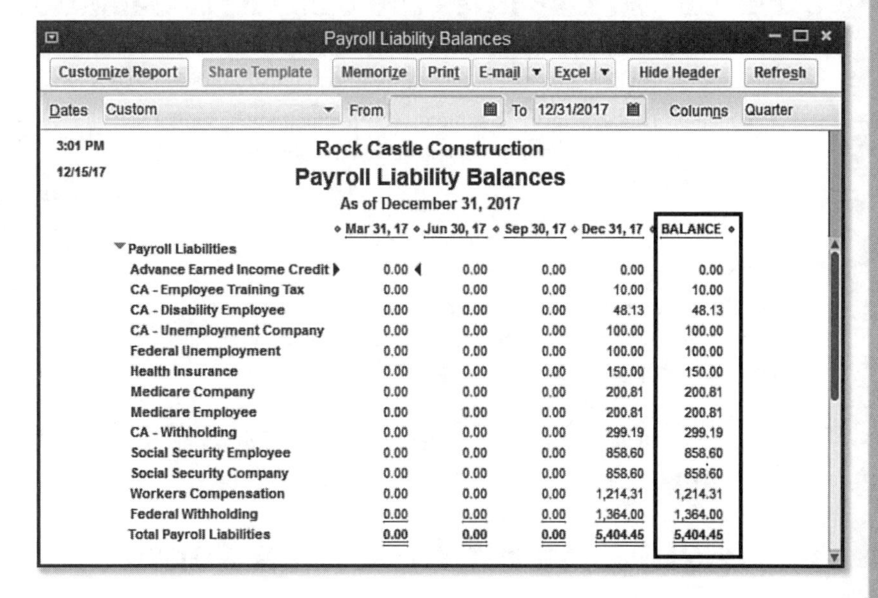

Rock Castle Construction
Payroll Liability Balances
As of December 31, 2017

	Mar 31, 17	Jun 30, 17	Sep 30, 17	Dec 31, 17	BALANCE
Payroll Liabilities					
Advance Earned Income Credit	0.00	0.00	0.00	0.00	0.00
CA - Employee Training Tax	0.00	0.00	0.00	10.00	10.00
CA - Disability Employee	0.00	0.00	0.00	48.13	48.13
CA - Unemployment Company	0.00	0.00	0.00	100.00	100.00
Federal Unemployment	0.00	0.00	0.00	100.00	100.00
Health Insurance	0.00	0.00	0.00	150.00	150.00
Medicare Company	0.00	0.00	0.00	200.81	200.81
Medicare Employee	0.00	0.00	0.00	200.81	200.81
CA - Withholding	0.00	0.00	0.00	299.19	299.19
Social Security Employee	0.00	0.00	0.00	858.60	858.60
Social Security Company	0.00	0.00	0.00	858.60	858.60
Workers Compensation	0.00	0.00	0.00	1,214.31	1,214.31
Federal Withholding	0.00	0.00	0.00	1,364.00	1,364.00
Total Payroll Liabilities	0.00	0.00	0.00	5,404.45	5,404.45

Sales Tax Payable

The Sales Tax Payable balance on the Balance Sheet report should agree with the Sales Tax Liability report balance. You might need to change the Sales Tax Payable report date to match that of your Balance Sheet.

To create the Sales Tax Liability report, from the menu bar, select **Reports**, **Vendors & Payables**, **Sales Tax Liability**.

caution

If you have set up your Sales Tax Preference as Cash Basis, you cannot compare this balance to an Accrual Basis Balance Sheet report.

Make sure the To Date matches that of the Balance Sheet report date. The total, shown in Figure 15.11, should match the Sales Tax Payable total on your Balance Sheet report.

Figure 15.11
The Sales Tax Liability report total should match the Sales Tax Payable balance on your Balance Sheet report.

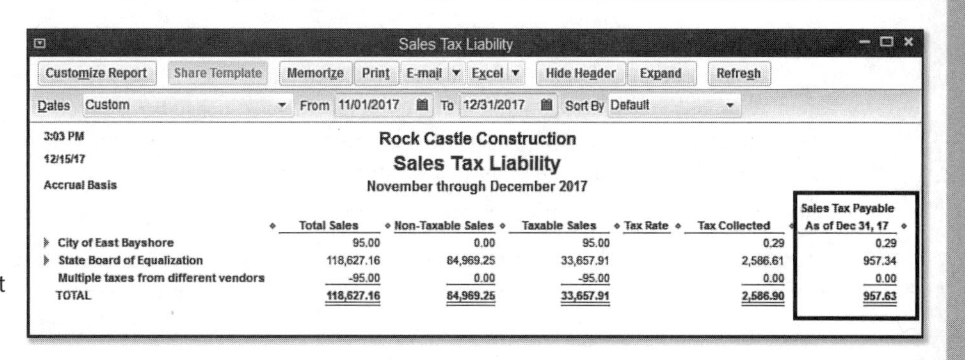

Rock Castle Construction
Sales Tax Liability
November through December 2017

	Total Sales	Non-Taxable Sales	Taxable Sales	Tax Rate	Tax Collected	Sales Tax Payable As of Dec 31, 17
City of East Bayshore	95.00	0.00	95.00		0.29	0.29
State Board of Equalization	118,627.16	84,969.25	33,657.91		2,586.61	957.34
Multiple taxes from different vendors	-95.00	0.00	-95.00		0.00	0.00
TOTAL	118,627.16	84,969.25	33,657.91		2,586.90	957.63

Other Current Liabilities and Long-Term Liabilities

Any other accounts you might have in the Other Current Liabilities and Long-Term Liabilities account types should be compared with outside documents from your lending institutions.

Reconcile these accounts the same as you reconcile your bank account to verify that your balances agree with the lending institution's records.

note

If you have an account called Opening Balance Equity with a balance, this account should have a zero balance after the data file setup is completed. For more information, see "Closing Opening Balance Equity to Retained Earnings," p. 568.

Equity

Equity accounts differ for each company. These account balances should be reviewed by your accountant and might have tax adjustments made to them at year-end or tax time.

The reports discussed in this chapter do not make up an exhaustive, end-all list for reviewing your Balance Sheet, but they are a great start to reviewing your own data or your client's data.

Reviewing the Profit & Loss Report

My experience over the years has been that business owners do not look at the Balance Sheet report often, if at all. However, nearly every business owner I have worked with has reviewed the Profit & Loss Standard report for their business. The reason might be that the Profit & Loss report is easier to interpret than the Balance Sheet report.

Even with the simple organization (money in, money out) of the Profit & Loss report, a careful review is prudent for the business owner who wants to track how well the business is doing financially. To create a Profit & Loss Standard report, from the menu bar, select **Reports**, **Company & Financial**, **Profit & Loss Summary** (or **Profit & Loss Detail**).

There are two methods for reviewing your Profit & Loss:

- **Cash Basis**—Income is recognized when received. Expenses are recognized when paid.
- **Accrual Basis**—Income is recognized as of the date of the customer's invoice. Expenses are recognized as of the date of the vendor's bill.

Cash basis reporting offers an incomplete snapshot in time because it shows what cash has changed hands, but doesn't show unpaid bills from vendors or uncollected invoices from customers. Additionally, many companies file their annual tax returns using cash basis reports. There is nothing wrong with looking at reports prepared with cash basis accounting. However, I encourage all my clients to consider reviewing the Profit & Loss Standard report in accrual basis.

Accrual basis, although more complex, provides so much more information about the business:

- **Matching Principle**—Revenue (customer invoice) is recorded in the same accounting period as the expenses (vendor bills, paychecks, and the like) associated with services or products sold on the customer's invoice.

- **Seasonal Variations**—Track how your business performs financially, for example, by comparing the same month across multiple years.
- **Tracking Receivables and Payables**—This information helps with both short-term and long-term forecast planning.

To review recurring monthly charges, it is useful to prepare your Profit & Loss by the month. From the Profit & Loss report, Columns drop-down menu at the top of the report, select **Month.**

With QuickBooks, you can easily change the report from cash to accrual basis by clicking the Customize Report button and manually selecting Cash or Accrual Basis on the Display tab of the Modify Report dialog box.

When reviewing the details of your Profit & Loss Detail report, you might want to look for these types of transactions:

- Monthly charges, such as rent, utility, equipment lease expenses, or other recurring expenses. Verify that the correct number of these charges is recorded, such as 12 monthly payments for rent.
- Credit card expenses reported to the proper expense accounts.
- Nonpayroll payments to owners, which normally are recorded to draw or equity type accounts.
- Purchase of equipment with a significant cost, which should have been recorded to an asset account.
- The principle portion of loan payments for vehicles or equipment; these should have been recorded to liability accounts.

A business owner who takes the time to review the Profit & Loss Detail report can feel more confident that business decisions founded on financials are as accurate as possible.

Other Reviews

You have completed the basic Balance Sheet and Profit & Loss Report reviews. These are important, and you are well on your way to being more confident about the information. There are, however, other equally important reviews that are detailed in this section.

Tracking Changes to Closed Accounting Periods

Did you know that you can "lock" your QuickBooks data and prevent users from making changes to prior accounting periods? This process is what we accountants call a "soft close." This means that at any time if you do need to add or modify a transaction in a prior period, the Admin user (or someone with security rights) can return and "unlock" the accounting period.

To have QuickBooks track information for the Closing Date Exception report, you first have to set a closing date and optionally set specific users' access to adding or modifying transactions on or before this date.

If you have compared your own or your clients' data to prior year financials or tax returns and the ending balances prior to the closing date have changed, you should view the Closing Date Exception report to see exactly who made the change and what specific transactions were affected. For more information on working with clients' files, see Chapter 16, "Sharing QuickBooks Data with Your Accountant."

To create the Closing Date Exception report (see Figure 15.12), from the menu bar, select **Reports**, **Accountant & Taxes**, **Closing Date Exception**. If you have not set a closing date, a warning prompt will display.

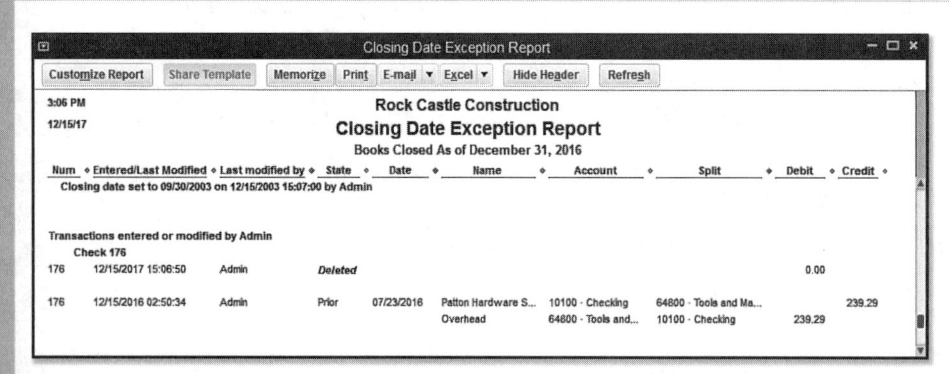

Figure 15.12 Review the Closing Date Exception Report for changes made to transactions dated on or before a closing date.

This report enables you to identify changes that were made to transactions dated on or before the closing date. For modified transactions, the report details both the latest version of a transaction and the prior version (as of the closing date). If your QuickBooks access rights allow you to change closed period transactions, you can then re-create the original transaction or change the date of added transactions so you can again agree with the ending balance from the previously closed period.

For accounting professionals, see Appendix A, "Client Data Review," for details on using the Troubleshoot Beginning Balances feature in QuickBooks Accountant.

Using the Audit Trail Report

The Audit Trail report provides details of additions and changes made to transactions, grouping the changes by username. The detail on this report shows the prior and latest version of the transaction, if it was edited. You can filter the report to show a specific date range to narrow the amount of detail.

The Audit Trail report is available in all desktop versions of QuickBooks. To create the Audit Trail report shown in Figure 15.13, from the menu bar, select **Reports**, **Accountant & Taxes**, **Audit Trail**.

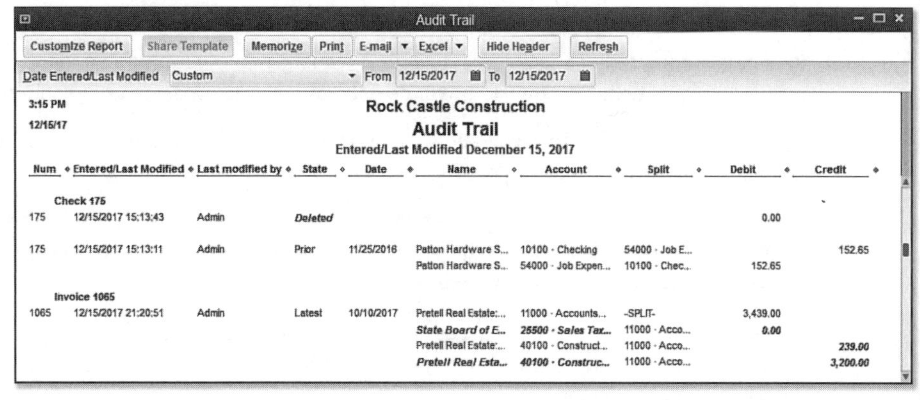

Figure 15.13 The QuickBooks Audit Trail report helps to identify what changes were made to transactions and by which user.

If you find undesired transaction changes, consider setting a closing date password and limiting user security privileges.

For more information, see "Set a Closing Date," p. 587.

Using the Credit Card Audit Trail Report

QuickBooks users can stay in compliance with credit card industry security requirements by enabling security around who can view, add, or edit your customers' credit card numbers.

Individual users can be included or excluded from accessing customers' sensitive credit card information. Also, for the company accountant, there is a user type called External Accountant. When this type is assigned to your accountant, she cannot view these sensitive customer credit card numbers.

Additionally, when enabled, you can track which user viewed, edited, added, or removed a customer's credit card number with the Credit Card Audit Trail report.

These three steps provide an overview of how to use this feature correctly:

1. Enable the customer credit card protection feature.
2. Select which users are given security rights to view the credit card numbers and which users are not given this privilege.
3. View the new Credit Card Audit Trail report to track viewing, editing, adding, and deleting activity with your customers' credit cards.

The first step to viewing details on the Credit Card Audit Trail report is to enable Customer Credit Card Protection in QuickBooks. To do so, follow these steps:

1. Log in to the data file as the Admin user. From the menu bar, select **Company**, **Customer Credit Card Protection**.
2. Click the Enable button to open the Customer Credit Card Protection Setup dialog box. Type a complex password. The complex password must be at least seven characters, including one

number and one uppercase character. For example, coMp1ex is a complex password. This complete password now replaces the previous Admin password.

3. You are also required to choose a Challenge Question from the drop-down menu and provide an answer to a question. This question will be used to reset your password if you forget it. Click OK.
4. A message box opens letting you know the next steps and that you will be reminded in 90 days to change the password. Click OK.
5. QuickBooks notifies you that you have enabled Customer Credit Card Protection and details how to allow access by user to the credit card numbers (see step 6). Click OK. You are returned to QuickBooks logged in as the Admin user.
6. To select which employees have access to view the full credit card numbers, or to add or change customer credit card numbers, from the menu bar select **Company**, **Set Up Users and Passwords**, and select the **Set Up Users** option.
7. The QuickBooks login dialog box displays, requiring you to enter the Admin password to gain access to user security settings. Click OK to open the User List dialog box.
8. Select a username and click the Edit button. (Optional) Edit the username or password, or click Next to accept these fields as they are.
9. The Access window for the specific user opens. Choose the Selected Areas of QuickBooks option. Click Next.
10. The Sales and Accounts Receivable access options display. Choose either Full Access or Selective Access; either of these choices combined with a checkmark in the View Complete Credit Card Numbers box (as shown in Figure 15.14) enables the user to view and add, delete, or modify the credit card number. If no checkmark is placed, the user sees only the last four digits of the customer's credit card when recording transactions that use this sensitive information.
11. Click Finish if this is the only setting you want to modify, or click Next to advance through additional security settings.

You have now properly enabled the customer credit card protection and granted or removed user access to these confidential credit card numbers.

With this feature enabled, your data file is now tracking critical user activity about your customers' credit card numbers. QuickBooks records when the credit card security was enabled, and maintains records of when a user enters a credit card number, modifies a credit card, or even views the credit card audit trail report (see Figure 15.15).

tip

When creating a login user for your accountant, select the user type External Accountant. By default, this user type cannot view your customers' stored sensitive credit card numbers.

This Customer Credit Card Audit Trail report is always tracking customer credit card activity as long as the feature remains enabled. This report can be viewed only by logging into the file as the Admin user. However, you can use your mouse to select all or part of the report and then press Ctrl+C to copy the report to the Windows Clipboard. You can then paste the report into Excel or another program if you want to search or filter the report.

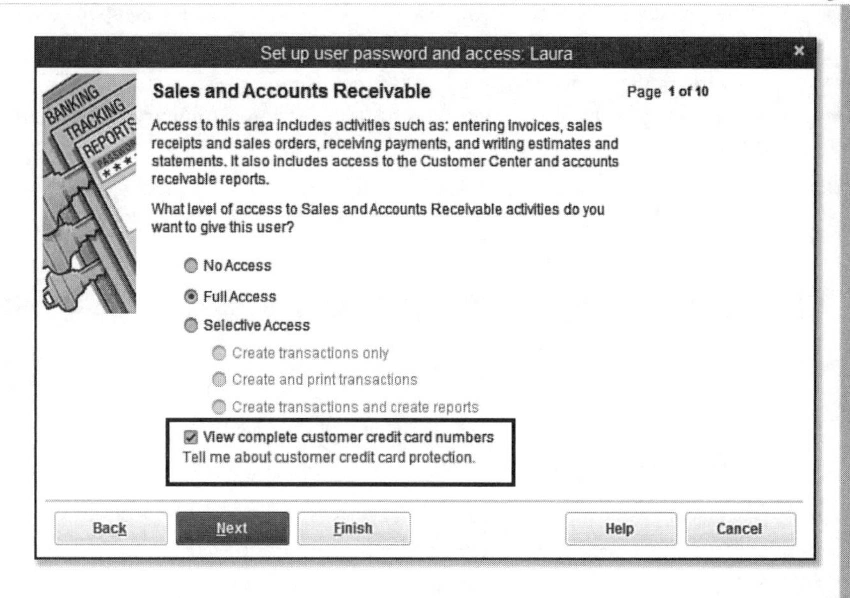

Figure 15.14
User-specific access to viewing complete customer credit card numbers.

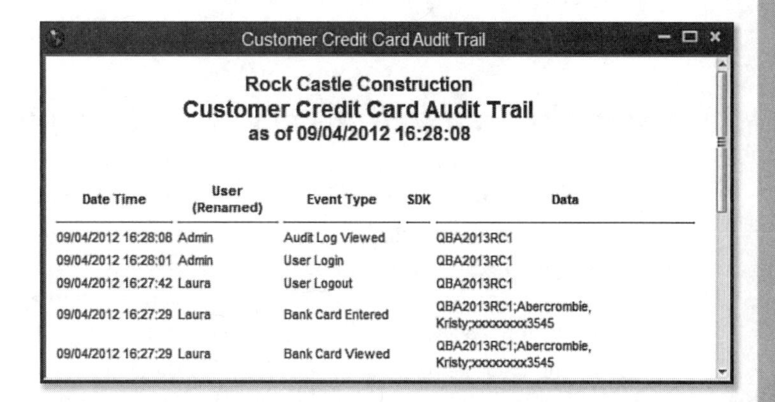
Customer Credit Card Audit Trail

Rock Castle Construction
Customer Credit Card Audit Trail
as of 09/04/2012 16:28:08

Date Time	User (Renamed)	Event Type	SDK	Data
09/04/2012 16:28:08	Admin	Audit Log Viewed		QBA2013RC1
09/04/2012 16:28:01	Admin	User Login		QBA2013RC1
09/04/2012 16:27:42	Laura	User Logout		QBA2013RC1
09/04/2012 16:27:29	Laura	Bank Card Entered		QBA2013RC1;Abercrombie, Kristy;xxxxxxxx3545
09/04/2012 16:27:29	Laura	Bank Card Viewed		QBA2013RC1;Abercrombie, Kristy;xxxxxxxx3545

Figure 15.15
The Customer Credit Card Audit Trail report cannot be modified, filtered, or purged.

If you want to disable this setting, you must first log in to the data file as the Admin user, enter the complex password that was created when you enabled the protection. From the menu bar, select **Company**, **Customer Credit Card Protection**, and select the **Disable Protection button**. Click Yes to accept that your customers' credit card number viewing, editing, and deleting activity by QuickBooks users is no longer being tracked for audit purposes.

Reporting on Voided/Deleted Transactions

QuickBooks offers flexibility for handling changes to transactions. If you grant users rights to create transactions, they also have rights to void and delete transactions. Don't worry—you can view these voided transaction changes in the Voided/Deleted Transactions Summary (see Figure 15.16) or Voided/Deleted Transactions Detail reports.

To create the Voided/Deleted Transactions Summary report, from the menu bar, select **Reports**, **Accountant & Taxes**, **Voided/Deleted Transactions Summary** (or **Voided/Deleted Transactions Detail**).

Use this report to view transactions before and after the change, and to identify which user made the change.

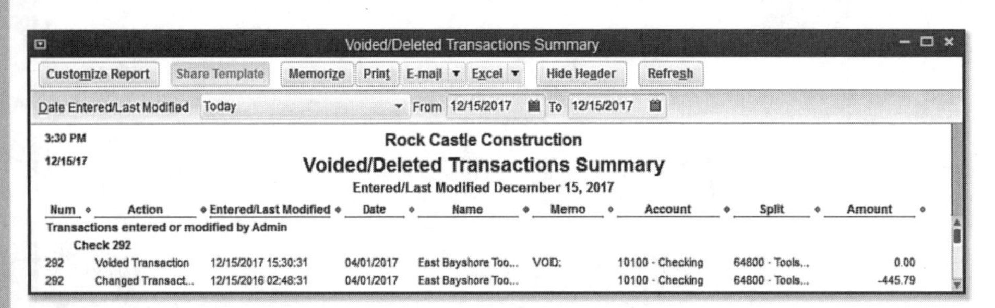

Figure 15.16
The QuickBooks Voided/Deleted Transactions Summary report quickly identifies which transactions were either voided or deleted, making troubleshooting easy!

Viewing the Transactions List by Date Report

Although the title of Transaction List by Date report doesn't indicate as much "power" as the other reports discussed in this chapter, I use this report most often when reviewing a data file.

If you are new to QuickBooks, you will soon learn that the date you enter for each transaction is important. The year you assign to the transaction is the year QuickBooks reports the transaction in your financials. For example, if you record a transaction with the year 2071 instead of 2017, this date can cause your financials not to show the effect until year 2071.

To create the Transaction List by Date report, as shown in Figure 15.17, from the menu bar, select **Reports**, **Accountant & Taxes**, **Transaction List by Date**. In the Dates drop-down menu, select **All**.

You can use this report to see both the oldest dated transaction (when the file was started) and the furthest out dated transaction (to identify whether date errors have been made). Then, as with all other QuickBooks reports, double-click a specific transaction to change the date if needed.

Fortunately, QuickBooks preferences help avoid transaction dating errors by enabling you to set a warning for date ranges.

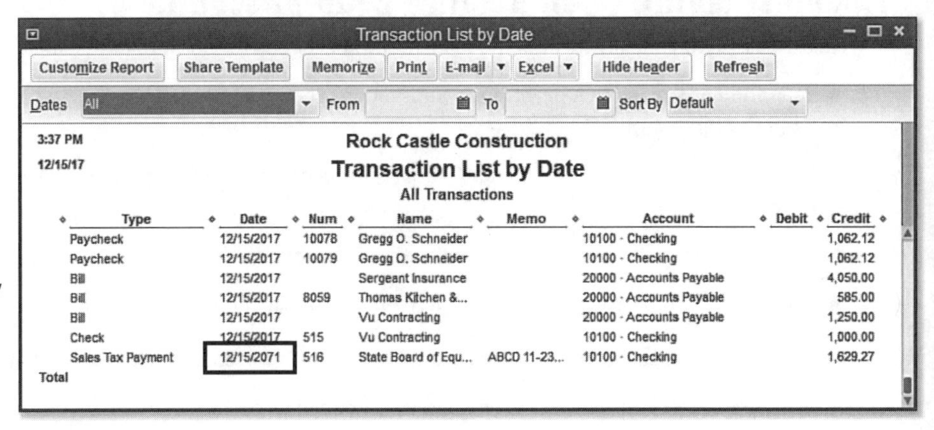

Transaction List by Date

Customize Report | Share Template | Memorize | Print | E-mail | Excel | Hide Header | Refresh

Dates All | From | To | Sort By Default

3:37 PM
12/15/17

Rock Castle Construction

Transaction List by Date

All Transactions

Type	Date	Num	Name	Memo	Account	Debit	Credit
Paycheck	12/15/2017	10078	Gregg O. Schneider		10100 · Checking		1,062.12
Paycheck	12/15/2017	10079	Gregg O. Schneider		10100 · Checking		1,062.12
Bill	12/15/2017		Sergeant Insurance		20000 · Accounts Payable		4,050.00
Bill	12/15/2017	8059	Thomas Kitchen &...		20000 · Accounts Payable		585.00
Bill	12/15/2017		Vu Contracting		20000 · Accounts Payable		1,250.00
Check	12/15/2017	515	Vu Contracting		10100 · Checking		1,000.00
Sales Tax Payment	12/15/2071	516	State Board of Equ...	ABCD 11-23...	10100 · Checking		1,629.27
Total							

Figure 15.17
The QuickBooks Transaction List by Date report can be used to identify whether any incorrectly dated transactions exist.

To open the date warning preference, follow these steps:

1. Log in to the QuickBooks data file as the Admin or External Accountant user.
2. From the menu bar, select **Edit**, **Preferences**. In the Preferences dialog box, choose the Accounting preference on the left.
3. Click the Company Preferences tab.
4. Type in the user-defined date warning range you want to work with for past-dated transactions and future-dated transactions. QuickBooks sets the default warnings at 90 days in the past and 30 days in the future. An attempt to enter transactions dated before or after this date range prompts QuickBooks to give the user a warning message, as shown in Figure 15.18.

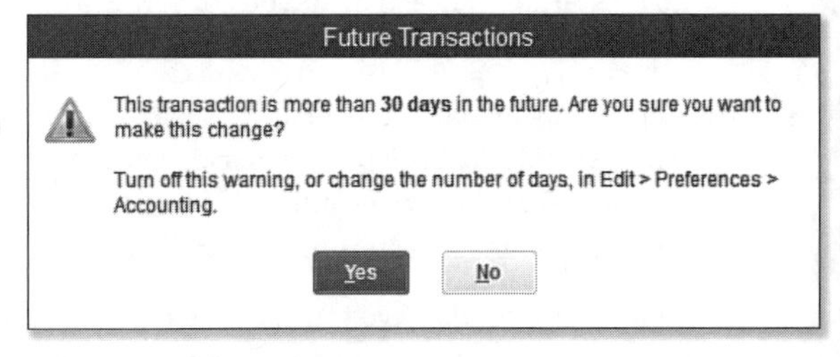

Figure 15.18
Set the Date Warning preference so users will be warned when dating a transaction outside an acceptable date range.

Be cautious when making changes to the dates, especially if the year in question has already had a tax return prepared on the existing information.

Troubleshooting Open Balance Equity Account

QuickBooks automatically records the following transactions to the Opening Balance Equity account:

- Your ending bank statement balance transaction when you created a new bank account in the Express Start setup
- Opening balances for other Balance Sheet report accounts created in the Add New Account dialog box
- Inventory total value balances entered in the New Item dialog box
- Bank reconciliation adjustments for older versions of QuickBooks

Other common transactions that a user might assign to this account include the following:

- Accrual basis opening accounts payable transactions as of the start date
- Accrual basis opening accounts receivable transactions as of the start date
- Uncleared bank checks or deposits (accrual or cash basis) as of the start date

Closing Opening Balance Equity into Retained Earnings

The Opening Balance Equity account should have a zero balance when a file setup is complete and done correctly. When I refer to a completely and correctly set up QuickBooks file, I assume the following:

- You *are not* converting your data from Quicken, Sage 50 (formerly Peachtree), Small Business Accounting, or Office Accounting. Each of these products has an automated conversion tool available free from Intuit, which eliminates the need to do startup transactions if you convert the data and not just lists.
- Your company *did not* have any transactions prior to the first use of QuickBooks. In this case, you simply enter typical QuickBooks transactions after your QuickBooks start date with no need for unusual startup type entries.

Although Intuit offers certain ready-made tools to convert other software to QuickBooks, some may not convert the data as expected. You would be prudent to verify that the information is correct after the conversion.

- Your company *did have* transactions prior to the first use of QuickBooks. You have chosen to enter these transactions one-by-one as regular transactions. You will not need to record any transactions to the Opening Balance Equity account.
- Your company *did have* transactions prior to the first use of QuickBooks, but there are so many it is not feasible to re-create them in QuickBooks. Instead, follow the directions in Chapter 3, "Setting Up a QuickBooks Data File for Accrual or Cash Basis Reporting," p. 88.
- You have entered each of your unpaid customer invoices, unpaid vendor bills, and uncleared bank transactions and dated them prior to your QuickBooks start date.

- You have entered and dated your trial balance one day before your QuickBooks start date. (You might need to request the trial balance numbers from your accountant if you are not converting from some other financial software that provides you with a trial balance.)
- When you create a Trial Balance report in QuickBooks dated one day before your QuickBooks start date, it agrees with your accountant's trial balance or with the trial balance from your prior financial software with the exception that you have a balance in the Opening Balance Equity account.

If you answered yes to each of these assumptions, I would expect that your Opening Balance Equity account is equal to the Retained Earnings balance from your accountant's financials or from your prior software. If it doesn't agree, you need to continue to review the data to determine what the errors are. If it does agree, you are prepared to make the final entry in your startup process.

Leave the first line of any Make General Journal Entries transaction blank because QuickBooks uses this line as the source line. Any list item in the name column on the first line (source line) of a general journal entries transaction will also be associated in reports with the other lines of the same general journal entries transaction. For more information about working with multiple line journal entries, see the caution on page 363 of Chapter 10, "Managing Customers."

To create this closing entry using a General Journal Entries transaction, follow these steps:

1. From the menu bar, select **Company**, **Make General Journal Entries**.
2. Enter a Date (it should be one day before your QuickBooks start date).
3. Type an **Entry No**.
4. Leaving line 1 of the transaction blank, on line 2 of the Make General Journal Entries transaction (using the example as shown in Figure 15.19), decrease (debit) Opening Balance Equity by $38,773.75 and increase (credit) Retained Earnings by the same amount. This action "closes" Opening Balance Equity to Retained Earnings. Click Save & Close.

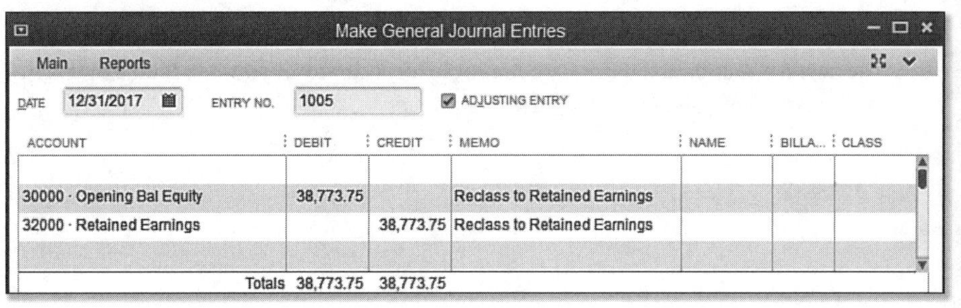

Figure 15.19 Use a Make General Journal Entries transaction to close Opening Balance Equity to Retained Earnings.

5. Click OK to the QuickBooks warning that displays; QuickBooks saves the transaction. The warning advises that you are posting to a Retained Earnings account and that QuickBooks has a

special purpose for this account. It is appropriate to post this entry to Retained Earnings. This warning is a result of a preference setting you can access from the menu bar by selecting **Edit**, **Preferences**, **Accounting**. Select the **Company Preferences** tab and choose the option to enable Warn When Posting a Transaction to Retained Earnings prompt. (You must be logged in as Admin or External Accountant user and in single-user mode to modify this preference.)

When the transaction is saved, create the Balance Sheet Standard report as explained earlier in this chapter and verify that your ending numbers are accurate; that is, that they match your accountant's or your prior software trial balance for the same period. Figure 15.20 now shows the proper Retained Earnings balance, and you no longer have a balance in Opening Balance Equity.

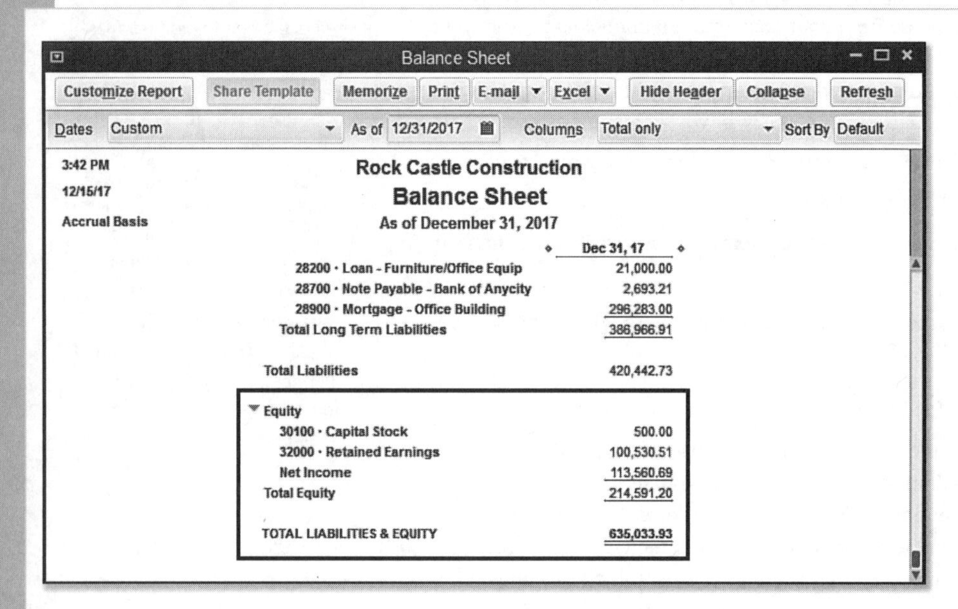

Figure 15.20 The Balance Sheet viewed after "closing" Opening Balance Equity to Retained Earnings.

Reviewing your data file can help improve the accuracy of your tax filings and provide more reliable information for making management decisions.

16

SHARING QUICKBOOKS DATA WITH YOUR ACCOUNTANT

One feature that truly sets QuickBooks apart from other business accounting software is the ease and flexibility of sharing a copy of the data between the business owner and the accounting professional. This chapter shares useful details for both the business owner and the accountant.

Overview

Accounting professionals can work more profitably with their client's files by partnering the Accountant's Copy functionality with the robust Client Data Review feature. The Client Data Review feature is available in QuickBooks Accountant 2013 and QuickBooks Enterprise Solutions Accountant 13.0.

For more information, refer to Appendix A, "Client Data Review."

Benefits for the Business Owner

As a business owner, you will want to have your accounting professional review your data. After all, you are using this data to make important management decisions. Additionally, you need to provide your data to your accountant for preparation of your federal and state tax returns.

So what might be some of the benefits of sharing your QuickBooks business data with your accountant? Benefits include the following:

- You can share an Accountant's Copy of your data, which allows your accountant to review and provide timely feedback without interrupting your daily workflow.

- You have less stress because you do not need to prepare multiple reports for your accountant to review.
- You can delegate critical tasks to your accountant, such as reconciling a bank account. (Use the Accountant's Copy file-sharing method.)
- Your accountant can use your data to compile the information needed for your tax returns.
- You can choose from multiple sharing methods and select one that is right for your business.
- Periodic review of your data by your accountant can save precious time at year's end and provide more accurate financials during the year.

Benefits for the Accountant

Periodically reviewing your client's data has become more important in recent years, as strict accounting guidelines tighten further. Often your clients are even unaware of these changes.

As an accountant, you can benefit from access to your client's data by doing the following:

- Review your client's data at your office at a time convenient for you or your staff.
- Complete key reviewing tasks while enabling your clients to continue their day-to-day transactions. (Use the Accountant's Copy file-sharing method.)
- Use the many accountant-specific tools to facilitate this review offered in the QuickBooks Accountant or QuickBooks Enterprise Solutions Accountant including the Client Data Review feature.
- Complete critical tasks for your client, such as reconciling a bank account, making your services more valued by the client. (Use the Accountant's Copy file-sharing method.)
- Provide your clients with more frequent and timely analysis of their data.

This chapter is a guide for how both the business owner and the accountant can share QuickBooks data.

QuickBooks File Types

QuickBooks offers much flexibility in how a business owner or accountant can share a common QuickBooks data file. Some of the benefits of sharing data using the Accountant's Copy file were previously listed. This chapter discusses details of all the choices offered in facilitating this sharing.

Table 16.1 lists the common QuickBooks file types used for sharing data. Knowing these file types is important as you make decisions on the best method for your business or your clients' data sharing needs.

Table 16.1 QuickBooks File Types

Extension	File Type	Description	QuickBooks Editions*
.QBW	QuickBooks for Windows regular working file	This is the working data file type created when a user creates a new QuickBooks file.	Pro, Premier, Professional Bookkeeper, Accountant, Enterprise
.QBB	QuickBooks for Windows backup file	The most secure and complete method for protecting your data with a backup.	Pro, Premier, Professional Bookkeeper, Accountant, Enterprise
.QBM	QuickBooks for Windows portable company file	This is a compressed version of your QuickBooks .QBW data file. Used primarily to email or move the file to another location.	Pro, Premier, Professional Bookkeeper, Accountant, Enterprise
.QBX	Accountant's Copy (export file)	This is created by the business owner to save or send data to the accountant.	Pro, Premier, Professional Bookkeeper, Accountant, Enterprise
.QBA	Accountant's Copy (converted .QBX file)	QuickBooks creates this file when open/convert an .QBX file is performed (usually by the accountant).	Professional Bookkeeper, Accountant, Enterprise Accountant
.QBY	Accountant's Copy (import file)	This is the file the accountant sends to the business owner after making changes.	Professional Bookkeeper, Accountant, Enterprise Accountant

**Not shown in Table 16.1 are QuickBooks Online and QuickBooks for Mac. Both of these versions have a different file structure, and neither of them supports the Accountant's Copy feature discussed at length in this chapter.*

Choosing a Method to Share Data

QuickBooks offers flexibility in how data is shared between a business owner and the accountant. Different methods can be used at different times during the year, depending on the nature of the changes to be made.

Options available might also be determined by the edition of QuickBooks you use and whether your data is in an older version of QuickBooks. The enhancements made in recent years for sharing your data with your accountant make it a perfect time to upgrade to the newest release.

To compare different QuickBooks products, go to http://quickbooks.intuit.com/product/accounting-software/quickbooks-comparison-chart.jsp

You might even choose to use multiple data sharing methods during the course of a year, after you know the advantages and limitations associated with each type.

Before choosing an option, review the details of each file type (shown earlier in Table 16.1) and in the sections that follow.

How the QuickBooks Year and Version Affect Your Data Sharing Choices

The choices of how you can share your data with your accountant depend on the version and release year of QuickBooks you and your accountant use.

The QuickBooks product line includes Pro, Premier (general and industry-specific versions), Professional Bookkeeper, Accountant, Enterprise (general and industry-specific versions), QuickBooks for Mac, and QuickBooks Online.

Additionally, Intuit releases a new QuickBooks version each year, often represented by the year included in the name. For example, QuickBooks Premier 2013 is the Premier version usually released in the fall prior to the stated year. This version is separate from the maintenance release updates QuickBooks provides throughout a year to add functionality and fix issues discovered with a version.

To determine your current version and release, with QuickBooks open, press F2 or Ctrl+1. At the top of the Product Information dialog box that displays is the product name (and industry edition if Premier or Enterprise), year, and release number.

So you can see how the version year can affect your choices for sharing data, in this chapter I discuss the Accountant's Copy features, which are not available for QuickBooks Online, the QuickBooks for Mac edition, or for any QuickBooks product prior to the 2007 version.

.QBW: Regular Working Copy of the Data

Each client file is originally created in this file type. Here is a list of some of the advantages and limitations of sharing this type of data file:

- The accountant *cannot* take the file to his office, work in the file, and later merge changes into the business owner's file unless the client agrees not to work in the file while the accountant has possession of it.
- New for QuickBooks 2013—if both the client and accountant are using QuickBooks 2013, the accountant can electronically transfer journal entries to clients. The transactions are attached to an email and imported by clicking on the attachment. Additionally, such journal transactions are not subject to the Dividing Date restrictions found in the Accountant's Copy file-sharing method.
- The accountant has access to all transaction activities.
- The accountant can access this file at the business owner's office or with a remote Internet-assisted program. QuickBooks partners with Remote Access by WebEx, but there are several others in the market, including LogMeIn or GoToMeeting.
- The file can often be too large to send as an attachment in an email.

To open a working copy of the data from the menu bar, select **File**, **Open or Restore Company** and select the **Open a Company File** option.

.QBB: QuickBooks Backup File

This file type remains as it has for years—it's the best choice for securing a data backup of your work. If needed, this file can be restored to a .QBW file. Here is a list of some of the advantages and limitations of sharing this type of data file:

- The file cannot be opened first without being restored.
- When restored, the file extension becomes a .QBW (see the pros and cons listed earlier).
- Changes made to a restored version of this file type *cannot* be merged later into the original data file.

To restore a backup file from the menu bar, select **File**, **Open or Restore Company** and select the **Restore a Backup Copy** option.

.QBM: QuickBooks Portable Company File

This file type has been offered for the past few years; however, it does not replace the usefulness of the QuickBooks .QBB file type. Here is a list of some of the advantages and limitations of sharing this type of data file:

- The compressed file size makes a .QBM a perfect choice for attaching to an email or moving from one computer location to another.
- The file type does not replace a .QBB backup because it lacks some of the needed transaction logs.
- The file cannot be opened until it is restored.
- When restored, the file extension becomes a .QBW (see the pros and cons listed earlier).
- Changes made to a restored version of this file type *cannot* be merged later into the original data file.

To restore a portable company file from the menu bar, select **File**, **Open or Restore Company** and select the **Restore a Portable File** option.

.QBX: Accountant's Copy (Export File)

As a business owner, if you choose to share your data with your accountant using the Accountant's Copy functionality, you will send this file type to your accounting professional. Here is a list of some of the advantages and limitations of sharing this type of data file:

- This file type is created by the business owner and enables your accountant to review and make needed changes to your data while you continue recording your day-to-day transactions in the file at your office.
- Any changes or additions your accountant makes *can* be imported (merged) into your company's data file.
- The accountant's work is protected by a required Dividing Date, preventing the business owner from making changes to transactions dated on or before the Dividing Date.
- The compressed file size makes it a perfect choice for attaching to an email or moving from one computer location to another.

- The file type does not replace a .QBB backup because it lacks some of the needed transaction logs.
- The file cannot be opened; it must be converted to a .QBA file type.

Using QuickBooks Accountant software, from the menu bar, select **File**, **Accountant's Copy** and select the **Open & Convert Transfer File** option.

.QBA: Accountant's Copy (Working File)

Only the accountant will work with this type of file. Listed here are some of the advantages and limitations of sharing this type of data file:

- This file type is a converted .QBX file and is created by the accountant from within the QuickBooks Accountant or QuickBooks Enterprise Solutions Accountant.
- The .QBA file type is the file the accountant will make changes to. It will be converted to a .QBY file for the client to import.
- The file can be saved to the accountant's computer and be opened and closed as needed while the accountant reviews the file.

.QBY: Accountant's Copy (Import File)

The business owner receives this file from the accountant, and it includes any accounting changes made to the original .QBX file. Here is a list of some of the advantages and limitations of sharing this type of data file:

- This file type is created by the accountant using QuickBooks Accountant or QuickBooks Enterprise Solutions Accountant software.
- The file includes the changes made by the accountant to the original .QBX file the business owner provided the accountant.
- The file cannot be opened; it must be imported into the data file that *originally created* the Accountant's Copy data file.

QuickBooks offers your business many options in how you want to share your data with your accountant. Select a solution that works for you and your accountant.

Send General Journal Entries

With QuickBooks Accountant 2013, you have flexibility in choosing what method of file sharing works best for you and your client. When considering a method, your client needs to continue the daily accounting tasks while allowing you to review the data and create journal entries.

With the new Send Journal Entry feature, your clients send you either a copy of their working file (.QBW), a backup (.QBB), or a portable company file (.QBM). Your clients can continue to work in their files while you review their copy at your office. This avoids the restrictions imposed when sharing an Accountant's Copy file.

See the section titled "Send General Journal Entries" later in this chapter for more details.

Data Sharing for the Business Owner

Few business owners with whom I have worked over the years have a college degree in accounting. That situation is exactly what makes QuickBooks so appealing to a growing business—you don't need to be an accountant to use it. However, you will need an accountant to review your financials, perhaps at tax time or when you need a statement of your business's financial condition to give to a bank when requesting a business loan.

QuickBooks provides several methods of sharing data with your accountant. Refer to Table 16.1 for details on the QuickBooks file types the business owner can choose.

When Your Accountant Is Using QuickBooks Accountant 2013

If you are using a version of QuickBooks 2012 or 2013 or Enterprise Solutions version 12.0 or 13.0, and you choose to share your data using the Accountant's Copy feature, your accountant can use the QuickBooks 2013 Accountant or Enterprise Solutions Accountant 13.0 version to open your 2012 or 2013 company file and make changes. Enterprise Solutions Accountant 13.0 can open a Pro or Premier Accountant's Copy (2012 or 2013) and can return the file to clients to open in their Pro or Premier software.

When the file is returned with the accountant's changes, you will be able to import the changes back into your QuickBooks file, even though the accountant used a newer version of QuickBooks. The QuickBooks Accountant 2013 and Enterprise Solutions Accountant 13.0 offer a degree of backward compatibility.

If you are sharing any other file type (other than the Accountant's Copy) with your accountant, there is no backward compatibility. When your accountant restores a .QBB (backup) or .QBM (portable) company file in a 2013 version, the file will be updated to 2013; if the file is returned to you, you need to update your QuickBooks version to the same release year as your accountant.

For example, suppose you are currently using a QuickBooks 2012 version. Your accountant is using QuickBooks 2013 Accountant. When your accountant restores a QuickBooks file backup, she will have to update the file to the QuickBooks 2013 release. If your accountant returns the data to you, you will not be able to open it with your QuickBooks 2012 software.

So, as you decide which method to use, consider discussing with your accountant the QuickBooks version and release year you are using. QuickBooks accountants who have serviced companies for many years often have several versions of QuickBooks installed.

Keep in mind that QuickBooks Enterprise Solutions presents its own set of special requirements. If you open a backup or portable company file from a Pro or Premier data file with the Enterprise Solutions software, you will no longer be able to open the same data file in its original QuickBooks Pro or Premier edition.

For the most flexibility in sharing data with your accountant, consider using the Accountant's Copy file type, discussed at length in this chapter.

Reviewing Your QuickBooks Data

No matter what method you choose to share your data file with your accountant, one of the most important things you can do is review your data for accuracy, especially in the areas of Accounts Payable and Accounts Receivable—areas that you will know better than your accountant.

To begin, pick a chapter of this book that covers the area of QuickBooks you need to review. You might want to start with Chapter 15, "Reviewing Your Data." This chapter shows you quick and easy data checks you can do before your accountant formally reviews your data. Performing this quick review can also help you identify any potential errors for which you will need your accountant's guidance when correcting.

Creating an Accountant's Copy of Your Data

The Accountant's Copy method of sharing your data is the most efficient because it enables your accountant to work in the data file from her office without interrupting your day-to-day work pattern.

caution

Only the Admin or new External Accountant user can create an Accountant's Copy or import the .QBY Accountant's Copy import file that contains the changes the accountant made to your data.

You must consider the following before making the choice to use the Accountant's Copy file-sharing type:

- If you choose to create an Accountant's Copy, you need to determine how to get the Accountant's Copy data file to your accountant. QuickBooks offers these options:
  - Send an encrypted copy of your data to your accountant via Intuit's secure Accountant's Copy File Transfer Service.
  - Attach the saved file to an email.
  - Copy it to a storage device such as a USB drive or CD.
  - Use an online file sharing service like YouSendIt or Dropbox.
- You also will be required to set a dividing date, as shown in Figure 16.1. The dividing date is a specific date in the past, which determines the restrictions you and your accountant will have when adding or editing transactions.

caution

When a dividing date is set, the business owner cannot add, modify, delete, or void any transaction dated prior to the dividing date, including nonposting documents such as estimates, sales orders, and purchase orders. This limitation can be terribly inconvenient for the business owner, so discuss it ahead of time with your accountant. If appropriate, you should change the date of these pending "nonposting" documents to a date after the expected dividing date.

The following list briefly identifies the date restrictions with a dividing date in place when you share an Accountant's Copy of your data with your accountant. For example, if you choose a sample dividing date of 12/31/16, the following restrictions exist:

- **On or Before the Dividing Date**—You (the business owner) cannot add, delete, or modify transactions. The accountant can add, delete, or modify transactions.
- **After the Dividing Date**—You (the business owner) can add, delete, or modify transactions. The accountant can add transactions, but cannot delete or modify them.

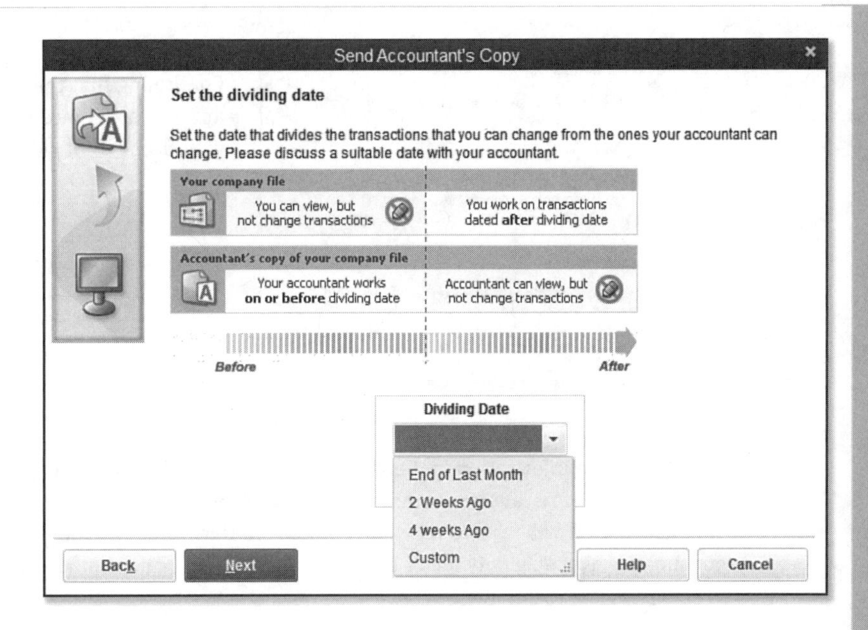

Figure 16.1
Setting a dividing date is required when creating an Accountant's Copy.

For more information, see "What the Business Owner Can and Cannot Do" later in this chapter for any restrictions that affect you, the business owner.

The business owner has these options for delivering the QuickBooks data file to the accountant:

- **Send to Accountant**—Send an encrypted copy of your data to your accountant via Intuit's Accountant's Copy File Transfer Service (free for the business owner). Included for the accountant who subscribes to the QuickBooks ProAdvisor program.
- **Save File**—Use this option to attach the file to an email or copy to USB or other portable medium.

Method 1: Using the Send File Method Via the Web

Offered with QuickBooks Pro, Premier, and Enterprise is the option to use a secure, Intuit-hosted site to encrypt and transfer data to your accountant without needing to create a file and attach it to an email.

To send data to your accountant with the secure encrypted file service, follow these steps:

1. From the menu bar, select **File**, **Accountant's Copy**, **Client Activities**, **Send to Accountant**. The Confirm Sending an Accountant's Copy dialog box displays, shown in Figure 16.2. This message details the service and what types of shared work are and are not recommended with this type of file .
2. Click Next. The Set the Dividing Date dialog box displays.
3. From the Dividing Date drop-down list, choose one of the date options shown in Figure 16.1, or choose Custom to select your own specific dividing date.

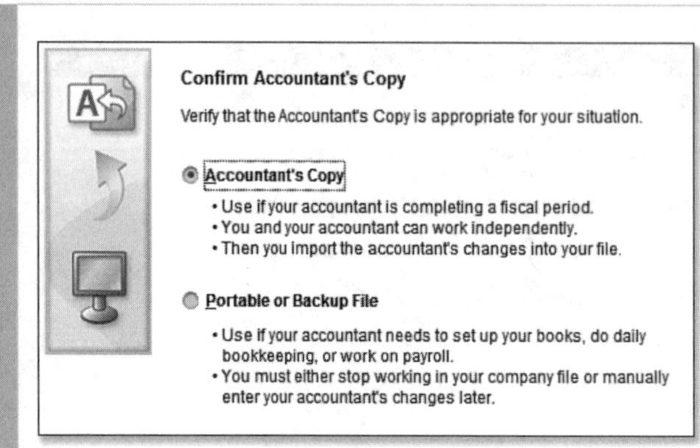

Figure 16.2
Confirming that the Accountant's Copy is the appropriate choice for the shared work you and your accountant will be doing.

4. Click Next. The Information for Sending the File (1 of 2) dialog box displays, as shown in Figure 16.3. Type the email address to notify your accountant, and include your name and return email. Your accountant will receive an email notification that your data file is ready to download. The download is available only for 14 days.

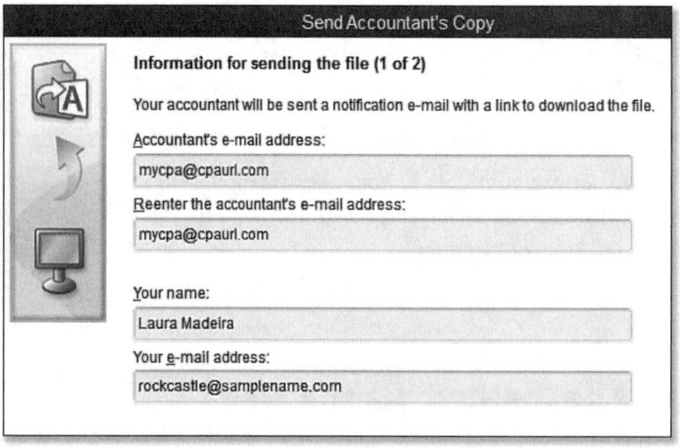

Send Accountant's Copy

Information for sending the file (1 of 2)

Your accountant will be sent a notification e-mail with a link to download the file.

Accountant's e-mail address:
mycpa@cpaurl.com

Reenter the accountant's e-mail address:
mycpa@cpaurl.com

Your name:
Laura Madeira

Your e-mail address:
rockcastle@samplename.com

Figure 16.3
Identify the email address where your accountant should be notified, as well as your own name and email address.

5. Click Next. The Information for Sending the File (2 of 2) dialog box displays, as shown in Figure 16.4.
6. Enter a strong password that is at least seven characters long and contains at least one capital letter and one digit. (Optional) Type a note to your accountant, but do not include the password in the communication.
7. Click Send.
8. Click OK to the message that QuickBooks has to close all windows to create the Accountant's Copy. Note: QuickBooks also provides an information message only (no action to be taken) that the transfer might take a few minutes, so don't worry if QuickBooks seems unresponsive.

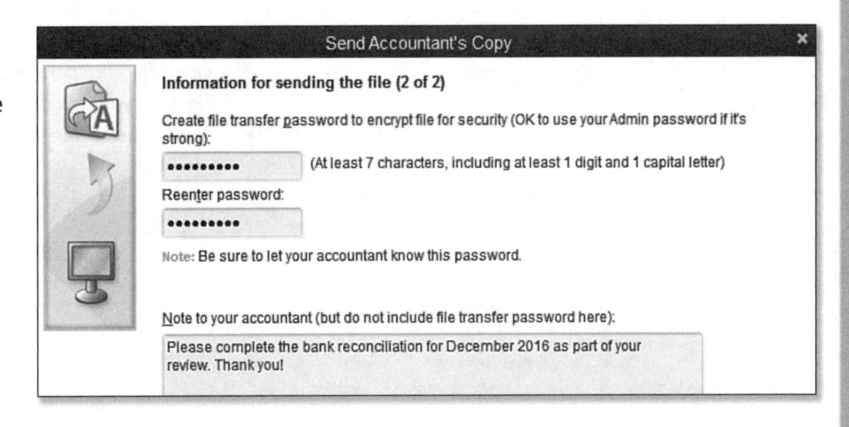

Figure 16.4
Set a strong password and add an optional note for your accountant.

9. Click OK on the QuickBooks Information dialog box that displays, which indicates the file was uploaded to the Intuit Accountant's Copy File Transfer server successfully.

The QuickBooks title bar identifies your file as having Accountant's Changes Pending, as shown in Figure 16.5. This title bar change indicates you have successfully created a file for your accountant to review, edit, modify, and later return the changes to you without interrupting your work.

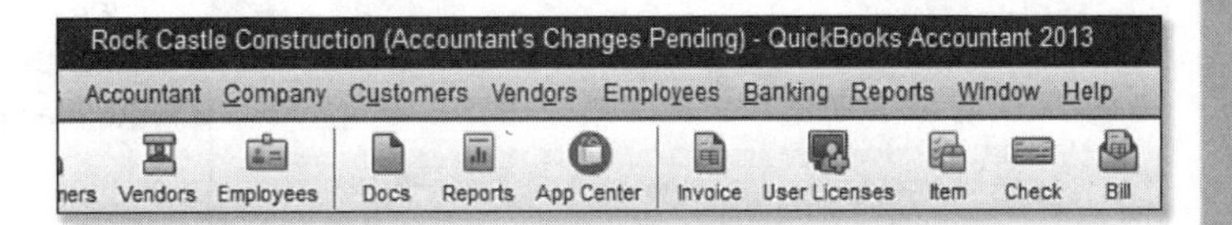

Figure 16.5
Your QuickBooks title bar will indicate whether you have accountant's changes pending.

Method 2: Using the Save File Method

Another method is to create the file, save it to your computer, and then email it or provide the file to your accountant on a USB device. To create an Accountant's Copy file of your data that your accountant can review and modify while you continue to do your daily transactions, follow these steps:

1. Close all your active QuickBooks windows. From the menu bar, select **File**, **Accountant's Copy**, **Client Activities**, **Save File**.
2. Choose the Accountant's Copy option, as shown in Figure 16.6. (The other option includes the Portable or Backup File. These methods will not allow the accountant to export any changes made or you to import the changes.)
3. Click Next. The Set the Dividing Date dialog box opens.
4. From the Dividing Date drop-down list, select one of the date options as previously shown in Figure 16.1, or choose Custom to select your own specific dividing date. For more information on the importance of this date, see "What the Business Owner Can and Cannot Do," p. 583.

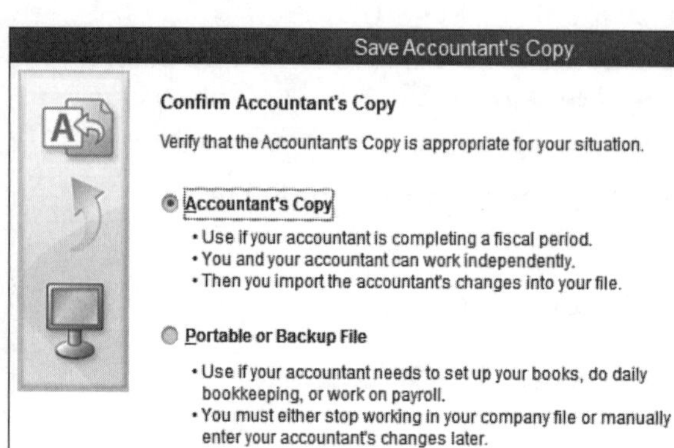

Figure 16.6
Saving a file as an Accountant's Copy creates a file that your accountant can work in and later merge the changes with your file.

5. Click Next. QuickBooks opens the Save Accountant's Copy dialog box, where you can browse your computer for the location where you want to save the Accountant's Copy export file (.QBX file).
6. Click the Save button. QuickBooks provides the message shown in Figure 16.7, indicating that you successfully created an Accountant's Copy and telling you where the file was saved, as well as other useful information.

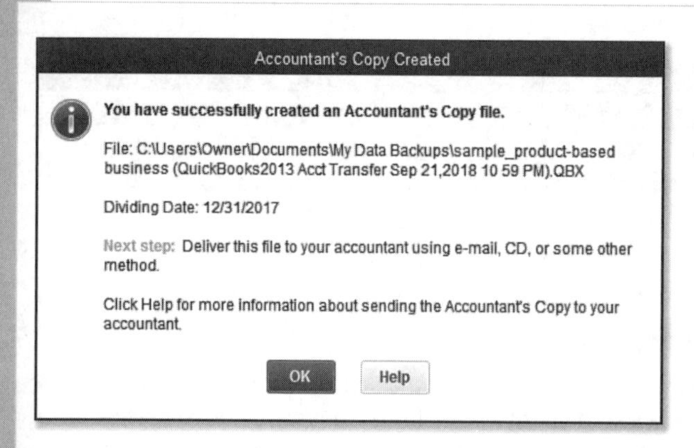

Figure 16.7
QuickBooks provides information about where the file was saved.

7. Click OK. As previously shown in Figure 16.5, the QuickBooks title bar now identifies your file as having Accountant's Changes Pending.
8. Send this .QBX file to your accountant as an email attachment, or copy it to a removable data storage device.

What the Business Owner Can and Cannot Do

With the useful features of Accountant's Copy, your accountant can be assured the information in the file she is working in will not change for dates prior to the dividing date.

The following list details what you can and cannot do with your data file while an Accountant's Changes are pending:

- **Transactions**—You can add, edit, and modify transactions with a date after the dividing date.
- **Accounts**—You can add a new chart of accounts list item.
- **Subaccounts**—You cannot add a subaccount to an existing account.
- **Editing, merging, or inactivating accounts**—You cannot edit, merge, or inactivate a chart of accounts item (your accountant can).
- **Editing lists (other than the chart of accounts)**—You can add, edit, and inactivate your list items. If you and your accountant make changes to the same item, the accountant's changes will override your changes.
- **Deleting lists**—You cannot delete or merge list items (your accountant can).
- **Reconciling the bank account**—In the .QBW file with pending Accountant's Copy, if the statement date and all transactions involved into the reconciliation are *after* the dividing date and the accountant didn't reconcile this account in the Accountant's Copy, reconciliation work remains in the .QBW file after the import. Bank reconciliations for dates *on or before* the dividing date are removed when you incorporate your accountant's changes file.

Reconciling While an Accountant's Copy Is Pending

When choosing to use the Accountant's Copy to share your data, you can complete the bank reconciliation only for reconciliations where the bank statement date and all transactions to be cleared are dated after the selected dividing date.

From the menu bar, select **Banking, Reconcile,** and select your bank account. The bank reconciliation dialog box opens. In this dialog box, dates entered must follow these guidelines:

- **Statement Date**—Must be a date after the specified dividing date.
- **Service Charge Date**—Must be a date after the specified dividing date.
- **Interest Earned Date**—Must be a date after the specified dividing date.

Your bank reconciliation work will remain after the import of your accountant's changes if

- None of the transactions you mark as cleared are dated on or before the Accountant's Copy dividing date.
- Your accountant did not also complete the bank reconciliation for the same bank account.
- Your accountant doesn't undo any bank reconciliations for this account in the Accountant's Copy.

There can be value in reconciling, even if the accountant's copy import will undo it, simply to verify that your bank balances are correct.

Importing Your Accountant's Changes

When you make an Accountant's Copy from your data file, QuickBooks creates a file for you to give to your accountant. Your accountant then works in this file, adding and editing transactions, and even reconciling your bank account. When the accountant finishes with the review, she exports the changes for you, which generates a .QBY file, also referred to as an Accountant's Copy Import File.

Your accountant has two options for sending you the file with her changes:

- **Send Changes to Client**—This method allows the business owner to incorporate the changes from a menu in QuickBooks. There is no charge to the business owner for this service and only a nominal fee for the accounting professional (included free for the accountant with a subscription to the QuickBooks ProAdvisor program).
- **Create Change File**—This method can be attached to an email or stored on a removable device. There is no fee for the business owner or the accountant when using this method.

Encourage your accountant to use the Send Changes to Client method—of the two methods, it is the easiest for the business owner.

Method 1: Importing Changes from the Web

You can tell if your accountant used this method if you receive an email from Intuit, providing instructions for incorporating the changes your accountant made to your file. This method does not require attachments to emails or files on flash drives, making it the simplest method to use.

To import changes from the Web, follow these steps:

1. With your QuickBooks data file open, verify that the title bar indicates that the accountant's changes are pending (refer to Figure 16.5). You might also see the message shown in Figure 16.8 when you open your data file.

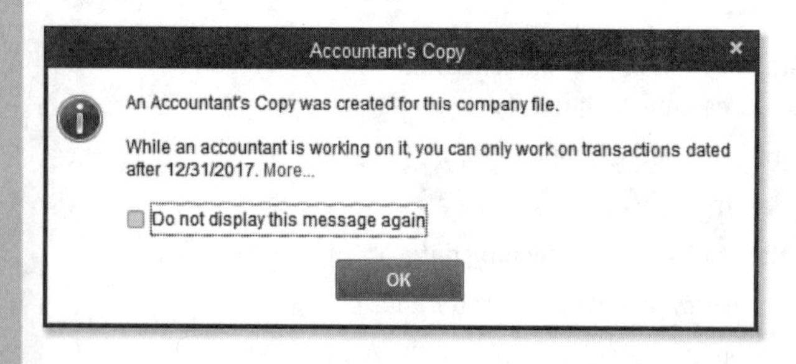

Figure 16.8
Message when you open the data file indicating that your accountant's changes are pending.

2. From menu bar, select **File**, **Accountant's Copy**, **Import Accountant's Changes from Web**. The Incorporate Accountant's Changes dialog box opens, enabling you to view the details of the changes to be imported (see Figure 16.9).

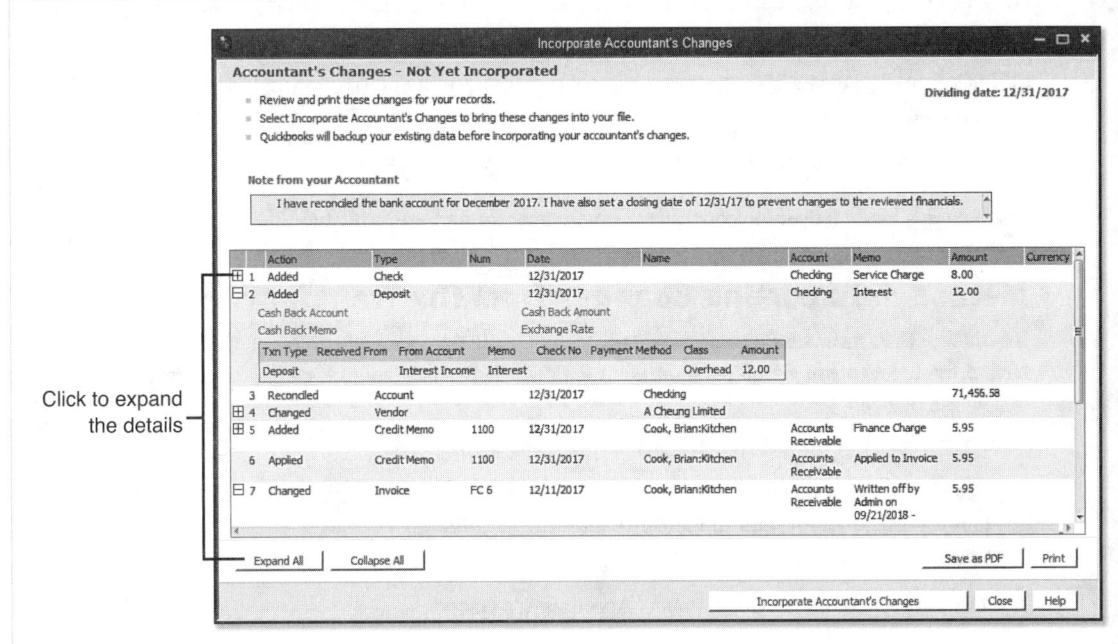

Figure 16.9
View the accountant's changes and notes before they are incorporated into your data.

3. Click the plus sign (+) in front of a transaction to see more details about that specific transaction, or click Expand All to see the details of all the transactions.
4. Click Save as PDF or Print to save the details for your future reference.
5. Click the Incorporate Accountant's Changes button when you have finished reviewing the changes.
6. The Accountant Import dialog box opens, instructing you to close any open QuickBooks windows. Click OK.
7. The Save Backup Copy dialog box opens, indicating that you must first make a backup of your data before the import. In the Save In drop-down menu select a location to save the backup file and in the File Name field, type a name if you don't want to accept the default name provided.
8. If a message displays about backing up your data to the same location as your data, read the message and select **Change Location** or **Use This Location**.
9. Click OK to close the message that informs you where the backup was stored. QuickBooks displays a progress indicator while it is incorporating the changes. When QuickBooks finishes, the Accountant's Changes Incorporated dialog box displays.
10. Click OK in the QuickBooks Information dialog box, which informs you about the PDF file of the changes that QuickBooks created and stored in the same location as your company file.

11. Click OK to close the message that your accountant has been notified that you have imported the changes.

12. Click Print or Save as PDF to store a copy of the changes in addition to the PDF automatically created in step 11.

13. Click Close to close the Incorporate Accountant's Changes dialog box.

The changes made by your accountant are now incorporated into your file.

Method 2: Importing Changes from the Transfer File

Use this method if the accountant provided you with a file with an extension of .QBY. She might have provided it to you via an email attachment or brought it by your office on a flash drive or other removable device.

To import changes from the transfer file, follow these steps:

1. With your QuickBooks data file open, verify that the title bar indicates that the accountant's changes are pending (refer to Figure 16.5). If the Accountant's Copy message displays, click OK to close.

2. Click File, Accountant's Copy, Import Accountant's Changes.

3. Browse to the location where you stored the .QBY Accountant's Copy (import file) your accountant sent you.

4. Select the file and click Open. The Incorporate Accountant's Changes dialog box opens, enabling you to view the details of the changes to be imported (refer to Figure 16.9).

5. Click the plus sign (+) in front of a transaction to see more details about that specific transaction, or click Expand All to see the details of all the transactions.

6. Click Print or Save as PDF to save the details for your future reference.

7. Click the Incorporate Accountant's Changes button when you have finished reviewing the changes.

8. The Accountant Import dialog box opens, instructing you to close any open QuickBooks windows. Click OK.

9. The Save Backup Copy dialog box opens, indicating that you must first make a backup of your data before the import. In the Save In drop-down menu, select a location to save the backup file, and in the File Name field, type a name if you don't want to accept the default name provided. Click Save.

10. Click OK to close the message that informs you where the backup was stored. QuickBooks displays a progressive message that it is incorporating the changes. When QuickBooks finishes, the Accountant's Changes Incorporated dialog box displays.

11. Click OK to the QuickBooks Information dialog box about the PDF file of the changes that was created and stored in the same location as your company file.

12. Click Close after viewing the Accountant's Changes—Incorporated dialog box. (Optional) Click Print or Save as PDF to store a copy of the changes in addition to the PDF automatically created in step 11.

13. Click Close to close the Incorporate Accountant's Changes dialog box.

Set a Closing Date

When the accountant's changes are imported, the dividing date and all the restrictions associated with it are removed. The accountant can include with his changes a closing date that transfers to your file so you do not inadvertently add, delete, or modify transactions prior to the closing date. If a closing date was set, you will see the details in the Incorporate Accountant's Changes report you view prior to importing the changes.

If your accountant did not send back a closing date and password, I recommend that you set a closing date the same as the dividing date to protect the accountant's work.

To set a closing date for your file, follow these steps:

1. Log in as the Admin user and from the menu bar, select **Company**, **Set Closing Date**.

2. The Preferences dialog box displays. Click the Set Date/Password button. The Set Closing Date and Password dialog box displays.

3. Select a closing date, typically the same date used for the dividing date.

4. (Optional) Select the **Exclude Estimates, Sales Orders, and Purchase Orders from Closing Data Restrictions** checkbox shown in Figure 16.10.

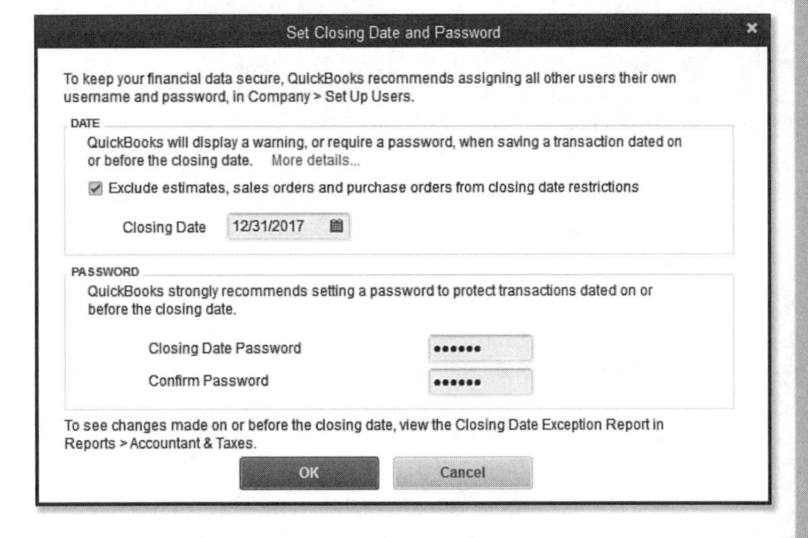

Figure 16.10
Setting a closing date will help protect the work done by the accountant.

5. Enter an optional password (recommended).

6. Click OK to accept the closing date and optional closing date password.

Setting Employee Security

To be certain the Closing Date control is managed properly, review all users for their specific rights for changing transactions prior to a closing date.

1. From the menu bar, select **Company**, **Set Up Users and Passwords**, **Set Up Users**. This is the menu path for QuickBooks Pro, Premier, or Accountant; QuickBooks Enterprise Solutions has more robust security setting options discussed in detail in Chapter 1, "User Security in QuickBooks Enterprise," p. 52.

2. To view existing security by user, from the User List dialog box opened in the previous step, select the user with your cursor and click the View User button.

3. The View User Access dialog box opens, as shown in Figure 16.11. Any user who should not have rights to change closed period transactions should have an "N" appearing in the last menu option in the Create column.

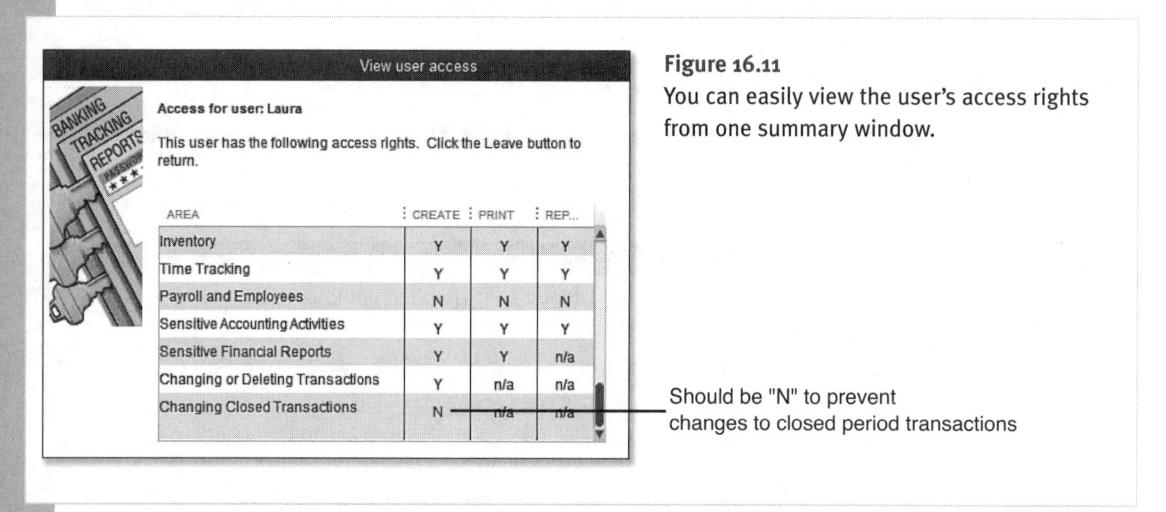

Figure 16.11
You can easily view the user's access rights from one summary window.

4. After reviewing the access for each employee, if you need to edit this setting for an employee, click Leave to close the View User Access dialog box.

5. You are returned to the User List dialog box. With your cursor, select the employee and click Edit User.

6. The Access for User dialog box opens. Choose the Selected Areas option and click Continue through the screens until you reach page 9 of 10, as shown in Figure 16.12. Click Next (page 10 of 10) to see a summary of the employee's security settings or click Finish to return to the User List dialog box.

7. Click Close.

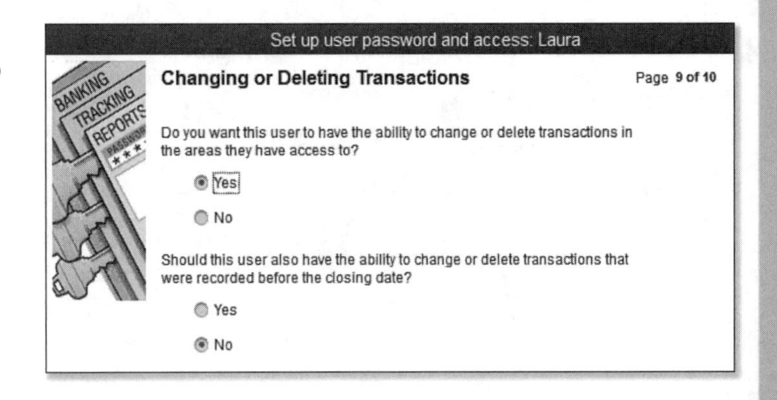

Figure 16.12
On the second option, click No to prevent the user from changing transactions in closed periods.

Canceling an Accountant's Copy

It is possible for you to cancel an accountant's copy of your data if necessary. Be sure to discuss this action with your accountant before you make this change. The following are some reasons you might need to cancel the accountant's changes:

- Your accountant has delayed the review of your file.
- You have found corrections you would like to make prior to the dividing date.
- You cannot modify nonposting documents (purchase orders, sales orders, and estimates) dated prior to the dividing date.
- Your accountant needs to work in your file without any transaction restrictions and makes an appointment to come to your office to work or perform the work remotely via the Internet.

Before canceling or removing restrictions on your data file, discuss this option with your accountant. After the Accountant's Copy is canceled, your accountant's changes file cannot be imported into your data file.

To remove the restrictions placed on your file by an Accountant's Copy, select **File**, **Accountant's Copy**, **Remove Restrictions** from the menu bar. The Remove Restrictions dialog box displays, warning you that your accountant will no longer be able to import changes back into your file, as shown in Figure 16.13.

After you remove the restriction from the file, no more data restrictions are imposed by the dividing date, and the top bar of your data file no longer displays the Accountant's Changes Pending message.

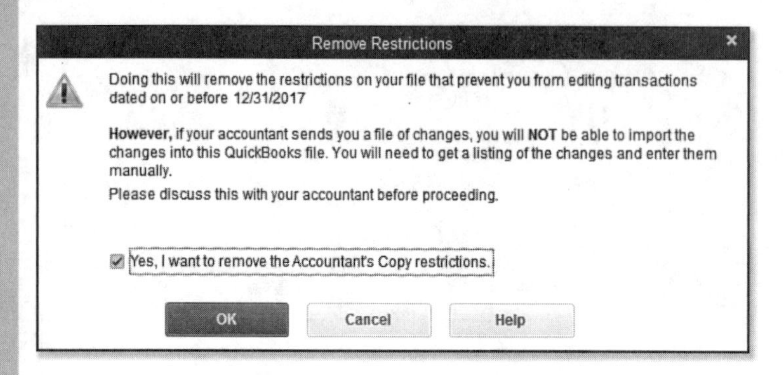

Figure 16.13
The Remove Restrictions warning displays when canceling an Accountant's Copy file.

Data Sharing for the Accountant

Earlier, Table 16.1 listed the types of QuickBooks files that business owners and accountants have the options of working with. This section discusses the options from the perspective of the accountant.

As the accountant, you will want to review the variety of file types and the pros and cons of using each file type for sharing data with your client.

For more information, see "QuickBooks File Types," p. 572.

File Manager 2013

QuickBooks File Manager 2013 (see Figure 16.14) is automatically installed with your QuickBooks Accountant 2013 and Enterprise Accountant 13.0 software. With File Manager accounting professionals can:

- Build a client list that creates a virtual view of your hard drive where your client files are stored. Files can be stored on a server, on a local hard drive, or both!
- Create user-definable client groups such as Annual Review Clients, Monthly Review Clients, or Payroll Clients to name just a few suggestions for grouping your client files.
- Save your client file passwords in one place, and QuickBooks File Manager will open the clients' files without requiring input of the password.
- View important information about your clients' without opening them, information includes:
    - Upgrade client files in batch to the newest release, a real time saver!
    - Open your client files from within File Manager and the correct year's version of QuickBooks opens automatically (must have that version installed).
    - Backup and restore your File Manager settings, useful when you buy a new computer or want to share one employee File Manager settings with another.

There are multiple ways to launch QuickBooks File Manager:

- Click the QuickBooks File Manager desktop icon.
- From the Accountant Center in your Accountant version of QuickBooks.
- From the menu bar, selecting **Accountant**, **QuickBooks File Manager**.
- Click the Start button in Windows, and then select Programs, QuickBooks, and File Manager.

Using File Manager takes the guesswork out of working with your client's file. It is easy to use and included with your Accountant version software.

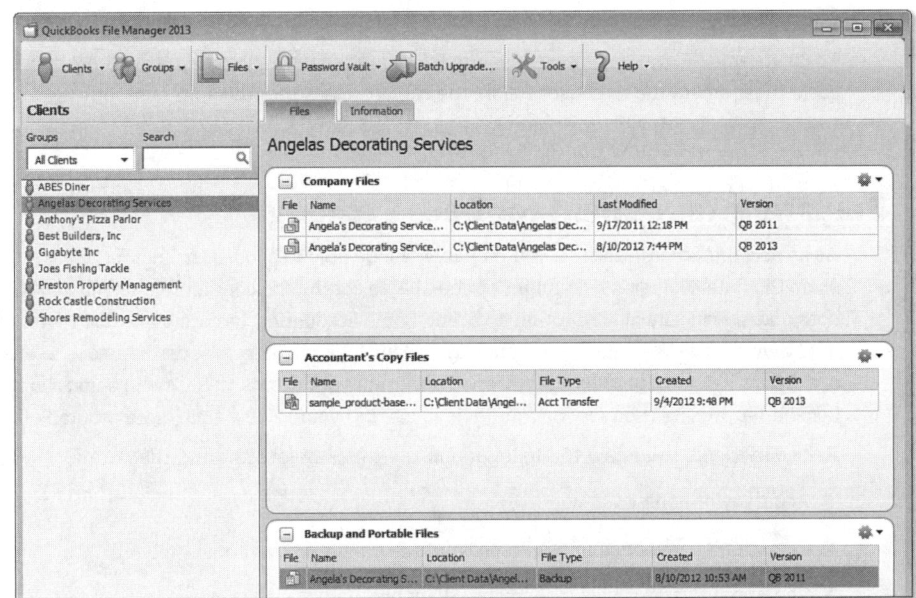

Figure 16.14 File Manager, included with QuickBooks Accountant, manages multiple client files, stores clients' passwords, and can upgrade client files in batch.

Creating an External Accountant User Type

When you work in a client's file, request that the client create a username specific for you and assign that username the External Accountant type, as shown in Figure 16.15. Benefits and controls available when working in a client's file as the External Accountant user type include the following:

- The capability to separate the changes you make in the data file from the changes your client makes.
- The option to use the Client Data Review feature efficiently. For more information, see "Client Data Review," p. 659.
- Access to all areas of QuickBooks, except creating new users or viewing sensitive customer credit card numbers.

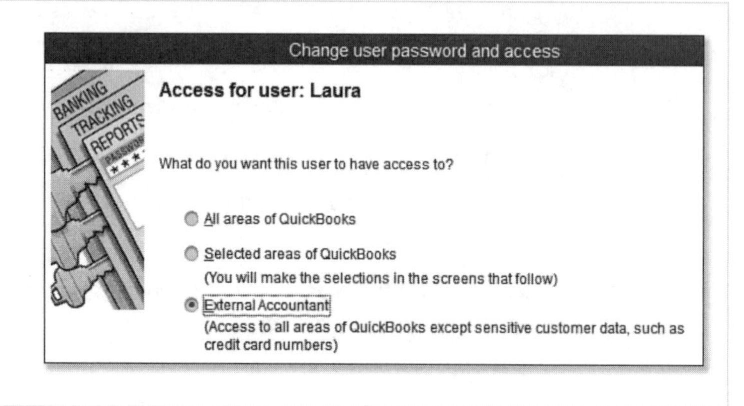

Figure 16.15
Ask your client to create an External Accountant user type for you as the company accountant.

To create this unique type of user, you must be logged in to the data file as the Admin user, and you or the client must create the new user *before* the client creates the Accountant's Copy file for your use.

You will then use this new login when you begin working with the client's data file.

Preparing Your Client for Data Exchange

As an accounting professional, you probably will be able to choose the method you and your client use to share the data. However, you might not be able to control the condition in which you receive the file. I am speaking specifically of accounting accuracy. Some accounting professionals don't worry much about this until they receive the data file; others might want their client to take certain steps to ensure the accuracy of the data before beginning the review. Encourage your clients to review specific chapters in this book to help better prepare their file for your review, making your review time more profitable!

Ask your clients to review the following in their files before sharing the data with you:

- Accuracy of bank balances
- The open customer invoices in Accounts Receivable
- The unpaid vendor bills in Accounts Payable

Other critical numbers to review are usually easier to reconcile by asking for documents from banks, such as a bank loan payoff statement or comparing the business financials with filed payroll returns.

After your client has reviewed the information and provided the documents you requested, you are ready to choose a method for sharing the data with your client.

Receiving an Accountant's Copy File

After reviewing the advantages or limitations of each file type in the section titled "QuickBooks File Types," you can see that the most effective method is the QuickBooks Accountant's Copy file feature. Using this file type, your clients can continue their day-to-day accounting tasks, and from the convenience of your office you can review and make needed changes to their data, later importing these changes into the files they have been using.

Discuss the following with your clients before they prepare an Accountant's Copy of their QuickBooks data:

- The Dividing Date selected. As their accounting professional, communicate what date this should be.
- How current are the bank reconciliations in the data file? In the Accountant's Copy, your bank reconciliation work is returned to the client only for statement dates on or before the dividing date. Additionally, the client can only mark as cleared items dated after the Dividing Date.
- Verify that the user settings in the data file include restrictions for editing or modifying transactions prior to the closing date. This step is optional, but when you are working in the Accountant's Copy file, you can send back the closing date with your changes.
- Instruct clients *not* to cancel or remove restrictions on the Accountant's Changes Pending file without first consulting you.
- Discuss the options for sending this file to you. Owners have these options:
  - Send you an encrypted copy of their data via Intuit's secure Accountant's Copy File Transfer Service, a free service to your client. Accounting professionals pay a nominal fee annually for an unlimited number of uses of the service (free if you are a QuickBooks ProAdvisor). Be sure your client knows the email address where you would like to be notified.
  - Attach the saved file to an email.
  - Copy it to a storage device, such as a USB drive or CD.

tip

If you are using QuickBooks Premier Accountant 2013 or QuickBooks Enterprise Solutions Accountant 13.0, you can convert your clients' QuickBooks 2012 or 2013 Accountant's Copy files (.QBX file extension); work with them in your Premier Accountant 2013 or Enterprise Solutions Accountant 13.0; and return them to your clients to import back into their QuickBooks 2012 or 2013 versions! This feature is available only with the Accountant's Copy file-sharing feature and does not apply to other file types.

QuickBooks Premier can open a Pro or Premier industry-specific edition, and when the files are returned to the clients, they will be able to work again with the files in their product edition.

QuickBooks Enterprise Solutions can open an Accountant's Copy File from a Pro, Premier, or Enterprise file and return the file back to the client for use in a Pro, Premier, or Enterprise product.

Method 1: Receiving Accountant's Copy from Client via Web

If your client chooses the Intuit's Accountant's Copy File Transfer secure server to get the data to you, you are notified at the email address the client provides in the transfer process, and you are directed to a secure site to download your client's file. This service offers your client simplicity in getting the data to you while aiding in the encrypted security of the transfer of sensitive data over the Internet. Downloading the client's file is only available for 30 days, so don't delay!

After downloading the file, follow the instructions in the next section for opening and converting the Transfer File (.QBX file extension) to an Accountant's Copy file (.QBA file extension).

Method 2: Receiving Accountant's Copy from Client via File

Have your client follow the steps to create and send you the Accountant's Copy file of the data as outlined in the section "Create an Accountant's Copy of Your Data."

To work with your client's Accountant's Copy (.QBX) file type your client sent you or that you downloaded, follow these steps:

1. From the menu bar, select **File**, **Accountant's Copy**, **Open & Convert Transfer File**. The Open and Convert Accountant's Copy Transfer File dialog box displays, as shown in Figure 16.16. This summary provides you with an overview of the workflow when using an Accountant's Copy of your client's data.

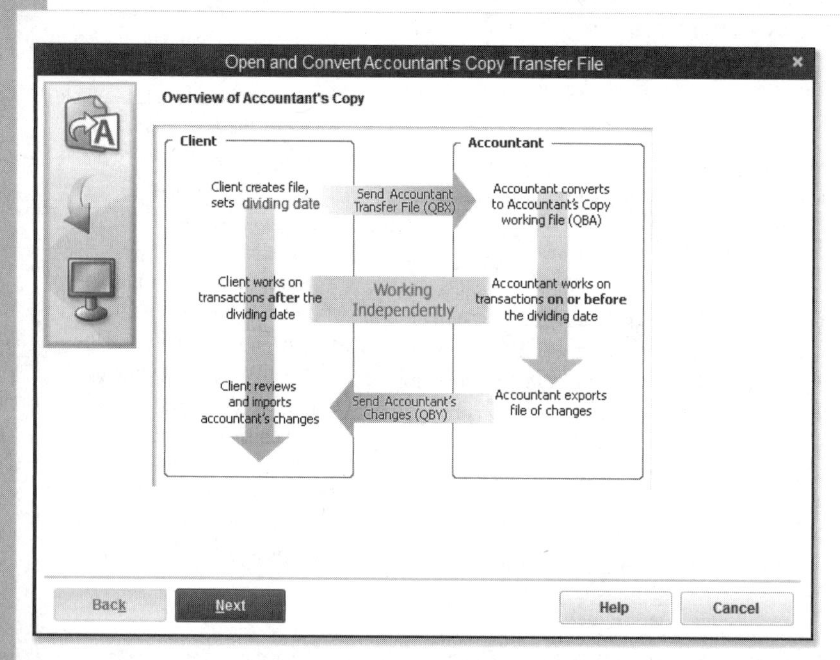

Figure 16.16 Overview of the Accountant's Copy workflow when working with your client's data.

2. Click Next. The Open Accountant's Copy Transfer File dialog box displays. This provides details on what tasks you can and cannot do when working with an Accountant's Copy. See Figure 16.17. Click Next.

3. Browse to the location where you stored your client's QuickBooks transfer file. Select the file and click Open. If displayed, click OK to the message that you have chosen an Accountant's Copy transfer file.

4. In the Save Accountant's Copy dialog box, select a location and name for the new file. I usually put the accounting period being reviewed in the name, such as <Company Name_YE_12_31_XX.QBA>. Click Save and QuickBooks shows a message that the conversion is taking place.

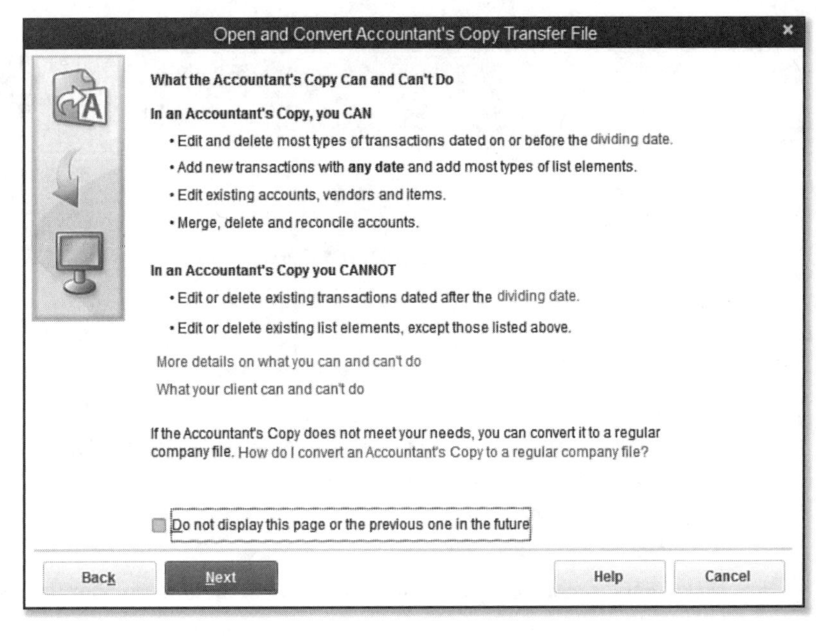

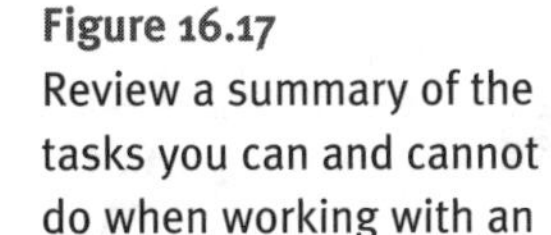

Figure 16.17
Review a summary of the tasks you can and cannot do when working with an Accountant's Copy file.

5. If you have not previously disabled this warning, you will see the message that indicates you are opening an Accountant's Copy, and it shows you the dividing date that was chosen by your client, as shown in Figure 16.18. Click OK to close.

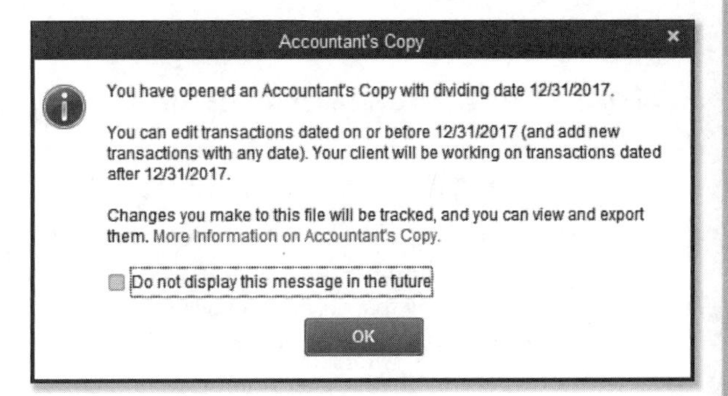

Figure 16.18
Notification that you are opening an Accountant's Copy file, providing details of the selected dividing date.

6. Your QuickBooks Accountant title bar will show that you are working with an Accountant's Copy and what the dividing date for that file is (see Figure 16.19).

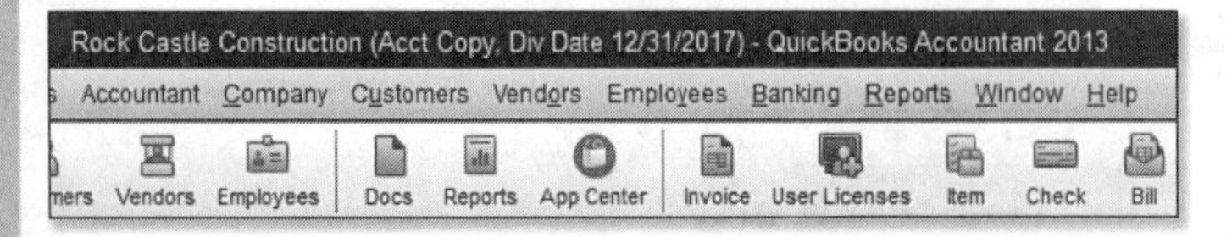

Figure 16.19
You can be certain you are working in the correct file by looking at the title bar of your Accountant's Copy .QBA file.

As the company's accounting professional, you can now review, add, and edit the data file and be secure that your clients cannot modify the balances prior to the dividing date that was set—all while the clients continue their day-to-day accounting tasks.

Reinstate Warnings

If you do not see some of the dialog boxes mentioned in this chapter, a user might have selected the Do Not Display This Message (or Page, and so on, depending on which dialog box is open), causing future users not to see these messages.

To turn these one-time messages back on, log in to the file as the user you want to reinstate the warnings for and follow these steps:

1. From the menu bar, select **Edit, Preferences.** In the dialog box that displays, select **General** on the left side.
2. Click the My Preferences tab.
3. Place a checkmark in the Bring Back All One-Time Messages box and click OK.

I often do this task in my client's file (prior to making an Accountant's Copy), especially if I have found errors that might have been prevented if the user had heeded the warning of a previously dismissed message.

What the Accountant Can Do

Recent releases of the QuickBooks software have greatly improved the capabilities you have with an Accountant's Copy of your client's data.

The restrictions invoked by the dividing date set by your client affect your ability to add or edit transactions. If these restrictions prevent you from completing your tasks, you can convert the Accountant's Copy to a working QuickBooks data file (.QBW file extension). However, your changes cannot be imported into your client's file.

For more information, see "Converting the Accountant's Copy to a Regular Company File," p. 603.

The Accountant's Copy provides a unique feature that will help you determine whether your changes will be sent back to the client's file. Any field that is colored beige will transfer back to your client. If the field is white, you might be able to modify it for your own purposes, but the change will not be sent back to your client.

For example, if part of your correction to your client's file was to modify an existing list item, only the fields identified in Figure 16.20 would be sent back to your client's data file. All other fields can be modified for your purposes, but would not transfer back to your client's file. If you and your client make changes to details on the same item, your changes will override the client's when the changes are imported.

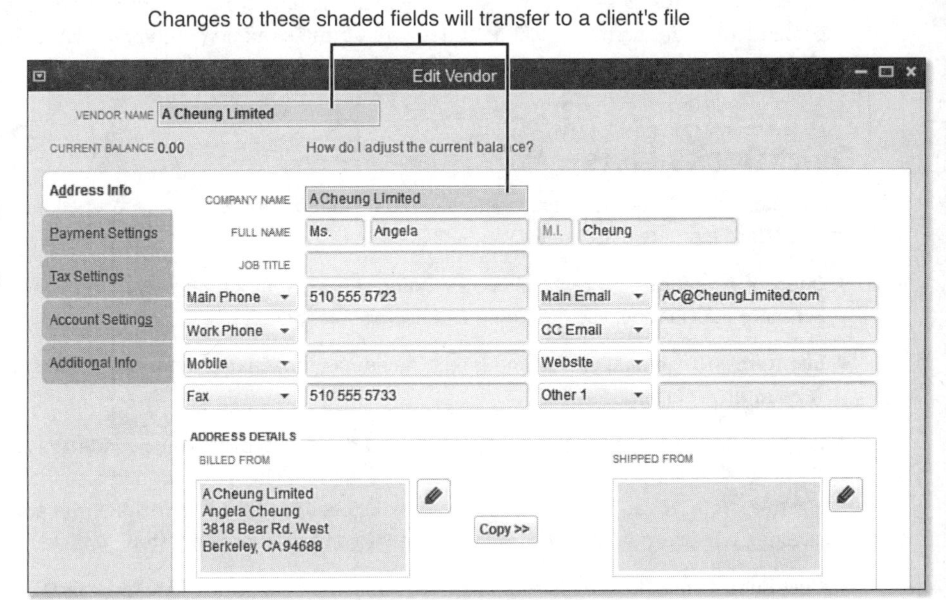

Figure 16.20 When adding or modifying details in the Accountant's Copy, any fields shaded beige (non-white) will be sent back to your client's file.

The following sections describe more specifically what you, the accountant, can do (with noted limitations) while working in the Accountant's Copy of your client's file.

Accounting Activities

Recent versions of QuickBooks enhance the accounting activities you can do with the client's data when sharing an Accountant's Copy file type:

- **Reconcile the bank statements for dates prior to the Dividing Date**—You can create and edit transactions necessary to perform the bank reconciliation. Additionally, your changes to a reconciled item will also be sent back to the client.

  Your client can reconcile the bank account when the statement date and all cleared transactions are dated after the selected dividing date. However, if you *also* reconcile this account, the client's bank reconciliation work will be rolled back to the transactions cleared status as of the time the Accountant's Copy was created.

- **Set 1099 account mappings**—You can assign the proper chart of account to the Federal Form 1099-MISC Income box.
- **Reconcile the bank statements for dates after the Dividing Date**—You can do this if it helps your review. However, these reconciliations will not be sent back to the client's data. Any transactions added will be sent back to the client.
- **Set tax-line mappings**—Used to assign the tax form line to a chart of accounts. Use this feature if you are integrating the QuickBooks data with Intuit's tax preparation software ProSeries or Lacerte.

QuickBooks Lists

Also enhanced with recent QuickBooks releases is your ability to manage your client's list items when performing data corrections:

- **Chart of Accounts**—No restrictions, including the capability to merge charts of account list items. For more information, see "Merging Duplicated Accounts," p. 127.
- **List Items**—In general you can add, edit, delete, and inactivate list items you create in the Accountant's Copy.
- **Items List**—For lists with items dated before the dividing date, you can edit the Item Name/Number, Subitem, Expense Account, Tax Code, and Income Account and also make the item inactive. Note: If you and your client both make changes to the same item, the accountant's changes will override that of the client when the changes are imported.
- **Customer, Other Names List**—Add a new Name, edit the Name field, or make the name inactive.
- **Vendor**—Add a new vendor or edit the Vendor Name, Tax ID, and identify vendor as an eligible to receive a 1099-MISC Income form at year-end. Additionally, you can assign up to three general ledger accounts on the Account Prefill tab. Your changes will override the same information in the client's file when imported.
- **Employee List**—Add a new employee or edit the Name and Social Security fields only.
- **Class List, Fixed Asset Item**—The capability to merge class list items. Additionally, you can add a new list item or edit the Name, assign Subclass of field, or make the class inactive.
- **Sales Tax Code**—Add a new sales tax code or edit the Name, Tax Agency, and make the item inactive. New sales tax items can be created, but the tax rate assigned will not transfer to the client's file.

Transactions

Generally, you can add any transaction type before or after the dividing date with the following limitations on editing, voiding, or deleting:

- **Bills and checks**—Add these types of transactions with dates before or after the dividing date. Edit, void, or delete is limited to those dated before the dividing date.

- **Vendor credits**—Add these types of transactions with dates before or after the dividing date. Edit, void, or delete is limited to those dated before the dividing date.
- **Item receipts**—Add or delete, but you will be unable to edit or void before and after the dividing date.
- **Bill payments by credit card**—Add or delete, but you will not be able to edit or void before and after the dividing date.
- **Inventory quantity/value adjustments**—Add or delete, but you will not be able to edit or void before and after the dividing date.
- **Customer payments**—Add or delete, but you will not be able to edit or void before and after the dividing date.

What the Accountant Cannot Do

Here is what you, the accountant, *cannot do* while working in the Accountant's Copy of your client's file:

- Add or modify payroll transactions.
- Add or modify nonposting transactions, such as estimates, sales orders, or purchase orders.
- Add or modify transfers of funds between accounts. Although you cannot use the transfer transaction, you can create the same effect on the accounts with a journal entry or deposit transaction.
- Add or modify the build assembly transaction.
- Add or modify the sales tax payment transaction.

Although you cannot make changes to these types of transactions in your client's file with an Accountant's Copy file type, you can conveniently make these changes in the client's file using remote access via tools such as Webex, LogMeIn, GoToMyPC, or others.

Returning the Accountant's Copy Change File to the Client

One of the most important features of using the Accountant's Copy to share your clients' data is that when your changes are complete, you can send back updated files for your clients to import into their files.

 **note**

If you are working with a client's Accountant's Copy file created from a QuickBooks 2012 version, you can open the file with your QuickBooks Accountant 2013 and return the data to the client in the original QuickBooks 2012 version.

Set a Closing Date

When your clients import the changes you have made to the Accountant's Copy of their files, the dividing date restrictions are removed. If you do not want a client to add or edit transactions prior to the dividing date, make sure you also set a closing date prior to exporting the data for the client.

To set a closing date while working in the Accountant's Copy of your client's data, follow these steps:

1. Log in to the client's Accountant's Copy file. From the menu bar, select **Company**, **Set Closing Date**.
2. The Company Preference dialog box displays. Click the Set Date/Password button. The Set Closing Date and Password dialog box displays.
3. Enter an optional password and a closing date—typically the same date that was used for the dividing date.
4. Click OK to accept the closing date and optional closing date password.

note

If you do not set a closing date as part of your changes, when the client incorporates the changes file, a message will display asking if the client wants to set a closing date.

The closing date will transfer back to the client's file, and the client will not be asked to set the closing date. The fact that a closing date was set is included in the information the client previews before incorporating the accountant's changes.

If you want your client to have the ability to modify your changes, you might not need to set a closing date for the file.

Review the details of setting a closing date and reviewing each employee's access rights to changing transactions prior to the closing date.

For more information, see "Setting Employee Security," p. 588.

Method 1: Send Changes to Client via Web

The Send Changes method is the simplest for your client to use to import. This service is included with a QuickBooks ProAdvisor membership or is available for a nominal annual fee. No fee is charged to the client to accept this file from you.

To return the corrected file to your client after you make all your changes, follow these steps:

1. From the menu bar, select **File**, **Accountant's Copy**, **View/Export Changes for Client**. The View/Export Changes for Client dialog box displays as shown in Figure 16.21.
2. Review your changes and add an optional note for your client.
3. If you need to make additional changes or edit the changes you have made to the file, click the X in the top-right corner.
4. If your changes are complete, click Send Changes to Client.
5. Enter your client's email address, your name, and your email address.
6. Click Send.

note

If you have already exported these changes for the client, a message will display informing you that if your client has already imported the previously exported changes file, the client will not be able to import these changes. Click OK if you still want to export the changes.

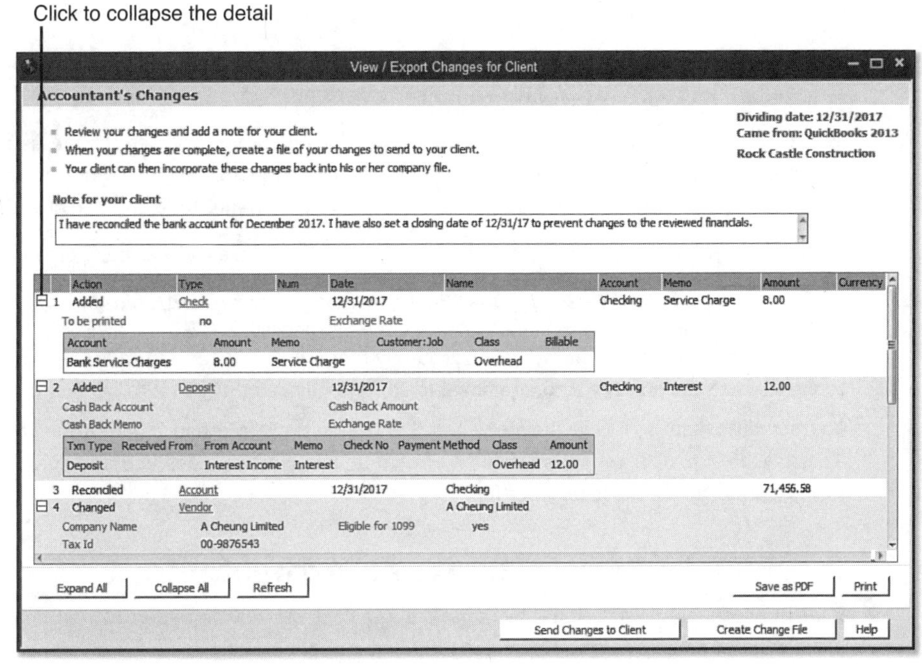

Figure 16.21 The View/Export Changes for Client dialog box, where you can review your changes and include a note for your client.

Intuit will send you an email notifying you that the file was uploaded to the Intuit Accountant's Copy File Transfer secure server. Your client will also receive an email notification that the file is available for downloading for 30 days. Encourage your client to follow the instructions in the email to easily incorporate your changes into the data file.

Method 2: Send Changes to Client via File

You might also choose to send the Changes File to the client via a file you can attach to an email or store on a flash drive or other storage device. This method requires more effort on the part of your customers. They must access the file, save it to their computer, and then import the changes into QuickBooks. Consider using the first method of sending the file via the Web, which does not require as many steps.

To create the Changes File (.QBY extension) to give to your client, follow these steps:

1. From the menu bar, select **File**, **Accountant's Copy**, **View/Export Changes for Client**. The View/Export Changes for Client dialog box displays (refer to Figure 16.21).

2. Review your changes and optionally add a note for your client.

3. If you need to make additional changes or edit the changes you have made to the file, click the X in the top-right corner.

4. If your changes are complete, click Create Change File. The Save Accountant Changes File to dialog box displays.
5. Browse to the location where you want to save the file and optionally edit the filename to be saved. QuickBooks creates a file with .QBY extension.
6. If you have already exported these changes for the client, you will see the message informing you that if your client has already imported the previously exported changes file, the client will not be able to import these changes. Click OK if you still want to export the changes.
7. Click Save. A message displays, letting you know the file was successfully created.
8. Click OK to close the message. QuickBooks returns you to the .QBA file.

To complete the process, simply give this newly created .QBY (Accountant's Copy import file) back to the client. You can copy it to a removable storage device or attach it to an email.

Instruct your client to follow the steps listed in the section, "Method 2: Importing Changes from the Transfer File," p. 586. Your client will be able to review your changes in detail before accepting or incorporating the changes into her file.

QuickBooks Remote Access for Accountants

If, as the accountant, you would like to take more control over the import of your changes into your client's file as well as setting the closing date, you might want to consider using a remote access program to log in to your client's file through the Internet.

QuickBooks partners with WebEx to bring you a solution that makes it easy to work remotely in your file or your clients' files. You can use this option if you need to make data changes that are not allowed in an Accountant's Copy—for example, making changes to payroll transactions. You can also use this tool to perform the import of your changes into your client's data file.

I find working in the remote environment a perfect choice for simplifying the entire process for clients. For more information, select **Accountant**, **Remote Access** from the menu bar in QuickBooks Accountant or QuickBooks Enterprise Accountant.

What to Request from the Client When the Import Is Complete

Clients can import your changes with simple, easy-to-follow instructions if you used the Send Changes to Client method. However, you might want to request a few items from the client after the import to be sure the process was completed successfully:

- **Trial Balance**—You should review the Trial Balance report as of the dividing date to compare with the same information from your copy of the client's file. From the menu bar, select **Reports**, **Accountant**, **Trial Balance**. Request that clients prepare the report in accrual or cash basis. They may have one or the other as the default setup in their file.
- **Closing Date**—If you want to verify that the closing date was incorporated with your changes, instruct your client to select **Company**, **Set Closing Date** from the menu bar. Doing so opens the Company Preference tab for Accounting Preferences. Have your client verify the closing date (or any date at all). Refer to Figure 16.10.

- **User Security Rights**—Verify with your client the access rights each employee has for changing transactions dated prior to the closing date. Instruct your client to select **Company**, **Set Up Users and Passwords**, **Set Up Users** from the menu bar. In the User List dialog box that opens, select the employee and the View User tab on the right. A "Y" in the Changing Closed Transactions permission allows that user to add or edit transactions dated prior to the closing date. If a closing date password was set, the user will have to type that password first. A creative password that I have used is "call laura," prompting the client to call me first before making the change!

Converting the Accountant's Copy to a Regular Company File

What can you do if, after beginning to work in the Accountant's Copy, you determine some of the changes that need to be made cannot be accommodated with this file type? You can convert the client's Accountant's Copy (.QBX) file type to a regular QuickBooks (.QBW) file type following these steps.

From the menu bar, select **File**, **Accountant's Copy**, **Convert Accountant's Copy to Company File/QBW**. A message displays, recommending that you contact your client to discuss this change.

You have to make the following decisions:

- Have the client manually repeat your changes in the client's file.
- If the client is going to use your file, the client must stop working in the file she has.

QuickBooks 2013 offers accountants more flexibility than in prior versions in how you choose to share and work in your client's data. These improvements help make the workflow for you and your client more efficient, making your accounting business more profitable.

Other Methods of Sharing Data

With QuickBooks Accountant 2013, you have flexibility in choosing what method of file sharing works best for you and your client. When considering a method, your client needs to continue daily accounting tasks while allowing you to review the data and create journal entries.

Send General Journal Entries

The Send General Journal Entries is new for QuickBooks 2013 and allows your accountant to share changes to your date easily with an email attachment.

The best practice when using this new feature would be to have the business owner send the accountant either a copy of the working file (.QBW), a backup (.QBB), or a portable company file (.QBM). Business owners can continue to work in their files while that accountant reviews the copy at his office. This avoids the restrictions imposed when sharing an Accountant's Copy file.

note

To use the Send General Journal Entries method, the business owner must be using a Windows version of QuickBooks 2013, and the accountant must be using QuickBooks Accountant 2013 or QuickBooks Enterprise Accountant 13.0.

The accountant's journal entries are emailed directly from QuickBooks, with no messy file transfers to worry about. Clients simply click the attachment to import the entries automatically into their file.

The best part about this new feature is that there are no new "tools" to learn for the accountant or your client. For the accountant, just follow these simple steps:

1. For the accounting professional, open or restore the file you have received from the client.
2. From the menu bar, select **Company**, **Make General Journal Entries**. Create the Journal Entry as you normally would. Click Save on the Main tab of the ribbon toolbar.
3. From the displayed Make General Journal Entries transaction, on the Main tab of the ribbon toolbar, click Send GJEs icon. See Figure 16.22.

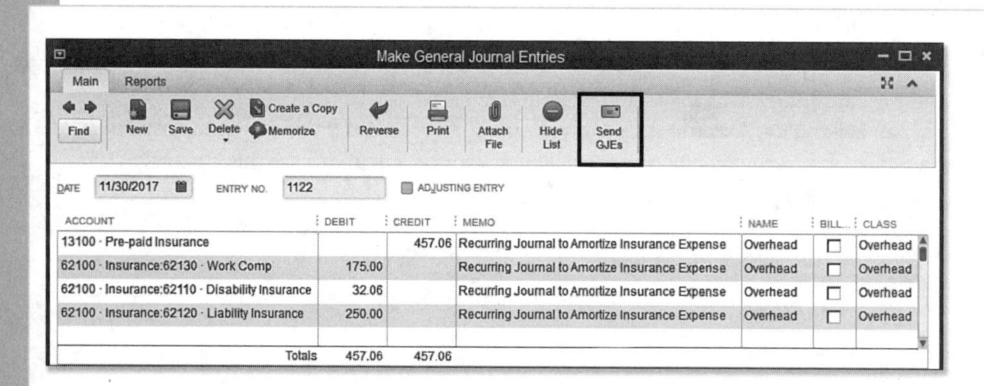

Figure 16.22 Click the Send GJEs icon to send to your client.

4. The Send General Journal Entries dialog box displays. Select a single journal entry or multiple journal entries. If needed, use the Dates or From and To fields to filter the displayed journal entries. See Figure 16.23.
5. Place a check in the box in front of each journal entry you want to send to the client. (Optional) Click Select All or Deselect All.
6. Click the Email as Attachment button. QuickBooks utilizes the email program specified within your QuickBooks preferences. In the example in Figure 16.24, an Outlook email is created with instructions for your client. The journal entries are attached automatically.

QuickBooks creates a ready-made email communication complete with instructions and attaches the journal entry or entries. You do not need to browse to find and attach the entries.

The business owner receives the email and clicks the attachment to add to the business owner's file.

Recommend this method to your accountant, if the accountant has been sending a list of journal entries for you to enter manually.

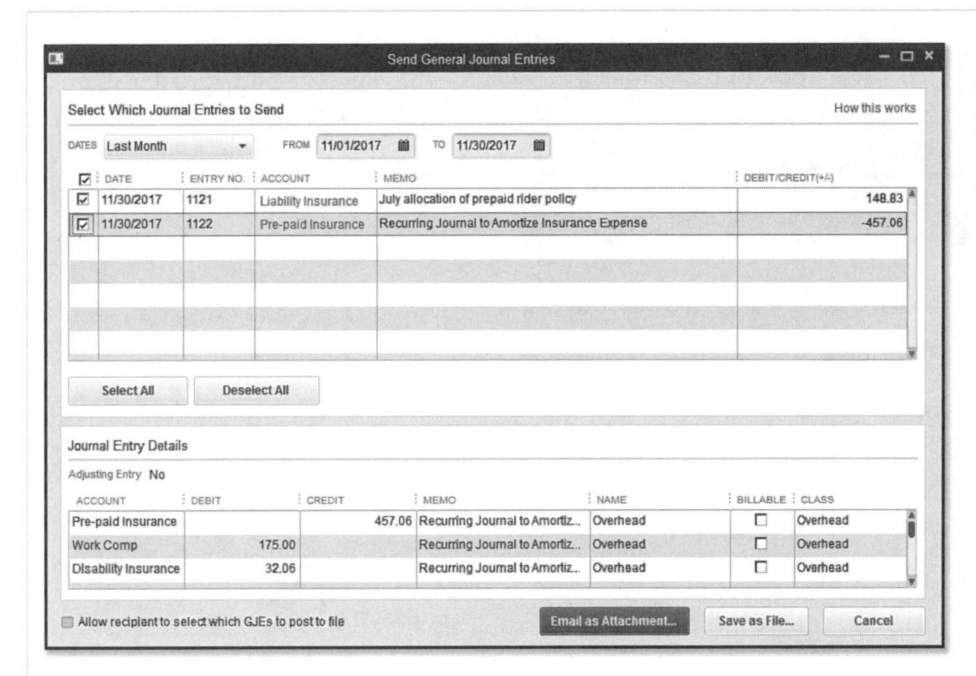

Figure 16.23
Select a single journal entry or multiple entries.

caution

Care should be taken not to click more than once on the attachment. QuickBooks allows the import of the attachment more than once, misstating the financials from what the accountant provided. If this should happen to you, prepare a report that shows the duplication and click one of the duplicated entries. From the Edit menu, select **Void**.

If a new general ledger account (chart of account), vendor, customer, or other list item is included in the journal entry, this new list item will be created in the business owner's file automatically.

If you have more than one QuickBooks company file, it works best to have that company file open before clicking the attachment. If you have the wrong file open, QuickBooks provides a warning message but will not prevent you from incorporating the changes into the wrong file.

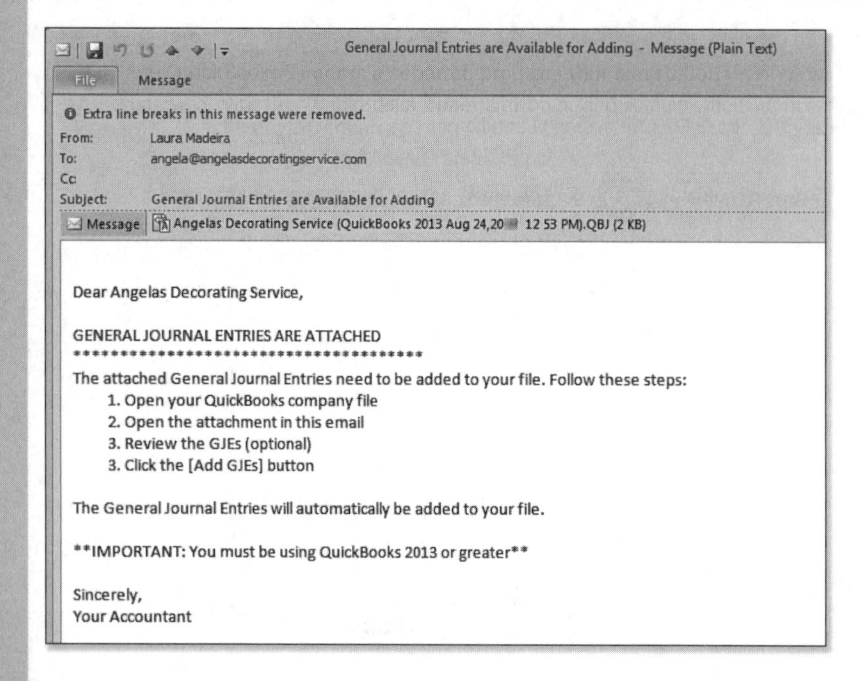

Figure 16.24
Click the attachment to add to the currently open QuickBooks file.

Batch Enter Transactions

The new batch transaction entry feature offers accounting professionals a way to streamline data entry tasks. This feature is included only with QuickBooks Professional Bookkeeper 2013, QuickBooks Accountant 2013, and QuickBooks Enterprise Solutions Accountant 13.0.

Use Batch Enter Transactions for adding the following to a QuickBooks data file:

- Checks
- Deposits
- Credit Card Charges or Credits

caution

The batch transaction entry feature *does not* allow the accountant to work in the file at the same time the client is working in the file at her office. If you choose to offer this service, make sure that only one of you (the business owner or accountant) is working in the file.

Typically, accounting professionals offer services helping clients enter data into QuickBooks. With the Batch Enter Transactions feature you can do the following:

- Enter transactions in batches on a screen designed for power data entry.
- Paste 1,000+ transactions from Excel and save all at once.
- Enter after-the-fact transactions easily into a customizable data entry grid.
- Configure the batch entry screen, including specifying data fields and column order.

Accounting professionals, follow these steps to use this helpful feature:

1. From the menu bar, select **Accountant**, **Batch Enter Transactions**. A dialog box of the same name displays.
2. From the Transaction Type drop-down menu, select **Checks**, **Deposits**, **Credit Card Charges & Credits**. I'll demonstrate entering checks, but the procedure is similar for other permitted transaction types.
3. Select the appropriate Bank Account or Credit Card account.

> **tip**
>
> If your transactions are in Excel, customize the columns of the Batch Enter Transactions dialog box to match those of your Excel spreadsheet. You can then copy the transaction data from Excel and paste it into the Batch Entry screen in QuickBooks.

4. Click the Customize Columns button as shown in Figure 16.25.
   You can add or remove data fields and rearrange the order of the fields. This is particularly useful if you are using Excel's copy and paste functionality.

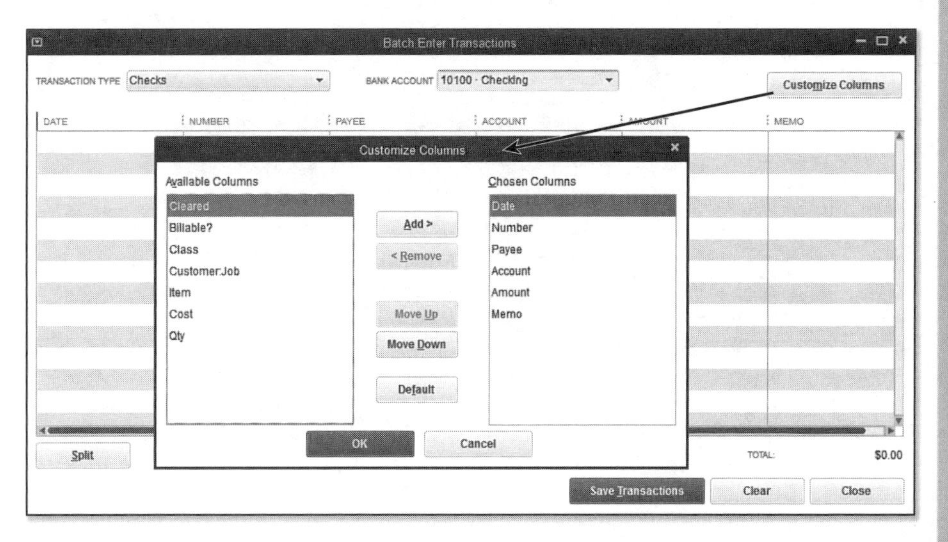

Figure 16.25 Customize the columns to aid in data entry or to match the Excel worksheet you are copying from.

5. Add transactions to the Batch Enter Transactions dialog box by manually entering them or from an Excel worksheet (see Figure 16.26) using the Windows copy and paste functionality.

> **caution**
>
> For best results, avoid blank fields when copying and pasting from an Excel file.
>
> If you choose to add transactions from an Excel worksheet, if any row does not have data, QuickBooks by default will copy the data from the cell adjacent to the left of the cell without data. This data will be displayed in red and should be reviewed and possibly corrected before saving the new transactions. See Figure 16.27.

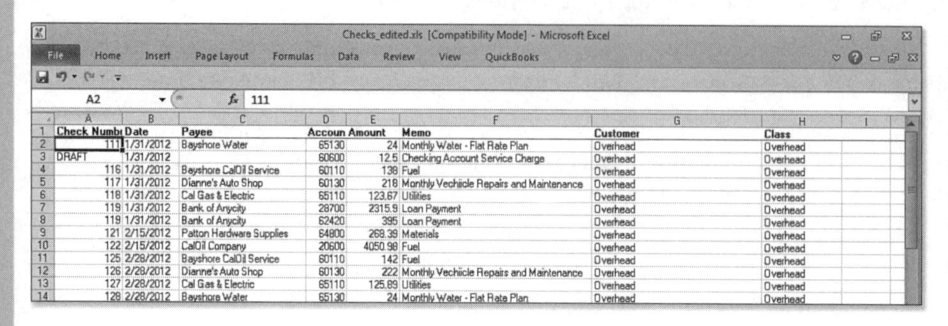

Figure 16.26 Copy and paste transactions from Excel to add to the Batch Enter Transactions dialog box.

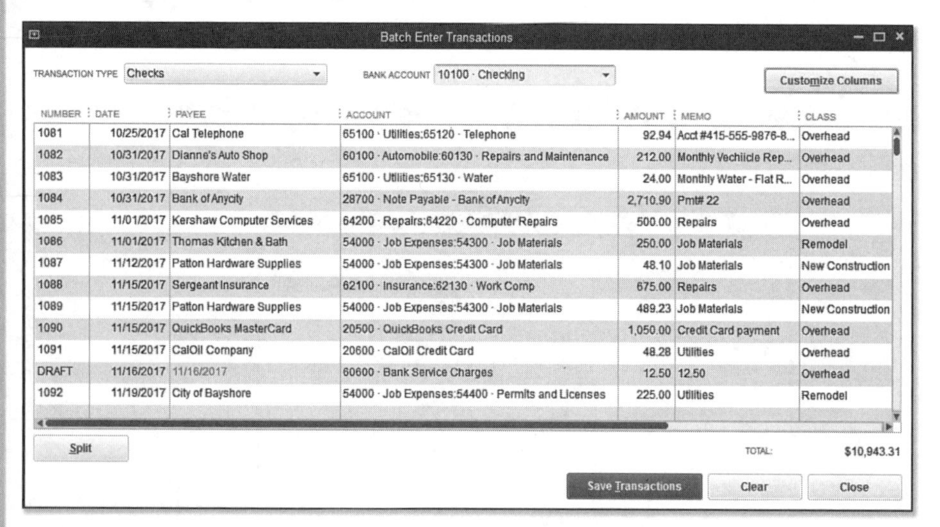

Figure 16.27 When adding data from an Excel spreadsheet, blank fields will have the adjacent cells' data copied into them and the text will be colored red.

This feature supports transaction entry using the Expense tab details (as shown in these figures) and also supports the Item tab details. However, you can use only one or the other in the same Batch Enter Transactions session.

In effect, this feature allows accounting professionals to automate the process of entering large amounts of data into a client's QuickBooks data file.

17

MANAGING YOUR QUICKBOOKS DATABASE

This reference guide would be incomplete without a detailed discussion of the QuickBooks database and managing it. This chapter provides both the business owner and computer professional guidelines for managing the QuickBooks database and any issues that can arise.

The QuickBooks Database

If you are the typical QuickBooks user, you purchased the software to track the income and expenses of your business. By selecting software for this task, you have advanced from a manual recordkeeping system into the world of database technology.

A database is an automated version of a big file room, with information of different types stored in different cabinets, drawers, and files. Years ago, companies employed file clerks to keep track of the company's paperwork. QuickBooks uses a Database Server to perform similar tasks to a file clerk; organizing and storing the data you create.

Depending on the number of licenses you purchased, you can choose to install the software as a single user application or install it in a network environment for use by multiple users (see Figure 17.1).

Based on your installation selection, QuickBooks either installs the personal Database Server or the network Database Server to control the flow of data from the QuickBooks application to your QuickBooks Company file. During the install, the computer operating system creates a Windows user account for this server in order to assign administrative-level access rights to the computer's resources and the QuickBooks files. When you view your list of users for your computer, included will be QBDataServiceUserxx (where xx defaults to 23 for all QuickBooks 2013 versions). During installation, the QuickBooks Database Server Manager is also installed. This utility is discussed later in this chapter.

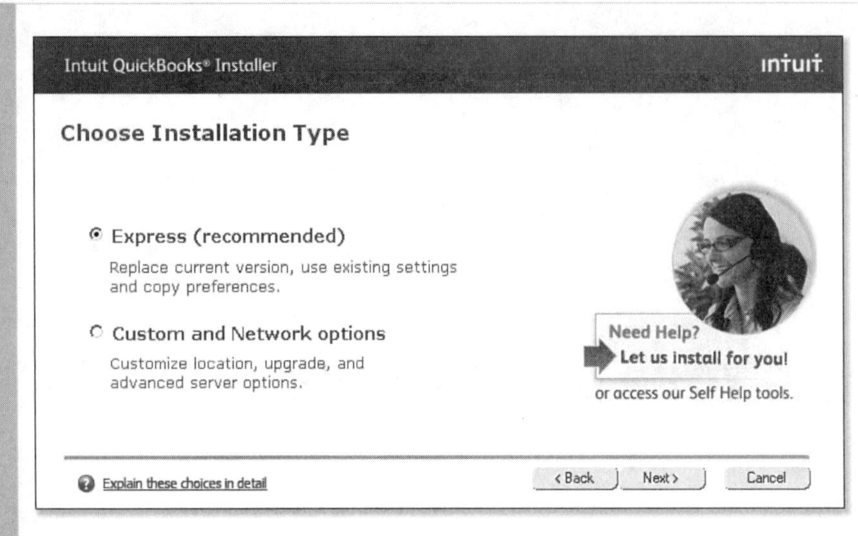

Figure 17.1
QuickBooks guides you through the installation of the software.

System Requirements

Verify that your computer and network hardware meets the minimum requirements for QuickBooks. This list is applicable to QuickBooks 2013 versions, but you might want to check the requirements for your specific version.

caution

Do not delete the QBDataServiceUser23 (or whatever version you are running) from the User's applet within the Control Panel.

Following are supported operating systems for QuickBooks for Windows products:

- Windows 8, either 32-bit or 64-bit versions (note must be on R4 or newer maintenance patch)
- Windows 7, either 32-bit or 64-bit versions
- Windows Vista, Service Pack 1 including either 32-bit or updated LM64-bit version
- Windows XP, Service Pack 3 and later

Computer processor, memory, and disk space requirements are the following:

- Minimum of a 2.0GHz processor; 2.4GHz is recommended.
- Minimum of 1GB of RAM for single-user configurations, 2GB of RAM recommended for multiple users.
- Minimum of 2GB of RAM for multiuser configurations; 4GB (or more) is recommended.
- Minimum of 2.5GB of disk space for the application.
- 250MB for Microsoft .NET 4.0 Runtime. Additional space is required for your QuickBooks data files.

Additional hardware, software, and Internet connectivity requirements include the following:

- Hardware
  - 4×4 CD-ROM drive required for CD installations
  - 1024×768 or higher screen resolution, 16-bit or higher color
- Multiuser—Microsoft Windows XP (SP3), Vista (SP1 with UAC on), Windows 8 (with UAC on), Windows 7 (with UAC on), Windows Server 2003 (SP2), Windows Server 2008, Small Business Server 2008
- Internet connectivity
  - Internet access with at least 56Kbps connection speed
  - Cable or DSL modem is highly recommended over dial-up service
  - Internet Explorer 7, 8, or 9
- Minimum browser requirement—Internet Explorer 7, 8, or 9
- Software for Integration Capabilities
  - Microsoft Word and Excel integration requires Word and Excel 2003, 2007, or 2010 (including 64-bit).
  - Synchronization with Outlook requires QuickBooks Contact Sync for Outlook 2003, 2007, and 2010 (including 64-bit) (downloadable for free at www.quickbooks.com/contact_sync).
- To learn more about synchronization with Outlook, see "Using Other Planning and Management Tools," p. 639.
  - Email Estimates, Invoices, and other forms with Windows Outlook, Outlook Express, and Mozilla Thunderbird, as well as web mail services such as Gmail, Yahoo! Mail, and Hotmail.
  - Compatible with QuickBooks Point of Sale version 8.0 and later
- Import data from Excel and other programs
  - Transfer data from Peachtree 2008–2011; Microsoft SBA 2006; and Microsoft Office Accounting 2007–2009 using the free tool available at http://quickbooks.intuit.com
  - Transfer data directly from Quicken 2011 through current version, QuickBooks 4.0 through current version, and Microsoft Excel 2000–2010.

Antivirus and firewall compatibility considerations include the following:

- Antivirus products (with/without firewalls) software compatibility
  - Symantec/Norton Antivirus, Internet Security, Norton 360
  - McAfee Internet Security, Total Protection, Antivirus Plus

- Trend Micro Titanium or Trend Micro Worry-Free Business Security
- ZoneAlarm

- Windows firewall compatibility
  - Windows 8 firewall (all versions)
  - Windows 7 firewall (all versions)
  - Windows Vista firewall (all versions)
  - XP firewall (all versions)

Express Installation of QuickBooks

Select the **Express** option (as shown in Figure 17.1) when you need to use QuickBooks from a single computer and you want to replace your original version of the software with the new software. QuickBooks Pro and Premier installs the application and database manager in the `C:\Program Files\Intuit\QuickBooks 2013` folder. QuickBooks Enterprise Solutions defaults to `C:\Program Files\Intuit\QuickBooks Enterprise Solutions 13.0` folder.

By default, QuickBooks uses the following locations for storing your data file, although you can select a different directory if desired:

- **Windows 8**—`C:\Users\Public\Documents\Intuit\QuickBooks\Company Files`
- **Windows 7**—`C:\Users\Public\Public Documents\Intuit\QuickBooks\Company Files`
- **Windows XP**—`C:\Documents and Settings\All Users\Documents\Intuit\QuickBooks\Company Files`
- **Windows Vista**—`C:\Users\Public\Public Documents\Intuit\QuickBooks\Company Files`

QuickBooks prompts you to enter the license and product numbers; these numbers are provided on a bright yellow sticker on the QuickBooks CD sleeve, or if you have downloaded the software, you will receive an email with the license details. Follow the remaining instructions for installing the QuickBooks software.

Installing QuickBooks for Multiuser Mode

QuickBooks 2013 streamlines the process of installing QuickBooks for multiuser simultaneous access to your company data. As discussed in the introduction, when QuickBooks is going to be used in a multiuser configuration there must be one computer on your network that will act as the QuickBooks Server to host your data files and the QuickBooks Database Server.

It is not necessary to use an actual computer running Windows Server software as your QuickBooks host because QuickBooks runs equally well on peer-to-peer and client/server domain networks. When you install QuickBooks on a network, you should always perform the installation on the computer that will function as the server before installing QuickBooks on any workstations.

During installation, QuickBooks prompts you to select the installation type, as shown in Figure 17.1. Select **Custom and Network Option** for all network installations, including server (host) and workstations (clients). Follow the remaining prompts to select the installation options that best fit your network requirements for the specific computer you are installing. The choices include

- **I'll Be Using QuickBooks on This Computer—**Use this if you are installing QuickBooks on a computer that will access only the Company files across the network.
- **I'll Be Using QuickBooks on This Computer, AND I'll Be Storing Our Company File Here So It Can Be Shared Over Our Network—**You will possibly run QuickBooks from this machine and have it act as your QuickBooks Server, which hosts your company files.
- **I Will NOT be Using QuickBooks on This Computer...—**You can elect to install only the QuickBooks Database Server and QuickBooks Database Server Manager Utility on the hosting computer. This install does not require a license.

You will then be prompted to enter your license and product numbers. Follow all additional prompts to complete the install process.

When all your settings are correct for your network, click Install from the Ready to Install dialog box. As with the Express install, QuickBooks displays a progress bar indicating the status of the install process. The Congratulations dialog box displays when the installation is finalized. You can either launch QuickBooks to begin creating a new file or open an existing file or a practice file.

tip

Using the I'll Be Using QuickBooks on This Computer, AND I'll Be Storing Our Company File Here... option is the preferred server option, even if QuickBooks will not routinely be used on this machine. Selecting this option allows the QuickBooks application to be opened on the server to perform certain file-related functions, including backup activities.

caution

If you selected the I Will NOT be Using QuickBooks... option, you should also review the section "The QuickBooks Database Server Manager" in this chapter.

For more information, see "Getting Started with QuickBooks," p. 31.

The QuickBooks Database Server Manager

Automatically installed is the QuickBooks Database Server Manager Utility, if you selected the option I Will NOT Be Using QuickBooks on This Computer. I Will Be Storing Our Company File Here So It Can Be Shared Over Our Network (A License Is Not Required For This Option). This utility launches automatically after the installation is complete.

Changing to Multiuser Access

If you initially installed QuickBooks for single-user access and want to change it to multiuser access, follow these steps to enable the Database Server Manager utility:

1. From the menu bar, select **File**, **Utilities**, **Host Multiuser Access**.
2. Click Yes to the Start Hosting Multiuser Access message that displays.

note

The QuickBooks Database Server Manager is needed only if you are using QuickBooks in multiuser mode.

3. Click Yes to the Company file must be closed. If prompted, click Continue to allow Windows administrator permissions and Yes to allowing the changes to be made to your computer.

4. Read the information on the Multiuser Setup Information message that displays. Click OK to close.

QuickBooks installs the network database server as a Windows service/process, and it is configured to run under the QBDataServiceUser23 Windows user account. (This is the user account assigned to QuickBooks 2013.)

The QuickBooks Database Server Manager utility provides users access to configure the database server. It is critical that this utility run and be properly configured to permit multiuser simultaneous access to your QuickBooks Company data files.

Opening the QuickBooks Data Server Manager

Your computer might display the utility in your system tray in the lower right of your computer taskbar. If not, you can open the QuickBooks Data Server Manager by following these steps:

1. From the Windows Orb or Windows Start button (lower-left corner of Windows taskbar), click All Programs.

2. Scroll to find and select the QuickBooks folder.

3. Click the QuickBooks Database Server Manager. If prompted, click Yes to the User Account Control Message. The Database Server Manager is launched, as shown in Figure 17.2. The data path displayed in this figure might differ from your own data path.

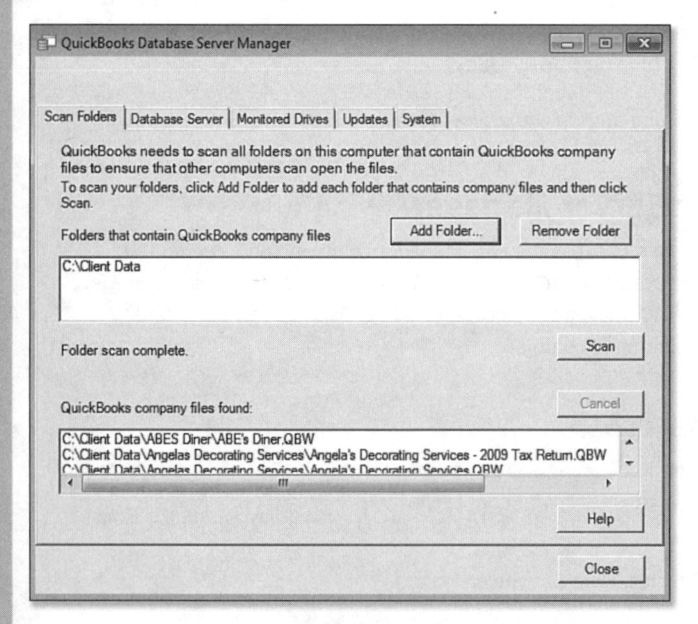

Figure 17.2
The Database Server Manager is used to configure proper multiuser hosting.

The Scan Folders tab consists of two main panels, each performing critical functions. The first is to identify the various windows folders on the QuickBooks server computer that contain QuickBooks data files. To add folders, click the Add Folder button and use the Windows directory service display to locate all folders appropriate for your network configuration.

When all folders containing QuickBooks data files are displayed in the top panel, perform a scan of those folders to locate your QuickBooks files; these files will then appear in the lower panel. A result of this scanning process, the Database Server creates a *.QBW.ND file for every QuickBooks Company file. This Network Description file contains critical information about the Database Server's location on your network, including the server name and IP address. When a QuickBooks workstation accesses the Company file, the companion *QBW.ND file advises QuickBooks where and how to find the Database Server.

The QuickBooks Administrator should also configure the Monitored Drives tab, selecting the computer disk drive(s) containing the folders where QuickBooks Company files are located. The utility then monitors these drives to identify new *.QBW or *.QBA files that might be added to those drives and directories.

For more information about these named QuickBooks file types, see "Choosing a Method to Share Data," p. 573.

The Database Server tab displays information about the Database Server, the current QuickBooks Company file(s) in use, and the name of the user logged in. The Updates tab provides information about the current version of the QuickBooks Database Server; it is essential the Database Server version always match the QuickBooks version in use.

For QuickBooks to operate properly, you should never close the QuickBooks Database Server Manager unless you must also shut down the server for other reasons. A best practice is to minimize the utility instead.

tip

If your QuickBooks network suddenly starts suffering from an inability to connect one or more workstations in multiuser mode to your Company file, you should promptly check to ensure that the QuickBooks Database Server Manager is running and still configured on the hosting computer.

Some Windows updates require a reboot of the computer. The QuickBooks Database Server Manager Service might have been stopped in the process. Contact your IT professional to restart the process. You might also need to perform the Scan function again to locate the data files on your computer.

Windows Permissions Required for QuickBooks

Simply installing QuickBooks for single-user or multiuser configuration does not guarantee that it will work properly. Certain Windows user permissions must be established to ensure proper access. All QuickBooks users must have full control, including read/write privileges for any directory from which Company data files will be accessed.

Setting Permissions in Windows 7 or Windows Vista

To properly configure Windows 7 or Windows Vista user permissions, follow these steps:

1. Using Windows Explorer, locate the folder containing your QuickBooks Company files.

2. Right-click the folder and select **Properties**.
3. Click the **Sharing** tab, and then click the **Share** button.
4. In the File Sharing window, use the drop-down list to select each user needing access to QuickBooks, and then click Add.
5. In the Permission Level column, click the Read drop-down list and select **Read/Write**.
6. Click the Share button to close the File Sharing window, and then click the Security tab in the Properties window.
7. Click the Edit button for the Group or usernames section.
8. Select the **QBDataServiceUser23 User.**
9. In the Permissions for QBDataServiceUser23, select the **Full Control** checkbox in the Allow column, and click OK.
10. Click Close.

note

As of the writing of this book, Windows 8 was just released. The instructions provided here are for Windows 7 or Vista. The steps could vary with Windows 8.

Setting Permissions in Windows XP Professional

To properly configure Windows XP Professional user permissions, follow these steps:

1. Using Windows Explorer, locate the folder containing your QuickBooks Company files.
2. Right-click the folder and select **Properties.**
3. Click Sharing, Share This Folder option.
4. Click the Permissions button.
5. In the Group or usernames section, select **Everyone.**
6. In the Permissions for Everyone section, select the **Full Control** checkbox in the Allow column.

Using the QuickBooks Connection Diagnostic Tool

The QuickBooks Connection Diagnostic Tool assists users in diagnosing and correcting various problems preventing proper connections between the QuickBooks application, the Database Manager, and QuickBooks Company files. This tool can troubleshoot the most common networking and multiuser errors (including H-series or 6000-series errors) that occur when trying to open a Company file.

To download this free tool, visit the QuickBooks support website http://support.quickbooks.intuit.com and search for Connection Diagnostic Tool. Click the supplied link for the tool.

After it is downloaded, click the .exe file and follow the install prompts. To launch the tool (see Figure 17.3), follow these steps:

1. Click the QuickBooks Connection icon from your desktop.

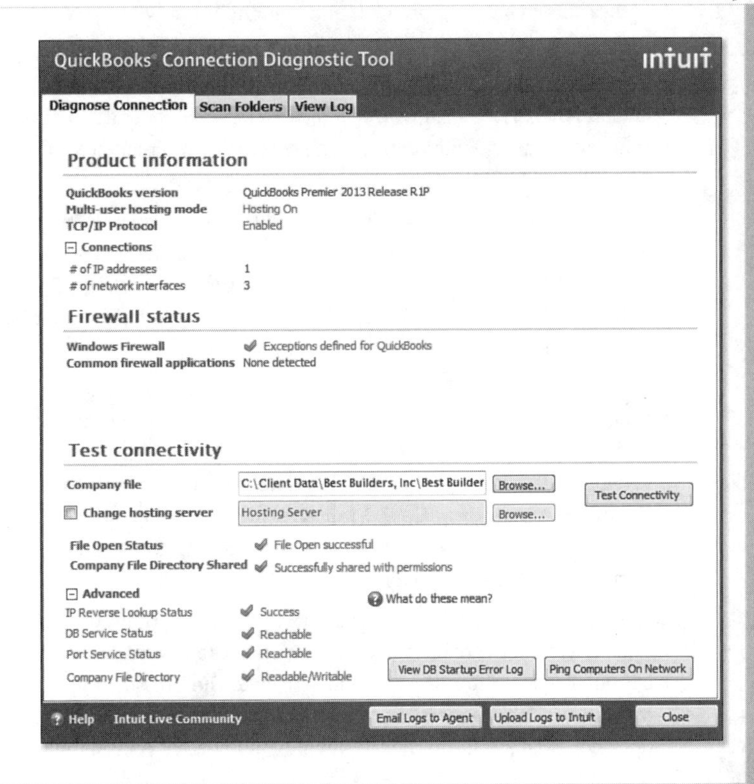

Figure 17.3
The QuickBooks Connection Diagnostic Tool helps you investigate network connection issues.

2. Click OK, if an information message displays, and click Yes to the User Account Control message.
3. Browse to the location of your QuickBooks file and click the Test Connectivity button. QuickBooks will perform certain diagnostics. If any error messages display, click the appropriate links for more information or for help.

Keeping Your Software Current

Intuit has a service discontinuation policy on its software. Live technical support and add-on business services such as payroll, credit card processing, QuickBooks Email, and online banking will be discontinued for versions three years or older.

Typically, you need to upgrade your software by May 31 for each year for versions of QuickBooks three years or older to retain these active services.

Upgrading Your QuickBooks Version

To keep your QuickBooks software supported, you need to upgrade at least every three years, or if you are like me, you may want to upgrade each year to take advantage of the newest features. I post a document on my website each fall detailing the newest features with each release. You can access this by visiting my blog and searching for "What's New" in the blog title at www.quick-training.com/blog.

If you are using QuickBooks Enterprise and you subscribe to the annual Full Service Plan, you will receive the newest software version each year, in addition to having access to elite technical support.

If you have used QuickBooks before, and then you purchase the newest year edition, you will be upgrading your QuickBooks file. QuickBooks Pro and Premier both can be upgraded to a QuickBooks Enterprise Solutions file. QuickBooks Enterprise Solutions cannot be downgraded to a QuickBooks Pro or Premier file.

The upgrade process is quite simple. If a prior installation of QuickBooks is detected, you will have the option to Upgrade or Change Installation location. If you want to upgrade the prior version, select **Replace the Version Selected Below with the Version I'm Installing Now**. From the drop-down list, select the version you want to upgrade. The Windows path for your current version of QuickBooks displays.

However, if you want to install QuickBooks 2013 without upgrading any existing version, select the **Change the Install Location** option. Select a different location by clicking the Browse button and locating a new installation folder. If the folder you want to use does not exist, click the Create New Folder icon for your installation. Follow the instructions for completing the install process.

tip

I recommend selecting the Change the Install Location during the install. This will retain the previous version of QuickBooks in the event you run into any issues with the new install.

After you have successfully upgraded your data to the newest version, you can then uninstall the prior version of the software using Windows uninstall.

note

Are you worried about changes made to the software when upgrading? No worries, for QuickBooks 2013, you can easily review improvements with the What's New tips.

At any time, from the menu bar, select **Help, What's New** to see the overlay of tips for working with the newest version of QuickBooks.

Installing a QuickBooks Maintenance Release

After a version is released, changes, improvements, and fixes are provided in the form of a maintenance release. Often, Intuit offers the release as a manual download only. This is usually during the testing phase, and you may not want to install the update in this phase.

To choose how QuickBooks detects whether a maintenance release exists, follow these steps:

note

An Internet connection is required to download and install the release patches.

1. From the menu bar, select **Help**, **Update QuickBooks**.
2. The Overview tab displays on the Update QuickBooks dialog box. Read the provided information. (Optional) Click Update Now if you want to complete the task.
3. Click the Options tab and select from the following:
   - **Automatic Update**—If you select Yes, QuickBooks automatically downloads the update and provides a dialog box for you to install the update the next time you launch QuickBooks.

- **Shared Download**—If you work with multiusers accessing QuickBooks, you should select Yes to share the download with the others. This will save time and ensure that other users can access the newly updated file.
- **Download Location**—QuickBooks displays the location and name of the downloaded file.

4. You can then choose which updates to install:
   - Payroll, Federal, Forms Engine
   - Employee Organizer
   - Maintenance Releases
   - Help and Other Updates
5. Click Save if you have made your changes, Revert to return to the original settings, or Close if you have not made any changes. (Optional) Click Help for more guidance.
6. Click the Update Now tab. From this tab, you can choose which updates to install, learn when they were last checked, and view the status.
7. (Optional) Select **Reset Update** to reinstall the entire update or select **Get Updates**.
8. A progress message displays. Click Close when finished.

To confirm that the newest maintenance release installed, you may need to close QuickBooks and relaunch the software. You can also check the product information window from an open QuickBooks file by selecting F2 or pressing Ctrl+1 on your keyboard; then you can read the Product line at the top (see Figure 17.7).

Protecting Your QuickBooks Database

It is a good practice to protect your QuickBooks data and safeguard it against some unforeseen catastrophic event. In addition to making a backup of your data regularly, you might also consider including power protection, virus protection, and computer disk defragmentation.

Creating a QuickBooks Backup

Even with the best planning and safeguards, unforeseen catastrophic events can happen. Safeguard your company data by creating a regular backup.

Ideally, you should back up your company files at the end of each session. However, if you are working in a multiuser environment, you should routinely wait until the end of each workday to back up. If your computer has more than one drive, you can back up onto a different disk drive from the one where your QuickBooks data is normally stored. If you have only one hard drive, you should back up onto some type of removable media, such as a USB flash memory drive.

note

You can perform a backup with multiple users logged in to the file. However, the backup process will not perform the recommended verification of the data as part of the backup.

To make a backup of your QuickBooks data, follow these steps:

1. From the menu bar, select **File**, **Back Up Company**, **Create Local Backup**. The Create Backup dialog displays with Local Backup selected.
2. (Optional) Click the Options button. The Backup Options dialog box displays as shown in Figure 17.4. Setting these options enables preferences for this and future backups.

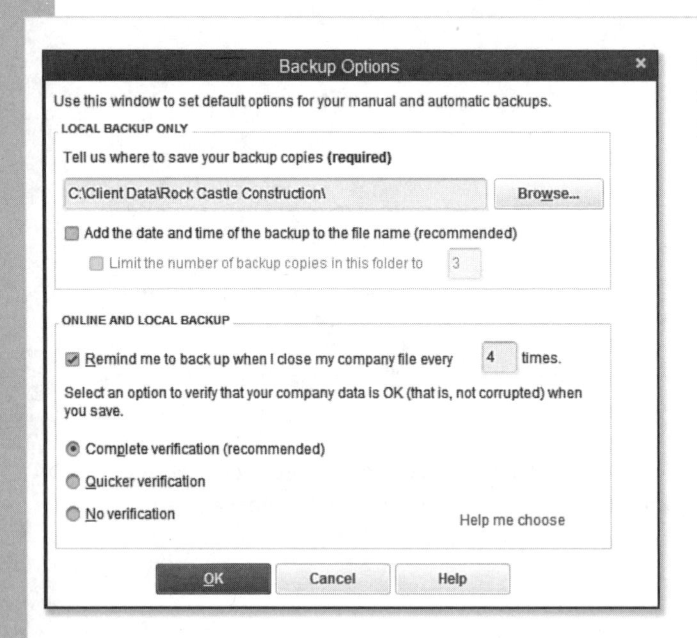

Figure 17.4
Create a backup of your QuickBooks file for safekeeping.

caution
Complete Verification is available only when the file is in single-user mode when performing the backup.

3. Choose the Browse button and browse to select a location to save your backup. It is recommended that you save your backup file to a location other than the location where the data is stored.
4. (Optional) Choose to Add the Date and Time, and to Limit the Number of Backup Copies in the selected folder.
5. Select the **Complete Verification (recommended)** option. For more information, see the section titled "Using the Verify Data Utility" in this chapter.

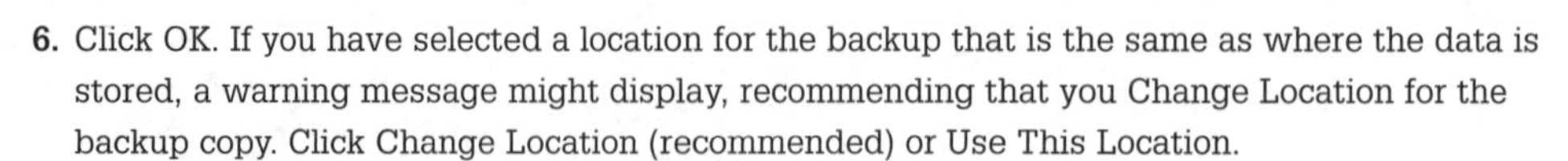

6. Click OK. If you have selected a location for the backup that is the same as where the data is stored, a warning message might display, recommending that you Change Location for the backup copy. Click Change Location (recommended) or Use This Location.
7. From the Create Backup dialog box, click Next.

8. Select **Save It Now** and click Next.

9. Type a filename for your backup, or accept the default filename.

10. Click Save.

Automating Your QuickBooks Backup

To create a schedule for automatically backing up your QuickBooks data file, follow these steps:

1. Follow steps 1–7 listed in the previous section titled "Creating a QuickBooks Backup."

2. Select one of the following options: **Save It Now and Schedule Future Backups** or **Only Schedule Future Backups**. The Where Do You Want to Backup Your Company File? message will display if you have not previously set your file to backup automatically.

3. If you want to define the number of times to do the automatic backup select **Save Backup Copy Automatically**....

4. To set a backup on a schedule, click the New button to display the schedule details as shown in Figure 17.5. Type a description for the backup, browse to the desired location, and define the number of Backup Copies to Keep.

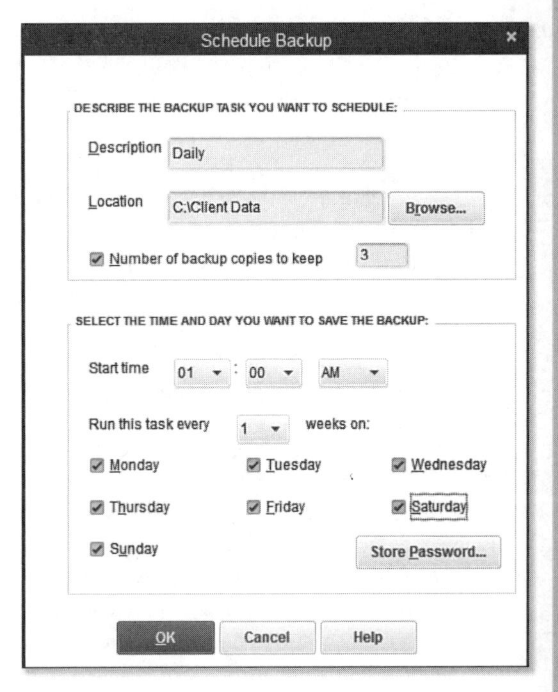

Figure 17.5
Schedule an automatic backup of the QuickBooks file.

5. Specify the Start Time, how often the task is run, and on what specific days.
6. (Optional) Click Store Password if your computer is password protected. Click OK to return to the Schedule Backup dialog box.
7. Click OK to close the Schedule Backup dialog box.
8. Click Finish to save the schedule.
9. Click OK to close the confirmation message that a backup has been scheduled.

Restoring a Backup

If you find you need to restore your data from a backup, follow these steps:

1. From the menu bar, select **File**, **Open** or **Restore Company**.
2. Select **Restore a Backup Copy**. Click Next.
3. Select **Local Backup**. Click Next.
4. Locate the backup file and click Open.
5. Click Next after reading the message about Where Do You Want to Restore the File.
6. Browse to select the location and type a name to be given to the restored file. Click Save.
7. QuickBooks provides a progress bar as the file is being restored. Click OK to the information window that the file was restored successfully.

Protecting the QuickBooks Operating Environment

To prevent an unexpected or unattended shutdown, you should install an uninterruptable power supply (UPS) on each of your computers running QuickBooks, as well as all network components that connect those computers. An adequately sized UPS can prevent power blackouts, brownouts, and surges. A Smart-UPS that automatically begins closing open programs and powering down the computer prior to depletion of the UPS battery should be used when QuickBooks must be left running during unattended periods.

Power Protection

Even if a UPS protects your server and workstation, if the connecting network hardware (switches, hubs, or routers) are not protected, a sudden power event will produce a loss of connection between the QuickBooks client and QuickBooks server, which might result in data corruption. It is recommended that all network hardware also be UPS protected.

Keep your computer safe by preventing power-related corruptions to your QuickBooks and not overloading your UPS with any nonessential computing components.

 **tip**

Do not plug printers or other appliances into any UPS protecting your computers and network components. Often when a printer or other appliance launches, it pulls a significant load of power that can produce a brownout condition within your UPS itself and compromise power protection.

Virus Protection

The Internet has changed our lives, but one unfortunate side effect has been the contagion of computer viruses sent via email (or other data transfers). Because of the Internet, computers and networks are not immune from attack. Malware programmers look for weaknesses in the computers not only of big corporations, but small businesses and individuals, in order to steal financial information or create havoc and destruction of our computer applications. Because QuickBooks is the leading financial software on the market, it is a favorite target of many who would seek to invade Company files for personal gain.

Good behavior on the part of computer users is not enough to protect your QuickBooks data from attacks. Although surfing certain kinds of websites puts users at higher risks of infection, even legitimate websites can be compromised. Seemingly innocent results in a search engine can open hostile sites that immediately download a computer virus. Some of these viruses collect information from your computer (spyware) and some install malicious (malware) software, but they almost all disguise themselves just long enough to take down your data or your network. Even if you never surf the Web, you are still vulnerable as long as you have an open Internet connection or ever access a flash drive or CD.

A high-quality antivirus program is essential if you are running QuickBooks on your computer or over a network. There are effective programs that can run with a minimum of computer resources and will block the overwhelming majority of threats. Set your antivirus program to run in an always-on mode and to perform a regular (preferably daily) scan of your computer. Ensure these programs are up-to-date; you should update your antivirus software to the most current virus definitions prior to each complete scan. Do not turn your antivirus software off unless you unplug your computer from the Internet and your network.

Many antivirus programs are sold in combination with a variety of Internet and network security features. Be advised that some of these features create additional layers of security that can restrict the capability to connect QuickBooks in a multiuser environment. A list of compatible antivirus and firewall programs is included in the "System Requirements" section of this chapter.

Windows Disk Defragmentation Utility

Fragmentation refers to any condition where data is not recorded in a logical continuous order. QuickBooks is subject to two different kinds of fragmentation—disk fragmentation and database fragmentation.

For more information on the latter, see "Database File Fragments," p. 627.

An example of disk fragmentation is when a QuickBooks invoice is recorded on your hard drive adjacent to a picture of your pets. Although it seems ridiculous to anyone who ever worked as a file clerk, this is the normal function of the Windows operating system.

Your QuickBooks company file can be fragmented on your computer's disk drive just like any of your other files. This occurs when the operating system cannot create or insert new information into the file in one logically contiguous space. Because the Windows operating system does not restrict the writing of data to only contiguous areas of your disk drive, as the total amount of data on your disk drive increases, fragmentation also increases.

Because of fragmentation, the hard drive's disk head must repeatedly move back and forth over the disk when reading and writing various parts of the file. The more the disk head must move from one area to another, the less efficient the disk drive is, lengthening the response time of QuickBooks trying to find your data.

To correct this type of fragmentation, we must force our Windows computer to rewrite all the parts of files to contiguous space on the hard drive. This is called *defragmentation*, and QuickBooks users should routinely run the Disk Defragmentation tool included with Windows software. After running this tool, QuickBooks users should see an increase in the speed of file access and data retrieval.

If your disk drive is less than 10% full, run defragmentation three or four times per year. If your disk drive is running at 25% to 30% of capacity, perform a monthly defragmentation. If your disk drive is at 50% or more of capacity or you have a QuickBooks Company file in excess of 50MB, you might need to run defragmentation once a week.

Defragmenting Your Windows 7 Computer

Choosing to defragment your computer can lead to a more responsive data file, providing quicker retrieval of data for reporting.

1. In the lower-left corner of your screen, click the Windows Orb or Start button.
2. Click All Programs.
3. Open the Accessories folder.
4. Open the Systems Tools folder.
5. Click Disk Defragmenter to open the utility displayed in Figure 17.6.

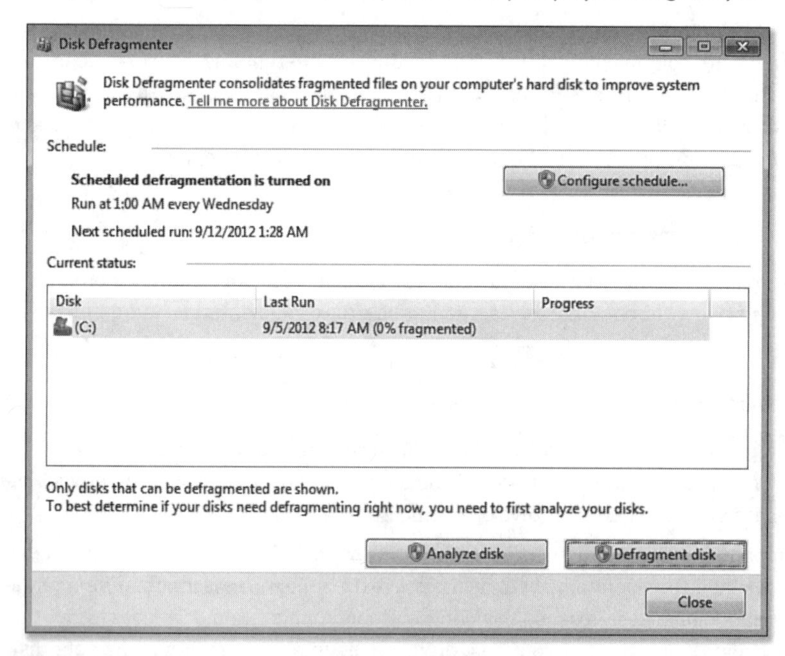

Figure 17.6
Run the defragmenter tool on your computer often.

6. Select the drive you want to defragment.
7. Click Analyze. A dialog box displays after the disk is analyzed, detailing if you need to perform the defragmentation.
8. To defragment the selected drive(s), click the Defragment Disk button. You can monitor the process in the Current status area (under the Progress column). After the process is complete, the results will be displayed.
9. To display more detailed information, click View Report.
10. To close the Disk Defragmenter, click Close.

Using Intuit Data Protect Online Backup Service

Intuit Data Protect is a subscription service that automatically backs up your company file(s) and optionally other important files from your computer. When you use Intuit Data Protect as your backup method, all your data needed to restore your company file is saved to Intuit's secure server. The backup files created by Intuit Data Protect are stored for 45 days, enabling you to not only restore the most recent backup but also any prior backup during the past 45 days.

After you have set up your Intuit Data Protect subscription you do not need to establish a backup schedule or perform manual backups. Intuit Data Protect will perform a once-a-day backup of every QuickBooks file you have configured for backup. This is unlike the manual backups, which should be done when no one is working in the file. The Intuit Data Protect backups run in the background, enabling you to continue working normally in QuickBooks. If a scheduled backup is missed because your computer is off or can't access the Internet, Intuit Data Protect will start a backup as soon as your computer is turned back on or Internet service becomes available.

To restore a backup made using the Intuit Data Protect Backup service, follow these steps:

1. From the menu bar, select **File**, **Back Up Company**, **Open Online Backup**: **Intuit Data Protect**.
2. From the Backup Status dialog box, click Restore from Backup.
3. Select the File you want to restore, and select the Version (Date and Time) of the backup. Click Continue.
4. Browse to the location where you want your file restored to (original or new location). Click Select.

   Intuit Data Protect begins the process of restoring your file(s) to the designated location. This process can take a substantial period of time depending on the size and number of files you are restoring. Do not attempt to close either Intuit Data Protect or QuickBooks during the restore process.
5. Upon completion, Intuit Data Protect will display a message that the restore completed. Click OK to close the dialog box.

Monitoring Your QuickBooks Database

Because QuickBooks is composed of a series of tables that store your accounting records, it is important to monitor your data file from time to time to ensure your data has integrity and is the proper size and configuration. There are a couple of methods in QuickBooks to monitor the database, including the Product Information dialog box and the Verify Data utility.

The Product Information Dialog Box

The Product Information dialog box provides valuable information about the health of your QuickBooks file. From an open QuickBooks file, press Ctrl+1 or F2 on your keyboard. The Product Information dialog box provides a wealth of information, including version, product license number, versions used, and much more. See Figure 17.7.

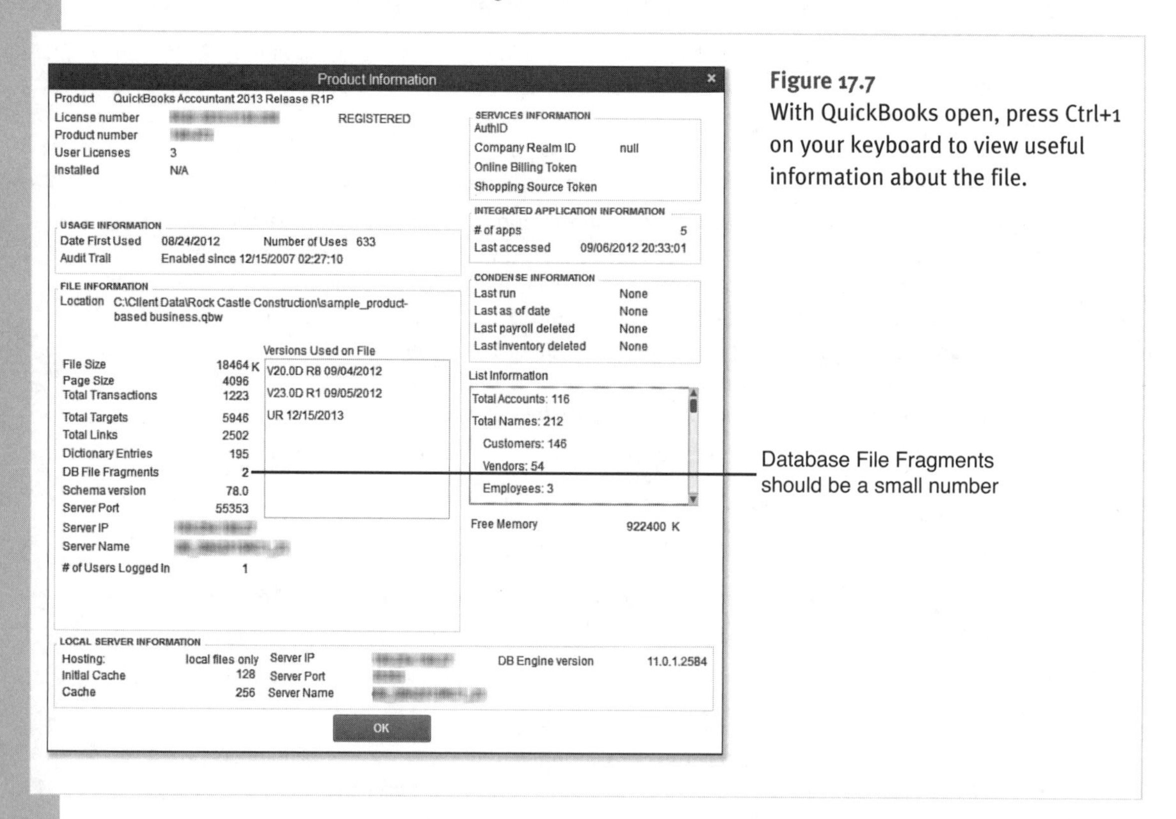

Figure 17.7
With QuickBooks open, press Ctrl+1 on your keyboard to view useful information about the file.

File Size

In Figure 17.7, about halfway down the left side is a section that provides data about the File Size, Total Transactions, Total Targets, Total Links, and DB File Fragments. This information can help you judge whether your data file is becoming too large for efficient processing of transactions and reports.

Many experts debate over the maximum file size of QuickBooks data, and Intuit has not published any formal guidelines regarding file size limits.

To calculate the anticipated growth of a data file, follow these steps:

1. Take the number of transactions each month times 2KB to get the monthly growth rate.
2. Take that amount times 12 for the annual KB growth per year.
3. Divide that amount by 1024 for the number of MB per year.

Typically, the file should grow by 30MB per year or less for Pro or Premier and 50 MB per year or less for Enterprise to maintain reasonable performance. Specialized condense features are available in the QuickBooks Accountant editions that can help in removing data from prior years; contact your accounting professional for this service. The age and processing speed of the computer, along with other factors, may also affect the software's performance.

Factors such as the number of lines of detail for each transaction significantly increase the number of links per transaction—this factor alone can greatly impact the size of the database. Based on personal experience, QuickBooks Pro or Premier data files in excess of 200MB or QuickBooks Enterprise files in excess of 450MB might experience sluggish performance. QuickBooks file performance is impacted by so many variables; it is not possible to name specifics.

note

If you would like more information about QuickBooks file size restrictions, from the QuickBooks support site http://support.quickbooks.intuit.com search for Knowledge Base article INF12412.

If you find your data file is becoming sluggish, you might consider starting a new data file or find companies listed on www.marketplace.intuit.com that will "shrink" your current file. You can contact me at info@quick-training.com for more information on this type of service.

Database File Fragments

As mentioned earlier, file fragmentation can negatively affect the performance of QuickBooks. Because file fragmentation is a normal part of using Windows, we must assume some fragmentation is also normal. The question becomes how many file fragments is too many? Some experts say more than 10 fragments is too many, others say 20, and still others say 50.

As a general rule, if the file is performing without issue and file fragments are fewer than 50, you don't need to be alarmed; however, anytime your file exceeds 50 fragments, it is time to reduce fragmentation.

For more information, see "Reducing Database File Fragments," p. 634.

QuickBooks List Limitations

As shown previously in Figure 17.7, the Product Information dialog box includes the List Information section. This section includes the size of the various QuickBooks lists (both active and inactive entries) and is another important database statistic to monitor. QuickBooks lists have been preconfigured to limit the number of entries the database can support.

One of the most significant limitations deals with the number of names you can have in QuickBooks Pro or Premier—the combined limit of customers, employees, vendors, and other names is 14,500.

QuickBooks does not permit you to delete any names that have been used in a transaction, and the list limits include both active and inactive entries. This list size restriction can be a serious limitation to a growing business. According to Intuit, QuickBooks Enterprise can support up to 1 million combined names, although they note some performance degradation is likely as you approach this upper limit.

Similar list limits exist for the Items list—14,500 in Pro or Premier and 100,000 from a functional standpoint for Enterprise. Most other lists in QuickBooks Pro, Premier, or Enterprise are limited to 10,000 entries. One noted exception is the Price Levels list, which is limited to 100 entries in Pro and Premier and 750 entries in Enterprise.

For QuickBooks Enterprise Solutions 13.0, there are new list limits for these specific lists, as detailed in Table 17.1:

Table 17.1 QuickBooks Enterprise 13.0 Larger List Limits

List	Previous	New
Chart of Accounts	10,000	100,000
Classes	10,000	100,000
Customer Types	10,000	100,000
Vendor Types	10,000	100,000
Memorized Transactions	29,000	50,000
To Do's	10,000	100,000
Customer Messages	10,000	100,000
Items in a Group or Sales Tax Item (also for Pro, and Premier)	20	50

Using the Verify Data Utility

Although the Verify Data utility can detect many forms of data corruption and test the integrity of the database, it also can be used to monitor the health of your Company file. Select this option when creating a backup of your QuickBooks Company file.

Additionally, if you use an external backup or Intuit Data Protect, run the Verify Data utility periodically to check the integrity of your Company file.

caution

When running the Verify Data utility, if the Not Responding message displays, do not attempt to close QuickBooks. Let the utility finish before closing it. More information about the Not Responding message can be found in the following section.

To Run the Verify Data Utility

To check the health of your QuickBooks data file, follow these steps for using the Verify Data utility:

1. Close all open windows in QuickBooks.
2. From the menu bar, select **File, Switch to Single-User Mode**. If this option is not displayed, you are currently using the file in Single-user Mode.
3. From the menu bar, select **File, Utilities, Verify Data**.

QuickBooks begins to verify your data. The technical results are reported in the QBWin.log file. For more information, see "The QBWin.log File," p. 631. If data integrity issues are not detected, QuickBooks displays the prompt shown in Figure 17.8.

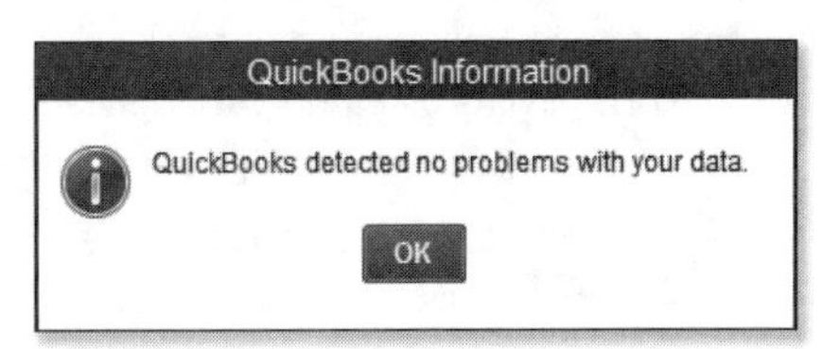

Figure 17.8
Message when the Verify Data utility detected no problems with the file.

The length of time the process takes depends on the size of your Company file.

Monitoring QuickBooks Performance Using Windows Task Manager

Have you ever encountered the Windows alert that QuickBooks is Not Responding? This can occur during any prolonged operation, such as compiling a lengthy or complex report, running one of the internal utilities, or even adding entries to large lists. This usually is a problem with the way Windows reports activity, rather than with QuickBooks itself.

Follow these steps to see if QuickBooks is still properly working by viewing the process in Windows Task Manager:

1. Place your cursor on an empty section of the Windows taskbar (typically at the bottom) of your computer. Right-click, and then select **Start Task Manager**.
2. From the Windows Task Manager, select the **Processes** tab.
3. Place a checkmark in the box Show Processes from All Users, located near the bottom of the list of processes.
4. Click the header of the Image Name column to sort the list of processes in alphabetical order.
5. Scroll down the list to the process QBW32.EXE. Observe both the numbers listed in the CPU and Memory columns. If either or both of them are changing even slightly, QuickBooks is still active and working.
6. To close the Windows Task Manager, click the X in the top-right corner.

After verifying that the process is running and the information referred to in step 5 is valid for your file, you can feel confident that when the task you started is finished, QuickBooks will return to full operation and will no longer display the (Not Responding) windows message.

QuickBooks Database Corruption

On occasion, your QuickBooks Company file can become corrupted. Database corruption is any damage to a database that impacts its integrity or functionality.

Common Causes of Corruption

Database corruption can result from improper shutdown of QuickBooks, as well as power issues (surges, spikes, and outages). It can also occur as a result of a fatal application (program) error. System hardware, such as bad disk drives or raid controllers, can corrupt data. Your operating system can produce QuickBooks data fragmentation.

In a multiuser environment, networking components (such as wireless routers) might produce corruption because their failure can break the connection between the Application and Database Server.

A large QuickBooks file size does not necessarily cause data corruption, although there is more data in which corruptions can occur. Larger files will also have more fragmentation and performance issues if your hardware is not meeting the reported minimum requirements.

For more information, see the section titled "System Requirements" in this chapter.

Signs of Data Corruption

QuickBooks might report data corruption by displaying specific problem messages or error codes. Often the first sign of data corruption does not appear until a QuickBooks user sees an accounting transaction irregularity—for example, when an out-of-balance balance sheet or accounts receivables or payables subledger reports don't reconcile to the general ledger.

If you run the Verify Data utility and your Company file has lost integrity, QuickBooks will display a warning such as the one shown in Figure 17.9, indicating you should run the Rebuild Data utility. In addition to the displayed message, additional information is provided in the QBWin.log file.

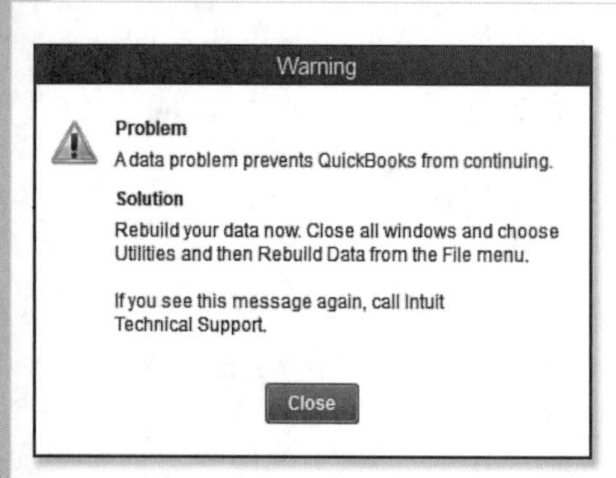

Figure 17.9
Some database corruption errors require using the Rebuild Data utility.

The QBWin.log File

If the Verify Data utility detects an error in your data, you might want to get more information about the specific problem(s) within your data. QuickBooks records operational data, including information related to the Verify Data and Rebuild Data utilities within a log file called the QBWin.log.

To view the QBWin.log file, follow these steps:

1. With your QuickBooks Company file open, press the F2 key (or Ctrl+1) to display the Product Information dialog box.
2. Now press the F3 key (or Ctrl+2) to display the Tech Help dialog box.
3. Select the **Open File** tab.
4. Scroll down the list and click the QBWIN.LOG file; then click Open File. The file opens in Windows Notepad (see Figure 17.10).

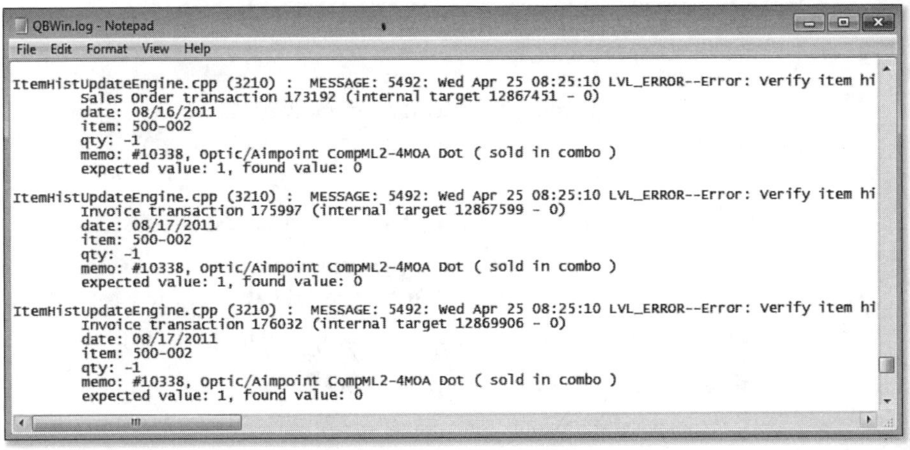

```
QBWin.log - Notepad
File Edit Format View Help
ItemHistUpdateEngine.cpp (3210) :  MESSAGE: 5492: Wed Apr 25 08:25:10 LVL_ERROR--Error: Verify item hi
        Sales Order transaction 173192 (internal target 12867451 - 0)
        date: 08/16/2011
        item: 500-002
        qty: -1
        memo: #10338, Optic/Aimpoint CompML2-4MOA Dot ( sold in combo )
        expected value: 1, found value: 0
ItemHistUpdateEngine.cpp (3210) :  MESSAGE: 5492: Wed Apr 25 08:25:10 LVL_ERROR--Error: Verify item hi
        Invoice transaction 175997 (internal target 12867599 - 0)
        date: 08/17/2011
        item: 500-002
        qty: -1
        memo: #10338, Optic/Aimpoint CompML2-4MOA Dot ( sold in combo )
        expected value: 1, found value: 0
ItemHistUpdateEngine.cpp (3210) :  MESSAGE: 5492: Wed Apr 25 08:25:10 LVL_ERROR--Error: Verify item hi
        Invoice transaction 176032 (internal target 12869906 - 0)
        date: 08/17/2011
        item: 500-002
        qty: -1
        memo: #10338, Optic/Aimpoint CompML2-4MOA Dot ( sold in combo )
        expected value: 1, found value: 0
```

Figure 17.10 Review the QBWIN.LOG to determine errors that might be causing the error messages.

5. The Verify Data section should be near the bottom of the log, so scroll to the bottom and then scroll back up until you find the Verify portion of the log file, which begins with the following:

   = = = = = = = = = = = * BEGIN VERIFY LOG * = = = = =

   The QBWIN.LOG file will end with:

   = = = = = = = = = = == = * END VERIFY LOG * = = = = = =

You can scroll through the log file to view errors detected with the file. I recommend that you contact Intuit technical support or a local QuickBooks professional for reading and correcting any errors listed.

The QBWIN.LOG is a snapshot of technical details during the current session of QuickBooks. It contains information about how the program performed when it was started, if it successfully connected with your Company file, and any errors experienced during operations or while performing the verify/rebuild utilities. Many different messages might be contained in your QBWin.log; some might represent minor errors and others might represent more severe forms of database corruption. The QuickBooks Support website contains many knowledge-based articles that correspond to the various errors. A few common error messages and possible solutions have been included in this section.

You might want to complete a rebuild of the company file after performing the suggested repairs.

For more information, see "Rebuilding Your Company File," p. 636.

Error: Verify Memorized Report List...

A corrupted Memorized Report is usually associated with this error. QuickBooks normally repairs this problem if you re-sort the Memorized Report List followed by running the Rebuild Data Utility. To do so, follow these steps:

1. From the menu bar, select **Reports**, **Memorized Reports**, **Memorized Report List**.
2. In the Memorized Report drop-down list, select **Re-Sort List**.
3. To continue, click OK to the Re-sort prompt.

In some cases these steps will not correct the corruption; it then becomes necessary to "delete" the affected memorized report, then re-sort the list, and rebuild the data file.

Error: Verify Names List (Such As Customers)...

This form of corruption occurs when one of the Names lists has a database index error. Try re-sorting the Names List followed by running the Rebuild Data utility to resolve this type of error.

To access the Names List, follow these steps while logged in to the file in single-user mode:

1. From the menu bar, select **Banking**, **Write Checks**.
2. Place your cursor in the Pay to the Order of field.
3. On your keyboard, press Ctrl+L.
4. The Name List displays. In the Name drop-down list, select **Re-sort List**.
5. In the Re-sort List? message, click OK.

Error: Verify Name (Specific List): Duplicate Name Encountered...

QuickBooks might encounter a duplicate name. This might occur if you import data using the IIF (Intuit Interchange Format) import file type or you use a third-party application. Frequently one name might be marked as inactive, or QuickBooks might have inserted an asterisk (*) in front of the duplicate name.

To locate and merge the duplicate names, follow these steps:

1. Find the names that are duplicated.

2. Edit one of the names to first change it to be unique; if QuickBooks has inserted an asterisk (*) remove that character from the name as part of this change. Save the new name.

3. Return to the name you just changed and edit it again to change it to be identical to its duplicate; then click Save.

4. QuickBooks displays the Merge dialog box, as shown in Figure 17.11. Confirm the merge of both names by clicking Yes.

Figure 17.11
Certain lists in QuickBooks will let you merge duplicate names.

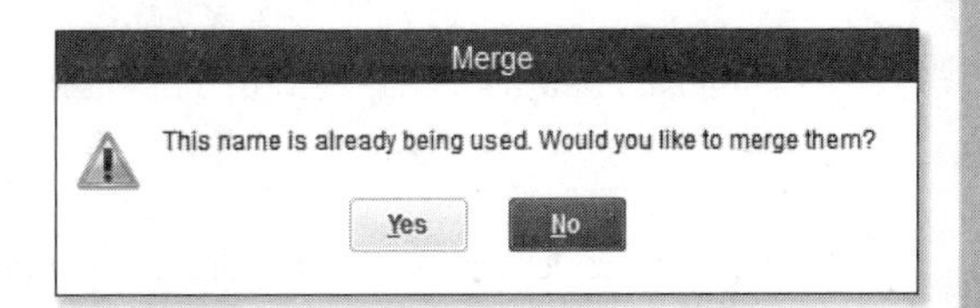

5. Run the Rebuild Data utility.

Error: Verify Target: Transaction Out of Balance...

This error usually results when the target record (such as the check detail lines) does not equal the amount of the source record (such as the check total).

To correct this type of error, follow these steps:

1. Open the transaction identified in the QBWin.log report.

2. Verify whether the amount in the header (such as check amount) is identical to the total of the amounts in the detail lines. If these amounts are different, you need to correct the erroneous amount(s).

3. Save the corrected transaction.

4. Run the Rebuild Data utility.

Error: Verify Target: Invalid Open Quantity...

This error can result when the link between an Estimate and Sales Order and its associated Invoice (for partial quantities) is broken.

To relink the transactions, follow these steps:

1. Open the transaction, reported in the QBWin.log.

2. Add a period (.) to an empty detail line of the transaction; this will not change any values for the transaction. However, doing so can help relink the source and target transactions.

3. Save the transaction.

4. Run the Rebuild Data utility.

For more information, see "Rebuilding Your Company File," p. 636.

Repairing List Corruptions

Several of the symptoms associated with data corruption, and QBWin.log messages detailed previously, involve problems with the various QuickBooks lists. For many lists, you can re-sort the list simply by opening the list and clicking the list's menu button located at the bottom of the list (such as Items). Prior to actually resorting the list, check the box labeled Include Inactive (if available) and select the option to change the list view from Hierarchical to Flat (not all lists offer a hierarchical view).

One of the major lists in QuickBooks is a hidden list called the Name List, which is a combined list of all the names (customers, employees, vendors, and other names).

To sort all the name lists at once, follow these steps:

1. From the menu bar, select **Banking**, **Write Checks**.

2. Place your cursor in the Pay to the Order of field.

3. On your keyboard, press Ctrl+L.

4. The Name List displays. From the Name drop-down list, select **Re-sort List**.

5. In the Re-sort List? message, click OK.

Reducing Database File Fragments

The highly compressed QuickBooks Portable Company File can be useful in dealing with some forms of index corruption as well as fragmentation. When a Portable Company (*.QBM) File is restored, QuickBooks re-creates all indexes associated with the database. In addition, the extreme level of compression applied when the file is produced eliminates file fragments. Therefore, creation and restoration of a Portable File might resolve many file-related issues.

Follow these steps to create and restore a Portable Company File:

1. From the menu bar, select **File**, **Create Copy**. The Save Copy or Backup dialog box displays, as shown in Figure 17.12.

2. Choose Portable Company File and click Next.

3. Accept the default location and filename or select a location to save the file and type a desired name for the file.

4. A few individual progress messages will display; click OK on each of them.

5. Upon completion, QuickBooks displays an Information message indicating the file has been saved and details the designated location. Click OK.

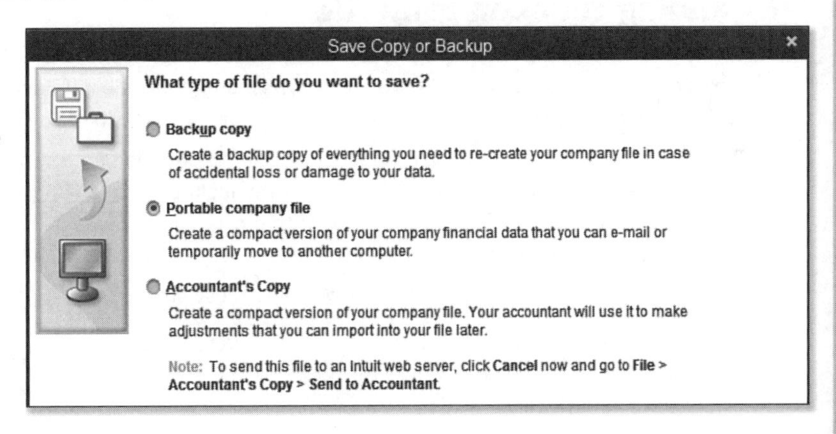

Figure 17.12
Create and restore a Portable Company File to help reduce database file fragments.

6. To restore the Portable Company File, select **File**, **Open or Restore Company** from the menu bar.
7. Select **Restore a Portable File** and click Next.
8. Select the Portable Company File (ending in .QBM) you saved to the desktop (or your alternative location), and click Open.

> **caution**
> Always create a backup of your file before attempting this type of file restore.

9. In the Open or Restore Company dialog box, the Where Do You Want to Restore the File dialog displays. Review the message details regarding overwriting your current file and click Next, as shown in Figure 17.13.

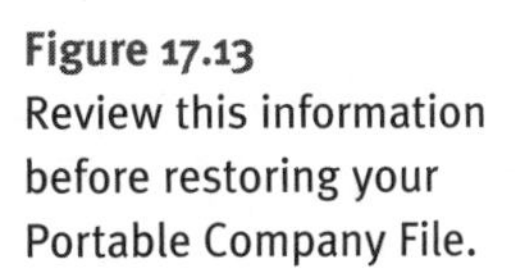

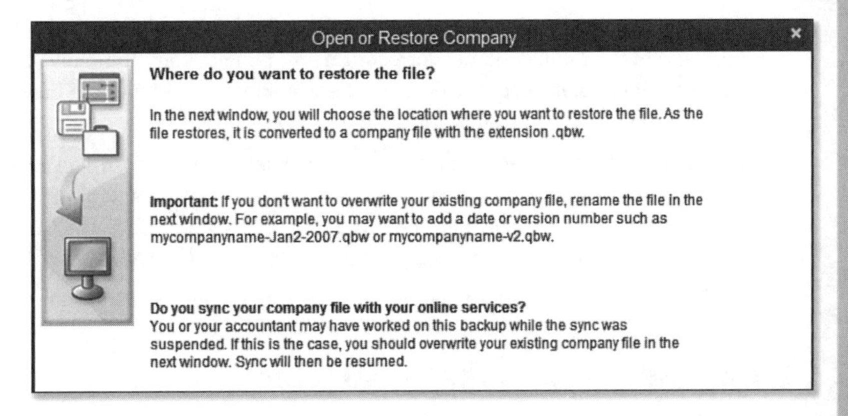

Figure 17.13
Review this information before restoring your Portable Company File.

10. Click Save and select a save location. Because you are intending to replace your current file, select your current file location and current filename.
11. Click Save. QuickBooks replaces your current file with the data restored from the QuickBooks Portable Company File.

Rebuilding Your Company File

The Rebuild Data utility can repair many QuickBooks Company file issues. The utility attempts to repair or update data found to be corrupted, which might include permanently deleting transactions or list entries that are damaged beyond repair or that compromise the overall integrity of the file.

Before running the rebuild utility, you should gather information for comparison after the rebuild is complete. This should include all summary reports, including the Balance Sheet Standard and Profit & Loss Standard Report. You might also want to process additional reports, such as those for payroll details or checkbook registers, and so on.

To use the QuickBooks Rebuild Data utility, follow these steps:

1. If you use your file in a multiuser install, you need to log in to the file in single-user mode. From the menu bar, select **File**, **Switch to Single User**.
2. From the menu bar, select **Utilities**, **Rebuild Data**.
3. QuickBooks displays a warning message requiring a backup of the company file before actually starting the rebuild process. Follow the prompts to save a backup copy of your data.
4. When the backup is completed, the Rebuild Data utility starts. The time required to rebuild the database can vary depending on the size of your Company file. It is extremely important to permit the utility to finish completely.
5. QuickBooks displays a Rebuild Has Completed message. Click OK.

Never rebuild a company file on a remote drive or across a network. You should always copy the file to a local computer before running the Rebuild Data utility.

Close all unnecessary programs and turn off your Windows screen saver and any power-saver functions before starting a rebuild.

After the Rebuild Data utility finishes, the data file might still have corrupted transactions that the first pass of the rebuild did not correct. It might be necessary to rebuild your data more than once. As a general rule, if the utility does not resolve an issue within three passes, the database error cannot be fixed using the Rebuild Data utility.

Although severely damaged transactions are usually removed during the rebuild process, you might need to manually correct or delete other transactions that Rebuild Data could not correct, and then reenter them. Transactional data removed or corrected is listed in the QBWin.log file along with corrupted transactions, which the Rebuild Data utility cannot correct.

For severe cases of database integrity issues, you need to contact Intuit's Technical Support.

Using the QuickBooks File Doctor

The QuickBooks File Doctor tool helps to diagnose and repair several forms of damage that prevent company files from opening. The tool must be run locally on a corrupted QuickBooks file; you cannot run this tool across a network or a mapped drive.

The QuickBooks File Doctor tool replaces and provides improved problem-solving features over the formerly available QuickBooks Company File Diagnostic tool.

The Company File Doctor tool requires the following:

- Internet connection.
- Company file must be smaller than 2GB.
- You must be logged in as the Administrator to run the network diagnose functions.
- QuickBooks must be in hosting mode. To start hosting from the menu bar, select **File**, **Utilities**, **Host Multiuser Access**.
- If Windows User Account Control is turned on, the File Doctor tool will be relaunched with elevated administrator privileges.
- Network diagnose and repair functionality may not work properly if multiple QuickBooks versions are installed on your computer.

Download the tool from QuickBooks technical support site:
http://support.quickbooks.intuit.com/support/articles/HOW17836
The referenced knowledgebase article includes general instructions for using the tool.

1. Install the downloaded QuickBooks Company File Diagnostic Tool, following the instructions provided by Intuit within the knowledgebase article.
2. Click the installed icon to launch the tool. If you receive a message that the tool will be relaunched with elevated permissions, click OK. Click Yes to the User Account Control message. Figure 17.14 shows the dialog box that displays.

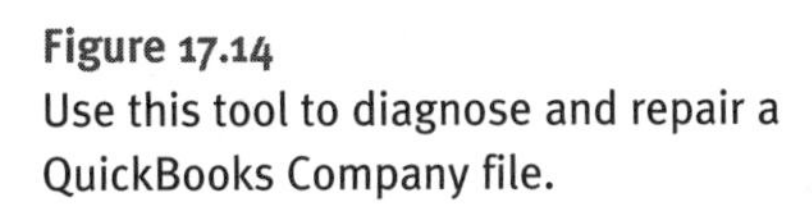

Figure 17.14
Use this tool to diagnose and repair a QuickBooks Company file.

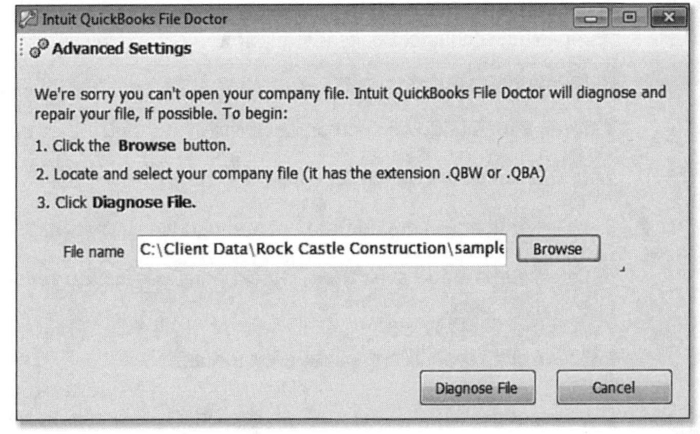

3. Click the Browse button to select the QuickBooks Company (*.QBW) file or QuickBooks Accountant's Copy File (*.QBA) that needs to be diagnosed and/or repaired.
4. Click Diagnose File. If required, enter the Admin password. Click OK. QuickBooks displays a Diagnosing Company File progress bar.

5. Select **Yes** if you access your company file from other computers on the network or No to the same message. When the tool has finished the process, there are three possible outcomes:
   - Problem was found and was fixed.
   - Problem was found but was not fixed. Instructions are provided for different methods of handling this.
   - No problem was found. Instructions are provided for additional tools to try, including detailed instructions for network connectivity issues.

note

If the File Doctor finds and fixes a problem, a new copy of your file is created automatically for you to open and use.

The File Doctor also offers advanced settings that can help with the following errors, although it is recommend you use these advanced settings only with the assistance of Intuit's Technical Support.

- **-6130 Errors**—These errors often occur when you are opening a company file and the database server terminates.
- **Data Sync Errors**—These errors are related to the QuickBooks Sync Manager that manages the data housed in your desktop software and the data maintained in the "Intuit Cloud" for those applications you have granted this access.

Resolving QuickBooks Program File Corruption Issues

Some corruption can be the result of problems with the QuickBooks program files. This can occur during installation. A conflict occurs with some required component, such as Microsoft.NET or even the Windows Registry. Generally, QuickBooks runs normally but at some point the program experiences fault errors or might not install an update properly. Usually, these problems can be resolved by repairing the QuickBooks installation.

To repair your QuickBooks program files, follow these steps:

1. From your Windows taskbar, click the Windows Orb or Start button, and select **Control Panel**.
2. In the Control Panel, double-click Programs.
3. In Programs, select **QuickBooks** and choose **Uninstall/Change**.
4. Select **Repair** and click Next. QuickBooks begins the repair, displaying a progress bar during the process.
5. When the repair is complete, click Finish.

This procedure usually, not always, resolves file issues. In the event that it does not work, you will need to Uninstall QuickBooks and then reinstall it. Use the preceding steps to remove QuickBooks by selecting the Uninstall option rather than Repair.

18

USING OTHER PLANNING AND MANAGEMENT TOOLS

There is much to be said about properly setting up your QuickBooks file and recording transactions correctly. However, for this chapter I wanted to share with you some lesser known features that can truly help you manage your business and work more efficiently with QuickBooks.

Planning and Budgeting

Like most business owners I have met, you probably know where your money will be spent each month, yet you might not see the value in writing it down. There is an old saying that is very appropriate here: "When you fail to plan, you plan to fail." This saying couldn't be truer than when it comes to watching your business financials.

QuickBooks makes the task of creating and tracking a financial budget for your business easy. Just follow a few steps and in no time you can print useful reports that track actual financial performance and compare it to your original budget.

Create a Budget

The first step is to set up a budget. Follow these steps to begin using this feature in QuickBooks:

1. From the menu bar, select **Company**, **Planning & Budgeting**, **Set Up Budgets**. The Create New Budget dialog box displays, as shown in Figure 18.1.

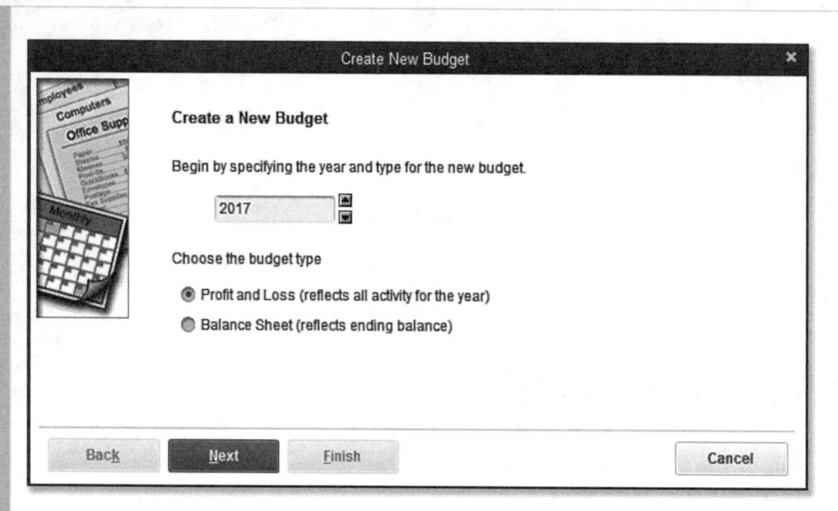

Figure 18.1
Create a Profit and Loss or Balance Sheet budget easily with QuickBooks.

2. Select the year you want to create the budget for.
3. Choose the budget type:
   - Profit and Loss
   - Balance Sheet
4. Click Next. Select from the following choices, as shown in Figure 18.2:
   - **No Additional Criteria**—Simplest form of budgeting. I recommend you start with this choice.
   - **Customer:Job**—You can create a budget for your customers or jobs here, but a better method might be to use a QuickBooks estimate. For more information, see "Using QuickBooks Estimates," p. 331.
   - **Class**—If you are using classes (department tracking), you might want to select the Class budget report. For more information on classes, see "Class," p. 111.

note
If you have previously created a budget, click the Create New Budget button in the Set Up Budgets dialog box (see Figure 18.4).

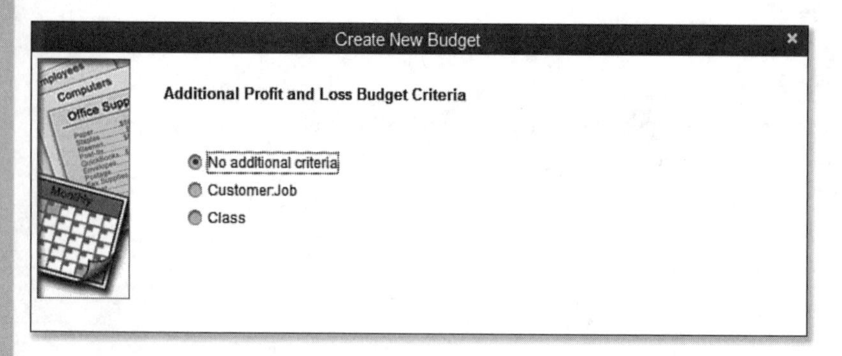

Figure 18.2
Choose the type of budget to create.

5. Click Next.
6. Choose how you want to create a budget from the choices displayed in Figure 18.3.

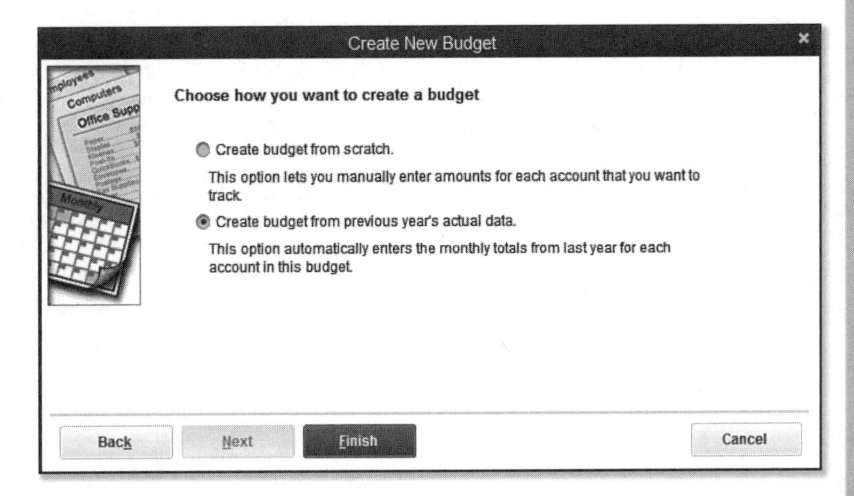

Figure 18.3
Choose from two methods for creating the new budget.

- **Create Budget from Scratch**—You will manually enter the budget amounts. This method requires the most effort on your part.
- **Create a Budget from Previous Year's Actual Data**—I recommend starting with this option. The budget is created using the prior year's data, allowing you to modify the budgeted amounts as needed.

7. Click Finish. QuickBooks creates the new budget. In Figure 18.4, a new budget has been created using actual revenue and expenses from the prior year.
8. Click Save. To close the newly created budget, click OK.

Edit a Budget

Budgets can be edited at any time to accommodate changes in your business. Additionally, if you created the budget using last year's actual numbers, you can follow these steps to revise the budget information:

1. From the menu bar, select **Company**, **Planning & Budgeting**, **Set Up Budgets**. Your previously saved budget displays.
2. To view a different budget, click the drop-down list to select the desired budget.
3. To create a new budget, click Create New Budget and follow the steps listed in the previous section.
4. With your cursor, click in any cell to change the amount budgeted for that category and month.

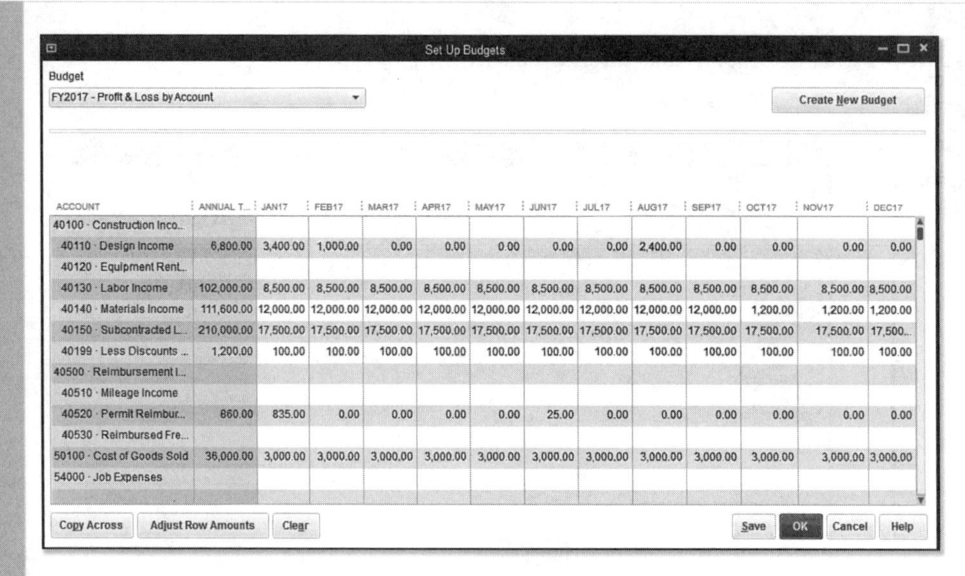

ACCOUNT	ANNUAL T...	JAN17	FEB17	MAR17	APR17	MAY17	JUN17	JUL17	AUG17	SEP17	OCT17	NOV17	DEC17
40100 · Construction Inco...													
40110 · Design Income	6,800.00	3,400.00	1,000.00	0.00	0.00	0.00	0.00	0.00	2,400.00	0.00	0.00	0.00	0.00
40120 · Equipment Rent...													
40130 · Labor Income	102,000.00	8,500.00	8,500.00	8,500.00	8,500.00	8,500.00	8,500.00	8,500.00	8,500.00	8,500.00	8,500.00	8,500.00	8,500.00
40140 · Materials Income	111,600.00	12,000.00	12,000.00	12,000.00	12,000.00	12,000.00	12,000.00	12,000.00	12,000.00	12,000.00	1,200.00	1,200.00	1,200.00
40150 · Subcontracted L...	210,000.00	17,500.00	17,500.00	17,500.00	17,500.00	17,500.00	17,500.00	17,500.00	17,500.00	17,500.00	17,500.00	17,500.00	17,500...
40199 · Less Discounts ...	1,200.00	100.00	100.00	100.00	100.00	100.00	100.00	100.00	100.00	100.00	100.00	100.00	100.00
40500 · Reimbursement I...													
40510 · Mileage Income													
40520 · Permit Reimbur...	860.00	835.00	0.00	0.00	0.00	0.00	25.00	0.00	0.00	0.00	0.00	0.00	0.00
40530 · Reimbursed Fre...													
50100 · Cost of Goods Sold	36,000.00	3,000.00	3,000.00	3,000.00	3,000.00	3,000.00	3,000.00	3,000.00	3,000.00	3,000.00	3,000.00	3,000.00	3,000.00
54000 · Job Expenses													

Figure 18.4 QuickBooks can create the budget quickly using actual information from the prior year.

5. (Optional) With your cursor in a specific cell, click Copy Across and QuickBooks will copy that amount to all the columns to right of your current cursor position.
6. (Optional) With your cursor in a specific cell, click Adjust Row Amounts. You can choose to increase or decrease by a specific percentage or dollar amount. See Figure 18.5. You can choose to update the following:
   - **1st Month**—Update budget amounts beginning with the first month in the year.
   - **Currently Selected Month**—Update budget amounts beginning with the currently selected month.
7. Click OK to close the Adjust Row Amounts dialog box. QuickBooks calculates new budget amounts depending on your selections in step 6.
8. (Optional) Click Clear and answer Yes or No to the warning message about clearing this page of the budget.
9. Click Save to save your changes as you work.
10. To close the budget, click the X in the top-right corner. You might be asked if you want to record your budget changes. Choose from Yes, No, or Cancel.

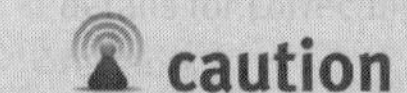

caution

If you select Clear and then choose Yes, QuickBooks removes all the budgeted amounts for the currently displayed budget.

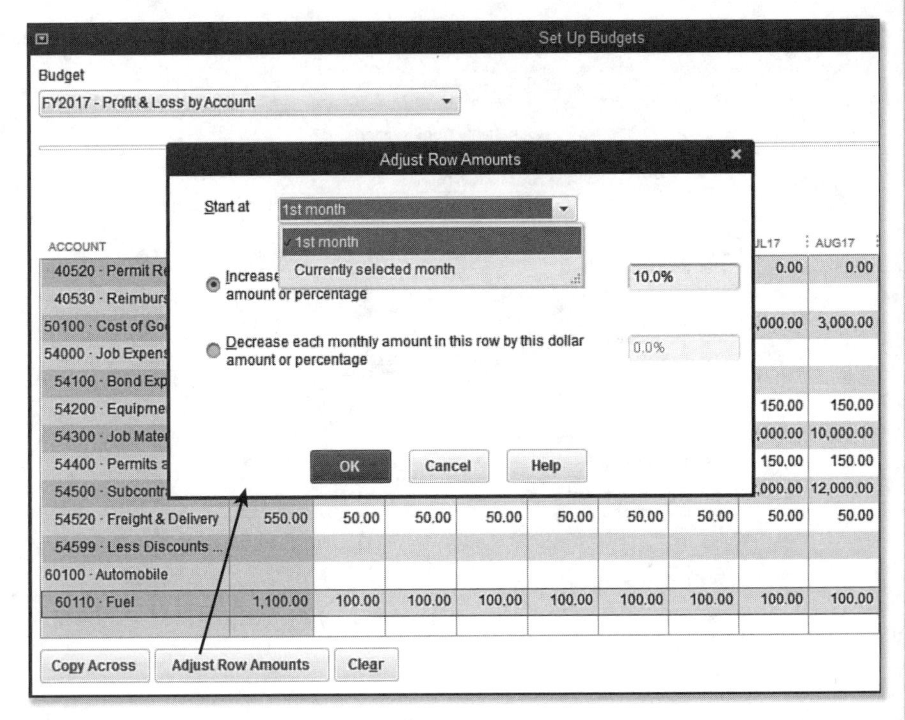

Figure 18.5
Use the Adjust Row Amounts dialog box to quickly change your budget amounts.

Print Budget Reports

You now have a budget prepared. So let's see how your current year is progressing by viewing the budget reports included with QuickBooks. From the menu bar, select **Reports**, **Budgets & Forecasts** where you will find these reports:

- Budget Overview
- Budget vs. Actual
- Profit & Loss Budget Performance
- Budget vs. Actual Graph
- Forecast Overview
- Forecast vs. Actual

Figure 18.6 shows a Profit & Loss Budget vs. Actual report.

To display a budget report, follow these steps:

1. From the menu bar, select **Reports**, **Budgets & Forecasts**, and choose a report.
2. In the drop-down list, select the year's budget you want to review.

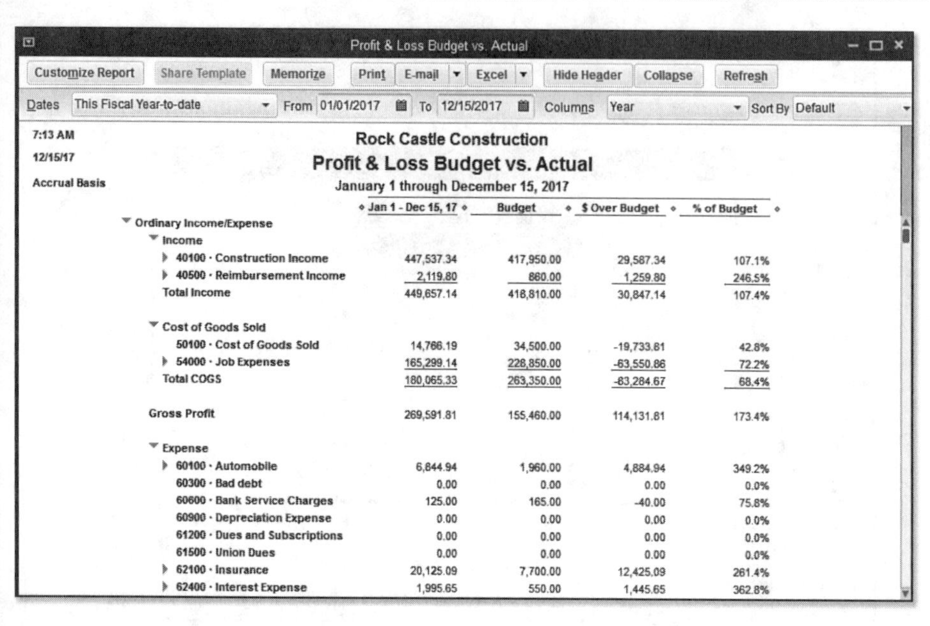

7:13 AM
12/15/17
Accrual Basis

Rock Castle Construction
Profit & Loss Budget vs. Actual
January 1 through December 15, 2017

	Jan 1 - Dec 15, 17	Budget	$ Over Budget	% of Budget
Ordinary Income/Expense				
Income				
40100 · Construction Income	447,537.34	417,950.00	29,587.34	107.1%
40500 · Reimbursement Income	2,119.80	860.00	1,259.80	246.5%
Total Income	449,657.14	418,810.00	30,847.14	107.4%
Cost of Goods Sold				
50100 · Cost of Goods Sold	14,766.19	34,500.00	-19,733.81	42.8%
54000 · Job Expenses	165,299.14	228,850.00	-63,550.86	72.2%
Total COGS	180,065.33	263,350.00	-83,284.67	68.4%
Gross Profit	269,591.81	155,460.00	114,131.81	173.4%
Expense				
60100 · Automobile	6,844.94	1,960.00	4,884.94	349.2%
60300 · Bad debt	0.00	0.00	0.00	0.0%
60600 · Bank Service Charges	125.00	165.00	-40.00	75.8%
60900 · Depreciation Expense	0.00	0.00	0.00	0.0%
61200 · Dues and Subscriptions	0.00	0.00	0.00	0.0%
61500 · Union Dues	0.00	0.00	0.00	0.0%
62100 · Insurance	20,125.09	7,700.00	12,425.09	261.4%
62400 · Interest Expense	1,995.65	550.00	1,445.65	362.8%

Figure 18.6
This report can be displayed for many time periods, including day, month, and year.

3. Click Next.

4. If the report offers multiple layout options, select the layout of your choice and click Next.

5. Click Finish to prepare the report.

You can also modify the information displayed on this report. Click Customize Report to modify these settings:

- **Report Date Range**—Settings that determine the dates included in the budget details.
- **Report Basis**—Accrual or cash basis.
- **Columns and Rows**—Settings that determine what data is included in the budget.

(Optional) Click the Advanced button and choose to Display only Nonzero rows or columns. You may also want to click the Show Only Rows and Columns with Budgets checkbox. See Figure 18.7.

Delete a Budget

If you find it necessary to delete a budget and start over, follow these steps:

1. From the menu bar, select **Company**, **Planning & Budgeting**, **Set Up Budgets**. Your previously saved budget will display in the Set Up Budgets dialog box.

2. From the menu bar, select **Edit**, **Delete Budget**.

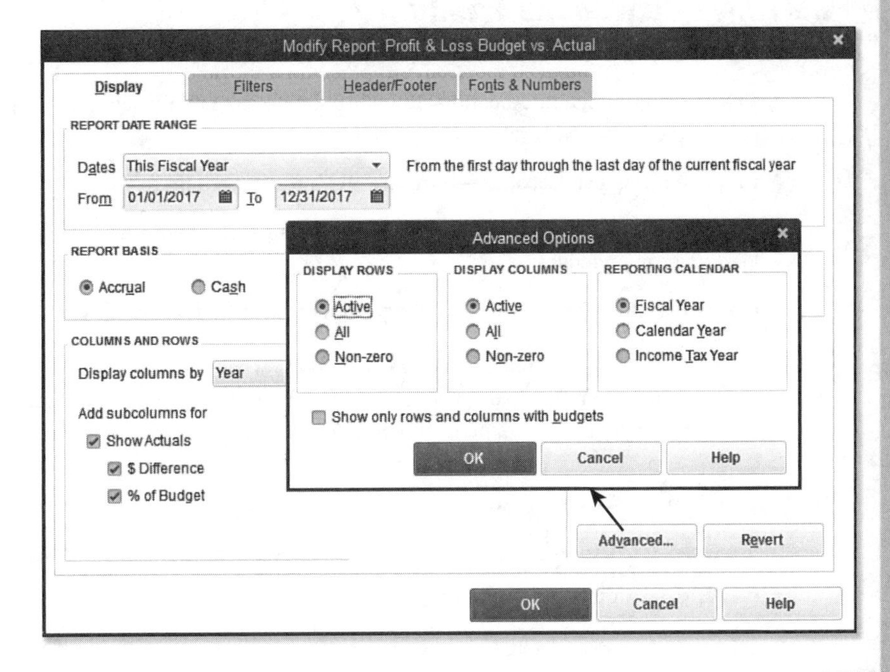

Figure 18.7
Modify the information displayed in the Budget vs. Actual report.

QuickBooks Loan Manager

Use the Loan Manager in QuickBooks to track loans you have created in QuickBooks. The Loan Manager helps you track all your loans in one convenient location.

With the Loan Manager you can

- View payment schedules
- Set up loan payments
- Analyze different loan payoff scenarios

Information to Collect

Before adding a loan to the Loan Manager, you should have the following information about your loans available. This information is usually included on your original finance documents:

- Origination Date
- Payment Amount
- Payment Term
- Escrow Amount (if any)
- Interest Rate

Getting QuickBooks Ready

Before setting up a loan in the Loan Manager in QuickBooks, you will want to set up the following:

- **Create a Loan Payable Account**—Usually a long-term liability account. This account displays the balance owed on the loan.
- **Create an Expense Account**—To record the interest paid on the loan.
- **(Optional) Create an Escrow Account**—Create an escrow account if required for your specific loan reporting needs.
- **Create a Vendor Record**—This is the person or institution to which you'll make payments.

If you have previously been using these QuickBooks accounts, make sure the balances in these accounts are up to date and agree with your lending institution's balances for the loan. Most businesses use a single interest expense account for all loans.

Setting Up a New Loan

To use QuickBooks to track your loan payment, follow these steps:

1. From the menu bar, select **Banking**, **Loan Manager**.
2. Click Add a Loan and complete the information as displayed in Figure 18.8.

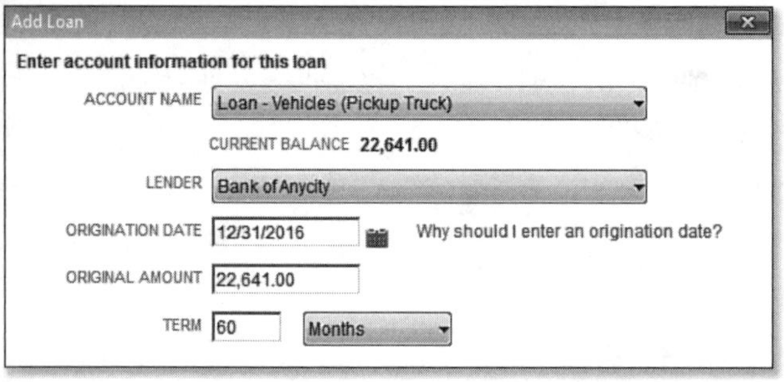

Add Loan
Enter account information for this loan
ACCOUNT NAME Loan - Vehicles (Pickup Truck)
CURRENT BALANCE 22,641.00
LENDER Bank of Anycity
ORIGINATION DATE 12/31/2016 Why should I enter an origination date?
ORIGINAL AMOUNT 22,641.00
TERM 60 Months

Figure 18.8
Complete the account information for the loan.

3. In the Account Name drop-down list, select the long-term liability account for the loan.
4. In the Lender drop-down list, select the payee.
5. Enter the loan Origination Date.
6. In the Terms drop-down list, select **Weeks**, **Months**, or **Years**. Click Next.
7. Enter the Due Date of Next Payment, Payment Amount, and optionally, Next Payment.
8. Select the **Payment Period**.

9. (Optional) Choose Yes or No to making an escrow payment and complete the fields for Escrow Payment Amount and Escrow Payment Account.
10. (Optional) Select the box to be alerted 10 days before the payment is due. Click Next.
11. Enter the Interest Rate and select a **Compounding Period**.
12. Choose a bank account from the Payment Account drop-down list.
13. Choose the Interest Expense Account and the account for Fees and Charges.
14. Click Finish. QuickBooks displays information in the Loan Manager about the newly created loan. See Figure 18.9.

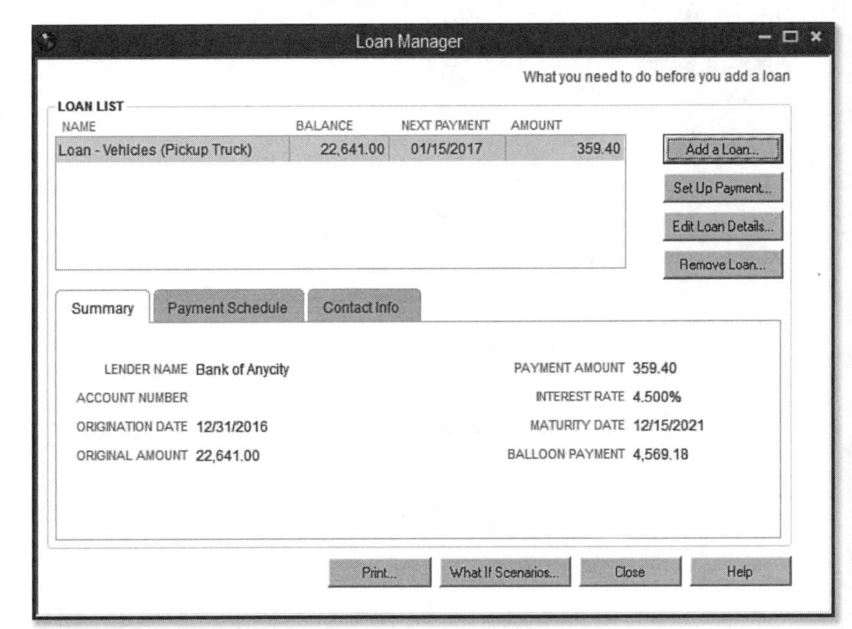

Figure 18.9
Use the Loan Manager to track long-term loan details.

Setting Up a Loan Payment

To set up a payment for the loan, follow these steps:

1. Select the loan from the list and click the Set Up Payment button. The Set Up Payment dialog box displays as shown in Figure 18.10.
2. In the This Payment Is drop-down list, select one of the following options: **A Regular Payment** or **An Extra Payment**.
3. View the Account Information and Payment Information. Modify the Payment Information if necessary.

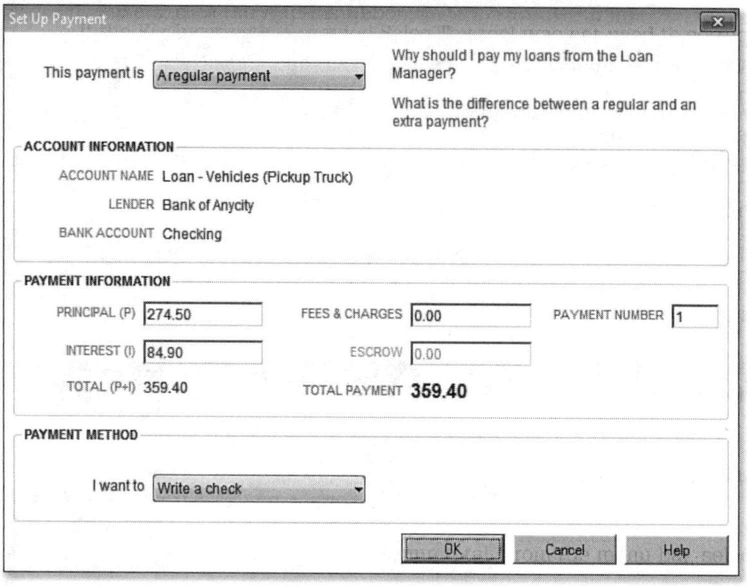

Figure 18.10
The Loan Manager can create the payment for the loan.

4. Select a **Payment Method** choosing between Write a Check or Enter a Bill.
5. Click OK and QuickBooks prepares a check or bill with the correct payment information.

Additionally from the Loan Manager, you can do the following:

- Edit the loan details or remove the loan.
- View summary information about the loan.
- View the payment schedule by payment number.
- Access contact information for the vendor, as set up with the original vendor record.
- Print the details of the loan.
- View multiple What If Scenarios, as shown in Figure 18.11.

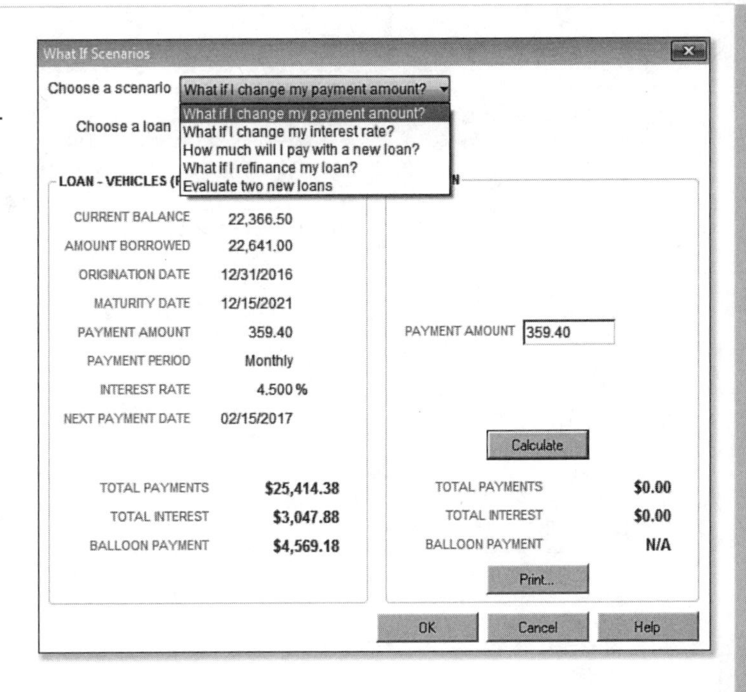

Figure 18.11
Use the QuickBooks Loan Manager to analyze different loan payoff scenarios.

Using the Year-End Guide

QuickBooks offers a ready-made Year-End Guide and checklist to help with your year-end tasks, as shown in Figure 18.12. Keep track of your progress as you get your file ready for your accountant or for tax time.

From the menu bar, select **Help**, **Year-End Guide**. Each task offers a link to more detailed help information. (Optional) Click the Save Checkmarks button so you can keep track of completed tasks.

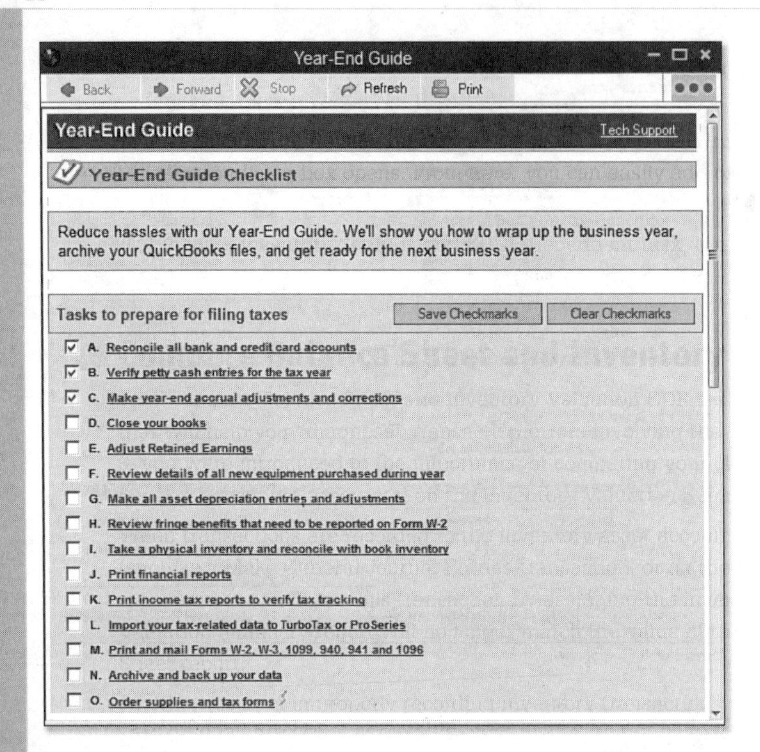

Figure 18.12
Use the Year-End Guide to help prepare your file for tax time.

Synchronizing QuickBooks Lists with Microsoft Outlook

If you use Microsoft Outlook to manage contact information, you can synchronize your contact data with QuickBooks. The information that can be synchronized includes the following:

- Customer and Job contact information
- Vendor contact information
- Other Names list contact information

To begin synchronizing your QuickBooks lists with Microsoft Outlook, follow these steps:

1. Before proceeding with this task, make sure you have a backup of your QuickBooks data and your Outlook contacts.
2. If you have previously installed the Contact Sync tool, you will be prompted to synchronize your contacts.

note

If you delete a contact in Outlook, that name will not be deleted in QuickBooks.

note

If you need help backing up your Outlook Contacts, from the QuickBooks Help search box on the icon bar, type **back up Outlook data** and select to search Help. Follow the appropriate links for more detailed information.

3. If you have not previously installed the free Contact Sync tool, from the menu bar, select **File**, **Utilities**, **Synchronize Contacts**. The Synchronize Contacts message displays. Select **OK** to be directed to the website (Internet connection required) to download the tool.

4. Click the file that was downloaded and follow the instructions to install. You will need to close Outlook before proceeding with the install.

If you want to have your QuickBooks contacts in a unique folder separate from your other contacts, create the new contact folder in Outlook and select the folder in step 7.

5. After installing, open Outlook. The Contact Sync Setup Assistant displays. See Figure 18.13.

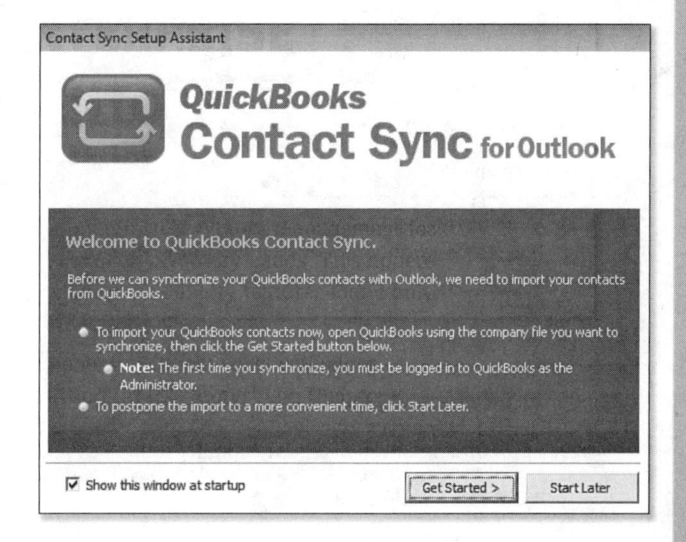

Figure 18.13
Setup of the QuickBooks Contact Sync is easy with step-by-step instructions.

6. Click Get Started and review the Begin Setup information. Click Setup.

7. QuickBooks Contact Sync displays the available Outlook Folder. If more than one is detected, select the appropriate folder. Click Next.

8. Select from Customer, Jobs, and Vendors to Synchronize. Click Next.

9. (Optional) Select to exclude from synchronization Outlook contacts marked as Personal or Private in Outlook. Click Next.

10. Review the defaults in the Mapping Fields window, as shown in Figure 18.14. Modify as needed or select **Restore Defaults**. Click Next.

11. If you selected to import Jobs or Vendors, complete the same information as detailed in step 10. Click Next.

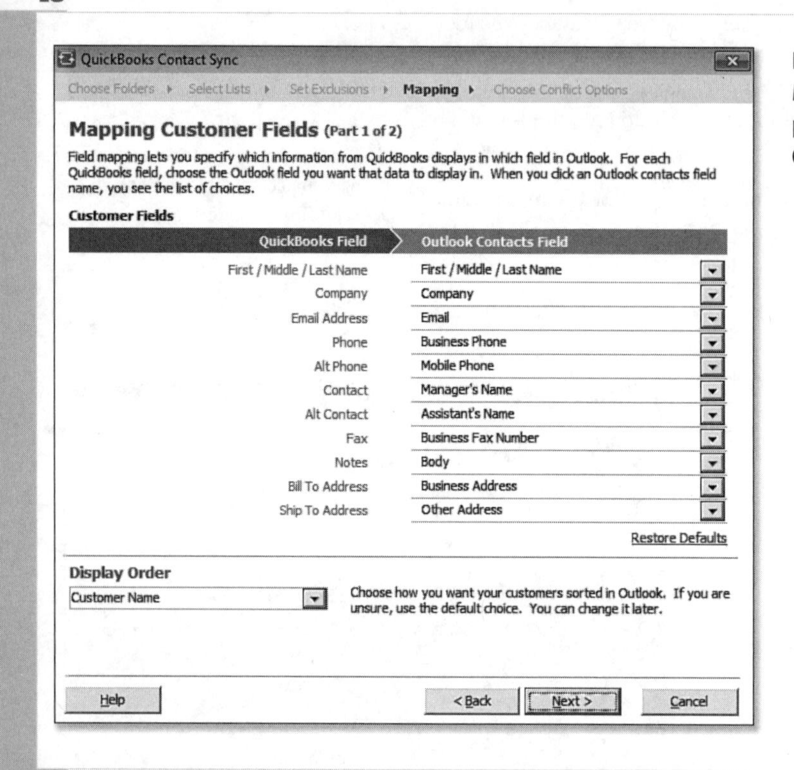

Figure 18.14
Modify the default mapping of fields from Outlook to QuickBooks.

12. Set an option for resolving any conflicts. Choices include
    - Let Me Decide Each Case
    - Outlook Data Wins
    - QuickBooks Data Wins
13. Click Save. Click Sync Now.
14. QuickBooks displays a Contact Overview Complete. If you selected the Let Me Decide Each Case in step 12, click Next to review the list of contacts to be imported.
15. Click to Accept the changes, which is not shown in Figure 18.15, and import the contacts. QuickBooks displays a progress bar.
16. Click Accept. QuickBooks displays a Synchronization Complete Message, click OK to close.
17. You can now view your contacts in Outlook, or your Outlook contacts in QuickBooks. See Figure 18.16.

The tool automatically installs in Outlook a QuickBooks Add-Ins tab (Outlook 2010) or a QuickBooks Toolbar (Outlook 2007 and earlier). From the Add-Ins you can change your synchronizing settings or Synchronize Contacts.

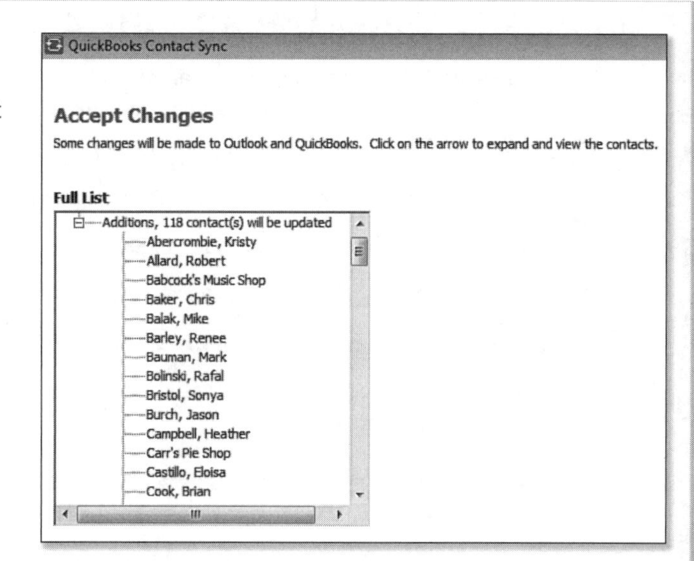

Figure 18.15
Review the contacts to be imported, if you selected the option in step 12 to Let Me Decide Each Case.

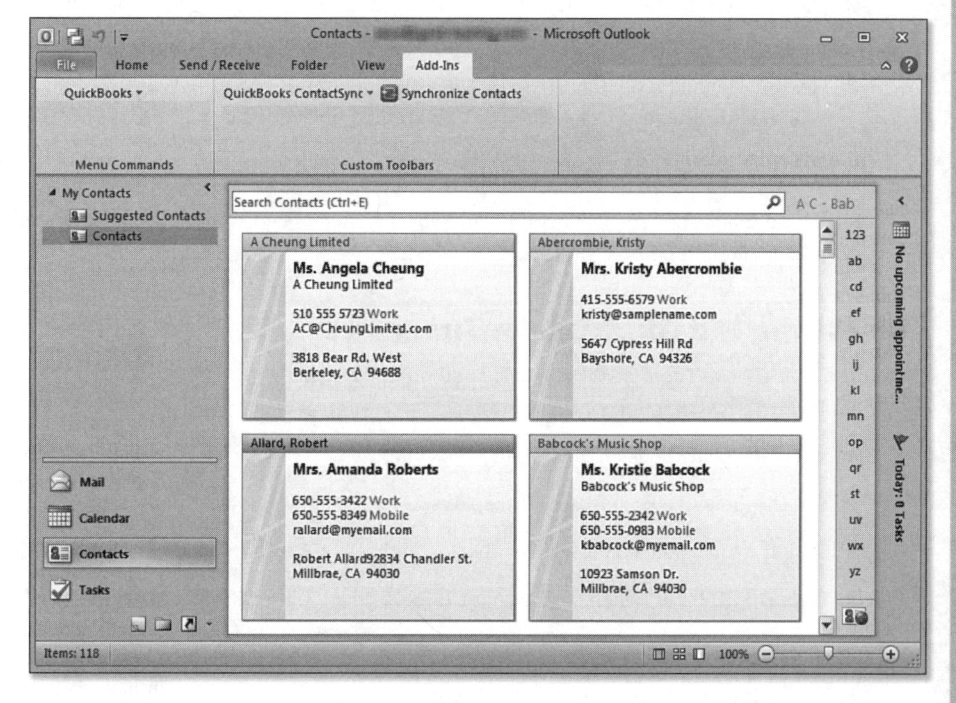

Figure 18.16
QuickBooks and Outlook will update with changes to contact details.

Using the QuickBooks Timer

The QuickBooks Timer is a separate program that can run on its own without QuickBooks. Time recorded with the QuickBooks Timer can be added to customer invoices when you do Time and Expense invoicing.

 *For more information, see "Time and Expense Invoicing," p. 346.*

Features of the QuickBooks Timer include the following:

- Track time spend on a task using a clock timer, or enter the time after you have done the work.
- Track time without having access to the QuickBooks data.
- Give a copy of the QuickBooks Timer program to people whom you want to track time, such as employees or subcontractors.

The basic workflow for using the QuickBooks Timer requires some manual processes, so be sure it is the right solution for you. The process includes the following four steps:

1. Once installed, the administrator of the QuickBooks file exports the current list of Service Items, Customers and Jobs, Vendors, and Employees.
2. The timekeepers receive this file via email or on a removable storage device like a USB flash drive. The lists are imported into each individual QuickBooks timer file.
3. The timekeepers track their time on their own computer and then when completed export the time to a file attached to an email or USB storage device.
4. The QuickBooks file administrator receives the file(s) and imports the time.

Each time the customers, jobs, vendor, employees, or service list items change, a new export file must be sent and imported by each timekeeper.

Installing the QuickBooks Timer

The QuickBooks Timer install file is located on the program CD-ROM. To install it, follow these steps:

1. Insert the QuickBooks CD-ROM into the computer.
2. Exit the QuickBooks startup if it displays.
3. Click the Microsoft Windows Start button and select **Run**.
4. Enter **D:\QBTimer** (where D:\ is your CD-ROM drive). Click OK.
5. Double-click the Setup file.
6. Follow the Timer installation instructions.

You can create a CD-ROM with the same install file and provide this CD to other timekeepers who might or might not have access to QuickBooks.

 **note**

You can also download the program from the Intuit support website http://support.quickbooks.intuit.com if you did not install your QuickBooks software from a CD-ROM. On the support website, type **QuickBooks Timer** into the search box. Scroll and click the link for Install the QuickBooks Timer instructions. Included in the instructions is a link to download the file. Click the setup.exe file and follow the install instructions on the screen.

Preparing the Timer for Activities

Before timekeepers can track their time, you need to import the QuickBooks Timer Lists. To do so, follow these steps:

1. Launch the QuickBooks Timer. If you recently installed the timer, you can launch it by clicking the Start button in Windows, All Programs, QuickBooks Timer, QuickBooks Pro Timer.
2. The No Timer File Is Open dialog box opens. Click Create New Timer File and click OK.
3. Type a name for the file (I use the QuickBooks company name) and select the proposed location for the file, or browse to a location of your choice. Click Save.
4. Click Yes, after reading the message about importing lists from QuickBooks.
5. The QuickBooks Timer help instructions display. Read the information or click the X in the top-right corner to close.
6. From your open QuickBooks file, select **File**, **Utilities**, **Export**, **Timer Lists** from the menu bar.
7. The Export Lists for Timer displays. Click OK.
8. QuickBooks opens a default location for the Timer Lists to be stored. This file will need to be updated as new customers, jobs, timekeepers, and so on are added to the file.
9. Provide a name for the file. Click Save. Click OK to the message that the data was exported successfully.
10. Launch the QuickBooks Timer as instructed in step 1.
11. From the File menu in QuickBooks Timer, select **Import QuickBooks Lists**.
12. Click Continue. Select the .IIF file to import, or browse to the location where you stored the file in step 9. Click Open.
13. Click OK to close the Data Imported Successfully message.

You are now ready to begin tracking time with the QuickBooks Timer.

Tracking Time with the Timer

Timekeepers can track time using the QuickBooks Timer even if they do not have access to the QuickBooks data file. However, to be current with the list of customers, jobs, or service items, the QuickBooks Administrator should frequently export the lists as detailed in the previous section.

To begin tracking time using the QuickBooks Timer, follow these steps:

1. Launch the QuickBooks Timer. If you recently installed the timer, you can launch it by clicking the Start button in Windows, All Programs, QuickBooks Timer, QuickBooks Pro Timer.

tip

Time format can be in decimal (10.20) or minutes (10:12). Log in to the QuickBooks data as the Admin user and then from the menu bar, select **Edit, Preferences, General, Company Preferences** tab.

2. In the QuickBooks Pro Timer window, click New Activity.

3. Select the Date, Your Name (timekeeper), Customer:Job, Service Item, optionally Class, and then enter an optional Note as displayed in Figure 18.17.

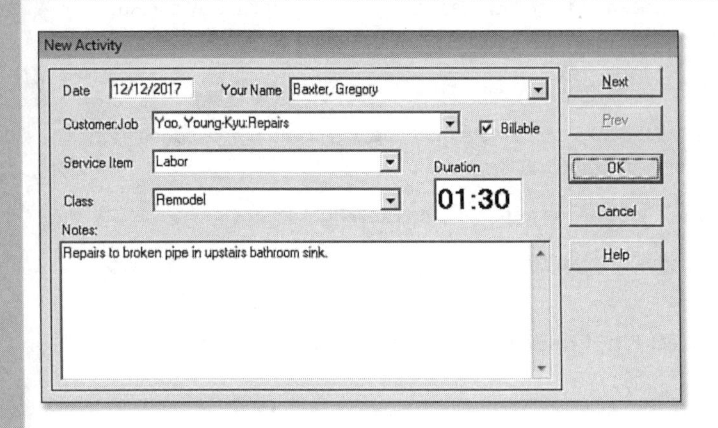

Figure 18.17
Enter your time after the service is performed, or click OK to start a "stop-watch" type of timer for the activity.

4. (Optional) Select **Billable** if this item will be included on a customer's invoice.

5. Click OK. The Timer shows the current activity. Click Start.

6. The QuickBooks Timer now begins a stopwatch type of timer. If instead you are entering your time after the service is performed, enter the time in the Duration field.

7. Click Edit at any time you need to change the time recorded.

8. Click Stop to stop the timer and Resume to begin timing again. See Figure 18.18.

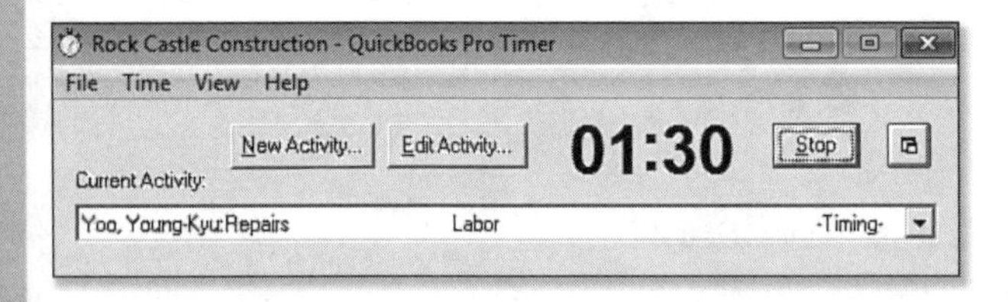

Figure 18.18
You can choose to use a stopwatch timer to track activities.

9. Click Stop when you are done with the selected task.

Exporting Timer Activities

If you are not entering your time directly into the QuickBooks file, the file administrator will need you to export your timer activities so that they can be imported into the QuickBooks file. When you are instructed by the QuickBooks administrator to export the Timer activities, follow these steps:

1. From the QuickBooks Timer file menu, select **Export Time Activities**. Click Continue.
2. Select the date you will be exporting activities through. Click OK.
3. Provide a filename and accept the default location for storing the exported lists, or browse to select a location of your choosing. The file will have the extension of .IIF (Intuit Interchange Format). Remember this location because you will need to attach this file to an email or copy it to a removable storage device such as a USB flash drive. Click Save.
4. Click OK to close the Data Exported Successfully message.

Each timekeeper will need to provide this saved file to the QuickBooks administrator for importing into the QuickBooks file.

tip

New for QuickBooks 2013 you can set a preference to have all time activities marked as billable. From the menu bar, select **Edit, Preferences, Time and Expenses** on the Company Preferences tab.

You would mark a time activity as billable only if your company wants to include line detail on a customer's invoice for the employee's or vendor's time activities. This is referred to as Time & Expense or Cost Plus billing.

Importing Timer Activities into QuickBooks

One of the features of using this free timer program is that the user does not need to have QuickBooks installed.

When you want the timer activities included in your QuickBooks data file, you need to import the Exported Timer Activities. Ask each of your timekeepers to follow the instructions listed previously for exporting their timer activities.

note

The next time you import timer activities, QuickBooks will remember where the lists were stored.

To import the Timer Activities received from your timekeepers, follow these steps:

1. Receive your timekeepers' individual QuickBooks Timer Exported Lists files. They will have an extension of .IIF (Intuit Interchange Format).
2. Launch QuickBooks. From the menu bar, select **File**, **Utilities**, **Import**, **Timer Activities**.
3. Click OK to the Import Activities from Timer message.
4. Browse to the location where you stored the Exported Timer Activities from your timekeepers.
5. Select the file. Click Open. QuickBooks displays the QB Pro Timer Import Summary. Click View Report (see Figure 18.19) to see a listing of the time activities imported. See Figure 18.20.

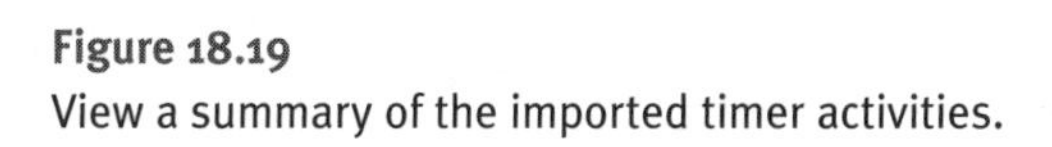

Figure 18.19
View a summary of the imported timer activities.

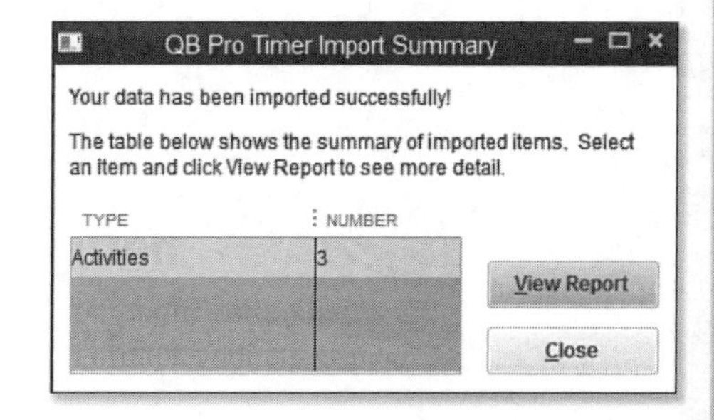

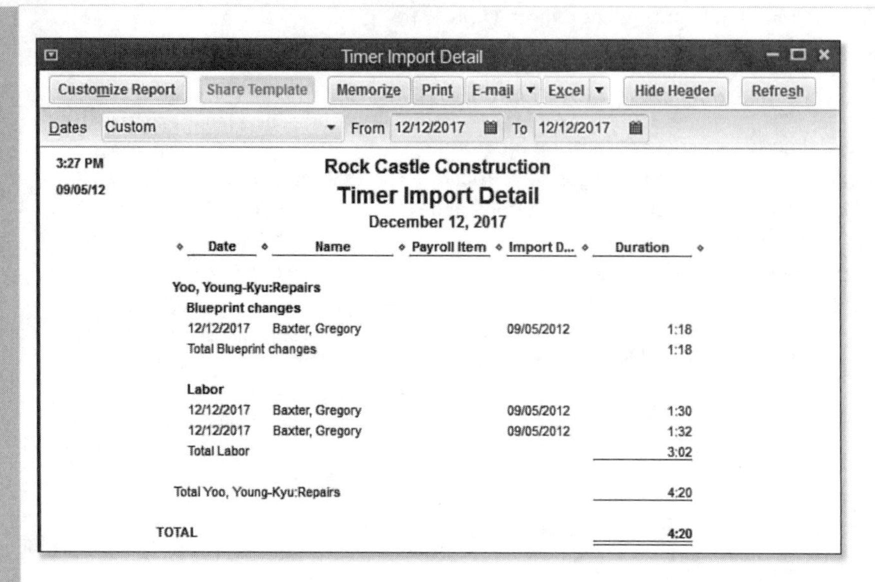

Figure 18.20
Details of the imported activities.

You can now include these imported timer activities on customer invoices, or issue vendor checks or employee checks using the timer activity totals.

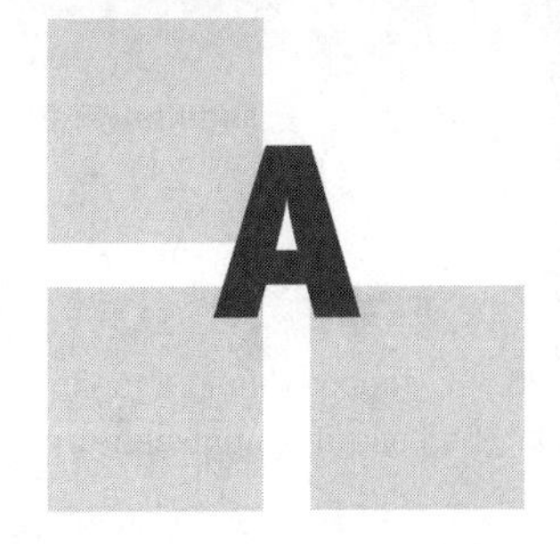

CLIENT DATA REVIEW

This appendix is provided for accounting professionals using QuickBooks Accountant 2013 or QuickBooks Enterprise Solutions Accountant 13.0. Client Data Review is a tool available with these editions of the QuickBooks software.

Reviewing client's files can be a time-consuming process. Accounting professionals can save time working with their clients' files using these features of Client Data Review:

- Reclassify hundreds of transactions all at once
- Write-off multiple open customer invoice balances at once
- Fix incorrectly recorded sales tax payments
- Quickly troubleshoot inventory issues
- Identify changes clients made to the lists in QuickBooks
- Troubleshoot beginning balance changes from year-to-year
- Apply open vendor and customer credits in batch to with charges/invoices
- Clear up balances left in the Undeposited Funds account

After working with the Client Data Review tools you will never want to review a client's file the "old fashioned way" again!

Introduction: Features and Benefits

Available with QuickBooks Accountant 2013 is the Client Data Review (CDR) feature, shown in Figure A.1. Accessing CDR tools and features is easier than ever with the customizable Accountant's Center. CDR is a collection of tools and reports used primarily by accounting professionals to streamline the many tasks involved in reviewing, troubleshooting, and correcting a client's QuickBooks data.

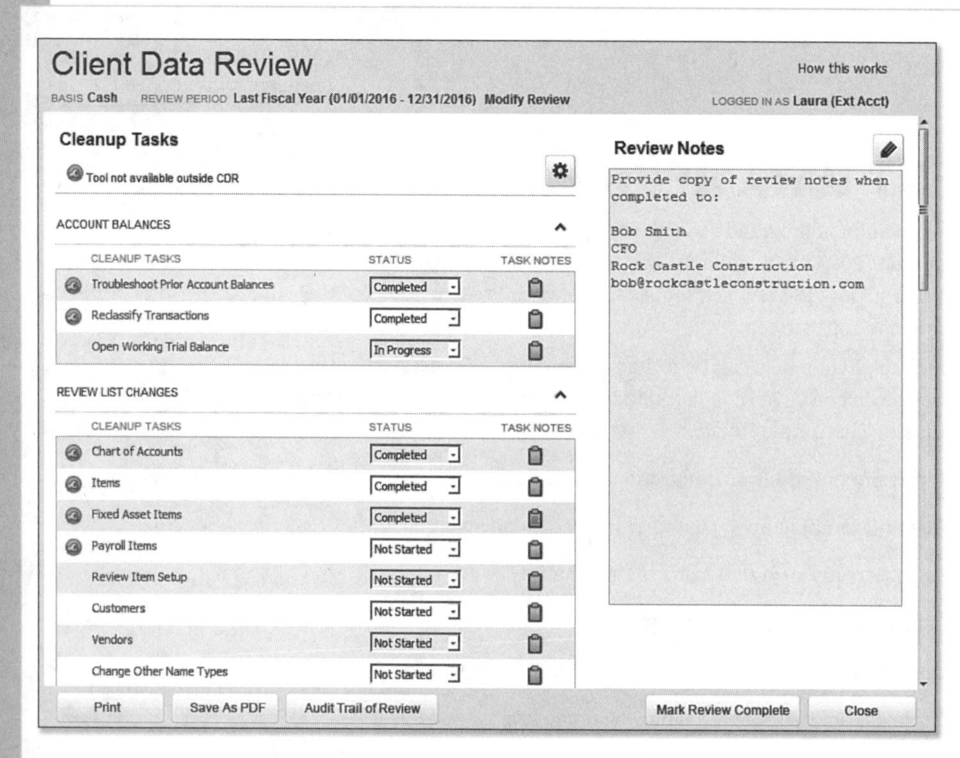

Figure A.1 Client Data Review (CDR) is helpful for finding and fixing your client's QuickBooks data entry errors.

The CDR feature is not available for use with QuickBooks Professional Bookkeeper, QuickBooks Online, or QuickBooks for Mac.

With QuickBooks Accountant software, all the features of CDR will work with a QuickBooks Accountant's Copy of your client's file. See Chapter 16, "Sharing QuickBooks Data with Your Accountant."

CDR can be used when working with a client's Accountant's Copy file type (.QBX file extension), but some feature limitations apply. Refer to Chapter 16 for more details on the benefits of working with this file type.

note

QuickBooks offers a version of its software titled QuickBooks Professional Bookkeeper 2013. This software solution does not include the Client Data Review feature discussed in this appendix.

Typically, a best practice workflow using CDR tools is as follows:

1. Review with the client open Accounts Receivable, Accounts Payable, and other balances for which the client has current information.
2. Review your client's data file using the CDR-specific tasks and reports.
3. Make data corrections using CDR tools and set a QuickBooks closing date.
4. If completing a formal review, Mark Review Complete, letting CDR "store" your period reviewed balances. (The client cannot change these reviewed balances!)
5. Save as PDF details of the review.
6. Print the details from the Client Data Review dialog box. Save the details as a PDF. You can also print an Audit Trail of Review, listing those transactions that were added or modified.
7. Begin your next review and let QuickBooks detail for you any and all changes to balances, transactions, and lists since your last completed review!

tip

CDR features can be used when QuickBooks is in multiuser mode. This means other users in the QuickBooks file can continue with their daily tasks while the accounting professional uses the CDR tools or features to review or make changes to the client's file.

However, only one user can access Client Data Review at a time.

Your steps might differ slightly if you are working in a client's Accountant's Copy file type. For more information on sharing data with your accountant using the Accountant's Copy, see Chapter 16.

There are specific tasks and reports that are available only with CDR. These tasks are indicated with the CDR icon. For example, see the icon next to the Troubleshoot Prior Account Balances task, as shown in Figure A.1. Other tasks listed without the icon indicate a feature or report that is available within and outside of the CDR functionality.

CDR offers robust tracking of the changes your client makes to the data between your reviews. CDR also offers the following:

- Powerful time-saving tools for finding and fixing client entry errors: Reclassify Transactions, Write-Off Invoices, Fix Incorrectly Recorded Sales Tax, Inventory Troubleshooting, Identify Changes to Lists, Troubleshoot Beginning Balance Differences, Match Unapplied Vendor and Customer Credits, and Clear Up Undeposited Funds.
- Troubleshooting beginning balances "saves" the previously reviewed debit and credit balances; the tool then compares this stored balance to the same prior-dated balances in QuickBooks as of today. Your previously reviewed and stored QuickBooks balances cannot be modified by the client!
- QuickBooks suggests an adjusting journal entry to make so your prior period reviewed balances agree with the current QuickBooks data for that period. You remain in control, deciding if you want to modify the detail in the journal entry.
- Identify what chart of accounts balances differ and the amount of the difference when compared to your prior period of reviewed financials.
- Track changes to the items lists, such as additions, name changes, and even tracking accounts or list items that were merged.

- Track changes made to list items, accounts assigned, or for payroll items when a change to a payroll tax rate is made.
- While working with CDR activities, if you have the Open Windows dialog box displayed, you can move efficiently between activities in QuickBooks and the CDR activities. For more information about navigating QuickBooks, see Chapter 2, "Getting Around QuickBooks."
- Conveniently work on CDR in QuickBooks and modify or add transactions as normal with an immediate refresh of the data in your review.
- Access the CDR while working in a client's Accountant's Copy file-sharing format. All CDR tools and features work with an Accountant's Copy. There are other restrictions when working with an Accountant's Copy, and these are detailed in Chapter 16.

If you are an accounting professional and want to work most efficiently with your client's file, use QuickBooks Accountant 2013 or QuickBooks Enterprise Solutions Accountant 13.0.

tip

As an accounting professional, would you like to "try" CDR even if you don't have the Accountant's edition of QuickBooks? Have your client create a User Log In for you in the client's file and assign the External Accountant user type. For more information, see "Creating an External Accountant User Type," p. 591.

When you log in to the client's Pro or Premier 2013 or Enterprise 13.0 data file as an External Accountant user, you will have access to the Accountant Center (which either opens automatically or you can access it from the Company menu). Although this Accountant Center is not customizable, you do have *limited* access to some of the features found only in QuickBooks Accountant software and selected CDR tools, including the following:

- Create a Working Trial Balance
- Reclassify Transactions
- Fix Unapplied Payments and Credits
- Write Off Invoices

In addition, your Accountant Center provides easy access to other common QuickBooks tasks, memorized reports, reconciliation details, and updates especially for the accounting professional.

Accessing Client Data Review Tools and Features

With QuickBooks Accountant 2013, accounting professionals can access common CDR tools and features in the software multiple ways, including the following:

- **Accountant Center**—Customize to include the tools you use most with your client's files.
- **Accountant Menu**—Use individual CDR tools and features without starting a review, or launch a formal dated review.

Before you use CDR, determine whether you need to do a formal review or just efficiently work on troubleshooting and fixing client data entry errors.

If your client has engaged you simply to clean up data entry errors, you might not need to open a review to complete these CDR-specific tasks:

- Reclassify Transactions
- Fix Unapplied Customer and Vendor Credits
- Clear Up Undeposited Funds Account
- Write Off Invoices
- Fix Incorrectly Recorded Sales Tax
- Compare Balance Sheet and Inventory Valuation
- Troubleshoot Inventory
- Find Incorrectly Paid Payroll Liabilities

tip

You can use many of the CDR tools without opening a dated review. The date range that will default when using CDR tools is your last fiscal year. However, with most of the tools you can change the date range manually if needed.

However, if part of your engagement with the client includes using the following CDR tools (detailed later in this chapter); you will need to Start Review formally using CDR:

- Troubleshoot Prior Account Balances
- Review List Changes

If your client sends you an Accountant's Copy file with data, you will be able to access the features available with CDR. The benefit of using the Accountant's Copy file is that your client can continue day-to-day operations while you make changes to the data. The file is then sent back to the client to import your changes.

Chapter 16 discusses the benefits of using the Accountant's Copy file, a preferred data-sharing method if you need to use the CDR while your client continues day-to-day work in the file.

If your client sends you a QuickBooks 2013 backup file (.QBB extension) or portable company file (.QBM file extension), both of these files when restored will enable you to use the CDR, but your changes will not be able to be merged into the client's data file.

note

New for QuickBooks 2013, if you are using the QuickBooks Accountant software and your client is using a version of the QuickBooks 2013 for Windows, you can send your adjusting journal entries by email for your client to import. For more information, see "Other Methods of Sharing Data," p. 603.

Customizing the Accountant Center

For the accounting professional, a great benefit of using the Accountant versions of QuickBooks 2013 or Enterprise 13.0 is the Accountant Center, as displayed in Figure A.2. The Accountant Center offers easy access to Client Data Review tools and other accountant features.

The Accountant Center can also be accessed from a client's 2013 Pro or Premier (non-accountant) and Enterprise 13.0 file when you, the accounting professional, log in to the file as an External Accountant user.

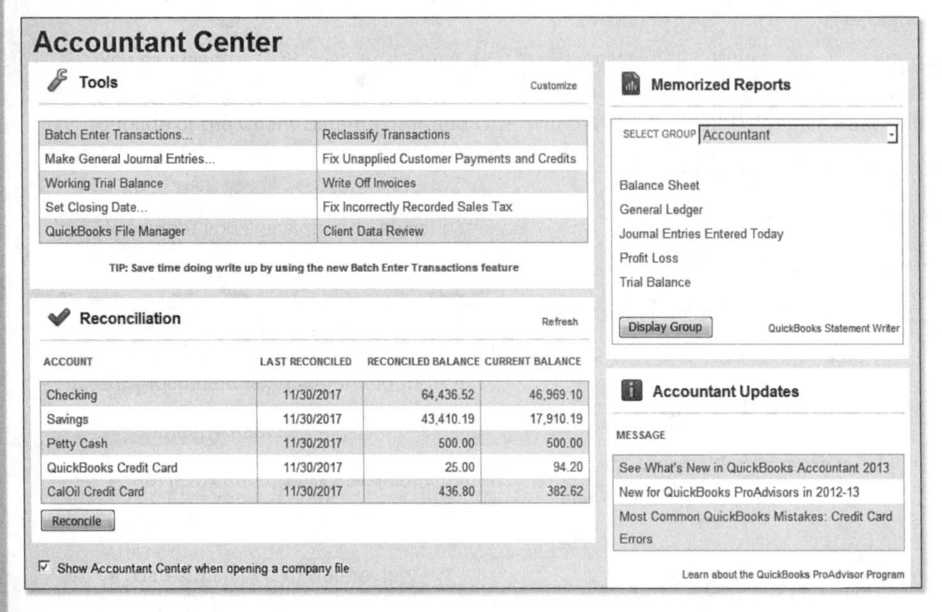

Figure A.2 Customize the Accountant Center to include those tools and features you use most when working with your client's data.

By default, a preference is set to have the Accountant Center open automatically. The Accountant Center can also be accessed from the Accountant menu. In a non-accountant edition of QuickBooks, you can log in as the External Accountant user type and access the Accountant Center from the Company menu. When you log in to the file this way, you will have some of the Accountant Center features available, but not all.

The Accountant Center also provides easy access to Memorized Report Groups. You can learn about working with reporting in QuickBooks in Chapter 14, "Reporting in QuickBooks."

For accounting professionals, create your own memorized report group and access it from the Accountant Center when working with each client's file.

tip

You need to customize the Accountant Center only once, and your customized view will display with each unique client file opened with your Professional Bookkeeper or Accountant 2013 software. However, a shortcut won't appear on the Accountant Center if the feature it points to is not enabled in a particular client's file.

The Reconciliation panel includes timely information about your client's last reconciliation date—reconciled balance and current balance for all bank and credit card type accounts. Click Refresh to reflect recent changes to the client's data. More information about working with banking activities is included in Chapter 13, "Working with Bank and Credit Card Accounts."

The Accountant's Update section helps accounting professionals stay informed with important alerts, practice development tips, and links to training opportunities.

If you are using QuickBooks Accountant 2013 or Enterprise Accountant 13.0, practice customizing the Accountant Center with these instructions:

Customize the Accountant Center

Open the Accountant Center from the Accountant menu to customize the Tools section:

1. From the menu bar, select **Accountant, Accountant Center.**
2. Click the Customize link in the Tools panel of the Accountant Center. The Customize Your List of Tools dialog box displays. See Figure A.3.

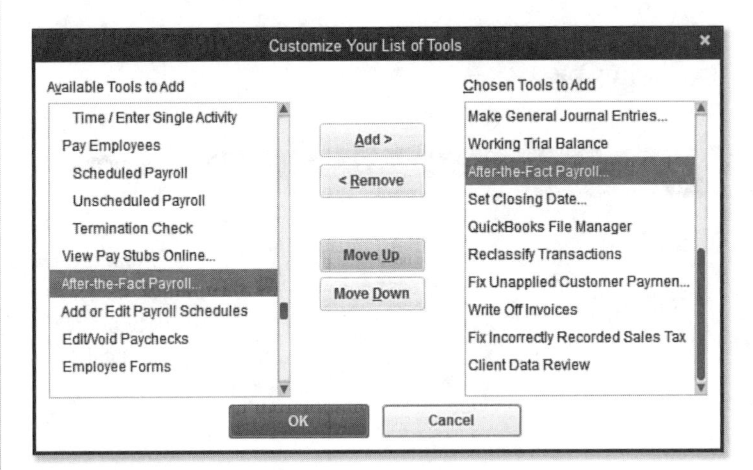

Figure A.3
Customize the Accountant Center to include those tools you use most often.

3. From the Available Tools to Add list, select an action you want to add to the Chosen Tools to Add section and click the Add> button.
4. Rearrange the order of the selected tools by selecting one in the Chosen Tools to Add list and then clicking the Move Up or Move Down button.
5. (Optional) To remove a tool, click the tool in the Chosen Tools to Add and then click the <Remove button.
6. Click OK to close the Customize Your List of Tools dialog box and your changes will now be displayed in your very own Accountant Center.

Customizing the Client Data Review Center

You can customize the list of displayed clean-up tasks in CDR. However, the changes you make affect only the QuickBooks file currently opened. Additionally, some CDR tasks will display only if the related feature in QuickBooks is enabled (Sales Tax, for example).

To gain access to the customizing feature, launch the CDR feature. To do so, follow these steps:

1. From the menu bar, select **Accountant**, **Client Data Review**, **Client Data Review**. You can also launch CDR from the QuickBooks icon bar if you are using QuickBooks Accountant 2013 or Enterprise Solutions Accountant 13.0.

2. If this is your first review for this client, the Client Data Review—Start Review dialog box displays, as shown in Figure A.4. From this dialog box, accept the default Review Date Range shown, or select a date range from the following options in the drop-down list:

   - Last Fiscal Year (your default fiscal year is defined in the QuickBooks Company, Company Information menu)
   - Last Fiscal Quarter
   - Last Month
   - Custom (you choose the From and To dates)

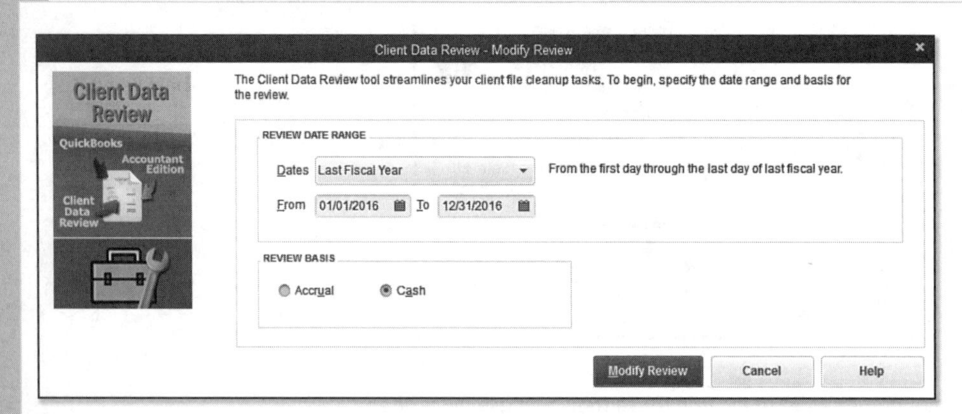

Figure A.4 When you choose to do a formal review, you select the date range and basis.

3. Select the appropriate **Review Basis—Accrual** or **Cash**. This basis defaults from the Reports & Graphs preference setting in the QuickBooks file.
4. (Optional) Click to select to have Task Notes from previous reviews follow to the new review.
5. Click Start Review, and the Client Data Review tasks display as previously shown in Figure A.1.

If you find you need to change your default reporting basis, you can do so on the Reports and Graphs tab of the Preferences dialog box (select **Edit, Preferences** from the menu bar). You will need to be logged in as the Admin or External Accountant user in single-user mode to change the global preference for reporting basis.

Modifying the Review Date and Basis

The basis shown in the CDR defaulted from the QuickBooks data file preferences when the CDR was first launched, or the basis was manually selected on the Client Data Review—Start Review or Modify Review dialog box.

After beginning a review, if you need to change either the review period or basis, click the Modify Review link in the CDR, top center, to be returned to the dialog box (refer to Figure A.1).

Customize Cleanup Tasks

You might have some clients who do not need a review of some of the task groups in their QuickBooks data. For example, you are working in a client's file that does not have to track or pay sales tax.

With CDR, you can remove those tasks that are not needed for the specifically open client file. The changes made in one client's file will not be made to another client's file CDR tasks.

With Client Data Review open, follow these steps to remove the sales tax task group (or any of the other tasks) from the CDR:

1. Click the Customize Cleanup Tasks link in the center of the CDR dialog box (refr to Figure A.1).
2. The Client Data Review—Customize dialog box displays as shown in Figure A.5.

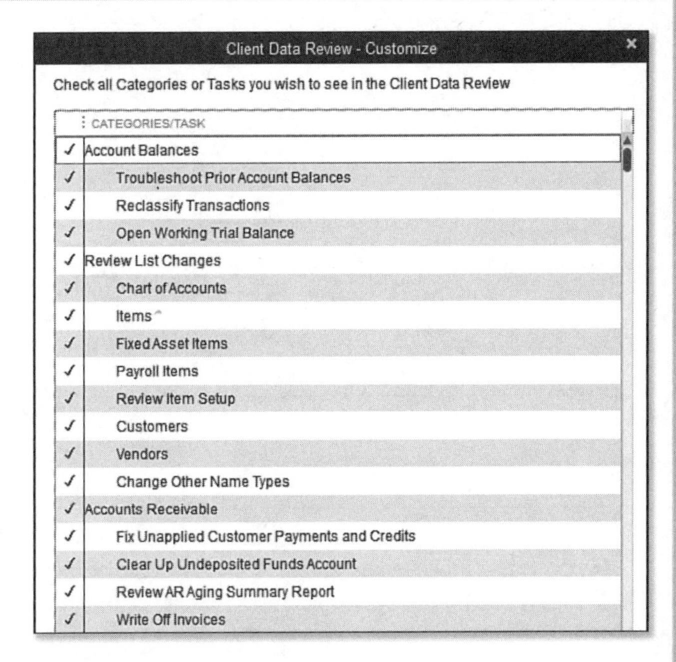

Figure A.5
Remove CDR tasks from being displayed in this currently selected client file.

3. Place your mouse pointer on any list item and click once to unselect that specific task or group of tasks. Clicking again will reselect the list item.
4. Click the Restore Defaults button to return to the original settings.
5. Click Help to open the help topic specific for CDR.
6. Click Save Changes or Cancel if you do not want to make the changes.

tip

If the desired Categories/Task is not displayed in the Client Data Review—Customize dialog box, it is because for the currently opened QuickBooks file that feature is not currently enabled.

You have successfully changed the lists of tasks that displays for this client's data file only.

Minimize or Expand Task Groups

You might not want to remove a task completely, but minimize it instead:

Figure A.6 shows the task group before being minimized. Figure A.7 shows the same group after being minimized. The Hide and Show Task state for each task group on the CDR is company file-dependent. The changes you make in one company file will not be made in other QuickBooks client files.

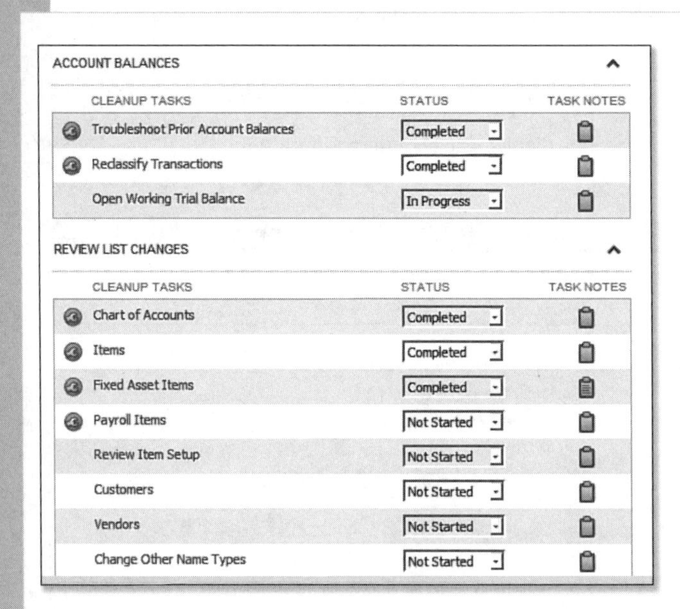

Figure A.6
View before minimizing the Review List Changes task.

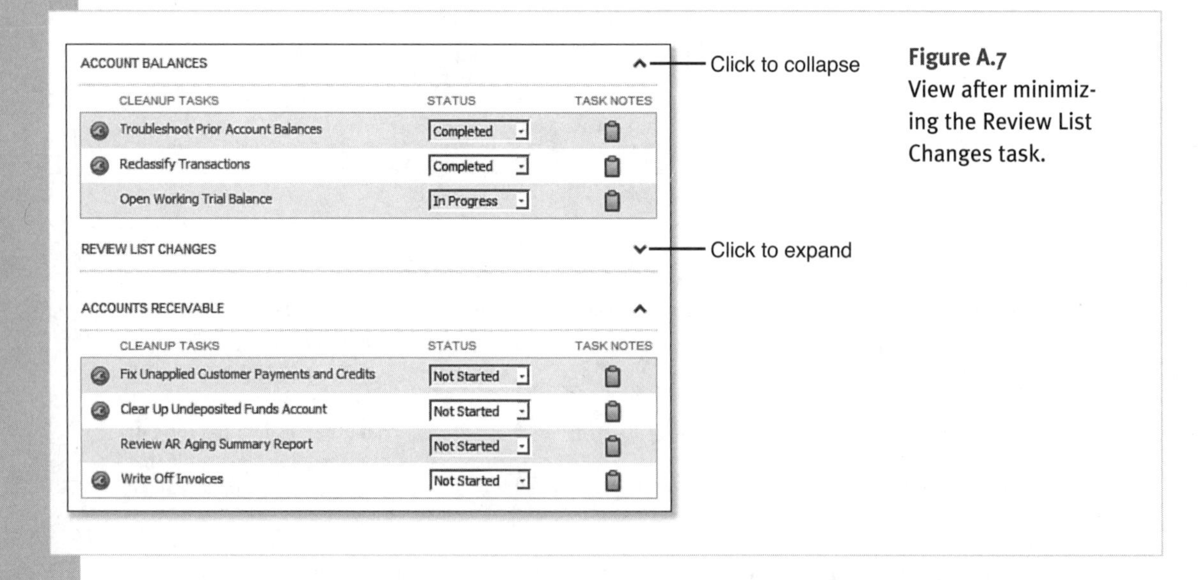

Figure A.7
View after minimizing the Review List Changes task.

Assigning Status and Notes to Review Tasks

To help in managing the review of a client's file, you have an associated status you can optionally assign to each task. This feature is useful for your own reference or if several accounting professionals are reviewing the same file.

To assign a new status or change an existing status, click the Status drop-down list and choose from one of the available choices:

- Not Started (this is the default status assigned to all tasks when a review is started)
- In Progress
- Completed
- Not Applicable

(Optional) You can record a note about a particular task. Click the task note icon to the right of a task; see Figure A.8. The Task Notes dialog box will display, and you can document specific review notes for that task. These notes are included in the CDR notes when Save as PDF is selected.

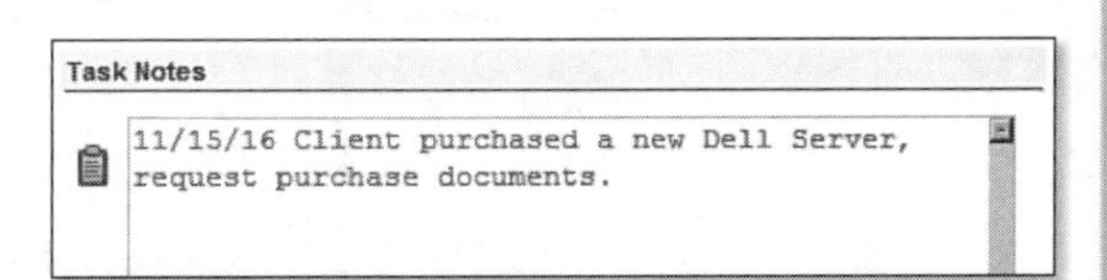

Figure A.8
Conveniently store specific task notes as you review the file.

When you return to a CDR in progress, or if you share the review with other accounting professionals at your firm, each individual can see the progress of a particular task in review.

After customizing the CDR to show or hide specific task groups, you should take one more precaution.

Before beginning the review and making changes to a client's file, make sure you are logged in as an External Accountant type user. This ensures that your changes can be tracked separately from those made by the client and also gives you complete access to the Admin activities available in the CDR. For more information, read the "Creating an External Accountant User" section later in this chapter.

To see the currently logged-in user, look to the top-right corner of the CDR. CDR identifies the username and whether the user is an External Accountant, as displayed in Figure A.1.

You are now ready to begin the review process. The following sections provide more details about the unique features and results you can expect when reviewing and correcting your client's data file using this innovative feature. You will never want to do a review the "old fashioned" way again!

Account Balances

Although you do not have to do the review task groups in any particular order, I do recommend you begin with the Account Balances task group. A reliable client data file review depends on accurate balance sheet reporting, which includes financial numbers from prior periods.

If a closing date was not set previously, or if the user was granted access to adding, modifying, or deleting prior year transactions, your ending balances that QuickBooks reports now might be different from those you used to prepare financials or tax return documents. Setting a closing date and password can help control changes to prior period transactions. More information about setting a closing date can be found in Chapter 16.

Troubleshoot Prior Account Balances

The first task included in Account Balances review, Troubleshoot Prior Account Balances, displays the trial balance in debit and credit format, as shown in Figure A.9.

Troubleshoot Prior Account Balances - Review Period: Last Fiscal Year (01/01/2016 - 12/31/2016)

Prior Review Period: From 01/01/2015 To 12/31/2015 Basis Cash | View Changed Transactions | View List Changes

Differences shown below may be due to changed transactions, list changes that affected accounts, or unentered transactions. How this works

Tips for entering balances	Balances in Accountant's Records		Balances in Client's File		Difference	
Account	Debit	Credit	Debit	Credit	Debit	Credit
ASSETS						
10100 · Checking	24,342.03		25,542.03			1,200.00
10300 · Savings	15,600.00		15,600.00			
10400 · Petty Cash	500.00		500.00			
11000 · Accounts Receivable	2,891.35		2,891.35			
12000 · Undeposited Funds						
12100 · Inventory Asset	17,903.00		17,903.00			
12800 · Employee Advances	770.00		770.00			
13100 · Pre-paid Insurance	4,050.00		4,050.00			
13400 · Retainage Receivable	1,796.72		1,796.72			
15000 · Furniture and Equipment	22,826.00		22,826.00			
15100 · Vehicles	78,936.91		78,936.91			
15200 · Buildings and Improvements	325,000.00		325,000.00			
15300 · Construction Equipment	15,300.00		15,300.00			
16900 · Land	90,000.00		90,000.00			
TOTAL	628,918.06	628,918.06	628,918.06	628,918.06	1,200.00	1,200.00

Only show accounts with different balances | View Suggested Adjustments

Figure A.9 Use Troubleshoot Prior Account Balances to correct any changes to prior period balances efficiently.

The Troubleshoot Account Balances tool displays these columns:

- **Accounts**—Grouped by account type:
  - Assets
  - Liabilities
  - Equity

- Income
- Cost of Goods Sold
- Expenses
- Other Income
- Other Expense

- **Balances in Accountant's Records**—Debit and credit columns, these amounts are fixed as of the previous review by the accounting professional. They do not change even when a customer makes a change to a transaction in the review period.
- **Balances in Client's File**—Debit and credit columns, these amounts are the currently calculated balances in the client's file for the reported review period.
- **Difference**—Debit and credit columns, any amounts displayed in these columns represent differences between the Balances in Accountant's Records and the Balances in Client's File.

The primary purpose of this task is to provide a window where QuickBooks can compare the prior year's ending balances (as you used to prepare financials, tax returns, or monthly and quarterly reviews) with what QuickBooks currently shows for that same prior date range.

Your work will be complete in this window when there are no amounts left in the difference columns—indicating that the Balances in Accountant's Records agree with the Balances in Client's File for that same prior period date.

Entering Balances in Accountant's Records

If this is your first time using CDR with your client's data, you will need to enter the Balances in Accountant's Records columns in debit and credit spreadsheet format. You have two options for completing this task:

- Select **Yes** to the message that displays when you begin your first CDR of this file. CDR will now copy the columns of data from the Balances in Client's File to the Balances in Accountant's Records columns. Simply change any of the values copied to agree with your prior financials. If you select **No** to this message, a Copy Balances button is available on the top left for you to click to complete the task automatically.
- Or, manually enter the amounts in the Balances in Accountant's Records columns to agree with your last reported financials or filed tax return.

This is the only time you will be required to enter the balances. For future reviews, QuickBooks will populate the Balances in Accountant's Records columns with the reviewed balances as recorded when you selected the Mark Review as Complete at the bottom-right of the CDR center.

The Troubleshoot Prior Account Balances task compares these prior balances to the current balances QuickBooks has for each account for the same prior date range. QuickBooks is determining for you which accounts have a discrepancy from the last review! Spend less time on clean-up tasks with CDR.

Any reported balance differences might have been less likely to occur if a closing date and password had been entered in your client's data file.

In Figure A.9 a difference is shown for the account Checking (and there is also a difference for the account Rent, not shown). The next section will detail how these CDR-dependent tasks will help you locate these differences.

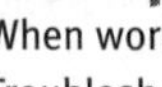

tip

When working with the Troubleshoot Prior Account Balances task, if a chart of account was marked as inactive in QuickBooks but has a balance in the account as of the date range in the review, the CDR will include that account listing.

View Changed Transactions

If this is your first time using the CDR for a client's data file, QuickBooks will not be able to detail the specific changed transactions in the Differences columns. However, after you choose Mark Review as Complete for the first CDR, QuickBooks begins tracking specific changed transactions from that time forward.

To determine what transactions dated on or before your last completed review date have been modified, double-click any amount displayed in the Differences column. A transaction listing report is displayed as shown in Figure A.10. The report identifies for you the specific transactions dated on or before the end of the last review period that have been added, modified, or deleted.

If you double-clicked a difference amount on a specific line, the resulting report is filtered for transactions modified after your last review. You can limit what you see on the report by selecting the Customize Report button on the displayed report. You can filter for Entered/Last Modified dates to see only those transactions that were changed after you finished your review.

This one feature alone is why accountants should use QuickBooks Accountant 2013. Think of all the time you will save on future reviews of your client's data!

8:10 AM
12/15/17

Rock Castle Construction - Account: 10100 · Checking
Transactions on/before 12/31/2015 - Changed on/after 01/01/2016
No list changes affect this account.

Last modified by	State	Date	Name	Account	Split	Debit	Credit
Laura (External Accountant)	*Deleted*					0.00	
Admin	Prior	12/01/2015	Reyes Properties	10100 · Checking	63900 · Rent		1,200.00
			Reyes Properties	63900 · Rent	10100 · Checking	1,200.00	

Figure A.10
Using CDR can help you easily identify changes to transactions that affect the beginning balances.

tip

Select the **Only Show Accounts with Different Balances** checkbox if you want to view fewer rows of detail in the Troubleshoot Prior Account Balances task in CDR.

View Suggested Adjustments

When QuickBooks detects any difference between the Balances in Accountant's Records and the Balances in Client's file, CDR suggests an adjusting journal entry for you to review.

To have QuickBooks assist in the preparation of this adjusting journal entry, follow these steps:

1. If differences are detected, click the View Suggested Adjustments button. QuickBooks opens the Make General Journal Entries dialog box marked as an adjusting entry and dated as of the last date of the period under review (see Figure A.11). If your debits and credits are equal in the Review Last Balances columns, this journal entry should also have debits equal to credits for any differences that were detected.

Make General Journal Entries

Main Reports

DATE 12/31/2015 ENTRY NO. 1001 ADJUSTING ENTRY

ACCOUNT	DEBIT	CREDIT	MEMO	NAME	BILL...	CLASS
10100 · Checking		1,200.00	Troubleshoot Balances Adjustment - As of 12/31/2015			
63900 · Rent	1,200.00		Troubleshoot Balances Adjustment - As of 12/31/2015			
Totals	1,200.00	1,200.00				

Figure A.11
QuickBooks prepares an adjusting journal entry to agree with your reviewed balances for the prior period.

2. If you are working in an Accountant's Copy file, you might also get a notice that any changes made to shaded fields in the journal entry will transfer back to the client. Click OK to close this message.
3. Click OK to close the message about automatically numbering your journal entries.
4. Click Save & Close to close the Make General Journal Entries dialog box.
5. Click View Suggested Reversing Entries if after these adjustments are made you need to reverse them; it is useful if the client corrected the error in a future accounting period. Or, click the Don't Reverse button to close the Reversing Entries dialog box.
6. Click the X in the top-right corner to close the Troubleshoot Prior Account Balances dialog box.

The Troubleshoot Prior Account Balances task is complete when there are no amounts in the Differences column. (Optional) Enter a task note for the Troubleshooting Prior Account Balances task to document your work or note other necessary actions.

note

You will not be able to save the journal entry unless the totals of the debits and credits are equal.

caution

If you selected View Suggested Adjustments and you had adjustments to an Accounts Receivable and Accounts Payable account, you will receive a warning message that you cannot adjust accounts receivable and accounts payable in the same journal entry. Instructions are given to remove one of the lines and the corresponding balancing line and enter it in a separate journal entry.

When the Mark Review Complete button is selected on the CDR dialog box, CDR will take the Balances in Client's File columns and transfer them to the Balances in Accountant's Records columns in the Troubleshoot Prior Account Balances dialog box. The Balances in Accountant's Records amounts *will not* change when clients add, modify, or delete transactions dated in your completed review period.

Reclassify Transactions

How often have you reviewed your client's QuickBooks data to see multiple transactions posted to the incorrect general ledger account? As an accountant, you will probably not want to spend the time needed to correct each individual transaction. A preferred method might be to create a journal entry transaction, which in effect "reclassifies" the amount out of the incorrect account and into the correct account.

With CDR in QuickBooks Accountant 2013 or Enterprise Solutions Accountant 13.0, you can use the Reclassify Transactions feature. You access this tool from the Accountant Center, Accountant menu, or from an opened review using CDR.

From the Accounts panel on the left side of the Reclassify Transactions dialog box, you can do the following:

- Accept or change the defaulted date range. These dates control the transactions that will display for reclassifying.
- Accept or change the defaulted basis. This basis defaults from the setting found on the Company Information dialog box (select **Company**, **Company Information** from the menu bar).
- From the View drop-down list, choose to view Expense, Profit & Loss, or Balance Sheet accounts.

After selecting a chart of account listing on the left in the Accounts panel, you can filter the transactions displayed on the right in the Transactions panel with these options:

- From the Name drop-down list, leave the default of All, which is all active list items. Or select a specific list item from Customers, Employees, Vendor, or Other Names list.
- From the Show Transactions drop-down list, the default of Non-Item-Based (can be reclassified) is selected. Other options include Item-Based (can change only the class) or All to show all transactions.

tip

When you select **Include Inactive Names** from the Name drop-down list in the Reclassify Transactions task, you will not affect the transactions displayed. Instead, the list now includes any inactive list items for you to select from.

If you select an inactive name from the list, you will get a message from QuickBooks asking if you would like to use it once, make it active, or cancel.

More information about working with lists can be found in Chapter 4, "Understanding QuickBooks Lists."

After reviewing the detailed transactions, you might find that a certain vendor had all transactions assigned to the wrong expense account. For example, in Figure A.12 vendor Cal Gas & Electric had the transactions assigned to the Utilities:Water expense account. This was a mistake made on each of the checks all year. The proper account should have been the Utilities:Gas and Electric expense account.

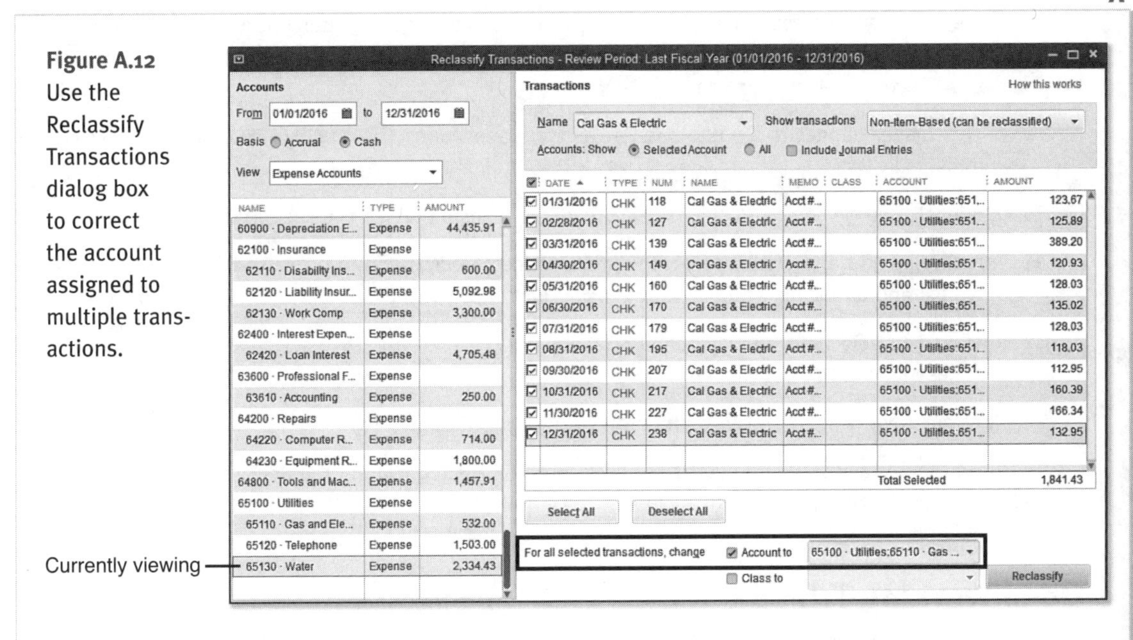

Figure A.12 Use the Reclassify Transactions dialog box to correct the account assigned to multiple transactions.

Prior to using CDR, accounting professionals would have created a journal entry reducing expenses recorded to the Utilities:Water account and increasing expenses for Utilities:Gas and Electric account. With this CDR feature, reclassifying the transactions is made easy by following these steps:

1. With the Reclassify Transactions dialog box displayed as shown in Figure A.12, select a date range for which you want to review and possibly reclassify transactions.
2. Accept the default Basis or change if needed.
3. From the View drop-down list, select the account types you want to review for reclassification.
4. With a chart of accounts item selected in the Accounts panel on the left, you will see displayed to the right transactions assigned to that account for the selected date range and basis.
5. (Optional) From the Name drop-down list, select a specific vendor, customer, employee, or other name for which you want to filter the displayed transactions.
6. The Show Transactions drop-down list will default to display only those transactions you can reclassify with this feature. (Optional) Select to show Item-Based transactions. For item-based transactions, you can reclassify only the Class assigned. Or select All to see both.
7. (Optional) Select the Include Journal Entries checkbox.

caution

Only non-item-based transactions can be reclassified with the CDR tool. If you want to edit the account assigned on item-based transactions, you need to edit the individual item in the original transaction. For more information about working with QuickBooks items, refer to Chapter 4.

8. In step 5, if you selected a specific name from the drop-down list, you might want to select in the Accounts: **Show All**. CDR will display all transactions for the Name selected for All accounts (not just the account selected on the left).
9. As you make changes to the filters in Reclassify Transactions, the displayed transactions refresh automatically.
10. (Optional) Choose Select All or Deselect All when choosing which transactions to reclassify.
11. For all selected transactions, select the proper general ledger account from the Account To drop-down list and optionally assign a new Class if desired.
12. Review your selections and click the Reclassify button. The window will refresh, displaying the changes made to the transactions.
13. Continue reviewing all the accounts until your review is complete.
14. Press the Esc key on your keyboard or click the X on the top right of the Reclassify Transactions dialog box when you are ready to close.

Open Working Trial Balance

The Working Trial Balance is a tool that has been available for years and is included with the Professional Bookkeeper, Accountant, and Enterprise Solutions Accountant versions of QuickBooks.

The Working Trial Balance, as shown in Figure A.13, displays the following details:

- Account
- Beginning Balance
- Transactions (for the selected date range)
- Adjustments (total of adjusting journal entries)
- Ending Balance
- Workpaper Reference (where you can record specific notes)

The Working Trial Balance provides a window to manage changes to a client's ending balances. You normally use this tool after you have matched the prior year balances in the Troubleshoot Prior Account Balances task with your records and you need to review and correct the next accounting period.

Click the Make Adjustments button to create an adjusting journal entry and watch the net impact to your client's Net Income with each saved journal entry change. When you are finished, click the Print button to prepare a report of your work.

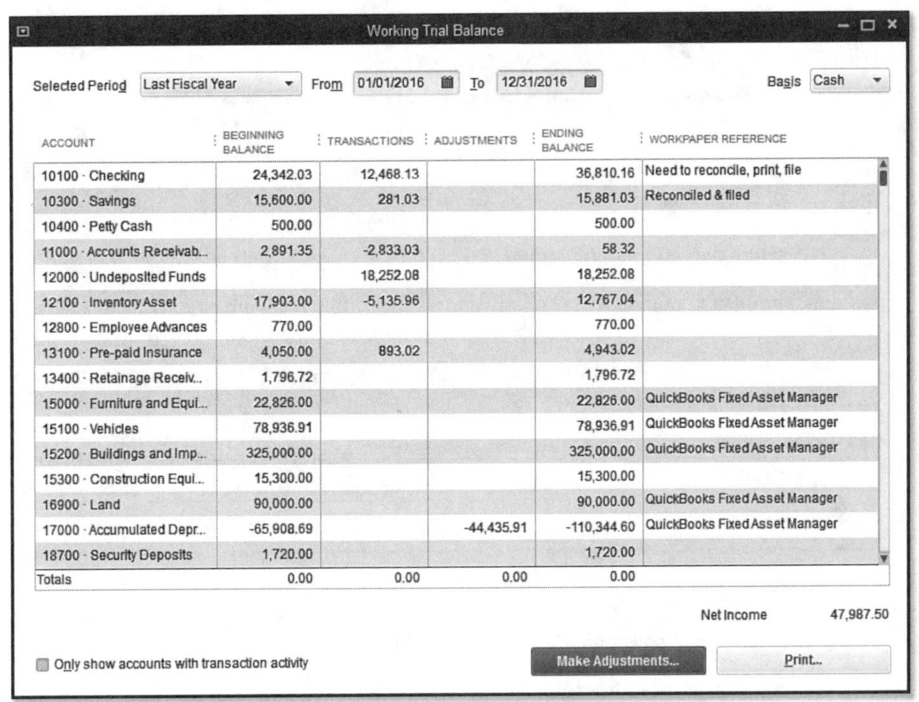

ACCOUNT	BEGINNING BALANCE	TRANSACTIONS	ADJUSTMENTS	ENDING BALANCE	WORKPAPER REFERENCE
10100 · Checking	24,342.03	12,468.13		36,810.16	Need to reconcile, print, file
10300 · Savings	15,600.00	281.03		15,881.03	Reconciled & filed
10400 · Petty Cash	500.00			500.00	
11000 · Accounts Receivab...	2,891.35	-2,833.03		58.32	
12000 · Undeposited Funds		18,252.08		18,252.08	
12100 · Inventory Asset	17,903.00	-5,135.96		12,767.04	
12800 · Employee Advances	770.00			770.00	
13100 · Pre-paid Insurance	4,050.00	893.02		4,943.02	
13400 · Retainage Receiv...	1,796.72			1,796.72	
15000 · Furniture and Equi...	22,826.00			22,826.00	QuickBooks Fixed Asset Manager
15100 · Vehicles	78,936.91			78,936.91	QuickBooks Fixed Asset Manager
15200 · Buildings and Imp...	325,000.00			325,000.00	QuickBooks Fixed Asset Manager
15300 · Construction Equi...	15,300.00			15,300.00	
16900 · Land	90,000.00			90,000.00	QuickBooks Fixed Asset Manager
17000 · Accumulated Depr...	-65,908.69		-44,435.91	-110,344.60	QuickBooks Fixed Asset Manager
18700 · Security Deposits	1,720.00			1,720.00	
Totals	0.00	0.00	0.00	0.00	

Figure A.13 Use the Working Trial Balance to make and review adjustments to the client's file in preparation for tax filings.

Review List Changes

The Review List Changes feature is available only with your QuickBooks Professional Bookkeeper and Accountant software and is available only when you launch a review using the Client Data Review feature. The type of changes tracked are specific to each task, as detailed in the next several sections. Remember, if a task has the CDR icon in front of it, it indicates that the task can only be accessed using CDR. If any other tasks are listed, they link to the respective menu in QuickBooks for that activity.

Chart of Accounts

Reviewing the chart of accounts, correcting setup errors, making an account inactive, and merging like accounts were covered in detail in Chapter 4. When a CDR is marked as Completed, these list changes are also marked with an "R" for reviewed so that in future reviews, you can conveniently hide those changes.

Click the Chart of Accounts task in the Review List Changes task group. QuickBooks displays the Review List Changes dialog box as shown in Figure A.14.

The Chart of Accounts tab on the Review List Changes dialog box tracks the following types of changes:

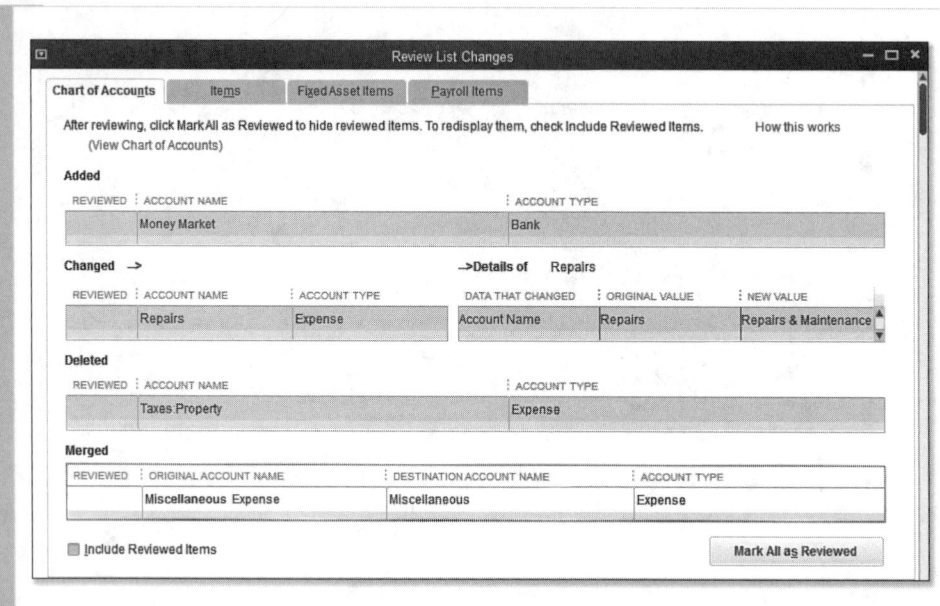

Figure A.14 Easily track your client's changes to the chart of accounts.

- **Added**—Account Name and Account Type
- **Changed**—Marked Inactive, Name or Account Number changed, Account Type changed, Parent:Subaccount relationship changed, or Tax-Line Mapping changed
- **Deleted**—Account Name and Account Type
- **Merged**—Original Account Name, Destination Account Name, and Account Type

For changes your client has made, which you want to indicate as "Reviewed," click the Mark All as Reviewed button. Changes you make to the lists while logged in as the new External Accountant user are automatically marked as reviewed.

The tabs at the top enable easy access to the remaining tracked list changes. Press the Escape key on your keyboard or click the X on the top right of the Review List Changes dialog box when you have completed this task.

Items

Chapter 4 details methods to find and troubleshoot item setup errors. This feature tracks changes made to items. When the review is completed, an "R" is placed next to each line item change to indicate it has been reviewed. In future Client Data Reviews, you can conveniently hide these previously reviewed changes.

Click the Items task in the Review List Changes task group. QuickBooks displays the Review List Changes dialog box, as shown in Figure A.15.

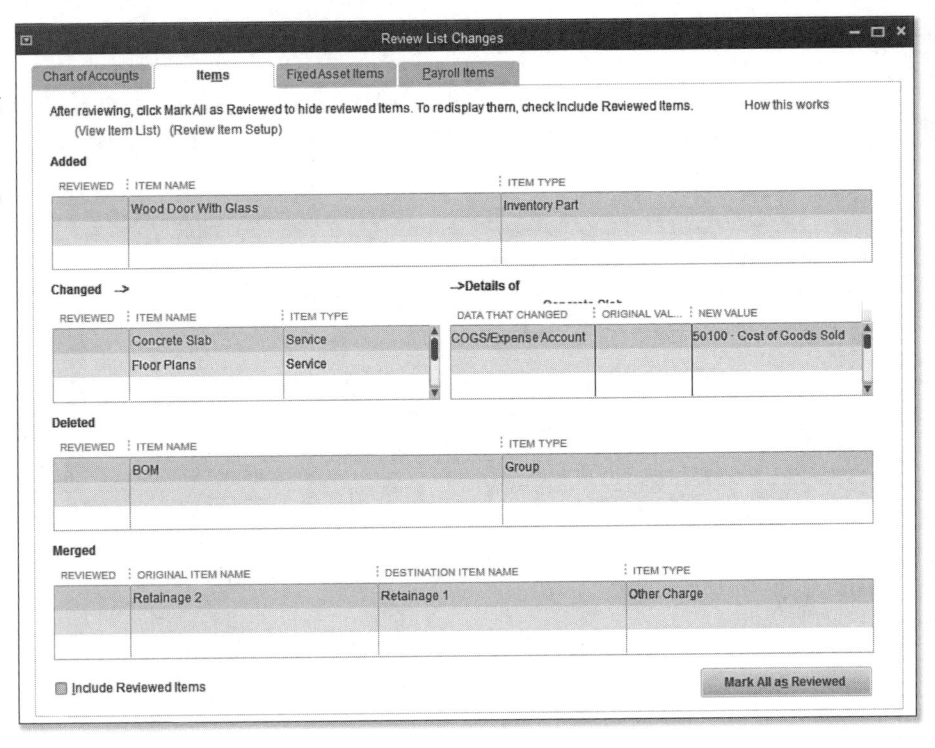

Figure A.15 Items affecting accounting and reviewing changes to these will help in a client's file review.

The Items tab on the Review List Changes dialog box tracks the following:

- **Added**—Item Name and Item Type
- **Changed**—Displays the data that Changed with Original Value and New Value
- **Deleted**—Item Name and Item Type
- **Merged**—Original Item Name, Destination Item Name, and Item Type

When the Mark All as Reviewed button is selected, the CDR feature will place an "R" in the Reviewed column for each item list change your client made. Changes you make to the list while logged in as the External Accountant user are automatically marked as reviewed.

Tabs at the top enable easy access to the remaining tracked list changes. Press the Esc key on your keyboard or click the X on the top right of the Review List Changes dialog box when you have completed this task.

Fixed Asset Items

The business owner using QuickBooks can create a Fixed Asset item type from the Fixed Asset Item List (select **Lists**, **Fixed Asset Item List** from the menu bar). Then when a purchase is made for the asset, the respective Fixed Asset item can be recorded on a purchase order, or on the Items tab of the Enter Bills dialog box or the Write Checks dialog box. This tab tracks changes made to the list of fixed assets.

Click the Fixed Asset Items task in the Review List Changes task group. QuickBooks displays the Review List Changes dialog box, as shown in Figure A.16.

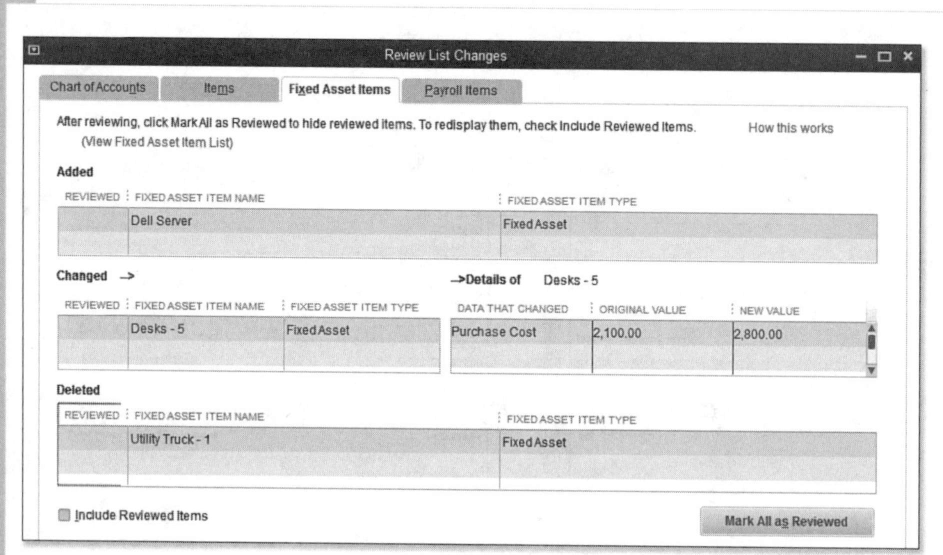

Figure A.16 Easily track additions, deletions, and changes to the client's Fixed Assets.

The Fixed Asset Items tab on the Review List Changes dialog box tracks the following fixed assets:

- **Added**—Fixed Asset Item Name and Fixed Asset Item Type
- **Changed**—Displays the data that Changed with Original Value and New Value
- **Deleted**—Fixed Asset Item Name and Fixed Asset Item Type

When the Mark All as Reviewed button is selected, the Client Data Review will place an "R" in the Reviewed column for each fixed asset item list change your client made. If you are logged in to the file as an External Accountant user type, as you make list changes, they are automatically marked as Reviewed.

Tabs along the top of the Review List Changes dialog box enable easy access to the remaining tracked list changes. Press the Esc key on your keyboard or click the X on the top right of the Review List Changes dialog box when you have completed this task.

Payroll Items

Reviewing the purpose of Payroll Items was covered in detail in Chapter 11, "Setting Up Payroll." Details were also provided in Chapter 12, "Managing Payroll" to correct payroll setup errors. This feature tracks changes made to payroll items. When the review is completed, an "R" is placed next to each payroll item change to indicate that it has been reviewed. In future client data reviews, you can conveniently hide these.

This task will display only in a file that has the payroll preference enabled.

Click the Payroll Items task in the Review List Changes task group. QuickBooks displays the Review List Changes dialog box, as shown in Figure A.17.

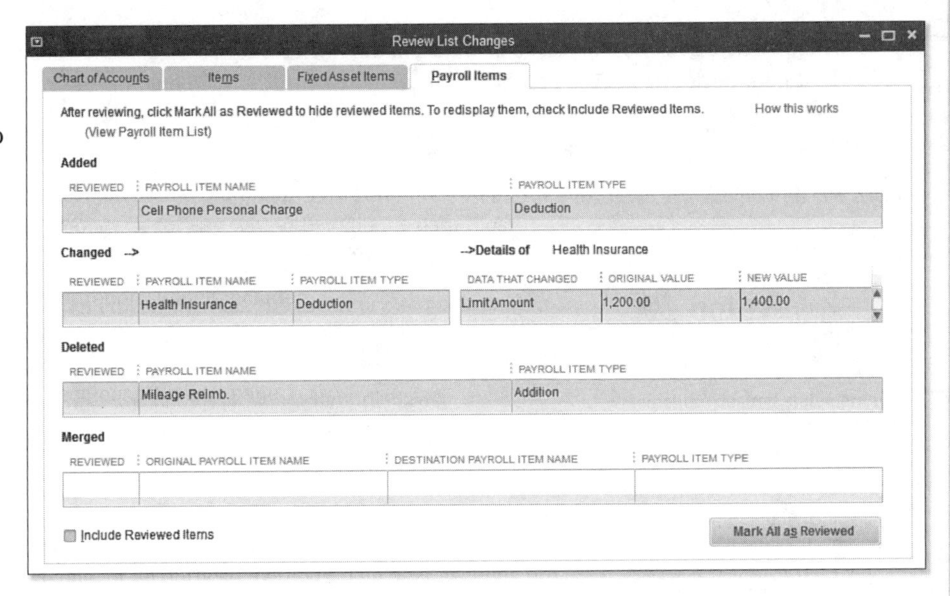

Figure A.17 See the changes the client made to payroll items throughout the year.

The Payroll Items tab on the Review List Changes dialog box tracks the following payroll items:

- **Added**—Payroll Item Name and Payroll Item Type
- **Changed**—Displays the data that Changed with Original Value and New Value
- **Deleted**—Payroll Item Name and Payroll Item Type
- **Merged**—Original Payroll Item Name, Destination Payroll Item Name, and Payroll Item Type

When you click the Mark All as Reviewed button, CDR will place an "R" in the Reviewed column for each item list change your client made. If you are logged in to the file as an External Accountant user type, as you make list changes, they are automatically marked as Reviewed.

Tabs at the top enable easy access to the remaining tracked list changes. Press the Escape key on your keyboard or click the X on the top right to close the Review list Changes dialog box when you have completed this task.

Review Item Setup

Click the Review Item Setup in the Review List Changes task group. The Add/Edit Multiple List Entries dialog box displays.

From this dialog box, you can make changes to selected item types. More detail about working with the Add/Edit Multiple List Entries feature was included in Chapters 4 and 5.

Customers

In Figure A.18, note that the Customers task in the Review List Changes pane does not have a Client Data Review icon in front of the name, indicating that CDR is linking you back to the original Customer Center.

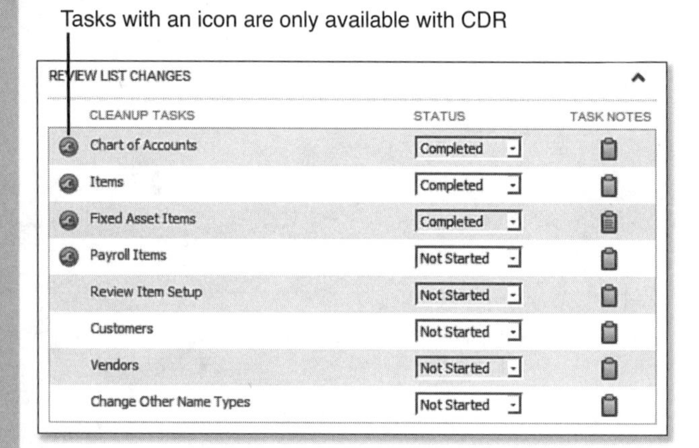

Figure A.18
Tasks without the CDR icon provide quick access to the same menu in QuickBooks.

Refer to Chapter 9, "Setting Up Customers," for more details on how to use the Customer Center to gather information and easily find specific transactions.

Vendors

The Vendors task in the Review List Changes task group also does not have a CDR icon in front of the name, indicating that CDR is linking you back to the original Vendor Center.

Refer to Chapter 7, "Setting Up Vendors," for more details on how to use the Vendor Center to gather information and easily find specific transactions.

Change Other Name Types

QuickBooks includes another names list that is useful when you are paying a supplier or service provider one time and you are not required to provide a 1099-MISC Income document at the end of the year.

This list is titled Other Names List. If you previously added a name to this list and later need to change the list name to a vendor or even a customer record, click this task link and make the change as desired.

The change is not reversible, so care should be taken with this task.

Accounts Receivable

Reviewing open Accounts Receivable with your client is an important part of a successful review of a client's file. When errors exist in accounts receivable, the balance sheet and income statement accounts could be misstated.

A complete review of Accounts Receivable, including the proper process to use in QuickBooks for potentially avoiding the corrections detailed in this section, can be found in Chapter 9, "Setting Up Customers" and Chapter 10, "Managing Customers."

The tasks listed in the Accounts Receivable task group of the CDR will help you easily correct client mistakes made when the client recorded a customer payment or completed a deposit but *did not* properly complete the transaction.

Recent versions of QuickBooks help discourage this error with messaging that warns the user not to use a Make Deposits transaction to record a customer payment. When recording a customer payment without assigning the payment to an open invoice, QuickBooks will provide a message that a credit will be left in the customer's account.

You might want to review the AR Aging Summary report first and then begin the process of using the CDR tools. Properly reviewing your client's data will help you make the most informed decisions about the corrections that might be needed.

Fix Unapplied Customer Payments and Credits

If your client entered a customer payment, but did not apply the payment to an invoice, this tool will help simplify the task of assigning the unapplied payment to the proper invoice.

Review the Open Invoices report (select **Reports**, **Customers & Receivables**, **Open Invoices** from the menu bar) before beginning to make corrections. This is especially important if you have more than one Accounts Receivable account in your chart of accounts.

To fix unapplied payments and credits, follow these steps:

1. If you are completing these changes as part of a dated review; from the menu bar, select **Accountant**, **Client Data Review** and launch **Client Data Review**. You will then launch the Fix Unapplied Customer Payments and Credits task in the Accounts Receivable group.
2. If you are not completing these changes as part of a dated review; from the menu bar, select **Accountant**, **Client Data Review** and launch the Fix Unapplied Customer Payments and Credits task.
3. If you have more than one Accounts Receivable account, review the details for each by selecting the appropriate Accounts.

4. Select any of the customers on the list, as shown in Figure A.19. With a customer selected on the left, the Invoices and Charges tab will display any unapplied payments and credits (left side) and open invoices (right side) for that specific customer.

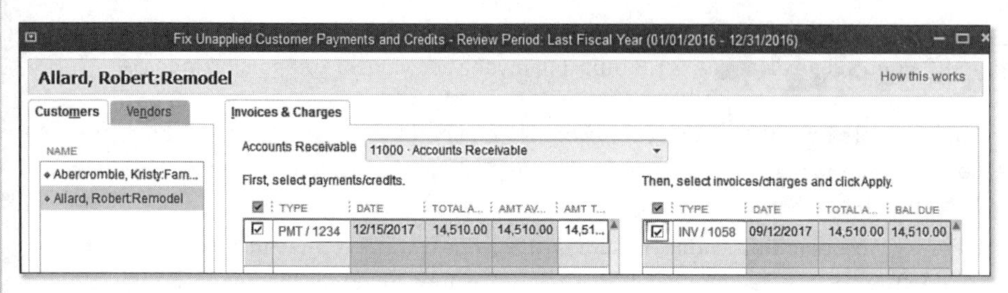

Figure A.19 Assign unapplied customer payments or credits to an open customer invoice.

5. On the Invoices and Charges tab, place a checkmark next to the payment or credit on the left pane and place a checkmark next to the associated open invoice on the right pane to which you want to apply the payment.

6. If you would like to apply only part of the credit or payment, enter the partial amount in the Amt to Apply column.

7. Click the Apply button to assign the payments or credits selected on the left to the selected open invoices on the right. The items are then grayed out to indicate that you have already assigned them.

8. (Optional) Click the Auto Apply All button to apply all the unapplied payments and credits to the invoices on the right.

9. Click Save to begin working on another customer record or Save & Close to complete the task.

Recent editions of QuickBooks make recording unapplied credits and payments less likely to occur because of the many warnings that are provided when the transactions are entered.

Clear Up Undeposited Funds Account

Have you ever worked with a client's data file that had an incorrect undeposited funds balance? Did your client create a separate deposit transaction without assigning the receive payment to the deposit?

caution

Cash basis reporting taxpayers should proceed with caution when using this tool. In cash basis reporting, the date of the Receive Payments transaction is the date that revenue is recorded. If a customer payment was dated in the prior filed tax year and was *not* applied to the customer's open invoice, the income from the invoice would not have been included in cash basis reporting.

When you use CDR to assign the payment to the open invoice, QuickBooks will report the revenue associated with that invoice as of the *date* of the customer payment.

This correction will change prior period financials. The CDR *does not* recognize the controls associated with setting a closing date. Additionally, QuickBooks *does not* provide any warnings that you are modifying a transaction dated on or before the closing date.

The undeposited funds account is a current asset type on the Balance Sheet. It's like using a safe to store checks prior to taking them to the bank. Customer payments are recorded in QuickBooks, increasing the amount in Undeposited Funds on the Balance Sheet. Later the checks are gathered and added to a single deposit ticket taken to the bank account (more details are provided in Chapter 9).

The Clear Up Undeposited Funds Account task can help you assign those undeposited funds to the deposit transaction that was created incorrectly.

Recent releases of QuickBooks make this error less likely to occur with the many warnings that are provided when the transactions are entered.

It is important to know that this feature will work when any of the following conditions apply:

- Receive Payments transaction was recorded and assigned to the Undeposited Funds account without including the payment in a Make Deposits transaction.
- Make Deposits transaction was recorded, the Received From column included the Customer or Customer:Job name, and the Account From column has an account assigned, which is typically an income account. See Figure A.20.

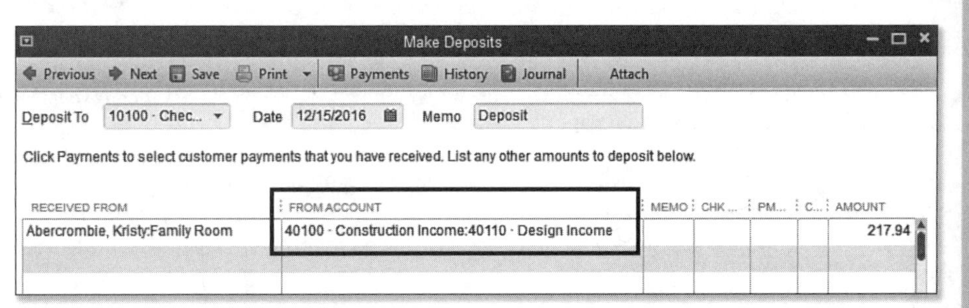

Figure A.20 Example of a customer payment recorded improperly on the Make Deposits dialog box.

- If the Make Deposits transaction did not include a name in the Received From column, CDR will report that deposit transaction in the Clear Up Undeposited Funds Account CDR task assigned to a customer named "No Name in Deposit."

To clear up the Undeposited Funds account, follow these steps:

1. If you are completing these changes as part of a dated review; from the menu bar, select **Accountant**, **Client Data Review** and launch Client Data Review. You will then select the **Clear Up Undeposited Funds** task in the Accounts Receivable group.
2. If you are not completing these changes as part of a dated review; from the menu bar, select **Accountant**, **Client Data Review, Clear Up Undeposited Funds** task.
3. The Show Deposits From field defaults to the review period selected when you started a client data review, or if you did not start a formal review, the dates default to your last fiscal year. If needed, change the selected dates and click Refresh to display the changes.
4. The Payers pane on the left displays any customers with transactions meeting the criteria listed previously. With a customer selected, review the payment transaction types on the right.

5. With a customer selected, place a checkmark next to the DEP transaction and also to the PMT transaction on the right with which you want to associate the payment, as shown in Figure A.21.

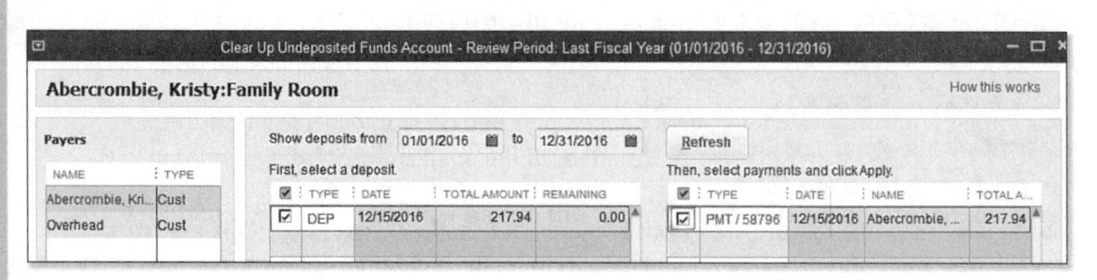

Figure A.21
Associate the customer payment in Clear Up Undeposited Funds Account to the incorrectly recorded Make Deposits transaction.

6. Click the Apply button to assign. The list items are grayed out, indicating they have been applied to each other.

7. Click Save to begin correcting records for the next customer or click Save & Close to complete the task.

Do you need to return to the original transaction in QuickBooks during your review? Simply double-click the selected transaction.

You are now ready to move on with your review or continue with additional clean up tasks. I recommend reviewing the AR Summary Report first to get a general idea of the types of corrections you might need to make with the remaining accounts receivable CDR tasks.

Reviewing the AR Aging Summary Report

Check the AR Aging Summary Report before fixing transactions. An individual transaction can be deceiving if you don't see its relationship with other related transactions.

When you select the Review AR Aging Summary Report link, QuickBooks opens the same titled report.

What exactly are you looking for on the aging report? You might be looking for customer credits that are aged and have not been applied to current open customer invoices. Or, perhaps as explained in Chapter 10, you might want to remove an open balance from a customer's invoice.

I suggest you use the Open Invoices report instead of the Aging reports. The Open Invoices report shows the transactions listed separately instead of in summary form. The Open Invoices Report is not part of the CDR tool set. It is, however, a regularly used QuickBooks report. Because the Open Invoices Report shows the current A/R status, if you are reviewing it for a previous date, you will need to modify the report to show the open balances as of that prior date. To do this, follow these steps:

1. From menu bar, select **Reports**, **Customers & Receivables**, **Open Invoices**. This report includes all open invoices, credits, and payments for your customers as of today's computer system date.

2. Review the report with today's date first. This will help you identify what corrections you might want to make using the tasks defined in this section. Reviewing it with today's date will also show if the correction you might have needed on a previous date has already been entered.

3. If you are reviewing for some date in the past, you can adjust the report to that date by clicking Customize Report at the top-left corner of the report window.

4. From the Display tab, click the Advanced button. In the Open Balance/Aging pane of the Advanced Options dialog box, change the selection to the Report Date option (see Figure A.22). This modification to the report enables you to see each customer's balance detail (see Figure A.23) as of a date in the past.

caution

If you do not modify this report as instructed here, QuickBooks will display the date you selected on the report, but will also reduce the balances owed for payments made after the report date.

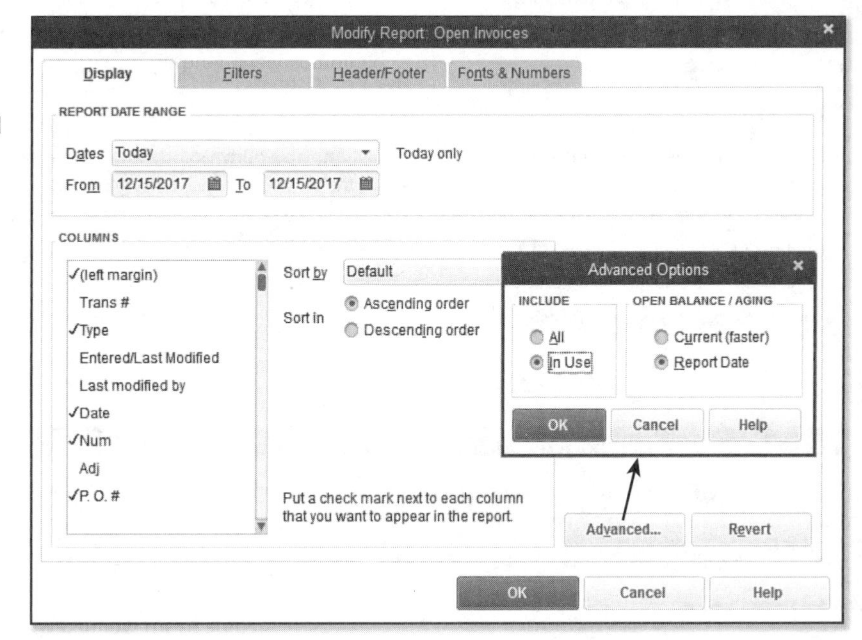

Figure A.22
The Open Invoices report, when modified, can be compared to the totals on your Balance Sheet report for some time in the past.

9:46 AM
12/15/17

Rock Castle Construction
Open Invoices
As of December 15, 2017

Type	Date	Num	P. O. #	Terms	Due Date	Class	Aging	Open Balance
Remodel								
Payment	12/15/2017	1234						-14,510.00
Invoice	09/12/2017	1058		Net 15	09/27/2017	Remodel	79	14,510.00
Total Remodel								0.00
Total Allard, Robert								0.00
Burch, Jason								
Room Addition								
Invoice	11/25/2017	1083		Net 30	12/25/2017	New Co...		1,005.00
Total Room Addition								1,005.00

Figure A.23
The Open Invoices report easily shows unpaid balances and any unapplied customer credits or payments.

Write Off Invoices

Often, as accounting professionals, we need to adjust our client's Accounts Receivable balances. Perhaps there were several small unpaid finance charge invoices, or over the year our client's customers paid their invoices short of what was due.

Creating a customer credit memo and assigning the credit memo to the original open invoice was time-consuming for the accounting professional. Often a journal entry was created, correcting the accounts receivable balance on the Balance Sheet but leaving the QuickBooks user with extra line details in the A/R Aging Summary or Detail reports.

The Write Off Invoices feature shown in Figure A.24 is one convenient window where you can write off balances, review the suggested transaction, and print the details for your customer.

tip

Earlier in this chapter, I recommended that you review the AR Aging Summary report before using the Accounts Receivable CDR tools. However, even if you do not review the report, the Write Off Invoices dialog box will show the word "CREDITS" in the Avail Credit/Pmt column if the customer with the open invoice balance also has unapplied credits.

Click the CREDITS link to open the Fix Unapplied Customer Payments and Credits dialog box. Here you can apply the payment to the open invoice as instructed previously.

It might be more appropriate to assign the available credit rather than to write off the open balance.

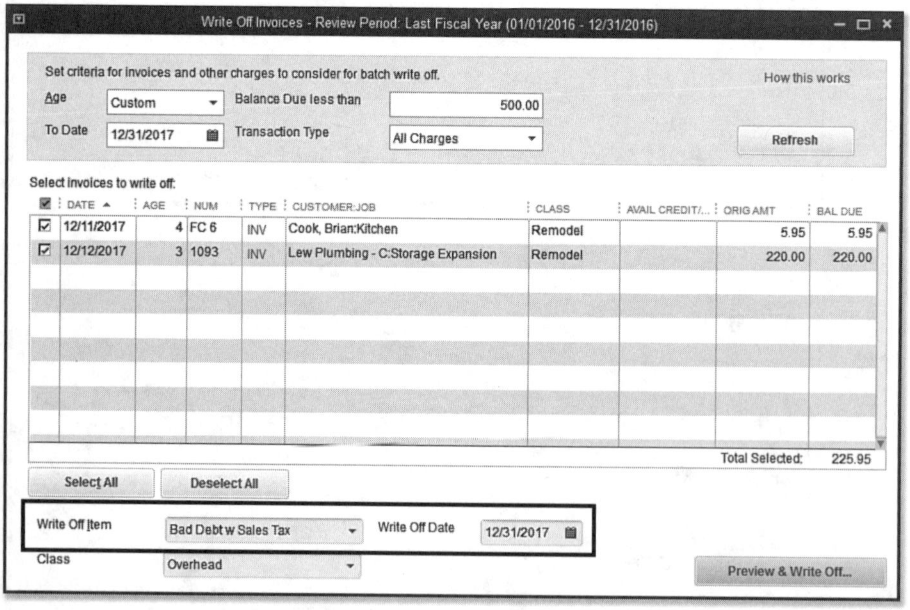

Write Off Invoices - Review Period: Last Fiscal Year (01/01/2016 - 12/31/2016)

Set criteria for invoices and other charges to consider for batch write off. How this works

Age: Custom — Balance Due less than: 500.00

To Date: 12/31/2017 — Transaction Type: All Charges — Refresh

Select invoices to write off:

☑	DATE	AGE	NUM	TYPE	CUSTOMER:JOB	CLASS	AVAIL CREDIT/...	ORIG AMT	BAL DUE
☑	12/11/2017	4	FC 6	INV	Cook, Brian:Kitchen	Remodel		5.95	5.95
☑	12/12/2017	3	1093	INV	Lew Plumbing - C:Storage Expansion	Remodel		220.00	220.00

Total Selected: 225.95

Select All — Deselect All

Write Off Item: Bad Debt w Sales Tax — Write Off Date: 12/31/2017

Class: Overhead — Preview & Write Off...

Figure A.24 Using CDR's Write Off Invoices makes removing open A/R uncollected balances easy!

To write off invoices, follow these steps:

1. If Client Data Review isn't already open, select **Accountant**, **Accountant Center** from the menu bar.
2. Select the **Write Off Invoices** task in the Accounts Receivable task group.
3. If presented with the warning that one or more customers in the list have available credits, click OK to close the message. Be sure to do a thorough review of your client's Open Invoices reports as previously recommended.

tip

If the customer's invoice being written off included sales tax, make sure the item selected for the write-off is a taxable item. This ensures that the sales tax payable account also shows the credit, which is important when sales tax is paid on Accrual basis.

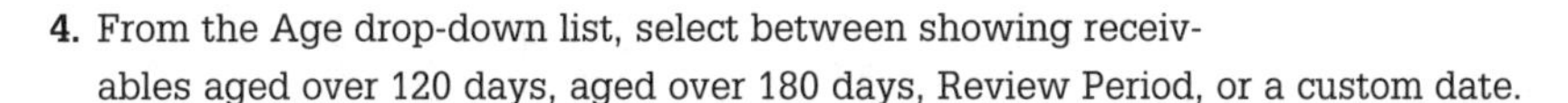

4. From the Age drop-down list, select between showing receivables aged over 120 days, aged over 180 days, Review Period, or a custom date.
5. (Optional) Enter an amount in the Balances Due Less Than box to limit the transactions that are displayed, which is particularly useful when writing off small balances only.
6. Select a **To Date**.
7. From the Transaction Type drop-down list, select **All Charges**, **Invoices**, **Finance Charges**, or **Statement Charges**.
8. Click Refresh if changing the filters.
9. Place a checkmark next to each transaction for which you want to write off the open balance. (Optional) Click the Select All button or Deselect All button at the bottom of the screen to simplify the process.
10. From the drop-down lists, select the **Write-Off Item** and **Write-Off Date**. (Optional) Select a **Class**.
11. Click the Preview & Write-Off button. CDR displays the Confirm Write-Off dialog box, as shown in Figure A.25.
12. Click Write Off when you are done reviewing the invoices, or click Cancel.
13. CDR returns you to the Write Off Invoices dialog box. Press the Esc key on your keyboard to view the Write-Off Completed details.
14. Click Save as PDF to print for your records.

QuickBooks creates a Credit Memo transaction using the item and date you selected at the time you created the write-off and applies this credit to the original invoice.

You are now finished with the Accounts Receivable tasks. There are many QuickBooks preferences that will guide your clients as they manage undeposited funds and accounts receivable transactions. Review Chapters 9 and 10 for more details and other Accounts Receivable troubleshooting suggestions.

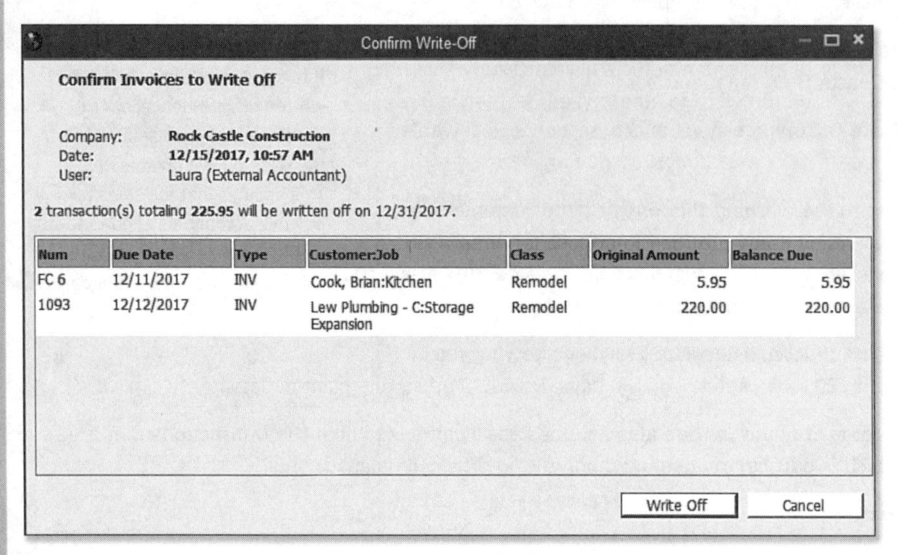

Figure A.25
You stay in control of the write-off, confirming the balances to be removed.

Accounts Payable

A complete review of Accounts Payable, including the proper process to use in QuickBooks, which potentially avoids the corrections detailed in this section, can be found in Chapters 7 and 8.

The tasks listed in the Accounts Payable section of the CDR feature can help you easily correct client mistakes made when the client has created a vendor credit or bill payment and did not assign it to the open vendor bill.

The Review Unpaid Bills Report is listed last in the Accounts Payable task group. I recommend reviewing this report as well as other reports prior to making corrections with the CDR. Properly reviewing your data will help you make the most informed decision on the corrections that might be needed.

caution

Item receipts do not display in the CDR tools, but these transaction types are included in your client's open accounts payable balances. Review the Unpaid Vendor Bills report (select **Reports, Vendors & Payables** from the menu bar) for any aged item receipts.

Chapter 6 offers more specific details for correcting aged item receipts.

Fix Unapplied Vendor Payments and Credits

Chapter 7, "Setting Up Vendors," detailed the proper accounts payable process, which is to use the Pay Bills dialog box to pay vendor bills. Some QuickBooks users might have used the Enter Bills transaction type and later paid that vendor bill using the Write Checks transaction instead of properly using the Pay Bills dialog box.

To fix unapplied vendor payments and credits, follow these steps:

1. If you are completing these changes as part of a dated review, from the menu bar select **Accountant**, **Client Data Review** and launch Client Data Review. You then select the **Fix Unapplied Vendor Payments and Credits task** in the Accounts Payable group.
2. If you are not completing these changes as part of a dated review, from the menu bar select **Accountant**, **Client Data Review** and launch the Fix Unapplied Vendor Payments and Credits task.
3. The Vendors tab on the top left and the Bills tab on the right are selected by default. Select any of the vendors on the list to the left. The Bills pane displays all unapplied vendor credits for the vendor selected on the left. On the right of the Bills pane, any open vendor bills for that specifically selected vendor display.
4. Place a checkmark next to the credit on the left and the open vendor bill on the right to which you want to apply the payment (see Figure A.26).

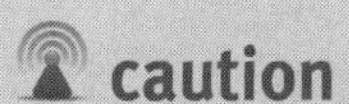
caution

If any of the checks listed in the left side of the Bills detail have an asterisk(*) in front of the word CHK, this indicates that the expense is marked as billable to the customer. CDR warns you that when you assign the check to an open vendor bill, the expense will no longer be marked as billable.

More details about working with billable expenses are included in Chapter 9, in the section titled "Time and Expense Invoicing."

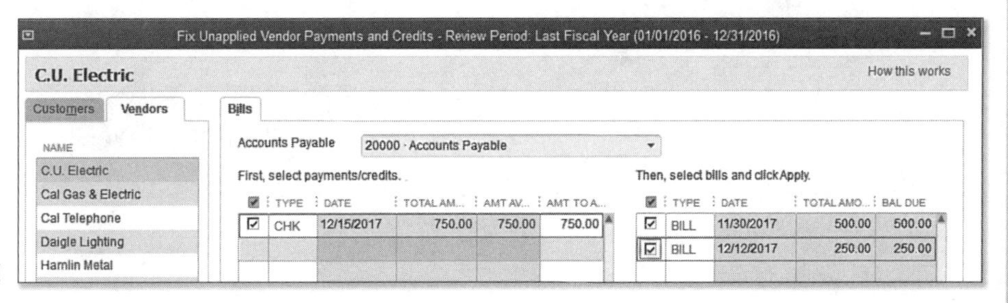

Figure A.26 Using CDR to assign a check written to a vendor as payment of an open vendor bill saves time!

5. Click the Apply button to assign that specific vendor credit transaction with that specific vendor bill. The items selected will be grayed out, indicating that you have assigned them properly.
6. You must click Save to begin correcting transactions for another vendor or click Save and Close to complete the task.

Evaluate and Correct 1099 Account Mapping

Setting up your vendors for proper 1099 status is important. However, be assured that if after reviewing this information you determine the original setup was incorrect, any changes made here will correct prior- and future-dated reports and forms.

When you select the link in the Accounts Payable task group for Evaluate and Correct 1099 Mapping, the Preferences dialog box for 1099s is displayed.

In the preference setting for Tax:1099, you can click the Yes button to select the Do You File option to let QuickBooks know you will be providing 1099 forms to your vendors at the end of the year. A new QuickBooks file will default with the preference set to Yes for filing 1099-MISC forms.

If this is your first time setting up 1099s in your file, click the link next to If You're Ready to Prepare... and the QuickBooks 1099 Wizard displays as shown in Figure A.27.

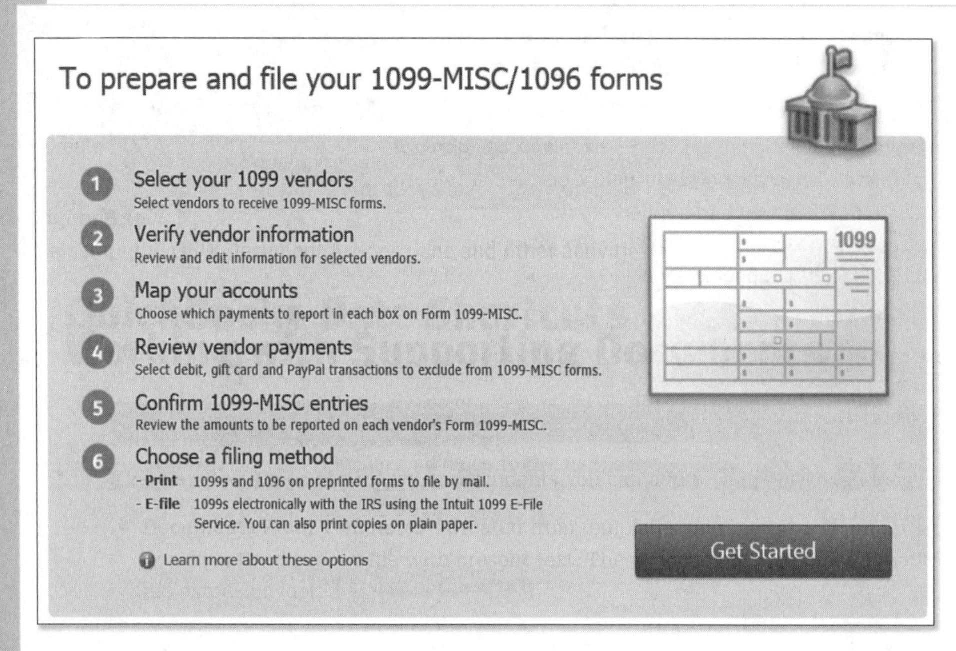

Figure A.27 Easily setup and process year-end forms with the 1099 Wizard.

More detailed information about setting up your 1099s in QuickBooks is included in Chapter 7.

Reviewing the Unpaid Bills Report

One of the first tasks you should do with your client is review the Unpaid Bills Report, primarily because the client will know best if the bills that are open are still due and payable to the vendor.

What exactly are you looking for on the aging report? You might be looking for vendor credits that are aged and have not been applied to current open vendor bills. Or, as Chapter 7 "Setting Up Vendors," and Chapter 8 "Managing Vendors" documented, you might see several aged item receipts for vendors you know your client has paid.

Use the information collected from this report to help determine the corrections that should be made with the tasks listed in the Accounts Payable task group of the CDR.

Sales Tax

This CDR feature not only identifies errors with using the incorrect payment transaction, but also fixes the transaction automatically for you!

More information about properly setting up and using sales tax is included in Chapter 9, "Setting Up Customers."

Before beginning the tasks listed in this section, you should review the client's settings (preferences) for sales tax, as shown in Figure A.28. Additionally, the Sales Tax task group will not display in the CDR if the Sales Tax feature has not been enabled.

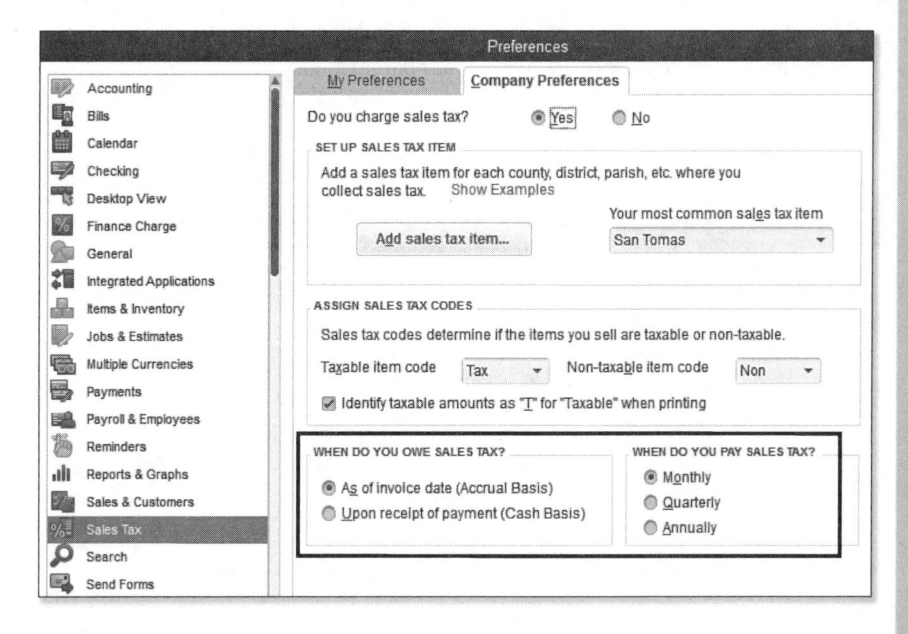

Figure A.28
Review Sales Tax preferences before making any corrections.

After reviewing and correcting your client's sales tax preference settings, you are prepared to begin the following CDR tasks.

Fix Incorrectly Recorded Sales Tax

QuickBooks uses a special Pay Sales Tax dialog box (as shown in Figure A.29) to record the sales tax liability payments properly. When payments are made using other transaction types, such as Write Checks, Pay Bills, or Make General Journal Entries, the Pay Sales Tax dialog box might not reflect the payments accurately.

The Fix Incorrectly Recorded Sales Tax task will help you identify and correct the transaction when a client paid the sales tax liability outside of the Pay Sales Tax dialog box. Figure A.30 shows the negative line entry that will be included in the Pay Sales Tax dialog box when a Write Checks transaction was created, assigned to the sales tax payable liability account, and payable to the sales tax vendor. Properly recorded sales tax payments will have a transaction type of TAXPMT in the checkbook register.

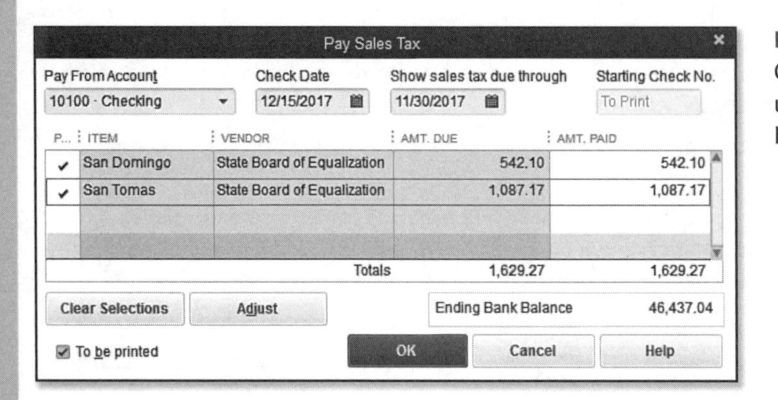

Figure A.29
Create properly paid sales tax using the Pay Sales Tax dialog box.

When sales tax is paid using a non-sales tax payment transaction type

Pay Sales Tax
Pay From Account
10100 · Checking
Check Date
12/15/2017
Show sales tax due through
11/30/2017
Starting Check No.
520

P...	ITEM	VENDOR	AMT. DUE	AMT. PAID
	San Domingo	State Board of Equalization	542.10	0.00
	San Tomas	State Board of Equalization	1,087.17	0.00
		State Board of Equalization	-1,629.27	0.00
		Totals	0.00	0.00

Pay All Tax
Adjust
Ending Bank Balance 46,437.04
To be printed
OK
Cancel
Help

Figure A.30
The Pay Sales Tax dialog box when an improperly recorded sales tax payment was made.

What exactly is this tool fixing? The tool will identify and fix non-sales-tax payable type transactions used to pay sales tax liability using Void and Replace functionality.

The tool will identify any Write Checks transactions where the payee is the same as an assigned payee for any sales tax item.

This tool *will not* identify any vendor bills, vendor bill payment checks, or journal entries recording payment for the Sales Tax Liability.

If this is your first incorrectly recorded sales tax transaction fix, you might want to change the "to" date to include today's date. This ensures you are seeing all sales tax payable transactions that were improperly recorded using the wrong transaction in QuickBooks.

caution

This might be a good time to review with your client the vendor names associated with different types of tax payments. Some states might have the same vendor name for multiple agency tax payments.

Suggest that your client use a unique vendor name for each different type of tax being paid. This will avoid CDR possibly correcting a non-sales-tax type of payment made to vendor.

To fix incorrectly recorded sales tax, follow these steps:

1. If you are completing these changes as part of a dated review, from the menu bar select **Accountant**, **Client Data Review** and launch Client Data Review. You then select the **Fix Incorrectly Recorded Sales Tax** task in the Sales Tax group.
2. If you are not completing these changes as part of a dated review, from the menu bar select **Accountant**, **Client Data Review** and launch the Fix Incorrectly Recorded Sales Tax task as shown in Figure A.31.
3. Double-click any transaction to see the originally created non-sales-tax payment transaction to make sure it should be changed to a Sales Tax Payment. Make note of the check number or check date.
4. Place a checkmark in each transaction to be fixed. (Optional) Use the Select All button or Deselect All button to streamline the process.

caution

If your client has multiple lines recorded on sales tax payable checks, such as including an additional fee for late payment penalty or other adjustment lines, you might want to use the link for making a manual Sales Tax Adjustment.

The Fix Incorrectly Recorded Sales Tax tool assumes all lines of the incorrect transaction belong in the Sales Tax Payable account.

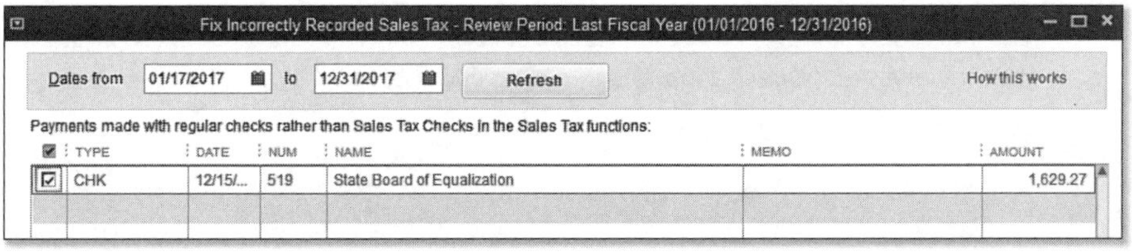

Figure A.31 Automatically find and fix incorrectly recorded sales tax payment transactions.

Fix Incorrectly Recorded Sales Tax - Review Period: Last Fiscal Year (01/01/2016 - 12/31/2016)

Dates from 01/17/2017 to 12/31/2017 Refresh How this works

Payments made with regular checks rather than Sales Tax Checks in the Sales Tax functions:

✔	TYPE	DATE	NUM	NAME	MEMO	AMOUNT
☑	CHK	12/15/...	519	State Board of Equalization		1,629.27

5. Click Void & Replace (not shown in Figure A.31). CDR then creates a new Sales Tax Payment transaction and voids the original Write Checks transaction or Make General Journal Entries transaction.
6. Click Proceed to the Fix Sales Tax message that displays to continue with the change, or click Cancel to return to the CDR tool.
7. Click OK to close the message indicating that the transaction(s) have been fixed.
8. Click the X in the top-right corner to return to the CDR Center.
9. Return to your checkbook register (icon on the Home page) and look for the check number or date (or both) to view the original transaction voided and the new transaction created as a Sales Tax Payment type.

With the Void and Replace functionality included in the Fix Incorrectly Recorded Sales Tax tool, you are assured that if your original transaction was marked as cleared in a bank reconciliation, the newly created Sales Tax Payment transaction will also be marked as cleared.

Adjust Sales Tax Payable

If the Fix Incorrectly Recorded Sales Tax tool was not used to correct the client's sales tax records, you might instead want to use this manual Adjust Sales Tax Payable link.

In addition to reviewing fixing transactions, I recommend you review the Sales Tax Liability reports and your Balance Sheet balance for Sales Tax Payable before and after making corrections to your sales tax payable balances in QuickBooks.

When comparing these reports and the Pay Sales Tax dialog box, make sure each report is using the same Accrual or Cash Basis and is prepared with the same reporting date. More information on working with the sales tax payable reports in QuickBooks can be found in Chapter 10, "Managing Customers."

Compare the following reports to each other for sales tax payable balances:

- **Balance Sheet**—Sales Tax Payable balance. From the menu bar, select **Reports**, **Company & Financial**, **Balance Sheet Standard**. (Optional) Click the Modify button to change the report basis and date.
- **Sales Tax Liability Report**—Sales Tax Payable as of <date> column total. From the menu bar, select **Vendors**, **Sales Tax**, **Sales Tax Liability**.
- **Pay Sales Tax**—Amt. Due column total. From the menu bar, select **Vendors**, **Sales Tax**, **Pay Sales Tax**.

The end result of a properly made sales tax correcting entry or adjustment is that the totals listed in the previously mentioned reports agree with each other.

To adjust sales tax payable, follow these steps:

1. If you are completing these changes as part of a dated review, from the menu bar select **Accountant**, **Client Data Review** and launch Client Data Review. You then select the **Adjust Sales Tax Payable** task in the Sales Tax group.
2. If you are not completing these changes as part of a dated review, from the menu bar select **Vendors**, **Sales Tax**, **Adjust Sales Tax Due**.
3. The Sales Tax Adjustment dialog displays as shown in Figure A.32.

Figure A.32
Use the Sales Tax Adjustment dialog box to adjust QuickBooks Sales Tax Payable properly.

4. Select the Adjustment Date.

5. Type in an Entry No if desired.

6. Select your Sales Tax Vendor from the drop-down list.

7. Select the Adjustment Account from the drop-down list. As an accounting professional, you should recommend the proper account type to your customer to use for these adjustments.

8. In the Adjustment pane, select the **Increase Sales Tax By** or **Decrease the Sales Tax By** option button. Enter an amount for the adjustment.

9. Enter a Memo or select the default memo.

10. Click OK to save the transaction.

QuickBooks will create a Make General Journal Entries transaction with a decrease (debit) or increase (credit) to Sales Tax Payable account with the resulting debit or credit in the account that was selected in step 7.

The adjustments created remain unapplied in the Pay Sales Tax dialog box until you assign them to your next Sales Tax Payment.

Manage Sales Tax

Click the Manage Sales Tax task to properly set up and work with Sales Tax in your QuickBooks data file. Manage Sales Tax is also available from a shortcut on the Home page. For more information, see Chapters 9 and 10.

Pay Sales Tax

Click the Pay Sales Tax task to pay your sales tax properly in QuickBooks. For more information, see Chapter 9.

Sales Tax Preferences

Click the Sales Tax Preferences task to define sales-tax-specific preferences affecting your QuickBooks data file. For more information, see Chapter 9.

Inventory

For the accounting professional, this is commonly one area of QuickBooks that is the least understood. Often when working with a client's file with inventory tracking, I will see a journal entry used to adjust inventory. Although this does make the adjustment to the inventory account balance on the Balance Sheet report, it does not reflect the adjustment in the Inventory Valuation Summary or Detail report.

Why is it that a journal entry shouldn't be used to adjust inventory? Consider that the inventory value on a balance sheet is the quantity of an item multiplied by a cost. When you create a journal entry, you can enter an amount for the adjustment, but you cannot associate it with an actual inventory item.

The following sections detail several inventory troubleshooting tools.

Review Inventory Setup

Chapter 6, "Managing Inventory," discusses several topics about the proper processes needed when your clients track inventory in their business.

When you click the Review Inventory Setup link in the CDR Inventory pane, the Add/Edit Multiple List Entries dialog box opens. From here, you can easily add or edit individual or multiple inventory or non-inventory items on the inventory list, as well as other lists.

The Review Inventory Setup is not a CDR-dependent task, but the link in the CDR center makes it easy to correct your client's inventory items.

Compare Balance Sheet and Inventory Valuation

This Compare Balance Sheet and Inventory Valuation CDR task is an inventory troubleshooting tool that will help you "diagnose" transaction errors involving the inventory asset account. In Chapter 6, you were introduced to the importance of comparing your client's Inventory Asset on the Balance Sheet report to the asset total on the Inventory Valuation Summary report.

When transactions are recorded to the inventory asset account without assigning an inventory item (such as a Make General Journal Entries transaction, or on the Expenses tab of a Write Checks transaction or an Enter Bills transaction by assigning the inventory asset account), the Inventory Valuation Summary report will no longer match the value of the Inventory Asset on the Balance Sheet report.

Another result of improperly recording inventory transactions is the potential for a misstatement of the value of the Cost of Goods Sold, or the cost of the inventory sold to a customer, which would affect job costing reports.

To compare the balance sheet and inventory valuation, follow these steps:

1. From the menu bar, select **Accountant**, **Client Data Review** and launch Client Data Review.
2. In the Inventory group, select the **Compare Balance Sheet and Inventory Valuation** task.
3. The CDR tool displays the Inventory Asset account balance from the Balance Sheet for the selected As Of date. (Optional) Click the Balance Sheet link to review the report.
4. The CDR tool displays the total asset value from the Inventory Valuation Summary report for the selected As Of date. (Optional) Click the Inventory Valuation Summary link to review the report.
5. A warning message is displayed (see Figure A.33) if there is a difference between the asset value reported on the two reports.
6. (Optional) Click the Transactions Using Inventory Asset Account But Not Inventory Items link, and the report in Figure A.34 displays. The report displays transactions that affect the Inventory Asset balance on the Balance Sheet, but are not properly affecting an inventory item.
7. (Optional) Click Review Inventory Setup to open Add/Edit Multiple List Entries.
8. (Optional) Click New Item to create a new inventory item.
9. (Optional) Click Adjust Inventory Quantity/Value on Hand to properly adjust inventory.

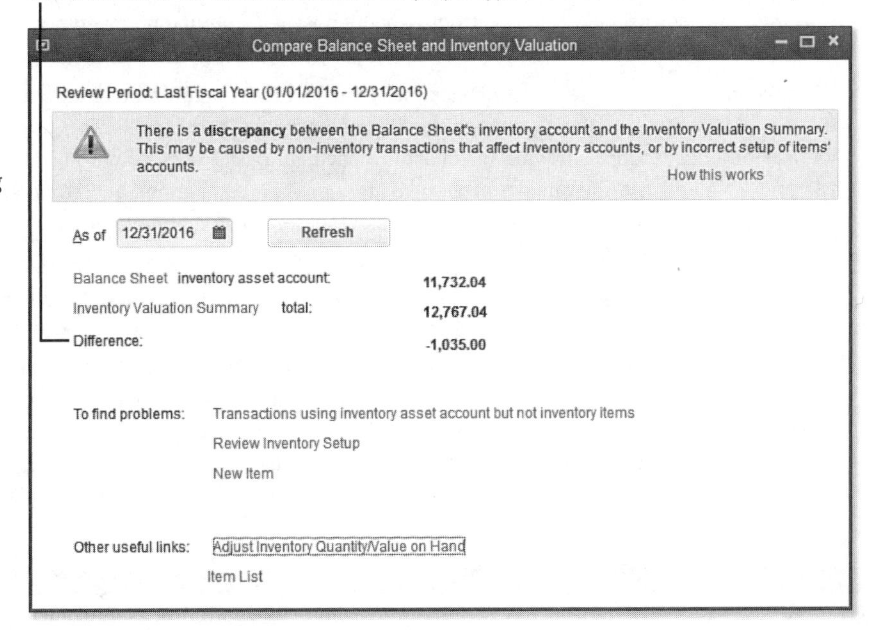

Figure A.33 Compare Balance Sheet and Inventory Valuation is useful when troubleshooting inventory asset discrepancies.

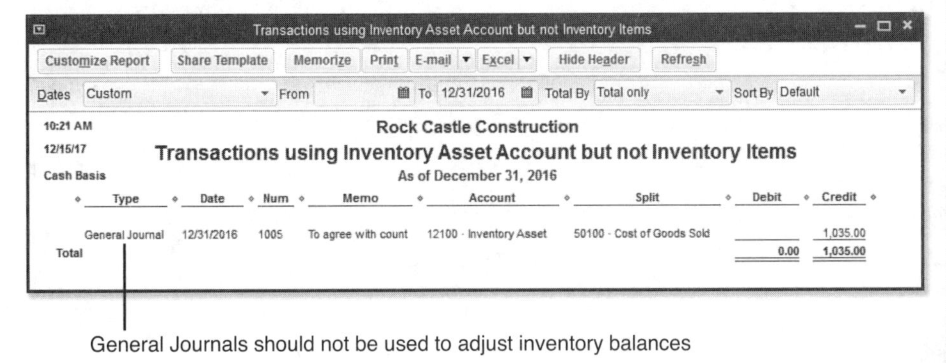

Figure A.34 CDR makes it easy to locate transactions that are affecting the Inventory Asset but not using the proper transaction type.

10. (Optional) Click Item List to modify an item.
11. To close, press the Esc key on your keyboard or click the X in the top-right corner when finished.

If you find these types of errors in your accounting for inventory, you instead should create an inventory adjustment to replace them with. QuickBooks will continue to report a difference between the reports if Journal Entries are recorded to the Inventory Asset account.

Troubleshoot Inventory

Chapter 6 provides useful content on troubleshooting issues surrounding inventory. One of the issues discussed in that chapter is the effect on the company's financials when inventory goes negative.

Negative inventory is caused when QuickBooks has recorded a higher quantity of inventory sold than is available to sell. This process might seem acceptable for some clients if they are waiting for back-ordered product but want to collect the payment from the customer in advance. Chapter 5, "Setting Up Inventory," details better methods for handling back orders and other issues, which can result in negative inventory values and the misstated financials that can result.

Also, Chapter 6 explained that if an inventory item is marked as "inactive" the resulting inventory value will not appear on the Inventory Valuation Summary report. If a client truly has inventory in stock but is not selling it, the Inventory Valuation Summary report would be misstated.

With the Troubleshoot Inventory feature (see Figure A.35) in QuickBooks Accountant, many of the reports and processes that had to be reviewed for diagnosing inventory valuation errors can be replaced by the new Troubleshoot Inventory CDR task. In fact, this tool is so valuable in detecting errors such as negative inventory and finding inactive items with a quantity on hand (to name just a couple), as accounting professionals we should encourage our clients to upgrade to QuickBooks 2013.

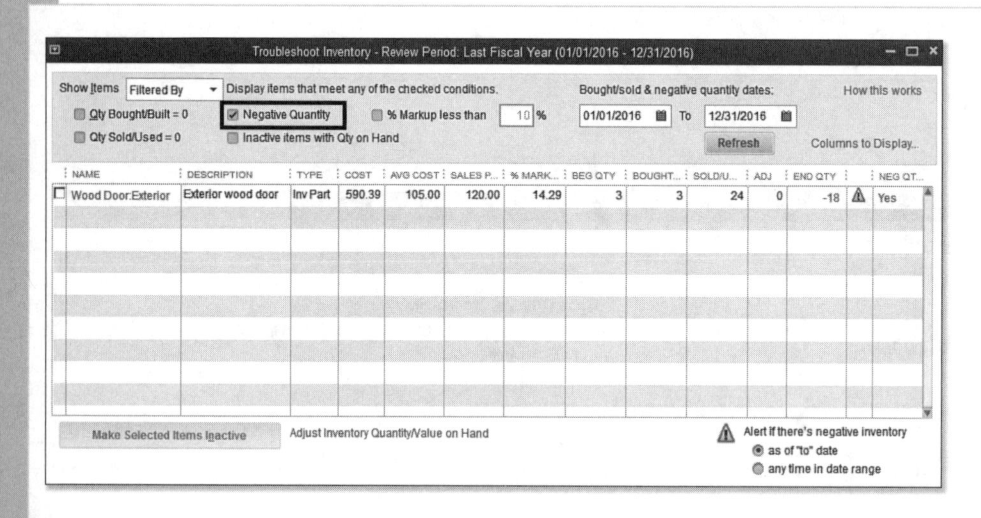

Figure A.35 Easily identify inventory with a negative quantity, and help your clients better manage their inventory processes.

All users in QuickBooks Premier 2013 and QuickBooks Enterprise Solutions 13.0 have access to the Inventory Center, which offers the ability to list any items that have negative inventory.

To review your client's inventory using the Troubleshoot Inventory CDR task, follow these steps:

1. If you are completing these changes as part of a dated review, from the menu bar select **Accountant**, **Client Data Review** and launch Client Data Review. Then, in the Inventory group, select the **Troubleshoot Inventory** task.

2. If you are not completing these changes as part of a dated review, from the menu bar select **Accountant**, **Client Data Review** and launch the Troubleshoot Inventory task.
3. From the Show Items drop-down list, select **Filtered By**, **All**, **or All Active**. This helps to display specific data for your review of your client's inventory.
4. Place a checkmark in any combination or all of the following:
   - Qty Bought/Built = 0
   - Qty Sold/Used = 0
   - Negative Quantity
   - Inactive Items with Qty on Hand
   - % Markup less than <enter the %>
5. The default date range is the same as the selected Review Period. (Optional) You can change the dates.
6. Click Refresh if you are changing the filters or dates to show current data.
7. (Optional) Click Columns to Display to modify the content that is displayed.
8. Inventory items that match your selected filter criteria are displayed. The column End Qty displays the number of units in stock as of the To date selected. Next to the End Qty column, a green circle symbol displays if there is no negative inventory. A yellow caution symbol displays if inventory items have a negative inventory quantity.
9. Select the option for Alert If There's Negative Inventory **As Of The "To" Date** or **Any Time in Date Range**.
10. (Optional) Place a checkmark in the box in front of any inventory item and then click the Make Selected Items Inactive button to mark the inventory item as inactive.
11. (Optional) Click the Adjust Inventory Quantity/Value on Hand to adjust the ending inventory balances to the client's physical inventory counted totals. More information is provided in the next section.

If your review using the CDR tools and features has identified inventory errors, you should read Chapter 6, which has sections on troubleshooting inventory in QuickBooks.

Adjust Inventory Quantity/Value on Hand

Before you perform this task, you need to know what the actual ending quantity and value for each inventory item is currently. This is determined by completing a physical inventory count. Without this important step, you might make an adjustment that is not supported by the actual count. To create a list used by the warehouse personnel to count inventory, select **Vendors**, **Inventory Activities**, **Physical Inventory Worksheet** from the menu bar.

Quantity Inventory Adjustment

The most common type of inventory adjustment is the Quantity Inventory Adjustment.

The Adjust Quantity/Value on Hand is not a CDR tool, but is accessible from the Vendors, Inventory Activities menu or from an opened Client Data Review. (Optional) If you use this feature often, you can also add this to your Accountant Center.

More details about properly using the Quantity Inventory Adjustment transaction can be found in Chapter 6.

The next section discusses a different type of inventory adjustment called a Value Adjustment.

Value Inventory Adjustment

When deciding whether to use a Quantity on Hand or Value Adjustment only, be sure of the net result you want to obtain. A value adjustment will not change the quantity on hand, but it will assign a new average cost by dividing the units in inventory by the new value.

Timing is important when doing a valuation adjustment. Value adjustments, if appropriate, should be carefully considered for their impact on the company's resulting financials.

The Value Inventory Adjustment is a less-common type of inventory adjustment. The Adjust Quantity/ Value on Hand is not a CDR tool, but is accessible from the Vendors, Inventory Activities menu or from an opened CDR. (Optional) If you use this feature often, you can add this to your Accountant Center.

Payroll

To have QuickBooks automatically calculate payroll, you or your client will need to purchase a payroll subscription from Intuit. When payroll is not prepared properly, many of the QuickBooks payroll transactions and calculations will not work correctly or at all.

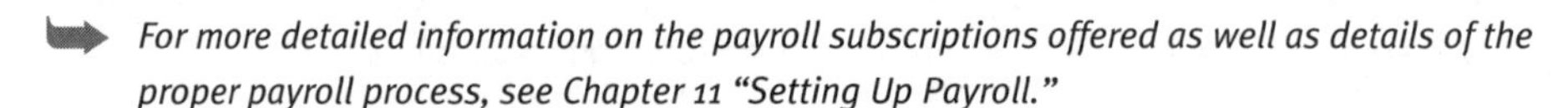

For more detailed information on the payroll subscriptions offered as well as details of the proper payroll process, see Chapter 11 "Setting Up Payroll."

The CDR tasks for payroll will help you find payroll errors and set defaults in your client's file, which will help to avoid future mistakes.

 **tip**

Your ability as the accountant to make changes in a client's payroll setup as well as adjust payroll transactions is only possible when

- You are working in a client's working data file (.QBW file extension). You cannot make changes to payroll transactions when working in an Accountant's Copy file copy.
- You are working onsite or remotely logged in to the client's file (via the Internet) and your client has a current paid payroll subscription. The payroll features available will be limited by the payroll subscription the client owns.
- You are working with the client's file at your place of business and you have a paid payroll subscription from Intuit. Accounting professionals providing payroll services for their clients will benefit from using the QuickBooks Enhanced Payroll for Accountants subscription. See Chapter 11 for more details.

Find Incorrectly Paid Payroll Liabilities

Details about the proper methods to prepare payroll and how to pay the accrued liabilities are provided in Chapter 11. Some QuickBooks users might choose to use the Write Checks transaction when preparing their payroll liability payments. Incorrectly prepared payments will adjust the balance sheet balances, but will not be reflected accurately in the Payroll Center. However, over the past several years, payroll liability payment errors are less likely to occur because of improved error messaging that encourages the QuickBooks user to prepare these liability payments properly.

This CDR task delivers another timesaving tool—helping the accounting professional easily and quickly find payroll liability payments that were recorded incorrectly.

When you select the menu or link in CDR to Find Incorrectly Paid Payroll Liabilities (Payroll group), QuickBooks prepares a report titled Payroll Liabilities Paid by Regular Check. See Figure A.36, which displays the results in true debit and credit format for each item found. This report will find a Write Checks transaction that was payable to a payroll item vendor.

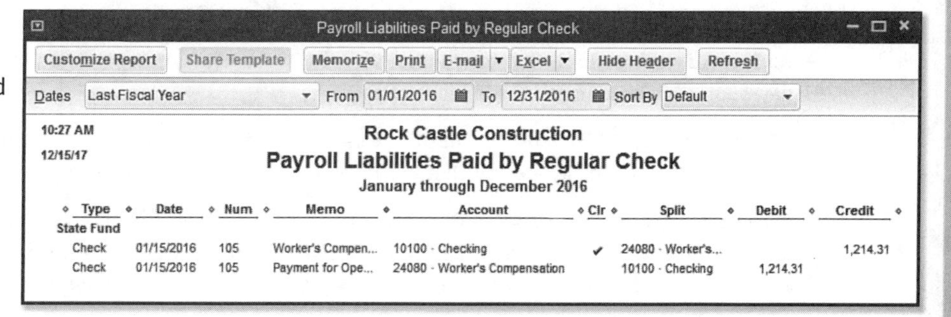

Type	Date	Num	Memo	Account	Clr	Split	Debit	Credit
State Fund								
Check	01/15/2016	105	Worker's Compen...	10100 · Checking	✔	24080 · Worker's...		1,214.31
Check	01/15/2016	105	Payment for Ope...	24080 · Worker's Compensation		10100 · Checking	1,214.31	

Figure A.36 This CDR report will find incorrectly paid payroll liability payment transaction types.

Use the details from this report to determine to which account your client has recorded these payroll liability payments. Did the client record them to the payroll liabilities account or select an expense account by mistake? More details about troubleshooting payroll can be found in Chapter 12.

After you determine what account the original entries were posted to, you can complete a Payroll Liability Adjustment by following these steps:

1. From the menu bar, select **Employees**, **Payroll Taxes and Liabilities**, **Adjust Payroll Liabilities** to open the Liability Adjustment dialog box shown in Figure A.37.
2. Enter the Date and Effective Date. Both should be dated in the quarter you want to effect the change.
3. Select **Company** for the adjustment. You would not select Employee here because the amounts calculated and paid were correct, just the type of transaction used to make the payment is incorrect.
4. Assign a Class if your business tracks different profit centers.

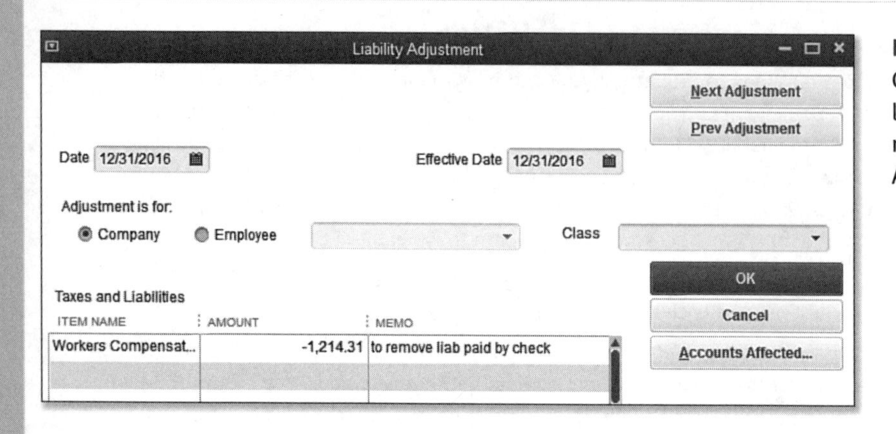

Figure A.37 Correct payroll liabilities paid incorrectly with a Liability Adjustment.

5. Click the Accounts Affected button. When determining which option button to select in the Affect Accounts? dialog box, take these suggestions into consideration:

   - **Do Not Affect Accounts**—Select whether the original transaction was assigned to the correct payroll liability account on the balance sheet.
   - **Affect Liability and Expense Accounts**—Select whether the original transaction was assigned to the expense account that is assigned to the payroll item used.
   - **Select Affect Liability and Expense Accounts**—Select whether the original transaction was assigned to any other account other than those stated above. You will want to review your financials after making this adjustment and might need to create an adjusting journal entry to correct the balance in the account that was originally used.

6. Click OK.
7. QuickBooks might open another dialog box with the default account that is going to be affected. You can specify the account used on the original tax payment transaction being corrected.
8. Click OK to save the transaction.
9. Review the balances in the affected accounts to make sure the adjusting transactions have been entered correctly.

You can check this and other details of your client's payroll setup by completing the Run Payroll Checkup as discussed in Chapter 11.

Review Payroll Liabilities

Conveniently, from within CDR you have access to the Employee Center: Payroll Center. From the displayed dialog box, you can view multiple month calendars; your upcoming scheduled payroll processing dates; due dates and amounts for paying your payroll liabilities in a timely fashion; and even links to processing the quarterly and annual forms for federal filings and most state filings.

To learn more about using the Payroll Center, read Chapter 11.

Review Employee Default Settings

QuickBooks CDR provides easy access to another feature that has been well hidden! Reviewing employee defaults will help your client process payroll with fewer mistakes, making future payroll reviews less time consuming.

 *You can learn more about setting these employee defaults in Chapter 11.*

Enter After-the-Fact Payroll

No longer is entering after-the-fact payroll time consuming! From within CDR, the accounting professional has access to this important feature. You or your client must have an active payroll subscription. If you or your client does not have an active payroll subscription, the After-the-Fact Payroll task will not display in the Payroll task group. Keep this in mind if you are working at the client's site or are remotely logged in to the client's data file.

Payroll entered through the After-the-Fact Payroll processing will also be included in all the federal and state forms QuickBooks payroll subscriptions prepare.

Bank Reconciliation

There are many ways to troubleshoot bank reconciliation issues with your client's data. With QuickBooks Accountant 2013 you have access to the Accountant Center (see Figure A.2), which displays timely information about your client's bank and credit card reconciliations.

 *Learn more about completing and troubleshooting your client's bank reconciliations in Chapter 13.*

Reconcile Accounts

You can use the Reconcile Accounts link in the Bank Reconciliation task group of the CDR feature to troubleshoot or complete your client's monthly bank reconciliation. If you are working with a client's Accountant's Copy file, you will be able to reconcile the bank account and these reconciliations will be incorporated into your client's data.

 *More details about this topic can be found in Chapter 16, "Sharing QuickBooks Data with Your Accountant."*

In my years of working with clients' QuickBooks files, the bank reconciliation is the task I most frequently see not completed at all or not done correctly, yet it is one of the most important tasks when you want to look at trusted financials. The CDR feature helps you, the accountant, work with your client's data file when reviewing or completing the bank reconciliation.

Locate Discrepancies in Bank Reconciliation

After reviewing the client's previous bank reconciliations, you might determine that the beginning balance, which was once correct, is no longer correct. Perhaps your client modified, voided, or deleted a previously cleared transaction.

The Locate Discrepancies in Bank Reconciliation report will help you to easily find these. The report is added to the CDR, Bank Reconciliation group:

1. From the menu bar, select **Accountant**, **Client Data Review** and launch the Client Data Review feature.
2. In the Bank Reconciliation group, select the **Locate Discrepancies in Bank Reconciliation** task.
3. The Previous Reconciliation Discrepancy report displays. For each transaction on this report, you see the modified date, reconciled amount, type of change (amount added or deleted), and the financial effect of the change (see Figure A.38) grouped by bank statement date.

10:33 AM
12/15/17

Rock Castle Construction

Previous Reconciliation Discrepancy Report

10100 · Checking

Type	Date	Entered/Last Modified	Num	Name	Reconciled Amount	Type of Change	Effect of Change
Statement Date: 11/30/2017							
Check	10/31/2017	12/15/2017 10:33:09	435	Dianne's Auto Shop	-212.00	Uncleared	212.00
Total 10/31/2007							212.00

Figure A.38
View details of previously cleared transactions that have been modified or deleted.

You can add the username to the report details to help in identifying who made the change to the transaction:

1. From the displayed Previous Reconciliation Discrepancy report, click Customize Report.
2. On the Display tab, place a checkmark on Last Modified By in the Columns box.
3. Click OK.

After reviewing the Previous Reconciliation Discrepancy report, you can prepare the Voided/Deleted report to help determine how to correct the transaction(s). To prepare this report, from the menu bar select **Reports**, **Accountant & Taxes**, **Voided/Deleted Transactions Summary (or Detail)**.

The Voided/Deleted report will not track discrepancies caused by changing the bank account associated with a transaction or changing a transaction amount. However, now the Client Data Review, Review List Changes task will track changes made from adding, deleting, or even merging charts of accounts and other list items in QuickBooks.

caution

Troubleshoot your beginning balance differences with the Previous Reconciliation Discrepancy report before completing the next month's reconciliation. Doing so is important because QuickBooks removes all details from the discrepancy report when you complete a new reconciliation. This is due to QuickBooks determining that you have solved the issue or you would not have completed the next month's bank reconciliation.

Reviewing Missing Checks

The Missing Checks report is useful when reviewing the accuracy of your client's bank account data. This report can help you determine whether any check transactions are missing or duplicated.

The Review Missing Checks link is conveniently included in the Bank Reconciliation cleanup tasks. In the Specify Account dialog box, select the appropriate bank account from the drop-down list.

The resulting Missing Checks report shows all transactions that are withdrawals from (that is, credits to) the bank account and that have a reference number. Transaction types include check, bill payment, sales tax payment, liability payment, paycheck, and general journal entry type transactions, presented in order by their reference number (see Figure A.39).

Figure A.39 The Missing Checks report can help you determine whether you need to enter any missing transactions before you reconcile.

10:36 AM
12/15/17

Rock Castle Construction
Missing Checks
All Transactions

Type	Date	Num	Name	Memo	Account	Split	Amount
Check	04/30/2016	150	Bayshore Water	Monthly Wat...	10100 · Checking	65130 · Water	-24.00
Check	04/30/2016	151	Cal Telephone	Flat Rate Ph...	10100 · Checking	-SPLIT-	-80.00
Check	04/30/2016	152	Bank of Anycity	Pmt# 4	10100 · Checking	-SPLIT-	-2,710.90
*** Duplicate document numbers ***							
Check	05/01/2016	152	Vu Contracting		10100 · Checking	-SPLIT-	-7,500.00
*** Missing numbers here ***							
Bill Pmt -Check	05/13/2016	154	East Bayshore Au...	Monthly Truc...	10100 · Checking	20000 · Acco...	-532.97
Check	05/15/2016	155	Patton Hardware S...		10100 · Checking	64800 · Tools...	-950.23
Check	05/15/2016	156	QuickBooks Maste...		10100 · Checking	20500 · Quic...	-1,400.00
Sales Tax Paym...	05/15/2016	157	State Board of Equ...	ABCD 11-23...	10100 · Checking	25500 · Sales...	-318.02
Check	05/31/2016	158	Bayshore CalOil S...	Fuel	10100 · Checking	60110 · Fuel	-143.00
Check	05/31/2016	159	Dianne's Auto Shop	Monthly Vec...	10100 · Checking	60130 · Repa...	-232.00

You should look for any breaks in the detail with a `***Missing` or `***Duplicate` warning.

Miscellaneous

This section of the CDR can be one of the most useful to you because it shows you how to set preferences to make your client's work more accurate and how to set a closing date, which will prevent or discourage a user from making changes to your reviewed data. If you are working with a client's Accountant's Copy, you will be able to set the Closing Date and optional Closing Date Password, which will be incorporated into the client's file.

Setting Closing Date and Password

QuickBooks offers flexibility for accounting professionals who want to protect prior period data and those who need or want to make changes to prior period accounting records.

What exactly is a "closed" accounting period? Well, a business can decide to close a month when a task such as a bank reconciliation is done or a sales tax return is filed, or a business can close once a year when the data is finalized for tax preparation. Because QuickBooks does not require you to close the books, it is a decision of the accounting professional and business owner (see Chapter 16).

The option of setting a closing date and password makes it easy to protect prior period transactions from unwanted modifications. With additional user-specific security settings, the business owner and accountant can also manage who has the privilege to make changes to transactions dated on or before a specific closing date.

Step One—Setting the Date and Assigning the Password

The first step in controlling changes to closed accounting periods is to set a closing date and optionally (although recommended) a closing date password the user must provide when adding, deleting, or modifying a transaction dated on or before the closing date.

Another important reason for setting a closing date is to track additions, modifications, or deletions to transactions dated on or before a closing date. The Closing Date Exceptions report will not track these changes when a closing date is not set.

To set the closing date and optionally a password (different from the Admin or External Accountant password) from an open Client Data Review, follow these steps:

1. Click the Set Closing Date and Password link in the Miscellaneous group of the CDR center. The Accounting—Company Preferences tab of the Preferences dialog box opens.
2. Click the Set Date/Password button. The Set Closing Date and Password dialog box displays.
3. (Optional) Select the following checkbox: **Exclude Estimates**, **Sales Orders**, **and Purchase Orders from Closing Date Restrictions**. These transactions are nonposting, and changes made will not affect your financials.
4. Enter a closing date and optional password. Consider using your phone number as the password or **Call Accountant** to encourage your client to call you before making changes to closed period transactions.
5. Click OK to close the Set Closing Date and Password dialog box.
6. If the No Password Entered warning displays, select **Yes** to add or edit users or **No** to close the warning.
7. Click OK to close the Preferences dialog box.

Setting a closing date is only step one. Next, you must set user-specific privileges for users to whom you want to allow access to adding, deleting, or modifying a transaction dated on or before the closing date.

Step Two—Setting User-Specific Security

To be certain the closing date control is managed properly, review all users for their specific rights to change transactions up to and including a closing date. To view the following menu, you need to be logged in to the file as the Admin user (External Accountant user type does not have the capability to create new users or change permissions for existing users):

1. From the menu bar, select **Company**, **Set Up Users and Passwords**, **Set Up Users**. The User List dialog box opens.
2. To view a user's existing security privileges (other than the Admin or External Accountant user) from the User List dialog box, select the **user** and click the View User button. You will be able to view in summary form the security settings for that user, as shown in Figure A.40.

Figure A.40
Review in summary form the user's security privileges.

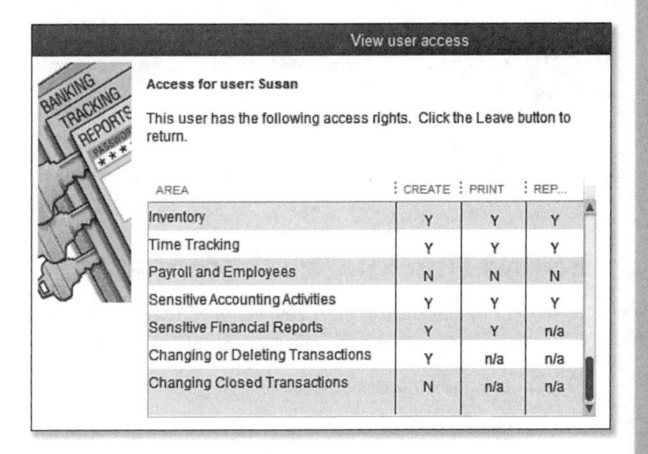

3. Any user who should not have rights to changing closed period transactions should have an "N" placed in the last setting of Changing Closed Transactions.
4. After reviewing a user's existing security privileges, if you need to edit the setting referenced earlier, click Leave to close the View User Access dialog box.
5. QuickBooks returns you to the User List dialog box. Select the username and click the Edit User button.
6. On the Change User Password and Access dialog box, optionally modify the username or password. Click Next to continue.
7. The User Access dialog box for the specific user displays. Choose **Selected Areas** and click Next to continue through each of the security selections until you reach the selections on Page 9 of the dialog box as shown in Figure A.41.

With the ease of doing client reviews, and now the security of knowing your hard work is documented and protected with a closing date, your future reviews should take even less time to complete, giving you more time to help your client with important management decisions.

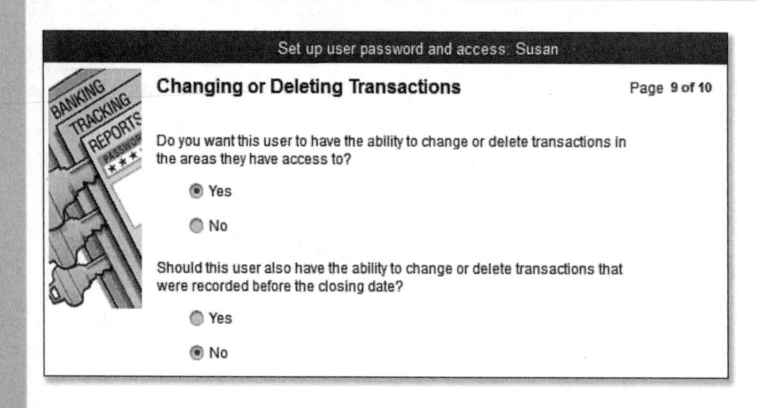

Figure A.41
With QuickBooks you set controls not to allow users to change transactions on or before a set closing date.

Review QuickBooks Preferences

Don't forget during your review to manage properly the many useful preferences that will help you and your client work more efficiently and accurately in the QuickBooks data file.

QuickBooks offers two types of preferences:

- **My Preferences**—Choices selected on this tab are being defined only for the currently logged-in user. If you are setting preferences for your client, you should log in with the client's username, and then set the My Preferences. These settings can be changed while in a multiuser environment (when others are in the data file).
- **Company Preferences**—Preferences set on these tabs are global for all users in the QuickBooks data file. Often, these preferences can be set only when you are in single-user mode, meaning other users cannot be working in the file when you set Company preferences. Both the Admin and the new External Accountant type user can modify Company Preferences.

There are preferences specific for accounting you should review. As the trusted accounting professional for your client, you benefit by reviewing each of the available preferences, including the following:

- Accounting
- Bills
- Calendar
- Checking
- Desktop View
- Finance Charge
- General
- Integrated Applications
- Items & Inventory
- Jobs & Estimates
- Multiple Currencies
- Payments
- Payroll & Employees
- Reminders
- Reports & Graphs
- Sales & Customers
- Sales Tax
- Search
- Send Forms
- Service Connection
- Spelling
- Tax: 1099
- Time and Expenses

Of the preferences, those that can enhance the accounting accuracy of a QuickBooks file are discussed in more depth in the related chapter. For example, the Sales & Customer preferences that improve the client's accuracy in QuickBooks are detailed in Chapter 9.

Condense Data from Previous Periods

If you find the client's data has become "sluggish" or has grown too large to be managed efficiently, you may want to consider using the Condense Data feature. This feature was improved in QuickBooks 2012. The Condense Data feature is greatly enhanced for the QuickBooks Accountant and QuickBooks Enterprise Solutions Accountant editions. Specifically, these software versions can

- Remove transactions before a specific date and optionally create a report showing which transactions were removed.
- Remove all transactions but keep lists and preferences.
- Remove transactions outside of a date range (to prepare a period copy of the company file).

After choosing from one of these data removal options, the accounting professional can then choose from these options:

- Create One Summary Journal Entry For All Transactions Prior To The Specified Cut-Off Date.
- Create A Summary Journal Entry For Each Month.
- Don't Create A Summary removes all transactions before the stated date regardless of status. Removed transactions are not replaced with a journal entry.

When condensing involves inventory, the accounting professional will have these choices:

- Summarize inventory transactions (recommended if goal is to reduce file size).
- Keep inventory transaction details.

As with any process of removing data, a backup should be created first in the event that the process does not provide the expected results. There are some limitations when using this tool—namely, current year payroll transactions are not removed.

> *For more information, see Chapter 17, "Managing Your QuickBooks Database," for details on file size management.*

With a password set and preferences reviewed, your next review of your client's data should take even less time using the CDR.

Finishing a Client Data Review

You can leave a CDR open for as long as it takes you to finish. When you close out of a task, your work is saved. Additionally, as you are working, you can conveniently select a QuickBooks menu outside of the Client Data Review and CDR will refresh automatically, including transactions created and modified.

(Optional) As you work through the many tasks, you can record an overall note for the review or individual notes assigned to specific tasks.

Saving the Review as a PDF

You can print the details of your CDR to paper or save as a PDF file. The information included with this document is shown in Figure A.42:

- Company name
- Review Period (Last Fiscal Year, Quarter, Month, or Custom)
- Date Printed
- Dates included in this review
- Basis: Accrual or Cash
- Client Data Review Notes
- Cleanup Tasks and Subtasks
- Status
- Task Notes
- Filename and path where the report is stored if prepared in PDF format

Marking Review Complete

When you have completed all tasks in the CDR and you select the Mark Review Complete button, QuickBooks does the following:

- Provides the option to set a closing date and password.
- Changes the Prior Review Period Dates in the Troubleshoot Account Balances Task.
- In the Troubleshoot Account Balances tasks, QuickBooks transfers your final reviewed balances to the Last Review Balances column. (These amounts will not change even if a customer makes a change to a transaction dated in that review period!)
- Provide the option to carry over task notes to the next review.

Figure A.42
Print or Save to PDF the details of the review for your paper files.

Rock Castle Construction

Review Period: **Last Fiscal Year** | Date Printed: **12/15/2017**

Dates: **01/01/2016 - 12/31/2016** | Basis: **Cash**

Review Notes:

```
Provide copy of review notes when completed to:

Bob Smith
CFO
Rock Castle Construction
bob@rockcastleconstruction.com
```

Cleanup Tasks	Status	Task Notes
Account Balances		
Troubleshoot Prior Account Balances	Completed	
Reclassify Transactions	Completed	
Open Working Trial Balance	In Progress	
Review List Changes		
Chart of Accounts	Completed	
Items	Completed	
Fixed Asset Items	Completed	11/15/16 Client purchased a new Dell Server, request purchase documents.
Payroll Items	Completed	
Review Item Setup	Not Started	
Customers	Not Started	
Vendors	Not Started	
Change Other Name Types	Not Started	
Accounts Receivable		
Fix Unapplied Customer Payments and Credits	Completed	
Clear Up Undeposited Funds Account	Completed	
Review AR Aging Summary Report	In Progress	
Write Off Invoices	Completed	Provide list of invoices to client
Accounts Payable		
Fix Unapplied Vendor Payments and Credits	Completed	
Evaluate and Correct 1099 Account Mapping	Completed	
Review Unpaid Bills Report	Completed	
Sales Tax		
Fix Incorrectly Recorded Sales Tax	Completed	
Adjust Sales Tax Payable	Completed	
Manage Sales Tax	Completed	
Pay Sales Tax	Completed	
Sales Tax Preferences	In Progress	
Inventory		
Review Inventory Setup	Not Started	
Compare Balance Sheet and Inventory Valuation	Completed	
Troubleshoot Inventory	Completed	
Adjust Inventory Quantity/Value On Hand	In Progress	
Payroll		
Find Incorrectly Paid Payroll Liabilities	Completed	
Review Payroll Liabilities	Completed	
Review Employee Default Settings	Completed	
Enter After-The-Fact Payroll	Completed	
Bank Reconciliation		
Reconcile Accounts	Completed	
Locate Discrepancies in Bank Reconciliation	Completed	
Review Missing Checks	Completed	
Miscellaneous		
Set Closing Date and Password	Completed	
Review QuickBooks Preferences	Completed	
Condense Data from Previous Periods	Completed	

Specific to the Troubleshoot Account Balances task, you do not have to Mark the Review as Complete for each review. However, your ending balances will be recorded only in the Last Review Balances column when you mark the review as completed. Marking a review as completed still gives you the option to reopen a previously closed review.

Reopening a Client Data Review

After marking a review as complete and before you start the next review, you will have the option to reopen the previously marked completed review as shown in Figure A.43. After you start a new review, you will no longer have the option to reopen the previously completed review.

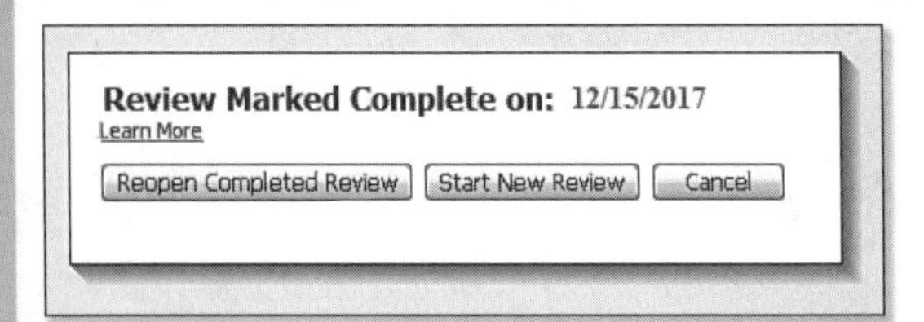

Figure A.43
Before starting a new review, you will have the option to open a previously closed review.

Reporting on Review Activity

Also available on the CDR center is a link to the Audit Trail of Review report (see Figure A.44). You can use this report to detail the transactions you have added, modified, or deleted during your review. The Audit Trail report will not report on changes made to list items.

12:58 PM
12/15/17

Rock Castle Construction
Audit Trail
Entered/Last Modified December 15, 2017

Num	Entered/Last Modified	Last modified by	State	Date	Name	Account	Split	Debit	Credit
General Journal 1006									
1006	12/15/2017 12:58:43	Laura (External A...	Latest	11/30/2016		60600 · Bank Serv...	10100 · Chec...	8.00	
						10100 · Checking	60600 · Bank...		8.00
Invoice 1100									
1100	12/15/2017 10:24:26	Laura (External A...	Latest	12/31/2016	Bauman, Mark:Hom...	11000 · Accounts...	-SPLIT-	2,586.00	
					Bauman, Mark:Hom...	40100 · Construct...	11000 · Acco...		2,400.00
					State Board of Equ...	25500 · Sales Tax...	11000 · Acco...		186.00

Figure A.44
The QuickBooks Audit Trail report helps identify what changes were made to transactions and by which user.

Additionally, if you used the new External Accountant type of login access, you were given all the rights of the Admin user (except adding or modifying users and viewing sensitive customer credit card information) and you can see your changes separate from the Admin or other users on this report.

The Audit Trail report provides details of additions and changes made to transactions, grouping the changes by username. The detail on this report shows the prior versions of the transaction and the latest version of the transaction, if it was edited. The Audit Trail report defaults to changes made as of today's date. This filter date can be modified for your needs.

The Audit Trail report can be lengthy to review. However, if as an accountant you try to track down specific user activity with transactions, this can be a useful report to review because the changes are grouped by username.

If you find undesired transaction changes, consider setting a closing date password and setting specific user security privileges as detailed earlier in this chapter.

Creating an External Accountant User

Setting up a QuickBooks user for each person who enters data provides a level of control over the sensitive data to be viewed by this user and gives access to specific areas in QuickBooks. For additional control, a user-specific password can also be assigned.

When you create a new user (or edit an existing user) in QuickBooks, you can assign that user as an External Accountant.

As an accounting professional using the CDR, you will want to request that your client create a username for you and assign the new External Accountant Type. If you then log in to the client file with this new user type, you will benefit from the following:

- Complete Admin access, except that you cannot create or edit users or view sensitive customer credit card numbers.
- Reports such as the Audit Trail can be filtered in Excel for a specific username, enabling you to see your transactions separate from the client's transactions.
- Client Data Review distinguishes in the dialog box if your login is the new External Accountant type (see Figure A.1).
- Access to Accountant Center, plus limited accountant and CDR tools when logging in to a client's QuickBooks Pro, Premier, or Enterprise 2013 non-accountant edition file.

If you are reviewing your client's data using the Accountant's Copy file type, or if you are not given the Admin login, this new External Accountant will have to be created before your client creates the Accountant's Copy or has you review data files.

To create an External Accountant, follow these steps:

1. Open the QuickBooks data file using the Admin user (the default user QuickBooks creates with a new QuickBooks file) and enter the appropriate password if one was created.
2. From the menu bar, select **Company**, **Set Up Users and Passwords**, **Set Up Users**.
3. Enter the Admin user password if one was originally assigned. Click OK.
4. The User List dialog box opens; it lists the current users set up for this file.

5. Click the Add User button to create a new user, or select an existing username and click the Edit User button.
6. The Set Up (or Change) User Password and Access dialog box opens.
7. In the User Name field, type the name you want the user to be identified by in the file.
8. In the Password field, enter an optional password, and in the Confirm Password field, retype the password for accuracy.
9. (Optional) Click the box to Add This User to My QuickBooks License. (See the Explain link for more details.)
10. Click Next. You might receive a No Password Entered message, click Yes or No to creating a password. If you select **Yes**, you will be taken back to step 8. (Optional) Select **Do Not Display This Message in the Future**. The Access for User:<username> dialog box opens.
11. Select the option for **External Accountant**, as shown in Figure A.45.

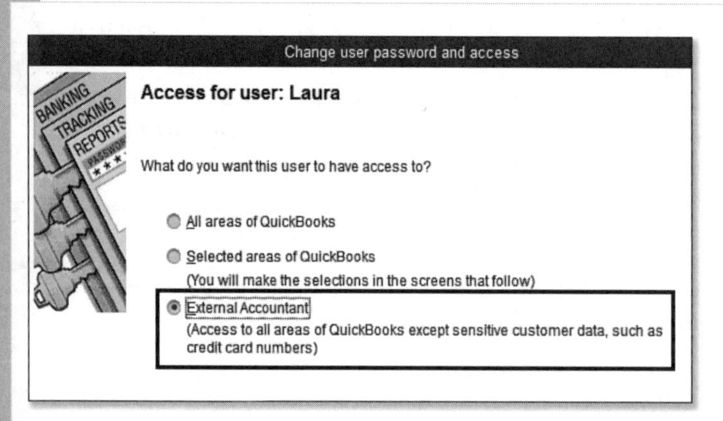

Figure A.45
Ask your client to create an External Accountant type user for your login.

12. Click Next.
13. QuickBooks provides a warning message, confirming that you want to give this new user access to all areas of QuickBooks except customer credit card numbers. Select **Yes** to assign the new External Accountant type privileges to this new or existing user.
14. The Access for User:<username> dialog box opens. The message restates that the new External Accountant user will have access to all areas of QuickBooks except sensitive customer credit card data. Click Finish to complete the process.

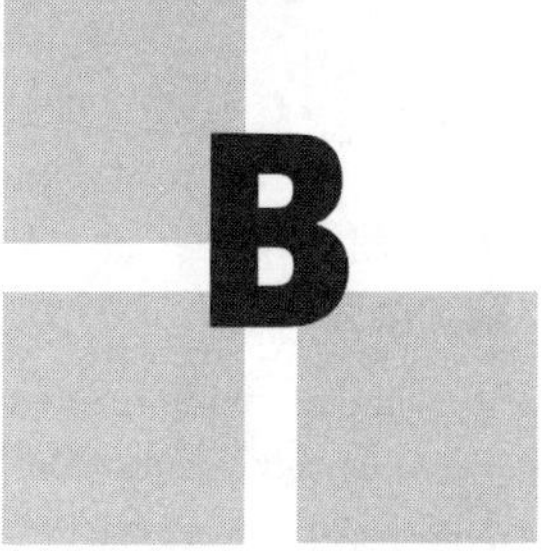

QUICKBOOKS STATEMENT WRITER

Overview

QuickBooks Statement Writer, formerly known as Intuit Statement Writer, is an extremely powerful and flexible reporting tool available for no additional fee with QuickBooks Accountant 2013 and all QuickBooks Enterprise Solutions 13.0 versions. Accounting professionals can use QuickBooks Statement Writer to prepare professional Generally Accepted Accounting Principles (GAAP)–compliant financials from QuickBooks data.

QuickBooks Statement Writer uses Microsoft Excel as the platform for creating customized financial reports from QuickBooks data. Additionally, QuickBooks Statement Writer keeps the statements synchronized with changes in the QuickBooks data. You can also add supporting documents created in Word and include them in your customized financials.

QuickBooks Statement Writer works with Excel 2003 or newer. (Note: It will *not* work with Microsoft Office 2003 Standard, 2003 Student Edition, or 2003 Small Business Edition.) Improved for QuickBooks 2013, QSW works with both the 32-bit and 64-bit install of Excel 2010.

Terms

The following terms will help you when working with the QuickBooks Statement Writer:

- **QSW**—Refers to QuickBooks Statement Writer.
- **Statement**—Specific financial statement, such as a Balance Sheet or Income Statement.
- **Documents**—Created with Word, such as a cover sheet or letter.
- **Statement Writer Report**—Collection of statements and documents.

note

The QuickBooks Statement Writer feature replaces the Intuit Statement Writer (ISW) and Financial Statement Designer (FSD) reporting tools used in earlier versions of QuickBooks.

If you are migrating from ISW or FSD to QuickBooks Statement Writer before preparing statements, visit http://accountant.intuit.com/ISW
Go to "Product Support" for details and tools to help with the conversion.

Workflow

There are three main steps when working with the QSW tool:

1. Open the QuickBooks file that contains the data using your QuickBooks Accountant 2013 or QuickBooks Enterprise Solutions 13.0 software (all editions).
2. Use the Report Designer for a step-by-step approach to creating a Statement Writer report.
3. Output the customized financial to Microsoft Excel, and use common Excel features or functions to add additional customization.

Benefits

Benefits of using QSW include the ability to:

- Create customized, professional financial statements from your client's QuickBooks data without manually typing data into Excel.
- Include multiple financial statements and supporting documents in a single QSW report.
- Use one of the many templates provided to create your own statements. Templates come in a variety of formats for the Balance Sheet, Income Statement, Cash Flow Statement, Retained Earnings Statement, and Budget to Actual Statements.
- Use Microsoft Excel (2003 or newer) as the platform for customizing and utilizing all the additional features and reporting flexibility available in Excel.
- Refresh customized financials with current QuickBooks data without leaving the Excel QSW report.
- Combine multiple QuickBooks account lines into one line on financial statements without changing your client's QuickBooks data.
- Add your own rows or columns of detail.
- Drill down to QuickBooks data and make changes to transactions within the QSW tool.

- Easily view and add any missing accounts not included in the current statement.
- Create charts and graphs using Excel functionality.
- Add supporting documents, such as a cover sheet or compilation letter, created in Microsoft Word and you have a complete set of financials ready to print.
- Share your customized reports with clients as an Excel spreadsheet or PDF formatted document.

Getting Started

To launch QSW from your QuickBooks Accountant 2013 or QuickBooks Enterprise Solutions 13.0 software, follow these steps:

1. From the menu bar, select **Reports**, **QuickBooks Statement Writer**. If you are using QuickBooks Accountant or QuickBooks Enterprise Accountant software you can also launch QSW from the Accountant Menu or the Accountant Center.

For more information, see "Customizing the Accountant Center," p. 663.

2. If prompted, select **Download Update** and then **Install Update**. If you are not prompted, skip to step 5.
3. Some computer systems require additional setup. If prompted with the User Account Control or other messages, follow the prompts to run QSW. You will only have to do these additional setup steps once.
4. Select **Yes** to the Install Shield Wizard and follow all prompts to install the update. Click Close to the QSW Update Manager message that you have the most current version.

5. The main QSW screen displays as shown in Figure B.1.

> **note**
> If you are prompted to install an update, you might need to restart your computer to finish the update process.

The following sections will detail the different global preferences that can be set in QSW.

Preferences & Formats

From the Preferences & Formats menu you will set global preferences and settings for customized reports prepared from all of your client's files.

General Preferences

The General Preference settings dialog box opens when you launch the Preferences & Formats from the main QSW screen. These settings permit you to:

- Accept the default location for your stored reports or browse to a location of your choice.
- Accept the default location for storing QSW templates or browse to a location of your choice.

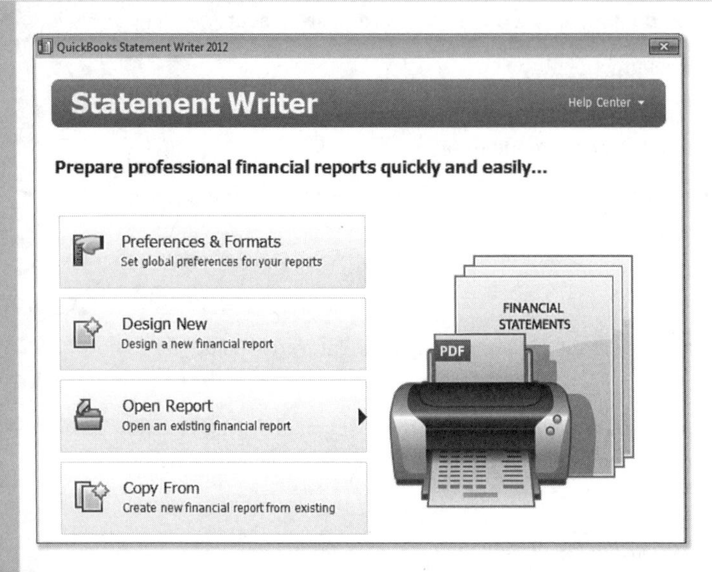

Figure B.1
The QuickBooks Statement Writer main screen offers easy access to all the features.

- Advanced setting for choosing to manually configure network permissions.
- Run Diagnostics Now, which will check if your system, QuickBooks, and QSW are configured correctly.
- Reset all warnings.
- Reset defaults.

note
Selecting OK on the General Preferences dialog box closes Preferences and returns you to the main QSW screen.

Optionally select **Apply** as you make changes. Next, select the **Your Details** menu tab to the left.

Your Details

Complete your Firm Name, Address, and other fields on the Your Details tab. The information entered here appears for all client files you open with this registered copy of QuickBooks. See Figure B.2.

Click the blue-colored text to access help content about the currently displayed window.

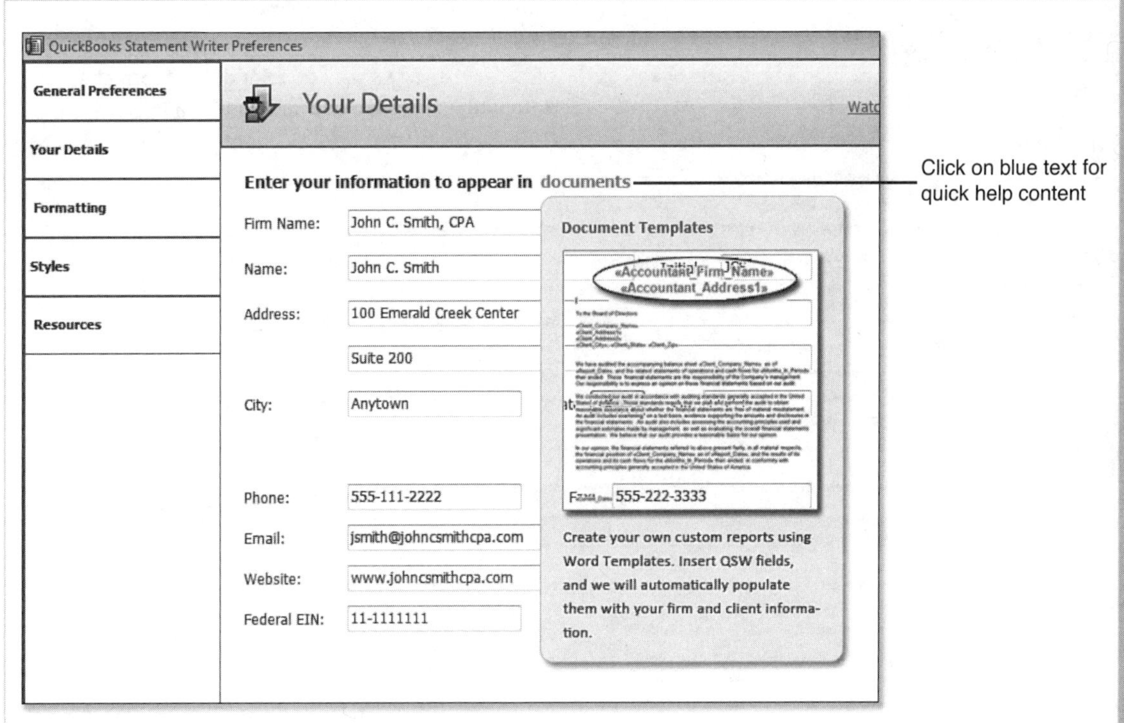

Figure B.2
Enter your firm information once and it will be included with each client's customized financial reports.

Formatting

On the Formatting tab, you can define the following global settings (see Figure B.3) for formatting all QSW statements. You can override these settings on individual statements when needed.

- **Automatic Underlines**—When total or subtotal rows are added to a statement, upon refresh underlines will be added.
- **Show**—Set defaults for displaying or not displaying of decimals, column headers, inactive accounts, and zero-balance accounts.
- **Show Zero Balances As**—Default the format for displaying any cell with a zero balance.
- **Show Negative Numbers As**—Choose from several options.
- **Divide All Data By**—Option to round (or not) the displayed amount.

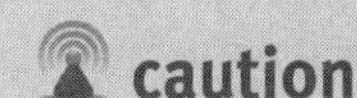

caution

Data formatting preferences will be displayed in Excel, but not while working in the QSW Report Designer.

Click the Reset Defaults button to return to the original formatting settings. Click Apply to save your changes. Click OK to close and save changes.

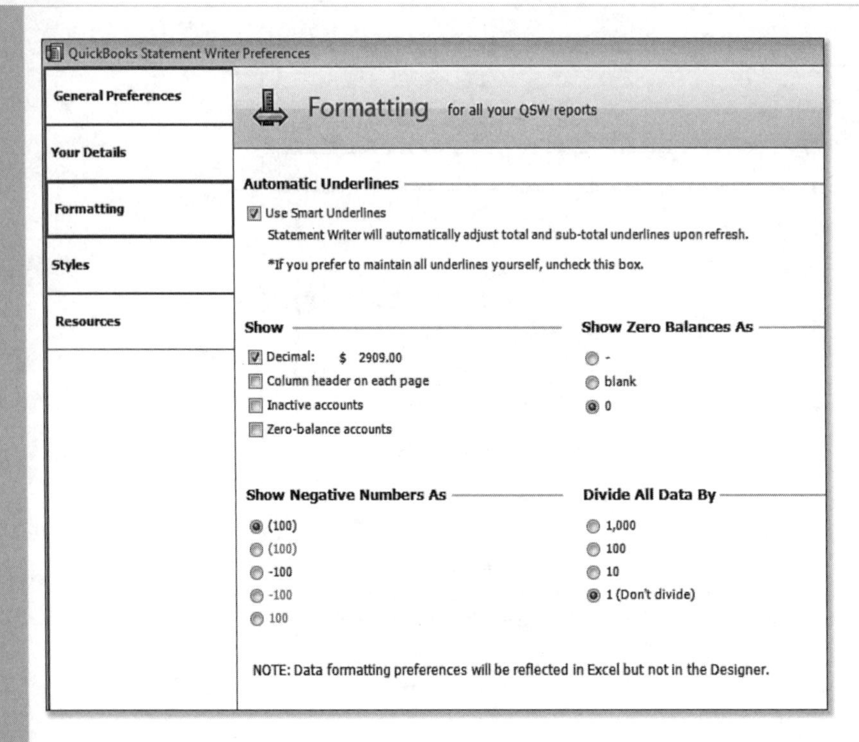

Figure B.3
Set default format settings for all QSW statements.

Styles

Styles are used for formatting the font, font size, bold, italic, and justification of the text as shown in Figure B.4.

On the Styles tab, select any style(s) and change the format as desired.

To change the style for multiple headers, labels or cells all at once, right-click with your mouse after selecting the content and choose the desired style.

tip

To assign a style for multiple rows, hold down the Ctrl key on your keyboard when selecting multiple headers, labels, or cells.

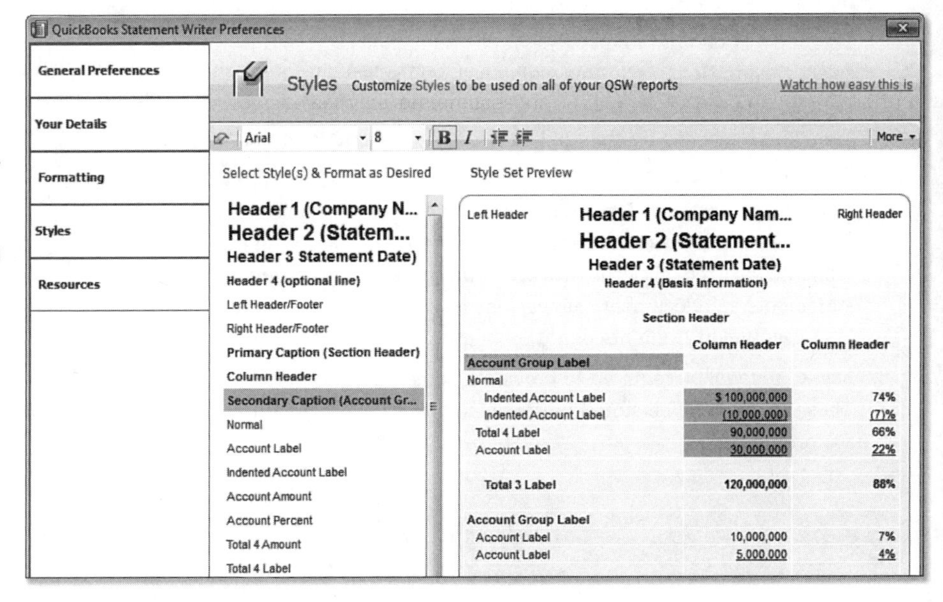

Figure B.4 Styles are used to set default font type and size. Style settings can be saved for reuse with other statements.

After customizing your style, from the More drop-down list select **Save as New Style Set**. Enter a Style Set Name, and this customized Style will be available the next time you create a new QSW statement.

Resources

Select the Resources tab for a listing of QSW resources and contact information. Additionally use this menu to download Intuit-provided statement and document templates.

Using the Report Designer

With the global preferences set, you are now prepared to create customized financials for your clients using QSW.

To begin using QSW, open your client's file in your QuickBooks Accountant 2013 or QuickBooks Enterprise 13.0 software (all versions) and launch QSW (as previously instructed).

You can use the ease of the QSW Report Designer to customize the financial report before creating it in Excel. You can further customize the report once you've exported it to Excel from the QSW.

Report Content

The Report Content tab displays when you launch QSW and select **Design New**. From this dialog box, you select your Report Date from pre-defined periods or choose a Custom Date range. This date range can be changed later without returning to this dialog box.

Select from Accrual or Cash Basis. From the Statement and Document Templates panel select the desired template. With the template selected, click the arrows in the center to add or remove statements and documents as well as arrange their order in the Financial Report Contents pane. See Figure B.5.

Lastly, you will be required to provide a name for the report. These reports will be stored in the default location defined in preferences.

Each template in the Financial Report Contents column will become a worksheet within a single Excel workbook.

You do not need to worry about the order the statements or documents are added to the Financial Report Contents. When you are ready to print the financials, you specify the print order within Excel.

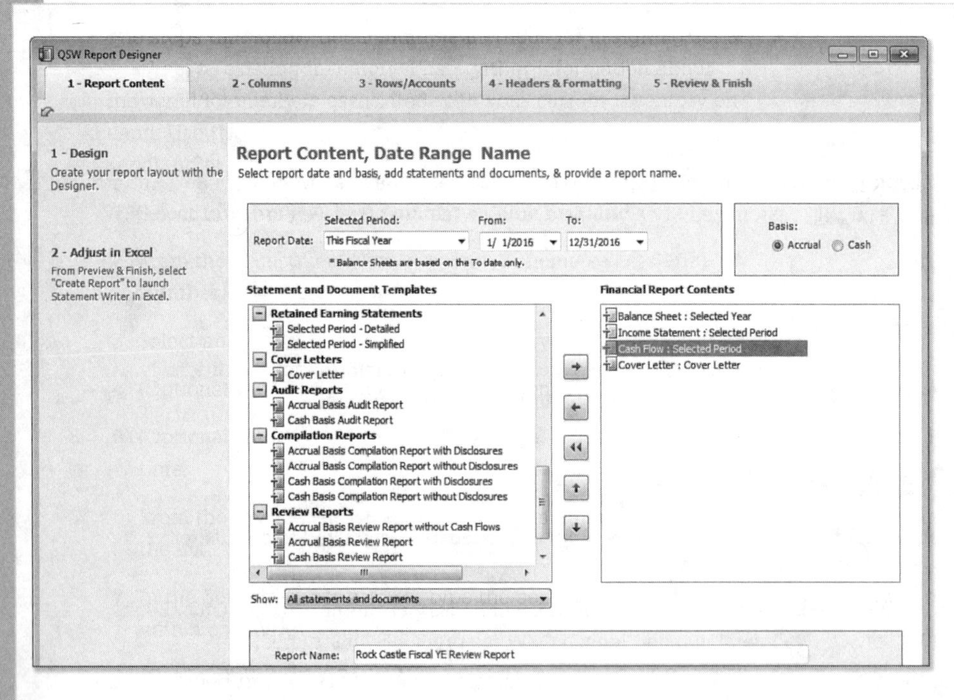

Figure B.5 The Report Date and Basis defined here can be modified later in the Statement Writer report.

For more information, see "General Preferences," p. 719.

Click Next to advance to the next task of customizing the columns of data to be included in the report.

Columns

tip

A short-cut menu containing many of the functions will appear when you right-click a column within a report.

Figure B.6 shows the Columns tab. A separate tab is created for each included statement or document. Click a specific statement to display data from the currently opened QuickBooks file (if a document is selected, instructions for modifying documents is provided).

Features of customizing columns include the ability to:

- Drag to insert columns, choosing from several types of columns including a Blank, QuickBooks Data, Variance, and Total columns to mention just a few.
- Refresh the data displayed in the QSW Report Designer, change the position of columns, remove columns, and modify the column header or dates from the toolbar.

Click the Undo icon on the toolbar (see Figure B.6) to undo the last action. Click Next to advance to the Rows/Accounts tab. Alternatively, click the Rows/Accounts tab at the top the QSW Report Designer dialog box to access this tab directly.

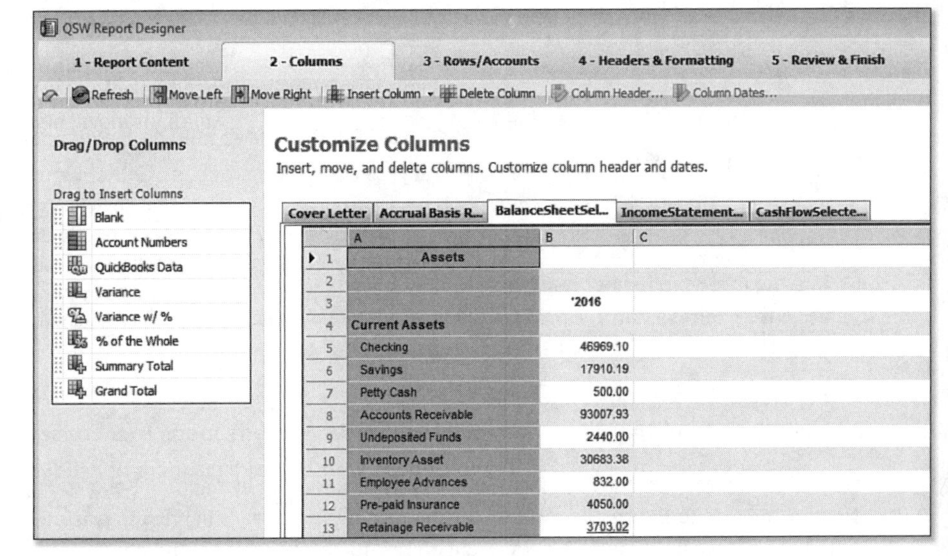

Figure B.6 Use the QSW Report Designer to customize the column properties in the selected statement.

Rows/Accounts

Figure B.7 shows the Rows/Accounts tab. A separate tab (worksheet) is created in Excel for each included statement or document. Click a specific statement to display data from the currently opened QuickBooks file (if a document is selected, instructions for modifying documents is provided).

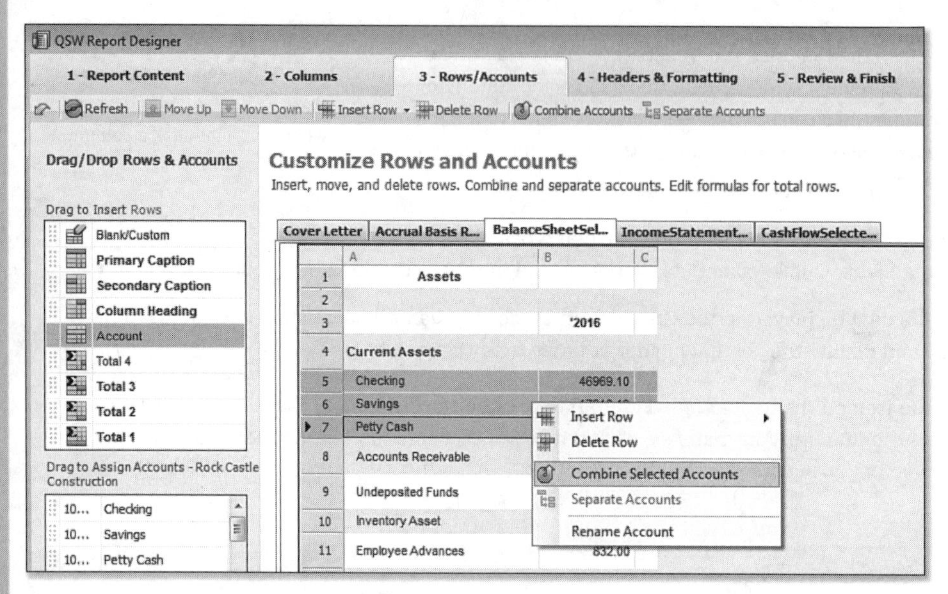

Figure B.7 Right-click to modify the currently selected row(s).

Features of this tab include the ability to:

- Drag to insert rows, choosing from several types of rows including a Blank/Custom, Account, and a variety of Total row options.
- Use the following toolbar buttons to modify rows and accounts: Refresh, Move Up, Move Down, Insert Row, Delete Row, Combine Accounts, or Separate Accounts.
- Easily identify missing or new rows by selecting the Show: Missing/New option button in the lower-left corner.

tip

Combine rows together by selecting multiple rows with the Ctrl key on your keyboard. From the Rows/Accounts toolbar, select **Combine Accounts.**

Click the Undo icon on the left side of the toolbar to undo the last action. Refer to Figure B.6. Click Next to advance to the Headers & Formatting tab. Alternatively, click the Headers & Formatting tab at the top of the QSW Report Designer dialog box to access this tab directly.

Headers & Formatting

Figure B.8 shows the Headers/Footers Formatting tab. A separate tab is created for each included statement (tab) or document. Click a specific statement to display data from the currently opened QuickBooks file (if a document tab is selected, instructions for modifying documents is provided).

Features of this tab include the ability to:

- Drag to insert header and footer fields, choosing from several types of fields including Statement Ending Date, Date Prepared, Basis, and Page # to name just a few.

- Use the Header & Formatting toolbar buttons to cut, copy, and paste fields and change the font, size, and properties of a field.
- Use QSW Smart Underlines. For more information, click the blue text to display help content.

Click the Undo icon on the toolbar to undo the last action as shown in figure B.6. Click Next to advance to the Review & Finish tab. Alternatively, click the Review & Finish tab at the top of the QSW Report Designer to access this tab directly.

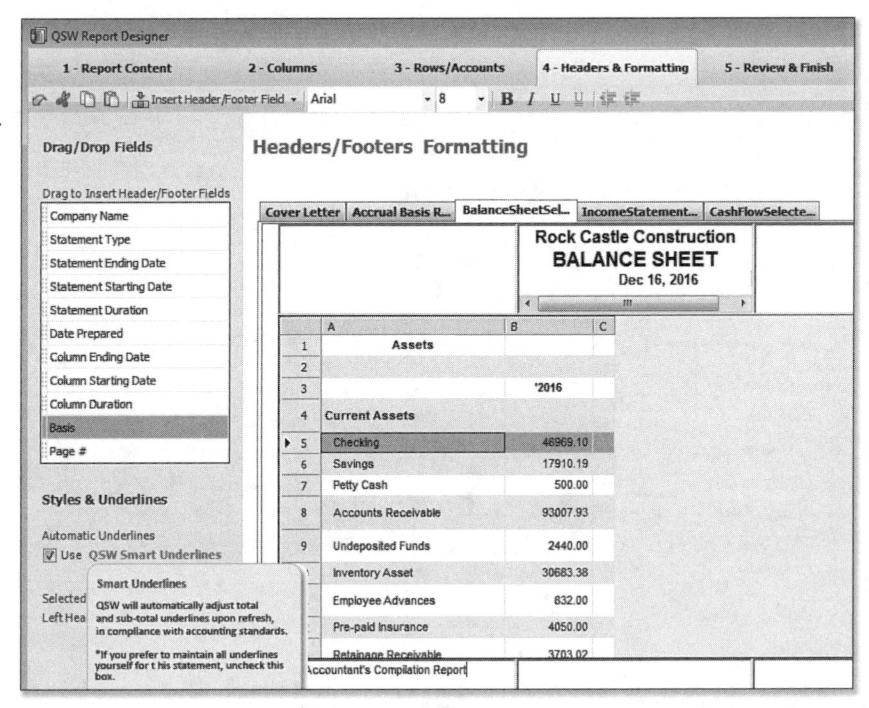

Figure B.8
Hover your cursor over blue text to view help content for that feature.

Review & Finish

If this is your first time creating the report using Report Designer, on the Review & Finish tab a separate tab is created for each included statement or document for review. Click a specific statement to display the customized formatting (if a document is selected, instructions for modifying documents is provided).

Select a specific statement and from the toolbar choose the Memorize Current Statement. You can then reuse this customized statement with new financial reports.

Choose Memorize Report Group from the toolbar to save the group of selected statements for use with a newly created financial report from another client's data.

note

If you are returning to the Report Designer from a previously prepared QSW report you will not see the individual statement tabs at the top. Instead, you will have to select the desired statement in the Excel QSW then select the Report Designer icon from the QSW Document Actions pane toolbar to modify.

Click Create Report to send your customization into Excel. QuickBooks will launch Excel and add the customized formatting you created in the Designer. Each statement will be an individual worksheet tab in a single Excel workbook. See Figure B.9.

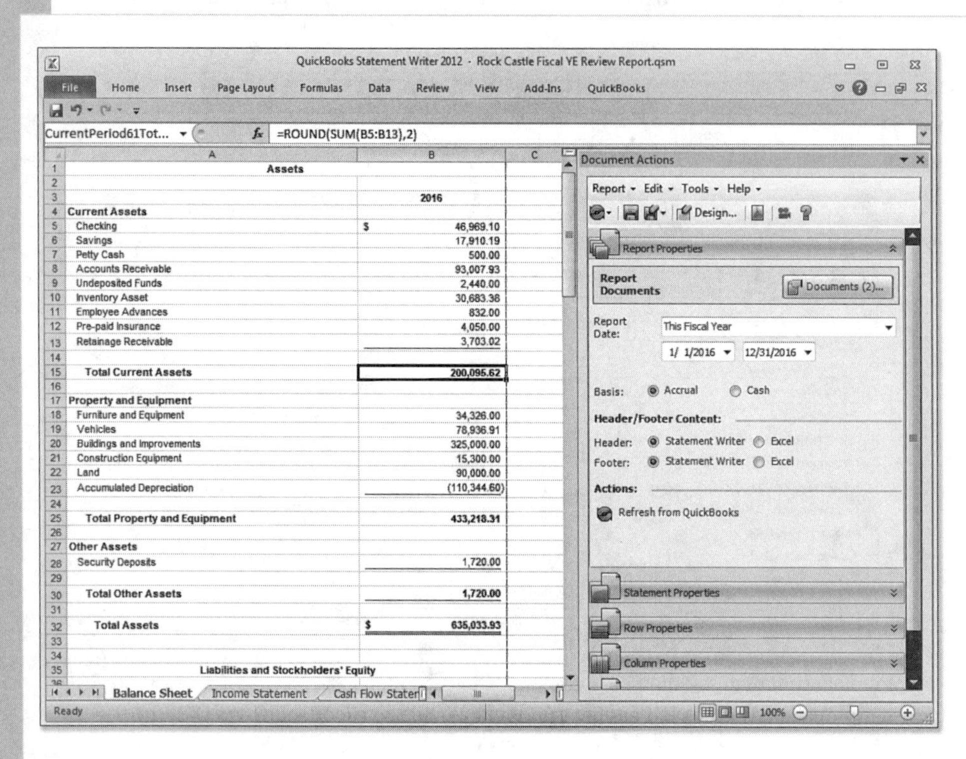

Figure B.9 QSW uses Excel for the completed report.

Opening a Previously Created Report

When a user clicks Open Report from the main QSW dialog box, the five most recently accessed reports for the currently opened company file will display. Optionally, a user can select Browse to Open, which by default looks to the same folder where the current reports are stored.

After selecting a report from the list or browsing to a report, QSW will launch the report in Excel. If prompted by your system, select Yes to any prompts to trust the source of the file. (Your version of Excel might have security settings that will not recognize the .QSM extension of the QSW stored report without your granting permission to trust the file type.)

Creating a New Report from a Memorized Report

Click the Copy From button on the main QSW dialog box to reuse a previously memorized statement or report group.

Click Browse, and QSW will default to the location where the most recent QSW report was stored. If necessary, browse to another location to find the report with the .QSM extension.

With the Source Report selected, click Open. The Copy From dialog box displays the Source Report location and the Destination Folder. Provide a New Report Name and click Copy.

Select or deselect the option to Open New Report.

Modifying a Statement Writer Report in Excel

Now that you have created a Statement Writer report, you might find the need to customize the content for future reports or for use with other client's data files.

There are several methods you can use to edit an existing Statement Writer report, which include:

- Returning to the Report Designer
- Using the Document Actions pane
- Using the QSW icons on the Excel Add-Ins ribbon (or Excel 2003 toolbar)
- Right-clicking a report column, row, or cell in Excel.

You might use one, or all of these methods. The next sections provide additional details on working with each of these methods.

 **note**

If you have multiple statements in your report, you will need to select the desired statement in Excel that you want to modify in Report Designer. Only the first time you created your QSW report will each statement display as an individual tab on the Report Designer, Review & Finish tab.

Method 1: Using the Report Designer

When creating the original Statement Writer report, you most likely used the Report Designer. You can return to this familiar tool to make edits to your existing Statement Writer report.

From a displayed Statement Writer report in Excel, click the Design icon on the Document Actions pane toolbar, as shown in Figure B.10.

If you have made formatting edits while in Excel, answer Yes or No to the warning message that displays. If you select Yes, the Report Designer for the current Statement Writer report opens.

For more information, see "Using the Report Designer," p. 723.

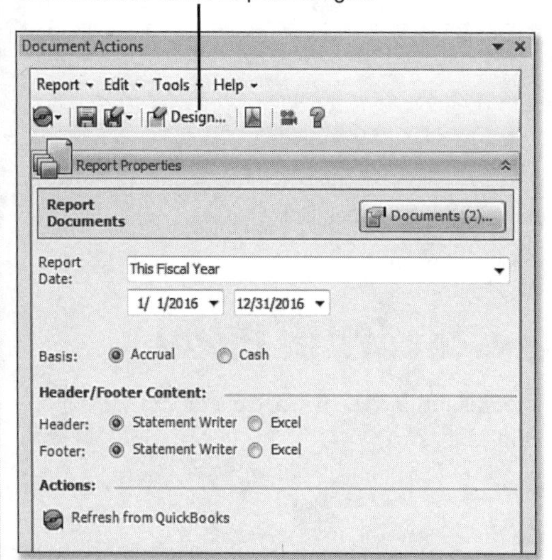

Figure B.10
Access the Report Designer from the toolbar in the Document Actions pane.

Method 2: Using the Document Actions Pane

There are several methods for editing an existing Statement Writer report; one method is accessing the many edit tools from the Document Actions pane.

The Document Actions pane, shown in Figure B.11, will only display when you launch QuickBooks and then open a Statement Writer report from within the QSW. The file extension of .QSM is assigned to these reports by QSW and cannot be opened directly with Excel.

Most, if not all, of the functionality detailed to this point in the chapter can be found by selecting one of the drop-down menus from the menu bar in the Document Actions pane.

Frequently used actions are included on the Documents Action toolbar, as shown in Figure B.11.

More detailed edits can be made by selecting one of the expandable panes for Report, Statement, Row, Column, and Cell Properties depending on the change you need to make.

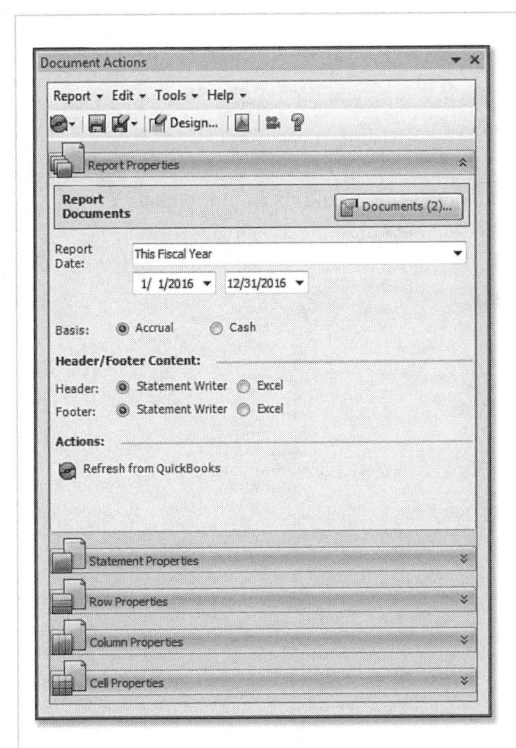

Figure B.11
Use the Document Actions pane to add or edit the Statement Writer report.

note

Are you having trouble viewing the Statement Writer pane in Microsoft Excel as shown in Figure B.11? First, be sure you have opened the QSW report from within the QuickBooks file. If you still do not see the Statement Writer pane you might have inadvertently closed it.

Depending on which version of Excel you have, reopening the Statement Writer pane requires different steps. In Excel 2010, select the Add-Ins ribbon and click the QSW Toolbar: Show Statement Writer Pane icon. In Excel 2007 and 2003, select the **Add-Ins** tab, select **View, Toolbars,** and place a checkmark next to QuickBooks Statement Writer. With Excel 2003, you might have to make the toolbar visible. Hover your mouse over the icons to find the icon that will reinstate your Statement Writer pane as shown in Figure B.19.

Find Missing Accounts

Identifying new accounts created by your client since the last time you prepared a Statement Writer report used to be a daunting task. Now, it is easier than ever.

From the toolbar in the Document Actions pane, select **Edit, Show All Accounts.** The All Accounts dialog box displays as shown in Figure B.12. Any missing accounts from the customized financials will be displayed in red. Optionally select to show only the Missing accounts.

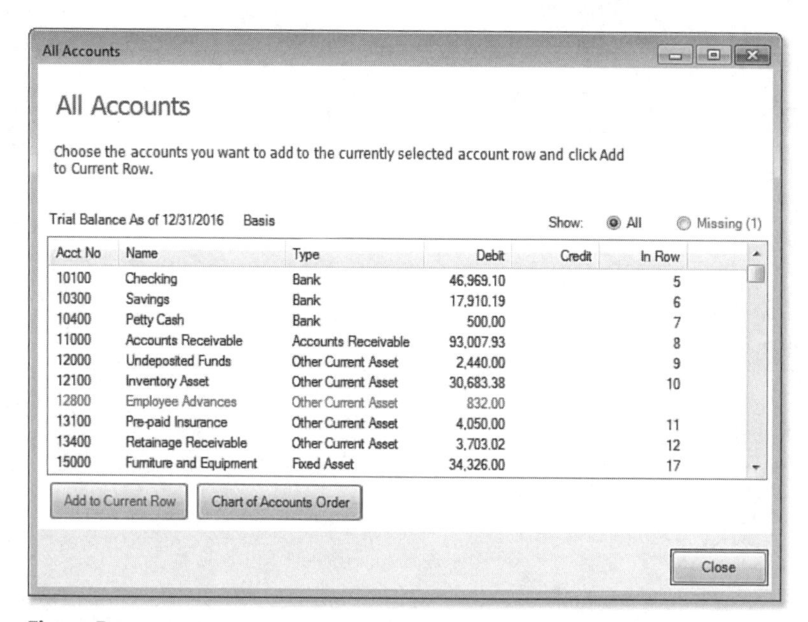

Figure B.12
Has your client added new accounts since preparing your last report? Locate them efficiently with the All Accounts dialog box.

To review or add the missing account(s), follow these steps:

1. After reviewing the missing accounts, click Close on the All Accounts dialog box.
2. From the Row Properties, choose to add a new account row or highlight with your cursor an existing row you want to add the missing account(s) to.
3. With your cursor on the row you want to add the account(s) to, from the toolbar in the Document Actions pane, select **Edit, Show All Accounts.**
4. Select the missing account(s).
5. Click the Add to Current Row button. As you complete this for each missing account(s) there will no longer be any accounts in red.
6. Click Close to return to the modified Statement Writer report.

Report Properties

The term used by QSW for a collection of statements is a Statement Writer report. When you need to make global changes to all statements within a report, use the Report Properties. With report properties (previously shown in Figure B.10) you can manage the following:

- **Documents**—Add or modify supporting documents. See, "Working with Supporting Documents," p. 740.
- **Report Date**—Select from predetermined dates or choose a custom date.
- **Basis**—Specify whether you want to use accrual basis or cash basis reporting.
- **Header/Footer Content**—Designate if you want your changes in Excel to supersede changes you made in Report Designer.
- **Refresh from QuickBooks**—Restate the entire QSW Report (multiple statements) with updated QuickBooks data.

Statement Properties

When you need to modify properties that affect a single statement, not just a specific row or cell, use the Statement Properties task from the QSW Document Actions pane.

The Statement Properties task (shown in Figure B.13), controls changes made to the currently selected financial statement:

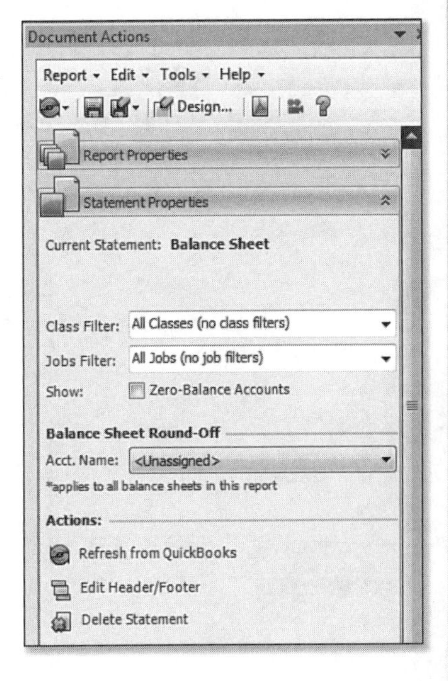

Figure B.13
Modify a selected statement from the Statement Properties panel.

- **Title**—Modify the currently selected title in the Statement Properties pane or optionally modify the title directly in the appropriate Excel data cell.
- **Class Filter**—Filter for all classes, a specific class, or for multiple classes.
- **Jobs Filter**—Filter for all jobs, specific jobs, or for multiple jobs.
- **Zero-Balance Accounts**—When selected, show accounts with a zero balance; when not selected, accounts with a zero balance are hidden.
- **Balance Sheet Round-Off**—Assign the account you will use for any rounding differences.
- **Refresh from QuickBooks**—Restate the currently selected statement with updated QuickBooks data.
- **Edit Header/Footer**—Change to the Header/Footer.
- **Delete Statement**—Remove a statement from a QSW Report.

Row Properties

To make a change to a specific row, and not affect other rows, review the features of the Row Properties task of the QSW Document Actions.

The Row Properties, shown in Figure B.14, affect formatting for the selected row and offer the following functionality when selecting a blank row:

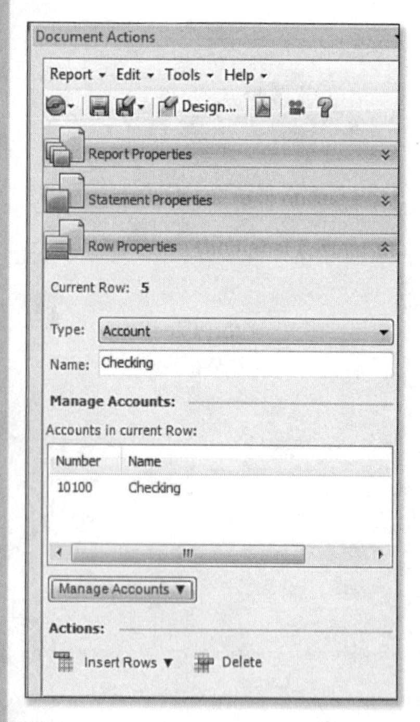

Figure B.14
Use the Row Properties options to control the data you view in a particular row.

- **Type**—Change the type of data that is represented in the cell, including Blank, Captions, Headings, Account (QuickBooks data), or Total types. For more information see Table B.1 "Row Total Specifications" in this chapter.
- **Name**—Change the label of the cell (with the cell selected); the default is the account name.
- **Manage Accounts**—Select from the following:
  - Combine accounts from selected rows
  - Add accounts by number, type, or name
  - Separate accounts that were previously combined
  - Remove accounts
  - Override zero-balance settings (from Statement Properties)
  - Reverse all the positive and negative numbers in the row.
- **Insert Rows**—Choose from Blank, Captions, Headings, Account (QuickBooks data), or Total types.
- **Delete**—Delete currently selected row. You have to use the QSW Delete Column function because the Excel worksheet is protected from using the Excel Delete command.

Did you know that to change the text in a row label, you can make the change directly in the Row Properties pane with the row selected, or simply type the new text directly into the appropriate cell of the spreadsheet? Entering new text using either of these options updates the Row Properties pane and the row label viewed for the statement.

Combine Account Rows

QuickBooks offers users a lot of flexibility when working with a chart of accounts. Often, several chart of account list items might have been created since your last review of the data. The QSW tool enables you to create customized financials grouping accounts together without affecting the client's original chart of accounts.

To combine account rows, follow these steps:

1. With the QSW statement open, click to highlight any two or more cells you want to combine into a single row. In the example shown in Figure B.15, the cells for Checking, Savings, and Petty Cash are selected.

Use the control key on your keyboard to select multiple rows.

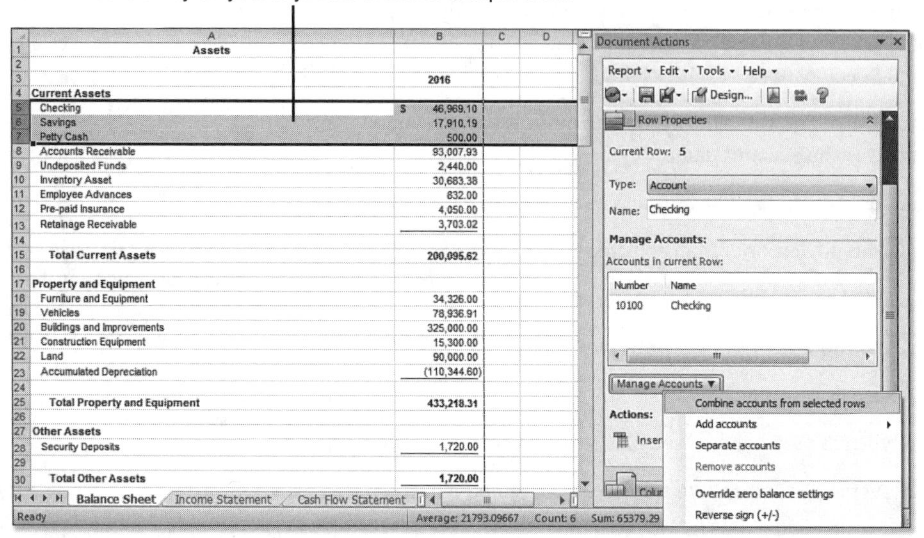

Figure B.15
Combine multiple QuickBooks account rows into one in the customized financials. No change is made to the QuickBooks file.

2. With multiple cells selected that you want to "roll up," select **Combine Accounts** from Selected Rows from the Manage Accounts drop-down list. (Optional) Click the Combine Accounts icon from the Excel Add-Ins ribbon.
3. Rename the label either in the Row Properties task or directly in the Excel cell. Figure B.16 shows that the row was renamed to Cash and Cash Equivalents.
4. Hover your mouse over the row to see a note of the accounts that are included in the new cell total.

To separate the accounts, in step 2 choose the Separate Accounts menu choice.

One of the most efficient uses in customizing your client's financials is the capability to combine "like" rows of data into a single row. Your financials will be more professional in appearance, while not affecting the client's chart of accounts.

A5 Cash and Cash Equivalents

	A	B	C	D
1	Assets			
2				
3		2016		
4	Current Assets			
5	Cash and Cash Equivalents	$		
6	Accounts Receivable			
7	Undeposited Funds			
8	Inventory Asset			
9	Employee Advances	832.00		
10	Pre-paid Insurance	4,050.00		
11	Retainage Receivable	3,703.02		
12				
13	Total Current Assets	200,095.62		

Accounts in this row:
10100 Checking
10300 Savings
10400 Petty Cash

Figure B.16
Multiple cash rows are now included in a single row. Mouse over the row to see the accounts included.

New for QuickBooks Statement Writer 2013 is improved row Total types. Table B.1 provides some technical information on the characteristics of the different Total types:

Table Appendix B.1 Row Total Specifications

Total Row Type	Behavior
Total 4	Inserts a Total 4 row The row is inserted and the total is the sum of all accounts above this line and after the previous total. An underscore appears below the last value in the Total 4 group of accounts. The row takes on the Total 4 STYLE.
Total 3	Inserts a Total 3 row All accounts and Total 4s above the current row and below the previous secondary caption or Total 3 row are included. An underscore appears below the last value in the Total 3 group of accounts. A blank row is inserted above the Total 3 row. The row takes on the Total 3 STYLE.
Total 2	Inserts a Total 2 row All Total 3s above the current row and below the previous secondary caption are included. An underscore appears below the last account and Total 3 value in the secondary group. A blank row is inserted above the Total 3 row. The row takes on the Total 2 STYLE.
Total 1	Inserts a Total 1 row All accounts and Total 2s, 3s, and 4s within the group above the new row and below the previous Total 1 or primary caption are included. A double underscore appears below the last value in the Total 1. A blank row is inserted above the Total 1 row. The row takes on the Total 1 STYLE.

Column Properties

Use the Column Properties pane (see Figure B.17) to change the properties of the selected column in the QSW statement. The options available in the Column Properties pane change depending on the type of column that is current when the pane is selected.

- **Type**—Choose the type of data in the column: Blank, Accounts (the column or statement header), Variance, % of the Whole, Summary Total, and Grand Total. Each type has its own unique column property options.
- **Heading**—Control the heading title of the currently selected column.

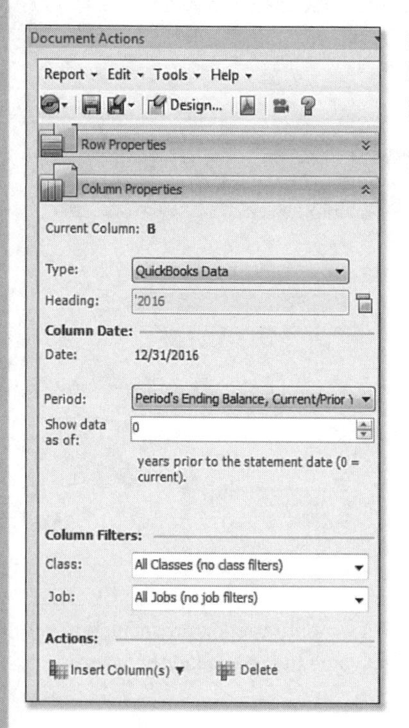

Figure B.17
Place your cursor in a column and then from the Column Properties panel control the contents of that column.

Depending on what type of column you have selected, the following menu options change:

- **Period**—Change the accounting period for the currently selected column.
- **Show Data**—Select to display past years for the same accounting period; used side-by-side analysis.
- **Filter for Class**—If you are using class tracking, select all classes, combination of classes, or a single class.
- **Filter for Job**—Filter for all jobs, combination of jobs, or a single job.
- **Insert Column(s)**—Use to add columns from the specified allowed types. Types include Blank, Account Numbers, QuickBooks Data, Variance, % of the Whole, Summary Total, and Grand Total.
- **Delete**—Click to select the column you want to delete and then click the Delete Column button on the Column Properties pane. You have to use the QSW Delete Column function because the Excel worksheet is protected from using the Excel Delete command.

Cell Properties

The Cell QSW actions will vary by the type of cell selected. In Figure B.18 an account amount cell is selected. Cell Properties include:

- **Current Cell**—Indicate the cell reference for the currently selected cell.
- **Cell Type**—Determined and set by either row or column properties.
- **Temporary Balance Override**—Define a manual amount for an account cell.
- **Override Date**—Override the selected date for a specific cell, so the date range differs from the rest of the statement data.
- **Reset Date**—Return the cell date to match the date assigned to the entire statement.
- **Insert Field(s)**—Add any of the following information to a selected blank cell:
  - Accountant Information
  - Client Information
  - Basis
  - Statement "From" Date
  - Statement "To" Date
  - Formatted Statement Date

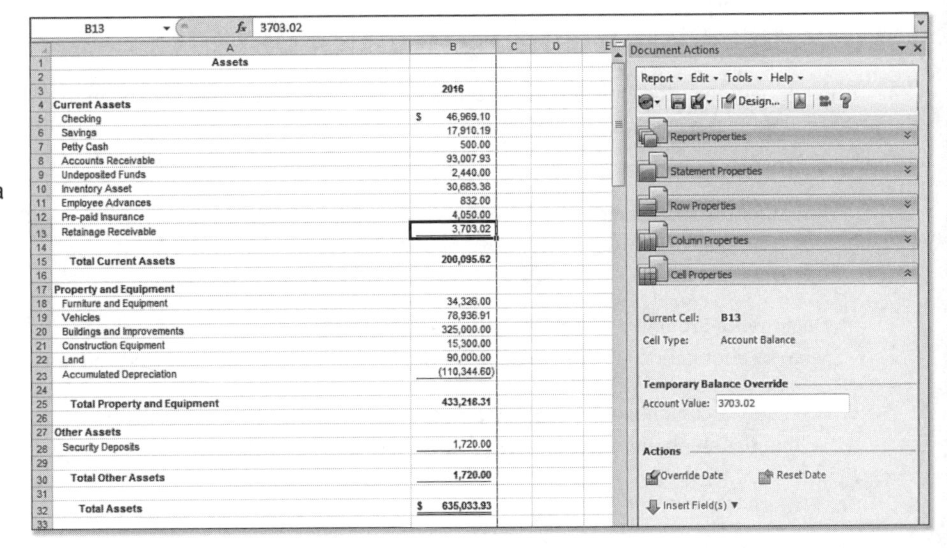

Figure B.18 Use the Cell Properties to manage the information displayed in a specific data cell.

Method 3: Using the Excel Add-Ins Ribbon Icons

You can also access selected editing functions from the Excel Add-Ins ribbon icon shown in Figure B.19.

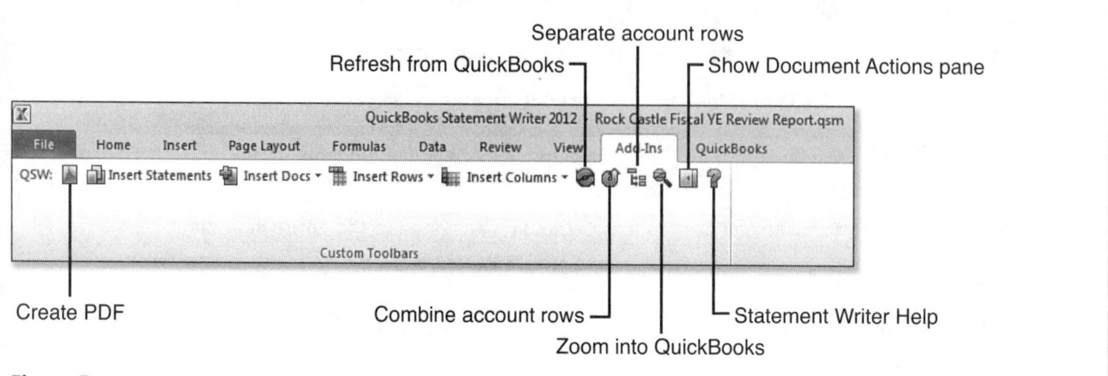

Figure B.19
Reinstate the QSW Document Actions pane and other activities available from the QSW toolbar.

Working with Supporting Documents

Another feature of the QuickBooks Statement Writer 2013 tool is the capability to create supporting documents to the customized statements.

There are two types of supporting documents you can add to your QSW statement:

- **Documents From Templates**—Created from templates that merge accountant and client information from the company file with present text. These documents are created with Word and have a file extension .dot.
- **Documents From My Computer**—Word documents you have already created and do not contain merged information. There are no limitations to the content of these documents.

You can add documents from templates or documents stored on your computer. Templates are both those that are shipped with the QSW product and those you can download directly from Intuit.

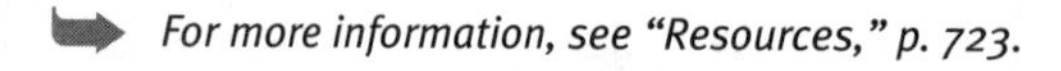
For more information, see "Resources," p. 723.

The following sections detail how to create or modify existing document templates and then attach them to your Statement Writer report. When you complete your client's customized financials, you can specify the order the documents are to print in.

Overview

You can add or modify the provided supporting document templates or you can create them on your own using Microsoft Word. Supporting documents can be a combination of both text (your own manually typed content) or dynamic data fields from the QuickBooks file, which are selected from a predefined list. For example:

"We have audited the accompanying statement of assets, liabilities, and equity—(cash, income tax basis) of «Client Company Name»."

In the text above, the first part of the sentence is manually typed text. The field name is Client Company Name. The chevrons («») are required and are added automatically by Microsoft Word. When the final report is printed, the data from QuickBooks (in this example, the Client Company Name) is replaced where the field name is listed in the template.

When you are creating a template with merged fields, you use a Microsoft Word .dot file. The only time you open the .dot file is when you need to modify the template details. When the final report is prepared, the field names will look for current data from the QuickBooks file you are using with QSW.

Adding or Modifying a Supporting Document

You might have added a supporting document when you created the Statement Report using the Report Designer. In Figure B.5 a Cover Letter document was added to the Financial Report Contents in Report Designer. If you did not add documents during the Report Designer setup, you can add them from the Document button in the Report Properties panel as shown in Figure B.20.

Figure B.20
View, add, open, rename, and delete supporting documents.

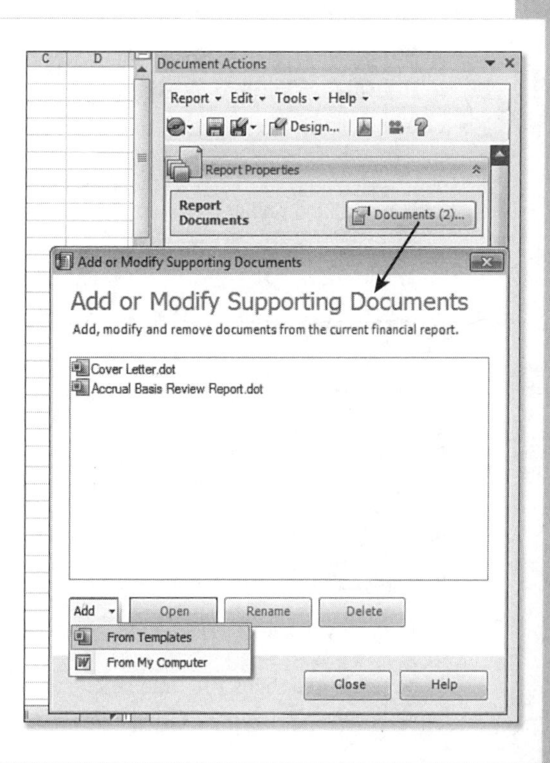

To add or modify a supporting document, follow these steps:

1. Open a Statement Writer Report. From the Document Actions pane, expand the Statement Properties panel.

2. Click the Documents button. The Add or Modify Supporting Documents dialog box displays any documents currently included in the Statement Report.

3. Click Add, to choose to add From Templates or From My Computer.
4. If you select From Templates, the Insert Documents dialog box displays as shown in Figure B.21.

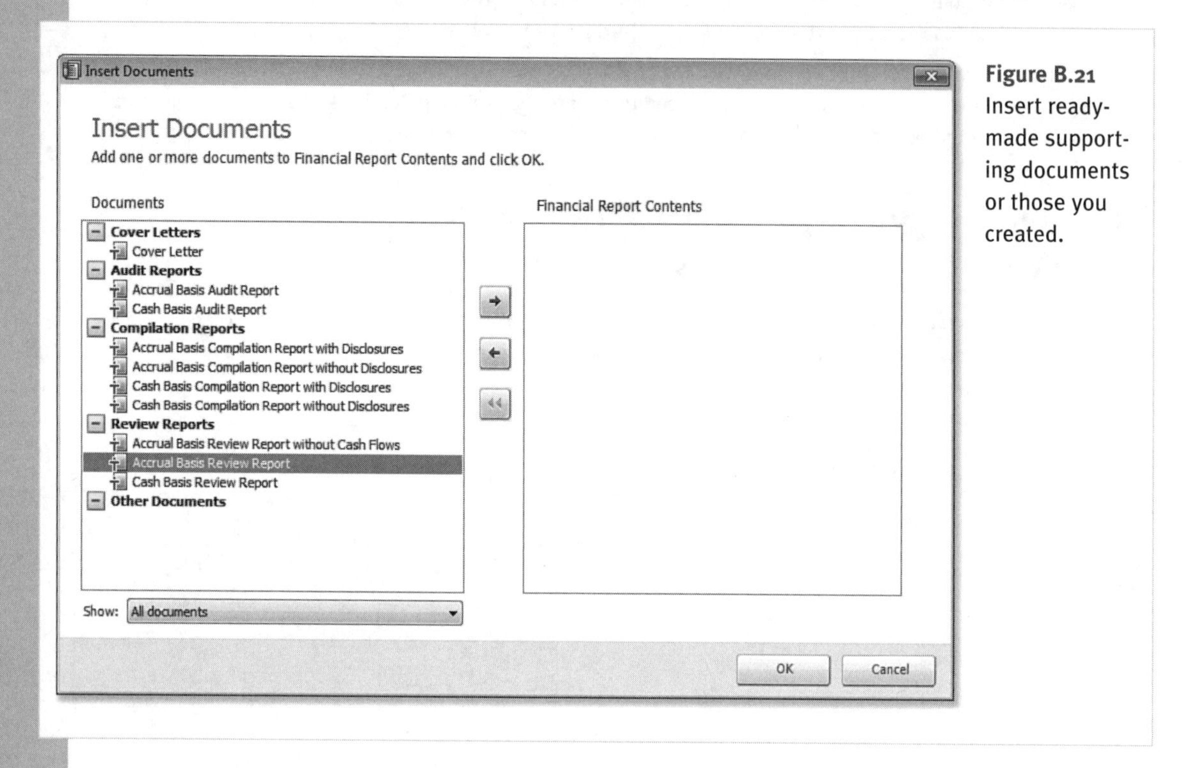

Figure B.21 Insert ready-made supporting documents or those you created.

5. Select the desired document template on the left and click the arrow pointing to the right to include the document in the Financial Report Contents.
6. Click OK. The new document displays in the Add or Modify Supporting Documents dialog box.
7. (Optional) With a document selected, click Rename or Delete.
8. To modify a selected document, click the Open button. QSW automatically launches Word.

Using templates saves you time by creating customized financial templates you can use with multiple clients Statement Writer reports.

Using the QSW Toolbar in Word

QSW adds a toolbar to Word to help you properly create supporting documents.

To access the toolbars in Word 2003, select **View**, **Toolbars**, and place a checkmark next to QuickBooks Statement Writer. In Word 2007 select the Add-Ins ribbon and the QSW toolbar displays as shown in Figure B.22.

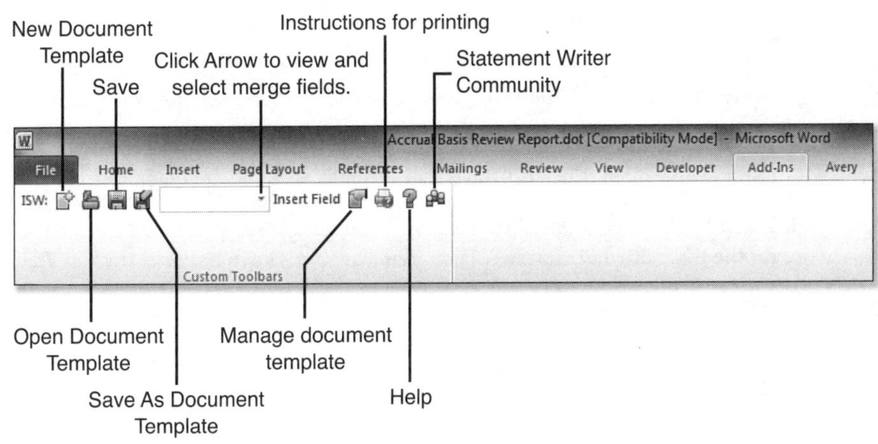

Figure B.22 Use the QSW toolbar in Word to create supporting documents with merged fields from the client's data.

Editing an Existing QSW Supporting Document

You might find it necessary to edit the text or fields in an existing QSW supporting document. You can access the Microsoft Word .dot templates directly from a QSW Report or you can browse to the stored templates directly from within Word.

To edit an existing QSW supporting document, following these steps:

1. Launch the QSW tool from within QuickBooks.
2. From the Document Actions pane, Report Properties, click the Documents button.
3. A list displays any supporting documents currently assigned to this QSW Report (see previous Figure B.20). Select a supporting document then click the Open button and skip to step 9. If no supporting documents are listed, go to step 4.
4. Click the Add button, and select **From Templates.**
5. The Insert Documents dialog box displays as shown in Figure B.21. Select a specific document and in the center of the window, click the arrow pointing to the right to add the selected document to the Financial Report Contents pane.
6. (Optional) Select **Show**, **All Documents**, **Intuit Documents**, **Custom Documents**, or **Custom Template Groups** to filter for specific documents to choose from.
7. Repeat step 5 until you have added the necessary documents to your QSW report. Click OK to close the Insert Documents dialog box.

The Add or Modify Supporting Documents dialog box displays with a list of added documents.

8. Click the Rename button if you want to give the document a new name for this QSW report.
9. Click the Open button. QSW opens the .dot template in Microsoft Word.
10. Edit the text as needed using Word's editing functions.

11. To add or edit merged data fields in Word 2003, click the QSW toolbar. For Word 2007 and 2010 users, click the Add-Ins ribbon.

12. With your mouse in the location on the document where you want to add the merged field, select the desired field from the Insert Field drop-down menu as shown in Figure B.23.

13. When you are finished with your edits on the QSW toolbar, click the Save button to save over the original document. Click the Save As button to save the document with a different name.

14. When you click Save As, the Save As—Document Template dialog box displays. Provide a Name for the template and choose a Type from the drop-down list as shown in Figure B.24.

15. Click OK to close the Save As—Document Template dialog box.

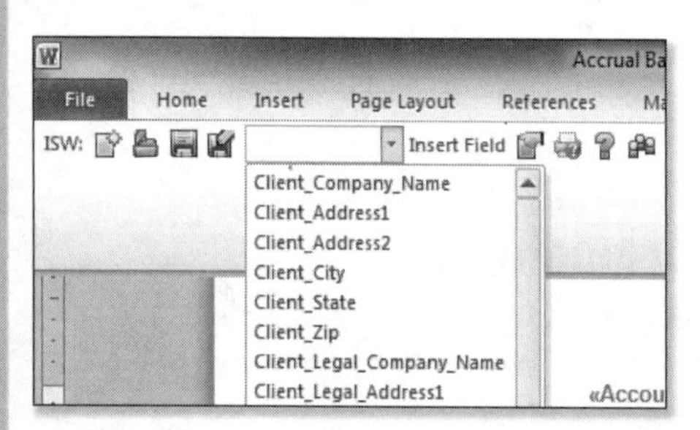

Figure B.23
Add QuickBooks data fields to customized document templates.

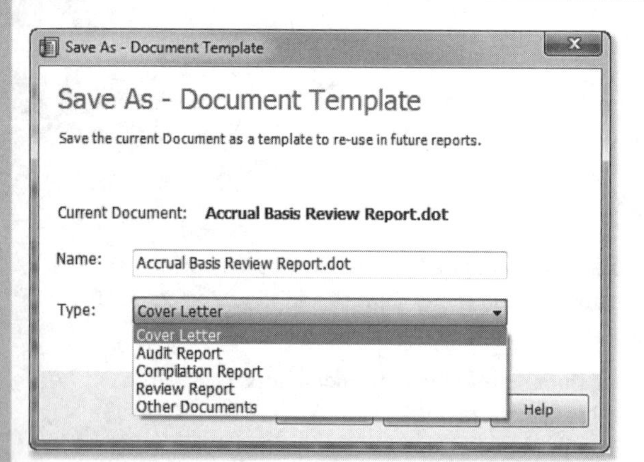

Figure B.24
Save your new supporting document as a template to be used with other client files.

Creating a New QSW Supporting Document

You can optionally create your own supporting document templates and store them on your computer.

To create a new QSW supporting document, follow these steps:

1. Open Microsoft Word.
2. Add the text or images as needed using Word editing functions.
3. To add or edit merged data fields in Word 2003, click the QSW toolbar. For Word 2007 or 2010 users, click the Add-Ins ribbon.
4. With your mouse in the location on the document where you want to add the merged field, select the desired field from the drop-down list items.
5. Click the Insert Field link (see previous Figure B.23) on the QSW toolbar.
6. When you are finished with your edits on the QSW toolbar, click the Save button to save over the original document. Click the Save As button to save the document with a different name.
7. When you click Save As, the Save As—Document Template dialog box displays (refer to previous Figure B.24). Provide a Name for the template and choose a Type from the drop-down list.

Now that you have created a new supporting document, you can attach the document to your QSW report so you can print a complete set of customized financials for your clients. Read on to the next section to learn more about attaching supporting documents.

Printing or Exporting a Statement Writer Report

In the previous section you learned how to add or modify supporting documents to your QSW report, making it a complete set of custom financials ready to print. QSW creates a PDF of the complete report set so you can print, send via email, and store for future reference.

To print or export a Statement Writer report, follow these steps:

1. Launch the QSW tool from within QuickBooks.
2. If you have just opened your QSW Report, the QuickBooks data has automatically refreshed. If you have been modifying the QSW report or QuickBooks data, refresh the data by clicking the Refresh button on the Document Actions pane.
3. From the Document Actions pane, select **Save As**, **QSW Report**, **Excel Workbook**, **Template Group**, or **PDF**.
4. If you selected Save as PDF, the Create PDF dialog box displays as shown in Figure B.25. The Available Report Contents show each of the statements and supporting documents you have included in this QSW report. On the left pane, select a statement or document to include in your PDF.
5. Use the arrow pointing to the right to include the selected statement or document in the PDF Contents pane.
6. Select an item in the PDF Contents pane, and use the up or down arrow to organize the print order for your financials.

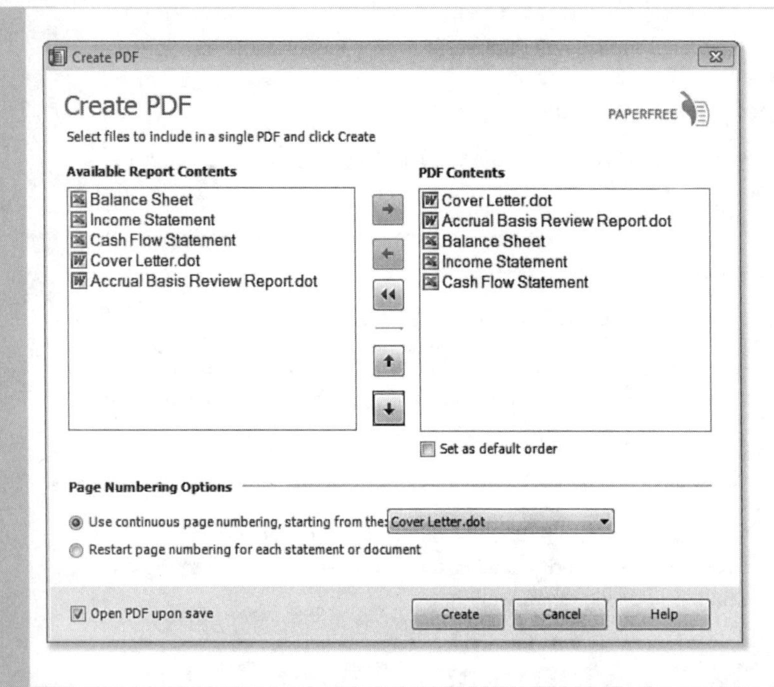

Figure B.25
You define the print order of the documents when creating a PDF.

7. (Optional) Select Set as Default Order so you do not have to make these choices again.
8. (Optional) Select Open PDF upon Save.
9. Click Create.
10. Select **Save as Excel Workbook**, QSW opens a Windows Explorer window.
11. Browse to the computer folder to which your Excel workbook should be saved and give the workbook a filename. Click Save.

caution

When you export your QSW report to Excel, it is no longer linked to QuickBooks and therefore cannot be updated or refreshed.

Accounting professionals can use QSW to create financial reports that include statements and supporting documents. These reports can be saved as templates for use with other client files and for updating with future dated information.

C

QUICKBOOKS ENTERPRISE SOLUTIONS INVENTORY FEATURES

QuickBooks Enterprise Solutions offers robust inventory management features for growing businesses with complex inventory needs. This appendix provides details for using these unique inventory features found only in the QuickBooks Enterprise Solutions software.

If you are new to inventory management in QuickBooks, you might want to first review Chapter 5, "Setting Up Inventory," and Chapter 6, "Managing Inventory." These two chapters provide the basics for managing inventory in QuickBooks.

For businesses that currently process inventory transactions in QuickBooks Pro or Premier, you can review this appendix to see what additional inventory features would be available to you if you upgraded to QuickBooks Enterprise Solutions software.

For more information see, "Upgrading Your QuickBooks Version," p. 617.

QuickBooks Enterprise

In addition to the inventory features discussed in detail in this appendix, other features exclusive to QuickBooks Enterprise include the following:

- Customizable reports using QuickBooks Statement Writer: harnessing the power of Microsoft Excel.

To learn more, see "QuickBooks Statement Writer," pg. 717.

- QuickBooks Enterprise offers ODBC connectivity for applications such as Microsoft Access, Microsoft Excel, and other ODBC-aware programs. To get started, in QuickBooks Enterprise select **File**, **Utilities**, **Configure ODBC**, and follow the onscreen documentation. Existing ODBC users report that the functionality works well with Microsoft Excel.
- Support more users, locations, and company files. QuickBooks Enterprise scales up to 30 simultaneous users and tracks thousands of customers, vendors, and inventory items.

For more information, see Table 17.1, "QuickBooks Enterprise 13.0 Larger List Limits," p. 628.

- Safeguarded business data that is sensitive. This allows more granular control over QuickBooks security settings for employees, which allows you to finely tailor access to just the information employees need to do their jobs.

To learn about user security, see "User Security in QuickBooks Enterprise," p. 52.

Custom Fields

Custom fields are offered in QuickBooks Pro, Premier, and Enterprise. However, in Enterprise users have more options when creating custom fields, including the following, as shown in Figure C.1:

- **Choose Field Attributes**—Text, numbers with or without decimals, date, phone, and user-defined multichoice list.
- **Required Field**—Requiring the field on a transaction, list, or both.

Custom fields provide the flexibility to add specialized information to data that QuickBooks already tracks about your customers, vendors, employees, and items that you purchase and sell. An advantage is the capability to create a user-defined drop-down list of values.

When using QuickBooks Enterprise software, you can create the following total number of custom-defined fields:

- **Items List**—Up to 15 custom-definable fields.
- **Customer/Vendor/Employee Lists**—Up to 12 custom-definable fields, limited to a total of 30 for these three lists combined.

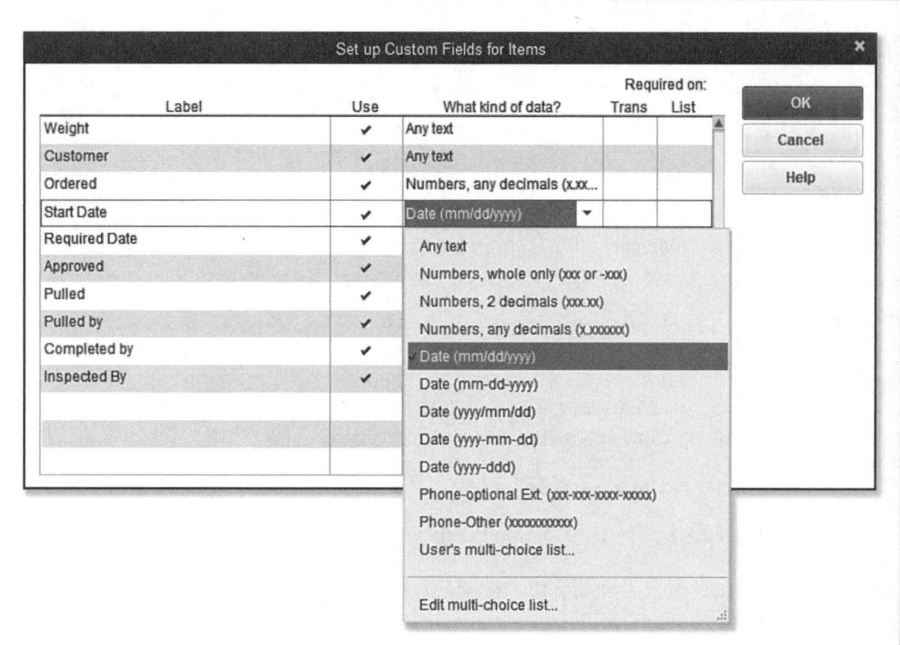

Figure C.1 QuickBooks Enterprise permits you to define custom fields with specific attributes.

You might consider using custom fields for tracking weight, color, or size for products you buy and sell. Some uses for custom fields within the customer list might include recording a route number or preferred shipping method. The uses are really endless!

caution

Keep in mind that custom fields can be added only to the following: estimates, sales orders, sales receipts, invoices, customer credit memos, and purchase orders. They cannot be added to vendor bills, item receipts, checks, or journal entries.

The following instructions detail how to add a custom field to an item. Follow these basic instructions if you are adding a custom-defined field to a vendor, customer, or employee list name.

1. From the menu bar, select **Lists**, **Item List**.
2. With your cursor select the item you want to define custom fields for; on your keyboard press **Ctrl+E** to edit the item.
3. Select the **Custom Fields** button to the right. The Custom Fields For (name of item) displays.

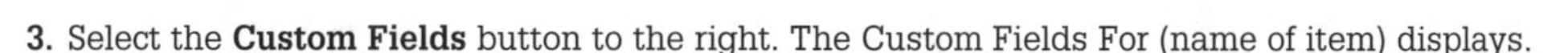

4. Select the **Define Fields** button to the right. The Set Up Custom Fields for Items displays.

note

Custom fields can be used to hold special values that you enter in a customer's invoice. Some QuickBooks-compatible programs use custom fields to hold calculated values. For example, CCRQInvoice (by CCRSoftware) can calculate the total quantity of items ordered in an invoice, or the total weight of items in an invoice, using custom fields to hold the item weight and to store the calculated totals: http://www.ccrsoftware.com/CCRQInvoice/InvoiceQ.htm

5. In the Label field, type a name to identify the field on transactions.
6. Place a checkmark in the Use column for fields you want to use.
7. From the What Kind of Data drop-down list, choose the attribute for the Defined Field.
8. Place a checkmark in the Trans field to require use on sales transactions. The Select Required Item Types dialog displays.
9. Place a checkmark next to the item types you want this newly custom-defined field to be used with. Click OK to close.
10. Place a checkmark in the List field to require data when creating new items. Click OK to close the Set Up Custom Fields for Items dialog box.
11. Complete any required fields.
12. Click OK to close the Custom Fields for the selected item.

caution

A checkmark in the Use column of the Custom Fields dialog box cannot be removed if the same field is included in a sales transaction template. First, remove the field from the template, then remove the checkmark from the Use column.

Information you enter into the fields can be for your use only, or could prefill fields within certain transactions when you enter a name or item on the form, as shown in Figure C.2. You can also include data from customized fields in your reports.

For more information, see "Customizing QuickBooks Forms," p. 322.

QuickBooks treats the information you enter into a custom field the same way it treats information entered into any other field. If you memorize a transaction that has a custom field, QuickBooks memorizes what you entered in the field along with the other details of the transaction. If you export a list that contains data in custom fields, QuickBooks exports that data along with the other data from the list.

caution

Including custom fields in reports can be tricky. There are two types of reports—summary and detail. A summary report shows only the value of a custom field associated with the list record. A detail report shows the custom field associated with a transaction. Because the custom fields can be changed on the transaction, you may find the value in a custom field assigned to the list to be different than what was used on a transaction.

Accessing Inventory Features and Reports

QuickBooks Enterprise makes it easy to access the many tasks and reports needed to manage the inventory needs of your business. Flexibility in accessing these task permits you to pick a method that works best for you!

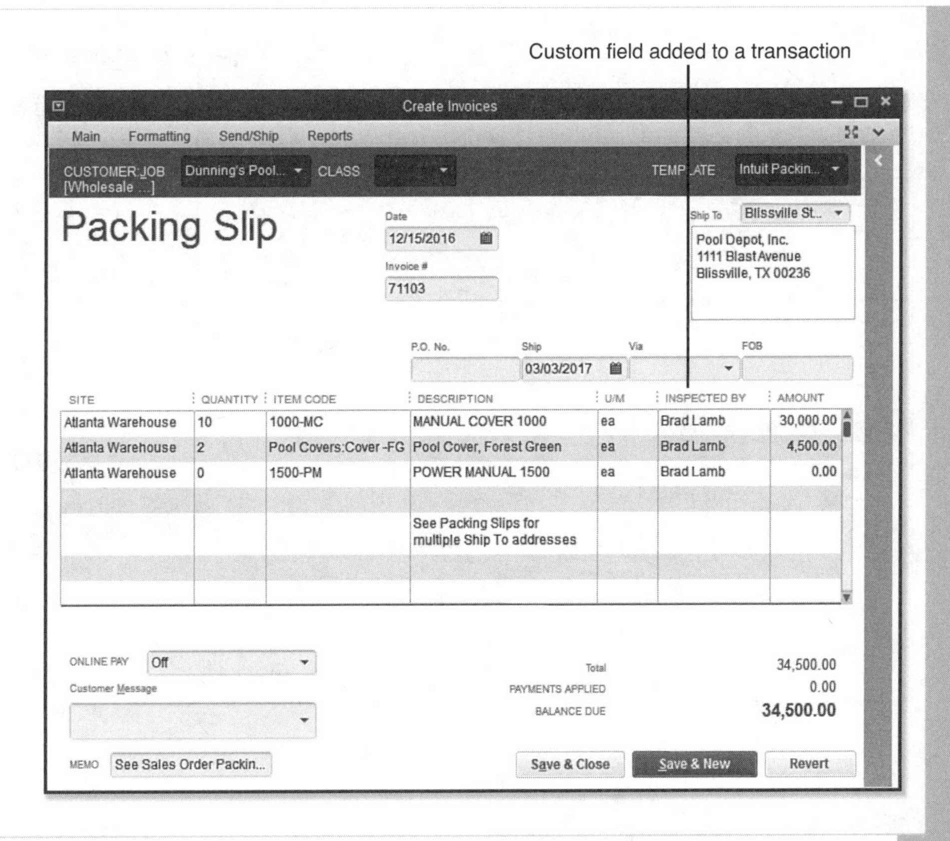

Figure C.2 Custom fields can be added to transactions and included in reports.

Inventory Center

The Inventory Center is available in QuickBooks Premier, Bookkeeper, Accountant, and QuickBooks Enterprise Solutions. In QuickBooks Enterprise, the Inventory Center includes the option to store an image of the item, as shown in Figure C.3. However, currently you cannot use this image on transactions or include in reports.

To learn more, see "Inventory Center," p. 201.

Inventory Access from the Menu Bar

QuickBooks Enterprise users can access features and reports from an Inventory-specific menu on the menu bar as shown in Figure C.4.

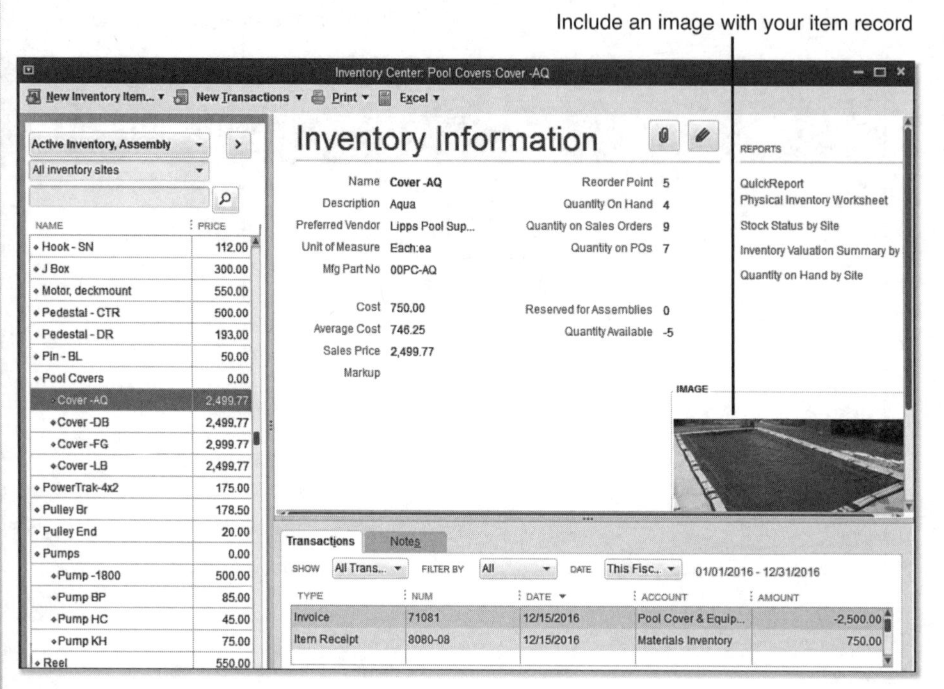

Figure C.3
Use the Inventory Center for all your inventory needs.

Figure C.4
QuickBooks Enterprise includes an Inventory-specific menu on the menu bar.

Auto Create Purchase Orders

The new Auto Create Purchase Orders feature in QuickBooks will help you restock your items in record time. In prior versions of QuickBooks you would review your inventory reorder reports, and then create a single purchase order at a time.

Follow these instructions for creating multiple purchase orders from the inventory stock reports:

1. From the menu bar, select **Reports**, **Inventory**, **Stock Status By Vendor** or any of the other stock status reports. You may also access this feature from the Inventory Reorder reports found in the Manufacturing and Wholesale edition of Enterprise. See Figure C.5.

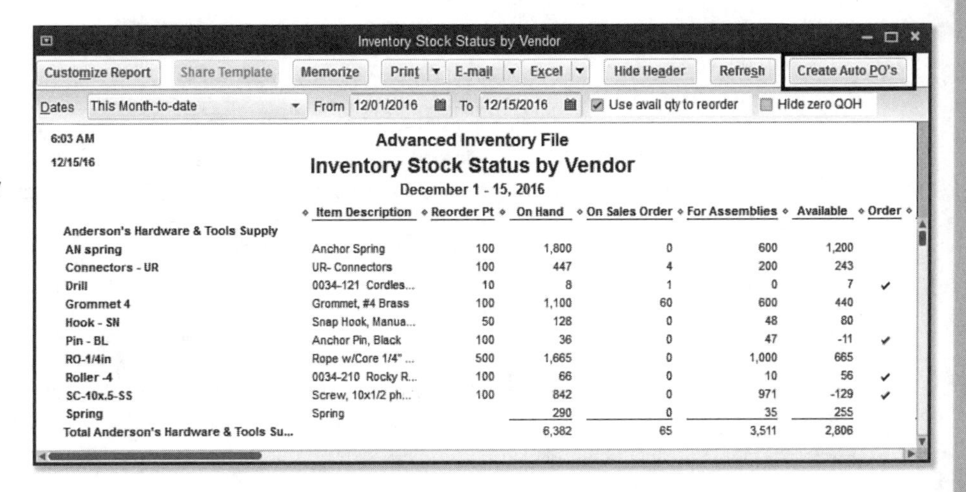

Figure C.5 Access the Auto Create Purchase Orders from the inventory stock status or reorder reports.

2. (Optional) Select the **Use Avail Qty To Reorder** checkbox. Selecting this checkbox may include additional items needing to be reordered.

3. Click the Create Auto PO's button at the top of the displayed report. A dialog box of the same name displays as shown in Figure C.6.

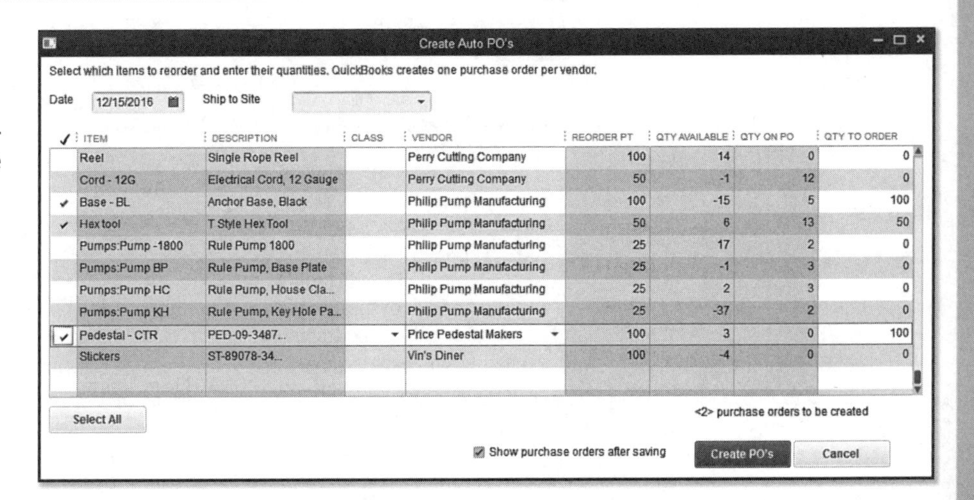

Figure C.6 Select the items you will be creating purchase orders for.

4. Select a date to assign to the multiple purchase orders.
5. If you are tracking multiple inventory locations, optionally select a Ship To Site. If you do not select a **Ship To Site** at this time, you will be required to select the Ship To Site when receiving the items into inventory.
6. Place a checkmark next to the item(s) you will be creating purchase orders for.
7. Select a **Class** if you are tracking departmental profit centers.
8. Accept the default vendor selected (this default is the vendor assigned to the item record) or optionally select a different vendor from the drop-down menu in the Vendor column.
9. In the Qty to Order column, enter the number of items you want to order.
10. In the lower right, place a checkmark if you choose to Show Purchase Orders After Saving.
11. Click Create PO's. The Create Auto PO's dialog closes automatically.

note

When multiple items are selected with the same vendor assigned, QuickBooks will create a single purchase order for that vendor including each of the selected items.

If you selected to Show Purchase Orders After Saving, QuickBooks displays the Open Purchase Orders report filtered for today's date. QuickBooks adds the memo "Auto created" to each purchase order. See Figure C.7. This helps users identify which purchase orders were created using the Auto Create PO's feature.

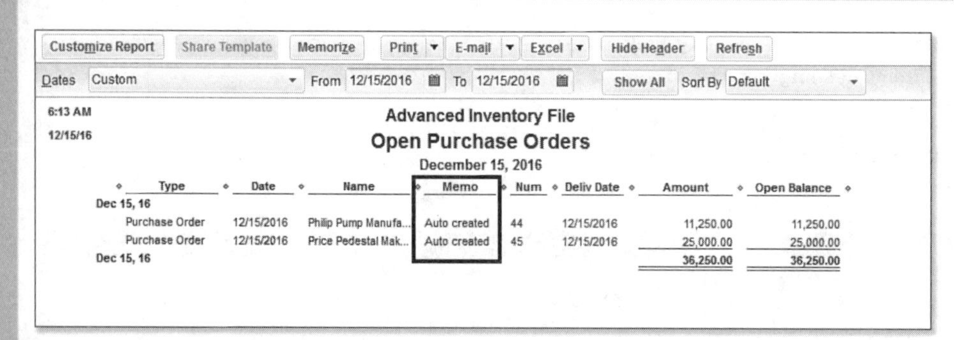

Figure C.7 View the Open Purchase Orders report, the memo line will indicate if they were auto created.

Sales Order Fulfillment Worksheet

If you track inventory items in QuickBooks and use sales orders, the Sales Order Fulfillment Worksheet (see Figure C.8) can help you decide which sales orders to fulfill when you don't have enough quantity on hand to fulfill them all. It does this by letting you create different "what if?" scenarios to see how fulfilling one set of sales orders affects your ability to fulfill others.

The Sales Order Fulfillment Worksheet is available with the following editions of QuickBooks:

- QuickBooks Enterprise (all editions)
- QuickBooks Accountant
- QuickBooks Premier Manufacturing and Wholesale
- QuickBooks Premier Retail

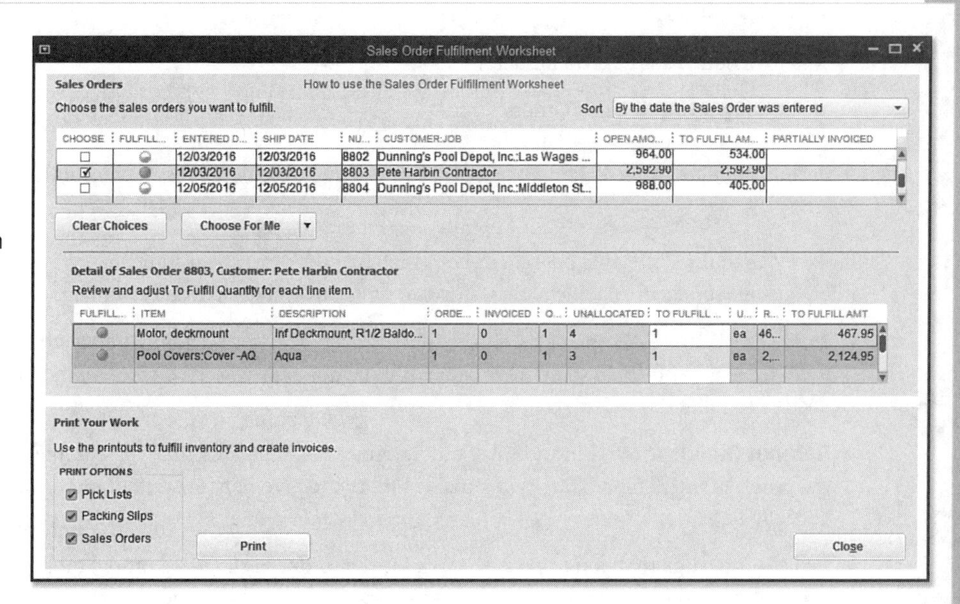

Figure C.8 The Sales Order Fulfillment Worksheet can help you choose which orders to fulfill first.

Enable Inventory and Sales Orders

To use this feature, you need to first enable Inventory and Sales Orders. From the menu bar, select **Edit**, **Preferences**, **Items & Inventory**. On the Company Preferences tab select **Items and Purchase Orders Are Active**. You must be logged in to the file as the Admin or External Accountant User.

Using the Sales Order Fulfillment Worksheet

You can use the Sales Order Fulfillment Worksheet to see at a glance which sales orders can be fulfilled.

To access the Sales Order Fulfillment Worksheet, from the menu bar select **Customers**, **Sales Order Fulfillment Worksheet**. The worksheet includes the following tables of data:

- **Sales Orders**—Provides a single row listing of all sales orders not yet fulfilled. This table of data can be sorted by any of the following:
    - Sales Orders Chosen for Fulfillment First

- Sales Orders That Can Be Completely Fulfilled First
- By the Date the Sales Order Was Entered
- By Ship Date
- By Order Number
- By Customer:Job
- By Open Amount
- By Amount That Can Be Fulfilled
- Partially Invoiced Sales Orders First

- **Details of Sales Order**—QuickBooks displays the line item detail for the currently selected sales order.

Status icons in the Fulfillable column in both tables in the worksheet indicate whether the sales order, specific items, or specific assemblies can be completely or partially fulfilled:

- **Solid Green Circle**—In the sales orders table, this indicates that you have enough inventory to fulfill the entire order. In the details table, it indicates that you have all of an individual item needed to fulfill the order.
- **Half-full Orange Circle**—In the sales orders table, this indicates that you can fulfill only part of the order. In the details table, this indicates that you have only enough of an individual item to partially fulfill the order.
- **Red X**—Indicates that you are out of stock for that order in the sales orders table or for an individual item in the details table.

Follow these steps to complete the process:

1. Place a checkmark next to the sale order(s) you want to fulfill.
2. In the Print Your Work section, select to print **Pick Lists**, **Packing Slips** and/or **Sales Orders**. You will use these printouts to fulfill inventory and create invoices.
3. Select **Print**. QuickBooks opens the Print dialog for you to select your printer. Click Print.
4. QuickBooks displays a message confirming that the documents printed successfully. Place a checkmark in the Reprint column next to any document you need to reprint. Click OK.
5. QuickBooks displays a warning message about invoicing your sales order to decrease your inventory levels. Click OK after reading the message.
6. Gather the printed documents and locate the individual sales orders in QuickBooks.
7. Click Create Invoice from the Main tab of the ribbon toolbar for each individual sales order.

Enhanced Inventory Receiving

Enhanced Inventory Receiving (EIR) is a preference that enables an optional workflow for improving how you receive and pay for inventory. With Enhanced Inventory Receiving, item receipts increase inventory and the inventory offset (current liability) account until the vendor bill is received and entered.

caution

If you turn on EIR, you can't turn it off. You should read and understand these important considerations before you turn it on.

When you turn on EIR, you receive and pay for items in QuickBooks in a completely different way. With EIR:

- Item receipts don't increase accounts payable.
- Vendor bills don't affect inventory.
- Vendor bills associated with item receipts no longer replace item receipts.

note

When EIR is not enabled QuickBooks does the following:

- Inventory asset account is increased when a vendor bill including inventory items is recorded.
- When a vendor bill is associated with an item receipt, the item receipt no longer is a separate document. Instead it is converted to a vendor bill.

To set your file up to track purchasing this way, QuickBooks changes the effect on accounting for past transactions during the EIR setup. It is recommended that you first evaluate whether EIR is right for you. To help you decide, ask yourself the following questions:

- Do you receive one bill that covers multiple item receipts?
- Do you receive multiple bills for one item receipt?
- Are your inventory quantities skewed when you enter a bill and QuickBooks automatically changes the date of the item receipt?
- Do you pay for items before you receive them but don't want your inventory quantities to increase? If you don't use EIR, QuickBooks increases inventory quantities when you enter a bill for inventory items.
- Do you want to separate the receiving department (item receipts) from the accounts payable department (enter and pay bills)? If you don't use EIR, QuickBooks converts item receipts to a bill when you receive the bill.

If you answered yes to any of these questions, consider using EIR. However, it's important that you read the following cautionary points before you begin because you can't turn EIR off:

- When you turn on EIR, QuickBooks changes past transactions. Converting to EIR may take up to a few hours depending on the size of your company file. If you have a large company file, you might consider condensing your company data before turning on EIR.

For more information about the size of a company data file, see Chapter 17, "Managing Your QuickBooks Database."

caution

Third-party applications that affect inventory may not work as expected with EIR. Check with the vendor before enabling this feature.

- EIR separates item receipts from bills. This creates a new process for receiving and paying for items. This new process also comes with some restrictions.
- You can't turn EIR off; see Figure C.9. After it's on, you must use the new EIR process for receiving and paying for items. A safe practice would be to create a backup of your file before you begin. If after trying EIR you find that it doesn't work for you, restore your backup.

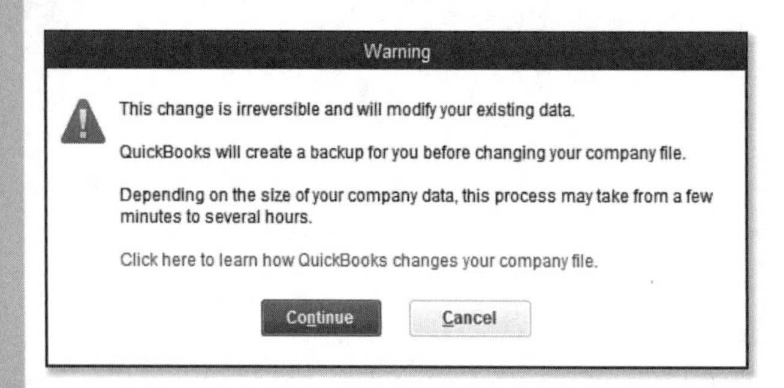

Figure C.9
The Enhanced Inventory Receiving setting cannot be reversed, so be sure to back up your data prior to the conversion.

- When using EIR, if you receive a bill with different item costs compared to the related item receipt, QuickBooks automatically changes the item cost on that item receipt. QuickBooks makes this change even if the item receipt is in a closed period.

Changes Made When You Enable EIR

Care should be taken when making the decision to use Enhance Inventory Receiving. These considerations include the following:

- **Past Transactions**—With EIR turned on, bills do not increase inventory quantities. This means that QuickBooks has to create an item receipt for every bill that included items. This increases the number of transactions in your company file.
- **Accounts Payable Balance**—If you haven't received a bill for an open item receipt, the amount no longer shows up in Accounts Payable. This is correct because you haven't received the bill yet. QuickBooks only shows the amount in Accounts Payable when you receive the bill. To understand what QuickBooks does with the value of open item receipts, review "The Accounting Behind EIR" section in this appendix.
- **Small Rounding Error to Average Cost**—When QuickBooks creates the new item receipts, it recalculates inventory average cost. These item receipts change the order of inventory transactions within each day. This change in transaction order can sometimes result in minor changes to the average cost of an item.

Workflow When Using EIR

Enabling Enhanced Inventory Receiving requires a slightly different workflow, as detailed next:

note

This new process applies only to vendor bills. You can still increase inventory quantities and pay for items with checks and credit card charges.

- **Without EIR**—You can receive and pay for inventory in two ways:
  - **A single transaction**—Enter a bill for inventory items that increases your inventory on hand and increases accounts payable.
  - **Two transactions**—Enter an item receipt to receive the inventory. Inventory is increased along with accounts payable; however, the item receipts are not displayed in the Pay Bills dialog. When the vendor bill is recorded, the same item receipt is converted to a vendor bill.
- **With EIR**, you must enter two separate transactions, and they can be entered in any order:
  - An item receipt to receive items
  - A bill to pay for the items

Restrictions When Using EIR

Enhanced Inventory Receiving imposes the following restrictions:

- You can't enter negative items on item receipts or bills.
- The Item Receipt transaction no longer includes an Expenses tab, as shown in Figure C.10.
- If you create a purchase order for non-inventory items, you must receive them with an item receipt to close the PO.
- You can no longer mark items as billable on item receipts.

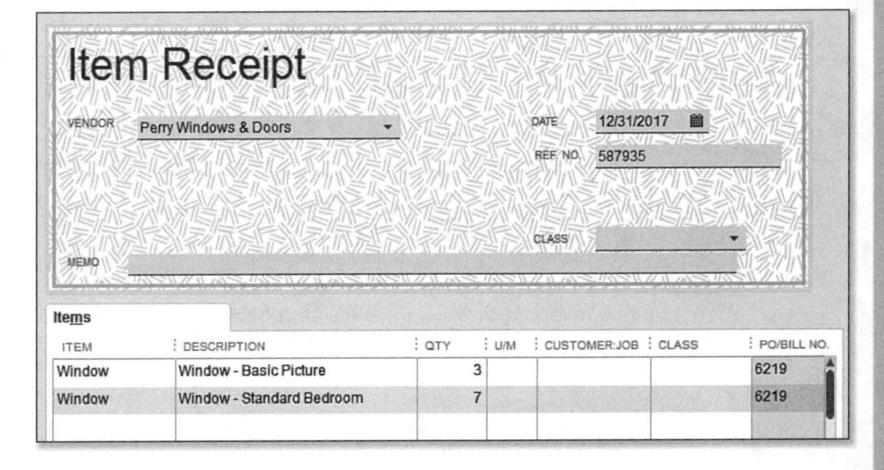

Figure C.10
Item receipts created using EIR enabled do not include the Expenses tab.

The Accounting Behind EIR

QuickBooks automatically creates a new account (Other Current Liability) called the Inventory Offset account. QuickBooks completes the following accounting with an item receipt and vendor bill, detailed in Tables C.1 and C.2:

Table C.1 Item Receipt accounting

Debit	Credit
Inventory Asset account	Inventory Offset account

Table C.2 Vendor Bill accounting

Debit	Credit
Inventory Offset account	Accounts Payable

After enabling EIR, QuickBooks provides a summary of the transactions and their value affected by the change, as shown in Figure C.11.

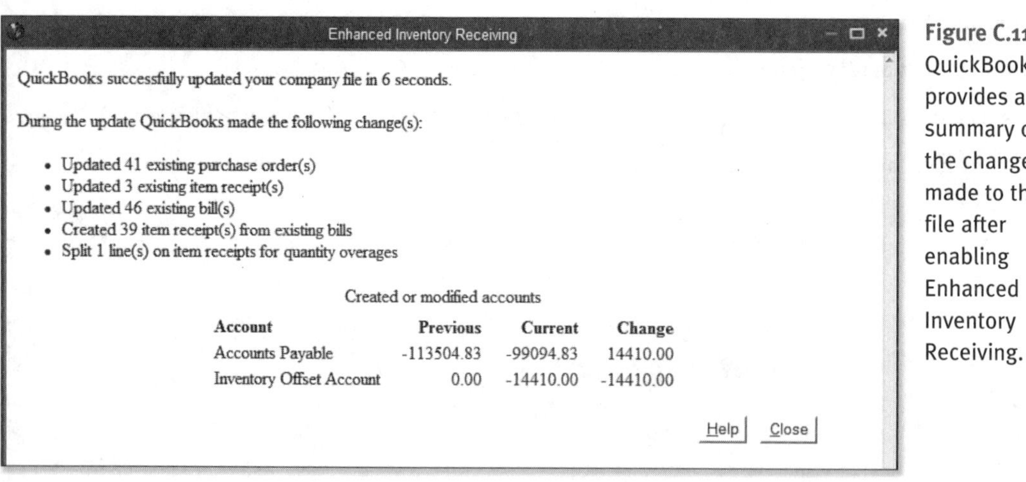

Figure C.11 QuickBooks provides a summary of the changes made to the file after enabling Enhanced Inventory Receiving.

If you enter items directly on a check or credit card charge, QuickBooks does the same accounting as before: debiting Inventory Asset and crediting the bank or credit card account.

Automatic Cost & Price Updates

As shown in Figure C.12, you can use the Automatic Cost & Price Updates Preference to determine how you handle item cost changes.

To set preferences for handling cost and price updates, follow these steps:

1. Log in to the file as the Admin User or External Accountant User in single-user.
2. From the menu bar, select **Edit**, **Preferences**, **Items & Inventory**, and then the **Company Preferences** tab.
3. Click the Automatic Cost & Price Updates button. The Automatic Cost & Price Updates dialog displays.
4. The following global preferences, as shown in Figure C.12, can be set:
   - **If Item Cost Changes on a Purchase**—Always Update the Item Cost, Never Update Item Cost, or Ask About Updating the Item Cost.
   - **When Item Cost Changes**—For the sales price: Always Update Sales Price, Never Update Sales Price, or Ask About Updating Sales Price.
   - **Markup**—Choose between Percent Over Cost or Amount Over Cost. This preference can be overridden individually within individual inventory item records.

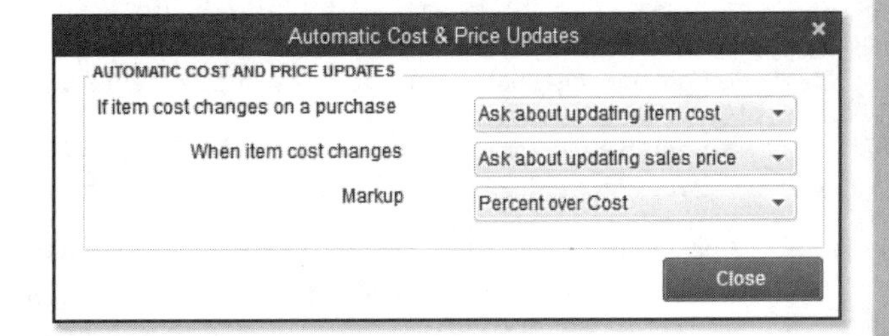

Figure C.12
Set global preferences for automatically handling cost and sales price changes. You can override these settings on the individual item record.

Assigning Markup Defaults per Item

The previous section detailed the options for setting a global preference for handling markups when a cost of item changes. This helps your business make sure you are earning the expected markup on your products and services.

Follow these steps to manage the markup individually for each item on your item list, as shown in Figure C.13:

1. From the menu bar, select **Lists**, **Item List**.
2. Double-click an item to display the Edit Item dialog. You can also define these settings when creating a new item.

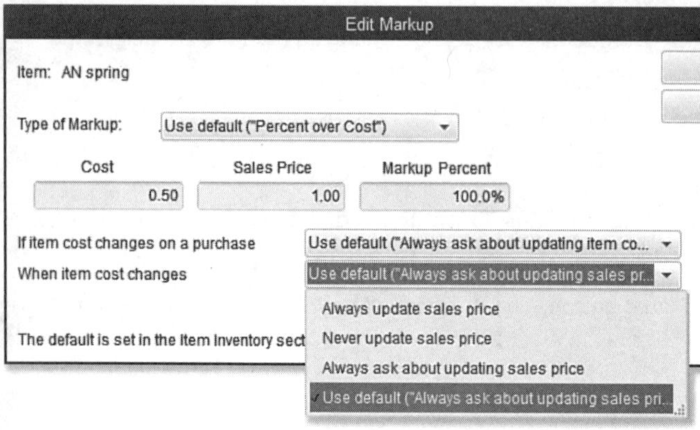

Figure C.13
Enterprise includes the capability to manage markup defaults individually with each unique item.

3. Select the **Edit Markup** button to the right. The Edit Markup dialog displays.
4. From the Type of Markup drop-down list, choose from the following:
   - Percent Over Cost
   - Amount Over Cost
   - Use Default ("Percent Over Cost"), or whatever your preference setting was.
5. Edit the Cost, Sales Price, and Markup Percent fields as desired.
6. From If Item Cost Changes on a Purchase, choose from Always Update Item Cost, Never Update Item Cost, Ask About Updating the Item Cost, or Use Default.
7. When Item Cost Changes, for the sales price choose from Always Update Sales Price, Never Update Sales Price, Always Ask About Updating Sales Price, or Use Default.
8. Click OK twice to save your changes.

QuickBooks Enterprise with Advanced Inventory

Advanced Inventory is a collection of advanced inventory management features, which are detailed in this section of the appendix. Advanced Inventory is an annual subscription and requires the user to also have an active Full Service Plan for QuickBooks Enterprise. More details on current pricing for Advanced Inventory and the Full Service Plan can be found on Intuit's website at http://enterprisesuite.intuit.com/

Your Advanced Inventory subscription enables additional features within QuickBooks Enterprise. There is no additional software to install or learn, and you can manage a number of sophisticated inventory scenarios.

Multiple Inventory Locations

In additional to tracking inventory in multiple warehouses, you can track inventory in different staging areas within a single warehouse, on service trucks, and on consignment, for example.

Prior to using Enterprise or before Multiple Inventory Location tracking was available, you might have used one of these alternative methods of tracking multiple inventory locations:

- Using multiple items (or subitems) for the same part
- Using a custom-defined field
- Using class tracking
- Using Microsoft Excel

Although this list is not exhaustive, note that you should take care when you begin to use the Multiple Inventory Locations feature when you have been tracking it in some other fashion.

To find more details about making the switch to using Multiple Location Inventory, from the menu bar select **Help**, and in the search field type **Multiple Inventory Locations**. Click the How to Switch from Another Method of Tracking Multiple Inventory Sites link.

Assign a Starting Inventory Site

When you first set up Multiple Inventory Locations in QuickBooks Enterprise, you will have to create a temporary site (for example, you might name it **Starting Inventory**). QuickBooks assigns all past inventory transactions to this site when you first enable Multiple Inventory Locations. You can later transfer items to their actual sites and bin locations. You can also rename this temporary site later.

To enable Multiple Inventory Locations, follow these steps:

1. Log in to the file as the Admin or External Accountant User in single-user mode.
2. From the menu bar, select **Edit**, **Preferences**, **Items & Inventory** and choose the Company Preferences Tab.
3. Select the **Advanced Inventory Settings** button to display a dialog box of the same name.
4. Click the Multiple Inventory Locations tab if it is not already selected.
5. Place a checkmark in the Multiple Inventory Sites Is Enabled checkbox.
6. QuickBooks displays the Enable Multiple Inventory Sites dialog box (see Figure C.14). Read the information and then assign your Beginning Inventory Site.
7. From the Inventory Site drop-down menu, select **Add New**. QuickBooks displays the New Inventory Site dialog box..
8. Type a name for the site; as mentioned previously, you might want to name this site **Starting Inventory**. Complete any of the remaining fields as desired. Click OK to close.
9. You are returned to the Enable Multiple Inventory Sites. Select the **Continue** button. You are returned to the Advanced Inventory Settings preferences.

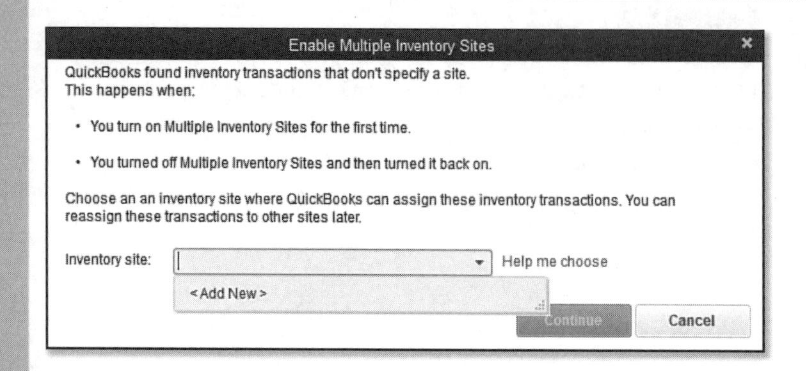

Figure C.14
When enabling Multiple Inventory Sites, you need to create a startup location to assign to existing transactions.

10. (Optional) Select any or each of the following:

- Warn About Duplicate Inventory Transfer Numbers
- Warn per Site if Not Enough Inventory to Sell
- Track Locations Within Inventory Sites (row, shelf, or bin) and the additional Warn Per Location if Not Enough Inventory to Sell. If selected, a message displays that to get started, QuickBooks will assign all the items to a bin named "Unassigned." Later you can transfer your items to their correct bins. See Figure C.15.

note
You can add more sites or rename existing sites later from the menu bar by selecting **Lists, Inventory Site List.**

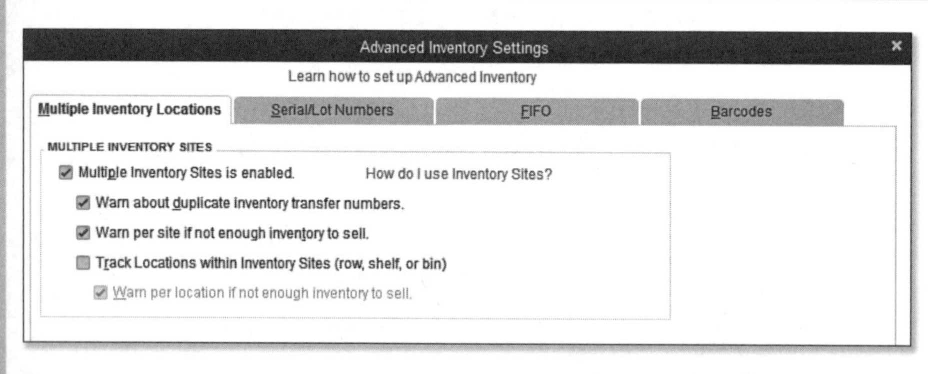

Figure C.15
Define warning preferences and the capability to track subsite locations for row, shelf, or bin tracking.

 **note**

You might encounter a message that items were automatically placed in an Unassigned (row, shelf, or bin). QuickBooks found inventory transactions that don't specify a site (or bin location, if you track bin locations). Reasons you might see this message include the following:

- You imported your accountant's changes. When you created the accountant's copy of your file, QuickBooks required you to turn off Multiple Inventory Locations. However, your accountant modified or added inventory transactions in the accountant's copy. Now QuickBooks must assign these transactions to a site (and bin location, if you track bin locations).
- You turned Multiple Inventory Locations back on. Multiple Inventory Locations was turned off in this file. Since then, QuickBooks hasn't assigned a site (or bin location, if applicable) to any inventory transactions.

Add an Inventory Site and Bin Locations

After creating your initial starting inventory site, you can add additional sites and bin locations, if you track bin locations.

1. From the menu bar, select **Lists**, **Inventory Site List**.
2. From the Inventory Site drop-down, select **New**.
3. In the Name field, type the name of the location.
4. If this is a bin location (row, shelf, or bin), select the This Is a Location Within Site checkbox. Then click the drop-down arrow and select a site (warehouse). See Figures C.16 and C.17.
5. Enter the appropriate information.
6. Click Next to add another location, or click OK if you're finished.

New for QuickBooks 2013, maintenance release 3 or later, you can add multiple Inventory Sites using the Add/Edit Multiple List Entries. From the menu bar select **Lists, Add/Edit Multiple List Entries** and select **Inventory Sites** from the List drop-down.

What if you're not sure what maintenance release you are on? On your keyboard, press the F2 key; the release is listed at the top of the production information dialog box. More about maintenance releases can be found in Chapter 17, "Managing Your QuickBooks Database."

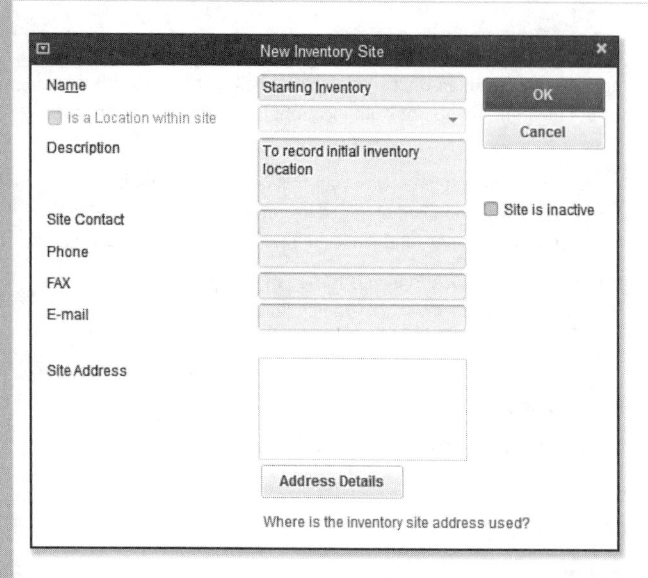

Figure C.16
Add inventory sites.

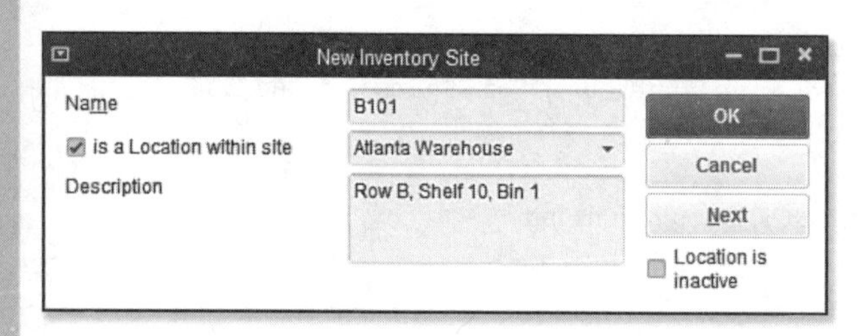

Figure C.17
Row, shelf, or bin tracking using sublocations of inventory sites.

Edit an Inventory Site and Bin Locations

You might find it necessary to edit an existing inventory site. You can even rename an existing site if necessary. Follow these steps:

1. From the menu bar, select **Lists**, **Inventory Site List**.
2. Double-click an inventory site or bin location from the list.
3. Change the information as needed.
4. Click OK.

tip

You can also choose to use the Lists, Add/Edit Multiple List Entries feature from the menu bar to efficiently add or edit the inventory site list.

Transferring Between Locations

Use the Transfer Inventory dialog to transfer inventory between locations, as shown in Figure C.18.

You can do this between sites (warehouses) to

- Replenish items at a location.
- Transfer items from your "home" warehouse to your "satellite" locations.
- Transfer items to a loading dock or ship.

You can also do this between bin locations (row, shelf, or bin) to replenish items in a row, shelf, or bin.

Follow these instructions to transfer inventory from one location to another:

1. From the menu bar, select **Inventory**, **Transfer Inventory**.
2. In the Date field, enter the date of the transfer.
3. In the Reference No. field, enter the appropriate transfer number. If you have a physical form for the transfer, use the number in this field.
4. (Optional) Click the Class drop-down arrow and select a class.
5. Click the Transfer from drop-down arrow and select an inventory site (warehouse).
6. Click the drop-down arrow and select the other inventory site (warehouse).

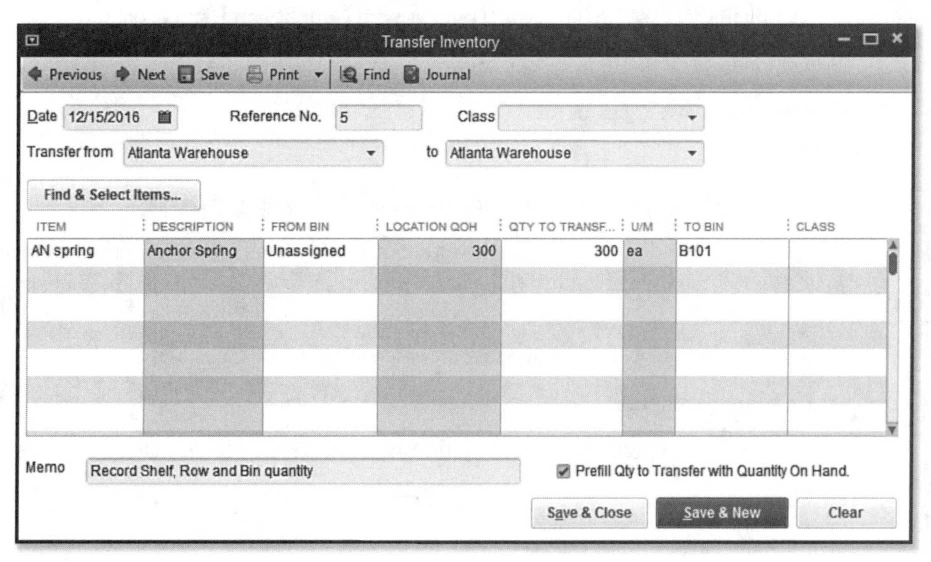

Figure C.18 Use the Transfer Inventory dialog for moving inventory from one location, row, shelf, or bin to another.

7. Select the inventory items to transfer to the site:
   - To select individual items
     - Click in the Item column.
     - Click the drop-down arrow and select an inventory item.
   - To search for or select multiple items
     - Click Find & Select Items.
     - (Optional) Enter a search term in the Find field and click Search.
     - Click the left column to select or clear inventory items.
     - Click Add Selected Items.

 **note**

If you're transferring between bin locations, you still need to enter a site in the Transfer From and To fields (in most cases, this will be the same site). You specify the bin locations in the fields below.

8. If you track bin locations, click the drop-down arrow in the first Location column and select the bin you're transferring from.
9. In the Qty to Transfer column, enter the number to transfer for each item.
10. If you track bin locations, click the drop-down arrow in the second Location column and select the bin you're transferring to.
11. (Optional) In the Memo field, enter the reason for this transfer, such as **Transfer opening quantity to site**.
12. (Optional) Click the Prefill Qty to Transfer with Quantity on Hand checkbox.
13. (Optional) Click the Print button to print a copy of the transfer for your records.
14. Click the Save & Close button.

Duplicating Inventory Transfer Transactions

You cannot transfer inventory from one site to multiple sites in the same transfer transaction. If you need to enter multiple inventory transfers, QuickBooks lets you duplicate previously recorded inventory transfers.

To duplicate a previously recorded inventory transfer, follow these steps:

1. Open an existing transfer.
2. With the transfer displayed, select **Edit**, **Duplicate Inventory Transfer**.
3. Change the details of the transfer as necessary.
4. Click the Save & Close button.

Reporting Inventory by Site

QuickBooks Enterprise makes it easy to report on inventory by site, shelf, bin, or row.

1. From the menu bar, select **Reports**, **Inventory**.
2. Choose from the following reports:
   - Serial Numbers in Stock by Site
   - Items by Bin Location (see Figure C.19)
   - Quantity on Hand by Site
   - Inventory Valuation Summary by Site
   - Inventory Stock Status by Site
   - Pending Builds by Site

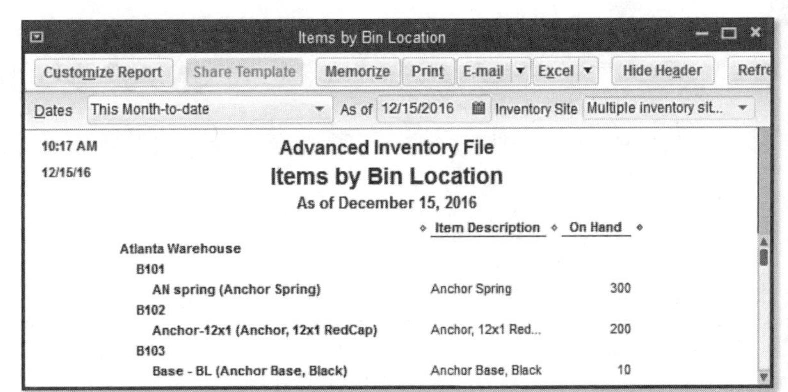

Figure C.19
Report on inventory by warehouse, row, shelf, and bin

Serial/Lot Numbers

With a subscription to QuickBooks Enterprise with Advanced Inventory, you can track serial numbers or lot numbers. You can't track both, so decide which you want before you begin.

Select serial numbers if the following applies to your business:

- You buy and sell inventory items that have unique serial numbers.
- You keep track of which customers bought specific serial numbers.
- You want to know which serial numbers are in stock.
- You need a report that shows the invoices related to a specific serial number (this helps you track down a serial number's history for a warranty).

Select lot numbers if the following applies to your business:

- You buy items in lots.
- You keep track of which customers bought items from a specific lot.
- You need a recall report in case you have to track all the items from a specific lot (such as which items are in inventory and which customers purchased them).

Turn On Serial or Lot Number Tracking

Follow these instructions to begin using this feature:

1. Log in to the file as the Admin or External Accountant user in single-user mode.
2. From the menu bar, select **Edit**, **Preferences**, **Items and Inventory,** and then select the **Company Preferences** tab. See Figure C.20. Make sure Inventory and Purchase Orders Are Active is selected.

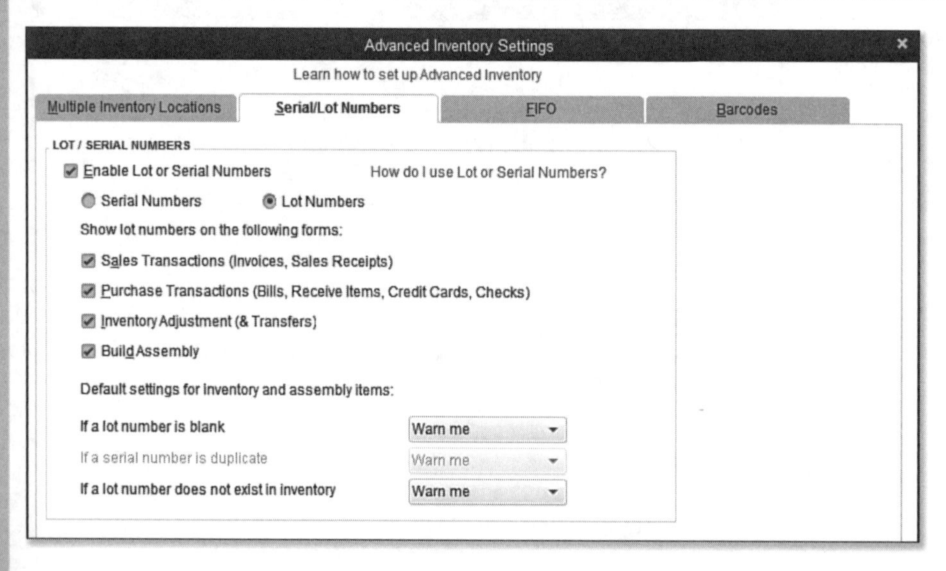

Figure C.20 Preferences when enabling Serial or Lot Number-tracking.

3. Click the Advanced Inventory Settings button. A dialog box with the same name displays, as shown in Figure C.20.
4. Click the Serial/Lot Numbers tab.
5. Click Enable Lot or Serial Numbers.
6. Select **Serial Numbers** or **Lot Numbers**.

7. (Optional) Select which transactions should display serial or lot numbers.
8. (Optional) Under Default settings for inventory and assembly items, click the drop-down arrows to set your preferences for warnings for all inventory and assembly items.
9. Click OK.
10. In the Preferences dialog, click OK to save your changes and close.

note

You can override global warnings set in preferences for each inventory and assembly item in the New or Edit Item dialog box.

note

You can edit templates to add or remove serial/lot numbers on printed forms. Serial/lot numbers always appear on the screen.

On printed forms, multiple serial numbers appear in the description separated by commas. The lot number appears in its own column.

After you turn on serial or lot number tracking, QuickBooks adds a serial or lot number field to most transaction types (see Figure C.21), including the following:

- Purchase Transactions
  - Item Receipts
  - Bills
  - Credit Card Transactions
- Write Checks
- Sales Transactions
  - Invoices
  - Credit Memos

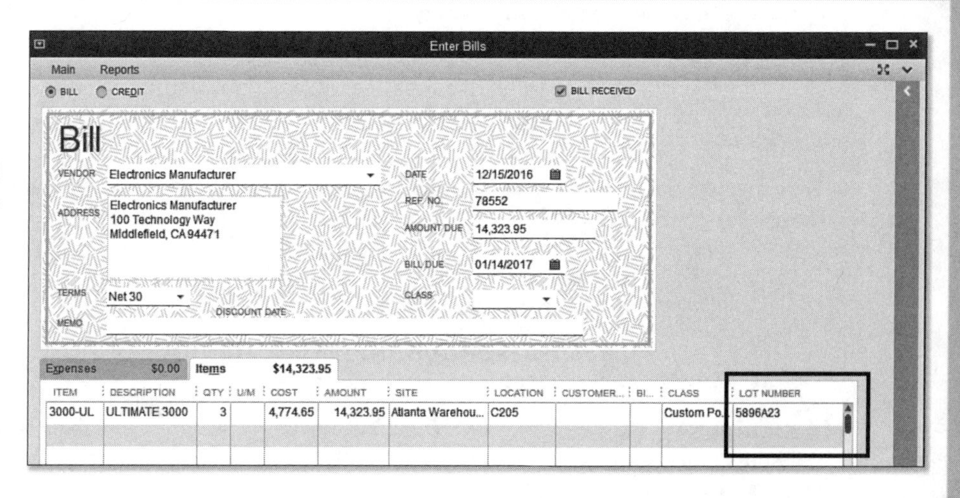

Figure C.21 The serial number or lot number field is added automatically to transactions when the feature is enabled.

- Sales Orders and Pending Invoices. However, QuickBooks doesn't remove these numbers from what's available to sell. The serial/lot number moves to the invoice or sales receipt when the sale becomes final.

You can also assign serial/lot numbers when you build assemblies and adjust inventory.

tip

If you buy or sell multiple items with serial numbers, enter all the serial numbers on the same line. Separate serial numbers with a space or comma.

Beginning to Track Serial or Lot Numbers

You don't have to assign serial or lot numbers to existing inventory to start tracking serial or lot numbers. If you have lots of items with serial numbers in stock, you may choose not to enter all your serial numbers in QuickBooks right away. It's okay to continue your current method of tracking while slowly moving to QuickBooks by entering all newly purchased or assembled items with serial numbers as you acquire them. Eventually, QuickBooks will have all your serial numbers.

The steps that follow detail multiple methods for assigning serial numbers to existing inventory. First, gather information about the serial/lot numbers associated with your current inventory on hand. Use the Adjust Quantity/Value on Hand window to assign serial (or lot numbers) to existing inventory:

tip

For another method useful for adding your initial serial numbers, from the menu bar select **Lists, Add/Edit Multiple List Entries.**

1. Select **Inventory**, **Adjust Quantity/Value on Hand**.
2. From the Adjustment Type drop-down menu, select **Serial Number**.
3. Select an **Adjustment Date** and **Inventory Site**.
4. (Optional) Assign a Reference No., Customer:Job, and Class.
5. (Optional) Select the **Find & Select Items**, a useful feature for selecting multiple items at one time.
6. From the Item field, begin typing the item name, or click the drop-down arrow and select it from the list.
7. In the Serial Number column, type the serial number, or if multiple serial numbers, separate them with a comma. See Figure C.22.
8. (Optional) From the Serial Number drop-down, select Quick View and copy and paste serial numbers from Excel or manually type them. See Figure C.23.
9. If you are instead transferring inventory that already has serial (or lot) numbers assigned, select the Add Multiple Serial (or Lot) Numbers to select which items are being transferred. See Figure C.24. Click Add Selected Numbers to add them to the Transfer Inventory dialog box.
10. Repeat steps 6 through 8 for each item as needed. When finished, click Save & Close.

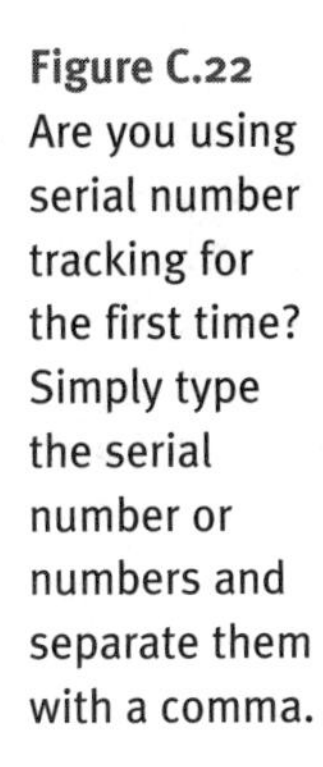

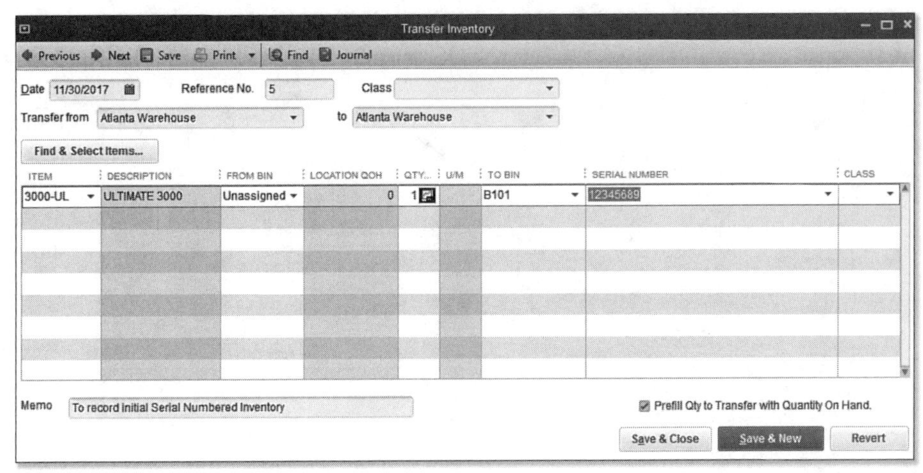

Figure C.22
Are you using serial number tracking for the first time? Simply type the serial number or numbers and separate them with a comma.

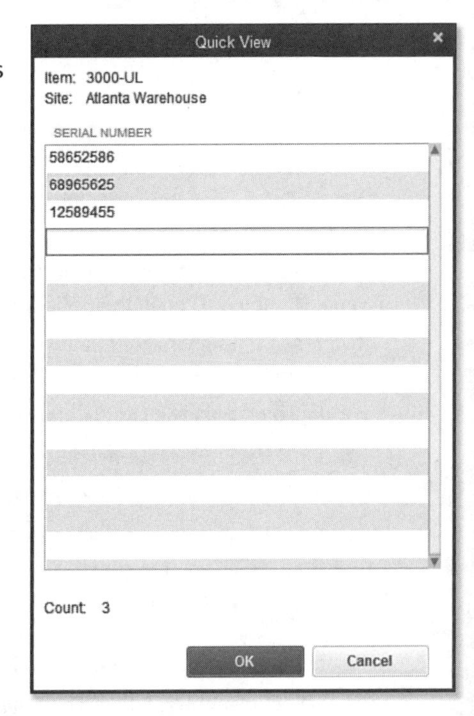

Figure C.23
Use the Quick View to efficiently add multiple Serial Numbers (or lots) for a single inventory item.

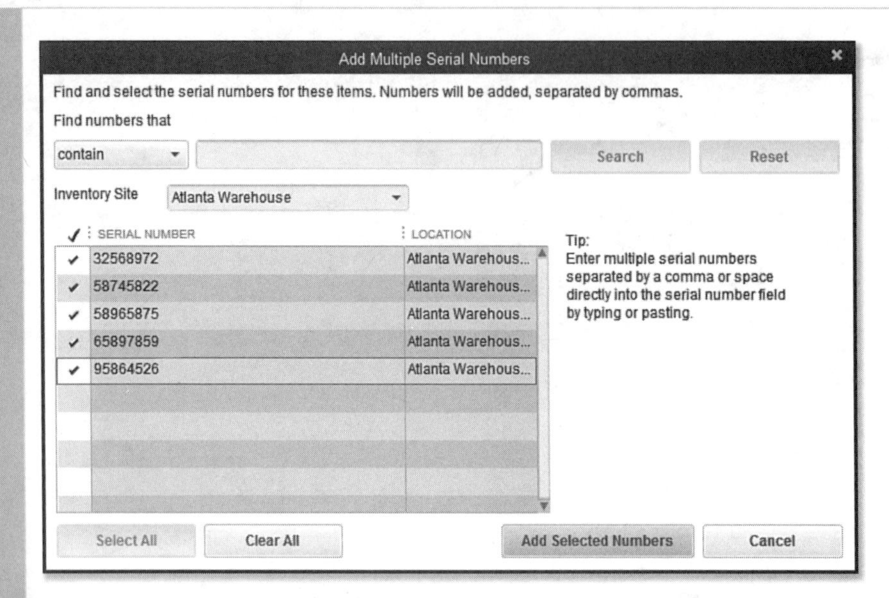

Figure C.24
To select multiple serial numbers for transfer, use the Add Multiple Serial Numbers from the Serial Number drop-down menu.

Paste Serial or Lot Numbers from Excel

You can paste serial numbers from Excel or a comma-delimited file into a QuickBooks transaction. In Excel, copy the serial numbers. In QuickBooks, click the Add Serial Numbers column.

If your serial numbers are separated by commas or spaces, paste them directly into the field. If your serial numbers are a column in Excel, click the drop-down arrow and select Quick View for Serial Numbers. Then in the Serial Numbers column, right-click and select Paste.

If your serial numbers are in a row in Excel, you can easily transpose them into a transaction column in Excel. To copy and paste serial numbers from Excel, follow these steps:

1. In Excel, copy the serial numbers.
2. Click the Excel column where you want to put the serial numbers.
3. Right-click and select **Paste Special**.
4. Select **Transpose**. You will have to use the Transpose function outside of the block of cells from which you are copying data.
5. Click OK to accept.

To manually update lot numbers in QuickBooks, follow these steps:

1. Select **Inventory, Adjust Quantity/Value on Hand**.
2. Click the Adjustment Type drop-down arrow and select **Lot Number**.
3. Click the Item field. Enter the item name, or click the drop-down arrow and select it from the list.
4. Enter the lot number.

5. In the New Count column, enter the number of items in that lot.
6. To assign a different lot number to more of the same item, or to assign a different lot number to a different item, repeat steps 3 to 6.
7. When finished, click Save & Close.
8. To verify your setup, run the Serial/Lot Numbers in Stock report.

Reporting on Lot Numbers

If you track lots and need to know where items from a specific lot are, follow this two-step process:

1. Find out how many items from a particular lot are still in inventory.
   - From the menu bar, select **Inventory, Inventory Center** to open the Inventory Center.
   - From the list on the left, select the item.
   - On the right side of the window below Recall Information, click Quantity on Hand by Lot Number. The Quick View window appears and shows the quantity on hand for each lot number associated with the item. See Figure C.25.
   - When finished, click Close.

If you are tracking Serial Numbers (and not Lot Numbers), you can use these same steps for reporting on serial numbers.

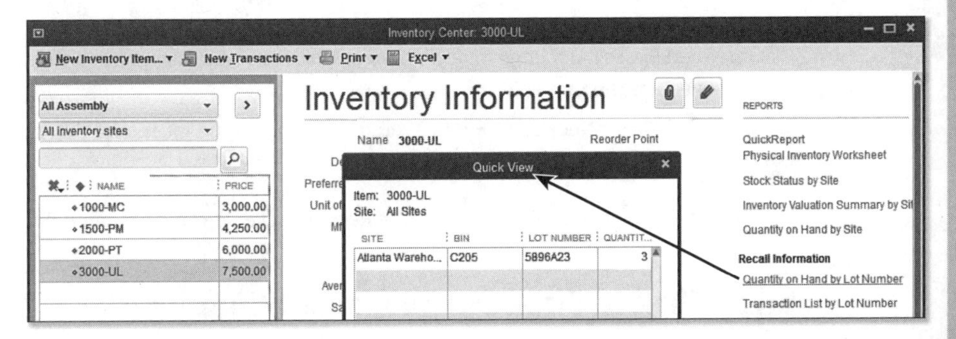

Figure C.25 Use the Inventory Center to gather information about where Lots are currently stored.

2. Research which customers purchased items from the lot:
   - Under Recall Information, click Transaction List by Lot Number.
   - Click the Item drop-down arrow and select the item from the list.
   - Click the Lot drop-down arrow and select a lot number.
   - Click OK. QuickBooks lists all transactions that include the lot, including assemblies and subassemblies.

You may also report on Lots (or Serial Numbers). From the menu bar select **Reports**, **Inventory**, **Lot Numbers in Stock by Site**, as shown in Figure C.26. Other reports include the Transaction List by Lot Number report, click the Sort By drop-down arrow, and select **Name**. This groups invoices by customer.

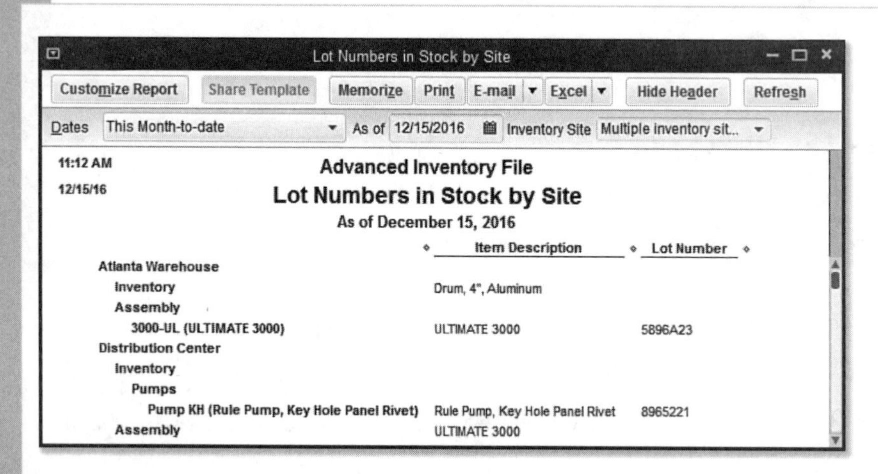

Figure C.26
Prepare reports detailing lot or serial number inventory details.

First In First Out (FIFO) Inventory Costing

FIFO (first in, first out) is a method of calculating the value of inventory sold and on hand. When you turn FIFO on, QuickBooks calculates inventory values based on the assumption that the first inventory items received are the first sold.

Without turning on FIFO, QuickBooks uses Average Costing as the means for determining the cost of inventory sold.

For more information, see "Reviewing the Recorded Average Cost Valuation," p. 206.

Enabling First In First Out Inventory Costing

1. From the menu bar, select **Edit**, **Preferences**, **Company Preferences** tab.
2. On the left side of the Preferences window, select **Items & Inventory**.
3. Click the Advanced Inventory Settings button.
4. In the Advanced Inventory Settings dialog, select **Use FIFO Starting On** and choose a date. QuickBooks recalculates all inventory-related transactions starting on the date you enter.

note

You can start tracking FIFO on any date. If you later decide to turn off FIFO, click to clear the Use FIFO Starting On checkbox, and QuickBooks again calculates inventory value using the average cost method.

5. Click OK.
6. In the Preferences window, click OK.

Reports Affected by FIFO Inventory Costing

When you enable FIFO inventory costing, the following report values will be adjusted:

- Inventory valuation reports
- Balance sheet reports
- Profit and Loss reports (cost of goods sold)
- *New*! FIFO Cost Lot History Report

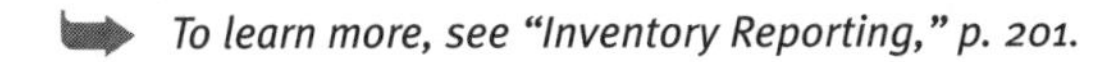
To learn more, see "Inventory Reporting," p. 201.

note
The FIFO Cost Lot History by Item report will be included in your inventory reports only if FIFO costing has been enabled.

QuickBooks 2013 provides a new report, the FIFO Cost Lot History by Item. Users can efficiently track the inventory acquisition (purchase, customer return, inventory adjustment, and so on) along with its cost. This provides users with information so they can see that the oldest (first in) cost lot is being disbursed first.

To prepare this report after enabling FIFO Costing, follow these instructions:

1. From the menu bar, select **Reports**, **Inventory**, **FIFO Cost Lot History by Item**. See Figure C.27.

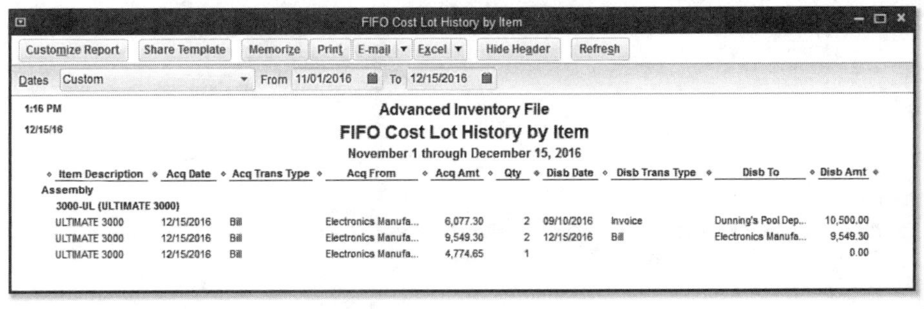

Figure C.27 *New!* For QuickBooks 2013 the FIFO Cost Lot History report provides details about the calculations done behind the scenes.

2. To filter for specific item(s), click the Customize Report button on the top left of the displayed report. The Modify Report dialog box displays.
3. Click the Filters tab. In the Filter pane, select **Item**.
4. From the Item drop-down, scroll to find the specific item or Multiple Items.
5. Click OK on the Modify Report dialog box to prepare the report filtered for the select Item or Items.

Barcodes

Increase efficiency and reliability for all inventory data entry by scanning items and serial numbers without touching a keyboard. QuickBooks automatically puts the information into the right field. If you don't have barcodes, QuickBooks will create them for you.

Overview—Working with Barcodes

Using barcodes in QuickBooks makes data entry faster and easier. You assign barcodes to items. Then you can scan barcodes when you buy or sell items. You can also scan barcodes to adjust the quantity of items on hand.

What barcode scanners does QuickBooks support?

QuickBooks supports most USB and Bluetooth scanners. When you purchase or evaluate a scanner, look for the following specifications:

- Support for EAN-13 and Code-128 barcodes
- Capability to produce a single carriage return at the end of the barcode

To test your scanner using Windows Notepad, follow these steps:

1. On the Windows desktop, select **Start**, **Accessories**, **Notepad**.
2. Scan an item with your barcode scanner. You should see the barcode number, one per line in Notepad, like Figure C.28.

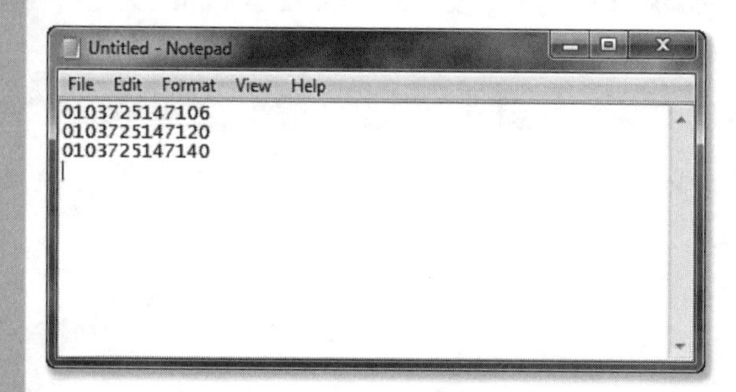

Figure C.28
Test the bar code scanner first in Notepad, making sure it scans with a hard return after each item.

QuickBooks accepts UPC/EAN-13 barcodes. Specifically, a valid barcode can be between 5 and 30 characters in length and contain the following character types:

- Numbers (0–9)
- Letters (a–z and A–Z)
- Space
- Minus sign (-)

- Plus sign (+)
- Period (.)
- Full stop (.)
- Colon (:)
- Forward slash (/)

Important: If the barcode is to be used as a serial or lot number,

- It can't contain spaces.
- It can't be composed entirely of numbers. That is, it must contain other character types (for serial or lot numbers only).
- It must be between 6 and 13 characters in length.

note

Barcodes are case sensitive. For example, 123456A is different from 123456a.

Barcodes generated by QuickBooks begin with "QB:". You can't create your own barcodes that begin with "QB:".

Set Up Barcode Scanning

Before you can begin scanning items into QuickBooks, you need to enable the Barcode Scanning feature. Follow these instructions:

1. From the menu bar select the **Edit**, **Preferences**, **Company Preferences** tab.
2. Select **Items & Inventory** from the left side.
3. Select **Advanced Inventory Settings** and click the Barcodes tab.
4. Select the **Enable Barcode Scanning** checkbox.
5. Click Open Barcode Wizard. If you already track barcodes in QuickBooks, QuickBooks will move the barcode you currently track in a custom-defined field for you. Just click the drop-down arrow and select the field you currently use for barcodes.
6. If you don't currently track barcodes in QuickBooks, leave the selection as I Don't Currently Track Barcodes in QuickBooks.

tip

Barcodes that QuickBooks generates begin with "QB:". You will need to edit the barcode name to remove the QB: and also change or remove barcodes that QuickBooks automatically generated for parent (top-level) items.

Importing Barcodes

If you track barcodes outside of QuickBooks (in Excel, for example), you can import them using Add/Edit Multiple List Entries. From the menu bar, select **Lists**, **Add/Edit Multiple List Entries,** as shown in Figure C.29.

For more information, see "Add/Edit Multiple List Entries," p. 115.

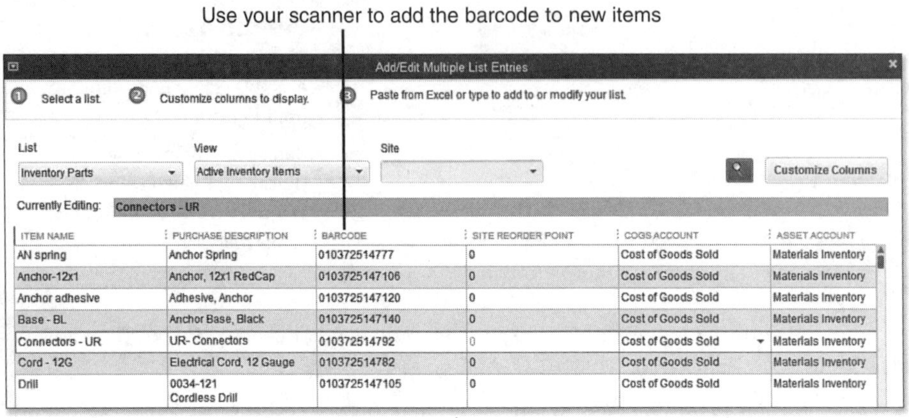

Use your scanner to add the barcode to new items

Add/Edit Multiple List Entries

1 Select a list. 2 Customize columns to display. 3 Paste from Excel or type to add to or modify your list.

List: Inventory Parts | View: Active Inventory Items | Site: | Customize Columns

Currently Editing: Connectors - UR

ITEM NAME	PURCHASE DESCRIPTION	BARCODE	SITE REORDER POINT	COGS ACCOUNT	ASSET ACCOUNT
AN spring	Anchor Spring	010372514777	0	Cost of Goods Sold	Materials Inventory
Anchor-12x1	Anchor, 12x1 RedCap	0103725147106	0	Cost of Goods Sold	Materials Inventory
Anchor adhesive	Adhesive, Anchor	0103725147120	0	Cost of Goods Sold	Materials Inventory
Base - BL	Anchor Base, Black	0103725147140	0	Cost of Goods Sold	Materials Inventory
Connectors - UR	UR- Connectors	010372514792	0	Cost of Goods Sold	Materials Inventory
Cord - 12G	Electrical Cord, 12 Gauge	010372514782	0	Cost of Goods Sold	Materials Inventory
Drill	0034-121 Cordless Drill	0103725147105	0	Cost of Goods Sold	Materials Inventory

Figure C.29 Use the Add/Edit Multiple List Entries feature to quickly scan in new barcodes or manually enter them.

Using Barcodes to Complete Transactions

You can scan barcodes while filling out sales or purchasing forms to speed data entry. While working in a sales or purchasing form, simply scan a barcode, and QuickBooks automatically places the barcode in the correct field on the form.

If QuickBooks doesn't automatically place the barcode in the correct field, QuickBooks may not support your scanner. However, you can still use your scanner for data entry by following these steps:

1. Turn off barcode scanning.
2. From the menu bar, select the **Edit**, **Preferences**, **Company Preferences** tab.
3. Click Advanced Inventory Settings.
4. Click the Barcodes tab.
5. Click to remove the checkmark from the Enable Barcode Scanning checkbox.
6. In the Advanced Inventory Settings window, click OK.
7. In the Preferences window, click OK.
8. From the menu bar, select the **Edit**, **Preferences**, **Company Preferences** tab.
9. On the left of the Edit Preferences window, click General.
10. On the My Preferences tab, select the **Pressing Enter Moves Between Fields** checkbox.
11. In the Preferences window, click OK.

To use your barcode scanner, click the field you want to enter information into, and then scan the barcode.

Print Barcodes to a Report

Follow these steps to print a report that lists the barcodes in your company file for ease in scanning:

1. From the menu bar, select **Reports**, **Inventory**, **Item Barcodes**.
2. At the top of the report window, click Print. See Figure C.30.
3. In the Print Reports window, change your printer settings as needed.
4. When you're ready to print the report, click Print.

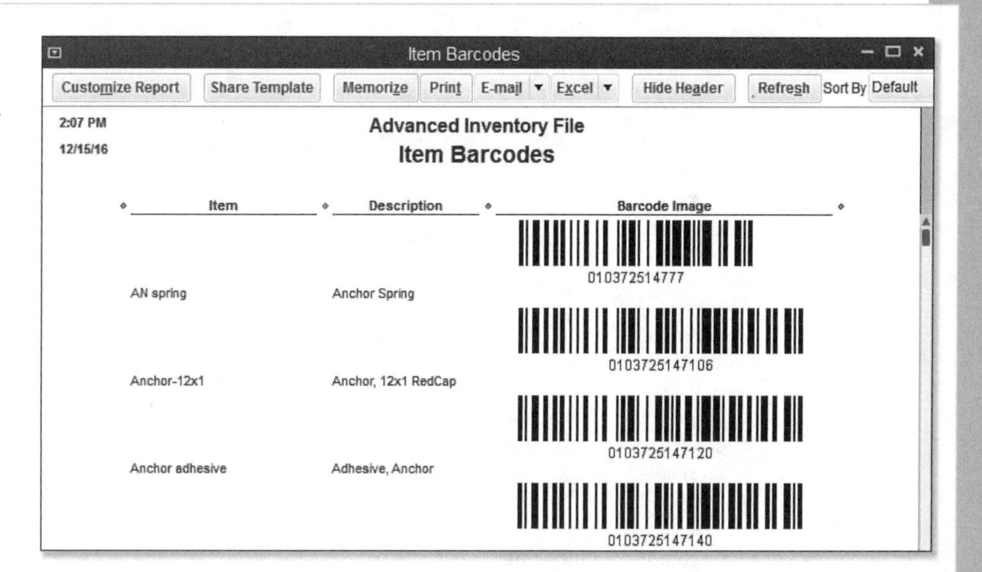

Figure C.30 Work efficiently, scanning from a printed list of Item Barcodes.

Print Barcode Labels

Follow these steps to print barcodes to affix to your products:

1. From the menu bar, select **File**, **Print Forms**, **Labels**. The Select Labels to Print dialog box displays.
2. Select the **Item Barcodes** option. From the drop-down list select the item you want to print barcodes to labels for. You can also choose to print, as shown in Figure C.31.
   - All Items
   - Multiple Items
   - All Items by type including All Services, All Inventory Items, and so forth.

note

Printing barcodes labels was an enhancement made to maintenance release 4 in QuickBooks Enterprise 13.0. If you do not have this choice in your file you will need to install the update. For more information see, "Installing a QuickBooks Maintenance Release," p. 618.

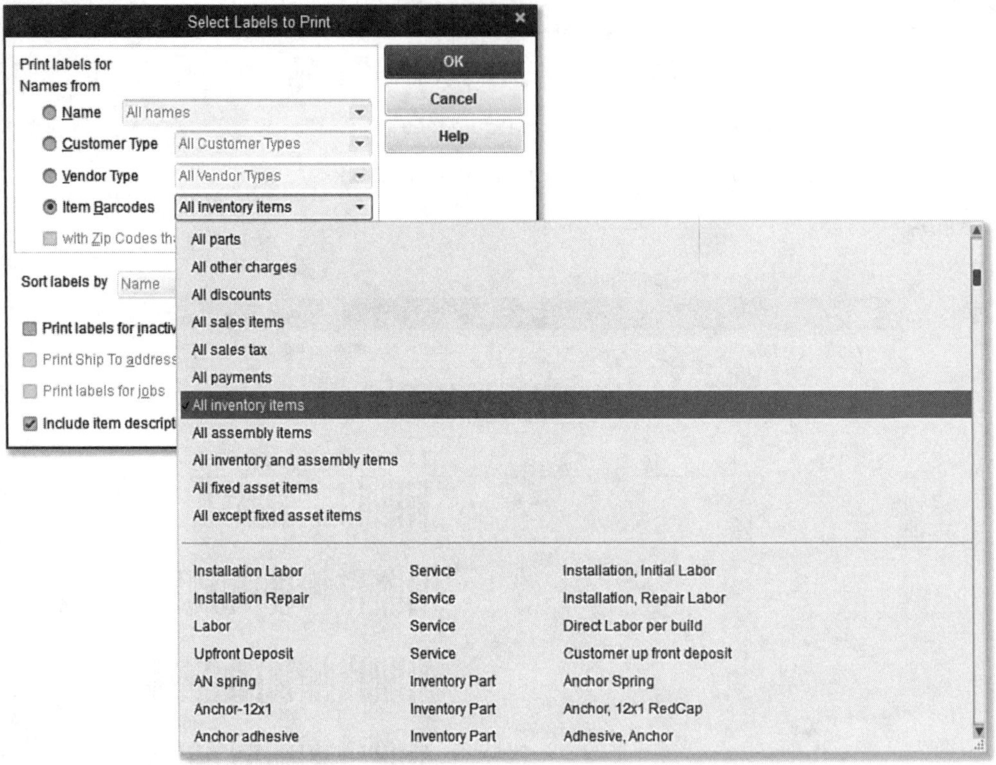

Figure C.31
After updating your data to maintenance release 4 or newer, you can print barcode to label stock.

3. Click OK to open the Print Labels dialog.
4. From the Label Format drop-down list select the type of label being printed. See Figure C.32.
5. Click Print.

note

This barcode printing capability includes only basic barcode printing functionality. For example, users cannot specify the size of the barcode, add a box around the barcode or assign characteristics like spacing and density to the barcode. Additionally, there is no capability to add other fields such as the manufacturer's part number or other information.

Figure C.32
QuickBooks will print basic label styles.

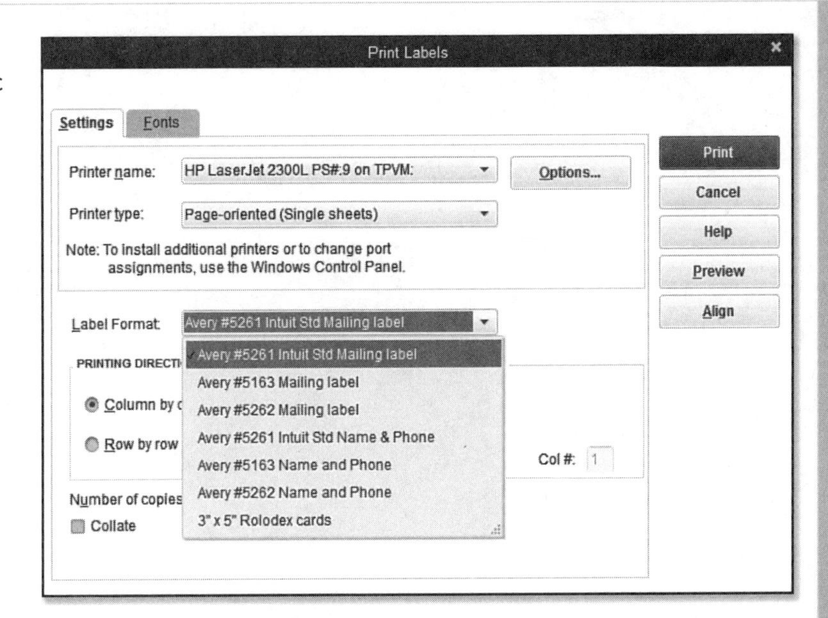

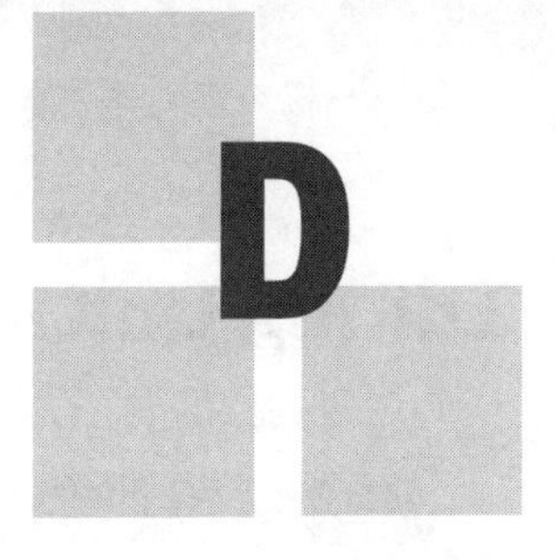

QUICKBOOKS SHORTCUTS

These Windows and QuickBooks keyboard shortcuts are provided to help you work efficiently in QuickBooks. With these shortcuts, you can keep your hands on the keyboard and minimize the time you might otherwise waste when using a computer mouse to activate a command or move to field on a transaction.

Editing QuickBooks Transactions and Lists

Use these shortcuts to save time editing a transaction or list in QuickBooks.

Key	Action
Ctrl+Del	Deletes the selected line in a transaction
Ctrl+Insert	Inserts a blank detail line in a transaction above the selected line
Ctrl+N	Creates a new transaction or list item when you have a list or transaction window open
Ctrl+D	Deletes the current transaction or list item
Ctrl+E	Edits the selected list item or transaction within an item list or register
Alt+S	Saves the selected transaction
Alt+N	Saves the selected transaction and advances to the next same-type transaction
Alt+P	Saves the selected transaction and advances to the previous same-type transaction
+	Within date fields, increments the date one day at a time; within other fields, such as check or invoice number, increments the transaction number by one
–	Within date fields, decreases the date one day at a time; within other fields, such as check or invoice number, decreases the transaction number by one
Ctrl+right arrow	Advances to next word in a field
Ctrl+left arrow	Advances to previous word in a field

Opening QuickBooks Dialog Boxes and Lists

With an open QuickBooks file, use these shortcuts to open a variety of dialog boxes and lists.

Key	Action
F1	Opens QuickBooks Help
F2	Displays QuickBooks diagnostic information
F3	Opens Search dialog box for company file information and transactions (different from the Ctrl+F search)
F4	Opens the QuickBooks Technical Support Helper, where you can provide technical information to an Intuit QuickBooks support agent when troubleshooting a database issue
Ctrl+W	Opens the Write Checks dialog box
Ctrl+Q	Opens a QuickReport for the selected saved transaction or list item

Key	Action
Ctrl+Y	Opens a Transaction Journal report for the selected transaction
Ctrl+L	From a displayed transaction, with a data field selected, opens the drop-down fields belonging to that list
Ctrl+J	Opens the Customer Center
Ctrl+A	Opens the Chart of Accounts list
Ctrl+I	Opens the Create Invoices dialog box
Ctrl+R	Opens the Use Register dialog box
Ctrl+P	Displays print options on an open transaction, report, or list
Ctrl+D	Deletes the selected transaction or list item
Ctrl+F	Launches the Find dialog box, or with an open transaction, displays Find filtered for that specific transaction type
Ctrl+H	Opens the Transaction History dialog box on an displayed transaction

Memorized Transactions

Use these keyboard shortcuts to save repeating transactions or to open the Memorized Transaction List.

Key	Action
Ctrl+M	Opens the Memorize Transaction dialog box from a displayed transaction
Ctrl+T	Opens the Memorized Transaction List

Standard Text Editing

These shortcuts make adding or modifying text more efficient.

Key	Action
Ctrl+Z	Undo typing or changes made in a field
Ctrl+X	Cut (delete selected text)
Ctrl+C	Copy selected text
Ctrl+V	Paste selected text
Del	Delete a character to the right
Backspace	Delete a character to the left

Opening QuickBooks Data Files

These shortcuts change how QuickBooks starts.

Key	Action
Ctrl	Before launching QuickBooks, press and hold the Ctrl key on your keyboard when clicking on the QuickBooks icon on your desktop. The No Company Open dialog box displays, where you can select from other listed data files. This shortcut is useful if you have trouble opening the last company file you accessed.
Alt	Before launching QuickBooks, press and hold the Alt key on your keyboard when clicking on the QuickBooks icon on your desktop. QuickBooks launches without opening the dialog boxes that were open when you exited QuickBooks. This can be useful if your file takes a long time to open.

QuickBooks Date Shortcuts

Use these shortcuts to efficiently change dates on transactions or reports.

Key	Action
+	Plus key, advance to the next day
–	Minus key, previous day
T	Today
W	First day of the week
K	Last day of the week
M	First day of the month
H	Last day of the month
Y	First day of the year
R	Last day of the year
Alt+down arrow	In a date field, opens the calendar, and in a list field, displays the drop-down list
[	For same date in previous week
]	For same date in next week
;	For same date last month
'	For same date next month
Date Fields	Dates can be entered into date fields without manually typing the date format

Miscellaneous Shortcuts

Be sure to try these! They are sure to save you time as you work with QuickBooks transactions.

Key	Action
Shift+Tab	Returns to prior field
Esc	Closes most open windows
Alt+Tab	Toggles between open windows
Ctrl+Enter	Saves the currently displayed transaction
Alt+F4	Closes QuickBooks
Ctrl+F4	Closes a QuickBooks dialog box when Esc will not close it
Ctrl+Tab	Advances through your open QuickBooks dialogs
Home	Returns to first character in a field
End	Advances to the last character in a field
Tab	Advances to next field
Ctrl+Tab	Advances to the next open dialog box
Ctrl+Page Up	Returns to the top of a long dialog box
Ctrl+Page Down	Advances to the bottom of a long dialog box
Ctrl+F6	Toggles between open dialog boxes (moves between items on the Open Windows list)
Shift+Ctrl+F6	Advances to the previous open dialog box

INDEX

Numbers

A

C

D

F

How can we make this index more useful? Email us at indexes@quepublishing.com

J

K

L

M

P

Q

How can we make this index more useful? Email us at indexes@quepublishing.com

R

S

T

U

V

W

X-Z

How can we make this index more useful? Email us at indexes@quepublishing.com